Vernacular Documents of Medieval Sardinia

The Medieval Mediterranean

PEOPLES, ECONOMIES AND CULTURES, 400–1500

VOLUME 147

The titles published in this series are listed at *brill.com/mmed*

Vernacular Documents of Medieval Sardinia

Editions and English translations of the Carte volgari, the condaghes of Silki and Bonárcado, and the Carta de Logu of Arborea

By

Alex Metcalfe
Hervin Fernández-Aceves
Maurizio Virdis

BRILL

LEIDEN | BOSTON

ISSN 0928-5520
ISBN 978-90-04-74113-3
ISBN 978-90-04-75095-1 (PDF)
DOI https://doi.org/10.1163/9789004750951

Library of Congress Control Number: 2026933239

Brill and Koninklijke Brill BV are part of De Gruyter Brill.
www.degruyterbrill.com

Questions about General Product Safety Regulation: productsafety@degruyterbrill.com

Cover illustration: Folio from the Condaghe of San Pietro di Silki, BUS, ms. 95 (fol. 8v). With kind permission of the Ministero della Cultura—Biblioteca universitaria di Sassari.

Contents

Acknowledgements

The editors would like to thank the UK's Arts and Humanities Research Council for their generous support of the project 'Power, society, and (dis)connectivity in medieval Sardinia' with a Standard Grant Award (2019–2024) that allowed the research and writing necessary for completion of this volume. The editors are also grateful to the following for their help and assistance: Davide Deiana, Giovanni Fiore, and Sergio Monagheddu from the Biblioteca Universitaria di Sassari; the archivists and staff at the Biblioteca Universitaria, Cagliari, and don Ferdinando Loddo from the Archivio storico diocesano in Cagliari.

Provisional List of the Rulers of the Sardinian *iudicatos*

Iudikes of Cálari[1]

- Salusi(?) aka Mariani or Mariano-Salusio I (pre-1058)
- Trogodori de Ugunali I aka Orzocco-Torchitorio I (1058–c. 1081)
- Salusi I aka Costantino I–Salusio II (c. 1081–c. 1103)
- Turbini aka Torbeno (c. 1103–c. 1107)
- Trogodori de Ugunali II aka Mariano II–Torchitorio II (c. 1107–c. 1130)
- Salusi de Lacon II aka Gostantinus II or Costantino II–Salusio III (c. 1130–c. 1168)
- Trogodori(?) aka Petrus or Pietro-Torchitorio III (c. 1168–c. 1188)
- Salusi de Lacon III aka William of Massa or Guglielmo I–Salusio IV (c. 1188–1214)
- Benedicta de Lacon aka Benedetta di Massa (1214–1232)
- Trogodori de Unali III aka Barisone-Torchitorio IV (1215–1217)

Iudikes of Torres

- Barisone I (c. 1063–c. 1073)
- Mariano I (1065–c. 1110)
- Costantino I (c. 1082–1127)
- Gonnario (1127–c. 1153)
- Barisone II (1147–1191)
- Costantino II (1170–1198)
- Comita (1198–1218)
- Mariano II (1204–1232)
- Barisone III (1232–1235)
- Adelasia (1235–1246) with Ubaldo Visconti (1235–1238) and with Enzo of Swabia (1238–1246).
- Enzo of Swabia (1246–1272)

Iudikes of Arborea

- Gonnario Comita I (c. 1015–c. 1038)
- Torchitorio Barisone de Lacon Gunale (c. 1038–c. 1060)
- Mariano I de Lacon-Thori (c. 1060–1070)
- Orzocco I de Lacon-Thori (c. 1070–c. 1100)

---

1 Such is the survival of source material that many of the dates for the rulers, especially for the eleventh and early twelfth century, are tentative and not firmly established.

- Torbeno di Arborea (1100–1133)
- Orzocco II de Lacon-Thori (1133–1147)
- Comita II de Lacon-Thori (1100–1116)
- Gonnario II de Lacon-Serra (1116–1131)
- Costantino I de Lacon (1131) with Orzocco III and Costantino II
- Comita III de Lacon-Serra (1131–1146)
- Barisone I de Lacon-Serra (1146–1186)
- Pietro I de Lacon-Serra (1185–1195) with Costantino III de Serra
- Ugone I de Serra Bas (1178–1195)
- Guglielmo–Salusio I de Lacon Massa (1195–1206)
- Ugone I de Serra Bas (1206–1211)
- Pietro II de Serra Bas (1211–1241)
- Guglielmo I de Capraia (1241–1264)
- Mariano II de Serra Bas (1264–1297)
- Giovanni I de Serra Bas (1297–1304)
- Andreotto de Serra Bas (1304–1309) with Mariano III de Serra Bas (1304–1321)
- Ugone II de Serra Bas (1321–1335)
- Pietro III de Serra Bas (1335–1347)
- Mariano IV de Serra Bas (1347–1375)
- Ugone III de Serra Bas (1375–1383)
- Eleonora de Serra Bas (1383–1392)

Iudikes of Gallura
- Manfredus Pisanus di Gallura (mid-1000s)
- Ubaldo I (–1065)
- Costantino I (later 1000s)
- Torchitorio de Zori (late 1000s / early 1100s?)
- Saltaro de Zori-Gunale (early 1100s)
- Ittocorre de Gunale (early 1100s)
- Costantino II Spanu (earlier 1100s)
- Comita Spanu (earlier 1100s)
- Costantino III de Lacon-Gunale (–c. 1171/3)
- Barisone I de Lacon-Gunale (later 1100s–1203)
- Elena de Lacon (1203–1218)
- Lamberto Visconti (–1225)
- Ubaldo Visconti (1225–1238)
- Adelasia di Lacon de Thori (1238–1246)
- Giovanni Visconti (–1275)
- Ugolino 'Nino' Visconti (1275–1296)

Maps and Figures

Maps

Figures

Figs. 1 and 2 are reproduced with the kind permission of the Archivio storico diocesano di Cagliari. Fig. 3 is reproduced with the kind permission of the Biblioteca Universitaria di Sassari. Figs. 4 and 5 are reproduced with the kind permission of the Biblioteca Universitaria di Cagliari.

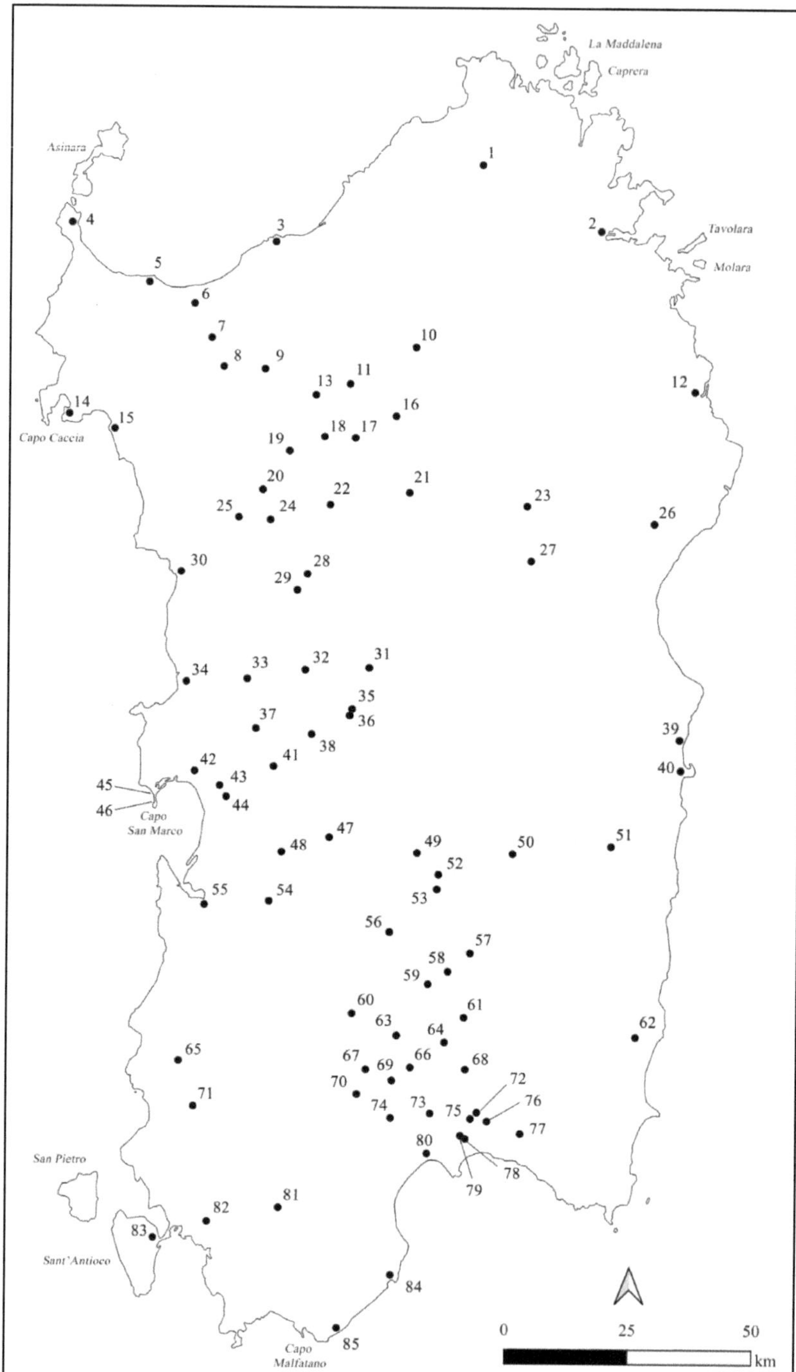

MAP 1 Medieval Sardinia

Legend to Map 1 in alphanumerical order

1. Luogosanto
2. Olbia (Civita)
3. Castelsardo
4. Stintino
5. Porto Torres (Torres, Ore, Turris Libisonis)
6. San Michele di Plaiano
7. Sassari
8. Ossi
9. Codrongianos, Saccargia
10. Oschiri, Nostra Signora di Castro
11. Ozieri, Sant'Antioco di Bisarcio
12. Posada
13. Ardara, Santa Maria del Regno
14. Alghero, Porto Conte
15. Alghero
16. Ozieri
17. Ittireddu, Santa Croce
18. Mores
19. Borutta, San Pietro di Sorres
20. Cossoine Santa Maria Iscalas
21. Anela, San Giorgio
22. Bonorva, Sant'Andrea Priu
23. Orune, Sant'Efisio
24. Semestene, San Nicola di Trullas
25. Padria
26. Galtellì, San Pietro
27. Nuoro
28. Mulargia
29. Macomer
30. Bosa
31. Bidonì
32. Abbasanta, Nuraghe Losa
33. Bonarcado
34. Cuglieri, Santa Caterina di Pittinuri (Cornus)
35. Ula Tirso
36. Busachi
37. Bauladu, Nuraghe Santa Barbara
38. Fordongianus (Forum Traiani)
39. Santa Maria Navarrese
40. Arbatax
41. San Vero Congius, San Vero
42. Cabras
43. Oristano (Aristianis)
44. Santa Giusta (Othoca)
45. Cabras, San Giovanni di Sinis
46. Tharros
47. Usellus (Uselis)
48. Mount Arci
49. Nuragus, Santa Maria di Valenza (Valentia)
50. Esterzili
51. Jerzu
52. Isili
53. Serri, Santa Vittoria
54. Uras, Nuraghe Sa Domu Beccia
55. Guspini, Santa Maria di Nabui (Neapolis)
56. Villanovafranca, Nuraghe Su Mulinu
57. Siurgus Donigala, Nuraghe Su Nuraxi
58. Suelli, San Giorgio
59. Ortacesus
60. Samassi
61. Sant'Andrea Frius
62. Villaputzu (Pubuzzi)
63. Nuraminis
64. Donori
65. Fluminimaggiore, Antas (Metalla)
66. Monastir
67. Villasor
68. Dolianova, San Pantaleo
69. San Sperate
70. Decimoputzu, San Giorgio
71. Iglesias
72. Sinnai
73. Sestu
74. Assemini
75. Settimo San Pietro
76. Maracalagonis
77. Quartucciu, Pixina Nuxedda
78. Quartucciu
79. Selargius
80. Cagliari (Calari, Santa Igia, Carales)
81. Nuxis, Sant'Elia
82. Tratalias, Santa Maria di Monserrato
83. Sant'Antioco (Sulci, Solky)
84. Nora
85. Domus de Maria, Chia (Bithia)

Legend to Map 1 in alphabetical order

32. Abbasanta, Nuraghe Losa
15. Alghero
14. Alghero, Porto Conte
21. Anela, San Giorgio
40. Arbatax
13. Ardara, Santa Maria del Regno
74. Assemini
37. Bauladu, Nuraghe Santa Barbara
31. Bidonì
33. Bonarcado
22. Bonorva, Sant'Andrea Priu
19. Borutta, San Pietro di Sorres
30. Bosa
36. Busachi
42. Cabras
45. Cabras, San Giovanni di Sinis
80. Cagliari (Calari, Santa Igia, Carales)
3. Castelsardo
9. Codrongianos, Saccargia
20. Cossoine Santa Maria Iscalas
34. Cuglieri, Santa Caterina di Pittinuri (Cornus)
70. Decimoputzu, San Giorgio
68. Dolianova, San Pantaleo
85. Domus de Maria, Chia (Bithia)
64. Donori
50. Esterzili
65. Fluminimaggiore, Antas (Metalla)
38. Fordongianus (Forum Traiani)
26. Galtellì, San Pietro
55. Guspini, Santa Maria di Nabui (Neapolis)
71. Iglesias
52. Isili
17. Ittireddu, Santa Croce
51. Jerzu
1. Luogosanto
29. Macomer
76. Maracalagonis
66. Monastir
18. Mores
48. Mount Arci
28. Mulargia
84. Nora
27. Nuoro
49. Nuragus, Santa Maria di Valenza (Valentia)
63. Nuraminis
81. Nuxis, Sant'Elia
2. Olbia (Civita)
43. Oristano (Aristianis)
59. Ortacesus
23. Orune, Sant'Efisio
10. Oschiri, Nostra Signora di Castro
8. Ossi
16. Ozieri
11. Ozieri, Sant'Antioco di Bisarcio
25. Padria
5. Porto Torres (Torres, Ore, Turris Libisonis)
12. Posada
78. Quartucciu
77. Quartucciu, Pixina Nuxedda
60. Samassi
6. San Michele di Plaiano
69. San Sperate
41. San Vero Congius, San Vero
61. Sant'Andrea Frius
83. Sant'Antioco (Sulci, Solky)
44. Santa Giusta (Othoca)
39. Santa Maria Navarrese
7. Sassari
79. Selargius
24. Semestene, San Nicola di Trullas
53. Serri, Santa Vittoria
73. Sestu
75. Settimo San Pietro
72. Sinnai
57. Siurgus Donigala, Nuraghe Su Nuraxi
4. Stintino
58. Suelli, San Giorgio
46. Tharros
82. Tratalias, Santa Maria di Monserrato
35. Ula Tirso
54. Uras, Nuraghe Sa Domu Beccia
47. Usellus (Uselis)
56. Villanovafranca, Nuraghe Su Mulinu
62. Villaputzu (Pubuzzi)
67. Villasor

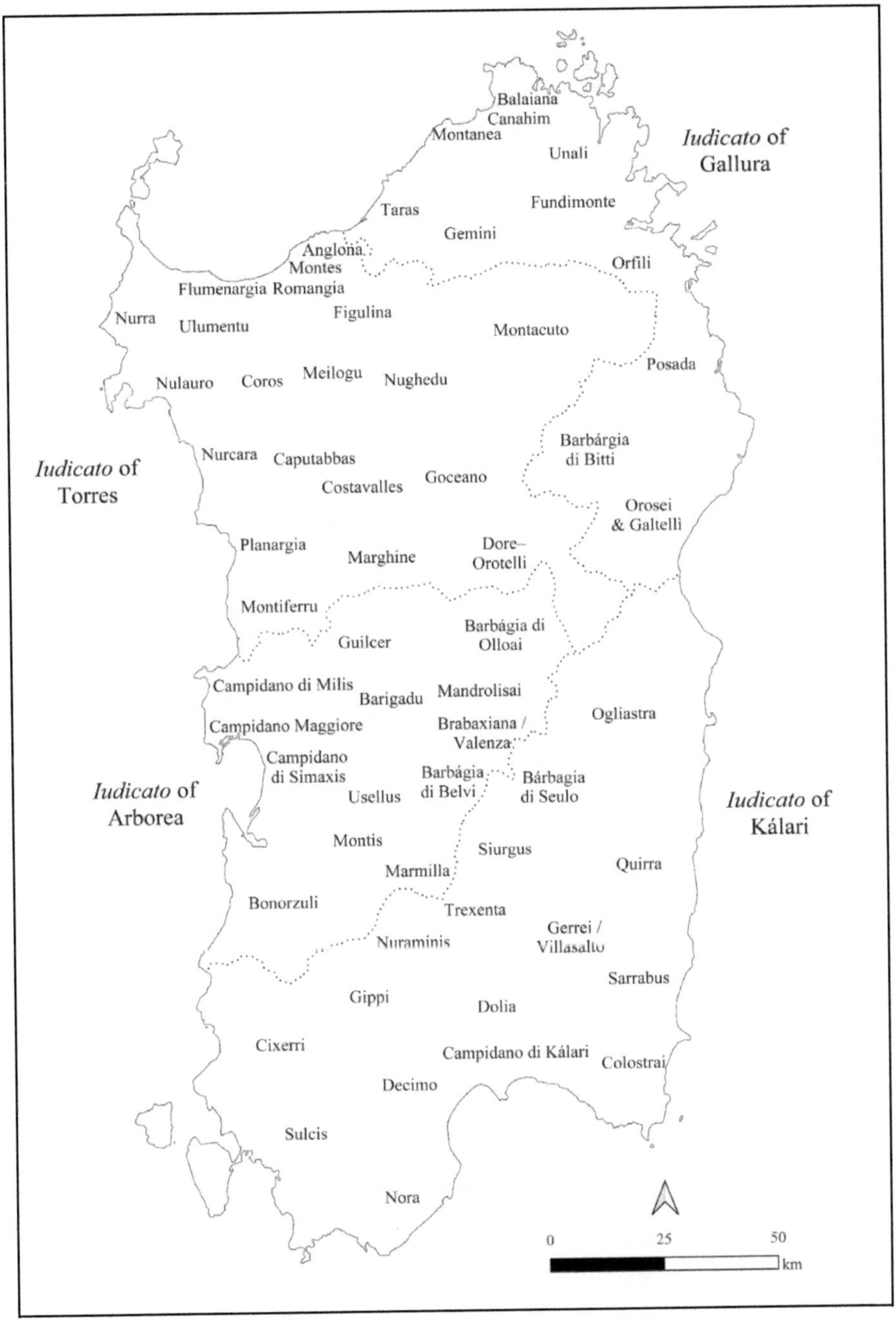

MAP 2 Relative locations of the *curatorías* within the four Sardinian realms (*iudicatos*)

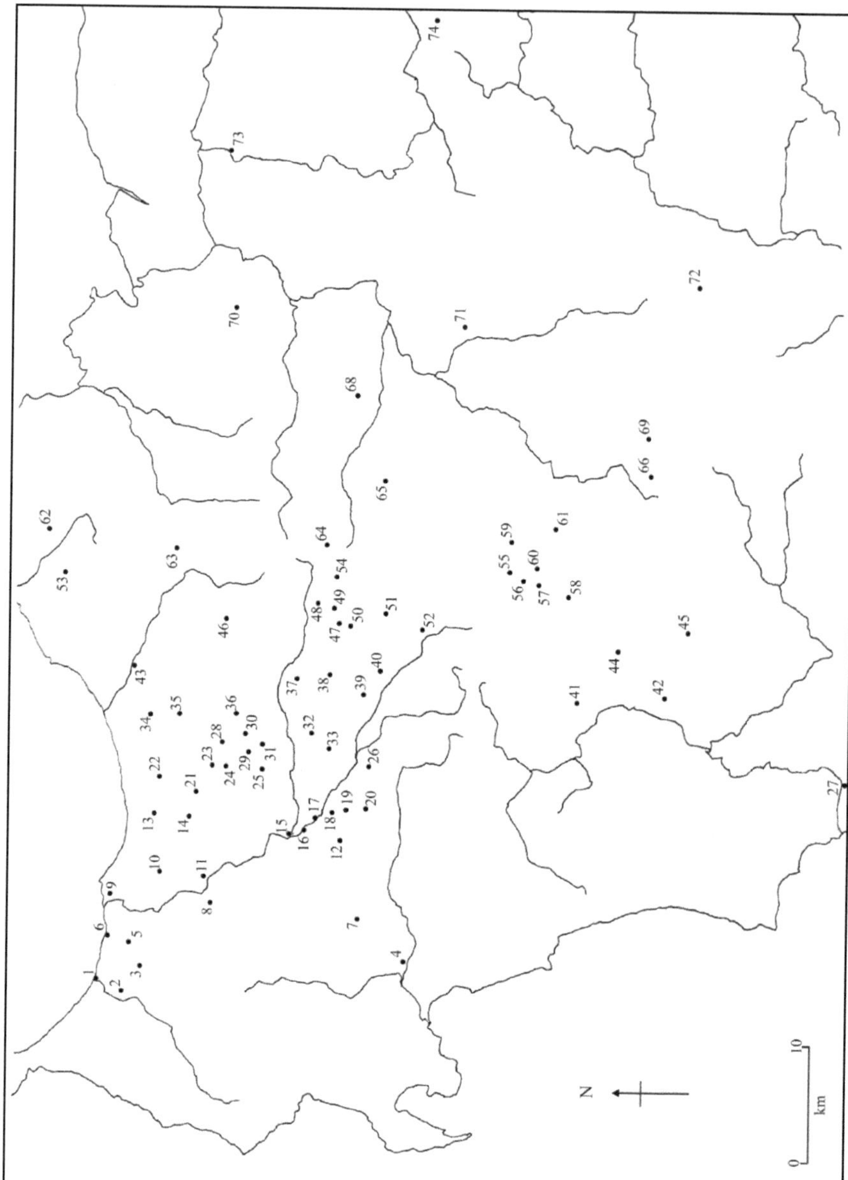

MAP 3 Places in the condagne of San Pietro di Silki

Legend to Map 3 in alphanumerical order

1. Flumen Sanctu (Fiume Santo)
2. Elba (Monte Elva)
3. Bisonis (Bisonis)
4. Nulabros (Lunafras)
5. Nuracati (Nuragaddu)
6. Iannanu (Gennano)
7. Ulumetu (Olmedo)
8. Erças (Ertas)
9. Turres (Porto Torres)
10. Kerki (Cherchi)
11. Curcaso (La Crucca)
12. Biosevi (Giusei)
13. Septupalmas (Fontana Sette Palme)
14. Ottave (Ottava)
15. Taverra (Taberra)
16. S. Iorgi d'Oiastreta (S. Giorgio di Oleastreto)
17. Tamarikes (Tamarighes)
18. Arave (Monte Pedralonga)
19. Banios (Banzos)
20. Urin (Uri)
21. Eristala (S. Giovanni)
22. Plaianu (S. Michele di Plaiano)
23. Murusas (nr. Sant'Orsola)
24. Innoviu (Sa Mandra 'e Noi Noi)
25. Canache (Caniga)
26. Padule (S. Maria di Paulis)
27. Bosa (Bosa)
28. Bosove (Latte Dolce)
29. Kitarone (Cadderoni–S. Eusebio)
30. Thathari (Sassari)
31. Silki (S. Pietro di Silki)
32. Tissi (Tissi)
33. Usune (Usini)
34. Sorso (Sorso)
35. Gereti (Geridu)
36. Enene (Eba Ciara)
37. Irbosa (Badde Ilvosa)
38. Carieke (S. Petru di Carieke)
39. Silvori (Silvaru)
40. Briave (Briai)
41. Teclata (Trigiada)
42. Favules (S. Pietro)
43. Gennor (Zennos)
44. Bonuvichinu (Bonuighinu)
45. Puthu Maiore (Pozzomaggiore)
46. Ogosilo (Osilo)
47. Quotrorianu Josso (Codronzani 'e josso)
48. Saccaria (Saccargia)
49. Contronianu (Codrongianus)
50. Ficulnas (Florinas)
51. Urieke (Urgeghe)
52. Seve (S. Maria de Sea)
53. Thergu (S. Maria de Thergu)
54. Salvénnor (Salvénnero)
55. Tigesi (Thiesi)
56. Sabren (Sarene)
57. Ibili (Ibili)
58. Puthu Passaris (S. Nenaldu)
59. Sorra (Sorres)
60. Kelemule (Cheremule)
61. Caputabbas (Cabuabbas)
62. Salasa (Salasgiu)
63. Nugulbi (Nulvi)
64. Plovake (Ploaghe)
65. Ardar (Àrdara)
66. Valles (Cantaru Addes)
67. Billalba (nr Viddalba)
68. Gisarclu (Bisarcio)
69. Abriu (Abriu)
70. Tula (Tula)
71. Guthule (Buttule)
72. Isporlathu (Esporlatu)
73. Ogothi (Otti)
74. Gullusò (Buddusò)

Legend to Map 3 in alphabetical order

69. Abriu (Abriu)
18. Arave (Monte Pedralonga)
65. Ardar (Àrdara)
19. Banios (Banzos)
67. Billalba (nr Viddalba)
12. Biosevi (Giusei)
3. Bisonis (Bisonis)
44. Bonuvichinu (Bonuighinu)
27. Bosa (Bosa)
28. Bosove (Latte Dolce)
40. Briave (Briai)
25. Canache (Caniga)
61. Caputabbas (Cabuabbas)
38. Carieke (S. Petru di Carieke)
49. Contronianu (Codrongianus)
11. Curcaso (La Crucca)
2. Elba (Monte Elva)
36. Enene (Eba Ciara)
8. Erças (Ertas)
21. Eristala (S. Giovanni)
42. Favules (S. Pietro)
50. Ficulnas (Florinas)
1. Flumen Sanctu (Fiume Santo)
43. Gennor (Zennos)
35. Gereti (Geridu)
68. Gisarclu (Bisarcio)
74. Gullusò (Buddusò)
71. Guthule (Buttule)
6. Iannanu (Gennano)
57. Ibili (Ibili)
24. Innoviu (Sa Mandra 'e Noi Noi)
37. Irbosa (Badde Ilvosa)
72. Isporlathu (Esporlatu)
60. Kelemule (Cheremule)
10. Kerki (Cherchi)
29. Kitarone (Cadderoni–S. Eusebio)
23. Murusas (nr. Sant'Orsola)
63. Nugulbi (Nulvi)
4. Nulabros (Lunafras)
5. Nuracati (Nuragaddu)
46. Ogosilo (Osilo)
73. Ogothi (Otti)
14. Ottave (Ottava)
26. Padule (S. Maria di Paulis)
22. Plaianu (S. Michele di Plaiano)
64. Plovake (Ploaghe)
45. Puthu Maiore (Pozzomaggiore)
58. Puthu Passaris (S. Nenaldu)
47. Quotrorianu Josso (Codronzani 'e josso)
16. S. Iorgi d'Oiastreta (S. Giorgio di Oleastreto)
56. Sabren (Sarene)
48. Saccaria (Saccargia)
62. Salasa (Salasgiu)
54. Salvénnor (Salvénnero)
13. Septupalmas (Fontana Sette Palme)
52. Seve (S. Maria de Sea)
31. Silki (S. Pietro di Silki)
39. Silvori (Silvaru)
59. Sorra (Sorres)
34. Sorso (Sorso)
17. Tamarikes (Tamarighes)
15. Taverra (Taberra)
41. Teclata (Trigiada)
30. Thathari (Sassari)
53. Thergu (S. Maria de Thergu)
55. Tigesi (Thiesi)
32. Tissi (Tissi)
70. Tula (Tula)
9. Turres (Porto Torres)
7. Ulumetu (Olmedo)
51. Urieke (Urgeghe)
20. Urin (Uri)
33. Usune (Usini)
66. Valles (Cantaru Addes)

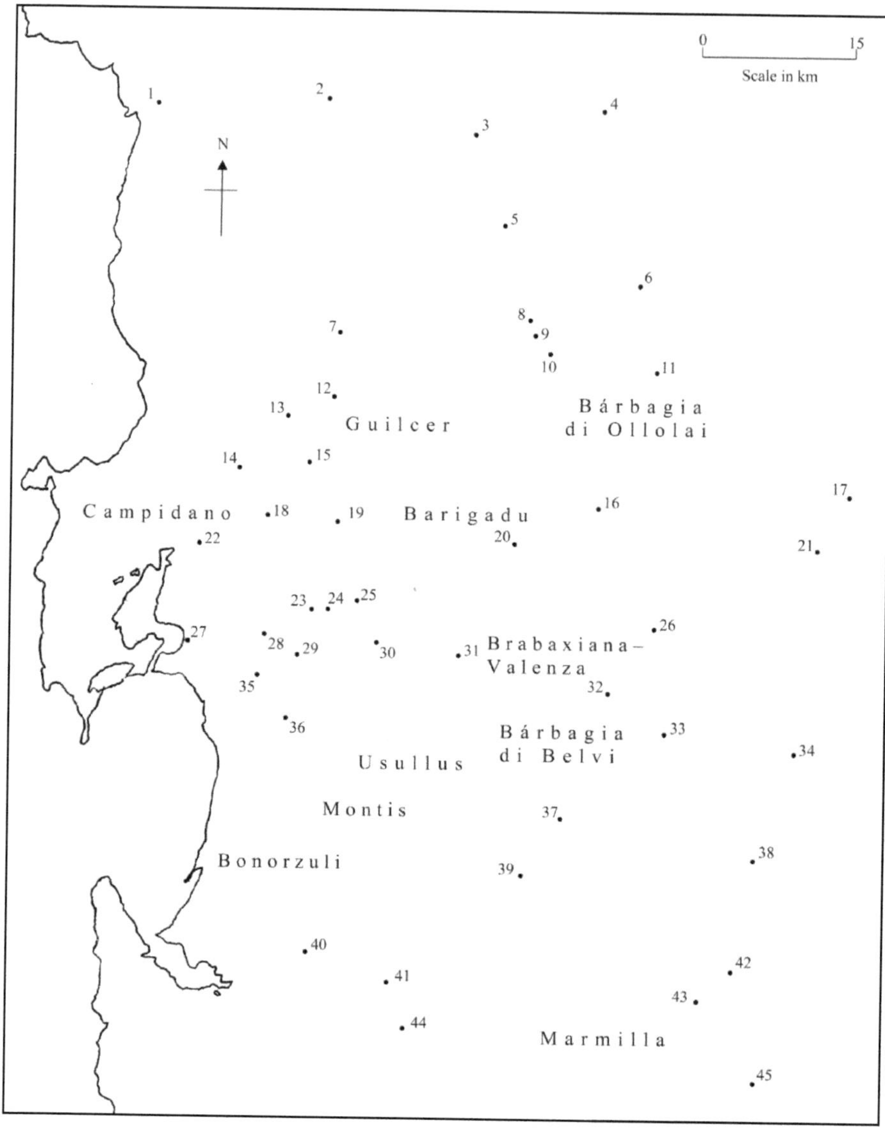

MAP 4 Places from the condaghe of Bonárcado in the *iudicato* of Arborea

Legend to Map 4 in alphanumerical order

1. Bosa
2. Sindia
3. Macomer
4. Silanus
5. Borore
6. Sedilo
7. Santu Lussurgiu
8. Nuraghe Suei (at Norbello)
8. Norbello
9. Villalonga
10. Ghilarza
11. Bidonì
12. Bonárcado
13. Seneghe
14. Narbolia
15. Milis
16. Busachi
17. Sorgono
18. San Vero Milis
19. Tramatza
20. Fordongianus
21. Atzara
22. Riola
23. Nuraxinieddu
24. Siamaggiore
25. Solarussa
26. Samugheo
27. Cabras
28. Dongala Fenughedu
29. Silì
30. Simaxis
31. Siamanna
32. Ruinas
33. Asuni
34. Láconi
35. Oristano
36. Santa Giusta
37. Usellus
38. Genoni
39. Ales
40. Terralba
41. Uras
42. Barumini
43. Las Plassas
44. Marmilla Castle
45. Villanovafranca

Legend to Map 4 in alphabetical order

39. Ales
33. Asuni
21. Atzara
42. Barumini
11. Bidonì
12. Bonárcado
5. Borore
1. Bosa
16. Busachi
27. Cabras
28. Dongala Fenughedu
20. Fordongianus
38. Genoni
10. Ghilarza
34. Láconi
43. Las Plassas
3. Macomer
44. Marmilla Castle
15. Milis
14. Narbolia
8. Norbello
8. Nuraghe Suei (at Norbello)
23. Nuraxinieddu
35. Oristano
22. Riola
32. Ruinas
26. Samugheo
18. San Vero Milis
36. Santa Giusta
7. Santu Lussurgiu
6. Sedilo
13. Seneghe
24. Siamaggiore
31. Siamanna
4. Silanus
29. Silì
30. Simaxis
2. Sindia
25. Solarussa
17. Sorgono
40. Terralba
19. Tramatza
41. Uras
37. Usellus
9. Villalonga
45. Villanovafranca

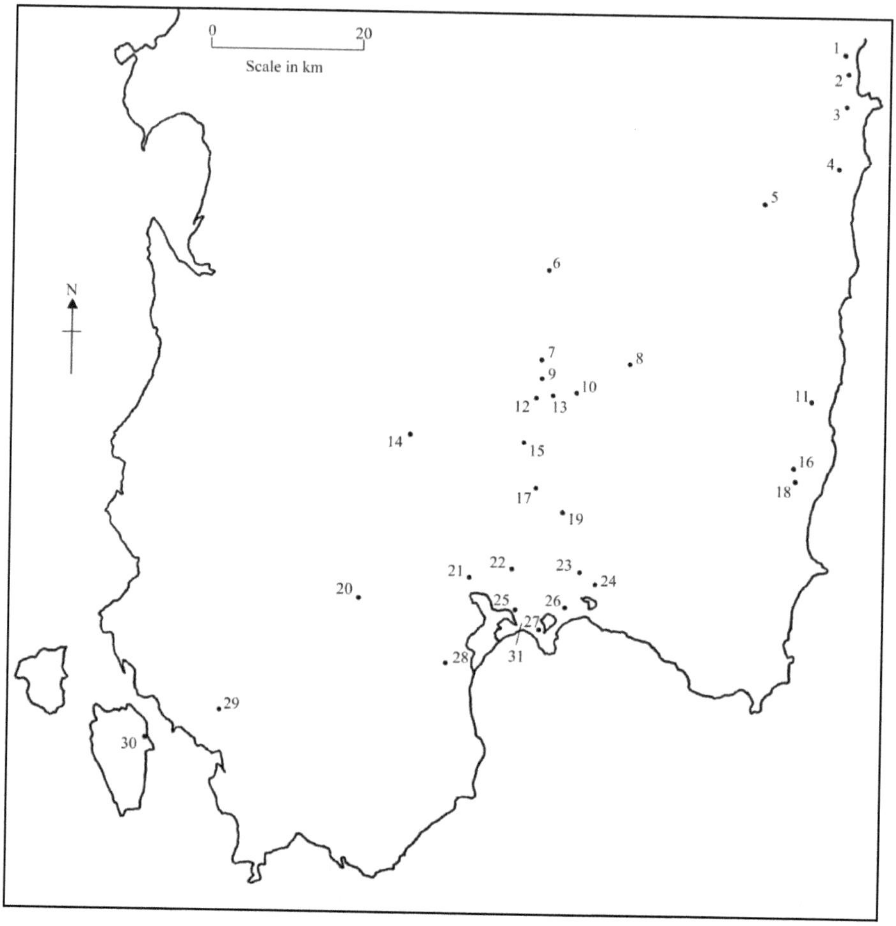

MAP 5 Places cited from the *Carte volgari* in the *iudicato* of Cálari

Legend to Map 5 in alphanumerical order

1. Lotzorai
2. Girasole
3. Tortolì
4. Barì
5. Jerzu
6. Serri
7. Piscu (nuraghe)
8. Goni
9. Suelli
10. San Basilio
11. Quirra
12. Senorbì
13. Arixi
14. Samassi
15. Barrali
16. Villaputzu (Pubuzzi)
17. Donori
18. Muravera
19. Dolionova
20. Acquafredda (castle)
21. Assemini
22. Sestu
23. Sinnai
24. Maracalagonis
25. Santa Gilla
26. Quartu Sant'Elena
27. San Saturnino (basilica)
28. Capoterra
29. Tratalias
30. Sant'Antioco
31. Cálari

Legend to Map 5 in alphabetical order

20. Acquafredda (castle)
13. Arixi
21. Assemini
4. Barì
15. Barrali
28. Capoterra
19. Dolionova
17. Donori
2. Girasole
8. Goni
5. Jerzu
31. Cálari
1. Lotzorai
24. Maracalagonis
18. Muravera
7. Piscu (nuraghe)
26. Quartu Sant'Elena
11. Quirra
14. Samassi
10. San Basilio
27. San Saturnino (basilica)
30. Sant'Antioco
25. Santa Gilla
12. Senorbì
6. Serri
22. Sestu
23. Sinnai
9. Suelli
3. Tortolì
29. Tratalias
16. Villaputzu (Pubuzzi)

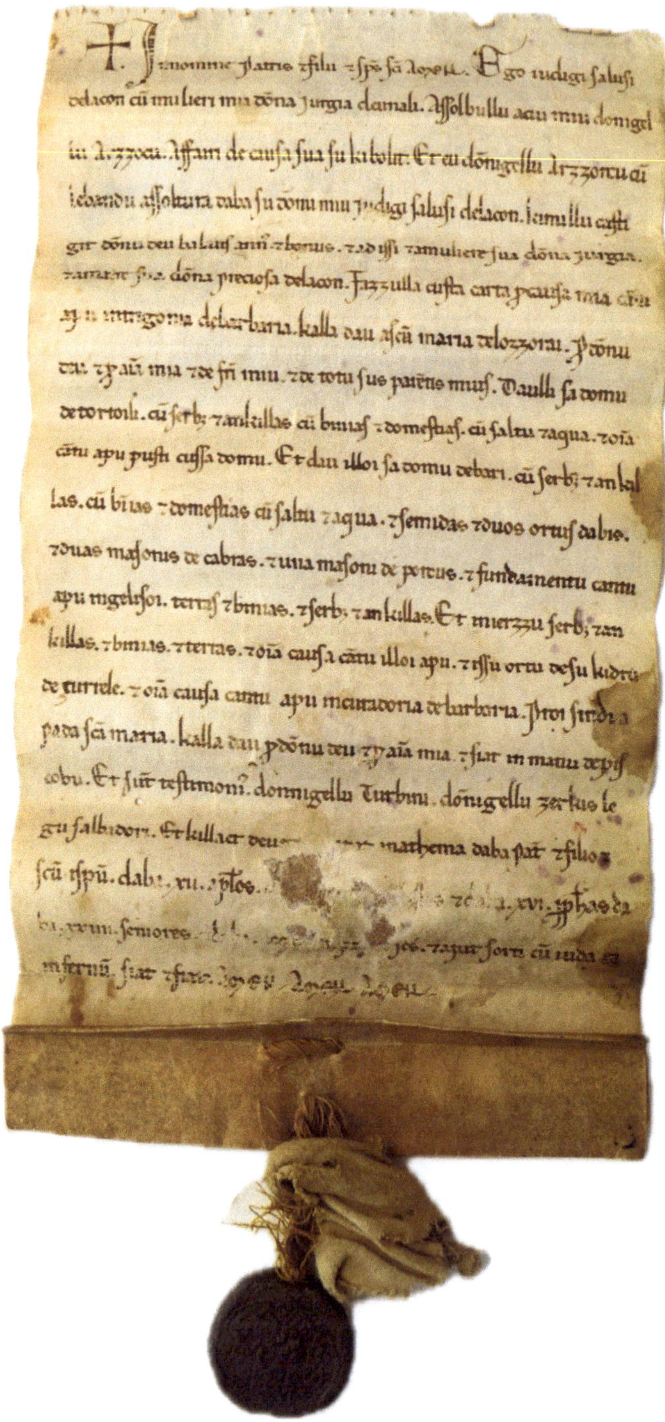

FIGURE 1
Charter number 6 from the *Carte volgari*

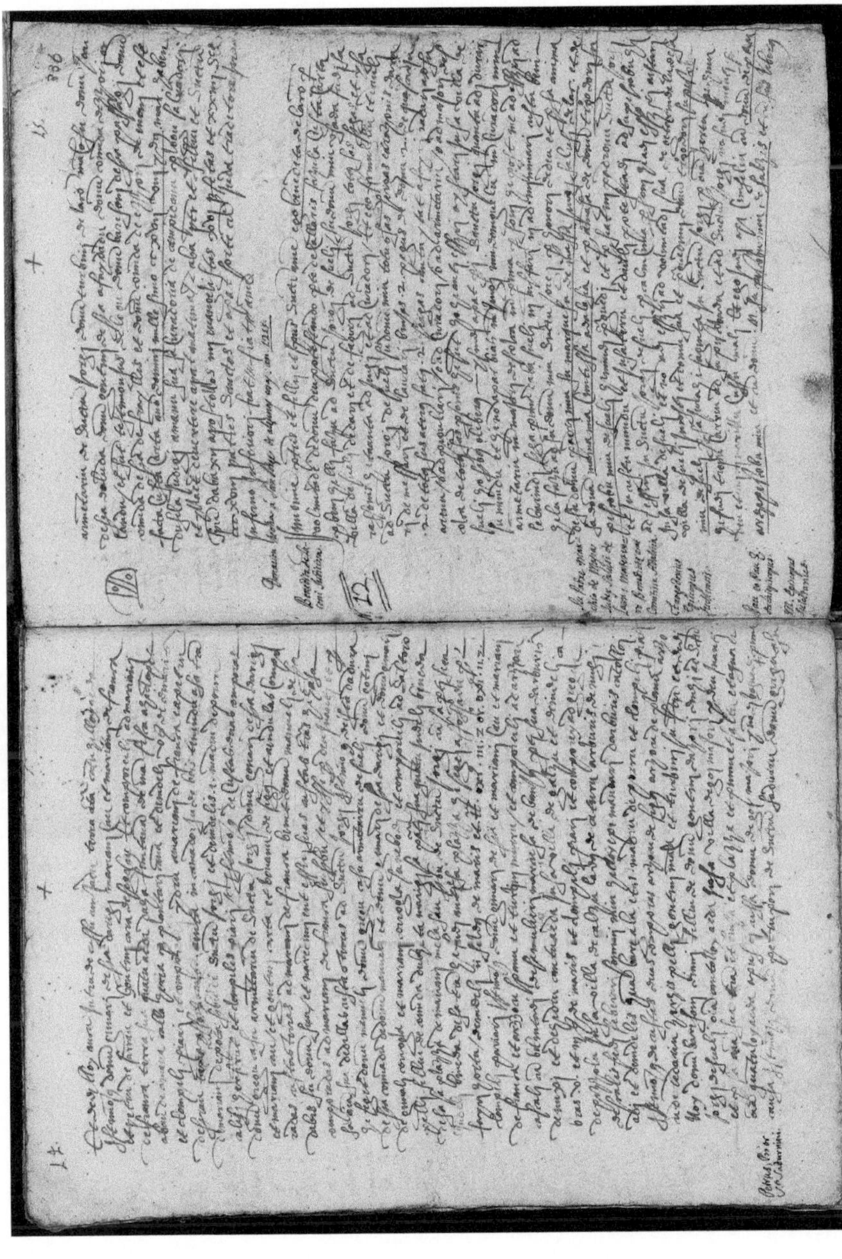

FIGURE 2 Transumpts of the *Carte volgari* from the *Liber Diversorum* (DigiLib., pp. 317; CVII)

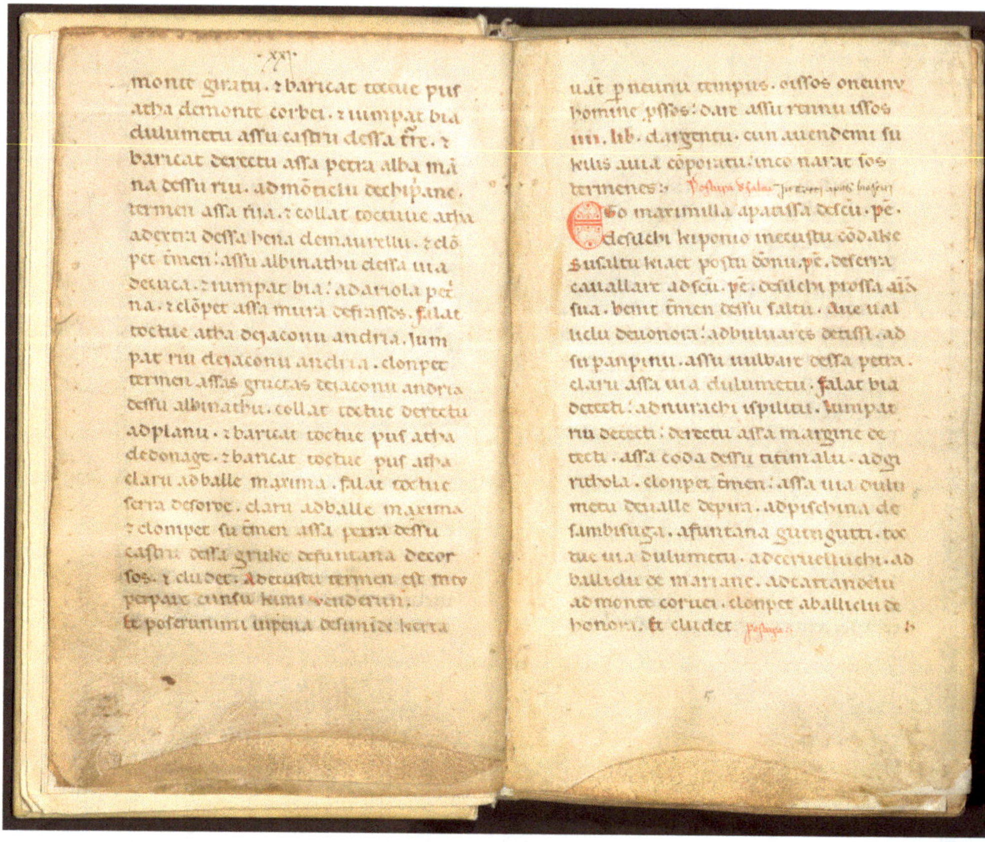

FIGURE 3 Folios 4^v and 5^r from the Condaghe di San Pietro di Silki

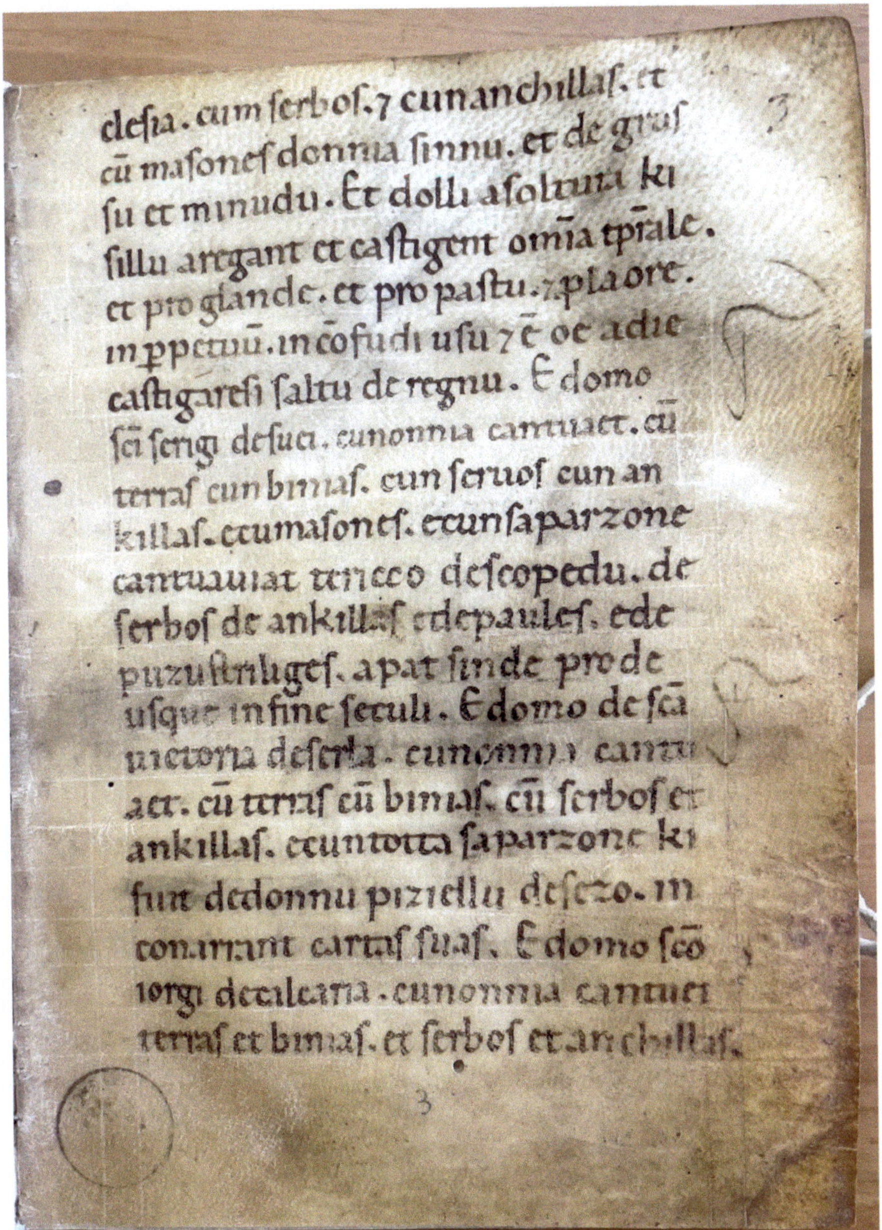

FIGURE 4 Folio 3r from the Condaghe of Santa Maria di Bonárcado

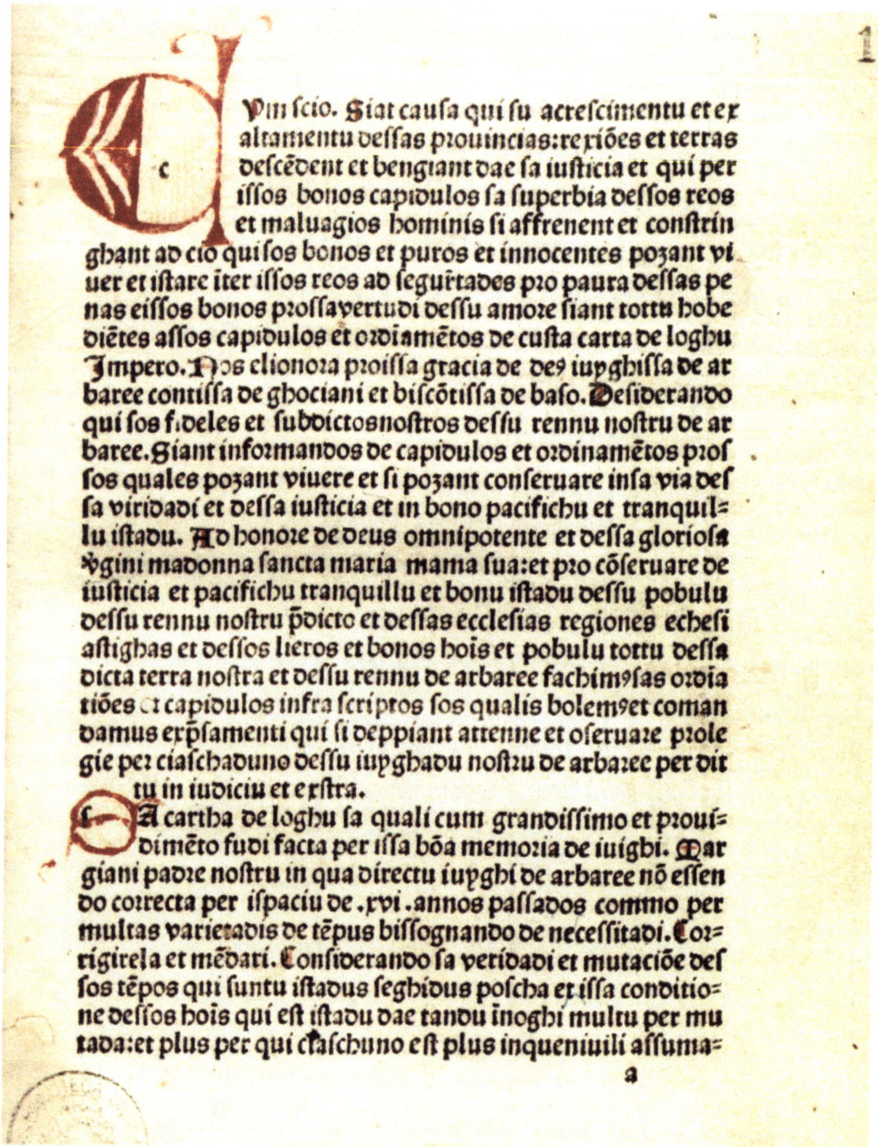

1

Cpin scio. Siat causa qui su acrescimentu et ex
altamentu dessas prouincias: rexiões et terras
descẽdent et bengiant dae sa iusticia et qui per
issos bonos capidulos sa superbia dessos reos
et maluagios hominis si affrenent et constrin
ghant ad cio qui sos bonos et puros et innocentes pozant vi
uer et istare iter issos reos ad segur̃tades pro paura dessas pe
nas eissos bonos pro ssa vertudi dessu amore siant tottu hobe
diẽtes assos capidulos et ordiamẽtos de custa carta de loghu
Impero. Nos elionora pro issa gracia de de9 iuyghissa de ar
baree contissa de ghociani et biscõtissa de baso. Desiderando
qui sos fideles et subdictos nostros dessu rennu nostru de ar
baree. Siant informandos de capidulos et ordinamẽtos pros
sos quales pozant viuere et si pozant conseruare insa via des
sa viridadi et dessa iusticia et in bono pacifichu et tranquil=
lu istadu. Ad honore de deus omnipotente et dessa gloriosa
vgini madonna sancta maria mama sua: et pro cõseruare de
iusticia et pacifichu tranquillu et bonu istadu dessu pobulu
dessu rennu nostru p̃dicto et dessas ecclesias regiones echesi
astighas et dessos lieros et bonos hois et pobulu tottu dessa
dicta terra nostra et dessu rennu de arbaree fachim9 sas ordia
tiões et capidulos infra scriptos sos qualis bolem9 et coman
damus expsamenti qui si deppiant attenne et oseruare prole
gie per ciaschaduno dessu iuyghadu nostru de arbaree per dit
tu in iudiciu et extra.

La cartha de loghu sa quali cum grandissimo et proui=
dimẽto fudi facta per issa bõa memoria de iuighi. Mar
giani padre nostru in qua directu iuyghi de arbaree nõ essen
do correcta per ispaciu de .xvi. annos passados commo per
multas varietadis de tẽpus bissognando de necessitadi. Cor=
rigirela et mẽdari. Considerando sa veridadi et mutaciõe des
sos tẽpos qui suntu istadus seghidus poscha et issa conditio=
ne dessos hois qui est istadu dae tandu inoghi multu per mu
tada: et plus per qui ciaschuno est plus inqueniuili assuma=

a

FIGURE 5 Folio 1r from the *Carta de Logu* of Arborea

Introduction

Sardinia's journey out of long Late Antiquity came via the Byzantine empire's African Exarchate of which it was a part until its fall to the Muslims with the conquest of Carthage in 698. From that time, the trail of evidence for the island and its relations with the Eastern Roman Empire grow increasingly faint. Sardinia appears to have entered a period of relative disconnection during which it was under occasional attack from Muslim fleets, but nonetheless maintained and developed limited contacts with the continental regions around it. Even as early as the 740s, the Sardinian mint, which had issued Byzantine gold and silver coinage, ceased to operate and no further coins were struck on the island until the late thirteenth century. And while other eastern imperial territories began to be reorganised into 'themes,' there is no clear evidence of this in Sardinia. That is not to say that Sardinia's political development within a roughly defined Byzantine framework had stagnated, but it remains difficult to describe in the historical record. The presence of an archon of Sardinia by the mid-950s, if not much sooner, as first attested in the *De Cerimoniis* of Constantine VII Porphyrogenitos is suggestive of important administrative reform of which we know precious little. Archons were also attested in Greek inscriptions on the island from the late 900s or early 1000s as well as on seals. The dates and authenticity of the latter are difficult to establish, but they probably relate to a similar period. In any event, centuries after the fall of Carthage, insular sigillography and epigraphy still emulated imperial models. Longer-term Byzantine heritage was visible in Sardinia's built environment too; for example, in the design of its pre-Romanesque churches which were often associated with saints from Christian Africa, while the onomastic record also continued to disclose many names of Byzantine Greek origin, often reshaped into Sardinianised forms, such as Gosantine, Goantine or Gantine for Konstantinos. When the first extant documentary records appeared in the later 1000s, they contained echoes of older forms of diplomatic, most obviously in the use of Greek script.[1] However, the choice of language was no longer Greek, but 'rustic' Latin and, most often, Sardinian. Indeed, chancery documents in Sardinian were the earliest in western Europe to be composed in the local vernacular.[2] Although this robust writing tradition endured under the Pisans,

1 For a comprehensive palaeographic reassessment of Greek-character Sardinian charters, see Giovanni Strinna, '"Litteris *semigraecis ac barbaris exarata monumenta*": sulla scripta sarda in caratteri greci', *Archivio Storico Sardo* 52 (2017), pp. 9–47.

2 For a catalogue of the extant eleventh-century diplomatic evidence, see Giovanni Strinna,

 | DOI:10.1163/9789004750951_002

Genoese and Aragonese, it is partly in virtue of language choice that the island's charters have remained inaccessible and understudied relative to their Latin counterparts from the rest of medieval Europe.[3]

The documentary record in medieval Sardinian can be broadly divided into three: charters, condaghes (or in-house record-books from churches and monasteries), and law codes, all of which were known in varying degrees to the island's main early modern scholars. The Sardinian prelate and historian, Giovanni Francesco Fara (1543–1591), whose *De rebus sardois* and *De chorographia Sardiniae* were composed in the 1580s, but were not fully published until between 1835 and 1838, was fully aware of the importance of the condaghes. Although countless condaghes have now been lost without trace, and the few that have survived to the present day were copied out, often multiple times, in subsequent periods either in Sardinian or Spanish, they would have been of little help to Fara whose interest lay in reconstructing the narrative framework of Sardinia's political history in the absence of any grand narrative of the island bar its passing mention in the histories of surrounding powers.

By the 1600s, the impact of Spanish scholars such as Francisco de Vico had marked a shift towards studies of legal and constitutional issues arising from Catalan colonial rule.[4] Here, one thinks of De Vico's description and evaluation of the *Carta de Logu*, the vernacular law code of Arborea, which remained a working document of fundamental importance until 1827.[5] In De Vico's era at least some of the island's scattered charter records were also known to historians. Here, one thinks of Jorge Aleo's translation into Spanish of Sardinian charters now known as the *Carte volgari* that also existed in transumpts collected in a (now lost) codex called the *Mare Magnum* which was itself a source for the *Libri Diversorum*, a multi-volume collection of miscellaneous records copied out between the 1600s and 1800s. The systematic study of these legal and diplomatic texts is a relatively recent undertaking.[6] It is unfortunate that

---

'The Earliest Charter Sources from Medieval Sardinia', in *The Making of Medieval Sardinia*, eds A. Metcalfe, H. Fernández-Aceves and M. Muresu (Leiden, 2021), pp. 319–323. Cf. Francesco Cesare Casula, 'Sulle origini delle Cancellerie giudicali sarde', in *Studi di Paleografia e Diplomatica*, eds F.C. Casula and L. D'Arienzo (Padua, 1974), pp. 1–99.

3 For a documentation overview, see Alberto Boscolo, ed., *Le fonti della storia medioevale. Orientamenti* (Sassari 1964).

4 Francisco de Vico, *Historia general de la isla y reyno de Sardeña* (Barcelona, 1639; repr. Cagliari, 2010, ed. F. Manconi); *Leyes y Pragmaticas reales del reyno de Serdeña* (Naples, 1640).

5 For an early Romantic narrative of Sardinian history, see Jean-François Mimaut, *Histoire de Sardaigne*, vol. 1 (Paris, 1825).

6 See Olivetta Schena, 'Archives and Documents Pertaining to the History of Medieval Sardinia', in *A Companion to Sardinian History, 500–1500*, ed. M. Hobart (Leiden, 2017), pp. 51–67, for a survey of surviving collections and their editorial history.

Sardinia in the mid-1800s was caught up in a scandal of forged documents. As in the case of the Vella scandal in Sicily from a slightly earlier time, forged documents focused attention on the importance of the medieval period as the oldest stratum of 'modern' history and identity.[7] However, they also lent an urgency to publish reliable editions of authentic materials.[8] The Sardinian forgeries, known as the *Falsi di Arborea*, comprised a series of charters, poems, legal texts, and chronicle extracts that purported to relate events of the eighth century on the island.[9] They had begun to appear from 1845 and were composed in Latin, Italian and a faux version of medieval Sardinian. Although the texts were crudely executed, they were sufficiently convincing to split the academic community on the island at the time, famously deceiving the historian, Pietro Martini, into publishing a two-volume edition of them.[10] The forgeries were not debunked until 1870, by which time two volumes of genuine Latin and Sardinian *diplomata* spanning from the eleventh to the end of the seventeenth century had been published by Pasquale Tola.[11] These have retained their importance as a work of reference to the present day.[12] By the 1870s, historians of the island were able to draw on a range of medieval Latin chronicles, mainland Italian sources, papal correspondence, Muratori's *Rerum Italicarum Scriptores*, and early volumes of the *Monumenta Germaniae Historica* among

7 Cf. Antonello Mattone, 'Le Carte d'Arborea nella storiografia europea dell'800', in *Le carte d'Arborea: falsi e falsari della Sardegna nel XIX secolo*, ed. L. Marrocu (Cagliari, 1997), pp. 25–152. For an analysis of how nineteenth-century Italian nationalists enlisted the *Falsi d'Arborea* to construct an Italianised and glorified Sardinian historical identity—and how later scholarship has dismantled that edifice—see Hervin Fernández-Aceves, Alex Metcalfe and Marco Muresu, 'Discovery, Invention, and Supposition: Three Case Studies from Medieval Sardinia', in *The Making of Medieval Sardinia*, pp. 17–41 (at 24–29).

8 See also earlier critical editions of charter materials, such as Carlo Baudi di Vesme, ed., *Codex diplomaticus Ecclesiensis* (Turin, 1877); Dionigi Scano, ed., *Codice Diplomatico delle Relazioni fra la Santa Sede e la Sardegna*, 2 vols. (Cagliari, 1940–1941), both of which remained references for charter records into the early twentieth century.

9 For the scholarly debate surrounding the credibility and historiographical consequences of these forgeries, see Aldo Accardo, 'L'invenzione della storia sarda nelle Carte d'Arborea', in *Le carte d'Arborea*, pp. 331–343.

10 Pietro Martini, *Pergamene, codici e fogli cartacei di Arborea* (Cagliari, 1863); *Appendice alla raccolta delle pergamene dei codici e fogli cartacei di Arborea* (Cagliari, 1865).

11 See Maria Giuseppina Cossu Pinna, 'Le carte d'Arborea alla Biblioteca Universitaria di Cagliari', in *Le carte d'Arborea*, pp. 195–210, for an overview of the physical documents preserved from the scandal.

12 Pasquale Tola, *Codex Diplomaticus Sardiniae*, vols. 1–2 (Turin, 1861–1868). For an updated diplomatic overview, see Francesco Cesare Casula, 'Aggiornamento e note storico-diplomatistiche al *Codex Diplomaticus Sardiniae* di Pasquale Tola', in *Codex Diplomaticus Sardiniae*, I, 2nd edn (Sassari, 1984), pp. ix–xxxvi.

others. It would seem, however, from Tola's introduction to the *Codex Diplomaticus Sardiniae* (CDS) that he had not consulted the near-contemporary, three-volume, *Storia dei musulmani di Sicilia* (1854–1872) by Michele Amari, which would have alerted him to the range and importance of Arabic sources for Sardinia. Only in the 1880s was Amari's *Biblioteca arabo-sicula* of Arabic sources in Italian translation published.[13]

The turn of the twentieth century was a watershed period that witnessed the publication of landmark editions of the *Carta de Logu* and of the *Carte volgari* by Enrico Besta and Pier Enea Guarnerio (d. 1952) and Arrigo Solmi (d. 1944), respectively.[14] Around the same time, Solmi also founded the *Archivio storico sardo* (1905–present). Both authors were keystones in the material and intellectual establishment of medieval Sardinian studies with publications on the political and constitutional history of the island that sought, inter alia, to trace the emergence of the iudikes from the end of the 'Byzantine' period and into the period of Pisan and Genoese control, thus tending to emphasise the island's Byzantine heritage in terms of political institutional infrastructure.[15] Their outputs also included the first printed edition of the condaghes of Trullas and Bonárcado.[16]

Post-war studies on medieval Sardinia have remained to this day closely associated with scholarship rooted in the universities of Sassari and Cagliari, such that by the end of the 1900s, almost all extant charter and condaghe collections had been published at least once.[17] Consequent analysis and interpret-

---

13 Michele Amari, *Biblioteca arabo-sicula; ossia Raccolta di testi arabici che toccano la geografia, la storia, le biografie e la bibliografia della Sicilia* (Turin, 1880–1889).

14 Enrico Besta, and Pier Enea Guarnerio, *La Carta de Logu de Arborea. Testo con prefazioni illustrative* (Sassari, 1905); Arrigo Solmi, 'Le carte volgari dell'Archivio Arcivescovile di Cagliari: testi campidanesi dei secoli XI–XIII', *Archivio storico italiano* 5, no. 35 (1905): 273–330; 'Le carte volgari dell'Archivio Arcivescovile di Cagliari. Note illustrative', *Archivio storico italiano* 5, no. 36 (1905), pp. 3–65.

15 Enrico Besta, *La Sardegna medioevale: le vicende politiche dal 450 al 1326*, vol. 1 (Palermo, 1908); *Le istituzioni politiche, economiche, giuridiche, sociali*, vol. 2 (Palermo, 1909); Arrigo Solmi, *Studi storici sulle istituzioni della Sardegna nel Medio Evo* (Cagliari, 1917; 2nd edn, Nuoro, 2001); Salvatore Cosentino, 'Potere e istituzioni nella Sardegna bizantina', in *Ai confini dell'impero. Storia, arte e archeologia della Sardegna bizantina*, eds P. Corrias and S. Cosentino (Cagliari, 2002), pp. 1–13.

16 Enrico Besta and Arrigo Solmi, *I condaghi di San Nicola di Trullas e di Santa Maria di Bonarcado* (Milan, 1937). See also Giuliano Bonazzi, ed., *Il condaghe di San Pietro di Silki: testo logudorese inedito dei secoli XI–XIII* (Sassari, 1900); Raffaele di Tucci, ed., *Il condaghe di S. Michele di Salvenor. Testo inedito* (Cagliari, 1912); Raimondo Carta Raspi, *Condaghe di S. Nicola di Trullas* (Cagliari, 1937); *Condaghe di S. Maria di Bonarcado* (Cagliari, 1937).

17 On the development of medieval history at the University of Cagliari, see Francesco Cesare Casula, 'Rassegna dell'Istituto di Storia medioevale della Facoltà di Lettere dell'Università di Cagliari', *Medioevo: Saggi e Rassegne* 1 (Cagliari, 1975), pp. 61–140.

ation, especially from juridical, constitutional and institutional perspectives has been considerable, stimulated not least by the seminal works of 'founding-father' figures such as Alberto Boscolo (d. 1987) and Francesco Cesare Casula.[18] Less attention has been paid to the social, cultural and economic history arising from the same documents. In this respect, the present generation has also seen a shift towards studies of the archaeological record for which the priorities have hitherto strongly focused on *nuragic* Sardinia, but for which much remains to be discovered from the medieval period.

The primary aim of this current undertaking is thus to present a substantial corpus of the earliest and most important vernacular texts to open up this fertile ground to historians who are not specialists in Sardinian history, language and culture, but who wish to understand more of the former western Byzantine outpost in the middle of Mediterranean which, from the 1000s, was the central pivot around which overseas forces—the Pisans, Genoese and Aragonese—came to reshape the commercial, cultural, and political frontiers of the wider region. The present volume includes complete sets of transcriptions made from the original documents and fitted with English translations, but they are not intended as full critical editions with historical commentaries. A glossary of Sardinian terms has been added to provide the necessary apparatus for researchers to access and analyse the primary sources for themselves. Since the established historiography for Sardinia has largely been a product of Italian scholarship, personal names from medieval Sardinian that appear in secondary literature have usually been adapted to fit an Italianised version. This has led to a rough standardisation of orthography which is otherwise characterised by variation. Thus, the frequently found personal name, Torchitorio (in Italian historiography) is found in the original texts as Torkitorios, Trogodori, Turgodori, Troodori, Drogotori and so on. We have adopted a compatibilist approach which leaves the primary source version intact in the transcription and English translation, but which adopts a standard Italian rendition in footnotes or discussion.

1 From Archons to Iudikes to Reges

By the second half of the eleventh century, from when the earliest extant charters date, the island comprised four distinct polities: Cálari (till 1258),

18 For example, see Boscolo, *Le fonti della storia medioevale*; Francesco Cesare Casula, 'Sulle origini delle Cancellerie giudicale sarde', in *Studi di Paleografia e Diplomatica*, eds F.C. Casula and L. D'Arienzo (Padua, 1974), pp. 1–100; 'Giudicati e curatorìe', in *Atlante della Sardegna*, eds R. Pracchi, A. Terrosu and M. Riccardi (Rome, 1980), pp. 94–109.

Arborea (till around 1404), Torres (till 1259), and Gallura (till 1296). Each was governed by a ruler called a 'iudike,' literally 'a judge,' and these have come to be regarded as the constitutional heirs of the archons.[19] Important evidence for this murky transition comes from the island's Greek epigraphy that reveals a distinctive and repeating nomenclature practice between successive Calaritan archons: namely, the use of two intercalating dynastic names: Torchitorio and Salusio.[20] The Calaritan iudikes maintained this same practice of alternating the rulers' dynastic name (sometimes in addition to their given names) in a display of continuity and tradition that lent stability and legitimacy to their rulership.[21] By the mid-1000s, the iudikes had also come to refer to themselves as *reges* ('kings'), each in his own *regnu* or *rennu* ('realm'). These territorial terms were loosely synonymous with *parte* and *loco* (or *logu*) that referred to their own lands as self-contained 'countries' within Sardinia. So, to some extent, the iudikes can be considered as kings within kingdoms, although they did not develop monarchies in the same sense as their contemporaries in the medieval West. For all intents and purposes, the Sardinian rulers were autonomous, and continental powers sometimes echoed their claims of royal status when it suited their agendas and alliances.[22] But outside their own realms, they were politically and economically weak relative to overseas forces, most notably the Pisans and Genoese, who invested vital capital to exploit insular resources, won over political control, and used Sardinia as a stepping-stone to reach the lucrative markets of the southern Mediterranean between the eleventh and thirteenth centuries.

The vocabulary of politics, governance and administration found in the early charter materials provides many important planks for reconstructing aspects of the iudikes' rulership. A key example is the role of the 'curators' or administrative officials overseeing the *curatorías*, a term which was derived from the Byzantine Greek κουρατωρία ('administrative district'). In the documentary record,

---

19 Luciano Gallinari, 'The *Iudex Sardiniae* and the *Archon Sardanias* between the Sixth and Eleventh Century', in *The Making of Medieval Sardinia*, pp. 219–226.

20 On dynastic naming practices and sociolinguistic change, see Giulio Paulis, 'Sociolinguistic Dynamics and Dynastic Names in Byzantine and Early Medieval Sardinia', in *The Making of Medieval Sardinia*, pp. 293–313.

21 Regarding the question of long-term memory and identity of the iudikes, see Luciano Gallinari, 'The Sardinian *Giudici* between Historical Memory and Identity. A Matter of *Longue Durée*?', in *Sardinia from the Middle Ages to Contemporaneity*, ed. L. Gallinari (Bern, 2018), pp. 29–44.

22 For a synthetical view of royal authority, see Alessandro Soddu, 'Il potere regio nella Sardegna giudicale', in *Linguaggi e rappresentazioni del potere nella Sardegna medievale*, ed. A. Soddu (Rome, 2020), pp. 31–88.

we can infer that the Sardinian *curatorías* were loosely defined territorial units that circumscribed settlements and villages (Sardinian: *biddas* from the Latin *villae*) under the authority of a 'curator' or *curatore* in Sardinian. The textual sources reveal that these functionaries exercised organisational duties for the iudike and oversaw the administration of justice at their own local assemblies or assize courts known as *coronas*. The Sardinian realms, divided into *curatorías*, were thus integral to the iudikes' administration. The surviving evidence does not allow us to claim that the *curatorías* had played similar roles in the time of the archons, but it is certainly plausible. Nor does the evidence allow the claim that Byzantine practices characterised the administration of Sardinia in the eleventh century, even if their presence was a characteristic of it. Instead, they perhaps reveal more about the political and ideological aspirations of its local rulers. In this respect, the employment of imperial-sounding language and administrative vocabulary, including a visual message in the use of Greek characters, allowed the iudikes to simulate a connective thread with the Byzantine Empire, regardless how weak political ties with Constantinople had become.[23] Even though Sardinian society had diverged politically, culturally, and linguistically from the Eastern empire by the turn of the millennium, the ruling class, especially in the south of the island, maintained a 'Byzantinesque' façade to help legitimise their authority.

For its part, the realm of Cálari (sometimes referred to as 'Pluminus' in contemporary sources) was organised around the ancient city of Káralis (modern Cagliari) at its political and ecclesiastical centre. It comprised the island's southern territories: that is to say, the Campidano plain; the region of Sulcis, and the eastern coast up towards the modern province of Nuoro. Torres, also known as the territory of Ore or Logu d'Oro (Logudoro), comprised a realm in the north-western quarter of the island whose ecclesiastical see and most important maritime town was the homonym town of Torres (modern Porto Torres). The seat of the iudike was not fixed at Torres, and his polycentric rulership developed residences in other towns, such as Àrdara, where a palace and royal church were founded. The realm of Arborea was located in the central-western part of the island, between Cálari and Torres, which expanded from Oristano and ancient Tharros to the borders of the mountainous central region known as Barbária. Finally, Gallura was the fourth *iudicato*, located in the north-eastern fringe of Sardinia with its most important centre being the port of Civita (modern Olbia).

---

23 On the Byzantine administrative vocabulary that filtered into Sardinian charters, see Michele Orrù, 'Byzantine Administrative Influence in Medieval Sardinia', in *The Making of Medieval Sardinia*, pp. 160–169.

The rulers of the *iudicatos* established their own ruling houses, and the title of iudike was passed on hereditarily in most instances to the first-born, but also to spouses, nephews and grandsons.[24] Some co-ruled with their elder sons with whom they shared the titles of iudike and *rege*. These ruling houses thus formed an upper sociopolitical echelon comprising their immediate relatives and their sons, and such kin-group status was recognised with the honorific epithet of *donikelo* or *donigellu* in Sardinian. This local aristocracy or 'royalty' was followed in the sociopolitical hierarchy by the *maiorales* or greater land-owning lords. Furthermore, the witness lists in our documents reveal the existence of a middle sociopolitical stratum composed of higher-ranking prelates and functionaries with official titles, but whose precise roles remain unclear. Besides the aforementioned *curatores*, we frequently encounter *armentarios* ('administrators') in charge of specific public and ecclesiastical bodies and production units, working alongside a wide array of officials/lords or 'those in charge' called *maiores*, who could be responsible for a town, a guard, or a group of people. Thus, for example, we find the *maiore de villa* ('of the village'), *d'ianna* ('of the gate'), or *de iscolca* ('of the ward') as well as numerous *mandatores* ('deputies') who were recognised representatives for communities, churches, and lords.

Male and female 'servants' (*servos* and *ankillas*) were situated towards the lower parts of the socioeconomic pyramid, and they emerge from the diplomatic evidence as an unfree rural labour force that underpinned agricultural production. The Sardinian *servos* were neither peasants attached to the land, nor serfs in the continental, feudal sense. Rather, they were under direct control of the landowners, both lay and ecclesiastical, as personal or collective property. Also, their offspring were tied to their parents' servile condition. The ownership of servants could be shared, and thus owners could hold, exchange, sell and buy shares of servants. Depending on who owned the servants and how they were shared, the nomenclature varied. For example, there were *servos de rennu* ('of the realm') owned by the iudike, and *servos de clesia* ('of the church'). Also, one can find *servos peguliares*, designated so as to suggest they were particularly owned by one person. Similarly, *servos intregos* ('full servants') were widely attested and belonged to a single entity and, consequently, their working week did not have to be divided between different owners. A distinction should be made, however, between the latter and the *servos de cadadie* ('daily servants') who tended to be female and whose duties may have consisted of everyday domestic chores instead of having to provide manual labour for a

24 See L.L. Brook, F.C. Casula, M.M. Costa, A.M. Oliva, R. Pavoni and M. Tangheroni (eds), *Genealogie Medioevali di Sardegna* (Cagliari and Sassari, 1984).

specific period of days per week, otherwise reckoned as a proportion of their time: a quarter, a half, three-quarters or full-time. Even though clear socioeconomic and political splits in Sardinian medieval society are evident, a range of ambiguous social descriptors reveal broad liminal margins between the 'unfree' *serbos* and *ankillas* and 'free' *liberus*. These include the *liberus de paniliu*, who, in spite of the name *liberus*, appear to have been granted as communal servants belonging to specific villages *de paniliu*—only attested in the *iudicato* of Cálari. Whereas the Calaritan *liberos de paniliu* appear locked into a rigid form of bonded tenancy, the Logudorese evidence—particularly the *Condaghe* of San Pietro di Silki—also records the pàperos the *pàperos*, who could accumulate modest surpluses and negotiate upward mobility, thereby blurring the boundary between servile and free status.[25] At the same level, the *colibertos* (or *colibertus*) and *liverus muniarius* are occasionally attested as those who appear to be unbound servants or as serfs closer to continental villeins. The difference, nonetheless, between *colibertos* and 'freed' people (*libertos*, also called *liberados*, *liberatos*, and *libertados*) is important, for the latter appear to have held prerogatives that the former are not attested as having, such as acting as witnesses to transactions, being part of a *corona*, and having their own legal representative (*mandatore*).[26] It would also seem that although freed servants were not acknowledged as completely free—that is to say, *liberus* without any qualifier—they had obtained a legal and political freedom that, as servants, they could have never held.

Public authority did not rest exclusively with the iudike, and each realm had its own collegiate body with both political and judicial functions. This was the *Corona de logu*, or the assembled audience of the realm. There were many other lesser *coronas* or local audiences which heard and adjudicated disputes and could be presided over by local functionaries, for the most part by a *curatore*. However, important disputes and business, and the ordinances that pertained to the entire territory, were discussed and passed on by the *Corona de logu*,

25 Alessandro Soddu, 'I *pàperos* ("poveri") nella Sardegna giudicale (XI–XII secolo): eredità bizantine, echi carolingi, peculiarità locali', *Acta Historica et Archaeologica Mediaevalia* 29 (2008), pp. 205–255; Pinuccia F. Simbula and Alessandro Soddu, 'Forme di servitù e mobilità dei servi in Sardegna nel basso Medioevo', in *Migrazioni interne e forme di dipendenza libera e servile nelle campagne bassomedievali. Dall'Italia nord-occidentale alla Catalogna*, eds R. Lluch Bramon, J.P. Garçon and P. Le Pogam (Cherasco, 2015), pp. 361–394 (at 370–372).

26 See Luciano Gallinari, 'Some voices on institutional, cultural and personal ties from within a Mediterranean island society with a Byzantine matrix: the Giudicati Sardinia (11th–14th centuries)', in *Forms of Unfreedom in the Medieval Mediterranean*, eds M.F. Lopes de Barros and C. Almagro Vidal (Évora, 2021), pp. 49–70.

over which the iudike often presided himself. This body not only acted as a court of justice, but also as a general council of *maiorales*, high prelates, and administrative functionaries with the authority to ratify acts, sentences, and agreements that concerned the entire territory or *logu*. The institution was, therefore, a keystone for governance of the *iudicatos*, and there are indications that the appointment of a iudike could be sanctioned, or even decided by election, by the *Corona de logu*.

The early iudikes of Cálari and Torres brought western monasticism to Sardinia by requesting monks from, and by makings donations to, influential monastic centres, such as Montecassino, St Victor in Marseille, and, later, to the Camaldolesi monasteries in Pisa.[27] They also exchanged correspondence with the pope as the island's rulers had done since before the time of Gregory the Great, mainly regarding the acceptability of nepotistic Sardinian practices of the rulers or Rome's claim to overlordship of the Mediterranean islands. This ecclesiastical rapprochement was not only supported by the papacy, but also by continental powers in Liguria and Tuscany who were looking to press control over the Tyrrhenian islands. Exposure to political and cultural influence from the mainland contributed to the gradual transformation of written and institutional practices, secular and religious, drawing the *iudicatos* towards the adoption of models, procedures and protocols of the Latin West, and away from Byzantine precedents.

In Cálari, we know of the existence of six iudikes before the arrival of the Tuscans and the Massa kin-group in 1188. These iudikes were part of the Gunali-Lacon dynasty, an indigenous kin-group that ruled Cálari for at least a century and a half. Iorgia de Lacon's marriage to Oberto Obertenghi, margrave of Massa, allowed a Pisan—William of Massa—to become the iudike of Cálari. His lineage, including his daughter, Benedicta de Lacon, and the marriage alliance with the house of the *iudicato* of Arborea, marked a distinct episode in terms of institutional developments in tandem with political and military rapports. The *iudicato* was thus dragged into internal disputes of the Tuscan lords which in

27 See Agostino Saba, *Montecassino e la Sardegna medioevale* (Montecassino, 1927), especially regarding early ecclesiastical and cultural links between Sardinia and the mainland. On royal patronage of monasteries beyond the island, see also Paola Serra, 'La donazione di Barisone I all'abbazia di Montecassino', in *S. Elia di Montesanto: il primo cenobio benedettino della Sardegna*, eds G. Strinna and G. Zichi (Florence, 2017), pp. 117–131. For the ecclesiastical frame within which these rulers operated, see Raimondo Turtas, 'The Sardinian Church', in *A Companion to Sardinian History*, pp. 177–214. Additionally, for an inventory of the possessions of Saint-Victor in and around Cagliari, see Édouard Baratier, 'L'inventaire des biens du prieuré Saint-Saturnin de Cagliari dépendant de l'Abbaye Saint Victor de Marseille', in *Studi storici in onore di Francesco Loddo Canepa*, 2 vols (Florence, 1959), vol. 2, pp. 41–74.

turn led to conflict between the Sardinian realms and a higher level of exposure to Pisan–Genoese rivalry. This period lasted around fifty years before the *iudicato* of Cálari was taken over and finally dismantled by the Pisans in 1258.

In the realm of Arborea, the succession of iudikes is not entirely clear, and the dynastic changes were more complex. Up to the early thirteenth century, around fifteen rulers of Arborea can be traced as the ruling houses shifted between several local and overseas families, including the Lacon, De Thori (also written Zori, Dezori etc.), the Serra, and the Aragonese Bas. Arborea was the only *iudicato* to outlive the thirteenth century becoming the sole independent Sardinian kingdom for more than a century and a half until the death of its famous ruler, Eleanor of Arborea around 1403, under whom the *Carta de logu* was promulgated. Late medieval Arborea developed into a divergent sociopolitical entity, which, without abandoning its Sardinian foundations, adapted to, and became part of, a wider changing suite of minor western European monarchies. The kingdom was ultimately subjected to the crown of Aragon by the beginning of the fifteenth century, and, upon its remains, the marquisate of Oristano was founded.

The *iudicato* of Torres also emerges from source obscurity in the second half of the eleventh century when, in 1065, Barusone the first iudike of the 'territory of Ore' (Logudoro), made a donation of churches in Sardinia to Montecassino on the south Italian mainland. Seven other iudikes of Torres are attested until the end of the twelfth century. The ruling houses included the local Lacon kin-group, together with another powerful aristocratic family that rose to power in the northern realm: the Athens. The thirteenth century witnessed a series of political convulsions, not least the pervasive conflict between Pisa and Genoa, incursions between the *iudicatos*, and the intervention of the German Hohenstaufen who, in 1238, elevated Torres to the rank of a kingdom under the suzerainty of the Holy Roman Empire. The kingdom came to an end in 1259 when queen Adelasia died without an heir and, thereafter, the political remnants of the erstwhile Torres *iudicato* were ruled by the Genoese Doria and Malaspina families and the enduring rulers of Arborea.

In the north-east of the island, the realm of Gallura was the smallest and least known of the Sardinian *iudicatos*. The documentary record for this realm is particularly thin, and the scarce sources that mention the iudikes of Gallura are all external to the island. Transactions from other *iudicatos* mention the presence of a iudike of Gallura, while papal and monastic letters provide some insights into this figure, such as the excommunication of the Gallurese '*iudex* Torquitor' by the late eleventh century. The larger corpus of surviving charters for Gallura are Pisan transactions in favour of the archbishopric and for works relating to the construction of Pisa's cathedral. There is no indica-

tion that the Sardinian eastern coast and or mountainous hinterland was very connected during the medieval period, leaving them remote from the political centres of Cálari, Torres, and Arborea. This geographical condition, which positioned Gallura closer to Corsica and the shores of Tuscany than to the rest of the Sardinian realms, facilitated the political proximity and even subordination of this *iudicato* to the papacy and to Pisa. Already by the early thirteenth century, Gallura's rulership had been taken over by the Visconti family of Pisa, who gradually placed the *iudicato* under direct Pisan control.

2 The Languages of Medieval Sardinia

Medieval Sardinian was a Romance language that had not been exposed to linguistic changes other continental Western languages had undergone as a result of the Carolingian Reform, which introduced a renovated and restored form of Latin around Europe.[28] Latin in Sardinia did not therefore occupy a prestige position in a diglossic situation vis-à-vis the local dialect as in the Latin West. Rather, in Sardinia, it co-existed alongside Byzantine Greek and Sardinian itself.[29] Besides this, the use of Latin in Sardinia was flexible, allowing a continuum between the oral and written forms of the language while also providing a high register that rivalled Greek as a key language of the Byzantine empire.[30] For its part, Greek is not thought to have been widely spoken on the island, but it nonetheless registered its presence through loan terms in both written and spoken forms.[31] Sardinia's isolation from Carolingian norms and

28 For a historical view of Sardinian, see Max Leopold Wagner, *Dizionario Etimologico Sardo*, 3 vols. (Heidelberg, 1960–1962; repr. Nuoro, 2008); Eduardo Blasco Ferrer, *Storia linguistica della Sardegna* (Tübingen, 1984).

29 For a comparative perspective on bilingualism south of the Alps, see Vera von Falkenhausen, 'Greek and Latin in Byzantine Italy (6th–11th Century)', in *A Companion to Byzantine Italy*, ed. S. Cosentino (Leiden, 2021), pp. 541–581. Cf. the early documents written in Greek with Latin letters, as discussed in Denis Feissel, 'Écrire grec en alphabet latin: le cas des documents protobyzantins', in *Bilinguisme gréco-latin et épigraphie*, eds F. Biville, J.C. Decourt and G. Rougemont (Lyon, 2008), pp. 213–230.

30 For a unique charter fragment in Byzantine Greek from Sardinia of the late sixth-early seventh century, see 'The Laudian Acts', Bodleian Library, MS. Laud Gr. fol. 227^{v}. See also, Virdis, 'Language and Vernacular Writing in Medieval Sardinia', in *The Making of Medieval Sardinia*, pp. 344–346.

31 Ignazio Efisio Putzu, 'Il repertorio linguistico sardo tra tardo-antico e alto medioevo. Un breve status quaestionis', in *Itinerando. Senza confini dalla preistoria ad oggi: studi in ricordo di Roberto Coroneo*, ed. R. Martorelli, vol. 1 (Perugia, 2015), pp. 497–518; Giulio Paulis, *Lingua e cultura nella Sardegna bizantina: testimonianze linguistiche dell'influsso*

its remote orbit of the Greek imperial world allowed the acceleration of insular vernaculars to language status by becoming the written languages of authority, a process that happened sooner than the use of written Romance elsewhere around the Latin West.[32] In good part, this was facilitated by the linguistic freedom in the provinces allowed by Constantinople, so that vernacular Sardinian came to be used as both the written and the spoken medium of public, political, and legal expression.[33] It is notable that medieval Sardinian scribes made sustained and conscious efforts to use a specific legal and administrative lexicon derived from the spoken language, which did not draw directly from precedents in either Latin or Greek.

Medieval written Sardinian also shows regional variations across the island. The Greco-Sardinian charters and the *Carte volgari*, for example, exhibited south Sardinian elements of Campidanese dialect.[34] These stand in contrast to the condaghe of San Pietro di Silki in Sassari that is marked by conservative Logudorese traits, while the condaghe of Santa Maria di Bonárcado and, later, the *Carta de Logu*, show tell-tale signs of an Arborense variety that can still be found today, *mutatis mutandis*, in the modern dialects of the Barigadu area. Unfortunately, with the exception of early administrative material in vernacular, a major obstacle for understanding medieval Sardinian is the acute absence of evidence before the 1300s. The first literary text of which we have notice is a brief and anachronistic late-thirteenth-century tale of the iudikes of Torres, the *Libellus Judicum Turritanorum*.[35] Hence, the charter material is of essential importance to historical linguists as well as to historians.[36]

---

greco (Sassari, 1983); *Studi sul sardo medioevale* (Nuoro, 1997); 'Greco e superstrati primari', in *Manuale di linguistica sarda*, eds E. Blasco Ferrer, P. Koch and D. Marzo (Berlin—Boston, 2017), pp. 104–118.

32 On the earliest evidence of the *scripta sarda*, see Armando Petrucci and Antonino Mastruzzo, 'Alle origini della *scripta sarda*: il *Privilegio Logudorese*', *Michigan Romance Studies* 16 (1996), pp. 201–214.

33 For the Latin and vernacular literary milieu, see Paolo Maninchedda, *Medioevo latino e volgare in Sardegna* (Cagliari, 2007; 2nd edn 2012). On historical sociolinguistics in medieval Sardinia, see Maurizio Virdis, 'Sociolinguistica storica nella Sardegna medievale: fra dialettologia e filologia', in *Il sardo medioevale*, eds G. Paulis, I. Putzu and M. Virdis (Milan, 2018), pp. 11–34.

34 On the earliest Cagliaritano scripts, see Maurizio Virdis, 'Le prime manifestazioni della scrittura nel Cagliaritano', in *Judicalia*, ed. B. Fois (Cagliari, 2004), pp. 45–54.

35 Patrizia Serra (ed.), *Libellus Judicum Turritanorum* (Cagliari, 2024).

36 For the linguistic profile of Sardinian, see Maurizio Virdis, 'Language and Vernacular Writing in Medieval Sardinia', and Eduardo Blasco Ferrer, *Crestomazia sarda dei primi secoli*, 2 vols (Nuoro, 2003).

3 Early Sardinian Charters and the *Carte volgari*

The earliest extant recorded transactions date from c. 1064–1066 and appeared almost simultaneously in Torres and Cálari. Although the number of eleventh-century charters is limited to around twelve (including later transcriptions), twelfth-century documents are more numerous. Scholarship remains divided regarding the origins of earlier Sardinian charters: either they were a consequence of direct Benedictine influence and intervention brought by the newly arrived monks to an island with an almost absent diplomatic and written tradition;[37] or else they were the consequence of a later phase of cultural adaptation and learning that was possible due to an earlier scribal tradition of which there is no surviving evidence, but which had gradually shifted to satisfy the legal and normative expectations of their continental counterparts.[38]

The collection of charters drafted in the late twelfth and early thirteenth centuries from the archives of the archbishopric of Cagliari, known as the *Carte volgari* can be classified into two types. First, donations made by the iudike of Cálari, and second, legal authorisations granted by the iudike to bishops (and others) for confirming donations, exchanges, purchases, and property transactions. In both types, the Church was the beneficiary, most notably the bishops and archbishop and of the three Calaritan dioceses of Barbária–Sanctu Iorgi (at Suelli), Dolia–Sanctu Pantaleu (at Dolianova), and Sulcis–Sanctu Antiogu (at Sant'Antioco). The recorded acts of the *Carte volgari* span from c. 1114/20 to 1226. Furthermore, there are additional Calaritan medieval transactions, recorded in vernacular, that can only be found today transcribed in the early modern *Liber Diversorum* of the archbishopric of Cagliari. When Arrigo Solmi published his edition of the *Carte volgari* in 1905, he integrated many of these transcriptions, including the earliest known transaction of the collection, dated to c. 1066–

---

37 On the broader discussion regarding the shape and survival of the early charter corpus, see Massimo Roncaglia, 'Le origini', in *Storia della letteratura italiana. Le origini e il Duecento*, eds E. Cecchi and N. Sapegno (Milan, 1965), p. 208; P. Merci, 'Le origini della scrittura volgare', in *La Sardegna*, vol. 1, ed. M. Brigaglia (Cagliari, 1982), pp. 11–24 (at 19); Eduardo Blasco Ferrer, 'Sardo antico', in *Manuale di linguistica sarda*, p. 119–136; Antonino Mastruzzo, 'Una postilla sarda', *Bollettino Storico Pisano* 78 (2009), pp. 169–170; Jean-Marie Martin, 'Les actes sardes (XIe–XIIe siècle)', in *L'héritage byzantin en Italie (VIIIe–XIIe siècle)*, vol. I *La fabrique documentaire*, eds J.M. Martin, A. Peters-Custot and V. Prigent (Rome, 2011), pp. 194–195. Cf. Francesco Cesare Casula, 'Sulle origini delle Cancellerie giudicale sarde', in *Studi di paleografia e diplomatica* (Padua, 1974), pp. 1–99. For the earliest Sardinian use of a monastic *clausula defensionis*—i.e., forbidding secular deposition of the abbot and reserving his successor to Montecassino—see Giovanni Strinna, 'La carta di Nicita e la *clausula defensionis*', *Bollettino di Studi Sardi* 2 (2009), pp. 7–22.

38 Strinna, 'The Earliest Charter Sources from Medieval Sardinia', pp. 314–315.

1074. We have expanded the compendium of vernacular charters by including unpublished Calaritan transumpts from the *Liber Diversorum* that relate to the eleventh, twelfth, and thirteenth centuries, and by including charters from the archives of Pisa, Genoa, and St Victor in Marseille.[39]

The history of the *iudicato* of Cálari can be periodised into two phases: before and after the Pisan intervention.[40] As such, the *Carte volgari* can also be better understood if grouped into two sets. The earliest nine charters, whose acts date from the late 1000s to c. 1150, can be contrasted to the remaining sixteen charters dating from between 1190 and 1226. None of the charters of the first set is explicitly dated, and each shares the same diplomatic format and formulae. The two eleventh-century documents of this first group were not part of the original collection (one of them being a Greco-Sardinian charter held in Marseille)[41] and they are of the more dissimilar within their set. The documents of the second group are more extensive and detailed, but they share a more stable common format and administrative lexicon. Also, most of the charters of the second group include dating clauses. Indeed, all of the thirteenth-century charters are explicitly dated. All the documents of the *Carte volgari* that survived in the archbishopric's archive have been identified, palaeographically and codicologically, as products of the late-twelfth and thirteenth century.[42]

39 See Maria Giuseppina Cossu Pinna, 'La carta pisana del 1 marzo 1230', *Biblioteca Francescana Sarda* 1 (1987), pp. 41–49; Paola Crasta, Alessandro Soddu and Giovanni Strinna, 'Un'inedita carta sardo-greca del XII secolo nell'Archivio Capitolare di Pisa', *Bollettino di Studi Sardi* 3 (2010), pp. 5–42; Henrike Haug, 'The Struggle for Sardinia in the Twelfth Century: Textual and Architectural Evidence from Genoa and Pisa', in *A Companion to Sardinian History*, pp. 215–227; Pier Giorgio Spanu, 'I possedimenti vittorini in Sardegna', in *Committenza, scelte insediative e organizzazione patrimoniale nel Medioevo* (*De Re Monastica I*), ed. L. Pani Ermini (Spoleto, 2007), pp. 245–279.

40 Cf. Corrado Zedda, 'A Revision of Sardinian History between the Eleventh and Twelfth Centuries', in *A Companion to Sardinian History*, pp. 115–140, for a revised political chronology of eleventh- and twelfth-century Sardinia focused on the central role played by the Roman Church.

41 For the critical text, linguistic reassessment, and archival contexts of this Greco-Sardinian charter, see Eduardo Blasco Ferrer, 'La carta sarda in caratteri greci del secolo XI: revisione testuale e storico-linguistica', *Revue de Linguistique Romane* 66 (2002), pp. 321–365; Lidia Perria, 'La carta sarda di S. Vittore di Marsiglia: scrittura e tradizione bizantina in Sardegna nell'età giudicale', in *Chiesa, potere politico e culturale in Sardegna dall'età giudicale al Settecento*, ed. G. Mele (Oristano, 2005), pp. 361–366; Olivetta Schena, 'La carta sarda in caratteri greci: note diplomatistiche e paleografiche', in *Sardegna e Mediterraneo tra Medioevo ed età moderna: studi in onore di Francesco Cesare Casula*, eds M.G. Meloni and O. Schena (Genoa, 2009), pp. 329–343; Benjamin Guérard (ed.), *Cartulaire de l'abbaye de Saint-Victor de Marseille*, vol. 1 (Paris, 1857).

42 Ettore Cau, 'Peculiarità e anomalie della documentazione sarda tra XI e XIII secolo', in

For this reason, all the charters of the first set (excluding our addenda) were subsequent redrafted versions of now-lost originals. This 'redrafting', as Ettore Cau proposed, may have been completed in the turbulent years of Benedicta de Lacon's rule (1214–1232), when, after iudike William of Massa, her Pisan husband died, she formed an alliance with the papacy to defend Cálari from the growing expansion of the Visconti of Pisa.[43] Fearful of incipient regime-change, the archbishop and bishops of the *iudicato* perhaps resorted to revalidating their written instruments, even fitting them to the formal expectations of continental administrative culture to help safeguard the assets and rights of their dioceses.[44] What is certain is that the *Carte volgari* of the second group were paleographically contemporary to the acts they recorded and, even if two transactions dated to between 1190 and 1200 were redrafted as well, the remaining eleven charters were made under Benedicta de Lacon.

The content of the transactions in the *Carte volgari* consists mainly of two types of granted and acquired goods: lands and servants. The lands acquired by the church ranged from large extensions of open countryside and farm complexes to smaller and more specific units of production, such as vineyards, animal herds, gardens, water supplies or threshing floors. The *servos* ('servants') mentioned in these transactions were considered as property despite the wide variety of services they owed as well as their varying degrees of agency and differing sets of responsibilities. When servants were granted, exchanged, or sold, their full names and information on their kinship were often provided, as the status of their respective parents and marriages determined their own inherited obligations and ownership, which were passed on to their children. Such records, however, offer a rich mine for prosopography of the lower social stratas as well as for complex socioeconomic critiquing of Sardinian rural communities.

Boundary clauses are common in the dispositive section of the *Carte*, and provide insights into the toponymy, rustic vocabulary, and landscapes of the region. Boundary delimitations tend to be more detailed and descriptive in the later documents of the second group. The recorded sales and pecuniary exchanges also provide illuminating details on how they used purchasing

---

Giudicato d'Arborea e Marchesato di Oristano: proiezioni mediterranee e aspetti di storia locale, Atti del I Convegno Internazionale di Studi (Oristano, 5–8 dicembre 1997), ed. G. Mele (Oristano, 2000), pp. 313–422, nos 32–35.

43 On diplomatic strategies during the subordination to Pisan rule, see Antonino Mastruzzo, 'Un "diploma" senza Cancelleria, un "re" senza regno: strategie documentarie di penetrazione coloniale in Sardegna', *Bollettino Storico Pisano* 77 (2008), pp. 1–32; id., 'Una postilla sarda', *Bollettino Storico Pisano* 78 (2009), pp. 169–171.

44 Cau, 'Peculiarità e anomalie della documentazione sarda', nos 36–38.

goods, for example, cattle or grain that were valued in monetary terms, often using the *sollus* as a unit of account, derived from the *solidus* coin. The use of actual cash currency, that is *sollus de dinaris*, for purchases is only attested in the acts of the charters of the second group, post-1190. This invites comparison with the usage of the Byzantine gold *tremissis* as a unit of account in the condaghes, even as late as the twelfth and early thirteenth centuries.

Witness lists are another key diplomatic feature of all the *Carte volgari*, which always follow the dispositive section, at the end. These lists offer valuable prosopographical information and are one of the few elements at our disposal for elucidating the nobility's kinship relationships and networks across Calaritan medieval aristocracy. Likewise, the witnesses' titles, in particular the *armentariu* ('administrator') and *logusalbadori* ('deputy') as frequently recorded, offer a view of the nobility and their higher-level functionaries across the different periods of the *iudicato*.

Attached to fifteen of the *Carte volgari* are lead seals anachronistically made in the names of Torchitorio and Salusio, the erstwhile archons of Cálari. These dynastic names are known from epigraphy that probably dates to around from the later tenth/early eleventh centuries. However, given that there was a tradition of alternating these dynastic names, they may relate to any time from the seventh/eighth century. The basic message of the seals' inscriptions is clear, and each obverse reads in Greek: 'Salusio [or Torkotorio], archon of the region of Kalari.' On the reverse is a type v Byzantine invocative monogram: 'Mother of God, help your servant!' This well known and widely diffused model in Byzantine sigillography is associated with very numerous examples from the eighth to tenth centuries, with a particular prevalence in the earlier half of that timeframe. This would suggest a dating for archons with the names of Torchitorio and Salusio to between roughly the eighth and tenth centuries. However, there is a problem. First, the documents on which they are hung are safely dated by their palaeography to the late twelfth or thirteenth century. And while their inscriptions adhere to models of that time, their weight alone is at least twice as much as a contemporary Byzantine seal of similar diameter. A full study of these seals is currently being undertaken by this volume's authors in collaboration with Marco Muresu, but it would seem that the extant *Carte volgari* seals cannot be authentic in the sense that they do not date from the period of composition as the documents to which they are appended.[45] One persuasive suggestion is that they are replicas of original and authentic seals from the

45 See Fernández-Aceves, Metcalfe, and Muresu, 'Discovery, Invention, and Supposition', pp. 35–40; see also Pier Giorgio Spanu and Raimondo Zucca, *I sigilli bizantini della Σαρδηνία* (Rome, 2004).

eighth to eleventh century that were copied and appended to the documents when they were rewritten in the late-twelfth/thirteenth centuries. Certainly, several transumpts from the 1400s and 1500s describe the presence of pendent seals—even if the scribes could not then decipher their legends or monograms. However, to dismiss the seals as unimportant on the grounds that they are inauthentic would be to undervalue their importance to both the history and the historiography of the archons-to-iudikes transition that links and spans both the Byzantine period and that of the iudikes/*reges* as more clearly autonomous rulers.

4 The Sardinian Condaghes from Torres and Arborea

A unique corpus of monastic record-keeping codices, written in vernacular and known as condaghes, compiled records of donations, purchases, exchanges, and legal disputes that involved the patrimony, both material and human, of several monasteries in the *iudicatos* of Torres and Arborea. Three condaghes are extant in the vernacular: that of San Pietro di Silki; the condaghe of Santa Maria di Bonárcado, and the condaghe of San Nicola di Trullas.[46] To these may be added the condaghe di San Michele di Salvénnor, which has come down to us in a Spanish translation from the sixteenth century, except for short fragments in Sardinian language that have come to light more recently.[47]

The condaghes recall European cartularies that collected and reproduced charters relating to the foundation, privileges, and grants of their institutions. The comparison provides a useful approximation, albeit imperfect.[48] The condaghe of San Pietro di Silki did not reproduce charters, but the condaghe from Bonárcado, on occasion, did. In their current form, the manuscripts were composed as an already established record, not as a work-in-progress compilation of diplomatic material. From time to time, we are told that the entire codex had been recopied due to its decrepit condition, for which permission was

---

46 The most recent Italian editions are by Alessandro Soddu and Giovanni Strinna (eds), *Il condaghe di San Pietro di Silki* (Nuoro, 2013); Maurizio Virdis (ed.), *Il condaghe di Santa Maria di Bonarcado* (Nuoro, 2003); Paolo Merci (ed.), *Il condaghe di San Nicola di Trullas* (Nuoro, 2001).

47 See Mauro Maxia (ed.), *Il condaghe di San Michele di Salvennor: edizione e commento linguistico* (Cagliari, 2012).

48 Cf. Bianca Fadda and Mariangela Rapetti, 'Cartulari del Mediterraneo occidentale: il caso dei condaghi sardi', in *From Charters to Codex: Studies on Cartularies and Archival Memory in the Middle Ages*, eds R. Furtado and M. Moscone (Turnhout, 2019), pp. 135–158.

sought and obtained from the iudike himself. Their script and local linguistic variations suggest that each was composed by 'in-house' monastic scribes.

The condaghes were written in book-hand, not in a chancery script. Even though they do not tend to reproduce chronicles or narrative prolegomena, as it is the case with the Abruzzese cartularies of Carpineto and Casauria, some of the acts they recorded are extensive enough to include important narrative accounts about the monastery's life and its connection to the lay authority.[49] These compendia were not exclusively legal texts or administrative records: the condaghes were also a textual space for dramatisation and for ideological legitimation, at times adding moral, emotional, and even theatrical elements in first-person speech to recorded acts and events, showing a degree of orality in their composition.[50]

The records in the condaghes are not itemised chronologically, although the most extensive ones are divided into discrete booklets that correspond to a given period, abbotship, or sister church. Nonetheless, related transactions to the same estate or town tend to be grouped together. The types most represented in these records are those of the economic act and the *notitia iudicati*, that is to say, a summarised account of a legal dispute, including the debate and the sentence pronounced at a *corona* or judicial court. However, the entries in the condaghes do not present the complete structure of a charter, but instead record an abridged version of the transaction. The focus of these entries is naturally on the dipositive section of what might have been included in the original document (if there was one) and only a handful give an *intitulatio* of the protocol or *arenga* and *narratio*. The typical Sardinian *sanctio* that is found in the *Carte volgari* and other early Sardinian charters is even rarer. Striking anathema clauses present in the *Carte volgari* can also be found in the condaghe of Bonárcado. Finally, and notably different from the European cartulary, is that barely any of the entries in the condaghes reproduce a *datatio* clause, and very few provide any indication of either the time the action had occurred or when the act was composed.

Witness lists are a common feature in the condaghes. Almost all the recorded transactions and judicial notices conspicuously included named wit-

49 Flora Di Donato, *La costruzione giudiziaria del fatto: il ruolo della narrazione nel processo* (Milan, 2008).

50 Ignazio Delogu, 'Introduzione', in *Il Condaghe di San Pietro di Silki: testo logudorese inedito dei secoli XI–XIII*, ed. G. Bonazzi. (Sassari, 1997), pp. 38–41; Ettore Cau, 'Oralità e scrittura nel Medioevo', in *La Sardegna*, vol. 1, ed. M. Brigaglia (Cagliari, 1982), pp. 5–24; Giampaolo Mele, 'I condaghi: specchio storico di devozione e delle tradizioni liturgiche nella Sardegna medievale', in *La civiltà giudicale in Sardegna nei secoli XI–XIII. Fonti e documenti scritti. Atti del Convegno Nazionale (Sassari–Usini, marzo 2001)* (Sassari, 2002), pp. 143–174.

nesses, hence revealing the legal, and symbolic, importance these actors played in the administrative–political culture as well as the collective memory of Sardinian institutions. Typically, witnesses were recorded by reference to both first- and second-name elements, and, where appropriate, they included the addition of an official title.

Boundary descriptions are present in many of the records of the condaghes as the delimitation of the church's lands was as important as attesting its contents for securing the integrity of the material asset. Brief circumscriptions were made in the form of point-to-point demarcations with references to roads, trees, plantations, threshing floors, farm complexes, ancient *nuraghi* and prehistoric dolmens, tombs, outcrops and mountain tops, hillsides, water-resources, rivers, streams and crossing points. There was no attempt to calculate the area of lands, nor was there any mention of productivity or taxable value of the plot. The boundary clauses are so generic and short that it is difficult to discern precedents for them. However, the occasional mention of a rope-length as a unit of measurement, for example, recalls a distinctively Byzantine tradition. Indeed, another precious and fleeting hint of Byzantine land-registry practice may be found in the presence of syntactical reduplication, as in the loan phrase *derectu derectu*, found on one occasion in the *Carte volgari* and several times with various nouns in a treaty of 1206 that fixed the borders of Arborea and Calari.[51] Finally, one of the richest elements found in the condaghes is the information about the *servos* ('servants'), which is far more extensive than those found in the *Carte volgari*.[52] Together with unworked land and farm complexes, servants were one of the most common and coveted possessions, perhaps especially on an island where the medieval population levels were low. We find *servos* being granted, exchanged, purchased, and carefully recorded throughout these monastic records. It is evident here that servants were fundamental and widespread drivers of the economic life of the monasteries, as they must also have been for the other primary economic actors across the island. Indeed, it is not uncommon to find entire families of servants recorded in the condaghes, and questions about their allocation and ownership are a characteristic of these documents.

---

51 For this example, see E. Blasco-Ferrer, *Crestomazia sarda*, vol. 1, pp. 77–84 (at 77). On the origins of the noun deduplication of this type, see Alex Metcalfe, 'Language and the written record: loss, survival and revival in early Norman Sicily', in *Multilingual and multigraphic manuscripts and documents of East and West*, eds G. Mandalà and I. Pérez Martín (Piscataway NJ, 2018), pp. 3–31.

52 For an illustrative case study of the *servos* in the conaghes, see Ignazio Delogu, 'Donnos, servos, appatissas e priores nella più grande "Cronaca" del Medio Evo sardo: il *Condaghe di S. Pietro di Silki*', *Sacer* 8 (2001), pp. 145–171.

5 The *Carta de Logu*

Promulgated by Eleanor of Arborea (Eleonora d'Arborea, d. c. 1403), this abiding territorial statute and criminal–legal code, which incorporates the customs of Sardinia, stands as a claim of identity for the island along with its cultural and legal tradition, not least as it was drawn up at a time of war against the Aragonese.[53] It is witnessed today by a manuscript preserved at the Biblioteca Universitaria di Cagliari,[54] produced in the third quarter of the fifteenth century, and by two incunabula of the *editio princeps*.[55] Of this, two copies are preserved: one at the Biblioteca Universitaria di Cagliari and the other at the Biblioteca Reale di Torino, both of which are part of a single edition dating from around 1480.[56] The two witnesses, although similar, are by no means the same. In particular, the printed edition, which is the result of a later revision of the late-fifteenth century under the Aragonese, incorporated the so-called *Rural Code* of Eleanor's father, Mariano IV.[57] This is absent in the manuscript version which legislates on the working and socioeconomic life of the countryside. It also contained important clauses that removed the possibility of subjection to torture in judicial inquisitions for men of good repute (*de bona fama*)—that is to say, who were from the nobility.[58] Likewise, it extended to widows, orphans and the poor the possibility of free legal aid which, in the manuscript version, was limited to religious institutions that could not afford it.

53 On Eleanor's war against the Crown of Aragon and the 1388 armistice, see Italo Bussa, 'L'armistizio tra regno d'Aragona e giudicato d'Arborea (1388)', *Quaderni Bolotanesi* 41 (2021), pp. 103–128; Alessandro Soddu, 'Il trattato di pace tra Giovanni I d'Aragona ed Eleonora d'Arborea (1388–1390)', *Pandemos* 2 (2024), pp. 1–33.

54 Biblioteca Universitaria di Cagliari, BUC 211. For a modern translation and historical commentary, see Francesco Cesare Casula, *La Carta de Logu del Regno di Arborèa: traduzione libera e commento storico* (Cagliari, 1994); cf. Jesús Lalinde Abadía, 'La "Carta de Logu" nella civiltà giuridica della Sardegna medievale', in *La Carta de Logu d'Arborea nella storia del diritto medievale e moderno*, eds I. Birocchi and A. Mattone (Rome and Bari, 2004), pp. 13–49.

55 On the manuscript witness and its textual tradition, see Giovanni Lupinu (ed.), *Carta de Logu dell'Arborea: nuova edizione critica secondo il manoscritto di Cagliari* (*BUC 211*) *con traduzione italiana* (Oristano, 2010); Giulia Murgia (ed.), *Carta de Logu d'Arborea: edizione critica secondo l'*editio princeps (BUC, Inc. 230), (Milan, 2016).

56 Biblioteca Universitaria di Cagliari, BUC Inc. 230; Royal Library of Turin, BRT Inc. I 44.

57 On the fifteenth-century revision that grafted Mariano IV's Rural Code into the printed text, see Pinuccia F. Simbula and Alessandro Soddu, 'Nuove riflessioni sulla Carta de Logu di Arborea', in *Medioevo e Mediterraneo: incontri, scambi e confronti. Studi per Salvatore Fodale* (Palermo, 2020), pp. 179–194.

58 For the Roman-law clauses on torture, widows and legal aid, see Francesco Sini, 'Influssi del diritto romano sulla "Carta de Logu" di Arborea', in *La Carta de Logu d'Arborea nella storia*, pp. 983–1012.

The *Carta* was promulgated in the last decade of the fourteenth century during a fertile period of legislative production in Sardinia which had issued the Statutes of Castelsardo, the *Breve di Villa di Chiesa*, and the Statutes of Sassari, the latter of which exerted a particular influence on the Arborense *Carta*.[59] Also, a Calaritan counterpart—the *Carta de Logu* enacted in Cálari under Pisan domination—frames these insular codifications within a wider late-medieval contest over political authority and written law.[60] The *Carta de Logu* also merged customary law of Sardinia with contributions from Roman Justinian law codes and canon law while also incorporating contemporary legal notions from the Italian mainland, especially from Tuscan Pisa.[61] It sought to order social life in both civil and criminal spheres, establishing relations between state power and people of the *judigadu*, while regulating rural, agricultural and pastoral pursuits. In this respect, it also anticipated modern 'constitutional' values of the *res publica* (*Sardescha*).[62] The *Carta de Logu* of Eleanor was itself an update of an earlier (and now lost) *Carta* of her father, Mariano IV, and the provisions of her brother, Ugone III.[63] It seems certain that there had been earlier legislative provisions that remain unknown to us, but presumably of a more embryonic form and value.

---

59 For the intellectual milieu of late-fourteenth-century Arborea, see Alessandro Soddu, 'Il *decretorum doctor* Filippo Mameli tra Papato, Regno di Ungheria e Giudicato di Arborea (XIV secolo)', *Rivista Storica Italiana* 136 (2024), pp. 888–939.

60 See Marco Tangheroni, 'La "Carta de Logu" del Giudicato di Cagliari', in *La Carta de Logu d'Arborea nella storia*, pp. 204–236. For the transition from customary to written law across the iudicati, see Angelo Aldo Castellaccio, 'I regni giudicali e il diritto statuale: le *Carte de Logu*', in *Scritti editi e inediti* (Sassari, 2022), pp. 197–212.

61 For further Roman-law borrowings in the appellate chapters, see id., 'Diritto romano nella Carta de Logu d'Arborea: i capitoli "De appellationibus" e "De deseredari"', in *Giudicato d'Arborea e Marchesato di Oristano*, pp. 983–1012; Soddu, 'Nuove riflessioni sulla Carta de Logu'. On the move from custom to written statute, and on late-medieval legislative practice, see Angelo Aldo Castellaccio, 'Il diritto della Sardegna medioevale: dalle consuetudini alla forma scritta', in *La civiltà giudicale in Sardegna nei secoli XI–XIII* (Sassari, 2002), pp. 127–142; 'I regni giudicali e il diritto statuale: le Carte de Logu', in *Scritti editi e inediti* (Sassari, 2022), pp. 197–212; Ennio Cortese, *Appunti di storia giuridica sarda* (Milan, 1964); *Il diritto nella storia medievale*, II *Il basso Medioevo* (Rome, 1995), pp. 613–620.

62 For the wider family of Sardinian urban statutes and *cartas de logu*, see Alessandro Soddu, 'Brevi, Statuti e "Cartas de logu" nella Sardegna tardomedievale', in *La libertà di decidere: Da Cento a Cento 1993–2024. Trent'anni di studi sugli statuti*, eds E. Angiolini et al (Florence, 2025), pp. 409–422.

63 On authorship and earlier redactions, see Antonio Marongiu, 'Sul probabile redattore della Carta de Logu d'Arborea', *Studi economico-giuridici della R. Università di Cagliari* 27 (1939), pp. 19–32; Salvatore Orunesu, *Quale Carta de Logu: nuove ipotesi sul codice arborense* (Lecce, 2024).

As far as language is concerned, the *Carta de Logu* was written in Sardinian of the Arborean variety and, while it had inherited a traditional oral style of Sardinian writings, it also displayed a tendency towards a fluid, articulate style, based on Italianate models with a more elaborate and arranged syntax. Ultimately, the *Carta de Logu* is a keystone in Sardinian legal and social history insofar as it is an organic text that synthesised, in an up-to-date and orderly manner, customs and previously issued provisions. It also fixed in writing the legal–administrative organisation of what could already be called 'a state' in all aspects of its social life. This dictate of the law was public and could be consulted by all. Indeed, it is important to note that the *Carta* stipulated that each *curatore* or district administrator should possess a copy. The longer-term value of the *Carta* of Arborea is reaffirmed by the fact that, after the Aragonese conquest of Sardinia, the king of Aragon maintained the *Carta* and extended it as the law for the whole of Sardinia—albeit as the law of a conquered state and subjugated people. Indeed, it remained in force after the long colonial period under Spanish rule, enduring into the Savoyard period until 1827 when a renewed code of civil and criminal law, promulgated by king Charles Felix came into force.[64] Several editions of the *Carta de Logu* were made after the fifteenth century, alongside several glosses, hermeneutic works and interpretations of the text, among which the most notable was the *Commentaria et glosa in Cartam de Logu* by Girolamo Olives, the renowned jurisconsult from Sassari, which was published in Madrid in 1567.

64 For legal and constitutional structures that bridged medieval and modern Sardinia, see Gian Giacomo Ortu, 'Establishing Power and Law in Medieval and Modern Sardinia', in *A Companion to Sardinian History*, pp. 228–251.

The Carte volgari

 | DOI:10.1163/9789004750951_003

Introduction

The corpus of documents known as the *Carte volgari* or Sardinian vernacular charters include the oldest-known medieval charters from the island. They record concessions made by the iudikes of Cálari in favour of the bishopric of Cagliari between the late eleventh and early thirteenth century. For the most part, their survival is due to repeated processes of copying and transcribing, such that most exist in late twelfth or early thirteenth-century transumpts, identifiable by their palaeography. When the bulk of the corpus was published by Arrigo Solmi in 1905, it is clear that many were more legible than they are today.[1] Indeed, some are in poor condition with signs of water damage and extensive mould. However, many also exist in accurate transcriptions made between the fifteenth and seventeenth centuries, and found in the cartulary known as the *Liber Diversorum*. Their survival allows a careful reconstruction and corroboration of the oldest material by comparison with the later copies. In some cases, a *deperditum* can be entirely recovered—with a high degree of trust—from an early modern transumpt. Given that this diplomatic corpus is essential for our understanding, *inter alia*, of the governance of the medieval Calaritan iudikes, there is good reason to preserve the documents in their fullest-known forms, as presented here. Both the *Carte volgari* and the volumes of the *Liber Diversorum* are kept in the Archivio diocesano storico di Cagliari. In the early 2020s, all these documents were digitised and fitted with citations beginning with 'DigiLib.,' thus adding a modern, but extra, level of referencing to an already complex and convoluted system. They are supplemented here by loose charters from archives in Archivio Capitolare di Pisa, the Archivio Capitolare della Chiesa di San Lorenzo in Genoa, and the Archives départementales des Bouches-du-Rhône in Marseille.

1 A. Solmi, 'Le carte volgari dell'Archivio Arcivescovile di Cagliari: testi campidanesi dei secoli XI–XIII', *Archivio Storico Italiano* 5, no. 35 (1905), pp. 278–330. Solmi's readings can be contrasted with the lacunose online edition of Marietta Falchi, which does not make full use of the later transumpts from the *Liber Diversorum* or documents from outside the Archivio diocesano di Cagliari. See www.reisar.eu/category/carte-volgari-dellarchivio-arcivescovile-di-cagliari/ [Accessed: 14 June 2024].

Document List

- *Carta volgare* 1. Transumpt. Date: c. 1066–1074.
- *Carta volgare* Suppl. A (Marseille): Greco-Sardinian. Date: c. 1081–1089.
- *Carta volgare* Suppl. B (Pisa) Greco-Sardinian. Date: c. 1107–1130.
- *Carta volgare* Suppl. C (Genoa). Date: c. 1108.
- *Carta volgare* Suppl. D (Genoa). Date: 29 June c. 1108–1109.
- *Carta volgare* 2. Date: c. 1114–1120.
- *Carta volgare* 3. Date: c. 1114–1120.
- *Carta volgare* 4. Date: c. 1121–1129.
- *Carta volgare* Suppl. E (Sant'Antioco). Date: 1124.
- *Carta volgare* 5. Date: c. 1130.
- *Carta volgare* 6. Date: c. 1130–1140. 'Authentic copy.'
- *Carta volgare* 7. Transumpt. Date: c. 1140.
- *Carta volgare* 8. Date: c. 1150.
- *Carta volgare* 9. Date: c. 1190–1200.
- *Carta volgare* 10. Date: c. 1190–1200.
- *Carta volgare* Suppl. F (Marseille). Date: c. 1190–1206.
- *Carta volgare* Suppl. G (Pisa). Date: 10 May 1211.
- *Carta volgare* 11. Date: June 1215.
- *Carta volgare* 12. Date: 30 September 1215.
- *Carta volgare* 13. Date: 6 November 1215.
- *Carta volgare* 14. Date: 7 November 1215.
- *Carta volgare* 15. Transumpt. Date: 22 May 1216.
- *Carta volgare* 16. Date: 22 February 1217.
- *Carta volgare* 17. Date: 22 February 1217.
- *Carta volgare* 18. Date: 21 March 1217.
- *Carta volgare* Suppl. H (Pisa): Date: 30 May 1225.
- *Carta volgare* 19. Date: 10 July 1225.
- *Carta volgare* 20. Transumpt. Date: 21 June 1226.
- *Carta volgare* 21. Transumpt. Date: 23 May 1226.

Texts

Carta volgare 1. Transumpt. Date: c. 1066–1074. Donation of villeins (*liberus de paniliu*) and their villages to the archbishopric of Cagliari by Trogodori de Ugunali (Orzocco-Torchitorio I), iudike of Cálari (c. 1058–1089), with his wife and son. Known from a 15th-century transumpt in the Archivio diocesano storico di Cagliari, *Liber Diversorum*, 1/I serie [A], ff. 101r–v; DigiLib., pp. 107–108. Editions: Tola, *CDS*, vol. 1, pp. 154–155; Solmi, 'Le carte volgari', no. 1, pp. 13–15; Monteverdi, *Testi volgari*, pp. 25–38; Lazzeri, *Antologia*, pp. 32–38; Blasco-Ferrer, *Crest.*, vol. 1, pp. 43–50, including a 17th-century Spanish translation by Aleo in *Sucessor generales*, ff. 304–307.

(1)Hoc est tra[n]sumptu[m] fidelit[er] su[m]ptu[m] a quada[m] carta pergamenea vetustissima (2)in li[n]gua Sardischa, c[uiu]s tenor t[a]lis e[st]: + In nomini de Pat[er] et Filiu et Sp[irit]u[m] S[anc]tu[m]. (3)Ego iudigi Trogodori de Ugunali, cum mulieri mia donna Bera et cum filiu miu (4)donnu Go[n]stantini, p[er] bolu[n]tate de do[n]nu Deu, potesta[n]du p[ar]te de Caralis, fage[mus] (5)illi custa carta p[ro] beni ki fagemus ass'archiepiscopadu n[os]tru de Caralis, (6)ad honore de Deu et in gratia de S[anc]ta Maria matrige D[omi]ni, et in g[rat]ia de S[anc]to Michali (7)archa[n]gelo, et de tota sa milicia de sus Angelus et de sus Archa[n]gelus, et i[n] g[rat]ia (8)de S[anc]tu Ioha[n]ni Baptista et o[mn]es s[anc]tos P[ro]ph[et]as, et i[n] g[rat]ia de S[anc]tu Petru princeps Ap[ostolo]rum, (9)et i[n] g[rat]ia de S[anc]tu Stephanu p[ri]mo Martiru, et i[n] g[rat]ia de S[anc]tu Saturno n[os]tru et (10)o[mne]s s[anc]ti Martires, et i[n] g[rat]ia de S[anc]ta Cecilia Virgini et o[mne]s s[anc]tos et s[anct]as Dei, ca lli dam[us] (11)ass'archiepiscobatu n[os]tru de Caralis, et p[ro] remissione dessos peccados n[os]tros et (12)de ssos maiorales dessa t[er]ra n[os]tra totu ssus liberus de paniliu cantu su[n]t p[er] totu (13)Caralis, ki servia[n]t assu archiepiscopatu n[os]tru de Caralis de tres setmanas una (14)in serbiciu cali abet voler s'archiepiscobu ki aet esser in s'archiepiscopadu in co (15)asserbiant usq[ue] m[od]o assu Re[n]nu, et serbia[n]t illi in terra et i[n] mari p[er] tota sa Sar-(16)dinga in s[er]biciu cale aet voler s'archiepiscobu ki aet e[ss]er in s'archiepiscopadu. (17)Custus lib[er]us de paniliu arint et messi[n]t et seident et trebule[n]t et i[n]cunge[n]t, (18)et fazzant o[mn]ia serbiciu et purilis et maistrus i[n] pedra et i[n] calcina et in ludu (19)et in li[n]na et i[n] o[mn]ia fatu ka[n]tu ad esser opus ass'archiepiscopadu. Et no[n] ausit s'archi-(20)episcopu ki aet esser p[ro] te[m]p[or]ale a llebarillis aliu et no[n] fazant messas mulieres (21)issoru et no[n] disponiat pastores kena fachi issoru. Et totu custu serbiciu fage[n]ta (22)fina ad icomo ad su R[en]nu. Et sunt sas villas, ubi sunt ad istari sus lib[er]us (23)de paniliu: sa villa de S[anc]ta Ilia. Et Quartu Iossu. Et S[anc]ta Maria de Paradisu (24)Et villa dearchiep[iscop]o

Carta volgare 1. Transumpt. Date: c. 1066–1074. Donation of villeins (*liberus de paniliu*) and their villages to the archbishopric of Cagliari (Caralis) by Trogodori de Ugunali (Orzocco-Torchitorio I), iudike of Cálari (c. 1058–1089), with his wife and son. Known from a 15th-century transumpt in the Archivio diocesano storico di Cagliari, *Liber Diversorum*, 1/I serie [A], ff. 101r–v; DigiLib., pp. 107–108. Editions: Tola, *CDS*, vol. 1, pp. 154–155; Solmi, 'Le carte volgari', no. 1, pp. 13–15; Monteverdi, *Testi volgari*, pp. 25–38; Lazzeri, *Antologia*, pp. 32–38; Blasco-Ferrer, *Crest.*, vol. 1, pp. 43–50, including a 17th-century Spanish translation by Aleo in *Sucessor generales*, ff. 304–307.

(1)This is a copy faithfully taken from a very old parchment charter (2)in the Sardinian language, the content of which is as follows: + In the name of the Father, the Son, and the Holy Spirit. (3)I, iudike Trogodori de Ugunali, with my wife lady Bera and my son (4)lord Gostantine, by the will of Lord God, ruling Caralis' territory (*parte*), (5)write them this charter for benefices we make to our archbishopric of (6)Caralis for the honour of God and in the grace of Holy Mary, Mother of the Lord, and in the grace of St Michael the Archangel (7)and all the Host of Angels and Archangels, and in the grace (8)of St John the Baptist and all the Holy Prophets, and in the grace of St Peter, first of the Apostles, (9)and in the grace of St Stephen, the first Martyr, and in the grace of our St Saturnus and (10)all the Holy Martyrs, and in the grace of St Cecilia the Virgin, and all the holy men and women of God!

We grant (11)to our archbishopric of Caralis, for the remission of our sins and for those (12)of the major lords (*maiorales*) of our land, all the *paniliu* villeins (*liberus de paniliu*) who live throughout (13)Caralis so they may serve our archbishopric one in [every] three weeks, (14)serving the archbishop in whatever he may wish in the archbishopric, in the same way as (15)they serve the realm. They shall give him service on land and sea, across all (16)Sardinia, serving the archbishop in whatever he may wish in the archbishopric. (17)These *paniliu* villeins shall till, reap, thresh, and gather, (18)and do all the services, whether apprentice or master in stone, mortar, clay, (19)or wood or in any other work for the archbishopric. (20)The archbishop should not dispose of them seasonally and take them somewhere else, nor should he make their women (21)reap or displace shepherds from their work. All this service is to be done (22)in this way for the realm.

The villages where the *paniliu* villeins are and dwell: (23)the village of Sancta Ilia (Santa Igia), and Quarto Iossu (Quartu Sant'Elena), and Sancta Maria de Paradisu, (24)and the village of the archbishop, Tolostrai, and the village

de Tolostrai. Et issa villa de Sancta Agatha de Zulkes. Et (25)Bau de Ca[n]nas. Et Marga[n]ni. Et Barau de Murakessus. Et issa villa de S[anc]ta (26)Agatha de Rutulas. Et damus illas custas villas c[um] ho[m]i[n]es cantu sunt et (27)cantu aent esser ad istari i[n]tru de custas billas p[ro] cantu adi durari su segulu. (28)Et dam[us] illas custas billas cu[m] fundame[n]tus et saltus, aquas et padrus et (29)domestigas et semidas et binias quantu se apartenet (a billas cu[m] fundame[n]tus (30)et saltus, aquas et padrus)[2] apusti custas villas, qui ll'apat s'archiepiscopadu de (31)Caralis cantu a durari su segulu. Et custu ordiname[n]tu fagemus i[n] manu (32)dess'archiepiscobu n[os]tru maistru Alfrede, et cu[m] bolu[n]tate de sus ep[iscop]os n[ost]ros et (33)de totu su clericadu, et de totu ssus maiorales fr[at]es n[ost]ros de Caralis. Et no[n] de-(34)bea[n]t serbire custus lib[er]us de panilio assu Re[n]nu, et ni a curadore, et ni a ar-(35)me[n]tario, et ni a maiori de scolca et ni a genezzario farce turbet tres arro-(36)batias de arari et tres de messari assu Re[n]nu. Et si benit p[ru]inas in sa t[er]ra, (37)de[n]t dato et opera. [Et] de curatore ki lli aet gittari i[n] iusticia, ki ssiat i[n] boli[n]tadi dess'ar-(38)chiep[iscop]o ki aet esser a po[n]ner curadores et maiores suos i[n] totas billas dessus (39)paniliu[s]. Et no[n] apat ausanzia Iudice et ni[n] Do[n]na et ni[n] nullo h[om]i[n]e carnale ki (40)pus nos aet e[ss]er, a llebarinde dessos líberos de panilio cantu sunt et cantu (41)ae[n]t e[ss]er, a poniri[n]de su serbiciu suu p[er]unu et ni a prearinde kena bolu[n]tate (42)dess'archiep[iscop]u, et no[n] ausent intrare p[er]unu curatore et ni[n] p[er]unu maiore de-(43)ssu Rennu ad iudigare, et ni a preare in istas villas de panilio kena bolu[n]tate (44)dess'archiep[iscop]o, daba si non bolet ma[n]dare h[o]m[in]e suo s'archiep[iscop]o a preare ki siat sa prea, (45)aut p[ro] morti d'omine, aut p[ro] sas op[er]as, aut p[ro] parime[n]tu de kertu. Custu fagimus et confirmamus ad honorem Dei et S[anc]te Marie matrige D[o]m[inis] et de totu ssus s[anc]tos, (46)et p[ro] remissione dessos peccados n[os]tros et de pare[n]tes n[ost]ros. Et no[n] appat au-(47)sanzia Iudiki et ni Donna et ni p[er]unu h[o]m[ini] carnali ad isbertere custu ormi[n]iu (48)k'aemus fattu pro do[n]nu Deu et p[ro]ssas an[im]as n[os]tras et de pare[n]tes nostrus, (49)et ka fudi minimadu s'archiepiscopadu de p[ru]inas ki be[n]int in sa t[er]ra, li fegimus (50)custu beni. Et sunt desti[m]onius, donnigellu Zerkis et donnigellu Gomita, Gosta[n]tine (51)de Rubo logusalbatori, et totu sa t[er]ra n[os]tra de Caralis. Ki l'aet devertere, (52)appat anathema daba Pat[er] et Filiu et S[anc]tu Sp[irit]u, daba .XII. Apostolos et daba (53).IIII. Evva[n]gelistas, daba .XVI. P[ro]ph[eta]s, daba .XXIIII. Seniores, daba .CCCXVIII. (54)S[anc]tos Patres, et sorti appat cu[m] Iuda in inferno inferiori. Fiat. Fiat. Ame[n].

2 *a billas cu[m] fundame[n]tus et saltus, aquas et padrus* is struck through with a single line.

of Sancta Agatha de Zulkes, and (25)Bau de Cannas ('ford of reeds'), Marganni, Barau de Murakessus, and the village of Sancta (26)Agatha de Rutulas. We grant these villages with as many villeins (*homines*) as there are and (27)will be, such that they dwell within these villages till the end of time. (28)We grant these villages together with real estate (*fundamentus*), unworked lands (*saltus*), water resources, meadows, (29)farmsteads, enclosed lands (*semidas*), and as many vineyards (30)as belong to these villages, so that the archbishop of (31)Caralis has them till the end of time. We put this order in the hands (32)of our archbishop, Maistru Alfrede, with the consent of our bishops and (33)of all the clergy and of all the lords of Caralis, our brothers.

And (34)let not these *paniliu* villeins provide service to the realm (*rennu*), nor to a curator (*curador*), nor to an (35)administrator (*armentario*), nor to heads of the ward (*maiori de scolca*), nor to a iudike's supervisor (*genezzario*), unless they owe the realm three [days of] farming obligations of (36)ploughing (*arrobatias de arari*) and three of sowing. If the land becomes barren, (37)they shall provide manual labour. Concerning the curator who can summon them to justice, let (38)the archbishop, by his own will, appoint his curators and heads (*maiores*) in all villages (39)of the *paniliu* villeins. No iudike, nor lady [of the realm], nor other mortal man (40)who may succeed us, shall dare remove those *paniliu* villeins, however many there are and (41)will be, in order to make use of their services or to remove them without the permission (42)of the archbishop! No curator nor leading functionary (43)of the realm (*maiore dessu rennu*) shall dare enter to arbitrate or make confiscations in these *paniliu* villages without the permission (44)of the archbishop if the archbishop does not want to send one of his men to take something away, whatever the seizure may be, either because (45)of a man's death or for work or regarding the settlement of a dispute. We issue and confirm this for the honour of God and Holy Mary, Mother of the Lord, and of all the saints, (46)and for the remission of our sins and of those of our relatives. (47)And no iudike nor lady [of the realm], nor any mortal man, shall dare controvert this order that we have issued (48)for God our Lord and for our souls and those of our relatives! (49)Since the assets of the archbishopric had deteriorated due to the barrenness that occurs in the soil, we have granted him (50)this benefit.

The witnesses are *donnigellu* Zerkis, and *donnigellu* Comita, Gosantine (51)de Rubo the deputy (*logusalbadori*), and all our land (*terra*) of Caralis. Whosoever dares to controvert it, (52)may the Father and the Son and the Holy Spirit curse him, and the twelve Apostles, (53)the four Evangelists, the sixteen Prophets, the twenty-four Elders, and the 318 (54)Holy Fathers, and may he have his lot with Judas in the depths of Hell! Let it be! Let it be! Amen.

Carta volgare Suppl. A (Marseille): Greco-Sardinian. Date: c. 1081–1089. Donation of landed properties along with male and female servants to the church of San Saturnino in Cagliari by Trogotori de Ugunali (Orzocco–Torchitorio I), iudike of Cálari (c. 1058–1089). Archives départementales des Bouches-du-Rhône, Fond Saint-Victor, 1 H 88, no. 427, Greca. Editions: Blancard & Wescher, 'Charte sarde', pp. 255–267; Monteverdi, *Testi volgari*, pp. 34–36; Lazzeri, *Antologia*, pp. 50–58; Blasco-Ferrer, 'La carta', pp. 321–365; Blasco-Ferrer, *Crest.*, vol. 1, pp. 51–62.

(1)Ην (ν)όμ(ινη) δε πάτρη ετ φιλ(ιο ε) σσάντω ἡσσπίιτο. Εγω, ἰούδ(ικι Σαλουση, περ βολουντ)άτε δε δόννου Δ(εου ποτεστ)ανδω πάρτη δε (2)Κ(αραλης) κ(ουν) Κα(μπι)δ(ανου δε Πλουμίνους, ισκρί)σσι ιστα καρτα πρὸ καωσα κη δέδητι πά-(3)τρε μιου ἰούικι Τρογ(ο)τόρη ἀ σάντου Σατουρνη (...) κη σα δοννιλακια σοῦα δε Κουσω κο(υ)ν σέρβους σούους, (4)ἐ κουν α(ν)κίλας σούας, ἀ Φοράτου Κορσου κ(ουν μουλ)ἰέρε σοῦαμ, ε κου(ν φ)ίλιους σούους, σενε Σοφία κη λασσέ(ι) (5)λίβερα πρὸ ανημα δε φίλια μια δόννα Ἑλένη, ε δο(λι ...) α τΤολ(...)ελο, ἐ α μουλιέρε σοῦα ἐ α φίλιους σού(ους) (6)ἐ α μουλέρη σοῦα, ε α φίλι(α) (...)αβ(.), ἐ δόλη βερβεκάριου ἀ τΤουρβηνῆ Κεκερέος (7)ἐ α μουλιέρε σοῦα ἐ α φίλιους σούους, ἐ α Γιάνη (8)Ὀρκεσό ἐ λλάτους δὲ φίλιους σούους κ(η), φούητι (...)λο, σούα λίβερα (δ)ε Μοντισούνου σουπερ Κλουκαβία λα-(9)τους ἀ ησα μάμα, ἐ α Φοράτα Κορσου, φίλια (δε) Κωσταντίνου Κόρσου, ἐ Κόμητα Κόκκας φίλιο δε (10)Κωνσταντίνη Κόκκας. Ε δολη βήνια ην Τέρτριω ε (η)σα δομίστι(α) δε Κανάλε δὲ Τούφου, ἐ ην παρτζόνε (11)κάντου άπω ήν Σετζάλε έ ην Τέρτριω, ε σάλτο ἐδ ἄουσα ἐ ττέρτα ἀκατόρια κή ἄπω ἀβ ἄωα μία (12)δόννα Γεωργία δε Σετζάλε κ(η) πάρτ(ζ)ω κουν φράτες μίους, ἐ ησα δομεστία δε Γρ(εγωρη) δε άκκουα (13)τόττα κάντου άπο, ε ησα δομεστία μία δε Κάστρω δε Μουγέτη, ἐ πλάτζας δὲ δον(ν)ιλέλου Πέτρου (14)κη σσούνου ἄντε κλήσια δε σάντου Σατούρνη, ἐ δομεστία δε Κελλάριους κή μι τραμουτέη, ἐδ ἄργιο-(15)λας κή σούντου σοῦπρα δόνν(ι)λάλια δὲ Κλούσω, ε παρτζόνες μίας κή παρτζω κουν Τζέργις δε (16)Γουνάλη ή Πλάταγες ἐ ην Κούρβας. Ἐ δόλλη σέμητα δε Κανάλη δε Σίνναη κη φούη δάόυ μέου (17)ἰουδικε Μαριάνη, ἐ δε ητίλλα φράττε μέου (δοννου) Γουνάρη ἀ τΤορβεννὴ δὲ Κούρκας, ε σσε καστη(κατ) κοῦσ-(18)α σέμητα δάβα πράδη ἐ δαβα βου(ρ)δουρι ε (...)ελκέρε, ἐ δαβα σίτη. Ετ έγω ἰούδικε (19)Σαλούση πρὸ ἀμάντζα δὲ πάτρε μέου δέηλλ(ηβι)λλα δε Τουρβενὴ δε Κοῦρκασο α Νησασέλη (ε) σέμιτα (20)μία δε Τηρία κη φούητι δε ρεν(ν)ου δε αρμενταρι(ου), εδ ἀπασίνδε πρόδε σάντου Σάτούρνου ἐ κόνδε (21)μανδετέ κουν πανήλιου δὲ Σίνναη κουν (σερβ)ίτζιου, ε σσίαντα ην μάνους δὲ δόννου (22)Δέου, ε σίατ ίλλης δουλίας ἰούδικη, ε σιαντα ην (μαν)ους δὲ (π)ρεσβήτερε κι αετ έσερε. Ε

Carta volgare Suppl. A (Marseille): Greco-Sardinian. Date: c. 1081–1089. Donation of landed properties along with male and female servants to the church of San Saturnino in Cagliari by Trogotori de Ugunali (Orzocco–Torchitorio I), iudike of Cálari (c. 1058–1089). Archives départementales des Bouches-du-Rhône, Fond Saint-Victor, 1 H 88, no. 427, Greca. Editions: Blancard & Wescher, 'Charte sarde', pp. 255–267; Monteverdi, *Testi volgari*, pp. 34–36; Lazzeri, *Antologia*, pp. 50–58; Blasco-Ferrer, 'La carta', pp. 321–365; Blasco-Ferrer, *Crest.*, vol. 1, pp. 51–62.

(1)In the name of the Father, the Son, and the Holy Spirit. I, iudike Salusi, by the will of Lord God, ruling over the territory (*Parti*) of (2)Karalis with Campidanu (Campidano) de Pluminus, wrote this charter for the assets that (3)my father iudike Trogotori gave to Santu Saturni (San Saturno in Cagliari) [...] that his domain (*donnicalia*) of Cluso with his servants (*serbus*) (4)and female servants (*ankilas*); Foratu Corsu with his wife and children, without Sofia whom I made (5)free (*libera*) for the soul of my daughter lady Eleni; and Doli[...] a To[...]elo, and his wife and children; and sScarfaru (6)and his wife and daughter [...]ab[.]. And I give the shepherd (*berbecarius*) tTourbini Kekereos (7)and his wife and children, and Costafu CKorsu (8)and his wife and children, and Giani (9)Orkeso and half (*llatus*) of his children who were [...]lo, his free woman (*libera*) from Montisunu beyond Clucabia [and] half-(10)share of her mother, and Forata Corsu daughter of Constantinu Corsu, and Comita Coccas son of (11)Constantini Koccas.

I give a vineyard in Tertrio and the farmstead (*domistia*) of Canale de Tufu, and the share (*partzone*) of what I have (12)in Setzale and in Tertrio, and the unworked land (*salto*), water resource (*acua*) and ploughed land (*aratoria*) that I have from my grandmother, (13)lady Georgia de Setzale, which I share with my brother, and all that I have at the farmstead of Gregori de Accua, and my farmstead of Castro de Mugeti ('fortress of Mugeti'), and the landed plots (*platzas*) of donnikelu Petru (14)that are in front of the church of Santu Saturni, and the farmstead of Kellárious that I exchanged, and the threshing (15)floors (*ariolas*) that are on the domain (*donnicalia*) of Cluso, and my shares that I divide with Tzergis de (16)Gunali in Platages and in Curvas.

I also give the enclosed land (*semita*) of Canali at Sinnai, which was that of my grandfather, (17)iudike Mariani, and which my brother, lord Gunari, gave to Torbenni de Curcas. This (18)farm land is protected from scrubs and wild bushes and [...] and drought. And I, iudike (19)Salusi, for the love of my father, give the village (*villa*) of Turbeni de Curcaso to Niaseli, and my farm land (20)of Tiria that was of the realm's administrator (*rennu de armentariu*). I have endowed Santu Saturnu and bestowed it (21)with the *paniliu* villeins of Sinnai in service (*serbitziu*), [it now] being in the hands of Lord (22)God, under the power (*dulias*) of the iudike and in the hands of the priest, whoever he

ἠνπερ(α)τόρ(η) κι λ'α-(23)τη κασστικάρη ἤστα δελεγάντζια ἐ φάγερε κάντου νάρατ ἤστα κάρτα, σίατ βενεδίττου (24)δάβα Δέους ἐ δαβα σσάντα Μαρία, ε δαβ(α σσαντ)ου (Σα)τουρνου. Εδ ες τεστιμόνιους δον(ν)ικέλου Μαριάνη (25)δον(ν)ικέλου Ὀρζόκορ, δον(ν)ικέλου Τζέργις λόκουσαλ(βα)τόρη, δον(ν)ικέλου Κομητὰ, δον(ν)ικι Γουρνάρη, δο-(26)ν(ν)ικέλου Πέτρου, δον(ν)ικέλου Τουρβενὼ, δον(ν)ικέλου Μαριάνη, δον(ν)ικέλου Τρογοτόρη. Ἐ κη λ'ατ α ἠνβέρτερε (27)άπατα ἀνάθεμα ἀβα Πάτρη ἐδ Φίλιου ε σΣπήριτου σάντου Μάρια ἐ δὲ δώδεκη α-(28)πόστολους ἐ ΙS προφέτας, ΚΔ σενιούρες, Τ(ΙΗ) σάντο(υς) πάτρες, ε σσόρτη κουν Ιούδα τραδιτόρη. (29)Φίατ. Φίατ. Ἄμεν. Ἐ φάτζαντα μίσσας σοῦας πρὸ άνημα δὲ πάτρη μέου (30)ἰουδικε Ὀρτζόκορ α σσάντου Σατούρνου ην (ησας) δίες δε αγούσου κάντου φούτι μόρτου, ἐ ἀ να-(31)τάλε δὲ σάντου Σατούρνου, ἐ ἀ ννατάλε Δομηνου, (ε Α) σσάβ(α)το δε καρρισεκ(άρη ε α) λλουνις δὲ-(32)πους Πάσχα πιτζῖν(ν)α ἐ δε τόττα (η)σ'άττερα κάωσα, ε (φ)άτζαντ σερβίτζιο (α)ντε δὲ Δ(εου)ς ἐ ππρο σσέδε-(33)η σάντα δε κλήσια. Ἄμην, γένοιττο, γενοιτο.

Carta volgare Suppl. B (Pisa): Greco-Sardinian. Date: c. 1107–1130. Charter fragment recording permission granted by Trogudori de Gunali (Mariano-Torchitorio II), iudike of Cálari (1108–1130), and his daughter, to Gosantine Frau to draw up a deed of purchase made between them for a landed plot. Archivio Capitolare di Pisa, Fondo Diplomatico, no. 69. Edition: Crasta, Soddu and Strinna, 'Un'inedita carta', pp. 33–38.

(1)+ Ηνομην δε Πατερ ετ Φηλησυ ετ σαντου Ησπη-(2)ρητου. Εγυο ηουδηγη Τρογυοδορη δε Γυναλη ξουμ (3)φηλησ μηα δυοννα Ηυργια δε Ξυορη, περ βουλην-(4)ταδη δε δυοννου Δεου ποτεστανδου παρτη (5)δε Γαλαρης, ασσυολβουλλου α Γυοσαντηνη Φραου. Ε (6)δεου Γυοσαντηνη Φραου, κυμλ(*corr.* κυμ) λεβανδου ασσουλ-(7)τουρα δαβα σσου δυοννου μηυ ηουδηγη Τρυογυο-(8)δορη δε Γουναλη, κη μη λλου καστηγηδη δυον-(9)νου Δεου βαλαγος αννος ετ βονους α ησση ετ (10)δα (*corr.* α) φη‹λησ›ς σουας, φαξουμη καρτα πρυο γονπορα καν-(11)του φεγη κουμ μουλλγερη μηα Ησπηλουρξα δε (12)Υργυ: κυονπορεηλλη α Φουραδα δε Υργυ τερρα δε (13)πλαξα θ' βηργας α λλονγυ ετ ζ' a λλαδου τενε-(14)νδυ α πλαξα μηα ετ δεηνδελλη α' βακυονι (15)ε α' μογηυ δε τρηηγυ ετ κλονπηλλη παργιαρη. (16)Αντε στημονγιυς Μαργηανη δε Σεερης μαιο-(17)ρη δε σκολκα, Μουντανεσου μαηορη δε βηλ-(18)λα, Τρυογυοδυορη Μυρηα. Ε κονπορεηλλη α Γυο-(19)σαντ[ηνη .... ετ α φ]ραδης σουους Β[......]

might be. May the ruler (*inperatori*) who will (23)protect this concession and does that which the charter states, be blessed (24)by God, Holy Mary, and St Saturnus!

The witnesses are *donnikelu* Mariani, (25)*donnikelu* Ortzocor, *donnikelu* Tzergis the deputy (*locusalbatori*), *donnikelu* Comita, *donniki* Gunari, *donnikelu* (26)Petru, *donnikelu* Turbeno, *donnikelu* Mariani, and *donnikelu* Trogotori.

Whoever dares to controvert it, (27)may the Father and the Son and the Holy Spirit curse him, and the twelve (28)Apostles, the four Evangelists, the sixteen Prophets, the twenty-four Elders, and the 318 Holy Fathers, and have his lot with the traitor Judas! (29)Let it be! Let it be! (*fiat, fiat*) Amen. Also, [they are] to hold Masses (*missas*) for him for the soul of my father, (30)iudike Ortzocor at Santu Saturnu during the days of August when he died; on the birthday of St Saturnus; at (31)Christmas; on Saturday of Carnival, and (32)Easter Monday (*Pasca Pitzinna*) or for any other reason. Also, may the service owed (*serbitzio*) be done before God and for the (33)Holy See of the Church. Amen! Let it be! Let it be! (*genoitto, genoito*).

Carta volgare Suppl. B (Pisa): Greco-Sardinian. Date: c. 1107–1130. Charter fragment recording permission granted by Trogudori de Gunali (Mariano-Torchitorio II), iudike of Cálari (1108–1130), and his daughter, to Gosantine Frau to draw up a deed of purchase made between them for a landed plot. Archivio Capitolare di Pisa, Fondo Diplomatico, no. 69. Edition: Crasta, Soddu and Strinna, 'Un'inedita carta', pp. 33–38.

(1)+ In the name of the Father, the Son, and the Holy Spi-(2)rit, amen. I, iudike Trogodori de Gunali, (3)with my daughter lady Iurgia de Zori, by the will (4)of Lord God, ruling the territory (5)of Garalis (Cálari), grant permission to Gosantini Frau. And (6)I, Gosantine Frau, with permission (7)from my lord, iudike Trogo-(8)dori de Gunali—may the Lord (9)God protect him for me for many good years, him and (10)his daughters!—make a charter regarding a purchase which (11)I made with my wife Ispilurza de (12)Urgu. I bought from Furada de Urgu a plot (13)of land, nine poles long and seven wide, adja-(14)cent to my plot. I gave him one [cured piece of] ham (15)and one bushel of wheat, and I completed the payment (16)before the witnesses Mariani de Seeris, head (17)of the ward (*maiore de skolka*); Muntanesu, head of the vi-(18)llage (*maiori de billa*); and Trogodori Muria. Also, I bought from Go-(19)san[tini] [...] [and from his b]rothers B[...]

Carta volgare Suppl. C (Genoa).[3] Date: c. 1108. Donation of the church of San Giovanni Battista at Assemini made by Trogotori de Gunali (Mariano-Torchitorio II), iudike of Callari (1108–1130), with his son, Constantini, to the church of San Lorenzo at Genoa, and renewal of a promise of an annual pound of gold. Transcription in a 13th-century cartulary from the Archivio Capitolare della Chiesa di San Lorenzo di Genova: PA, cc. 17b–18a (34b–35a); PB, cart. 9b, 2; duplicate in PA, cc. 18a (35a–35b); PB, c. 9b, 3. Edition: Tola, *CDS*, vol. 1, pp. 180–181 (from PB); *Liber Privilegiorum*, by Puncuh, *Liber Privilegiorum*, no. 35, p. 53 (from PA); duplicate: no. 36, p. 54 (from PA).

In nomine Dei Patris, et Filii, et Spiritus Sancti. Ego Iudice Trogotori de Gunali cum filio meo domnu Constantini per voluntate de domnu Deus, potestando parte Karalis, fazo custa carta pro S. Joanne de Arsemin, qui dabo ad sancto Laurentio de Ianua pro Deus, et pro anima mea, et de parentes meos, et pro una libra de auro qui plagitara ad sanctum Laurentium ad dari omni anno; et non capat ausantia Imperatore et executore, non una persona ad deverter ista carta chi ordine ego pro Deus, et pro anima mea, et de muliere mea domna Preciosa de Lacon. Et sunt testimonios domnicello Cerchius, et domnicello Orzocho locu Salvatore, et ser Guido Ruffo [*corr.* Russo?], et ser Otto Fornario. Et chi la deberteret capata anathema dab Patri et Filio et Sancto Spiritu, dab XII Apostolos, et quatuor Evangelistas, et XVI prophetas, et XX Seniores, dab CCCXVIII Patres Sanctos, et sorte cum Juda in inferno. Fiat, et fiat, amen, amen.

Carta volgare Suppl. D (Genoa). Date: 29 June c. 1108–1109. Exchange made by Trogotori de Gunale, also known as Marianus (Mariano-Torchitorio II), iudike of Cálari (1108–1130), with his wife Pretiosa de Lacon and son, Constantini, with the church of San Lorenzo in Genoa of farm complexes with appurtenances and servants in Quarto, Capoterra and Acquafredda. Transcription in a 13th-century cartulary from the Archivio Capitolare della Chiesa di San Lorenzo di Genova: PA, cc. 18a–18b (35b–36a); PB, cc. 9b–10a. Edition: Tola, *CDS*, no. 6, p. 181 (from PB, with some reference to PA); Puncuh, *Liber Privilegiorum*, no. 37, pp. 54–55 (from PA), on which the following reading is also based.

In nomine Patris et Filii et Spiritus Sancti. amen. Ego iudice Trogotori de Gunale, qui Marianus vocor, per voluntatem Dei potestando parte de Karalis, et cum muliere mea Preciosa de Lacon, et cum filium meum donnu Constantini,

3 Transcription based on Archivio Capitolare della Chiesa di San Lorenzo di Genova, version PB.

Carta volgare Suppl. C (Genoa).[4] Date: c. 1108. Donation of the church of San Giovanni Battista at Assemini made by Trogotori de Gunali (Mariano-Torchitorio II), iudike of Callari (1108–1130), with his son, Constantini, to the church of San Lorenzo at Genoa, and renewal of a promise of an annual pound of gold. Transcription in a 13th-century cartulary from the Archivio Capitolare della Chiesa di San Lorenzo di Genova: PA, cc. 17b–18a (34b–35a); PB, cart. 9b, 2; duplicate in PA, cc. 18a (35a–35b); PB, c. 9b, 3. Edition: Tola, *CDS*, vol. 1, pp. 180–181 (from PB); *Liber Privilegiorum*, by Puncuh, *Liber Privilegiorum*, no. 35, p. 53 (from PA); duplicate: no. 36, p. 54 (from PA).

In the name of the Father, the Son, and the Holy Spirit. I, iudike Trogotori de Gunali, with my son lord Constantini, by the will of Lord God, ruling Karalis' territory (*parte*), make this charter for San Joanne de Arsemin (Assemini), which I gave to San Laurentio de Ianua (San Lorenzo di Genova), for God, and for my soul, and for those of my relatives, for one pound of gold that San Lorenzo had pledged to give every year. May no ruler (*imperatore*), functionary (*executore*) or anyone controvert this charter that I order for God and for my soul, and for that of my wife, lady Preciosa de Lacon! The witnesses are: *domnicello* Cerchius; *domnicello* Orzocho, deputy (*locu salvatore*); Guido Ruffo (or Russo?); and lord (*ser*) Otto Fornario. Whosoever dares to controvert it, may the Father and the Son and the Holy Spirit curse him, as well as the twelve Apostles, the four Evangelists, the sixteen Prophets, the twenty-four Elders, and the 318 Holy Fathers, and have his lot with Judas in Hell! Let it be done and be done! Amen. Amen.

Carta volgare Suppl. D (Genoa). Date: 29 June c. 1108–1109. Exchange made by Trogotori de Gunale, also known as Marianus (Mariano-Torchitorio II), iudike of Cálari (1108–1130), with his wife Pretiosa de Lacon and son, Constantini, with the church of San Lorenzo in Genoa of farm complexes with appurtenances and servants in Quarto, Capoterra and Acquafredda. Transcription in a 13th-century cartulary from the Archivio Capitolare della Chiesa di San Lorenzo di Genova: PA, cc. 18a–18b (35b–36a); PB, cc. 9b–10a. Edition: Tola, *CDS*, no. 6, p. 181 (from PB, with some reference to PA); Puncuh, *Liber Privilegiorum*, no. 37, pp. 54–55 (from PA), on which the following reading is also based.

In the name of the Father, the Son, and the Holy Spirit. I, iudike Trogoroti de Gunali, who is called Marianus, by the will of Lord God, ruling Karalis' territory (*partem*), and with my wife lady Pretiosa de Lacon, and with my son lord

4 Transcription based on Archivio Capitolare della Chiesa di San Lorenzo di Genova, version PB.

facio carta ad Sancto Laurentio pro tramuta chi facio per sas domos chillis dera cando, migi tortarant. Et ego cum bulintate de clericus meus et de fratres meos, et de totu logu daulis sas missas de donnicella Maria; et isus cum bolintate de su piscopu de Genua et de su prepositu et de totu clerus de sa calonica, et de sus consulus, et de totu sus gomuni de Genua simi danti; cusas utres domos a Quartu, et a Caputerra, et Aquafrigida cum serbos et ancillas et saltu et semita et culia de custas tres domos, qui mi danti sine centu porcos da Quartu et daulis, et Aquafrigida a Constantini Cirinda cum filios suos, et Iani Buca et Mariani Zapula, et duas sorres suas, et Constantini de Camarada et Gunnari Zapulu cum sorre sia, et Mariani Zapuladu et Albuchi Zapulu et isus derunt mi a Cumita de Nuchis cum muliere sua, et filios suos, et Maria Zapulu, et ego daulis a Sebazu et a Pau et a Barrala et Tracasil et a Fucilla et Sancta Bictoria de Billa Pupuci cum servos et ancillas, et cum mansiones et saltus et semitas et omnia cantu bi pertinet ad icussas domos. Et istas domos chillis dau non siant in manu de curatore, aut per alius a fatu donnicu si non aserbiri a sas clesias a chillis dau de Sanctu Laurentiu, et siant dare casu in quo furunt sas chillis dera, et si ponet aliquis certu decertarindi mecum, et binchimmi, de torraris sas domos chi mi derunt. Et sunt testimonios: donnicellu Cerchis, et Arzoco de Lacun, curatore de Zulchis, Arzoco de Ruco, Furatu de Gunale et Comita de Gunale, Arzoco de Curcas, Comita Castai, Comita de Arzedi, Torbeni de Curcas, Cerchis de Zori et Cerchis Descala, Mariani Descala, donnicello Arzoco, locu Salvatore, et ista carta iscripta est in die Natale Sancti Petri.

Carta volgare 2. Date: c. 1114–1120. Donation made by Trogotori de Unali (Mariano-Torchitorio II), iudike of Cálari (1108–1130), of lands around Dolia to the church of San Saturnino in Cagliari. Archivio diocesano storico di Cagliari, DigiLib., no. 1; 15th-century transcription from the Archivio diocesano storico di Cagliari, *Liber Diversorum*, 2/I serie, f. 140; DigiLib., p. 150; 17th-century Spanish translation in Aleo, *Sucessos generales*, ff. 302–303. Editions: Solmi, 'Le carte volgari', no. 2, pp. 15–16; Falchi, *reisar.eu*, carta II.

(1)+ In nomin de Pater [et] Filiu [et] S[an]cto Isp[irit]u. Ego iudigi Trogotori de Unali, cu[m] (2)(m)uliere mia donna P[re]ciosa de Lacon, p[er] boluntate (de) Donnu Deu podestandu Pa[r]ti de Karalis, (3)fazzulli custa carta ad S[an]c[t]u Sadurru de Giida pr[o] beni ki lloi fazzu p[ro] Deu Innanti (4)[et] p[ro]ssa anima mia. Daulloi ladus dessa semida mia de Zalia in Montis de Olia. Et (5)ingenzzatsi custa semida daba su Pizzariu de Murabera; tudui sa

Constantini, make a charter for Sancto Laurentio (San Lorenzo in Genoa) for the exchange (*tramuta*) that I made, so that the farm complexes (*domos*) I had given would be restored to me. I, with the consent of my clerics, and of my brothers, and of the entire realm (*logu*), to give the Masses of *domnicella* Maria. And they, with the consent of the bishop of Genua (Genoa), of the provost, of all the canons of the cathedral's house, and of the consuls, and of all the trusted men of Genua, gave us those three farms complexes in Quartu (Quarto), in Caput Terra (Capoterra), and in Aqua Frigida (Acquafredda), with male and female servants (*servos et ancillas*), unworked land (*saltu*) and enclosed lands (*semitas*), and courtyards (*culia*) of these three complexes, which they gave me without [including] one hundred pigs from Quartu. And at Aqua Frigida I gave Constantini Cirinda with his sons; and they gave me Cumita de Nuchis with his wife and his sons, and Mariane Zapula. I gave them Sabazu, and Pau, and Barala, and Tracasil, and Fucilla, and Sancta Victoria de Villa Pupia, with male and female servants, and with dwellings (*mansiones*), unworked lands (*saltos*), and farm lands, and all that belonged to those complexes. These farms that I give them may not be in the hands of a curator, nor have any other lord than would serve the churches that I gave to San Lorenzo. And if it were the case that the exchanged assets were disputed in a suit raised against me, and I were defeated, I would return the complexes they gave me! The witnesses are: *donnicellu* Cerchius, Azzocco de Lacuni, Muratore de Zurchiis, Arzocco de Recco, Comita Castai, Zerku de Zerkis, Zerkius de Mota, Mariani de Scala, *donnicellu* Arzocco the deputy (*locu Salvatore*). And this charter was written on the day of the Feast of St Peter (29 June).

Carta volgare 2. Date: c. 1114–1120. Donation made by Trogotori de Unali (Mariano-Torchitorio II), iudike of Cálari (1108–1130), of lands around Dolia to the church of San Saturnino in Cagliari. Archivio diocesano storico di Cagliari, DigiLib., no. 1; 15th-century transcription from the Archivio diocesano storico di Cagliari, *Liber Diversorum*, 2/I serie, f. 140; DigiLib., p. 150; 17th-century Spanish translation in Aleo, *Sucessos generales*, ff. 302–303. Editions: Solmi, 'Le carte volgari', no. 2, pp. 15–16; Falchi, *reisar.eu*, carta II.

(1)+ In the name of the Father, the Son, and the Holy Spirit. I, iudike Trogotori de Unali, with (2)my wife, lady Preciosa de Lacon, by the will of Lord God, ruling Karalis' territory (*parti*), (3)make them this charter for Sanctu Sadurru de Giida (San Saturnino at Cagliari) for benefices I make to them for God Almighty (4)and for my soul. I grant half my enclosed land (*semida*) at Zalia in the mountains of Olia (Dolia).

(5)This enclosed land (*semida*) starts from the plot (*pizzariu*) of Murabera; [it goes] along the road towards the field (*campu*) of Tiirri and, from the field

bia derectu ad campu de Tiirri, (6)[et] daba campu de Tiirri falat tudui sa biaderectu ad s'Iscla de Maso[n]i Maiori, [et] daba (7)Masoni Maiori tenitsi sa bia de pei de Scoba derectu ad Ienna de L'Istincu, [et] daba Genna de (8)Listincu tenitsi s'erriu derectu assa Bega de sus Sueri[us] ubi torra[n]t b[er]begarius, [et] daba custa (9)bega badi derectu ad Cucuru de Berbeis, [et] daba Cucuru de Berbeis badi tudui serra derectu (10)ad Orriina de Muscadoriu, [et] badi tudui serra de Muscadoriu derectu ad bia de Logu, [et] badi tudui bia (11)derectu ad Pedra de Caballu, [et] daba Pedra de Caballu badi derectu ad Jenna de Cuerrantu et daba (12)Jenna de Cuerrantu badi derectu ad Ienna de Mindigi, [et] daba Jenna de Mindigi, badi (13)tudui bia, [et] clonpit ad su Pizzariu de Murabera daundis [et] cuminzzat [et] cum beni ki lu fazzu (14)ad S[an]c[t]u Sadurru de Giida p[ro] Deu Innanti [et] p[ro] anima mia [et] de parentis (mius) (…) (15)mi inpadronu S[an]c[t]u Sadurru ante Deu p[ro] lla peccada mia. Et [sunt testimonius donnu] Alib[er]tu piscobu de Olia, Cumidai de Frailis, (…) (16)(C)astai, Orgodori Dezzori. Istimoni[us] de Logu: Cumidai de Serra (…) (17)de Serra de Frailis. Et ki ll'aet debertiri appat hanazzema daba Pat[er] [et] Filiu [et] S(anctu Ispiritu), (18)daba XII Apostolos et quatuor Ebangelistas, daba XVI P[ro]phetas [et] XXIIII Sen(iores), (19)daba CCCXVIII S[an]c[t]os Patres [et] sorti cu[m] Juda appat in infernu[m]! Siat [et] fiat, amen! Genitosi fiat! Amen. Amen.

Carta volgare 3. Date: c. 1114–1120. Trogodori de Unali (Mariano-Torchitorio II), iudike of Cálari (1107–1129) with his son, grants permission to Petru Pintori, bishop of San Giorgio di Suelli, to draw up a deed of purchase for his own benefit. Archivio diocesano storico di Cagliari, DigiLib., no. 2. Fitted with a 'Byzantine' lead seal (51 g) and seal tag of brown chord: Obv. +TOPK / O(TO)PHW / APXUNTH / MEPEHCK / (A)PAVEWC. Rev. Cruciform invocative monogram (Type V), Θεοτόκε βοήθει; in the quarters: TW-ΣW ΔOY-ΛW (τῷ σῷ δούλῳ). Also known from a 15th-century transcription in *Liber Diversorum*, 2/I serie, Appendix 'Quaderno,' no. 4, DigiLib., p. 313. Editions: Solmi, 'Le carte volgari', no. 3, p. 16; Falchi, *reisar.eu*, carta III.

(1)+ In nomin de Pater [et] Filiu [et] S[an]c[t]u Isp[irit]u. Ego iudigi Trogodori (2)de Unali, cu[m] filiu miu donnu Gostantini, per boluntate de (3)Donnu Deu potestandu parti de Calaris, assolbullu a piscopu (4)Petru a ffagirisi carta in co bolit. [Et] ego piscopu Petru Pintori, (5)cum lebandu assoltura daba ssu donnu miu iudigi Trogodori, (6)ki mi llu castigit Donnu Deu balaus annus [et] bonus, [et] ad issi (7)[et] a muliere sua donna Preciosa de Lacon, fazzumi carta p[ro]

of Tiirri, (6)it descends along the road towards the islet (*iscla*) of Masoni Maiori ('large flocks'); (7)from Masoni Maiori it keeps to the path of Scoba, [goes] towards the pass (*ienna*) of Linstincu (Villa Lustincho), and from the pass of (8)Linstincu, it keeps to the stream [going] towards Bega de sus Suerius ('valley of the cork oaks') where the shepherds return; and from this (9)valley it goes straight to Curcuru de Berbeis ('sheep's summit'), and from Curcuru de Berbeis, it goes along the ridge (*serra*) towards (10) Orriina de Muscadoriu ('shack of Muscadoriu'), and goes along the ridge of Muscadoriu towards the main road (*via de Logu*); it [then] goes (11)straight along the road towards Pedra de Caballu ('rock of the horse'), and from Pedra de Caballu it goes towards the pass (*jenna*) of Cuerrantu; from (12)Cuerrantu pass, it goes towards to the pass of Mindigi, and from Mindigi pass (13)it goes along the road and joins the plot (*pizzariu*) of Murabera.

These donations I make (14)for Sanctu Sadurru de Giida, [are] for God Almighty, and for my soul, and for those of my relatives (…) (15)I place myself under the patronage of Sanctu Sadurru before God for my sins. The witnesses are: Alibertu bishop of Olia (Dolia), Cumidai de Frailis, (…) (16)Castai, Orgodori Dezzori. Witnesses of the realm (*Istimonius de logu*) [are]: Cumidai de Serra (…) (17)de Serra de Frailis. Whoever dares to controvert this, may the Father, the Son, and the Holy Spirit, (18)the twelve Apostles and the four Evangelists, the sixteen Prophets, the twenty-four Elders, (19)the 318 Holy Fathers curse him, and have his lot with Judas in Hell! Let it be and be done! Amen. May it happen (*genitosi*) and let it be (*fiat*)! Amen. Amen.

Carta volgare 3. Date: c. 1114–1120. Trogodori de Unali (Mariano-Torchitorio II), iudike of Cálari (1107–1129) with his son, grants permission to Petru Pintori, bishop of San Giorgio di Suelli, to draw up a deed of purchase for his own benefit. Archivio diocesano storico di Cagliari, DigiLib., no. 2. Fitted with a 'Byzantine' lead seal (51g) and seal tag of brown chord: Obv. +TOPK / O(TO)PHW / APXUNTH / MEPEHCK / (A)PAVEWC. Rev. Cruciform invocative monogram (Type V), Θεοτόκε βοήθει; in the quarters: TW-ΣW ΔOY-ΛW (τῷ σῷ δούλῳ). Also known from a 15th-century transcription in *Liber Diversorum*, 2/I serie, Appendix 'Quaderno,' no. 4, DigiLib., p. 313. Editions: Solmi, 'Le carte volgari', no. 3, p. 16; Falchi, *reisar.eu*, carta III.

(1)+ In the name of the Father, the Son, and the Holy Spirit. I, iudike Trogodori (2)de Unali, with my son lord Gostantine, by the will of (3)Lord God, ruling Cálari's territory (*parti*), permit (*assolbullu*) bishop (4)Petru to make himself a charter as he wishes. So, I, bishop Petru Pintori, (5)with permission (*assoltura*) from my lord, iudike Trogodori—(6)may Lord God protect him for me for many good years, him (7)and his wife, lady Preciosa de Lacon—make myself a char-

co[n]pora (8)ki fegi in Serriga. Conporei a Trogodori de Muntigi [et] a mulieri (9)sua, parçzoni cantu habeant in Serriga, pus mama [et] pus padri, (10)[et] deilli sollu de cabras [et] sollu de triigu, [et] clo[m]peilli pariari. (11)An(te) testimoni[us] Amirai de Muntigi, [et] Trogodori Boe, et Iorgi Manca, (12)et Trogodori Littera. Et sunt destimoni[us] Arzzocu de Lacon, et Furadu (13)de Unali, donnigellu Artzocu logu salbadori. [Et] ki ll'aet dever(te)re (14)appat anathema dabba Pater et Filiu et S[an]c[t]u Isp[irit]u, dabba XII Ap[os]t[ol]os, (15)IIII Evang[e]listas, XVI P[ro]ph[et]as, XXIIII Seniores, CCCXVIII S[an]c[to]s Patres, [et] (16)appat sorti cum Iuda in inferno. Siat [et] fiat. Amen.

Carta volgare 4. Date: c. 1121–1129. Permission granted by Trogotori de Unali (Mariano-Torchitorio II), iudike of Cálari (1107–1129), and his son, to Petru Pintori, bishop of San Giorgio di Suelli to make a charter for the acquisition of a church and its appurtenances. Archivio diocesano storico di Cagliari, DigiLib., no. 3. Fitted with a 'Byzantine' lead seal (53.5 g) with a seal tag of brown chord: Obv. [+TOPK / OTOP]HW / [APXUNT]H / [MEPE]HCK / [KAPAVE]WC. Rev. Cruciform invocative monogram (Type V), Θεοτόκε βοήθει; in the quarters: TW-ΣW ΔOY-ΛW (τῷ σῷ δούλῳ). Also known from a 15th-century transcription from the Archivio diocesano storico di Cagliari, *Liber Diversorum*, 2/I serie, Appendix 'Quaderno', no. 6, DigiLib., p. 314. Editions: Solmi, 'Le carte volgari', no. 4, pp. 16–17; Falchi, *reisar.eu*, carta IV.

(1)+ In nomine Patris [et] Filii [et] Sp[iritu]s S[an]c[t]i, amen. Ego judigi Trogotori de (2)Unali, cu[m] filiu miu do[n]nu Gostantini, p[er] bolintadi de Do[n]nu Deu potestandu parti de Caralis, assolbullu a piscobu (3)Petru Pintori a ffagirisi carta in co bolit. Et ego piscobu Petru, cu[m] lebandu assoltura (4)daba su do[n]nu miu iudigi Trogotori de Unali, ki mi llu castigit Do[n]nu Deu balaus ann[us] [et] (5)bon[us], [et] a issi [et] a mulieri sua do[n]na P[re]tiosa de Laco[n], fazzumi carta p[ro] S[an]c[t]a Lukia d'Arigi, ki fabricarat (6)Mariani Mellu, s[er]bu de Cumida de Serre[n]ti, ki fudi eniu. [Et] dedibi sa die ki lla secrabat (7)plazza [et] binia [et] t[er]ra a essiri pus S[an]c[t]u Petru de Suelli, cu[m] bulintadi de Cumida de Serre[n]ti, do[n]nu suo. (8)Et fraigaru[n]t s[er]b[us] de do[n]nu Arzzocu de Laco[n], Basili [et] fr[ad]is suus, a S[an]c[t]u Biniitu [et] issa die ki (9)lla segraru[n]t, deru[n]t ibi t[er]ra [et] bacas et b[er]begis [et] porc[us]. [Et] dedibi do[n]nu Arzzocu de Laco[n] a Bera, (10)filia de Basili Arrasu, ankilla sua peguliari, ad ankilla de cadadie, [et] siat in potestadi

ter regarding a purchase (8)that I made in Serriga. I bought from Trogodori de Muntigi and from his wife the share (*parçzoni*) of all they had in Serriga, from the mother's side and the father's side. (9)I gave them one soldo (*sollu*) of goats and one soldo (*sollu*) of wheat, and I completed the payment (10)before the witnesses Amirai de Muntigi, and Trogodori Boe, Iorgi Manca, (11)and Trogodori Littera.

The witnesses [to this] are Arzzocu de Lacon, and (12)Furadu de Unali, and *donnigellu* Artzocu the deputy (*logu salbadori*). Whoever dares to controvert this, (13)may the Father, the Son and the Holy Spirit, the twelve Apostles, (14)the four Evangelists, the sixteen Prophets, the twenty-(15)four Elders, and the 318 Holy Fathers curse him, and (16)may he have his lot with Judas in Hell! Let it be and amen!

Carta volgare 4. Date: c. 1121–1129. Permission granted by Trogotori de Unali (Mariano-Torchitorio II), iudike of Cálari (1107–1129), and his son, to Petru Pintori, bishop of San Giorgio di Suelli to make a charter for the acquisition of a church and its appurtenances. Archivio diocesano storico di Cagliari, DigiLib., no. 3. Fitted with a 'Byzantine' lead seal (53.5 g) with a seal tag of brown chord: Obv. [+TOPK / OTOP]HW / [APXUNT]H / [MEPE]HCK / [KAPAVE]WC. Rev. Cruciform invocative monogram (Type V), Θεοτόκε βοήθει; in the quarters: TW-ΣW ΔOY-ΛW (τῷ σῷ δούλῳ). Also known from a 15th-century transcription from the Archivio diocesano storico di Cagliari, *Liber Diversorum*, 2/I serie, Appendix 'Quaderno', no. 6, DigiLib., p. 314. Editions: Solmi, 'Le carte volgari', no. 4, pp. 16–17; Falchi, *reisar.eu*, carta IV.

(1)+ In the name of the Father, the Son, and the Holy Spirit, amen. I, iudike Trogotori de (2)Unali, with my son lord Gostantini, by the will of Lord God, ruling Caralis' territory (*parti*), permit (*assolbullu*) bishop (3)Petru Pintori to make himself a charter as he wishes. So, I, bishop Petru Pintori, with permission (*assoltura*) (4)from my lord, iudike Trogodori—may Lord God protect him for me for many (5)good years, him and his wife, lady Pretiosa of Lacon—make myself a charter for Sancta Lukia (Santa Lucia) d'Arigi (Arìxi) which (6)Mariani Mellu, a servant (*serbu*) of Cumida of Serrenti, built and who was childless (*eniu*). He [Mariani] provided it on the day of its consecration with (7)the plot of land (*plazza*), vineyard (*binia*) and land beyond Sanctu Petru of Suelli with the approval of Cumida of Serrenti, his lord. (8)The servants (*serbus*) of lord Arzzocu de Lacon, Basili and his brothers, built Sanctu Biniitu (St Vinicius); on the same day that (9)they consecrated it, they granted it land, cows, sheep, and swine.

Also, lord Arzzocu de Lacon donated Bera, (10)daughter of Basili Arrasu, his own (*peguliari*) female servant (*ankilla*) as a daily female servant (*ankilla de

de piscabu (11)ki aet essiri in Suelli. Et dedigi do[n]nu Arzzocu de Laco[n] a S[an]c[t]u Petru de Suelli a fFurada, (12)filia de Turbini de Fraili, ad ankilla de cadadie, p[ro] Do[n]nu Deu [et] p[ro] a[n]i[m]a sua. Et su[n]t destimo[n]ius (13)do[n]nigellu Arzzocu, do[n]nigellu Zerkis, do[n]nigellu Gosta[n]tini logu salbadori. Et ki ll'aet dev[er]tere (14)apat anathema daba Pat[er] [et] Filiu [et] S[an]c[t]u Isp[irit]u, et daba XII Ap[osto]los, IIII Eva[n]g[e]listas, XVI (15)P[ro]-ph[et]as, XXIIII Seniores, [et] daba CCCXVIII S[an]c[to]s Patres, [et] h[abe]at sorti cu[m] Iuda in inferno. Siat [et] fiat. (16)Amen.

Carta volgare Suppl. E (Sant'Antioco). Transumpt. Date: 1124. Donation of the island (*tota insula sulcitana*) of Sant'Antioco along with an estate to the church of Sant'Antioco by Trogotori de Gunali (Mariano-Torchitorio II), iudike of Cálari (1108–1130). Known from at least five Latin transumpts, a 14th-century transcription and four 17th-century copies, most likely taken from a lost Sardinian cartulary known as the *Mare Magnum*. These five Latin transumpts are conserved in the Archivio diocesano storico di Cagliari, *Liber Diversorum*, 2/I serie, ff. 122–125, 263; DigiLib., pp. 119–122, 255. Editions: B.R. Motzo, 'La donazione'; Lai & Marco, *S. Antioco*, pp. 141–142.

(1)In nomine Patris et Filii et Spiritus Sancti, amen. Ego Iudex Torquitor qui est Mari-(2)anus vocor, per voluntatem Dei potestandu regnum Calaritanum cum filio meo, dominu (3)Costantino et cum uxore mea, domina Preziosa, pro remissione omnium pecc-(4)atorum meorum omniumque parentum nostrorum, facio donationem ad sanctum Antiochum (5)de tota insula[5] Sulcitana et de semitta que appellatur Sikirbi que michi per (6)ex parte domine Gitite et ex parte domicellus Terki pervenit[6] (7)at dominum Furatum de Gonale et a frate suo et dederunt michi et (8)omnium que michi per quocumque ordine pertinere videretur, et absolvo fratres (9)meos et sorores meas, qui sunt dominum Otorku, dominum Terkis, et dominam (10)Maria, et dominam Vera, facere de causa sua que volunt. (11)Et ego domicellus Othorkus et domicellus Terkis et domina Maria et (12)domina Vera, cum absoltura de Mariano Iudice, quem Dominus (13)multos annos nobis cunsservat et deffendat facimus similiter (14)cartam ad sanctum Antiochum de ipsas portiones nostras de eadem in-(15)sulam et semitam que nobis pertinebantur ut nullus imperatur vel (16)curator aut alia persona magna sive parva qui post nos venturi (17)sunt habeat potestatem sive audaciam tolendi sive minuendi de supra (18)dicta insula et semitta

5 The clear sense of this phrase cannot be that the entire island was donated to the church. Rather, *insula* is either a hypercorrection of *iscla* ('wetland'), which is ultimately derived from *insula* ('island') or *insula* here refers to 'wetlands.'

6 The copyist has mistakenly repeated the phrase '*per venit*.'

cadadie); she shall be under the custody of the bishop, (11)whosoever he is,at Suelli. Also, lord Arzzocu de Lacon gave to Sanctu Petru de Suelli fFurada, (12)daughter of Turbini de Fraili, as a daily female servant, for Lord God and for his soul.

The witnesses are *donnigellu* Arzzocu, *donnigellu* Zerkis, (13)*donnigellu* Gostantini the deputy (*logusalbadori*). Whosoever dares to controvert this, (14)may the Father and the Son and the Holy Spirit, the twelve Apostles, the four Evangelists, the sixteen (15)Prophets, the twenty-four Elders, and the 318 Holy Fathers curse him, and may have his lot with Judas in Hell! Let it be and be done! (16)Amen!

Carta volgare Suppl. E (Sant'Antioco). Transumpt. Date: 1124. Donation of the island (*tota insula sulcitana*) of Sant'Antioco along with an estate to the church of Sant'Antioco by Trogotori de Gunali (Mariano-Torchitorio II), iudike of Cálari (1108–1130). Known from at least five Latin transumpts, a 14th-century transcription and four 17th-century copies, most likely taken from a lost Sardinian cartulary known as the *Mare Magnum*. These five Latin transumpts are conserved in the Archivio diocesano storico di Cagliari, *Liber Diversorum*, 2/I serie, ff. 122–125, 263; DigiLib., pp. 119–122, 255. Editions: B.R. Motzo, 'La donazione'; Lai & Marco, *S. Antioco*, pp. 141–142.

(1)In the name of the Father, of the Son and of the Holy Spirit, amen. I, iudex Torquitor, called (2)Marianus, by the will of God, ruling the Calaritan realm with my son, lord (3)Costantino and my lady wife, Preziosa, for the remission of all our (4)sins, and of all our ancestors, make a donation to St Antiochus (5)of the entire island of Sulci (*insula sulcitana*) and of the enclosed land (*semitta*) that is called Sikirbi which came to me (6)through the share belonging to lady Gitita and from the share of *donnicellu* Terki (Zerkis), (7)with the share of lord Furatu de Gonale and his brother, who donated it to me, as well as (8)all the other things that were given to me by whatever order it may appear that they belong to [us], I give permission to my brothers (9)and sisters, who are lord Otorku, lord Terkis, lady (10)Maria and lady Vera, so that they can dispose of their assets in the way that they wish.

(11)So I, *donnicellu* Othorkcus, *donnicellu* Terkis, lady Maria and (12)lady Vera, with the permission of the iudike, Mariano—may the Lord (13)preserve and defend him for many years—likewise draw up (14)a charter for [the church of] St Antiochus of the parts of the said (15)islet and of the lands that belonged to us, so that no ruler (*imperator*), nor curator (16)nor any other person of great or little authority that will succeed us, (17)might have the authority or audacity to remove or diminish [any part] of the aforesaid (18)islet and the lands that we

quam damus ad sanctum Antiochum. Et similiter (19)absolvo domicellos meos de causa sua facere que volunt. Et ego (20)domicellus G[onarius] et domicellus Petrus et domicellus Marianus et (21)domicellus Torquitor et domina Georgia de Gonale facimus cartam (22)ad sanctum Antiochum de supra dicta insula et semitta de Sikirbi que (23)nobis pertinere videbatur. Similiter dedit domicellus Turbini portionem (24)suam de eadem insula et semitta ad supra dictum sanctum Antiochum de (25)Surkes. Et non liceat nec habeat audaciam nullus imperator sive (26)curator neque filii aut alias personas qui post nos venturi sunt de omnia (27)que dedimus ad supra dictum sanctum Antiochum. Et ego domicellus Terkis, (28)testis, et ego domicellus Comitta testis, et ego donnicellus Otorcho (29)testis, et ego lodo salvatore (*corr.* locu salvatore) testis, et alii plurimi testes. Qui autem (30)cartam istam sive supra dictas donationes everterit vel minuere (31)voluerit sit excomunicatus, et cetera. (32)MCXXIIII[7]

Carta volgare 5. Date: c. 1130. Donation of lands by Salusi de Lacon (Costantino-Salusio), iudike of Cálari (1130–1162), with his mother, to the church of Santa Cristina in the bishopric of Suelli. Archivio diocesano storico di Cagliari, DigiLib., no. 4. Fitted with a 'Byzantine' lead seal (49.2 g) and seal tag of brown chord: Obv. [...] / AP[X]ONTI / [ME]I(?)PE[...] / [...]ΛEW[C]. Rev. Cruciform invocative monogram (Type V), Θεοτόκε βοήθει; in the quarters: TW-ΣW ΔOY-ΛW (τῷ σῷ δούλῳ). Also known from 15th- and 16th-century transcriptions from the Archivio diocesano storico di Cagliari, *Liber Diversorum*, E old serie, fol. 144; 2/I serie, Appendix 'Quaderno,' no. 5, DigiLib., pp. 313–314; 17th-century Spanish translation in Aleo, *Sucessos generales*, ff. 295–296. Editions: Solmi, 'Le carte volgari', no. 5, pp. 17–18; Falchi, *reisar.eu*, carta V.

(1)+ In nomine Patris [et] Filii [et] Sp[iritu]s S[an]c[t]i, am[en]. Ego judigi Salusi de Laco[n], cu[m] matre mia (2)do[n]na Prizzosa Dezzori, p[er] bolintate de Do[n]nu Deu potesta[n]du parti de Karalis, fazzulla custa (3)carta pro parzzoni de saltu de Marzzana, ki dau a S[an]c[t]a Cristina, ki e[st] pesada in su saltu. Daullillu (4)daba s'erriu des Garan[us] deretu ass'erriu de fFogis, daba bia in iossu fisca Flumini, [et] ca[m]pu [et] semida (5)[et] aradoriu [et] binias ca[n]tu bi su[n]t; [et]cu ki dau a S[an]c[t]a Xr[ist]ina p[ro] Do[n]nu Deu [et] p[ro] a[n]i[m]a mia [et] de (6)padri miu. Et no[n] apat ausantia inp[er]adori, ki p[us]

7 Year added in a different hand.

gave to St Antiochus. And, in the same way, (19)I grant permission to my family members to dispose of their assets as they wish. So I (20)*donnicellu* G[onarius], *donnicellu* Petru with *donnicellu* Marianus, (21)*donnicellu* Torquitor and lady Georgia de Gonale, draw up a charter (22)to St Antiochus for the aforesaid islets and the lands of Sikirbi which (23)we believe belong to us. Similarly, *donnicellu* Turbini gave his share (24)from the same islet and the land to the aforementioned St Antiochus (25)de Surkes ('of Sulcis'). Let no one be allowed to have the audacity—neither a ruler, (26)nor a curator, nor sons or other people who will come after us, to oppose all (27)that we have given to the aforementioned St Antiochus! I *donnicellu* Terkis (28)am a witness; I, *donnicellu* Comitta witness; I *donnicellu* Otorcho (29)witness, and I the deputy (*loci salvator*) am a witness, alongside many others witnesses. Whoever (30)has the audacity to overrule this charter and the aforementioned donations or who wishes to diminish [them] (31)let him be excommunicated! And so on. (32)[Year] 1124.[8]

Carta volgare 5. Date: c. 1130. Donation of lands by Salusi de Lacon (Costantino-Salusio), iudike of Cálari (1130–1162), with his mother, to the church of Santa Cristina in the bishopric of Suelli. Archivio diocesano storico di Cagliari, DigiLib., no. 4. Fitted with a 'Byzantine' lead seal (49.2 g) and seal tag of brown chord: Obv. [...] / ΑΡ[Χ]ΟΝΤΙ / [ΜΕ]Ι(?)ΡΕ[...] / [...]ΛΕΩ[C]. Rev. Cruciform invocative monogram (Type V), Θεοτόκε βοήθει; in the quarters: ΤΩ-ΣΩ ΔΟΥ-ΛΩ (τῷ σῷ δούλῳ). Also known from 15th- and 16th-century transcriptions from the Archivio diocesano storico di Cagliari, *Liber Diversorum*, E old serie, fol. 144; 2/I serie, Appendix 'Quaderno,' no. 5, DigiLib., pp. 313–314; 17th-century Spanish translation in Aleo, *Sucessos generales*, ff. 295–296. Editions: Solmi, 'Le carte volgari', no. 5, pp. 17–18; Falchi, *reisar.eu*, carta V.

(1)+ In the name of the Father, the Son, and the Holy Spirit, A[men]. I, iudike Salusi de Lacon, with my mother (2)lady Prizzosa Dezzori, by the will of Lord God, ruling Karalis' territory (*parti*), make them this (3)charter regarding the share (*parzzoni*) of the unworked land (*saltu*) of Marzzana, which I give to Sancta Cristina that is built on the land. That which I give is (4)from s'Erriu des Garanus ('the stream of Garanus'), towards s'Erriu de fFogis ('the stream of Fogis'), from the road in the lower part up to Flumini with everything there: a field, enclosed land (*semida*), (5)ploughed land (*aradoriu*) and vineyards (*binias*). That which I grant to Sancta Cristina [is] for Lord God and for the salvation of my soul and of (6)my father's. May no ruler (*inperadori*) who suc-

8 Year added in a different hand.

me aet essiri, a disbertiri custu orminiu ki (7)fegi p[ro] Do[n]nu Deu [et] p[ro] a[n]i[m]a mia et de pat[er] miu; [et] no[n] apat ausantia no[n] genezzariu [et] no[n] porcariu (8)a nogiri ellus sus s[er]b[us] de clesia, et po[n]iullus in manu de Deu [et] de S[an]c[t]a Xr[ist]ina [et] de piscobu Petru (9)Pi[n]tori. Et su[n]t destimo[n]i[us] do[n]nigellu Zerkis logusalbadori, do[n]nigellu Turbini ki fuit (10)curadori, Torgodori Dezzori arme[n]tariu, Arzzoccu de Laco[n]. Et ki ll'aet devertere apat anath[em]a (11)daba Pat[er] [et] Filiu et S[an]c[t]u Isp[irit]u, daba XII Ap[osto]los, IIII Eva[n]g[e]listas, [et] XVI P[ro]ph[et]as, XXIIII Seniores, (12)[et] daba CCCXVIII S[an]c[tu]s Patres, [et] apat sorti cu[m] Juda in infernu[m]. Siat [et] fiat. A[men].

Carta volgare 6. Date: c. 1130–1140. Grant of permission by Salusi de Lacon (Costantino-Salusio), iudike of Cálari (1130–1162), with his wife, to allow his uncle to record his donation of various lands and resources in the '*trigonía* of Barbária' to the church of Santa Maria di Lotzorai. Archivio diocesano storico di Cagliari, DigiLib., no. 5; two copies of this charter are extant; one is in very poor condition and the other is considered an 'authentic copy.' Both are fitted with a 'Byzantine' lead seal (50.7 g) with a seal tag of brown chord. Obv. [...] / ΛOVC(IW) / APK(?)ON[...] / [...]EHCK / [...]ΛEW[C]. Rev. Cruciform invocative monogram (Type V), Θεοτόκε βοήθει; in the quarters: TW-ΣW ΔOY-ΛW (τῷ σῷ δούλῳ). CV6 authentic copy: Fitted with a 'Byzantine' lead seal (51 g) with a seal tag of brown chord. Obv. [...] / ΛOVC(IW) / APK(?)ON[...] / [...]EHCK / [...]ΛEW[C]. Rev. Cruciform invocative monogram (Type V), Θεοτόκε βοήθει; in the quarters: TW-ΣW ΔOY-ΛW (τῷ σῷ δούλῳ). DigiLib., no. 6; 15th-century transcription in the Archivio diocesano storico di Cagliari, *Liber Diversorum*, 2/I serie, Appendix 'Quaderno,' no. 8, DigiLib., p. 314. Editions: Tola, *CDS*, 1, p. 227; Solmi, 'Le carte volgari', no. 6, pp. 18–19; Falchi, *reisar.eu*, carta VI.

(1)+ In no[m]ine Patris [et] Filii et Sp[iritu]s S[an]c[t]i, amen. Ego iudigi Salusi (2)de Lacon cu[m] mulieri mia do[n]na Jurgia de Unali, assolbullu a ciu miu (3)donigellu Arzzocu a ffairi de causa sua su ki bolit. Et eu do[n]nigellu Arzzorcu cu[m] (4)lebandu assoltura daba su do[n]nu miu judigi Salusi de Lacon ki mi llu castigit (5)Do[n]nu Deu balaus ann[us] [et] bonus, [et] ad issi [et] a muliere sua do[n]na Jurgia (6)[et] a matre sua do[n]na Preciosa de Lacon, fazzulla custa carta p[ro] causa mia ca[n]tu (7)apu in trigonia de Barbaria ka lla dau a S[anct]a Maria de Lozzorai p[ro] Do[n]nu (8)Deu [et] p[ro] a[n]i[m]a mia et de fr[ad]i miu [et] de totu sus pare[n]tis mius. Daulli sa domu (9)de Tortoili cu[m] serb[us] [et] ankillas cu[m] binias [et] domestias cu[m] saltu [et] aqua [et] o[mn]ia (10)ca[n]tu apu pusti cussa domu. Et dau illoi sa domu de Bari cu[m] serb[us] [et] (11)ankillas cu[m] bi[n]ias [et] domestias cu[m] saltu

ceeds us dare controvert this order that (7)I have made for Lord God and for my soul, and my father's. And no iudike's supervisor (*genezzariu*) nor [even] a swine-keeper (*porcariu*) (8)shall themselves misuse the church servants (*serbus de clesia*); I then commit them [the servants] into the hands of God and of Sancta Cristina and of bishop Petru (9)Pin[tori].

The witnesses are: *donnigellu* Zerkis the deputy (*logusalbadori*), *donnigellu* Turbini, who was (10)curator (*curadori*), Torgodori Dezzori the administrator (*armentariu*), [and] Arzzoccu de Lacon. Whosoever dares to controvert it, may (11)the Father and the Son and the Holy Spirit curse him, and the twelve Apostles, the four Evangelists, the sixteen Prophets, the twenty-four Elders, (12)and the 318 Holy Fathers, and may he have his lot with Judas in Hell! Let it be and let it be! Amen.

Carta volgare 6. Date: c. 1130–1140. Grant of permission by Salusi de Lacon (Costantino-Salusio), iudike of Cálari (1130–1162), with his wife, to allow his uncle to record his donation of various lands and resources in the '*trigonía* of Barbária' to the church of Santa Maria di Lotzorai. Archivio diocesano storico di Cagliari, DigiLib., no. 5; two copies of this charter are extant; one is in very poor condition and the other is considered an 'authentic copy.' Both are fitted with a 'Byzantine' lead seal (50.7 g) with a seal tag of brown chord. Obv. [...] / ΛΟVC(IW) / ΑΡΚ(?)ΟΝ[...] / [...]ΕΗCΚ / [...]ΛΕW[C]. Rev. Cruciform invocative monogram (Type V), Θεοτόκε βοήθει; in the quarters: TW-ΣW ΔΟΥ-ΛW (τῷ σῷ δούλῳ). CV6 authentic copy: Fitted with a 'Byzantine' lead seal (51 g) with a seal tag of brown chord. Obv. [...] / ΛΟVC(IW) / ΑΡΚ(?)ΟΝ[...] / [...]ΕΗCΚ / [...]ΛΕW[C]. Rev. Cruciform invocative monogram (Type V), Θεοτόκε βοήθει; in the quarters: TW-ΣW ΔΟΥ-ΛW (τῷ σῷ δούλῳ). DigiLib., no. 6; 15th-century transcription in the Archivio diocesano storico di Cagliari, *Liber Diversorum*, 2/1 serie, Appendix 'Quaderno,' no. 8, DigiLib., p. 314. Editions: Tola, *CDS*, 1, p. 227; Solmi, 'Le carte volgari', no. 6, pp. 18–19; Falchi, *reisar.eu*, carta VI.

(1)+ In the name of the Father, the Son, and the Holy Spirit, amen. I, iudike Salusi (2)de Lacon, with my wife lady Jurgia de Unali, permit (*assolbullu*) my uncle (3)*donnigellu* Arzzocu to arrange his assets (*causa*) as he wishes. So, I, *donnigellu* Arzzorcu (4)with permission (*assoltura*) from my lord, iudike Salusi of Lacon—may (5)Lord God protect him for me for many good years, [both] him and his wife, lady Jurgia, (6)and his mother, lady Preciosa of Lacon—make this charter regarding the assets (*causa*) of all (7)I have in the district (*trigonia*) of Barbária that I grant to Sancta Maria de Lozzorai (Lotzorai) for Lord (8)God, for my soul and my brother's and the souls of all my relatives. I grant it the farm complex (*domu*) (9)of Tortoili (Tortolì), with servants (*serbus*) and female servants (*ankillas*), with vineyards (*binias*) and farmsteads (*domestias*),

[et] aqua [et] semidas [et] duos ortus d'abis (12)[et] duas masonis de cabras [et] una masoni de porcus [et] fundamentu cantu (13)apu in Gelisoi, terras [et] binias [et] serb[us] [et ankillas]. Et in Ierzzu (Ertho) serb[us] [et] (14)ankillas [et] binias [et] terras [et] o[mn]ia causa ca[n]tu illoi apu [et] issu ortu de su Kidru (15)de Çurrele [et] o[mn]ia causa cantu apu in curadoria de Barbaria, proi si'ndi (16)apada S[an]c[t]a Maria, ka lla dau p[ro] Do[n]nu Deu [et] p[ro] a[n]i[m]a mia [et] siat in manu de piscobu. (17)Et su[n]t testimoni[us] donnigellu Turbini, do[n]nigellu Zerkis logu salbadori. (18)Et ki ll'aet dever(tere) apat anathema daba Pat[er] [et] Filio [et] (19)S[an]c[t]u Isp[irit]u, daba XII Ap[osto]los, (daba IIII Evangeli)stas [et] daba XVI P[ro]ph[et]as (20)daba XXIIII Seniores, et daba (CCCXVIII) Pa(tres Sanct)os. [Et] apat sorti cu[m] Iuda (21)in infernu. Siat [et] fiat, amen, amen, amen.

Carta volgare 7. Transumpt. Date: c. 1140. Permission granted to Turbini de Sillii (Sijillu) by Salusi de Lacon (Costantino-Salusio III), iudike of Cálari (1130–1162), and his wife, to draw up a charter of affiliation with, and grant of land to, the church of San Giorgio di Suelli. Known from a 15th-century transcription in the Archivio diocesano storico di Cagliari, *Liber Diversorum*, 2/1 series [E], Appendix 'Quaderno,' no. 7, DigiLib., p. 314. Edition: Solmi, 'Le carte volgari', no. 7, pp. 19–20.

(1)+ In nomine Patris et Filii et Sp[irit]us Sancti, ame[n]. Ego Iudigi Salusi de Laco[n], p[er](2)boluntadi de Do[n]nu Deu potestandu p[ar]ti de Callaris, assolbullu a Turbini (3)de Sillii (Sijllu) affagirisi de causa sua su ki bolit. Et ego Turbini de Sili (Sijllu), cum lebandu (4)assoltura daba su do[n]nu miu Iudigi Salusi, ki mi liti castigit Do[n]nu Deu balaus a[n]nus (5)et bonus, et a issi et a mulieri sua do[n]na Sardinia de Laco[n], fazzumi carta ca mi a-(6)filliu a Sanctu Jorgi de Suelli. Et daulloi ladus de fundame[n]tu miu et de causa mia (7)cantu apu: sa plazza mia de Barrala tota, ki la dau ad Sanctu Jorgi, daba sa (8)domu ki lloi anti serbus de S[anc]ta Lukia in foras, dab[a] indi tota sa plazza siat de Sanctu (9)Jorgi; et ladus de fundame[n]tu miu [et] de causa mia ca[n]tu apu fisca anno, [et] daba anno (10)in foras su cantu apu p[ar]i p[ro] ki si 'ndi apat Sa[n]ctu Jorgi de Suelli. Eccu ki lloy (11)dau p[ro] Do[n]nu Deu et p[ro] a[ni]ma mia, et p[ro] honori de donnu Alibertu su piscobu (12)de Suelli. Et sunt testimonius Arzzoco de Laco[n], Costantini de Unali, et donnigellu (13)Zerchis

with unworked land (*saltu*), water supply (*aqua*), and (10)all I have at that farm. I also grant the farm at Bari (Barì Sardo), with servants and (11)female servants, with vineyards and farmhouses, with unworked land, water supply, farm land, two bee yards (*ortus d'abis*), (12)two goat herds (*masonis*), one swine herd, and any property (*fundamentu*), (13)lands, vineyards, male and female servants that I have at Gelisoi (Girasole), as well as the male and female servants, vineyards, lands, and all the assets (*causa*) I have at Ierzzu (Jerzu), including (14)male and female servants, vineyards, lands, and any asset I have, and the plantation of su Kidru ('the cedar') (15)de Çurrele and all the assets (*causa*) I have in the district (*curadoría*) of Barbária, insofar as it (16)pertains to Sancta Maria, which I give for Lord God and for my soul. So let it be in the hands of the bishop!

(17)The witnesses are: *donnigellu* Turbini, and *donnigellu* Zerkis the deputy (*logu salbadori*). (18)Whosoever dares to controvert it, may the Father and the Son and (19)the Holy Spirit curse him, as well as the twelve Apostles, the four Evangelists, the sixteen Prophets, (20)the twenty-four Elders, and the 318 Holy Fathers, and have his lot with Judas (21)in Hell! Let it be and be done! Amen. Amen. Amen.

Carta volgare 7. Transumpt. Date: c. 1140. Permission granted to Turbini de Sillii (Sijillu) by Salusi de Lacon (Costantino-Salusio III), iudike of Cálari (1130–1162), and his wife, to draw up a charter of affiliation with, and grant of land to, the church of San Giorgio di Suelli. Known from a 15th-century transcription in the Archivio diocesano storico di Cagliari, *Liber Diversorum*, 2/1 series [E], Appendix 'Quaderno,' no. 7, DigiLib., p. 314. Edition: Solmi, 'Le carte volgari', no. 7, pp. 19–20.

(1)In the name of the Father, the Son, and the Holy Spirit, amen. I, iudike Salusi de Lacon, by (2)the will of Lord God, ruling Callaris' territory (*parti*), permit (*assolbullu*) Turbini (3)de Siillu to arrange his interests (*causa*) as he wishes. So, I, Turbini de Siillu, with (4)permission (*assoltura*) from my lord iudike, Salusi—may Lord God protect him for me for many (5)good years, him and his wife, lady Sardinia of Lacon—make myself a charter to (6)affiliate me with Sanctu Jorgi de Suelli. So, I grant it half (*ladus*) of my real estate (*fundamentu*) and assets (*causa*) (7)I have: my entire plot (*plazza*) of Barrala (Barrali), which I grant to Sanctu (8)Jorgi, [extending] from the farm complex (*domu*) where there are servants (*serbus*) of Sancta Lukia (Santa Lucia in Arìxi) henceforth. Let the entire plot belong to Sanctu (9)Jorgi! Also, half of my estate (*fundamentu*) and assets that I have up to this year, (10)equal to that which I will acquire from this year onwards (*in foras*)—so let Sanctu Jorgi de Suelli hold it! This is what (11)I donate for Lord God, and for my soul, and for the honour of lord Alibertu, the bishop (12)of Suelli. The witnesses are Arzzoco of Lacon, Costantini de Unali, and *don-*

logusalbadori. Et ki ll' aet dev[er]tere apat anath[em]a daba pat[er] et filiu et sp[irit]u s[a]nctu, daba XII apostolos, IIII evangelistas, et XVI prophethas, (14)XXIIII seniores, et daba CCCXVIII patres sanctos, et apat sorti cu[m] Juda (15)in infernum. Fiat et fiat.

Carta volgare 8. Date: c. 1150. Grant of permission by Salusi de Lacon (Costantino-Salusio III), iudike of Cálari (1130–1162), to Petru Macis, the bishop of Suelli, to draw up a charter for benefices made to the church by Turbini de Serra, including donations of male and female servants with their shares. Archivio diocesano storico di Cagliari, no. 7, DigiLib., no. 7. Fitted with a 'Byzantine' lead seal (53.2 g) and seal tag of brown braided chord: obv. [...] (Λ)OVCIW / APXONT(I)/ [-M?]EPEHC[K]A / [...]PAΛEW[C?]. Rev. Cruciform invocative monogram (Type V), Θεοτόκε βοήθει; in the quarters: TW-ΣW ΔOY-LW (τῷ σῷ δούλῳ). Also exists as a 16th-century transumpt in the Archivio diocesano storico di Cagliari, *Liber Diversorum*, 2/I serie, f. 68, DigiLib., pp. 70–71. Editions: Solmi, 'Le carte volgari', no. 8, pp. 20–21; Cannas, *San Giorgio*, no. 4, p. 196; Falchi, *reisar.eu*, carta VIII.

Hoc est translatum bene et fideliter sumptum in civitate et castro Callaris die xxvi, mensis Januarii an[n]o a nat[ivitat]e d[omi]ni Millesimo quingentesimo septuagesimo quarto a quadam carta pergamenea sigillo plumbeo a quibusdam cordulis canopinis in penden[te] munita non rasa no[n] viciata neq[ue] in aliqua sui parte suspecta sed ab eius vetustatem in aliquibus partibus corrosa in aliquis vicio et suspictione caren[te] cuius tenor seguitur sub his verbis:[9]

(1)+ In nomine Patris [et] Filii [et] Sp[iritu]s S[an]c[t]i, am[en]. Ego judigi Salusi de Laco[n], p[er] bolintate de Do[n]nu Deu potesta[n]du (2)parti de Karalis, assolbullu a piscobu Petru Macis a ffagirisi carta in co bolit. Et ego piscobu Petru, cu[m] leba[n]du (3)assoltura daba su do[n]nu miu judigi Salusi de Laco[n], ki mi llu castigit Do[n]nu Deu balaus ann[us] [et] bon[us], e a issi e a (4)mulieri sua do[n]na Sardinia Deççori, façcumi carta p[ro] beni ki fegit Turbini de S[er]ra a S[an]c[t]u Jorgi de Suelli. Dedi ella (5)ad Aleni Cabillu, filia de Cumida Ispanu, su de Sarasi, ad ankilla de cadadie, p[ro] Deu [et] p[ro] a[n]i[m]a sua [et] p[ro] darilli Deus (6)[et] S[an]c[t]u Jorgi sanidadi assa filia, [et] positi ella cu[m] totu parççoni sua. Et dedilloi Gu[n]nari Deççori a S[an]c[t]u Jorgi a Ja[n]ni (7)Meloni, filiu d'Arççocu Meloni, a s[er]bu de cadadie

9 Proemium taken from a 16th-century transumpt in the *Liber Diversorum*, 2/I serie, f. 68, DigiLib., pp. 70–71.

nigellu (13)Zerchis the deputy (*logusalbadori*). Whoever dares to controvert it, may the Father and the Son and the Holy Spirit curse him, and the twelve Apostles, the four Evangelists, the sixteen Prophets, (14)the twenty-four Elders, and the 318 Holy Fathers, and may he have his lot with Judas (15)in Hell! Let it be done and let it be done!

Carta volgare 8. Date: c. 1150. Grant of permission by Salusi de Lacon (Costantino-Salusio III), iudike of Cálari (1130–1162), to Petru Macis, the bishop of Suelli, to draw up a charter for benefices made to the church by Turbini de Serra, including donations of male and female servants with their shares. Archivio diocesano storico di Cagliari, no. 7, DigiLib., no. 7. Fitted with a 'Byzantine' lead seal (53.2 g) and seal tag of brown braided chord: obv. [...] (Λ)OVCIW / APXONT(I)/ [-M?]EPEHC[K]A / [...]PAΛEW[C?]. Rev. Cruciform invocative monogram (Type V), Θεοτόκε βοήθει; in the quarters: TW-ΣW ΔOY-LW (τῷ σῷ δούλῳ). Also exists as a 16th-century transumpt in the Archivio diocesano storico di Cagliari, *Liber Diversorum*, 2/I serie, f. 68, DigiLib., pp. 70–71. Editions: Solmi, 'Le carte volgari', no. 8, pp. 20–21; Cannas, *San Giorgio*, no. 4, p. 196; Falchi, *reisar.eu*, carta VIII.

This is well and faithfully translated, [being] made in the city and citadel of Callaris (Cagliari) on the 26th day of the month of January in the year from the birth of the Lord 1574, from a certain parchment charter fitted with a lead seal hanging by hemp cords; [it is] not itself suspect in any part but, because of its great age, it is in some parts corroded. The content of it, which is not flawed nor suspect, follows beneath these words:[10]

(1)+ In the name of the Father, the Son, and the Holy Spirit, amen. I, iudike Salusi de Lacon, by the will of Lord God, ruling (2)Karalis' territory (*parti*), permit (*assolbullu*) bishop Petru Macis to make himself a charter as he wishes. So, I, bishop Petru, with (3)permission (*assoltura*) from my lord, iudike Salusi of Lacon—may Lord God protect him for me for many good years, [both] him and (4)his wife, lady Sardinia Deççori—make myself a charter for benefices that Turbini de Serra made to Sanctu Jorgi de Suelli. He granted (5)to Aleni Cabillu, daughter of Cumida Ispanu from Sarasi, as a daily female servant (*ankilla de cadadie*), for God and for his soul, and in order to entrust his daughter's health to God (6)and Sanctu Jorgi. He gave her together with her entire share (*parççoni*). Also, Gunnari Deççori granted Janni (7)Meloni, son of Arççocu Meloni, to

10 Taken from the transumpt in *Liber Diversorum*, 2/I serie, f. 68, DigiLib., pp. 70–71.

cu[m] totu parçҫoni sua, p[ro] Deu [et] p[ro] a[n]i[m]a sua [et] de pare[n]tis suus. (8)Et posit a Sanctu Jorgi, Maria Deçҫori, neta de do[n]nu Turbini, unu s[er]bu a Mariani Carboni, filiu d'Arçҫocu Carboni, (9)p[ro] Deu [et] p[ro] a[n]i[m]a sua, [et] dedi ellu cu[m] totu parçҫoni sua. Et dedilloi a S[an]c[t]u Jorgi do[n]na Muscu de Scala una (10)ankilla a Bera P[er]ra ad cadadie, p[ro] Deu [et] p[ro] a[n]i[m]a sua. Et deru[n]t a S[an]c[t]u Jorgi Cumida d'Orruu Malusinnu et (11)Zerkis d'Orruu su de Segog[us] unu s[er]bu a Gosta[n]tini Devedu, filiu de Saraginu Devedu ki aiant inpari, [et] deru[n]t (12)iellu a s[er]bu de cadadie p[ro] Deu [et] p[ro] a[n]i[m]a issor[u] [et] deru[n]t illu cu[m] totu parçҫoni sua. Et posit iellu a S[an]c[t]u Jorgi d[on]nu (13)Petru Castai, filiu de do[n]nu Furadu de Unali, a Gosta[n]tini d'Ortu a s[er]bu de cadadie cu[m] tota parçҫoni sua. (14)Et posit do[n]na Muscu de S[er]ra a S[an]c[t]u Jorgi una ankilla a Marcusa Dusala, filia de Bera Dusala, a cadadie, (15)p[ro] Deu [et] p[ro] a[n]i[m]a sua, [et] dedi ella cu[m] totu parçҫoni sua. Et posit a S[an]c[t]u Jorgi Cumida d'Orruu una ankilla (16)a Furada Zalis, filia d'Aleni Zalis, ad ankilla de cadadie, p[ro] Deu et p[ro] a[n]i[m]a su(a) (Et posit) a S[an]c[t]u Jorgi Arçҫocu (17)de Laco[n], filiu de do[n]nu Gu[n]nari, unu s[er]bu a Mariani Co[n]tu, filiu de Petru Co[n]tu, a s[er]bu de cadadie, et (18)Sardinia, sa neta, posit a S[an]c[t]u Jorgi a Mariani Ma[n]ca, filiu de Petru de Ca[m]pu, [et] posit illu a s[er]bu de cadadie. Et su[n]t (19)testimomo[n]i[us] Gosta[n]tini de S[er]ra, Arçҫocu de Laco[n], et do[n]nigellu Petru logusalbadori, et ki ll'aet devert[er]e apat (20)anathema daba Pat[er] [et] Filiu [et] S[an]c[t]o Sp[irit]u, daba XII Ap[osto]los, IIII Eva[n]g[e]listas, XVI P[ro]ph[et]as, XXIIII Seniores, CCCXVIII (21)(Pa)dris S[an]c[tu]s, [et] apat sorti cu[m] Juda in infernu. Siat [et] fiat, amen, amen, amen.

Carta volgare 9. Date: c. 1190–1200. Grant of permission by Salusi de Lacon (Costantino-Salusio III), iudike of Cálari (1130–1162), with his wife, to Paulu, the bishop of Suelli to draw up a charter for purchases and donations of lands and resources made for the benefit of the church. Archivio diocesano storico di Cagliari, no. 10, DigiLib., no. 8. Fitted with a 'Byzantine' lead seal (60 g) and seal tag of brown chord: obv. + CA / ΛOVCIW / A]PXONTI/ [ME]PEHC[K]A / [...]. Rev. Cruciform invocative monogram (Type V), Θεοτόκε βοήθει; in the quarters: TW-ΣW ΔOY-ΛW (τῷ σῷ δούλῳ). Also exists as a 15th-century transcription in the Archivio diocesano storico di Cagliari, *Liber Diversorum*, 2/I serie, Appendix 'Quaderno,' no. 9, DigiLib., pp. 314–315. Editions: Solmi, 'Le carte volgari', no. 9, pp. 21–23; Falchi, *reisar.eu*, carta IX.

Sanctu Jorgi as a daily servant (*serbu de cadadie*) together with his entire share, for God and for the salvation of his soul and of his relatives. (8)Also, Maria Deççori, the granddaughter of lord Turbini, granted to Sanctu Jorgi, a servant (*serbu*) [called] Mariani Carboni, son of Arççocu Carboni, (9)for God and for her soul, and she granted him together with his entire share. Also, lady Muscu de Scala granted to Sanctu Jorgia (10)a female servant (*ankilla*), Bera Perra, as a daily servant, for God and for her soul. Also, Jorgi Cumida de Orruu Malusinnu, and (11)Zerkis de Orruu from Segogus, gave to Sanctu Jorgi a servant (*serbu*), Gostantini Devedu, son of Saraginu Devedu, whom they have together, and they granted him (12)as a daily servant (*serbu de cadadie*), for God and for their souls, together with his entire share. Also, lord (13)Petru Castai, son of lord Furadu de Unali, presented Sanctu Jorgi with a daily servant, Gostantini d'Ortu, together with all his share. (14)Also, lady Muscu de Serra granted Sanctu Jorgi with a female servant, Marcusa Dusala, daughter of Bera Dusala, as a daily servant, (15)for God and for her soul, and she donated her together with her entire share. Also, Cumida de Orruu presented Sanctu Jorgi with a female servant, (16)Furada Zalis, daughter of Aleni Zalis, as a daily female servant, for God and for her soul. Arççozu (17)de Lacon, son of lord Gunnari, also granted to Sanctu Jorgi a servant, Mariani Contu, son of Petru Contu, as a daily servant. Also, (18)Sardinia, his [lord Gunnari's] granddaughter, gave Sanctu Jorgi with Mariani Manca, son of Petru of Campu, as a daily servant.

(19)The witnesses are Gostantini de Serra, Arççocu de Lacon, and *donnigellu* Petru the deputy (*logusalbadori*). Whosoever dares to controvert it, (20)may the Father and the Son and the Holy Spirit curse him, and the twelve Apostles, the four Evangelists, the sixteen Prophets, the twenty-four Elders, and the 318 (21)Holy Fathers, and may he have his lot with Judas in Hell! Let it be and be done! Amen. Amen. Amen.

Carta volgare 9. Date: c. 1190–1200. Grant of permission by Salusi de Lacon (Costantino-Salusio III), iudike of Cálari (1130–1162), with his wife, to Paulu, the bishop of Suelli to draw up a charter for purchases and donations of lands and resources made for the benefit of the church. Archivio diocesano storico di Cagliari, no. 10, DigiLib., no. 8. Fitted with a 'Byzantine' lead seal (60 g) and seal tag of brown chord: obv. + CA / ΛOVCIW / A]PXONTI/ [ME]PEHC[K]A / [...]. Rev. Cruciform invocative monogram (Type V), Θεοτόκε βοήθει; in the quarters: TW-ΣW ΔOY-ΛW (τῷ σῷ δούλῳ). Also exists as a 15th-century transcription in the Archivio diocesano storico di Cagliari, *Liber Diversorum*, 2/I serie, Appendix 'Quaderno,' no. 9, DigiLib., pp. 314–315. Editions: Solmi, 'Le carte volgari', no. 9, pp. 21–23; Falchi, *reisar.eu*, carta IX.

(1)+ In nomin de Pat[er] [et] Filiu [et] S[an]c[t]o Yspirity. Ego judigi Salusi de Lacon, cu[m] muliere mia (2)do[n]na Adalasia, p[er] voluntate de Do[n]nu Deu potestandu parti de Karalis, assolbullu (3)a piscobu Paulu a ffagirisi carta in co bolit. Et ego piscobu Paulu, cu[m] lebandu (4)assolt[ur]a daba su do[n]nu miu judigi Salusi de Laco[n], ki mi llu castigit Do[n]nu Deu (5)bala[us] ann[us] [et] bon[us] [et] ad issi [et] a muliere sua, fazzumi carta pro conporas ki fegi (6)prossu piscobadu miu S[an]c[t]u Georgii de Suelli. Conporeilli in Sestu a Maria d'Arzola (7)sa plazza sua tenendu a Marzzu de Siuni su frau, [et] calatsi tudui usca a chi clo[n]pit (8)assa via dessu muristeri de S[an]c[t]u Petru, daba s'atera parti batsi tudui sa bia usca (9)assa via dessa ieca de Gontini Cicia, [et] deindelli xxv bias[n]tis et clo[m]pi'lli pariari. Istimo[n]ius, (10)p[res]b[ite]ru Gontini de Mo[n]tis, Cumida de Zori de Enoni, Trogotori de Zori de Sestu, e Marzu, (11)Cumida de Pira Ma[n]nu, Mariani de Orrù maiori de villa. Co[m]poreillis a Go[n]tini de (12)Mo[n]tis Buliariu [et] a Mariani Co[n]cas I cu[r]ria de t[er]ra costas assa plazza ki co[m]porej a Maria (13)d'Arzzola [et] cabiza assa plazza de Marzu [et] dei[n]dellis x soll[us] de dinaris i[n]t[er] pari, [et] clo[m]pi'l-(14)lis pariari. Co[m]poreillis a p[re]b[ite]ru Go[n]tini de Mo[n]tis [et] a Cumida su fr[ad]i sa plaza issor[u] ca[nt]u lloi (15)abe[n]ta, tenendu a Marzu, [et] clo[m]pit assa co[m]pora ki fegi a Cumida de Sikiu et clompit assa pla(z)-(16)za de Mariani de Orrù maiori de illa, [et] der[un]tmi sa domu cu[m] iscala debus domu [et] lad[us] dessa (17)fu[n]tana, [et] dei[n]dell[is] int[er] pari viiii bias[n]tis et clo[m]pill[is]. Istimo[n]i[us]de custa co[m]pora p[re]sbi[t]er Ma(r)-(18)iani Cavana, Mariani de Orrù maiori de illa, Gontini Cicia Marzu, Arzocu de Mo[n]tis. Et (19)d(e)milloi Cumida de Sikiu intru de custa plaza, una domu totu fabrigada [et] cob[er]ta cu[m] pl(a-)(20)za sua in co si falat usca a ki clo[m]pit assa plazza ki co[m]porei a Maria Arzola. Et ego c(o)[m]poreilli (21)plaza ubi mi kerfit issi subra plaza de Marzu [et] fraigei elli una domu [et] cob[er]ssi cali [et]issa domu (22)ki mi dedi issi, [et] plachit[us] nos appari. Istimo[n]i[us] de custa ca[m]bia, p[re]sbi[t]er Go[n]tini de Mo[n]tis Marzu, (23)Mariani de Orrù, Trogotori Dezori de Sestu, Mariani Co[n]cas serbu de do[n]nu Ia[n]ni de Siillu. (Co[m])poreilli (24)ad Aleni Grega sa parzoni ca[n]tu elli bi n'eda sua e de fr[ad]is suus, cui tene[n]du assa domu (25)ki mi ca[m]biedi Cumida de Sikiu, [et] levedisi i[n] pala de spiliarimilla da ki comindiedi kertari (26)[et] dei[n]delli iiii soll[us] de dinaris, [et] clo[m]pilli pariari. E[t] sunt destimo[n]i[us], p[re]sbi[t]er G(o)n(ti)ni de Monti[s], Ki(rbiu) (27)de Pira, Juenalis Frau, Furadu Mudis, Basili Cicia. Co[m]poreilli a Ia[n]ni Mudis una curria de (28)t[er]ra de plaza, tene[n]du assa ca[m]-

(1)+ In the name of the Father, the Son, and the Holy Spirit. I, iudike Salusi de Lacon, with my wife, (2)lady Adalasia, by the will of Lord God, ruling Karalis' territory (*parti*), permit (*assolbullu*) (3)bishop Paulu to make himself a charter as he wishes. So, I, bishop Paulu, with (4)permission (*assoltura*) from my lord, iudike Salusi of Lacon—may Lord God protect him for me for (5)many good years, [both] him and his wife—make myself a charter for the purchases that I have made (6)on behalf of (*prossu*) my bishopric of Sanctu Georgii de Suelli.

I bought in Sestu, from Maria d'Arzola, the (7)plot of land (*plazza*) that bordered [that of] Marzzu su Frau ('the blacksmith') of Siuni, which goes along until it reaches (8)the road of the monastery of Sanctu Petru; from the other part, it goes along the road until reaching (9)the road of the entrance (*ieca*) of Gontini Cicia. I gave her twenty-five bezants (*bisantis*), and completed the payment. The witnesses are: (10)priest Gontini de Montis, Cumida de Zori from Enoni (Genoni), Trogotori de Zori from Sestu, and Marzu, (11)Cumida de Pira Mannu, [and] Mariani de Orrù, head of the village (*maiori de villa*).

I bought from Gontini de (12)Montis Buliariu and Mariani Concas one rope-length (*curria*) of land, adjacent to the plot (*plazza*) that I bought from Maria (13)d'Arzzola; it reaches its end at the plot of Marzu. I then gave them ten soldi in cash (*sollus de dinaris*) between them equally (*inter pari*), and completed (14)the payment. I bought from priest Gontini de Montis and his brother Cumida their plot (15)they had bordering [that of] Marzu; also, I completed the purchase I made with Cumida de Sikiu and bought the plot of (16)land from Marianu d'Orrù, head of the village.

Also, they gave me the farm complex (*domu*) with its own hillside (*iscala*) and half (*ladus*) of (17)its spring (*funtana*). I gave them eight bezants between them equally, and completed the payment. The witnesses of this purchase are priest Mar-(18)iani Cavana, Mariani de Orrù head of the village, Gontini Cicia, Marzu, Arçozu de Montis. (19)Also, Cumida de Sikiu gave me, within this plot, a fully built and roofed house (*domu*) (20)with its plot of land, down the road towards the plot that I bought from Maria Arzola. I bought this (21)plot where I wanted it, below the plot of Marzu, and [where] he had a farm built and roofed; that was the farm (22)that he gave me; and we were both equally satisfied.

The witnesses of this transaction are priest Gontini de Montis, Marzu, (23)Mariani de Orrù, Trogotori de Zori from Sestu, Mariani Concas servant (*serbu*) of lord Ianni de Siilu. I bought (24)from Aleni Grega all the share (*parzoni*) he had that was his and his brothers', and which bordered the farm (25)that Cumida de Sikiu gave me in exchange, and he assumes the burden of proof against whomever may sue me for this in future. (26)I gave him [Aleni] four soldi in cash; I completed the payment. The witnesses are: priest Gontini de Montis, Kir[biu] (27)de Pira, Juenalis Frau, Furadu Mudis, [and] Basili Cicia. I bought from Ianni Mudis a rope-length (28)of a landed plot bordering the land

bia ki fegi cu[m] Cumida de Sikiu [et] tene[n]du assa co[m]por(a) ki fegi (a Iur)gia (29)de Kerki, [et] dei[n]delli VI soll[us] de dinaris [et] clo[m]pilli pariari. Isti(mo[n]i[us]) p[re]sbi[t]er Go[n](ti)ni (Cicia), Ior-(30)gi de Mo[n]tis, Gontini Cicia, [et] Golorgi de Kibullas. Conporeilli a Iurgia de Kerki fi(li)a de (Lan)-(31)dulfellu su ki fuit maiori de portu, su lad[us] dessa plaza ki lli (be)n(nit) dessa partizoni cu[m] do[n]nu (32)Ia[n]ni de Siillu, dessa plaza ki fuit de Basili Ca[m]ba, ki partea[n]t i[n]pari lad[us] a do[n]nu Ia[n]ni [et] lad[us] a Iur-(33)gia de Kerki, [et] dei[n]delli p[ro] cussu lad[us] IIII bisa[n]tis [et] clo[m]pilli pariari. Et su[n]t destimo[n]i[us] p[re]sbi[t]er Go[n](ti)-(34)ni de Montis, Masedu Muria maiori de scolca, Go[n]tini Cicia, Petru de Casta[n]ia de (B)a(radili), T(rogo)tori (35)Dezori, filiu de Trogotori Dezori de Giippi, Gidi[n]bili de Cabut[er]ra e(t dedilloi a sanctu Georgii de) (36)Suelli, p[ro] a[n]i[m]a sua, do[n]nu Ia[n]ni de Siillu su lad[us] dessa plaza ki parteat cu[m] (Jurgia sa filia de Lan-)(37)dulfellu maiori de portu. Istimo[n]i[us] calonigu Petru Furca, p[re]sbi[t]er Petru (Manca de Sigussuni, ja-)(38)g(u)nu Furadu Ma[n]nu, clerigu Ia[n]ni de Lugunu, clerigu Guielminu de S[an]c[t]a Ilia, Cumida (de Pira) (39)(de) Sestu, (et) Kirbiu su f[ra]di, Maria(ni) Co[n]cas serbu de do[n]nu Ia[n]ni de Siillu, Arçocu Frau. Co[m]p(oreilli) (40)a Petru de Scali, filiu d'Aleni Argulesa, sa parzoni ca[n]tu bi aeat sua [et] de fr[ad]is suu(s) et es[t] (ass'una parti) (41)(te)ne[n]du assa co[m]pora ki fegi a Cumida de Sikiu, [et] issu at[er]u lad[us] tenen(du as)sa plaza (chi conporei a prebiteru) (42)Go[n]tini de Mo[n]tis [et] deindelli II bisantis [et] clo[m]pilli pariari. Eleued(isi) (Petru de Scali in pala de) (43)spi(li)arimil(l)a da ki comindiedi kertari. Istimo[n]i[us] de custa co[m]pora p[re]sbi[t]er (Gontini de Montis), (44)(Kirbiu de Pira), Fu(r)adu de Ierrei, Petru Corsu de Sestu, Ma[r]iani de Sestu de Scala. Et (sunt destimonius: (45)Gunnari de Lacunu Mancosu) Arzocu de Maru[n]iu Pedru d'Arcedi. Et es[t] fata (custa carta abendusilla iudigi a manu) (46)sua sa curatoria de Ca[m]pitanu p[ro] (Et ki ll'aet devertere appat (47)anathema daba Pater et Filiu) [et] S[an]c[t]o Yspiritu, daba XXII Apostolos [et] IIII (Evangelistas et XVI P[ro]phetas, et) (48)XXII(II Seniores, CCCXVIII) s[an]c[t]os patris, [et] (apat) sorti cu[m] Iuda (in inferno, amen. Siat et fiat. Amen).

Carta volgare 10. Date: c. 1190–1200. Grant of permission by Salusi de Lacon (Costantino-Salusio III), iudike of Cálari (1130–1162), with his wife, to Paulu, the bishop of Suelli to draw up a deed of purchase for landed plots, vineyards and water resources bought for the benefit of the church. Archivio diocesano storico di Cagliari, DigiLib., no. 9; this

I exchanged with Cumida de Sikiu, and bordering the land I purchased from Iurgia (29)de Kerki, and I gave him six soldi in cash; I completed the payment. Witnesses are priest Gontini Cicia(?), (30)Iorgi de Montis, Gontini Cicia, and Golorgi de Kibullas. I bought from Iurgia de Kerki, daughter of Lan-(31)dulfellu, who was harbour master (*maiori de portu*), half of the plot which came from the partition made with lord (32)Ianni de Siilu, [extending] from the partition that was of Basili Camba, which they divided between them one half from lord Ianni and the other half from Iur-(33)gia de Kerki; I gave her, for her half, four bezants and completed the payment. The witnesses are priest Gont-(34)ini de Montis, Masedu Muria, head of the ward (*maiori de scolca*), Gontini Cicia, Petru de Castania of Baradili, Trogotori (35)Dezori, the son of Trogotori Dezori de Giippi, [and] Gidinbili de Cabuterra (Capoterra). [Also, Ianni de Siillu granted to Sanctu Georgii de] (36)Suelli, for his soul, half of the plot that he divided with [Iurgia, the daughter of Lan-](37)dulfellu the harbour master. The witnesses are: canon (*calonigu*) Petru Furca, priest (*clerigu*) Petru [Manca de Sigussini, (38)deacon (*iagunu*) Furadu Mannu, canon Ianni de Lugunu, priest Guielminu of Sancta Ilia, Cumida [de Pira] (39)of Sestu, his brother Kirbiu, Mariani Concas, servant of lord Ianni de Siillu, [and] Arçocu Frau.

(40)I bought from Petru of Scali, son of Aleni Argulesa, all the shares (*parzoni*) that they held, both of his and his brothers; one of its parts (41)borders the property I purchased from Cumida de Sikiu, and the other half borders the plot of land (*plaza*) I bought from priest (42)Gontini de Montis. I gave him two bezants and completed the payment. [Petru de Scala assumes] (43)the burden of proof against anyone who may sue me for this in the future. The witnesses of this purchase are priest [Gontini of Montis,] (44)[Kirbiu de Pira,] Furadu de Ierrei, Petru Corsu from Sestu, [and] Mariani de Sestu from Scala.

The witnesses (of this charter): are (45)[Gunnari de Lacunu Mancosu,] Arozcu de Maruniu, [and] Pedru de Arcedi. This charter was made [as the iudike has in his hands] (46)the district (*curatoría*) of Campitanu (Campidano) on behalf of (*pro*) [the deputy (*logusalbadori*)]. Whoever dares to controvert it, (47)may the Father and the Son and the Holy Spirit curse him, and the twelve Apostles, the four Evangelists, the sixteen Prophets, (48)the twenty-four Elders, and the 318 Holy Fathers, and may he have his lot with Judas in [the depths of Hell! Amen! Let it be and be done! Amen].

Carta volgare 10. Date: c. 1190–1200. Grant of permission by Salusi de Lacon (Costantino-Salusio III), iudike of Cálari (1130–1162), with his wife, to Paulu, the bishop of Suelli to draw up a deed of purchase for landed plots, vineyards and water resources bought for the benefit of the church. Archivio diocesano storico di Cagliari, DigiLib., no. 9; this

charter also exists as two 15th-century transcriptions in the Archivio diocesano storico di Cagliari, *Liber Diversorum*, 2/1 serie [E], f. 202, DigiLib., pp. 104–105; App. no. 10, DigiLib., p. 316. Editions: Solmi, 'Le carte volgari', no. 10, pp. 23–24; Falchi, *reisar.eu*, carta x.

(1)In nomin de Pat[er] [et] Filiu [et] S[an]c[t]u Isp[irit] Ego iudigi Salusi de Lacon, (2)cu[m] mulieri mia donna Adalasia, p[er] voluntate de Do[n]nu Deu potestando parte (3)de Karalis, assolbullu a donnu Paulu su piscopu miu de Suelli a ffagirisi karta (4)in co bolit. E[t] eu piscopu Paulu levandu assoltura dava ssu do[n]nu miu judigi (5)Salusi de Lacon, ki mi llu kastigit Donnu Deu balaus ann[us] [et] bonus [et] ad issi [et] ad (6)mulieri sua, fazzumi karta pro conpora ki mi fegi. Conporeillis ad Cumida de (7)Castania [et] assus fradis Gontini et Mariani, filius d'Arzzocu Duda [et] de Jurgia de Kastania, (8)pro ssu kantu illoi abeanta in Goi ka mi deru[n]t plazza [et] terras [et] vinias [et] saltus (9)et aquas, parzzoni issoru [et] de (d)onnu Petru de Kastania su preidi ki torrabat a icustus, (10)ca fuit ciu issoru, ki non mi 'ndi bogaruntu farçi sas II t[er]ras ki suntu in Iscobedu, (11)atara in Turzuala [et] atara I in erriu Gettadu. Et eu deindellis XXXIIII bisantis et (12)unu cavallu arzzu ambulanti, [et] clonpillis pariari. An(te) testimo[n]i[us], Mariani Dezzori. (13)Orlandu, ki fudi curatori de Tregenta, [et] Juanni de Serra, Forastiu de Kabut[er]ra, [et] Cumida (14)Stadigu, Gostantini Flori pikinnu, Frau d'Arcu, [et] Gostantini Traccucu. Istimoni[us] de logu: (15)Arzzocu de Maroniu, Petru d'Arzeti, Gunnari de Lacon Mancosu. Et est fata custa (16)karta habendusilla judigi ha manu sua sa curatoria de Kanpitanu pro logu[salbatori] (17)(Et) ki ll'aet devertere happat hanathema daba Pat[er] [et] Filiu [et] S[an]ctu Isp[irit]u, (18)daba XII appos[t]olos, daba IIII Eva[n]g[e]listas, daba XVI P[ro]ph[et]as, daba XXIIII Seniores, (19)daba CCCXVIII S[an]c[t]us Patris, et sorte appat cu[m] Iuda in inferno i[n] Ame[n] [et] fiat.

Carta volgare Suppl. F (Marseille). Date: c. 1190–1206. Permission granted by Salusi de Lacunu (William of Massa/Guglielmo I–Salusio IV), iudike of Cálari (1187–1214), with his wife, to Arresmundu, prior of San Saturnino in Cagliari to draw up a charter to confirm a judicial settlement with the people of Maara (Maracalagonis). Archives départementales des Bouches-du-Rhône, Fond Saint-Victor, 1 H 88, no. 428. Editions: Contini, 'La seconda carta,' pp. 61–79; Blasco-Ferrer, *Crest.*, vol. 1, pp. 72–76.

charter also exists as two 15th-century transcriptions in the Archivio diocesano storico di Cagliari, *Liber Diversorum*, 2/I serie [E], f. 202, DigiLib., pp. 104–105; App. no. 10, DigiLib., p. 316. Editions: Solmi, 'Le carte volgari', no. 10, pp. 23–24; Falchi, *reisar.eu*, carta x.

(1)In the name of the Father, the Son, and the Holy Spirit. I, iudike Salusi de Lacon, (2)with my wife, lady Adalasia, by the will of Lord God, ruling the territory (*parte*) (3)of Karalis, permit (*assolbullu*) lord Paulu, my bishop of Suelli, to make himself a charter (4)as he wishes. So, I, bishop Paulu, with permission (*assoltura*) from my lord, iudike (5)Salusi of Lacon—may Lord God protect him for me for many good years, both him and (6)his wife—make myself a charter for the purchase that I have made. I bought from Cumida de (7)Castania and his brothers Gontini and Mariani, sons of Arzzocu Duda and Jurgia de Kastania, (8)for all that which they held in Goi (Goni); they gave me their plot (*plazza*), lands (*terras*), vineyards (*vinias*), unworked lands (*saltus*), (9)and water resources (*aquas*), [and] their own shares (*parzzoni*) as well as those of lord Petru de Kastania the priest (*preidi*) who returned to them (10)that which belonged to their uncle, but who did not recall any from me except for two lands that are located in Iscobedu, (11)one in Turzuala and the other in Erriu ('stream') Gettadu. I gave them thirty-four bezants (*bisantis*) and (12)one dappled riding horse.

I completed the payment before the witnesses Mariani Dezzori (13)Orlandu who was curator (*curatori*) of Tregenta (Trexenta), Juanni de Serra, Forastiu de Kabuterrra (Capoterra), Cumida (14)Stadigu, Gostantini Flori Pikinnu ('small'), Frau de Arcu, and Gonstantini Traccucu. Witnesses of the realm (*Istimonius de logu*): (15)Arzzocu de Maroniu, Petru d'Arzeti, [and] Gunnari de Lacon Mancosu. This (16)charter was issued as the iudike has in his hands the district (*curatoría*) of Kanpitanu (Campidano) on behalf of the deputy (*logusalbadori*). (17)Whoever dares to controvert it, may the Father and the Son and the Holy Spirit curse him, and (18)the twelve Apostles, the four Evangelists, the sixteen Prophets, the twenty-four Elders, and the (19)318 Holy Fathers, and may he have his lot with Judas in Hell! Amen and let it be done!

Carta volgare Suppl. F (Marseille). Date: c. 1190–1206. Permission granted by Salusi de Lacunu (William of Massa/Guglielmo I–Salusio IV), iudike of Cálari (1187–1214), with his wife, to Arresmundu, prior of San Saturnino in Cagliari to draw up a charter to confirm a judicial settlement with the people of Maara (Maracalagonis). Archives départementales des Bouches-du-Rhône, Fond Saint-Victor, 1 H 88, no. 428. Editions: Contini, 'La seconda carta,' pp. 61–79; Blasco-Ferrer, *Crest.*, vol. 1, pp. 72–76.

(1)In nomine de Pater et Filiu et Sanctu Ispiritu. Ego Iudigi Salusi de Lacunu, cun muiere mea donna Ad-(2)alasia, per voluntate de donnu Deu potestandu parte de kKaralis, assolbullu Arresmundu (3)priori de Sanctu Saturru a fagirisi carta in cobolit. Et ego Arresmundu, lebandu assoltura daba su (4)donnu miu Iudigi Salusi de Lacunu, ki mi llu castigit donnu Deu balaus annus et bonus et a issi et a muiere (5)sua, fazzumi carta pro kertu ki fegi cun isus de Maara pro su saltu ubi si partzint appari Zizimi et Maa-(6)ra, ki est de Sanctu Saturru. Intrei in kertu cun isus de Maara, ca mi machelaant in issu saltu miu. Canpa-(7)niarunt si megu, c'avea cun me istimonius bonus ki furunt armadus a iurari pro cantu kertaa cun issus, ca fuit totu de Sanctu Satur-(8)ru su saltu, et derunt mi in issu canpaniu daa Petra de Mama et Filia derectu assu Runcu dessa terra de Gosan-(9)tini de Baniu, et derectu a Bruncu de Argillas, et derectu a Piskina d'Arenas, et levat cabizali derectu assa Bia de (10)Carru de su mudeglu, et clonpit assu cabizali de Ventu d'estru dessa domestia de donnigellu Cumitai, (11)et levat tudui su cabizzali et essit assas zinnigas de Moori de Silba, lasandu a manca s'erriu, et clon-(12)pit deretu assu Pizariu de Sellas ubi posirus sa dii su tremini et levat sa Bia Maiori de Genna [...] terra al[...], (13)et lebat su moori [...] a sa terra de Sanctu Saturru, lassandulla issa a manca, et lebat su moori lassandu a manca sas (14)Cortis de Orruinas de [.a.]si. Et apirus cummentu in su canpaniu ki fegirus d'arari issus sas terras ipsoru ki sunt (15)in saltu miu et llu castiari su saltu, et issus hominis mius de Sinnai arari sas terras mias et issas terras issoru (16)ki sunt in saltu de 'ssus, et issus castiari su saltu issoru. Custu fegirus plagendu mi a mimi et a issus homi-(17)nis mius de Sinnai et de totu bi[l]la de Maara. Istimonius ki furunt a ssegari su saltu de pariari (18)et a poniri sus treminis, donnu Cumita de Lacun ki fut curatori de Canpitanu, Cumita d'Orru [...] (19)du, A. Sufreri et Iohanni de Serri filiu de su curatori Petru Soriga, et Gosantini Toccu Mullina, M[....-](20)gi Calcaniu de Pirri, C. de Solanas, C. Pullu de Ergei, Iorgi Cabra de Kerarius, Iorgi Sartoris, Laurenzu de Kerar-(21)ius, G. Toccu de Kerarius et P. Marzu de Quartu Iossu, et prebiteru Albuki de Kibullas, P. de zZipari, et M. Gre-(22)gu, M. Desogus de Palma, et G. Corsu de Sancta Ilia, et A. Carena, G. Artea de Palma, et Oliveri de kKarda[....] (23)Pisanu, et issu gonpanioni. Et sunt istimonius de logu, Arzzoccu de Maroniu, et Gonnari de Lacon (24)Mancosu, et Trogotori Dezzori de Dolia. Et est facta custa

In the name of the Father, the Son, and the Holy Spirit. I, iudike Salusi de Lacon, with my wife, lady Adalasia, by the will of Lord God, ruling Karalis' territory (*parte*), permit (*assolbullu*) Arresmundu, prior of Sanctu Saturru (San Saturnino in Cagliari), to make himself a charter as he wishes. So, I, Arresmundu, with permission (*assoltura*) from my lord, iudike Salusi of Lacon—may Lord God protect him for me for many good years, him and his wife—make myself a charter about legal dispute (*kertu*) that I had with the people of Maara, regarding the unworked land (*saltu*) where Zizimi and Maara are divided into two equal parts, which belongs to Sanctu Saturru. I entered into a dispute with the people of Maara because they slaughter cattle for me in that land of mine. They agreed on a settlement with me because I had with me good witnesses who were prepared to testify under oath regarding everything that I disputed with them, because all that unworked land was of Sanctu Saturru, and by that settlement they conceded me [the land] from Petra de Mama et Filia ('mother and child rock') towards Piskina d'Arenas ('sand pool'), which then goes to top boundary (*cabizali*) towards the road of Carru de su Mudeglu ('cart of the cairn'), and connects with the top boundary of Ventu d'Estru from the farmland (*domestia*) of *donnigellu* Cumitai, and goes up along the top boundary and leaves at the rushes of Moori de Silba, reaching the river at the left side, and continuing towards Pizariu de Sellas, where the boundary is, it goes up the main road of Genna [...] land al[...], and goes up the bordering path [...] to the land of Sanctu Saturru, leaving it by the left side, and goes up the bordering path leaving by the left side Cortis de Orruinas from [.a.]si. We agreed on the settlement we reached that they would plough their lands that are in my unworked land and take care of the land, and that my men from Sinnai would plough my land and their lands that are in their unworked lands and take care of their land. I, my men from Sinnai and all the village of Marra, were satisfied with what we did.

Witnesses who went to alienate (*ssegari*) the unworked land in equal parts and to set the boundaries: lord Cumita de Lacun who was curator (*curatori*) of Canpitanu (Campidano), Cumita d'Orru [...]du, A. Sufrei and Iohanni de Serri son of the curator Petru Soriga, and Gosantini Toccu Mullina, M[...]gi Calcaniu de Pirri, C. de Solanas, C. Pullu de Ergei, Iorgi Cabra de Kerarius, Iorgi Sartoris, Laurenzu de Kerarius, G. Toccu de Kerarius, and P. Marzu de Quartu Iossu ('Lower Quarto', Quartu Sant'Elena), and priest Albuki de Kibullas, P. de zZipari, and M. Grego, M. Desogus de Palma, and G. Corsu de Sancta Ilia, and A. Carena, G. Artea de Palma, and Oliveri de kKarda[...] Pisanu, and his companion.

The witnesses of the realm (*istimonius de logu*) are: Arzzoccu de Maroniu, and Gonnari de Lacon Mancosu, and Trogotori Dezzori from Dolia. This char-

carta abendusilla Iudegi a ma-[25]nu sua sa curatoria de Canpitanu pro logus-albatori. Et ki ll'aet devertere apat anathema daba [26]Pater et Filiu et Sanctu Ispiritu, daba XII Appostolos et IIII Evangelistas, XVI Prophetas, XXIV Seniores, CCCXV-[27]III Sanctus Patris, et sorti apat cun Iuda in infernum inferiori. Siat et Fiat.

Carta volgare Suppl. G (Pisa). Date: 10 May 1211. Permission granted by Salusi de Lacon (William of Massa/Guglielmo I–Salusio IV), iudike of Cálari (1187–1214), together with his daughter Benedicta, to the *domus* of Sanctu Iorgi de Sebollu, dependent on the monastery of San Gorgonio on the island of Gorgona and on the Pisan monastery of San Vito, exempting it from the payment of any tribute. Archivio di Stato di Pisa, Fondo Diplomatico, R. Acquisto Coletti, 10 maggio 1212, p. corta. Editions: Solmi, *Studi storici*, App. V, pp. 422–423; Tanfani Centofanti, 'Due Carte inedite', pp. 357–376; Fadda, 'Le pergamene nel Coletti', no. 6, pp. 123–125.

[1]In nomine Patris et Filii et Spiritus Sancti, Amen. [2]Ego Iudigi Salusi de Lacon cun filia mia Bene-[3]dicta, per bolintate de donnu Deu potestando [4]parti de Kalaris, fazzulla custa carta pro beni [5]ki fazzu a onori de Deu et de Sanctu Iorgi et de Sanctu [6]Gorgonii et de Sanctu Vitu, martirus de Cristu, et pro [7]remissioni de sus peccadus mius et de parentis [8]mius, et pro pregu ki mi'ndi fegit, candu andei [9]ad Pisas, donnu Albertu su abbadi de Gorgona et [10]de Sanctu Vitu cun issus fradis suus. Assolbulla sa [11]domu de Sanctu Iorgi de Sebollu, ki si clabat ad pusti [12]su monasteriu de Gorgona et de Sanctu Vitu, et assolbu [13]sus serbus et is ankillas de cussa domu, et totu sus [14]hominis ki anti stari ad sirbitiu de cussa domu; ki [15]non denti aligandu dadu, ni issa domu ni is serbus, [16]ni is sirbidoris suus, ni ad Iuigi ni ad curadori, ni [17]ad maiori de scolca, ni ad armentariu et ni ad peruna per-[18]soni ki siat, nin pro nomini de Iudigi, nin pro nomini [19]alienu, farci siat si libera et assolta, et icussa domu de [20]Sanctu Iorgi de Sebollu et totu sus hominis suus de non [21]dari aligandu perunu dadu nin pro personis, nin pro [22]causa issoru peruna. Et icustu beni ki apu fatu ad sa do-[23]mu de Sanctu Iorgi de Sebollu et ad totu sus hominis suus de [24]nollis lebari aligandu dadu, non apat balia nin po-[25]testadi perunu Iuigi et nin peruna personi, ki ad benni pust [26]mei, a isfairillu ni ad minimari llu aligandu cantu [27]adi durari su segulu. Et icustu beni fegi sendu in Pi-[28]sas in sa clesia de Sanctu Pedru ad vincula, ante testimon-[29]ius Nigola

ter was made as the iudike has in his hands the curator's district of Canpitanu (Campidano) on behalf of the deputy (*logusalbadori*). Whosoever dares to controvert it, may the Father and the Son and the Holy Spirit curse him, and the twelve Apostles, the four Evangelists, the sixteen Prophets, the twenty-four Elders, and the 318 Holy Fathers, and have his lot with Judas in the depths of Hell! Let it be and be done!

Carta volgare Suppl. G (Pisa). Date: 10 May 1211. Permission granted by Salusi de Lacon (William of Massa/Guglielmo I–Salusio IV), iudike of Cálari (1187–1214), together with his daughter Benedicta, to the *domus* of Sanctu Iorgi de Sebollu, dependent on the monastery of San Gorgonio on the island of Gorgona and on the Pisan monastery of San Vito, exempting it from the payment of any tribute. Archivio di Stato di Pisa, Fondo Diplomatico, R. Acquisto Coletti, 10 maggio 1212, p. corta. Editions: Solmi, *Studi storici*, App. V, pp. 422–423; Tanfani Centofanti, 'Due Carte inedite', pp. 357–376; Fadda, 'Le pergamene nel Coletti', no. 6, pp. 123–125.

(1)In the name of the Father, the Son, and the Holy Spirit, amen. (2)I, iudike Salusi de Lacon, with my daughter Bene-(3)dicta, by the will of Lord God, ruling (4)Kalaris' territory (*parti*), write her this charter for the benefices (5)I make for the honour of God, and of Sanctu Iorgi, and of Sanctu (6)Gorgonii, and of Sanctu Vitu, martyrs of Christ, and for (7)the remission of my sins and of my relatives (*parentis*), (8)and for the plea that lord Albertu the abbot of Gorgona and Sanctu Vitu and his brothers made to me when I went (9)to Pisa. I absolve (*assolbulla*) the house of Sanctu Iorgi de Sebollu, affiliated to the monastery of Gorgona and (10)Sanctu Vitu with their brothers. I absolve (11)the house of Sanctu Iorgi de Sebollu, and all that is included at (12)the monastery of Gorgona and of Sanctu Vitu, and I absolve (13)the servants (*serbus*) and female servants (*ankillas*) of that house, and all the (14)men (*homines*) who will be in the service of that house, (15)from ever paying tax (*dadu*), whether of the house or its servants (16)or retainers (*sirbidoris*), either to the iudike or to a curator (*curadori*), or (17)to a head of the ward (*maiori de scolca*), or to an administrator (*armentariu*), or to any other person, (18)either in the name of the iudike or in the name of anyone (19)else.

Thus, may this house of (20)Sanctu Iorgi de Sebollu and all its villeins (*hominis*) (21)be free and exempt (*assolta*), either for any of its people (22)or for any of its assets (*causa*). (23)I have made this for the house of Sanctu Iorgi de Sebollu and to all its men, (24)so they are never due to pay tax (25)And no iudex nor any person (26)may diminish any of this (27)till the end of time. I made these benefices while being in (28)Pisa at the church of Sanctu Pedru ad Vincula (San

nodaiu et Barlecta de Luca filiu de Brunec-(30)tu, Gualteroto filiu de Gilardinu Castagnaccii, et Bandi-(31)nu filiu de Bonaiuncta de Philipu, et Brunectu filiu (32)de Villanu Follaiu. Et sunt destimonius, Petru d'Arcedi, (33)Barisoni Passagi, et Comita de Serra de Frailis. Et est (34)facta custa carta Anno Domini MCCXII, Indictione XIIII (35)sexto idus Madii, habendumilla sa curadoria de Campida-(36)nu ad manu mia pro logusalbadori. Et ki ll'aet devertere, (37)apat anathema daba Patre et Filio et Sancto Spiritu, daba XII (38)Apostolos et IIIIor Evangelistas, daba XVI Prophetas et XXIIII Se-(39)niores, daba CCCXVIII Sanctos Patres, et sorte habeat [cu]m (40)Iuda traditore in inferno inferiori. Amen et Fiat.

Carta volgare 11. Date: June 1215. Confirmation by Benedicta de Lacon (Benedetta di Massa), iudike of Cálari (1214–1233), of benefices made by Troodori (Mariano-Torchitorio II), iudike of Cálari (1103–1130) to the church of San Giorgio di Suelli. The confirmation includes an account in Latin of the miraculous healing of the iudike by St George of Suelli (d. 1117), taken from his *Life*. Archivio diocesano storico di Cagliari, no. 1, DigiLib., no. 10. Fitted with a 'Byzantine' lead seal (50.4g) and seal tag of brown chord. Obv. +T(O)PK / OTOPHW / [A]PXUNTH / (M]EP[E]HCK / (A)PAVEW[C]. Rev. Cruciform invocative monogram (Type V), Θεοτόκε βοήθει; in the quarters: TW-ΣW ΔOY-ΛW (τῷ σῷ δούλῳ). Also known from 15th- and 16th-century transcriptions in the Archivio diocesano storico di Cagliari, *Liber Diversorum*, 1/I serie, ff. 130–131r, DigiLib., pp. 120–121; 2/I serie, f. 141, DigiLib., pp. 150–151; Appendix 'Quaderno,' no. 1, DigiLib., pp. 310–311; no. 12, DigiLib., pp. 317–318; 17th-century Spanish translation by Aleo in *Sucessos generales*, ff. 149–152. Editions: Tola, *CDS*, p. 323; Solmi, 'Le carte volgari', no. 11, pp. 24–26; Cannas, *San Giorgio*, no. 5, p. 197; Falchi, *reisar.eu*, carta XI.

Hoc es[t] tra[n]sumptu[m] fidelit[er] s[u]mptu[m] a q[ua]da[m] p[u]blico instrume[n]to pergamineo s[um]ptu[m] in li[n]gua Sardisca plu[m]bo cu[m] q[ui]busda[m] litteris et caracterib[us] in pe[n]de[n]ti sigillato cu[ius] tenor talis e[st]:[11]

(1)In nomine Patris [et] Filii [et] Sp[irit]us S[an]c[t]i, amen. Ego Benedicta de Lacon, per boluntade de do[n]nu Deu potestando (2)(parti de) Kalaris, f(azzulli) carta ad Sanctu Jorgi de Suelli su donnu miu, p[ro] beni ki lli fegit juigi Troodori ad s[an]c[t]u Jorgi, insendur(u) (biu (3)et pisco)bu de (Barbaria, pro miragula ki fegit) Deus in juigi Troodori, p[ro] amantia [et] pregu de s[an]c[t]u Jorgi, d'una pestilentia (4)(de) ki llu iscapedi s[an]c[t]u Jorgi ad

11 Taken from *Liber Diversorum*, 1/I serie, ff. 130–131r, DigiLib., pp. 120–121.

Pietro in Vincoli) in front of the witnesses: (29)Nigola the notary; Barlecta de Luca, son of Brunectu; (30)Gualteroto, son of Gilardinu Castagnaccii; (31)Bandinu, son of Bonaiuncta de Philipu, and Brunectu, son (32)of Villanu Gollaru. The witnesses [to this charter] are Petru d'Arcedi, (33)Barisoni Passagi, and Comita de Serra from Frailis.

(34)This charter was made in the year of our Lord 1212 of the 14th Indiction on the (35)6th day before the Ides of May (10 May), as I have in my hands the curator's district (*curadoría*) of Campidanu (36)on behalf of the deputy (*logusalbadori*). Whosoever dares to controvert it, (37)may the Father and the Son and the Holy Spirit curse him, and the twelve (38)Apostles, the four Evangelists, the sixteen Prophets, the twenty-four (39)Elders, and the 318 Holy Fathers, and may he have his lot with (40)Judas the traitor in the depths of Hell! Amen and let it be done!

Carta volgare 11. Date: June 1215. Confirmation by Benedicta de Lacon (Benedetta di Massa), iudike of Cálari (1214–1233), of benefices made by Troodori (Mariano-Torchitorio II), iudike of Cálari (1103–1130) to the church of San Giorgio di Suelli. The confirmation includes an account in Latin of the miraculous healing of the iudike by St George of Suelli (d. 1117), taken from his *Life*. Archivio diocesano storico di Cagliari, no. 1, DigiLib., no. 10. Fitted with a 'Byzantine' lead seal (50.4g) and seal tag of brown chord. Obv. +T(O)PK / OTOPHW / [A]PXUNTH / (M]EP[E]HCK / (A)PAVEW[C]. Rev. Cruciform invocative monogram (Type V), Θεοτόκε βοήθει; in the quarters: TW-ΣW ΔOY-ΛW (τῷ σῷ δούλῳ). Also known from 15th- and 16th-century transcriptions in the Archivio diocesano storico di Cagliari, *Liber Diversorum*, 1/I serie, ff. 130–131r, DigiLib., pp. 120–121; 2/I serie, f. 141, DigiLib., pp. 150–151; Appendix 'Quaderno,' no. 1, DigiLib., pp. 310–311; no. 12, DigiLib., pp. 317–318; 17th-century Spanish translation by Aleo in *Sucessos generales*, ff. 149–152. Editions: Tola, *CDS*, p. 323; Solmi, 'Le carte volgari', no. 11, pp. 24–26; Cannas, *San Giorgio*, no. 5, p. 197; Falchi, *reisar.eu*, carta XI.

(1)[Sardinian]: In the name of the Father, the Son, and the Holy Spirit, amen. I, Benedicta de Lacon, by the will of Lord God, ruling (2)Kalaris' territory (*parti*), make a charter for [the church of] Sanctu Jorgi de Suelli, my lord, for the benefices that iudike Troodori made to St George while alive and being the (3)bishop of Barbária, for the miracle that God made in favour of iudike Troodori, by the love and intercession of St George, regarding a pestilence (4)from which God relieved the iudike through [the person of] St George. That pesti-

juigi Troodori esti custa sigundu (ind' esti seritu) (5)(i)n sa legen(da dessa bida de sanctu Jorgi: Preterea supradictus) kalaritan[us] Iude(x) incurrit gravissima[m] [et] miserabile[m] calamitate[m] nam cu[m] (hora) (6)pr[and]dii sive (mensa referta multis ciborum) ferculis (statim omnes cibi scarabeis atque scabronib[us] et) varii op[er]ieba(ntur) (sord)ib[us] (7)cu[m] (tantum creuisset hec persecutio, ut iam non) posset sumere cibu[m] nisi quasi abscondite manu tenendo, tande[m] sa(u)b(ri) (8)(reperti) consil(io venit ad servum Dei Jeorgium et retulit ei miseriam qua cotidie) affligebat[ur], dep[re]cat[us] es[t] etia[m] multis p[re]cib(us et lacrimis, ut sibi sub-(9)veni)re dig(naretur et suis cum precibus a presenti liberaret) exitio. (Quod cum audisset) beat[us] Jeorgi[us], mis[er]icordia mot[us] sup[er] eu[m], iussit eu[m] secu[m] venire ad pr(an)-(10)dium. Cu[m](que ventum esset, ad mensa) p[re]cepit illu[m] discu[m]b(ere, accipiensque) pane[m] benedixi[t] ac fregit [et] dedit illi, [et] parit[er] co[m](ederunt. Ex (11)illa igi[t]u]r hora (liberatus est) iudex a sup[ra]-dicta miseria [et] ia[m] nu(lle) sordes in eius) convivio apparueru[nt]. Vide[n]s aute[m] se p[re](cibus et meritis beati (12)J)orgii e[ss]e salva(atum), dedit villa[m] Suellense[m] cu[m] t[er]ris [et] silvis, servis (et anc)illis [et] om[n]i suppelletili, ut ipse om[n]esque sui su(ccessore)s (eam) (13)sine lite possidere[n][t]. Coniux (vero) ei[us] no[m]i[n]e Sinispella optulit s[an]c[t]o Jeorgio villa[m] Simeri cu[m] o[mn]ib[us] suis p[er]tinentiis [et] delegavit ei (14)om[n]em sua[m] portione[m] ut post morte[m] sua[m] ipse om[n]esque sui successores ea[m]possidere[n]t. C(u)st(a) esti sa miragula ki fegit Deu [et] s[an]c[t]u Jor-(15)gi cun juigi Troodori p[ro] ki lli dedi ad s[an]c[t]u Jorgi sa billa de Suelli, cun su ca[n]tu si p[er]tineda a icussa billa [et] a issa mulieri do[n]na Nispella (16)illi dedi sa billa de Simieri. Et icusta(s) billas ancu si llas airit in pag(i) su piscobadu de Barbaria daba senduru biu s[an]c[t]u Jorgi, sem-(17)piri illi llas firmu ego [et] inde lli bullu carta ad S[an]c[t]u Jorgi, tenendulli terminis ad su saltu dessa billa de Suelli, ki si cum(e[n]zat) d(a)-(18)ba su bau de T[er]ra Alba dess'aqua des Passaris, [et] tenit sa bia de Logu, fisca a issu erriu ki falat daba Funtana noa, [et] tenit su er(riu) ad Ca-(19)bu iossu deretu ad Nuragi descoriadu, [et] deretu ad su bru[n]cu dessu Mudeglu, pare[n]du ad pischina de Bois, [et] lebat sa serra dessu (Mude)-(20)glu i[m]plassandullu ad pauli de Mela, deretu a orriina de nonzu Pedru, [et] junpat erriu deretu ad su masuniu de (Jorgi Muria) (21)clo[m]pit ad su bau d'Aq[ua] salsa, [et] tenit tudui su erriu ki falat daba bau de Godi kena llu lassari, fisca a issu bau ki (iunpat daba Suelli)(22)ad Siuni [et] daba cundi collat treessu margini deretu ad sa corona,

lence from which St George relieved iudike Troodori is as follows, according to that which is written in (5)the legend of the *Life* of St George.

[Latin:] The Calaritan iudike experienced a very serious and pitiful calamity, for when (6)lunch or dinner was to be prepared, if a table was packed with many dishes, all the food was immediately covered with beetles, scarabs, and other filthy creatures. This torment had worsened to the point (7)that he could no longer eat any food except by keeping it hidden in his hand. Finally, after being wisely advised, (8)he came to George, servant of God, and told him the agony with which he was afflicted daily; he also begged, with many pleas and tears, that he would agree to come to his aid, and, with his pleas, to relieve him of his present ruin. (9)When holy George heard this, being moved with compassion for him, he demanded him to join him for dinner, and (10)when he came, he ordered him to sit down at the table. He then took the bread, blessed it, broke it, gave it to him, and they ate together. (11)From that moment, the iudike was freed from the aforesaid agony, and no filth appeared at his meal-times anymore. Seeing that he was saved by the pleas and virtues of (12)George, he granted him the village of Suelli with lands and woods, male and female servants, and all furnishings, so that he and all his successors would possess it (13)without litigation. Moreover, his wife Sinispella offered to Santu Jorgi the village of Simeri, with all its belongings, and granted (14)him all her shares so that, after her death, he and all his successors would possess it.

[Sardinian] This is the miracle that God and St George made (15)for iudike Troodori, for which he granted to Sanctu Jorgi the village of Suelli, together with all that belonged to this village. Also, his wife lady Nispella (16)gave him the village of Simieri. And these villages, additionally, have always been held peacefully by the bishopric of Barbária since St George was alive. (17)I confirm them to him and seal a charter to Sanctu Jorgi regarding them. These villages border the confines of the unworked land (*saltu*) of the village of Suelli which began from (18)Bau de Terra Alba ('the ford of white land') to the water of Passaris, bordering the main road (*bia de Logu*), until it reaches the stream that descends from Funtana Noa ('new spring'), and borders it along the stream to Cabu (19)Iossu towards Nuraghe Descoriadu, towards the hilltop of su Mudeglu ('the cairn'), stopping at the Pischina de Bois ('pool of oxen'), and then carries on along the ridge of su Mudeglu ('the cairn') and then descends until (20)reaching the marsh of Mela, going towards the Orriina de Nonzu Pedru ('shack of notary Peter'), and then crosses the stream straight up to the paddock of Jorgi Muria, and (21)arrives at su Bau d'Aqua Salsa ('the ford of salt water'), and then borders it all along the stream that descends from Bau de Godi ('ford of Godi') without leaving it, [then] up to the ford that one crosses to go from Suelli (22)to Sinui, and from there it ascends across the ridge towards sa Corona ('the crown'), stopping

parendu ad Siuni (et clompit a sa bia et tudui sa bia deretu) (23)ad nuragi de (pisco)bu [et] lebat cussa bia ki badi ad Seerri kena lla (lassa)ri [et] i[m]plassat illa a orriina d'Iizu [et] calat(si) (adsu flumini de)-(24)retu deretu (ad baniu) d'Aseni, [et] calat tudui su flumini (deretu ad concas) d'Aseni [et] clo[m]pit ad bau de piscobu, inui si (ingenzat s'ateru) (25)saltu ki ll(oi dedi Juigi) Gontini, aioni miu ad S[an]c[t]u (Jorgi) (...) dessa billa de Suelli de ki si 'ndi apat p[ro]i s[an]c[t]u (Jorgi. Et illu esti su saltu dessa billa de Suelli de ki si 'nde apat proi Santu (Jorgi cantu a)-(26)di dura(ri su mun)du, ki no[n] apat b(al)ias nin juigi, ki pus (me ad esse, nin) do[n]nigellu, nin p[er]una p[er]soni dessu mundu a isfairillu, ni (a) (27)minimarillu custu beni ki lli fudi dadu ad s[an]c[t]u Jorgi in (in bida sua. Et ego) illi llu firmu p[ro] honori de Deus, [et] p[ro] siat mi issi padron(u) (28)[et] in icustu mundu [et] in (s'ateru) [et] p[ro] s'anima dessu do[n]nu padri miu su marchesu de Massa juigi Salusi de Laco[n] [et] dess(a) do[n]na (ma)ma (29)mia cuntissa Adalasia, [et] p[ro] ama[n]tia de do[n]nu Troodori su piscobu miu de Suelli. Et firmulli ad S[an]c[t]u Jorgi su saltu (de Calcaria) (30)ki si segat daba gut[ur]u des Nugis, deretu ad cucuru de Forru de mo[n]t(...)riu, et calat deretu ad sa ie[n]na de sas teson(is) (inter montis, et essit) (31)p[er] bia deretu ad su mulume[n]tu de Cipari Carsada, [et] collat deretu ad s(u ar)cu de sa ie[n]na de Rugi, [et] benit deretu ad s'arb(uri ki tennit Sanctu) (32)Jorgi de su bakellu suu, ki fissit in t[er]ra candu t[er]minaat custu saltu s[an]c[t]u Jorgi cun sus maioralis, [et] fegitsi arburi sinbilianti d('iligi et) (33)collat deretu ad bru[n]cu de Saltu piki[n]nu, [et] essit deretu ad su bru[n]cu de Riu de paboru, [et] calat deretu ad su planu de nonzu Gulpis, [et] c(a)-(34)lat derectu ad Padru de Tiricu, [et] lebat su erriu de gut[ur]u d'Esquilla (et cal)at su erriu dessa coa iossu de fu[n]tana (longa et le)bat sa bia d[e] (mo)-(35)oris de Porru, tudui su erriu de Cortis de bituru, deretu ad Gi(di)li int[er] (s)altus [et] essit ad su erriu d'aqua de Go(sti Mikina) [et] calat su (36)(er)riu de Mandara, deretu a iscla de s'Ortiada, [et] calat deretu a Ariola Mella, (et) torrat deretu ad su gut[ur]u des Nugis (daundi se et ingenzat). (37)Ki si 'ndi appat p(ro)i S[an]c[t]u Jorgi cantu adi durari su mundu. (Istestimonius a)nte ki lli firmu ad S[an]c[t]u Jorgi (de Suelli, et de totu cantu) (38)narat ista carta, do[n]nu Riccu su archipiscobu (m)iu (de Pluminus), do[n]nu Mariani su piscobu miu de (de Zulkis; prebiteru Johanni Spina capellanu) miu (de) su mo[n]ti d'Aqua Friida, [et] Comida (Dezo)ri de Ienoni [et] Joh[ann]i de Serra Daluda,

at Sinui, then it reaches the road and borders it along (23)to the Nuraghe de Piscobu ('of the bishop'; modern Nuraghe Su Piscu), and then takes up the road that goes towards Seerri without leaving it, and it reaches Orriina d'Iizu ('the shack of Iizu'), and then it descends towards the river, along the way (24)towards Baniu d'Aseni ('the bath of Aseni'), and goes down along the river towards Concas d'Aseni ('the basins of Aseni'), and then it reaches Bau de Piscobu ('the ford of the bishop'), where it connects with the other (25)unworked land (*saltu*) that iudike Gontini granted to him, to my dear St George. And this is the land of the village of Suelli which Sanctu Jorgi may hold (26)till the end of time. And no iudike, whoever may succeed me, nor any other person of the world, shall undo this or (27)diminish this benefit that was given to St George in life!

I confirm this for the honour of God, and for that I may be forgiven (28)in this world and in the next, and for the salvation of the soul of the lord my father, the marquis of Massa, iudike Salusi de Lacon, and of the soul of the lady my mother, (29)countess Adalasia, and for the love of lord Troodori, my bishop of Suelli.

Also, I confirm to Sanctu Jorgi the unworked lands (*saltus*) of Calcaria; (30)[the boundary] crosses Guturu des Nugis ('the gorge of Nugis'), then continues towards the hill (*cucuru*) of Forru de Munturiu, and then descends towards the pass (*ienna*) of sas Tesonis inter Montis ('the weavers in the mountains'), and leaves (31)by the road towards su Mulumentu ('the tomb') of Cipari Carsada, and descends towards the arch of Rugi's pass, and continues towards the tree that St (32)George had as his staff (*bakellu*)—which St George planted in the earth when he finished [surveying] this land with his lords (*maioralis*), and made a tree grow from it—then (33)it crosses towards the hilltop of Saltu Pikinnu ('little land'), and leaves towards the hilltop of Riu de Paboru ('Paboru river'), and descends towards the plain of Nonzu Gulpis, and then (34)descends towards Padru de Tiricu ('meadow of Tiricu'); it [then] carries along the stream of the Guturu d'Esquilla ('gorge of Esquilla'), then it descends towards the stream of the lower extension of Funtana Longa ('long spring'), and carries on along the road of the bordering (35)path of Porru, along the stream of Cortis de Bituru, towards Gidili crossing over unworked lands, and then leaves towards the stream of Gosti Mikina, then descends along the (36)stream of Mandara towards the islet (*iscla*) of s'Ortiada, and then descends towards Ariola Mella ('Mella threshing floor'), and then turns back towards Guturu des Nugis where it started. (37)May all this Sanctu Jorgi hold till the end of time!

The witnesses before whom I confirm this to Sanctu Jorgi de Suelli, and of all that is (38)narrated in this charter, are: lord Riccu my archbishop of Pluminus (Cálari), lord Mariani my bishop of Sulcis, priest Johanni Spinna my chaplain (39)from su Monti d'Aqua Friida ('the mountain of cold water'), Comida Dezori

[et] Comida d(e Serrabura portus. Et sunt) (40)destimoni[us] Barisoni de Serra Passagi, [et] Comida de Serra de Frailis, [et] Mariani Dezori Orlan(do. Et est facta custa carta) (41)anno do[m]i[n]ice incarnatio[n]is MCCXV (in me)[n]se Junio,[12] habendumilla ego sa curadoria de Ca(mpidanu pro logusalbatori) (42)Et ki ll'aet devert[er]e appat anat(hema, daba Pater et Filiu et Spiritu Sancto), daba XII Apos[t]olos [et] IIII Eva[n]gelistas, (daba XVI Prophetas (43)et) XIIII s(eniores, daba) CCCXVIII Patres s[an]c[t]os, [et] sorte[m] habeat cu[m] Juda p[ro]ditore in inferno inferiori. Amen (et fiat).

Carta volgare 12. Date: 30 September 1215. Grant of permission by Trogodori de Unali (Barisone–Torchitorio IV) iudike of Cálari (1214–1217), with his wife, to Trogodori, the bishop of Suelli, to make a charter confirming the acquistion of servants, lands and farms for the benefit of the church in the time of the former iudike of Cálari, Pedru de Pluminus (Cosantino-Salusio III, c. 1130–1163). Archivio diocesano storico di Cagliari, no. 3, DigiLib., no. 11. Fitted with a 'Byzantine' lead seal (39.7 g) and seal tag of dark red braid. Obv. +TOPK / [O]T[O]PHW / APXUNTH / MEPCHCK / APAVEWC. Rev. Cruciform invocative monogram (Type V), Θεοτόκε βοήθει; in the quarters: TW-ΣW ΔOY-ΛW (τῷ σῷ δούλῳ). Also known from a 15th-century transcription in the Archivio diocesano storico di Cagliari, *Liber Diversorum*, 2/I serie, Appendix 'Quaderno,' no. 10, DigiLib., pp. 315–316. Editions: Solmi, 'Le carte volgari', no. 12; Spanu, *Ortografia Sarda*, vol. 1, pp. 91–92; Tola, *CDS*, pp. 325–326; Falchi, *reisar.eu*, carta XII.

(1)In nomine patris [et] Filii [et] Sp[irit]us S[an]c[t]i, amen. Ego iuigi Trogodori de Unali, cu[m] do[n]na Ben(edic)ta (2)de Lacon m[u]liere mia, p[er] boluntade de do[n]nu Deu podestando parti de Kalaris, assolbullu a do[n]nu Tr(ogo)dori (su) (3)piscobu miu de Suelli, ad fagirisi carta in co bolit. Et ego Trogodori, p[er] issa mis[er]icordia de Deu pi(sco)bu (de) Suel(li cu[m]) (4)lebando assoltura daba su do[n]nu miu iuigi Trogodori de Unali [et] daba sa do[n]na mia do[n]na Benedicta de (Lacon), (5)ki mi llus castigit donnu Deu balaus ann[us] [et] bon[us], fazzumi carta p[ro] beni ki fegit iuigi Pedru de Pluminus ad (6)s[an]c[t]u Jorgi de Suelli su do[n]nu miu, p[ro] s'anima sua [et] de filias suas. Dedilloi su cantu habeat in Sinorbì [et] in Ca(7)stania, serbus [et] ankillas, [et] t[er]ras [et] binias, [et] saltus [et] aquas [et] o[mn]ia cantu si clabaat ad pusti cussas ambas dom[us], (ki fu)di (8)paru suu de sa co[m]pora ki fegerat a do[n]nu Gontini Spanu, [et] do[n]nu Gontini Spanu illu habeat binkidu a (don)nu (9)Barisoni de Serra de Cabuderra. Et habendusil-

12 2/I serie, DigiLib., p. 318: *mense Madio*.

de Ienoni, Johanni de Serra Saluda, and Comida de Serrabura Portus. (40)The witnesses are Barisoni de Serra Passagi, and Comida de Serra from Frailis, and Mariani Dezori Orlandu.

This charter was made (41)in the year of our Lord 1215, in the month of June, as I hold the curator's district (*curadoría*) of Campidanu (Campidano) on behalf of the deputy (*logusalbadori*). (42)Whosoever dares to controvert it, may the Father and the Son and the Holy Spirit curse him, and the twelve Apostles, the four Evangelists, the sixteen Prophets, (43)the twenty-four Elders, and the 318 Holy Fathers, and may he have his lot with Judas in the depths of Hell! Amen and let it be done!

Carta volgare 12. Date: 30 September 1215. Grant of permission by Trogodori de Unali (Barisone–Torchitorio IV) iudike of Cálari (1214–1217), with his wife, to Trogodori, the bishop of Suelli, to make a charter confirming the acquistion of servants, lands and farms for the benefit of the church in the time of the former iudike of Cálari, Pedru de Pluminus (Cosantino-Salusio III, c. 1130–1163). Archivio diocesano storico di Cagliari, no. 3, DigiLib., no. 11. Fitted with a 'Byzantine' lead seal (39.7 g) and seal tag of dark red braid. Obv. +TOPK / [O]T[O]PHW / APXUNTH / MEPCHCK / APAVEWC. Rev. Cruciform invocative monogram (Type V), Θεοτόκε βοήθει; in the quarters: TW-ΣW ΔOY-ΛW (τῷ σῷ δούλῳ). Also known from a 15th-century transcription in the Archivio diocesano storico di Cagliari, *Liber Diversorum*, 2/I serie, Appendix 'Quaderno,' no. 10, DigiLib., pp. 315–316. Editions: Solmi, 'Le carte volgari', no. 12; Spanu, *Ortografia Sarda*, vol. 1, pp. 91–92; Tola, *CDS*, pp. 325–326; Falchi, *reisar.eu*, carta XII.

(1)In the name of the Father, the Son, and the Holy Spirit, amen. I, iudike Trogodori de Unali with lady Benedicta (2)de Lacon my wife, by the will of Lord God, ruling Kalaris' territory (*parti*), permit (*assolbullu*) lord Trogodori, (3)my bishop of Suelli, to make himself a charter as he so wishes. So, I, Trogodori, by the mercy of God, bishop of Suelli, (4)with permission (*assoltura*) from my lord, iudike Trogodori de Unali and from my lady Benedicta de Lacon—(5)may Lord God protect them for me for many good years—make me a charter for the benefices that iudike Petru of Pluminus (Cálari), my lord, made to (6)Sanctu Jorgi de Suelli for the salvation of his soul and of his daughters. I grant to it all that he used to have in Sinorbi (Senorbì) and (7)Castania, servants (*serbus*) and female servants (*ankillas*), lands, vineyards, unworked lands (*saltus*) and water resources (*aquas*), and all that is enclosed in the place of both farm complexes (*domus*) that were (8)part of the purchase he made from lord Gontini Spanu. Lord Gontini Spanu had them after having won a legal dispute against lord (9)Barisoni de Sera from Cabuderra (Capoterra).

las custas dom[us] s[an]c[t]u Jorgi su do[n]nu miu, inde 'lli pidii merk(ei) (10)ad su do[n]nu miu juigi Barisoni [et] ad sa donna mia sa muliere, ki mi 'ndi fagiri[n]t carta bullada pro llas sigu(n)du (11)in co furu[n]t dadas ad s[an]c[t]u Jorgi su do[n]nu miu. Et ca no. 'ndi furu[n]t issus sigurus de custa dadura, kerfiru[n]t mi 'ndi (12)beridadi come[n]ti illas habeat S[an]c[t]u Jorgi custas dom Et ego batusindi livrus maioralis, ad do[n]nu Mariani Dezo(ri)(13)Orlandu, [et] ad do[n]nu Joh[ann]i de Serra Daluda, [et] a do[n]nu Saltoro de Unali Corrogla, [et] ad do[n]nu Turbini de Siiki, [et] ad Ma(r)-(14)iani de Zoli d'Ozzorkesus, ki juraru[n]t ad bangeliu de Deu, ante iuigi, in sa billa de Quartu, ad corona de (sanctu Mi)aili, (15)ca custas ambas domus juigi Pedru illas habeat dadas sendu in Plumin[us] ad S[an]c[t]u Jorgi de Suelli, p[ro] (s'ani)ma (16)sua [et] de filias suas. Et pusco co[n]noschit juigi Barisoni su do[n]nu miu [et] issa do[n]na mia sa m[u]liere custa (beri)dadi, (17)bullaru[n]tmindi custa carta, [et] affirmaru[n]tmillas custas ambas domus de Sinorbì [et] de Castania (cu[m]) (18)o[mn]ia cantu si p[er]tenit ad pusti 'llas, ki si 'ndi appat p[ro]i s[an]c[t]u Jorgi su do[n]nu miu ca[n]tu adi durari su mundu. E(t) inui (19)iuraru[n]t custus liberus co illas habeat dadas custas dom[us] juigi Pedru ad S[an]c[t]u Jorgi, fudi do[n]nu Mariani (su pis)cobu (20)de Zulkis, [et] do[n]nu Barisoni de Serra Passagi, [et] do[n]nu Furadu Dezori Zurru[m] Et sunt destimon(i[us]) (21)Barisoni de Serra Passagi, [et] Comida de Serra de Frailis, [et] Mariani Dezori Orlandu. Et est facta cust(a car)ta (22)anno do[m]ini MCCXV II k[a]l[endas] Octubri, habendusilla juigi ad manu sua sa curadoria de Ca[m](pidanu pro) (23)(l)ogusalbadori. Et ki ll'aet divert[er]e apat anathema daba P(ater et Filiu et) S[an]c[t]o Sp[irit]u, daba XII Apos[t]olos (et IIII Evangelist)as (24)daba XVI P[ro]ph[et]as [et] XXIIII Seniores, daba CCC(XVIII) P(adre)s Sanctos. Et sorte[m]habeat cu[m] Juda p[ro](ditore) i[n] inf(erno) (in)f(eriori, amen).

Carta volgare 13. Date: 6 November 1215. Grant of permission by Trogotori de Unali (Barisone-Tochitorio IV), iudike of Cálari (1214–1217), and his wife, to Trogodori, bishop of Suelli to draw up a charter confirming lands, servants, and resources acquired for the benefit of the church. Archivio diocesano storico di Cagliari, no. 2, DigiLib., no. 12. Fitted with a 'Byzantine' lead seal (50.7 g) and modern seal tag of dark red braid. Obv. +TOPK / [O]T[O]PHW / APXUNTH / [---MEPC]HCK / [A]PAVEWC. Rev. Cruciform invocative monogram (Type V), Θεοτόκε βοήθει; in the quarters: TW-ΣW ΔOY-ΛW (τῷ σῷ δούλῳ). Also known from a 16th-century transcription in the Archivio diocesano storico di Cagliari, *Liber Diversorum*, 2/I serie [E], ff. 56–58, DigiLib., pp. 58–61. Editions: C. Baudi di Vesme, *Codex Diplomaticus Ecclesiensis*, p. 249; Solmi, 'Le carte volgari', no. 13, pp. 28–32; Falchi, *reisar.eu*, carta XIII.

And having these farms in the possession of my lord, Sanctu Jorgi, I request, regarding these, the favour (10)of my lord, iudike Barisoni, and my lady his wife, so they have made me a charter with a seal (*carta bullada*) for these just (11)as they were given to my lord, Sanctu Jorgi. And because there were no assurances regarding this donation, they wanted me (12)to tell the truth about how Sanctu Jorgi came to have these farms. I brought forth free lords (*liverus maioralis*), calling on lord Mariani Dezori (13)Orlandu and lord Johanni de Serra d'Aluda and lord Saltori de Unali Corrogla and lord Turbini de Siiki, and Mariani (14)de Zoli Dozzorkesus, who swore on the gospels of God in front of the iudike in the village of Quartu at the hearing (*corona*) of Sanctu Miaili (in October), when iudike Pedru, while being in Pluminus (Cálari), granted (15)both these farms to Santu Jorgi de Suelli, for his soul (16)and that of his daughter. After my lord, iudike Barisoni, and my lady, his wife, learnt this truth, they made me this (17)sealed charter, and confirmed both farms of Sinorbi and Castania (18)with all that belongs to those places—may Sanctu Jorgi hold them till the end of the world!

Those who joined these freemen (*liberus*) and (19)swore that iudike Pedru had granted these farms to Sanctu Jorgi were: lord Mariani the bishop (20)of Zulkis (Sulcis), lord Barisoni de Serra Passagi, and lord Furadu Dezori Zurrum. And the witnesses are: (21)Barisoni de Serra Passagi, Comida de Serra Frailis, and Mariani Dezori Orlandu.

This charter was made (22)in the year of our Lord 1215, in the 2nd day before the kalendas of October (30 September), as the iudike has in his hands the *curatore*'s district (*curadoría*) of Campidanu (Campidano) on behalf of (23)the deputy (*logusalbadori*). Whoever dares to controvert it, may the Father and the Son and the Holy Spirit curse him, and the twelve Apostles, the four Evangelists, (24)the sixteen Prophets, the twenty-four Elders, and the 318 Holy Fathers, and may he have his lot with Judas in the depths of Hell! Amen.

Carta volgare 13. Date: 6 November 1215. Grant of permission by Trogotori de Unali (Barisone-Tochitorio IV), iudike of Cálari (1214–1217), and his wife, to Trogodori, bishop of Suelli to draw up a charter confirming lands, servants, and resources acquired for the benefit of the church. Archivio diocesano storico di Cagliari, no. 2, DigiLib., no. 12. Fitted with a 'Byzantine' lead seal (50.7 g) and modern seal tag of dark red braid. Obv. +TOPK / [O]T[O]PHW / APXUNTH / [---MEPC]HCK / [A]PAVEWC. Rev. Cruciform invocative monogram (Type V), Θεοτόκε βοήθει; in the quarters: TW-ΣW ΔOY-ΛW (τῷ σῷ δούλῳ). Also known from a 16th-century transcription in the Archivio diocesano storico di Cagliari, *Liber Diversorum*, 2/I serie [E], ff. 56–58, DigiLib., pp. 58–61. Editions: C. Baudi di Vesme, *Codex Diplomaticus Ecclesiensis*, p. 249; Solmi, 'Le carte volgari', no. 13, pp. 28–32; Falchi, *reisar.eu*, carta XIII.

Hoc est translatum bene et fideliter sumptum in civitate et castro Callaris die XXVI menses Januarii anno a nat[ivitate] D[o]m[in]i MDLXXIIII a quadam carta pergamenea sigillo plumbeo a quibusdam vetis cericeis(?) rubei coloris in penden[ti] munita non rasa non viciata neq[ue] in aliqua sui parte suspecta sed ab eius vetustatem in aliquibus partibus corrosa in aliquis vicio et suspictione caren[te] cuius tenor sequitur sub his verbis:[13]

(1)In nomine Patris [et] Filii [et] Sp[irit]u S[an]c[t]i, amen. Ego iudigi Trogotori de Unali cu[m] do[n]na Biniita de Laco[n] mulieri mia, p[ro] bolintate de do[n]nu Deu (2)potestandu parti de Calaris, assolbullu a do[n]nu Trogotori, su piscopu miu de Subelli, a ffagirisi carta in co bolit. Et ego Trogotori, p[er] issa m[isericord]ia de Deu piscobu (3)de S(u)elli, cu[m] leba[n]du assoltura daba su do[n]nu miu judigi Trogotori de Unali [et] daba sa do[n]na mia do[n]na Biniita de Laco[n] sa mulieri, ki mi llus castigit Do[n]nu Deu balaus (4)ann[us] [et] bonus, cu[m] habe[n]du fili[us] bon[us], fazzulla custa carta p[ro] beni ki fegiru[n]t a S[an]c[t]u Jorgi de Suelli. Dedilloy do[n]nu Trogodori de Zebera, cu[m] bulintadi de sus fili[us], a ora (5)de sa morti sua, sa filiadura ki ll'aeda a issi facta do[n]nu Gu[n]nari de Serra, filiu de do[n]nu Cumida de Serra de do[n]na Bera. Istimoni[us], p[re]bi[t]eru Mariani de Quartu [et] p[re]bi[ter]u (6)Arzzocu Porkella, ki furu[n]t assa penede[n]tia sua, [et] do[n]nu Guilgemu priori de Kirra, Gu[n]nari Caliu, Go[n]tini Niellu [et] Et dedilloi a S[an]c[t]u Jorgi de Suelli (7)Aleni de Curcas de Do[n]nigalia Alba, filia de Mariani de Curcas [et] de Bera Castay, a ora de morti sua, ca fudi enia [et] no[n] aeda filiu, o[mn]ia cantu aeda, plazza(s) [et] terras aradorias (8)[et] binias [et] pumu [et] saltus [et] semidas [et] aquas, [et] o[mn]ia ca[n]tu abeat in sa billa de Do[n]nigalia alba. Et su[n]t destimo[n]i[us], p[re]bi[t]eru Turbuu de Onori ki lla penede[n]tiedi, [et](9)do[n]nu Go[n]tini Curria de Sibiola, Trogotori Inboy, [et] Cumida de Laco[n], filiu d'Arzzocu de Laco[n] muciu, [et] Arzzocu de Lacon, filiu de do[n]na P[re]tiosa d'Azzeni, [et] Turbini (10)su fr[adu]. Et be[n]nit do[n]nu Cumida de Serra de Frailis assa festa de s[an]c[t]u Jorgi de Suelli, malaidu d'unu dolu ki lli fudi scudu; [et] p[er] 'ssa mis[ericord]ia de Deu, innanti ki 'ndi andarit (11)daba sa festa, fudi sanu. E[t] pro custu beni ki lli aeda Deu fatu, ad honori de Deu [et] de s[an]c[t]u Jorgi, dedi ellu a serbu de cadadie su lad[us] ki aeda in Petru Ladu, filiu (12)de Bitoria Spana ankilla

13 Proemium taken from the transumpt in the *Liber Diversorum*, 2/I serie [E], ff. 56–58, DigiLib., pp. 58–61.

This is well and faithfully translated, [being] taken from the city and citadel of Callaris (Cagliari) on the 26th day of the month of January in the year of the birth of the Lord 1573 from a certain parchment charter—fitted with a lead seal and old wax suspended by a red-coloured [chord], not effaced, not flawed, nor suspect in any part of itself, but corroded by its age in some areas—the content of which follows beneath these words [that are] lacking no flaw nor doubt:[14]

(1)In the name of the Father, the Son, and the Holy Spirit, amen. I, iudike Trogotori de Unali with my wife lady Biniita de Lacon, by the will of Lord God, (2)ruling Cálari's territory (*parti*), permit (*assolbullu*) lord Trogodori, my bishop (3)of Suelli (Subelli), to make himself a charter as he wishes. So, I, Trogodori, by the mercy of God, bishop of Suelli, with permission (*assoltura*) from my lord, iudike Trogodori de Una and from his wife, my lady Biniita de Lacon—may Lord God protect them for me for (4)many good years, while having fine children—make her a charter for benefices that they made to Sanctu Jorgi de Suelli.

On his deathbed, (5)lord Trogodori de Zebera granted, with consent of his children, the part of the succession inheritance (*filiadura*) that he had made to him by lord Gunnari de Serra, son of lord Cumida de Serra and lady Bera. Witnesses: priest (*prebiteru*) Mariani de Quartu, and priest (6)Arzzocu Porkella who were at his confession, and lord Guilgemu, prior of Kirra; Gunnari Caliu, and Gontini Niellu.

Also, (7)Aleni de Curcas from Donnigalia Alba, daughter of Mariani de Curca, and Bera Castay, gave to Sanctu Jorgi de Suelli, on her deathbed, because she was unmarried and had no children (*ca fudi enia et non aeda filiu*), all that she had—landed plots (*plazzas*), arable lands, (8)vineyards, a fruit orchard (*pumu*), unworked lands (*sultus*), enclosed lands (*semidas*), and water resources (*aquas*) that she held in the village of Donnigalia Alba. The witnesses are priest Turbuu de Onori, who administered her confession; (9)lord Gontini Curria de Sibiola; Trogotori Inboy; Cumida de Lacon, son of Arzzocu de Lacon 'Muciu'; Arozzocu de Lacon, son of lady Pretiosa d'Azzeni, and his (10)brother, Turbini.

Also, lord Cumida de Serra from Frailis came to the feast of Sanctu Jorgi de Suelli suffering from pain that was taken away. By the mercy of God, before (11)he left the feast, he was cured. And for this benefit that God made for him, for the honour of God and St George, he granted a daily servant (*serbu de cadadie*), half (*ladus*) [the services] of Petru Ladu, son (12)of Bitoria Spana, her

14 Taken from the transumpt in the *Liber Diversorum*, 2/1 serie [E], ff. 56–58, DigiLib., pp. 58–61.

sua, [et] de Mariani Ladu, serbu de S[an]c[t]u Jorgi. Istimoni[us], do[n]nu Joh[ann]i Spina, p[re]idi de su mo[n]ti, do[n]nu Go[n]tini Dezzori de Siillu, Gu[n]nari (13)Corsu, [et] Go[n]tini su fr[ad]i, [et] Arzzocu d'Arcedi, ie[n]niru de do[n]nu Cumida de Serra, [et] Petru de Serra Pinna, [et] Turbini de Scala de Cizzerra, [et] Basili P[er] Et kertei cu[m] (14)do[n]nu Saltoro de Unali corrogla, p[ro] sa binia d'orriina de Flumini, ki aeda de co[m]pora da do[n]nu Forastiu, [et] p[ro] sa binia ki aeda d'Arzzocu d'Orruu flocu, [et] p[ro] sa binia ki (15)fudi de Cumida Medas, ca fudi in fundame[n]tu de sa dadura de do[n]nu Cumida d'Orruu de Serra [et] de fFrailis, ki ll'aenta dadu a Sa[n]c[t]u Jorgi, p[ro] 'ndi adi S[an]c[t]u Jorgi carta (16)E[t] supra totu custu kertu ca[m]paniar[us] nos inpari, [et] bogeimi de totu custu kertu p[ro] Deu [et]p[ro] s[an]c[t]u Jorgi, [et] p[ro] p[re]gu ki mi 'ndi fegiru[n]t ho[m]i[n]is bon[us] ki lloi furu[n]t, (17)[et] p[ro] essiri indi issi fideli a S[an]c[t]u Jorgi, in ca[m]paniu [et] in cu[m]be[n]tu de ma[n]diarisilla issi custa binia p[ro] ki lli kertaa in bida sua, [et] daa k'edi morri do[n]nu Saltoro airisilla S[an]c[t]u (18)Jorgi in pagi sa binia d'orriina de Flumini sa ca[n]tu aeda co[m]porada a do[n]nu Forastiu. Istimo[n]ius, do[n]nu Contini d'Orruu Daluda curadori de Treie[n]ta ante ki kertam[us], (19)[et] do[n]nu Mariani Dezzori Orla[n]du, [et] do[n]nu Cumida Dezzori de Enoni, [et] do[n]nu Joh[ann]i de Serra, [et] do[n]nu Arzzocu de Unali de Segariu [et] do[n]nu Petru de Unali su(20)(frad)i [et] do[n]nu Turbini de Siiki, [et] do[n]nu Mariani Dezoli. Et ca[m]biei cu[m] su do[n]nu miu judigi Barusoni [et] cu[m] sa do[n]na mia do[n]na B(i)niita de Laco[n] sa mulieri, (21)deru[n]tmi issus a mimi a Furadu Baca de Goni, filiu de Jorgi Pili s[er]bu issoru, cu[m] sus fili[us]; [et]ego deillis a issus a Cumida Calca[n]iu de Ma[n]das, filiu de Maria Fiori, (22)ankilla de S[an]c[t]u Jorgi, cu[m] sus fili[us]. Istimoni[us], do[n]nu Barusoni Passagi, do[n]nu Mariani Dezzori Orla[n]du, do[n]nu Joh[ann]i de Serra Daluda, do[n]nu Furadu Dezzori Zuru[m] (23)Et donedilloy do[n]na Maria de Laco[n], filia de do[n]nu Turbini de Laco[n] de Donori, a S[an]c[t]u Jorgi de Suelli, p[ro] Deu [et] p[ro] a[n]i[m]a sua, in sa billa de Jana I orroglu de (24)t[er]ra ubi nara[n]t Binia Senega, cabizza a binia de Masedu [et] cabizza a Piskina Durca, ki fudi intru de t[er]ra de S[an]c[t]u Jorgi. Istimo[n]i[us], do[n]nu Gontini Madellu arme[n]tariu (25)de s'arkipiscobu [et] do[n]nu Contini Cauli, p[re]idi de s[an]c[t]u Lare[n]zzu, [et] Mariani Zalis, [et] Cumida de Carra, [et] Cipari Devedi, [et] Joh[ann]i su terali suu. Et dedilloi (26)do[n]na Muscu de Unali, filia de do[n]nu Arzzocu de Unali manufalki, a S[an]c[t]u Jorgi, p[ro] Deu [et] p[ro] a[n]i[m]a sua. Cu[m]

female servant (*ankilla*), and of Mariani Ladu, servant of Sanctu Jorgi. Witnesses: lord Johanni Spina, priest of Su Monti, lord Gontini Dezzori de Siilu, Gunnari (13)Corsu, and his brother Gontini, and Arzzocu D'Arcedi son-in-law of lord Cumida de Serra, and Petru de Serra Pina, and Turbini de Scala from Çizzerra, and Basili Perra.

Also, I contested a piece of land with (14)lord Saltoro de Unali concerning the vineyard at Orriina de Flumini ('river shack'), which he had purchased from lord Forastiu, and concerning the vineyard that he had from Arzzocu d'Orru Flocu, and concerning the vineyard that (15)used to belong to Cumida Medas, because they were among the real estate (*fundamentu*) donated by lord Cumida d'Orruu from Serra and from Frailis, who had given it to Sanctu Jorgi, for which Sanctu Jorgi had a sealed charter. (16)And regarding this entire dispute, we agreed on a settlement together, and I withdrew myself from (*bogeimi*) the whole of this issue (*kertu*), for God and for St George, and for theprayers that some trusted men who were there (17)addressed to me, and for their loyalty to Sanctu Jorgi. And we agreed and settled on the fact that the vineyard, which was the subject of the dispute, would be conceded to him while he lived, and that, after lord Saltoro's death, the vineyard of Orriina de Flumini, which he had bought from lord Forastiu, would pass into the possession of Sanctu (18)Jorgi in peace. Witnesses: lord Contini d'Orruu d'Aluda *curatore* of Terienta (Trexenta) before we were in dispute, and (19)lord Mariani Dezzori Orlandu, and lord Cumida Dezzori de Enoni, and lord Johanni de Serra, and lord Arzzocu de Unali de Segariu, and his (20)brother, lord Petru de Unali, and lord Turbini de Siiki, and lord Mariani de Zoli.

Also, I made an exchange with my lord iudike Barusoni and my lady, his wife, lady Biniita de Lacon, who (21)gave me Furadu Baca de Goni, son of Jorgi Pili their servant, together with his sons. I gave them in return Cumida Calcaniu de Mandas, son of Maria Fiori, (22)a female servant of Sanctu Jorgi, with his sons. Witnesses: lord Barusoni Passagi, lord Mariani Dezzori Orlandu, lord Johanni de Serra d'Aluda, lord Furadu Dezzori Zurum.

(23)Also, lady Maria de Lacon, daughter of lord Turbini de Lacon from Donori, gave to Sanctu Jorgi de Suelli, for God and for her soul, one piece of land (*orroglu*) in the village of Jana, (24)called Binia Senega ('Senega vineyard'), reaching, at one end, the vineyard of Masedu and, at the other, Piskina d'Urea ('pool of Urea'), which was within the land of Sanctu Jorgi. Witnesses: lord Gontini Madellu administrator (*armentariu*) (25)of the archbishop, and lord Contini Cauli, priest of Sanctu Larenzzu (San Lorenzo), and Mariani Zalis, and Cumida de Carra, and Cipari Devedi, and his tenant farmer (*terali*) Johanni.

Also, (26)lady Muscu de Unali, daughter of lord Arzzocu de Unali Manufalki, gave to Sanctu Jorgi, for God and for her soul, with the consent of her husband

buli[n]tadi de do[n]nu Go[n]tini d'Abis su maridu, o[mn]ia ca[n]tu (27)lloi aeda in sa billa d'Arigi, [et] sua [et] de serb[us] suus, plazzas [et] t[er]ras et binias [et] salt[us] [et] semidas [et] aquas, [et] o[mn]ia ca[n]tu si p[er]tineda a icussa domu. Istimoni[us], do[n]nu (28)(An)astasi, p[re]idi de S[an]c[t]a Aleni de Tolostrai, [et] Jorgi de Calagonis, p[re]idi de S[an]c[t]u Arca[n]gelu, [et] do[n]nu Mariani de Quartu, p[re]idi de billa de Pubuzzi, [et] Cumida de Mizzuzzi, (29)clerigu de s'archipiscobu, [et] Go[n]tini de Serra. Et co[m]poreilli a do[n]na P[re]tiosa, filia de do[n]nu Arzzocu de do[n]nigellu, cu[m] buli[n]tadi de do[n]nu Go[n]tini de Laco[n] su (30)maridu, o[mn]ia ca[n]tu aeda in sa billa de Sigii, [et] suu [et] de serb[us] suus, plazzas [et] t[er]ras [et] binia [et] saltu [et] semida [et] aqua, [et] o[mn]ia ca[n]tu si p[er]tineda a icussa domu, (31)[et] o[mn]ia causa ki edi airi p[er]didu o ki ell'e[n]ti airi levadu o minimadu de su ca[n]tui deveda airi dep[us] pare[n]tis suus, in sa billa de Sigii, o d[e] ho[m]i[n]is, o de fundam[en]tu, (32)o de p[er]una at[er]a causa, o p[er]una arrasoni ki airit in sus fili[us] de Petru Magia. Kerrimillu eu totu p[ro] S[an]c[t]u Jorgi, et deindelli XX berbeis de madriedu, calis (33)si seberaru[n]t sus ho[min]is suus daa sa masoni de S[an]c[t]u Jorgi in Iana, [et] una egua [et] IIII libras [et] mesu, [et] clo[m]pilli pariari. Istimo[n]i[us], do[n]nu Go[n]tini de Serra (34)af(ai)dadu, [et] Joh[ann]i filiu de do[n]nu Forastiu de Cabuderra, [et] do[n]nu Turbini de Siiki [et]Mariani Dezoli, [et] Mariani Demo[n]tis de Sigii, [et] Cumida Eci de Sigii, [et] Petru (35)(Corsu). Et kertemi Jorgi Lepuri de parti de judigi p[ro] Jorgi de Margini [et] p[ro] sas sorris, k'enti essiri muniari[us] [et] ego batusi a corona a do[n]na Muscu de S[er]-(36)(ra) filia de do[n]nu Barusoni Ma[n]nu ki llus aeda dad[us] a S[an]c[t]u Jorgi a serb[us] de cadadie, [et] carta fata [et] Et issa posit a do[n]nu Petru de Sii su jenniru a ttorra(ri) (37)berbu de parti sua. E[t] kertaru[n]t illi de parti de judigi, p[ro] Jurgia Cucu aba de Jorgi de Margini [et] de ssorris, k'edi essiri mu[n]iaria [et] issi torredi berbu (de) parti (38)de do[n]na Muscu sa sogra, ca Jurgia Cucu no[n] fudi mu[n]iaria, antis fudi ankilla de padri miu. Juigaru[n]t illi destimo[n]i[us] a Jorgi Lepuri ca fu(di) Jurgia Cucu (mun)taria. (39)Istimo[n]i[us] no[n] d'apit. Posiru[n]t inde 'lla a do[n]na Muscu a iurari in S[an]c[t]u Jorgi de Suelli, [et]issa juredi in S[an]c[t]u Jorgi, ca Jurgia Cucu ankilla p(e)guliari de padr(i mi)u (40)fudi, k'aliga[n]du muniaria no[n] Istimo[n]i[us] ante ki iuredi do[n]na Muscu, ispilia[n]dusi a sii [et] a s[an]c[t]u Jorgi, Seri Iogulu, arme[n]tariu de judigi de sa billa de Ba[n]iu, (41)[et] do[n]nu Mariani Dezoli, ki lla pone[n]ta a iurari de parti de judigi; do[n]nu Petru de Unali de Segariu, [et] Cogori de Fu[n]tanas de Segolai, [et] Petru Baca, maiori de (42)(equa)s

lord Gontini d'Abis, all that (27)which she had in the village of Arigi (Arixi), of hers and of her servants: plots, lands, vineyards, unworked lands, farm lands, water resources, and everything that belongs to that farm complex (*domu*). Witnesses: lord (28)Anastasi, priest of Sancta Aleni de Tolostrai; Jorgi de Calagonis (Maracalagonis), priest of Sanctu Arcangelu; lord Mariani de Quartu, the village priest of Pubuzzi; Cumida de Mizzuzzi, (29)priest of the archbishop, and Gontini de Serra.

Also, I bought from lady Pretiosa, daughter of lord Arzzocu de Onnigellu, with the consent of her (30)husband lord Gontini de Lacon, all that she had in the village of Sigii, of hers and her servants: plots, lands, vineyards, unworked land, farm land and water resources, and everything that belongs to that farm complex, (31)and all the assets (*causa*) that might have been lost, taken away or diminished, which she should have had from her relatives in the village of Sigii, either from men (*hominis*) or real estate (*fundamentu*) (32)or any other asset or obligations (*arrasoni*) that she had from the sons of Petru Magia. I wanted all this for Sanctu Jorgi, so I gave her twenty ewes, (33)which their men can have from the flock of Sanctu Jorgi at Iana, and one mare, and four and a half pounds [of silver?] (*libras*), and I completed the payment. Witnesses: lord Gontini de Serra (34)Afaidadu; Johanni, son of lord Forastiu de Cabuderra (Capoterra); lord Turbini de Siiki; Mariani de Zoli; Mariani de Montis from Sigii; Cumida Eci de Sigii, and Petru (35)[Corsu].

Also, I had a dispute with Jorgi Lepuri, on the part of the iudike, over Jorgi de Margini and his sisters, who owed certain duties (*muniarius*). I brought forth to a hearing (*corona*) lady Muscu de Serra, daughter (36)of lord Barusoni Mannu, who had given them to Sanctu Jorgi as daily servants (*serbus de cadadie*) for which a charter was made and sealed. And she made the son-in-law (*jenniru*) lord Petru de Sii (37)respond on his part. Also, they raised a dispute, on the part of the iudike over Jurgia Cucu grandmother of Jorgi de Margini and his sisters, who owed certain duties. He responded (38)on the part of lady Muscu, his mother-in-law, [saying] that 'Jurgia Cucu did not owe certain duties; she was previously a female servant of my father!' They adjudicated the testimony from Jorgi Lepuri, who said that 'Jurgia Cucu was someone who owed certain duties!' (39)The testimony was not accepted. They made lady Muscu take an oath at Sanctu Jorgi de Suelli, and she swore at Sanctu Jorgi that 'Jurgia Cucu was her father's own (*peguliari*) female servant,' (40)contending that she was not someone who owed certain duties. Lady Muscu swore an oath, defending herself and Sanctu Jorgi before the [following] witnesses: Seri Iogulu—the iudike's administrator of the village of Baniu—(41)and lord Mariani de Zoli—who made her take an oath on the part of the iudike, lord Petru de Unali from Segariu, Cogoru de Funtanas from Segolai, and Petru Baca, master of (42)the horses on the plain of Donnigalia.

de planu de Do[n]nigalia. Et dedilloi Petru Morrocu a S[an]c[t]u Jorgi, p[ro] Deu [et] p[ro] a[n]i[m]a sua, o[mn]ia ca[n]tu aeda in sa billa d'Arigi, plazza [et] t[er]ra [et] binia [et] saltu [et] s(e)mida (43)(et aqua, et o)[mn]ia ca[n]tu aeda apusti cussa domu. Istimo[n]i[us], do[n]nu Cumida de Serra de Frailis, [et] do[n]nu Gontini de Serra afaidadu, [et] Mariani su fr[ad]i, [et] Petru de S[er]ra Calag(o)nesu, (44)[et] Gu[n]nari su fr[ad]i, [et] Petru de Serra Pi[n] Et afiliessi a S[an]c[t]u Jorgi do[n]na Jurgia de Cabuderra, filia de do[n]nu Turbini de Cabuderra de Paulis. A darilloi ad S[an]c[t]u (45)Jorgi parzzoni d'unu filiu suu d'o[mn]ia ca[n]tu aeda, de ho[m]i[n]is bo[n]is [et] de plazzas [et] de t[er]ras [et] d[e] binia [et] d[e] pumu [et] de salt[us] et d'aquas, [et] de causa d'intru [et] de foras, (et omnia cant)u (46)aeda in totu Plumin[us]. E[t] ca moriit do[n]na Jurgia, apit i[n]di S[an]c[t]u Jorgi p[ro] parti sua deho[m]i[n]is ad Turbini Pirdigi, filiu de Mariani Pirdigi [et] de VI una de Pisin(...) (47)su fr[ad]i, [et] de tres una de totu s'at[er]u suu ca[n]tu aeda, [et] d'intru [et] de foras. Istimo[n]i[us], do[n]nu Petru d'Arcedi, [et] do[n]nu Mariani Castay, [et] do[n]nu Barusoni (d'Ac)eni [et] do[n]nu (48)Cumida de Serra. Et dedilloi a S[an]c[t]u Jorgi, p[ro] Deu [et] p[ro] a[n]i[m]a sua, do[n]nu Cumida Curria filiu de do[n]nu Zerkis Curria, o[mn]ia ca[n]tu aeda in sa billa de Sestu, [et] plazza [et] (terra)(49)[et] bini(a) [et] saltu [et] Istimo[n]i[us] Go[n]tini Curria, [et] Mariani sus fili[us], [et] do[n]nu Cumida d'Orruu de Sibiola, [et] do[n]nu Petru Tro[n]ki, [et] do[n]nu Go[n]tini de Mo[n]tis, p[re]idi de Sestu, [et] (50)(Pe)tru Corsu. Et dedilloi do[n]na Cucusa de Sii, mulieri de do[n]nu Saltoro de Unali corrogla, a S[an]c[t]u Jorgi de Suelli, a ora de morti sua, omnia (cantu aeda in) sa billa de (51)Se(stu et domu) [et] t[er]ra(s) [et] binias [et] saltu [et] aqua, [et] o[mn]ia ca[n]tu aeda apusti cussa domu. Istimo[n]i[us], do[n]nu Saltoro de U(nali) su maridu, [et] do[n]nu Gu[n]nari su fr[ad]i, [et] do[n]nu (52)(Johanni Spina), p[re]idi de su Mo[n]ti d'Aqua friida, [et] do[n]nu Cumida d'Asteri, p[re]idi de Segolai, [et]do[n]nu Petru Calagonesu, [et] do[n]nu Gu[n]nari su fr[ad] E(t) dedill(oi a S[an]c[t]u) Jorgi do[n]na (53)Prizzosa de Scala, filia de do[n]nu Turbini de Scala faturosu a Marcusa Loru, filia de Gol-orgi Cau s[er]bu suu ad ankilla (de) ca(dadie p[ro]) Deu [et] (pro anima sua. Istimoni)[us], (54)do[n]nu Mariani de Quartu, p[re]idi de billa de Pub-uzzi, [et] do[n]nu Mariani Dezzori Guzubiu, [et]Gu[n]nari de Ba[n]iaria, [et] Gu[n]n(ari) (d'Arzedi et Traiosu. Et derunt illoi donnu) (55)Petru d'A(zen)i [et] do[n]nu Cumida su fr[ad]i, fili[us] de do[n]nu Trogotori Dezzori de Urgu, a S[an]c[t]u Jorgi, p[ro] a[n]i[m]a issoru [et] des pare[n]tis, s(...) (56)ki lloi aenta in sa billa de Goni, [et] daa sa plazza in foras deru[n]t o[mn]ia ca[n]tu illoi aenta a partirisi paris Sa[n]c[t]u Jorgi cu[m] S[an]c[t]u (Pantaleu, terra) [et]

Also, Petru Morrocu gave to Sanctu Jorgi, for God and for his soul, all that which he had in the village of Arigi, plot and land and vineyard and unworked land and farm land (43)and a water resource, and everything which he had at that farm complex. Witnesses: lord Cumida de Serra de Frailis, and lord Gontini de Serra Afaidadu, and his brother Mariani, and Petru de Serra Calagonesu, (44)and his brother Gunnari, and Petru de Serra Pinna. Also, lady Jurgia de Cabuderra (Capoterra), daughter of lord Turbini de Cabuderra from Paulis, affiliated herself to Sanctu Jorgi, so she gave to Sanctu (45)Jorgi one of his son's shares (*parzzoni*) of all that she had: all the trusted men (*hominis bonis*), plots and lands, vineyard and fruit orchard, unworked land, a water resource, and assets both in the village and the countryside, and all that (46)she had throughout Pluminus (Cálari). When lady Jurgia died, Sanctu Jorgi had these from its share of men: Turbini Pirdigi, son of Mariani Pirdigi, and one-sixth of Pisinagiseti, (47)his brother, and a third of all the rest of what she had, both in the village and in the countryside. Witnesses: lord Petru d'Arcedi, and lord Mariani Castay, and lord Barusoni d'Aceni, and lord Cumida de Serra.

Also, lord (48)Cumida Curria, son of lord Zerkis Curria, gave to Sanctu Jorgi, for God and for his soul, all that which he had in the village of Sestu, and plot and land and (49)vineyard and unworked land (*saltu*) and a water resource. Witnesses: Gontini Curria, and his sons Mariani, and lord Cumida d'Orruu from Sibiola, and lord Petru Tronki, and lord Gontini de Montis priest of Sestu, and (50)Petru Corsu.

Also, lady Cucusa de Sii, wife of lord Saltoro de Unali Corrogla, gave to Sanctu Jorgi de Suelli, on her deathbed, all that she had in the village of (51)Sestu—farm complex, lands, vineyards, unworked land and water resource, and all that she had at that farm complex. Witnesses: her husband, lord Saltoro de Unali; his brother, lord Gunnari, lord Johanni Spina, (52)priest of Su Monti d'Aqua Friida; lord Cumida d'Asteri, priest of Segolai; lord Petru Calagonesu, and his brother, lord Gunnari.

Also, lady (53)Prizzosa de Scala, daughter of lord Turbini de Scala Faturoso, gave to Sanctu Jorgi Marcusa Loru, the daughter of her servant Golorgi Cau, as a daily servant, for God and for her soul. Witnesses: (54)lord Mariani de Quartu, priest of the village of Pubuzzi; lord Mariani Dezzori Guzubiu; Gunnari de Baniaria; Gunnari d'Arzedi, and Traiosu.

Also, lord (55)Petru d'Azeni and his brother lord Cumida, sons of lord Trogotori Dezzori de Urgu, gave to Sanctu Jorgi, for their souls and of their relatives, all that (56)they had in the village of Goni, and from the plot outside [of Goni] they gave all that they had to be divided between Sanctu Jorgi and Sanctu Pan-

binia (et saltu et aqua). (57)Istimo[n]i[us], do[n]nu Joh[ann]i de S[er]ra Daluda, [et] Petru de Allari su fr[ad]i, [et] do[n]nu Mariani de S[er]ra Daluda, [et] Petru su fr[ad]i, [et] Bonanu de Figus. Et (dedilloi) do[n]nu Ma(nu)eli (d'Abis, fil)iu (58)d[e] (d)o[n]nu Go[n]tini d'Abis a S[an]c[t]u Jorgi, p[ro] Deu [et] p[ro] a[n]i[m]a sua, in Funtana de Figu, parzzoni d'unu filiu suu. Istimo[n]i[us] do[n]nu C(umi)da (de Serra de Frailis (59)et donnu Gontini de Serra Afaidadu), et Mariani su fr[ad]i, [et] do[n]nu Petru de S[er]ra Calagonesu, [et] Gu[n]nari su fr[ad]i, [et]Petru de S[er]ra Pi[n] Et su[n]t destimo[n]i[us], Barusoni (de Serra) P(assa)gi, [et] (60)Cu(mida de Serra de) Frailis, [et] Mariani Dezzori Orlandu. Et est fata custa carta anno do[m]ini MCCXVVIII id[us] Nove[m]bris, habe[n]dusilla ju(di)gi (a) m(an)u su-(61)(a sa curadoria de) Ca[m]pidanu p[ro] logusalba(to)ri. Et ki ll'aet devertere apat anathe[m]a daba Pat[er] [et] Filiu [et] S[an]c[t]u Isp[irit]u, [et] daba XII Apos[t]olos, IIII Eva[n]gelistas, (XVI (62)p[ro]phetas), XXIIII Seniores, CCCXVIII Patres s[an]c[t]os, [et] apat sorte[m] cu[m] Juda p[ro]ditore in inferno inferiori. Siat (et fiat), amen.

Carta volgare 14. Date: 7 November 1215. Grant of permission by Trogotori de Unali (Barisone-Torchitorio IV), iudike of Cálari, (1214–1217), with his wife, to Trogotori, the bishop of Suelli, to make a confirmation charter of various lands, resources, and servants acquired for the benefit of the church. Archivio diocesano storico di Cagliari, no. 6, DigiLib., no. 13. Fitted with a 'Byzantine' lead seal (50.6 g) and modern seal tag of dark red braid. Obv. +TOPK / OTOPHW / APX[UN]TH / MEP[C]HCK / APAVEWC. Rev. Cruciform invocative monogram (Type V), Θεοτόκε βοήθει; in the quarters: TW-ΣW ΔOY-ΛW (τῷ σῷ δούλῳ). Also known from a 16th-century transcription in the Archivio diocesano storico di Cagliari, *Liber Diversorum*, 2/I serie, Appendix 'Quaderno,' no. 13, DigiLib., p. 318. Editions: Solmi, 'Le carte volgari', no. 14, pp. 32–36; Falchi, *reisar.eu*, carta XIV.

(1)In nomine patris [et] Filii [et] Sp[irit]o S[an]c[t]i, amen. Ego (iudi)gi T(rog)otori de Unali, cu[m] do[n]na Biniita de Laco[n], mulieri mia, [per] bolintadi de (2)Do[n]n(u) Deu potestandu parti de Caralis, assolbullu a do[n]nu Trogotori, su piscobu miu de Suelli, ad fagirisi carta in co bolit. Et ego Trogotori, (3)p[er] issa m[isericord]ia de Deu piscobu de Suelli, cu[m] leba[n]du assoltura daba su do[n]nu miu iudigi Trogotori de Unali, [et] daba sa do[n]na mia do[n]na Biniita de Laco[n] (4)sa mulieri, ki mi llus castigit Do[n]nu Deu balaus a[n]nus [et] bon[us], fazzulla custa carta p[ro] beni ki fegiru[n]t a S[an]c[t]u Jorgi de Suelli. Deru[n]t illoi do[n]nu Ar-(5)zzocu Dezzori [et] do[n]na Jurgia sa sorri, fili[us] de do[n]nu Trogotori Dezzori de Urgu, a S[an]c[t]u Jorgi, p[ro] Deu [et] p[ro] a[n]i[m]a issoru [et] des pare[n]tis, o[mn]ia ca[n]tu

taleu: land, vineyard, unworked land and a water resource. (57)Witnesses: lord Johanni de Serra Saluda and his brother, Petru de Allari; lord Mariani de Serra d'Aluda and his brother, Petru, and Bonanu de Figus.

Also, lord Manueli d'Abis, son (58)of lord Gontini d'Abis, gave to Sanctu Jorgi, for God and his soul, a share of one of his sons at Funtana de Figu. Witnesses: lord Cumida de Serra Frailis, lord Gontini de Serra Afaidadu (59)and his brother, Mariani, lord Petru de Serra Calagonesu and his brother, Gunnari, and Petru de Serra Pinna. The witnesses are Barusoni de Serra Passagi, (60)Cumida de Serra from Frailis, and Mariani Dezzori Orlandu.

This charter was made in the year of our Lord 1215, in the 8th day before the Ides of November (6 November), as the iudike has in his hands (61)the curator's district (*curadoría*) of Campidanu on behalf of the deputy (*logusalbatori*). Whoever dares to controvert it, may the Father and the Son and the Holy Spirit curse him, and the twelve Apostles, the four Evangelists, the sixteen (62)Prophets, the twenty-four Elders, and the 318 Holy Fathers, and have his lot with Judas in the depths of Hell! Let it be and be done! Amen.

Carta volgare 14. Date: 7 November 1215. Grant of permission by Trogotori de Unali (Barisone-Torchitorio IV), iudike of Cálari, (1214–1217), with his wife, to Trogotori, the bishop of Suelli, to make a confirmation charter of various lands, resources, and servants acquired for the benefit of the church. Archivio diocesano storico di Cagliari, no. 6, DigiLib., no. 13. Fitted with a 'Byzantine' lead seal (50.6 g) and modern seal tag of dark red braid. Obv. +TOPK / OTOPHW / APX[UN]TH / MEP[C]HCK / APAVEWC. Rev. Cruciform invocative monogram (Type V), Θεοτόκε βοήθει; in the quarters: TW-ΣW ΔOY-ΛW (τῷ σῷ δούλῳ). Also known from a 16th-century transcription in the Archivio diocesano storico di Cagliari, *Liber Diversorum*, 2/I serie, Appendix 'Quaderno,' no. 13, DigiLib., p. 318. Editions: Solmi, 'Le carte volgari', no. 14, pp. 32–36; Falchi, *reisar.eu*, carta XIV.

(1)In the name of the Father, the Son, and the Holy Spirit, amen. I, iudike Trogotori de Unali with my wife lady Biniita de Lacon, by the will of (2)Lord God, ruling Caralis' territory (*parti*), permit (*assolbullu*) lord Trogodori, my bishop of Suelli, to make himself a charter as he wishes. So, I, Trogodori, (3)by the mercy of God bishop of Suelli, with permission (*assoltura*) from my lord, iudike Trogodori de Unali, and from his wife Biniita de Lacon (4)his wife—may Lord God protect them for me for many good years—make her a charter for benefices they made to Sanctu Jorgi de Suelli. (5)Lord Arzzocu Dezzori and her sister lady Jurgia, son and daughter of lord Trogotori Dezzori de Urgu, gave to Sanctu Jorgi, for God and for their souls and those of their relatives, all that which their father

illoi abe[n]ta in sa (6)billa de Goni de padri issor[u], plazza [et] t[er]ras et binias [et] saltu [et] aqua Et su[n]t desti(moni)[us] do[n]nu Cumida Pullu, arme[n]tariu de S[an]c[t]u Pa[n]taleu, [et] (7)do[n]nu Tiricu, p[re]idi d'Arcu [et] Cumida Soliu, [et] do[n]nu Mariani de Zoli, [et] Cumida Dardu d'Orzzokesus. Et dedilloi do[n]nu Manueli d'Abis, filiu de do[n]nu (8)Go[n]tini d'Abis a S[an]c[t]u Jorgi, p[ro] Deu [et] p[ro] a[n]i[m]a sua, in Fu[n]tana de Figu, parzzoni d'unu filiu suu. Et dedilloi do[n]nu Furadu Dezzori Zoro[m]pis a S[an]c[t]u Jorgi, (9)cu[m] buli[n]tadi [et] cu[m] paraula de sa mulieri do[n]na Maria Duliketa, filia de do[n]nu Cumida de Serra Pinna de Loguori, parzzoni d'unu filiu suu in Por-(10)(ta)sillas. Istimo[n]i[us], do[n]nu Cumida d'Orruu de Sibiola, do[n]nu Cumida Dezzori de Enoni, do[n]nu Petru d'Arcedi, [et] do[n]nu Mariani Castiai, do[n]nu Gontini (11)d'Orruu Daluda. Et dedilloi a S[an]c[t]u Jorgi, do[n]na Sardinia de Serre[n]ti, filia de do[n]nu Turbini de Serre[n]ti, cu[m] bulintadi de d(o[n]nu) Mariani Dezzori su maridu, (12)a Bera Tillia, filia de Malfidana Corbu ankilla sua, ad ankilla de cadadie, p[ro] Deu [et] p[ro] a[n]i[m]a sua. Istimo[n]ius, do[n]nu Joh[ann]i Spina, capellanu de su mo[n](ti d'Aqua) (13)Friida, [et] Turbini Piligas, [et] Joh[ann]i de Giida, p[re]idis de S([an]c[t]u Jor)gi, [et] Go[n]tini Pruzza, ki fraigaat a S[an]c[t]u Jorgi, [et] Gontini Co[n] Et dedilloi Bera Tuveri, mulieri (14)(de Cum)ida Lollu, ad S[an]c[t]u Jorgi de Suelli, p[ro] Deu [et] p[ro] a[n]i[m]a sua, ad ora de morti sua, sa parti sua ca[n]tu illi gitaat in sus fili[us] de Mariani de Bani[us], ki fudi s[er]bu suu, (15)(ea s'atera part)i de S[an]c[t]u Jorgi si fudi, p[ro] sa mulieri de Mariani de Bani[us], Furada de Barbaria, ki fudi ankilla de S[an]c[t]u Jorgi, [et] dedi ellus a serb[us] de cadadie. Istimo[n]i[us] (16)(preidi Gontini Zu)ca capellanu de Barcudi, [et] p[re]idi Go[n]tini de Quartu, capellanu de Sedaunu, [et] p[re]idi Go[n]tini Ulisinda, capellanu de Quartu susu, [et] Philipu [et] Cu(mida) (17)(Cuca). Et co[m]poreillis a Petru Flori, [et] assu fr[ad]i, [et] assa mama, sa binia de Pisadu k'esti costas ass'at[er]a binia de S[an]c[t]u Jorgi de Basili de Barbaria, ki no[n] anti (18)(ante pari faki su f)lumin(i et) deindellis sollus xxv, [et] clo[m]pillis pariari. Istimo[n]i[us], Bonanu de Fig[us], Cumida Ladu, Mariani Ladu, Petru de Serra Dardu, Joh[ann] i (19)de S(egolay). Et daulloi su do[n]nu miu judigi Guilielmu su markesu de Massa, in sa billa de Sestu, a S[an]c[t]u Jorgi de Suelli, una domestia k'esti cabizza assa(20){assa} bia ki ba[n]ti daa Sestu a nNuracadi daa estru, [et] daundi i[n]trat soli es[t] costas a Ciculelis [et] ferit ad t[er]ra de do[n]nu Joh[ann]i de Siillu [et] de Go[n]tini P[er]ra, [et] parta a ma-(21)ri ferit cabizza a t[er]ra de sus f[ra]dis P[er]ras,

had in the (6)village of Goni: a plot (*plazza*), lands (*terras*), vineyards, unworked land (*saltu*), water (*aqua*) and enclosed lands (*semidas*). The witnesses are lord Cumida Pullu, administrator (*armentariu*) of Sanctu Pantaleu (San Pantaleo at Dolianova), and (7)lord Tiricu priest of Arcu, Cumida Soliu, lord Mariani de Zoli, and Cumida Dardu d'Orzzokesus.

Also, lord Manueli d'Abis, son of lord (8)Gontini d'Abis, gave to Sanctu Jorgi, for God and for his soul, a share of one of his sons in Funtana de Figu ('spring of the fig'). Lord Furadu Dezzori Zorompis gave to Sanctu Jorgi, (9)with the consent and permission (*paraula*) of his wife lady Maria Duliketa, daughter of lord Cumida de Serra Pinna de Logu Ori (Logudoro), a share of one of his sons in (10)Portasillas. Witnesses: lord Cumida d'Orruu de Sibiola, lord Cumida Dezzori de Enoni, lord Petru d'Arcedi, and lord Mariani Castiai, [and] lord Gontini (11)d'Orruu d'Aluda.

Also, lady Sardinia de Serrenti, daughter of lord Turbini de Serrenti, gave to Sanctu Jorgi, with the consent of his husband lord Mariani Dezzori, (12)Bera Tillia, daughter of her female servant (*ankilla*) Malfidana Corbu, as a daily servant, for God and for her soul. Witnesses: lord Johanni Spina, chaplain at Su Monti d'Aqua (13)Friida ('the mountain of cold water'), and Turbini Piligas, and Johanni de Giida priest of Sanctu Jorgi, and Gontini Pruzza who is a builder for Sanctu Jorgi, and Gontini Concas.

Also, Bera Tuveri, wife of (14)Cumida Lollu, gave to Sanctu Jorgi de Suelli, for God and for her soul, on her deathbed, her part that she expected from the sons of Mariani de Banius, who was his servant, because the other part belonged (15)to Sanctu Jorgi, since the wife of Mariani de Banius, Furada de Barbaria, was a female servant of Sanctu Jorgi, therefore she donated them [i.e. her part of Mariani's sons] as everyday servants. Witnesses: (16)priest Gontini Zuca, chaplain of Barcudi; priest Gontini de Quartu, chaplain of Sedauni; priest Gontini Ulisinda, chaplain of Quartu Susu; Philipu, and Cumida Cucu.

(17)Also, I bought from Petru Flori and his brother and his mother the vineyard of Pisadu which borders on another vineyard of Sanctu Jorgi, of Basili de Barbaria, (18)by the river which had not previously been divided equally, and I gave them twenty-five soldi (*sollus*), and I completed the payment. Witnesses: Bonanu de Figus, Cumida Ladu, Mariani Ladu, Petru de Serra Dardu, and Johanni (19)de Segolay.

Also, my lord iudike Guilielmu, the marquis (*markesu*) of Massa, gave to Sanctu Jorgi de Suelli, at the village of Sestu, a farmstead (*domestia*) which it borders at one end (20)at the road that goes from Sestu to Nuracadi on the right side, and, where the sun sets, it borders Ciculelis and continues towards the land of lord Johanni de Siillu and Gontini Perra, and then goes towards the sea (21)to border with the land of the Perras brothers at another end; and

[et] daa s'at[er]a parti es[t] costas ass'at[er]a t[er]ra de judigi daundi si segad. Istimo[n]i[us] an[t]e ki fegi(t) su do[n]nu miu su markesu custu (22)beni ad S[an]c[t]u Jorgi, p[re]bi[t]eru Gontini de Mo[n]tis, capellanu de Sestu, [et] Furadu Frau jenezzariu de iudigi, ki lla daat a parti de su markesu [et] Petru Corsu, [et] Cumi-(23)(da de) Ecca afaidadu, [et] Furadu d'Arge[n] Et dedilloy a S[an]c[t]u Jorgi su p[re]idi de Sestu, do[n]nu Go[n]tini de Mo[n]tis, [et] Jorgi su fr[ad]i, in Sestu una binia k'esti parta a d'estru (24)costas assa binia de Furadu Spiga [et] de Basili Tivani daundi intrat soli, ferit costas a bi[n]ia de Joh[ann]i Frau, [et] falatsi 'nki fini a flumini, [et] parta a mari (25)(f)erit cab(izz)a a flumini, [et] daa s'at[er]a parti ferit cabizza ad s'iscla. Et su[n]t destimo[n]i[us], Gidi[n]bili d'Orruu, Cumida de (...)ga, Masedu Muria, Maria(ni) de Scala, Cumida (26)Corsu. Et dedilloi do[n]nu Joh[ann]i de Serra Daluda, filiu de do[n]nu Cumida de Laco[n], a S[an]c[t]u Jorgi de Suelli sa domu sua de Figu Orrubia, cun o[mn]ia ca[n]tu lloi aeda, (27)ho[m]i[n]is [et] plaçça [et] t[er]ra [et] binia [et] saltu [et] semida [et] aqua, [et] o[mn]ia ca[n]tu lloi aeda apusti cussa domu, [et] dedilloi ancu ad S[an]c[t]u Jorgi, kena custa domu, parççoni d'unu (28)filiu suu, in salt[us] [et] in semidas [et] in pastu [et] in landi [et] in aquas, ca[n]t'adi p[er] totu logu [et] dep[us] mama [et] dep[us] Eccu su beni ki lloi fegit do[n]nu Joh[ann]i de Serra (29)ad S[an]c[t]u Jorgi ki ll'apat S[an]c[t]u Jorgi p[us] morti sua, p[ro] Deu inna[n]ti [et] p[ro] a[n]i[m]a sua. Istimo[n]ius, Petru de Serra Dardu, [et] Cumida de Cabuderra, [et] Petru de Cabuderra (30)de Castania, t[er]rali suu de fitu, [et] Go[n]tini Isquirru, [et] Cumida su co[n]nadu, [et] Mariani de Unali, [et] Arççocu su fr[ad]i, [et] Joh[ann]i de Cabuderra. Et dedilloi do[n]na Muscu (31)(de) Serra, mulieri de do[n]nu Go[n]tini d'Orruu Daluda, ad S[an]c[t]u Jorgi de Suelli, a ora de morti sua, o[mn]ia ca[n]tu lloi aeda in sa domu sua de Figu Orrubia, ho[m]i[n]is [et] plaçça (32)(et terr)a [et] binia [et] saltu [et] semida [et] aqua, [et] o[mn]ia ca[n]tu aeda adpusti cussa domu. Eccu beni ki lloi fegit do[n]na Muscu de Serra ad Sanctu Jorgi, p[ro] Deu inna[n]ti [et] p[ro] (33)s'a[n]i[m]a su(a). Istimo[n]ius, do[n]nu Joh[ann]i de Serra su fradi carrali, [et] do[n]nu Mariani Deççori Orlandu, [et] do[n]nu Mariani de Serra Daluda, filiu de cussa stissa do[n]na (34)Muscu, [et] do[n]nu Turbini de Siiki, [et] do[n]nu Cumida de Unali de Billa de Ca[m] Et dedilloi do[n]nu Arççocu de Laco[n], filiu de do[n]nu Gu[n]nari de Laco[n] Ma[n]cosu [et] de do[n](na) (35)Maria Duliketa, a S[an]c[t]u Jorgi de Suelli, a ora de morti sua, ca fudi eniu [et] no[n] aeda filiu, o[mn]ia ca[n]tu aeda in tota t[er]ra de Plumin[us], ad partiri cu[m] s'arkipiscoba(du) (36)et cu[m] Sancta Maria de Clusu, ki si partirint custas tres clesias,

from the other part, it borders other land of the iudike from where it was alienated (*si segad*). The witnesses before whom my lord the marquis made these (22)benefices to Sanctu Jorgi [are]: priest Gontini de Montis chaplain of Sestu, and Furadu Frau, the iudike's supervisor (*jenezzariu*) who gave it on behalf of the marquis, and Petru Corsu, and Cumida (23)de Ecca Afaidadu, and Furadu d'Argenti. Also, lord Gontini de Montis the priest of Sestu, and his brother, gave to Sanctu Jorgi a vineyard in Sesto that goes towards the right side, bordering where the sun sets, (24)with the vineyard of Furadu Spiga and Basili Tivani, along the border of the vineyard of Johanni Frau, and continues until reaching the river, and goes towards the sea (25)and makes a border at the river, and from the other side it borders at the islet (*iscla*). The witnesses are Gidinbili d'Orruu, Cumida de Rega, Masedu Muria, Mariani de Scala, [and] Cumida (26)Corsu.

Also, lord Johanni de Serra d'Aluda, son of lord Cumida de Lacon, gave to Sanctu Jorgi de Suelli his farm complex (*domu*) of Figu Orrubia, together with all that he had: (27)men, and a plot, and land, vineyard, and unworked land, farm land, and a water resource, and all that he had at that farm complex. And he also gave to Sanctu Jorgi, apart from this farm, one of (28)his son's shares (*parççoni*) of unworked land, farm land, pannage (*in pastu et in landi*), and water, which he has across the entire country (*logu*), from both his mother's and father's side. These are the benefices that lord Johanni de Serra made (29)to Sanctu Jorgi (St George) which may be granted to Sanctu Jorgi after his death, for God before all else and for his own soul. Witnesses: Petru de Serra Dardu, and Cumida de Cabuderra (Capoterra), and his tenant farmer (*terrali de fitu*) Petru de Capuderra (30)de Castania, and Gontini Isquirru, and his brother-in-law Cumida, and Mariani de Unali, and his brother Arççocu, and Johanni de Cabuderra (Capoterra).

Also, lady Muscu (31)de Serra, wife of lord Gontini d'Orruu of Aluda, gave to Sanctu Jorgi de Suelli, on her deathbed, all that she had at her farm complex of Figu Orrubia: men, and plot, (32)and land, and vineyard, and unworked land, and farm land, and a water resource, and all that he had at that farm complex. These are the benefices that lady Muscu de Serra made to Sanctu Jorgi, for God before all else and (33)for her soul. Witnesses: his carnal brother, lord Johanni de Serra; lord Mariani Deççori Orlandu; lord Mariani de Serra of Aluda, son of this same lady (34)Muscu; lord Turbini de Siiki, and lord Cumida de Unali from Billa de Campu.

Also, lord Arççozu de Lacon, son of lord Gunnari de Lacon Mancosu and lady (35)Maria Duliketa, gave to Sanctu Jorgi de Suelli, on his deathbed, because he was unmarried and had no children, all that he had across the land (*terra*) of Pluminus (Cálari), to divide amongst the archbishopric [of Cálari] and (36)with Sancta Maria de Clusu (Santa Maria di Cluso at Cagliari), so these three

Sanc[t]u Jorgi de Suelli, [et] S[an]c[t]a Cecilia, [et] S[an]c[t]a Maria de Clusu, totu su suu co fradis bonus, [et] dom[us] [37](et) serb[us] et ankillas, et t[er]ras aradorias et domestias et binias, et padrus et salt[us], et semidas et aquas et o[mn]ia quaturpenna, et o[mn]ia ca[n]tu aeda per totu logu et d'intru et [38]de foras. Eccu beni ki lloi fegit do[n]nu Arççocu de Laco[n] ad S[an]c[t]u Jorgi, p[ro] Deu [et] p[ro]s'a[n]i[m]a sua. Istimo[n]ius, do[n]nu Mariani de Quartu, p[re]idi de billa {de billa}de Pubuççi, [39](k)i llu p(ene)de[n]tiedi (et) Arççocu Porkella, p[re]idi de Sirigariu, do[n]nu Gu[n]nari de Laco[n] su padri, do[n]nu Gu[n]nari de Çebera su tadaiu, [et] Mariani su filiu, [et] do[n]nu [40]Trogotori de Çebe(ra) et (Bar)isoni su filiu, [et] Gu[n]nari d'Orruu [et] kertei cu[m] do[n]nu Joh[ann]i de Curcas, filiu de do[n]nu Turbini de Curcas, p[ro] Petru Baca, ki fud(i) [41]s[er]bu de S[an]c[t]u Jorgi, [et] arreedasillu issi in serbitiu suu, [et] subra su kertu ca[m]paniedisi 'ndi megu, [et] dedimindi in ca(m)paniu lad[us] de Maria P[er]ra, filia de Cumida [42]Lo[n]gu s[er]bu suu, [et] c sollus. Istimo[n]i[us] p[re]idi Mariani de Quartu, do[n]nu Furadu Deççori de Çorro[m]pis, do[n]nu Turbini de Laco[n], curadori de Tolostrai, Gu[n]nari de [43]Cabu(d)err(a et) Gu[n]nari d'Orruu caliuu. Et dedilloi do[n]na Maria de Çebera, filia de do[n]nu Trogotori de Çebera, ad Sanctu Jorgi a Bera Orru[n]kina, filia de Mariani Orru[n](kina) [44](serbu) suu de sa billa de Kirra, ad ankilla de cadadie. Eccu beni ki lloi fegit do[n]na Maria de Çebera ad S[an]c[t]u Jorgi a ora de morti sua, p[ro] Deu inna[n]ti [et] p[ro] s'a[n]i[m]a [45](sua. Istimo[n]i[us]) p[re]idi Mariani de Quartu, [et] do[n]nu Petru d'Arcedi, [et] do[n]nu Pisanellu su fr[ad]i, [et] Çerkis Braga, [et] Saltoro Palia. Et dedilloi do[n]na Muscu de Serra, [46](filia de donnu) Barusoni Ma[n]nu ad S[an]c[t]u Jorgi, o[mn]ia ca[n]tu lloi abeda in sa billa de Sigii, plaçça t[er]ras aradorias [et] binias [et] salt[us] [et] aqua [et] o[mn]ia ca[n]tu si p[er]tineda a-[47](pusti cussa domu. Eccu beni) ki lloi fegit do[n]na Muscu ad S[an]c[t]u Jorgi, p[ro] Deu inna[n]ti [et] p[ro]s'a[n]i[m]a sua. Istimo[n]ius, do[n]nu Petru de Sii su ienniru, [et] Barusoni de Ser(ra) [48](Mudasclu), Go[n]tini Meloni, [et] Petru Kerbu. Et ca[m]bieilli a Go[n]tini Ma[n]ca, filiu de Maria Ma[n]ca, una parçoni sua de bi[n]ia, ki aeda intru [49](de binia de domestia de sanctu) Jorgi [et] deindelli intesiga de tres una de sa binia de S[an]c[t]u Jorgi de Pira Pedrosa, [et] p[ro] su ki mi subereledi ipsi a mimi adiu[n]xi inde lli [50](una molenti et binissir[us] nos apari). Istmoni[us] p[re]idi Turbini de Onori, [et] p[re]idi Arççocu de Molaria, [et] Bonanu de Fig[us], [et] do[n]nu Petru d'Aceni, [et] Cumida de La-[51](con de donnigalia alba. Et) dedilloi do[n]nu Mariani de Unali Orrudundu filiu de do[n]nu Go[n]tini de Unali

churches—Sanctu Jorgi de Suelli, and Sancta Cecilia (the cathedral of the archbishopric of Cálari) and Sancta Maria de Clusu—divided amongst them all that was for the good brothers: farm complexes, (37)male and servants, ploughed lands (*terras aradorias*), farmsteads, vineyards, meadows (*padrus*), unworked lands and farm lands, water resources, all the livestock (*quaturpenna*), and all that which he has across the whole country, both in the village (38)and beyond. These are the benefices lord Arççocu de Lacon made to Sanctu Jorgi, for God and for his soul. Witnesses: lord Mariani de Quartu priest of the village of Pubuççi (Villaputzu), who administered (39)his confession; Arççocu Porkella, priest of Sirigariu (Sirigraxu); his father, lord Gunnari de Lacon; his distant uncle, Gunnari de Çebera; his son, Mariani; lord (40)Trogotori de Çebera, and his son Barisoni; Gunnari d'Orruu, and Traiosu.

Also, I was in dispute with lord Johanni de Curcas, son of lord Turbini de Curcas, over Petru Baca who was (41)a servant of Sanctu Jorgi, and who kept him in his service; and regarding the dispute, he agreed with me and gave me half (*ladus*) of [the service of] Maria Perra, daughter of Cumida (42)Longu his servant and 100 soldi (*sollus*). Witnesses: priest Mariani de Quartu; lord Furadu Deççori de Çorrompis; lord Turbini de Lacon *curatore* of Tolostrai; Gunnari de (43)Cabuderra (Capoterra), and Gunnari d'Orruu Caliuu.

Also, lady Maria de Çebera, daughter of lord Trogotori de Çebera, gave to Sanctu Jorgi, as a daily servant, Bera Orrunkina, daughter of Mariani Orrunkina. (44)These are the benefices that lady Maria de Çebera made to Sanctu Jorgi on her deathbed, for God before all else and for the salvation of her soul. (45)Witnesses: priest Mariani de Quartu; lord Petru d'Arcedi, and his brother, lord Pisanellu; Çerkis Braga, and Saltoro Palia.

Also, lady Muscu de Serra, daughter of (46)lord Barusoni Mannu, gave to Sanctu Jorgi all what she had in the village of Sigii: plots, lands, ploughed lands, vineyards, unworked lands, water resources, and all that is found at that farm complex. (47)These are the benefices that lady Muscu made to Sanctu Jorgi, for God before all else and for the salvation of her soul. Witnesses: the son-in-law (*ienniru*) lord Petru de Sii, Barusoni de Serra (48)Mudasclu, Petru Meloni, Gontini Meloni, and Petru Kerbu.

Also, I exchanged with Gontini Manca, son of Maria Manca, one of his shares of a vineyard that he had within (49)a vineyard of a farmstead of Sanctu Jorgi; and, in exchange of three, I gave him one of [the shares of] the vineyard of Sanctu Jorgi of Pira Pedrosa, and he added a donkey to that which I received for the one he conceded me. (50)We were both mutually satisfied. Witnesses: priest Turbini de Onori; priest Arççocu de Molaria; Bonanu de Figus; lord Petru d'Aceni, and Cumida de (51)Lacon de Donnigalia Alba. Also, lord Mariani de Unali Orrudundu, son of lord Gontini de Unali Orrudundu, gave to Sanctu Jorgi

Orrudu[n]du, ad S[an]c[t]u Jorgi, sa parti sua de (52)(su salti d'Ardilli et de semi)da, et de pastu [et] d'aqua, in cu[m]bentu si fili[us] suus indi kere[n]ta ca[m]bia p[ro] custu saltu, ki learint a iuriu ca[m]bia de su suu (53)(peguliari. Eccu) beni ki lloi fegit do[n]nu Orrudu[n]du a Sanctu Jorgi, p[ro]Deu inn(anti) [et] p[ro] s'anima sua. Et dedilloi do[n]nu I(liççu) (54)(Dinki, filia de donnu Iliççu) de Laco[n] Isculççu ad S[an]c[t]u Jorgi sa parti sua de custu stissu saltu d'Ardilli, [et] de semida [et] de pastu [et] aqua, p[ro] Deu in-(55)(nanti et pro s'anima sua. Istimonius de cus)tas amb(a)s daduras, do[n]nu Mariani Deççori Orlandu, do[n]nu Barusoni Dinki, do[n]nu Gontini d'Orruu d'A(bis) (56)(Cumida d'Arcedi de Semassi, et) Turbini su fradi. Et su[n]t destimo[n]i[us] Brusoni de Serra Passagi [et]Cumida de Serra de Frailis, [et] Mariani Deççо(ri) (57)(Orlandu). (Et est fata custa car)ta anno do(mi[n]i) (MCCXV. VII.) id[us] Nove[m]bris, habe[n]dusilla judigi a manu sua sa curadoria de Campidanu (58)(pro logusalbadori. Et ki ll'aet devertere apat anathema daba) Pater [et] Filiu [et] S[an]c[t]u Isp[irit]u, daba XII Apos[t]olos IIII Eva[n]gelistas XVI P[ro]p[et]has XXIIII (59)(Seniores et CCCXVIII Patres Sanctos et) apat sorti cu[m] Juda in inferno inferiori. Siat et fiat. Amen, amen, amen.

Carta volgare 15. Transumpt. Date: 22 May 1216. Grant of permission by Trogotori de Unali (Barisone-Torchitorio IV), iudike of Cálari (1214–1217), with his wife, to Mariani, the bishop of Sulchis, to draw up a confirmation for an exchange of plotted enclosures (*cuniadus*) made with the first lady of the realm (*donna de logu*), Biniita de Lacon (Benedetta de Lacon), the iudike of Cálari (1214–1233) and wife of Barisone-Torchitorio IV. Known from two 15th-century transumpts in the Archivio diocesano storico di Cagliari, *Liber Diversorum*, 2/I serie [E], ff. 116–117r, DigiLib., pp. 124–125, and f. 234v, DigiLib., p. 249. Editions: Solmi, 'Le carte volgari', no. 15, pp. 36–37.

Hoc est translatum copia et exemplum bene et fideliter sumptum in castro Callari, die IIII, mensis Augusti anno a nativitate Domini MCCCCLXXVI a quodam libro appellato Mare Magnum, episcopati Sulcitanis non vitiato, non cancellato, nec in aligua sui parte suspecto, sed omni prorsus vitio et suspectione carente, cuius tenor sequitur sub his verbis:[15]

---

15 The proemia found in the *Liber Diversorum*, 2/I serie [E], ff. 116v, DigiLib., pp. 124 and at f. 234v, DigiLib., p. 249 are the same except for trivial variants in their use of abbreviations.

his part of (52)su Saltu d'Ardilli: farm land, unworked land, and a water resource. We agreed on this with his sons who wanted an exchange for this unworked land, who took legal action on the exchange of their (53)particular [servant] for this land. These are the benefices that lord Orrudundu made to Sanctu Jorgi, for God before anything else and for the salvation of his soul.

And lord Iiççu Dinki, son of lord (54)Iiççu de Lacon Isculççu, gave to Sanctu Jorgi his part of the same Saltu d'Ardilli: farm land, unworked land, and water resources, for God (55)before all else and for the salvation of his soul. Witnesses of these two donations: lord Mariani Deççori Orlandu, lord Barusoni Dinki, lord Gontini d'Orruu d'Abis, (56)Cumida d'Arcedi de Semassi, and his brother Turbini. The witnesses are: Barusoni de Serra Passagi, and Cumida de Serra de Frailis, and Mariani Deççori (57)Orlandu.

This charter was made in the year of our Lord 1215, on the 7th day before the Ides of November (7 November), as the iudike has in his hands the curator's district (*curadoría*) of Campidanu (Campidano) (58)on behalf of the deputy (*logusalbadori*). Whosoever dares to controvert it, may the Father and the Son and the Holy Spirit curse him, and the twelve Apostles, the four Evangelists, the sixteen Prophets, the twenty-four (59)Elders, and the 318 Holy Fathers, and may he have his lot with Judas in the depths of Hell! Let it be and be done! Amen, amen, amen.

Carta volgare 15. Transumpt. Date: 22 May 1216. Grant of permission by Trogotori de Unali (Barisone-Torchitorio IV), iudike of Cálari (1214–1217), with his wife, to Mariani, the bishop of Sulchis, to draw up a confirmation for an exchange of plotted enclosures (*cuniadus*) made with the first lady of the realm (*donna de logu*), Biniita de Lacon (Benedetta de Lacon), the iudike of Cálari (1214–1233) and wife of Barisone-Torchitorio IV. Known from two 15th-century transumpts in the Archivio diocesano storico di Cagliari, *Liber Diversorum*, 2/I serie [E], ff. 116–117^{r}, DigiLib., pp. 124–125, and f. 234^{v}, DigiLib., p. 249. Editions: Solmi, 'Le carte volgari', no. 15, pp. 36–37.

This is a transumpt copy and exemplum, faithfully and well made in the citadel of Callari on the 4th day of August, in the year of the birth of the Lord 1476, from a certain book called the *Mare Magnum*, in the bishopric of Sulcis. [It is] neither damaged, nor abrogated, nor is any part of it suspected of any fault, but [is] entirely without suspicion, the content of which follows under these words:[16]

16 The proemia found in the *Liber Diversorum*, 2/I serie [E], ff. 116^{v}, DigiLib., pp. 124 and at f. 234^{v}, DigiLib., p. 249 are the same except for minor variants in their use of abbreviations.

In nomine Domini, amen. Ego iuigi Trootori de Unali, cum do[n]na Biniita de Lacon, mulieri mia, per bolintadi de donnu Deu potestandu parti de Caralis, assolbullu a donnu Mariani, su piscobu miu de Sulchis ad fagirisi carta in co bolit. Et ego Mariani, per issa misericordia de deu piscobu de Sulchis, cum assoltura daba su donnu miu iudigi Trogotori de Gunali et dessa donna mia donna Biniita de Lacon sa mulieri, ki mi llus castigit donnu Deu balaus annus et bonus, façςumi carta pro tramuda ki fegit megu sa donna mia donna Biniita de Lacon, donna de logu. Kerfidimi issa a mimi sus cuniadus cantu furunt bagantis kena plantari a binia, daba sa bia ki badi daba bau de s'errema [a] sa bilia de Pardu, fisca a pischina de Ladiri a cabizza sua fisca a bau de Bituni; k' ellas keredas ad darilas a s'obera de sanctu Maria de Pisas: et icustus cuniadus auiat mi llus issa dadus in cambia pro sus cuniadus cantu auiat sanctu Antiogu suus et de seruus suus, intru de sus cuniadus de Padru maiori; et eo fegii 'nd 'elli boluntadi a sa donna mia, et deis illus. Et issa, cum boluntadi de su donnu miu iuigi Barusoni su maridu, dedi illoy a sanctu Antiogu d'iscla, su donnu miu, intesiga s'orriina sua de Carrarius de bogada et a bogari, ki fudi apusti sa domu sua d'Urradoli. Et segatsi custa orriina de Carrarius daba bau de serra, et collat tudui su bau de serra deretu a sa bia de corti de porchus, et leuat tudui sa bia deretu a sspiuntadoriu de pulledrus, et iumpat bia deretu a pedra lampadorza, et badit frangenduru aqua de monti pichinnu deretu assa bia d' Entergenna, et collat tudui sa bia deretu a bau de serra, da undi si ingençat. Custa orriina de Carrarius ylloi dedi sa donna mia donna Biniita de Lacon a sanctu Antiogu su donnu miu, intesiga de su cantu auiat sanctu Antiogu ad terra baganti daba bau de s'erremas fisca a bau de Bituni; et daba bau de Bituni tudui su erriu ki essit assa bia de logu, ki banti daa billa de Padru a bau de s'erremas da undi si in gençat; pro su ki apat indi proi sanctu Antiogu dessa orriina de Carrarius cantu adi durari su mundu, kena briga nin molestia de perunu homini dessu mundu. Destimonius, presbiter Mariani Saltizu, et clerigu Contini de Siuni, Arççocu de Sii, curadori de Sigerri, et Grunnari su fradi, curadori de Sulchis, et Benitu, castellanu de su monti d'Aqua friida. Et sunt testimonius Barisoni de Serra Passagi, et Cumida de Serra de Frailis, et Mariani Dezori Orlandu. Et

In the name of the Lord, amen. I, iudike Trootori de Unali, with my wife lady Biniita de Lacon, by the will of Lord God, ruling Caralis' territory (*parti*), permit (*assolbullu*) lord Mariani, my bishop of Sulchis (Sulchi), to make himself a charter as he wishes. So, I, Mariani, by the mercy of God bishop of Sulchis, with permission (*assoltura*) from my lord, iudike Trogodori de Gunali, and from his wife my lady Biniita de Lacon—may Lord God protect them for me for many good years—make me a charter for the exchange that I made with my lady, [first] lady of the realm (*donna de logu*), lady Biniita de Lacon.

She wished me to give her the plotted enclosures (*cuniadus*) that were uncultivated without a planted vineyard, [starting] from the road that goes from Bau de s'Errema ('ford of the ruin') to the village of Pardu, until reaching Pischina de Ladiri ('pool of Ladiri') and reaching its end at Bau de Bituni ('ford of Bituni'); she wishes to give them for the construction works of [the cathedral of] Santa Maria of Pisa (Opera della Primaziale Pisana). She had given me the plotted enclosures in agreed exchange for the plotted enclosures that Sanctu Antiogu had and for its servants (*servus*) inside the plotted enclosure of Padru Maiori ('great meadow'). I did so by the will of my lady, and I gave them. And she, with the consent of his husband, my lord iudike Barusoni, gave to Sanctu Antiogo d'Iscla, my lord, in agreed exchange, her [property at] Orriina de Carrarius (lit. 'cartwright's shack'), for collection and to collect (*de bogada et a bogari*), which was located at his farm complex of Urradoli. Orriina of Carrarius borders with Bau de Serra ('ford of the mountain range'), [the boundary] goes up, keeping to Bau de Serra, towards the road of Corti de Porchus ('yard of pigs'), and keeps to that road towards s'Spiuntadoriu de Pulledrus, then crosses the road towards Pedra Lampadorza and keeps to the edge of Aqua de Monti Picchinu ('pond of Small Hill') towards the road of Entergenna, then it goes up the road towards Badu de Serra from where it started. Orriina de Carrarius, which my lady, lady Biniita de Lacon gave to Sanctu Antiogu, my lord, in agreed exchange for all that Sanctu Antiogu had in uncultivated land, [extending] from the Bau de s'Erremas ('ford of the ruins') up to Bau de Bituni ('ford of Bituni'); from Bau de Bituni, it goes along the stream that leads to the main road (*bia de logu*), which goes from the village of Padru to Bau de s'Erremas, from where it started. This is in order that Sanctu Antiogu has its property in Orriina de Carrarius till the end of the world, without any quarrel or trouble from any man of this world. Witnesses: priest Mariani Saltizu; cleric Contini de Siuni, Arççocu de Sii, *curatore* of Sigerri (Cixerri valley), and his brother Grunnari the *curatore* of Sulchis (Sulcis), and Benitu, castellan at Monti d'Aqua Friida ('the mountain of cold water'). The witnesses are Barisoni de Serra Passagi, Cumida de Serra de Frailis, and Mariani Dezori Orlandu.

fudi fata custa carta anno domini MCCXVI XI. kal. junii, habendusilla su iuigi a manu sua sa curadoria de Campidanu pro logu salbadori, et ki ll'aet deuertere apat anathema etc.

Carta volgare 16. Date: 8 March 1217. Grant of permission by Trogotori de Unali (Barisone-Torchitorio IV) iudike of Cálari (1214–1217), with his wife, Biniita de Lacon (Benedetta de Massa), iudike of Cálari (1214–1233), to Trogodori, the bishop of Suelli, to draw up a charter for exchanges and donations of servants and landed properties made for the benefit of the church. Archivio diocesano storico di Cagliari, no. 9. DigiLib., no. 14. Fitted with a 'Byzantine' lead seal (49.3 g) and seal tag of plaited brown chord. Much of the charter is severely water-damaged and barely legible. Obv. +TOPK / OTOPHW / APXUNTH / MEPEHCK / [A]P[AVE]WC. Rev. Cruciform invocative monogram (Type V), Θεοτόκε βοήθει; in the quarters: TW-ΣW ΔOY-ΛW (τῷ σῷ δούλῳ). Transumpt in the *Liber Diversorum*, E, cc. 155–156 v. (n.n. 172–173v). Editions: Solmi, 'Le carte volgari', no. 14, pp. 37–40; Falchi, *reisar.eu*, carta XVI.

(1)In nomine Patris et Filii et Spiritus Sancti, am[en]. Ego judigi Trogotori de Unali cum donna Biniita de Lacon (2)mulieri mia, per bolintadi de donnu Deu podestandu parti de Caralis, assolbullu a donnu Trogotori, piscobu de Suelli, (3)a ffagirisi carta in co bolit. Et ego Trogotori, piscobu de Suelli, cum levandu assoltura daba su donnu miu judi-(4)gi Trogotori de Unali et daba sa donna mia donna Biniita de Lacon sa mulieri, ki mi llus castigit donnu Deu balaus (5)annus et bonus, façςumi custa carta pro cambias ki fegi et pro daduras ki fegirunt ad Sanctu Jorgi de Suelli. Cambiei [cum su (6)donnu miu judigi Barusoni, et cum sa donna mia Biniitaa de Lacon sa mulieri, deillis eo ad issus in Barbaria (7)ad Maria Dadu, filia de Cumida Dadu, et ad Johanni su filiu, et issus deruntmi a mimi in Barbaria, in sa bilia de (8)Gairu, una condoma ad Cumida Dorruu, filiu d' Arççocu Cucii, et ad Aleni Coçça sa mulieri, filia de Petru Cozza. Et derunt-(9)millus ad serbus de cadadia, cum filius et filias issoru, et cantu aenta fatus et cantu enti fairi, et deruntumillus cum fundamentu de parentis issoru. (10)Istimonius, donnu Turbini Corsu, calonigu de sancta Maria de Clusu, et preidi Mariani de Setimu, et preidi Arççocu Loki, et donnu Cumida de Serra de Frailis, (11)et donnu Turbini de Lacon Mancosu, et Petru Meli de Cidu. Et cambiei cum donnu Barusoni (12)de Çebera, filiu de donnu Troodori de Zebera: deilli eo ad issi in Sarrabus ad Aleni de Margini, filia de Bera de Margini, ankilla (13)piguliari de sanctu Jorgi de sa bilia de Siuni, cum parti de filius suus ki aeda fatus daa

This charter was made in the year of our Lord 1216, in the 11th day before the kalends of June (22 May), as the iudike has in his hands the curator's district (*curadoría*) of Campidanu (Campidano) on behalf of the deputy (*logu salbadori*). Whosoever dares to controvert it, may be cursed, *et cetera*.

Carta volgare 16. Date: 8 March 1217. Grant of permission by Trogotori de Unali (Barisone-Torchitorio IV) iudike of Cálari (1214–1217), with his wife, Biniita de Lacon (Benedetta de Massa), iudike of Cálari (1214–1233), to Trogodori, the bishop of Suelli, to draw up a charter for exchanges and donations of servants and landed properties made for the benefit of the church. Archivio diocesano storico di Cagliari, no. 9. DigiLib., no. 14. Fitted with a 'Byzantine' lead seal (49.3g) and seal tag of plaited brown chord. Much of the charter is severely water-damaged and barely legible. Obv. +TOPK / OTOPHW / APXUNTH / MEPEHCK / [A]P[AVE]WC. Rev. Cruciform invocative monogram (Type V), Θεοτόκε βοήθει; in the quarters: TW-ΣW ΔOY-ΛW (τῷ σῷ δούλῳ). Transumpt in the *Liber Diversorum*, E, cc. 155–156 v. (n.n. 172–173^{v}). Editions: Solmi, 'Le carte volgari', no. 14, pp. 37–40; Falchi, *reisar.eu*, carta XVI.

(1)In the name of the Father, the Son, and the Holy Spirit, amen. I, iudike Trogotori de Unali with Biniita de Lacon, (2)my wife lady, by the will of Lord God, ruling Caralis' territory (*parti*), permit (*assolbullu*) lord Trogodori, bishop of Suelli, (3)to make himself a charter as he wishes. So, I, Trogodori, bishop of Suelli, with permission (*assoltura*) from my lord, iudike (4)Trogodori de Unali, and from his wife Biniita de Lacon his wife—may Lord God protect them for me for (5)many good years—make me a charter for the exchanges I made, and for the donations they made to Sanctu Jorgi de Suelli. I made an exchange with (6)my lord iudike Barusoni and my lady, his wife, lady Biniita de Lacon. In Barbaria, I gave them (7)Maria Dadu, daughter of Cumida Dadu, and her son Johanni, and they gave me, in Barbaria, in the village of (8)Gairu, a married couple of servants (*condoma*): Cumida de'Orruu, son of Arççocu Cucci, and his wife Aleni Cozza (Coçça), daughter of Petru Cozza. They also gave (9)me everyday servants together with their sons and daughters, and any they have or will have. And they gave them to me together with the real estate (*fundamentu*) of their relatives. (10)Witnesses: lord Turbini Corsu, canon of Sancta Maria de Clusu (Santa Maria di Cluso in Cagliari); priest Mariani de Setimu (Settimo San Pietro); priest Arççocu Loki; lord Cumida de Serra from Frailis; (11)lord Turbini de Lacon Mancosu, and Petru Meli de Cidu.

I made an exchange with lord Barusoni de Çebera, son of lord Troodori (12)de Çebera. In Sarrabus, I gave him Aleni de Margini, daughter of Bera de Margini, (13)a female servant (*piguliari ankilla*) of Sanctu Jorgi from the village of Siuni,

Mariani Cariga serbu suu; et deillilla (14)cum fundamentu suu. Et issi dedimi a mimi in sa bilia de Bary ad Aleni Loki, cum ii. filius suus, Cumida et Siona; et fudi custa (15)Aleni Loki filia de Maria Loki, ankilla sua piguliari de sa villa d'Osono, depusti sa mama donna Furada de Serra, et dedimilla (16)cum fundamentu suu. Istimonius, donnu Turbini Corsu, calonigu de sancta Maria de Clusu, et Arççocu Loki, preidi de Kirra, et donnu (17)Cumida de Serra de Frailis, et donnu Petru de Serra su filiu, et donnu Gontini Deççori de Sijllu, et Gunnari Zapuladu. Et bennit sa donna (18)mia donna Benedicta de Lacon, donna de logu, ad sanctu Jorgi de Suelli ad orationi; et donedilloi ad sanctu Jorgi, cum bulintadi (19)bona de su donnu miu iudigi Barusoni su maridu, pro deu innanti et pro s'anima sua, una condoma, in sa villa de Sisini, ad (20)Petru de Segedi, filiu de Gontini de Segedi, et ad Bera de Kerki sa mulieri, filia de Troolzzu de Kerki, et dedi ella custa (21)condoma ad sanctu Jorgi ad serbus de cadadie, cum filius et filias issoru, et cantu aenta fatus et cantu enti fairi, et dediellus cum fundamentu de (22)parentis issoru. Et arregordarunt illi ad sa donna mia, pro una terrazzola de Barbaria ki fudi mii in Suelli, ad ki naraant Aleni (23)de Urguri, filia de Dominada Magau, ankilla sua d'Ulaççai, et de Iiççu Manca, serbu de sanctu Jorgi de sa villa de Urgu, (24)ki aeda ladus ladus cum sanctu Jorgi; et issa, pro Deu innanti et pro s'anima sua, dedi ellu ad sanctu Jorgi su ladas suu ki 'nd' elli gitaat d'Aleni (25)de Urguri. Istimonius de custu beni, ki fegit sa donna mia ad sanctu Jorgi, donnu Gregu Casu, armentariu de sanctu Jorgi, donnu Cumida (26)de Serra de Frailis, et donnu Petru de Serra buccaporcu, et donnu Gontini de Serra affaidadu, et Cumida Calcaniu, et Mariani de Cidu. (27)Et kertei cum Troodori de Urgu, filiastru de Cumida de Cabras, de Sisini, pro duus filius de Justa Lada, filia de Petru Ladu, serbu (28)de sanctu Jorgi, ki s'arreeda kena 'ndi dari ad sanctu Jorgi; et tenealli kertu candi fudi binkidu pro minimançça in corona de sa (29)kida, in bida de su Markesu, suta piscobu Paulu. Tassiaruntmi a mimi destimonius ca fudi beru su cantu naraa. Et subra (30)baturi sus istimonius nos campaniarus inpari pro pregu ki mi 'ndi fegirunt, et leuei 'ndi eo su maschi pro sanctu Jorgi, a (31)ki narant Furadu, et a issi lasseilli sa femina a ki narant Marcusa. Custu lii fegi pro deu innanti et pro sanctu Jorgi, et pro essirigi[17] (32)issi fideli in sa domu de sanctu Jorgi. Istimonius de custu campanili ki fegirus inpari, donnu Masedu, armentariu de Olia, et prebiteru Tiricu, capellanu d'Arcu, et Gunnari de Serra, filiu de donnu (33)Cumida de Serra de [d]onna Bera, et Mariani Frau, et Cumida Cabras. Cerga antiga li fudi candu ca

17 The left-hand side of the manuscript and the foot of it become increasingly illegible. The transcription of these parts is based on Solmi's edition.

together with its share of her sons that she had with its servant Mariani Cariga. And I gave her along (14)with her built property. In the village of Bary, he gave me Aleni Loki together with two of her sons: Cumida and Siona. And this (15)Aleni Loki, daughter of Maria Loki, her own (*piguliari*) female servant from the village of Osono, was inherited from his mother lady Furada de Serra; and he gave her to me with (16)her built property. Witnesses: lord Turbini Corsu, canon of Sancta Maria de Clusu; Arççocu Loki, priest of Kirra; lord (17)Cumida de Serra from Frailis, and his son, lord Petru de Serra; lord Gontini Deççori de Sijllu, and Gunnari Zapuladu.

Also, my lady, (18)[the first] lady of the realm (*donna de logu*), lady Benedicta de Lacon, came to pray and she gave to Sanctu Jorgi, with the (19)good will of her husband, my lord, iudike Barusoni, for God before all else, and for her soul, a couple of servants, in the village of Sisini: (20)Petru de Segedi, son of Gontini de Segedi, and his wife Bera de Kerki, daughter of Troolzzu de Kerki. She donated this (21)couple of servants to Sanctu Jorgi as everyday servants, together with their sons and daughters, and any [children] they have and will have. She granted them along with the built property of (22)their relatives. And they reminded my lady of one plot of land from Barbaria which was mine in Suelli, regarding which Aleni (23)de Urguri—daughter of Dominada Magau, her female servant from Ulaççai, and of Iiççu Manca, servant of Sanctu Jorgi from the village of Urgu—says (24)that she had half and Sanctu Jorgi the other half. And she, for God before all else and for her soul, gave her half to Sanctu Jorgi, which she recalled from Aleni (25)de Urguri. Witnesses of these benefices that my lady made to Sanctu Jorgi: Gregu Casu, administrator (*armentariu*) of Sanctu Jorgi; lord Cumida (26)de Serra from Frailis; lord Petru de Serra Buccaporcu ('pig mouth'); lord Gontini de Serra Affaidadu, Cumida Calcaniu, and Mariani de Cidu.

(27)I also had a dispute with Troodori de Urgu, stepson of Cumida de Cabras from Sisini, over two children of Justa Lada, daughter of Petru Ladu, servant (28)of Sanctu Jorgi, whom he kept for himself without giving any [of the children] to Sanctu Jorgi. I contended that he had already been defeated [legally] for having been in contempt (*minimanzza*) at the summons' court (*corona de sa kida*), (29)when the marquis was alive, during the bishopric of Paul. They made me (30)present witnesses who could confirm all that I say. And upon having brought witnesses forth, we agreed together on the plea that was made to me: I took for Sanctu Jorgi the male, (31)named Furadu, and I left him the female, named Marcusa. I agreed on this for God before all else and for St George, and because (32)he was faithful at the house of Sanctu Jorgi. Witnesses of this settlement that we agreed together: lord Masesu, administrator of Olia; priest Tiricu, chaplain of Arcu; Gunnari de Serra, son of lord (33)Cumida de Serra; lady Bera; Mariani Frau, and Cumida Cabras.

seeda Iudigi nou in sa terra, (34)dari una condoma a sancta Maria de Lozzorai, su Iudigi et issa donna de logu, su maschi pro su Iudigi, et issa femina (35)pro sa donna de logu; et icustus donnus mius Iudigi Barusoni et donna Benedita sa mulieri, pro deu innanti et pro s'anima issoru, (36)et pro custa cerga ki fudi et usada et antiga, derunti illoy ad bolia de pari, ad sancia Maria de Loççorai, una condoma in[18] (37)sa billa de Tortoeli, ad Gontini Zacca, filiu de Petru Zacea, et ad Florida Lua sa mulieri, filia de Golorgi Lua, et derunti ellus cum fundamentu issoru, pro serbias de cadadie. Istimonius, donnu Barusoni de Serra Passagi, et donnu Johanni de Serra Daluda, et donnu Cumida de Serra de Frailis, et Arççocu Boy, et Cipari d'Arzedi, et Janni Guleri. Et sunt testimonies de logu donnu Barusoni de Serra Passagi, donnu Cumida de Serra de Deççori de Enoni. Et est facta custa carta anno domini MCCXVII VIII idus Martii, habendusilla iudigi ad manu sua sa curadoria de Campidanu pro logu salbadori. Et ki ll'aet deuertere apat anathema daba pater et filiu et semeio ispmtu, et daba XII Apostolos, et IIII Evangelistas, et XVI Prophetas, XXIIII Seniores, CCCXVIII Patres Sanctos, et habeat sortem cum Juda proditore in inferno inferiori. Siat et fiat. Amen.

Carta volgare 17.[19] Date: 8 March 1217. Grant of permission by Trogotori de Unali (Barisone-Torchitorio IV) iudike of Cálari (1214–1217), with his wife, Biniita de Lacon (Benedetta de Lacon, iudike of Cálari, 1214–1233), to Trogodori, the bishop of Suelli, to make a confirmation charter for various purchases, exchanges and donations of land made for the benefit of the church. Archivio diocesano storico di Cagliari, no. 7, DigiLib., no. 15. Fitted with a 'Byzantine' lead seal (47.5 g) and seal tag of brown chord. Obv. +TOPK / OTOPHW / APXUNTH / MEP(E)HCK / [A]PAV(EWC). Rev. Cruciform invocative monogram (Type V), Θεοτόκε βοήθει; in the quarters: TW-ΣW ΔOY-ΛW (τῷ σῷ δούλῳ). Also known from two 16th-century transcriptions in the Archivio diocesano storico di Cagliari, *Liber Diversorum*, 2/I serie, Appendix 'Quaderno,' no. 11A, pp. 316–317; no. 17, DigiLib., p. 323. Edition: Solmi, 'Le carte volgari', no. 17, pp. 40–43.

18 The final section of the charter is lacunose and has been reconstructed from the transumpt from the *Liber Diversorum*.

19 The entire manuscript is severely water-damaged and is almost completely illegible. However, it seems to have been read by Solmi without difficulty for his edition of 1905. The transcription given below is reconstructed from the transumpts in the *Liber Diversorum* in tandem with his edition.

By ancient duty (*cerga*), when a new iudike came to power, the iudike and the [first] lady of the realm must give (34)a couple of servants to Sancta Maria de Lozzorai: the male [was] donated in the name the iudike, and the female (35)in the name of the [first] lady of the realm. And these lords of mine, iudike Barisone and his wife lady Benedita, for God before all else and for their souls, and as a result of (36)this duty that has been customary and ancient, jointly gave to Santa Maria di Lozzorai a couple of servants in (37)the village of Tortoeli (Tortolì): Gontini Zacca, son of Petru Zacca, and his wife Florida Lua, daughter of Golorgi Lua. They donated them together, as everyday servants, with their built property. Witnesses: lord Barusoni de Serra Passagi, lord Johanni de Serra d'Aluda, lord Cumida de Serra de Frailis, Arççocu Boy, Cipari d'Arzedi, and Janni Guleri. The local witnesses are lord Barusoni de Serra Passagi, lord Cumida de Serra de Deççori from Enoni.

This charter was made in the year of our Lord 1217, in the 8th day before the Ides of March (8 March), as the iudike has in his hands the curator's district (*curadoría*) of Campidanu (Campidano) on behalf of the deputy (*logu salbadori*). Whosoever dares to controvert it, may the Father and the Son and the Holy Spirit curse him, and the twelve Apostles, the four Evangelists, the sixteen Prophets, the twenty-four Elders, and the 318 Holy Fathers, and may he have his lot with Judas in the depths of Hell! Let it be and be done! Amen.

Carta volgare 17.[20] Date: 8 March 1217. Grant of permission by Trogotori de Unali (Barisone-Torchitorio IV) iudike of Cálari (1214–1217), with his wife, Biniita de Lacon (Benedetta de Lacon, iudike of Cálari, 1214–1233), to Trogodori, the bishop of Suelli, to make a confirmation charter for various purchases, exchanges and donations of land made for the benefit of the church. Archivio diocesano storico di Cagliari, no. 7, DigiLib., no. 15. Fitted with a 'Byzantine' lead seal (47.5 g) and seal tag of brown chord. Obv. +TOPK / OTOPHW / APXUNTH / MEP(E)HCK / [A]PAV(EWC). Rev. Cruciform invocative monogram (Type V), Θεοτόκε βοήθει; in the quarters: TW-ΣW ΔOY-ΛW (τῷ σῷ δούλῳ). Also known from two 16th-century transcriptions in the Archivio diocesano storico di Cagliari, *Liber Diversorum*, 2/I serie, Appendix 'Quaderno,' no. 11A, pp. 316–317; no. 17, DigiLib., p. 323. Edition: Solmi, 'Le carte volgari', no. 17, pp. 40–43.

20 The entire manuscript is severely water-damaged and is almost completely illegible. However, it seems to have been read by Solmi without difficulty for his edition of 1905. The transcription given below is reconstructed from the transumpts in the *Liber Diversorum* in tandem with his edition.

+ In nomine patris et filii et spiritus sancti, amen. Ego iudigi Trogotori de Unali, cum donna Biniita de Lacon mulieri mia, per bolintadi de donnu deu potestandu parti de Caralis, assolbullu a donnu Trogotori, piscobu de Suelli, affagisi (*corr.* a ffagirisi) carta in co bolit. Et ego piscobu Trogotori, cum levandu assoltura daba su donnu miu iudigi Trogotori de Unali, et daba sa donna mia donna Biniita de Lacon sa mulieri, ki mi llus castigit Donnu Deu balaus annus et bonus, façḉulla custa carta pro comporas et pro tramudas ki fegi in sa billa d'Arigi, et pro daduras ki lloy fegirunt a sanctu Jorgi de Suelli. Posimi in coru de plantarilla ad binia a sanctu Jorgi sa domestia sua, a ki narrant domestia de bau de piscabu; et ca mi pareda pagu custa domestia, de no. mi bastari ad fagiri binia cantu bolea fairi ad sanctu Jorgi, comporeilloy, in giru de cussa domestia, et tramudei et pidii terras a hominis[21] bonus ki ellas aenta, et fegimi cuniadu cantu mi parsit de podiri plantari su cantu m'aea postu in coru de plantari. Comporeilloi intru de cussu cuniadu a Petru de Sarrau su ladus dessa terra sua de bau de piscabu, tenendu a icussa istissa domestia de sanctu Jorgi de bau de piscobu, et dei nd'elli III. sollus de inaris, et clompilli pariari. Istimonius, Saltoro de Unali corrogla, et Gunnari de Serra, filiu de donnu Cumida de Serra de donna Bera, el M[ariani] Cau d'Arigi, et Mariani Franca, et Bonanu de Figus. Et camieillis a Maria Sirigu et a ffilius terra cantu lloy aenta, intru de cussu istissu cuniadu, et dei nd'ellis terra de sanctu Jorgi ki mi kerferunt, ki fudi ad cabizza dessa nuella issoru, tenendu ad Mariani Cau, et biniissirus nos appari. Istimonius, Gunnari de Serra, filiu de donnu Cumida de Serra de domna Bera, et Mariani Cau d'Arigi, et Petru de Sarrau et Gontini Cara, et Mariani de Franca. Et dedilloy donnu Cumida de Serra de Frailis ad sanctu Jorgi, pro deu innanti et pro s'anima sua, intru de cussu cuniadu, terra cantu lloi aeda; et dedilloy donnu Gunnari de Serra, filiu de donnu Cumida de Serra de donna Bera, ad sanctu Jorgi, pro deu innanti et pro s'anima sua, terra cantu lloy aeda intru de cussu cuniadu. Istimonius de custas duas daduras, donnu Gregu Casu, ki fudi armentariu de sanctu Jorgi, et donnu Manueli de Serra su fradi, et donnu Cumida de Serra corcu. Et dedilloy donnu Manueli de Serra d'Abis ad sanct'u Jorgi, pro deu innanti et pro s'anima sua, terra cantu lloy aeda intru de cussu cuniadu. Et aendulla dada donnu Manueli custa terra ad sanctu Jorgi, bennit donnu Petru de Serra, filiu de donnu Cumida de Serra de donna Bera, ad baratarimi ndi narrandu c' "a mimi ill'aeda innanti dada donnu Manueli." Et eo, pro airi pagi, cum donnu Petru de Serra, et pro non airi barata donnu Petru de Serra cum donnu Manueli, campanieimi ndi cum donnu Petru de Serra, cum

---

21 Text of transumpt from DigiLib., p. 323 ends abruptly here. Text of transumpt from App. no. 11A, DigiLib., p. 316 begins here.

In the name of the Father, the Son, and the Holy Spirit, amen. I, iudike Trogotori de Unali with Biniita de Lacon, my wife lady, by the will of Lord God, ruling Caralis' territory (*parti*), permit (*assolbullu*) lord Trogodori, bishop of Suelli, to make himself a charter as he wishes. So, I, Trogodori, bishop of Suelli, with permission (*assoltura*) from my lord, iudike Trogodori de Unali, and from his wife Biniita de Lacon his wife—may Lord God protect them for me for many good years—make me a charter for the purchases and exchanges I made in the village of Arigi, and for the donations they made to Sanctu Jorgi de Suelli.

I dearly wished to plant a vineyard for Sanctu Jorgi at its farmstead (*domestia*) that they call Bau de Piscabu ('bishop's ford'), but because this farmstead seems too small to me, for it was not enough for making a vineyard I wanted to make for Sanctu Jorgi, I bought, exchanged and requested land from trusted men who had [land] around that farmstead, and made a plotted enclosure (*cuniadu*) as large as to allow me to plant all that I had dearly wished. Within that plotted enclosure, I bought from Petru de Sarrau half (*ladus*) of his land of Bau de Piscabu, which borders that same farmstead of Sanctu Jorgi from Bau de Piscobu. I gave him three soldi in cash, and I completed the payment. Witnesses: Saltoro de Unali Corroglai; Gunnari de Serra, son of lord Cumida de Serra; lady Bera; Mariani Cau d'Arigi; Mariani Franca, and Bonanu de Figus.

Also, I exchanged with Maria Sirigu and her four sons all the land that they had within that same plotted enclosure, and I gave them the land of Sanctu Jorgi that they wished from me, which reached its end at ours and borders [the land of] Mariani Cau. We were both satisfied. Witnesses: Gunnari de Serra, son of lord Cumida de Serra; lady Bera; Mariani Cau d'Arigi; Petru de Serrau, Gontini Cara, and Mariani de Franca.

Also, lord Cumida de Serra from Fraills gave to Sanctu Jorgi, for God before all else and for his soul, all the land he had within that plotted enclosure. Also, lord Gunnari de Serra son of lord Cumida de Serra and lady Bera gave to Sanctu Jorgi, for God before all else and for his soul, all the land that he had within that plotted enclosure. Witnesses of these donations: lord Gregu Casu, who was administrator (*armentariu*) of Sanctu Jorgi, and his brother, lord Manueli de Serra, and lord Cumida de Serra Corcu.

Also, lord Manueli de Serra d'Abis gave to Sanctu Jorgi, for God before all else and for his soul, all the land he had within that plotted enclosure. When lord Manueli had granted this land to Sanctu Jorgi, then lord Petru de Serra, son of lord Cumida de Serra and lady Bera, came to contest (*baratarimi*) me over it, saying that 'lord Manueli had given it to me before!' So I, to be at peace with lord Petru de Serra and so that lord Petru de Serra would not have a legal contest with lord Manueli, reached an agreement with lord Petru de Serra with

bolintadi bona de su piscobu de Olia a ki fudi affiliadu, et deilli sa binia de s'iligi de sanctu Jorgi, pro mandiarisilla cantu edi essiri biu, et daa g'adi morri, torritsi sanctu Jorgi ad sa binia sua. Et icusta terra de su cuniadu, pro ki baratáat, lassedilla ad sanctu Jorgi in sinpiderru, ki perunu homini no. nd'elli fairit aligandu nin briga ni molestia. Istimonius, et de sa dadura de donnu Manueli, et de su campaniu ki fegi cum donnu Petru de Serra, donnu Johanni de Serra Daluda et ambus nebodis suus, donnu Mariani de Serra, et donnu Petru, et Petru de Cabuderra, et donnu Gunnari de Serra d'Arigi, et Mariani Cau. Et dedilloy Arççocu Sirigu ad sanctu Jorgi, pro deu innanti et pro s'anima de sa mama, intru de cussu cuniadu, sa terra cant'esti apus flumini, daa sa binia de donnu Petru de Serra, filiu de donnu Cumida de Serra de donna Bera, fisca a ki clompit assa terra de Gontini de Turri, serbu de sanctu Jorgi; et dedilloy ancu intru de cussu cuniadu terra atera cantu lloy aeda. Istimonius, donnu Gunnari de Serra d'Arigi, Mariani Cau, et Mariani de Franca, et Petru de Sarrau, et Gontini Cara de Segolai. Et comporeilli ad Mariani de Franca terra sua cantu aeda, daa funtana de ebba, fisca a ki clompit a bau decimana, ka lla kerea pro plantari canna, et dei nd'elli v. sollus de dinaris, et clompilli pariari. Et comporeilli idru a Mariani de Franca et a Petru de Serrau terra de Mariani de Porta, serbu de sanctu Jorgi, et dei nd'ellis I. madrii de porcu cali si kerfirunt, et clompillis pariari. Istimonins de custas duas comporas, donnu Gunnari de Serra d'Arigi, et Mariani Cau, et Gontini Cara, et Bonanu de Figus. Et aendullas comporadas custas terras ad Mariani de Franca, bennit donnu Manueli de Serra d'Abis su donnu suu, et naredimi k'ant essiri suas custas terras, ki aia comporadas ad Mariani de Franca su serbu; et issi, pro deu innanti et pro s'anima sua, dedillas custas terras ad sanctu Jorgi. Istimonins d'esta dadura ki fegit donnu Manueli, donnu Gregu Casu, armentariu de Suelli, donnu Gontini de Serra, connadu de donnu Manueli, et donnu Gunnari de Serra d'Arigi, et donnu Gunnari de Unali Corrogla, et Mariani Corrogla su nebodi. Et comporeilli ad Saltoro Pelli, filiu de Cumida Duliketa, in Arigi, sa parti sua cantu inde lli bineda de sa plaçça, ki fudi ante sa plaçça ki segei a ffossadu pro fairi ortu, et dei nd'elli II sollus de inaris, et triticu moins III, et o riu moius II, et clompilli pariari. Istimonius, donnu Gunnari de Serra, et Mariani Cau, et Mariani de Franca, et Arççocu Spanu, et Turbini Murrit. Et comporeilli ad Arççocu Cascali, cum bulintadi de sa mulieri Marcusa de Banius, parti sua d'arburis de nugi et de kidru cantu aeda in sa villa de Galzu, et dei nd'elli cabras v., et III. solius de inaris, et clompilli pariari. Et comporei ad Gregu de Pizzolu,

the consent of the bishop of Olia (Dolia)—with whom he had previously been affiliated: I gave the vineyard at s'Iligi ('the holly oak') of Sanctu Jorgi, on the understanding that he would make use of it for as long as he lived and that it would return to Sanctu Jorgi after his death. And this land of the plotted enclosure, which he disputed, was left to Sanctu Jorgi forever, so that no one in relation to it would ever present any dispute or nuisance. Witnesses to lord Manueli's donation and of the agreement I reached with lord Petru de Serra [are]: lord Johanni de Serra d'Aluda and both of his grandchildren; lord Mariani de Serra; lord Petru; Petru de Cabuderra (Capoterra); lord Gunnari de Serra d'Arigi, and Mariani Cau.

Also, Arççocu Sirigu gave to Sanctu Jorgi, for God before all else and for his mother's soul, the land that is by the river, within that plotted enclosure, extending from the vineyard of lord Petru de Serra, son of lord Cumida de Serra and lady Bera, up to where it reached the land of Gontini de Turri, servant (*serbu*) of Sanctu Jorgi. He also gave, within that plotted enclosure, other land that he had. Witnesses: lord Gunnari de Serra d'Arigi, Mariani Cau, Mariani de Franca, Petru de Sarrau, and Gontini Cara de Segolai.

Also, I bought from Mariani de Franca all the land he had extending from Funtana de Enna ('Enna's spring') reaching to Bau Decimana ('Decimana ford'), which I wanted for planting cane, so I gave him five soldi in cash and completed the payment. I also bought from Mariani de Franca and Petru de Serrau the land of Mariani de Porta, a servant of Sanctu Jorgi, and I gave them one breeding sow of their choice, and completed the payment. Witnesses to these two purchases: lord Gunnari de Serra d'Arigi, Mariani Cau, Gontini Cara, and Bonanu de Figus. And, having bought these lands from Mariani de Franca, lord Manueli de Serra d'Abis, his lord, came and told me that those lands were his, which he had bought from his servant Mariani de Franca. Then, for God before all else and for his soul, he conceded these lands to Sanctu Jorgi. Witnesses of this donation made by lord Manueli: lord Gunnari de Serra d'Arigi, lord Gunnari de Unali Corrogla, and his nephew Mariani Corrogla.

Also, in Arigi I bought from Saltoro Pelli, son of Cumida d'Uliketa, his share that was due to him from the plot (*plaza*) that used to be the plot which I dug (*affossadu*) to make an orchard, and I gave him two soldi in cash, three bushels (*moius*) of wheat, and two bushels of barley, and completed the payment. Witnesses: lord Gunnari de Serra, Mariani Cau, Mariani de Franca, Arççocu Spanu, and Turbini Murrit.

Also, I bought from Arççocu Cascali, with the consent of his wife Marcusa de Banius, his part of walnut trees and cedars that he had in the village of Galzu, and I gave him five goats and three soldi in cash, and completed the payment.

in sa villa de Calzu, ladns de quaturu arburis de nugi, des calis fedi seberari s'omini miu ki lloy epi mandari, d'arburis cantu lloy adi, et dei n'elli I bargala et I madrii de porcu, et clompilli pariari. Istimonius de custas duas comporas, Arççocu de Figus, Arççocu de Planu, Arççocu de Redariu, Zerkis Pelli, Gontini Manca, et Turbini su fradi. Et dedilloy donnu Barisoni Dinki, filiu de donnu Gontini Dezzori Dinki, ad sanctu Jorgi de Suelli, omnia cantulloy aeda in sa villa de Goy maiori, pro deu innanti et pro s'anima sua, terra et binia et plaçça, et pumu et saltu et aqua, et omnia cantu lloy aeda apusti cussa domu de Goy maiori, ki no. ndi bogedi peruna causa. Istimonins, donnu Petru, priori de sanctu Sadurru, donnu Gregu Casu, armentariu de sanctu Jorgi, donnu Turbini de Lacon mancosu, donnu Johanni de Serra daluda, donnu Gontini de Serra affaidadu, donnu Cumida Dezzori Orlandu. Et sunt destimonius de logu, donnu Barusoni de Serra Passagi, donnu Cumida de Serra Frailis, et donnu Cumida Deççori de Enoni. Et est facta custa carta anno domini MCCXVII. VIII. idus martii, habendusilla iudigi a manu sua sa curadoria de Campidanu pro logu salbadori. Et ki ll'aet deuertere apat anathema daba pater et filiu et sanctu [ispiritu], daba XII. appostolos, IIII. euangelistas, XVI prophetas, XXIIII seniores, CCCXVIII sanctos patres, et habeat sortem [cum Juda] proditore in inferno inferiori. Siat et fiat, amen

Carta volgare 18. Date: 21 March 1217.[22] Confirmation issued by Trogotori de Unali, (Barisone-Torchitorio IV), iudike of Cálari (1214–1217), with his wife, Benedicta de Lacon, to concede labour services to the church of San Giorgio di Suelli, and to absolve witnesses for the church from having to swear oaths in minor legal disputes. Archivio diocesano storico di Cagliari, no. 11, DigiLib., no. 16. The lower half of the charter is water-damaged and large sections are illegible. Fitted with a 'Byzantine' lead seal (49.5g) and seal tag of brown chord. Obv. +TOPK / OTOPHW / APXUNTH / MEPEHCK / [APAVE]WC. Rev. Cruciform invocative monogram (Type V), Θεοτόκε βοήθει; in the quarters: TW-ΣW ΔOY-ΛW (τῷ σῷ δούλῳ). Also known from 15th- and 16th-century transcriptions in *Liber Diversorum*, 1/I serie [A], ff. 131^{v}–132^{r}, DigiLib., p. 122; 2/1 serie [E], ff. 60–61^{r}, DigiLib., pp. 62–63; Appendix 'Quaderno,' no. 16, DigiLib., pp. 322–323. Edition: Solmi, 'Le carte volgari', no. 18, pp. 43–44.

22 Solmi mistakenly dated the charter to 20 April, but may have confused the *kalendas aprilis* for *kalendas mai*.

I also bought from Gregu de Pizzolu, in the village of Calzu, an eighth [part] of walnut trees; of the trees which are all mine, they are to be separated and checked, and I gave him one grindstone and one breeding sow, and completed the payment. Witnesses of these two purchases: Arççocu de Figus, Arççocu de Planu, Arççocu de Iiedariu, Zerkis Pelli, Gontini Manca, and his brother, Turbini.

Also, lord Barisoni Dinki, son of lord Gontini Dezzori Dinki, gave to Sanctu Jorgi de Suelli all that which he had in the village of Goy Maiori, for God before all else and for his soul: land, vineyard, a plot (*plazza*), a fruit orchard (*pumu*), unworked land (*saltu*), a water resource (*aqua*), and everything he had at that farm complex (*domu*) of Goy Maiori, which should not have any asset (*causa*) removed [from it]. Witnesses: lord Petru, prior of Sancti Sasurru (San Saturnino); lord Gregu Casu, administrator (*armentariu*) of Sanctu Jorgi; lord Turbini de Lacon Mancosu; lord Johanni de Serra d'Aluda; lord Gontini de Serra Affaidadu, and lord Cumida Dezzori Orlandu. The witnesses of the State (*destimonius de logu*) are lord Barusoni de Serra Passagi, lord Cumida de Serra Frailis, and lord Cumida Deççori from Enoni.

This charter was made in the year of our Lord 1217, in the 8th day before the Ides of March (22 February), as the iudike has in his hands the curator's district (*curadoría*) of Campidanu (Campidano) on behalf of the deputy (*logu salbadori*). Whosoever dares to controvert it, may the Father and the Son and the Holy Spirit curse him, and the twelve Apostles, the four Evangelists, the sixteen Prophets, the twenty-four Elders, and the 318 Holy Fathers, and may he have his lot with Judas in the depths of Hell! Let it be and be done! Amen!

Carta volgare 18. Date: 21 March 1217.[23] Confirmation issued by Trogotori de Unali, (Barisone-Torchitorio IV), iudike of Cálari (1214–1217), with his wife, Benedicta de Lacon, to concede labour services to the church of San Giorgio di Suelli, and to absolve witnesses for the church from having to swear oaths in minor legal disputes. Archivio diocesano storico di Cagliari, no. 11, DigiLib., no. 16. The lower half of the charter is water-damaged and large sections are illegible. Fitted with a 'Byzantine' lead seal (49.5g) and seal tag of brown chord. Obv. +ТОРК / ОТОРНW / АРХUNТН / МЕРЕНСК / [АРАVЕ]WС. Rev. Cruciform invocative monogram (Type V), Θεοτόκε βοήθει; in the quarters: ΤW-ΣW ΔΟΥ-ΛW (τῷ σῷ δούλῳ). Also known from 15th- and 16th-century transcriptions in *Liber Diversorum*, 1/I serie [A], ff. 131^{v}–132^{r}, DigiLib., p. 122; 2/1 serie [E], ff. 60–61^{r}, DigiLib., pp. 62–63; Appendix 'Quaderno,' no. 16, DigiLib., pp. 322–323. Edition: Solmi, 'Le carte volgari', no. 18, pp. 43–44.

23 Solmi mistakenly dated the charter to 20 April, but may have confused the *kalendas aprilis* for *kalendas mai*.

Hoc e[st] tra[n]su[m]ptu[m] fidelit[er] s[u]mptu[m] a q[ua]da[m] p[u]blico instr[ument]o vetustissi[m]o in pergameno su[m]ptu[m] in li[n]gua Sardischa, plu[m]bo cu[m] q[ui]busda[m] litteris et caracterib[u]s in pe[n]de[n]ti sigillato, cu[ius] tenor talis e[st]:[24]

Hoc est translatum bene et fideliter sumptum in civitate et castro Callari die XXVI mensis Januarii anno a nat[ivitate] domini MDLXXIIII a quadam carta pergamenea sigillo plumbeo a quibusdam vetis cericeis(?) rubei coloris in penden[ti] munita no[n] rasa non viciata neq[ue] in aliqua sui parte suspecta sed omni prorsus vitio et suspictione caren[te], cuius tenor sequitur sub his verbis:[25]

(1)+ In nomine patris et filii et spiritus sancti amen. Ego iudigi Trogotori de Unali, cum donna Benedicta (2)de Lacon mulieri mia, per bolintadi de donnu deu potestandu parti de Caralis, fagemus illa custa carta pro beni ki lli (3)fagemus ad sanctu Jorgi de Suelli su donnu nostru. Usada fudi sa villa de Suelli de dari et de fairi ad sanctu Jorgi totu sas cergas (4)et is arrasonis ki gittaant ad iudigi et a curadori. Et nos illa firmamus et damus illi ad sanctu Jorgi de Suelli, su donnu (5)nostru, totu sas cergas et is arrasonis d'arari et de messari et de laurari binias, et de pegus de donu et de quasquariu, (6)et de totu sus aterus factus et cergas, cantu gittat a ffairi o a dari ad su a renu, o ad piguliari, o ad curadori, o ad arm-(7)entariu, o ad maiori de scolca, de totu sas personis ki sunt o ki anti essiri a istari in sa villa de Suelli, o suus o alienus, (8)o serbus o liberus, ki si 'ndi apat proi sanctu Jorgi, cantu adi durari su mundu. Et cali naramus pro sus serbus de sanctu Jorgi de sa villa (9)de Suelli, naramus et pro sus serbus de sanctu Jorgi cantu anti istari in sa villa de Sigii, ki totu sas cergas et is arrasonis, cant'anti (10)gitari ad iudigi, o ad curadori, ad maiori de scolca, o ad perunu ateru maiori, totu illas façcant ad sanctu Jorgi (11)cali et issus serbus de Suelli, ki non apat bias nin iudigi, nin donnigellu, nin curadori, ni armentariu, ni maiori de scolca, (12)nin peruna personi, ki depus essiri, ad leuari, ndi cerga peruna dava Suelli, nina dava serbus de sanctu Jorgi de sa villa de Sigii, ni (13)a iffairi ni ad minimari custu beni ki lli fagemus ad donnu nostru sanctu Jorgi, ca pro honori deus et pro s'animas nostras, et pro amantia (14)de donnu Trogotori su piscobu nostru de Suelli ki nos inde pregedi; et pro siat nos padronu sanctu Jorgi, et in icustu mundu et in s' ateru, (15)illi emus fatu custu beni ad sanctu Jorgi. Et damus illi

24 Taken from *Liber Diversorum*, 1/1 serie [A], ff. 131v–132r, DigiLib., p. 122.
25 Taken from *Liber Diversorum*, 2/1 serie [E], ff. 60–61r, DigiLib. p. 62.

This is a faithfully and well made transumpt from a certain very old public document of parchment made in the Sardinian language with a hanging lead seal with letters and designs. Its content is as follows:

This was well and faithfully translated, [being] taken from the city and citadel of Callaris [Cagliari] on the 26th day of the month of January in the year of the birth of the Lord [1573] from a certain parchment charter fitted with a lead seal and old wax suspended by a red-coloured [chord], not effaced, nor damaged, nor suspect in any part of itself, but totally devoid of all vice and suspicion, the content of which follows beneath these words:

(1)+ In the name of the Father, the Son, and the Holy Spirit, amen. I, iudike Trogotori de Unali with my wife, lady Benedicta (2)de Lacon, by the will of Lord God, ruling Caralis' territory (*parti*), (3) make this charter for the benefices we make to our lord Sanctu Jorgi de Suelli. It was customary for the village of Suelli to give to, and to do all the duties (*cergas*) (4)and obligations (*arrasonis*) for, Sanctu Jorgi that were due to the iudike and the curator (*curadori*). So we confirm and give to our lord, Sanctu Jorgi de Suelli, (5)all the duties and the farming obligations of ploughing, reaping, working the vineyards, taking care of livestock for breeding and slaughtering, (6)and all other work and duties that are due to be given to, or made for, either the realm or a particular functionary (*piguliari*), or for a curator, administrator (*armentariu*), or (7)head of the ward (*maiori de scolca*) by all the people who are in the village of Suelli or will settle there, whether locals or outsiders, (8)servants or freemen (*liberus*). May Sanctu Jorgi make use of it for as long as the world lasts! And this that we declare regarding the servants of Sanctu Jorgi in the (9)village of Suelli, we say it for the servants of Sanctu Jorgi who there will be in the village of Sigii—that all the duties and farming obligations that would (10)be due either to the iudike or the curator or head of the ward or some other chief functionary (*maiori*), will be made for Sanctu Jorgi (11)and the servants of Suelli. No iudike, nor princely overlord (*donnigellu*), nor curator, nor administrator, nor head of ward, (12)nor any person who will come after us, shall dare subtract any duties from Suelli, nor grant servants from Sanctu Jorgi from the village of Sigii, (13)nor to undo nor diminish these benefices we make to our lord Sanctu Jorgi in honour of God and for our souls, and for the love of (14)lord Trogotori, our bishop of Suelli, who prayed for us. We have made these benefices to Sanctu Jorgi so that St George would be our patron saint, in this world and in the next. (15)And we grant authority to the bishop, whomsoever he is, at Sanctu Jorgi de Suelli,

potestadi ad su piscobu ki ad essiri[26] [in sanctu Jorgi de Suelli, pro] (16)calincuna personi, ki ad essiri a istari in sa villa de Suelli, et non ad essiri [ad bolintadi sua; de getari 'nd' ellu de sa villa de Suelli in co] (17)'st et domu sua, et si no. 'ndi bolit andari pro paraula de su [piscobu lei di 'lli iudigi omnia cant' a dairi et getit inde 'llu. Et] (18)pregedi nos donnu Trogotori su piscobu [nostru de Suelli, pro sa iura ki fagenta in sanctu Jorgi pro omnia kertu pikinnu, ki fudi] (19)et tropu carriu ad su piscobadu, [et ad sanctu Jorgi non fudi honori, ki imponi remas menti pro deu, et minimaremus illu cussu mali]. (20)Et nos, cum cunsiliu de sus hominis [bonas de sa terra nostra, ordinarus ki non iurarit perunu homini in sanctu Jorgi de Suelli pro perunu] (21)kertu nin campaniu ki balirit minas de C. solus Junuinus, [non adprezzandu su pro k' edi] (22)kertari. Et ordinarus ki non lloi iurarint sa dii de su besperu, [nin de sa festa sua, et ni in peruna pasca. Et ordinarus ki] (23)niunu homini de sa villa de Suelli, nin clerigu, [ni n laigu, non bengat a istimoniu pro niunu homini ki adi iurari in sanctu Jorgi;] (24)e[27] ki c' adi essiri postu ad sagramentu ad sanctu Jorgi et kerradi istimonius de sa villa de Suelli, issus non siant tentus de beniri pro peruna nunzza ki llis anti fairi; et issu homini, k'illus ad kerri pro stimonias, perdatsi su kertu suu, si non batiit ateras istimonius. Et icustu ordinamentu cumandamus in corona de logu ki llu tengant totu firmu, et gasi inde 'lli bullamus carta ad sanctu Jorgi su donnu nostru. Et sunt destimonias, ante k' illi fegirus ad sanctu Jorgi de Suelli custu beni, cantu narat custa carta, donnu Ricu s'archipiscobu nosiru, et donnu Gontini su piscobu nosiru de Olia, et donnu Mariani su piscobu nosiru de Zulchis, et prebtieru Pisanu Pullu de Zulchis, et Barusoni de Serra Passagi, et Gontini Dezzori de Sijllu. Et sunt destimonitus Barusoni de Serra Passagi, et Cumida de Serra de Frailis, et Cumida Dezzori de Enoni. Et est facta custa carta anno domini M. CC. XVII., XII. kalendas aprilis, habendumilla ad manu mia sa curadoria de Campidanu pro logu salbadori. Et ki ll'aet deuertere abat anathema daba pater et filiu et sanctu yspritu, et daba XII. apostolos, IIII. evangelistas, XVI. prophetas, XXIIII. seniores, et daba CCCXVIII. sancios patres, et sortem habeat cum Juda proditore in inferno inferiori. Siat et fiat, amen.

26 The manuscript at this point becomes largely illegible; the remaining text is taken from the *Liber Diversorum* transcriptions.

27 The poor condition of the manuscript, especially at the start and end of lines, does not allow line divisions to be made. The remaining transcription of the charter is based on the transumpt version.

(16)over any person, to determine on his own who will settle in the village of Suelli and who may not, and to eject them from the village of Suelli where his farm complex (*domu*) is. (17)And if someone does not wish to get permission (*paraula*) from the bishop, then the decision is given to the iudike so everything can be given and taken away [accordingly]. (18)Also, lord Trogotori, our bishop of Suelli, favoured (*pregedi*) us regarding sworn testimonies made at Sanctu Jorgi for every minor legal dispute, causing (19)an excessive burden for the episcopate and no prestige for Sanctu Jorgi, for which he asked us to find a remedy from God and to reduce this bad thing. (20)And we, with the advice of trusted men of our land (*terra*), order that no one should testify under oath in the name of Sanctu Jorgi of Suelli regarding any dispute or agreement that is worth less than a hundred Genoese solidi (*solus*) with no evaluation of that which is (21)to be contested. Also, we order that no testimony under oath should be taken during a vigil or on feast days, nor over Easter. Also, we order that no men of the village of Suelli, either cleric or layman, may come to testify for anyone who had sworn at Sanctu Jorgi; (22) and any man who was under oath at Sanctu Jorgi and summoned as a witness from the village of Suelli may not have to come to any summons (*nunzza*) that he has received. And if a man who[28] was thus summoned as a witness loses his legal dispute, he should not be brought forth as a witness again. And we instructed this order at the hearing of the realm (*corona de logu*), which they fully endorse, and so we sealed the charter for our lord Sanctu Jorgi. The witnesses before whom we made these benefices to Sanctu Jorgi de Suelli, as described in this charter, are: lord Ricu, our archbishop; lord Gontini, our bishop of Olia (Dolia); lord Mariani, our bishop from Sulcis; priest Pisanu Pullu from Sulcis; Barusonu de Serra Passagi, and Gontini Dezzori de Siillu. The witnesses are: Barusoni de Serra Passagi, Cumida de Serra Frailis, and Cumida Dezzori from Enoni. This charter was made in the year of our Lord 1217, on the 12th day before the kalends of April (21 March), as I have in my hands the curator's district (*curadoría*) of Campidanu on behalf of the deputy (*logu salbadori*). Whoever dares to controvert it, may the Father and the Son and the Holy Spirit curse him, and the twelve Apostles, the four Evangelists, the sixteen Prophets, the twenty-four Elders, and the 318 Holy Fathers, and may he have his lot with the traitor Judas in the depths of Hell! Let it be and be done! Amen!

---

28 Henceforth, the poor condition of the MS, especially at the start and end of lines, does not allow line divisions to be made. The remaining transcription of the charter is based on the transumpt version.

Carta volgare Suppl. H (Pisa). Date: 30 May 1225. Permission and exemption granted by Benedicta de Lacon (Benedetta di Massa), ruler of Cálari (1214–1233), with her son Guglelmu, to the church of Sanctu Georgi dr Sebollu, consisting of free grazing and water rights. She also confirmed a previous exemption made by his father (William of Massa/Guglielmo I–Salusio IV). Archivio della Certosa di Calci, Pergamene, II serie/634, 30 maggio 1226 (according to the Pisan calendar). Unpublished diplomatic transcription by Ludovico Baille, in *Fondo Baille*, University Library of Cagliari, portafolio V,2, cartella 80/710, f. 2. Edition: Solmi, 'Studi sulla proprietà fondiaria', p. 445 (reproduced in *Studio storico sulle istituzioni*, p. 424); Blasco-Ferrer, *Crest.*, vol. 1, 93–96. Summary in Frank & Hartmann, *Inventaire systématique*, vol. 5, p. 60.

(1)In nomine Patris et Filii et Spiritu Sancti, Amen. Ego Benedicta (2)de Lacon cum filiu miu donnigellu Guglelmu, per bolintadi de donnu (3)Deu potestando parti de Calaris, fazzulli custa carta ad Sanctu (4)Georgi de Seppollu de Gurgu et ad Sanctu Gorgoni et ad Sanctu Vittu pro beni (5)ki llis fazzu pro Deu innanti et pro s'anima mia et de parentis mius. Dau pode-(6)stadi et assoltura de paschiri et a aquari sa causa de Sanctu Georgi de Sebollu (7)daa Serramanna fini ad s'oliastru de Semassi, k'esti paris cum s'ortu de (8)suta billa, berbeis et cabras, et porcus et baccas, et eguas et cavallus. (9)(Et) no'ndi levit pegus perunu pro terra maina et ni atera causa peruna (10)ni ad sa dommu de Sanctu Georgi et ni ad sus serbus, nin pro Iuigi, nin pro donni-(11)gellu et nin pro curadori et nin pro armentariu et ni ad peruna personi dessu mun-(12)du. Et icusta podestadi et icusta assoltura ki dau ad paschiri et a aquari (13)sa causa de Sanctu Georgi in icustu cuili ki narat custa carta, non ap-(14)pat ausancia perunu homini dessu mundu a isfairi llu ni ad minimaril-(15)lu cantu ad durari su mundu, nin ca lloi adi paschiri causa mia, et nin (16)ca non lloi adi paschiri causa mia, ca pro donnu Deu et pro s'anima mia et de (17)parentis mius illu appu factu, et pro honori de donnu Plachidu, s'abbadi de (18)Gorgona. Et confirmu su beni ki lloi fegit su donnu padri miu ad (19)Sanctu Georgi de Seppollu et ad Sanctu Gorgoni et ad Sanctu Vittu. Istimonius, (20)donnu Mariani s'archipiscobu miu, markesi Andrea Iuigi de fatu, prei-(21)di Cummida de Zori canonigu de Sancta Cecilia, et preidi Mariani Saltizu, et Arri-(22)gu Pintigosu, et Bartholomeu de Ludenti, et Barisoni Dinchi, et iagunu (23)Arzocu de sSufrau. Istimonius de logu, Cummida de Zori de Enoni, et Gunna-(24)ri de Sii et Cummida d'Açeni tadaiu miu. Et est facta custa carta Anno (25)Domini .MCCXXVI., .III. kalendas Iunii, habendumilla ad manu mia sa curado-(26)ria de Canpidanu pro logusalbadori. Et ki

Carta volgare Suppl. H (Pisa). Date: 30 May 1225. Permission and exemption granted by Benedicta de Lacon (Benedetta di Massa), ruler of Cálari (1214–1233), with her son Guglelmu, to the church of Sanctu Georgi dr Sebollu, consisting of free grazing and water rights. She also confirmed a previous exemption made by his father (William of Massa/Guglielmo I–Salusio IV). Archivio della Certosa di Calci, Pergamene, II serie/634, 30 maggio 1226 (according to the Pisan calendar). Unpublished diplomatic transcription by Ludovico Baille, in *Fondo Baille*, University Library of Cagliari, portafolio V,2, cartella 80/710, f. 2. Edition: Solmi, 'Studi sulla proprietà fondiaria', p. 445 (reproduced in *Studio storico sulle istituzioni*, p. 424); Blasco-Ferrer, *Crest.*, vol. 1, 93–96. Summary in Frank & Hartmann, *Inventaire systématique*, vol. 5, p. 60.

(1)In the name of the Father, the Son, and the Holy Spirit, amen. I, Benedicta (2)de Lacon, with my son *donnigellu* Gugelmu, by the will of Lord (3)God, ruling Cálari's territory (*parti*), make them this charter to Sanctu (4)Georgi de Seppollu de Gurgy, Santu Gorgoni, and Sanctu Vittu for the benefices (5)I make for God before all else and for the salvation of my soul and of my relatives. I grant authority (6)and permission (*assoltura*) to graze and to use water for the benefit of Sanctu Georgi de Sebollu's assets (*causa*), (7)from [the land extending from] Serramanna up to the wild olive of Semassi, which is shared with the garden (8)of the village below, [including] sheep and goats, pigs and cows, and mares and horses. (9)And no one shall take any farm animal away for fertile land, nor any other asset, (10)neither of the house of Sanctu Georgi nor of his servants (*serbus*), on behalf of neither iudike, (11)nor *donnigellu* nor *curatore* not administrator (*armentariu*) nor any other person from this world. (12)And this authority and permission (*assoltura*) that I grant to graze and use water (13)in benefit of Sanctu Georgi's assets in this pen, as described in this charter, (14)shall not be undone or reduced by the audacity of any man of this world, (15)till the end of the world, regardless whether I had grazed my livestock (*causa*) there (16)or not, for Lord God and for the salvation of my soul and of (17)my relatives, and for the honour of lord Plachidu, the abbot of (18)Gorgona. And I confirm the benefices that my father the lord made to (19)Sanctu Georgi de Seppollu, Sanctu Gorgoni, and Sanctu Vittu. Witnesses: (20)lord Mariani my archbishop, marquis Andrea Iugi de Fatu, priest (21)Cummida de Zori canon of Sancta Cecilia, and priest Mariani Saltizu, and (22)Arrigu Pintigosu, and Bartholomeu de Ludenti, and Barisoni Dinchi, and deacon (23)Arzocu de sSu Frau. Witnesses of the realm: Cummida de Zori from Enoni, and Gunnari (24)de Sii, and Cummida d'Azeni (Açeni) my distant uncle.

And this charter was made in the (25)year of our Lord 1226, in the 3rd day before the kalends of June (30 May), as I have the *curatore*'s district (*curadoría*) (26)of Campidanu (Campidano) in my hands on behalf of the deputy (*logusal-*

ll'aet devertere, appat ana-(27)thema daba Pater et Filiu et Sanctu Ispiritu, daba .XII. Apostolos et (28).IIII. Evangelistas, daba .XVI. Prophetas et .XXIIII. Seniores, daba .CCC-(29)XVIII. Patres Santos. Et sorti appat cum Iuda traditori in inferno in-(30)feriori. Fiat. Fiat. Fiat. Fiat. Fiat. A[m]en. [Am]en.

Carta volgare 19. Date: 10 July 1225. Grant of various lands, resources and appurtenances by Benedicta de Lacon (Benedetta di Massa), iudike of Cálari (1214–1233), with her son, Gugelmu, to the church of San Giorgio di Suelli, including the village of Jana with exemption from labour service, taxes and obligations for those living there. Archivio diocesano storico di Cagliari, DigiLib., no. 17. Fitted with a 'Byzantine' lead seal (44 g) and seal tag of dark red chord. Obv. +T[OP]K / OT[OP]HW / [APXU]NTH / [MEPE]HCK / [...]. Rev. Cruciform invocative monogram (Type V), Θεοτόκε βοήθει; in the quarters: TW-ΣW ΔOY-ΛW (τῷ σῷ δούλῳ). Also known from a 15th-century transumpt in *Liber Diversorum*, 2/I serie, Appendix 'Quaderno', no. 3, DigiLib., p. 313. Edition: Solmi, 'Le carte volgari', no. 19, pp. 45–46; Falchi, *reisar.eu*, carta XIX.

(1)In nomine Patris et Filii [et] Sp[irit]u S[an]c[t]i, am[en]. Ego Benedicta de Laco[n], (cu[m] filliu) (2)meu do[n]nigellu Gugelmu, p[er] bolintadi de donnu Deu podestando part(i) de C(alaris) (3)fazzulli custa carta ad ssu donnu miu s[an]c[t]u] Jorgi de Suelli, p[ro] (be)ni ki lli fazzu. Daulli (4)assu donnu miu S[an]c[t]u Jorgi de Suelli sa domestia mia, k'esti intru de (saltu) de S[an]c[t]u Jorgi dessa billa (5)de Suelli, ad ki narant domestia de padru de Sisini. E[t] est parta a Suelli, cabizza ad sa do[m]mes(tia) de (6)S[an]c[t]u Jorgi ad ki narant terra de Gontini Ala, [et] parta a nuragi de Seti badi tudui sa bia ki badi daa (7)Suelli ad Sisini, [et] clompit ad s'aqua des Passaris de S[an]c[t]u Jorgi, in bau de Terra alba, [et]cal(at)si tudui (8)s'erriu fisca ad Funtana de Corbu, [et] clonpit ad ssa bia ki badi daa Sisini ad Arcu, ([et]) coll(at) tudui (9)bia parta a nuragi descoriadu, [et] clonpit ad sa terra de S[an]c[t]u Jorgi de Go(n)tini Ala d(...)ençat. (10)Et daulli in Jana ad ssu do[n]nu miu s[an]c[t]u Jorgi de Suelli totu su fundam[en]tu dessa (billa) errema de (11)Iana Iossu de Liurus, ki fudi arregnada, [et] dau ella cu[m] totu sas p[er]tinentias suas, plazas [et] ter(ras arador)ias (12)[et] saltu [et] aqua, [et] cu[m] totu su cantu si ap[er]tineda ad icussa billa. E[t] si p[er]unu tempu(s), (...) bolint (13)torrari hominis ad istari in icussa billa, sus cantu lloi anti istari, totu sas arrasonis [et] issas cergas k'enti (14)debiri fairi de p[er]soni o de causa ad ssu regnu, o ad peguliari, o ad

badori). Whosoever dares to controvert it, (27)may the Father and the Son and the Holy Spirit curse him, and the twelve Apostles, (28)the four Evangelists, the sixteen Prophets, the twenty-four Elders, and the 318 (29)Holy Fathers, and have his lot with Judas in the depths of Hell! (30)Let it be done! Let it be done! Let it be done! Let it be done! Let it be done! Let it be done! Let it be done! Amen! Amen!

Carta volgare 19. Date: 10 July 1225. Grant of various lands, resources and appurtenances by Benedicta de Lacon (Benedetta di Massa), iudike of Cálari (1214–1233), with her son, Gugelmu, to the church of San Giorgio di Suelli, including the village of Jana with exemption from labour service, taxes and obligations for those living there. Archivio diocesano storico di Cagliari, DigiLib., no. 17. Fitted with a 'Byzantine' lead seal (44 g) and seal tag of dark red chord. Obv. +T[OP]K / OT[OP]HW / [APXU]NTH / [MEPE]HCK / [...]. Rev. Cruciform invocative monogram (Type V), Θεοτόκε βοήθει; in the quarters: TW-ΣW ΔOY-ΛW (τῷ σῷ δούλῳ). Also known from a 15th-century transumpt in *Liber Diversorum*, 2/I serie, Appendix 'Quaderno', no. 3, DigiLib., p. 313. Edition: Solmi, 'Le carte volgari', no. 19, pp. 45–46; Falchi, *reisar.eu*, carta XIX.

(1)In the name of the Father, the Son, and the Holy Spirit, amen. I, Benedicta de Lacon, with my son, (2)*donnigellu* Gugelmu, by the will of Lord God, ruling Cálari's territory (*parti*), make them (3)this charter for my lord, Sanctu Jorgi de Suelli, for the benefices that I make for it. I give (4)to my lord Sanctu Jorgi de Suelli my farmstead (*domestia*), which is within the unworked land (*saltu*) of Sanctu Jorgi in the village (5)of Suelli, which they call the farmstead of Padru de Sisini ('meadow of Sisini'). It starts from Suelli and reaches its end at the farmstead of (6)Sanctu Jorgi that they call Terra de Gontini Ala ('land of Gontini Ala'). It begins from Nuraghe de Seti and goes along the road that leads from (7)Suelli to Sisini; then it reaches s'Aqua des Passaris ('water of sparrows') of Sanctu Jorgi at Bau de Terra Alba ('ford of white land'); it keeps to (8)the stream until Funtana de Corbu ('crow's spring'), then keeps to the road that goes from Sisini to Arcu, and passes along the (9)road starting from Nuraghe Descoriadu; it reaches the land of Sanctu Jorgi at Gontini Ala, from where it started.

(10)Also, in Jana, I give to my lord Sanctu Jorgi de Suelli all the built property from the abandoned village of (11)Iana Iossu de Livrus ('of the freemen'), which had been expropriated (*arregnada*), and I give it with all its belongings, plots (*plazas*), ploughed lands (*aradorias*), (12)unworked lands, water resources (*aquas*), and with everything that pertained to that village. And if, over time, (13)men want to return to this village, all the farming obligations (*arrasonis*) and duties (*cergas*) which those who live there owe in person (14)or for their assets (*causa*) to the realm (*regnu*), to a particular functionary (*peguliari*), to a cura-

curatori, o ad maiori de scolca, o (15)ad'arme[n]tariu, totu llas fazzant ad su donnu miu s[an]c[t]u Jorgi de Suelli. Et totu sus serbus [et] isas ankillas (16)de S[an]c[t]u Jorgi de Suelli, ki sunt o ki anti essiri a istari in Jana; siant assoltus [et] liberadus (d'omnia) sirbitiu (17)de p[er]sonis [et] de causa issoru, ki non fazzant sirbitiu p[er]unu de p[er]sonis, [et] non denti int(r)ad(ia) nin (18)trauda p[er]una de (cau)sa issor[u], ni ad regnu, ni ad peguliari, ni ad curadori, ni ad maiori de scolca, (19)ni ad armentariu, ni ad p([er])unu homini dessu mundu, si non totu su cantu furunt usadus de fairi (20)de dari, o assu regnu o a peguliari, o ad curadori, o ad maiori de scolca, o ad armentariu, totu illu (21)fazzant [et] denti ad s[an]c[t]u Jorgi de Suelli su donnu miu, ad bulintadi dessu piscobu do[n]nu issoru. (cu)stu (22)beni, ki fazzu ad s[an]c[t]u Jorgi su donnu miu, non appat balia p[er]unu juigi, ki pus me adi e(sser, nin) (23)donn(a), nin donnigellu, nin p[er]una p[er]soni dessu mundu, a (istr)umarillu, ni ad minimarillu ad (s[an])c[t]u (Jorgi) (24)ci appat si 'ndi p[ro]i cantu adi durari su mundu, ca p[ro] donnu Deu illu apu f(at)u, [et] a s'anima (mia [et] de marke)su (25)Gugelmu padri miu, [et] de cu[n]tissa Adalasia mama mia, [et] p[ro] siat mi ku[m] Jorgi padronu ante Deu (26)[et] (in icustu) mundu ([et] in s'ate)ru (et p[ro]) amantia de do[n]nu Cerchis, piscobu miu de Suelli, ki mi fudi padri (27)[et] amigu b(onu). Et sunt destimoni[us] donnu Mariani s'archipiscobu miu, [et] donnu Gontini Madi-(28)lu, (archi)p[re]idi de S[an]c[t]a Maria de Clusu, [et] do[n]nu Pedru, priori de S[an]c[t]u Sadurru de Chiida, [et] p[re]idi C(umi)da De-(29)zori canonicu (de) S[an]c[t]a Giulia, [et] p[re]idi Mariani (Salitz)u [et] conti (Bertoldu). Istimonius de logu (30)(Cu)mida Dezori de Eno(ni) [et] Gunnari de Sii, [et] Cu[m]mida d'Aceni tadaiu. Et est facta custa carta (31)anno do[m]ini MCCXXV VI idus Iulii, habendumilla sa curadoria de Campidanu ad (manu mia) (32)p[ro] logusalbadori. Et ki ll'aet devertere apat anathema daba Pater (et Fil)iu ([et] S[an]c[t]u Ispiritu, daba XII) (33)Apostolos [et] (IIII) Evangelistas, (daba XVI Prophetas, et XXIIII Seniores daba CCCXVIII Patres Sanctos, et sorti (34)apat cum Juda traditori in inferno inferiori. Siat et fiat, amen).

Carta volgare 20. Transumpt. Date: 21 June 1226. Grant of various lands and the rights to benefit from them, made by Benedicta de Lacon (Benedetta di Massa), iudike of Cálari (1214–1233), and her son, in favour of the church of Sant'Antioco and bishopric of Sulchis. Known from a 15th-century transumpt in the Archivio diocesano storico di Cagliari, *Liber Diversorum*, 2/I serie, f. 131–132^{r}, DigiLib., pp. 140–141. Edition: Solmi, 'Le carte volgari', no. 20, pp. 46–48.

tor (*curatori*), to a head of the ward (*maiori de scolca*), or (15)to an administrator (*armentariu*), will have to be made to my lord Sanctu Jorgi de Suelli. All the servants (*serbus*) and female servants (*ankillas*) (16)of Sanctu Jorgi de Suelli who are or who will stay in the village of Jana are to be excused (*assoltus*) or released from any (17)personal service and any performance related to their assets, and not to be in the service of any person and not to pay any income (*intradia*) or (18)tribute (*trauda*) for their assets to the realm (*regnu*), to a particular functionary (*peguliari*), to a curator, to a head of the ward (*maiori de scolca*), or (19)to an administrator (*armentariu*), or to any men of this world, but whatever they were used to doing (20)and giving either to the realm, a functionary, a *curatore*, a heard of the ward, or an administrator, all this (21)they should do it and give it to my lord Sanctu Jorgi de Suelli, according to the will of their lord bishop. These (22)benefices that I make to my lord Sanctu Jorgi shall not be undone or reduced by any iudike, whoever he may be, nor by any lady, (23)*donnigellu*, or person of the world, so may Sanctu Jorgi (24)hold them till the end of the world; because I made this for Lord God, and for my soul and that of marquis (25)Gugelmu, my father, and of my mother, countess Adalasia, and, before God, (26)so to be in this world and in the next with Jorgi as patron, and for the love of lord Cerchis my bishop of Suelli, who was [as a] father to me (27)and a good friend.

And the witnesses are lord Mariani my archbishop, and lord Gontini (28)Madilu archpriest of Sancta Maria de Clusu (Santa Maria di Cluso in Cagliari), and lord Pedru prior of Sanctu Sadurru de Chiida (San Saturnino of Civita/Cagliari), and priest Cumida (29)Dezori canon of Sancta Giulia, and priest Mariani Salitzu, and count Bertoldu. Witnesses of the realm (*Istimonius de logu*): (30)Cumida Dezori de Enoni, and Gunnari from Sii, and Cummida d' Açeni Tadaiu ('distant uncle').

This charter was made (31)in the year of our Lord 1225, in the 6th day before the Ides of July (10 July), as I have in my hands the curatorial district (*curadoría*) of Campidanu (32)on behalf of the deputy (*logusalbadori*). Whoever dares to controvert it, may the Father and the Son and the Holy Spirit curse him, and the twelve (33)Apostles, the four Evangelists, the sixteen Prophets, the twenty-four Elders, and the 318 Holy Fathers, and have his lot (34)with the traitor Judas in the depths of Hell! Let it be and be done! Amen.

Carta volgare 20. Transumpt. Date: 21 June 1226. Grant of various lands and the rights to benefit from them, made by Benedicta de Lacon (Benedetta di Massa), iudike of Cálari (1214–1233), and her son, in favour of the church of Sant'Antioco and bishopric of Sulchis. Known from a 15th-century transumpt in the Archivio diocesano storico di Cagliari, *Liber Diversorum*, 2/I serie, f. 131–132r, DigiLib., pp. 140–141. Edition: Solmi, 'Le carte volgari', no. 20, pp. 46–48.

Hoc est translatum copia et exemplum bene et fidel[itu]r suptum in castro Callari die IIII. mens[i]s Aug[ust]i anno a nat[ivitate] D[omi]ni Millesimo CCCCLXXVI, a quodam libro appellato Mare Magnu[m] ep[iscop]ati Sulsitan[i] non viciato, no[n] cancellato, nec in aliqua sui parte suspecto, sed omni p[ro]rsus vicio et suspectione carente, cuius tenor seguitur sub hiis verbis: In nomine domini, amen. Ego Benedicta de Lacon donna de logu cum filiu miu donnigellu Guillelmu, per boluntade de donnu deu podestandu parti de Callaris, fazu custa carta pro beni ki fazu assu donnu miu sanctu Anthiogu d'iscla de Sulchis. Dau illoy a yscla de Finugu, he a iscla de Jogos, he a Cortinas, et a iscla Masonis et a iscla mayori ki est inter aquas, et a corru de ponti, ki sunt custas isclas dae su ponti innoghi, in co intrant a intru de s' iscla de sanctu Anthiogu, et sunt da incili dessa clesia de sanctu Speradu de ponti fini assa terra firma. Custas isclas illoy dau, cum aquas dulchis, et cum aquas salsas, et cum omnia causa cantu si apartenit apusti custas isclas, ki 'ndi fazat su donnu su piscobu miu de Sulchis Maistru Bandinu su ki Ili at plakiri a boluntadi sua, segundu in c' at fagiri dessas ateras causas dessu piscobadu suu, ki sunt in balya sua, et issu et totus sus piscobus, cantu ant essiri pusti issu in su piscobadu de Sulchis, bollant pasquiri cum peguliu issoru, bollant arari, bollant fayri illoy silva, ho fayri chirras, ho piscari, ho fayri peruna atera causa, ki torrit a proy a sanctu Anthiogu et assu piscobadu de Sulchis. Et dau illoy su saltu miu de genna de Codrigla totu in qua si segat. Et segatsi custu saltu daba sus coronius, et tenit serra de monti d'asayiu, in qua partit aqua deretu ad iscolca et deretu a grutta de nanus, et tenit sa bia deretu assa bucca de cabudaqua, et essit deretu ass'aqua de kellariu, et collatsi s'erriu deretu a bia de logu, et leatsi sa bia deretu assas ariolas, et torratsi deretu assus corongius daundi si comensat. Custas isclas et icustu saltu dau assu donnu miu sanctu Antiogu d'iscla de Sulchis ad ispiliadu, ki non loy apat perunu homini a ifairi, non pro su regnu, et non pro peruna atera personi, exceptu ki essirit a boluntadi dessu donnu su piscobu miu de Sulchis Maistru Bandinu, a fayri 'ndi su ki ll'at plakiri a issu et assus aterus piscobus ki ant essiri pusti issu in su piscobadu de Sulchis. Et apant balya de poniri illoy castyu a guisa ki si castiaat suta su donnu padri miu Guillermu markesi.

Et daulloy assu donnu miu sanctu Antiogu d'iscla de Sulchis omnia et cantu apu dessu saltu miu et de ssemidas de Baniuy cum aquas et cum linna et cum totas sas causas cantu si apartenint apusti custu saltu. Et segatsi custu saltu

This is a transumpt copy and exemplum, faithfully and well made in the citadel of Callari on the 4th day of the month of August in the year of the birth of the Lord 1476, from a certain book called the *Mare Magnum* in the bishopric of Sulcis. [It is] neither damaged, nor abrogated, nor is any part of it suspected of any fault, but [is] entirely without suspicion, the content of which follows under these words: In the name of the Lord, amen. I, Benedicta de Lacon [first] lady of the realm (*donna de logu*), with my son, *donnigellu* Guillelmu, by the will of Lord God, ruling Callaris' territory (*parti*), make this charter for the benefices I make to my lord, Sanctu Anthiogu of the islet (*iscla*) of Sulchis (Sant'Antioco, i.e., the bishopric of Sulci). I give it the islet (*yscla*) of Finugu, and the islet of Jogos, and [that of] Cortinas, and the islet (*iscla*) of Masonis, and the islet (*iscla*) of Mayori, which are between the waters (*aquas*) at Corru de Ponti ('horn of the bridge'). These islets extend from the bridge there and enter the island of Sanctu Antiogu, and they extend from the church of Sanctu Speradu up to the *terra firma*. I grant these islets with freshwater and saltwater resources, and with all the assets that are found at these islets, so that my bishop of Sulchis, 'Maistru' Bandinu does that which he pleases with them according to his will, as he does for other assets of his bishopric that are in his possession. I give them to him and to all the bishops who will be there after him in the bishopric of Sulchis should they wish to graze their cattle (*peguliu*), plough, make use of the forest (*silva*), collect duties (*chirras*), fish or do anything else that benefits Sanctu Anthiogu and the bishopric of Sulchis.

Also, I give it my unworked land (*saltu*) at Genna de Codrigla ('pass of Codrigla'), all which is alienated from my estate. I grant from my estate this unworked land from Coronius ('the baths') that borders the hills of Monti d'Asayiu, from which water leaves towards the hillside (*iscolca*) and Grutta de Nanus ('cave of Nanus'), and borders the road towards Bucca de Cabudaqua ('mouth of Water's Cape'), and leaves towards s'Aqua de Kellariu ('the water of Selargius'), and joins the stream towards the main road (*bia de logu*), and keeps to the road towards the threshing floors (*ariolas*), and then comes back towards Coronius, from where it started. I grant these islets and this unworked land to my lord, Sanctu Antiogu d'Iscla at Sulchis, for its protection. No man shall undo this, either on behalf of the realm (*regnu*) or for any other person, except by the will of my bishop of Sulchis, lord 'Maistru' Bandini, as he and the other bishops who may succeed him in the bishopric may do whatever they please to them. And may they have the courage to protect this in the same way in which it was protected under my father, lord marquis Guillermu!

Also, I give to my lord Sanctu Antiogu of the island (*iscla*) of Sulchis all that I have in my unworked land (*saltu*) and my enclosed land (*semidas*) of Baniuy with water resources and timber, and with all the assets that are found in that

de Baniuy daba Genna maiori, et calatsi gutturu a Sulibuzu et deretu a bau de serri, et intrat a gutturu d'arriu, et intrat in su gutturu d'aquabona, et essit assa arjola de Fadarta, et essit a gutturu de sorigella, et leuatsi serra de genna d' iligis cum totu monti d'Enbalba, et calat deretu a jenna de porta, et calat gutturu de cungiadura, et essit mizas de Gennari, et torrat a genna de tesonis, et calat deretu a mortu Basili, et pesatsi a guturu pizinnu, et leuatsi sa serra de Candellaççu, et torrat a Genna maiori da undi se començat.

Et daulloy assu donnu miu sanctu Antiogu d'iscla de Sulchis omnia et cantu dessu saltu et de ssemidas Desulegi, cum aquas, et cum linna, et cum totus sas causas cantu si apartenit apusti custu saltu. Et segatsi custu saltu daa ssu flumini dessa uilla de Flumentebidu, in qua essit a masuniu depintu, et essit a corongiu de maialis, et essit ad gennas d'Assulla, et tenit sa bia deretu ad Canamenda, et torrat a giba orrubia, et falat ad giba de maçarus, et essit ad giba de Marcu, et iunpat ad Oru de Forru, et essit assa bia de Flumentebidu, et torratsi deretu ad Creadis. Anno domini M.CC.X[X]VI, XI. Kal. junii. Presbiter Marianus Scartellus testis, Petrus acolitus testis.

Carta volgare 21. Transumpt. Date: 23 May 1226.[29] Exemption from taxes and labour services, and a grant of lands, made by Benedicta de Lacon (Benedetta di Massa), iudike of Cálari (1214–1244), with her son, to the church of San Pantaleo di Dolia. Known from three 15th- and 16th-century-copies in the Archivio diocesano storico di Cagliari, *Liber Diversorum*, 2/I serie [E], f. 65, DigiLib., pp. 67–68; Appendix 'Quaderno,' no. 2, DigiLib., pp. 311–312; Appendix 'Quaderno,' no. 15, DigiLib., pp. 321–322. Edition: Solmi, 'Le carte volgari', no. 20, pp. 48–50.

Hoc est transuptu[m] sive translatu[m] aut exemplu[m] cuiusdam privilegii sive carte p[er]gaminea sigillati sigillo plumbeo apendito cu[m] cordulis canapi sive canami in quoquidem sigillo plumbeo ex una p[ar]te est quaedam crux et sunt alique littere inlegibiles et ex alia p[ar]te alique litere inlegibiles

29 Solmi mistakenly dated it to 22 June, possibly by confusing the *kalendas iunii* for *kalendas iul.*

land (*saltu*). I then granted from my estate this unworked land of Baniuy from Genna Maiori ('large pass'): [the boundary] goes down the gorge (*gutturu*) to Sulibuzu and towards Bau de Serri ('Serri's ford'), and goes onto Arriu track, and onto Aquabona track, then leaves to Fadarta's threshing floor, and leaves to Sorigella's track, and goes up Serra de Genna d'Iligis ('ridge of Iligis's pass') through all the hills of Enbalba, then descends towards Jenna de Porta ('pass of the gate'), and goes down the track of Cungiadura, and leaves Mizas de Gennari ('springs of Gennari'), then goes back to Genna de Tesonis ('weavers' pass'); it descends towards Mortu Basili, crosses Pizinnu track, and leads to Serra de Candellazzu ('the ridge of Candellazzu'), then comes back to Genna Maiori, from where it started.

Also, I give to my lord Sanctu Antiogu of the island (*iscla*) of Sulchis all that I have in the unworked land and the farm lands of Sulegi, with water resources and timber, and with all the assets that are found at that unworked land. I granted from my estate this unworked land from the river of the village of Flumentebidu, through which one goes out to Masuniu Depintu; then it goes out to Corongiu de Maialis ('pigs' bath'), and goes out to Assulla's passes, bordering the road towards Canamenda, it returns to Giba Orrubia and continues towards Giba de Maçarus, it comes out at Giba de Marcu, crosses Oru de Forru, then goes out to the road of Flumentebidu, and comes back towards Creadis. In the year of the Lord 1226, on the 11th day before the kalends of June (10 July). Priest Marianus Scartellus, witness; assistant Petrus, witness.

Carta volgare 21. Transumpt. Date: 23 May 1226.[30] Exemption from taxes and labour services, and a grant of lands, made by Benedicta de Lacon (Benedetta di Massa), iudike of Cálari (1214–1244), with her son, to the church of San Pantaleo di Dolia. Known from three 15th- and 16th-century-copies in the Archivio diocesano storico di Cagliari, *Liber Diversorum*, 2/I serie [E], f. 65, DigiLib., pp. 67–68; Appendix 'Quaderno,' no. 2, DigiLib., pp. 311–312; Appendix 'Quaderno,' no. 15, DigiLib., pp. 321–322. Edition: Solmi, 'Le carte volgari', no. 20, pp. 48–50.

This is a transcript, translation or otherwise a copy of a certain privilege or parchment charter sealed with a lead seal attached with hemp cords or string, on which the lead seal on has a cross one side and there are some illegible letters and on the other [some illegible letters] (*sic* the phrase is repeated). It has been

30 Solmi mistakenly dated it to 22 June, possibly by confusing the *kalendas iunii* for *kalendas iul.*

sumptu[m] sive tra[n]slatu[m] per me Jo[annem] Polla Sardum not[arium] publicum auct[oritat]e regia per tota[m] insula[m] Sardinae et Corsice de verbo ad verbum bene [et] legaliter ac bene [et] fedeliter nil ad[d]endo vel minuendo aut muta[n]do cuius siquidem privilegii sive carte p[er]gaminee teno[r] sic se habet ut infra scribitur:[31]

+ In nomine patris et filii et spiritus sancti, amen. Ego Benedicta de Lacon, cum filiu miu donnigellu Gugellmu, per boluntadi de donnu deu potestandu parti de Cálaris, faççula custa carta ad sanctu Pantalea de Olia, pro beni ki lloi faççu, pro deu innanti et pro s'anima mia et de parentis mius. Faççula franca sa bilia de sanctu Basili de Montis, ki est apusti sa domu de sanctu Pantaleu de Olia, de cergas cantu se apartenit adpusti su regnu in manu dessu donnu su piscobu donnu Gontini Pizzolu, ki est oy, et de sus aterus piscabus cantu i anti a beniri apusti, et ki siat [in] custa domu de sanctu Basili; et pro iudigi, et pro curadori, et pro maiori de scolca et pro armentariu, o ateru seniori, ki gi at essiri in sa terra, no'nd'elli façςat grauitia ad su piscobadu de Olia peruna, pro custa domu de sanctu Basili, dessu cantu narat custa carta; no. 'ndi leint arrobadia, nin pro regnu, nin pro peguliari, et ni curadori, et ni ad maiori de scolca; et no. llis leinti binu, et ni laori d'olbezas, et ni orriu de caballus, et no. indi leinti dadu, ni sendu ego bia et ni supra perunu ateru seniori ki gi at essiri pus me in terra; si non per manu de su piscobu ki gi at essiri in sanctu Pantaleu de Olia, siat ponendu su piscobu su dadu a sus hominis ki i anti essiri in sa bilia, segundu sa força issorti. Et non baiant ad silbas donnigas, et ni de curadori, et nin de maiori de scolca; et si i banti, ad boluntadi issoru, d'omnia cantu i anti occhyri, lebintsi 'nde 'lias et pezzas et pellis; et non turbint gimilioni de manus perunu, et nin de messari, et nin de binia, et ni ad regnu, et ni ad peguliari, et ni a curadori, et ni a peruna personi, pro cerga ki ad essiri pro su seniori de sa terra, et non façςant peruna munia mala plus secundu in co fagenta. Et pro sus ķertus dessa terra sus cantu anti gittari ad Iuigi, ante Iuigi bengant; et sus ki gittant ad curadori o a maiori de scolca, bollu ki bengant totus ante su piscobu et ante su piscobu si iuigint, in cantu est seniori dessa billa. Et in cali

31 Proemia taken from the 16th-century transumpts in *Liber Diversorum*, 2/I serie [E], f. 65, DigiLib., pp. 67–68, and Appendix 'Quaderno', no. 2, DigiLib., pp. 311–312; these are identical, except for a few trivial variations in orthography.

taken and translated well by me, Joannis Polla the Sardinian, a public notary by royal authority throughout the entire island of Sardinia and Corsica, word for word, legally, well and faithfully, without adding, subtracting or changing anything. The content of the privilege or parchment charter is as written below:

+ In the name of the Father, the Son, and the Holy Spirit, amen. I, Benedicta de Lacon, with my son *donnigellu* Gugellmu, by the will of Lord God, ruling Cálari's territory (*parti*), make her this charter for my lord Sanctu Pantaleu de Olia (San Pantaleo, the cathedral of Dolianova; i.e., the bishopric of Dolia), for the benefices that I make to him, for God before all else and for my soul and of my relatives. I make free (*franca*) the village of Sanctu Basili de Montis, which is located by the farm complex (*domu*) of Sanctu Pantaleu de Olia, from the duties (*cergas*) that are due to the realm, which should now be put in the hands of their lord, bishop lord Gontini Pizzolu, who is the current bishop, and of any other bishop who may succeed him, and who may be at that farm complex of Sanctu Basili. And for the benefit of the iudike, *curatore*, head of the ward (*maiori de scolca*), administrator (*armentariu*), or any other lord (*seniori*) who may be on this earth, no burden should be imposed on the bishopric of Olia (Dolia), regarding this farm complex at Sanctu Basilia in relation to what been declared in this charter. No farming obligation (*arrobadia*) is exacted from them, neither for the realm (*rennu*), nor for a particular functionary (*peguliari*), nor for a *curatore*, nor for a head of the ward.

Also, neither wine, grain for consumption, nor barley for the horses should be exacted, and no tax (*dadu*) should be exacted from them, either by me in life, or by any other lord (*seniori*) who may succeed me on earth, but only by the hand of the bishop who will be there in San Pantaleo de Olia (Dolia) the bishop must impose a tax on the men who may be in the village, according to their abilities. And they should not go on lordly hunts (*silbas donnigas*), neither for the curator, nor for the head of the ward, and if they go there of their own free will, they may take the flesh and skins of all the animals they kill; and they should not divert any work obligation (*gimilioni*) of manual work, harvesting or vineyard tending, neither to the realm (*regnu*) nor to a particular functionary (*peguliari*), nor to a curator, nor to any person for the duties that may be for the lord of the land; and they should no longer provide any inappropriate service, as they had done until then.

Also, regarding legal disputes of this land, all that pertains to the iudike, should be submitted to the iudike; and I mandate that those who submit to the curator or head of the ward come before the bishop, and be judged before the bishop, as he is the lord (*seniori*) of the village. Also, I order the village of

l'apu dada custa frankidadi, bollu ki l'appat sa bilia de sanctu Basili de Montis, et in bida mia et de pusti morti mia. Et daulloi ad sanctu Pantaleu de Olia su saltu miu de Yduna, cantu Yduna, cantu si apartenit adpusti su regnu, et saltu et semida; et ingençcatsi custu saltu de Prima, essit de planu de Moguru daa pey d'alburu, et leuat su Rumini de Sibizori, et essit deretu a ccodis de marzallia, et essit deretu a sa perda de sa kida, et clompit assa bia de jenna de furca, et falat derectu a su cucuru d'arjola, et essit derectu assa jenna de sa tesonis, et de pedra de cavallu, et leuat sa bia de nuragi de paulis, et leuatsi sa bia a pei d' album da undi se ingençcat. Eccu beni ki fazzu ad sanctu Pantaleu de Olia pro deu innanti et pross'anima mia et de parentis mius, et pro siat mi padronu sanctu Pantaleu ante deu, pro sus peccadus mius. Et sunt destimonius donnu Gontini Madellu, archipreidi de sancta Maria, el preidi Turbini Corsu, canonigu suu, et preidi Dominigu et jagonu Kidru canonigus de sancta Cegilia; et laigus, Pedru de Serra Passagi, Arzoccu de Sii, Pedru de Unali tronchi, et Comida Dezori de Siillu, Pedru d'Azeni, et Arzocu d'Azeni su fradi, et Cumida de Unali de Sextu, et Gontini Curria. Istimonius de logu, Cumida Dezzori de Jenoni, et Gunnari de Sii, et Cumida d'Açeni tadaiu miu. Et est facta custa carta anno domini MCCXXVI. X. kalendas iunii, habendumilla sa curadoria de Campidanu ad manu mia pro logu salbadori. Et ki ll'aet deuertere appat anathema daba pater et filiu et saneio ispmiu, daba XII. apostolos, et IIII. evangelistas, daba XVI. prophetas, et XXIIII. seniores, daba CCCXVIII. patres sanctos, et sorti appat cum Juda traditore in infermi inferiori. Siat et fiat, amen.

Sanctu Basili to have that which has been granted in this free village charter (*frankidadi*), while I am alive and after my death.

Also, I give to Sanctu Pantaleu de Olia my unworked land of Yduna, both Yduna and what pertains to the realm, and unworked land and farm land. This unworked land starts from Prima, leaves the plain of Moguru from Pey d'Alburu, then goes up Rumini de Sibizori, and leaves towards cCodis de Marzallia, then leaves towards sa Perda de sa Kida ('the rock of the end'), and joins the road of Furca's pass (*jenna*), and descends towards su Cucuru d'Arjola ('the hill of the threshing floor'), and leaves towards the pass (*jenna*) of sa Tesonis ('the weavers') and of Pedra de Cavallu ('rock of the horse'), and then goes up the road of Nuraghe de Paulis up to Pei d'Album, from where it started. These are the benefices I make to Sanctu Pantaleu de Olia (Dolia), for God before all else and for my soul and of my relatives, and so may Sanctu Pantaleu be my patron saint before God and intercede for my sins!

The witnesses are: lord Gontini Madelli archpriest of Sancta Maria (de Clusu), and his canon priest Turbini Corsu, and priest Domingiu, and deacon Kidru the canon of Sancta Celigia, and the laymen Pedru de Serra Passagi, Arozoccu de Sii, Pedru de Unali Tronchi, and Comida Dezori de Siilu, Pedru d'Azeni, and his brother Arzocu d'Azeni, and Cumida de Unali from Sextu, and Gontini Curria.

Witnesses of the realm (*Istimonius de logu*): Cumida Dezzori de Jenoni, Gunnari de Sii, and Cumida d'Açeni, my distant uncle. This charter was made in the year of our Lord 1226, in the 10th day before the kalends of June (23 May), as I have in my hands the *curatore*'s district (*curadoría*) of Campidanu (Campidano) on behalf of the deputy (*logusalbadori*). Whoever dares to controvert it, may the Father and the Son and the Holy Spirit curse him, and the twelve Apostles, the four Evangelists, the sixteen Prophets, the twenty-four Elders, and the 318 Holy Fathers, and may he have his lot with Judas the traitor in the depths of Hell! Let it be and be done! Amen!

The Condaghe of San Pietro di Silki

 | DOI:10.1163/9789004750951_004

Introduction to the Text and Translation

The single codex of the condaghe di San Pietro di Silki (SS) is held at the Biblioteca Universitaria in Sassari (BUS, ms, 95). It is a compilation of three condaghes from several Benedictine monasteries in the iudicato of Torres, covering a period from c. 1065 to c. 1250. It comprises 135 well preserved and legible parchment folios measuring approximately 24 cm by 14.5 cm, and its most substantial part is formed of two condaghes from the monastery of Sanctu Petru de Silki. It also contains condaghes from the dependent monasteries of Sanctu Imbricu di Sauren (San Quirico, Cheremule-Thiesi) and Sancta Maria at Cotronianu (Codrongianos). The booklets that comprise the codex were drafted between the second half of the twelfth century and the middle of the thirteenth century. The text was drafted by multiple hands which changed from booklet to booklet. The short rubric that introduces different entries was also made in a different hand to the main text. Several simple illuminations can be found in the margins and capital letters; likewise, late medieval and early modern notes specifying the names of recorded lands were subsequently added in the margins. The entries of the condaghe relate to Silki's legal, economic and administrative transactions, including donations, purchases, judicial disputes, settlements, exchanges, and resolutions related to the monasteries' properties and rights. The original entries were not numbered, but for ease of reference, each entry has been numbered in both text and translation. There are two editions of the text: Giuliano Bonazzi (ed.), *Il condaghe de San Pietro di Silki. Testo Logudorese inedito dei secoli XI–XIII* (Sassari, 1900; repr. 1997), and Alessandro Soddu and Giovanni Strinna (eds), *Il condaghe di San Pietro di Silki* (Nuoro, 2013), which includes a scholarly introduction and an Italian translation.

Text

Colophon in 17th-century Spanish
Condague, y registro del monasterio de las monjas de la orden de San Benito, fundado junto á la antiquíssima Iglesia de San Pedro de Sirchi, villa del districto de Sacer, Diocesi Turritana, y datado cerca de los años de 1112 por la madre de Mariano, juez y Rey de la Provincia de Logudoro, en el qual registro se escrivian y notavan las donaciones, legados pios, herencias, compras, permutas y vencimentos de bienes a favor de la dicha iglesia y monasterio, cuyas Abadessas eran señores temporales de la dicha villa y administravan las rentas del monasterio suso dicho y de otras iglesias y monasterios agregados, de que se haçe mención en este libro y registro fecho por las Abadessas y bienhechores. Este libro está empeçado cerca del año de 1118. Y aunque se faltan las primeras 17 hojas o folio y otros al último, contiene la data del mes y año de sus addiciones del año 118[0], como se lee en el folio 109. Y es digno de ser [con]servado.

1r 1. [... T[este]s: ...][1] e fFuratu de Cotinas su d'Innoviu, e Gunnari d'Akettas.

2. *Kertu p[ro] S[anct]u Johanne de Usune.*
Ego appatissa Massimilla. Kertait mecu s'arkipiscopu de Turres, donnu Athu, sa die de sinotu in Turres, in corona de iudike Gu[n]nari e dessos piscopos, plakendeli ad isse, ass'arkipiscopu, e dandelila sa corona p[ro] sua a iudike [et] assos piscopos ki vi furun p[ro] fakernos iustithia a mimi et ad isse. Naraitimi: 'Eccola s'apatissa, naret p[ro]gitteu li lu levat a S[an]c[t]u Gaviniu a S[anct]u Juanne d'Usune, ki est pecuiare de S[anct]u Gaviniu?' Et ego naraili ca 'S[an]c[t]u Juanne et S[an]c[t]a Maria et S[an]c[t]a Caterina ecclesias de rennu furun, et iudike Mariane las deit assu monasteriu nostru cando li deit totu s'ateru, candu lu deit a S[an]c[t]a Maria de Nasca.' Judikarun ass'arkipiscopu a battuier destimonios et S[an]c[t]u Gaviniu inco kertait, destimonios non poteit batuier. [Derunili iura] assu p[re]b[iteru] meu, p[re]b[iteru] Ithokor de Fravile cun [...] e binki ca S[anct]u Juanne d'Usune [non fuit] de S[anct]u Gaviniu in co mi kertait s'arkipiscopu [...]

1 Incomplete entry of which only the final section of the witness list survives.

Colophon in seventeenth-century Spanish
Condaghe (*condague*) and register of the monastery of nuns from the order of San Benito, founded next to the old church of San Pedro of Sirchi, a town (*villa*) of the district (*districto*) of Sacer (Sassari) [in the] diocese of Turres (Torres), and dated around 1112 by the mother of Mariane, iudike (*juez*) and king of the province of Logudoro, in which were written and noted donations, pious legacies, inheritances, purchases, exchanges and sales of benefices for the said church and monastery of which the abbesses were worldly lords of the said town (*villa*), and administered the revenues of the said monastery and of other attached churches and monasteries, which are mentioned in this book and register dated by the abbots and benefactors. This book began around the year 1118, and although the first seventeen sheets or folios are missing, and others are missing from the end, it contains the date of the month and year of additions from the year 118[0], as can be read on folio 109. It is worthy of conserving.

1. [... Witnesses: ...] and Furatu de Cotinas from Innoviu, and Gunnari d'Akettas.

2. *Dispute regarding Sanctu Johanne de Usune* (Usini)
I, abbess Massimilla. There was a dispute between myself and the archbishop of Turres (Torres), lord Athu, on the day of the assembly (*sinotu*) at Turres at the hearing (*corona*) of iudike Gunnari and the bishops. The archbishop himself was pleased to hand over the hearing to the iudike and to the bishops who were present to oversee justice for me and for him. He said to me, 'Here's the abbess! Let her say why property (*peculare*) of Sanctu Gaviniu (San Gavino di Torres) has been taken away from the church of Sanctu Gaviniu and from Sanctu Juanne d'Usune (Usini)!' I said that the churches of Sanctu Juanne, Sancta Maria and Sancta Caterina were [once] property of the realm (*rennu*), but that iudike Mariane gave them to our monastery at the time he gave everything else when he made donations to Sancta Maria de Nasca (Santa Maria di Asca). They decided (*iudikarun*) that the archbishop and Sanctu Gaviniu bring witnesses. In this case, it was not possible to bring witnesses. They asked my priest, priest Ithokor de Fravile with [...], and I won because Sanctu Juanne d'Usune [was not the property] of Sanctu Gaviniu about which the archbishop had sued me [...].

1v 3. *Pro ansilla.*

Ego apatissa Maria. Kertait mecu Ga[n]tine Canbella [et] Ithoccor Thanthalu p[ro]ssa mukere[2] d'Istefane de Nussu in corona de iudike Ga[n]tine ca vi keriat su latus [et] ego torraili verbu ca non bi aviat parte. Iudicarunili ad issos a destimonios, destimonios non apperun. Iurait su servu meu Ga[n]tine Tra[m]pas a .+. et binki. T[es]tes: Iudike Ga[n]tine in cuia corona binki [et] Barusone Punga su de Torricla, [et] Iorgi̦ de Lenthas su arm[en]tariu de Salamatter.

4.[3] *Saltu de Cop[er]clatas.*

Ego[4] judike Mariane de Laccon chi do ad issu muristere de Santa Julia de Kitarone su saltu de Coperclatas. Et est termen de custu saltu su guttur josso d'iscala de Macaricas, et baricat derectu ad su badu dessa pruna, collat toctue pus flumen ad badu porosu, et collat ad iscla de Galleta, et collat toctue pus flumen ad su badu d'Uthikeor, et girat ad sa funtana priga dessu Cannisone, et collat ad nurake Pithi[n]nu, et baricat toctue pus fronte ad su nuracke d'A[n]navos, et baricat ad corona rubia, et collat toctue termen ad su
2r saltu de planu de Kitarone | et essit toctue ad sa via maiore dessa gruke, et falat toctue sa via maiore de valle torta, et termen ad oiastros de Parthimale, et adfliscat ad iscala de Macaricas. Et doli dessu saltu de Thela de tres partes una, et ecustos saltos li do ki los adpat c'a ssecatura de re[n]nu. Custu bene bi fatho ad su muristere de Santa Julia de Kitarone p[ro] Deu inna[n]ti et p[ro]ssa anima mia et de pare[n]tes mios, [et] siat custu firmu [in fine seculi, amen]. Et su[n]t testes: primus Barusone de Laccon, et Gu[n]nari de Maro[n]iu, et Ga[n]tine d'Athen, et Ithoccor de Navithan, et Gantine de Laccon. T[este]s.

5.[5] *In su saltu de Arave.*

Ego apatissa Massimilla. Conporaili ad Gu[n]nari de Thori Pista[n]ca su lat[us] dessu saltu d'Arave, et deivili i libra d'arge[n]tu. Venit term[en] dave badu de P[re]viteru, falat pus flum[en] ad badu de Labros, et collat s'iscala derectu ad sa via travessaria ki vaet a Banios, et clo[m]pet assa petra longa d'Arave, et falat su valliclu derectu ad rivu, avi[n]de rivu falat isc'a badu de P[re]viteru et clu-

2 *sic* for muliere.

3 Duplicated in entries 6 and 12.

4 Change of hand.

5 Duplicated in entries 7, 12 and 379.

3. *Concerning a female servant.*
I, abbess Maria. Gantine Canbella and Ithoccor Thanthalu sued me concerning the wife of Istefane de Nuss at the hearing (*corona*) of iudike Gantine, over a claim of half [her services], and I replied that he did not have that share. They decided to bring witnesses to them; witnesses were not apparent. My servant, Gantine Trampas, swore on the cross, and I won. Witnesses: iudike Gantine at whose hearing I won; Barusone Punga from Torricla (Torrija), and Jorgi de Lenthas the administrator (*armentariu*) of Salamatter.

4. *The unworked land* (saltu) *of Coperclatas.*
I, iudike Mariane de Laccon, give to the monastery of Santa Julia de Kitarone (Caddaroni-Sant'Eusebio), the unworked land (*saltu*) of Coperclatas ('dolmens'). The boundary of this estate is [from] the lower track of Iscala de Macaricas (the hillside of Macaricas); it passes towards Badu dessa Pruna ('crossing-ford of the plum'); it runs along the flow of the stream to Badu Porosu ('sieve crossing-ford'); it passes Iscla de Galleta ('the islet of Galleta') and runs along the flow of the stream to the crossing-ford of Othikeor. It turns to Funtana Priga ('the weak spring') below Cannisone, passes to nuraghe Pithinnu ('little nuraghe'), follows the flow ahead to Nuracke d'Annavos ('the nuraghe at Annavos'), and passes [the locality of] Corona Rubia ('red hilltop'). The boundary passes along the land (*saltu*) on the plain (*planu*) of Kitarone, then along Via Maiore dessa Gruke ('the main road of the cross'), it descends by the main road from Valle Torta ('twisted valley') and the boundary at the wild olives of Parthimale, then reaches Iscala de Macaricas ('hillside of Macarias'). I [also] give one-third part of the land (*saltu*) of Thela, and these lands (*saltos*) I give are alienated (*a ssecatura*) from the realm. This benefit I make to the monastery of Santa Julia de Kitarone for God, for my soul and for that of my parents (*parentes*). Let this be fixed to the end of time! Amen. The witnesses are: first, Barusone de Laccon, Gunnari of Maroniu, Gantine d'Athen, Ithoccor of Navithan, and Gantine de Laccon. Witnesses.

5. *On the unworked land* (saltu) *of Arave.*
I, abbess, Massimilla, bought from Gunnari de Thori Pistanca, half the unworked land (*saltu*) of Arava, and I gave him one pound (*libra*) of silver. The boundary begins from Badu de Previteru ('priest's crossing-ford'), it descends with the flow of the stream to Badu de Labros ('laurel ford'), and runs straight along the hillside (*iscala*) to the road-crossing that goes to Banios; and [then] it reaches Petra Longa ('the long rock') at Arave. It goes down the little valley (*valliclu*) straight to the stream (*riu*), from there the stream descends to Badu de

2v det. T[este]s: Mariane de Ca[n]nas, [et] do[n]nu | Petru d'Athen, cu[n] ken lu parthimus de pare, et Comi[ta] d'Arthacan, et Comita Bardane. T[este]s.

6.[6] Saltu *de Cop[er]clatas.*
Ego judike Mariane de Laccon ki do ad su muristere de Santa Julia de Kitarone su saltu de Coperclatas. Et est term[en] de custu saltu su guttur josso d'iscala de Macaricas, et baricat derectu ad su badu dessa Pruna, collat toctue pus flum[en] ad badu Porosu, et collat ad iscla de Galleta, et collat toctue pus flum[en] ad su badu d'Uthikeor, et girat ad sa fu[n]tana priga dessu Cannisone, et collat ad nurake Pithi[n]nu, et baricat toctue pus fronte ad su nuracke d'A[n]navos, et baricat ad corona rubia, et collat toctue term[en] ad su saltu de planu de Kitarone, et essit toctue ad sa via maiore dessa gruke, et falat toctue sa via maiore de valle Torta, et term[en] ad oiastros de Parthimale, et adfliscat ad iscala de Macaricas. Et doli dessu saltu de Thela de tres partes una, et ecustos saltos li do ki los adpat c'a ssecatura de re[n]nu. Custu bene li fatho
3r ad su muristere de Santa | Julia de Kitarone p[ro] deu inna[n]ti et p[ro]ssa anima mia et de parentes mios, et siat custu firmu [in fine seculi, amen]. Et sunt testes: primus do[n]nicellu Petru, Gantine d'Athen, Dorgotori d'Ussan, Mariane d'Ussan, Ithoccor de Thori, Petru Pinna, Gitilesu de Gitil et Furatu su frate, Niscoli de Thori, Niscoli d'Ussan, Gantine de Sogostos, Dorgo[to]ri de Capatthennor, Mariane su frate, Jorgi de Canpu. T[este]s.

7.[7] *In su saltu de Arave.*
Ego apatissa Massimilla. Comporaili ad Gunnari de Thori Pistanca su lat[us] dessu saltu d'Arave, et deivili I libra d'argentu. Venit termen dave badu de Previteru, falat pus flum[en] ad badu de Labros, et collat s'iscala derectu ad sa via travessaria ki vaet a Banios, et c[l]onpet ad sa petra longa d'Arave, [et] falat su valliclu derectu ad rivu, avinde rivu falat isc'a badu de Previteru et cludet. T[este]s: Mariane de Cannas, et do[n]nu Petru d'Athen, cu[n] ken lu parthi[amus].

6 Duplication of no. 4, repeated also in entry 12.

7 Duplication of no. 5, repeated also in entries 13 and 379. The transcription is abridged, as in entry 13.

Previteru and [the boundary] closes. Witnesses: Mariane de Cannas; lord Petru d'Athen, with whom we have an equal share [of the land]; Comita d'Arthacan, and Comita Bardane. Witnesses.

6. *Estate of Coperclatas.*
I, iudike Mariane de Laccon, give to the monastery of Santa Julia de Kitarone (Caddaroni-Sant'Eusebio), the unworked land (*saltu*) of Coperclatas ('dolmens'). The boundary of this estate is [from] the lower track of Iscala de Macaricas ('the hillside of Macaricas'); it passes straight on to Badu dessa Pruna ('crossing-ford of the plum tree'); it runs along the flow of the stream to Badu Porosu ('leaky crossing-ford'); it passes Iscla de Galleta ('the islet of Galleta') and runs along the flow of the stream to the crossing-ford of Othikeor. It turns to Funtana Priga ('the weak spring') below Cannisone, passes to Nuraghe Pithinnu ('little nuraghe'), follows the flow ahead to Nuracke d'Annavos ('Annavos nuraghe'), and passes Corona Rubia ('red hilltop'). The boundary passes along the land (*saltu*) on the plain (*planu*) of Kitarone, then along Via Maiore dessa Gruke ('the main road of the cross'), it descends by the main road from Valle Torta ('twisted valley') and the boundary at the wild olives of Parthimale, and reaches Iscala de Macaricas. I [also] give one-third part of the land (*saltu*) of Thela, and these lands (*saltus*) I give are alienated (*a ssecatura*) from the realm. This benefit I make to the monastery of Santa Julia de Kitarone for God, for my soul and that of my parents (*parentes*). Let this be fixed to the end of time! Amen. The witnesses are: *donnikellu* Petru, Gantine d'Athen, Dorgotori d'Ussan, Mariane d'Ussan, Ithoccor de Thori, Petru Pinna, Gitilesu de Gitil, and Furatu his brother, Niscoli de Thori, Niscoli d'Ussan, Gantine de Sogostos, Dorgotori de Capatthennor, Mariane his brother, and Jorgi de Canpu. Witnesses.

7. *In the unworked land* (saltu) *of Arave.*
I, abbess Massimilla, purchased from Gunnari de Thori Pistanca, half the unworked land (*saltu*) of Arave, and gave him a pound (*libra*) of silver. The boundary begins from Badu de Previteru ('priest's crossing-ford'), it descends with the flow of the stream to Badu de Labros (laurel ford), and runs straight along the hillside (*iscala*) to the road-crossing that goes to Banios; it [then] reaches Petra Longa ('long rock') at Arave, goes down the little valley (*valliclu*) straight to the stream (*riu*); from there, the stream descends to Badu de Previteru and [the boundary] closes. Witnesses: Mariane de Cannas, and lord Petru d'Athen with whom we share it.

3v 8.

Ego Massimilla apatissa de San[c]tu Pe[tru] de Silchi, ki ponio in ecustu co[n]dake accordiu ki feki cun fiios de donnu Therchis Mastru p[ro]ssu saltu de Sanctu Imbiricu de Biosevi.

In Biosevin.

Kertarunimi fiios de do[n]nu Therchis, Ith[occ]or [et] Gant[ine], ca naravan ca avia baricatu sos t[er]menes in su saltu de Biosevi, in corona de judike Varusone Mannu. Et donnikellu Ith[occ]or ki fuit donnu [et] arm[en]tariu dessa domo de S[anct]u Pe[tru] de Silki, binchitindelos in corona de judike Varusone Ma[n]nu ca fuit pecuiare de S[an]c[t]u Pe[tru] de Silki ad uve furun sos termenes. T[es]t[e]s: ho[m]i[n]es ki vi furun in corona uve binkit: Gunn[a]ri de Maroniu, [et] Comita de Navithan, [et] Gun[na]r[i] de Lacchon, [et] Ith[occ]or d'Athen su connatu. T[es]t[e]s.

9.[8] Conporu. *In Biosevin.*

Et appus custa binchitura ki lis feki, bennerun issos ad mimi [et] benderun-
4r imi omnia cantu vi avian in su saltu de Biosevi. Et ego dein[de]lis | ad ambos
fr[at]es, ad Ith[occ]or et ad Gant[ine] III libras d'argentu lavoratu. T[es]t[e]s ki vi furun uve conporai [et] mi deru[n] issos: Gun[n]ar[i] de Lachon, [et] Ith[occ]or d'Athen su co[n]natu, [et] Pe[tru] de Roma, [et] Co[mita] Vardane, [et] Barusone Masala, [et] Gant[ine] Manutha. Custos destimo[n]ios vi furu[n] uve adterminavan su saltu, andandeli ave termen in termen, homines ki connoschian su saltu: Pe[tru] Lorica, [et] Kipriane de Vare, servos ki furun dessos d'Athen.

10. Termen. *In Biosevin.*

Est termen dessu saltu de S[anct]u Imbiricu de Biosevi, dessu ki conporai ad sos de Thori fiios de donnu Therchis Mastru. Benit t[er]men dessu meu, [et] ki mi derun issos, ave sa petra dessu castru uv'est sa gruke de funtana de Corsos, jumpat rivu a dextra dessu Tectinosu assu valliclu dessu Furru, [et] baricat p[us] fronte, [et] clonpet assu valliclu de Vonora, [et] collat toctuve
4v valliclu adcatandelu toctu ad | monte giratu, [et] baricat toctue pus atha de
monte Corbei, [et] iumpat bia d'Ulumetu assu castru dessa T[ur]re, [et] baricat derectu assa petra alba ma[n]na dessu riu ad mo[n]ticlu de Chip[ri]ane, termen assa tija [et] collat toctuve atha a dextra dessa hena de Maurellu, [et]

8 Cf. entry 202.

8. *At Biosevi* (*Giusei*).
I, Massimilla, abbess of Santu Petru de Silchi, put in this condaghe accordingly that which I concluded with the sons of lord Therchis Mastru ('maestro') regarding the unworked land (*saltu*) of Sanctu Imbiricu at Biosevi (Giusei).

Biosevi (*Giusei*).
Ithoccor and Gantine, the sons of lord Therchis, sued me at the hearing (*corona*) of iudike Varusone Mannu ('the elder') saying that I had gone beyond (*baricare*) the boundaries [of what is mine] in the unworked land (*saltu*) of Biosevi (Giusei). *Donnikellu* Ithoccor, who was lord (*donnu*) and administrator (*armentariu*) of the house of Sanctu Petru de Silki, won at the hearing of iudike Varusone Mannu regarding the boundaries which were the property of Sanctu Petru de Silki. Witnesses: the men (*homines*) who were at the hearing in which he won were: Gunnari de Maroniu, Comita de Navithan, Gunnari de Lacchon, and Ithoccor d'Athen his brother-in-law. Witnesses.

9. Purchase. *At Biosevi* (*Giusei*).
After this victory I had over them, they came to me and sold me everything they had in the unworked land (*saltu*) of Biosevi (Giusei). I gave the two brothers, Ithoccor and Gantine, three pounds (*libra*) of worked silver. Witnesses who were there when I made the purchase and gave them [the silver]: Gunnari de Lachon, Ithoccor d'Athen his brother-in-law, Petru de Roma, Comita Vardane, Barusone Masala, and Gantine Manutha. These were [also] witnesses, men (*homines*) who knew the estate and who were there when they delimited the estate going from boundary to boundary: Petru Lorica and Kirpiane de Vare, who were servants of d'Athen.

10. Boundary limit. *At Biosevi* (*Giusei*).
The boundary of this unworked land (*saltu*) of Sanctu Imbiricu de Biosevi (Giusei) which I purchased from the De Thori sons of lord Therchis Mastru. The start of my boundary and that which they gave me has a rock below the outcrop (*castru*) where there is the cross (*gruke*) at Funtana de Corsos ('Corsos' spring'). It crosses the stream to the right of Tectinosu in Valliclu de Furru ('the little valley of Furru, lit. 'of the oven''); it passes in front and reaches Valliclu de Vonora ('the little valley of Bonora'); it goes along the valley keeping close to Monte Giratu (Monte Iradu, Uri), passing along beyond the crag (*atha*) de Monte Corbei (Monte Chelvei), it goes over the Ulumetu (Olmedo) road to Castru dessa Turre ('outcrop of the tower'). It goes straight along to the large white rock in the stream (*riu*) at Monitclu Chipriane ('Chiprane hill'). Boundary: from the lime tree (*sa tija*), it passes along to the crag to the right of Hena

clo[m]pet t[er]men assu albinathu de sa via de Cuca, [et] iumpat bia ad ariola Pet[ri]na, [et] clo[m]pet assa mura de frassos, falat toctuve atha de jaconu Andria, jumpat riu de jaconu Andria, clonpet termen assas gructas de jaconu Andria dessu albinathu, collat toctue derectu ad planu [et] baricat toctue pus atha de Donage, [et] baricat toctue pus atha claru ad balle Maxima, falat toctue serra de Soroe claru ad balle Maxima, [et] clompet su t[er]men assa petra dessu castru dessa gruke de funtana de Corsos, [et] cludet. Ad ecustu termen est meu per pare cun su ki mi venderun. Et poserunimi in pena de, si mi'[n]de
5r kertava[n]t | p[er] neunu tempus, o issos o neunu homine p[ro] 'ssos, dare assu rennu issos IIII lib[ras] d'argentu, cun avendemi su ki lis avia co[m]poratu, in co narat sos termenes.

11. Postura d[e] saltu. *In Tecti apus Biosevi.*
Ego Maximilla apatissa de S[an]c[t]u Pe[tru] de Silchi ki ponio in ecustu co[n]dake su saltu ki aet postu do[n]nu Pe[tru] de Serra Cavallare ad S[anc]t[u] Pe[tru] de Silchi p[ro]ssa a[n]i[m]a sua. Benit t[er]men dessu saltu de ave valliclu de Vonora, ad bulvares de Tissi, ad su Panpinu, assu vulbare dessa petra, claru assa via d'Ulumetu, falat bia de Tecti, ad nurachi Ispilitu, jumpat riu de Tecti, derectu assa margine de Tecti, assa coda dessu Titimalu, ad Girithola, clompet t[er]men assa via d'Ulumetu de valle de pira, ad pischina de s'Ambisuga, a funtana gutti-gutti, toctue via d'Ulumetu, ad Cervelluchi, ad valliclu de Mariane, adcattandelu ad monte Corvei, clonpet a valliclu de Honora et cludet.

5v 12.[9] Postura. | *Saltu de Cop[er]clatas.*
Ego iudike Mariane de Laccon ki do ad su muristere de S[an]c[t]a Julia de Kitarone su saltu de Coperclatas. Et est t[er]men de custu saltu su guttur josso d'iscala de Macaricas, [et] baricat derectu ad su badu dessa pruna, collat toctue pus flumen ad badu porosu, [et] collat ad isc[a]la de Galleta, [et] collat toctue pus flum[en] ad su vadu d'Othikeor, [et] girat ad sa funtana p[ri]ga dessu Ca[n]nisone, [et] collat ad nurake Pithi[n]nu, [et] baricat toctue pus fronte ad

9 Duplication of nos 4 and 6.

de Maurellu ('the spring of Maurellu'). The boundary goes from the limestone rock (*terra calcarea*) on the Cuca road, passes the track to the threshing floor (*ariola*) of Petrina, reaches the line (*mura*) of ash trees, descends along Atha de Jaconu Andria ('the crag of deacon Andria'), crossing Iaconu Andria stream (*riu*), it reaches the boundary at sas Gructas ('the crosses') of Iaconu Andria ('deacon Andria') by Albinathu ('the limestone rocks'). It goes straight along to the plain (*planu*), and goes along Atha de Donage ('the crag of Donage'), then passes across to Balle Maxima ('Maxima valley'); it descends along Serra de Soroe ('Soroe ridge') across Balle Maxima, and reaches the boundary at the rock of the outcrop (*castru*) at the cross of Funtana de Corsos. Then it closes. Up to this boundary is mine along with that which they sold me. If they ever contest this, either they or anyone else, they should give as a forfeit four pounds of silver to the realm that I paid them as it says in the boundary definition.

11. Grant of an estate. *In Tetti at Biosevi* (*Giusei*).
I, Massimilla, abbess of Sanctu Petru de Silchi, put in this condaghe the unworked land (*saltu*) that lord Petru de Serra Cavallare gave to Sanctu Petru de Silchi for [the salvation of] his soul. The boundary of the estate is from Valliclu de Vonora ('the little valley of Bonora'), to the animal enclosures (*bulvares*) at Tissi, to Panpinu, to the enclosure of Petra, towards the Ulumetu (Olmedo) road; it goes down the Tecti road to Nurachi Ispilitu, crosses Tecti stream (*riu*), goes straight to the outer part of Tecti [and then] to the end by Titimalu ('euphorbia plant'). [From there], to Girithola, the boundary reaches the Ulumetu road in Valle de Pira ('pear valley'); to Pischina de s'Ambisuga ('pool of the leech'), to Funtana Gutti-Gutti, ('dripping spring') along the Ulumetu road to Cervelluchi, to Balliclu de Mariane ('the little valley of Mariane'), it reaches Monte Corvei, joins Balliclu de Honora ('the little valley of Honora'), and closes.

12. Grant. *Unworked land* (saltu) *of Coperclatas*.
I, iudike Mariane de Laccon, give to the monastery of Santa Julia at Kitarone (Caddaroni-Sant'Eusebio), the unworked land (*saltu*) of Coperclatas ('dolmens'). The boundary of this estate is [from] the lower track of Iscala de Macaricas ('the hillside of Macaricas'); it passes straight on to Badu dessa Pruna ('crossing-ford of the plum'); it runs along the flow of the stream to Badu Porosu ('sieve crossing-ford'); it passes Iscala de Galleta ('the hillside of Galleta') and runs along the flow of the stream to Vadu d'Othikeor ('the crossing-ford of Othikeor'). It turns to Funtana Priga ('the weak spring') of Cannisone, passes to Nuraghe Pithinnu ('the small nuraghe'), follows the flow ahead to Nuracke

su nuracke d'Annavos, [et] baricat ad corona rubia, [et] collat toctue t[er]men
ad su saltu de planu de Chitarone, et essit toctue ad sa via maiore dessa gruke,
[et] falat toctue sa via maiore de valle torta, et terme[n] ad oiastros de Parthi-
male, et adfliscat ad iscala de Macaricas. Et doli dessu saltu de Thela de III
partes una, et ecustos saltos li do ki los appa[n] co a ssecatura de rennu. Custu
6r bene | li fatho ad su muristere de Sancta Julia de Kitarone p[ro] deu innanti [et]
p[ro]ssa a[n]i[m]a mea [et] de parentes m[e]os, [et] siat custu firmu [usque
in fine seculi, amen]. T[es]t[e]s: donnichellu Petru, [et] Gant[ine] d'Athen, [et]
Barusone de Lachon, [et] Gun[na]r[i] de Maroniu, [et] Ith[occ]or de Navithan,
[et] Gantine de Lachon, [et] Dorgotori d'Ussan, [et] Mariane d'Ussan, [et]
Itho[cc]or de Thori, [et] Pet[ru] Pinna, [et] Gitilesu de Gitil, [et] Furatu su frate,
[et] Niscoli de Thori, [et] Niscoli d'Ussan, [et] Gantine de Sogostos, [et] Dorgo-
tori de Capathe[n]nor, [et] Mariane su frate, [et] Jorgi de Campu. T[es]t[e]s.
T[es]t[e]s. T[es]t[e]s.

13.[10] Comporu. *In su saltu de Arave.*
Ego apatissa Massimilla. Conporaili ad Gunnari de Thori Pistanca su latus dessu
saltu d'Arave, [et] deivili una libra d'argentu. Benit t[er]men dave vadu de
p[re]viteru, falat pus flumen ad badu de Lavros, [et] collat s'iscala derectu ad sa
6v via travessaria ki vaen | a Banios, [et] clompet assa petra lo[n]ga d'Arave, [et]
falat su valliclu derectu ad riu, avinde riu falat ischi badu de previteru et clu-
det. T[es]t[e]s: Mariane de Ca[n]nas, et do[n]nu Pe[tru] d'Athen, cu[n] ken lu
parthin. T[es]t[e]s.

14. *De s[er]vis.*
Ego Susanna Pinna p[ri]orissa de S[an]c[t]u Petru de Silchi, et Ogulinu dessa
Rocha p[ri]ore de Silchi, parthivimus con Dorgotori Pinna [et] cun sos fr[at]es
cantos vi avian parte, [et] intraitimi a mimi apus patre Susanna Achetu [et]
apus mama mi intrait pede d'Elene Achetu. Giraimus manu a parthire sos
chi aviamus romasitos [et] intraitimi Ga[ntine] Achetu, [et] apus mama mi
intrait pede de Victoria Achetu. Et ecusta parthithione fechimus cun Dorgo-
tori Pinna [et] cun toctu fr[at]es de 'sse chi avian parte in Maria Sella, ca fuit
meu ad intreu Ith[occ]or Achetu, [et] c'avia pede in Maria Sella sa muiere.
T[es]t[e]s uve parthivim[us]: Gunnari de serra Brunchuchiu, [et] Bortholu
7r de Serra, [et] Gantine de Nurechi | [et] Gantine de Varru, [et] Ith[occ]or su
fr[at]e.

10 Duplication of nos 5 and 7.

d'Annavos ('the nuraghe at Annavos'), and passes [the locality of] Corona Rubia ('red hilltop'). The boundary passes along the land (*saltu*) on the Plain (*planu*) of Chitarone, then along the main road of the cross[road] (*dessa gruke*), it descends by the main road from Valle Torta (twisted valley) and the boundary at the wild olives of Parthimale, and reaches Iscala de Macaricas. I [also] give one-third part of the land (*saltu*) of Thela, and these estates I give them are alienated from the realm. This benefit I make to the monastery of Sancta Julia at Kitarone for God, for my soul and that of my parents (*parentes*). Let this be fixed to the end of time! Amen. Witnesses: *donnikellu* Petru, Gantine d'Athen, Barusone de Lachon, Gunnari de Maroniu, Ithoccor de Navithan, Gantine de Lachon, Dorgotori d'Ussan, Mariane d'Ussan, Ithoccor de Thori, Petru Pinna, Gitilesu de Gitil, and Furatu his brother, Niscoli de Thori, Niscoli d'Ussan, Gantine de Sogostos, Dorgotori de Capathennor, and Mariane his brother, and Jorgi de Campu. Witnesses. Witnesses. Witnesses.

13. *In the unworked land* (saltu) *of Arave.*
I, abbess Massimilla, purchased from Gunnari de Thori Pistanca half the unworked land (*saltu*) of Arave, and gave him a pound (*libra*) of silver. The boundary begins from Badu de Previteru ('priest's crossing-ford'), it descends with the flow of the stream to Badu de Labros ('laurels' ford'), and runs straight along the hillside (*iscala*) to the road-crossing that goes to Banios; and [it then] reaches Petra Longa ('the standing stone') at Arave. It goes down the little valley (*valliclu*) towards the stream (*riu*), from there the stream descends to Badu de Previteru and [the boundary] closes. Witnesses: Mariane de Cannas, and lord Petru d'Athen with whom we share it.

14. *Concerning servants.*
I, Susanna Pinna, prioress of Sanctu Petru de Silchi, and Ogulinu dessa Rocha, prior of Silchi, make a division with Dorgotori Pinna and with all his brothers who have a share: there belonged to me Susanna Achetu from the father's side, and from the mother's side there belonged a quarter share [of the services] of Elene Achetu. We took turns in dividing [the services] of those we have who remained, and there belonged to me Gantine Acetu, and from the mother's side a quarter share of Victoria Achetu. We made this division with Dorgotori Pinna and with all his brothers who had a share of Maria Stella, as Ithoccor Achetu was entirely mine and I had a quarter [share] in Maria Stella, his wife. Witnesses when we made the division: Gunnari de Serra Brunchuchiu, Bortholu de Serra, Gantine de Nurechi, Gantine de Varru, and Ithoccor, his brother.

15. *De s[er]vis.*

Ego Susanna Pinna p[ri]orissa de S[anct]u Petru de Silchi, [et] Ogulinu dessa Rocha p[ri]ore de Silchi, parthivimus cun donnu Ju[anne] de Balvasi, abbate de Padule, fiios chi aviat Jorgi Pithos in Susa[n]na Melone. Levarun issos apus mama in p[ri]mariu ad Maria Pithos, [et] nois levaimus apus patre ad Gant[ine] Pithos, romanende ad cumone Ju[anne] Pithos. Et parthivimus sos fiios de Furata Melone [et] de Comita de Piras; issos levaru[n] apus mama a Prethiosa, [et] nois levaimu[s] apus patre a Susanna, avendevi in Petru su latus, chi remaniat a parthire ca fuit pithinnu. T[es]t[e]s uve parthivim[us]: Mariane Solina arm[en]tariu de Canache, [et] Furatu Nurresu, [et] Mariane de Rosa, [et] Gantine de Nurechi, et Gant[ine] de Varru. T[es]t[e]s.

16. *De s[er]vis.*

Ego Susanna Pinna p[ri]orissa de S[anct]u Pet[ru] de Silchi, [et] Ogulinu dessa
Rocha, p[ri]ore de Silchi, parthivimus cun do[n]nu Ju[anne] de Malvasi apate
7v de Padule, fiios de Muscu Casole chi aviat in Mariane Solina, | [et] intratinos
apus mama Elene Solina, et ad issos intrait apus patre Ju[anne] Solina, [et]
intraitinos ad nois Gantine apus mama, [et] ad issos intrait apus patre Janne
Solina, [et] Petru romasit ad in cumone, lat[us] appare. T[es]t[e]s: Gant[ine]
de Nurechi, [et] Gant[ine] de Varru, [et] Ith[occ]or su fr[at]e, [et] Furatu Nur-
resu, [et] Mariane de Rosa. T[es]t[e]s.

17. *De s[er]vis.*

Ego Susanna Pinna priorissa de S[an]c[t]u Petru de Silchi, [et] Ogulinu dessa Rocha priore de Silchi, parthivimus cun do[n]nu Ju[anne] de Belvasi apate de Padule, sende armentariu Dorgotori Pi[n]na in Canache. Intraitinos ad nois Justa Pertethe, [et] ad Padule Istefania sa sorre. T[es]t[e]s uve parthivimus, Ju[anne] de Liios, [et] Mariane Corsellu, [et] Mariane de Rosa, [et] Petru Muthuru, [et] Furatu Nurresu.

18. *De s[er]vis.*

Parthivim[us] a Merchisa cun sos Casos, [et] cun donna Justa de Cleu, [et] cun
Dorgotori Pinna, [et] int[r]ait a S[anct]a Julia su latus [et] ad S[an]c[t]u Petru
8r su pede, [et] conporai ad Ju[anne] de Rosa [et] assos Casos | sas III dies de custu
pede chi mi '[n]de essiat, [et] a donna Iusta de Cleu et assu frate. T[es]t[e]s
uve conporait: su priore donnu Ogulinu dessa Rocha, [et] issa priorissa donna

15. *Concerning servants.*
I, Susanna Pinna, prioress of Sanctu Petru de Silchi, and Ogulinu dessa Rocha, prior of Silchi, divided with lord Juanne of Balvasi, abbot of Padule (Santa Maria di Paulis, Ittiri), the sons that Jorgi Pithos had with Susanna Melone. They took these in the first place from the mother's side, Maria Pithos; we took from the father's side, Gantine Pithos, leaving in common Juanne Pithos. We divided the sons of Furata Melone and Comita de Piras: they took from the mother's side, Prethiosa, and we took from the father's side, Susanna, having half [the services] of Petru that remain to be divided because he was a child. Witnesses when we made the division: Mariane Solina administrator (*armentariu*) de Canache (Caniga), Furatu Nurresu, Mariane de Rosa, Gantine de Nurechi, and Gantine de Varru. Witnesses.

16. *Concerning servants.*
I, Susanna Pinna, prioress of Sanctu Petru de Silchi, and Ogulinu dessa Rocha, prior of Silchi, divided with lord Juanne de Malvasi, abbot of Padule (Santa Maria di Paulis, Ittiri), the [services of the] sons of Muscu Casole which he had with Mariane Solina. We took from the mother's side, Elena Solina; to them from the father's side there belongs Juanne Solina; we took for ourselves Gantine from the mother's side, and to them there belongs Janne Solina from the father's side. Petru has remained in common, a half each. Witnesses: Gantine de Nurechi, Gantine de Varru, Ithoccor his brother, Furatu Nurresu, and Mariane de Rosa. Witnesses.

17. *Concerning servants.*
I, Susanna Pinna, prioress of Sanctu Petru de Silchi, and Ogulinu dessa Rocha, prior of Silchi, divide with lord Juanne of Balvasi, abbot of Padule (Santa Maria di Paulis, Ittiri), when Dorgotori Pinna was administrator (*armentariu*) at Canache (Caniga). We take for ourselves Justa Pertethe, and to Padule, Istefania, her sister. Witnesses when we made the division: Juanne de Liios, Mariane Corsellu, Mariane de Rosa, Petru Muthuru, and Furatu Nurresu.

18. *Concerning servants.*
We divided Merchisa between the Casos [family] and between lady (*donna*) Justa de Cleu, and between Dorgotori Pinna. Half was given to Santa Julia, and a quarter (*pede*) to Sanctu Petru. I purchased from Juanne de Rosa and the Casos family, three days of this quarter [service] for myself and for lady Iusta de Cleu and her brother. Witnesses to that which was purchased: the prior lord Ogulinu dessa Rocha, the prioress lady Susanna Pinna. Witnesses to that which

Susanna Pinna, [et] uve parthivimus: Ith[occ]or Casu chi fuit frate de parthone, [et] Ith[occo]r de Cleu, [et] donnu Petru Marthane, [et] donnu Gunnari de serra bruncuchiu, [et] Bortholu de Serra. T[es]t[e]s.

19. *Conporu in su saltu d'Arave.*

Conporali[11] a Gunnari de Thori Pistanka su latus dessu saltu d'Arave, et ego deindeli II l[i]b[ras] d'arientu. [Et] est t[er]men dessu saltu, ad sa petra longa d'Arave, et benit assa via dessa coda dessa Kersa, [et] falat tottuve via ad flum[en], [et] falat tottuve flum[en] ad Lavros, [et] falat tottuve flum[en] a badu de vervekes, [et] collat tottuve via ass'ariola de Petru de Vare, [et] benit tottuve via a ffu[n]tana de Corsos, [et] collat assu mo[n]ticlu de Sorove, [et] baricat tottuve serra de do[n]na e Ispathata, [et] falat i[n] sos balliclos derettu assu mo[n]ticlu de Casula, [et] collat a dextra de matta de Plave, derettu assu sueriu de mesa via chi vaen sos de Vanios ad Arave, derettu assa[12] // petra longa.[13] T[este]s: Mariane de Canas et do[n]nu Pet[ru] d'Athen, cum ken aviamus su saltu, [et] Comita de Itin d'Arthacan et Comita Vardane. T[este]s //[14]

8v [15]*In nomine D[omi]ni nostri Ih[es]u Chr[ist]i eterni D[e]i, am[en].*

20. Ego[16] Maximilla abbatissa de S[anct]u Petru de Silki ki lu renovo custu condake ad unore Deus innanti, e de S[anct]u Petru, e de S[anct]a Iulia, e ccun boluntate dessu do[n]nu meu iudike Gunnari, e dessu fiiu iudike Barusone, e dessos fr[ate]s, e dessos maiorales de Locudore, dandem'isse paragula de renobarelu su co[n]dake.

21. Postura. *De s[er]vis.*

Ego prebiteru Petru Iscarpis, ki ponio in ecustu co[n]dake de S[an]c[t]u Petru de Silki, parthithione d'omines ki feki cu nontho Pet[ru] de Kentu Istafla. Prebiteru Pet[ru] Calfe fuit suo, e matro[n]a fuit de S[anct]u Petru de Silki; fekerun IIII fiios, e pparthivimus a nnatias; isse levait a Gavini [et] a Gosantine, e S[anct]u Petru lebait a sSusanna [et] a Jannia.

11 Change of hand.

12 The entry in the manuscript breaks off here and continues at f. 115v.

13 See entry 412.

14 This last line of the entry is transcribed from f. 115v.

15 A second section of the manuscript starts here; it has been identified as a renewed version of the original *condaghe* of San Pietro di Silki, comprising eight *quaternioni* (ff. 8–71) and a *duerno* (ff. 96–99); for discussion see A. Soddu and G. Strinna (eds), *Il condaghe di San Pietro di Silki* (Nuoro, 2013), p. 66.

16 Change of hand.

was divided: Ithoccor Casu who was party (*frate*) to the division, Ithoccor de Cleu, lord Petru Marthane, lord Gunnari de Serra Bruncuchiu, and Bortholu de Serra. Witnesses.

19. *Purchase in the unworked land* (saltu) *of Arave.*
I purchased from Gunnari de Thori Pistanka half of the unworked land (*saltu*) of Arave, and I gave him two pounds (*libras*) of silver. The boundary of the estate is from Petra Longa ('long rock') of Arave, and it starts at the road of the deep-cut valley (*coda*) of sa Kersa ('the mastic shrub'), goes along the road to the stream, and descends along the stream to Lavros; it goes down along the stream to the Badu de Verkeves ('crossing-ford of the sheep'), and joins the road of Petru de Vare's threshing floor (*ariola*). It goes along the road to Funtana de Corsos ('the spring of Corsos'), and reaches the hill (*monticlu*) of Sorove, goes along the ridge of Donna e Ispathata, and descends to the little valleys directly below Casula hill. It passes on the right the *macchia* (*matta*) of Plave, [goes] towards the cork oaks half-way along the road that goes from Banios to Arave, and [then goes] towards Petra Longa. Witnesses: Mariane de Canas, and lord Petru d'Athen with whom we have the land (*saltu*), and Comita de Itin from Arthacan, and Comita Vardane.

(Latin): In the name of the Lord Jesus Christ, eternal God, amen.

20.
I, Massimilla, abbess of Sanctu Petru de Silki, update (*renovo*) this condaghe for the honour of God above all, and for Sanctu Petru and Sancta Julia, and with the permission of my lord iudike Gunnari, and of the son of iudike Barusone and his brothers, and the major lords (*maiorales*) of Locudore (Logudoro), having given me authorisation to update the condaghe.

21. Donation. *Of servants.*
I, priest Peter Iscarpis, put in this condaghe of Sanctu Petru di Silki the division of men (*omines*) which I made with the notary (*nontho*) Petru de Kenti Istafla ('hundred stables'): the priest Petru Calfe was his, and his wedded wife (*matrona*) belonged to Sanctu Petru de Silki. They had four children and we divided them by [their] birthdate: he took Gavino and Gostantine, and Sanctu Petru took Susanna and Jannia.

22. Postura. *De s[er]vis.*
9r Ego p[re]b[iteru] Petru Iscarpis, ki ponio | in ecustu co[n]dake p[ro] Petru Rasu ki fuit de S[an]c[t]u Petru de Silki, e Iusta Pettena fuit d'Ithoccor de Vosove e dessos fr[ate]s; [et] ego pettilila a ttottu fr[ate]s suos [et] ad isse, e derunimila e ccoiuvaimusilos cum Petru Rasu, a boluntate de pare.

23. *De s[er]vis.*
Petru Caste e Iusta de funtana coiuves furun, Iusta fuit de S[an]c[t]u Petru de Silki e Pet[ru] Caste fuit de S[an]c[t]a Barbara d'Erthas; fekerun II fiios, a Gavini et a Barbara, e cken'esser alicando parthitis est mortu Gavini, ramasit ad in cumone Barbara.

24. Parthitura. *De s[er]vis.*
Ego pr[e]b[iter]u Petru Iscarpis, ki parthibi cun pr[e]b[iter]u Gavini Pithale a ffiios de Istefane de Nussas e de Maria de Funtana, ki furun de S[an]c[t]u Pet[ru] de Silki, e de S[an]c[t]u Pet[ru] de Carieke. A Iusta [et] a Bona [et] ad Elene levaitilos S[an]c[t]u Pet[ru] de Silki; [et] a Migali, [et] a Petronella, [et] a Barbara, [et] a Pet[ru] levaitilos S[an]c[t]u Pet[ru] de Carieke.

25. *De s[er]vis.*
Ego pr[e]b[iter]u Pet[ru] Iscarpis, ki ponio in ecustu co[n]dake de S[an]c[t]u
9v Pet[ru] de Silki, p[ro] ca mi la furait Pet[ru] Tecas a nNastasia de | funtana ave domo dessu thiu, de Iuste de Silki, sene mi la peter, nen a mimi, nen a fr[ate]s suos, ki non fuit servu de S[an]c[t]u Petru, vorthe de paperos. [Et] ego torrainde verbu assu donnu meu, a iudike Gosantine de Sogostos, [et] isse, co do[n]nu bonu torraitililu tottu su fetu a sS[an]c[t]u Pet[ru] de Silki. T[es]t[e]s: Therkis de Nureki, e Barusone de Martis, e Jorgi d'Iscanu, [et] Egithu de Sevin, e Mariane de Nureki.

26. Parthitura. *De s[er]vos.*
Ego pr[e]b[iter]u Pet[ru] Iscarpis ki parthivi homines cu nontho Pet[ru] de Kentu Istafla, a fiios de Pet[ru] Calfe ki fuit suo, e matrona fuit de S[an]c[t]u Pet[ru]; fekerun IIII fiios, parthivi a nnatias, isse levait a Gavini, [et] a Gosantine; e sS[an]c[t]u Pet[ru] levaitila a sSusanna et ad Anania.

27. Levatura a llar[ga]. *De s[er]vos.*
Ego pr[e]b[iter]u Pet[ru] Iscarpis ki ponio in ecustu co[n]dake de S[an]c[t]u Pet[ru] de Silki p[ro] Elene de Fu[n]tana ki fuit ankilla de S[an]c[t]u Pet[ru] de Silki, e llevatila a llarga Ianne de Monte, e fekerun IIII fiios, a Maria, [et] a
10r Gavini, [et] a Iusta, [et] a cCaterini. E ssende su fetu fattu, | tenninde corona

22. Donation. *Of servants.*
I, priest Peter Iscarpis, put in this condaghe [an entry] about Petru Rasu who was [in the service] of Sanctu Petru di Silki, and Iusta Pettena was of Ithoccor de Vosove and his brothers. I asked him and all the brothers, and they gave me her and swore with Peter Rasu in mutual agreement.

23. Donation. *Of servants.*
Petru Caste and Justa de Funtana were spouses. Justa belonged to Sanctu Petru de Silki, and Petru Caste was of Sancta Barbara d'Erthas (Ertas). They had two children, Gavino and Barbara; Gavino died, and Barbara remained shared [between us].

24. Division. *Of servants.*
I, priest Peter Iscarpis, divided with the priest Gavini Pithale, the offspring of Istefane de Nussas and Maria de Funtana who belonged to Sanctu Petru de Silki and to Sanctu Petru de Carieke. Sanctu Petru de Silki took Iusta, Bona and Elene; Sanctu Petru de Carieke took Migali, Petronella, Barbara, and Petru.

25. *Of servants.*
I, priest Peter Iscarpis, put in this condaghe [an entry] about Nastasia de Funtana whom Petru Tecas took from me without asking either me or her brothers from the house of her uncle Juste de Silki, who was not a servant (*servu*) of Sanctu Petru, but was instead a smallholder (*papero*). I spoke with my lord Gostantine de Sogostos and he, being a good lord, restored all the offspring to Sanctu Petru de Silki. Witnesses: Therkis de Nureki, Barusone de Martis, Jorgi d'Iscanu, Egithu de Sevin, and Mariane de Nureki.

26. Division. *Of servants.*
I, priest Peter Iscarpis, divided men (*homines*) with the notary (*nontho*) Petru de Kentu Istafla; the sons of Petru Calfe were his; his wife was of Sanctu Petru. They had four offspring. I divided them by birthdate: he took Gavino and Gostantine; Sanctu Petru took Susanna and Anania.

27. Wrongful appropriation. *Of servants.*
I, priest Peter Iscarpis, put in this condaghe of Sanctu Petru de Silki [an entry] concerning Elene de Funtana who was a female servant (*ankilla*) of Sanctu Petru di Silki, and who was wrongfully appropriated by Ianne de Monte, and who had four children: Maria, Gavino, Iusta, and Caterina. When the children were born, [the matter] was brought to a hearing (*corona*) of iudike Barusone

de iudike Barusone, cun donnos de Ianne de Monte, cun Furatu de Sevin e ccun Comita de Gunale. Iudicarunimi a iura ca mi la levaran a llarga, [et] issara iurait su mandatore de clesia, ca ad Elene de funtana a llarga fekit levata, ki non fekit pettita alicando nen a do[n]nu, nen a cculivertu p[er] ista .+. [et] issara mi torrarun tottu su fetu, e llevaimi[n]delu. T[es]t[e]s: su do[n]nu meu iudike Barusone, e Mariane de Thori, e Pet[ru] de Serra, e Therkis de Nureki, ki 'nke fuit curatore in Romania, e Dorgotori de Sogostos, e Dorgotori de Oiun, e Dericcor de Capathennor, e Dorgotori de Vosove, e Furatu de Vosove, [et] totta corona in co vi fuit tottu locu Golletu, in Turres, sa die de sinotu.

28. Postura. *De s[er]vos.*

Ego pr[e]b[ite]ru Elias ki ponio in ecustu co[n]dake de S[an]c[t]u Pet[ru] de Silki, p[ro] fetu de Iorgia Manca ca la levarat a llarga Gosantine Tusu, servu de Nicola Regitanu, e fekitivi IIII fiios; [et] osca tenninde corona cun Sardos cun ken la aveat ad issa S[an]c[t]u Pet[ru], in corona de iudike in Kitarone, e iudi-
10v caruni | mi a iura, e iurainde a gruke .+. [et] ego, e no[n]tho Dorgotori de Martis ca no nos la petterun, e torraruninolla cun IIII fiios suos, e parthivi cun Sardos; levai ego a Barbara [et] a Maria, [et] issos levarunila a Natolia [et] ad Andria, sendevi a destimoniu su donnu meu iudike Pet[ru], e Gosantine de S[o]gostos curatore de Romania, e Gosantine de Martis, essendevi arm[en]tariu Gosantine de Valles.

29. *De s[er]vos.*

Ego pr[e]b[iter]u Elias ki ponio in ecustu co[n]dake de S[an]c[t]u Pet[ru] de Silki p[ro] ca li petti muiere a Ianne Rasu, ki fuit servu de S[an]c[t]u Pet[ru] de Silki; pettila a Iusta Pala, a Gosantine d'Erthas [et] a Donotho d'Urieke, [et] issos derunilos appare, e ccoiuvaimusilos a boluntate de pare.

30. *De s[er]vos.*

Ego pr[e]b[iteru] Elias ki ponio in ecustu co[n]dake de S[an]c[t]u Pet[ru] de Silki p[ro] homines. Iorgi Infante e Mendalo coiuves furun, anbos intregos de S[an]c[t]u Pet[ru] furun; fekerunila a Bittoria, e llevaitila a muiere Gosantine Muthuru; [et] issos fekerunila a cCulu[m]ba; [et] avendemila ego ad intro, diskit a ffuricare cun Andria Mollu, e fugivit cun illa a cCoraso. E ssende fugitos

between the lords of Ianne de Monte, Furatu de Sevin, and Comita de Gunale. They decided that I should swear to that which had been wrongfully appropriated from me, and the church's representative (*mandatore*) swore that Elene de Funtan had been wrongfully taken, and that no request had been made either to the lord or a servant (*culivertu*) for a sworn declaration. They returned to me all the offspring and I took [possession] of them. Witnesses: my lord iudike Barusone, Mariane de Thori, Petru de Serra, Therkis de Nureki who was *curatore* of Romangia, Dorgotori de Sogostos, Dorgotori de Oiun, Dericcor de Capathennor (Crabattennere), Dorgotori de Vosove, Furatu de Vosove, and the whole hearing at which there was the whole of Gallura (*tottu locu Golletu*) at Turres (Torres) on the day of the assembly (*sinotu*).

28. Donation. *Of servants.*
I, priest, Elias, put [an entry] in this condaghe of Sanctu Petru de Silki regarding the offspring of Iorgia Manca whom Gostantine Tusu, a servant (*servu*) of Nicola Regitanu, wrongfully appropriated, and they had four children. Then, holding a hearing with the local people (*Sardos*) with whom Sanctu Petru had [a claim] at the hearing (*corona*) of the iudike at Kitarone (Caddaroni-Sant'Eusebio), they decided that I take an oath. I swore on the cross, both myelf and the notary Dorgotori de Martis, that no one had requested her from us, and that they had had four children, and I had divided [them] with the locals (*Sardos*). I took Barbara and Mari, and they took Natolia and Andria. As witnesses, there was my lord iudike Petru, Gostantine de Sogostos the *curatore* of Romangia, Gostantine de Martis, and also present [was] the administrator (*armentariu*) [of Sanctu Petru], Gostantine de Valles.

29. *Of servants.*
I, priest, Elias, note in this condaghe of Sanctu Petru de Silki the matter of seeking a wife for Ianne Rasu who was a servant (*servu*) of Sanctu Petru de Silki. Gostantine d'Ethas and Donotho d'Urieke approached Iusta Pala [for permission]. They both gave their consent and we married them with the permission of both.

30. *Of servants.*
I, priest Elias, put in this condaghe of Sanctu Petru de Silki [an entry] regarding men [owing service] (*homines*). Iorgi Infante and Mendalo were spouses (*coniuves*); both were entirely held (*intregos*) by Sanctu Petru. The child they had, Bittoria, was taken as a wife by Gosantine Muthuru with whom they had Culumba. While I had her in my service (*ad intro*), I learned of her adultery with Andria Mollu and [that] he fled with her to Coraso (Coros). As runaways,

11r umpare fekerun | totu fetu, e ssende tottu fetu fattu tenni[n]de ego corona de Mariane de Locu ki vi fuit curatore, e iurainde a gruke .+. ca alicando nen ego, nen mandatore de S[an]c[t]u Pet[ru], nen petterunnolla e nen darela deimus alicando.

31. Kertu. *De s[er]vos.*
Ego pr[e]b[iter]u Iorgi ki ponio in ecustu co[n]dake de S[an]c[t]u Petru de Silki. Tenni corona cun Comita de Gunale, e ccun sos fiiastros p[ro] Iusta Solina, ki fuit de S[an]c[t]u Pet[ru] de Silki, e llevaitimila a fura prebiteru Francu, kene mi la peter, [et] ego tenni[n]de corona dessu donnu meu, de iudike Barusone in Irbosa. Iudicarunili a iura ave latus de fiios de Maria de Kerki e non potterun iurare, e boluerunilu tenne su pr[e]b[iter]u ad ockiderelu, a pr[e]biteru Francu, ca 'tu nos mascasti ki la levasti kene la peter.' E ffugiuit su pr[e]b[iter]u, e tennit a patronu a iudike; e naraitili iudike ca 'fakemi volu[n]tate de parthirevos kene iura de 'ssos.' Parthirun issos primariu sos pr[e]biteros anbos, ego levailu apus
11v S[an]c[t]u Pet[ru] a pr[e]b[iter]u Istefane, [et] issos levarunilu a pr[e]biteru | Gosantine. Parthiui ego osca, posilu a Ianne ad una parte, ca fuit mastriu de fravica e de linna, [et] ass'atera parte posilu a Iorgi et a fFurata ca furun puriles; issos levarunilu a Ianne ca fuit mastriu e sS[an]c[t]u Pet[ru] de Silki levaitilos a Iorgi [et] a Furata ki furun puriles. T[es]t[e]s: su do[n]nu meu iudike Barusone, [et] Ithoccor de Sevi[n], [et] Egithu su fr[at]e, e Iorgi d'Iscanu, e Therkis de Nureki, e Mariane de Valles, e Gosantine de Cannas, e ckita sua.

32. Postura. *De s[er]vos.*
Bittoria de Nurra fiia ki fuit de p[re]biteru Gabini Pulla, e pettila a sSagio de Capriles, ki furun do[n]nos de Vittoria de Nurra, [et] a Maria de Valles ki fuit donna sua, e ccoiuvarunilos umpare. Fekerun v fiios, IIII feminas, [et] I masclu; [et] osca cando vennimus a parthire cun Sardos, levaimus dessas feminas cana II ca furun sinkeras, [et] issu masclu ca fuit semu lassaimusilu ad in cumone. Posimusilas appare, a Iorgia et a Greca, issos levarunila a Iorgia [et] ego a Greca; posimusilas appare a Maria et a Furata; issos levarunila a Maria, [et] ego
12r a Furata | apus S[an]c[t]u Pet[ru], [et] a Gavini dassaimusilu ad in cumone. T[es]t[i]s: su donnu suo.

33. Kertu. *De s[er]vos.*
Ego pr[e]b[iter]u Iorgi Maiule ki ponio in ecustu co[n]dake p[ro] ca tenni corona cun Gunnari d'Oiun e ccun Gunnari de Nureki e ccun Baru de Castavar,

they had all their offspring together. With all the offspring born, I brought the case [to] a hearing (*corona*) of Mariane de Locu who was the *curatore*. I swore on the cross that neither I, nor the representative (*mandatore*) of Sanctu Petru, had sought her [service], nor have we ever given her [services] away.

31. Dispute. *Of servants.*
I, priest Iorgi, put [an entry] in this condaghe of Sanctu Petru de Silki. I had recourse to a hearing (*corona*) with Comita de Gunale and his sons-in-law regarding Iusta Solina, who was held by Sanctu Petru de Silki, but who was wrongfully taken by priest Francu who had not sought permission. I appealed at the hearing of my lord, iudike Barusone, at Irbosa (Badde Ilvosa). They decided he should swear that he had a half-share of the children of Maria de Kerki. He was not able to swear, and they wanted to take the priest—priest Francu—and kill him on the grounds that 'you have offended us by taking him without seeking consent!' The priest fled and appealed to the iudike as [if he were] the owner [of the half share]. He told him, 'let me make the division [of services] by consent without them swearing on oath!' They divided first of all both priests: I took for Sanctu Petru the priest Istefane, and they took the priest Gosantine. Then, I made the division, and assigned Ianne to one part as he was skilled (*mastriu*) as a builder and carpenter. To the other part I assigned Iorgi and Furata who were youngsters (*puriles*); they took Ianne as he was a skilled worker (*mastriu*), and Sanctu Petru took Iorgi and Furata who were youngsters (*puriles*). Witnesses: my lord iudike Barusone, Ithoccor de Sevin, Egithu his brother, Iorgi d'Iscanu, Therkis de Nureki, Mariane de Valles, Gosantine de Cannas and his entourage (*e ckita sua*).

32. Donation. *Of servants.*
Bittoria de Nurra, who was daughter of priest Gabino Pulla, made a request to Sagio de Capriles and to Maria de Valles, who were the lords of Vittoria de Nurra, as she [and another] had got married together. They had five children: four girls and one boy. Then, when we came to divide [their services] with the local people (*cun Sardos*), we took the girls, two [females] for one [male], who were of sound mind. The boy, who was a juvenile, we left in common. We shared equally [the services] of Iorgia and Greca; they took Iorgia and I [took] Greca. We shared Maria and Furata equally; they took Maria, and I [took] Furata for Sanctu Petru. Gavino we left in common. Witness: his own lord (*su donnu suo*).

33. Dispute: *Of servants.*
I, priest Iorgi Maiule, note in this condaghe, recourse to a hearing (*corona*) against Gunnari d'Oiun, Gunnari de Nurecki and Baru de Castavar concerning

p[ro] fiios de Barbara Rasa, ca no[n] fuit pettita e mandicavansilos kene 'nde
dare a sS[an]c[t]u Pet[ru]. [Et] ego tenninde corona de iudike Barusone in
Ardar, e binkilos ca non fekerat pettita s'ankilla de S[an]c[t]u Pet[ru], vorthe a
ttuturo, ki la levarat; e pus co los vinki torraitimilos iudike tottos VI sos fiios de
Barbara Rasa, a Iorgi, [et] a Iorgia, [et] ad Aravona, [et] ad Iscurthi, [et] a Ianne,
et a lLeo. E cco morivit iudike Barusone, levarunimilos etro; [et] ego, tenninde
corona de donnikellu Pet[ru] in Kitarone, uve furun donnos ki 'nde kertavan
p[ro] 'llos, Baru de Castavar, e Mariane su nepote, [et] Egithu d'Urieke e generos
de Gunnari d'Oiun; [et] indulserunimi sa iura p[ro] S[an]c[t]u Pet[ru], et si 'nde
kertat alikis p[ro] 'llos, in anima mea 'nde iuren servos de S[an]c[t]u Pet[ru],
p[ro] fiios de Barbara Rasa, ca non bi abean bias in illos. T[este]s: primus De[us]
12v o[mn]ip[otens], | deinde su do[n]nu meu iudike Barusone, e donnu Petru de
Serra Cigulu, ki iudicavat su kertu in Ardar; e de cande tenni corona in Kitarone,
donnikellu Petru, e Bolorike de Trifiu.

34. *De s[er]vos.*

Ego piscopu Iorgi, ki ponio in ecustu co[n]dake de S[an]c[t]u Pet[ru] de Silki
a Iorgia Pala, [et] a Iscurthi, [et] a Barbara, fiios de Barbara Rasa, ca torran ad
issos sos donnos paperos, ki los inperavan inanti. [Et] ego te[n]ninde corona
de iudike Mariane de Laccon, ca mi las avean levatas e ccoiuvaranilas cu[n]
servos issoro, kene las petire, nen a do[n]nu, nen a ma[n]datore de S[an]c[t]u
Pet[ru], e nen a fr[ate]s issoro; [et] issos kertarunimi in Ardar ca 'pettitas vos
las aviamus a ccoiuvarelas cun servos n[ost]ros.' Iudicarunilis ad issos a des-
timonios ca las avean pettitas a donnos, [et] issos no los potterun aver; issara
lis poserun a cKitarone, no los potterun aver sos destimo[n]ios; derunili iura
assu mandatore de cl[es]ia, a Furatu de Savitanu, ca no[n] fekerun pettitas
p[er] ecusta .+. e torrait iudike tottu su fetu dessas colivertas meas. T[este]s:
su donnu meu iudike Mariane de Lacon, e do[n]nikellu Petru, [et] Ithoccor de
13r Thori, e Bosoveckesu de Gitil, maiore d'iscolca, e Gosantine de | Thori, e Dor-
gotori d'Ussan.

35. Parthitura. *De s[er]vos.*

Ego piscopu Iorgi ki partivi sos filios de pr[e]b[iter]u Migale e de Maria Capillu cum pr[e]b[iter]u Sursitanu e ccun Gosantine de Farfare, ki fuit maiore d'iscola

the children of Barbara Rasa [for the reason] that [permission] was not sought nor given by Sanctu Petru while they were being used [for work]. I, making recourse to the hearing of iudike Barusone in Ardar (Árdara), won [the case] against them as a request had not been made for the female servant of Sanctu Petru. In fact, it was the opposite: they had taken her. After I had defeated them, the iudike returned to me all six of the children of Barbara Rasa—Iorgi, Iorgia, Aravona, Iscurthi, Ianne, and Leo. When iudike Barusone died, they took them from me again, so I had recourse to a hearing of *donnikellu* Petru at Kitarone (Caddaroni-Sant'Eusebio) where the lords were who were arguing about them, [namely] Baru de Castavar, Mariane his nephew, Egithu d'Urieke, and the sons-in-law of Gunnari d'Oiun. They spared me from swearing on behalf of Sanctu Petru, but if there is any dispute about them, [then] upon my soul, the servants of Sanctu Petru will swear regarding the children of Barbara Rasa, [such] that they will have no way [to claim] them. Witnesses: before God Almighty, my lord iudike Barusone, lord Petru of Serra Cigulu, who judged the dispute in Árdara and, from the time I had recourse to the hearing at Kitarone, *donnikellu* Petru, and Bolorike de Trifiu.

34. *Of servants.*
I, bishop Iorgi, register in this condaghe of Sanctu Petru de Silki that Iorgia Pala, Iscurthi, Barbara—the children of Barbara Rasa—have returned to their smallholding lords (*donnos paperos*) who had made use of them beforehand. I had recourse to a hearing of iudike Mariane de Laccon because 'they have taken them from me, and have married [other] servants of theirs without having sought [permission] either from their lord or the representative (*mandatore*) of Sanctu Petru or from their brothers. They disputed [this with] me at Ardar (Árdara) because 'we sought your permission to marry them with our servants!'' They decided that they should bring witnesses about what they had sought for them from their lords. They were unable to bring them [as witnesses]. Then, they made a request for them at Kitarone (Caddaroni-Sant'Eusebio), but they were not able to have the witnesses [attend]. They called the representative (*mandatore*) of the church, Furatu de Savitanu, to swear on this cross that they had not made any requests, and the iudike returned all the offspring of my female servants (*colivertas*). Witnesses: my lord iudike Mariane de Lacon, *donnikellu* Petru; Ithoccor de Thori, Bosoveckesu de Gitil the head of the ward (*maiore d'iscolca*), Gosantine de Thori, and Dorgotori d'Ussan.

35. Division. *Of servants.*
I, bishop Iorgi, divided the offspring of the priest Migali and of Maria Capillu with the priest Sursitanu and with Gosantine de Farfare, who was the head of

in Ogosilo; parthinde a nnatias, S[an]c[t]u Pet[ru] levait a Gavini [et] a Matrona [et] ad Ithoccor, e S[an]c[t]a Barbara levait a Pet[ru] et a Juvanne [et] a Gosantine; [et] ad Anna, ki fuit in fascas, deim[us]ila a nnutricare, ca fuit orfana de mama e ed patre, e nnutricatila Iusta Gilligia, e deim[us]indeli su lat[us] ca la nutricait, [et] iss'ateru lat[us] remasit ad in cumone. T[este]s: sos cantos vi furon.

36. P[ro] Pet[ru] Infante. *De s[er]vos.*
Petru Infante intregu de S[an]c[t]u Petru fuit co coiuvait cun Biola, ankilla de S[an]c[t]a Maria d'Urgeke; fekerun II fiios, a Bonella, [et] ad Urgekitana; a Bonella levaitila S[an]c[t]a Maria, e sS[an]c[t]u Petru levaitila ad Urgekitana.

37. *De s[er]vos.*
Coivuait Urgekitana cun Furatu ki fuit servu de rennu; fekerun II fiios, a Pe[tru]
[et] a Gosantine; S[anct]u Pet[ru] de Silki levaitilu a Gosa[n]tine, e rrennu
levaitilu a Pet[ru]. E Gosantine coivuait cu[m] Maria Napulitana, ankilla de
13v do[n]na Iorgia, fekerun V fiios; a cKipriane | [et] ad Urgekitana, e llat[us] de
Maria levarun paperos; [et] a Ianne, [et] a Pet[ru], e llat[us] de Maria levaitilos
S[an]c[t]u Pet[ru] de Silki. E Ianne levaitila a Iusta Canio, ankilla de paperos;
fekerun IIII fiios; a Maria [et] ad Olisave, levarunilos paperos; a Pet[ru], [et] ad
Urgekitana levaitilos S[an]c[t]u Petru.

38. Coiuviu. *De s[er]vis.*
Petru coiuvait cun Iusta Vola ankilla de paperos; fekerun II fiios: a Maria levar-
unila paperos, [et] a cKipriane levaitilu S[an]c[t]u Pet[ru]. Maria coiuvait
cun Gosantine de Nurra ki fuit de paperos; fekerun VI fiios; levarun appus
patre a Ianne, [et] ad Anna, [et] a Iusta; sos III pus mama remaserun ad in
cumone cun paperos. Et osca parthivim[us] cun donnu Gosantine de Mularia,
parthivim[us] a boluntate de pare, isse levaitila a Bona, e sS[an]c[t]u Petru
levaitilu a Pet[ru]. Coiuvait Urgekitana cun Iorgi Carta, servu de paperos;
fekerun V fiios, a Maria [et] a Pet[ru] levarunilos app[us] patre, ki furun de ten-
ner opus; [et] issos III apus mama, sos II ca furun pithinnos fekeruni[n]de unu.
14r Parthivilos ego cun | iudike Mariane, e ccun do[n]nu Comita su fr[at]e, ante
su avu iudike Barusone in Salvennor; a Gosantine posilu ad una parte ca fuit
mannu, [et] a Ianne [et] a Bona posilos ad atera parte; issos levarunilu a Gos-
antine, e sS[an]c[t]u Pet[ru] levaitilos a Bona [et] a Ianne, ca furun pithi[n]nos

the ward (*maiore d'iscolca*) at Ogosilo (Osilo). Dividing by birthdate: Sanctu Petru took Gavino, Matrona, and Ithoccor; Sancta Barbara took Petru, Iuvanne, and Gosantine. Anna, who was in swaddling clothes, we gave to be brought up for she was orphaned of mother and father, so Iusta Gilligia is bringing her up; we gave her [services] to the part who brought her up, and the other part [of her services] remained in common. Witnesses: everyone who was there.

36. Concerning Petru Infante. *Of servants.*
Petru Infante, who was wholly serving (*intregu*) Sanctu Petru, married Biola, a female servant (*ankilla*) of Sancta Maria d'Urgeke (Urgeghe, in Florinas). They had two children, Bonella and Urgekitana. Sancta Maria took Bonella, and Sanctu Petru took Urgekitana.

37. *Of servants.*
Urgekitana married Furatu who was a servant of the realm (*servu de rennu*). They had two sons, Petru and Gosantine. Sanctu Petru took Gosantine, and the realm took Petru. Gostantine married Maria Napulitana, female servant of lady Iorgia. They had five children: Kipriane and Urgekitana. Half [the services] of Maria, the smallholders (*paperos*) took; Ianne, Petru, and [the other] half of [the services] of Maria, Sanctu Petru took. Ianne took [as wife] Iusta Canio, a female servant of the smallholders (*ankilla de paperos*). They had four children: the smallholders took Maria and Olisave; Sanctu Petru took Petru and Urgekitana.

38. Marriage. *Of servants.*
Petru married Iusta Vola, a female servant of smallholders (*ankilla de paperos*). They had two children. The smallholders (*paperos*) took Maria, and Sanctu Petru took Kipriane. Maria married Gostantine de Nurra who was one of the smallholders. They had six children. They took from the father's side, Ianne, Anna, and Iusta. The three on the mother's side remain shared with the smallholders. Later, we made a division [of services] with Gosantine de Mularia. We divided them both by consent: he took Bona, and Sanctu Petru took Petru. Urgekitana married Iorgi Carta, a servant of the smallholders. They had five children: they took Maria and Petru on the father's side, who were [old enough] to do work. Of the three from the mother's side, two were minors that made up one [share]. I divided them with iudike Mariane and with lord Comita, his brother, before his uncle, iudike Barusone, at Salvénnor. I gave Gostantine to one party because he was an adult (*mannu*), and Ianne and Bona I gave to the other party. They took Gostantine, and Sanctu Petru took Bona and Ianne. As

los levai p[ro] unu. T[e]st[es]: anbos iudikes, iudike Barusone, e iudike Mariane, e buiakesu maiore de ianna Mariane de Valles, sendevi su mandatore suo Simione Pinnithar.

39. *De s[er]vis.*
Coiuvait Maria Solina, cun servu de S[an]c[t]a Nastasia, cun pr[e]b[iter]u Ianne Macle; fekerun III fiios, a Iorgia, [et] a Mikine, [et] a Iusta. A Iorgia levaitila S[an]c[t]u Pet[ru], [et] a Mikine levait S[an]c[t]a Nastasia, e Iusta remasit ad in cumone.

40. Postura.
Ego, piscopu Iorgi, ki ponio in ecustu co[n]dake de S[an]c[t]u Pet[ru] de Silki, p[ro] cantu '[n]ke poserun a S[an]c[t]u Pet[ru] cantu l'appi ego sa cl[esi]a in manu. Positivi a S[an]c[t]u Pet[ru] Iusta d'Ortu fundam[en]tu cantu 'nke
14v aveat, [et] iss'ateru lat[us] ki fuit dessos nepotes | co[mp]orailillu. Deili ad Elene d'Ortu II baccones, e pannu intintu, e pannu albu, e llenthu, p[ro]ssa parthone sua, e p[ros]sa parthone dessos fr[ate]s, de Gosantine e de Gosma, ki morran enios. Pettitilila sa parthone sa mama a iudike, e iudike deitilila, e mandicaisila in bita sua; [et] ad ora de morte sua mandaitimi a mimi, e posili pannu a mortaia, e ccantaili XL missas, e benedisstimila sa parthone sua dessa corte [et] issu cuniatu suo de Gortoni, e bacante, e ppumu e fficu cantu vi aveat, e t[er]ras d'agrile ue [et] ue las aveat; [et] ego benedissilila assu do[n]nu meu S[an]c[t]u Pet[ru]. T[este]s: pr[e]b[iter]u Gavini Thanpuia su no[n]nu, [et] totta villa. Et ego armailu tottu su munistere ave novu, e pposiui o[mn]ia regenthia, [et] de aram[entu], [et] de vinias, [et] de ortu, e ccupas, e berbekes, e ccap[ra]s, [et] ebbas, tottu ego vi parai p[ro] a[n]i[m]a mea. Positivi do[n]nu Barusone, e donna Muscu a S[an]c[t]u Pet[ru], a cCumine Tropoti [et] a Iuste Savitanu.

41. *De s[er]vis.*
Positivi a S[an]c[t]u Pet[ru] do[n]na Iorgia ave Turthevi, a Bonisinda de Silki,
15r [et] Petru | Tianu, [et] a ffiiu d'Andria Pelegrine, cum parthone issoro.

42. Kertu. *De s[er]vos.*
Ego piscopu Iorgi ki ponio in ecustu co[n]dake de S[an]c[t]u Pet[ru] de Silki, a Muscu de Ioscla, [et] a lLukia d'Ispata ki furun fiias de Iulitta de Ioscla e de Pet[ru] Frabu, ki furun intregos de S[an]c[t]u Pet[ru] de Silki e ffugiruninke a Gallul; [et] ego posinkelis in fattu a iudike ki las aveat, [et] ego pettililas naran-

they were minors, I took them as a single share. Witnesses: both iudikes, iudike Barusone and iudike Mariane, Mariane de Valles chief house-guard (*buiakesu maiore de ianna*), and Simione Pinnithar his representative (*mandatore*) also being present.

39. *Of servants.*
Maria Solina married a servant of Sancta Nastais, priest Ianne Macle. They had three children: Iorgia, Mikine, and Iusta. Sanctu Petru took Iorgia, and Sancta Nastasia took Mikine. Iusta remained in common.

40. Donation.
I, bishop Iorgi, note in this condaghe of Sanctu Petru de Silki everything that [benefactors] gave to Sanctu Petru when I had the church in my charge (*in manu*). Iusta d'Ortu assigned to Sanctu Petru all the land he had; the other half, which was of his nephews, I purchased. I gave Elene d'Ortu two preserved hams (*baccones*), dyed cloth, white cloth, and linen cloth for her division and for the division of her brothers, Gostantine and Gosma, who both died childless (*enios*). The mother requested the division to the iudike, and the iudike gave her it, and she benefitted from it during her lifetime. At the hour of her death, she instructed me personally and I assigned funereal cloth [that was needed] for singing forty masses. She blessed me with the share of her farmyard (*corte*), her enclosure (*cuniatu*) at Gortoni, unused land (*bacante*), any pear or fig tree she had there, and wherever she had lands for cultivation (*terras d'agrile*). I faithfully committed it to my lord Sanctu Petru. Witnesses: his grandfather (*su nonnu*) priest Gavino Thanpuia, and the whole village. I furnished the monastery from the start and gave all types of equipment (*regenthia*), of ploughlands (*de aramentu*), vineyards, a vegetable garden (*ortu*), barrels (*cupas*), sheep, goats, and horses—I paid for all these for [the salvation of] my own soul. Lord Barusone and lady Muscu donated [this] to Sanctu Petru, Cumine Tropiti, and Iuste Savitanu.

41. *Of servants.*
I, lady Iorgia from Turthevi, grant to Sanctu Petru: Bonisina de Silki, Petru Tianu, and the son of Andria Pelegrine along with their share.

42. Dispute. *Of servants.*
I, bishop Iorgi, note in this condaghe of Sanctu Petru de Silki: Muscu de Ioscla and Lukia d'Ispata children of Iulitta de Ioscla and Petru Frabu, who were full servants (*intregos*) at Sanctu Petru de Silki, fled to Gallul (Gallura). I put this fact to the iudike who might have them [there], and I made a request for them

deli ca 'de S[an]c[t]u Petru sun tottos iiii intregos.' [Et] isse naraitimi ca 'a
tTherkis d'Orbei [et] ad Egithu su fr[at]e los dei.' [Et] ego andai a sSalasa ad
uve los iusserat, e naraili ca 'torratemi sas ankillas meas, ki sun pecuiares de
S[an]c[t]u Pet[ru], e no mi las torrait.' [Et] ego andai a ccorona dessu do[n]nu
meu, de iudike Barusone a cCurcaso e nnuntharunimilu e bennit, e kertai cun
ille, e binkilu ca furun servos de S[an]c[t]u Pet[ru] in co los tenni a nnum[en].
T[este]s de ca vinki e mi los torrait, su do[n]nu meu iudike Barusone, e do[n]nu
Mariane de tThori, e do[n]nu Dorgotori de Vosove, e do[n]nu Pet[ru] de Serra,
15v e maiorales cantos vi | furun. [Et] osca levaitimilas a llarga e ccoiuvaitilas cun
servos suos, sene mi las peter; a Muscu coiuvaitila cun Ianne Gemellu, [et] a
lLukia deitila a sSimione de Cuniatu. [Et] ego vocailos a ccorona dessu do[n]nu
meu, de iudike Barusone, ca las coiuvait ad tortu meu; [et] issos kertarunimi c'
'a bolu[n]tate de pare los coiuvaim[us].' Kerverunilis destimonios e no los pot-
terun aver; iurait a gruke .+. su mandatore meu, Bonellu, ca 'ad tutturo dessu
do[n]nu meu los coiuvarun, e meu;' torrarunimilas issara in corona cun fiios
cantos avean, ave[n]de Muscu duos fiios fattos, a Pet[ru] [et] a Iusta, [et] a
Ianne. T[e]st[es]: su do[n]nu meu iudike Barusone, e do[n]ne, Mariane de
Serra, [et] Ithoccor de Varru.

43. Kertu. *De s[er]vis.*
Ego piscopu Iorgi ki ponio in ecustu co[n]dake de S[an]c[t]u Pet[ru] p[ro]
cando 'nke fugivit Maria de Canake ki fuit ankilla intrega de S[an]c[t]u Petru
de Silki, e ffuraratinkela Migali Aketu, ki fuit servu de Mariane de Castavar iii
16r pedes e pede | de S[an]c[t]a Maria de Cotronianu; [et] a mimi ca mi par-
vit male ca mi la furarat, e cca vi aveat paperu, e cca fuit seneke, andavi e
llevaindela, e ttorraila assa domo de S[an]c[t]u Petru. [Et] avendemila levata,
se mi armait etro Migali Achetu, e llevaitimindela etro a llarga. Et a mimi ca mi
'nde aveat fattu turpe duas vias, andavi cun sos servos de S[an]c[t]u Pet[ru] e
llevaindela; [et] avendemila levata ave Cotronianu uve fuit cun illa, me secutait
in via Mariane de Castavar, e nnaraitimi ca 'dass(a)telos umpare, e ssi faken fetu
p[ro]de nd'appat S[an]c[t]u Pet[ru] dessa parte mea.' E kertande gasi umpare
andaim[us] a fFiculinas de Castellu, uve fuit su curatore do[n]nu Mariane de
Vosove, e posim[us]nollu a destimoniu, e dassaimusilos umpare, in fine de si
fakean fetu umpare d'esser tottu de S[an]c[t]u Pet[ru], e de no[n] bi aver bias
Mariane. T[este]s: Dorgotori de Gunale, [et] Ithoccor Manata arm[en]tariu de
S[an]c[t]u Gaviniu, e Gosantine de Nurdole, e Iorgi Locco, e Ianne Papusellu:

saying that, 'all four are full servants of Sanctu Petru de Silki!' He told me, 'I gave them to Therkis d'Orbei and to Egithu!' I went to Salasa where he had bid them [go] and I told him [Therkis d'Orbei], 'return my female servants to me as they are property of Sanctu Petru!' But they did not return them to me. I went to the hearing of my lord, iudike Barusone, at Curcaso (La Crucca). They summoned him and he came, and I sued him and won because they were servants of Sanctu Petru whom I could mention by name. Witnesses that I won and that they were returned: my lord iudike Barusone, lord Mariane de Thori, lord Dorgotori de Vosove, and lord Petru de Serra. All the major lords (*maiorales*) were present. Later, he [Therkis d'Orbei] wrongfully appropriated them and married them with his servants without having asked my permission. Muscu married Ianne Gemellu, and Lukia was given [in marriage] to Simione de Cuniatu. I brought this to the hearing of my lord, iudike Barusone, that he had married them to my disadvantage. They disputed this [saying] that, 'we married them both willingly!' They demanded witnesses, but they were unable to bring any. My representative (*mandatore*), Bonellu, swore on the cross that 'they married them against my will and that of my lord!' They returned them to me at the hearing with all the children they had, Muscu having had two (*sic*) children, Petru, Iusta, and Ianne. Witnesses: my lord iudike Barusone, lord Mariane de Serra, and Ithoccor de Varru.

43. Dispute. *Of servants.*
I, bishop Iorgi, [make a] note in this condaghe of Sanctu Petru de Silki concerning when Maria de Canake (Caniga), who was a full (*intrega*) female servant of Sanctu Petru de Silki, ran away, and Migali Aketu, who was a servant [giving] three-quarters [service] to Mariane de Castavar and one-quarter to Sancta Maria de Cotronianu (Codrongianos) snatched her away. It seemed to me wrong that he had taken her away and that he was a smallholder (*paperu*), so I went to take her back and return her to the church (*domo*) of Sanctu Petru. Having taken her back to me, Migali Aketu conspired to take her away again, and so he did me wrong twice. I went with the servants of Sanctu Petru and retrieved her. Having taken her from Contronianu where he was with her, Mariane de Castavar pursued me down the road and said to me, 'Leave them together as they will have offspring that Sanctu Petru will have from my share!' Arguing together in this way, we went to Ficulinas de Castellu where there was the *curatore*, lord Mariane de Vosove, and we called on him as a witness. In the end, we left it uneven so that if they would have children, they would all be of Sanctu Petru, and that Mariane would have no grounds [to claim them]. Witnesses: Dorgotori de Gunale, Ithoccor Manata administrator (*armentariu*) de Sanctu Gaviniu, Gosantine de Nurdole, Iorgi Locco, and Ianne Papusellu. If

16v e ssorti kertund'at esser no[n] dubitet ispiiarelu do[n]nu | ki bi aet esser in S[an]c[t]u Petru.

44. *De s[er]vis.*
Ego piscopu Iorgi ki tenni corona dessu do[n]nu meu iudike Barusone, p[ro] Muscu de Ioscla ki mi mandicavan a ffura Therchis d'Orvei, [et] Egithu; [et] ego tenni[n]de corona cun illos, e binkilos ca fuit ankilla intrega de S[an]c[t]u Pet[ru] de Silki; [et] ego iurainde a gruke .+. ca fuit de S[an]c[t]u Petru, e ttorraitimila issara su do[n]nu meu iudike Barusone, avende II fiios fattos, a Pet[ru] [et] a Iusta. T[e]st[es] ante ken iurai e binki, do[n]nu Mariane de Serra, [et] Ithoccor de Varru, e Pet[ru] de Serra, e maiorales ca[n]tos vi furun in sa corona. [Et] osca torrarun etro appare, a ffura co [et] innanti. E ssende umpare morivit su maritu, Ianne Gemellu; e pus co morivit Ianne Gemellu benneru[n] sos donos suos e llevarun totta sa casa issoro, canta pararan umpare, e domos, e binias, e II orrios plenos de lavore, e II cupas de vinu, e CL argenthola de linu, e XXX inter discos, e cconcas, [et] I serviente, [et] I mola; e iettaruni[n]dela, ad issa [et] assos fiios, kene 'nde lis dare dessa casa, e sS[an]c[t]u Pet[ru] levaitsi sos
17r homines. T[este]s: Dorgotori de Roma, [et] Ithoccor de Kerki | e Petru de Setilo; custos vi furun kerra 'nde levavan issos sa casa, e sS[an]c[t]u Pet[ru] levait sos homines.

45. Kertu. *De s[er]vis.*
Ego piscopu Iorgi Maiule ki ponio in ecustu co[n]dake de S[an]c[t]u Pet[ru] de Silki, p[ro] Maria de funtana ki fuit ankilla de S[an]c[t]u Pet[ru], e fforricatila Dericcor de Martis, e ffekitiuilu a Iuste Lassu, [et] andaivi e llevaindelu pus co se fekit de servire; [et] isse vennit osca e furatimindelu [et] ego andaivi p[ro] levarendelu e no mi lu voluit dare, narandemi ca 'fiiu meu est.' [Et] ego andai assu do[n]nu meu a iudike Barusone e nnunthaitimilu a ccorona; e kertai cun illu e binkilu, ca l'aveat fattu in furrithu, in s'ankilla de S[an]c[t]u Pet[ru]; [et] issara mi torrarun e mama e fiiu, uve fakeat corona in Curcaso. T[este]s: su do[n]nu meu iudike Barusone, e do[n]nu Mariane de Thori, e do[n]nu Pet[ru] de Serra, e Therkis de Nureki, curatore de Romania, e Dorgotori de Sogostos.

46. Kertu. *De s[er]vis.*
Ego piscopu Iorgi Maiule ki ponio in ecustu co[n]dake de S[an]c[t]u Pet[ru] de Silki ca mi la furait ad Inbenia Plana Gosantine de Nurki, e Gosantine d'Arcu-
17v liki a Borconani, [et] ego andavala | kerende in adteru locu; [et] ego p[ro]vaila a IIII annos de co l'avea fugita, ca fuit in Borconani, [et] ego andavi [et]

there is a dispute, let whoever is in charge (*donnu*) of Sanctu Petru be in no doubt to reject [any claim].

44. *Of servants.*
I, bishop, Iorgi, had recourse to a hearing of my lord, iudike Barusone, concerning Muscu de Ioscla [from] whom Therchis d'Orvei and Egithu had wrongfully benefitted. I appealed at the hearing against them and I defeated them as she was a full (*intrega*) female servant of Sanctu Petru de Silki, and I swore on the cross that she was of Sanctu Petru; my lord iudike Barusone then returned her to me, having had two children, Petru and Iusta. Witnesses before whom I had sworn and won: lord Mariane de Serra, Ithoccor de Varru, Petru de Serra, and all the major lords (*maiorales*) who were there at the hearing. Later, they [Muscu and her husband] returned again undercover as before. While they were together, the husband, Ianne Gemellu, died. After Ianne Gemellu died, his lords (*donnos*) came and took all the belongings they had acquired together: property, vineyards, two grain [containers] full of wheat, two barrels of wine, forty lengths (*argenthola*) of linen, thirty plates and pots in total, a grinder and a grindstone (*mola*). They drove her out and her children without giving them [a share] of the belongings. Sanctu Petru took the [services of the] men (*homines*). Witnesses: Dorgotori de Roma, Ithoccor de Kerki, and Petru de Setilo. These were there when they took the belongings and Sanctu Petru took the men.

45. Dispute. *Of servants.*
I, bishop Iorgi Maiule, note in this condaghe of Sanctu Petru de Silki that Maria de Funtana was a full (*intrega*) female servant of Sanctu Petru. Dericcor de Martis had an affair with her and they had [a child] Iuste Lassu. I went and took him after he reached [the age] to give service. Later, he [Dericcor] came and stole him back. I went to take him, but he did not want to give me him, saying that, 'he is my son!' I went to my lord iudike Barusone and he summoned me to a hearing (*corona*). I sued him [Dericcor] and won as he had done this secretly with a female servant of Sanctu Petru, and so the mother and son were returned to me when the hearing was held at Curcaso (La Crucca). Witnesses: my lord iudike Barusone, lord Mariane de Thori, lord Petru de Serra, Therkis de Nurecki *curatore* of Romangia, and Dorgotori de Sogostos.

46. Dispute. *Of servants.*
I, bishop Iorgi Maiule, note in this condaghe of Sanctu Petru de Silki [that] Gostantine de Nurki (La Corte) and Gostantine d'Arculiki stole Inbenia Plana from me [and was taken to] to Borconani. I went looking in various places, but I had evidence from three years before that she had fled and was in Bor-

accataimila, avende III fiios fattos, e giraitsemi [et] in mama [et] in fiios; [et] ego andai a iudike Barusone a [n]Nulabros, e nuntharunimilos a Gosantine de Nurki, [et] a Gosantine d'Arculiki, e kertarunimi ca 'mea intrega fuit Inbenia.' Iudicarunilis ad issos a destimonios [et] a ccarta ca fuit issoro intrega sa mama de Inbenia, e no[n] potterun aver nen carta, nen destimonios; derunili 'ssara iura assu mandatore de S[an]c[t]u Pet[ru], a fFuratu de Funtana, e iurait a gruke .+. e binki in Inbenia Plana, fiia ki fuit de Maria Plana intrega de S[an]c[t]u Pet[ru]. T[este]s: su do[n]nu meu iudike Barusone, ki mi la torrait issara in corona, e do[n]nikellu Pet[ru], maiore, [et] Itthoccor de Thori, e Bosovekesu de Gitil, maiore.

47. Pettitura. *De ancilla.*
Ego piscopu Iorgi Maiule ki li petti muiere a pr[e]b[iter]u Istefane Solina, ki fuit servu intregu de S[an]c[t]u Pet[ru] de Silki, pettilila a Bittoria de Cannas e derunilila sos do[n]nos suos.

18r 48. Kertu. *De s[er]vos.*
Ego piscopu Iorgi Maiule ki tenni corona cun Gunnari d'Oiun, e ccun Baru de Castavar, p[ro] fiios de Ianne Rasu, ki furun servos de S[an]c[t]u Pet[ru] de Silki ca mi los avean levatos, e iudike Barusone torraitimilos in Ardar. E cco morivit iudike levarunimilos etro; [et] ego tenninde corona de do[n]nikellu Pet[ru] in Kitarone, cun Baru de Castavar, e ccu[n] Mariane su nepote, e ccun Egithu d'Urieke, e ccun duos generos de Gu[n]nari d'Oiun, e binkilos, [et] issos indulserunimi sa iura p[ro] S[an]c[t]u Pet[ru]. E ssi es tantu e 'nde kertat alikis pus morte mea, in anima mea 'nde iuren ca no[n] bi avean bias in fiios de Ianne Rasu.

49. Ockisura d'omine. *In Turthei.*
Ockisitilu Gosantine Culurione a Pet[ru] Pippi, ki fuit servu de do[n]nikella Iorgia, depus Turthebi, e llevaruninde su lat[us] appus Turthevi; [et] osca positilu su lat[us], do[n]nikella Iorgia, de Gosantine, a S[an]c[t]u Petru, cu[n] bolu[n]tate dessos fiios.

50. Postura. *De ancilla.*
Positivi a S[an]c[t]u Pet[ru] de Silki do[n]na Porosa de Thori a Iusta Papis, cun parthone sua, ave Murusas.

conani. I went [there] and claimed her back. Having had three children, she refused me; both the mother and the children. I went to iudike Barusone at Nulabros (Nulauro/Lunafras) and denounced Gostantine de Nurki and Gostantine d'Arculiki. They disputed this [saying] that 'Inbenia was my full (*intrega*) female servant!' The decided that they should call witnesses and a document (*carta*) [to confirm] that Inbenia's mother was a full (*intrega*) female servant of theirs, but they were not able to produce either a document or witnesses. Then, they had the representative (*mandatore*) of Sanctu Petru, Furatu de Funtana, take an oath. He swore on the cross and I won, as Inbenia Plana, daughter of Maria Plana, was a full (*intrega*) female servant of Sanctu Petru. Witnesses: my lord iudike Barusone, who then returned her to me at the hearing; *donnikellu* Petru, the official (*maiore*); Itthoccor de Thori, and the official (*maiore*), Bosevekesu de Gitil.

47. Request. *Of a female servant.*
I, bishop Iorgi Maiule, requested the wife of priest Istefane Solina who was a full (*intregu*) servant of Sanctu Petru di Silki, requesting her from Bittoria de Cannas. Her lords (*donnos*) granted her.

48. Dispute. *Of servants.*
I, bishop Iorgi Maiule, had recourse to a hearing against Gunnari d'Oiun and Baru de Castavar about the children of Ianne Rasu who were servants of Sanctu Petru de Silki they had taken from me, and whom iudike Barusone had returned to me at Ardar[a]. When the iudike died, they took them from me again, so I had recourse to a hearing of *donnikellu* Petru, lord at Kitarone (Caddaroni-Sant'Eusebio) against Baru de Castavar, Mariane his nephew, Egithu d'Urieke, and against Gunnari d'Oiun's two sons-in-law (*generos*). I defeated them and they exempted me from swearing an oath for Sanctu Petru. If there is any dispute after my death, they will swear on my soul [instead] so that they have no grounds [to claim] Ianne Rasu's children.

49. Killing of a man. *In Turthe[v]i.*
Gostantine Culurione killed Petru Pippi who was a servant of *donnikella* Iorgia at Turthebi, half [of whom was taken] by Turthevi. Afterwards, donnikella Iorgia gave the half [share] of Gostantine to Sanctu Petru with the permission of the sons.

50. Donation. *Of a female servant.*
I, lady Porosa de Thori, granted to Sanctu Petru de Silki, Iusta Papis with her share [of services] at Murusas (Sant'Orsola).

18v 51. Postura. *De ancilla.*
Posit a S[an]c[t]u Pet[ru] iudike Gosantine a ffiios de Ia[n]ne Tillis, a Kipriane [et] I dessas feminas, a famiia, cum parthone issoro; sendenke arme[n]tariu Pet[ru] Canbella, e fFuratu de funtana ma[n]datore.

52. Postura. *Terras i[n] Turthei [et] in Norgia.*
Posit a S[an]c[t]u Pet[ru], Pet[ru] Tartasu terras tenende assa domo d'Istefane Lelle, ave secus.

53.
Posit a S[an]c[t]u Pet[ru] Gosantine d'Ennu II t[er]ras, I sutta Turthevi, [et] adtera in Norgia; sendenke arm[en]tariu Pet[ru] Canbella, e ma[n]datore Furatu de Funtana.

54. Postura. *In Turthei.*
Posit donnikella Iorgia a S[an]c[t]u Pet[ru] su petholu dessa terra ki fuit tenende assa vinia de S[an]c[t]u Pet[ru] in Turthevi, [et] issa matta dessa ficu, cu[n] boluntate dessos fiios, sendenke armentariu Gavini de Kerone.

55. Postura. *De s[er]vo.*
Posit donikellu Ithoccor a S[an]c[t]u Pet[ru] a fiiu de Forasticu Thinga, cu[n] parthone sua.

56. Tramutu. *De s[er]vos.*
Appit tramutu S[an]c[t]u Pet[ru] cun Comita de Thori p[ro] fiia d'Alanpi, p[ro] Maria Paraguri. Deitimi isse lat[us] de Istefane de Carros, e pede de Vittoria sa sorre, e p[ro]ssu pede ki mi restavat deitiminde su latus de Comita Paraguri, su
19r fiiu d'Alanpi ca fuit in fascas, p[ro] gatantu | mi deit su lat[us]. T[este]s: Pet[ru] Canbella, e cCristofore Iscarpa arm[en]tariu de S[an]c[t]u Pet[ru], e Pet[ru] su fr[at]e, e do[n]nikellu Comita ki fuit curatore de Romania.

57. P[ro] fetu de Iusta de Canake.
Ego piscopu Iorgi ki ponio in ecustu co[n]dake de S[an]c[t]u Pet[ru], p[ro]ssu fetu de Iusta de Canake, ki mi levavan a ckerbiclia Niscoli d'Erthas, [et] issos fr[ate]s. [Et] ego tenninde corona de iudike Barusone in Turres, sa die de sinotu, e binkilos iurandende a gruke .+. ca fuit tottu su fetu de Iusta de Canake de S[an]c[t]u Pet[ru], [et] issara mi torrarun sos homines a S[an]c[t]u Pet[ru].

51. Donation. *Of a female servant.*
Iudike Gostantine gave to Sanctu Petru, the sons of Ianne Tillis—Kipriane and one of the girls—with their division [of services] to the [church] community (*a famiia*). In the presence of Petru Canbella the administrator (*armentariu*), and Furatu de Funtana the representative (*mandatore*).

52. Donation. *Lands in Turthei and in Norgia.*
Petru Tartasu donated to Sanctu Petru lands adjacent to the house of Istefane Lelle, at the back.

53.
Gostantine d'Ennu granted two lands to Sanctu Petru: one below Turthevi and the other in Norgia, when there were the administrator (*armentariu*) Petru Canbella, and representative (*mandatore*) Furatu de Funtana.

54. Donation. *In Turthei.*
Donnikella Iorgia gave to Sanctu Petru the plot (*petholu*) which adjoins the vineyard of Sanctu Petru in Turthevi, and [also] the fig tree, with the consent of his sons in the presence of administrator (*armentariu*) Gavino de Kerone.

55. Donation. *Of a servant.*
Donnikellu Ithoccor gave to Sanctu Petru the child of Forasticu Thinga with his share.

56. Exchange. *Of servants.*
Sanctu Petru made an exchange of Comita de Thori for the daughter of Alanpi, Maria Paraguri. He gave me half share of Istefane de Carros, and a quarter (*pede*) of Vittoria his sister, and for the quarter that remains, he gave me the half share of Comita Paraguri, the son of Alanpi, who was [a baby] in swaddling (*in fascas*) on account of which he gave me half. Witnesses: Petru Canbella, Cristofore Iscarpa administrator (*armentariu*) of Sanctu Petru, and Petru his brother, and *donnikellu* Comita who was *curatore* of Romangia.

57. Concerning the offspring of Iusta de Canake.
I, bishop Iorgi, make a note in this condaghe of Sanctu Petru about the offspring of Iusta de Canake (Caniga) whom Niscoli d'Erthas (Ertas) and his brothers took from me by force (*a ckerbiclia*). I had recourse to a hearing (*corona*) of iudike Barusone in Turres (Porto Torres) on the day of the assembly (*sinotu*). I won, swearing on the cross that all the offspring of Iusta de Canake (Caniga) belonged to Sanctu Petru. Then, they returned the men (*homines*) to Sanctu

T[este]s: su do[n]nu meu iudike Barusone, e do[n]nu Mariane de Thori, e do[n]nikellu Pet[ru] de Serra, e Bosevekesu de Gitil, e Pet[ru] de Serra, e totu locu.

58. Postura. *De ancilla.*
Posit do[n]na Maria d'Arsum[en] a S[an]c[t]u Pet[ru] a Maria Furca, cun parthone sua.

59. Postura. *De s[er]vos.*
Posit a S[an]c[t]u Pet[ru] do[n]nu Pet[ru] de Thori a Petru Melone, cu[n] parthone sua.

60. Postura. *De ancilla.*
Posit donu Pet[ru] de Thori, [et] issa muiere, a S[an]c[t]u Pet[ru] a Greca Pistis, cu[n] parthone sua.

61. Postura. *De saltu de S[er]ra de Calcargia, in Iennanu.*
Ego piscopu Iorgi Maiule ki ponio in ecustu co[n]dake p[r]ossu saltu ki 'nke
19v posit iudike Barusone a S[an]c[t]u Pet[ru] de Silki. Positinke su | saltu de serra de calcaria, cun bolu[n]tate dessos fiios. Es term[en] dessu saltu: ave sa foke de Iannanu, assu bruncu dessu ferru clesu, avinde tottuve s'atha, assa T[er]ra Rubia dessa via ki vaen sos d'Elba a Turres, tottuve via, appede dessu ponte, avinde tottuve mare isc'a sa foke; secandelu su saltu do[n]nu Mariane de Thori ki fuit curatore de Roma[n]ia.

62. Postura. *Saltu de petra lata apus Iennanu.*
Positinke iudike Mariane a S[an]c[t]u Pet[ru] su saltu de Pet[ra] Lata [et] issu gulbare maiore de Nuracati, cu[n] bolu[n]tate dessos fr[ate]s. Sun t[er]menes dessu saltu: dave su gulbare assu castru, s'atha, assa gruke dess'ena ki est oru sa via, assa pet[ra] iunpatu, uve sun sos thithiclos, assu patronu longu sup[ra] sa padule, avinde tottuve su sulcu a destra de Pet[ra] Lata, avinde su sulcu collat a manca d'Ena de Nikifori, a derettu assas pet[ra]s dessu Munime[n]tu de Gulparios, avinde tottuve via de Verale, avinde tottuve sa via essit isca ad uve s'oviat

Petru. Witnesses: iudike Barusone, lord Mariane de Thori, *donnikellu* Petru de Serra, Bosevekesu de Gitil, Petru de Serra, and [others] from the whole country (*totu locu*)

58. Donation. *Of a female servant.*
Lady Maria d'Arsumen gave Maria Furca to Sanctu Petru with her division (*parthone*).

59. Donation. *Of a servant.*
Lord Petru de Thori gave Petru Melone to Sanctu Petru with his division (*parthone*).

60. Donation. *Of a female servant.*
Lord Petru de Thori and his wife gave Greca Pistis to Sanctu Petru with her division (*parthone*).

61. Donation. *Of unworked land* (saltu) *from Serra de Calcargia in Iennenu* (*Gennano, Porto Torres*).
I, bishop Iorgi Maiule, put [an entry] in this condaghe regarding the unworked land (*saltu*) that iudike Barusone gave to Sanctu Petru de Silki. He granted the land (*saltu*) of Serra de Calcargia ('limestone ridge') with the consent of his sons. The boundary of the land is: [from] the mouth (*foke*) of [the stream at] Iannanu (Gennano, Porto Torres), to the hill of Ferru Clesu, going along the crag (*s'atha*) to the reddish ground (*terra rubia*) of the road that goes from Elba (Monte Elva) to Turres, keeping to the road, [then] to the foot (*appede*) of the bridge, and along the sea [front] until the mouth [of the stream]; dividing the land (*saltu*) [was] Mariane de Thori, who was the *curatore* of Romangia.

62. Donation. *Unworked land* (saltu) *of Petra Lata at Iennanu* (*Gennano, Porto Torres*).
Iudike Mariane donated to Sanctu Petru the unworked land (*saltu*) of Petra Lata and the main enclosure (*su gulbare maiore*) at Nuracati (Nuragaddu) with the consent of his brothers. The boundaries of the land (*saltu*) are: from the enclosure to the outcrop (*castru*), [to] the crag (*atha*), to the cross of the spring (*ena*) which is at the side of the road, passing the mamillated standing stone (*sa petra ... uve sun sos thithiclos*) to the large field (*patronu*) above the marsh (*padule*), going along the depression (*sulcu*) to the right of Petra Lata; [then] from the depression to the left of Ena de Nikifori ('the spring of Nikiforos'), straight on to the rocks of Munimentu de Gulparios ('the tomb of Gulparios'), from there along the Verale road; from there, along the road until it meets the

cu[n] sa via maiore ki vaen sos de Bionis a Turres, ave 'lla de Vanaria, avinde tot-
20r tuve sa via ki essit isc'a su bruncu claru assa padule de Nuracati, avinde sa serra | tottuve, assu bruncu dessu iunpatoriu dess'Ulumu, ivi iumpat ribu, e ccollat a destra dessu puthu, derettu assu bulbare. Secandelu su saltu donikellu Pet[ru] ki fuit curatore de Romania, e pupillu dessu saltu, e sservos de rennu Pet[ru] de Nurake, e Iorgi de Bonike, e Pet[ru] de Malai.

63. Postura. *In Iennanu.*
Positinke do[n]nikellu Pet[ru] a S[an]c[t]u Pet[ru] de Silki sa parte sua dessu saltu de Iannanu, ki parthiat cun sa sorre, do[n]nikella Iorgia, cun bolu[n]tate de 'ssa, e dandenke issa su gulbare claru a mare, dandenos via assas baccas uve furun d'intrare assu gulbare, ave sa foke a derettu ad ivi, dandelilu issa assu fr[at]e, ca no[n] levarat isse dessos gulbares.

64. *In eode[m] loco.*
Ego Pet[ru] Muthuru, ki kertai cun Gosanti[ne] de Kerki p[ro]ssu istanivi de Iannanu, p[ro]ssa parte ki fuit de donikellu Pet[ru] Maiore, ki poserat a S[an]c[t]u Pet[ru]; [et] ego binkindelu in corona dessu donnu meu iudike Gosantine de Laccon in S[an]c[t]a Maria d'Agustu in Turres, iurandende a gruke .+. T[este]s: su donnu meu iudike Gosantine de Laccon, e donnikellu Comita, e Gosa[n]tine d'Athen.

20v 65. *De ancilla.*
Ego Pet[ru] Canbella ki ponio in su condake de S[an]c[t]u Pet[ru] de Silki, p[ro] Furata de funtana ki fuit intrega de S[an]c[t]u Pet[ru], e furaruninkela servos de paperos, e iusseruninkela a cCoraso, [et] ego posilis in fattu e llevaindela ligata; ponendeminde destimo[n]ios, a Pet[ru] Mankia, [et] a Dorgotori de Kerki, ki fuit maiore d'iscolca; [et] osca bennerun e ffuraruninkela kene lis la dare nen do[n]nu, nen maiore; e ssi 'nde faken plus kertu do[n]nos depus patre, in anima mea 'nde iuren a gruke .+. ca no[n] fekit pettita alicando.

66. Kertu. *De ancilla.*
Ego Iorgi d'Okeri ki ponio in ecustu co[n]dake p[ro] Susanna Thana ki mi lebait a llarga pr[e]b[iter]u Gosantine Pira; [et] ego andai a iudike Mariane, e torraindeli berbu p[ro]ssa larga; e iudike mandaitili a do[n]nu Ithoccor de Thori,

main road that goes from Bionis (Biunisi) to Turres (Porto Torres) and Vanaria; from there, along the road until the hill by the marsh of Nuracati; from there, along the ridge to the hill of Iunpatoriu dess'Ulumu ('elm tree crossing-point') where it crosses the stream (*ribu*), passes to the right of the well (*puthu*), and goes towards the enclosure (*bulbare*). Donikellu Petru, who was *curatore* of Romangia and proprietor (*pupillu*) of the land (*saltu*), alienated it [with] servants of the realm (*rennu*), Petru de Nurake, Iorgi de Bonike, and Petru de Malai.

63. Donation. *In Iennanu (Gennano, Porto Torres).*
Donnikellu Petru donated to Sanctu Petru de Silki his share of the unworked land (*saltu*) of Iannanu (Gennano, Porto Torres), which he divided with his sister, *donnikella* Iorgia with her consent, giving the animal enclosure (*gulbare*) by the sea, and gave access for the cows to enter the enclosure straight from the mouth [of the water], giving this to her brother as he did not have any enclosures.

64. *At the same place.*
I, Petru Muthuru, was in dispute with Gosantine de Kerki concerning the lagoon (*istaniu*) at Iannanu (Gennano, Porto Torres), part of which belonged to *donnikellu* Petru Maiore ('the elder') who granted it to Sanctu Petru. I won [the case] at the hearing (*corona*) of my lord iudike Gostantine de Laccon at Sancta Maria d'Agustu in Turres (Porto Torres) by swearing on the cross. Witnesses: my lord iudike Gostantine de Laccon, *donnikellu* Comita, and Gosantine d'Athen.

65. *About a female servant.*
I, Petru Canbella, make [an entry] in the condaghe of Sanctu Petru de Silki concerning Furate de Funtana who was a full (*intrega*) female servant of Sanctu Petru and whom servants of smallholders (*paperos*) stole and took her to Coraso (Coros). I searched [for her] and took her back tied up, having as witnesses Petru Mankia and Dorgotori de Kerki who was the head of the ward (*maiore d'iscolca*). Later, they came and stole her without either lord (*donnu*) or an official (*maiore*) having given her away; if lords further dispute her ownership, upon my soul, [witnesses] will swear on the cross that no request was sought.

66. Dispute. *About a female servant.*
I, Iorgi d'Okeri, make [an entry] in this condaghe regarding Susanna Thana whom priest Gosantine Pira wrongfully took from me. I went to iudike Mariane and spoke with him about the appropriation. The iudike summoned Ithoccor

e bennit; [et] ego kertai cun ille ca mi la aveat levata a llarga sa coliverta mea; e iudike naraitili ca 'torrala s'ankilla de S[an]c[t]u Pet[ru], ca no[n] ti la volen dare;' [et] isse naraitili ca 'no la potho iscoiuvare;' e iudike naraitili ca 'fiios cantos aen faker u[m]pare, tottu los apat S[an]c[t]u Pet[ru].' T[este]s: do[n]nu
21r Gosantine | d'Athen, e do[n]nikellu Pet[ru] maiore, e Barusone de Setilo.

67. Postura. *De s[er]vo.*
Positinke iudike Mariane a S[an]c[t]u Pet[ru] de Silki lat[us] de Gavini Lelle, p[ro]ssu pede de Nastasia sa sorre, ki fuit de S[an]c[t]u Pet[ru], e deitila iudike Mariane a do[n]nikellu Pet[ru] maiore, ca li armait su vestare de Bosove. T[este]s ca vi lu posit su latu[s]de Gavini Lelle, do[n]nikellu Pet[ru], e Bosovekesu de Gitil, e Dorgotori d'Ussan.

68.[17] Kertu. *De s[er]vos.*
Ego Pet[ru] Muthuru ki kertai cun Dorgotori de Carvia, e ccun sos fr[ate]s, in corona de iudike Mariane in Turres, p[ro] Furatu Gattu, ca 'p[ro]gitteu mi lu levas k'est intregu de S[an]c[t]u Petru?' [Et] isse naraitimi ca 'no[n] bi aet bias S[an]c[t]u Pet[ru], ca meu est intregu e de fr[ate]s meos.' Kerverunili destimo[n]ios a Dorgotori de Carbia, [et] assos fr[ate]s, a cCurcaso ad uve fuit iudike, ca fuit suo, e no[n] pottit aver destimo[n]ios; derunili iura assu mandatore de cl[es]ia, a Furatu de Funtana, e iurait a gruke .+. ca 'Furatu Gattu intregu de S[an]c[t]u Pet[ru] est, ki non bi aet bias nemos.' [Et] issa[ra] partihivim[us] su fetu ante iudike ca IIII | fiios aveat d[e] servire. Levait Dorgotori [et] issos fr[ate]s a Maria [et] a Gavini appus mama, e S[an]c[t]u Pet[ru] levait a Ianne [et] a Gosantine app[us] patre; parthindenos a nnatias iudike in corona. T[este]s: do[n]nu Gosantine d'Athen, e Dorgotori d'Ussa[n], e do[n]nu Bosovekesu de Gitil maiore, e donnikellu Pet[ru] maiore. E kerra istrumait iudike corona me posit in manu d'Antoni Tranpas, maiore suo de Murusas, e de Pet[ru] Masala, e de Gosantine d'Arculiki, p[ro] levarende uniskis parte n[os]tra, [et] issos levarunsinde issara parte issoro a Briave in co abiam[us] parthitu in corona.

21v (marginal folio marker for the line beginning "hivim[us]")

69. Postura. *De s[er]vos.*
Positinke iudike Mariane [et] issa muiere do[n]na Susanna de Thori, a S[an]c[t]u Pet[ru], a Gosantine de Savitanu, [et] ad Elias Falke, dav'Ardar [et] a ffiiu de Pet[ru] d'Erthi, cun parthone issoro.

17 Cf. entry 82.

de Thori, and he came. I argued with him because he had stolen my female servant (*coliverta*). The iudike said to him: 'Return the servant of Sanctu Petru because they do not wish to concede her to you!' He replied to him that I cannot dissolve the marriage! The iudike said that any children they have will belong to Sanctu Petru. Witnesses: lord Gosantine d'Athen, *donnikellu* Petru Maiore, and Barusone de Setilo.

67. Donation. *Of a servant.*
Iudike Mariane granted to Sanctu Petru de Silki half [the services] of Gavino Lelle for a quarter of Nastasia, his sister, who was [a servant] of Sanctu Petru. Iudike Mariane gave her to *donnikellu* Petru Maiore ('the elder') because he had furnished his house at Bosove (Latte Dolce). Witnesses that he gave the half [services] of Gavino Lelle: *donnikellu* Petru, Bosovekesu de Gitil, and Dorgotori d'Ussan.

68. Dispute. *Of servants.*
I, Petru Muthuru, was in dispute with Dorgotori de Carvia and his brothers at the hearing (*corona*) of iudike Mariane at Turres (Porto Torres) concerning Furatu Gattu [asking], 'Why do you take from me [a servant] who is a full servant (*intregu*) of Sanctu Petru?' He told me that Sanctu Petru has no grounds because he is a full servant of mine and my brothers! They asked Dorgotori de Carbia and his brothers to produce witnesses that he was theirs at Curcaso (La Crucca) where the iudike was, but it was not possible to bring witnesses. The representative (*mandatore*) of the church, Furatu de Funtana, gave an oath and swore on the cross that Furatu Gattu is a full servant of Sanctu Petru and no one has any grounds [to claim his services]. Then we divided the offspring before the iudike that four sons had to serve. Dorgotori and his brothers took Maria and Gavino on the mother's side, and Sanctu Petru took Ianne and Gosantine from the father's side [with] the iudike dividing them by birth at the hearing. Witnesses: lord Gosantine d'Athen, Dorgotori d'Ussan, lord Bosovekesu de Gitil Maiore ('the elder'), *donnikellu* Petru Maiore. When iudike had closed the hearing, he placed me in the charge of Antoni Tranpas, his official (*maiore suo*) at Murusas (Sant'Orsola) to Petru Masala and Gosantine d'Arculiki regarding each of us taking his own part; and so, they each took their own part at Briave (Briai) where we made the division at the hearing (*corona*).

69. Donation. *Of servants.*
Iudike Mariane and his wife, lady Susanna de Thori, donated to Sanctu Petru, Gosantine de Savinatu, Elias Falke from Ardar (Árdara), and the sons of Petru d'Erthi with their share.

70. *De s[er]vis.*
Pettitili donnikellu Pet[ru] a iudike Mariane, a pr[e]b[iter]u Basili [et] ad Elene de Savitanu, [et] isse deitililos cun parthone issoro, [et] isse positilos a S[an]c[t]u Petru.

71. Postura. *De ancillis.*
Positinke iudike Gosantine a S[an]c[t]u Pet[ru], a sSusa[n]na P[ro]feta [et] a Maria d'Ulumos, cun parthone issoro.

22[r] 72. Kertu. *De s[er]vos.*
Ego Pet[ru] Muthuru ki ponio in ecustu co[n]dake de S[an]c[t]u Pet[ru], p[ro] kertu ki appit noscus donnikellu Gunnari, e Gosantine de Roma, e cComita de Carbia Manos-Mannas, e cComita de Serra, p[ro] fiios d'Istefane Barbaru, ca los levavan a S[an]c[t]u Pet[ru] cuios furu[n]; [et] ego torrainde verbu a iudike Gosantine, cun sa donna mea donna Theodora; e iudike positinos a nnatale S[an]c[t]i Gavini; [et] issa die kertai cun sos do[n]nos d'Istefane Barbaru, ca la levarat a llarga a Iorgia Cocone ki fuit ankilla de cl[es]ia, e cca vi andai e lu tenni e bi lu fusticai, e cca 'nde avea torratu verbu a iudike, [et] assu curatore, a donnu Ithoccor de Kerki, ki fuit curatore in Nurra. [Et] issara mi essiron a destimo[n]ios iudike [et] issu curatore p[ro] ca 'nde lis torra verbu, e cca me vi poserun a fusticareuilu; [et] issos homines dessa corona narrun ca 'pus co li essites bois a destimoniu, dateli iura assu servu de cl[es]ia.' [Et] ego iurainde a gruke .+. ca vi lu fusticai e cca 'nde lu iettai; [et] issara delegaru[n] ad esser tottu su fetu a ccl[es]ia. T[este]s: iudike Gosantine, e Barusone de Setilo, e Pet[ru]
22[v] d'Athen, | [et] Ithoccor su fr[at]e, e Gunnari de Thori, [et] totta corona.

73. Kertu. *De s[er]vos.*
Ego Pet[ru] Muthuru tenni corona cun Donotho de Maroniu, p[ro] fetu d'Iscurthi Pala e de Iorgi Barbaru, ki fuit servu suo intregu, [et] Iscurthi fuit intrega de S[an]c[t]u Pet[ru], ca mi 'nde kereat parte dessu fetu; [et] ego vi[n]kilu in corona de iudike Gosantine cun destimo[n]ios meos, ca vi lu batti, e cca vi li feki turpe, iurandende a gruke .+. cun duos destimonios meos; torrarun issara tottu su fetu a S[an]c[t]u Pet[ru]. E ppus co lu vin[ki] andaitivi e llevaitindela ad intro a Maria Pala fiia d'Iscurthi Pala; [et] ego andai a iudike e ttorraindeli verbu ca mi largarun; [et] isse co do[n]nu bonu mandaitivilu a donnu Barusone de Setilo, e ppredaitilu, e deitimindela s'ankilla de S[an]c[t]u Pet[ru]. T[este]s: donnikellu Gunnari, e donnikellu Pet[ru], e Barusone de Setilo, e Pet[ru] d'Athen, e Niscoli de Carbia, e Mariane Thanca.

70. *Of servants.*
Donnikellu Petru sought [permission] from iudike Mariane for the priest Basili and Elene de Savitanu, and he gave me them with their share and granted them to Sanctu Petru.

71. Donation. *Of female servants.*
Iudike Gosantine donated to Sanctu Petru, Susanna Profeta and Maria d'Ulumos with their share [of services].

72. Dispute. *Of servants.*
I, Petru Muthuru, note in this condaghe of Sanctu Petru a dispute that happened between ourselves and *donnikellu* Gunnari, Gosantine de Roma, Comita de Carbia Manos-Mannas ('big hands') and Comita de Serra regarding the sons of Istefane Barbaru whom they took from Sanctu Petru to whom they belonged. I spoke to iudike Gostantine with my wife, lady Theodora. The iudike convened us on the feast day of St Gavino, and on that day, I raised the argument about the lords (*sos donnos*) of Istefane Barbaru whom Iorgia Cocone—a female servant (*ankilla*) of the church—had taken unlawfully, [saying] that I went [after him], caught him and whipped him, and that I had spoken to the iudike and to the *curatore*, lord Ithoccor de Kerki who was *curatore* at Nurra. Then, iudike and the *curatore* were witnesses to that which I had spoken to them about and that they had given me [grounds] to whip him. The men of the hearing (*corona*) said that 'notwithstanding you are here as witnesses, you [also] had a servant of the church give an oath!' I also swore on the cross that I whipped him and pursued him (*lu iettai*). Then, they assigned all the offspring to be of the church. Witnesses: iudike Gosantine, Barusone de Setilo, Petru d'Athen, Ithoccor his brother, Gunnari de Thori, and the whole hearing.

73. Dispute. *Of servants.*
I, Petru Muthuru, had recourse to a hearing (*corona*) against Donotho de Maroniu concerning the offspring of Iscurthi Pala and Iorgi Barbaru who was a full (*intregu*) servant, and Iscurthi a full female servant of Sanctu Petru, because he [Donotho] claimed my share of the offspring. I won at the hearing (*corona*) of iudike Gosantine with my witnesses; then they returned the offspring to Sanctu Petru. After I had defeated him, he went and took for himself (*ad intro*) Maria Pala, daughter of Iscurthi Pala. So, I went to iudike and told him what they had taken from me. He, as a good lord (*donnu*), dispatched lord Barusone de Setilo to take him back and to give the female servant to Sanctu Petru. Witnesses: iudike *donnikellu* Gunnari, *donnikellu* Petru, Barusone de Setilo, Peter d'Athen, Niscoli de Carbia, and Mariane Thanca.

74. Kertu. *De s[er]vos.*
Ego Pet[ru] Canbella ki tenni corona cun Therkis de Carbia, e ccun Donotho de
23r Gorare, p[ro] Ianne Plana, e p[ro]ssa sorre Maria, e binkindelos | in corona de
iudike Gosantine in S[an]c[t]u Migali de Plaianu, e iurainde a gruke .+. in fattu
dessa carta de S[an]c[t]u Pet[ru] de Silki. T[este]s: donnikellu Comita ki 'nke
fuit curatore in Romania, e Mariane d'Ussan, e Petru de Roma.

75. Kertu. *De ancilla.*
Ego Pet[ru] Muthuru ki tenni corona de do[n]nikellu Comita, p[ro]ssu fetu de Iusta de Canake, ki mi levarat Niscoli d'Erthas, e binkilu in corona de iudike Gosantine de Laccon, e iurainde a gruke .+. e derun issara tottu su fetu a S[an]c[t]u Pet[ru]. T[este]s: su do[n]nu meu iudike Gosantine de Laccon, e donikellu Comita ki 'nke fuit curatore in Romania, e donikellu Gunnari, e donnikellu Ithoccor, e donnikellu Pet[ru], e Barusone de Setilo.

76. Parthitura. *De s[er]vos.*
Ego Pet[ru] Muthuru ki parthivi sos fiios d'Istefane d'Urieke, cun Gosantine
Pullikina ki fuit armentariu de S[an]c[t]u Iorgi de Locu, cuia fuit sa muiere
d'Istefane. Levaitilu isse appus S[an]c[t]u Iorgi, a Mariane, [et] a pr[e]b[iter]u
Pet[ru], [et] a nNastasia; [et] ego levai appus S[an]c[t]u Pet[ru] de Silki, ad
Anna, [et] a Dorveni, [et] a sSimione, parthindenos do[n]nikellu Comita,
23v kinke | fuit curatore in Romania. T[este]s: Cristofore Iscarpa cun iscolca sua,
e Pet[ru] Ca[m]bella cu[n] iscolca sua.

77. Kertu. *Pro s[er]vos.*
Ego Pet[ru] Muthuru ki tenni corona cun do[n]nu Gosantine de Thori Mutatu, e ccun Marian[e] d'Ussan, su connatu, p[ro] Furatu Gattu, e p[ro]ssos fr[ate]s ki furun de S[an]c[t]u Pet[ru] de Silki, ki mandicavan a gratis, e binkilos in corona de iudike Gosa[n]tine de Laccon in Turres, e ttorrarunilos tottu a S[an]c[t]u Pet[ru]. T[este]s ki vi furun uve binki, donnikellu Comita, e donnikellu Ithoccor, e donnikellu Gunnari, e donnikellu Petru, e Gosantine d'Athen.

78. Postura. *De terras in Silki.*
Positinke a S[an]c[t]u Pet[ru] de Silki Ithoccor de Kerki totta sa parthone sua de Silki, e ccorte, e t[er]ras d'agrile, e ssaltos, e ffenarios, [et] ortales, e de cantu 'nke l'intravat de v partesɪ, p[ro]ss'anima sua.

74. Dispute. *Of servants.*
I, Petru Canbella, had recourse to a hearing (*corona*) against Therkis de Carbia and Donotho de Gorare concerning Ianne Plana and his sister, Maria. I defeated them at the hearing of iudike Gosantine at Sanctu Migali de Plaianu (San Michele di Plaiano), swearing on the cross about [the truth of] the facts (*in fattu*) in the document (*carta*) of Sanctu Petru de Silki. Witnesses: Comita, who was *curatore* in Romangia, Mariane d'Ussan, and Petru de Roma.

75. Dispute. *Of a female servant.*
I, Petru Muthuru, had recourse to a hearing (*corona*) of *donnikellu* Comita concerning the offspring of Isuta de Canake (Caniga) whom Niscoli d'Erthas (Ertas) took from me. I defeated him at the hearing of iudike Gosantine de Laccon, swearing on the cross. They then gave all the offspring to Sanctu Petru. Witnesses: my lord iudike Gosantine de Laccon, donikellu Comita who was *curatore* in Romangia, *donnikellu* Ithoccor, *donnikellu* Petru, and Barusone de Setilo.

76. Division. *Of servants.*
I, Petru Muthuru, divide the sons of Istefane d'Urieke with Gosantine Pullikina, who was the administrator (*armentariu*) of Sanctu Iorgi de Locu to which the wife of Istefane belonged. He took Mariane, the priest Petru, and Nastasia for Sanctu Iorgi; I took Anna, Dorveni, and Simone for Sanctu Petru. Dividing them was *donnikellu* Comita, who was *curatore* in Romangia. Witnesses: Cristofore Iscarpa with his guard (*iscolca*), and Petru Cambella with his guard (*iscolca*).

77. Dispute. *Concerning servants.*
I, Petru Muthuru, had recourse to a hearing (*corona*) against lord Gosantine de Thori Mutatu and against Mariane d'Ussan his brother-in-law (*connatu*) about Furatu Gattu and his brothers who belonged to Sanctu Petru de Silki, and whom they had claimed for free (*a gratis*). I defeated them at the hearing of iudike Gosantine de Lacon at Turres (Porto Torres), and they returned them all to Sanctu Petru. Witnesses who were there when I won: *donnikellu* Comita, *donnikellu* Ithoccor, *donnikellu* Gunnari, *donnikellu* Petru, and Gosantine d'Athen.

78. Donation. *Of lands in Silki.*
Ithoccor de Kerki donated to Sanctu Petru de Silki all his share (*parthone*) [held] at Silki: farmyards (*corte*), ploughlands (*terras d'agrile*), unworked lands (*saltos*), hayfields (*fenarios*), and vegetable gardens (*ortales*), and however much is due on one-fifth of his revenue. [Donation made] for [the salvation of] his soul.

79. Kertu. *De s[er]vos.*

Ego Pet[ru] Muthuru ki kertai in corona de iudike Gosantine, cun Ithoccor de Kerki, e ccun Ithoccor de Carbia, e ccun fiios de Mariane d'Ussan maiore, e ccun Thippari de Carbia, e ccun Mabrikellu d'Athe[n], e ccun Ithoccor de
24r Gunale, e ccun fratres suos |, e ccun Gunnari de Maroniu, e ccun Dorgotori de Maroniu, e ccun Dericcor de Maroniu, e ccun Comita Thancas Latas, in Turres, p[ro] fiios de Barbara Rasa, e pp[ro]ssos nepotes, ad inperaresilos ki ''nde furun binkitos parentes dunde naskites bois, de piscopu Iorgi Maiule.' [Et] issos kertarunimi ca 'alicando nen a pparentes n[ost]ros nen a nnois, no nd'apit kertu fattu, e nen bi[n]kitos in co nos kertas.' [Et] issara mi iudicait do[n]nikellu Gunnari a battuier su co[n]dake de S[an]c[t]u Pet[ru], dessa vinkitura; [et] ego battussi su co[n]dake issara a ccorona ki narabat sa binkitura in co 'nde los abeat binkitos piscopu Iorgi Maiule sos parentes avunde naskian ecustos. Derunili'issara iura assu mandatore de S[an]c[t]u Pet[ru], a Kipriane Murtinu, ca in co narat custu co[n]dake de S[an]c[t]u Pet[ru] gasi es veru; [et] issara torrarun a S[an]c[t]u Pet[ru] fiias feminas cantas aveat fattas Barbara [Ra]sa, ca los coiuvaran do[n]nos aienos. T[este]s: su donnu meu iudike Gosantine de
24v Lacco[n], in cuia corona binki, e donnikellu Gunnari, e donnikellu | Petru su fr[at]e, e donnu Mariane de Thori, e donnu Pet[ru] d'Athen, e do[n]nu Mariane su fr[at]e, e do[n]nu Pet[ru] de Serra, e donnu Gunnari de Thori.

80. Kertu. *De ancilla.*

Ego Pet[ru] Muthuru ki appi kertu cun Romanu de Serra, e ccun Ianne de Carbia, p[ro] Susanna Tatacke ki fuit intrega de S[an]c[t]u Pet[ru] de Silki, [et] ego kertainde cun illos in corona de iudike Gosantine de Laccon, in Turres, ca la levarat a llarga Pet[ru] Cacute, ki fuit servu issoro intregu; [et] ego vinkilos in tottu su fetu, e iurainde a gruke .+. ca fekerat levata a llarga. T[este]s: ki iudicavat su kertu do[n]nikellu Comita ki fuit curatore de Romania, [et] Ithoccor de Lacco[n], e Barusone de Setilo, e Pet[ru] d'Athen, e ccantos vi furun sa die in sinotu.

81. Kertu. *Pro su istaniu de Iennan[u].*

Ego Pet[ru] Muthuru ki appi kertu cun Gosantine de Kerki, p[ro]ssu istaniu de Iannanu, p[ro]ssa parte ki fuit de do[n]nikellu Pet[ru], maiore; [et] ego vinkindelu in corona de iudike Gosantine de Lacco[n] in S[an]c[t]a Maria d'Agustu in Turres, e iurainde a gruke .+. T[este]s: iudike Gosantine, e do[n]nik-
25r ellu | Comita, e Gosantine d'Athen.

79. Dispute. *Of servants.*
I, Petru Muthuru, was a dispute in the hearing (*corona*) of iudike Gosantine in Turres (Porto Torres) with Ithoccor de Kerki, Ithoccor de Carbia, the sons of Mariane d'Ussan Maiore (the elder), and with Thippari de Carbia, Mabrikellu d'Athen, Ithoccor de Gunale and his brothers, and with Gunnari de Maroniu, Dorgotori de Maroniu, Dericcor de Maroniu, and Comita Thancas Latas concerning the children of Barbara Rasa and her nephews for making use of them [saying that] 'the parents (*parentes*) from whom you were born belong to bishop Iorgi Maiule!' But they argued against me that 'never we nor our parents would ever raise a dispute, and [we have] never been defeated in our disputes either!' Then, *donnikellu* Gunnari pronounced that I bring as evidence of the [previous] victory, the condaghe of Sanctu Petru. I then brought the condaghe to the hearing which related the victory that bishop Iorgi Maiule had [when he] defeated the parents from whom they were born. Next, they made the representative (*mandatore*), Kipriane Murinu, take an oath [to the effect that] what it says in this condaghe is true as it is. Then, they returned to Sanctu Petru all the daughters of Barbara Rasa so that they marry husbands (*donnos*) from outside the area (*aienos*). Witnesses: my lord iudike Gosantine de Laccon at whose hearing (*corona*) I won, *donnikellu* Gunnari, *donnikellu* Petru his brother, lord Mariane de Thori, lord Petru d'Athen, lord Mariane his brother, lord Petru de Serra, and lord Gunnari de Thori.

80. Dispute. *Of a female servant.*
I, Petru Muthuru, had a dispute with Romanu de Serra and Ianne de Carbia concerning Susanna Tatacke who was a full servant (*intrega*) of Sanctu Petru de Silki. I raised the dispute with them at the hearing (*corona*) de iudike Gosantine de Laccon in Turres (Porto Torres) because Petru Cacute, who was a full servant of theirs, had taken her wrongfully. I defeated them [and] all of their offspring, swearing on the cross that he had taken her wrongly. Witnesses who adjudicated at the dispute: *donnikellu* Comita, who was *curatore* of Romangia, Ithoccor de Laccon, Barusone de Setilo, Petru d'Athen, and all who were there on the day of the assembly (*in sinotu*).

81. Dispute. *Concerning the lagoon of Iennanu* (*Gennano, Porto Torres*).
I, Petru Muthuru, was in dispute with Gosantine de Kerki concerning the lagoon (*istaniu*) at Iannanu (Gennano, Porto Torres), part of which was of *donnikellu* Petru Maiore (the elder) who granted it to Sanctu Petru. I won [the case] at the hearing of my lord iudike Gostantine de Laccon at Sancta Maria d'Agustu in Turres (Porto Torres) by swearing on the cross. Witnesses: my lord iudike Gostantine de Laccon, *donnikellu* Comita, and Gosantine d'Athen.

82. *Pro s[er]vis.*
Ego pr[e]b[iter]u Ithoccor de Fravile ki kertai cun Dorgotori de Carvia e ccun fr[ate]s suos, in corona de iudike Gosantine in Saccaria, p[ro] fiios de Furatu Gattu, ca 'p[ro]gitteu la vendisti sa parte de S[an]c[t]u Pet[ru] de Silki a do[n]nu Gunnari do[n]nikellu, ki aviamus parthitu ave cando te vinkeran in corona de iudike Mariane, p[ro]ssu patre, ki aveas tu parte tua levata, e fr[ate]s tuos, a Maria [et] a Gavini, e S[an]c[t]u Pet[ru] levait a Gosantine [et] a Ianne?' [Et] isse kertaitimi ca 'su fetu de Furatu Gattu no los parthivim[us].' Iudicarunimi a destimonios ca los aviam[us] parthitos in co li kertava ave sa vinkitura dessu patre; [et] ego vattussi destimonios a Iorgi Iscarpa su d'Eristala, e Dominike su de Domosnovas, [et] a Pet[ru] de Laverru, [et] a Pet[ru] de Seltas; e iurait a gruke .+. su mandatore de S[an]c[t]u Pet[ru] Kipriane Murtinu, cun III destimo[n]ios n[ost]ros, ca 'in co vo llos tennim[us] a nnum[en] sos fiios de Furatu Gattu, gasi los aviam[us] parthitos.' T[este]s: in cuia corona vi[n]ki, su do[n]nu
25v meu iudike Gosantine de | Laccon, e donnu Mariane de Thori, e donnu Mariane d'Athen, e donnu Pet[ru] de Serra, e do[n]nu Gunnari de Thori, e do[n]nu Gosantine de Thori. Ecco destimo[n]ios meos ki vi furun uve binki in Saccaria.

83. *De s[er]vo.*
Inprestait donna Sarra manaca a Dericcor de Gitil I libra d'argentu; keruitililu e no li lu deit; torraitinde berbu a iudike Gosantine in S[an]c[t]u Nicola de Thathari, e iudike positilu a Dericcor de Gitil a ppariarela, [et] isse deitindelilu in pariam[en]tu dess'argentu, a Dorgotori de Rosa intregu kene aver fiiu fattu, e donna Sarra positilu a S[an]c[t]u Pet[ru] de Silki. T[este]s: Gosantine de Gitil su fr[at]e e Pet[ru] de Nugula, e Furatu Canbella, e Furatu d'Oligula.

84. Postura. *In Silki.*
Posit a S[an]c[t]u Pet[ru] Dericcor de Gitil p[ro] anima sua lat[us] d'onnia cantu 'nke aveat in Silki, homines, e t[er]ras, e binias; fakendelos sos homines cantos aveat in Enene apus sa domo de Silki, ca non bi l'intrarat domo in Enene.

85. Postura. *De s[er]vos.*
26r Positinke lat[us] in Gosantine de Bare, e pede | in Elias su fr[at]e, [et] Istefane de Vare intregu, e Marcusa Labra intrega, e III pedes in Iusta sa thia, e III

82. *Concerning servants.*
I, priest Ithoccor de Fravile, was in dispute with Dorgotori de Carvia and his brothers at the hearing (*corona*) of iudike Gosantine at Saccaria (Saccargia) concerning the sons of Furatu Gattu [asking] 'why did you sell the share (*sa parte*) of Sanctu Petru di Silki to lord *donnikellu* Gunnari which we had divided when they defeated you at the hearing of iudike Mariane concerning his father whose share you and your brothers had taken, as well as that of Maria and Gavino, while Sanctu Petru took Gosantine and Ianne?' He argued against me that 'we did not divide the offspring of Furatu Gattu!' They decided that [I produce] witnesses [to show] that we had divided them in the disputed victory over the father. I brought as witnesses Iorgi Iscarpa of Eristala (San Giovanni, Sassari), Dominike of Domosnovas, Petru de Laverru, and Petru de Seltas. The representative (*mandatore*) of Sanctu Petru, Kipriane Murtinu, swore on the cross with three of our witnesses that 'we keep [a record of] the names of the sons of Furatu Gattu, thus we have divided them [previously]!' Witnesses at the hearing in which I won: my lord iudike Gosantine de Laccon, lord Mariane de Thori, lord Mariane d'Athen, lord Petru de Serra, lord Gunnari de Thori, and lord Gosantine de Thori. These were my witnesses that were there when I won at Saccaria.

83. *Of a servant.*
Lady Sarra, a nun (*manaca*), lent to Dericcor de Gitil one pound (*libbra*) of silver. She complained that he did not give it back. She explained to iudike Gosantine at Sanctu Nicola de Thathari (Sassari) and the iudike made Dericcor de Gitil pay her back; he gave as repayment of the silver, Dorgotori de Rosa, a full servant (*intregu*) who had no children. Lady Sarra granted her to Sanctu Petru de Silki. Witnesses: Gosantine de Gitil the brother [of Dericcor de Gitil], Petru de Nugula, Furatu Canbella, and Furatu d'Oligula.

84. Donation. *In Silki.*
Dericcor de Gitil donated to Sanctu Petru for [the salvation of] his soul, half of everything he had at Silki: men (*homines*), lands (*terras*), and vineyards, making all the men [servants] he had at Enene (Eba Ciara) belong to the church (*domo*) of Silki, so that none belong to the church (*domo*) at Enene.

85. Donation. *Of servants.*
[Dericcor de Gitil] donated half of Gosantine de Bare; one-quarter (*pede*) of Elias, his brother; Istefane de Vare, a full servant (*intregu*); Marcusa Labra, a

pedes in su fiiu de Iusta Tenera, in Ianne, [et] in Marcusa sa sorre III pedes, e llat[us] in Nastasia sa sorre, e llat[us] in anbas sas fiias de Gosantine de vare, in Marcusa [et] in Arabona, ki dittavan appus patre, e ppede in sa fiia d'Elias de Vare, in Sappatina, e II dies in Iusta de Vare, e II dies in su fiiu Ianne. Et a ora de morte narait Dericcor de Gitil, 'si morit fiiu meu eniu, appatila totta sa parthone S[an]c[t]u Pet[ru] p[ro] a[n]i[m]a mea.' T[este]s: prebiteru Gosantine Carta ki li davat penetenthia, e Gosantine su fr[at]e, e Petru Iscarpa, e Pet[ru] de Nugula, su de Nurra, e Gosantine Regitanu e Furatu Canbella, e cComita su fr[at]e. Pus morte sua largaitimi in sos ho[m]i[n]es Comita Manutha, e llevaitimilos. [Et] ego pr[e]b[iter]u Ithoccor de Fravile ki tenni corona de iudike Gosantine in Curcaso, cun Comita Manutha; kertaitimi isse ca 'no[n] ti los deit sos omines
26ᵛ d'Enene.' [Et] ego battussili destimonios in | co mi kertavat e iudicarun ca mi los deit sos ho[m]i[n]es d'Enene apus Silki, e binki e ttorrarunili issara sos ho[m]i[n]es a S[an]c[t]u Pet[ru]. T[este]s: Pet[ru] d'Ithir, ki fuit fr[at]e dessa parthone, e Pet[ru] Iscarpa, e Furatu Canbella, ki 'nde iurait in corona de iudike Gosantine. T[esti]s: donikellu Petru.

86. Postura. *De s[er]vos.*
Positinke donnikellu Gunnari a S[an]c[t]u Pet[ru], cando lu sacravan, a pPaganellu fiiu de Maria Thinnogesa, ki fuit depus sa domo de Puthu maiore, [et] a Pet[ru] Cotroske, su de Nurra. T[este]s: fr[ate]s meos cantos vi furu[n] et istranios.

87. Postura.
Positinke a S[an]c[t]u Pet[ru] Ithoccor de Gunale sa parthone sua, e de Dorgotori su fr[at]e, e dessu nepote Pet[ru] de Varru, lat[us] e bukellu de domos e de saltos; dessu saltu d'Albuthetu lat[us] e bukellu, e llat[us] e bukellu dessu saltu d'Ersitali, e llat[us] e bukellu dessu saltu de Iunketu, e llat[us] e bukellu dessu fenariu. 'E poniovi lat[us] e bukellu dessa parthone de Turthevi, ego e fr[at]e meu Dorgotori, e Pet[ru] de Barru nepote meu. [Et] iss'ateru bukellu, S[an]c[t]u
27ʳ Pet[ru] e S[an]c[t]a Iulia lu co[m]porarun | a Pet[ru] fr[at]e meu [et] a Iusta [et] a Muscu. Ave S[an]c[t]a Iulia lis derun ad tottos III sos ki venderun, I boe, [et] II vaccas; e dave S[an]c[t]u Pet[ru] I cavallu domatu, e I fargala, e II soll[os] de pannu.' T[este]s: Pet[ru] Canbella ki fuit maiore d'iscolca, e Dorgotori de Gunale, e Mariane de Bosove.

full female servant (*intrega*); three-quarters of Iusta, her aunt; three-quarters of Iusta Tenera's son, Ianne; three-quarters of Marcusa's sister; half of Nastasia her sister; half of both Gosantine de Vare's daughters, Marcusa and Arabona, who pertained to the father's side; a quarter of the daughter of Elias de Vare at Sappatina; two days [of work] of Iusta de Vare, and two days of her son, Ianne. And at the hour of his death, Derricor de Gitil said, 'if my son dies childless (*eniu*), Sanctu Petru will have all the share [of his services] for [the salvation of] my soul!' Witnesses: priest Gostantine Carta, who conducted his confession; Gosantine, his brother; Petru Iscarpa; Petru de Nugula from Nurra; Gosantine Regitanu; Furatu Canbella, and Comita, his brother. After his death, Comita Manutha stole men (*homines*) from me and took them away. So, I, priest Ithoccor de Fravile, had recourse to a hearing (*corona*) of iudike Gosantine in Curcaso (La Crucca) against Comita Manutha. He disputed me [saying] that 'he did not give you the men of Enene (Eba Ciara)!' I called for witnesses for what I was arguing and they decided that he did give me the men of Enene [who were] at Silki, so I won and they returned the men to Sanctu Petru forthwith. Witnesses: Petru d'Ithir, who was party to (*frate de*) the division, Petru Iscarpa, and Furatu Canbella, who took an oath at the hearing of iudike Gosantine. Witness: *donnikellu* Petru.

86. Donation. *Of servants.*
Donnikellu Gunnari donated to Sanctu Petru when they consecrated it, Paganellu, son of Maria Thinnogesa, who was at the farm (*domo*) of Puthu Maiore (Pozzomaggiore), and Petru Cotroske from Nurra. Witnesses: all my brothers were there, as well as outsiders (*istranios*).

87. Donation.
Ithooccor de Gunale gave to Sanctu Petru his division [of lands], and that of Dorgotori his brother, and of his nephew Petru de Varru, three-quarters (*latus e bukellu*) of [his] farms (*domos*) and uncultivated lands (*saltos*); of the land (*saltu*) of Albuthetu, [he gave] three-quarters, and three-quarters of the land of Ersitali, and three-quarters of the land of Iunketu (Giuncheddu) and three-quarters of a hayfield (*fenariu*). 'I, my brother Drogotori and Petru de Barru, my nephew, gave three-quarters of [our] share of Turthevi. For the other quarter, Sanctu Petru and Sancta Iulia purchased it from my brother, Petru, and from Iusta and Muscu. From Sancta Iulia, they gave to all three of the buyers, one ox and two cows; and from Sanctu Petru [they gave] one tamed horse, one millstone (*fargala*), and two soldi of cloth!' Witnesses: Petru Canbella, who was head of the ward (*maiore d'iscolca*), Dorgotori de Gunale, and Mariane de Bosove (Latte Dolce).

88. Postura. *In Enene.*
Ego Ithoccor de Gunale, e Dorgotori fr[at]e meu, kinke ponemus a S[an]c[t]u Pet[ru] sa parthone nostra in co nos intravat in Enene, p[ro]ss'anima nostra.

89. Kertu. *De s[er]vos.*
Ego pr[e]b[iter]u Ithoccor de Fravile, ki kertai cun Ithoccor de Kerki, curatore de Nurra, e ccun Furatu de Gunale, e ccun Ithoccor de Kerki Murris, generu de Dorgotori de Locu, p[ro] fetu ki fekerun servos issoro cun ankillas de S[an]c[t]u Pet[ru], Ianne Gemellu cun Muscu, e sSimione de Cuniatu cun Lukia, fiios ki furun de Muscu de Ioscla e de Lukia d'Ispata, ki furun custas fiias de Iulitta de Ioscla e de Pet[ru] Frabu, ki furun intregos de S[an]c[t]u Pet[ru] de Silki. [Et] ego vi[n]kilos, ca los aveat binkitos piscopu Iorgi Maiule ad Egithu d'Urieke, 27v [et] assu frate | Therkis, in corona de iudike Barusone; e iurait a gruke .+. su mandatore de S[an]c[t]u Pet[ru] Kipriane Murtinu, ca 'in co narat su co[n]dake de S[an]c[t]u Pet[ru] gasi est veru.' T[es]t[e]s: su donnu meu iudike Gosantine de Laccon, in cuia corona vinki in Sorra, torrandemi tottu su fetu a S[an]c[t]u Pet[ru], e donnu Comita d'Athen manacu, e Mariane d'Athen, e Gunnari de Thori, e do[n]nu Pet[ru] su fr[at]e.

90. Postura. *De ansilla.*
Positinke a S[an]c[t]u Pet[ru] de Silki do[n]nu Mariane de Thori a Bera Pilio, fiia de Mariane Pilio depus Ogosilo.

91. Postura. *De ansillas.*
Positinke a S[an]c[t]u Pet[ru] donna Susanna d'Ussa[n] ad Anna Titu, fiia de Pet[ru] Titu, [et] a Barbara Lekeri, dandela dave Bionis a famiia.

92. *De s[er]vo.*
Positinke a S[an]c[t]u Pet[ru] donnu Mariane de Thori Aspru ad Andria Serata, fiiu de Maria Serata, ki fekerat in furrithu in Gosantine de Magar, p[ro] servire i[n] famiia.

93. Postura. *De s[er]vos.*
Positinke a S[an]c[t]u Pet[ru] Iorgi d'Iscanu lat[us in Ianne Pica, e llat[us] de Iusta de Gogon, ave sa domo d'Enene. T[es]t[e]s: su fr[at]e Gosantine de Gitil,

88. Donation. *In Enene* (*Eba Ciara*).
I, Ithoccor de Gunale and Dorgotori my brother, give to Sanctu Petru our division of what we have at Enene (Eba Ciara), for the [benefit of] our soul.

89. Dispute. *Of servants.*
I, priest Ithoccor de Fravile, was in dispute with Ithoccor de Kerki, the *curatore* of Nurra, and with Furatu de Gunale and Ithoccor de Kerki Murris, son-in-law (*generu*) of Dorgotori de Locu, concerning the offpring they made their own servants with the female servants of Sanctu Petru—Ianne Gemellu from Muscu, and Simione de Cuniatu from Lukia who were sons of Muscu de Ioscla and of Lukia d'Ispata who were [themselves] the daughters of Iulitta de Ioscla and Petru Frabu, who were full servants (*intregos*) of Sanctu Petru de Silki. I defeated them because bishop Iorgi Maiule had defeated Egithu d'Urieke and his brother Therkis at the hearing (*corona*) of iudike Barusone. The representative (*mandatore*) of Sanctu Petru, Kipriane Murtinu, swore on the cross that 'what the condaghe of Sanctu Petru states in it is indeed true!' Witnesses: my lord iudike, Gosantine de Laccon at whose hearing at Sorra (Sorres) I won with all the offspring of Sanctu Petru returned to me, and lord Comita d'Athen the monk, Mariane d'Athen, Gunnari de Thori, and lord Petru his brother.

90. Donation. *Of a female servant.*
I, lord Mariane de Thori, grant to Sanctu Petru de Silki, Bera Pilio, daughter of Mariane Pilio from Ogosilo (Osilo).

91. Donation. *Of female servants.*
I, lady Susanna d'Ussan, grant to Sanctu Petru, Anna Titu, daughter of Petru Titu, and [I grant] Barbara Lekeri giving her to the community [of the church] (*famiia*) from Bionis (Biunisi).

92. *Of a servant.*
I, lord Mariane de Thori Aspru, grant to Sanctu Petru, Andria Serata, son of Maria Serata, who was born from an illegitimate relationship (*fekerat in furrithu*) with Gosantine de Magar, in order to serve the church community (*famiia*).

93. Donation. *Of servants.*
I, Iorgi d'Iscanu grant to Sanctu Petru, half [the services] of Ianne Pica, and half of Iusta de Gogon from the [religious] house (*domo*) of Enene (Eba Ciara).

e Bosovekesu de Gitil, a ken lu narait su fr[at]e ca 'homine intregu 'nke posit
28[r] fr[at]e meu a S[an]c[t]u | Pet[ru],' [et] a Gosantine Regitanu, dandelos a sser-
vire in famiia.

94. Postura.
Positinke Iusta d'Ortu a S[an]c[t]u Pet[ru] su lat[us] dessa corte sua, [et] issu pede d'Istefane Lelle p[ro]ss'anima sua.

95. Kertu. *De s[er]vos.*
Ego pr[e]b[iter]u Ithoccor de Fravile ki ponio in ecustu co[n]dake, p[ro] ca kertait mecu Mariane de Nugula, [et] issu nepote Comita de Castavar, e fr[ate]s suos, [et] ego battussi su co[n]dake de S[an]c[t]u Pet[ru], e destimonios ca la levarat a llarga sa coliverta mea, su servu; [et] ego levaindela sa coliverta mea, battendevilu su servu; e bennit su do[n]nu suo Mariane de Castavar, e naraitili a piscopu Iorgi, ca 'do[n]nu, dassatelos umpare, e ffiios cantos aen faker umpare p[ro]de nd'appat S[an]c[t]u Pet[ru] dessa parte mea.' E iurait a gruke .+. su mandatore de S[an]c[t]u Pet[ru] in corona de donikellu Pet[ru], c'a bolu[n]tate sua la deit sa parte sua dessu fetu do[n]nu Mariane de Castavar a S[an]c[t]u Pet[ru] p[er] ista .+. T[e]st[e]s: Pet[ru] d'Ithir, e Gosantine de Maiorica, e Gosantine de Martis maiore d'iscolca.

96. Conporu. Saltu *de Puthu ruviu apus Sauren.*
28[v] Ego apatissa Theodora, co[m]p[or]ailis assos ho[m]i[n]es | de Tigesi, [et] a lli-
veros [et] a sservos, su saltu de Puthu ruviu. Ave t[er]me[n] d'agitu de Seuni, [et] essit via maiore de [Kentu] Istafla, a derettu a domo istrumosa, e cclompet a t[er]me[n] dessu de S[an]c[t]a Elena, e moliat sutta su castru de Valisandra, e falat a rrivu, assa funtana dessa ficu nigella; ivi iunpat bia, e collat assu monte claru a Puthu Passaris, e moliat tottuve s'atha, a t[er]me[n] dessu de Puthu Passaris, assa iscala ki falat a billa; ivi iu[m]pat via assa margine, e baricat tottuve margine a ssupra funtana de Tongone, e baricat tottuve margine ass'ena de Ca[m]pulongu, e cclonpet a ffuntana Guttiosa, e moliat a rivu de Ianne Corbu, e cclompet assu acclaratoriu de littu de mela, e moliat serra de funtana de murta, a derettu ad agitu d'Arulas, tottuve atha ad agitu de Seuni, uve parthim[us] de

Witnesses: his brother, Gosantine de Gitil, and Bosovekesu de Gitil of whom his brother said that 'my brother granted a full servant (*homine intregu*) to Sanctu Petru;' and Gosantine Regitanu, giving them to serve in the church community (*famiia*).

94. Donation.
Iusta d'Ortu granted to Sanctu Petru half of his farmyard (*corte*), and a quarter [of the services] of Istefane Lelle, for [the salvation of] his soul.

95. Dispute. *Of servants.*
I, priest Ithoccor de Fravile, note in this condaghe concerning that which I contested with Mariane de Nugula, his nephew Comita de Castavar and his brothers. I produced [as evidence] the condaghe of Sanctu Petru and witnesses that the servant (*servu*) had taken away my female servant (*coliverta*). I, taking my female servant back, beat the servant. His lord, Mariane de Castavar, came and he told bishop Iorgi, 'lord, leave them both, and any sons they have together will be a benefit to Sanctu Petru from my share [of their services]!' The representative (*mandatore*) of Sanctu Petru swore on the cross at the hearing (*corona*) of *donnikellu* Petru that lord Mariane de Castavar gave the share of the offspring to Sanctu Petru with his consent, [swearing] on this cross. Witnesses: Petru d'Ithir, Gosantine de Maiorica, and Gosantine de Martis, head of the ward (*maiore d'iscolca*).

96. Purchase. *Unworked land* (saltu) *of Puthu Ruviu at Sauren.*
I, abbess Theodora, purchased from the men (*homines*) of Tigesi (Thiesi), both freemen (*liveros*) and servants (*servos*), the unworked land (*saltu*) of Puthu Ruviu (red well). The boundary is from the entrance (*aylitu*) of Seuni and goes [along] the main road of Kentu Istafla ('hundred stables'), towards Domo Istrumosa ('delapidated house'), it reaches the boundary of Sancta Elena, turns beneath Castru de Valisandra ('the outcrop/ruin of Valisandra'), and descends to the river; [then] to Funtana dessa Ficu Nigella ('spring of the black fig, Sa Figu Niedda'). There, it crosses the road and passes to the hill towards Puthu Passaris ('sparrows' well, San Nenaldu, Cheremule') and turns along the crag to the boundary of Puthu Passaris, [then it goes] to the hillside that descends to the village. There, it passes the road to the side, and passes along the wayside to [a point] above Funtana de Tongone ('spring of Tongone'); it passes along the border to s'Ena de Campulongu (the spring of Campulongu) and reaches Funtana Guttiosa ('dripping spring'), [then] it turns to the stream (*rivu*) of Ianne Corbu, reaches the clearing of Littu de Mela ('apple wood'), turns [along] the ridge of Funtana de Murta ('myrtle spring') towards the entrance of Arulas, [and

pare cun su de S[an]c[t]a Maria de Tigesi. Aterminande pupillos dessu saltu,
Gunnari de Castavar, e Gunnari de Lella, e Nicola Salluri, e Gosantine su fr[at]e,
29r e Gunnari de Torricla, e pPet[ru] Furca, e Gosantine Massilla, e Mariane | de
Pathata, e Gosantine Sella, e Furatu Pithu, e Thipari Cothane. Dande XL mai-
ales, e II verve[ke]s per porcu, a parthiresi uniskis cun kella sua; dassandelu
s'atteru a bolu[n]tate de pare p[ro] a[n]i[m]a issoro. T[e]st[e]s: donnu Petru de
serra de Ierusalé ki fuit curatore, e Pet[ru] Tha[n]kis maiore d'iscolca, e Pet[ru]
Caprinu maiolariu maiore de iudike, e Gosantine de Tola porcariu n[ost]ru, ki
lis davat sos porcos.

97. Tramutu. *De s[er]vos.*
Ego apatissa Massimilla. Tramutai homines cun donnu Gosantine de Cannetu visdominu dess'arkipiscopatu. Ego deili lat[us] in Gosantina, fiia de Maria Pithiris e de Ianne Albu, [et] isse deitimi lat[us] d'Elene Culurione, fiia de Furata Culurione e de Gavini Kitera; tramutande a bolu[n]tate de donnu Ithoccor de Laccon curatore de Romania [et] arm[en]tariu dess'arkipiscopatu, e ccun bolu[n]tate dessas manacas sorres meas. T[e]st[e]s: donnu Gosantine de Martis su de Silki, e Pet[ru] de Lella.

98. Kertu. *De ansilla.*
Ego pr[e]b[iter]u Ithoccor de Fravile ki ponio in ecustu co[n]dake ca mi la
29v levait Juvanne | Cane a llarga a Iusta Calfone, e deitila a Gosantine Pira ki fuit
servu suo. [Et] ego andaivi cun culivertos meos, e giraitsemi supra 'lla e no mi la voluit dare. [Et] ego andai assu curatore, a do[n]nu Ithoccor de Laco[n], ki fuit curatore i[n] Nurra, e nu[n]thaitimilu, e kertaili ca mi la levarat a llarga sa coliverta mea; [et] isse kertaitimi ca 's'apatissa mi la deit a coiuvarela cun su servu meu.' Iudicarunili a battuger destimo[n]ios bonos de Romania, ante ken lila derat s'apatissa, e no los potit aver; iurait a gruke .+. su mandatore de S[an]c[t]u Pet[ru] Kipriane Murtinu ca no[n] fuit pettita nen ad apatissa, nen ad arm[en]tariu, e nen a fr[ate]s suos. T[e]st[e]s: su curatore, e Furatu d'Orane, e Gosa[n]tine Thipircu, e Iuvanne Pirella, e Ia[n]ne Locco, e Dericcor Calva, e Domitri de Vosa; iudicande su kertu in sa corte d'Ottave, de S[an]c[t]u Iorgi, e delegaru tottu su fetu, cantu ain faker umpare, a S[an]c[t]u Pet[ru] de Silki.

goes] along the crag to the entrance of Seuni where we have the boundary in common with that of Sancta Maria de Tigesi (Thiesi). Defining the boundary were the proprietors (*pupillos*) of the land (*saltu*), Gunnari de Castavar, Gunnari de Lella, Nicola Salluri, Gosantine his brother, Gunnari de Torricla (Torrija), Petru Furca, Gosantine Massilla, Mariane de Pathata, Gosantine Sella, Furatu Pithu, and Thipari Cothane. I gave forty pigs (*maiales*) and two sheep for every pig (*porcu*) for each person to share with his own kin (*kella*), leaving the rest at the consent of them both for [the salvation of] their own souls. Witnesses: lord Petru de Serra from Ierusalé who was *curatore*; Petru Thankis, the head of the ward (*maiore d'iscolca*); Petru Caprinu, the iudike's head swineherd (*maiolariu maiore*), and Gosantine de Tola, our pig-farmer (*porcariu*) who gave them the pigs.

97. Exchange. *Of servants.*
I, abbess Massimilla, exchanged men (*homines*) with lord Gosantine de Cannetu, delegate of the See (*visdominu dess'arkipiscopatu*). I gave a half-share [of the services] of Gosantina, daughter of Maria Pithiris and Ianne Albu, and he gave me half-share of Elene Culurione, daughter of Furata Culrione and Gavini Kitera, exchanging [them] with the consent of lord Ithoccor de Laccon, *curatore* of Romangia and administrator (*armentariu*) of the See, and with the consent of my sister nuns. Witnesses: lord Gosantine de Martis from Silki, and Petru de Lella.

98. Dispute. *Of a female servant.*
I, priest Ithoccor de Fravile, note in this condaghe that Iuvanne Cane stole from me Iusta Calfone and gave her to Gosantine Pira, who was her servant. I went with my servants (*culivertos*), but he turned against me over her and did not want to give me her. I went to the *curatore*, lord Ithoccor de Lacon, who was *curatore* of Nurra; I explained myself to him and argued that he had taken away my female servant (*coliverta*). He argued with me that 'the abbess gave me her to marry with my servant (*servu*)!' They decided that I produce sound witnesses from Romangia before whom the abbess had granted her, but it was not possible to have them [appear]. The representative (*mandatore*) Kipriane Murtinu of Sanctu Petru swore on the cross that no one had sought [permission] from the abbess, nor from the administrator (*armentariu*), nor from their brothers. Witnesses: the *curatore*, and Furatu d'Orane, Gosantine Thipircu, Iuvanne Pirella, Ianne Locco, Dericcor Calva, and Domitri de Vosa, arbitrating (*iudicande*) the dispute at the court (*corte*) of Sanctu Iorgi d'Ottave (Ottava); and they assign all the offspring, as many as they will have together, to Sanctu Petru.

99. Kertu. *De s[er]vos.*
30r Tennit mecu corona Gunnari de Thori | p[ro] Bittoria Aketu, e p[ro]ssos fr[ate]s,
ca 'p[ro]gitteu mi los levas?' [Et] ego kertaili ca 'Mical Aketu la levarat a llarga sa
mama de Vittoria.' Kerverunimi destimonios a mimi, e ccarta, de ca la aveat las-
sata sa parte ca[n]ta vi l'intravat dessu fetu a Mariane de Castavar dessos fiios
de Migali Aketu, [et] dessa muiere. [Et] ego vattussi su co[n]dake de S[an]c[t]u
Pet[ru], ki naravat in co li kertava, e binkilu in corona de do[n]nu Mariane de
Maroniu, a Gunnari de Thori, [et] a fiios de Mariane de Castavar; e iuraitinde
a gruke .+. Dericcor d'Okeri ki fuit mandatore de S[an]c[t]u Pet[ru]. T[e]st[e]s:
su curatore donu Mariane de Maroniu, e do[n]nu Mariane de Thori, e donnu
Pet[ru] su fr[at]e.

100. Kertu. *De s[er]vos.*
Ego pr[e]b[iter]u Ithoccor de Fravile, ki kertai cun Furatu de Gallu, e ccun Mari-
ane de Lella, e ccun fr[ate]s suos, p[ro] fiios de Furatu Tranpas, ki furun de
S[an]c[t]u Pet[ru]. [Et] isse kertaitimi ca 'fiios de Barbara Palas levastis vois.'
[Et] ego kertaili ca 'Barbara Palas intrega de S[an]c[t]u Pet[ru] fuit, [et] a llarga
30v la levastis assu servu nostru, kene la peter | nen a donna, nen ad arm[en]tariu.'
Et isse kertaitimi c', 'a boluntate mi la derun.' Kerberunili destimo[n]ios, e no
los potti aver; iurait a gruke .+. su mandatore de S[an]c[t]u Pet[ru], Kipriane
Murtinu, in corona de iudike Gosantine in Turres, ca lu vinki a Thipari de
Carvia, [et] a Mabrikellu d'Athen, [et] a Dericcor de Maroniu; [et] issara mi
essivit a destimo[n]iu Dorgotori de Maroniu, fr[at]e de 'ssos ki kertavan mecu,
e cComita de Matrona, e Furatu de Matrona, e Furatu Canbella, e cComita
su fr[at]e; [et] issara nos torrait su curatore do[n]nu Mariane de Maroniu a
pparthirenos lat[us] a llat[us], sos fiios de Furatu Trampas ca no 'nde fekit nen
iettatu e nen battitu, e cca los coiuvarat do[n]nu aienu s'ankilla de S[an]c[t]u
Pet[ru], [e] su servu de 'ssos.

101. Kertu. *De s[er]vos.*
Appimus kertu appare kerra vennimus a parthire ca aveat IIII fiios, [et] isse
narait ca 'sos III fiios sun bivos, [et] iss'ateru kene esser de servire es mortu.'
[Et] ego battussili destimonios ca morivit servindeli ad isse in cap[ra]s, e
31r iuraitinde a gruke .+. | Gosantine Sikule, e Furatu Caste, [et] issu mandatore
de S[an]c[t]u Pet[ru], Dericcor d'Ockeri. Nois levaim[us] appus S[an]c[t]u
Pet[ru], a Iorgi [et] a Muscu. T[e]st[e]s de ca vinki: donnu Mariane de Maroniu

99. Dispute. *Of servants.*
I, Gunnari de Throi, had recourse to a hearing (*corona*) about Bittoria Aketu and about her brothers about 'why have you taken them from me?' I argued that 'Mical Aketu took by stealth Vittoria's mother!' They disputed my own witnesses (*kerverunimi destimonios a mimi*), and a document (*carta*) that all the division of the due services (*vi l'intravat*) of the offspring of Migali Aketu and his wife had been given (*lassata*) by Mariane de Castavar. I brought forth the condaghe of Sanctu Petru which spoke of the disputed matters, and I won at the hearing of lord Mariane de Maroniu, Gunnari de Thori, and the sons of Mariance de Castavar; Dericcor d'Okeri, who was representative (*mandatore*) of Sanctu Petru, swore on the cross. Witnesses: the *curatore*, lord Mariane de Maroniu; lord Mariane de Thori, and lord Petru, his brother.

100. Dispute. *Of servants.*
I, priest Ithoccor de Fravile, was in dispute with Furatu de Gallu and with Mariane de Lella and his brothers regarding the sons of Furatu Tranpas, who belonged to Sanctu Petru. He argued with me that 'you have taken the sons of Barbara Palas!' I retorted that 'Barbara Palas was a full female servant (*intrega*) of Sanctu Petru, and that you took away our servant without seeking [permission] from either the lady [abbess] nor the administrator (*armentariu*)!' He opposed me [saying] that 'they gave me her by consent!' They called for witnesses, but did not have any. The representative (*mandatore*) of Sanctu Petru, Kipriane Murtinu swore on the cross at the hearing (*corona*) of iudike Gosantine in Turres (Porto Torres) where I defeated Thipari de Carvia, Mabrikellu d'Athen, and Dericcor de Maroniu. Then, there came as witness for me Dorgotori de Maroniu, the brother of those who were suing me, Comita de Matrona, Furatu de Matrona, Furatu Canbella, and Comita his brother. Next, the *cura tore*, lord Mariane de Maroniu came back to us to divide the sons of Furatu Trampas half-and-half as no one had caught or beaten [the culprit], and as a stranger (*aienu*) had married the female servant of Sanctu Petru and the servant of theirs.

101. Dispute. *Of servants.*
We fell into dispute together when we came to divide [the services] that the four sons [of Furatu Trampas] had. He told me, 'three sons are alive, but the other is dead and does not give service!' I called for witnesses that he had died in service to them as a goat-herder. Gosantine Sikule, Furatu Caste, and the representative (*mandatore*) of Sanctu Petru, Dericcor d'Ockeri, swore on the cross. We took for Sanctu Petru, Iorgi and Muscu. Witnesses that I had won: Mari-

in cuia corona binki in Kitarone, e Furatu Canbella, e cComita Canbella, e Dorgotori de Maroniu, e cComita de Matrona.

102. Kertu. *De s[er]vos.*
Ego Ithoccor de Fravile ki ponio in ecustu co[n]dake, ca tennit mecu corona Pet[ru] de Varru su d'Usune, in Kitarone, p[ro] Bonellu, e p[ro]ssos nepotes ca 'servos meos sun.' [Et] ego kertaili ca 'Bonellu in uve mi kertas, piscopu Iorgi Maiule los vinkerat a parentes tuos, avunde vas tu in parentes de Vonellu?' Iudicarunimi a battuger codike in co li kertava, [et] ego vattussi su condake de S[an]c[t]u Pet[ru] in co li kertava, ki narait tottu su kertu in co li kertai ego in corona; e iurait Kipriane Murtinu mandatore de S[an]c[t]u Pet[ru], e binki in corona dessu curatore, de do[n]nu Mariane de Maroniu. T[e]st[e]s:
31v donn'Antine de Martis, e Pet[ru] de Varda, e Furatu | Canbella, [et] issu fr[at]e Comita, e Gosantine de Varda, [et] issu fr[at]e Mariane.

103. Kertu. *De s[er]vo.*
Ego Ithoccor de Fravile ki tenni corona cun fiios de Barusone de Setilo, cun Gosantine e ccun Comita, p[ro] Pet[ru] Corsu ca 'p[ro]gitteu mi lu inperas tu, k'est de S[an]c[t]u Pet[ru]?' [Et] isse kertaitimi ca '[e]s meu e de parentes meos.' [Et] ego kertaili ca 'a patre tuo 'nde vi[n]keran in su patre de Pet[ru] Corsu.' Iudicarunimi a destimo[n]ios uve 'nde vi[n]kerat arm[en]tariu de S[an]c[t]u Pet[ru], Pet[ru] Iscarpa; [et] ego battussi destimo[n]ios, ad Andria Corsu, [et] a Furatu de Fravile, [et] a Furatu Urule; e iurait su mandatore de S[an]c[t]u Pet[ru], Kipriane Murtinu, a gruke .+. e binki in corona de do[n]nu Pet[ru] donnikellu. T[e]st[e]s: su curatore donnikellu Pet[ru], [et] issos destimo[n]ios ki 'nde iurarun, e donnu Ithoccor de Kerki, curatore de Nurra, e ccantos vi furun in sa corona.

104. Kertu. *De s[er]vo.*
Ego pr[e]b[iter]u Ithoccor de Fravile. Bocaitime a ccorona Gunnari de Liios su de Sorso, e Gunnari de Vosove, fiiu de Pet[ru] Iscarpa, su de Thathari, p[ro]
32r Kipriane Murtinu | ca 'iudike Gosantine nos lu aveat datu a nnois.' [Et] ego kertailis ca 'veru narates ca vollu derat a bois, sene se ricordare ca lu aveat datu a S[an]c[t]u Pet[ru]; e cco se 'nde recordait, iudike deitibollu a cComita de Contra, bicanu de Kipriane, e cKipriane remasit a S[an]c[t]u Pet[ru].' Iudicarunimi

ane de Maroniu, at whose hearing in Kitarone (Caddaroni-Sant'Eusebio) I had won; Furatu Canbella, Comita Canbella, Dorgotori de Maroniu, and Comita de Matrona.

102. Dispute. *Of servants.*
I, Ithoccor de Fravile, note in this condaghe that I had recourse to a hearing of Petru de Varru from Usune (Usini) [convened] at Kitarone (Caddaroni-Sant'Eusebio), concerning [a claim about] Bonellu and his nephews that 'they are mine!' I argued that 'the parents of Bonellu whom I am contesting, bishop Iorgi Maiule won [the rights to]; what [rights] do you have over the parents of Vonellu?' They decided to produce a document [*codike*] as evidence for what I was arguing, so I brought forth the condaghe of Sanctu Petru that [related] to what I was arguing, and which told of every dispute I had contested at a hearing. Kipriane Murtinu, the representative (*mandatore*) of Sanctu Petru took an oath, and I won at the hearing of the *curatore*, lord Mariane de Maroniu. Witnesses: lord Antine de Martis, Petru de Varda, Furatu Canbella and his brother Comita, and Gosantine de Varda and his brother, Mariane.

103. Dispute. *Of a servant.*
I, Ithoccor de Fravile, had recourse to a hearing against the sons of Barusone de Setilo, Gosantine and Comita concerning Petru Corsu [and the reason] 'why have you taken advantage of him when he belongs to Sanctu Petru?' He argued that 'he is mine and from my parents!' I argued that 'they defeated your father over the matter of Petru Corsu's father!' They decided that I would find witnesses who were there when the administrator (*armentariu*) of Sanctu Petru, Petru Iscarpa, had won. I brought as witnesses Andria Corsu, Furatu de Fravile, and Furatu Urule. The administrator (*armentariu*) of Sanctu Petru, Kipriane Murtinu, swore on the cross and I won at the hearing (*corona*) of lord Petru *donnikellu*. Witnesses: the *curatore donnikellu* Petru, and the witnesses who swore there, and lord Ithoccor de Kerki *curatore* of Nurra, and all those who were at the hearing.

104. Dispute. *De servo.*
I, priest Ithoccor de Fravile: Gunnari de Liios from Sorso, Gunnari de Vosove, son of Petru Iscarpa from Thathari (Sassari) summoned me to a hearing (*corona*) concerning Kipriane Murtinu on the grounds that, 'iudike Gosantine had given him to us!' I argued that 'what you say is true that he gave him to you, but without recalling that he had been given to Sanctu Petru, and that the iudike recalled giving you Comita de Contra in place of Kipriane, and that Kipriane had remained at Sanctu Petru!' They decided that I call witnesses, so I produced

a destimo[n]ios, e battussi destimo[n]ios, a Kitrike, [et] a Furatu de Fravile, [et] a Furatu Urule ki furun buiakesos de iudike, e iurait a gruke .+. Dericcor d'Okeri mandatore de S[an]c[t]u Pet[ru], cun ecustos destimo[n]ios e binki, in corona de donnu Mariane de Thori. T[este]s: Dorgotori Iscarpa su d[e] Gereti, e Gosantine de Lella, e Furatu Canbella su de Silki.

105. Kertu. *De s[er]vo.*

Ego pr[e]b[iter]u Ithoccor de Fravile. Tennerun mecu corona fiios de donnu Therkis, Ithoccor de Thori, e Gosantine su fr[at]e, p[ro] Maria de funtana ki mi levavan. Kertarunimi issos c', 'a bolu[n]tate de pare los coiuvaim[us].' [Et] ego kertailis c', 'a tortu e de donna e d'arm[en]tariu 'nke la levasti.' Iudicarunimi a
32v mimi a battuger destimo[n]ios; [et] ego | battussi destimo[n]ios meos, a Gosantine Regitanu, [et] a Mariane de Garba, e iurait su mandatore de S[an]c[t]u Pet[ru] a gruke .+. Kipriane Murtinu, cun ecustos destimonios, e binki in corona d'Ithoccor de Laccon. T[estes]: su curatore, [et] issu fr[at]e Barusone, e Gosantine de Martis, e cComita Canbella, e cantos vi furun in sa corona.

106. Kertu. *De s[er]vos.*

Tennit mecu corona Pet[ru] de Roma, p[ro] fiias de Furatu Boricke, a Barbara [et] ad Amata, et a Iorgia. 'P[ro]gitteu mi los levates apus S[an]c[t]u Pet[ru], ca mi lu desti tu a Furatu Boricke cando parthivimus, levande tu a Gavini Albu?' Iudicarunimi a mimi a destimonios, [et] ego battussilos ad Istefane de Nurake, [et] a cComita Tussia, [et] a Ianne Foiola e iurait a gruke .+. su mandatore de ccl[esi]a, Kipriane Murtinu, cun ecustos destimo[n]ios, e binki in corona de Petru de Thori. T[estes]: Ithoccor Urse, e Pet[ru] Iscarpa, e ccantos vi furun in sa corona.

107. Kertu. *De s[er]vos.*

Ego pr[e]b[iter]u Ithoccor de Fravile. Tenni corona de do[n]nu Mariane de
33r Maroniu, cun Ithoccor Manutha ca 'Comita Catroske | p[ro]gitteu lu vendisti a do[n]nu Pet[ru] do[n]nikellu, ki fuit intregu de S[an]c[t]u Pet[ru]?' [Et] isse kertaitimi ca 'si vendi, casa mea vendi, e de fr[ate]s meos.' Et ego kertaili ca 'vinkitos vi setes in sos parentes davunde nasket Comita, a parentes vostros.' Positimi iustithia a battuger su co[n]dake de S[an]c[t]u Pet[ru], [et] ego vattussi su co[n]dake issara de cand'aveat binkitu piscopu Iorgi Maiule in pare[n]tes dunde naskeat Comita, a parentes d'ecustos, ki 'nde kertan como mecu. Derunili iura assu mandatore de S[an]c[t]u Pet[ru], a Kipriane Murtinu e iurait in fattu dessu co[n]dake, ca 'in co narat su co[n]dake de S[an]c[t]u

as witnesses Kitrike, Furatu de Fravile, and Furatu Urule who were iudike's personal guards (*buiakesos*). The representative (*mandatore*) of Sanctu Petru, Dericcor d'Ockeri, swore on the cross along with the witnesses, and I won at the hearing of lord Mariane de Thori. Witnesses: Dorgotori Iscarpa from Gereti (Geridu), and Gosantine de Lella, and Furatu Canbella from Silki.

105. Dispute. *Of a servant.*
I, priest Ithoccor de Fravile: the sons of lord Therkis, Ithoccor de Thori and Gosantine his brother, had recourse to a hearing (*corona*) with me over Maria de Funtana whom they had taken from me. They argued that 'we married them with the consent of both!' I argued that 'you took her wrongfully from the lady [abbess] and the administrator [*armentariu*].' They decided that I should call forth witnesses, so I produced as witnesses Gosantine Regianu and Mariane de Garba. The representative (*mandatore*) of Sanctu Petru, Kipriane Murtinu, swore on the cross with the other witnesses, and I won at the hearing of Ithoccor de Laccon. Witnesses: the *curatore* and his brother, Barusone, as well as Gosantine de Martis and Comita Canbella, and all who were at the hearing.

106. Dispute. *Of servants.*
Petru de Roma had recourse to a hearing (*corona*) against me over the daughters of Furatu Boricke, Barbara, Amata, and Iorgia because 'you took them from me to Sanctu Petru when you gave me Furatu Boricke at the time we made a division [of services], taking for yourself Gavini Albu!' They decided that I bring witnesses, so I called Istefane de Nurake, Comita Tussia, and Ianne Foiola. The representative (*mandatore*) of the church, Kipriane Murtinu, swore on the cross with the witnesses, and I won at the hearing of Petru de Thori. Witnesses: Ithoccor Urse, Petru Iscapra, and all who were at the hearing.

107. Dispute. *Of servants.*
I, priest Ithoccor de Fravile had recourse to a hearing (*corona*) of Mariane de Maroniu against Ithoccor Manutha about 'why you sold to lord *donnikellu* Petru, Comita Catroske, who was a full servant of Sanctu Petru?' He argued that 'if I sold him, [then it was when] I sold my property (*casa*) and my brothers!' I argued that 'your parents lost [the case] as parents when Comita was born!' The justice [process] (*iustithia*) had me produce the condaghe of Sanctu Petru, so I brought out the condaghe at the time when bishop Iorgi Maiule had won against the parents from whom Comita was born, the very parents who were in dispute with me. They made the representative (*mandatore*) of Sanctu Petru, Kipriane Murtinu, swear and he swore to the facts [written] in the condaghe—'that which the condaghe of Sanctu Petru states as such is true,' and I won. Wit-

Pet[ru], gasi e[st] veru,' e binki. T[este]s: su curatore Mariane de Maroniu, in cuia corona vinki in sa Padule de Sila, [et] Ithoccor de Carvia, fiiu de Comita de Carvia, e Gosa[n]tine de Valles, [et] issu nepote, e ccantos vi furu in sa corona.

108. Kertu. *De s[er]vos.*

Ego Ithoccor de Fravile. Tennit mecu corona Pet[ru] de Carbia, e nNiscoli d'Erthas, p[ro] Iorgi Pirastru, e p[ro] fiios suos, ca 'p[ro]gitteu los aet S[an]c[t]u
33v Pet[ru], ki furun meos pecuiares?' | Et ego kertaili ca 'kertande in co 'nde kertas como tu, 'nde kertarun e parentes tuos, in corona de iudike Gosantine, cun Pet[ru] Muthuru,' e cande vinkit Pet[ru] Muthuru in corona de iudike Gosantine. [Et] ego vattussi su co[n]dake de S[an]c[t]u Pet[ru] dessa vinkitura, e iurait Kipriane Murtinu in fattu dessu co[n]dake, e binki in corona de do[n]nu Mariane de Thori ki nos fuit curatore. T[estes]: su curatore, [et] issu fr[at]e, e Gosa[n]tine de Maiorica, e Ianne Thanca, e cca[n]tos vi furun in sa corona.

109. Kertu. *De s[er]vos.*

Tenni corona cun pr[e]b[iter]u Pet[ru] Romanu, ki fuit depus Saccaria, ca mi largait in Martina. Avende parthitu, isse levaitilu a Ianne, e S[an]c[t]u Pet[ru] a Martina, [et] in Balsamu aveat Pet[ru] III pedes, [et] iss'ateru pede fuit de Sancta Maria d'Altasar, e de S[an]c[t]u Kiprianu; fekerun VI fiios, III a mama, e III a patre; intraitiminde a mimi Martina intrega, e pede in Susanna, parthindenos a bolu[n]tate de pare donnos de mama, e donnos de patre. Iudi-
34r carunimi a destimo[n]ios in co li kertava in corona dessu curatore | de Gunnari de Laccon. Derunilu su kertu iudicatu p[ro] ispiiarelu [a] Pet[ru] de Torricla, [et] ego iussili sos destimo[n]ios, a Iuste d'Olgan, [et] a Gavini de Iovola, a ccorona de Pet[ru] de Torricla, e iurait Kipriane Murtinu servu de S[an]c[t]u Pet[ru] a gruke .+. cun destimonios suos, e binkit. T[este]s: su maiore d'iscolca, e Ianne Suveione, e Comita de Tutar, e Gosantine de Tutar.

110. Kertu. *De s[er]vos.*

Okisit ho[m]i[n]e de iudike Pet[ru] Manata, servu ki fuit d'Ithoccor de Athen. Bocaitilu a ccorona iudike ad Ithoccor d'Athen p[ro] custu ho[m]i[n]e ca 'pariamilu!' [Et] Ithoccor d'Athe[n] naraitili a iudike ca 'non pario solus. Nunthatemilu a cKipriane Murtinu mandatore de S[an]c[t]u Pet[ru] de Silki, ca cun livertu suo l'ockisit su servu vostru su servu meu, cun Balsamu.' Nunthar

nesses: the *curatore* Mariane de Maroniu at whose hearing at Padule de Sila I won, and Ithoccor de Cavia, son of Comita de Carvia, as well as Gosantine de Valles and his nephew, and all who were at the hearing.

108. Dispute. *Of servants.*
I, Ithoccor de Fravile. Petru de Carbia and Niscoli d'Erthas (Ertas) had recourse to a hearing (*corona*) against me concerning Iorgi Pirastru and his sons [about] 'why does Sanctu Petru have those who are my property?' I argued 'that which you are disputing now, your parents disputed at the hearing of iudike Gosantine against Petru Muthuru when Petru Muthuru won at the hearing of iudike Gosantine.' I produced as evidence the condaghe of Sanctu Petru concerning the victory. Kipriane Murtinu had sworn to the facts in the condaghe, and I won at the hearing of lord Mariane de Thorki who was our *curatore*. Witnesses: the *curatore* and his brother, Gosantine de Maiorica, Ianne Thanca, and all who were at the hearing.

109. Dispute. *Of servants.*
I had recourse to a hearing (*corona*) against Petru Romanu, who was from Saccaria (Saccargia), as he had taken Martina from me. When the division [of servants] was made, he took Ianne, and Sanctu Petru took Martina. [Sanctu] Petru also had three-quarters [share] of the [services] of Balsamo, and the other quarter was [given] to Sancta Maria d'Altasar and to Sanctu Kipirianu. They had six children: three from the [side of] the mother, and three from the father's side. Martina, a full servant [*intrega*], and a quarter of Susanna, belonged to me. Making the division for us, by even consent, were the lords (*donnos*) of the mother and the lords of the father. They decided that I bring witnesses about that which I was arguing at the hearing of the *curatore*, Gunnari de Laccon. The dispute was adjudged according to the resolution (*pro ispiiare*) of Petru de Torricla (Torrija). I brought Iuste d'Olgan and Gavin de Iovola as witnesses at the hearing of Petru de Torricla. Kipriane Murtinu, servant (*servu*) de Sanctu Petru swore on the cross with his witnesses, and he won. Witnesses: the head of the ward (*maiore d'iscolca*), and Ianne Suveione, and Comita de Tutar, and Gosantine de Tutar.

110. Dispute. *Of servants.*
A servant (*servu*), who was of Ithoccor de Athen, killed a man (*homine*) of iudike Petru Manata. The iudike called Ithoccor d'Athen to a hearing (*corona*) regarding this man [saying] 'compensate me for him (*pariamilu*)!' Ithoccor d'Athen said to the iudike that 'I am not the only one who will pay!' Kipriane Murtinu, the representative (*mandatore*) of Sanctu Petru de Silki was summoned for me [to testify] that 'with his freeman (*livertu*), Balsamo, your ser-

unilu a Kipriane a sSacaria, e kertait cun illu Ithoccor d'Athen, ca 'su servu de iudike, cun su servu meu l'ockisit su culivertu tuo Balsamu.' E Kipriane kertaitili ca 'kerra clo[n]pit Balsamu, Pet[ru] Manata mortu l'aveat s'omine.' Iudicarun
34v a destimonios | ca kerra clonpit Balsamu mortu fuit s'omine: essivitimi a destimo[n]iu Comita de Campu, e iuraimus ambos a gruke .+. e binki; [et] in fatu n[os]tru iurait Pet[ru] Manata ca 'solus l'ockisi s'ho[m]i[n]e,' in corona de iudike Gosantine. T[estes]: Mariane de Thori Mannu, [et] issu fr[at]e Pet[ru], e Pet[ru] de Laccon, e Gosantine de Thori Coke.

111. Kertu. *De s[er]vos.*
Ego Kipriane Murtinu, ki tenni corona cun Pet[ru] de Carbia Cossa Silli, ca 'p[ro]gitteu mi los levas a fiios de Ianne Tarai?' [Et] isse kertaitimi ca 'fiios de servu meu sun.' [Et] ego kertaili c', 'a llarga la levait su servu tuo sa coliverta mea, ki non fekit pettita nen a do[n]na, nen ad arm[en]tariu, nen a ma[n]datore.' [Et] isse mutaitimi kertu 'cun S[an]c[t]u Migali lu partho.' E Ianne Tarai, e Gu[n]nari de Thori, [et] Andria de Fravile narrunili ca 'in Dominica mi desti a S[an]c[t]u Migali de Kerki, ma in Ianne no nos desti.' [Et] ecustos destimonios iurarun mecu a gruke .+. ca a llarga la levait Ianne Tarai s'ankilla de S[an]c[t]u
35r Pet[ru], e binki in corona dessu curatore do[n]nu Mariane de Thori. | T[estes]: Gosantine de Martis, e Gosa[n]tine de Maiorica.

112. Kertu. *De s[er]vo.*
Tenni corona cun do[n]nu Dorgotori de Thori, p[ro] Gavini Tenneru ki mi levauat, [et] isse vidit ca vi fakeat kertu in favula, ca los voleat levare in gratis, no 'nde iskiuit faker kertu, narait ca 'appattinde prode S[an]c[t]u Pet[ru].' [Et] ego iurai a gruke .+. e binki in corona de iudike Gosantine. T[estes]: donnu Pet[ru] d'Athen, e donnu Ithoccor su fr[at]e, e Gosantine de Martis, e ccantos vi fur[u]n i[n] sa corona.

113. Postura. *In su saltu de Ersitali.*
Posit a S[an]c[t]u Pet[ru] Dorgotori de Bosove, in sa sacrathione, sa parte sua in co vi l'intravat in su saltu d'Ersitali, p[ro]ss'anima sua.

114. Co[m]po[r]u. *In Ersitali.*
Co[m]p[or]alis a fiios de Furatu Canbella sa parte issoro in co vi lis intravat in su saltu d'Ersitali, [et] ego deindelis I cavallu domatu cale si keruerun issos atrasattu. T[estes]: Gosantine de Martis, e Mariane de Varda, e Gosantine Regitanu.

vant killed my servant!' They summoned Kipriane to Sacaria (Saccargia) and he argued with Ithoccor d'Athen that 'the servant of the iudike, with my servant (*servu*), killed your freeman (*culivertu*), Balsamu!' Kipriane argued back that 'when Balsamu arrived, the man was dead!' I proceeded to call to witness Comita de Campu; we both swore on the cross, and I won. For our case, Petru Manata swore that 'only one person killed him' at the hearing of iudike Gosantine. Witnesses: Mariane de Thori Mannu and his brother Petru, and Petru de Laccon, and Gosantine de Thori Coke.

111. Dispute. *Of servants.*
I, Kipriane Murtinu, had recourse to hearing (*corona*) against Petru de Carbia Cossa Silli about 'why you took from me the sons of Ianne Tarai?' He argued that 'the sons of the servant (*servu*) are mine!' I disputed this because 'your servant, who did not make a request, either to the abbess (*donna*) or the administrator (*armentariu*), or to the representative (*mandatore*), took my female servant (*coliverta*)!' Then, he changed the argument against me [saying] that 'I divided [his services] with Sanctu Migali!' Ianne Tarai, Gunnari de Thori and Andrea de Fravile said that 'you gave to Sanctu Migali de Kerki, Dominica. You did not give us Ianne!' These witnesses swore with me on the cross that Ianne Tarai took the female servant (*ankilla*) from Sanctu Petru. I won at the hearing of the *curatore* Mariane de Thori. Witnesses: Gosantine de Martis, and Gosantine de Maiorica.

112. Dispute. *Of a servant.*
I had recourse to a hearing against lord Dorgotori de Thori concerning Gavini Tenneru whom he took from me. It was obvious that he had invented the dispute as he wanted to take them gratis, but, not knowing how to argue a legal case (*faker kertu*), he said that 'Sanctu Petru has the offspring!' I swore on the cross and won at the hearing of iudike Gosantine. Witnesses: lord Petru d'Athen, lord Ithoccor his brother, Gosantine de Martis, and all those who were at the hearing.

113. Donation. *In the unworked land* (saltu) *of Ersitali.*
Dorgotori from Bosove gave to Sanctu Petru, at its consecration, his share of that which he possessed in the land (*saltu*) of Ersitali, for [the salvation of] his soul.

114. Purchase. *In Ersitali.*
I purchased the share of the sons of Furatu Canbella who gave services in the unworked land (*saltu*) of Ersitali. I gave for them a trained (*domatu*) horse, which they asked to be tacked up (*atrasattu*). Witnesses: Gosantine de Martis, Mariane de Varda, and Gosantine Regitanu.

115. Canbiu. *In eodem loco.*
Canbiai cun Furatu Canbella, e ccun Comita su fr[at]e; derunimi 'ssos sa parte issoro dessu saltu d'Ersitali, in co vi l'avean, [et] ego deilis ad issos in sa Petrosa supra Silki. T[estes]: sos vikinos n[ost]ros.

116. Postura.
35v Posit a S[an]c[t]u Pet[ru] Nikifori de Osta sa parte sua e dessa muiere, in co vi lis intravat in Ersitali.

117. Conporu.
Conp[or]aili a Gosantine Regitanu su vinia sua in co vi l'intravat in Ballare, e binia, e pumu; [et] ego deindeli I cavallu domatu atrasattu. T[estes]: Gosantine de Martis, e Natalesu, [et] anbos Comitas de Liios.

118. Postura. *In Ersitali.*
Poserun a S[an]c[t]u Pet[ru] Iuste Canbella, [et] issa muiere, sa parte issoro in co vi lis intravat in Ersitali, p[ro] a[n]i[m]a issoro.

119. Postura. *In Ersitali.*
Posit p[ro] a[n]i[m]a sua, Anna, sa muiere de Iannellu, sa parte sua d'Ersitali, [et] issu ki vi li remasit de pone a S[an]c[t]u Pet[ru] co[m]p[or]aitilu Gosantine de Martis, [et] isse positilu a S[an]c[t]u Pet[ru] p[ro] a[n]i[m]a sua.

120. Kertu d[e] pr[e]b[iter]u Furatu. *De s[er]vos.*
Ego pr[e]b[iter]u Furatu de Vosa ki kertai cu[n] Comita de Varda p[ro] fiios de Gosantine Cocone, ki fuit servu intregu de S[an]c[t]u Pet[ru], [et] issa muiere fuit livera de Roma[n]ia, e binki in su fetu, e derunilos a sservos a S[an]c[t]u
36r Pet[ru] in corona de iudike Gunnari in Nurra. T[estes] ki iudicavat su kertu: | Mariane de Maroniu, [et] Ithoccor d'Atthen curatore de Nurra, [et] Ithoccor de Laccon, e Mariane de Serra, ki fuit iuratu de narre iustithia. Et aveat binde coiuvatu cun livera de Flumenariu, e iudike mandaitivi avunde fakeat corona in Ottave, p[ro] andarende sa livera e no 'nde volit andare, e iudike narait ca 'pus co lis plaket esser umpare cun su servu, fiios cantos aen faker umpare tottu sian servos de S[an]c[t]u Pet[ru] de Silki.' T[estes] ki vi furun in sa corona: Mariane de Maroniu, [et] Ithoccor de Laccon, [et] Ithoccor d'Athen, e Mariane de Serra, [et] totta sa curatoria.

115. Exchange. *In the same place.*
I made an exchange with Furatu Canbella and Comita, his brother. They gave me their share they had at the unworked land (*saltu*) of Ersitali, and I gave them [lands] in Petrosa above Silki. Witnesses: our nearest (relatives or neighbours) (*sos vikinos nostros*).

116. Donation.
Nikifori de Osta donated to Sanctu Pertru the share of his [services] and that of his wife that they had in Ersitali.

117. Purchase.
I bought from Gosantine Regitanu his vineyard that he possesses there in Ballare, both vines and fruit trees. I gave him one trained horse with tack (*atrasattu*). Witnesses: Gosantine de Martis, Natalesu, and both [those called] Comita from Liios.

118. Donation. *In Ersitali.*
Iuste Canbella and his wife gave to Sanctu Petru their share of what they had in Ersitali, for [the benefit of their] souls.

119. Donation. *In Ersitali.*
For [the salvation of] her soul, Anna, the wife of Iannulla, granted her share (*parte*) of Ersitali. Gosantine de Martis bought it, so that which remains is assigned to Sanctu Petru and is donated to Sanctu Petru for her soul.

120. Dispute of priest Furatu. *Of servants.*
I, priest Furatu de Vosa, had a dispute with Comita de Varda about the sons of Gosantine Cocone who was a full servant (*intregu*) of Sanctu Petru, and his wife, a free servant (*liverta*), from Romangia. I won in [the matter of] the offspring, and they gave me them as servants (*servos*) of Sanctu Petru at the hearing (*corona*) of iudike Gunnari at Nurra. Witnesses who adjudicated the dispute were: Mariane de Maroniu; Ithoccor d'Athen, *curatore* of Nurra; Ithoccor de Laccon; and Mariane de Serra, who was sworn to give justice (*iustithia*). There was a marriage with a free servant (*livera*) from Flumenatiu, so iudike ordered there to be a hearing (*corona*) at Ottave (Ottava) for the free servant to attend, but she did not want to go. Iudike said that 'as it pleases her to be together with the servant, all her sons they will have together will all be servants of Sanctu Petru de Silki!' Witnesses: all who were at the hearing, Mariane de Maroniu, Ithoccor de Laccon, Ithoccor d'Athen, Mariane de Serra, and the whole district (*curatoría*).

121. Postura. Saltu *d'Erginas*.
Positinke donna Iusta d'Athen sa parte sua dessu saltu d'Erginas. Testes: do[n]nu Comita de Capathennor cun ken lu parthiat, e Furatu d'Olivula, e Petru de Varda.

122. Postura.
Positinke a sS[an]c[t]u Pet[ru] do[n]na Furata de Lella sa parte sua dessa terra ki fekimus a binia, tenende assa de Gosantine Saraca; [et] issa parte dessos
36v fiios conporailila | e deivilis ad in cumone I voe. T[estes] e de donnu[18] e de co[m]poru: Furatu Canbella, e cComita Ca[m]bella, e Gosa[n]tine Fra[n]cu.

123.
Comporaili a Ianne d'Olivas sa parte sua dessa t[er]ra, t[er]m[en] assa de Comita de Liios, [et] ego deindeli I voe domatu. T[estes]: Simione Muthuru, e Gosantine Tussia su connatu, e cComita de Liios.

124. Tramutu. *Terra in Ia[m]pula*.
Tramutai cun Gosantine Iscarpa, [et] assos fr[ate]s, a Pet[ru] et a Nicola [et] a Furatu et a Iusta, sa t[er]ra canta vi lis intravat in Ianpula; [et] ego deindelis a Furatu [et] a Nicola ad in cumone sa parthone dessa vi[n]ia de Gortoni, ki posit Iusta d'Ortu a S[an]c[t]u Pet[ru]; [et] a Pet[ru] deili sa de Pithuru, vinia ki fuit de Gavini Tenneru, ki fuit servu de S[an]c[t]u Pet[ru]; [et] a Gosantine [et] a Iusta deilis sa lintha de Ponte, ki posit Dorgotori Tussia a S[an]c[t]u Pet[ru], vocandendeli sa de Dorgotori de Vosove, ki poserat a S[an]c[t]u Pet[ru].

125. Postura. *In eodem loco*.
Positinke Pet[ru] de Nugula sa parte sua ki vi aveat dessa terra in Ia[m]pula.

126. *In eodem loco*.
Posit a S[an]c[t]u Pet[ru] Gosantine de Maiorica, e cComita d'Iscanu, sa parte
37r issoro | de sa t[er]ra de Ianpula p[ro] a[n]i[m]a issoro.

127. *In eode[m] loco*.
Posit a S[an]c[t]u Pet[ru] Furatu de Varca sa parte sua des sa t[er]ra de Ia[m]pula p[ro] a[n]i[m]a sua.

18 (*sic* for *donu*).

121. Donation. *Unworked land* (saltu) *of Erginas.*
Lady Iusta d'Athen grants her share (*parte*) of the land (*saltu*) at Erginas. Witnesses: lord Comita de Capathennor (Crabattennere) with whom the division was made, Furatu d'Olivula, and Petru de Varda.

122. Donation.
Lady Furata de Lella granted to Sanctu Petru her share (*parte*) of the land (*terra*) that we prepared for a vineyard bordering that of Gosantine Saraca. I bought the share from the sons and gave them an ox between them. Witnesses to both the gift and the purchase: Furatu Canbella, Comita Canbella, and Gosantine Francu.

123.
I bought from Ianne d'Olivas his share (*parte*) of the land [whose] boundary is that of Comita of Liios. I gave them a trained ox. Witnesses: Simione Muthuru, and Gosantine Tussia his brother-in-law, and Comita de Liios.

124. Exchange. *Land in Iampula.*
I exchanged with Gosantine Iscarpa and his siblings, Petru, Nicola, Furatu and Iusta, all the land (*terra*) that belonged to them at Ianpula. I gave Furatu and Nicola a [half-]share to have between them of Gortoni's vineyard that Iusta d'Ortu gave to Sanctu Petru. To Petru I gave from Pithuru a vineyard that used to belong to Gavini Tenneru who was a servant (*servu*) of Santu Petru. To Gosantine and to Iusta, I gave the strip of land (*sa lintha*) at Ponte which Dorgotori Tussia gave to Sanctu Petru, prior to which it was Dorgotori de Vosove who had given it to Sanctu Petru.

125. Donation. *In the same place.*
Petru de Nugula donated his share (*parte*) that he had in the land (*terra*) in Ianpula.

126. *In the same place.*
Gosantine de Maiorica and Comita d'Iscanu gave to Sanctu Petru their share (*parte*) of the land (*terra*) of Ianpula for [the salvation of] their souls.

127. *In the same place.*
Furatu de Varca gave to Sanctu Petru his share (*parte*) of the land (*terra*) of Ianpula for his soul.

128. *Terra in Nervosa.*
Tramutai cun Gosantine de Gitil t[er]ra p[ro] t[er]ra; isse deitimi sa de Nervosa, tenende assa d'Ithoccor de Gunale, [et] ego deindeli sa de Therganianu.

129. Postura. *In Silki.*
Positinke Muscu de Varru, fiia de Gosantine de Martis, su de Planu, parthone canta 'nke aveat in Silki.

130. Postura. *In Gortoni.*
Positinke Dorgotori de Carvia sa vinia sua de Gortoni p[ro] a[n]i[m]a sua.

131. Postura. *Ortale sutta funtana.*
Positinke a S[an]c[t]u Pet[ru] Furatu Canbella et issa sorre Iorgia s'ortale dessa ficu de Sutta funtana p[ro] a[n]i[m]a sua.

132. Tramutu. *In su ortu longu.*
Tramutai cun Furatu Canbella; deitimi isse sa parte sua dess'ortu longu, [et] ego deili ad isse II ordines de vinia ki furun de Ianne Tenneru, ki aveat in sa vinia sua de Vallari.

133. Postura. *Saltu de Conca maiore.*
Positinke Dorgotori de Roma, su d'Usune, connatu de Pet[ru] de Varru, e Iusta sa sorre, su saltu de Conca maiore, in co falat cun s'iscla. T[estes]: pr[e]b[iter]u
37v Pet[ru] de tT[ho]ri ki li | levait penetenthia, e Petru de Varru, e cComita Vardane.

134. Postura. *In Planu.*
Positinke Gosantine de Martis, su de Silki, a S[an]c[t]u Pet[ru] su saltu suo de Planu. T[er]m[en] dessu saltu, in sa valle ki parthimus de pare cu[n] donnikella Iorgia, accatande tottu su monte d'Albuthetu, [et] essit assa via maiore ki vam[us] a Gusalai.

135. Co[m]p[or]u. *In eode[m] loco.*
Conp[or]aili a Mariane de Gallu Thurungone, su de Gereti, sa parte sua dessu saltu de Planu, ki parthiat cun Gosantine de Martis; [et] ego deindeli I voe domatu. T[estes]: Gosantine de Martis, fr[at]e suo de parthone, e cComita de Liios Tocca, e cComita d'Iscanu.

128. *Land in Nervosa.*
I exchanged with Gosantine de Gitil land for land (*terra pro terra*). He gave me his at Nervosa next to that of Ithoccor de Gunale, and I gave him that at Therganianu.

129. Donation. *In Silki.*
Muscu de Varru, daughter of Gosantine de Martis from Planu, gave all the division (*parthone*) she had at Silki.

130. Donation. *In Gortoni.*
Dorgotori de Carvia gave his vineyard at Gortoni for [the salvation of] his soul.

131. Donation. *The vegetable garden* (ortale) *below the spring.*
Furatu Canbella and his sister, Iorgia, gave to Sanctu Petru s'Ortale dessa Ficu ('the vegetable garden of the fig tree') at Sutta Funtana ('lower spring').

132. Exchange. *In su Ortu Lungu.*
I made an exchange with Furatu Canbella; he gave me the share (*parte*) of Ortu Lungu ('long garden') and I gave him two rows of vines which belonged to Ianne Tenneru who had his vineyard at Vallari.

133. Donation. *Unworked land* (saltu) *at Conca Maiore.*
Dorgotori de Roma from Usune (Usini), brother-in-law of Petru de Varru, and Iusta his sister, gave the unworked land (*saltu*) of Conca Maiore that descends to the islet (*iscla*). Witnesses: priest Petru de Thori who gave them confession, Petru de Vallu, and Comita Vardane.

134. Donation. *In Planu*
Gosantine de Martis from Silki gave to Sanctu Petru his share (*parte*) at Planu. The boundary of the unworked land (*saltu*) in the valley (*valle*) that we share equally with *donnikella* Iorgia includes all Monte d'Albuthetu and ends at the main road that we take to Gusalai.

135. Purchase. *In the same place.*
I bought for them from Mariane de Gallu Thurungone from Gereti (Geridu), his share (*parte*) of the unworked land (*saltu*) at Planu which we share with Gosantine de Martis. I gave them a tamed ox. Witnesses: Gosantine de Martis [who was] party to the division, Comita de Liios Tocca, and Comita d'Iscanu.

136. Postura. *Saltu de Mola Fratta in Pla[n]u.*
Positinke a sS[an]c[t]u Pet[ru] Dericcor d'Urieke su saltu de Mola Fratta, sa parte sua. T[estes]: su pr[e]b[iter]u ki li deit penetenthia, donnu Furatu Gaspis.

137. Postura. *Terra de Forkillos.*
Positinke Dericcor de Gitil, e Gosantine su fr[at]e, sa t[er]ra de Forkillos ave 'lla de S[an]c[t]u Simione.

138. Tramutu. *In N[er]vosa.*
Tramutai cun Ianne Galle sa t[er]ra de Sancta Margarita ki aveat in sa vinia sua.
38r Deitimi | isse sa t[er]ra sua de Nervosa, tenende assa dessos de Lella; [et] ego
deili cussa ki aveat intro dessa vinia sua, e deitimi s'attera t[er]ra tenende assa
dessos de Gitil, [et] assa de Gosantine Tolis.

139.
Ego Maximilla abbatissa dessu monasteriu de S[an]c[t]u Pet[ru] de Silki, ki ponio in ecustu co[n]dake p[ro] o[mn]ia ca 'nke parai in sa domo, ave co 'nke venni ad esserinke do[n]na, [et] ad 'ver sa domo in manu mea.

140. Conpo[r]u. *De Pedra[s] Niedas.*
Conp[or]aili a Barusone de Serra, fr[at]e de Cok'-e-Mandica, e de do[n]nu
Gunnari de tThori, sa t[er]ra de Pet[ra]s Nigellas, su lat[us] part'ave Via alva;
[et] iss'ateru lat[us] positinkelu donna Sanna de Thori, sa sorre, a sS[an]c[t]u
Pet[ru]; [et] iss'ateru positilu do[n]nu Comita Gardis a sS[an]c[t]a Iulia.
T[estes] e de donu e de co[m]p[or]u: Gosantine de Martis su de Silki, ki fuit
maiore d'iscolca, e Pet[ru] de Varda, e Gosantine su fr[at]e, e Petru Lavirru
maiore de gulvare d'Innoviu, e Furatu de Gallu, e Gavini Mannias, [et] arm[en]-
38v tariu meu Simione Muthuru, | e mandatore Ianne Muthuru.

141. Conporu. *Sediles.*
Conp[or]aili a Frevari IIII fustes de virga dessu fenariu de vadu de Coltu, [et] ego deindeli IIII sol[los] de lavore. Testes: Gosantine Solina, e Mariane su fr[at]e, e Furatu Cocoriata.

136. Donation. *Land* (saltu) *of Mola Fratta at Planu.*
Dericcor d'Urieke gave to Sanctu Petru his share (*parte*) [of] the land (*saltu*) of Mola Fratta ('broken grindstone'). Witnesses: the priest who gave them confession, lord Furatu Gaspis.

137. Donation. *Terra de Forkillos.*
Dericcor de Gitil and his brother Gosantine gave the land (*terra*) at Forkillos adjacent to that of Sanctu Simione.

138. Exchange. *At Nervosa.*
I exchanged with Ianne Galle the land (*terra*) of Sancta Margarita that he had in their vineyard. He gave me his land at Nervosa alongside one of those at Lella. I gave them that which he had in their vineyard, and he [also] gave me the other land bordering one of those at Gitil, and the one of Gosantine Tolis.

139.
I, Maximilla, abbess of the monastery of Sanctu Petru, make an entry in this condaghe about everything that I bought for the monastery (*domo*) since the time I came to be abbess (*donna*) and the monastery was under my control.

140. Purchase. *At Pedra Niedas.*
I bought from Barusone de Serra, brother of Cok'-e-Mandica and of lord Gunnari de Thori the land of Petras Nigellas ('black rocks', Pedra Niedda, Codrongianos), one part (*latus*) of which was along Via Alva ('white road'); another part (*latus*) lady Sanna de Thori, his sister, gave to Sanctu Petru; another part (*latus*), lord Comita Gardis gave to Sancta Iulia. Witnesses of the gift and the purchase: Gosantine de Martis from Silki, who was the head guard (*maiore de iscolca*); Petru de Varda; Gosantine, his brother; Petru Lavirru, supervisor of the enclosure (*maiore de gulvare*) at Innoviu; Furatu de Gallu; Gavini Mannias; my administrator (*armentariu*), Simione Muthuru, and representative (*mandatore*) Ianne Muthuru.

141. Purchase. *Sediles.*
I bought from Frevari four pole-lengths (*fustes de virga*) of the hayfield (*fenariu*) at Vadu de Coltu ('the crossing-ford at Coltu'). I gave him four soldi of grain. Witnesses: Gosantine Solina; Mariane his brother, and Furatu Cocoriata.

142. Conporu.
Conp[or]aili ad Ithoccor de Seltas iiii fustes de virga dessu fenariu tenende appare cun su ki co[m]porai a Fervari; [et] ego deindeli iiii sollos inter pannu e llavore. Testes: ambos fr[ate]s Solinas, Gosantine e Mariane.

143. Conporu. *De s[er]vos.*
Conp[or]aili a Furatu Cocoriata, [et] a Mariane Kerunthu iiii fustes de virga dessu fenariu tenende appare cu[n] su d'Ithoccor de Seltas, [et] ego deindelis iiii sol[los] inter pannu e llavore. Teste[s]: Mariane de Varda, e Mariane Solina, e Gavini de Vare.

144. Conporu.
Conp[or]aili ad Ithoccor de Seltas, [et] a Gosantine d'Urieke iiii fustes de virga
dessu fenariu ivi tenende appare, [et] ego deindelis iiii sol[los] inter pannu
39r e llavore. T[estes]: Dorgotori Corsu, | maiore de gulbare, e Mariane Solina;
iukendevi su maiore d'iscolca Petru de Varda minore, a bider et ad app[re]thare
e ffenu e p[re]thu, [et] arm[en]tariu su previteru donnu Petru Contena, e
ma[n]datore Petru Marcu.

145.[19] Conp[or]u. *In su saltu de Sediles in Montes de Ogosilo.*
Conp[or]aili a Mariane de Thori Grassu fiiu de Gosantine de Thori, su latus
dessu saltu de Sediles, [et] ego deindeli iii libras d'argentu e mesa; [et] es
term[en] dessu saltu: ave su monticlu dessu Ferulariu, a ffundu dess'elike, assu
monticlu dessu pirastru; ivi iunpat via assu valliclu, e ccollat p[er] meiu monte
de Rolacki, derettu assu valliclu dessa ficu alva, accatande s'ariola dess'ab[b]a
salsa, e ttorrat assa funtana, e ffalat tottuve rivu derettu a padu dessu Carvone,
ivi moliat sa via ki vamus ad Ogosilo, a derettu a t[er]m[en] dessu de S[an]c[t]a
Maria, e falat tottuve t[er]en assu kercu mannu, lassandenollu a ma[n]ca su
39v kercu et a dextra su termen, | derettu assu rivu de Varatu; tottuve rivu 'nde
falat intro assu badu dessa via ki vamus ad iscala de vaccas, ave cunde torrat assu monticlu dessu ferulariu, assu fundu dess'elike. T[estes] ki furun uve conp[or]ai custu saltu: Gosantine de Martis su de Silki, [et] anbos fr[ate]s Can-

19 Duplicated in entry 381.

142. Purchase.
I bought from Ithoccor de Seltas four pole-lengths (*fustes de virga*) of the hayfield (*fenariu*) adjacent to that which I bought from Fervari. I gave him [the value of] four soldi (*sollos*) in cloth and grain. Witnesses: both the Solina brothers, Gosantine and Mariane.

143. Purchase.
I bought from Furatu Cocoriata and Mariane Keruthu four pole-lengths (*fustes de virga*) of the hayfield (*fenariu*) adjacent to that of Ithoccor de Seltas. I gave them [the value of] four soldi (*sollos*) in cloth and grain. Witnesses: Mariane de Varda, Mariane Solina, and Gavini de Vare.

144. Purchase.
I bought from Ithoccor de Seltas and Goasantine d'Urieke four pole-lengths (*fustes de virga*) of the hayfield (*fenariu*) that is adjacent to it there. I gave them [the value of] four soldi (*sollos*) in cloth and grain. Witnesses: Dorgotori Corsu, head of the animal pen (*maiore de gulbare*); Mariane Solina; Petru de Varda Minore ('the younger') when he was the head of the ward (*maiore d'iscolca*) there to oversee and to value both the hay and the price; and the priest, lord Petru Contena as administrator (*armentariu*); and Petru Marcu representative (*mandatore*).

145. Purchase. *In the land* (saltu) *of Sediles in the hills of Ogosilo* (*Osilo*).
I bought from Mariane de Thori Grassu ('fat'), son of Gosantine de Thori, the half-(share) of the unworked land (*saltu*) at Sediles. I gave him three and a half pounds of silver. The boundary of the land (*saltu*) is from Monticlu dessu Ferulariu ('the hill of hayfield'), down to the holm oak, to Monticlu dessu Pirastru ('the hill of the wild pears'); there, it cross the road to the small valley (*valliclu*), procedes between [that and] Monte de Rolacki ('hill of Rolacki', Orolacche, Osilo), [going] towards Valliclu dessa Ficu Alva ('the small valley of the wild fig tree'), reaching s'Ariola dess'Aba Salsa ('the threshing floor of salty water'), it turns at the spring and descends along the stream towards Padu dessu Carvone ('ford of Carvone', Funtana su Carvone, Osilo). There, it turns with the road we take for Ogosilo (Osilo); [it goes] towards the boundary of Sancta Maria and descends along the boundary to the large oak tree, leaving the oak on the left and the boundary on the right, [it goes] towards the stream of Varatu; along the stream, descending to the crossing-ford at the road we take to Iscala de Vaccas ('hillside of the cows') from where it turns towards Monticlu dessu Ferulariu and down to the holm oak. Witnesses who were there when I purchased this land (*saltu*): Gosantine de Martis from Silki; both the Canbella brothers, Furatu

bellas, Furatu e cComita, [et] ho[m]i[n]es ki andavan cun illu, anbos fr[ate]s suos de cuncuba, Pet[ru] de Mocor, e Gitimel, e Barusone de Sogostos, e Dorgotori de Liios.

146.
Morivitili sa mama a Mabrikellu, fiiu de Dericcor de Gitil, e llevaitilu Bera sa thia ad averelu in manu; [et] avendelu issa in manu vennit cun illu e bendit sa vinia d'Ortu Donnicu a Petru Serette ad ascuse mea, uve fuit pupillu S[an]c[t]u Petru; [et] ego pismaimende cun illu; e cco vidit Pet[ru] Serette ca mi 'nde pareat male, bennit a mimi e nnaraitimi ca 'donna, pus co vio ca vos inde paret male, torratemi su ki vi dei, e gollitevos sa vinia.' Et ego deindeli I libra d'argentu,
40r cantu vi derat | et isse, [et] aiunsili I varrellu, ca mi fekit voluntate de torraremi
sa vinia. T[este]s: Furatu d'Olivula, e Pet[ru] de Varda, e cComita Ispanu; e de Silki, Gosantine de Martis, e Furatu Canbella, e cComita su fr[at]e, e cComita d'Iscanu.

147. Kertu. *De vingia de Tor[ra]si.*
Kertait Bosovekesu de Laccon Malkidu cu[n] Petru de Sune su de Thathari, fiiu de Romanu Tussia, p[ro]ss'ankilla sua d'intro, ki li furarat, e benderatila a pPisanos; e binkitindelu, e derunindeli in pariamentu sa parte sua dessa vinia de Torasi. E donnu Bosovekesu deitilila a donnu Mariane de Maroniu, p[ro] devitu ki li aveat sende curatore in Romania. E do[n]nu Mariane de Maroniu deitila custa vinia a sS[an]c[t]u Pet[ru] p[ro] a[n]i[m]a sua. T[estes]: Gosantine de Castellu, maiore d'iscolca de Thathari, e Migali de Cotinas, mandatore de liveros, e Furatu Ca[m]bella, e Furatu d'Olivula. Eremait sa vinia. Bennerun sos
40v fiios de Dorgotori e benderunimila sa parte issoro, pus morte dessu patre, | ven-
neru sas fiias cun sa mama, e benderunimila, [et] ego deindeli IIII sol[lo]s de pannu. T[es]t[es]: Petru de Ca[n]nas, e cComita de Setilo.

148. Conporu. *In Torasi.*
Conp[or]aili ad Ubertellu doctore, [et] assa muiere Maria de Sune, sa parte sua dessa vinia de Torasi, [et] ego dei[n]deli VI sol[los] IIII de pannu e II de casu. T[es]t[e]s: Comita de Setilo, e Ianne Corellu, e Gosantine Pullialvu.

and Comita; the men (*homines*) who went with him together with his brothers from a mistress (*de cuncuba*); Petru de Mocor; Gitimel; Barusone de Sogostos, and Dorgotori de Liios.

146.
The mother of Mabrikellu, son of Dericcor de Gitil, died and his aunt Bera took him under her control. Having him thus, she came with him and sold the vineyard of Ortu Donnicu to Petru Serette, unbeknown to me, when Sanctu Petru was the owner. I objected about this to him, and when Petru Serette realised that I thought it was wrong, he came to me and said: 'My lady, as I see that this seems wrong to you, return to me that which I gave you, and allocate the vineyard for yourselves!' So, I gave him one pound of silver, the total that he had given me, and I added a garment (*varrellu*) because he had voluntarily returned me the vineyard. Witnesses: Furatu d'Olivula; Petru de Varda; Comita Ispanu; and from [Sanctu Petru di] Silki, Gosantine de Martis; Furatu Canbella; Comita his brother, and Comita d'Iscanu.

147. Dispute. *About a vineyard at Torrasi.*
Bosovekesu de Laccon Malkidu was in dispute with Petru de Sune from Thathari (Sassari), the son of Romanu Tussia, over a female servant (*ankilla*) of his who was taken away and sold to the Pisans. He won [the case] and gave in recompense his share (*parte*) of the vineyard at Torasi. Lord Bosovekesu then gave it to lord Mariane de Maroniu for a debt (*devitu*) that he had when he was *curatore* of Romangia. Lord Mariane de Maroniu then gave this vineyard to Sanctu Petru for [the salvation of] his soul. Witnesses: Gosantine de Castellu, head of the ward (*maiore d'iscolca*) at Thathari (Sassari); Migali de Cotinas, representative of freemen (*mandatore de lıveros*); Furatu Canbella, and Furatu d'Olivula. The vineyard is overgrown. The sons of Dorgotori came and sold me their share and, after the death of their father, the daughters with the mother came to sell me it. I gave them four soldi (*sollos*) of cloth. Witnesses: Petru de Cannas, and Comita de Setilo.

148. Purchase. *In Torasi.*
I bought from Ubertellu Doctore ('the learnèd') and his wife Maria de Sune, his share (*parte*) of the vineyard at Torasi. I gave him six soldi (*sollos*): four in cloth and two in cheese. Witnesses: Comita de Setilo; Ianne Corellu, and Gosantine Pullialvu.

149. Conp[or]u. *In eode[m] loco.*
Conp[or]aili a cComita Musuri sa parte sua dessa vinia de Torasi ki fuit de Iusta de Iaca, [et] ego deindeli VI sol[los] T[e]st[e]s: Gosantine Isclafu, e Ianne Corsellu, e cComita de Iannu.

150. Conporu. *In eode[m] loco.*
Conp[or]araili a Maria Tussia, fiia de Comita Tussia, sa parte sua dessa vinia de Torasi, [et] ego deindeli VII sol[los]. T[e]st[e]s: Comita Canbella, e Pet[ru] d'Iscanu su fiiu, e Gosantine de Martis; e de Kitarone, Pet[ru] Tumbas, e Fotine Ocli ruiu. Et issu ki vi fuit foras de muru, sa parte de Furatu Ca[m]bella,
41r co[m]p[or]aililu assu fiiu, pus morte sua, [et] ego deindeli | I FARGA, [et] issa via ki andavat assa vinia de Ianne de Carros. T[e]st[e]s: Mariane de Varda, e lLabrenthu. Et issu ki remasit foras de muru de Torasi, de Comita Ispanu, derunila sos fiios a S[an]c[t]u Pet[ru] pus morte dessu patre. T[e]st[e]s: Ithoccor d'Olivula, e lLabrenthu.

151. Conporu.
Conp[or]aili a Gosantine Regitanu sa vinia canta vi aveat in cuniatu de Tussia sa parte sua, e de binia, e de pumu, cu[n] bolu[n]tate de sos fiios. [Et] ego deindeli I cavallu, app[re]thandelu a mesa libra d'argentu. T[e]st[e]s: Comita de Liios Mannu, e cComita de Liios Tocca, e Dorgotori d'Iscanu.

152. Postura.
Vennit ad ora de morte Comita d'Iscanu, e positinke a sS[an]c[t]u Pet[ru] sa vinia sua de Norgia, [et] ego tramutaila cu[n] Gosa[n]tine de Martis; deitimi isse in cuniatu de Tussia, [et] ego deili sa de Norgia, e binia e pumu, cu[n] boluntate sua e mea. T[e]st[e]s: Comita Ca[m]bella, e Dorgotori d'Iscanu, su fratile, e cComita de Liios Ma[n]nu.

153. *Co[m]p[or]u.*
Conp[or]aili a cComita Pagiti sa binia de cuniatu de Tussia, e binia e pumu
41v ca[n]tu | vi aveat, [et] ego deindeli I mesa libra d'argentu. T[e]st[e]s: Gosantine de Martis, e cComita d'Iscanu, e cComita Ca[m]bella.

154. Postura. *De s[er]vos.*
Positinke donnu Gosantine de Thori Cok'-e-Mandica a Dericcor de Magar, fiiu de cuncuva de Gosantine de Magar, ki fekerat in ankilla de donnu Gosantine de

149. Purchase. *In the same place.*
I bought from Comita Musuri the share (*parte*) of his vineyard at Torasi that used to belong to Iusta de Iaca. I gave him six soldi (*sollos*). Witnesses: Gosantine Isclafu; Ianne Corsellu, and Comita de Iannu.

150. Purchase. *In the same place.*
I purchased from Maria Tussia, daughter of Comita Tussia, the share (*parte*) of her vineyard at Torasi. I gave her seven soldi (*sollos*). Witnesses: Comita Canbella; Petru d'Iscanu his son; Gosantine de Martis; from Kitarone (Caddaroni-Sant'Eusebio), Petru Tumbas, and Fotine Ocliruviu. The share of Furatu Canbella is that which is beyond the wall [of Torasi], and I bought it from his son after his death. I gave him a millstone (*farga*) and the road that goes to the vineyard of Ianne de Carros. Witnesses: Mariane de Varda, and Labrenthu. That which remained outside the wall of Torasi is Comita Ispanu's; his sons gave it to Sanctu Petru after the death of their father. Witnesses: Ithoccor d'Olivula, and Labrenthu.

151. Purchase.
I bought from Gosantine Regitanu all his share of the vineyard he had at the enclosure (*cuniatu*) of Tussia, including both vines and fruit orchard (*pumu*) with the consent of his sons. I gave them a horse, valued at half a pound of silver. Witnesses: Comita de Liios Mannu ('the elder'); Comita de Liios Tocca, and Dorgotori d'Iscanu.

152. Donation.
At the hour of Comita d'Iscanu's death, he donated to Sanctu Petru the vineyard of his at Norgia, and I exchanged it with Gosantine de Martis. He gave me the enclosure (*cuniatu*) at Tussia for that which I gave him at Norgia, of both vine and fruit orchard (*pumu*), with his consent and mine. Witnesses: Comita Cambella; Dorgotori d'Iscanu his cousin (*fratile*), and Cimota de Liios Mannu ('the elder').

153. Purchase.
I bought from Comita Pagiti the vineyard of the enclosure (*cuniatu*) at Tussia, including all the vines and fruit orchard (*pumu*) he had there. I gave him one pound of silver. Witnesses: Gosantine de Martis; Comita d'Iscanu, and Comita Cambella.

154. Donation. *Of servants.*
Lord Gosantine de Thori Cok'-e-Mandica gave to Dericcor de Magar, son of Gosantine de Magar's mistress, who was born from a female servant (*ankilla*)

Thori, cando 'nke la vattussit sa netta a Travesa; [et] ego tramutailu cun donnu Mariane de Maroniu. Isse deitimi sa muiere de Petru Marcu, a Iorgia Prias, ki li co[m]p[or]at a pPetru Fara, pede in illa e pede in fiios cantos aen dittare appust'issa; [et] ego deililu a Dericcor. T[e]s[te]s: su donnu meu iudike Gunnari de Laccon, et issu fiiu donnu Barusone rege, et ambos Comitas de Gunale, et Ithoccor de Laccon, curatore de fattu de Romania.

155. Conp[or]u. *De s[er]vos.*
Conp[or]aili a Dorovesa [et] assu fiiu Gosantine II dies in mese in Iorgia Prias, et in sos fiios ca[n]tos aen dittare appus issa, cantu vi aveat; [et] ego deindeli I boe domatu, [et] I pulletru. T[e]st[e]s: Petru de Varru su thiu, e Pet[ru] Matale,
42r e Gosa[n]tine | de Martis, e cComita Ca[m]bella.

156. Postura. *In Turthelas.*
Positinke a S[anct]a Iulia Comita Ispanu, et issa mama, su cantu vi lis intravat in Turthelas.

157. Conp[or]u.
Conp[or]aili a Furatu, fiiu de Comita Ispanu, sa pintana ki li remaserat de 'ssa ki poserat a cclesia, [et] ego deindeli III moios d'oriu assu mesinu.

158. Co[m]p[or]u. *In Turthelas.*
Conp[or]aili ad Andria Ispanu su ca[n]tu vi aveat in su cuniatu de Turthelas, sa parte sua e dessa sorre Muscu; [et] ego deindeli I cavallu domatu, caput appare. Inter co[m]p[or]u et in donu fekimilu tuttu su cuniatu ad intregu. T[e]st[e]s de co[m]p[or]u e de postura: Gosantine de Varda, e Mariane su fr[at]e, e lLabrenthu, e Dorgotori Corsu, maiore de gulbare, e Gosantine Gerule.

159. Co[n]p[or]u. *In Turthelas.*
Conp[or]aili a Gosantine de Varda, fiiu de Petru de Varda, sa vinia canta vi aveat su patre in su cuniatu in Turthelas, parthindesi cun sos frates, et intran-
42r deli ad isse cussa in parte, et ego deindeli I mesa libra d'argentu | lavorata, e XXV vervekes. T[e]st[e]s: Petru Pedes, maiore d'iscolca, e Petru de Valles, ma[n]datore de liveros, [et] Ithoccor de Varda, fr[at]e suo de parthone, e Mariane de Varda, e pPetru de Varda su fratile.

160. Co[m]poru. *In Ortu Donnicu.*
Conp[or]aili a Dericcor de Gitil, fiiu de Gosantine de Gitil, sa parte sua dessa vinia e dessu pumu e de cantu vi aveat in Ortu Donnicu; [et] ego deindeli I

of Gosantine de Thori, when he brought his nephew to Travesa. I exchanged him with lord Mariane de Maroniu: he gave me Iorgia Prias, the wife of Petru Marcu whom she had bought from Petru Fara, a quarter [of her services] and a quarter for each of the sons who will belong to her. I gave him to Dericcor. Witnesses: my lord iudike Gunnari de Laccon and his son, the lord king (*rege*) Barusone; both [of those called] Comita de Gunale, and Ithoccor de Laccon, the *curatore* of Romangia at the time (*de fattu*).

155. Purchase. *Of servants.*
I bought from Dorovesa and her son, Gosantine, two days [of services] per month for Iorgia Prias and for each and every child that she might herself have. I gave one tamed ox and one foal (*pulletru*).

156. Donation. *In Turthelas.*
Comita Ispanu and his mother donated to Sancta Iulia all that pertained to them at Turthelas.

157. Purchase.
I bought from Furatu, the son of Comita Ispanu, the remaining plot (*pintana*) of his which he gave to the church. I gave him three measures (*moios*) of barley accoding to the measure (*mesinu*).

158. Purchase. *In Turthelas.*
I bought from Andria Ispanu everything he had in the enclosure (*cuniatu*) at Turthelas—his own share and that of his sister, Muscu. I gave him a trained horse by mutual agreement (*caput appare*). Between the purchase and gift, all the enclosure was made entirely mine.

159. Purchase. *In Turthelas.*
I bought from Gosantine de Varda, son of Petru de Varda, the entire vineyard his father had in the enclosure (*cuniatu*) at Turthelas, making the division of their share with his brothers of that belonging to them. I gave one-half pound of hammered silver (*argentu lavorata*) and twenty-five sheep. Witnesses: Petru Pedes, the head of the ward (*maiore d'iscolca*); Petru de Valles, representative of the freemen (*mandatore de liveros*); Ithoccor de Varda, his partner (*frate suo*) in the division; Mariane de Varda, and Petru de Varda, his cousin.

160. Purchase. *In Ortu Donnicu.*
I bought from Dericcor de Gitil, son of Gosantine de Gitil, his share of the vineyard, fruit trees, and all else he had at Ortu Donnicu ('Donnicu vegetable

terrale, a Petru Carta, fiiu de servu suo e d'ankilla de S[anct]a Iulia. T[e]st[e]s: Petru Pedes, maiore d'iscolca, e cComita de Varru, e Ianne Corsellu, e donnu Gosantine de Martis su de Silki, e Mariane de Varda, e cComita Canbella.

161. Tramutu. *In sa pala de Nurailo, apus Junketu.*
Tramutai cu[n] donnu Bosovekesu de Gitil, su de Canake; deitimi isse sa t[er]ra dessa pala de Nurailo, tenende assu capitellu de Vallinas, [et] ego deili su cuniatu de Guriola, tenende assa sua. T[e]st[e]s: Gosantine de Martis, e cComita d'Iscanu, e sSimione Muthuru, servu [a]d in cumone.

162. Postura.
Positinke Gosantine Tussia sa vinia sua ki fuit inter issa n[os]tra e de Gos-
43r antine | Regitanu; et avendemila sa vinia 'nde kertait mecu Simione Muthuru, e cComita de Liios ca 'no ti la deit.' Iudicarunimi a battuger destimonios ante ken la deit a cclesia; et ego vattussi su p[re]viteru ki li deit penetenthia kerra moriat, a donnu Gosantine Carta, [et] a Gosantine de Martis [et] a Gosantine Regitanu, [et] ambos fr[ate]s de Lella, a Iorgi [et] ad Ithoccor, a ccorona de iudike Gunnari a cKitarone, e iuraitinde a .+. Kipriane Murtinu ca 'in co vos narat su p[re]viteru, [et] issos destimonios gasi est veru!'

163. Postura. *In Ianpula.*
Positinke donnu Gosantine de Martis ad ora de morte a sS[an]c[t]u Pet[ru] sa vinia de Ianpulla, cu[n] pumu cantu vi aveat, ki co[m]p[or]arat isse a Petru Iscarpa Thoppu. T[e]st[e]s: p[re]viteru Furatu de Vosa, e p[re]viteru Gosantine Catha, e p[re]viteru Tobias, e cComita de Varru; dandela custa vinia cu[n] bolu[n]tate dessa muiere e dessas fiias.

164. Postura. *Terra in Brunkiles.*
Positinke Bulsu, generu de Comita Canbella, sa parthone de Brunkile ki co[m]-
43v porait a sSusanna de Canake; positila | a sS[an]c[t]u Pet[ru] p[ro] a[n]i[m]a sua. T[e]st[e]s: Mariane Mankio, e cComita de Monte.

165. Postura.
Positinke Comita de Liios Mannu a sS[an]c[t]u Pet[ru] VI sol[los] de vinia, tenende assa de Gosantine Canbella, capithale assa n[os]tra. T[este]s: Comita Carta, e cComita de Liios su nepote; cu[n] bolu[nt]ate de sos fiios.

garden'). I gave him a tenant (*terrale*), Petru Carta, the son of his servant, and a female servant from Sancta Iulia. Witnesses: Petru Pedes head of the ward (*maiore d'iscolca*); Comita de Varru; Ianne Corsellu, lord Gosantine de Martis from Silki; Mariane de Varda, and Comita Canbella.

161. Exchange. *On the hillside of Nuarailo at Iunketu* (*Giuncheddu*).
I made an exchange with lord Bosovekesu de Gitil from Canake (Caniga). He gave me the land (*terra*) of Pala de Nurailo ('the hillside of Nurailo') adjacent to the boundary (*capitellu*) of Vallinas, and I gave him the cultivated plot (*cuniatu*) of Guriola, adjacent to his. Witnesses: Gosantine de Martis; Comita d'Iscanu, and Simione Muthuru, a servant [we hold] in common (*servu ad in cumone*).

162. Donation.
Gosantine Tussia donated his vineyard which was between ours and that of Gosantine Regitanu. Simione Muthuru and Comita de Liios sued me about my having the vineyard because 'he did not give you it!' They decided I call witnesses that he gave it to the church, so I brought the priest who confessed him (Gosantine Tussi) on his deathbed, [as well as] lord Gosantine Carta; Gosantine de Martis; Gosantine de Martis; Gosantine Regitanu, and both the de Lella brothers, Iorgi and Ithoccor, to the hearing (*corona*) of iudike Gunnari at Kitarone (Caddaroni-Sant'Eusebio). Kipriane Murtinu swore on the cross that 'what the priest tells you, and the witnesses (too), is indeed true!'

163. Donation. *In Ianpula.*
At the hour of his death, lord Gosantine de Martis gave to Sanctu Petru the vineyard of Ianpulla with all the fruit trees he had there which he had bought from Petru Iscarpa Thoppu ('lame'). Witnesses: priest Furatu de Vosa; priest Gosantine Catha; priest Tobias, and Comita de Varru. Giving this vineyard [was made] with the consent of his wife and daughters.

164. Donation. *Land* (terra) *in Brunkiles.*
Bulsu, the son-in-law of Comita Canbella, gave his share of Brunkile that he bought from Susanna de Canake (Caniga). He donated it to Sanctu Petru for [the salvation of] his soul. Witnesses: Mariane Mankio and Comita de Monte.

165. Donation.
Comita de Liios Mannu ('the old') gave to Sanctu Petru six soldi of vines adjacent to Gosantine Canbella's, the top part [of which is] as ours. Witnesses: Comita Carta; Comita de Liios, his nephew. With the consent of his sons.

166. Datura. *Terra in Nerbosa a prope dessa corte.*
Deitinos Gosantine d'Urieke sa t[er]ra sua de Nerbosa, tenende assa de Dericcor de Gitil, e nois dassaimusili sa muiere III annos sene poner opus. T[e]st[e]s: Ithoccor de Monte, e cComita de Varru, e cComita de Liios; dandenolla sa t[er]ra a ppecuiare.

167. Co[m]poru. *In Nerbosa.*
Conp[or]aili a Petru Tartasu, connatu de Gosantine Canbella, sa t[er]ra sua de Nerbosa, tenende assa de Gosantine d'Urieke; [et] ego deindeli I maiale, e II moios de tridicu. T[este]s: Comita Carta, e Ianne Regitanu, [et] Ithoccor de Monte.

168. Postura. *In eode[m] loco.*
Posit Lussuria a sS[an]c[t]u Pet[ru] sa t[er]ra sua de Nervosa, sa ki co[m]p[or]ait a Gosantine Canbella, cu[n] boluntate dessu maritu. T[este]s: p[re]viteru Gosantine Catha; e ccu[n] boluntate dessos co[n]natos, de Gu[n]nari e de Furatu.

44r 169.
[P]ositinke donnu Furatu d'Olivula sa terra de Nervosa, ki est tene[n]de assa de Gosantine Regitanu, p[ro] a[n]i[m]a sua. T[este]s: su p[re]viteru donnu Petru Contena; e ccun boluntate dessos fiios.

170. Postura. *In eode[m] loco.*
Posit Dericcor de Canake a sS[an]c[t]u Pet[ru] p[ro] a[n]i[m]a sua sa t[er]ra sua de Nervosa, tene[n]de assa d'Ithoccor de Varda, cum bolu[n]tate dessos fiios. T[e]st[i]s: su p[re]viteru donnu Pet[ru] Co[n]tena ki li deit penete[n]thia.

171. Postura. *In eode[m] loco.*
Positinke Ithoccor de Varda p[ro] a[n]i[m]a dessa muiere sa t[er]ra sua de Nerbosa, ki est tenende assa de Dericcor de Canake, cum boluntate dessos fiios.

172. *In Ersitali.*
Conp[or]aili ad Ithoccor de Thori, [et] a Gosantine, [et] a Mariane, tottos III fr[ate]s, in co vi l'avean sa parthone issoro in Ersitali; [et] ego deindelis IIII vaccas ave S[an]c[t]u Pet[ru], e II ave S[anct]a Iulia; [et] I colkitra in III sol[los], [et] I cunduri de rocca nobu muierile, in VII sol[los], [et] VII sol[los] de pannu tenneru. T[este]s ki app[re]thava[n] e ssaltu e pp[re]thu, donnu Gosantine de
44v Martis, e fFuratu Canbella, e Mariane | de Varda.

166. Gift. *Land* (terra) *in Nerbosa near the farmyard* (corte)
Gosantine d'Urieke gave us his land (*terra*) at Nerbosa, adjacent to that of Dericcor de Gitil, and we exempted his wife from having to give any labour (*ponere opus*) for three years.

167. Purchase. *In Nerbosa.*
I bought from Petru Tartasu, the brother-in-law of Gosantine Canbella, the land (*terra*) of his at Nerbosa, adjacent to [that] of Gosantine d'Urieke. I gave him one pig (*maiale*) and two measures (*moios*) of grain. Witnesses: Comita Carta; Ianne Regitanu, and Ithoccor de Monte.

168. Donation. *In the same place.*
Lussuria gave to Sanctu Petru, her land (*terra*) at Nervosa, which she had bought from Gosantine Canbella with the consent of her husband. Witnesses: priest Gosantine Catha with the consent of his brothers-in-law, Gunnari and Furatu.

169.
Lord Furatu d'Olivula granted the land (*terra*) of Nervosa, which is adjacent to that of Gosantine Regitanu, for [the salvation of] his soul. Witnesses: the lord priest Petru Contena and [with] the consent of his sons.

170. Donation. *In the same place.*
For his soul, Dericcor de Canake (Caniga) gave to Sanctu Petru the land (*terra*) of his at Nervosa adjacent to that of Ithoccor de Varda, with the consent of his sons. Witness: the lord priest Petru Contena who leads the confession.

171. Donation. *In the same place.*
Ithoccor de Varda gave for [the salvation of] his wife's soul, the land (*terra*) of his at Nerbosa which is adjacent to that of Dericcor de Canake (Caniga); with the consent of his sons.

172. *In Ersitali.*
I purchased from all three brothers, Ithoccor de Thori, Gosantine, and Mariane the [land] in which they had their share at Ersitali. I gave them four cows from Sanctu Petru; two from Sancta Iulia; one blanket (*colkitra*) [worth] three soldi; one new, female undergarment (*cunduri de rocca*) worth seven soldi, and seven soldi of soft cloth. Witnesses who evaluated the unworked land (*saltu*) and price: lord Gosantine de Martis; Furatu Canbella, and Mariane de Varda.

173. Tramutu. *In Nerbosa.*
Tramutai cum Comita de Varru; isse deitimi sas t[er]ras de Nervosa, ave t[er]m[en] dessa terra de Gosantine Regitanu, e benit assu kiiu de Gosantine Regitanu, e cclompet assa de clesia, e ssutta via, e ssupra via. T[e]st[e]s: Petru Pedes, e cComita de Liios Mannu, e Dorgotori de Nureki.

174. Postura. *In Gortoni.*
Positinke Petru de Farfare sa parte ki l'intravat in su cuniatu dessa Pruna de Gortoni, tenende assa de Gosantine Francu. T[e]st[i]s: su p[re]viteru donnu Tobias.

175. Postura. *In eode[m] loco.*
Positinke Petru de Carvia sa parte ki l'intravat dessu cuniatu dessa pruna, ki parthiat de pare cu[n] Petru de Farfare. T[esti]s: su p[re]viteru ki li deit penetenthia. E deitila custa t[er]ra a cclesia cum boluntate dessos fiios.

176. Postura.
Positinke Gosantine Francu sa t[er]ra sua de cuniatu de Murinu, t[er]m[en] assa dessos de Carvia. T[e]st[e]s: previteru Furatu de Vosa ki li deit penetenthia.

177. Postura. *In Nurailo.*
Positinke Dorgotori d'Utan sa t[er]ra de Nurailo, sa ki est tenende assa ki tramu-
45r tai | a donnu Bosovekesu. T[este]s: su p[re]viteru ki li deit penetenthia, donnu Ithoccor de Fravile; e ccu[n] bolu[n]tate de sos fiios.

178. Tramutu. *In eode[m] loco.*
Tramutai cu[n] Dorgotori Farrikellu; deitimi isse sa lintha de Nurailo ki est tenende assa de do[n]nu Pet[ru] d'Ispatha, [et] ego deili s'ortale de Vote ki est tenende assa sua. T[e]st[e]s: Iubanne de Thori, e nNatalesu, [et] issu mandatore de liveros Gosantine de Farfare.

179. Postura. *In eodem loco.*
Positinke donna Iusta Mannata sa lintha de Nurailo ki est tenende assa de Dorgotori Farrikellu. T[este]s ante ken mi lu narait su fiiu ca la posit sa mama a ccl[es]ia, Gosantine de Gerule, e Gosantine d'Olibas, serbu depus Canake.

173. Exchange. *In Nerbosa.*
I made an exchange with Comita de Varru: he gave me lands (*terras*) at Nervosa from the boundary of the land (*terra*) of Gosantine Regitanu which starts that the border (*kiiu*) of Gosantine Regitanu['s land] and reaches the church at both the top road and the road below. Witnesses: Petru Pedes; Comita de Liios Mannu, and Dorgotori de Nurecki.

174. Donation. *In Gortoni.*
Petru de Farfare gave the share of what he had in Cuniatu dessa Pruna ('enclosure of the plum tree') at Gortoni, adjacent to that of Gosantine Francu. Witness: the lord priest Tobias.

175. Donation. *In the same place.*
Petru de Carvia gave the share of what he had in Cuniatu dessa Pruna ('enclosure of the plum tree') which he held equally with Petru de Farfare. Witness: the priest who gives the confession. He gave this land to the church with the consent of his sons.

176. Donation.
Gosantine Francu gave his land (*terra*) in the enclosed plot (*cuniatu*) at Murinu, the boundary [being the same as] those at Carvia. Witnesses: priest Furatu de Vosa who gives the confession.

177. Donation. *In Nurailo.*
Dorogtori d'Utan gave his land (*terra*) at Nurailo adjacent to that which I exchanged with lord Bosovesku. Witnesses: the priest who gives the confession; lord Ithoccor de Fravile and with the consent of his sons.

178. Exchange. *In the same place.*
I made an exchange with Dorgotori Farrikellu: he gave me the strip [of land] (*lintha*) at Nurailo which is adjacent to that of Petru d'Ispatha. I gave him the vegetable garden (*ortale*) which is adjacent to his. Witnesses: Iubanne de Thori; Natalesu; and the representative of the freemen (*mandatore de liveros*), Gosantine de Farfare.

179. Donation. *In the same place.*
Lady Iusta Mannata donated the strip [of land] (*lintha*) at Nurailo which is adjacent to that of Dorgotori Farrikellu. Witnesses before whom the son told me that his mother had given it to the church: Gosantine de Gerule and Gosantine d'Olibas, a servant (*serbu*) at Canake (Caniga).

180. Datura. *In iscala de Fustes.*

Deitili do[n]nu Petru donnikellu assu servu, a Ianne de Sarule, sa t[er]ra d'iscala de Fustes, e nnois co[m]poraimusilila, e deimusindeli I boe domatu, cu[n] boluntate dessu do[n]nu suo ki li la derat sa t[er]ra. T[es]t[e]s: donnikellu Gunnari, curatore de Romania. Termen dessa t[er]ra; ave s'una parte sa de
45^v donnu Comita | do[n]nikellu, e d'ave s'attera muru tottuve, part'ave sa de donnu Comita de Laccon.

181. Postura. *In Silki.*

Bennit ad ora de morte Comita d'Iscanu, e positinke a sS[an]c[t]u Pet[ru] o[mn]ia ca[n]tu 'nke aveat in Silki, e t[er]ras, e binias, e dies d'omine ki nc'aveat, a pparthire cun S[an]c[t]u Gaviniu, lat[us] appare. T[e]st[e]s: su p[re]viteru donn'Antine Carta, ki li deit penetenthia, e do[n]nu Dorgotori su fr[at]e, e Gosantine de Martis su fratile. Vocandenosinde s'ortu suo ki est ave secus dessa corte de Gosantine de Martis. Vennimus a pparthire cun S[an]c[t]u Gaviniu e bennitinke donnu Mariane Carbone su calonicu: parthivimus sos ho[m]i[n]es; ego levai pede de Susanna Sella, e IIII dies de Mariane, e II dies in Pet[ru] Argillis; e sS[an]c[t]u Gaviniu levait pede de Furatu Calaresu, e ppede de Iorgia Frunia, e II dies in Pet[ru] Argillis. T[este]s ante ken parthivimus, Ackettore
46^r armentariu issoro, e cComita | de Varru, e Gosantine de Martis.

182. Postura.

Positinke Petru de Tissi in bita sua a sS[an]c[t]u Petru su buckel[lu] dessu lat[us] suo, ca su latus dessa muiere fuit, [et] iss'ateru bukellu deit assa fiia, cun sa corte. T[este]s: su p[re]viteru do[n]nu Tobias ki li levait penetenthia, e Ianne d'Ardu su fr[at]e, ki fuit uve fakeat custu testame[n]tu.

183.

Applaticaitinke mesa libra d'argentu donna Gedida de Rethas e cco li la kervi ad ora de morte e no la potti aver, positime in manu dessos nepotes [et] issos derunimi dessa binia sua cantu ait baler me[sa] libra d'argentu, [et] ego bendila ass'Ispitale, ad Ithoccor Pira cun ken l'avea.

184. *De s[er]vos.*

Pettitimi merkede Gispina d'Athen p[ro]ssa fiia de Gosantine de Muskianu p[ro] fakerla livera, [et] ego deilila cu[n] boluntate dessu donnu meu iudike

180. Gift. *At Iscala de Fustes.*
Lord *donnikellu* Petru gave to his servant (*servu*), Ianne de Sarule, the land (*terra*) of Iscala de Fustes ('hillside of the canes'). We purchased it from him and gave him one tame ox with the consent of his lord who had given him the land. Witness: *donnikellu* Gunnari, *curatore* of Romangia. The boundary of the land: one side (*parte*) [is] that of lord *donnikellu* Comita, and the other is along the wall, part of which is [the boundary] of lord Comita de Laccon.

181. Donation. *In Silki.*
Comita d'Iscanu reached the time of his death and donated to Sanctu Petru everything he had at Silki: lands, vines, and days [of service] of the men he had, to be shared half each with Sanctu Gavinu. Witnesses: the priest lord Antine Carta who gives the confession; lord Dorgotori, his brother, and Gosantine de Martis his cousin. [The donation] leaves aside his vegetable garden (*ortu*) which is behind the farmyard (*corte*) of Gosantine de Martis. We came to make the division with Sanctu Gaviniu, and lord Mariane Carbone the canon (*calonicu*) arrived. We divided the men (*homines*); I took a quarter [share] (*pede*) of Susanna Sella; four days [of service] for Mariane and two days for Petru Argillis. Sanctu Gaviniu took a quarter of Furatu Calaresu, a quarter for Iorgia Frunia, and two days for Petru Argillis. Witnesses before whom we made the division: Ackettore, their administrator (*armentariu*); Comita de Varru, and Gosantine de Martis.

182. Donation.
Petru de Tissi gave to Sanctu Petru during his life, quarter (*bukellu*) of his share; the share that was of his wife, and the other quarter he gave to his daughter with its farmyard (*corte*). Witnesses: the lord priest lord Tobias who gives the confession, and Ianne d'Ardu his brother who was there when he made this testimony.

183.
Lady Gedida de Rethas promised [to the church] half a pound (*libra*) of silver, but when I asked for it as she was on the point of death and unable to let me have it, she put it in the hands of her nephews and they gave me all her vineyard worth half a pound of silver. I sold it to the hospital (*ispitale*), to Ithoccor Pira, who did not have one.

184. *Of servants.*
Gispina d'Athen sought a favour from me regarding the daughter of Gosantine de Muskianu (Muscianu) about making her free (*livera*). I gave her the consent

Gunnari, e dessu fiiu donnu Barusone rege, e ccu[n] boluntate dessos clericos[20]
46v meos, e dessas manacas; e issa deitimindela | ad Elene Thinnogesa, e IIII libras d'argentu, plakitandemi Gosantine de Muskianu a dargli ass'ankilla ki davat a cclesia parte d'unu fiiu.

185. Kertu. *De s[er]vos.*
Vocaitime a ccorona Ithoccor de Laccon p[ro] Ithoccor de Seltas, e p[ro]ssos frates, ca los kereat a lliveros appus sos Cocoriatas. Nunthaitimenke iudike ad Ardar, sa die de S[anct]a Maria d'Agustu, [et] ego posilu a kertare su p[re]viteru meu a fFuratu de Bosa. Et isse kertaitili ca 'ad Ithoccor de Seltas p[ro]gitteu lu keres a lliveru, ki est servu de S[an]c[t]u Pet[ru]?' [Et] Ithoccor de Laccon naraitili ca 'est fiiu de Gosantine Cocoriata ki est liveru fr[at]e meu.' Et isse naraitili ca 'si fuit liveru Gosantine Cocoriata non ti vi kerto[21] [...]'

185bis.[22] [...] coiuvait cu[n] Masia ki fuit ankilla intrega de S[an]c[t]u Pet[ru], e ffekit VI fiios, ad Elene, [et] a Maria, et a Iusta, et a sSubia, et a Mariane, et ad Osilla. Nois levaimus ad Elene, [et] a Maria, [et] a sSubia; e donnikella Iorgia levait a Iusta, [et] a Mariane, [et] ad Osilla.[23] [...] Issara mi derun tottu su
47r fetu appus bulba; | e li vinkiat Ithoccor de Laccon sos nepotes de donnikella Iorgia, torrarelos a sS[an]c[t]u Pet[ru], ca furu fiios d'ankilla sua. T[es]t[e]s: su donnu meu iudike Gunnari de Laccon, [et] issu fiiu iudike Varusone, e donnikellu Petru, e donnikellu Ithoccor, e cComita de Gunale fr[at]e de iudike, e cComita de Gunale Ioculanu, e cComita de Navitha, [et] tottu locu in co vi furun sa die de S[an]c[t]a Maria d'Agustu in Ardar.

186. *Terra in Iscala de Fustes.*
Pettili a donna Maria de Thori Pala, fiia de donnikellu Comita, sa t[er]ra d'Iscala de Fustes p[ro] lavorarevi, [et] issa deitimila, a S[an]c[t]u Pet[ru], p[ro] a[n]i[m]a sua, cu[n] boluntate dessa fiia, e dessos nepotes, de Petru de Cupellu, e de Petru de Tian. T[este]s: Gunnari de Varru, e Gosantine Mollone, servu de iudike, e Petru Corsellu, su servu a cken mi deit ad amustraremi sos termenes: term[en] assa mea ki vi avea av'innanti, ki fuit de donnikellu Petru, tottuve falat via, ass'ariola, falat tottuve rivu, assu castru dess'elike, e ccollat su traginu tot-
47v tuve, parthinde de pare cun | su de donnu Iubanne de Thori, e cclonpet ad altu assa margine. Et ecusta t[er]ra deratilila iudike Mariane assu fiiu, a donnikellu Comita, a ssecatura de ren[n]u, sende curatore de Romania.

20 The manuscript reads *cloricos.*

21 The entry breaks off here.

22 Fragment of an entry, transcribed consecutively with entry 185.

23 The sentence breaks off here in an apparent transcription error.

of my lord iudike Gunnari and that of his son, the lord king (*rege*) Barusone, and with the consent of my clerics (*clericos*) and monks. She gave me Elene Thinnogesa and four pounds of silver. Gosantine de Muskianu promised me to assign him [the service of] the female servant (*ankilla*) which she would give to the church [as if it were] the share of a son.

185. Dispute. *Of servants.*
Ithoccor de Laccon summoned me to a hearing (*corona*) concerning Ithoccor de Seltas and his brothers because he took them for freemen (*liveros*) from the Cocoriata [family]. The iudike called me to Árdara on the feast of the Assumption (*sa die de Sancta Maria d'Agustu*), and I sent my priest Furatu de Bosa to put [the case]. He argued 'why do you take Ithoccor de Saltas, who is a servant of Sanctu Petru, as a freeman?' Ithoccor de Laccon said that 'he is a son of Gosantine Cocoriata, who is a freeman and my associate (*frate meu*)!' He replied that, 'if Gosantine Cocoriate were a freeman, I would not argue with you […]' he married Masia who was a full female servant (*intrega*) of Sanctu Petru, and he had six children: Elene, Maria, Iusta, Suvia, Mariance, and Osilla. We took Elene, Maria and Subia, and *donnikella* Iorgia took Iusta, Mariane, and Osilla […]. Then, they gave me all the offspring from the female line, and Ithoccor de Laccon won [the case] for returning the nephews of *donnikella* Iorgia to Sanctu Petru [on the grounds] that they were sons of her female servant. Witnesses: my lord iudike Gunnari de Laccon; his son, iudike Varusone; *donnikellu* Petru; *donnikellu* Ithoccor; Comita de Gunale, brother of the iudike; Comita de Gunale Ioculanu; Comita de Navitha, and the whole realm who were present in Ardar (Árdara) on the day of the Assumption.

186. *Land* (terra) *at Iscala de Fustes.*
I asked lady Maria de Thori Pala, daughter of *donnikellu* Comita for the land (*terra*) of Iscala de Fustes ('hillside of the canes') concerning its cultivation, and she gave me it for Sanctu Petru for her soul with the consent of her daughter and nephews, Petru de Cupellu and Petru de Tian. Witnesses: Gunnari de Varru; Gosantine Mollone, servant of iudike, and Petru Corsellu, the servant he assigned me to show me the boundaries. The boundary [is that of] mine at the front [and] which was *donnikellu* Petru's; it descends along the road to the threshing floor (*ariola*); it goes down along the stream to Castru dess'Elike ('outcrop of the holly oak'), and passes along the flow dividing [the land] equally with that of lord Iubanne de Thori, and [then] it arrives at the high part of the border (*margine*). This land iudike Mariane gave to his son, *donnikellu* Comita, as an alienation of the realm when he was *curatore* of Romangia.

187. Conporu. *Silvori.*
Conp[or]aili a Gosantine de Thori Titicca sa parte sua dessu saltu de Flume[n]
Minore, [et] ego deindeli I libra d'argentu lavorata. T[es]t[e]s: Gunnari de Varru,
e Gosantine Mollone, e Gosantine de Kerki, su de Tamarikes, [et] Ithoccor
d'Iscanu, e Gosantine de serra Mirkis. Termenes dessu saltu: ave su cucuthu
dess'iscala d'Orthole, avunde parthimus de pare cun sos de Thori, e ccollat
ass'elike de serras dessa Cotina, ass'ariola de monte de Petru, a ffuntana de lutu,
e iunpat derettu assos gulvares de Oreiu, tottuve sa via de serra isc'a Malusone,
e ttorrat assu rivu ki e[st] in derettu dessu kerku iunpatoriu, sutta su vadu ki
48r iunpamus ad Erthone, e ccollat tottuve flum[en] isca guttur | d'eslikes, e benit
termen assu saltu de Th[e]rkis de Thori.

188. Conporu. *In Silvori.*
Conp[or]aili a Petru de Nureki sa parte sua dessu saltu de flume[n] minore, [et] ego deindeli I mesa libra d'argentu lavorata, [et] I eba, [et] I boe. T[este]s: Gunnari de Varru, e Mariane de Kerki, e Petru Mutascu, e Furatu Mutascu. Term[en] dessu saltu: ave s'ariola cotinatha de Serras, ass'attera ariola susu de Lellagor, tottuve sa serra in co parthimus de pare cu[n] Thurrove, a ccorona pertusa, e falat assu badu ki iunpan a Gurtagine, e ttorrat a fundu dessa corona d'iscala d'ebbas, e ttorrat a funtana de lutu.

189. Co[m]po[r]u. Saltu *in Cleu.*
Conp[or]aili a cComita de Thori Gardis su saltu de Ribu de Turthebi, ki fuit
de secatura de rennu, cu[n] bolu[n]tate dessos fiios; e de V partes I de cuniatu
de Pilosu; [et] ego deindeli I mesa libra d'argentu, [et] I voe domatu. Term[en]
dessu saltu: ave su kiiu dessa vinia de Gosantine de Tureki, e benit sutta sa fun-
48v tana dassande sos II cuniatos | ki sun dessa corte dessa funtana, e benit per
meiu su gulbare, tottuve muru, tottuve margine, ass'agitu de valle de Petru; ivi
iunpat bia, tottuve via, e ttorrat assu kiiu dessa vinia de Gosantine de Tureki.
T[este]s: Gosantine Pacu-mi-restat maiore d'iscolca de Kitarone, e Gosantine

187. Purchase. *Silvori.*
I bought from Gosantine de Thori 'Titicca' his share of the unworked land (*saltu*) of Flumen Minore ('lesser river', Riu Minore, Ittiri), and gave him one pound (*libra*) of hammered silver (*argentu lavorata*). Witnesses: Gunnari de Varru; Gosantine Mollone; Gosantine de Kerki from Tamarikes (Tamarighes, near Usini); Ithoccor d'Iscanu, and Gosantine de Serra Mirkis. Boundaries of the estate are: from the top of Iscala d'Orthole ('hillside of Orthole') that we share together with the de Thori family it passes to the holly oak (*elike*) of Serras dessa Cotina ('ridges of the rocks'), to the threshing floor (*ariola*) of Monte de Petru ('hill of Petru'), to Funtana de Lutu ('muddy spring'), it crosses towards the enclosures (*gulbares*) at Oreiu, [goes] along the road of Serra as far as Malusone, turns at the stream which goes in the direction of Kerku Iunpatoriu ('oak tree crossing-ford') below the ford (*vadu*) that crosses to Erthone, and passes along the river as far as Guttur d'Elikes ('the path of the holly oaks'), and the boundary reaches the land (*saltu*) of Therkis de Thori.

188. Purchase. *In Silvori.*
I bought from Petru de Nureki his share of the unworked land (*saltu*) of Flumen Minore ('lesser river', Riu Minore, Ittiri), giving him a half-pound of hammered silver, one mare (*eba*) and an ox. Witnesses: Gunnari de Varru; Mariane de Kerki; Petru Mutascu, and Furatu Mutasanctu. Boundary of the estate: from the rocky threshing floor (*ariola*) at Serras to the other threshing floor higher up at Lellagor, [it goes] along the ridge which we share together with Thurrove, [then] to Corona Pertusa ('pierced hilltop'), and descends to the ford that crosses to Gurtagine, and [then] turns to the foot of Corona ('the hilltop') at Iscala d'Ebbas ('hillside of mares'), and turns to Funtana de Lutu ('muddy spring').

189. Purchase. *Unworked land* (saltu) *in Cleu.*
I bought from Comita de Thori Gardis the unworked land (*saltu*) at Ribu de Turthebi ('Turthebi river'), which was an alienation from the realm, with the consent of his sons, as well as one of five shares of the cultivated enclosure (*cuniatu*) at Pilosu, giving a half pound of silver and one tame ox. The boundary of the estate is from the border (*kiiu*) of the vineyard of Gosantine de Tureki, and starts beneath Funtana ('the spring') leaving behind the two cultivated plots (*cuniatos*) which are part of the farmyard (*corte*) at Funtana; it goes through the middle of the enclosure (*gulbare*), along the wall and along the border (*margine*) to the entrance (*agitu*) of Valle de Petru ('the valley of Petru'); there, it crosses the road, goes along the road and turns to the border of the vineyard of Gosantine Tureki. Witnesses: Gosantine Pacu-mi-restat,

de Varda, [et] ambos sos fr[ate]s, Ithoccor e Mariane. E de Cleu: Presnaki, e Gosantine de Tureki, e Gosantine de Martis su de Silki.

190. Term[en]. *Apus sa domo de Teclata.*
Termen dessu saltu depus sa domo de Teclata, ki fuit de donnu Petru de Serra, e de Mariane su fiiu: su saltu de Gureiu, via de valle Becla, margine de Molendinu, assu gulbare dessa mura, muru tottuve, ad ispelunca de Co[n]so, via tottuve de serra, assu muru de Suruge, muru falat tottuve, derettu assa petra dessos Lakellos, derettu a margine de Nurgoi, assu muru dessa funtana de term[en] de Survi, muru falat a flum[en], flumen tottuve a flum[en] maiore; flumen maiore
49r a Marikella, tottuve | flum[en], assu rivu ki falat ave Teclata; ivi dassat flum[en] maiore, assos kercos clopatos de co parthimus de pare cum Curin, assu furru de Sega, [et] torrat assu muru de Sega. Custu saltu partho cu[n] frates meos, appus sa domo de Teclata, e llat[us] dessa villa.

191. Postura. *De s[er]vos.*
Positinke Iusta de serra a S[an]c[t]u Pet[ru] de Silki cando se 'nke affersit, fiia de Pet[ru] de Capathennor, e de Maria de Serra, su lat[us] dessa domo de Favules cu[n] p[er]tenenthia canta vi aveat, saltos, t[er]ras, binias, corte [et] ho[m]i[n]es; parthone in su saltu de Sugugin, ki parthimus cu[n] fiios de Varusone de Setilo; e parthone in su saltu de planu de Murta, ki est ante Comata; e parthone in Kerkethanos; e parthone in Silva Manna; e pparthone in su saltu de Saressi, ki aveat apus donnu Petru de Carvia su avu, ki parthin umpare cu[n] fiios de Mariane de Caruia; e parthone in Ballenari, [et] in su
49v de codas de Bonanu; ecco sos de Nurcar; saltos de | Calabrike, in Gurri, de VI partes I; parthone in co mi vi dittavat dessu de padule de vaccas; e partho[ne] in su de valle de ruginas; e parthone in pratu de Mugore; e parthone in Puthu Pianis. Ecco custas parthones de Favules, [et] issu de Calabrike mi partho latus ego e llat[us] ambos sos frates. Et issa parthone canta vi li dittavat in Ficu nigella positila a sS[an]c[t]u Pet[ru] innanti de se vi offerre. Sa parthone de

the head of the ward (*maiore d'iscolca*) at Kitarone (Caddaroni-Sant'Eusebio); Gosantine de Varda with both his brothers, Ithoccor and Mariane; and from Cleu [there was] Presnaki and Gosantine de Tureki, and Gosantine de Martis from Silki.

190. Boundary. *At the farm* (domo) *of Teclata.*
Boundary of the unworked land (*saltu*) at the farm (*domo*) de Teclata (Trigiada, near Romana), which used to belong to lord Petru de Serra and to Mariance, his son: the land (*saltu*) of Gureiu [that is] along road of Valle Becla ('Becla valley'), the border (*margine*) of Molendinu (near Cossoine) to the enclosure (*gulbare*) of the wall, along the wall to Ispelunca de Conso ('cave of Conso'), the road along ridge to the wall of Suruge (near Cossoine); it descends along that wall in the direction of Petra dessos Lakellos ('the rock of the Lakellos [family]') towards the side of Nurgoi (Nergui), to the wall of the spring of the boundary of Survi; the wall goes down to river; along the river to Flumen Maiore ('great river'); [from] Flumen Maiore to Marikella, [and] along to the stream that descends from Teclata. There, it leaves Flumen Maiore, [goes to] the pair of covered oaks we share in common with Curin; to the communal oven (*furru*) at Sega [and] turns to the wall of Sega. This estate I divided with my brothers at the farm of Teclata, and with half [those] from the village.

191. Donation. *Of servants.*
Iusta de Serra, daughter of Petru de Capathennor (Crabattennere) and Maria de Serra donated to Sanctu Petru de Silki, when she avowed (*cando se'nke affersit*), a half share (*latus*) of the farm (*domo*) at Favules (San Pietro, Padria) with all the pertinences it has there: unworked lands (*saltos*), lands (*terras*), vineyards, farmyards (*corte*) and men (*homines*); a share (*parthone*) in the land (*saltu*) of Sugugin, which we divided with the sons of Varusone de Setilo, and a[nother] share in Silva Manna ('large wood', near Montresta), and a share in the land (*saltu*) of Saressi that she had from her grandfather, lord Petru de Carvia, which was shared together with Mariane de Carvia; and a share in Ballenari, and one in the Codas de Bonanu ('gorges of Bonanu'). These latter are at Nurcar and are unworked lands (*saltos*) of Calabrike (Calarighe) at Gurri (Burri). Of six shares, one share relates to Padule de Vaccas ('marsh of the cows'), one share is in Valle de Ruginas ('valley of the ruins,' Badde Ruinas, near Cossoine), one share is at Pratu de Mugore ('meadow of Mugore'), and one share is at Puthu Pianis ('Pianis well'). These divisions of Favules and that of Calabrike (Calarighe) I have a half share, and both brothers have the other half. All the share that relates to Ficu Nigella ('black fig', Figu Niedda), she [Iusta de Serra] donated to Sanctu Petru before she had made her offer. The share of Favules, belonging to lady

Favules, depus donn'Elene de Kerki, parthianila, su latus donna Sanna de Serra, et iss'ateru latus donna Elene de tThori, e ffiios de donnu Mariane de Serra Grassu.

192. Postura. *In Salvennor.*
Positinke Mariane de Thori p[ro]ss'anima dessa mama, sa domo sua de Salvennor; corte, e t[er]ras, e vinias, et ho[m]i[n]es, e ssaltos, [et] o[mn]ia cantu vi aveat appus isse, kene su dessu patre. Term[en] dessu saltu de Petronaki, ki
50r fuit depus sa domo de Salvennor, depus Mariane | de Thori: ave su kercu ub'es sa petra infurcata, termen de co parthiat cun sos Arracanes, ass'oiastru de co parthiat cun sos de Kerki; e ccollat su traginu a derettu assu tamarike dess'Ena, e benit assu pirastru dess'Ena, derettu assos oiastros dess'Ena, assu castru dessa funtana dess'ulumu, in co benit ass'oiastru dess'ariola, e ccollat derettu assu volitravu de monte de Vallatoriu, e ffiliat falande sa serra, a ccapithale de co venit termen dessu saltu de Iorgia de Roma; et oviat assa margine de co torramus a termen dessos Arracanes, in co falat assa via, derettu assu kercu de co ingetthamus in primariu ub'est sa petra infurcata. E ppositinke su saltu de Mafalu, sa parte sua canta vi li dittavat, ki parthiat cun su thiu Gosantine de Thori Divite. E ppositinke su saltu de valle de Niscoli, su latus ki parthiat cun su thiu Gosantine de Thori.

50v 193. Conporu.
Conporaili a Mariane Carbone, [et] ad Andria su connatu, sa terra de Pede de Nurake, term[en] assa de Capathennor, [et] ego deindelis x vervekes. T[es]t[e]s: Petru Pullikina, maiore d'iscolca, [et] ambos sos fr[ate]s, e pr[ev]iteru Dorgotori de Ca[m]pu.

194. Kertu. *De s[er]vos.*
Ego previteru Furatu de Vosa ki ponio in ecustu co[n]dake ca me bocait a ccorona s'apate de Nurki, do[n]nu Vinkenthu, p[ro] Petru de Ioscla, e pp[ro] Bera sa sorre, ca 'p[ro]gitteu non mi los das ki sun meos?' [Et] ego kertaili ca 'vicanos ind'aes levatos.' Gasi mi kerverun destimo[n]ios ca los aveat levatos bicanios. [Et] ego naraili ca 'p[ro]gitteu ti appo battuier destimonios? O iura, o iure ego!' Vattussi s'omine meu p[ro] iurare, [et] isse indulsitimi sa iura.

Elene de Kerki, was divided in half by lady Sanna de Serra, and Elene de Thori and the sons of lord Mariane de Serra Grassu ('the fat') the other half.

192. Donation. *In Salvénnor.*
Mariane de Thori gave, for the soul of his mother, the farm (*domo*) at Salvénnor—farmyard (*corte*), lands (*terras*), vines, men, and unworked lands (*saltos*), and everything that he had there except that of his father. The boundary of the land (*saltu*) of Petronaki, which used to belong to Mariane de Thori's farm (*domo*) at Salvénnor [is] from the oak at Petra Infurcata ('the standing stone'), the boundary of which is shared with the Arracanes [family], to the ogliastra tree from where it is shared with the Kerki [family], and [it] follows the flow [of water] towards the tamarisk at s'Ena ('the spring'); it goes to the pear tree of s'Ena ('the spring'), towards the wild olives of s'Ena, to the outcrop of the spring of s'Ulumu ('the elm') in which there is the wild olive tree at the threshing floor; it passes in the direction of the bog (*volitravu*) on Monte de Vallatoriu, descending along the ridge to the top [part] of the boundary of the estate of Iorgia de Roma. It meets the border (*margine*) where we turn to the boundary of the Arracanes where it descends to the road, [goes] towards the oak from which we set out at the start [and] where there is sa Petra Infurcata ('the embedded rock'). He also donated the unworked land (*saltu*) of Mafalu (Maffaru, Codrongianos), all his share that related to him there, which he shares with his uncle Gosantine de Thori Divite ('rich'). He also donated the land (*saltu*) of Valle de Niscoli ('valley of Niscoli'), the half-share that he has in common with his uncle, Gosantine de Thori.

193. Purchase.
I bought from Mariane Carbone and from Andria, his brother in law, the land (*terra*) of Pede de Nurake ('base of a nuraghe'), the limit of which is that of Capathennor (Crabattennere), and I gave them ten sheep. Witnesses: Petru Pullikina, head of the ward (*maiore d'iscolca*); both of the brothers, and priest Dorgotori de Campu.

194. Dispute. *Of servants.*
I, priest Furatu de Vosa, note in this condaghe that the abbot of Nurki, lord Vinkethu, called me to a hearing (*corona*) concerning Petru de Ioscla and Bera, his sister, [saying] 'why you don't give me them as they are mine?' I argued that 'others were taken in their place!' As such, they asked me for witnesses that they had taken others. I said: 'why do I have to bring you witnesses? Either take an oath or I will!' I brought forth a man [*omine*] of mine to swear and this [oath] exempted me from [having to swear] the oath. Witnesses: the *curatore*

T[e]st[e]s: su curatore in cuia corona kertavamus, e Gosantine de tThori Divite, e Gosantine de Nurdole, armentariu suo, e Petru de Valles, et totta sa corona.

195. Kertu. *De s[er]vos.*

51r Ego previteru Furatu de Vosa. Vocaitime a ccorona Pet[ru] de Martis | Gulpis, e Petru de Roma, e Dorgotori de Tureki, pro fiios d'Istefane Barbaru ca 'progitteu no mi 'nde das, ki sun fiios de servu meu?' Et ego narailis ca 'vinkitos inde sun parentes bostros.' Iudi[ca]runimi a destimonios ca 'nde furun binkitos sos parentes, et ego vatussi su co[n]dake de S[an]c[t]u Petru a ccorona e binki, in fattu dessu co[n]dake iurandende a .+. Petru de Ioscla, servu de clesia. T[e]st[e]s: su curatore Gosantine de Thori Divite, in cuia corona kertai e binki, e Petru de Carvia Bariu, maiore d'iscolca, e Gosantine de Nurdole, e totta curatoria, de co faken corona in esse[r].

196. Conp[or]u. *In Jennanu.*

Conp[or]ailis a ffiios de Melaki sa terra dessa corte, termen assa de Gosantine de Capriles, ave s'attera parte assa de Simione Bakillu, [et] essit a bia maiore ki vamus a fflumen S[an]c[t]u; [et] ego deindelis II sollos de lavore a pparthiresi, a sSusanna, [et] a Furatu, [et] a Marcusa, [et] a Iusta fiia de Ianne. Testes ki ap[prethavan ...][24]

51v 197. Datura. *Dessa iscla de Junketu.*

Ego iudike Barusone deili a S[an]c[t]u Pet[ru] de Silki p[ro]ssa a[n]i[m]a mea sa iscla de Junketu. Benit t[er]men dessa iscla assa vinia de do[n]nu Juva[n]ne de Thori, falat toctue sa iscla ad macta de Palonariu, et clonpet ad sa via ki collat de balle de boe, torrat toctue pus ena assu guttur de Latila, collat toctue pus ena, et junpat ad mo[n]ticlu Alvu, collat toctue pus ena, et affliscat assa vinia de do[n]nu Juva[n]ne de Thori. Test[e]s: do[n]nikellu Ithoccor su fr[at]e, et do[n]nikellu Comita su fr[at]e, et do[n]nu Ithoccor d'Athen su d'Usune, et do[n]nu Barusone Punca su de Torricla, et do[n]nu Petru de Maroniu su connatu.

198.[25] Datura. *Apus Cherki.*

In nomine Do[m]ini am[en]. Term[en] dessu saltu ki parthimu[s] de pare cu[n] Bosa: sa gruke ki am[us] in sa via, et falat capugosso sa via de Carru,

24 The entry breaks off here, at the end of f. 51r, and continues on f. 52r: *prethavan e ccorte, e prethu, Ianne de Campu, e Domitri de Bosa, e Ianne Pullikina, e Gosantine Melone mandatore de liveros.*

25 Duplicated in entry 404.

at whosehearing I won; Gosantine de Thori Divite; Gosantine de Nurdole, his administrator (*armentariu*); Petru de Valles, and the whole hearing.

195. Dispute. *Of servants.*
I, priest Furatu de Vosa. Petru de Martis Gulpis, Petru de Roma and Dorgotori de Tureki called me to a hearing concerning the sons of Istefane Barbaru [saying] 'why don't you give me [the service of] those who are sons of my servant? I told them that 'they were [lawfully] won from your parents!' They decided that I call witnesses from the time their parents were defeated, so I brought forth the condaghe of Sanctu Petru to the hearing and I won by way of the condaghe with Petru de Ioscla swearing on the cross. Witnesses: the *curatore*, Gosantine de Thori Divite at whose hearing I argued and won; Petru de Carvia Bariu, head of the ward (*maiore d'iscolca*); Gosantine de Nurdole, and the whole hearing.

196. Purchase. *In Iennanu (Gennano, Porto Torres).*
I bought from the sons of Melaki the land (*terra*) of the farmyard (*corte*), the boundary [of which is] to that of [the land of] Gosantine de Capriles, and from the other share (*parte*) [is] to that of Simione Bakillu, and goes out to the main road (*bia maiore*) that goes to Flumen Sanctu ('holy river', Fiume Santo). I gave them two minted (*de lavore*) soldi in payment to Susanna, Furatu, Marcusa, and to Iusta, daughter of Ianne. Witnesses who assessed both the farmyard (*corte*) and price: Ianne de Campu; Domitri de Bosas; Ianne Pullikin, and Gosantine Melone, representative of the freemen (*mandatore de liveros*).

197. Gift. *Of Iscla de Iunketu.*
I, iudike Barusone, gave to Sanctu Petru for [the salvation of] my soul, Iscala de Iunketu ('hillside of reeds'). The boundary of the marshland starts at the vineyard of lord Iuanne de Thori, it goes down to the islet (*iscla*), to the Macta de Palonariu ('*macchia* at Palonariu') and arrives at the road that leads to Balle de Boe ('valley of the ox'); it turns at the spring and goes along the vineyard of Guttur de Latila ('the path of Latila'), passes beyond the spring and crosses to Monticlu Alvu ('white hill'), passes beyond the spring and closes at the vineyard of lord Juvanne de Thori. Witnesses: *donnikellu* Ithoccor the brother; *donnikellu* Comita the brother; lord Ithoccor d'Athen from Usune (Usini); lord Barusone Punca of Torricla (Torrija), and lord Petru de Maroniu, his brother-in-law.

198. Gift. *At Cherki.*
In the name of the Lord, amen. The boundary of the unworked land (*saltu*) that we share in common with Bosa [goes from] the cross that we have on the road, it descends down the Carru road and goes down along the road to the bound-

[et] falat toctue sa via ad term[en] dessa gruke ki parthim[us] de pare cu[n] Gisarclu, derectu assa iscala lanci[n]osa, moliat cui assa gruke dessu Gisterru, dave sa gruke dessu Gisterru [...][26]

52r [...][27] prethavan e ccorte, e prethu, Ianne de Campu, e Domitri de Bosa, e Ianne Pullikina, e Gosantine Melone, mandatore de liveros.

199. Datura. *Salina in saltu.*
Deitinke a aS[an]c[t]u Pet[ru], sa donna de locu, mama de iudike Gunnari, sa salina sua d'Eriu, a parthirenos lat[us] appare cu[n] Saccaria, cu[n] bolu[n]tate dessu fiiu iudike Gunnari, e dessu nepote iudike Barusone. T[e]st[e]s: Gosantine Vacca, portorariu, maiore de saltu.

200.[28] *De s[er]vos.*
Kertait mecu Mariane de Kerki, fiiu de Comita de Kerki su de Gelesi, in Petru de Varda, et in Istephane su frate, et in sa sorre Furata, ca 'p[ro]gitteu mi los levas ki sun liveros fr[ate]s meos?' Et ego kertaili ca 'custu kertu ki mi fakes como tu, mi fekit Gosantine de Varda su thiu, e Mariane de Varda, in corona dessu donnu meu iudike Gunnari de Laccon, in Ottave, e derunimilos a sservos, ca furun fiios de Gosantine Cocone, ki fuit servu de S[an]c[t]u Petru de
52v Silki.' Judicarunimi | a destimonios ca nd'avea gosi binkitu in co kertava. Et ego battussilu assu curatore donnu Gosantine de Thori Divite, et ass'arkiprete de Turres donnu Gosantine de Lella, [et] a Iubanne de Maro[n]iu, maiore d'iscolca de Duos Nurakes, et a Petru Minninnu, mandatore de liveros. E iurarun a gruke .+. ca nd'avea binkitu, e cca mi los avean datos in corona a sservos, in co kertava, e iurait Jorgi Muris servu de S[an]c[t]u Pet[ru] de Silki in fattu dessos destimonios. T[este]s: su do[n]nu meu iudike Barusone de Laccon in cuia corona binki, e donnu Comita de Gunale Ioculanu, e donnu Ithoccor de Laccon Pinna, e do[n]nu Gosa[n]tine su fr[at]e.

201. Conp[or]u. *In Jennan[u].*
Conp[or]aili a Dericcor de Maroniu, fiiu de Juvanne de Maroniu, sa parte canta vi l'intravat in su saltu de Gulparios, ki fuit depus su socru Gosantine Pullikina, cu[n] boluntate dessa muiere do[n]na Nivata; [et] ego deindeli I cavallu, [et] I boe. T[este]s: Gosantine Cambulis, e Petru Muthurti, [et] Ithoccor Corsu, e
53r Iacunu, | e Ianu Petru Cosellu, e pr[e]biteru Gosantine Iscarpa, e Bukeri, maiore d'iscolca de Kitarone.

26 The entry breaks off here, at the end of f. 51v.
27 This is the continuation of entry 196 which breaks off at the end of f. 51r.
28 Duplicated in entry 274.

ary [marker] of the cross which we share in common with Gisarclu; [it goes] towards Iscala Lancinosa ('Lancinosa hillside') [and] from the cross of Gisterru [...] assessed both the farmyard (*corte*) and price: Ianne de Campu; Domitri de Bosas; Ianne Pullikin, and Gosantine Melone, representative of the freemen (*mandatore de liveros*).

199. Gift. *Salt-pan* (salina) *within the unworked land* (saltu).
The lady of the realm (*locu*) and mother of iudike Gunnari gave to Sanctu Petru her salt-pan (*salina*) at Eriu, half of which we share together with Saccaria (Saccargia), with the consent of her son, iudike Gunnari, and her grandson (*nepote*), iudike Barusone. Witnesses: Gosantine Vacca, the official assessor of land (*portorariu maiore de saltu*).

200. Of servants.
Mariane de Kerki, son of Comita de Kerki from Gelesi sued me over Petru de Varda and his brother Istephane and his sister Furata about 'why you deprive me of them when they are my free brothers (*liveros frates*)?' I argued that 'this dispute you have brought as you do, Gostantine de Varda the uncle [of theirs] and Mariane de Varda made at the hearing (*corona*) of my lord iudike Gunnari de Laccon at Ottave (Ottava), and they were given as servants (*servos*) because they were sons of Gosantine Cocone who was a servant (*servu*) of Sanctu Petru de Silki!' They decided that I bring witnesses [to say] that I had won [the case] about which the dispute was thus. I brought forth [as witnesses] the *curatore* lord Gosantine de Thori Divite, and the archpriest of Turres (Torres) lord Gosantine de Lella, and Iubanne de Maroniu, head of the ward (*maiore d'iscolca*) at Duos Nurakes ('two nuraghi', Due Nuraghe), and Petru Minninnu representative of the freemen (*mandatore de liveros*). They swore on the cross that I had won and that they had awarded me the servants at the hearing about which there was the dispute. Iorgi Muris, servant of Sanctu Petru de Silki, swore after the witnesses. Witnesses: my lord iudike Barusone de Laccon at whose hearing I won, and lord Comite de Gunale Ioculanu ('the jovial'), and lord Ithoccor de Laccon Pinna, and lord Gosantine his brother.

201. Purchase. *At Jennanu* (*Gennano, Porto Torres*).
I bought from Dericcor de Maroniu, son of Iuvanne de Maroniu, the whole share (*parte*) he had in the unworked land (*saltu*) of Gulparios, which was from the side of his father-in-law, Gosantine Pullikana, with the consent of his wife, lady Nivata. I gave them a horse and an ox. Witnesses: Gosantine Cambulis, Petru Muthurti, Ithoccor Corsu, and Iacunu, and Ianu Petru Cosellu, and priest Gosantine Iscarpa, and Bukeri the head of the ward (*maiore d'iscolca*) at Kitarone (Caddaroni-Sant'Eusebio).

202. *In Biosevin.*
Ego Massimilla abbatissa ki ponio in ecustu condake p[ro]ssu saltu de S[an]c[t]u Imbiricu de Biosei, ca mi kertavan in sos termenes fiios de donnu Therkis, Gosantine [et] Ithoccor, dandemi parte issoro, e parte dessu fr[at]e Mariane; [et] ego deindelis III libras d'argentu lavoratas. Test[es] ki vi furun uve mi davan su saltu: Gunnari de Laccon, [et] Ithoccor d'Athen su connatu, e Petru de Varru, e cComita Bardane, e Barusone Masala, e Gosantine Manutha. Custos destimonios vi furun uve atterminavan su saltu, andandeli ave term[en] in termen Petru Lorica, e Kipriane de Vare, ki furun servos d'Athen. Termenes dessu saltu, dessu meu, ki fuit de S[an]c[t]u Imbiricu, e dessu ki co[m]p[or]ai assos de
53v Thori, fiios de donnu Therkis mastriu: ave su castru de Gollettoriu, | parthinde s'Ena Dorta p[er] meia lege, e benit assu monticlu dessu gulbare dessu Castru, a derettu assu rivu dessa petra Alba, a pedale dessu monticlu de Kypriane; avinde valle collat tottuve a derettu ad uv'est mortu cane, a ccapithale dessu valliclu de Filicosu, a derettu assu bru[n]cu, claru ass'iscla de jacunu Andria, a ffundu dessu kercu dess'iscla de jacunu Andria; tottuve rivu falat isc'a su guttur de sSuveriu; tottuve margine a ccorona de Pilosu, avinde tottuve margine de Sutta Luianathos, assu muru dessu nassariu, e iunpat rivu, e ccollat tottuve su muru sutta coda dessu Pullialbu, tottuve su muru collat assu nurake de Gollettoriu.

203.[29] Kertu. *In Urin.*
Ego Massimilla appatissa de S[an]c[t]u Pet[ru] de Silki. Largaitimi donnu Mariane de Laccon su de Linthas, in su saltu de S[an]c[t]e Helias d'Urin, ca mi 'nde
54r kereat su lat[us]. Et ego tenninde | corona cun ille, in corona dessu do[n]nu meu iudike Gunnari de Laccon, sa die de S[an]c[t]u Simione in Nulabros; isse kereatinde su latus p[ro] se, et ego kerealu ad intregu, in co lu posit donnu Comita de Martis a sS[an]c[t]e Elias d'Urin. Iudicarunimi a destimonios ca lu posit donnu Comita de Martis a sS[an]c[t]'Elias, in co kertava; [et] ego battussilu a Dorgotori Palas, [et] a Pet[ru] de Funtana, ser(v)uos de rennu, [et] a Presnaki de Tutar, [et] a Bittorine Manicas, e iurarun a gruke .+. sos destimonios meos, e Dominike su mandatore meu. T[e]st[e]s: su do[n]nu meu iudike Gunnari de Laccon, in cuia corona binki, e donnu Saltaro su fr[at]e, curatore de Coraso, a ken mi deit su donnu meu ad andareli ave termen in termen dessu

29 Duplicated in entry 275.

202. *At Biosevin* (*Giusei*).
I, abbess Massimilla, put in this condaghe [an entry] regarding the unworked land (*saltu*) of Sanctu Imbiricu de Biosei (Giusei), the boundaries of which the sons of lord Therkis, Gosantine, and Ithoccor, contested [when] they gave me their own share and the share of their brother, Mariane, [for which] I gave them three pounds (*libras*) of worked silver. Witnesses who were there when they gave me the land (*saltu*) are: Gunnari de Laccon, and Ithoccor d'Athen his brother-in-law, and Petru de Varru, and Comita Bardane, and Barusone Masala, and Gosantine Manutha. These are the witnesses who were present when they delimited the land (*saltu*) going from boundary to boundary: Petru Lorica and Kipriane de Vare who were sevants of d'Athen. The boundaries of the land (*saltu*), [that is] of mine, which used to belong to Sanctu Imbiricu, and which the sons of lord Therkis de Thori Mastriu purchased, are: from the nuraghe (*castru*) of Gollettoriu, dividing s'Ena Dorta in half; [the boundary] arrives at the hill of the enclosure of the nuraghe, [then goes] towards Rivu dessa Petra Alba ('stream of the white rock'), [and] to the foot of the hill of Kypriane; from the valley, it passes along towards Mortu Cane ('dead dog'); [then] from the top of the small valley of Filicosu, towards the hill, in the direction of Iscla de jacunu Andria ('the islet of deacon Andria'), to the oak tree of Iscla de jacunu Andria, it descends along the stream as far as Guttur de Suveriu ('the track of the cork oak'), along the border (*margine*) at the hilltop (*corona*) of Pilosu; from there, along the border (*margine*) of Sutta Luianathos ('lower Luianathos'), to the wall of the weir (*nassariu*), it crosses the stream and passes along the wall below Coda dessu Pullialbu ('valley of Pullialbu'), it proceeds along the wall to the nuraghe (*nurake*) of Gollettoriu.

203. Dispute. *In Urin* (Uri).
I, Massimillla abbess of sanctu Petru de Silki. Lord Mariane de Laccon from Linthas took [land] from me in the unworked land (*saltu*) of Sancte Elias d'Urin (Uri) as he claimed half my share. I had recourse to a hearing (*corona*) with him at the hearing of the lord my iudike Gunnari de Laccon on the [feast] day of Sanctu Simione in Nulabros (Lunafras). He claimed half for himself and I claimed the whole of it because lord Comita de Martis gave it to Sancte Elias d'Urin. They decided that I call witneses [to say] that lord Comita de Martis had given it to Sancte Elias d'Urin which he was disputing. I brought Dorgotori Palas and Petru de Funtana, servants of the realm (*rennu*), also Presnaki de Tutar and Bittorine Manicas as witnesses, and they swore on the cross as well as my representative (*mandatore*) Domininke. Witnesses: the lord iudike Gunnari de Laccon at whose hearing I won [the case], and lord Saltaro his brother, *curatore* of Coraso (Coros) who my lord assigned me to go from boundary to

saltu; e do[n]nu Mariane de Thori d'Enticlas, e do[n]nu Dorgotori de Thori Camba-curtha. Ecco custos mi deit su do[n]nu meu iudike Gunnari de Laccon ad aterminarelu su saltu.

Saltu de S[an]cta Maria de Uri.[30]

54v Termen dessu saltu: ave Sancta | Maria assa funtana dessa corona, tottuve sa margine, assa corona iackitoria; avinde falat tottuve assa via, ave sa via falat a rrivu, su rivu collat a badu de piperas, e ccollat assa margine, et essit sa margine ass'agitu de co parthimus cun sos Aketos, e ccollat assu nurake, e ffalat p[er] meia sa serra, assa gruke, a su kercu uv'es sa petra infurcata, e falat assa coperclata; avinde collat sa via, e cclompet assu nuracke, girat ave su nuracke susu, a derettu assu nuracke de sutta via, ave su nurake assu gulbare dessa via ki vaet a lLinthas, e falat ribu assu badu ki iunpat a pPetretu, e ccollat tottuve assa corte de S[anct]a Maria. T[e]st[e]s: do[n]nu Saltaro su fr[at]e de iudike ki lu aterminait su saltu, e donnu Mariane de Thori d'Enticlas, e donnu Dorgotori de Thori Ca[m]ba-Curtha, e Dorgotori Pala servu de iudike, [et] ho[m]i[n]es bonos dessa curatoria de Coraso.

204. Kertu. *De s[er]vos.*

55r Kertait mecu Gosantine de Thori, fiiu | de Dorgotori de Thori Camba-Curtha, p[ro] fiios de Maria de Vare ca 'p[ro]gitteu no mi 'nde das, ki fuit coiuvata cum servu meu?' Et ego naraili ca 'non ti 'nde do ca mi la furait su servu tuo.' Et isse naraitimi c', 'a boluntate de pare los coiuvaimus, p[ro] parthire su fetu.' Issara li iudicarun a battuier isse destimonios ca los coiuvaramus a boluntate de pare, e no los appit; et issara mi essirun a mimi a destimonios totta sa villa d'Innoviu, ca vi andai e 'nde la levai, avunde mi l'avea furata su servu. Issara mi delegarun ad avermi tottu su fetu. Test[e]s: judike Barusone in cuia corona binki in Kitarone, sa die de letania maiore, e Petru Iscarpa Pedes, maiore d'iscolca, e Gosantine de Thori Manutha, e Pet[ru] de Matrona, et totta curatoria uve faken corona.

205. Kertu. *De s[er]vos et de ankillas.*

Kertai p[ro] servos de S[an]c[t]u Petru de Silki ki mi furun andatos p[ro] livertatos, e non bolean faker servithu ki fakean parentes issoro, in famiia, et | ego no
55v

30 This is not a separate entry in the manuscript, but a continuation of entry 203.

boundary in the land (*saltu*); and Mariane de Thori d'Enticlas, and lord Dorgotori de Thori Camba-Curtha ('short-leg'). My lord iudike Gunnari de Laccon assigned me these [people] to define the land (*saltu*).

Unworked land (saltu) *of Sancta Maria de Uri.*
The boundary of the land (*saltu*) [is]: from Sancta Maroa to Funtana dessa Corona ('the spring of the hilltop'), along the border (*margine*) to the summit [called] Iackitoria. From there, it descends along the road; from the road it descends to the stream; the stream proceeds to Badu de Piperas ('ford of snakes'), and passes along the border (*margine*), then goes from the border to the entrance [*agitu*] that we share with the Aketos [family]; it goes to the nuraghe, descends down the middle of the ridge to the cross, and to the tree where there is Petra Infurcata ('the standing stone'); it descends to Coperclata ('the dolmen'); from there, it passes along the road and reaches the nuraghe; it turns up from the nuraghe and towards the nuraghe of the lower road; from the nuraghe of the enclosure on the road that goes to Linthas, and descends [along] the stream to the ford that crosses at Petretu, then passes towards the farmyard (*corte*) of Sancta Maria. Witnesses: lord Saltaro, the brother of the of iudike who delimited the land (*saltu*), and lord Mariane de Thori d'Enticlas, and lord Dorgotori de Thori Camba-Curtha ('short-leg'), and Dorgotori Pala servant of iudike, and trusted men (*homines bonos*) from the *curatoría* of Coraso (Coros).

204. Dispute. *Of servants.*
Gosantine de Thori, son of Dorgotori de Thori Camba-Curtha ('short leg'), was in dispute with me over the sons of Maria de Vare, [demanding] 'why do you not give me [the woman] who was married with my servant?' I said that 'I do not give you [her], as your servant took her away from me!' He replied to me that 'we married them with the consent of both with regard to dividing the offspring!' Next, they decided to call witnesses that we had wed them both with their consent, but there was none. Then, witnesses from the whole village of Innoviu presented themselves for me [saying] that I went and took her, the servant having deprived me of her. Then, they assigned all the offspring for me to have. Witnesses: iudike Barusone, at whose hearing at Kitarone I won on the day of the Great Litany (*letania maiore*), and Petru Iscarpa Pedes, the head of the ward (*maiore d'iscolca*), and Gosantine de Thori Manutha, and Petru de Matrona, and trusted men from the *curatoría* of Coraso (Coros).

205. Dispute. *Of servants and female servants.*
I was in dispute over servants of Sanctu Petru de Silki who claimed to be freemen (*livertatos*), and who did not wish to do service that their own parents

'nde potti faker kerviclia, tenninde corona dessu donnu meu iudike Gunnari de
Laccon, ponendelu ego a kertare a donnu Mariane de Maroniu p[ro] S[an]c[t]u
Petru. E iudike torraitili berbu, ca 'curatore de Romania ses, nunthalos tu, [et]
issos atteros ki sun foras de curatoria de Romania ego los appo nunthare.' E
iudike nunthaitilos a nnatale de S[anct]i Gavini, a benner cum cartas avunde
bolean esser liberos ispesoniarios. E battusserun cartas sos ki las avean, e iudike
precontait sos dessa corona ca 'gitteu bos inde paret d'ecustas cartas?' [Et] issos
torrarunili berbu, ca 'malas nos paren, e non sun de crederelas.' E non parverun
bonas sas cartas nen a iudike, nen a lLocu. Poserunimi in manu sos homines
a sserviremi, e iudike naraitilis c', 'assa festa de Sanct'Elias siates in su Monte,
in corona mea, cum sas cartas p[ro]unde bolites esser liveros.' Et ego levailu
56r a do[n]nu Mariane de | Maroniu, [et] assu priore meu donnu Furatu Gaspis,
e mandailos assu Monte, a cco posit iudike; [et] issos non bi bennerun, nen
cum cartas, nen sene cartas a ccorona. E iudike narait ad totta corona, ca 'de
custos homines in uve kertat S[an]c[t]u Petru de Silki ki lis posi ecco accantas
coronas, e non bennerun, gitteu volites ca 'nde fatha?' [Et] issos liveros torrar-
unili verbu ca 'datende iura assos servos de S[an]c[t]u Petru, ca si se videren
c'arun poter vi[n]ker ad esser liveros, vennitos in esser a ccorona.' E iudike pos-
itinos ad isettare isc'a notte, e non bennerun; et issos homines ki kertavan custu
kertu, narrunili a iudike ca 'donnu, gitteu nos fakites?' E iudike naraitilis ca
'vattute servu de clesia, e iuret.' Bennit Gosantine de monte ki fuit servu de
clesia e iurait a .+. ca 'custos homines uve kertat donnu Mariane de Maroniu,
56v de fiios de servos de famiia de S[an]c[t]u Petru de Silki sun, ki | non furun liv-
ertatos.' E iudike naraitinos ca 'inperatelos avestara a famiia tottu su paniiu, ki
furun p[ro] livertatos de S[an]c[t]u Petru, e non iusserun cartas a ccorona a
cco lis ponean.' T[e]st[e]s: iudike Gu[n]nari de Laccon, e cComita de Gunale,
e Petru de Laccon, [et] Ithoccor de Laccon, e cComita de Laccon, e sSaltaro
Pinna, e Petru Pinna, e Dorgotori de Ponte, e Gosantine de Varca, e Gunnari
de Thori, e Dorveni de Carvia, [et] Ithoccor de Thori, e Gosantine de Thori, e
ccantos vi furu[n] in sa corona; e maiore de ianna Gosantine Palas, e ckita sua.
T[e]st[e]s. E nnara[it] iudike in corona p[ro]ssos ki non vatusserun sas cartas,
ca 'si vattun avestara de no las creder, o malas essere[nt], o bonas.' Numen
dessos homines ki se mi levavan p[ro] livertatos: Petru de Mukianu, e Gos-
antine su fiiu, [et] Istephane su fiiu, e cComita su fiiu, e llatus d'Andria su fiiu;

had done for the church (*in famiia*). I, unable to constrain them by force, had recourse to a hearing (*corona*) of my lord iudike Gunnari de Laccon, assigning lord Mariane de Maroniu to argue for Sanctu Petru. The iudike declared that 'you are the *curatore* of Romangia, so you summon them! The others who are outside the district (*curatoría*) of Romania, I will summon!' On the feast day (*nnatale*) of Sancti Gavino, iudike summoned them to come with documents (*cartas*) by which they had wished to be free tenants (*liberos ispesoniarios*). They brought forth the documents they had, and iudike asked at the hearing, 'what do you think about these documents?' They replied that 'they seem to us unsound (*malas*) and are not to be trusted!' The documents did not seem good either to the iudike or to those present (*a llocu*). [And so] they placed the men in my hands to serve me, and the iudike told them that 'at the feast of Sanct'Elias, be present at Monte, at my hearing (*corona*), with the documents by which you wish to be [considered] freemen!' I took lord Mariane de Maroniu and the prior lord Furatu Gaspis and sent them to Monte as iudike had indicated. But they did not come to the hearing either with documents or without documents. Iudike addressed the whole hearing: 'What do you want to do with these men over whom Sanctu Petru de Silki is in dispute and to whom I have allocated several hearings, and [yet] they do not come?' The freemen replied, 'have the servants of Sanctu Petru take an oath because if they think they can win [the case] of being freemen, they will come to the hearing!' The iudike had us wait until night-time, but they did not come. The men who were involved in this dispute said to iudike, 'lord, what will you have us do?' The iudike told them, 'call forth a servant of the church and he will take an oath!' Gosantine de Monte, who was a servant of the church, came and swore on the cross that 'these men about whom lord Mariane de Maroniu is in dispute are sons of servants of the church of Sanctu Petru de Silki who are not freemen!' Iudike told us, 'from now on, make use of all those who were [claiming] to be freemen of Sanctu Petru, but who did not produce documents at the hearing to which they were called, as required labour (*tottu paniiu*) for the church (*a famiia*)!' Witnesses: iudike Gunnari de Laccon, Comita de Gunale, Petru de Laccon, Ithoccor de Laccon, Comita de Laccon, Saltaro Pinna, Petru Pinna, Dorgotori de Ponte, Gosantine de Varca, Gunnari de Thori, Dorveni de Carvia, Ithoccor de Thori, Gosantine de Thori, and all who were present at the hearing as well as the chief guard (*maiore de ianna*) Gosantine Palas and his entourage (*ckita sua*). Witnesses: iudike said at the hearing concerning those who did not bring forth the documents as evidence that 'if they bring documents as evidence in future, whether they are good or bad, they are not to be trusted!'

The names of the men who took themselves from me as freemen were: Petru de Mukianu, and Gosantine his son, and Istephane his son, and Comita his son,

Mariane Arte, e fiios suos; Petru Corsu, e ffiios suos; Jorgi de Canake, e Deric-
57r cor su fr[at]e, e Gosantine | su fr[at]e, et Anna sa sorre, e Maria sa sorre, cum
fiios issoro; Dericcor d'Ockeri, e fiios suos; Gosantine d'Orane, e ffiios suos; Dor-
gotori Pettenatu e fiios suos; Gosantin'Arte, e Petru su fr[at]e, et Elene Arte,
e Maria Arte, e Iusta Arte cu[n] fiios issoro; e fiios de Petru d'Ockeri; e Gos-
antine Parithe, e ffiios suos; e Iusta Parithe cu[n] fiios suos; e Mariane Tillis,
e fiios suos tottu; Petru [...] e fiios suos; Comita Tussia, e fiios suos; Dorgotori
Tussia e fiios suos; Justa Tussia e fiios suos; Frevari Capillu e fiios suos, e llatus
de Gavini su fr[at]e; Garulittu e fiios suos; Gosantine su fr[at]e, e fiios suos;
Viventi de funtana e fiios suos; Maria sa sorre e fiios suos; Jorgi su frate, e fiios
suos; Gosantine Piticu e fiios suos; Furatu Piticu e fiios suos, et issa sorre cu[n]
fiios suos; Ithoccor de Seltas e fiios suos, e Ianne su frate; e Iorgi su fr[at]e de
57v Garulittu e fiios suos; Furatu Solina e fiios suos depus issa; | Istephane Pala e
fiios suos; Gosantine su frate e fiios suos; Petru Pala e fiios suos; Elene Pala sa
sorre e fiios suos; Gosantine d'Urieke cu[n] fiios suos, e Mariane su frate, e fiios
suos, e Maria sa sorre, cu[n] fiios, [et] Elene sa sorre e fiios suos; Maria de Soiu
cu[n] fiios suos; Petru de Soiu su frate, cu[n] fiios suos; Iusta de Soiu sa sorre,
cu[n] fiios; Gosantine Savitanu, e Matrona sa sorre, cu[n] fiios suos; Mariane
Savitanu su frate, cu[n] fiios suos, e Dorgotori Savitanu su frate; Jorgi Muris,
[et] issos fiios depus isse; Thaita Pala intrega e llatus de Martine Muris su mar-
itu, cu[n] parte canta mi dittavat dessu fetu; Bittorine de funtana cu[n] su fiiu;
Nastasia de Carros, cu[n] fiios suos; Bonosia cu[n] fiios suos depus issa; Vit-
toria de Soiu, cu[n] fiios suos; Jorgia Cocone cu[n] tottu fiios suos; Andria de
Soiu cu[n] fiios suos; Furatu Topparu, cu[n] parte sua dessu fetu; Gavini Ten-
58r neru, cu[n] fiios suos; Muscu Culurione, cu[n] parte sua dessu fetu; Susanna |
Carta, cu[n] parte sua dessu fetu; Pet[ru] de Seltas, [et] Elene sa sorre; Mariane
Cocone, cu[n] fiios suos, [et] Angela sa netta, Pet[ru] de Varda cu[n] fiios suos;
Istephane su fr[at]e, cu[n] fiios suos, e Furata de Varda sa sorre, [et] Elene fiia de
Comita, [et] Elene fiia de Gosantine; Elias Dente, [et] Ithoccor, [et] Iskemose, e
Pet[ru], tottos III frates, e Maria sa sorre, cu[n] fiios suos; e Maria Pinta, e Bona;
e Maria de Cannetu; Gavini d'Ariolas cu[n] fiios suos; Bonellu cu[n] fiios suos;
Maria Furca e fiios suos, e nepotes suos, ki fuit de postura de do[n]na Maria
d'Arsumen.

206. Postura. *In Gennor.*
Positinke Mariane de Thori a S[an]c[t]u Pet[ru] de Silki sa domo de Gennor, cu[n] servos [et] ankillas, e ccu[n] terras, e ccu[n] binias; e ppositinke su saltu de Bubui, ki fuit de secatura de rennu. Termen dessu saltu: ave su monticlu

and half [the share of] Andria his son; Mariane Arte and his sons; Petru Corsu and his sons; Jorgi de Canake (Caniga), and Dericcor his brother, and Gosantine his brother, and Anna his sister, and Maria his sister with their sons; Dericcor d'Ockeri and his sons; Gosantine d'Orane and his sons; Dorgotori Pettenatu and his sons; Gosantin'Arte, and Petru his brother, and Elene Arte, and Maria Arte, and Iusta Arte with their sons; and the sons of Petru d'Ockeri; and Gosantine Parithe and his son; and Iusta Parithe with her sons; and Mariane Tillis and all her sons; Petru [...] and his sons; Comita Tussia and his sons; Dorgotori Tussia and his sons; Iusta Tussia and his sons; Frevari Capillu and his sons, and half [the share] of Gavino his brother; Garulittu and his sons; Gosantine his brother and his sons; Viventi de Funtana and his sons; Maria his sister and her sons; Jorgi the brother and his sons; Gosantine Piticu and his sons; Furatu Piticu and his sons, and his sister with her sons; Ithoccor de Seltas and his sons, and Ianne his brother; and Iorgi the brother of Garulittu and his sons; Furatu Solina and the sons from her line; Istephane Pala and his sons; Gosantine his brother and his sons; Petru Pala and his son; Elene Pala the sister and her sons; Gosantine d'Urieke with his sons, and Mariane his brother and his sons; and Maria his sister with sons, and Elene the sister with her sons; Maria de Soiu with her sons; Petru de Soiu the brother with his sons; Iusta de Soiu his sister with sons; Gosantine Savitanu and Matrona his sister and her sons; Mariane Savitanu the brother with his sons; Dorgotori Savitanu the brother; Jorgi Muris and the sons from his line; Thaita Pala a full female servant (*intrega*), and half [the share] of Martine Muris her husband with all the share of her offspring that belongs to me; Bittorine de Funtana with her son; Nastasia de Carros with her sons; Bonosia with the sons from her line; Vittoria de Soiu with her sons; Jorgia Cocone with all her sons; Andria de Soiu with his sons; Furatu Topparu, with his share of offspring; Gavini Tenneru with his sons; Muscu Culurlon with her share of the offspring; Susanna Carta, with her share of the offspring; Petru de Seltas and Elene his sister; Mariane Cocone with his sons and Angela his niece; Petru de Varda with his sons; Istephane his brother with his sons; and Furata de Varda his sister; and Elene daughter of Comita, and Elene daughter of Gosantine; Elias Dente, and Ithoccor, and Iskemose, and Petru, all three [are] brothers, and Maria their sister with her sons; Maria Pinta, and Bona; and Maria de Cannetu; Gavini d'Ariolas with his sons; Bonellu with his sons; Maria Furca and his sons and nephews who were [part of] the donation of lady Maria d'Arsumen.

206. Donation. *In Gennor* (Zennos).
Mariane de Thori donated to Sanctu Petru de Silki the farm (*domo*) at Gennor (Zennos) with male and female servants, lands and vineyards. He also donated the unworked land (*saltu*) of Bubui which was alienated from the

dessa kersa dessa petra dess'Asinu, e ccollat tottuve sa via ki collat de valle de Iorgi Kercas, derettu assa sella maiore de Thilaccor, e benit assu càntaru dessu carru, e falat sa valle dessa murta, e benit ass'iscla de Pet[ru] de Nurki, de s'uvile de Gunnali, e iunpat assa petra dess'ape de Lenposti, e benit ivi ass'ariola de Lenposti, e benit assa sella dessu kercu de Mabrannu, e benit tottuve sa via, assu càntaru d'Abbas, e falat ass'iscla, parthinde s'iscla de Bubui, e benit assu monticlu dess'arenariu, a derettu assa petra dess'ape de fruscos, [et] aflis-cat assu gulbare dessa petra dess'asinu. Ecco saltu ki li deit iudike Barusone a donnu Comita de Martis su frate, de secatura de rennu.

207. Postura.
Positinke do[n]na Sikiia Tussia I mesa livra d'argentu a S[an]c[t]u Pet[ru], ki lis derat assos nepotes a ccasticare; et issos no la potterun aver sa mesa libra, derun inde su saltu de valle de Cucke. Termen dessu saltu: ave sa de Petru Longu, e iunpat travessu sa serra, a termen dessa de donnu Gosantine Thelle
59r su p[re]viteru, e ccollatin | de sa serra, term[en] assa de Petru de Capriles Prinkiu, et essit assa via travessaria de Ospitine; varicat sa via a term[en] dessa de Comita de Navitha, e ffalat a ssup[ra] s'ariola, e ffalat assa valle, e iunpat assu piskinale dessu muteclu, e ffalat tottuve s'atha a term[en] dessa de Petru Lo[n]gu.

208. Co[m]p[or]u.
Conporaili a Travesu Catha, intro d'ecustu saltu I lintha in sa valle, [et] ego deindeli IIII vardones de petha porkina in sollu.

209. Co[m]poru.
Conp[or]aili a pPetru de Serra Digititruncu I sol[lu] de t[er]ra sup[ra] custa ki conporai a Travesu Catha, [et] ego deindeli I sagu.

210.
Conp[or]aili a Petru Icalis I sol[lu] de t[er]ra tenende ad ecusta, ego deindeli I sol[lu] de pa[n]nu.

realm (*rennu*). The boundary of the land (*saltu*) [is]: from the hill of Kersa ('mastic tree'), from Petra dess'Asinu ('rock of the donkey'); it passes along the road that goes from the valley (*valle*) of Iorgi Kercas, [goes] towards the big saddle [of the hill] at Thilaccor, and arrives at Cántaru dessu Carru ('waterfall of the cart'), and [then] goes down the Valle dessa Murta ('valley of the myrtle'), and comes out at Iscla de Petru de Nurki ('islet of Petru de Nurki'); from the sheepfold of Gunnali it crosses to Petra dess'Ape ('rock of the bee') at Lenposti and reaches the threshing floor at Lenposti; it [then] comes to Sella dessu Kercu ('the saddle of the oak') a Mabrannu; it goes along the road to Càntaru d'Abbas ('waterfall of waters') and descends to the islet (*iscla*), dividing the islet (*iscla*) of Bulbui, and reaches Monticlu dess'Arenariu ('hill of the sandpit'), towards Petra dess'Ape ('rock of the bee') at Fruscos, and closes at the enclosure of Petra dess'Asinu ('rock of the donkey'). That is the land (*saltu*) which iudike Barusone gave to lord Comita de Martis, his brother [as] an alienation from the realm.

207. Donation.
Lady Sikiia Tussia donated one-half of a pound (*livra*) of silver to sanctu Petru which she her nephews to look after; they were unable to have [access to] the half-pound [of silver], so they gave the unworked land (*saltu*) of Valle de Cucke ('valley of Cucke'). The boundary of the land (*saltu*): from that of Petru Longu ('long rock'), it crosses the ridge, to the boundary of that of lord Gosantine Thelle the priest, and passes along the ridge; the [other] boundary is that of Petru de Capriles Prinkiu, and comes out at the crossroad for Ospitine. It passes the road to the boundary of [lands of] Comita de Navitha, and descends to [a point] above the threshing floor; it descends the valley and crosses Piskinale dessu Muteclu ('the pool of Muteclu'), then descends along the crag (*atha*) to the boundary of Petru Longu.

208. Purchase.
I bought from Travesu Catha, within this land (*saltu*), one length (*lintha*) [of land] in the valley, and I gave him the cash equivalent (*in sollu*) of four pieces of pork meat.

209. Purchase.
I bought from Petru de Serra Digititruncu ('chopped fingers'), one soldo of land (*terra*) above that which I bought from Travesu Catha, and I gave him a piece of rough cloth (*sagu*).

210.
I bought from Petru Icalis one soldo worth of land (*terra*) bordering on this, and I gave him one soldo of cloth (*pannu*).

211. Tramutu.
Tramutai cu[n] Bassu de Novaia; deitimi isse I lintha tenende ad ecustas ki
59v avea de co[m]p[or]u, et | ego deili sa corte ki fuit de Pet[ru] de Gunale, fiiu de Varusone Angata, ki poserat a S[an]c[t]u Petru de Silki, sa parte ki li dittavat ad isse. T[e]st[e]s ki vi furun ad app[re]thare su saltu et issu conporu, Petru d'Oia, e cComita de Carvia, e Petru de Cap[ri]les Prinkiu, e Petru de Cap[ri]les Longu, e nNiscoli su frate.

212. Conporu.
Conp[or]aili a fForasticu Bakillu sa t[er]ra dessu planu dessu Laccu Secatu, tenende assa de Petru de Cap[ri]les Longu; [et] ego deindeli II bardones de petha porkina, e II moios d'oriu, [et] I petha berbekina in s'annu dessu fam[en].

213. Co[m]p[or]u.
Conp[or]aili a Gosantine Siccule, sa t[er]ra dess'ariola de Cucumake, [et] ego deindeli bukellu de baccone, caput a pare, s'a[n]nu dessu famen.

214. Conporu.
60r Conp[or]aili a Iustu Tincu, sa t[er]ra dessu Palitortu, ki est term[en] | assa de S[an]c[t]a Maria de Thergu; [et] ego deindeli IIII clopa[s] de petha, s'annu dessu famen.

215. Conporu.
Conp[or]aili a Pet[ru] Soru I terra tenende ad ecussa ki co[m]p[or]ai a Iustu Tincu, [et] ego deindeli VI moios d'oriu s'a[n]nu dessu fam[en].

216. Co[mporu].
Conp[or]aili a Petru Gereiu sa parthone sua dessa vinia tenende assa de S[an]c[t]u Petru, [et] ego deindeli I sol[lu] de pannu.

217. Conp[or]u.
Conp[or]aili etro cuvi, tenende ad ecussa, a Iustu Tincu, [et] a sSimione su frate, [et] a Iorgi Soricone, sa parte canta vi avean intro dessa vinia, e deivilis VI moios d'oriu.

211. Exchange.
I made an exchange with Bassu of Novaia (Noazza); he gave me one length (*lintha*) [of land] bordering those which I had from a purchase, and I gave the farmyard (*corte*) which used to belong to Petru de Gunale, son of Varusone Angata, who donated the share that belonged to him to Sanctu Petru de Silki. Witnesses who were present to assesss the land (*saltu*) and the purchase: Petru d'Oia, and Comita de Carvia, and Petru de Capriles Prinkiu, and Petru de Capriles Longu, and Niscoli his brother.

212. Purchase.
I bought from Forasticu Bakillu the land (*terra*) of Planu dessu Laccu Secatu ('the plain of the broken drinking-trough') bordering on [the land of] Petru de Capriles Longu. I gave him two pieces of pork meat, two measures (*moios*) of barley, and one piece of sheep in the year of the famine (*famen*).

213. Purchase.
I bought from Gosatine Siccule, the land (*terra*) of the threshing floor of Cucumake, and I gave him a quarter ham (*bukellu de baccone*) by mutual agreement (*caput a pare*) in the year of the famine (*famen*).

214. Purchase.
I bought from Iustu Tincu, the land (*terra*) of Palitortu, which is the boundary [next to] Sancta Maria de Thergu. I gave them four sides (*clopas*) of meat in the year of the famine (*famen*).

215. Purchase.
I bought from Petru Soru a piece of land (*terru*) bordering on that which I bought from Iustu Tincu, and I gave him six measures (*moios*) of barley in the year of the famine (*famen*).

216. Purchase.
I bought from Petru Gereiu the share of his vineyard bordering with Sanctu Petru, and I gave him one soldo of cloth.

217. Purchase.
I also bought, bordering on this, from Iustu Tincu and from Simione his brother and from Iorgi Sorcicone, the whole share they had of the vineyard, and I gave them six measures (*moios*) of barley.

218. Conp[or]u.
Conp[or]aili a Mariane Volicke su terraticu tenende ad ecussa vinia, cantu posi sa clusura, term[en] assa de Comita d'Urieke, e deivili I pelle livastrina.

219. Tram[utu].
60v Tramutai cu[n] Mariane Volicke; deitimi isse sa t[er]ra dessu Capone | de Mariane Bolicke Pithinnu, cun I fundu de ficu. P[ro]ssa terra deili dessa de Ianne Gattu canta fuit sa sua, tenende assa domo sua; e p[ro]ssa ficu deili I moiu d'oriu. T[e]st[e]s de tottu custu co[m]p[or]u e tramutu ca[n]tu feki, Petru d'Oia [et] ambos fr[ate]s de Guin, e Pet[ru] de Cap[ri]les Prinkiu, e Petru de Capriles Longu, et issu frate Niscoli.

220. Kertu.
Vocaitime a ccorona Gunnari de Liios e Gosantine Mickinione p[ro]ssa nuke de Cafianu, cun cortaticu suo, e ccun sa vinia ki est ivi ante sa nuke, e ffekimusinde ca[m]pania in corona de Dericcor Ca[m]pule, ki fuit mandatore de liveros, e deindelis I petha cale si keruerun issos, e II moios de tridicu; custu lis dei p[ro]ssa vinia; e p[ro]ssa nuke, e p[ro]ssa terra deindeli I coriu de vacca, p[ro]ssa terra dessu piskinale de valle de piras. T[e]st[e]s: su mandatore de liv-
61r eros Dericcor Canpule, e Mariane Volicke Ma[n]nu, | e Manfrì; in platicu de si mi 'nde kertavat alikis, o fr[at]e suo, o istraniu, d'ispiiarela issos a S[an]c[t]u Pet[ru].

221. Datura dessu saltu d[e] M[ur]tetu.
Vennerun a parthire su saltu de M[ur]tetu, ki fuit populare dessa villa, e deruninde fune a S[an]c[t]u Petru de Silki. T[er]m[en]: assa de S[an]c[t]a Maria de Thergu ave s'una parte, e dave s'attera parte assa de S[an]c[t]a Maria de Gennor, a ccapithale de tottu sas adteras. T[e]st[e]s: Dorgotori de Kerki, curatore de Romania ki lu parthiat su saltu, [et] Ithoccor de Vanios, maiore d'iscolca, e fr[ate]s de Curcas, Gosantine, e Mariane, e cComita, et totta villa. Testes.

218. Purchase.
I bought from Mariane Volicke the arable land (*terracitu*) bordering on this vineyard, all [of which] I gave [with]in the delimitation (*sa clusura*), the border [of which] is [the land] of Comita d'Urieke. I gave him one whitened (*livastrina*) hide.

219. Exchange.
I made an exchange with Mariane Volicke: he gave me the land (*terra*) of Capone of Mariane Bolicke Pithinnu ('the little') and one fig tree for the land, Ianne Gattu gave him for all of which was his, bordering on his farm (*domo*) and for the fig tree, one measure (*moiu*) of barley. Witnesses of the whole purchase and all I exchanged: Petru d'Oia, both of the de Guin brothers, Petru de Capriles Prinkiu, Petru de Capriles Longu, and his own brother, Niscoli.

220. Dispute.
Gunnari de Liios and Gosantine Mickinione called me to a hearing over the walnut tree of Cafianu with his farmyard (*cortaticu*) and with his vineyard which there is in front of the walnut tree. We made an agreement (*campania*) at the hearing (*corona*) of Dericcor Campule, who was the representative of freemen (*mandatore de liveros*): I gave them any piece of meat that they wished and two measures (*moios*) of wheat (*triticu*); for the vineyard, walnut tree, and land (*terra*) of the marsh (*piskinale*) in Valle de Piras ('valley of pears'), I gave them a cow-hide (*coriu de vacca*). Witnesses: the representative (*mandatore*) of freemen, Dericcor Canpule, and Mariane Volicke Mannu ('the big/large/elder'), and Manfrì. It is on the promise (*plakitu*) that if anyone should contest this with me, whether an interested party (*frate*) or a stranger, then those at Sanctu Petru are free to decide the matter (*d'ispiiarela*).

221. Donation of unworked land (*saltu*) at Murtetu.
They came to divide the unworked land (*saltu*) of Murtetu which was a collective [property] (*populare*) of the village, and they gave a rope-length [of land] (*fune*) to Sanctu Petru di Silki. The boundary is that of Sancta Maria de Thergu on one side, and from the other side it is that of Sancta Maria de Gennor (Zennos) at the top of (*a ccapithale*) all the others. Witnesses: Dorgotori de Kerki, *curatore* of Romangia, who divided the land (*saltu*), and Ithoccor de Vanios head of the ward (*maiore de iscolca*), and the de Curcas brothers—Gosantine and Mariane—and Comita, and the whole village. Witnesses.

222. Conporu. *In Jennor.*

Conp[or]aili a Iorgi Mugra sa parte sua dessa vinia canta aveat intro dessa vinia de S[an]c[t]u Petru de Silki de Gennor, cu[n] boluntate dessos donnos suos; et ego deindeli thancas kervinas cositas, p[ro]ssa vinia, e p[ro] I fundu de mela.
61v T[e]st[e]s: | Comita de Thori de Curcas, e cComita de Carbia Carica, e Dorgotori Serrone mandatore de liberos.

223. *In Nerbosa.*

Tramutai cu[n] Janne Regitanu; deitimi isse sa t[er]ra sua de Nerbosa in co bi l'abeat isc'a sa via, e pparte sua e dessos frates, levande issos bicania; et ego deili sa t[er]ra dessu laccu ki mi derat Comita de Varru, pro tramutu; [et] aiunsim[us]li nois, ca fuit plus sa sua, cantu e[st] II fustes de birga dess'ortu ki ma[n]dicabat do[n]nu Ithoccor de Fravile. T[e]st[e]s: Comita de Varru, e cComita de Liios, [et] issu nepote Comita.

224. Co[m]p[or]u.

Conp[or]aili a pPet[ru] Murtinu sa parte sua de vinia e de pumu in co vi l'intravat, [et] ego deindeli II istaios d'oriu, [et] I de tridicu. T[este]s: Comita de Varru, manda[to]re de liveros, [et] tottu culivertos suos.

225.

Conp[or]aili a sSusanna sa sorre, ivi tenende ad ecussa, sa parte sua canta vi
62r l'intravat de vinia, | e de pumu; [et] ego deindeli II istaios d'oriu [et] I sol[lu] de pannu. T[este]s: previteru Furatu de Vosa ki li davat su p[re]thu, e Ianne su nepote.

226. Kertu.

Kertai cun Janne d'Olivas p[ro]ssa corte de Maria Furca, mama de donnu Ithoccor de Fravile su p[re]viteru; [et] ego vinkindelu in corona de Comita de Varru mandatore de liveros. T[este]s: sos ki vi furun in corona, e lliveros e sservos.

227. Postura.

Pos[i]tinke Pet[ru] de Murena sa t[er]ra ki e[st] tenende a ccuniatu de Varusone; e mandica[n]dela sa t[er]ra la vendit Janne Pili ad Ubertellu Frabu. Et ego kertainde cun ille in corona de Pet[ru] Iscarpa, e binkindelu. T[este]s: sos homines dessa villa.

222. Purchase. *In Jennor.*
I bought from Iorgi Mugra all the share he had of the vineyard that belonged to the vineyard of Sanctu Petru de Silki at Gennor (Zennos). [I made the purchase] with the consent of his lords, and I gave stitched leather gaiters (*thancas*) for the vineyard and for one apple tree. Witnesses: Comita de Thori from Curcas, Comita de Carbia Carica, and Dorgotori Serrone, representative of the freemen (*mandatore de liberos*).

223. *In Nerbosa.*
I made an exchange with Janne Regitanu: he gave me his land at Nerbosa, which he had up till the road, both his share and of his brothers, taking it in exchange. I gave them the land at Laccu ['drinking trough'] which Comita de Varru had given me as an exchange. We added for them, because his [land] was larger, two pole-lengths (*fustes de birga*) of the vegetable garden that lord Ithoccor de Fravile used. Witnesses: Comita de Varru, and Comita de Liios, and his nephew Comita.

224. Purchase.
I bought from Petru Mutinu his share of the vineyard and of fruit trees that belonged to it. I gave him two measures of barley (*istaios d'oriu*) and one of grain (*tridicu*). Witnesses: Comita de Varru representative of freemen (*mandatore de liberos*), and all the servants (*colivertos*).

225.
I bought from Susanna his sister all the share of hers that she had of the vineyard and of the fruit trees bordering on this. I gave her two measures of barley (*istaios d'oriu*) and one soldo of cloth. Witnesses: priest Furatu de Vosa, who evaluated it, and Ianne, his nephew.

226. Dispute.
I had a dispute with Janne d'Olivas concerning the farmyard (*corte*) of Maria Furca, mother of lord Ithoccor de Fravile the priest. I defeated him at the hearing (*corona*) of Comita de Varru, representative of the freemen (*mandatore de liberos*). Witnesses: those who were at the hearing, both freemen and servants.

227. Donation.
Petru de Murena gave the land (*terra*) which borders on the plot (*cuniatu*) of Varusone. Ianne Pili sold the land to Ubertellu Frabu who used to make use of the land. I was in dispute with him at the hearing (*corona*) of Petru Iscarpa, and I won [the case]. Witnesses: the men (*homines*) of the village.

228. Postura.
Positinke Comita d'Iscanu ad ora de morte s'ortu suo dessa funtana cun sa nuke e ccun sa parte sua dessa murikersa.

229. Canpania.
Ego p[re]viteru Furatu de Vosa ki ponio in ecustu co[n]dake p[ro]ssa bia dess'-
62v abba | ki falat ass'ortu de S[an]c[t]u Pet[ru], in sa vinia de Pet[ru] Tolis, ca no mi la voleat dare p[ro]ssu voe suo ki li ockiserant sos t[er]rales de fittu in Ortu Donnicu. Et ego fekinde ca[m]spania cun ille, cu[n] boluntate dessa donna mea, donna Massimilla, e torraili su voe; [et] isse deitinos sa via dessa abba a sse[m]piterru, vocandesemi dessu kertu dessu voe. T[es]t[e]s: Petru Iscarpa maiore d'iscolca, ante ken nos canpaniaim[us], e Mikine su fr[at]e.

230. Postura.
Positinke Elene de Platha a S[an]c[t]u Pet[ru] sa parte sua de Gogari, dessu cuniatu ki parthiat cu[n] Pet[ru] Cuccu, p[ro]ss'anima dessos fiios.

231. Postura.
Positinke Furata, fiia de Comita de Liios, sa parte sua in co vi l'intravat in Gogari.

232. Postura.
Positinke Ispethiosa sa parte sua ki vi l'intravat in su cuniatu dessa pruna de Gortoni.

233. Postura.
63r Positinke Petru de Carvia sa parte sua dessu cu[n]iatu de Gortoni | dessa pruna.

234. Postura,
Positinke Nikifori sa parte sua dessa pruna dessu cuniatu de Gortoni.

235. Postura.
Positinke Gosantine Francu sa t[er]ra sua de cu[n]iatu de Murinu.

228. Donation.
At the hour of his death, Comita d'Iscanu donated his vegetable garden of sa Funtana ('the spring'), with the walnut tree and with his share of the blackberry bushes (*murikersa*).

229. Compromise (*canpania*)
I, priest Furatu de Vosa, make an entry in this condaghe regarding the flow (*bia*) of the water that descends to the vegetable garden of Sanctu Petru in which there is the vineyard of Petru Tolis because he did not wish to give me it for [the matter of] his ox which tenant farmers (*terrales de fittu*) killed (*ockiserant*) at Ortu Donnicu. I made a deal (*campania*) with him, with the consent of my lady, lady Massimilla, and gave him back an ox; he gave us the flow (*via*) of the water for all time, revoking the dispute over the ox. Witnesses: Petru Iscarpa, head of the ward (*maiore d'iscolca*) before whom we made the compromise, and Mikine, his brother.

230. Donation.
For [salvation of] the souls of her sons, Elene de Platha gave to Sanctu Petru her share at Gogari of the enclosure (*cuniatu*) which he shares with Petru Cuccu.

231. Donation.
Furata, daughter of Comita de Liios, donated her share that belongs to her at Gogari.

232. Donation.
Ispthiosa donated her share that belongs to her of Cuniatu dessa Pruna ('enclosure of the plum tree') at Gortoni.

233. Donation.
Petru de Carvia donated his share of Cuniatu dessa Pruna ('enclosure of the plum tree') at Gortoni.

234. Donation.
Nikifori donated his share of Pruna dessu Cuniatu ('the plum tree of the enclosure') at Gortoni.

235. Donation.
Gosantine Francu donated his land at the enclosure (*cuniatu*) at Murinu.

236.
Positinke Ithoccor Castanna sa parte sua de[s]su fenariu sutta Musikennor.

237. Tramutu. *In Nerbosa.*
Tramutai cu[n] Pet[ru] Tolis t[er]ra p[ro] t[er]ra; deitimi isse a mimi sa t[er]ra sua de Nervosa, e nnois deimusili ad isse sa t[er]ra ki fuit de postura dessu co[n]natu. T[este]s: Ithoccor de monte e Ianne Regitanu.

238. Postura.
Positinke Jorgi Muris sa ficu ca[n]ta vi aveat in su cuniatu de Ianpulla a S[an]c[t]u Petru.

239. Tramutu. *In Nurailo.*
Tramutai cun Ithoccor d'Utan; isse deiti sa t[er]ra sua de Nurailo, parte sua e dessa sorre Bera, [et] ego deili ave secus dessa domo sua; [et] issa parte de Ior-
63v gia sa sorre, a cclesia la poserun sos fiios p[ro] a[n]i[m]a sua. T[es]t[e]s dessu |
tramutu, Juvanne Corsu, su de Kiterone.

240. *Terra de Nerbosa.*
Positinke Comita Iscarpa sa parte sua dessa t[er]ra de Nervosa, fiiu de Gosantine de Castellu. T[es]t[e]s: Comita Corsu su socru, e Jorgi Muris.

241. Dispute.
Furait Pet[ru] Melone sa keia dessu lavore de Gosantine Locco, e de Pet[ru] Corda sos d'Erças, e binkitindelu in corona d'Ithoccor de Laccon, ki 'nke fuit curatore, e llevavanili e t[er]ra, e binia, e domo, ki fuit de parthone dep[us] sa muiere; [et] ego petti merkede cando vennerun a llevare su pariam[en]tu, [et] indulserunimi ki no mi 'nde kerverun borthe II vaccas, in corona de Gosantine de Martis maiore d'iscolca. T[este]s: su maiore e cComita Canbella, e Gunnari Corsu, e Comita de Varru, ma[n]datore de liveros, e Gosantine Passare, totta corona.

242. Postura. *De s[er]vos.*
64r Positinke donna Iorgia de tThori a S[an]c[t]u Pet[ru] de Silki, | p[ro] anima
sua, I metatu de porcos cun sos porcarios ad Ithoccor d'Arestanis intregu, fiiu de Pet[ru] d'Arestanis su de Gullusò, [et] a Juste Murtinu intregu, et a cComita su fr[at]e fiios de Corsellu Murtinu, et a Maria Pirari fiia de Petru Pirari

236.
Ithoccor Castanna donated his share of the hayfield (*fenariu*) below Musikennor.

237. Exchange. *In Nerbosa.*
I exchanged land for land with Petru Tolis: he gave me his land (*terra*) at Nervosa; we gave him the land that was a donation from his brother-in-law. Witnessees: Othoccor de Monte and Ianne Regitanu.

238. Donation.
Jorgi Muris gave to Sanctu Petru all the fig trees he had in his enclosure (*cuniatu*) at Ianpulla.

239. Exchange.
I made an exchange with Ithoccor d'Utan: he gave me his land at Nurailo—his share and that of his sister, Bera, and I gave him [the land] from behind his house. The share of his [other] sister, Iorgia, their sons gave to the church for her soul. Witnesses of the exchange: Juvanne Corsu from Kiterone.

240. *Land at Nerbosa.*
Comita Iscarpa, son of Gosantine de Castellu, donated the share of his land at Nervosa. Witnesses: Comita Corsu, the father-in-law, and Jorgi Muris.

241. Dispute.
Petru Melone stole a container (*keia*) of grain of Gosantine Locco and Petru Cordo of Erças (Ertas), and he they won [their case] against him at the hearing (*corona*) of Ithoccor de Laccon, who was *curatore*, and [so] they took from the land, vineyards and house of which he had a share on his wife's side. I sought leniency (*merkede*) when they came to decide recompense, and they were let off by me, but for [the compensation of] two cows. [This was] at the hearing of Gosantine de Martis, head of the ward (*maiore d'iscolca*). Witnesses: the [said] official (*maiore*), and Comita Canbella, Gunnari Corsu, and Comita de Varru, representative of the freemen (*mandatore de liveros*), and the whole hearing (*coronas*).

242. Donation. *Of servants.*
Lady Iorgia de Thori gave to Sanctu Petru de Silki for her soul: one pen of pigs with their keepers; Othoccor d'Arestanis (Oristano) a full servant (*intregu*), son of Petru d'Arestanis from Gullusò (Buddusò); Juste Murtinu, a full servant; Comita, his brother; the sons of Corsellu Murtinu; Maria Pirari, daughter

su de Isporlathu, [et] de Sarakina Piana, ki mi derat iudike Gunnari, cu[n] parte sua dessu fetu ki dittavat app[us] issa; [et] issu saltu de Ysaia, ki fuit appus sa domo de Loccorro, de battor partes I.

243. Kertu. *De s[er]vos.*
Bocaitime a ccorona Pet[ru] de Roma in Turres sa die de sinotu, p[ro] fiios de Viventi ki fuit servu de S[an]c[t]u Petru, et issa muiere Maria Porkella kereatila ad ankilla, ca mi voleat levare su fetu. Et ego kertavali ca 'livera l'aveas fatta, vinkendetende in corona de iudike Gunnari, battuiende carta ca fuit livera
64v fatta, e pparendeli bona a iudike.' Poserunimi | a destimonios, [et] ego battussi destimonios a S[an]c[t]u Iorgi d'Oiastreta, de ca uinkerun sos frates ad esser livera, e cca la renovait iudike sa carta. E iurait a .+. cun destimonios meos su servu de S[an]c[t]u Petru Jorgi Muris, cu[n] Mariane de Varda, [et] Andria Corda, [et] Ithoccor de Vanios ki lu narait a bervos in corona de iudike Barusone. T[estes]: donikellu Petru curatore de Romania, e donnikellu Dorveni, e cComita de Laccon curatore de Nurcar, e Gosantine de Thori Manutha ki kertavat su kertu p[ro] S[an]c[t]u Petru, e derunimi tottu su fetu a sservos, vinkendelu a Gosantine de Thori de T[er]re, ki fuit generu de Gosantine Diuite, ki fuit pupillu in su kertu cale vinki, [et] a pPetru de Roma.

244. Tramutu. *De s[er]vos.*
Tramutai cun s'abbate de Plaianu donnu Rodulfu, e ccun su priore suo donnu Juvanne; ego deili lat[us] [et] I die in Dorgotori Mugra, [et] issos derunimi
65r lat[us] de Petru Unkinu, fiiu de | Gavini Tatake, [et] de Maria Mug[ra], ankilla issoro, et issu cantu vi avean in candalabru, ca fuit mastriu Dorgotori Mug[ra]. T[este]s: Mikinu Pinna maiore d'iscolca, [e] Mariane d'Iscanu, e Gitilesu de Kerki, e Dorgotori Ca[m]bella.

245. *De s[er]vos.*
[E]go Istephane Unkinu. Kertait mecu Petru de Kerki, nepote de Mariane de Castavar, p[ro] fiios de Migali Aketu, e de Maria e Canake, ca 'p[ro]gitteu mi los levas?' Et ego kertaili ca 'vinkitu te nd' aveat piscopu Jorgi Maiule ad avu tuo, a Mariane de Castavar, in corona de Mariane de Vosove curatore de Ficulinas de Castellu.' Poserunimi a battuger su co[n]dake, [et] ego battussilu a ccorona

of Petru Pirari from Isporlathu (Esporlatu), and Sarakina Piana whom iudike Gunnari gave me with the share of the offspring that belonged to her, and one-quarter of the unworked land (*saltu*) of Ysaia that belonged to the farm (*domo*) of Loccorro.

243. Dispute. *Of servants.*
Petru de Roma called me to justice at a hearing (*corona*) in Turres (Porto Torres) on the day of the assembly (*sinotu*), concerning the sons of Viventi who was a servant of Sanctu Petru and his wife Maria Porkella whom he supposed to be a female-servant (*ankilla*), [for the reason that] he wished to take from me the offspring. I argued that 'you made her free (*livera*),' winning [the case] at the hearing of iudike Gunnari by producing as evidence a document (*carta*) [to the effect] that she was made free, and it [the document] seemed sound to the iudike. They had me find witnesses, so I called forth witnesses at Sanctu Iorgi d'Oiastreta (San Giorgio di Oleastreto), and the monks won [the case] for her being free, and iudike confirmed the document (*renovait carta*). The servant Jorgi Muris of Sanctu Petru swore on the cross with my witnesses Mariane de Varda, and Andria Corda, and Ithoccor de Vanios, who gave oral testimony (*narait a bervos*) at the hearing of iudike Barusone. Witnesses: donikellu Petru *curatore* of Romangia, and *donnikellu* Dorveni, and Comita de Laccon *curatore* de Nurcar, and Gosantine de Thori Manutha, who led the case for Sanctu Petru. They gave me all the offspring as servants as the winning party was Gosantine de Thori from Terre, who was the son-in-law of Gosantine Divite who presided at the hearing (*pupillu in keru*) that I won, and Petru de Roma.

244. Exchange. *De servos.*
I made an exchange with the abbot of Plaianu (San Michele di Plaiano), lord Rodulfu, and with the prior, his lord, Juvanne. I gave them a day [of work] and half of Dorgotori Mugra; they gave me half of Petru Unkinu, son of Gavini Tatake and Maria Mugra their female servant (*ankilla*), and all [the share] they had in candlesticks (*in candelabru*) because Dorgotori Mugra was a craftsman (*maistru*). Witnesses: Mikinu Pinna, head of the ward (*maiore d'iscolca*), and Mariane d'Iscanu, Gitilesu de Kerki, and Dorgotori Cambella.

245. *Of servants.*
I, Istephane Unkinu, had a dispute with Petru de Kerki, nephew of Mariane de Castavar concerning the sons of Migali Aketu and Maria de Canake (Caniga) about 'why you have taken them from me?' I argued that 'Jorgi Maiule won [the rights to] your grandfather (*avu*), Mariane de Castavar, at the hearing of Mariane de Vosove, *curatore* of Ficulinas de Castellu!' They bid me bring forth

de Dorgotori de Ponte, e llesserunilu e pparvit bonu; e bolende iurare m'indulsit sa iura, e binki. T[este]s: su curatore, [et] issu camaralingu de Saccaria, e Dorgotori de Ca[m]pu, e Mariane su fr[at]e.

246. Conporu. *In Ortu Donnicu.*
Conporaili a cComita de Gitil, sa parte ca[n]ta vi l'int[ra]vat in Ortu Do[n]-
65v nicu; | [et] ego deindeli I mesa libra d'argentu, [et] II vaccas, [et] I boe, plakendenos appa[re]; [et] iss'ateru indulsitilu a sS[an]c[t]u Pet[ru] p[ro]ss'anima sua. Test[es]: Dorgotori de Nureki, e Petru Regitanu, e cComita de Varru.

247. Conp[or]u.
Co[m]p[or]aili a cComita de Thori sa t[er]ra sua ki e[st] ante s'ortu meu de corte, [et] ego deindeli I boe de duos fr[at]es. T[este]s: Ithoccor de serra Bardane, e Iorgi Tolis, e cComita de Natas.

248. Tramutu.
Tramutai cu[n] Marthu Pica; ego deili sa parthone ca[n]ta vi l'intravat a Bulsu in Brunkile, ki posit a S[an]c[t]u Petru; [et] isse deitimi su vaca[n]te ca[n]tu vi l'int[ra]vat in su cuniatu de Kip[ri]ane Murtinu, ki li co[m]porait, cu[n] sa matta dessa ficu lata.

249. Conporu.
Co[m]p[or]aili a Iorgia Murtina II soll[os] de vinia in Ballari, ki l'intravat depus su patre, [et] ego deindeli II sollos I de pannu, [et] adteru de lavore.

250. Co[m]p[or]u.
Co[m]p[or]aili a Petronella et assa sorre II soll[os] de vinia, intro d'ecussu cuni-
66r atu, [et] ego deindeli I bargala, [et] I | sollu de pannu.

251. Conporu.
Co[m]p[or]aili a cComita Murtinu II soll[os] de vinia intro de cussu cuniatu, [et] ego deivili I pulletru anniclu.

252. Co[m]p[or]u.
Co[m]p[or]aili a cCip[ri]ane Murtinu II soll[o]s de vinia. Et ego deivili I maiale, dassandelila s'attera ca[n]ta vi aveat a mandicare in bita sua, e ppus co aet morre torraresi a sS[an]c[t]u Petru.

the condaghe [as evidence], and I produced it for the hearing of Dorgotori de Ponte. They read it and it seemed sound. Wishing to take an oath, they excused me [from taking it], and I won [the case]. Witnesses: the *curatore* and his chamberlain (*camarlingu*) at Saccaria (Saccargia), and Dorgotori de Campu, and Mariane his brother.

246. Purchase. *At Ortu Donnicu*
I bought from Comita de Gitil all the share pertaining to him at Ortu Donnicu, and I gave him half a pound (*libra*) of silver, two cows, and an ox, pleasing us both. Of the other [payment] Sanctu Petru relieved him for the [sake of] his soul.

247. Purchase.
I bought from Comita de Thori his land (*terra*) which is in front of the vegetable garden (*ortu*) of my farmyard (*corte*). I gave him one of two oxen [who were] brothers. Witnesses: Ithoccor de Serra Bardane, Iorgi Tolis, and Comita de Natas.

248. Exchange.
I made an exchange with Marthu Pica. I gave him all the division (*parthone*) that belonged to Bulsu at Brunkile which he gave to Sanctu Petru. He gave me all he had in the enclosure (*cuniatu*) of Kipriane Murtinu who [had previously] bought it along with a white fig tree.

249. Purchase.
I bought from Iorgia Murtina two soldi of vines at Ballari that belonged to her father's line, and I have her two soldi: one of cloth and another of grain.

250. Purchase.
I bought from Petronella and her sister, two soldi of vines within this enclosure (*cuniatu*), and I gave them a millstone (*bargala*) and one soldo (*sollu*) of cloth.

251. Purchase.
I bought from Comita Murtinu two soldi (*sollos*) of vines inside this enclosure (*cuniatu*). I gave him a year-old foal.

252. Purchase.
I bought from Cipriane Murtinu two soldi (*sollos*) of vines. I gave him a pig, leaving the rest of what he had for his sustenance in his lifetime, to revert to Sanctu Petru after he dies.

253. Kertu. *De s[er]vos.*
Ego abbatissa Maximilla ki ponio in ecustu co[n]dake su kertu ki appit mecu Barusone Masala, e pPetru de Carvia Variu, p[ro]ssa kella dessos M[ur]tas d'Enene, fiios d'Elene Murta, ca los kereat a sservos tottu. Et ego ca[m]paniaim[en]de cun issos, e deruniminde su lat[us] ante iudike Gunnari. Et avendenollos lat[us] app[ar]e, kertait cun illos Dorgotori de Castavar in corona de iudike Barusone in Kitarone, e binkitilos. T[este]s: judike Barusone in cuia
66v corona vinkit, e donnikellu Petru e donnikellu Ithoccor | e Petru de Maroniu e Dericcor de Kerki.

De s[er]vos.
E D[o]rgotori de Castavar p[ro] honore de Deus, e p[ro]ssu p[re]gu ki 'nde li fakeat s'apatissa, [et] issa do[n]na maiore, torraitilos a sS[an]c[t]u Petru [et] sS[an]c[t]a Julia p[ro]ss'anima sua, e torrandelos Dorgotori a sS[an]c[t]u Pet[ru] cu[n] bolu[n]tate de tottu frates suos. T[este]s: judike Barusone [et] arkipiscopu Petru Manacu de Turres. Et ego p[ro] custa honore ki 'nde fekit a D[eu]s [et] a sS[an]c[t]u Petru, deindeli I libra d'arientu e mesa [et] I cavallu cale kervit dessos meos, [et] I eba. T[este]s ante ken li dei custu arientu: su plevanu de Thathari, donn'Antine de Martis, e p[re]viteru Forasticu e Gosantine de Risa e iacunu Gavini de Vare.

254. Kertu. *De s[er]vos.*
Kertait p[re]viteru Forasticu cun Ithoccor de Varda [et] issu fr[at]e Gosantine, p[ro] fiios de Frevari, p[ro] ca '[n]de li kerean parte, avendesi levatu su issoro, e mortu servinde ad issos. Et isse kertavatilis ca fuit mortu servinde ad issos s'issoro. Kerverunili destimo[n]ios, [et] isse battussit destimo[n]ios, assu ple-
67r vanu de Thathari | ki fuit pupillu co [et] issos, e Pet[ru] Pedes maiore d'iscolca, e iurait a .+. su mandatore meu Petru Marcu, in corona de Dorgotori de Kerki, ki fuit curatore de fattu de Roma[n]ia.

255. Conp[or]u. Saltu *de Co[n]ca maiore.*
Co[m]porait Istephane Unkinu a Barusone de Nurki sa parte sua dessu saltu de Co[n]ca maiore, [et] ego deivili II vaccas in VIII soll[os], in fine de si lu p[er]dea custu, de torraremi saltu antesicu. T[este]s: Dorgotori de Nureki, cun ken andai ad ap[re]tharemi su saltu, [et] Ithoccor de Varru e Iorgi Tolis e Gosantine de Carvia.

253. Dispute. *Of servants.*
I, abbess Maximilla, note in this condaghe the dispute I had with Barusone Masala and Petru de Carvia Variu over the kin of Murtas d'Enene (Eba Ciara), the sons of Elene Murta, because he wanted them as his servants. I reached an agreement with them in the presence of iudike Gunnari, and they gave me half (*latus*) of the servants. Having divided them in half, Dorgotori de Castavar sued for them at a hearing (*corona*) of iudike Barusone at Kitarone, and he won. Witnesses: iudike Barusone, at whose hearing I won; *donnikellu* Petru, *donnikellu* Ithoccor, Petru de Maroniu, and Dericcor de Kerki.

Of servants.
And Dorgotori de Castavar, for the honour of God and for the prayer that the abbess and lady superior (*donna maiore*) had made for him, restored them [the servants] to Sanctu Petru and Sancta Julia for [the salvation of] his soul. Dorgotori restored them to Sanctu Petru with the consent of all his brothers. Witnesses: iudike Barusone, and archbishop Petru Manacu of Turres (Torres). And I, for this honour made to God and Sanctu Petru, gave him one pound and a half of silver (*arientu*), one horse of his wish from among mine, and one mare. Witnesses in the presence of whom I give this silver: the parish priest (*plevanu*) of Thathari (Sassari), lord Antine de Martis; priest Forasticu; Gosantine de Risa, and deacon Gavini de Vare.

254. Dispute. *Of servants.*
Priest Forasticu sued Ithoccor de Varda and his brother Gosantine over the sons of Frevari for they claimed part of them, having already taken his and having one of them die in his service. He [Forasticu] disputed that he [the servant] had died in his service. He was requested to provide witnesses, and he brought forth as witnesses the local priest (*plevanu*) of Thathari (Sassari), who was a proprietor (*pupillu*) like them, and Petru Pedes, head of the ward (*maiore d'iscolca*). My representative (*mandatore*), Petru Marcu, testified under oath swearing on the cross at a hearing (*corona*) of Dorgotori de Kerki, who was then *curatore* of Romangia.

255. Purchase. *Unworked land* (saltu) *of Conca Maiore.*
Istephane Unkinu bought from Barusone de Nurki (La Corte) his part of the land (*saltu*) of Conca Maiore. I gave him two cows worth eight soldi (*sollos*), so that in the eventuality of any loss, he would restore the land (*saltu*) to me instead. Witnesses: Dorgotori de Nureki, with whom I went to the land (*saltu*) for its appraisal; Ithoccor de Varru; Iorgi Tolis, and Gosantine de Caruia.

256. Postura. *Domo d'Ogothi.*
Positinke Mariane de Thori Cavallare sa domo sua d'Ogothi, cu[n] p[er]tenentia ca[n]t'aveat appus sa domo, corte, t[er]ras, binias, saltos [et] ho[m]i[n]es. Term[en] dessu saltu de Gutherva: ave su castru de Mamusi, tottuve sa serra assa Pet[ra] infurcata, [et] essit oru sepe, travessande sa via dessu Mamuthologe, e fferitse assa via dessa Serra, tottuve via a badu de Goloppuma, avinde
67v appus | flum[en] intro assu castru de Mamuse.

257.
Term[en] dessu saltu de Surtallo: ave sa Piskina de Tamuri, travessu s'iscla, derettu assu suveriu dessu rivu, e ccollat tottuve a manu manca derettu assa Pet[ra] P[er]tusita, e iettat sende derettu assu nurake Curthu, assas kersas de Laccorria, derettu ass'ilike; avinde tottuve sepe, assu vadu de Sisia, falat tottuve flum[en] intro assas iunturas de vadu de Petru Piri. Ecco term[en] dessu saltu de Surtallo. Term[en] dessu saltu d'Ostitthe: ave agitu de Gattu, tottuve via, intro assu saltu de rennu de Villa Nova, s'urvitu levat derettu assu suveriu mannu dessa sella de Thurvali; ivi falat a destra dessu traginu de funtana de Gavini Lello, assa via de Cannabretu, tottuve via, isc'a Pet[ra] Sinnata, derettu a badu de tThuccone, via tottuve a balle de Gruke, avinde sa serra tottuve, derettu a Pet[ra]
68r Maiore, tottuve serra, derettu ad agitu de Gattu, e benit t[er]m[en] | dessu de rennu.

258. Postura.
Positinke donnu Pet[ru] de serra Cavallare a sS[an]c[t]u Petru de Silki in bita sua su saltu d'Arenosu, ki tramut[a]rat cun donnu Comita d'Athen Manucu[m]. Term[en] de custu saltu: ave badu de Tavellas, in co essit sa via, assu suveriu mannu, a derettu assu valiclu de Valle de Tanserata, serra tottuve, assu castru de Goloppuma, flum[en] tottuve a badu de Tavellas. T[este]s ante ken lu deit: Comita de Varru e Gosantine d'Ackettas, nepotes suos de cuncuva, e Gosantine de Martis e cComita d'Oskeri, su d'Ulumetu.

256. Donation. *Farm complex* (domo) *of Ogothi* (*Otti*).
Mariane de Thori Cavallare donated his farm complex (*domo*) of Ogothi (Otti) with all the belongings he had at the farm (*domo*): farmyard (*corte*), lands, vineyards, unworked lands (*saltos*), and men. Boundary of the land (*saltu*) of Gutherva: from Castru de Mamusi ('the outcrop of Mamusi'), [it goes] along the ridge towards Petra Infurcata ('the standing stone'), and keeps to the hedgerow, crosses the road of Mamuthologe, then joins the road of the ridge; [then it goes] along the road to Badu de Goloppuma ('crossing-ford at Goloppuma') and, from there, it goes along the river back to Castru de Mamuse.

257.
Boundary of the unworked land (*saltu*) at Surtallo: from Piskina de Tamuri ('the pool of Tamuri'), across the islet (*iscla*) towards the cork oaks at the stream; it passes to the left, towards Petra Pertusita ('the pierced rock'), extends towards nuraghe Curthu ('low nuraghe') to the mastic shrubs (*kersas*) of Laccorria, towards the holly oak; from there, along the hedgerow to Vadu de Sisia ('the ford of Sisia'), and along the river until the meeting points at Vadu de Petru Piri ('ford of Petru Piri'). The boundary of the unworked land (*saltu*) at Surtallo is thus. Boundary of the land (*saltu*) of Ostitthe: from the entrance (*agitu*) at Gattu, along the road into the land of the realm (*saltu de rennu*) at Villa Nova; the path leads towards the large cork tree at Sella de Thurvali ('the saddle of Thurvali'), there it goes down to the right of the flow from Funtana de Gavini Lello ('spring of Gavini Lello'), to the road of Cannabretu, along the road until Petra Sinnata ('marked rock') in the direction of Badu de Thuccone ('ford of Thuccone'), [and] along the road to Balle de Gruke ('cross valley'); from there, along the ridge towards Petra Maiore ('great rock'), along the ridge, towards the entrance (*agitu*) at Gattu, and then it reaches the boundary of that of the realm.

258. Donation.
Lord Petru de Serra Cavallare donated to Sanctu Petru de Silki, when he was still alive, the unworked land (*saltu*) of Arenosu, which he had received in exchange from lord Comita d'Athen Manucum ('monk'). Boundary of this land (*saltu*): from Badu de Tavellas ('ford of Tavellas'), where the road ends, to the big cork tree, towards the vale (*valiclu*) of Valle de Tanserata ('valley of Tanserata'), along the ridge, up to Castru de Goloppuma ('the outcrop of Goloppuma'), keeping to the river, back to Badu de Tavellas. Witnesses in the presence of whom he donated it: Comita de Varru and Gosantine d'Ackettas, his nephews (*nepotes*) on the side of a mistress (*concuva*); Gosantine de Martis, and Comita d'Oskeri from Ulumentu.

259. Tramutu. *In Nurailo, apus Junketu.*
Tramutai cu[n] su p[re]viteru d'Enene, donnu Janne Mollone; isse deitimi sa t[er]ra canta vi l'int[ra]vat i[n] Nurailo, depus donnu Pet[ru] d'Ispata, tenende assa valle dessu Favariu, [et] ego deili sas t[er]ras meas de Kitarone ki furun in Co[n]cas de Varu, T[este]s: Mariane de Varda [et] Ithoccor su fr[at]e, e Pet[ru] de Matrona.

260. Co[m]poru. *In eode[m] loco.*
68v Conp[or]aili a Iorgi Paraguri sas t[er]ras | cantas aveat in Nurailo, in su planu [et] in sa pala [et] ego deindeli in p[re]thu I boe domatu. T[este]s: Gavini Galle, e Dorgotori Galleta e Gosantine de Farfare; dandemilas cu[n] bolu[n]tate dessu donnu suo, Juvanne Persa.

261. Conporu. *Terra in plan[u] de Nurailo.*
Co[m]p[or]aili a Gosantine Latu, [et] ad Ithoccor de Ioscla, sa t[er]ra ki vi avean in su planu de Nurailo, [et] deivilis IIII moios d'oriu. T[este]s: Juvanne Galle e Gosantine Solina [et] issu fr[at]e Mariane.

262. Kertu.
Kertait mecu Comita d'Urieke p[ro]ssa t[er]ra ki poserat su patre a ccl[es]ia, ca naravat ca 'non bi la posit patre meu.' [Et] ego binkindelu in corona dessu maiore d'iscolca, de Dorgotori de Navitha, ca vi la poserat su patre, co [et] issos frates. T[este]s: su maiore e Dorgotori de Nureki e Niscoli.

263. Postura.
Posit Furatu de Varcca a ccl[es]ia su ki vi aveat in cuniatos de S[an]c[t]u Ianne, in s'Olivellu, ca[n]do andavat ad Ier[usa]l[e]m. T[este]s: Dorgotori de Nureki e Niscoli.

264. *Terra in Nervosa.*
69r Posit Dorgotori de Sune a ccl[es]ia, | e Pet[ru] su fratile, sa t[er]ra issoro de Nervosa, p[ro] anima issoro.

265. Postura.
Morivit Bera d'Utan e pposit a sS[an]c[t]u Pet[ru] sa parthone canta 'nke aveat in Silki, corte, t[er]ras, e binias.

259. Exchange. *In Nurailo, at Junketu.*
I made an exchange with the priest of Enene (Eba Ciara), lord Janne Mollone. He gave me the land that he held at Nurailo from lord Petru d'Ispata, bordering the valley (*valle*) of Favariu, and I gave him my lands of Kitarone (Caddaroni-Sant'Eusebio) that were in Concas de Varu ('vale of Varu'). Witnesses: Mariane de Varda; his brother, Ithoccor, and Petru de Matrona.

260. Purchase. *In the same place.*
I bought from Iorgi Paraguri all the lands that I had in Nurailo, in the plain and on the slope. I gave him in return one tamed ox. Witnesses: Gavini Galle; Dorgotori Galleta; and Gosantine de Farfare. He gave them to me with the consent of his lord, Juvanne Persa.

261. Purchase. *Land in the plain of Nurailo.*
I bought from Gosantine Latu and Ithoccor de Ioscla the land (*terra*) that he had in the plain (*planu*) of Nurailo. I gave them four measures (*moios*) of barley. Witnesses: Juvanne Galle; Gosantine Solina, and his brother, Mariane.

262. Dispute.
I was sued by Comita d'Urieke over the land (*terra*) that his father donated to the church because he said that 'my father did not donate it!' I defeated him at a hearing (*corona*) of the head of the ward (*maiore d'iscolca*), Dorgotori de Navitha, because the father, together with his brothers, had indeed donated it. Witnesses: the [said] official (*maiore*); Dorgotori de Nureki, and Niscoli.

263. Donation.
Furatu de Varcca donated to the church everything he had in the plotted enclosures (*cuniatos*) of Sanctu Ianne at s'Olivellu when he went to Jerusalem. Witnesses: Dorgotori de Nureki, and Niscoli.

264. *Land in Nervosa.*
Dorgotori de Sune and Petru his cousin (*fratile*) donated to the church their land at Nervosa for their souls.

265. Donation.
Bera d'Utan died and bequeathed to Sanctu Petru the share (*parthone*) she had in Silki: farmyard (*corte*), lands, and vineyards.

266. Postura.
Posit Elene de Farfare a S[an]c[t]u Pet[ru] sa parte sua dess'ortu de Ianpulla, cu[n] boluntate dessos fiios. T[este]s: p[re]viteru Furatu de Vosa, ki li deit penetenthia, e Juvanne Secke.

267. Postura.
Posit P[re]thiosa Iscarpa a S[an]c[t]u Pet[ru], p[ro] a[n]i[m]a dessu fiiu, sa t[er]ra ki aveat sup[ra] corte de Ianne Pili, su lat[us] dessa ki parthiat cun fiios de Ianne Furone.

268.
Posit Maria de Iannu a S[an]c[t]u Petru ad ora de morte, p[ro] a[n]i[m]a sua, o[mn]ia ca[n]tu 'nke aveat in Silki; corte, terras, e binias. T[este]s: p[re]viteru Furatu de Vosa e Gosantine Kerellu.

269. Kertu.
Kertai cun Gosantine de Thori de T[er]re, generu de Gosantine de Thori Divite, p[ro] Colatu, fiiu de Vallesu e de Justa Tecas, ki furun servos depus sa domo de
69v Teclata; [et] ego binkindelu | in corona de donnu Ithoccor d'Athen curatore de Nura, intro in Salinas de rivos. T[este]s uve lu vinki: su curatore e Gosantine de Nurdole, maiore d'iscolca, [et] issu fr[at]e donnu Pet[ru] de Laccon e Petru de Valles.

270. Kertu. *De s[er]vis.*
Kertaitimi p[ro] fiios de Romanesa, ca los kereat a sservos, [et] ego kertaili ca Romanesa livera fuit, e ccoiuvait cun servu meu, e ccun ille fekit tottu su fetu. Judicarunimi a battuier ego destimonios, [et] sende de battuier destimo[n]ios, bocaisemi dessu kertu [et] indulsitimi ante su curatore donnu Ithoccor d'Athen. T[este]s: Gosantine de Nurdole maiore d'iscolca, e Petru de Valles, e p[re]viteru Petru de Laccon.

271. Kertu. *De s[er]vis.*
Kertait mecu Petru Pinna p[ro] Vosoveckesu Gattu ca l'aveat su pethone ca 'fuit in sa morte de su servu, de Janne de Ca[m]piiolu.' Iudicarunili a destimo[n]ios, e no los appit. Jurait Istefane Unkinu a gruke, in corona de judike
70r Barusone in Nulabros, ca no[n] bi fuit | Bosoveckesu in sa morte de Janne de Ca[m]piiolu. T[este]s ki vi furun in sa corona: Mariane de Thori d'Enticlas,

266. Donation.
Elene de Farfare donated to Sanctu Petru her share of the vegetable garden (*ortu*) of Ianpulla with the consent of her sons. Witnesses: priest Furatu de Vosa who gives the confession, and Juvanne Secke.

267. Donation.
Prethosa Iscarpa donated to Sanctu Petru, for [the salvation of] her son's soul, the land that she had beyond the farmyard (*corte*) of Ianne Pili, half of which is shared with the sons of Ianne Furone.

268.
Maria de Iannu donated to Sanctu Petru on her deathbed, for the salvation of her soul, everything she had at Silki: farmyard (*corte*), lands, and vineyards. Witnesses: priest Furatu de Vosa, and Gosantine Kerellu.

269. Dispute.
I had a dispute with Gosantine de Thori de Terre, son-in-law (*generu*) of Gosantine de Thori Divite, over Colatu, son of Vallesu and Justa Tecas who were servants (*servos*) at the farm complex (*domo*) of Teclata (Trigiada, near Romana). I defeated him at a hearing (*corona*) of lord Ithoccor d'Aten, *curatore* of Nurra, at Salinas de Rivos ('salt-pans at Rivos'). Witnesses who were there when I defeated him: the *curatore*, and Gosantine de Nurdole head of the ward (*maiore d'iscolca*), and his brother lord Petru de Laccon, and Petru de Valles.

270. Dispute. *Of servants.*
I was sued over the sons of Romanesa because he wanted them as servants (*servos*). I claimed that Romanesa was a free woman (*livera*) and married a servant of mine with whom she had all her offspring. They decided that I bring witnesses, and, having brought forth witnesses, the dispute was dismissed and I was exonerated in front of the *curatore*, lord Ithoccor d'Athen. Witnesses: Gosantine de Nurdole, head of the ward (*maiore d'iscolca*); Petru de Valles, and priest Petru de Laccon.

271. Dispute. *Of servants.*
I had a dispute with Petru Pinna over Vosoveckesu Gattu because he claimed that 'he was involved in the death of his servant, Janne de Campiiolu'. They decided that he provide witnesses, but he did not have them. Istefane Unkinu testified under oath, swearing on the cross, at a hearing (*corona*) of iudike Barusone in Nulabros (Nulauro/Lunafras) that Bosoveckesu was not present when Janne de Campiiolu died. Witnesses who were at the hearing: Mariane

curatore de Nulabros, [et] Ithoccor de Lacco[n], curatore de Meiulocu, e Gosantine de Thori, curatore de Romania.

272. Kertu. *De s[er]vis.*
Kertait mecu su priore de Plaianu donnu Juvanne de Sevenes, pro fiios d'Ele[ne]
Gathia, ca 'p[ro]gitteu no[n] mi 'nde das, ki sun fattos in servu meu, in Lustri
de Cora?' Et ego kertaili ca 'Iuste de Cora coiuvatu fuit cu[n] Susanna Cotro-
ske, e ssende coiuvatos umpare cun Susanna Cotroske mi la furricait ad Elene
Gathia, ki fuit ankilla mea.' Judicarunimi a battuier destimo[n]ios de ca fuit coi-
uvatu Juste de Cora cun Susanna Cotroske e de ca fuit fattu in furrithu su fetu
in Elene Gathia, ki fuit ankilla mea; [et] ego battussilos, a Gosantine de Magar
[et] a Dorgotori Caia, [et] a Dericcor d'Innoviu, [et] a Mariane Caia, [et] ad
70v Ithoccor Pintu; [et] ego iurai cun illos a .+.ke, in corona de iudike Gunnari | in
Kitarone. T[este]s: do[n]nu Comita de Gunale e do[n]nu Mariane de Maroniu,
ki lu kertavat su kertu, e cComita de Thori e ttotta corona.

273. Kertu. *De s[er]vis.*
Kertai cun Petru Furca e ccun Gavini Papis, ponendevilos su piscopu suo a kertare, e ccun Dorgotori de Padules, e ccun su camaralingu de Saccaria, p[ro] fiios de Gosantine Mancu e de Susanna de Castra. Issos ker[tar]unimi ca 'xxx annos sun ki no[n] bi inperasti.' [Et] ego kertailis ca 'servindemi intro de xxx annos mi los levastis.' Iudicarunimi a battuier destimonios, ca vi mandicai intro de xxx annos, [et] ego vattussilos a corona de donnu Comita de Navitha, a Gunnari de Varru [et] a Pet[ru] Locco [et] ad Ithoccor Clacare [et] a cComita de Tutar, e iurai a .+.ke, cun illos, in corona, e binki in tottu su fetu; torrarunimi sos omines. T[e]st[e]s: su curatore et totta corona.

274.[31] *De s[er]vis.*
Kertait mecu Mariane de Kerki, fiiu de Comita de Kerki, su de Gelesi, in Pet[ru]
71r de Varda, [et] in Istephane | su fr[at]e, [et] in sa sorre Furata, ca 'p[ro]gitteu mi
los levas ki sun liveros fr[at]es meos?' Et ego kertaili ca 'custu kertu ki mi fakes
como tu, mi fekit Gosantine de Varda su thiu, e Mariane de Varda, in corona
dessu donnu meu judike Gu[n]nari de Laccon, in Ottave, e derunimilos a sser-
vos, ca furun fiios de Gosantine Cocone, ki fuit servu de S[an]c[t]u Petru de
Silki.' Judicarunimi a destimo[n]ios ca nd'avea gasi binkitu in co kertava. [Et]

31 Duplication of entry 200.

de Thori d'Enticlas, *curatore* of Nulabros; Ithoccor de Laccon, *curatore* of Meiulocu (Meilogu), and Gosantine de Thori, *curatore* of Romangia.

272. Dispute. *Of servants.*
I had a dispute with the prior of Plaianu (San Michele di Plaiano), lord Juvanne de Sevenes, concerning the sons of Elene Gathia about 'why do you not give me them since they were born to my servant Lustri de Cora?' I argued that 'Iuste Cora was married with Susanna Cotroske, and while married to Susanna Cotroske he had an affair with Elene Gathia who was my female servant (*ankilla*)!' They decided that I should bring forth witnesses to attest that Juste de Cora was married with Susanna Cotroske, and that he had offspring out of wedlock with Elene Gathia who was my female servant. I brought forth Gosantine de Magar, Dorgotori Caia, Dericcor d'Innoviu, Mariane Caia, and Ithoccor Pintu. I swore with them on the cross at the hearing (*corona*) of iudike Gunnari in Kitarone (Caddaroni-Sant'Eusebio). Witnesses: lord Comita de Gunale; lord Mariane de Maroniu, who was disputing the case; Comita de Thori, and the whole hearing (*corona*).

273. Dispute. *Of servants.*
I had a dispute with Petru Furca and Gavini Papis—their bishop had them bring the dispute—and with Dorgotori de Padules and his chamberlain (*camaralingu*) at Saccaria (Saccargia), over the sons of Gosantine Mancu and Susanna de Castra. They claimed that 'you have not made use of them in thirty years!' And I claimed that 'you took them away from me while they were serving me before thirty years had passed!' They decided that I should bring witnesses to testify that I had benefitted from them within the past thrity years. I brought forth Gunnari de Varru, Petru Locco, Ithoccor Clacare, and Comita de Tutar to a hearing (*corona*) of lord Comita de Navitha. I swore on the cross with them at the hearing; I won the dispute regarding the offspring, and they returned me the men. Witnesses: the *curatore*, and the whole hearing.

274. *Of servants.*
I had a dispute with Mariane de Kerki, son of Comita de Kerki from Gelesi, over Petru de Varda, his brother Istephane, and his sister Furata, who said 'why do you take them away from me as the siblings are my villeins (*liveros*)?' I claimed that 'this dispute you make with me as you do, I had with your uncle Gosantine de Varda and Mariane de Varda at a hearing (*corona*) of my lord iudike Gunnari de Laccon at Ottave (Ottava), and they granted them to me as servants (*servos*) because they were the sons of Gosantine Cocone who was a servant (*servu*) of Sanctu Petru de Silki!' They decided that I would bring forth witnesses who

ego battussilu assu curatore donnu Gosantine de Thori Divite, [et] ass'arkiprete de Turres do[n]nu Gosantine de Lella, [et] a Juvanne de Maro[n]iu, maiore d'iscolca de Duos Nurakes, [et] a Petru Minninnu, ma[n]datore de liveros. E jurarun a gruke .+. ca[n]d'avea binkitu, e cca mi los avean datos in corona a sservos, in co kertava, e jurait in fattu dessos destimo[n]ios Jorgi Muris servu de S[an]c[t]u Petru de Silki. T[este]s: su do[n]nu meu judike Barusone de Lac-
71v con in cuia corona binki, e do[n]nu Comita | de Gunale Ioculanu, e do[n]nu Ithoccor de Laccon Pinna, e do[n]nu Gosantine su fr[at]e.

275.[32]

Ego Massimilla appatissa de S[an]c[t]u Pet[ru] de Silki. Largaitimi do[n]nu Mariane de Lacc[on] su de Linthas, in su saltu de S[an]c[t]e Helias d'Urin, ca mi 'nde kereat su latus. Et ego tenninde corona cun ille, in corona dessu do[n]nu meu judike Gunnari de Lacc[on], sa die de S[an]c[t]u Simione in Nulabros; isse kereatinde su lat[us] p[ro] se, [et] ego kerealu ad intregu, in co lu posit do[n]nu Comita de Martis a sSant'Elias d'Urin. Judicarunimi a destimo[n]ios ca lu posit do[n]nu Comita de Martis a sSant'Elias, in co kertava; [et] ego battussilu a Dorgotori Palas, [et] a Petru de Funtana, servos de rennu, [et] a Presnaki de Tutar, [et] a Bittorine Manicas, e jurarun a .+. sos destimo[n]ios meos, e Dominike su ma[n]datore meu. T[e]st[e]s: su do[n]nu meu iudike Gunnari de Laccon, in cuia corona binki, e do[n]nu Saltaro su fr[at]e, curatore de Coraso, a ken
96r mi deit[33] | su donnu meu ad andareli ave t[er]men in t[er]men dessu saltu; e do[n]nu Mariane de Thori d'Enticlas, e do[n]nu Dorgotori de Thori Ca[m]ba-Curtha. E ccustos mi deit su do[n]nu meu judike Gunnari de Lacco[n] ad at[er]minarelu su saltu. Term[en] dessu saltu: ave S[an]c[t]a Maria assa funtana dessa corona, tottuve sa margine, assa corona iackitoria; avinde falat tottuve assa via, ave sa via falat a rrivu, su rivu collat a badu de piperas, e ccollat assa margine, [et] essit sa margine ass'agitu de co parthim[us] cun sos Aketos, e ccollat assu nuracke, e falat p[er] meia sa serra assa gruke, assu kercu uve est sa pet[ra] infurcata, e ffalat assa coperclata, avinde collat sa via, e cclompet assu nurake. Girat ave su nuracke susu, a derettu assu nurake de sutta via, ave su nuracke assu gulbare dessa via ki vaet a lLinthas, e falat ribu assu badu ki iunpat

32 Duplication of entry 203.

33 Last line of f. 71v. The entry in the manuscript breaks off here and continues on f. 96r.

were there when I won the case. I then brought forth the *curatore*, lord Gosantine de Thori Divite; the archpriest of Turres (Torres), lord Gosantine de Lella; Juvanne de Maroniu, head of the ward (*maiore d'iscolca*) of Duos Nurakes ('two nuraghi', Due Nuraghe), and Petru Minninnu representative of the freemen (*mandatore de liveros*). They swore on the cross that I had won and they had granted the servants at the hearing at which there was the dispute. Jorgi Muris, servant of Sanctu Petru de Silki, testified under oath with those witnesses. Witnesses: my lord iudike Barusone de Laccon, at whose hearing (*corona*) I won; lord Comita de Gunale Ioculanu; Ithoccor de Laccon Pinna, and lord Gosantine, his brother.

275.
I, Massimilla, abbess of Sanctu Petru de Silki. Lord Mariane de Laccon from Linthas appropriated from me [land in] the unworked land (*saltu*) of Sancte Helias d'Urin (Uri) of which he wanted half (*latus*). I then had an recourse to a hearing (*corona*) against him, at the hearing of my lord iudike Gunnari de Laccon on the day of Sanctu Simione in Nulabros (Nulauro/Lunafras). He wanted half of it for himself; I wanted it entirely as lord Comita de Martis had donated it to Sancte Helias d'Urin. They decided that I bring forth witnesses to testify that lord Comita de Marti had donated it to Sancte Helias as disputed. I brought forth Dorgotori Palas and Petru de Funtana, servants of the realm (*rennu*); Presnaki de Turar; Bittorine Manicas, and Dominike, my representative (*mandatore*). My witnesses swore on the cross. Witnesses: my lord iudike Gunnari de Laccon, at whose hearing I won; his brother lord Saltaro *curatore* of Coraso (Coros) to whom my lord entrusted me to go boundary by boundary around the land (*saltu*); lord Mariane de Thori d'Enticlas, and lord Dorgotori de Thori Camba-Curtha ('short leg'). These were whom my lord iudike Gunnari de Laccon entrusted me to delimit the land (*saltu*). Boundary of the land (*saltu*) [is]: from Sancta Maria to Funtana dessa Corona ('the spring of the hilltop'), along the border (*margine*), to Corona Iackitoria ('Iackitoria summit'); from there, it goes along the road and, from the road, it goes along the river; the river passes Badu de Piperas ('ford of the snakes'), passes the border (*margine*), and keeps to the border (*margine*) at the entrance (*agitu*) we share with the Aketos [family]; it [then] passes by the nuraghe and goes down the middle of the ridge to the cross and to the oak tree where there is sa Petra Infurcata ('the standing stone'); it descends to Coperclata ('the dolmen'); from there, it passes to the road and reaches the nuraghe. It turns from the nuraghe, goes up towards the nuraghe that is on the road below; from the nuraghe [it goes] to the livestock enclosure (*gulbare*) on the road that goes to Linthas, then it goes down the river towards the ford that crosses Petretu, and passes along to the farm-

a pPetretu, e ccollat tottuve assa corte de S[an]c[t]a Maria. T[este]s: do[n]nu
96v Saltaro | su fr[at]e de judike ki lu ate[r]minait su saltu, e do[n]nu Mariane de Thori d'Enticlas e do[n]nu Dorgotori de Thori Ca[m]ba-Curtha, e Dorgotori Pala servu de rennu, [et] ho[m]i[n]es.

276.
Ego appatissa Jena. Canbiai cu[n] su piscopu de Plovaki, cu[n] do[n]nu Gosantine de Lella, saltu p[ro] saltu. Ego deili ad isse a cCoda de Clesia, [et] isse deitimi a mimi a balle Savina. T[es]t[es]: p[re]viteru Furatu Solina, [et] Ithoccor de Liios su de Novaia, e Gosantine de Posia, e Barusone de Stere e Dorgotori de Valles e sSimione de Posia e Gosantine Thancute e Janne Cocone e Gunnari de Serra, su de Gelesi.

277.
Posit do[n]na Sanna de monte ad ora de morte, a S[an]c[t]a Julia de III par[t]es I dessa domestica de Solanas, p[ro] a[n]i[m]a sua e de parentes suos. Test[es]: Gosantine de Farfare e Furatu d'Olivula e Petru de Varda Mannu e Gosantine de Varda su socroniu.

278. Postura.
Posit Ithoccor d'Olivula, e Mariane su fr[at]e, a S[an]c[t]a Julia, sa parte issoro
97r dessa ter[ra] de Nuratholu, in co vi la avean. | T[e]st[e]s: Petru Ispanu e Furatu de Martis e Mickine Ca[m]bella.

279. Canpania. *In Torasi.*
Furait Frevari Gureiu sa puteca dessu Tiniosu, [et] issu Turiu deitindeli I mesa libra d'arientu assu Tiniosu in canpania, ponendevilu Frevari assu Turiu a darelila sa mesa libra p[ro] 'lle, p[ro] vocare se de 'lle, [et] assu Turiu derunindeli p[ro] custa mesa libra ki deit isse assu Tiniosu p[ro]ssa canpania de Frevari, s'ortu suo de Torasi, [et] iss'appatissa torraitilila sa mesa libra assu Turiu, [et] iss'ortu remasit appus S[an]c[t]u Petru. T[e]st[e]s ante ken li torrait s'apatissa assu Turiu sa mesa libra, e p[ro] ca remasit s'ortu a S[an]c[t]u Petru: Mariane de Varda et ambos sos fr[ate]s, Gosantine et Ith[o]ccor.

280. Postura.
Positinke a S[an]c[t]a Julia Pet[ru] Muthuru, p[ro] a[n]i[m]a sua, sa parte sua dessa t[er]ra de Nuratholu, tenende assa ki 'nke posit Ithoccor d'Oliuvla, e Mariane su fr[at]e. T[e]st[e]s: Mariane Selina e Gosantine Muthuru e Gosantine Mamalu.

yard (*corte*) of Sancta Maria. Witnesses: lord Saltaro, the iudike's brother who demarcated the land (*saltu*); lord Mariane de Thori d'Enticlas; lord Dorgotori de Thori Camba-Curtha; Dorgotori Pala, servant of the realm (*servu de rennu*), and [other] men (*homines*).

276.
I, abbess Jena, exchanged with the bishop of Plovaki, lord Gosantine de Lella, unworked land (*saltu*) for unworked land (*saltu*). I gave him Coda de Clesia ('gorge of the church'), and he gave me in return Balle Savina ('Savina valley'). Witnesses: priest Furatu Solina, Ithoccor de Liios from Novaia (Noazza), Gosantine de Posia, Barusone de Stere, Dorgotori de Valles, Simione de Posia, Gosantine Thancute, Janne Cocone, and Gunnari de Serra from Gelesi.

277. Donation.
Lady Sanna de Monte donated on her deathbed to Sancta Julia a third of the farmstead (*domestica*) of Solana for [the salvation of] her soul and that of her parents. Witnesses: Gosantine de Farfare, Furatu d'Olivula, Petru de Varda Mannu ('the elder'), and his in-law (*socroniu*) Gosantine de Varda.

278. Donation.
Ithoccor d'Olivula and his brother Mariane donated to Sancta Julia their share (*parte*) of the land at Nuratholu that they held. Witnesses: Petru Ispanu, Furatu de Martis, and Mickine Cambella.

279. Compromise. *In Torasi.*
Frevari Gureiu stole [from] the storehouse (*puteca*) of su Tiniosu ('the mangy'). Then, su Turiu gave half a pound of silver to su Tiniosu in a deal (*canpania*), so Frevari was forced to give to su Turiu half a pound for it in order to compensate him. By Frevari's deal, he gave to su Turiu for that half pound which he gave to su Tiniosu, his vegetable garden (*ortu*) at Torasi. The abbess then reimbursed the half pound to su Turiu, and the garden remained with Sanctu Petru. Witnesses before whom the abbess reimbursed the half pound to su Turiu, for which the garden remained with Sanctu Petru: Mariane de Varda and both of his brothers, Gosantine and Ithoccor.

280. Donation.
Petru Muthuru donated to Sancta Julia, for his soul, the share of his land at Nuratholu which borders with the one that Ithoccor d'Olivula and his brother Mariane donated. Witnesses: Mariane Selina, Gosantine Muthuru, and Gosantine Mamalu.

281. Postura.
97v Posit Gosantine Lelle, a S[an]c[t]a Julia, p[ro] | a[n]i[m]a sua, sa parte sua dessa t[er]ra de Nuratholu, tenende assa ki 'nke posit Petru Muthuru. T[es]t[e]s: Ithoccor de Seltas e Jorgi Kerellu e sSimione Masala.

282. *De s[er]vos.*
Ego[34] apatissa Ispethiosa. Inprestaitimi Porca Pala IIII libras d'arientu, [et] ego deindeli IIII omines a serbire p[ro]ssu pr[o]de, isc'a co li a torrare IIII libras d'arie[n]tu; deili a sserbire a Gabini Pettenatu intregu, [et] a fFurata Murta intrega, e llat[us] de Janne Corsu, e llat[us] dessa fiia, e llat[us] in Ianne Argillis, e llat[us] in sa fiia, ecco IIII omines. Sendenke arm[en]tariu donnikellu Ithoccor in sa domo, isdebitaitindeli donnikellu Ithoccor a Porca Pala, XII porcos p[ro] I libra d'arientu, et I mesa libra laborata, e p[ro]ss'atera libra e mesa, lebait totta sa calkina dessu calkinariu ki fekim[us] in Atilike, in platicu de torrare a cclesia III dessos omines ~~e llat[us]~~[35] ki li serbian p[ro]ssu prode. T[este]s: Mariane de Barru portorariu de donnikellu, ante ken se clamait pariatu de III libras d'arientu ~~e mesa~~.[36]

98r 283. Abbatissa Maria. *De s[er]vos.*
Ego[37] abbatissa Maria. Canbiai cu[n] donnu Juvanne Aspru, cu[n] boluntate dessas manacas sorres meas. Deili ego ad isse latus de Janne Cucu, kene aver fiiu factu, [et] isse deitimi lat[us] de Binkenthi, kene aver fiiu factu, canbiande a boluntate de pare. Test[e]s: Mariane de Kerki, arm[en]tariu dessa domo, et Ithocor su fiiu, et previteru Ithoccor de Liios.

284. Kertu. *De s[er]vos adpus sa domo de Teclata.*
Kertaitili su donnu meu judike Gosantine de Laccon, ki fuit armentariu dessa domo de S[an]c[t]u Petru de Silki, assu priore de S[an]c[t]u Nicola de Guthule, a do[n]nu Nicola, p[ro]ssa isclatta dessos Barithos, ca 'p[ro]gitteu 'de keres ki sun de S[an]c[t]u Petru de Silki, appus sa domo de Teclata ad intregu?' Et issu priore donnu Nicola clamaitilu a donnu Comita de Navithan, ki fuit arm[en]tariu dessa domo, et torraitili verbu ca 'sa isclacta dessos Varithos de donnu Petru de serra Caballare furun, et pro 'lle 'de kerem[us] su latus.' Et issu
98v donnu meu rispositili, ca 'p[ro]gitteu | li los levas e 'nde keres, ki cando la deit donnu Petru de serra Cavallare, pus morte dessu fiiu, sa domo de Teclata a

34 Change of hand.
35 *e llat[us]* has been cancelled by surrounding dots in the manuscript.
36 *e mesa* has been cancelled by surrounding dots in the manuscript.
37 Change of hand.

281. Donation.
Gosantine Lelle donated to Sancta Julia, for his soul, the share of his land at Nuratholu which borders the one that Petru Muthuru donated. Witnessses: Ithoccor de Seltas, Jorgi Kerellu, and Simione Masala.

282. *Of servants* (servos).
I, abbess Ispethiosa. Porca Pala lent me four pounds of silver, and I gave him four people (*omines*) to serve him as surety (*prossu prode*) until I gave him back the four pounds of silver. I gave Gabini Pettenatu to serve him in his entirety; Furata Murta [to serve] in her entirety; half of Ianne Corsu; half of his daughter; half of Janne Argillis, and half of his daughter. These were all of the four people. While *donnikellu* Ithoccor was administrator (*armentariu*) of the farm complex (*domo*), Ithoccor paid off the debt to Porca Pala with twelve pigs worth one pound of silver and with labour worth one pound and a half. For the remaining pound and a half, he delivered all the lime for the mortar that we had made at Atilike with the commitment on his part to return to the church three of those people who were in his service as security. Witnesses: Mariane de Barru, revenue collector (*portorariu*) of the *donnikellu* in the presence of whom the debt of three pounds was declared fulfilled.

283. Abbess Maria. *Of servants.*
I, abbess Maria. I made an exchange with lord Juvanne Aspru with the consent of my sisters the nuns. I gave him half of Janne Cucu who had not had a child, and he gave in return half of Binkenthi who has not had a child. We made this exchange by mutual consent. Witnesses: Mariane de Kerki, administrator (*armentariu*) of the farm complex (*domo*); his son Ithocor, and the priest Ithoccor de Llos.

284. Dispute. *Of servants* (servos) *from the farm complex* (domo) *of Teclata* (*Trigiada, near Romana*).
My lord iudike Gosantine de Laccon, who was administrator (*armentariu*) of the farm complex (*domo*) at Sanctu Petru de Silki, sued the prior of Sanctu Nicola de Guthule (Buttule, Ozieri), lord Nicola, over the descent of the Barithos family, [arguing] 'why do you want in its entirety that which Sanctu Petru de Silki holds at the farm of Teclata?' The prior, lord Nicola, brought forth lord Comita de Navithan, who was administrator (*armentariu*) of the farm (*domo*) and declared that 'the line of the Varithos belonged to lord Petru de Serra Caballare ('knight'), and because of that we want half!' My lord replied to them: 'why do you take away what you want when lord Petru de Serra Cavallare donated, after his son's death, the farm (*domo*) of Teclata to Sanctu Petru de Silki, which

S[an]c[t]u Petru de Silki, sa isclatta dessos Varithos apus sa domo de Teclata furun ad intregu?' Et do[n]nikellu Mariane ki regiat corona p[ro] iudike, p[er]contait sos homines de corona, [et] iudicarun a bature destimonios sos de S[an]c[t]u Petru, ca furun appus sa domo de Teclata. Et iudike clamaitilu a Dorgotori Pithirubiu et a donnu Barusone Punga, et a donnu Petru de Martis, su de Canpulongu, et iurarun a gru.+.ke ca 'sa isclatta dessos Varithos, servos de S[an]c[t]u Petru de Silki furun appus sa domo de Teclata ad intregu.' Et in factu issoro iurait su servu de S[an]c[t]u Petru Jorgi Tonto et binkit. Test[e]s: donnikellu Mariane, in cuia corona binkit, et donnu Bosovekesu de Navithan, et donnu Mariane de Kerki Rubiu, et totta corona, in co vi furun in S[an]c[t]u Petru de Sorra. Test[e]s.

285. Postura. *Apus sa domo de Cotronianu.*
99r Positinke Comita de Gunale, fiiu de iudike Mariane [e] de cuncuva, | su lat[us] dessu saltu de Interrivora ki co[m]porait a Comita de Kerki, et isse positilu ad ora de morte p[ro]ssa anima sua a S[an]c[t]a Maria de Cotronianu. Term[en] dessu saltu: assa padule dessu pullialbu, assu derectu dessu monim[en]tu dessa Seneca, termen assu bulvare d'iscalas d'Alaterru, term[en] assa iscala dessa mela, et baricat tottuve sa margine maiore assu laccu de Migili, et baricat tottuve sa atha ischi a golletoriu de Silva, ad derettu assu monte dessa ficu, a ffuntana de Martine, et baricat tottuve sa margine d'Uraressi, ischi a cherra clompet assu monte dessu Caprufìcu, et clompet assa padule. Test[e]s: Comita Tortolle et Comita de Martis et Comita de Canpu. Test[e]s.

286.[38] Canbiu. *De s[er]vos.*
Canbiai cu[n] Ithoccor de Kerki, su de Cotronianu. Deitimi isse a mimi su cantu bi aveat in sa muiere de Petru Porkinu, et in tottu sos fiios de Istefane Unkinu, dandemi parte sua et parte dessos frates, in platicu de ispiiaremilos isse; et ego
99v deili ad isse a Martine | avendela facta a Maria. Test[e]s: previteru Gosantine Muthike et previteru Ithoccor de Liios. Test[e]s.

287. Postura.
Posit[39] donna Bera d'Athen, muiere ki fuit de donnu Petru Seche Barbate, a S[an]c[t]u Petru pross'anima sua de III partes I de donnia cantu aveat, ed intro de domo, e foras de domo; domos, serbos, saltos, terras, binias, battorpedia.

38 Duplicated in entry 288.
39 Change of hand.

included in its entirety the offspring of the Varithos?' *Donnikellu* Mariane who presided over (*regiat*) the hearing (*corona*) for the iudike, consulted the men of the hearing (*corona*), and decided to bring forth as witnesses the men of Sanctu Petru who were at the farm (*domo*) of Teclata. The iudike brought forth Dorgotori Pithiruviu, lord Barusone Punga, and lord Petru de Martis from Canpulongu, and they swore on the cross that 'the offspring of the Varithos were servants (*servos*) of Sanctu Petru de Silki in their entirety at the farm (*domo*) of Teclata!' After them, a servant of Sanctu Petru, Jorgi Tonto, testified under oath, and he [the iudike] won. Witnesses: *donnikellu* Mariane, at whose hearing he won; lord Bosovekesu of Navithan; lord Mariane de Kerki Rubiu, and the whole hearing of those present at Sanctu Petru de Sorra (San Pietro di Sorres). Witnesses.

285. Donation. *At the farm complex* (domo) *de Cotronianu* (*Codrongianos*).
Comita de Gunale, son of iudike Mariane and his mistress (*de cuncuva*), donated half of the unworked land (*saltu*) of Interrivora which he had purchased from Comita de Kerki. He donated it on his deathbed for his soul to Sancta Maria de Cotronianu (Codrongianos). Boundary of the land (*saltu*): from the marsh (*palude*) of Pullialbu towards Monimentu dessa Seneca ('Seneca's tomb'), bordering with the livestock pen at Iscalas d'Alterru ('the hillsides at Alterru') and Iscala dessa Mela ('hillside of the apple tree'), it passes the border of Laccu de Migil ('drinking trough of Migil'), and goes beyond the cliff up to the meeting place (*gollotoriu*) at Silva, towards Monte dessa Ficu ('hill of the fig tree'), to Funtana de Martine ('spring of Martine'); it then passes along the border of Uraressi, and reaches Monte dessu Capruficu ('hill of the wild fig tree'), and then reaches the marsh. Witnesses: Comita Tortolle, Comita de Martis, and Comita de Canpu. Witnesses.

286. Exchange. *Of servants.*
I made an exchange with Ithoccor de Kerki from Cotronianu (Codrongianos). He gave me all [the share] he had of Petru Porkinu's wife and of all [the share] of the sons of Istefane Unkinu, including both his shares and his brothers' shares, with the promise to relinquish them to me (*de ispiiaremilos*). I gave him in return Martine, having had [a daughter] Maria. Witnesses: priest Gosantine Muthike, and priest Ithoccor de Liios. Witnesses.

287. Donation.
Lady Bera d'Athen, who was the wife of lord Petru Seche Barbate ('bearded'), donated to Sanctu Petru, for her soul, a third of all she had both within and outside her farm complex (*domo*): buildings (*domos*), servants (*serbos*), unworked

T[este]s: prebiteru Barusone Casu, ki la penetenthiait, et issu maritu donnu Petru Seche, e iudike Barusone, e donnikellu Ithoccor e Bernagallu e Juvanne Seche su de Silki. Test[e]s.

288.[40] *De s[er]vos.*
Canbiai cun Ithoccor de Kerki, su de Cotronianu. Deitimi isse a mimi su cantu bi aveat in sa muiere de Petru Porkinu [et] in totu sos fiios [et] issu cantu abiat in sos fiios d'Istefane Unkinu, dandemi parte sua et parte dessos fr[ate]s, in platicu de ispiiaremilos isse; et ego deili ad isse a Martine abendela fatta a Maria. T[este]s: prebiteru Gosantine Muthike, e prebiteru Ithoccor de Liios e donnu Mariane de Kerki Rubiu [et] Comita de Martis. T[este]s.[41]

72ʳ [*Condake de Sanctu Imbiricu de Sauren*]

289. *Apus Sauren.*
Ego[42] Massimilla abb[a]tissa de Sanctu Petru de Silki ki renovo custu co[n]dake de S[an]c[t]u Imbiricu de Sauren, ki fuit de te[m]p[us] meta. Et ego pettili boluntate assu do[n]nu meu judike Barusone de Lacc[on] p[ro] renovaremilu, [et] isse, co do[n]nu bonu, deitiminde assoltura de fakerlu novu, [et] ego fatholu novu cu[n] boluntate de Deus e dessa sua.

290. Postura. *Apus sa domo de Sauren.*
Ego Thunthule de Salvennor ki fatho custu co[n]dake p[ro] ca la fatho sa domo de S[an]c[t]a Elena; e poniovilu a manacu Gavini [et] a Gelandru [et] a Pelaki [et] issa muiere Barbara de Remuia; e poniovi tottu su saltu de Sega; e poniovi su saltu de Pagines, isc'a flum[en], ki mi derat su do[n]nu meu judike Gunnari de Lacco[n], sendenke curatore Ithoccor d'Urieke [et] arm[en]tariu Petru de Gunnannor; e po[n]iovi sa t[er]ra d'agitu d'Ibili [et] issa de Valle, [et] issa t[er]ra d'Ispilita, [et] issa secatura de monte de Valisandra, ave su nurake isc'a
72ᵛ rivu, e falat flum[en] isc'a badu de cote, e ccollat assu nuracke; e po[n]iovi | sa t[er]ra d'Ena de Liios, [et] issu dessa Bathaburi, ave sa mandra, [et] essit a bia isc'a badu de flum[en], e falat ribu isc'a badu de Gulturiu, e ccollat a mo[n]ticlu formicosu, e ccollat assa mandra, ave in co parthim[us] cu[n] Marcusa Urule,

40 Duplicated in entry 286.
41 End of f. 99ᵛ. The following entries continue in a different section of the text, that is to say, the condaghe of San Quirico (Sanctu Imbiricu) de Sauren, which begins on f. 72ʳ.
42 Change of hand.

lands (*saltos*), lands (*terras*), vines, and livestock (*battorpedia*). Witnesses: priest Barusone Casu, who administered her confession; her husband, lord Petru Seche; iudike Barusone; *donnikellu* Ithoccor; Bernagallu, and Juvanne Seche from Silki. Witnesses.

288. *Of servants.*
I made an exchange with Ithoccor de Kerki from Cotronianu (Codrongianos). He gave me all [the share] he had of Petru Porkinu's wife and of all Istefane Unkinu's sons, including both his shares and the shares of his brothers with the promise to relinquish them to me (*de ispiiaremilos*). I gave him in return Martine, having had Maria. Witnesses: priest Gosantine Muthike, priest Ithoccor de Liios, lord Mariane de Kerki Rubiu, and Comita de Martis. Witnesses.

[Condaghe of Sanctu Imbricu di Sauren (San Quirico, Cheremule-Thiesi)].

289. *At Sauren (Sarene, Cheremule-Thiesi).*
I, Maximilla, abbess of Sanctu Petru de Silki, renew (*renovo*) this condaghe (*condake*) of Sanctu Imbiricu de Sauren (Sarene, Cheremule-Thiesi) which was made some time ago. I sought the consent (*boluntate*) of my lord iudike Barusone de Laccon for me to renew it (*renovaremilu*), and he, good lord that he is, granted me permission (*assoltura*) to write it out again (*fakerlu novu*), so I thus renew it (*fatholu novu*) with God's will and with his.

290. Donation. *At the farm complex* (domo) *of Sauren (Sarene, Cheremule-Thiesi).*
I, Thunthule de Salvénnor, make (*fatho*) this condaghe (*condake*) for what I did regarding the farm complex (*domo*) of Sancta Elena which I grant to the monk Gavini, and to Gelandru, and to Pelaki and his wife Barbara de Remuia. I also donate the entire unworked land (*saltu*) at Sega, and the unworked land (*saltu*) of Pagines, up to the stream, which had been given me by my lord iudike Gunnari de Laccon when Ithoccor d'Urieke was *curatore*, and Petru de Gunnannor was administrator (*armentariu*). I grant the land at the entrance (*agitu*) of Ibili, and that of Valle ('valley'), the land (*terra*) at Ispilita, and the alienated portion (*secatura*) of Monte de Valisandra ('Valisandra hill'), from the nuraghe to the stream, it goes down the stream as far as Badu de Cote ('dish ford') and passes to the nuraghe. I also grant the land of Ena de Liios ('spring of Liios') and that of Bathaburi extending from the cattle stall (*sa mandra*), it continues on the road until the ford of the stream, then it goes down the stream to Badu de Gultieru ('ford of Gulturiu'), reaching Monticlu Formicosu ('ant hill') and back to the cattle stall; from there, we share it with Marcusa Urule and beyond it with

e dave susu cu[n] S[an]c[t]u Petru; e poniovi sa t[er]ra de T[er]ra Rubia cu[n] sa de badu de s'Aginariu [et] issa d'Ariolas, cu[n] anbas sas ariolas de Pelaki, [et] issa vinia de vadu de Tracla cun radicariu suo, isc'a bia maiore; [et] issu radicariu d'iscala de Urbeni, [et] a manca [et] a destra dessa funtana; e binia de Calbai, isc'a iunpatu rivu; [et] issu radicariu de Revesiiu, [et] iss'ortu de Piligine, isc'assa funtana pithinna; [et] iss'iscla de fustes albos, in co collat a destra [et] a manca de rivu; [et] issu lat[us] de monticlu de nukes, isc'assa vinia de Gosantine de Carbia, e falat assa pet[ra] dessa nuke, e falat a rrivu, e ccollat assa pet[ra] dessu kerku, e ccollat a badu de nuke; e poniovi sa vinia de Garulatho, [et] a balle de Vona, e cclompet isca ad s'iscala d'Urse, e
73r falat assa | sa pet[ra] dessa gruke d'ulumos de Murtina, e falat a rrivu, a balle de Sorike, cu[n] tottu cortes de Vikinos: [et] issa corte de Sabren, e cCoda de Tamuseli, e t[er]ra de Rubos, e t[er]ra de Golormena, e t[er]ra de vinia de manacu, e balle de ruginas, e ccuniatos de silicas, e ccuniatu de mela, e domestica de filistru, e ssup[ra] bia, e ssutta bia [e] t[er]ra de Iorgi Coppiu, e t[er]ra de Codas de Casta, e t[er]ra de Ferruchesos, in co essit isc'a balliclos; [et] issa de Viniolas, cun codas suas; e ccodas de Tedore, e ccu[n]iatu de Thunthula, e t[er]ra de Suriaca, e t[er]ra de Calabrikes, e t[er]ra de Mathuccar; cuniatos de cl[es]ia, cuniatos de Calvai, ortu de manacu, cuniatu de piskinale, cuniatu longu, lintha petrosa, agru de valle e planu de gruke, ruginas de manacu, e secatura de Sega, ave iscala de ficos, e rradicariu d'Urbitu d'Agustine, ambas sas cortes de Sega. Ecco ca[n]tu vi ponio ispiiatu d'atteros fr[ate]s meos, a parthiresi, lat[us] Sancta Elena, e lat[us] Iuste de Salvennor, fiiu meu.

291.

73v Ego piscopu Iuste de Salvennor, ki mi essivit | in sonnu p[ro] thuccarendela sa cl[es]ia ave Thilica, ki fekerat patre meu; [et] ego thuccaindela a ccuniatos de Pagines, uve se kervit issa; e gollessimilu a Garulittu Troccu p[ro] servirebi I die in settumana, e golligobilu a Bonose de Birrillo, cun sa muiere Albina Luthis, p[ro] serbirebi I die in settumana, e golligobilu a Mical de Bessute [et] I die dessa muiere Nastasia Argalia, e ssi no li servit a S[an]c[t]a Elena de no[n] bi aver bias in su saltu; e ssi vi aet alikis kertu, fiios meos li sian defensores.

Sanctu Petru. I also grant the land of Terra Rubia ('reddish earth'); the ford of s'Arginariu and that of Ariolas with both threshing floors at Pelaki; the vineyard at Vadu de Tracla ('ford of Tracla') with its cane field (*radicariu*) up to the main road; the cane field at Iscala de Urbeni ('hillside of Urbeni') both to the right and left of the spring; the vineyard of Calbai up to the stream's bank; the cane field of Revesiiu; the vegetable garden (*ortu*) of Piligine; the spring of Pithinna; the islet (*iscla*) of Fustes Albos ('white poles'), both on the right and left sides of the stream, and half (*latus*) of Monticlu de Nukes ('hill of the walnut trees'), which extends from the vineyard of Gosantine of Carbia, goes down to Petra dessa Nuke ('rock of the walnut'), descends to the stream, passes Petra dessa Kerku, and passes Badu de Nuke. I also donate the vineyard of Garulatho and that in the valley of Vona that reaches as far as Iscala d'Urse ('the hillside of Urse'), then goes down to Petra dessa Gruke ('the rock of the cross') at Ulumos de Murtina, and down the stream to Balle de Sorike ('Sorike valley'), with all the farmyards (*cortes*) at Vikinos (Bighinza), and the farmyard (*corte*) of Sabren (Sarene, Cheremule-Thiesi), Coda de Tamuseli ('Tamuseli gorge'), the land (*terra*) of Rubos; the land of Golormena; the land at Manacu's vineyard; the enclosures (*cuniatos*) of Silicas; the enclosure of Mela; the farmstead (*domestica*) of Filistru, both above the road and below the road; Jorgi Coppiu's land; the land of Codas de Casta ('gorges of Casta'); Ferruchesos' land, which extends up to the valleys; that of Viniolas with its deep-cut valleys (*codas*); the valleys (*codas*) of Tedore; Thunthula's enclosure, Suriaca's land, Calabrikes's (Calarighe) land; Mathuccar's land; the enclosures of Clesia; Calvai's enclosures; Manacu's vegetable garden (*ortu*); Piskinale's enclosure; Cuniatu Longu ('long enclosure'); Lintha Petrosa ('stony strip of land'); Agru de Valle ('valley field') and Planu de Gruke ('plain of the cross'); Manacu's ruins (*ruginas*); Sega's granted portion from Iscala de Ficos ('hillside of figs'); Urbitu d'Agistine's cane field, and both Sega's farmyards (*cortes*). All these I donate free from any claim (*ispiiatu*) from my other brothers, to be divided in half between Sancta Elena and my son, Iuste de Salvénnor.

291.

I, bishop Iuste de Salvénnor, had a dream (*in sonnu*) about relocating the church [of Sancta Elena] my father built at Thilica. Hence, I relocated it to Cuniatos de Pagines ('enclosures of Pagines') as he wished. I dispensed Garulittu Trocci to serve there for one day a week; Bonose de Birrillo with his wife, Albina Luthis, to serve one day a week; Mical de Bessute and, for one day a week, his wife Nastasia Argalia; and if he does not serve Sancta Elena, he will not have access to the unworked land (*saltu*). If any dispute (*kertu*) arises, it is my children who will act as defenders.

292. Parthiu. *Apus Sauren.*
Partho ave Sabren cun Comita de Tenore. Abe iscala d'Urse, isc'a ad ariola de mo[n]ticlu de Mariane, a ffundu de mo[n]te, e falat in Petr[as] Suparpare, a cCoda de Casta, a fFerrukesos, ad iscala de Gurgusa, ad iscala de Vonorcatu, ad iscala de ficu, e pplanu de pithu, ad iscala de porcu, a badu de T[ra]cla, e ccollat tottuve flum[en] a petra de laccu, tottuve bia, a Pet[ra] Betrana, ad ulumos de M[ur]tina, ad iscala d'Urse. Ecco saltu meu ki vi posi kene nullu kertu.

74r 293. Postura. *In avitu de Ibeli; apus Sauren.*
Ego judike Dorgotori de Kerki, ki 'nde seco dessu saltu de Nuresa, d'agitu d'Ibili, e poniolu a S[an]c[t]u Inbiricu de Sabren: ave sa via d'agittu d'Ibili, ki baet ad Uras, e benit assa funtana dessu gulbare, ube iaken sos boes de Kelemule, e ccollat tottuve s'atha, assu puthu dessu mo[n]te d'Ithomor, e benit assu castru d'Int[er]mo[n]tes, [et] afliscat appare cun su ki vi aveat ave innanti S[an]c[t]u Imbiricu.

294. Postura. *Saltos de Mu[r]gokia et de Nuresa, apus Sauren.*
Ego judike Dorgotori ki 'nde seco dessu saltu de Murgokia, ki fuit de rennu, depus Caputabas, e poniolu a S[an]c[t]u Imbiricu de Sauren, ave su badu de s'Aginariu, e ccollat assu castru dessa Serra, a t[er]m[en] dessu de S[an]c[t]u Petru, avinde bia maiore de T[er]ra Rubia; e poniovi dessu saltu de Nuresa, ave sa via ki vaet ad Uras, e benit assa funtana ante su gulbare de Kelemule, e ccollat assu castru d'Int[er]montes; e poniovilu a Petru d'Annunthia [et] a sSusanna Bubate cun totta domo sua e fiios suos.

295. Tramutu.
74v Ego p[re]viteru Janne Papis. Tramutai | binia cu[n] Petru M[ur]tinu, e ccun sos fr[ate]s, e binia e pumu. Derunim'issos in Gargulathu, ave corona isc'a rribu, [et] ego deilis in Theppage, cu[n] pumu ca[n]tu vi aveat. T[este]s: Marginesu [et] totta villa de Kelemule. E p[ro]ssu ki lis sup[er]claict ad issos deilis I boe domatu.

292. Division. *At Sauren* (*Sarene, Cheremule-Thiesi*).
I divide [the land (*saltu*)] at Sabren with Comita de Tenore, [which goes] from Iscala d'Urse ('hillside of Urse') up to the threshing floor (*ariola*) of Monticlu de Mariane ('hill of Mariane'), to the foot of the hill, descending to Petras Suparpare ('piled stones'), to Coda de Casta ('gorge of Casta'), to Ferrukesos, to Iscala de Gurgusa ('hillside at Gurgusa', Domus de Janas di Birgusa, Thiesi), to Iscala de Vonorcatu ('hillside at Bonorcatu', San Giorgio, Thiesi), to Iscala de Ficu ('hillside of Ficu') and Planu de Pithu ('plain of Pithu'), to Iscala de Porcu ('pig hillside'), to Badu de Tracla ('ford of Tracla'), passing along the stream to Petra de Laccu ('stone drinking trough'), [goes] along the road to Petra Betrana, to Ulumos de Murtina ('elms of Murtina'), to Iscala d'Urse ('hillside of Urse'). This is my unworked land (*saltu*) which I donated free of any dispute (*kertu*).

293. Donation. At the entrance (*agitu*) of Ibeli at Sauren (Sarene, Cheremule-Thiesi).
I, iudike Dorgotori de Kerki, grant from the unworked land (*saltu*) of Nuresa the entrance (*agitu*) of Ibili, and donate it to Sanctu Inbiricu de Sabren. It starts from the road of the pass of Ibili which goes towards Uras (S'Ena Uras) and arrives at Funtana desse Gulbare ('the spring of the enclosure') where there are oxen from Kelemule; it passes along the cliff to the well (*puthu*) on Monte d'Ithomor ('Ithomor hill') and reaches Castru d'Intermontes ('outcrop of Intermontes') and ends at the land that belonged to Sanctu Imbiricu before.

294. Donation. *Unworked lands* (saltos) *of Murgokia and Nuresa at Sauren.*
I, iudike Dorgotori, alienate from the realm the unworked land (*saltu*) at Murgokia, and donate it to Sanctu Imbiricu de Sabren; it is from Badu de s'Aginariu ('the ford of the donkey') and passes Castru dessa Serra ('the outcrop of the ridge') to the boundary of Sanctu Petru along the main road of Terra Rubia ('reddish earth'). I also donate the land (*saltu*) of Nuresa; from the road that goes to Uras (S'Ena Uras), it reaches the spring (*funtana*) in front of the livestock enclosure (*gulbare*) at Kelemule, and passes to Castru d'Intermontes ('the outcrop at Intermontes'). I also donate Petru d'Annunthia and Susanna Bubate with her entire household (*domo*) and their sons.

295. Exchange.
I, priest Janne Papis, exchanged a vineyard with Petru Murtinu and, with his brothers, a vineyard and a fruit orchard (*pumu*). They gave me in return [land] in Gargulathu from the hilltop (*corona*) up to the river. I gave them [land] at Theppage with all the fruit orchard (*pumu*) he had there. Witnesses: Marginesu and the whole village of Kelemule. And because that which they gave me was more valuable, I gave them a tamed ox.

296. Parthitura. *De s[er]vis.*
Parthivi fiios de Gavini T[r]occu cu[n] Iorgi de Tanar, a Maria [et] a Justa; issos levarun a Maria, e ccl[es]ia a Justa.

297. Parthitura. *De s[er]vis.*
Coiuvait Ianne Cucuma cun Elene Pinna, cu[n] boluntate de piscopu Francu e de do[n]nos paperos. Fekerun IIII fiios et parthivim[us]inos in corona de Comita de Gallu, ki 'nke fuit curatore. Levarun issos ad Aravona [et] a Petru, e nois a Iusta et a Chr[is]pina, a S[an]c[t]u Imbiricu. Et osca aper[un] kertu in parthon[e] de S[an]c[t]u Inbiricu, [et] ego e Mical Sarakinu, tenni[n]de corona de iudike Mariane in Padule de Kerketu, e iurainde a .+. ca furun parthitos. T[este]s: donnikellu Pet[ru] e Mariane de Capathennor, ki 'nke fuit curatore.

298. *De s[er]vis.*
75r Levaitila Migali Ape ad Elene Marras | assu maritu a ken fuit plakitata, e fugivitinke cun illa a Pluminos, e fekitivi fiios. Andaitivi Ianne Cuccu, ki 'nke fuit mandatore, e bocaitindela, a mama e fiios; [et] osca pettitinolla, e deim[us] lila, e no[n] bi fekit fíios, e si e[st] mortu Migali.

299. *De s[er]vis.*
Positilu Comita de Baragai su pede de Gosantine Cucusole, [et] am[us]lu como ad intregu, a sS[an]c[t]u Inbiricu.

300. Parthitura. *De s[er]vis.*
Coiuvaim[us] a bolu[n]tate de pare a Iorgi Sarakinu ki fuit s[er]bu de cl[es]ia cun Elene Thite ankilla d'Ithoccor de Kerki. Feker[un] V fiios, a Gosantine [et] a Petru [et] a Migali [et] a Bera [et] a Maria. Ego levailu a Migali [et] a Bera, a ccl[es]ia, e pap[er]os a Gosantine, ki fuit maiore, [et] a Pet[ru]; e Maria remasit ad in cumone, parthinde a bolu[n]tate de pare in corona de iudike, in Ardar. T[este]s: do[n]nu Bosoveckesu e do[n]nikellu Petru e Mariane de Thori.

301. Postura. *In Sauren, saltu de Segadon.*
Ego iudike Gunnari, ki 'nde seco dessu saltu de Segadon, ad una parte, a sS[an]c[t]u Inbiricu de Sabren, p[ro] t[er]ras ki appo intro dessu saltu meu,
75v e dolis ave | sa funtana de valle de Gargalio, e collat assa serra accatande su

296. Division. *Of servants.*
With Iorgi de Tanar, I divided the children of Gavini Troccu—Maria and Justa; they took Maria, and the church took Justa.

297. Division. *Of servants.*
Ianne Cucuma married Elene Pinna with the consent of bishop Francu and the smallholder lords (*donnos paperos*). They had four children and we divided them at a hearing (*corona*) presided over (*regiat*) by Comita de Gallu who was *curatore*. They took Aravona and Petru, and we [took] Iusta and Chrispina for Sanctu Imbiricu. Thereafter, they began a dispute (*kertu*) about the share of Santu Inbiricu, so I, Mical Sarakinu, had recourse to a hearing (*corona*) of iudike Mariane at Padule de Kerketu, and I swore on the cross that they had been divided. Witnesses: *donnikellu* Petru, and Mariane de Capathennor (Crabattennere) who was the *curatore*.

298. *Of servants.*
Migali Ape took Elene Marras from the husband (*marito*) to whom she was engaged and ran away with her to Pluminos (Cagliari), and had children. Ianne Cuccu, who was [our] representative (*mandatore*), went looking for them and retrieved the mother and her children. Her hand was then requested in marriage, and we gave her away. They had no children of their own, and Migali died.

299. *Of servants.*
Comita de Baragai donated his share of Gosantine Cucusole, and thus we held him in full (*ad intregu*) for Sanctu Imbiricu.

300. Division. *Of servants.*
We married by mutual consent, Iorgi Sarakinu, who was a servant (*serbu*) of the church, with Elene Thite, a female servant (*ankilla*) of Ithoccor de Kerki. They had five children: Gosantine, Petru, Migali, Bera, and Maria. I took Migali and Bera for the church, and the smallholders (*paperos*) took Gosantine, who was the eldest, and Petru. Maria continued to be shared. We divided them by mutual agreement at a hearing (*corona*) of the iudike at Ardar (Árdara). Witnesses: lord Bosoveckesu, *donnikellu* Petru, and Mariane de Thori.

301. Donation. *At Sauren. unworked land* (saltu) *of Segadon.*
I, iudike Gunnari, granted from the unworked land (*saltu*) of Segadon a part for Sanctu Inbiricu at Sabren (Sarene, Cheremule-Thiesi), and donate lands that I have in my land (*saltu*). [The boundary is] from the spring (*funtana*) of Valle

planu de Sem[en]siccu, e falat parthinde paris su castru ma[n]nu de valle de Tirri, derettu assu ribu de pet[ra] dura, in co collat assu rivu maiore de vadu de iaca.

302. Tramutu. *De s[er]vis.*
Tramutai ho[m]i[n]es cu[n] Gosantine Marthane: deitimi isse lat[us] in Gosantine Mingiris, [et] ego deili ad isse lat[us] in Iusta sa sorre, [et] apitsila intrega, [et] ego a Gosantine intregu, ap[us] S[an]c[t]u Inbiricu. T[este]s: do[n]nu Petru de serra Girusale, ki 'nke fuit curatore, et totta curatoria.

303. Parthitura. *De s[er]vis.*
Coiuvait Ianne Cuccu cun Iusta Marke; Ianne fuit de S[an]c[t]u Imbiricu, e Iusta de pap[er]os; coiuvaim[us]ilos a bolu[n]tate de pare, petindelila a Dorgotori de Sethales.[43] Fekerun III fiios, a Pet[ru] [et] ad Elene, [et] a sSusanna. Parthivim[us] su fetu; cl[es]ia levait ad Elene, e Dorgotori de Sethales et issos fr[ate]s levarunilu a Pet[ru], e sSusanna remasit ad in cumone. T[este]s: Sal-
76r taro Pinna, maiore d'iscolca, e Dorgotori Manicas, e Gunnari Taras. Et osca | pus cussa parthitura, tennit corona Dorgotori de Sethales e fr[ate]s suos cun serbos de cl[es]ia, sendevi arm[en]tariu Mariane de Capathennor. Kertait Mariane de Capathennor, ki fuit arm[en]tariu de S[an]c[t]u Imbiricu, cun Dorgotori de Sethales e ccun fr[ate]s suos, in corona de iudike Mariane, in Amendulas, e binkitilu Mariane de Capath[e]nnor a Dorgotori de Sethales [et] a fr[ate]s suos, ca levait cl[es]ia ad Elene e latus de Susanna, e Dorgotori e frates suos, a Petru Cuccu e lat[us] de Susanna; e iura[i]tinde a gruke Mical Flaca, mandatore de cl[es]ia, e Iorgi Sarakinu e Gosantine Flaca. T[este]s: Gosantine d'Athen e Mariane d'Ussan e Dorgotori de Capath[e]nnor.

304. Parzi[tura]. *De s[er]vis.*
Parthivi sos fiios de Ianne Cuccu cun pap[er]os; cl[es]ia lebait a Iusta [et] ad Andria,[44] e pap[er]os a Gosantine [et] a Margarita. T[este]s: p[re]viteru Ianne Bikio e sSaltaro Pinna e p[re]viteru Iuste.

305. Kertu. *P[ro] saltu dessu Asinargiu, apus Sauren.*
Kertarun sos ho[m]i[n]es de Sabren e d'Ibili cun Petru Cap[ra] ki fuit arm[en]-
76v tariu, e ccun Furatu Solina, sendenke do[n]na apatissa | Massimilla, p[ro]ssu

43 Manuscript reads *Sethalezales.*
44 Manuscript reads *Adndria.*

de Gargalio ('Gargalio valley'), it passes the ridge next to Planu de Semensiccu ('the plain of dry seed'), then it descends, splitting in half Castru Mannu ('the big outrop/nuraghe') of Valle de Tirri (Badde Tirri, near Thiesi), towards the stream of Petra Dura ('hard rock'), it passes to the main stream (*rivu maiore*) at Vadu de Iaca ('ford of the gateway').

302. Exchange. *Of servants.*
I made an exchange of 'men' (*homines*) with Gosantine Marthane; he gave me half of Gosantine Mingiris, and I gave him in return half of his sister, Iusta, so he held her in full (*intrega*) and I held Gosantine in full (*intregu*) at Sanctu Inbiricu. Witnesses: lord Petru de Serra Girusalé, who was the *curatore*, and the whole district (*curatoría*).

303. Division. *Of servants.*
Ianne Cuccu married Iusta Marke; Ianne was of Sanctu Imbiricu, and Iusta was of the smallholders (*paperos*). We married them by mutual consent following a request sought by Dorgotori de Sethales. They had three children: Petru, Elene, and Susanna. We divided the offspring: the church took Elene; Dorgotori de Sethales and his brothers took Petru, and Susanna remained in common. Witnesses: Saltaro Pinna the head of the ward (*maiore d'iscolca*), Dorgotori Manicas, and Gunnari Taras. After the division was made, Dorgotori and his brothers had recourse to a hearing (*corona*) against the servants (*serbos*) of the church when Mariane de Capathennor (Crabattennere) was administrator (*armentariu*). Mariane de Capathennor, who was the administrator of Sanctu Imbiricu, sued Dorgotori de Sethales and his brothers at a hearing (*corona*) of iudike Mariane at Amendulas (Mendulas). Mariane de Capathennor defeated Dorgotori de Sethales and his brothers, and the church took Elene and half (*latus*) of Susanna; Dorgotori and his brothers took Petru Cuccu and half of Susanna. Mical Flaca, the church's representative (*mandatore*), and Iorgi Sarakinu, and Gosantine Flaca swore on the cross. Witnesses: Gosantine d'Athen, Mariane d'Ussan, and Dorgotori de Capathennor.

304. Division. *Of servants.*
I divided the children of Ianne Cuccu with smallholders (*paperos*). The church took Iusta and Andria, and the smallholders (*paperos*) took Gosantine and Margarita. Witnesses: priest Ianne Bikio, Saltaro Pinna, and priest Iuste.

305. Dispute. *Regarding the unworked land* (saltu) *of s'Aginariu at Sauren.*
When Massimilla was the lady abbess, the men (*homines*) of Sabren (Sarene, Cheremule-Thiesi) and Ibili had a dispute with Petru Capra, who was an admin-

saltu de s'Aginariu, ca lu kerean a populare. E Petru Capra e Furatu Solina binkerunilas ambas sa[s] villas, ca fuit su saltu de S[an]c[t]u Imbiricu, ki no[n] bi aveat bias sas villas. T[este]s: su curatore do[n]nu Comita d'Athen, in cuia corona kertarun e binkerun, e Petru de Serra Boe, e Gosantine de Maroniu, e Petru de Martis de Ca[m]pulongu, e Furatu Bardane su de Sustan, et totta corona.

306. Kertu.
Kertait Gosantine de Seltas cun fiios de Gosantine Pithale, in sa corte de Parente, ki [est] ave secus de muristere, e p[ro]ssas t[er]ras de Pagine, [et] in sa binia d'Ulumos, e binkitilos in corona dessu curatore do[n]nu Comita de Athen, iurandende a destimo[n]iu Mariane Murtinu e Gosantine Backillu e Mariane Furca Porkellu.

307. Kertu. *De s[er]vis.*
Kertai cu[n] fiios de Gosantine Pithale, ca 'n[de] li los lebarun de serbos assa do[n]na mea, in parthone canta 'nke ma[n]dicavat su patre ki aveat de Mical Flaca, ki fuit patre de Gosantine Pithale. [Et] issos kertarunimi ca 'de co[m]-
77r poru l'am[us].' Poserunilis | a postu, a III [et] a IIII postos, e non battusserun beritate, gasi clonpit an'intregu; torrai a ccorona dessu curatore meu, do[n]nu Comita d'Athen, ki nos abeat iudicatu, e deitimi iura e binki. T[este]s: Gunnari Cap[ri]nu e Gosantine de Maroniu e Gosantine Pullikina e Gosantine de Rivora, et totta corona.

308. *De s[er]vis.*
Ego[45] apatissa Massimilla de S[an]c[t]u Petru de Silki. Parthivi sos omines cun judike Gunnari ki aviam[us] ad in cumone depus sa domo de Sabren k'istavan in Kelemule. Levait judike Gunnari, a Janne de Seltas, ki fuit arm[en]tariu de Capu[s]tabas, [et] ego levai a Gosantine de Seltas, porcariu [et] arm[en]tariu de Sabren, et a Furatu su fr[at]e, cun sos porcos ki aviat su patre Simione de Tola; e judike levait a Pet[ru] su fr[at]e, remanende Elene de Seltas ad in cumone. Parthivimus sos fiios d'Ithoccor Murtinu, e de Maria de Tola ki fuit ankilla de S[an]c[t]u Imbiricu. Levai ego ad Elene de Tola, e judike levait a
77v Pet[ru] [et] a Ianne; [et] ego | levai a Juste, remanende Gavini ad in cumone, lat[us] a judike e llat[us] a S[an]c[t]u Imbiricu. T[este]s: su piscopu de Sorra do[n]nu (*sic*) Iuvanne Sargu, ante ken parzivimus, [et] issu prio[re] suo

45 Change of hand.

istrator (*armentariu*), and with Furatu Solina regarding the land (*saltu*) of s'Aginariu which they supposed was held in common (*a populare*). Petru Capra and Furatu Solina defeated both the villages (*villas*) because the land (*saltu*) was of Sanctu Imbiricu and the villages did not have any grounds to claim it. Witnesses: the *curatore* lord Comita d'Athen, at whose hearing (*corona*) they sued and won; Petru de Serra Boe; Gosantine de Maroniu; Petru de Martis from Campulongu; Furatu Bardane from Sustan (S'Ustanu, Thiesi), and the whole hearing (*corona*).

306. Dispute.
Gosantine de Seltas sued the sons of Gosantine Pithale over the farmyard (*corte*) at Parente, which is behind the monastery and beyond the lands of Pagine in the vineyard of Ulumos. He defeated them at a hearing (*corona*) of the *curatore*, Comita de Athen. Witnesses taking an oath [were]: Mariane Murtinu, Gosantine Backillu, and Mariane Furca Porkellu.

307. Dispute. *Of servants.*
I had a dispute with the sons of Gosantine Pithale because they took my lady's servants (*serbos*) as part of the division his father, Mical Flaca, had enjoyed, and who was the father of Gosantine Pithale. They claimed that 'we have bought it [i.e. the share]!' They were required [to provide witnesses] once, three and then four times, but did not provide proper testimony throughout a whole year. I had recourse to a hearing (*corona*) of my *curatore*, lord Comita d'Athen, who judged us, had me testify under oath, and I won the case. Witnesses: Gunnari Caprinu, Gosantine de Maroniu, Gosantine Pullikina, Gosantine de Rivora, and all the hearing (*corona*).

308. *Of servants.*
I, abbess Massimilla of Sanctu Petru de Silki, divided with iudike Gunnari the men (*omines*) who were at Kelemule whom we have in common at the farm complex (*domo*) of Sabren (Sarene, Cheremule-Thiesi). Iudike Gunnari took Janne de Seltas who was the administrator (*armentariu*) at Caputabas (Cabuabbas), and I took Gosantine de Seltas, swineherd (*porcariu*) and administrator (*armentariu*) of Sabren, and his brother Furatu with the pigs that his father, Simione de Tole, has. The iudike took his [Gosantine's] brother. Elene de Seltas remained in common. We divided the children of Ithoccor Murtinu and Maria de Tola, who was a female servant (*ankilla*) of Sanctu Imbiricu. I took Elene de Tola, and iudike took Petru and Ianne; I also took Juste, leaving Gavini I common, half for iudike and half for Sanctu Imbiricu. Witnesses: the bishop of Sorra (San Pietro di Sorres), lord Iuvanne Sargu, before whom we made this division;

do[n]nu Ithoccor de Monte, e do[n]nu Comita de Gunale, fr[at]e de iudike, e do[n]nu Maroniu e do[n]nu Comita de Gunale Ioculanu.

309. *Adpus Sauren.*
Mandait[46] iudike Barusone a pparthire su saltu de monte de Kerketu, ki aviam-[us] ad in cumone Silki e pPlaianu, e judike [et] issos d'Athen. Parthirunilu dave sa funtana de monte de Kerketu, e falat tottuve serra, ass'Erva Frisa, e falat assu volitravu dessu Cleu, e girat assu vadu de tufu d'Aspilletu, e ccollat assu calkinariu, e ccollat su valliclu derettu assa Brunkitorta, e girat tottuve su margine d'Arkethi, a derettu ass'iscala de curatore de valle, e girat margine ass'ariola de valle de Curatore, e baricat sa via dess'iscala Alba, e girat margine ass'iscala dessu Manacu, e falat assa via maiore, e girat bia derettu assa funtana,
78r [et] affliscat. | Custu derun a sSilki, [et] a pPlaianu et issos levarun dave serra inoke. T[este]s: Petru de Serra Ossirosu, a ken bi mandait iudike ante sicu suo, e Pet[ru] de Martis de Campulongu, e Pet[ru] de serra dessa Cupa, et Ithoccor de Lella, serbu de rennu, ki at[er]minavat su saltu.

310. Kertu. *In Puthu Pasari.*
Kertarun mecu sos o[m]i[n]es dessa villa de Puthu Passaris in corona de donnu Comita d'Athen Arcatu, ki fuit curatore de Caputabas, p[ro]ssu saltu de Puthu Rubiu, ca lu kerean p[ro] populare dessa villa de Puthu Passaris. [Et] ego narailis ca 'co[m]poratu l'appo assos omines dessa villa de Tigesi.' Judicarunimi a mimi a batuier destimo[n]ios ca lu avea co[m]poratu, [et] ego batussilos issara sos destimo[n]ios a ccorona, e iurarun a .+.ke ca l'avea co[m]poratu, e binki. T[estes]: su curatore do[n]nu Comita d'Athen, in cuia corona kertarun issos mecu, e los binki ego ad issos, e cComita de Martis de Ca[m]pulongu, [et] is[su] frate Petru, e Pet[ru] de Serra dessa Cupa.

311. Termen de saltu. *In Teclata. In Bonuvichinu.*
Term[en] dessu saltu depus sa domo de Teclata, ki fuit de donnu Pet[ru] de
78v Serra | Cavallare, e de Mariane su fiiu: dave sa matta de Gureiu, sa via de valle

46 Change of hand.

his prior, lord Ithoccor de Monte; lord Comita de Gunale, brother of the iudike; lord Maroniu, and lord Comita de Gunale Ioculanu.

309. *At Sauren* (*Sarene, Cheremule-Thiesi*).
Iudike Barusone ordered the division of the unworked land (*saltu*) of Monte de Kerketu which we shared with Silki, Plaianu (San Michele di Plaiano), the iudike [himself], and the d'Athen [family]. They made the division from the spring (*funtana*) of Monte de Kerketu, descending along the ridge to s'Erva Frisa ('scorched grass'), then to Volitravu dessu Cleu ('swamp of the Cleu'), then it turns towards Vadu de Tufu ('the ford of Tufu') at Aspilletu, and passes the limepit (*su calkinariu*), then it passes the small valley (*valliclu*) towards Brunkitorta ('twisted hill'), and turns towards the border of Arkethi, [it then goes] towards s'Iscala de Curatore de Valle ('the hillside of the *curatore* of the valley'), and goes around the border of the threshing floor in Valle de Curatore ('valley of the *curatore*'), it crosses the road of s'Iscala Alba ('the white hillside'), turns around the border of s'Iscala dessu Manacu ('hillside of the monk'), then descends towards the main road and keeps to the road towards the spring where it ends. This was given to Silki and Plaianu, while the others took that which was from the ridge to here. Witnesses: Petru de Serra Ossirosu whom the iudike had sent in his stead; Petru de Martis from Campulongu; Petru de Serra from Sa Cupa, and Ithoccor de Lella, servant (*serbu*) of the realm (*rennu*) who delimited the land (*saltu*).

310. Dispute. *In Puthu Pasari*.
The men of the village of Puthu Passaris ('sparrows' well', San Nenaldu, Cheremule) sued me at a hearing (*corona*) of lord Comita d'Athen Arcatu who was the *curatore* of Caputabas (Cabuabbas) over the unworked land (*saltu*) of Puthu Rubiu ('red well') because they claimed it to be communal property (*populare*) of the village of Puthu Passaris. I said that 'I purchased it from the men of the village of Tigesi (Thiesi)!' They decided that I should bring forth witnesses that I purchased it, so I brought forth witnesses to a hearing (*corona*), and they swore on the cross that I had bought it, and I won the dispute. Witnesses: the *curatore* lord Comita d'Athen at whose hearing (*corona*) they sued me and I defeated them; Comita de Martis from Campulongu and his brother Petru, and Petru de Serra from Cupa.

311. Boundary of unworked land (*saltu*). *At Teclata. At Bonuvichinu*.
Boundary of the land (*saltu*) at the farm complex (*domo*) of Teclata (Trigiada, near Romana) that used to belong to lord Petru de Serra Cavallare ('knight') and Mariane, his son. [It starts] from Matta de Gureiu ('the *macchia* of Gureiu'),

becla, assa margine de Molendinu, assu gulbare dessa mura, su muru dessas petrosas, ass'ispelunca de Consons, sa via maiore ki benit de Surugel, ass'ariola Terrania, muru de Gitil tottuve, assa margine de coda de Pullis, su muru tottuve parthinde paris a monte d'oiastrai, falande flum[en] maiore, flumen tottuve, a Mabrikella, isc'a su flum[en] de Teclata, collat a kercos clopatos, uve parzit de pare cun S[an]c[t]a Maria de Curin, serra tottuve de pratu de cavallos, assas elikes de S[an]c[t]u Janne, cun lat[us] dessa villa de Teclata, e iunpat su vadu de Teclata, tottuve bia maiore a ffuntana salsa, assu badu maiore de vite, flum[en] tottuve ass'elike iscusoria de vadu d'elike, a rriu de Bonasiias, assu nurake de Guthoppor, ass'iscala dessu labru, assa petra de Thilomor, assu monticlu dess'iscopa libida, assa [ma]tta de Gureiu. E ccustu saltu partho cun fr[ate]s meos appus sa domo de Teclata, cun lat[us] dessa villa.

312. Co[m]poru.

79r Co[m]p[or]aili a Gosantine de Kerki su de | Tamarikes, su saltu suo dessu Musuleu d'Othila, tottu in co vi lu aviat; [et] e[st] t[er]men d'ecustu saltu: dave sa ficu de S[an]c[t]u Migali de Salvennor, [et] essit derettu tottube bia app'a Andria, e ffalatinke tottube bia maiore, accata[n]delu tottu a muros de Barusone, assu iunpatoriu d'Istuccu, e torrat totuve sa pala assa corona dessa Carica, e torrat assa ficu de S[an]c[t]u Migali de Salvennor [et] affliscat. [Et] ego deindeli a Jorgi de Fokile intregu. T[este]s: Gunnari de Varru e Gosantine Mollone e Petru de serra de tamarikes.

313. Conporu.

Co[m]p[or]aili[47] a ffiios de Comita de Ca[m]pu su de Valles, a Pet[ru] [et] a Jorgia [et] a Justa [et] a Bittoria [et] assu fiiu de Dorgotori de Ca[m]pu, [et] ad Ithoccor, sa parte issoro canta vi avian in su saltu de labrea, e binia, e ppu[mu] cantu vi avian. [Et] ego deindelis ad tottu ad in cumone, a pparthiresi paris, duas baccas, e duas petthas de pesentinu, e tres sollos de pannu.

47 Change of hand.

[goes to] the road of Valle Becla ('Becla valley'), to the border of Molendinu (near Cossoine), then to Gulbare dessa Mura ('the enclosure of the brambles'), [to] the rocky wall, then to the cave (*ispelunca*) at Consons, then to the main road that comes from Surugel (Suruge, near Cossoine), then to Terrania threshing floor, keeping to the wall of Gitil, then to the border of Coda de Pullis ('gorge of Pullis'), keeping to the wall that divides Monte Oiastrai ('the hill of Oiastrai', Monte Ozzastru, Cossoine) in half, and descends to the main river, keeping to it, [then it goes] to Mabrikella (Funtana Marighedda) and as far as the river of Teclata, passing Kercos Clopatos ('covered oaks'), where it divides [the land] equally with Sancta Maria de Curin; then to the ridge of Pratu de Cavallos ('horses' meadow'), towards the holly oaks at Sanctu Janne [where it borders] with half the village of Teclata, and then crosses Vadu de Teclata ('the ford at Teclata'), keeping to the main road towards Funtana Salsa ('salty spring'), towards Badu Maiore de Vite ('the main ford of Vite'), keeping to the river to s'Elike Iscusoria ('the hollow holm oak') of Vadu d'Elike ('holm oak ford'), then to the river of Bonasiias, to the nuraghe of Guthoppor, to Iscala dessu Labru ('hillside of the bay tree'), to Petra de Thilomor ('the rock of Thilomor', Monte Tiloromo, Cossoine), to the hill of Iscopa Libida ('the pale broom'), then back to Matta de Gureiu ('the *macchia* of Gureiu'). I divided this land (*saltu*) with my brothers of the farm complex (*domo*) of Teclata, and with half of the village.

312. Purchase.
I bought from Gosantine de Kerki from Tamarikes (Tamarighes, near Usini) his unworked land (*saltu*) of Musuleu d'Othila, all of it that he had. This is the boundary of the land (*saltu*): it starts from the fig tree of Sanctu Migali at Salvénnor and continues straight towards the road for Andria, then descends along the main road, keeping along the walls of Barusone until it reaches the crossing point (*iunpatoriu*) of Istuccu. It [then] turns along the slope of Corona dessa Carica ('the summit of the dried fig'), and returns to the fig tree of Sanctu Migali at Salvénnor where it ends. I gave him Jorgi de Fokile as a full servant (*intregu*). Witnesses: Gunnari de Varru, Gosantine Mollone, and Petru de Serra from Tamarikes.

313. Purchase.
I bought Petru, Jorgia, Justa, and Bittoria from the sons of Comita de Campu from Valles (Cantaru Addes). And from the son of Dorgotori de Campu, I bought Ithoccor and his share (*parte*) of that which they had in the land (*saltu*) of Labrea: vineyard, fruit orchard (*pumu*) and all they had there. I gave them two cows, two pieces of Piacenza-style fabric (*Pesentinu*), and three soldi

Testes: Gosantine Manata e pPetru de Varru, maiore d'iscolca, e Dorgotori de Porta e pPetru Gaspio.

79^{v} 314.[48]
Ego[49] Benevenuta apatissa de S[an]c[t]u Petru de Silki, ki ponio in ecustu condake bene ki 'nke fekerunt sendeke ego donna.

314bis[50] Postura. *Sa domo de Jennan[u]*.
Immalavidaitse su Turciu dessu male dunde morivit, [et] cu[m]bersaitse a S[an]c[t]u Petru de Silki. Sende i[n] sa domo de Silki, bennit Arrigu dessu Mare ad isse, [et] naraitili su Turciu ad Arrigu ca 'morio, [et] testam[en]tu voio facer dessu meu. Bocatemi dessa domo de Iannanu ki am[us] a ccumone p[ro] pinn[us], [et] tu leva dess'intica ki am[us] ad i[n] cumone atteru gota[n]tu.' Et ad Arrigu plakitili, [et] pariaisse dessa i[n]tica ki avian a ccumone, [et] issa domo de Iannanu remasit ad i[n]tregu assu Turciu. [Et] issu Turciu penetenthiaisse [e] positi[n]ke a sS[an]c[t]u Petru de Silki, p[ro] sa a[n]i[m]a sua, sa domo de Iannanu, ki aviat a pi[n]nus, cu[n] bolu[n]tate de Arrigu dessu Mare. Test[e]s ki furun uve se penetenthiait: previteru Forasticu et p[re]viteru Petru Corsellu [et] Dorgotori de Varru [e] Gosantine de Martis, su de Silki, [et] Terramannesos, Gelardinu de Cunitu [e] Guidu dessu Bullu [e] Jacopu de Scerbuna [e] Berrardu Pathu. Custos vi furun uve la torrait su Turciu sa domo de Iannanu a sS[an]c[t]u Pet[ru], ki aveat a ppinnus. Test[e]s.[51]

80^{r} [*Condake de Sancta Maria de Cotronianu*]

315.
Ego[52] Massimilla apatissa ki renovo custu co[n]dake de S[an]c[t]a Maria de Cotronianu, cu[n] bolu[n]tate de Deus e dessu do[n]nu meu judike Gu[n]nari de Lacc[on] [e] dessa muiere do[n]na Maria regina e dessu fiiu do[n]nu Barusone rege, ca fuit su vetere iskecatu.

316. Postura. *Domo de Cotro[n]gian[u]*.
Ego do[n]nikella Justa d'Oskeri ki fatho custu co[n]dake p[ro] o[mn]ia ca[n]tu 'nke ponio a sS[an]c[t]a Maria de Cotronianu. Ponionke su saltu de Pet[ra]

48 Cf. entry 382 where the first sentence has been reproduced.
49 Change of hand.
50 Cf. entry 383 where the same transaction is reproduced, but not verbatim.
51 End of f. 79^{v}.
52 Change of hand.

(*sollos*) of cloth to be shared between them. Witnesses: Gosantine Manata; Petru de Varru the head of the ward (*maiore d'iscolca*); Dorgotori de Porta, and Petru Gaspio.

[Condaghe of Sanctu Petru de Silki].

314.
I, Benevenuta, abbess of Sanctu Petru de Silki, put in this condaghe the benefices made at the time when I was in charge (*donna*).

314bis. Donation. *The farm complex* (domo) *at Jennanu.*
Su Turciu fell ill with the disease from which he would die, so he devoted himself to Sanctu Petru de Silki. While he was at the church (*domo*) of Silki, Arrigu dessu Mare came to him, and Su Turciu told Arrigu, 'I am about to die and I wish to make my last will and testament. Return to me the farm complex (*domo*) of Iannanu (Gennano, Porto Torres) whose property we share as a security payment (*pro pinnus*), and take a share of equal value of the storehouse (*intica*) we share!' Arrigo agreed to this, and was compensated with the storehouse they shared, and the farm of Iannanu was conceded in full to Su Turciu. Afterwards, Su Turciu received the last rites and donated to Sanctu Petru de Silki the farm of Iannanu that he had used as security, for [the salvation of] his soul, with the consent of Arrigu dessu Mare. Witnesses who were there when he received the last rites: priest Forasticu, priest Petru Corsellu, Dorgotori de Varru, Gosantine de Martis from Silki, and the mainlanders (*terramannesos*) Gelardinu de Cunitu, Guidu dessu Bullu, Jacupu de Scerbuna, and Berrardu Pathu. These were present when Su Turciu granted to Sanctu Petru the farmstead of Iannanu that he held as security. Witnesses.

[Condaghe of] Sancta Maria at Cotronianu (Codrongianos).

315.
I, abbess Massimilla copy out (*renovo*) this condaghe of Sancta Maria de Cotronianu (Codrongianos), with the consent of God and of my lord iudike Gunnari de Laccon, and of his wife, lady Maria the queen (*regina*), and of his son, lord Barusone the king (*rege*), because the old one had faded (*iskecatu*).

316. Donation. *Farm complex* (domo) *of Cotrongianu.*
I, *donnikella* Justa d'Oskeru, make this condaghe for everything I donate to Sancta Maria at Cotronianu (Codrongianus). I gave the unworked land (*saltu*) of Petra de Ponte ('rock of the bridge'). The boundary of the land (*saltu*) is: from

de Ponte. Term[en] dessu saltu: ave Pet[ra] de Ponte, e baet sa via a gulvare de Turre, de co parthimus de pare cun S[an]c[t]a Inbenia, e moliat sa via, e ccollat a nuracke de t[er]m[en], ed avinde baet a mo[n]ticlu de t[er]m[en], e falat balle ass'ariola Cotinatha, e falat assu rivu de ficos rankidas, ribu falat tottuve a Pet[ra] de Ponte: ecco co vaet t[er]m[en] dessu saltu ki 'nke ponio a S[an]c[t]a Maria; su lat[us] d'ecustu saltu, ca s'atteru lat[us] sorre mea Elene lu levait, cussu a destra de via, ki faket cantu, [et] ecustu ki levait cuke sorre
80v mea Elene, lat[us] e buckellu, ca | fuit lat[us] sa destra de via ki levait issa, e llat[us] sa manca ki parthiam[us] u[m]pare, ki posit issa a S[an]c[t]a Inbenia, e p[ro] cussu lu levai ego su saltu de Calkinata ad intregu, e poniolu a S[an]c[t]a Maria. Term[en] d'ecussu saltu de Calkinata: ave sa funtana, e ccollat s'ena dessos cannavarios, [et] essit a bia, e llevat bia tottuve isca ad uve se clompet, sa serra tottuve, tottuve falat sa serra dessu petrosu de Pelagesu, e torrat assa funtana de Calkinata. E ponionke lat[us] de t[er]ras d'agrile de villa; lat[us] dessa d'Iscolcatoriu, e lat[us] dessa valle de Gosantine, e lat[us] de valle Villaria, e lat[us] dessas Linthas de Ca[m]pu, e lat[us] dessa serra de Pet[ra] de Frates, e lat[us] dessas de Clusuras, e parte ca[n]ta mi 'nke int[ra]vat dessos ho[m]i[n]es, X int[er] intregos, e laterati e pedati. Ecco co levai ego lat[us], e lat[us] sorre mea Elene; e poniolu ego tottu meu a S[an]c[t]a Maria de Cotronianu, cu[n] bolu[n]tate de fr[ate]s meos. T[este]s: Albis de Nuracati [et] Egithu de Capriles e cComita de Cap[ri]les e cComita de Puthu Maiore, e Petru de Viniolas, e Pellio de Capriles.

81r 317. Postura. | *In Cotrongianu.*
Positinke Egithu de Silvori parthone ca[n]ta 'nke aveat in Cotronianu, e domo et ho[m]i[n]es: Andria Tunba cun IIII fiios suos, e previteru Pantaleo cun V fiios suos, [et] a Maria Argata [et] a Ianne Ungla su maritu cun VI fiios suos, e Dorveni Sarakina e Maria sa muiere, e III fiios suos, e Furatu Thinca et Elene Sardasa sa muiere, cun VI fiios suos; ecco p[us]p[ar]e XXXII; e binias II, sa d'Othias [et] issa de Narvone; e t[er]ras, su cuniatu de Cotinas, ki avea cuniatu a muru, [et] issa de valle de Piras, [et] issa de Iaccaria, [et] iss'Ariola T[er]rania, et a Mo[n]ticlu de Gosantinu. T[este]s: Ithoccor de Sevin, ki 'nke fuit curatore, e Gosantine de Castavar, [et] Egithu de Kerki e cComita de Cotronianu e ccolivertos meos, e fr[at]es meos de cuke fundamentales.

Petra de Ponte, it goes along the road to Gulvare de Turre ('livestock enclosure at Turre'), which we share with Sancta Inbenia, it then turns with the road and passes a nuraghe as a boundary [marker] (*termen*), and from there it continues to a hill as a limit, and goes down the valley to Ariola Cotinatha ('the rocky threshing floor'), and comes down to Rivu de Ficos Rankidas ('river of rotten figs'), [and] descends along the river towards Petra de Ponte. This is the boundary of the land (*saltu*) that I donate to Sancta Maria, which is half of the entire land (*saltu*) because the other half, which is at the right side of the road, was taken by my sister Elene. The part of the land (*saltu*) that my sister took is equal to three-quarters (*latus e buckellu*), for it was the half at the right side of the road that she took, while we split evenly the half at the left side, which I donate to Sancta Inbenia. In order to compensate for this, I took the entire land (*saltu*) of Calkinata, and I donated it to Sancta Maria. The boundary of this land (*saltu*) of Calkinata starts from the spring (*funtana*), passes s'Ena dessos Cannavarios ('the spring of the hemp fields'), comes out at the road and takes it until reaching the end; then [it goes] along the ridge, descends along the ridge of Petrosu de Pelagesu ('the rocky place at Pelagesu'), and turns at Funtana de Calkinata ('the spring of Calkinata'). I also donate half of the village's arable lands (*terras d'agrile*), half (*latus*) of Iscolcatoriu, half of lands of the Valle de Gosantine ('valley of Gosantine'), half of Valle Villaria ('Villaria valley'), half of the lands of Linthas de Campu ('land-strips at Campu'), half of the lands of Serra de Petra de Frates ('the ridge of brothers' rock'), half of Clusuras, and half the share (*parte*) of ten men who belong to me, including those whose service I claim in full (*intregos*), in half (*laterati*), and in quarter (*pedate*). I thus took half, and my sister Elena the other half, and I donated all my part to Sancta Maria de Cotronianu with the consent of my brothers. Witnesses: Albis de Nuracati (Nuragaddu), Egithu de Capriles, Comita de Capriles, Comita de Puthu Maiore (Pozzomaggiore), Petru de Viniolas, and Pellio de Capriles.

317. Donation. *At Cotrongianu.*
Egithu de Silvori donated all the share (*parthone*) he had in Cotronianu (Codrongianos), both farm complex (*domo*) and men (*homines*): Andria Tunba with his four children; priest Pantaleo with his five children; Maria Argata and her husband Ianne Ungla with their six children; Dorveni Sarakina, his wife Maria and their three children; Furatu Thinca and his wife Elene Sardasa with their six children. In total, thirty-two. Also, two vineyards: that of Othias, and that of Narvone. Also, lands: the walled enclosure (*cuniatu a muru*) at Cotinas; that of Valle de Piras; Iaccaria; s'Ariola Terrania; and Montiticlu de Gosantinu. Witnesses: Ithoccor de Sevin who was *curatore*, Gosantine de Castavar, Egithu de Kerki, Comita de Cotronianu, my servants (*colivertos*), and those there who were party to this arrangement (*frates fundamentales*) with me.

318. Fura. *In eode[m] loco.*
Ego Severu p[re]viteru. Furaitimi sa cl[es]ia Maria Flaca, e p[ro]vailila. Tenni corona de judike Petru de Serra, [et] apretharunimila a XL sol[los], et issara mi derun o[mn]ia cantu 'nke aveat in Cotronianu, e domo, e binias, e t[er]ras, [et] issu sepe ki co[m]p[or]arat a Dorgotori Floru, dandemilu in corona de
81v do[n]nu | meu, judike Petru de Serra. T[este]s: Comita d'Urieke, curatore de Ficulinas, [et] Ithoccor de Sevin, e ccantos vi furun in sa corona.

319. *De s[er]vis.*
Ego piscopu Iorgi Maiule. Kertait mecu Ithoccor de Sogostos p[ro]ssu fetu de Suvia Pullis, ki mi levarat a larga su servu Simione Cuccu, ca mi 'nde kereat parte. [Et] ego kertaili c', 'a larga mi la levait su servu tuo, andandevi e llevandemindela a fura; et ego andaivi e battivilu e lievaiminde s'ankilla mea. Andaitivi e furaitimindela.' Issara mi kerverun destimo[n]ios a mimi ca lu batti e cca 'nde lu gettai e cca mi 'nde la levai s'ankilla mea. Essivitimi a destimoniu Niscoli de Thori curatore d'Anglone, e Barusone de Kerki, cun ken lu secutai e lu batti, e iurait a .+. su mandatore de cl[es]ia, Gavini Pelle. T[este]s: su curatore Gosantine d'Athen e Niscoli de Thori, e Dorgotori d'Ussan, et totta corona. Et issara mi derun tottu su fetu, ass'ankilla mea, a Furatu [et] a sSarakina [et] a Forastica [et] a Gavini [et] a Ianne.

82r 320. *Pro s[er]vis.*
Parthivi ho[m]i[n]es cu[n] Petru de Kerki, a Margarita [et] a Bonita. Isse levait a Margarita, ca l'aveat ad amante, [et] ego a Bonita. Morivit sa sua e largaitimi in sa mea, [et] ego kertai cun isse, e binkilu in corona de Dorgotori d'Ussan, ki fuit curatore in Castellu sa die de Letania Maiore, e iurait a .+. su mandatore meu Gavini Pelle. T[este]s: Ithoccor de Vosoue e cComita su fr[at]e, [et] Ithoccor de Kerki.

321. Conporu. *Cotro[n]janu[m].*
Co[m]p[or]aili a Petru de Muskianu su saltu de Capathennor, ki parthiat lat[us] a ppare cun Ithoccor de Vanios, e deivili I boe, [et] I vacca e II maiales, e II sol[los] de pecuiu, p[us]p[ar]e XI sol[los]. T[este]s: Petru de Ca[m]pu e Gunnari de Vanios e cComita de Carvia e Baru de Castavar.

318. Theft. *In the same place.*
I, priest Severu. Maria Flaca stole from the church, and I could prove it. I had recourse to a hearing (*corona*) of iudike Petru de Serra, and [the theft] was evaluated at forty soldi (*sollos*), and for that I was given all that she had in Cotronianu (Codrongianos): farm complex (*domo*), vineyards, lands, and a hedgerow (*sepe*) that she bought from Dorgotori Floru. I was given this at a hearing (*corona*) of my lord iudike Petru de Serra. Witnesses: Comita d'Urieke *curatore* of Ficulinas, Ithoccor de Sevin, and all those who were at the hearing (*corona*).

319. *De servis.*
I, bishop Iorgi Maiule. I sued Ithoccor de Sogostos over the offspring of Suvia Pullis who was stolen from me by the servant (*servu*) Simione Cuccu because he wanted a share [of his services]. I argued with him by saying 'your servant took her away; when he came and stole her from me, I beat him and took my servant back. [But] he came and took her away from me!' I was requested to provide witnesses who could testify that I beat him and chased him, and that he took my female servant (*ankilla*). The witnesses who came were: Niscoli de Thori, *curatore* of Anglone (Anglona); and Barusone de Kerki with whom I chased and beat him. Gavino Pelle, the church's representative (*mandatore*), swore on the cross. Witnesses: the *curatore* Gosantine d'Athen, Niscoli de Thori, Dorgotori d'Ussan, and the whole hearing (*corona*). Hence, they gave me my female servant and all her offspring: Furatu, Sarakina, Forastica, Gavini, and Ianne.

320. *About servants.*
I divided the servants (*homines*) Margarita and Bonita with Petru de Kerki. He took Margarita because he had her as a lover (*amante*), and I took Bonita. [But] his female servant died, so he took mine. I sued him and I won at a hearing (*corona*) of Dorgotori d'Ussan who was the *curatore* in Castellu, on the day of the Major Litany (*letania maiore*). My representative (*mandatore*), Gavini Pelli, swore on the cross. Witnesses: Ithoccor de Vosove, his brother Comita, and Ithoccor de Kerki.

321. Purchase. *Cotronjanum* (*Codrongianos*).
I bought from Petru de Muskianu (Muscianu) the unworked land (*saltu*) of Capathennor (Crabattennere) which he divided in half with Ithoccor de Vanios; he gave him one ox, one cow, two pigs, and two soldi in cash (*sollos de pecuiu*) to a total value of eleven soldi (*sollos*). Witnesses: Petru de Campu, Gunnari de Vanios, Comita de Carvia, and Baru de Castavar.

322. Parthitura. *De s[er]vos*.
Ego Theodora appatissa de S[an]c[t]a Julia de Kitarone. Parthivi ho[m]i[n]es cun do[n]na Maria de Laccon muiere de donnikellu Ithoccor, a Gavini Cafia [et] a Ianne Papate. Gavini Cafia lat[us] fuit de S[an]c[t]a Maria de Cotronianu, e lat[us] de S[an]c[t]u Paulu, e gasi etro Ianne Papate. Naraitimi ca 'levatende
82v I cale volites, | a sS[an]c[t]a Maria, [et] issateru app[us] S[an]c[t]u Paulu.' Parthivilos ego e levait issa a Ianne Papate, app[us] S[an]c[t]u Paulu, e Gavini remasit a S[an]c[t]a Maria de Cotronianu. T[este]s ante ken parthiam[us]: do[n]nu Ianne Argenti, ki fuit p[re]viteru in S[an]c[t]u Paulu, e Mariane de Kerki, arm[en]tariu de S[an]c[t]a Maria, e Janne de Liios su de Sorso, e Pelaki de Carros, mandatore de S[an]c[t]a Julia, e Gosantine de Farfare, mandatore de liveros de Kitarone.

323. Postura.
Positinke Comita de Gunale, fiiu de iudike Mariane [e] de cuncuva su lat[us] dessu saltu d'Interrivora ki co[m]p[or]ait a cComita de Kerki, [et] isse positilu ad ora de morte a sS[an]c[t]a Maria de Cotronianu. T[este]s: Comita Tortolle e cComita de Martis e cComita de Ca[m]pu e Gosantine de Ca[m]pu.

324. Kertu.
Ego Massimilla apatissa. Kertai cu[n] fiios de Mariane de Castavar p[ro]ssa parthone de Maria Flaca, ki mi deran p[ro]ssa fura dessa cl[es]ia ki mi fekerat, ki mi aveat levata Mariane su patre, et posilu a do[n]nu Mariane de Maroniu a ckertare p[ro] me, e pro'ssos kertavat Petru de Nurdole, e sSaltaro de Navitha;
83r e binkitilos | do[n]nu Mariane de Maroniu, in corona de Gosantine de Thori Cok'e-Mandica, curatore de Ficulinas, e iuraitinde a .+. Janne Tatacke, mandatore de cl[es]ia. T[este]s: Ithoccor d'Athen e sSaltaro fr[at]e de judike, e cComita de Ca[m]pu, et totta corona.

325. Conporu. *Cotro[n]janu[m]*.
Co[m]p[or]aili a Gosantine de Iana [et] assa mama Justa de Valles sa parte sua dessa vinia de Funtana, cu[n] pumu e bacante cantu vi aveat, ki parthiat cu[n] Petru de Iana, [et] app[re]tharunila a xv sol[los]. [Et] ego deivili III boes domatos e II sol[los] de verbekes, a bolu[n]tate de pare, sende arm[en]tariu de clesia do[n]nu Mariane de Kerki, e ma[n]datore Ianne Tatacke. T[este]s: Comita de Martis e cComita Tortolle e Dorgotori Mug[ra] e sSimione Pede, ki nuverauat sa vinia.

322. Division. *Of servants.*
I, Theodora, abbess of Sancta Julia de Kitarone (Caddaroni-Sant'Eusebio) divided with lady Maria de Laccon, wife of *donnikellu* Ithoccor, the [following] men (*homines*): Gavini Cafia and Ianne Papate. Half (*latus*) of Gavini Cafia belonged to Sancta Maria de Cotronianu (Codrongianos), and the other was of Sanctu Paulu, and thus with Ianne Papate too. She [lady Maria] told me: 'take whichever you want for Sancta Maria, and [leave] the other one for Sanctu Paulu!' I divided them, and she took Ianne Papate for Sanctu Paulu; Gavini remained at Sancta Maria de Cotronianu. Witnesses before whom we made the division: lord Ianne Argenti, who was a priest at Sanctu Paulu; Mariane de Kerki, administrator (*armentariu*) of Sancta Maria; Janne de Liios from Sorso; Pelaki de Carros, representative (*mandatore*) of Sancta Julia, and Gosantine de Farfare, representative of the freemen (*mandatore de liveros*) at Kitarone.

323. Donation.
Comita de Gunale, son of iudike Mariane and a mistress (*cuncuva*), donated the half (*latus*) of the unworked land (*saltu*) of Interrivora that he bought from Comita de Kerki. He made the donation on his deathbed to Sancta Maria de Cotronianu (Codrongianos). Witnesses: Comita Tortolle, Comita de Martis, Comita de Campu, and Gosantine de Campu.

324. Dispute.
I, Massimilla, abbess, had a dispute with the sons of Mariane de Castavar over the share (*parthone*) of Maria Flaca which they gave me [to compensate] for the theft she had committed in the church [because] their father Mariane had taken them away. I sent lord Mariane de Maroniu to argue on my behalf; Petru de Nurdole and Saltaro de Navitha argued for the sons. Mariane de Maroniu defeated them at a hearing (*corona*) of Gosantine de Thori Cok'e-Mandica, *curatore* de Ficulinas. Janne Tatacke, the church's representative (*mandatore*), swore on the cross. Witnesses: Ithoccor d'Athen, Saltaro the brother of the iudike, Comita de Campu, and the whole hearing (*corona*).

325. Purchase. *Cotronjanum* (*Codrongianos*).
I bought from Gosantine de Iana and his mother Justa de Valles their share (*parte*) of Vinia de Funtana ('vineyard of the spring') with the fruit orchard (*pumu*) and all the empty land (*bacante*) they had and shared with Petru de Iana. They valued it at fifteen soldi (*sollos*). I gave them, in mutual agreement, three tamed oxen and two soldi of sheep when lord Mariane de Kerki was administrator (*armentariu*) of the church, and Ianne Tatacke [was] the representative (*mandatore*). Witnesses: Comita de Marti, Comita Tortolle, Dorgotori Mugra, and Simione Pede who counted the vines.

326. Conporu.
Co[m]poraili a Petru Marthane [et] a Gavini Marthane su cannavariu de Funtana, tenende assa vinia de cl[es]ia, e deivilis kis baccone e ccana II moios
83v d'oriu, a bolu[n]tate issoro. T[este]s: | Pismaki d'Oianu, maiore de gulbare, [et] Ithoccor de Gunale, mandatore de liveros, e Ianne Prinkis, mandatore de cl[es]ia, e Ianne Tatacke.

327. Kertu.
Kertait Petru Thuris e binkit in sol[lu] de vinia ki aveat intro dessu cuniatu de cl[es]ia, e deindeli novellu de sol[lu]. T[este]s: Gitimel Tortolle, maiore, in cuia corona binki, e Gosantine Turdu e Pet[ru] Papate.

328. Tramutu.
Tramutai cun Gosantine Turdu t[er]ra ki co[m]porarat assos [...] sup[ra] Funtana, e deindeli in binia de Pira. T[este]s: Dorgotori de Foke, maiore de gulbare, e Dorgotori de Gallu, e Furatu Thinca.

329. Conporu.
Co[m]p[or]aili a sSusanna de Tula t[er]ra in ariola T[er]rania, tenende assa de cl[es]ia, e deivili II t[re]m[isse]s de casu, a cca[n]tu valeat sa t[er]ra.

330. Co[m]po[r]u.
Co[m]po[r]aili ad Inbenia de Runda t[er]ra tenende ad ecussa in Ariola T[er]rania, e deivilis ad in cumone ad issa [et] assu fr[at]e Gosantine, II t[re]m[isse]s
84r de casu. T[este]s: Simione Rasu, maiore | de vulvare, e Dericcor d'Oianu.

331.
Co[m]poraili a fFurata Co[n]iu terra in badu de Muskianu, e deivili II t[re]m[isse]s de casu, a cca[n]tu l'app[re]tharun sa t[er]ra. T[este]s: Gavini Cafia e sSimione Rasu e Gosantine Turdu.

332. Tramutu. *In argiola Te[r]rangia.*
Tramutai cun Ianne Thoia. Ego deili cussa ki co[m]porara a Furata Co[n]iu, [et] isse deitimi in Ariola T[er]rania, paris cun sa ki co[m]porara a Gosantine P[ri]nkis. T[este]s: Simione Rasu, maiore de gulbare, e sSimione T[ra]npas.

326. Purchase.
I bought from Petru Marthane and Gavini Marthane the hemp field (*cannavariu*) at Funtana ('spring'), which borders on the church's vineyard; I gave each of them a cured ham (*baconne*), and two measures of barley with their consent. Witnesses: Pismaki d'Oianu, head of the livestock enclosure (*maiore de gulbare*); Ithoccor de Gunale, representative of the freemen (*mandatore de liveros*); Ianne Prinkis the church's representative (*mandatore*), and Ianne Tatacke.

327. Dispute.
Petru Thuris sued and won a soldi (*sollu*) of vines that he had within the church's enclosure (*cuniatu*); I gave him one soldi of veal (*novellu*). Witnesses: Gitimel Tortolle the official (*maiore*) at whose hearing (*corona*) he won; Gosantine Turdu, and Petru Papate.

328. Exchange.
I exchanged with Gosantine Turdu land that he had bought from [...] above Funtana ('spring'); I gave them land in Binia de Pirra ('vineyard of Pirra'). Witnesses: Dorgotori de Foke, head of the livestock enclosure (*maiore de gulbare*); Dorgotori de Gallu, and Furatu Thinca.

329. Purchase.
From Susanna de Tula, I bought land in Ariola Terrania bordering that of the church; I gave her two tremisses of cheese to the total that the land is worth.

330. Purchase.
I bought from Inbenia de Runda land bordering that in Ariola Terrania. I gave him and his brother, Gosantine, two tremisses of cheese, with whom he shared it. Witnesses: Simione Rasu, head of the livestock enclosure (*maiore de gulbare*), and Dericcor d'Oianu.

331.
I bought from Furata Coniu land at Badu de Muskianu ('ford of Muskianu', Muscianu); I gave him two tremisses of cheese, equal to their evaluation of the land. Witnesses: Gavini Cafia, Simione Rasu, and Gosantine Turdu.

332. Exchange. *In Argiola Terrangia.*
I made an exchange with Ianne Thoia. I gave him that land which I bought from Furata Coniu, and he gave me the one in Ariola Terrania, along with that which he had bought from Gosantine Prinkis. Witnesses: Simione Rasu, head of the livestock enclosure (*maiore de gulbare*), and Simione Tranpas.

333. Co[m]po[r]u.
Co[m]po[ra]ili a Dorveni Berreu t[er]ra in monticlu de Gosantinu, e deivili x thiriccas de casu. T[este]s: Gosantine Pira e Gosantine Vai.

334. Tramutu.
Tramutaila osca cussa t[er]ra cun Gavini Cafia: ego deili cussa, et isse deitimi in monticlu de Gosantinu, ki fuit in meia sa domestica. T[este]s: Andria Unkinu e Ianne Papate.

335. Tramutu. *In Argiola Te[r]rangia.*
Tramutai cu[n] p[re]viteru Gosantine Pala t[er]ra p[ro] t[er]ra. Ego deili in
84v Cunucla, [et] isse deitimi in Ariola | T[er]rania, [et] issa de Iaccaria, tenende assa domestica de cl[es]ia; e cca no[n] baleat sa sua ca[n]tu sa mea de Cunucla, mi aiunsit sa de Iaccaria. T[este]s: Mariane de Ca[m]pu, e Dericcor d'Oianu.

336. *Terra in Argiola Terra[n]gia.*
Tramutai cu[n] p[re]viteru Gosantine Tene t[er]ra p[ro] t[er]ra. Ego deili in sa petra longa de Ca[m]pu, [et] isse deitimi in Ariola T[er]rania, tenende assa domestica.

337. Kertu. *De s[er]vos.*
Ego Istefane Unkinu. Kertait mecu Mariane de Kerki e Gosantine su fr[at]e ca 'p[ro]gitteu no[n] mi das dessa fiia de Dorveni Berreu?' Et ego kertaili ca 'levatu aveas parte tua, dep[us] patre.' Judicarunimi a destimo[n]ios, [et] ego battussilos a ccorona de do[n]nu Ithoccor de Thori Calcafarre, e iurai a .+. cun destimo[n]ios meos, e binki. Destimo[n]ios meos Dericcor Gespula e sSimione Rasu e Pet[ru] Latu. T[este]s: su curatore in cuia corona binki, e Gunna[ri] de Kerki, t[er]rale suo de fittu, e Furatu Virde su servu. Testes.

85r 338. Kertu. | *De s[er]vis.*
Kertait mecu Petru Secke p[ro]ssos fiios de Petru Manutha ca mi los voleat levare app[us] sa mama. [Et] ego kertaili ca 'sa mama abu tuo la fekit livera.' Keruerunimi destimo[n]ios, [et] ego battussi destimonios a Dorgotori de Titale [et] assu fr[at]e Mariane, e ssende de iurare m'indulsit sa [i]ura, a mimi [et]

333. Purchase.
I bought from Dorveni Berreu land at Monticlu de Gosantinu ('hill of Gosantinu'). I gave him ten siliquae (*thiriccas*) of cheese. Witnesses: Gosantine Pira, and Gosantine Vai.

334. Exchange.
Next, I exchanged that land with Gavini Cafia; I gave him that piece, and he gave me land in Monticlu de Gosantinu ('the hill of Gosantinu'), which is in the middle of the farmstead (*domestias*). Witnesses: Andria Unkinu, and Ianne Papate.

335. Exchange. *In Argiola Terrangia.*
I exchange with priest Gosantine Pala land for land. I gave him [land] in Cunucla, and he gave me [land] in Ariola Terrania and at Iaccaria bordering with the church's farmstead (*domestica*). His [land] was not as valuable as mine in Cunucla, so he added that at Iaccaria. Witnesses: Mariane de Campu, and Dericcor d'Oianu.

336. *Land in Argiola Terrangia.*
I exchanged with priest Gosantine Tene land for land. I gave him [land] in Petra Longa de Campu ('the long stone of the field'), and he gave me [land] in Ariola Terrania bordering the farmstead (*domestica*).

337. Dispute. *Of servants.*
I, Istefane Ukinu [make this entry]. Mariane de Kerki and his brother Gosantine sued me because [he claimed] 'why do you not give me the daughter of Dorveni Berreu?' I argued that 'you have already taken your share from the father's line!' They decided that I provide witnesses, and I brought them forth to a hearing (*corona*) of lord Ithoccor de Thori Calcafarre, and I swore on the cross with my witnesses; I won the case. My witnesses: Dericcor Gespula, Simione Rasu, and Petru Latu. Witnesses: the *curatore* at whose hearing I won; Gunnari de Kerki, his tenant farmer (*terrale de fittu*), and Furatu Virde, his servant (*servu*). Witnesses.

338. Dispute. *Of servants.*
Petru Secke sued me over the children of Petru Manutha because he wanted to take them from me [on account of their being] from mother's side. I argued that 'their mother was freed by your grandfather!' They asked me to provide witnesses, so I brought forth as witnesses Dorgotori de Titale and his brother Mariane. When it came to swearing, I was excused from taking the oath—

assos destimonios meos, in corona dessu curatore do[n]nu Mariane de Ponte, uve fakeat corona in Urieke. T[este]s: Gitimel Tortolle, maiore d'iscolca, e Janne Siricu, maiore d'iscolca de Novaia, e Gitilesu maiore d'iscolca de Castellu; e binkilu p[ro] servos in sos fiios de Pet[ru] Manutha e de Iorgia de Nureki. E cca m'indulsit sa iura a mimi [et] assos destimo[n]ios meos, deindeli x berbekes [et] I barrellu de pesentinu.

339. Parthitura. *De s[er]vos.*

Iorgi Pistis e Maria P[er]sa coiuves furun; Maria P[er]sa fuit intrega de S[an]c[t]a Maria de Cotronianu, e Iorgi Pistis lat[us] de S[an]c[t]u Petru de Plovaki,
85v e lat[us] | e lat[us] de paup[er]os. Fekerun II fiios, a Plave [et] a Barvara. Vennim[us] a parthire fetu cu[n] piscopu Istefane Iscarpa, e ccu[n] pauperos. Plave fuit maiore, levaim[us]ilu a S[an]c[t]a Maria, [et] a Barvara levaitila S[an]c[t]u Petru e ppaup[er]os. T[este]s: su curatore Comita d'Urieke, e maiore d'iscolca Petru d'Ackettas, et totta curatoria.

340. *De s[er]vos.*

Gavini Pelle e Marcus[a] Pelle coiuves furun; Gavini fuit intregu de S[an]c[t]a Maria de Cotronianu, e Marcusa fuit de S[an]c[t]u Gaviniu. Fekerun IIII fiios, a Maria, [et] a Gosantine e Nikita e Marina. Maria fuit maiore, coiuvarunila cun servu de S[an]c[t]u Gaviniu, cun Iorgi Pupusellu; e cca[n]do parthivim[us] II fiios avean fattos, a fFurata [et] a Marina. Vennimus a pparthire; levarun a S[an]c[t]u Gaviniu a Maria [et] a Nikita, e lat[us] de Furata, fiia de Maria; e llevaim[us] a S[an]c[t]a Maria, a Gosantine [et] a Marina, e lat[us] de Furata
86r sa netta. Ecco parthitura ki fekim[us], ego episcopu | Jorgi Maiule, cun arkipiscopu Gosantine de Castra, et arm[en]tariu de S[an]c[t]u Gaviniu Petru de Fravile, e mandatore Gosantine de Tofilatte. T[este]s: Petru de Villabetere e cComita de Padules et Ithoccor de Gallu.

341. Kertu. *Pro servos.*

Previteru Petru e Furata Cocote coiuvarun u[m]pare a bolu[n]tate de donnos; fekeru III[I] fiios, ad Inbenia [et] a Plave, a Petru [et] a Iorgia; e kene parthire levarunila ad Inbenia, ki fuit p[ri]maria, [et] coivarunila cun servu issoro, [et] fekitivi I fiiu, ad Istefane, sende ad in cumone. [Et] ego levai ap[us] natia de patre, a Plave [et] a Pet[ru]. Vocarunime a ccorona Comita de Nurki e p[re]viteru Ianne, de curatore Comita de Therkillo, uve fuit totta curatoria,

both me and my witnesses—at a hearing (*corona*) of the *curatore*, lord Mariane de Ponte at Urieke. Witnesses: Gitimel Tortolle, head of the ward (*maiore d'iscolca*); Ianne Siricu, head of the ward (*maiore d'iscolca*) of Novaia (Noazza); Gitilesu, head of the ward (*maiore d'iscolca*) of Castellu. I won the case over the servants (*servos*) [who were] the sons of Petru Manutha and Iorgia de Nureki. Since I and my witnesses were excused from testifying under oath, I gave him [the *curatore*] ten sheep and one piece of cloth made of Piacenzan-style fabric (*de pesentinu*).

339. Division. *Of servants.*
Iorgi Pistis and Maria Persa were spouses. Maria Persa was [a servant] in full (*intrega*) of Sancta Maria de Cotronianu (Codrongianos); half (*latus*) of Iorgi Pistis belonged to Sanctu Petru de Plovaki, and the other half to smallholders (*pauperos*). They had two children, Plave and Barvara. We came to divide their offspring with bishop Istefane Iscarpa and the smallholders. Plave was the older and we took him for Sancta Maria; Sanctu Petru and the smallholders took Barvara. Witnesses: the *curatore*, Comita d'Urieke; the head of the ward (*maiore d'iscolca*), Petru d'Ackettas, and the whole district (*curatoría*).

340. *Of servants.*
Gavini Pelle and Marcusa Pelle were spouses. Gavini was [a servant] in full (*intregu*) of Sancta Maria de Cotronianu (Codrongianos), and Marcusa belonged to Sanctu Gaviniu. They had four children: Maria, Gosantine, Nikita, and Marina. Maria was the eldest. They married her to a servant (*servu*) of Sanctu Gaviniu, Iorgi Pupusellu. When we made the division, they had two sons: Furata and Marina. We came to divide them thus: Sanctu Gaviniu took Maria, Nikita, and half (*latus*) of Furata, daughter of Maria. We took for Sancta Maria: Gosantine, Marina, and half of Furata, their niece (*netta*). This was the division made by me, bishop Jorgi Maiule with archbishop Gosantine de Castra, and the administrator (*armentariu*) of Sanctu Gaviniu, Petru Fravile, and the representative (*mandatore*) Gosantine de Tofilatte. Witnesses: Petru de Villabetere, Comita de Padules, and Ithoccor de Gallu.

341. Dispute. *For servants.*
Priest Petru and Furata Cocote married one other with the consent of their lords. They had four children: Inbenia, Plave, Petru, and Iorgia. Without dividing the offspring, Inbenia was taken away and was married with a servant (*servu*) of theirs; they had one son, Istefane, who was shared among them. I took Plave and Petru from their father's line. Comita de Nurki (La Corte) and priest Ianne summoned me to a hearing (*corona*) of Comita de Therkillo where the

ca 'progitteu mi lu levas a Plave [et] a Pet[ru]?' 'Ca levasti tu a natia tua, ad Inbenia [et] a Iorgia, lu levai ego a Pet[ru] [et] a Plave.' Issara poserun a battuier a ccorona, e meos, e suos [destimonios], e no los voluerun battuier. Canpaniaruninos a pparthire in co aviam[us] levatu; levailu ego a Petru [et] a
86v Plave, [et] issos ad Inbenia | [et] a Iorgia. Et avende parthitu morivit Iorgia, [et] est natu Sagio. Bocarunime a ccorona dessu curatore Comita d'Urieke, p[re]viteru Janne e Dorgo[to]ri d'Olgadon, e Petru d'Olivula, sa die co fekit corona primaria in S[an]c[t]a Bittoria de Ficulinas de Castellu, calkinande sa cl[es]ia, ca 'progitteu mi levas fiios de p[re]viteru Gavini?' [Et] ego kertailis ca 'parthitu aviamus in corona de curatore Comita de Therkillo.' Derunimi iura, e iurai a .+. ca la levarun issos ad Inbenia [et] a Iorgia, e llat[us] de Sagio, ki fuit natu pus co parthiramus, et Inbenia sende in cumone est coiuvata. Issara mi derun lat[us] dessu fiiu Istefane. T[este]s: curatore Comita de Therkillo [et] totta corona.

342. Parthitura. *De s[er]vos.*
Petru de Sotonoti e Germana Tonse coiuves furun, Germana fuit de cl[es]ia; fekerun II fiios, a Nastasia, [et] a Plave. Vennerun a parthire cl[es]ia e paperos; cl[es]ia levait a Nastasia, e paperos a Plave, parthi[n]de ante maiore d'iscolca Comita de Nurki, [et] ante p[re]viteru Gosantin[e] Sp[an]u. E sservindelis Plave ad issos est mortu. Vennerun e llargarunimi sos paperos i (*sic*) Nastasia, e llevaruniminde su lat[us], Petru de Ca[m]pu e fFuratu de Castavar e cComita su fr[at]e, e cComita d'Urieke ki fuit curatore in Ficulinas de Castellu. E nunthaitilos a ccorona, e ckertai cun illos e binkilos ca m'intrait a mimi Nastasia, [et] ad issos Plave; e iurait a .+. Janne Argata, ki fuit mandatore de cl[es]ia ca 'in co vos naro sun parthitos.' Issara mi torrarun a Nastasia, ki mi avean levata. T[este]s ki vi furun in sa corona: Dericcor de Vosove e cComita de Martis e cComita de Puthumaiore e cComita de Cap[ri]les, [et] totta corona.

343. Co[m]po[r]u.
Co[m]p[or]aili a p[re]viteru Petru de Sorso t[er]ra in balle Votoi, de ca[n]ta vi aveat, e deivili II baccas, cu[n] boluntate dessu do[n]nu Pet[ru] de Serra; [et] issa die de co li dei sas baccas, andaim[us] assa t[er]ra, [et] istettitili in t[er]m[en], e naraitimi ca 'poneli muru e ccasticala a fferru co a ccasa de S[an]c[t]a Maria.'

whole district (*curatoría*) was present. They asked me 'why are you taking Plave and Petru?' [I replied:] 'Because you took Inbenia and Iorgia from the mother's side, so I took Petru and Plave!' We were requested to bring forth to a hearing (*corona*) witnesses for me and for them; but they did not want to produce any. They had us agree to the division of the offspring we had made: I took Petru and Plave, and they took Inbenia and Iorgia. After having divided them, Iorgia died and Sagio was born. Priest Janne, Dorgotori d'Olgadon and Petru d'Olivula summoned me to a hearing of the *curatore* Comita d'Urieke on the day the first hearing (*corona*) was held in Sancta Bittoria de Ficulinas at Castellu when they were plastering the church (*calkinande clesia*). They asked me 'why are you taking the children of priest Gavini?' I disputed that by replying: 'we had divided them at a hearing (*corona*) of Comita de Therkillo!' They gave me an oath, and I swore on the cross that they took for themselves Inbenia, Iorgia, and half of Sagio, who was born after we made the division. And also, Inbenia, who they shared, was married after the division. Then, they gave me half of Istefane's son. Witnesses: *curatore* Comita de Therkillo, and the whole district (*curatoría*).

342. Division. *Of servants*.
Petru de Sotonoti and Germana Tonse were spouses. Germana was [a servant] of the church, and they had two children, Nastasia and Plave. The church and [some] smallholders (*paperos*) came to divide [the children]. The church took Nastasia, and the smallholders (*paperos*) took Plave. The division was made in the presence of the head of the ward (*maiore d'iscolca*), Comita de Nurki, and priest Gosantine Spanu. Afterwards, Plave died while he was in their service. The smallholders—Petru de Campu, Furtatu de Castavar, his brother Comita, and Comita d'Urieke, who was *curatore* in Ficulinas de Castellu—came and stole Nastasia from me, taking away half (*latus*) [of her service]. They were summoned to a hearing (*corona*); I sued them and I won the dispute because Nastasia belonged to me, while Plave belonged to them. Janne Argata, who was the church's representative (*mandatore*), swore on the cross that 'I tell you they were divided thus!' Then, they returned Nastasia to me, who had been taken from me. Witnesses who were at a hearing (*corona*): Dericcor de Vosove, Comita de Martis, Comita de Puthu Maiore (Pozzomaggiore), Comita de Capriles, and the whole hearing (*corona*).

343. Purchase.
I bought from priest Petru de Sorso all the land that he had in Balle Votoi ('Votoi valley'). I gave him two cows with the consent of lord Petru de Serra. On the day I gave him the cows, we went to that land, established the boundary and he told me, 'put up a wall and protect it with an armed guard (*ccasticala afferru*) as part of the assets (*casa*) of Sancta Maria!'

344. Conporu. *Cotro[n]ianu[m].*
Co[m]p[or]aili a Gosantine de Kerki, [et] a Mari[a]ne su fr[at]e, sos de Tamarikes, lat[us] dessu | saltu de valle de Mariane, e deivilis a Iorgi de Fokile fiiu de Susanna Kerbu, ki fuit intrega de cl[es]ia, ca l'aveat fattu in furrithu cun su ieneru. T[este]s: Saltaro de Navitha, maiore d'iscolca, [et] Ithoccor de Gunale e Mariane de Ca[m]pu.[53]

87v

345. *S[er]vos appus sa domo de Teclata.*
Cando posit donnu Petru de serra Caballare a S[an]c[t]u Pet[ru] de Silki sa domo de Teclata, tando bi deit appus sa domo de Teclata totta s'isclatta dessos Barithos, cun perten[en]thia issoro. T[es]t[e]s: prebiteru de Cannetu e prebiteru Gosantine Plana et issu connatu Gosantine de Thori Dibite, et Ithoccor de Laccon, ante ken bi los deit appus sa domo de Teclata.

346.
Co[m]poraili a Pet[ru] de Liios Bucca, su de Silki, sa parte sua in co bi l'abeat in Ianpulla, t[er]m[en] assa binia de S[an]c[t]u Petru, et ego deindeli I bargala, e XXX moios de labore e IIII pecos. T[este]s: Mariane de Barru e cComita su frate, e Petru Regitanu, e nNiscoli. T[este]s.

88r [*Condake de Sanctu Petru de Silki*]
In[54] no[m]i[n]e Do[mi]ni n[ost]ri Ih[es]u [Christ]i Dei Eterni. Anno ab Incarnatione Eius M[illesimo] C[entesimo] Octogesimo, Indictione XIII.

347.
Ego Maximilla, abbadissa de S[an]c[t]u Petru de Silki, [et] soror Bulliafave, ki lu fatho custu condake, cu[n] bolu[n]tate de D[eu]s et dessu donnu meu judike Barusone de Laccon et dessa muliere do[n]na Prethiosa de Orrubu regina, et dessu filiu do[n]nu Gosantine rege, p[ro]ssu ka[nt]u appo paratu in su tempus meu [et] appo parare avestara ad honore de D[eu]s [et] de S[an]c[t]u Petru de Silki, [et] de co[m]poru [et] de datura; et p[ro]ssu ka[n]tu accattai scrittu in cartas ki fuit de S[an]c[t]u Petru, [et] no[n] bi aveat bacante in su condake vetere de S[an]c[t]u Petru de Silki uve lu ponne; et ego inde lu ponio in ecustu condake meu, ko 'nde appan veritate pus me.

53 Change of hand.
54 Change of hand.

344. Purchase. *Cotronianum* (*Codrongianos*).
I bought from Gosantine de Kerki and his brother Mariane [both] from Tamarikes (Tamarighes, near Usini), half (*latus*) the unworked land (*saltu*) in Valle de Mariane ('valley of Mariane'), giving them [in return] Iorgi de Fokile, son of Susanna Kerbu who was [a servant] in full (*intrega*) of the church and who was born from an illicit relationship (*fattu in furrithu*) with her son-in-law (*ieneru*). Witnesses: Saltaro de Navitha, head of the ward (*maiore d'iscolca*); Ithoccor de Gunale, and Mariane de Canpu.

345. *Servants at the farm complex* (domo) *of Teclata.*
When lord Petru de Serra Caballare donated to Sanctu Petru de Silki the farm complex (*domo*) of Teclata (Trigiada, near Romana), he also granted from the farm (*domo*) at Teclata all the offspring of the Barithos [family] with their belongings. Witnesses: priest Petru de Cannetu, priest Gosantine Plana, his brother-in-law Gosantine de Thori Dibite, and Ithoccor de Laccon before whom he granted them at the farm (*domo*) of Teclata.

346.
I bought from Petru de Liios Bucca from Silki, his share (*parte*) of what he had at Ianpulla, the boundary of which is the vineyard of Sanctu Petru. I gave him a millstone (*bargala*), thirty measures of wheat (*moios de lobore*), and four heads of cattle. Witnesses: Mariane de Barru and his brother Comita, and Petru Recitanu, and Niscoli. Witnesses.

Condaghe of Sanctu Petru de Silki.
In the name of our Lord Jesus Christ, Eternal God. Year 1180 of His Incarnation [In the] 13th Indiction.

347.
I, Maximilla, abbess of Sanctu Petru de Silki, with sister Bulliafave, compose (*fatho*) this condaghe with the consent of God and of my lord iudike Barusone de Laccon and his wife, lady Prethiosa de Orrubu, queen (*regina*), and of their son, lord Gosantine, king (*rege*), for all that I have acquired during my time and will acquire from now on for the honour of God and of Sanctu Petru de Silki regarding purchases and gifts (*dabatura*). Also, [it is] for all I found written in documents (*cartas*) that belonged to Sanctu Petru for which there was no space in the old condaghe of Sanctu Petru de Silki to include them. So, I put them in this condaghe of mine so that they will be taken as truthful after my time.

348. Postura. *In Sorso.*

Morivit do[n]na Jorgia Pinna, filia de do[n]nu Gosantine Pi[n]na su de Nugor,
muliere ki fuit de do[n]nu Dorgotori de Navithan Boe, kene aver filiu; et posit
88^{v} in sa penitentia | a S[an]c[t]u Petru de Silki, p[ro] a[n]i[m]a sua, sa domo
sua de Sorso cu[n] om[n]ia kantu vi aveat, [e] corte, [e] terra, [e] binia, [e]
pumu; [et] issa parte sua ka[n]ta li dittavat in su Ca[n]netu de Silasa, [et]
ho[m]i[n]es kantos vi aveat app[us] cussa domo. Et avendemila data, mi vi lar-
gait Gosantine de Thori Ispentumatu. Et ego andai assu do[n]nu meu, a judike
Barusone de Lacco[n], [et] pettili merkede p[ro] iudicareminde. Et isse nun-
thaitimilu a Gosantine de Thori Ispentumatu assa festa de S[an]c[t]u Nicola
de Silano[s]; et ego posilu a donnikellu Ithoccor a kertare p[ro] me, et Gos-
antine de Thori Ispentumatu positilu a do[n]nu Ithoccor de Laccon Pinna a
kertare p[ro] se. Et donnikellu Ithoccor kertaitili ka 'sa domo de Sorso, ki fuit
de do[n]na Jorgia Pinna, ki posit a S[an]c[t]u Petru, p[ro]gitteu mi la leva[s]?'
[Et] Ithoccor de Lacco[n] Pinna kertaitili ka 'non bi la posit, ka kene limba
morivit.' Et do[n]nikellu Ithoccor kertaitili ka 'sende bene in sinnu suo, la
89^{r} posit a S[an]c[t]u Petru de Silki sa domo sua de Sorso do[n]na | Jorgia Pinna,
cu[n] om[n]ia kantu vi aveat, in sa penitentia ki si levait.' Judicarunimi a bat-
tuger destimonios ka fuit in sinnu suo do[n]na Jorgia Pinna kando la posit a
S[an]c[t]u Petru de Silki sa domo sua de Sorso. Et ego battusi sos destimo-
nios atteru die de sinotu a Kitarone, a do[n]nu Petru Pirillu a ken vi mandait
do[n]nu Bernardu, su priore dessu Ispitale de Billalba, ki li levait penitentia,
[et] li coma[n]dait a iurare in a[n]i[m]a sua, ka la posit sa domo sua de Sorso
do[n]na Jorgia Pinna a S[an]c[t]u Petru de Silki p[ro] a[n]i[m]a sua in sa pen-
itentia ki li levait, [et] a cComita de Maro[n]iu Piu ki vi fuit in sa penitentia,
[et] a Pet[ru] de Maro[n]iu Albuscar, ki fuit armentariu suo appus sa domo
sua de Sorso, [et] bi fuit in sa penitentia, ka[n]do la posit a S[an]c[t]u Petru
de Silki do[n]na Jorgia Pinna sa domo sua de Sorso; [et] jurarun a gru .+. ke
custos destimonios meos, ka do[n]na Jorgia Pinna la posit a S[an]c[t]u Petru
de Silki sa domo sua de Sorso cu[n] om[n]ia ka[n]tu vi aveat, in sa penitentia
89^{v} sua, sende in sinnu | suo kando la penitentiarun, et Istephane Unkinti, servu
de S[an]c[t]u Petru de Silki, iurait in fattu dessos destimonios meos, [e] binki.
Test[e]s: su do[n]nu meu judike Barusone de Lacco[n], in cuia corona binki,
[et] issu filiu do[n]nu Gosantine rege [et] donnikellu Comita [et] do[n]nu
Petru de Maro[n]iu et do[n]nu Gitimel de Serra [et] do[n]nu Pet[ru] Secke,
[et] totta sa corona. Test[e]s.

349. *Pro s[er]vos.*

Coiuvait Nivata Tussia, filia de Dorgotori Tussia, ankilla intrega de S[an]c[t]u Petru, cu[n] Gosantine de Putholu, servu de do[n]na Muscu de Laccon, [e]

348. Donation. *In Sorso.*
Lady Iorgia Pinna, daughter of lord Gosantine Pinna from Nugor (Nuoro), who was the wife of lord Dorgotori de Navithan Boe, died without having a child. In her [final] confession, she donated to Sanctu Petru de Silki for her soul, her farm complex (*domo*) at Sorso with all that she had there: farmyard (*corte*), land, vineyard, and fruit orchard (*pumu*), [as well as] the share that belongs to her of Cannetu de Silasa ('the cane field of Silasa'), and the servants (*homines*) who were at this farm (*domo*). After she granted it to me, Gosantine de Thori Ispentumatu appropriated it, so I went to my lord iudike Barusone de Laccon and sought mercy in adjudicating for me. He summoned Gosantine de Thori Ispentumatu at the feast of Sanctu Nicola de Silanos. He bid *donnikellu* Ithoccor argue for me; Gosantine de Thori Ispentumatu had lord Ithoccor de Laccon Pinna argue for him. *Donnikellu* Ithoccor argued 'why do you appropriate the farm (*domo*) of Sorso which belonged to lady Jorgia Pinna that she donated to Sanctu Petru?' And Ithoccor de Laccon Pinna argued that 'she did not donate it because she died without saying a will (*kene limba*)!' Then, *donnikellu* Ithoccor argued that 'lady Jorgia Pinna, in her right mind (*bene in sennu suo*), donated her farm complex (*domo*) of Sorso to Sancti Petru de Silki with all its appurtenances when she took the confession!' It was decided that I should bring forth witnesses [to attest] that lady Jorgi Pinna was of sound mind when she donated her farm (*domo*) at Sorso to Sanctu Petru de Silki. The day after the assembly in Kitarone (Caddaroni-Sant'Eusebio), I brought forth witnesses: lord Petru Pirillu whom lord Bernardu, prior of the hospital of Billalba, who administered the confession, and was called on to swear on his soul that lady Iorgia Pinna had donated her farm (*domo*) at Sorso to Sanctu Petru de Silki for her soul during the confession. Comita de Maroniu Piu, who was at the confession, and Petru de Maroniu Albuscar, who was his administrator (*armentariu*) at the farm complex (*domo*) of Sorso, and was also at the confession when lady Iorgia Pinna donated her farmstead (*domo*) of Sorso to Sanctu Petru de Silki. These witnesses of mine swore on the cross that lady Jorgia Pinna had donated her farm (*domo*) of Sorso to Sanctu Petru de Silki with all it possessed when they led the confession and was of sound mind. Istephane Unkinu, servant (*servu*) of Sanctu Petru Silki, also swore after my witnesses. I won the case. Witnesses: my lord iudike Barusone de Lacco at whose hearing (*corona*) I won; his son lord Gosantine, king (*rege*); *donnikellu* Comita, and lord Petru de Maroniu, and lord Gitimel de Serra, and lord Petru Secke, and the entire hearing (*corona*). Witnesses.

349. *Concerning servants.*
Nivata Tussia, daughter of Dorgotori Tussia, female servant in full (*ankilla intrega*) of Sanctu Pettru, married Gosantine de Putholu, a servant (*servu*)

fekerun IIII filios, a Petru [et] a Barusone [et] ad Ithoccor [et] a Muscu. Et
levavatinollos do[n]nu Ithoccor de Laccon Pinna, filiu de do[n]na[55] Muscu
de Laccon. Et ego posilu a do[n]nikellu Ithoccor a kertarende cu[n]de. Et
do[n]nikellu Ithoccor kertaitinde cun ille in Padule de Kerketu, ka 'sos filios
de Nivata Tussia p[ro]gitteu mi los levas ki e[st] ankilla intrega de S[an]c[t]u
Petru, [et] aveat maritu bivu, [et] aetilos fattos in forrithu cu[n] Gosantine de
90r Putholu?' Et isse kertaitili | ka 'no[n] fuit coiuvata si non cu[n] su ho[m]i[n]e
meu.' Et do[n]nikellu Ithoccor naraitili ka 'coiuvata fuit cu[n] liveru, cu[n]
Dorgotori Trullari, [et] fugivitili assu maritu.' Judicarunili a destimo[n]ios a
do[n]nikellu Ithoccor ka fuit coiuvata inna[n]ti in ko kertavat. Et do[n]nu
Ithoccor de Laccon Pi[n]na narait ka 'o iuret, o iure!' Et judike narait ka 'fakite
bene, ka[m]paniateuos kene iura!' Et nois ka[m]paniaimusinos umpare, [et]
parthivimus su fetu. Isse levait Barusone, [et] nois a Petru; isse levait a Muscu,
[et] nois ad Ithoccor, in ko furun a natias. Test[e]s: su do[n]nu n[ost]ru judike
Barusone de Laccon, in cuia corona nos ka[m]paniaim[us], [et] do[n]nikellu
Comita [et] do[n]nikellu Ithoccor, ki lu kertait su kertu, [et] do[n]nu Petru de
Maro[n]iu, [et] do[n]nu Comita de Kerki Cafana, [et] do[n]nu Gunnari de Gitil
[et] do[n]nu Gosantine de Athen De[n]tenigella, [et] totta corona. Test[e]s.

350.
Conversaisse Pet[ru] de Valles, [et] Jorgia sa muliere, a S[an]c[t]u Petru de Silki,
90v et poserun a S[an]c[t]u Petru de Silki su latus de | om[n]ia kantu avean, [et]
latus assu filiu, [et] de domos [et] de terras [et] binias, [et] de om[n]ia kantu
avean. Et si moriat su filiu kene aver filiu, de torrare tottu su suo a S[an]c[t]u
Petru. Test[e]s: su do[n]nu meu judike Barusone de Lacco[n] [et] issu filiu
do[n]nu Gosantine rege, [et] do[n]nu Petru de Maro[n]iu, ante ken se con-
versarun, [e] Comita de Serra [e] Pet[ru] de Varru [e] Mariane Pithicatu, [e]
Dorgotori su fr[at]e. Test[e]s.

351. *Saltu de Serras et de Iscala* [*sic* for Iscla] *de Sale, et vingias una in Tingaru, et in Brunkiles, et in Ortu Donnicu, et anbas sas terras dessa Petrosa, et issa de Creskente, et issa terra de Laia.*
Conversaisse Susanna de Carvia [et] Maria sa filia a S[an]c[t]u Petru de Silki, [et] poseru[n] a S[an]c[t]u Petru de Silki om[n]ia kantu avean, [et] corte [et] terras [e] binias [e] saltos. Su saltu de Serras et issu saltu de iscla de Sale, usq[ue] a S[an]c[t]u Gaviniu de Arcave; e binias, una in Tingaru, tenende assa de do[n]nu Petru Secke, [et] attera in Brunkile tene[n]de assa de S[an]c[t]u

55 Manuscript reads *do*[*n*]*nu*.

of lady Muscu de Laccon, and they had four children: Petru, Barusone, Ithoccor, and Muscu. Lord Ithoccor de Laccon Pinna, son of lord Muscu de Laccon, took them away from us. I had *donnikellu* Ithoccor raise a legal dispute, and *donnikellu* Ithoccor sued him at Padule de Kerketu ('the marsh of Kerketu') [asking]: 'why do you take away the children of Nivata Tussia who is the female servant in full of Sanctu Petru, and who had an illegitimate child with Gosantine de Putholu when she had a husband who was alive?' He argued that 'she was not married, except to my servant (*homine*)!' *Donnikellu* Ithoccor said that 'she was married to a freeman (*liveru*), Dorgotori Trullari, but she fled from her husband!' They decided that *Donnikellu* Ithoccor should bring witnesses that the woman was married before the dispute. Lord Ithoccor de Laccon Pinna said 'let him swear or swear [yourself]!' Iudike said 'do the right thing! Reach an agreement without swearing!' Then, we reached a mutual agreement and divided the offspring. He took Barusone and we took Petru; he took Muscu and we took Ithoccor in order of birth. Witnesses: our lord, iudike Barusone de Laccon at whose hearing (*corona*) we reached agreement; *donnikellu* Comita, and *donnikellu* Ithoccor who argued this case, and lord Petru de Maroniu, lord Comita de Kerki Cafana, lord Gunnari de Gitil, lord Gosantine de Athen Dentenigella ('black tooth'), and the entire hearing (*corona*). Witnesses.

350.
Petru de Valles and his wife Jorgia devoted themselves to (*conversaisse*) Sanctu Petru de Silki and gave the church half (*latus*) of everything they owned: farmsteads (*domos*), lands, and vineyards; the other half they gave to their son with farms (*domos*), lands, vineyards, and everything they had. If the son died without a child, all of it would revert to Sanctu Petru. Witnesses: my lord iudike Barusone de Laccon; his son, lord Gosantine, king (*rege*); lord Petru de Maroniu, before whom they became devoted patrons; Comita de Serra; Petru de Varru, and Mariane Pithicatu and his brother, Dorgotori. Witnesses.

351. *Unworked land* (saltu) *of Serras, islet* (iscla) *at Sale, and vineyards, one in Tingaru in Brunkiles, and in Ortu Donnicu; and both lands of Petrosa: that of Creskente, and in the land of Laia.*
Susanna de Carvia and her daughter Maria devoted themselves to (*conversaisse*) Sanctu Petru de Silki and donated to the church everything they owned: farmyard (*corte*), lands, vineyards, and unworked lands (*saltos*): the land (*saltu*) of Serras; the islet (*iscla*) of Sale up to Sanctu Gaviniu de Arcave (San Baingiu Arca); the vineyards, one in Tingaru (Tingari) bordering that of lord Petru Secke, and that of Brunkile bordering that of Sanctu Petru; another [vineyard]

Petru; [et] attera in Ortu do[n]nicu, tene[n]de assa de S[an]c[t]u Petru; et ambas sas terras dessa Petrosa, supra Silki, [et] issa terra de Creskente, tenende assa bi[n]ia de do[n]nu Juva[n]ne Secke; [et] issas terras de Laia, in ko falan
91r assa bi[n]ia de Gu[n]nari | Corsu. In fine de, si fakeat filiu Maria de Carvia, de aver latus de om[n]ia casa ka[n]ta narat ave susu, in custa postura; et si non aveat filiu, de aversilu S[an]c[t]u Petru. Et si non aveat filiu su filiu ki ait aver Maria de Carvia, torrare tottu a S[an]c[t]u Petru; [et] si aveat filiu de aver latus appare cu[n] S[an]c[t]u Petru, [et] si furun tottu enios, de torrare tottu a S[an]c[t]u Petru. Test[e]s: su do[n]nu meu iudike Barusone de Laccon, in cuia boluntate [et] ante ken fuit Susanna de Carvia, [et] Maria sa filia, ka[n]do se conversait a S[an]c[t]u Petru de Silki, Susanna de Carvia [et] Maria sa filia [et] do[n]nikellu Comita [et] Petru de Maroniu [et] Juva[n]ne Secke [et] Niscoli de Carvia. T[este]s.

352. *In Nuracati, apus Jannanu.*
Co[m]p[or]aili a do[n]nu Dericcor de Maro[n]iu, su de Erkilo, cu[n] bolu[n]tate de do[n]na Nivata Pullikina, cuiu fuit su saltu, ki fuit muliere sua, su ka[n]tu li dittavat in su saltu de Nuracati, et deivili II unthas de argentu [et] V capras. Test[e]s: do[n]nu Augustine, ki fuit tando arkiprete in S[an]c[t]u
91v Gaviniu de Turres [et] pupillu in su saltu | [et] do[n]nu Petru Secke, [et] Ja[n]ne Pullikina, su thiu de do[n]na Nivata cu[n] ken parthiat su saltu, [et] Barusone su fr[at]e, [et] Dorgotori de Fravile, maiore d'iscolca in Bionis, [et] Iorgi de Rosa [et] Juva[n]ne Gulpio, sos de Bionis. Test[e]s.

353. Tramutu. *De s[er]vos.*
Tramutai cu[n] su abbate de Plaianu, do[n]nu Jacobu, cu[n] bolu[n]tate dessu priore suo do[n]nu Guilielemu, [et] cu[n] bolu[n]tate dessas manacas sorres meas. Ego deili lat[us] de Petru Pithos [et] tres pedes de Maria sa filia, ka su atteru pede suo si fuit, et isse deitimi tres pedes de Ja[n]ne Casole kene aver filiu fattu, filiu de Honoria Casole [et] de Juste Gureiu. Test[e]s: Mariane de Varru [et] Gosantine de Martis [et] Comita su fr[at]e. Test[e]s.

354. Tramutu. *De s[er]vos.*
Tramutai etro cu[n] su abbate de Plaianu do[n]nu Jacobu. Ego deili pede de Jettatu, [et] isse deitimi pede de Petru Pithos su fr[at]e. Test[e]s: Mariane de Varru [et] Gosantine de Martis [et] Comita su fr[at]e.

near Ortu Donnicu bordering [the land of] Sanctu Petru; both lands of Petrosa above Silki; the land of Creskente which borders the vineyard of lord Juvanne Secke, [and] the lands of Laia which descend to the vineyard of Gunnari Corsu. In the event that Maria de Carvia had a child, he would have half of each of the assets (*casa*) mentioned above in this donation. But if she had no child, everything is to revert to Sanctu Petru. And if the son of Maria de Carvia in turn had no child, everything is to be returned to Sanctu Petru. Should he have a child, it is to be divided in half with Sanctu Petru. But if all of them were unmarried and completely childless (*tottu enios*), everything is to return to Sanctu Petru. Witnesses: my lord iudike Barusone de Laccon, by whose consent and before whom Susanna de Carvia and her daughter Maria devoted themselves to Sanctu Petru de Silki; and Susanna de Carvia, and her daughter Maria, and *donnikellu* Comita, and Petru de Maroniu, and Juvanne Secke, and Niscoli de Carvia. Witnesses.

352. *In Nuracati (Nuragaddu), at Jannanu (Gennano, Porto Torres).*
I bought from lord Dericcor de Maroniu from Erkilo (Cuili Ercoli), with the consent of lady Nivata Pullikina, who was his wife, that which was his of the unworked land (*saltu*) of Nuracati (Nuragaddu). I gave him two ounces (*unthas*) of silver and five goats. Witnesses: lord Augustineo, who was then archpriest in Sanctu Gaviniu at Turres (San Gavino di Torres) and proprietor of the land (*saltu*); lord Petru Secke; Janne Pullikina the uncle of lady Nivata, with whom the land (*saltu*) was divided; his brother Barusone; Dorgotori de Fravile, head of the ward (*maiore d'iscolca*) at Bionis (Biunisi); Jorgi de Rosa, and Juvanne Gulpio, both from Bionis. Witnesses.

353. Exchange. *Of servants.*
I exchanged with the abbot of Plaianu (San Michele di Plaiano), lord Jacobu, with the consent of his prior, lord Guilielemu, and my sister nuns. I gave him half (*latus*) of Petru Pithos and three-quarters (*pedes*) of his daughter Maria; the other quarter already belonged to him. He gave me three-quarters [of the services] of Janne Casole who was without children and who was the son of Honoria Casole and Juste Gureiu. Witnesses: Mariane de Varru, Gosantine de Martis, and Comita, his brother. Witnesses.

354. Exchange. *Of servants.*
I made another exchange with the abbot of Plaianu (San Michele di Plaiano), lord Jacobu. I gave him a quarter (*pede*) of Jettatu and he gave me a quarter of Petru Pithos, his brother. Witnesses: Mariane de Varru, Gosantine de Martis and his brother, Comita.

355.
Tramutai cu[n] Alexandru [et] cu[n] su fr[at]e Gimbardu, et cu[n] Gemulina
92r sa sorre. Issos | derunimi su ka[n]tu vi avean in Ortu Do[n]nicu, [et] binia [et] pumu [et] bacante, tenende assa ki vi aveat dave inna[n]ti S[an]c[t]u Petru, et ego deilis su ka[n]tu mi dittavat in sa corte de Silki, ki posit Jorgia de Thori [et] Comita de Gitil su filiu, a S[an]c[t]u Petru, cu[n] sa oliva, [et] issos petholos dessa terra ki avean de foras, tenende assa corte, [et] issu ka[n]tu vi aveat su thiu in cu[n]iatu de Barusone. Test[e]s: Mariane de Varru [et] Falcone su de Thathari, [et] Petru Canu [et] Dorgotori Casu [et] Petru Mastinu. Test[e]s.

356.
Vennit Petru Caprinu, filiu de Gosa[n]tine Caprinu, et battussitila a Jorgia de Arsumen sa muliere, filia de Comita de Maro[n]iu [et] de Susanna de Arsum[en], a S[an]c[t]u Petru, sende malavida, [et] istettit malavida in sa domo de S[an]c[t]u Petru. Et Deus et S[an]c[t]u Petru sanaitila. Et Petru Caprinu [et] Jorgia de Arsum[en], sa muliere, ave ko viderun bene ka la sanait D[eu]s et S[an]c[t]u Petru, afferserunse a S[an]c[t]u Petru, ambos umpare;
92v Petru | Caprinu se affersit a S[an]c[t]u Petru in gotale tenore: de si li davat D[eu]s filiu de matrona o in custa muliere o in attera, de aver parthone S[an]c[t]u Petru de om[n]ia ka[n]tu aveat de unu filiu, si aveat filiu; o, si non aveat, [et] de t[er]ras [et] de binias [et] de cortes [et] de saltos [et] de ho[m]i[n]es [et] de battorpedia, [et] de o[mn]ia ka[n]tu aveat. Et Jorgia de Arsum[en], sa muliere, se affersit a S[an]c[t]u Petru in gotale tenore, de si li davat D[eu]s filiu, de aver S[an]c[t]u Petru parthone de unu filiu de om[n]ia ka[n]tu aveat, [et] de terras, [et] de bi[n]ias, [et] de cortes, [et] de saltos, [et] de battorpedia, [et] de o[mn]ia ka[n]tu aveat, et, si non aveat filiu, de aver S[an]c[t]u Petru om[n]ia ka[n]tu aveat, [et] terras, [et] binias, [et] cortes, [et] saltos, [et] ho[m]i[n]es, [et] battorpedia, [et] om[n]ia ka[n]tu aveat. Test[e]s: do[n]nu Petru de Kerki, su pr[e]b[iter]u de Tamarikes, [et] pr[e]b[iter]u Furatu de Bosa, et pr[e]b[iter]u Isperate, in cuia manu se miserun, [et] Gosa[n]tine Masala arm[en]tariu de do[n]nikellu Ithoccor in Favules, [et] Forasticu servu de
93r do[n]nikellu | Ithoccor, [et] Petru de Kerki su de Silki, [et] Mariane Secke, su ki si notavat a do[n]nikellu Ithoccor. Test[e]s.

357. Postura. *In Pirastru.*
Morivit Susa[n]na de Kerki, filia de Comita de Kerki, [et] posit a S[an]c[t]u Petru sa t[er]ra sua de Pirastru, ki aveat tenende assa de S[an]c[t]a Julia.

355.
I made an exchange with Alexandru and with his brother Gimbardu and his sister Gemulina. They gave me all they had at Ortu Donnicu: vineyard, fruit orchard (*pumu*) and unused land (*bacante*), bordering the lands in front of Sanctu Petru. I gave them what belonged to me in the farmyard (*corte*) of Silki which was donated to Sanctu Petru by Jorgia de Thori and her son Comita de Gitil with the olive tree (*sa oliva*), and those pieces (*petholos*) of land they had beyond it, bordering on the farmyard (*corte*), and everything his uncle had in the enclosure (*cuniatu*) of Barusone. Witnesses: Mariane de Varru, Falcone from Thathari (Sassari), Petru Canu, Dorgotori Casu, and Petru Mastinu.

356.
Petru Caprinu, son of Gosantine Caprinu, came to Sanctu Petru bringing with him his wife Jorgia de Arsumen, daughter of Comita de Maroniu and Susanna de Arsumen when she was ill. While ill, she stayed at the church (*domo*) of Sanctu Petru. God and St Peter restored her health (*sanaitila*). When Petru Caprinu and his wife Jorgia de Arsumen clearly saw that God and St Peter had restored her health, they both avowed themselves (*afferserunse*) equally to Sanctu Petru. Petru Caprinu vowed in this way: if God might give him a child (*filiu*) by this wife (*de matrona*) or by some woman or another (*o in custa muliere o in attera*), Sanctu Petru would have a share (*parthone*) of everything up to having a child (*filiu*). This is if he might have a child. But if not, then [Sanctu Petru will have a share of] lands, vineyards, farmyards (*cortes*), unworked lands (*saltos*), servants (*homines*), cattle (*battorpedia*) and every other thing that he has. Jorgia de Arsumen, his wife, made a vow to Sanctu Petru in this way: if God gives her a child, then Sanctu Petru would have a share equivalent to that of a child on everything she had: land, vineyards, farmyards, unworked lands (*saltos*), livestock, and all else she might have. If she were to have no child, then Sanctu Petru is to have all she had: land, vineyards, farmyards, unworked land (*saltos*), servants, cattle and all else she had. Witnesses: lord Petru de Kerki, priest of Tamarikes (Tamarighes, near Usini); priest Furatu de Bosa; priest Isperate, in whose hands they placed themselves; Gosantine Masala, administrator (*armentariu*) of *donnikellu* Ithoccor at Favules (San Pietro, Padria); Forasticu, servant (*servu*) of *donnikellu* Ithoccor; Petru de Kerki from Silki, and Mariano Secke who was present for *donnikellu* Ithoccor. Witnesses.

357. Donation. *In Pirastru.*
As she was dying, Susanna de Kerki, daughter of Comita de Kerki, donated her property in Pirastru, bordering that of Sancta Julia. Witnesses: Ithoccor Mankia

Test[e]s: Ithoccor Ma[n]kia su de Cleu, ki fuit fr[at]e carrale dessa mama, [et] Comita Ma[n]kia su fratile, [et] Niscoli de Carvia [et] Petru de Regitanu. Test[e]s.

358. Postura.

Vennit ad hora de morte Comita de Iscanu, [et] fekisse manacu in S[an]c[t]u Petru, [et] deitinke a S[an]c[t]u Petru sa parthone sua in ko 'nke la aveat in Silki, tene[n]dela a nnum[en] sa bi[n]ia de Laia, tenende assa de Gu[n]nari Ga[m]bella ave iosso, [et] ave susu tenende assa de filios de Gitilesu, et dave ambas sas atteras partes ave mo[n]te in mo[n]te; et issas terras de agrile, uve ed uve las aveat, ki furun dessu patre, [et] de Juva[n]ne su fr[at]e; [et] issos ortales in ko '[n]ke los aveat, [et] unu pedaniu, [et] una cupa, in gotale tenore, de si
93v 'nde davan sos fr[ate]s de 'sse una libra de argentu lavorata | a S[an]c[t]u Petru de Silki, de averla issos sa parthone, si lu davan su argentu usq[ue] assu annale suo; et si baricavat su annale, de aversinde p[ro]de S[an]c[t]u Petru de totta custa parthone. Et dave co baricait su annale, bennit Petru de Kerki su f[ra]tile, et kertaitinde in corona de Mariane de Varru, ki 'nke fuit maiore d'iscolca, [et] narait ka 'ecco, a bi boio dare su argentu.' Et issu maiore positili a darelu su argentu avinde usq[ue] ad octo dies. Et ad octo dies torraim[us] nois verbu in corona ka non nos davan su argentu. Et issu maiore accordaisse cu[n] sos ho[m]i[n]es ka[n]tos vi furun in sa corona, [et] narrun ka 'pus ko non bos dan su argentu, appatinde prode S[an]c[t]u Petru dessa parthone totta in ko volla deit Comita de Iscanu, cuia fuit.' Test[e]s: Juva[n]ne Secke [et] Niscoli de Carvia [et] Pet[ru] de Regitanu [et] Petru de Lella su fr[at]ile, [et] ambos fr[ate]s de Carvia, Comita [et] Mariane, [et] Petru de Nureki, [et] pr[e]b[iter]u Furatu
94r de | Bosa, [et] pr[e]b[iter]u Isperate, ki li levarun penitentia; custos vi furun uve la posit Comita de Iscanu totta custa parthone supra iscritta a S[an]c[t]u Petru de Silki, ka[n]do se manacait. Test[e]s. Et ka 'nde kertait Petru de Kerki su fr[at]ile, et ka li poserun de darenos su argentu, [et] non nollu deit, [et] nos narrun ka 'pus ko no[n] bos dat su argentu assu postu ki li posim[us], appatinde p[ro]de dessa parthone S[an]c[t]u Pet[ru] d'avestara.' Test[e]s: Mariane de Varru, maiore d'iscolca, [et] Niscoli de Carvia [et] Petru de Regitanu, [et] homines bonos ka[n]tos vi furun in sa corona.

359. Postura.

Vattussitilu do[n]na Vittoria de Iscanu assu filiu Comita malavidu a S[an]c[t]u Petru, et narait ka 'si mi lu sanat D[eu]s et S[an]c[t]u Petru a filiu meu, p[ro]de si 'nde appat S[an]c[t]u Petru dessu baca[n]te meu de Presnaki, [et] de tottu su pumu ka[n]tu vi aet, [et] meu et de fr[ate]s meos, tenende assa de Niscoli de Carvia, dave om[n]ia parte, [et] assa de Mariane de Varru, [et] assa

from Cleu, the carnal brother (*frate carrale*) of his mother; his cousin (*fratile*) Comita Mankia; Niscoli de Carvia, and Petru de Regitanu. Witnesses.

358. Donation.
Comita de Iscanu's hour of death came, so he committed himself to be a monk at Sanctu Petru and he donated to the church his division (*parthone*) at Silki citing specifically (*a numen*): the vineyard of Laia, which in the lower part bordering that [property] of Gunnario Gambella; in the upper part with that of the sons of Gitilesu, and on both sides from hill to hill. The arable lands (*terras de agrile*), wherever he might have them, which already belonged to his father and his brother, Juvanne; the vegetable gardens (*ortales*) that he had, and a keg-rest (*pedaniu*) and a barrel (*cupa*), such that if the brothers had given Sanctu Petru de Silki a pound of hammered silver (*libra de argentu lavorata*), they could have the share (*parthone*), handing over the silver within a year. If it goes beyond a year, his whole share is to be held by Sanctu Petru. After it surpassed one year, his cousin (*fratile*) Petru de Kerki came and raised a case at a hearing (*corona*) of Mariane de Varru, who was the head of the ward (*maiore d'iscolca*), and said: 'Here! I want to give you the silver!' This official (*maiore*) bid him to bring the silver in eight days. Eight days later, we explained at a hearing that he had not given us the silver. The official agreed with the men present at a hearing (*corona*) and said that 'since he did not give you the silver, Sanctu Petru shall have all the share that was donated by Comita de Iscanu, to which they belonged.' Witnesses: Juvanne Secke, Niscoli de Carcia, Petru de Regitanu, and his cousin Petru de Lella; both brothers of Carvia—Comita and Mariane; Petru de Nureki, priest Furatu de Bosa, priest Isperate, who administered him the confession—these were present when Comita de Iscanu donated all this share, as above, to Sanctu Petru de Silki when he made himself a monk. Wit nesses that cousin Petru de Kerki sued us and committed to give us the silver, but did not give it to us, told us 'since he did not give you the silver as agreed (*assu posto*), Sanctu Petru will own this share from now on!' Witnesses: Mariane de Varru, head of the ward (*maiore d'iscolca*); Niscoli de Carvia, and Petru de Regitanu, and all the trusted men (*homines bonos*) who were there at a hearing (*corona*).

359. Donation.
Lady Vittoria de Iscanu brought her son Comita, who was sick, to Sanctu Petru and said, 'if God and St Peter will heal my son, then Sanctu Petru may have my unused land (*bacante*) at Presnaki and the entire fruit orchard (*pumu*) that belongs to me and my brothers, bordering on every side (*parte*) with that of Niscoli de Carvia, and that of Mariano de Varru and with the main road

94v via maiore.' Et D[eu]s et S[an]c[t]u Petru | sanaitililu, [et] issa benedissitilu a S[an]c[t]u Petru, [et] issu baca[n]te, [et] issu pumu, in ko est iscrittu cuke ave susu. Test[e]s: Juva[n]ne Secke [et] Niscoli de Carvia, [et] Pet[ru] de Lena, su fr[at]e, [et] pr[e]b[iter]u Furatu de Bosa [et] pr[e]b[iter]u Isperate. Test[e]s.

360. Postura.
Posit Mariane de Nureki ad hora de morte a S[an]c[t]a Julia, sa terra sua de Nuratholu, tenende assa de Gosantine Lelle, cun boluntate de Ithoccor su fr[at]e, [et] dessos nepotes de Pet[ru] Ispanu, [et] de Juvanne su fr[at]e. Test[e]s: su pr[e]b[iter]u do[n]nu Forasticu ki li levait penitentia, [et] Ithoccor de Oliuvla su fr[at]e, [et] Petru Ispanu [et] Juva[n]ne, su fr[at]e. Test[e]s.

361. Postura.
Posit Gosantine Lelle ad hora de morte sa t[er]ra sua de Nuratholu, tene[n]de assa ki posit Mariane de Nureki a S[an]c[t]a Julia. Test[e]s: su p[re]b[iter]u do[n]nu Forasticu, ki li levait penitentia, [et] Simione Masila [et] Jorgi Kerellu. Test[e]s.

362. Postura.
Posit Pet[ru] Muthuru ad hora de morte sa terra sua de Nuratholu a S[an]c[t]a Julia, tene[n]de assa ki vi posit Gosa[n]tine Lelle. Test[e]s: su p[re]v[iter]u
95r do[n]nu Forasticu ki li | levait penitentia, et Gosa[n]tine su filiu, et Mariane Solina. Test[e]s.

363. Postura.
Posit Petru Contena a S[an]c[t]a julia, ad hora de morte, su latus dessa t[er]ra sua de Via Alba, tene[n]de assa domestica de S[an]c[t]a Julia. Test[e]s: su pr[e]b[iter]u do[n]nu Forasticu, ki li levait penitentia, [e] Gosa[n]tine Iscarpa su pr[e]b[iter]u, ki fuit filiu suo, [et] Gu[n]nari Contena, su atteru filiu, [et] Ithoccor de Ruta, [et] atteros ho[m]i[n]es ki vi furun. Test[e]s.

364. Conporu.
Co[m]p[or]aili a Martine Melone sa terra sua de Pantaleo, dave sa ficu berbekina in susu; et deivili II istaios de lavore, [et] misimila intro dessu cu[n]iatu meu de Utheri. Test[e]s: Furatu Cocoriata, su thiu, [et] Petru Capra, [et] Ba[n]dinu.

365.[56] *De s[er]vis.*
Kertait do[n]nikellu Ithoccor in filios de Dorgotori Tussia, cu[n] Gosantine Tussia ki fuit thiu issoro, torrande isse verbu p[ro] 'llos, ka 'p[ro]gitteu los keres

56 Cf. entry 374.

(*via maiore*)!' God and St Peter restored his health, so she offered, as a benefice to Sanctu Petru, the uncultivated land (*bacante*) and the fruit orchard as written above. Witneses: Juvanne Secke, Niscoli de Carvia and his brother Petru de Lella, and priest Furatu de Bosa, and priest Isperate. Witnesses.

360. Donation.
Mariane de Nureki, at the hour of his death, donated to Sancta Julia his land of Nuratholu bordering that of Gosantine Lelle, with the consent of his brother Ithoccor, the nephews of Petru Ispanu and his brother, Juvanne. Witnesses: lord Forasticu, the priest who took the confession; his brother, Ithoccor de Olivula, and Petru Ispanu, and his brother, Juvanne. Witnesses.

361. Donation.
Gosantine Lelle, at the hour of his death, donated his land of Nuratholu, bordering that which Mariano de Nureki donated to Sancta Julia. Witnesses: lord Forasticu, the priest who took the confession; Simione Masala, and Jorgi Kerellu. Witnesses.

362. Donation.
Petru Muthuru, at the hour of his death, donated to Sancta Julia his land at Nuratholu bordering that which Gosantine Lelle donated. Witnesses: lord Forasticu, the priest who took the confession; his son, Gosantine, and Mariane Solina. Witnesses.

363. Donation.
Petru Contena donated to Sancta Julia, at the hour of his death, half (*latus*) of his land at Via Alba ('white road'), bordering on the farmstead (*domestica*) of Sancta Julia. Witnesses: lord Forasticu, the priest who took the confession; priest Gosantine Iscarpa, who was his son; Gunnario Contena, the other son; Ithoccor de Ruta; and other men (*homines*) who were there. Witnesses.

364. Purchase.
I bought from Martine Melone his land in Pantaleo from Ficu Berbekina (a type of fig tree) and beyond. I gave him two measures of wheat and a part (*misimila*) of my enclosure (*cuniatu*) at Utheri. Witnesses: Furatu Cocoriata, his uncle; Petru Capra, and Bandinu.

365. *Of servants.*
Donnikellu Ithoccor brought a dispute over the sons of Dorgotori Tussia with Gosantine Tussia, who was their uncle, and explained about them: 'why do

a liveros, ki sun filios de servu intregu de S[an]c[t]u Petru?' Et isse kertaitili ka 'nde lu aveat binkitu a do[n]nu Mariane de Maro[n]iu in corona de iudike
95v Gu[n]nari. | Kerverunili destimo[n]ios ka 'nde aveat binkitu in ko kertavat. Et Gosa[n]tine Tussia battussit duos destimo[n]ios a natale de S[an]c[t]i Gavini, [et] no[n] parveru[n] bonos. Poserun ad Abriu a battuger atteros, [et] isse non bi vennit ne[n] cu[n] bonos, ne[n] cu[n] malos. Derun iura assu ho[m]i[n]e de S[an]c[t]u Petru, [et] iurait a gru .+. ke Gosa[n]tine Caprinu, servu de S[an]c[t]u Petru [et] arm[en]tariu de Sabren, ka 'Dorgotori Tussia servu intregu de S[an]c[t]u Petru de Silki fuit, et alica[n]do do[n]nu Mariane de Maro[n]iu binkitu no '[n]de fekit, in ko kertait Gosa[n]tine Tussia.' Et issara su do[n]nu meu iudike Barusone de Lacco[n] torraitimilos a S[an]c[t]u Petru sos filios de Dorgotori Tussia a servos, a Gedida [et] a Pet[ru] [et] a Nivata [et] ad Helene. Test[e]s: su do[n]nu meu iudike Barusone de Lacco[n], ki mi los torrait, [et] in cuia corona binki, [et] issu filiu do[n]nu Gosa[n]tine rege, [et] Ithoccor de Lacco[n] Pinna [et] Gosa[n]tine, su fr[at]e.

366. *De s[er]vis.*
[T]ramutai cu[n] su arkiprete de S[an]c[t]u Gaviniu de Turres, do[n]nu Augustine, cu[n] [...].[57]

367.[58]
// [... cun boluntate de Deus et dessu donnu meu judike Barusone de Lac-
100r con et dessa muliere donna Prethiosa de Or-] //[59] |[60] -rubu regina, [et] dessu filiu, do[n]nu Gosa[n]tine rege, bullaitiminde carta, p[ro] appati[n]de p[ro]de S[an]c[t]u Petru de Silki a secatura de rennu dessu saltu de Ruginas, in ko narat sos termenes ave susu, usq[ue] in p[er]petuu[m], am[en]. De kita de maiores de ja[n]na: Comita de Muru [et] kita sua. Test[e]s.

368. Co[m]po[r]u.
Co[m]poraitili Gosa[n]tine de Monte, sendevi arm[en]tariu in Usune, a Comita de Natas sa terra sua de Uresa, ki fuit intro dessa domestica n[ost]ra de S[an]c[t]a Maria, et deimusuili una vacca. Test[e]s: Petru de Varru, su thiu dessa muliere, [et] Petru Pinna. Test[e]s.

---

57 The entry abruptly ends here, at the final line of f. 95v.
58 Incomplete entry without heading.
59 Suggested text based on entry 347.
60 Change of hand.

you expect them to be freemen (*liveros*), since they are the sons of a servant in full (*servu intregu*) of Sanctu Petru?' He contested this by saying he had already defeated lord Mariane de Maroniu at a hearing (*corona*) of iudike Gunnari. They requested witnesses that he had won [the case] that was contested. Gosantine Tussia brought forth two witnesses on the feast day (*a natale*) of Sancti Gavini, but they were not considered valid. They bid him bring others to Abriu, but he did not come, either with good or bad witnesses. They called forth a man (*homine*) of Sanctu Petru, Gosantine Caprinu, a servant (*servu*) of Sanctu Petru, to swear on the cross, and the administrator (*armentariu*) of Sauren (Sarene, Cheremule-Thiesi) [to attest] that 'Dorgotori Tussia was a servant in full (*intregu*) of Sanctu Petru de Silki and, regarding what Gosantine Tussia [says], lord Mariane de Maroniu was never defeated in the dispute!' Then my lord iudike Barusone de Laccon returned the sons of Dorgotori Tussia to Sanctu Petru as servants: Gedida, Petru, Nivata, and Helene. Witnesses: my lord iudike Barusone de Laccon, at whose hearing (*corona*) I won and who gave me back the servants; his son Gosantine the king (*rege*); Ithoccor de Laccon Pinna, and Gosantine his brother.

366. *Of servants.*
I made an exchange with the archpriest of Sanctu Gaviniu de Turres (San Gavino di Torres), lord Augustine, with [...].

367.
[...] with the consent of my lord, iudike Barusone de Laccon, and his wife, lady Prethiosa de Or]rubu, queen (*regina*), and his son, lord Gosantine, king (*rege*), he issued me a sealed document (*bullaitiminde carta*) by which Sanctu Petru de Silki could enjoy forever the unworked land (*sultu*) of Ruginas, alienated (*a secatura*) from the realm, the boundaries of which are described above. Amen. From the guard of the senior house-guards (*kita de maiores de janna*): Comita de Muru, and his guard (*kita*). Witnesses.

368. Purchase.
Gosantine de Monte, when he was administrator (*armentariu*) in Usune (Usini), bought his land at Uresa from Comita de Natas which was within our farmstead (*domestica*) of Sancta Maria. We gave him a cow. Witnesses: Petru de Varru, uncle of his wife, and Petru Pinna. Witnesses.

369.
Posit Maria de Varru, filia de Petru de Varru, p[ro] a[n]i[m]a dessu patre, sa terra ki aveat in Uresa, tene[n]de assa de Comita de Natas, a Sancta Maria. Test[e]s: Gosa[n]tine de Roma su nepote [et] Comita de Natas. Test[e]s.

370. Postura.
Posit Comita de serra ad hora de morte sa bi[n]ia ki aveat in Bi[n]ias intro dessa n[ost]ra, a S[an]c[t]a Maria, p[ro] a[n]i[m]a sua. Test[e]s: do[n]nu Petru de Save, su pr[e]b[iter]u ki li levait penitentia, [et] Gosa[n]tine de Moco su servu. T[este]s.

371.
100v Poserun filios de Iorgi Tolis sa terra issoro | de Uresa tene[n]de assa n[ost]ra, p[ro] a[n]i[m]a dessu patre, a S[an]c[t]a Maria. Test[e]s: Brunu Mamalu [et] Petru Pinna [et] Gosa[n]tine Thenthere.

372. *De s[er]vos.*
Kertait su op[er]aiu de S[an]c[t]a Maria de Pisas, do[n]nu Juva[n]ne, cun Marinianu, ki 'nke fuit priore in S[an]c[t]u Petru, in corona de iudike Gu[n]nari, in sinotu, ka 'p[ro]gitteu no[n] mi 'nde das de Pretiosa de Mocon, ki e[st] filia de Istephane de Mocon, ki e[st] servu meu?' Et Marinianu naraitili ka 'veru naras ka fuit filia de servu tuo [et] de Maria Ramike, ankilla de S[an]c[t]u Petru, [et] coiuvata la avea cu[n] Juste Tu[n]faris, servu intregu de S[an]c[t]u Petru, [et] levandelila a larga Istephane de Mocon, la fekeru[n] a Pretiosa de Mocon, sendevi bivu Juste Tu[n]faris, su maritu.' Judicaru[n]nili a Marinianu a destimo[n]ios ka fuit gasi in ko kertavat et battusitilu a Gosa[n]tine de Varda, [et] a Petru su fr[at]ile, [et] a Gosantine Solina servu de iudike [et] arm[en]tariu suo in Kitarone, et iurarun a gru.+.ke custos destimo[n]ios meos, [et] in fattu
101r issoro Iorgi Muris, servu de S[an]c[t]u Petru ka levandelila | a larga Istephane de Mocon, a Juste Tu[n]faris, a Maria Ramike sa muliere, [et] fugindeli cu[n]da, la fekeru[n] a Pretiosa de Mocon, [e] binki. Test[e]s: su do[n]nu n[ost]ru, iudike Gu[n]nari de Lacco[n], in cuia corona binkim[us], [et] Ithoccor de Lacco[n] Pinna [et] issu fr[at]e Gosa[n]tine [et] Mariane de Maro[n]iu, ki fuit patronu de S[an]c[t]u Petru, [et] ho[m]i[n]es bonos ka[n]tos vi furun in sa corona, sa die in sinotu. Test[e]s.

369.
Maria de Varru, daughter of Petru de Varru, donated to Sancta Maria, for [the salvation of] her father's soul, the land she had in Uresa, bordering that of Comita de Natas. Witnesses: his nephew (*nepote*) Gosantine de Roma, and Comita de Natas. Witnesses.

370. Donation.
Comita de Serra, on the hour of death, donated to Sancta Maria the vineyard he had in Binias [which is] within ours, for her soul. Witnesses: lord Petru de Save, the priest who gave the confession, and Gosantine de Moco, his servant (*servu*). Witnesses.

371.
The children of Iorgi Tolis donated their land at Uresa bordering ours for his father's soul. Witnesses: Bruno Mamalu, Petru Pinna, and Gosantine Thenthere.

372. *Of servants.*
The supervisor of works (*su operaiu*) at Sancta Maria de Pisas (Santa Maria di Pisa), lord Juvanne, sued Marinianu, who was prior at Sanctu Petru at a hearing (*corona*) of iudike Gunnari on the day of the assembly (*in sinotu*) [arguing], 'why do you not give me Pretiosa de Mocon, the daughter of Istephane de Mocon who is my servant (*servu*)?' Marinianu said that 'it is true, as you say, that she was the daughter of your servant and of Maria Ramike, female servant (*ankilla*) of Sanctu Petru, but I had married her to Juste Tunfaris, a servant in full (*intregu*) of Sanctu Petru, and then Istephane de Mocon stole her away and they had Pretiosa de Mocon while Juste Tunfaris, her husband, was alive!' They decided that Marinianu bring witnesses [to attest] that it was as he argued. He brought forth Gosantine de Varda, his cousin Petru, and Gosantine Solina servant (*servu*) of the iudike and his administrator (*armentariu*) at Kitarone (Caddaroni-Sant'Eusebio). These witnesses of mine swore on the cross, and then Jorgi Muris, servant of Sanctu Petru, too, that Istephane de Mocon stole his wife Maria Ramike from Juste Tunfaris, fled with her and had [the child] Pretiosa de Mocon [together]. I won the dispute. Witnesses: our lord iudike Gunnari de Laccon at whose hearing (*corona*) we won; Ithoccor de Laccon Pinna; his brother Gosantine; Mariane de Maroniu, who was a patron (*patronu*) of Sanctu Petru, and the trusted men (*homines bonoss*) who were present at a hearing (*corona*) on the day of the assembly. Witnesses.

373.[61] Kertu. *De s[er]vos.*

Kertait do[n]nu Petru de Maroniu in filios de Petru Palu[m]ba ki se mi lebavan p[ro] liveros apus mama; issos kertavan ca furun fattos in furrithu, et do[n]nu Petru de Maroniu, ki fuit arm[en]tariu de S[an]c[t]u Petru, kertait ca fuit coiuvata sa mama issoro a cclaru [et] a facke cu[n] Petru Palu[m]ba. Kerveruninos destimonios ca furun coiuvatos a cclaru [et] a facke, e battussimus sos destimonios a ssinotu, a do[n]nu Petru Marke [et] a Mariane de Varda; e iurarun a .+. in corona dessu do[n]nu n[ost]ru, judike Barusone de Laccon, ambos sos
101v destimonios n[ost]ros, e Gosantine | de Monte, serbu de S[an]c[t]u Petru de Silki, ca furun fattos, Gosantine de Valle, [et] Istephane su fr[at]e, [et] issa sorre, sende coiuvatu a cclaru [et] a facke Petru Palu[m]ba cu[n] sa mama issoro, e binkimus. T[e]st[e]s: su do[n]nu n[ost]ru judike Barusone de Lacco[n], in cuia corona binkimus, [et] issu fiiu do[n]nu Gosa[n]tine rege, e do[n]nu Comita de Gunale Ioculanu, e do[n]nu Ithoccor de Lacco[n] Pinna, e Gosantine su fr[at]e.

374. Kertu. *De s[er]vis.*

Ego do[n]nikellu Ithoccor. Kertai in fiios de Dorgotori Tussia, cu[n] Gosantine Tussia ki fuit thiu issoro, torrande isse verbu p[ro] 'llos ka 'progitteu los keres a lliveros, ki sun filios de servu de S[an]c[t]u Pet[ru]?' Et isse kertaitimi ca 'do[n]nu Mariane de Maro[n]iu 'de binki in corona de judike Gunnari.' Kerverunili destimo[n]ios ca '[n]d'aveat binkitu in co kertavat. Battusit duos destimonios a nnatale de S[an]c[t]i Gavini, e no[n] parveru[n] bonos. Poserun ad Abriu a battuier adteros, [et] isse no[n] bi vennit ne[n] cu[n] bonos, ne[n]
102r cu[n] malos. Derunimi iura, e iurait a .+. Gosantine Caprinu, | servu intregu de S[an]c[t]u Petru [de] Silki fuit, [et] alica[n]do do[n]nu Mariane de Maroniu binkitu no '[n]de fuit, in co kertat Gosantine Tussia,' e binki. T[es]t[e]s: su do[n]nu meu judike Barusone de Lacco[n], in cuia corona binki, e mi los torrait assos fiios de Dorgotori Tussia, e Gedida [et] a Petru [et] a nNivata, [et] issu filiu do[n]nu Gosa[n]tine rege. T[e]st[e]s: Ithoccor de Lacc[on] Pinna e Gosantine, su fr[at]e, e Gunnari de Gitil.

375. Postura.

Morivit Dorgotori d'Uricke in Nugulbi, e bennitimi su fr[at]e Comita [et] issa sorre Bera, e nnarruninimi ca 'battugamusindelu e demusivos su ca[n]tu vi am[us]in Ianpulla, e nostru, e ssuo.' [Et] ego batussindelu, [et] issos derun-

61 Change of hand.

373. Dispute. *Of servants.*
Lord Petru de Maroniu raised a dispute about Petru Palumba's children who considered themselves freemen (*liveros*) from their mother's side. They argued that they were born out of wedlock (*in furrithu*). Lord Petru de Maroniu, administrator (*armentariu*) of Sanctu Petru, argued that their mother's marriage with Petru Palumba was clear and obvious (*a cclaru et a facke*). They requested us to bring witnesses [to attest] that this marriage was clear and obvious, so we brought forth Petru Marke and Mariane de Varda to the assembly (*a ssinotu*) as witnesses. Both of our witnesses, along with Gosantine de Monte, servant (*serbu*) of Sanctu Petru de Silki, swore on the cross at the hearing (*corona*) of our lord iudike Barusone de Laccon that Gosantine de Valles and his brother Istephane and his sister were born after Petru Palumba had married their mother in a clear and open way. We won the dispute. Witnesses: our lord iudike Barusone de Laccon at whose hearing (*corona*) we won; his son lord Gosantine, king (*rege*); lord Comita de Gunale Ioculanu; lord Ithoccor de Laccon Pinna, and Gosantine his brother.

374. Dispute. *Of servants.*
I, *donnikellu* Ithoccor, raised a dispute over the sons of Dorgotori Tussia with Gosantine Tussia, who was their uncle, saying about them 'why do you expect them to be freemen (*liveros*) since they are the sons of a servant in full (*servu intregu*) at Sanctu Petru?' He argued with me that 'regarding this, I have already defeated lord Mariane de Maroniu at a hearing (*corona*) of iudike Gunnar!' He was requested to bring witnesses to confirm that he had won in this dispute; he brought forth two witnesses on the feast day of Sancti Gavini, but they were not considered good. They ordered him to bring others to Abriu, but he did not appear either with good or bad witnesses. They called me to swear, and a ser vant of Sanctu Petru, Gosantine Caprinu, as well as administrator (*armentariu*) of Sauren (Sarene, Cheremule-Thiesi), swore on the cross that 'Dorgotori Tussia was a servant in full (*intregu*) of Sanctu Petru de Silki and, regarding what Gosantine Tussia argues, lord Mariane de Maroniu was not defeated'. I won. Witnesses: my lord iudike Barusone de Laccon who returned to me the sons of Dorgotori Tussia, Gedida, Petru, Nivata and his son Gosantine the king (*rege*), and at whose hearing I won. Witnesses: Ithoccor de Laccon Pinna; Gosantine, his brother, and Gunnari de Gitil.

375. Donation.
Dorgotori d'Urieke died at Nugulbi (Nulvi), and his brother, Comita, and his sister, Vera, came to me and said to me: 'allow us to bury him here and we will give you what we have in Ianpulla, both ours and his!' I had him brought here

imi sa parte de Dorgotori, cu[n] boluntate dessa muiere e dessas fiias, [et] issa parte issoro. T[e]st[e]s: Niscoli e Petru Regitanu, p[ro]ssa parte issoro; e p[ro]ssa parte de Dorgotori, Gosantine de Varru et Andria Corsu.

376. Postura.

Positinke a S[an]c[t]u Petru do[n]na Jorgia de Thori, mama ki fuit de do[n]nu
102v Comita | de Gitil, o[mn]ia cantu 'nke aveat in Silki, e ccorte, e t[er]ras e binias [et] ho[m]i[n]es. Et est sa corte ki nos deit tenende assa de Gosantine Regitanu, [et] assa de Petru de Murena. E deitinke sa vinia d'Ortu do[n]nicu, tenende ass'ortu de iudike part'ave iosso, e dave susu est tenende assa de Dorveni Musuri, e ccosta assa n[ost]ra de S[an]c[t]a Julia; [et] o[mn]ia ca[n]tu vi l'int[ra]vat in cuniatu de Varusone, e binia, e ficu, e pira, [et] oliva, in co vi est. E deitinke lat[us] d'Elene Labra, e Furatu su fiiu intregu, e pede in Jorgia sa fiia. T[este]s: p[re]viteru Furatu de Vosa e p[re]viteru Isperate, ki li davan penetenthia, dande sa parte ca[n]tu narat custu co[n]dake ave susu, cu[n] bolu[n]tate de do[n]nu Comita su fiiu, e dessas fiias, e dessos nepotes.

377. Postura.

Positinke a S[an]c[t]u Petru do[n]nu Comita de Gitil, fiiu ki fuit de do[n]na Jorgia de Thori, sa parte sua in co vi l'intravat in sa t[er]ra de Labros, ki parthiat
103r cu[n] do[n]na Maria sa sorre. T[este]s: do[n]nu | Pet[ru] de Save su p[re]viteru, e p[re]viteru Furatu Cathari, e Mariane de Varru, e Juvane de Serra, su generu.

378. Postura.

Positinke do[n]na Jorgia de Lacco[n], fiia de do[n]nikellu Petru, muiere ki fuit de do[n]nu Comita de Navitha, cu[n] bolu[n]tate dessos fiios, su saltu de ca[m]pu de boes, ad intregu; e llat[us] dessu saltu de Baniaria, ki parthim[us] cun judike Petru. Term[en] dessu saltu de ca[m]pu de boes: dave flum[en] collat tottuve pus muru isc'a planu, avinde baet tottuve pus margine, e benit ass'iscala dessu caprione, e falat derettu su valliclu assu Leporariu, e benit a flum[en], e ccludet. T[este]s: Petru de Thori [et] Ithoccor su fr[at]e, e Petru de Capathennor e Gosantine de Therkillo, servu de iudike.

379.[62] Conp[o]ru.

Co[m]p[or]aili a Gunnari de Thori Pistanca, su lat[us] dessu saltu d'Arave, [et] deivili I libra d'arientu. Term[en], dave badu de P[re]viteru, falat pus flum[en]

62 Duplication of entries 5, 7 and 13.

and they gave me the share (*parte*) of Dorgotori with the consent of his wife, daughters, and theirs. Witnesses: Niscoli and Petru Regitanu concerning their share, and Gosantine de Varru and Andrea Corsu for that of Dorgotori.

376. Donation.
Lady Jorgia de Thori, who was mother of lord Comita de Gitil, donated everything she owned at Silki to Sanctu Petru: farmyard (*corte*), lands, vineyards, and men (*homines*). The farmyard that she gave us borders that of Gosantine Regitanu and that of Petru de Murena. He also gave us the vineyard at Ortu Donnicu bordering in the lower part with Ortu de Iudike ('vegetable garden of the iudike') and in the upper part with that of Dorveni Musuri and on one side with ours at Sancta Julia, and everything that he had at the enclosure (*cuniatu*) de Varusone: vineyard, fig trees, pear trees, and olive trees that are there. She also gave us half (*latus*) of Elena Labra, her son Furatu in full (*intregu*), and a quarter (*pede*) of her daughter Jorgia. Witnesses: priest Furatu de Vosa, and priest Isperate who gave the confession when she donated the share described above in this condaghe with the consent of her son lord Comita and [the consent] of her daughters and nephews (*nepotes*).

377. Donation.
Lord Comita de Gitil, son of lady Jorgia de Thori, donated to Sanctu Petru the share (*parte*) that he had at the land of Labros which he divided with lady Maria, his sister. Witnesses: lord and priest Petru de Save, priest Furatu Cathari, Mariane de Varru, and Juvanne de Serra, his son-in-law.

378. Donation.
Lady Iorgia de Laccon, daughter of *donnikellu* Petru, wife of lord Comita de Navitha, donated, with the consent of her children, the unworked land (*saltu*) of Campu de Boes ('field of oxen'), in full (*intregu*), and half (*latus*) of the land (*saltu*) of Baniaria (Villanova Monteleone), which we share with iudike Petru. The boundary of the land (*saltu*) of Campu de Boes is from the river (*flumen*), [it] passes along the wall to the plain; from there it goes along its border and reaches Iscala dessu Caprione ('hillside of the wild fig'), then descends towards the valley until reaching Leporariu ('hares' nest'), and comes back to the river, and closes. Witnesses: Petru de Thori, and Ithoccor his brother, and Petru de Capathennor (Crabattennere), and Gosantine de Therkillo, servant (*servu*) of the iudike.

379. Purchase.
I bought from Gunnari de Thori Pistanca half (*latus*) of the unworked land (*saltu*) of Arave and I gave him one pound of silver (*libra d'arientu*). The

ad badu de Labros, et collat s'iscala derettu assa via travessaria ki vaet a Banios, e
103v cclo[m]pet | assa pet[ra] longa d'Arave, e falat su valliclu derettu a rrivu, avinde rivu falat isc'a badu de p[re]viteru et ccludet. T[este]s: Mariane de Ca[n]nas e do[n]nu Petru d'Athen, cu[n] ken lu parthim[us] de pare, e cComita d'Arthacan e cComita Bardane.

380. Cambiu.[63] *De s[er]vis.*
Cambiai ho[m]i[n]es cu[n] s'apate de Saccaria, cun donnu Juvanne Gramaticu, a bolu[n]tate de pare. Deili ego ad isse su lat[us] de Maria Kervu, sa fiia de Juvanne Kervu, ki fuit servu n[os]tru, ca Sidonia sa mama fuit ankilla de Saccaria; [et] isse deitimi su lat[us] de Maria Fara, fiia de Gosantine Fara e d'Elene Unkinu. T[este]s: ante ken ca[m]biaim[us] a boluntate de pare, previteru Istefane Piskella e Mariane de Kerki, su de Cotronianu, e Mariane de Capriles, su de Muskianu, e Gosantine de Sersa, e previteru Petru Keru.

381.[64] Conporu. *In montes de Osilo.*
Conporaili[65] ad Mariane de Thori Grassu, fiiu de Gosantine de Thori, su saltu de Sediles, et ego deindeli III libras d'argentu e mesa; [et] es termen dessu
104r saltu: ave su monticlu dessu ferulariu ad fundu | dess'elike, assu monticlu dessu pirastru; ivi iunpat via assu valliclu et ccollat p[er] meiu mo[n]te de Rolacki, derettu assu valliclu dessa ficu alva, accatande s'ariola dess'aba salsa, e torrat assa funtana e falat tottuve rivu derettu a padu dessu Carvone. Ivi moliat sa via ki vamus ad Ogosilo, a derettu a t[er]m[en] dessu de S[an]c[t]a Maria, e falat tottuve t[er]m[en] assu kercu ma[n]nu, lassandenollu a manca su kercu et a dextra su termen, derettu assu rivu de Varatu; tottuve rivu 'nde falat intro assu badu dessa via ki vamus ad iscala de vaccas, ave cunde torrat assu monticlu dessu ferulariu, assu fundu dess'elike. Testes ki furun uve conporai custu saltu: Gosantine de Martis, su de Silki, et anbos frates Canbellas, Furatu e cComita, et homines ki andavan cun illu, anbos frates suos de cuncuba, Petru de Mocor e Gitimel, et Barusone de Sogostos e Dorgotori de Liios.

63 Change of hand.
64 Duplication of entry 145.
65 Change of hand.

boundary is from Badu de Previteru ('priest ford'), it goes down along the river (*flumen*) to Badu de Labros ('ford at Labros'), passes the hillside towards the crossroad which goes to Banios, then reaches Petra Longa d'Arave ('the long rock/menhir of Arave'), descends along the valley towards the stream, and from there, following the stream, it descends to Badu de Previteru, and closes. Witnesses: Mariane de Cannas, and lord Petru d'Athen with whom we divided it, and Comita d'Arthacan, and Comita Bardane. Witnesses.

380. Exchange. *Of servants.*
I exchanged men (*homines*) with the abbot of Saccaria (Saccargia), lord Juvanne Gramaticu, by mutual agreement. I gave him half (*latus*) of Maria Kervu, daughter of Juvanne Kervu, who was our servant since his mother, Sidonia, was a servant (*ankilla*) at Saccaria. He gave me half (*su latus*) of Maria Fara, daughter of Gosantine Fara and Elene Unkinu. Witnesses before whom we agreed it by consent: priest Istefane Piskella, Mariane de Kerki from Cotronianu (Codrongianos), Mariane de Capriles from Muskianu (Muscianu), Gosantine de Sersa, and priest Petru Keru.

381. Purchase. *In the hills of Osilo.*
I bought from Mariane de Thori Grassu ('the fat'), son of Gosantine de Thori, the unworked land (*saltu*) at Sediles. I gave him three and a half pounds of silver. The boundary of the land (*saltu*): from Monticlu dessu Ferulariu ('hill of the staff') to the tree (*fundu*) of s'Elike ('the holm oak'), then to Monticlu dessu Pirastru ('hill of the pear orchard'), and there it crosses the road to the valley and passes the middle of Monte de Rolacki ('hill of Rolacki', Orolacche, Osilo), towards Valliclu dessa Ficu Alva ('vale of the white fig'), and reaches the threshing floor of s'Ab[b]a Salsa ('the salty water'), and turns to the spring and descends along the stream towards Padu dessu Carvone ('ford of Carvone', Funtana Su Carvone, Osilo). There, it takes the road that leads to Ogosilo (Osilo), [goes] towards the boundary of Sancta Maria, then descends along the boundary to Kerku Mannu ('big oak'), leaving the oak on the left and the boundary on the right, [then it goes] towards Rivu de Varatu ('the stream of Varatu'), and, keeping to the stream, it descends to the ford on the road that leads to Iscala de Vaccas ('hillside of cows', Nurague Accas and Necropolis di Iscalaccas) from where it returns to Monticlu dessu Ferulariu and to the holm oak tree. Witnesses present when I bought this land (*saltu*): Gosantine de Martis from Silki; the two Canbella brothers, Furatu and Comita; and the men who accompanied him; both of the brothers from his father's mistress (*cuncuba*), Petru de Mocor and Gitimel, and Barusone de Sogostos, and Dorgotori de Liios.

104v 382.
Ego[66] Benevenuta abbatissa ki ponio in ecustu condake de S[an]c[t]u Petru de Silki, conporu [et] testamentu cantu se 'nke fekit, sendeke ego donna.

383.[67] Postura.
Inmalavidaitse su Turciu dessu male dunde morivit, et cunbersaitse a S[an]c[t]u Petru de Silki. Et sende in sa domo de Silki, bennit Arrigu dessu Mare assu Turciu, [et] naraitili su Turciu ad Arrigu [c]a 'morio, et testam[en]tu voio faker p[ro] sa a[n]i[m]a mea. Bocatemi dessa domo de Iannanu ki am[us] p[ro] pinn[us] ad i[n] cumone, [et] tu leva per rathone dessa i[n]tica ki am[us] ad i[n] cumone, atteru gotantu cantu e[st] supr'unde amus sa domo de Iannanu.' Et a rRrigu plachitili, et pariaisse dessa i[n]tica ki avian ad i[n] cumone, et issa domo de Iannanu remasit ad i[n]tregu assu Turciu. Et issu Turciu penetenthiaisse et positinke a S[an]c[t]u Petru de Silki p[ro] a[n]i[m]a sua sa domo de Iannanu, ki aviat p[ro] pinnus, cu[n] boluntate de Arrigu dessu Mare. Testes
105r sos ho[m]i[n]es ki furun uve se fekit tottu su ki e[st] iscritu dave | susu: previteru Forasticu [et] previteru Petru Corsellu [et] Dorgotori de Varru et donnu Petru de Martis de Canpulo[n]gu [et] do[n]nu Petru de Thori su nepote [et] Gelardinu de Cunittu [et] Guidu de su Bullu [et] Jacubu de Cerbuna [et] Berrardu Pathu. Test[e]s.

384. Postura.
Cunbersarunse frates de Carvia, Mariane [et] Comita, assa batia de S[an]c[t]u Petru de Silki. Et derun a S[an]c[t]u Petru, sa die de co se cunbersarun, tottu su issoro, domos et binias [et] terras [et] o[mn]ia cantu avean, i[n] rathone de mandicarelu issos, i[n] bita issoro, kin[e] bi aver bias nen de vender nen de donare, [et] pus morte issoro averelu S[an]c[t]u Petru, secundu co li lu avean datu. Test[e]s: Dorgotori Pagiti et Dorgotori Pinna et Gunnari de Serra. Test[e]s.

385. Conporu.
Conporaili a Petru Reitanu sas t[er]ras suas ki sun sutta S[an]c[t]u Legori, i[n] co falat sa mura et clompet a bia, [et] baiet totuve pus via i[n]tro assa iaca de
105v Ianne de Vare, [et] collat to[tu]ve muru ad ave secus dessa domo | de Maria Pirastru, [et] collat totuve term[en] assa de S[an]c[t]u Iuvanne. [Et] ego deivili I boe [et] I terra sutta Turthebi. Test[e]s: Gosantine de Martis et Dorgotori Paiti et fr[ate]s de Carvia. Test[e]s.

66 Change of hand.
67 Duplication of entry 314bis.

382.
I, abbess Benevenuta, put in this condaghe of Sanctu Petru de Silki [each] purchase and testimony (*testamentu*) made when I was in charge (*donna*).

383. Donation.
Su Turciu fell ill with a sickness from which he would die, and devoted himself to Sanctu Petru de Silki. While he was at the church (*domo*) of Silki, Arrigu dessu Mare came to him, and Su Turciu told Arrigu that 'I am about to die, and I wish to make my last will and testament. Return to me the farm complex (*domo*) of Iannanu (Gennano, Porto Torres) whose property we share as a security payment (*pro pinnus*), and take a share of equal value of the storehouse (*intica*) we share!' Arrigo agreed to this, and was compensated with the storehouse they shared, and the farm complex (*domo*) of Iannanu was conceded in full to Su Turciu. Afterwards, Su Turciu received the last rites, and donated to Sanctu Petru de Silki the farm of Iannannu that he had used as security, for [the salvation of] his soul, with the consent of Arrigu dessu Mare. Witnesses: the men who were there when all of this was written above: priest Forasticu, priest Petru Corsellu, Dorgotori de Varru, lord Petru de Martis from Canpolongu, lord Petru de Thori his nephew, and Gelardinu de Cunittu Guidu from Bullu, Jacubu de Cerbuna, and Berrardu Pathu. Witnesses.

384. Donation.
The Carvia brothers, Mariane and Comita, devoted themselves to (*cunbersare*) the abbey (*batia*) of Sanctu Petru de Silki. On the day they devoted themselves, they donated everything they had to Sanctu Petru: farmsteads (*domos*), vineyards, lands, and all they had, on the understanding (*in rathone*) that they enjoy it while they are alive, without any reason to sell or give it away, but that, after their death, Sanctu Petru was to have it according to what they had donated. Witnesses: Dorgotori Pagiti, Dorgotori Pinna, and Gunnari de Serra. Witnesses.

385. Purchase.
I bought from Petru Reitanu his lands (*terras*) that were below Sanctu Legori, [the boundary of which] descends along the wall, reaches the road, goes along the road to the entrance (*iaca*) of Ianne de Vare, and passes along the wall behind the farmstead (*domo*) of Maria Pirastru, then passes along the boundary to that of Sanctu Iuvanne. I gave him an ox and a [piece of] land (*terra*) below Turthebi. Witnesses: Gosantine de Martis, Dorgotori Paiti, and the Carvia brothers. Witnesses.

386.[68]

Cambiai[69] cu[n] Petru de Thori Papitari omines: deitimi isse a mimi a Janne Thinga intregu, cu[n] parthone sua, [et] ego deili ad isse a Petru Bakillu, fravicatore, intregu, cu[n] parzone sua. T[es]t[e]s: Gosantine de Maroniu, curatore de Lerron, e Gosantine de Zori Pira, curatore de Ficulinas, e Pet[ru] de Seltas, e previteru Petru Carbone; [et] ecustu tramutu feki cun apatissaria, cu[n] boluntate e de manacas e de clericos e de ladicos.

387.[70]

Ego apatissa Tedora de S[an]c[t]a Maria de Nasca, ki ponio in ecustu co[n]dake tramutu d'omines ki feki cun Petru de Thori Papitari: deitimi isse a mimi a Gosantine Zinga intregu, remanende sa muiere [et] ambas sas fiias a S[an]c[t]u
106r Petru, e llat[us] de Petru Bakillu, cu[n] parzone | issoro; [et] ego deili ad isse a Janne Cocone intregu e llat[us] de Gavini Cucui cu[n] parzone issoro. T[es]t[e]s ante ken tramutaimus a boluntate de pare: Comita de serra Pirella, curatore de Frussia, e cComita de Serra, curatore de Sarule, e Gosantine de Ca[m]pu, curatore d'Ozan, e previteru Petru Carbone e previteru Jubanne Kerellu e previteru Furatu Marcu e Jorgi de Ca[m]pu. Custu tramutu fekim[us] a bolu[n]tate de totu sas manacas meas e de clericos e de ladicos.

388.

Narevos[71] p[ro]gitteu se condennait custu tramutu ki feki s'apatissa Tedora cu[n] Pet[ru] de Thori Papitari, ca no li parvit bonu custu tramutu a judike Comita, inde lu isforrait isse p[ro] no[n] esser fattu, e ka no[n] se fekit cu[n] boluntate sua, ki fuit armentariu de S[an]c[t]u Petru. Test[e]s: judike Comita, ki lu isgirait custu tramutu, [et] donnu Ithoccor de Navithan [et] donnu Conmita de Navithan [et] donnu Mariane de Maroniu [et] donnu Comita de Serra. Testes.

106v 389.

Ego[72] abbatissa Tedora ki ponio in ecustu condake de S[an]c[t]u Petru de Silki tramutu [et] postura et paru, kantu'[n]che est factu et se 'nke aiet faker in bita mea.

68 The entire entry has been cancelled by an undulating line under each line of text.

69 Change of hand.

70 The entire entry has been cancelled by an undulating line under each line of text.

71 Change of hand.

72 Change of hand.

386.
I exchanged men (*omines*) with Petru de Thori Papitari. He gave me Janne Thinga in full (*intregu*), with his share (*parthone*), and I gave him Petru Bakillu, a builder (*fravicatore*), in full, with his share. Witnesses: Gosantine de Maroniu *curatore* of Lerron, and Gosantine de Zori Pira, *curatore* of Figulinas, and Petru de Seltas, and priest Petru Carbone. I made this exchange with the abbey's council (*cun apatissaria*), with the consent of the nuns (*manacas*), clerics (*clericos*), and the laity (*ladicos*).

387.
I, abbess Teodora de Sancta Maria de Nasca (Santa Maria di Asca), put in this condaghe the number of servants (*omines*) I exchanged with Petru de Thori Papitari. He gave me Gosantine Zinga in full (*intregu*), as his wife and two daughters remained in Sanctu Petru, and half (*latus*) of Petru Bakillu, with their shares (*parzone*). I gave him Janne Cocone in full, and a half of Gavini Cucui, with their shares. Witnesses before whom we made the exchange by mutual agreement: Comita de Serra Pirella, *curatore* of Frussia; Comita de Serra, *curatore* of Sarule; Gosantine de Campu, *curatore* of Ozan (Ottana); priest Petru Carbone; priest Jubanne Kerellu; priest Furatu Marcu, and Jorgi de Campu. We made this exchange with the consent of all my nuns, clerics, and laity.

388.
'I tell you why this exchange (*tramutu*) that I, abbess Tedora, made with Petru de Thori Papitari, was annulled (*condennait*)—because this exchange was not seen as valid (*bonu*) by iudike Comita, and so he annulled it himself so that it would not happen, for it was not made with his consent, [when] he [Comita] was administrator (*armentariu*) of Sanctu Petru!' Witnesses: iudike Comita, who cancelled (*isgirait*) this exchange; lord Ithocor de Navithan; lord Comita de Navithan; lord Mariane de Maroniu, and lord Comita de Serra. Witnesses.

389.
I, abbess Tedora, put in this condaghe of Sanctu Petru de Silki [each] exchange, donation and purchase that has been made and that will be made in my lifetime.

390. Kertu. *De s[er]vis.*
Kertait donnu Comita de Serra, ki 'nche fuit armentariu dessa domo de S[an]c[t]u Petru, in corona de judike Comita; kertait cu[n] Ithoccor de Kerki, fiiu de Mariane de Kerki, su de Cotronianu, p[ro] Elene Titu, ca 'p[ro]iteu la keres ad Elene Titu, ki e[st] intrega sa mama Bittoria Porkina de S[an]c[t]u Petru de Silki, et latus dessu patre Juvanne Titu, ki e[st] Elene a nnatia de mama?' Et isse naraitimi ca 'su masclu, ki fuit a nnatia de patre, in ken avia ego su latus, tramutai cu[n] abbatissa Maria, cu[n] boluntate de Petru de Seltas, priore dessa domo, et de Petru Salvaru, ki fuit armentariu; ego dei latus dessu masclu ki fuit a nnatia de in cumone ca non aveat plus fiiu, et issos mi derun latus dessa femina, ki fuit a nnatia de mama.' Et ego torraili verbu ca 'non ti la potiat dare
107r nen abbatissa | et nen priore, kene boluntate de iudike, ki 'nde fuit armentariu et donnu dessa domo.' Et issu donnu meu judike Comita percontait insara in corona si ait poter tramutare sa abbatissa, nen issu priore, kene boluntate de judike ki 'nde fuit armentariu. Et parvit in corona iustithia non poter tramutare sa abbatissa nen issu priore kene boluntate de judike; et issara mi la derun in corona de sinotu ad intrega ad Elene Titu. Test[e]s: su donnu meu judike Comita, in cuia corona binchi, et donnu Ithoccor de Navithan et donnu Comita de Navithan et donnu Mariane de Maroniu et donnu Gosantine de Thori Pira. Test[e]s.

391. Kertu. *De s[er]vis.*
Ego Comita de Serra, kertai cu[n] donnu Mariane de Laccon, ieneru de donnikellu Ithoccor, p[ro] latus de Maria Kirione et latus dessa fiia Bittoria, in corona dessu donnu meu judike Comita in Sorra, et naraili ca 'p[ro]iteu li las levates
107v a S[an]c[t]u Petru de Silki sas a[n]killas | suas?' Et isse naraitimi ka 'abbatissa Maria las donait a ssocru meu, a donnikellu Ithocor.' Et ego narai ca 'percontet su donnu n[ost]ru si potet donare s'abbatissa servu o ankilla.' Et judike percontait issara i[n] corona, et narrunili sos ho[m]i[n]es de corona ca 'non potiat donare sa abbatissa nen servu, nen ankilla.' Et issara mi torrait su donnu meu judike Comita latus de Maria Kirione, et lat[us] i[n] sa fiia Bittoria. Test[e]s: su donnu meu judike Comita, i[n] cuia corona binki, et donnu Ithoccor de Navithan et donnu Mariane de Maroniu et donnu Gosantine de Athen et donnu Comita de Navithan. Test[e]s.

390. Dispute. *Of servants.*
Lord Comita de Serra, administrator (*armentariu*) of the church (*domo*) of Sanctu Petru, sued Ithocor de Kerki, son of Mariane de Kerki from Cotronianu (Codrongianos) at a hearing (*corona*) of iudike Comita concerning Elena Titu, and asked him: 'why do you want Elena Titu whose mother, Bittoria Porkina, is a [female servant] in full (*intrega*) of Sanctu Petru de Silki, just as half (*latus*) of her father Juvanne Titu, and Elena belongs to the maternal line?' He told me: 'I exchanged with abbess Maria the male child, for whom I had half as he was from the paternal line, with the consent of Petru de Seltas, prior of that house, and of Petru Salvaru, who was the administrator (*armentariu*). I gave him the male for that half which was shared since he was born as he had no children, and they gave me half of the female who was from the maternal line!' I then replied: 'neither the abbess nor the prior could give you this without the consent of the iudike who was administrator (*armentariu*) and lord of the house!' My lord iudike Comita then asked at a hearing (*corona*) if the abbess and the prior could make an exchange without the consent of the iudike, who was [once] administrator (*armentariu*) of Sanctu Petru. It seemed right (*iustithia*) to the hearing (*corona*) that neither the abbess, nor the prior, could make exchanges without his consent. Therefore, at the hearing (*corona*) [on the day] of the assembly, they gave me Elena Titu (*intrega*) in full. Witnesses: my lord iudike Comita, at whose hearing (*corona*) I won, and lord Ithoccor de Navithan, lord Comita de Navithan, lord Mariane de Maroniu, and lord Gosantine de Thori Pira. Witnesses.

391. Dispute. *Of servants.*
I, Comita de Serra, sued lord Mariane de Laccon, son-in-law of *donnikellu* Ithoccor, concerning half (*latus*) [the services] of Maria Kirionc and for half of those of his daughter, Bittoria, at a hearing (*corona*) of my lord iudike Comita at Sorra (Sorres). I said: 'why are you taking your female servants (*ankillas*) away from Sanctu Petru de Silki?' He said that 'abbess Maria gave them to my father-in-law, *donnikellu* Ithocor!' Then I said: 'ask our lord if the abbess is able to grant (*donare*) a servant (*servu*) or a female servant (*ankilla*)?' The iudike then asked this to a hearing (*corona*), and the men (*homines*) of the hearing (*corona*) said that 'the abbess cannot grant a servant or female servant!' Next, my lord iudike Comita returned to me half (*latus*) of Maria Kirio and half of her daughter, Bittoria. Witnesses: my lord iudike Comita at whose hearing (*corona*) I won, and lord Ithoccor de Navithan, lord Mariane de Maroniu, lord Gosantine de Athen, and lord Comita de Navithan. Witnesses.

392. *Anni Do[m]ini M[illesimo ducentesimo decimo]. Sa domo de Ogothi.*
Ego, abbatissa Tedora, accatai sa domo de Ogothi a judike Comita ki la aveat
a ppinnus su fr[at]e judike Gosantine p[ro] avere ki li deviat sa domo de
S[an]c[t]u Petru. Et ego petilila ki la torraret a S[an]c[t]u Petru, p[ro] sa
a[n]i[m]a sua et dessu fr[at]e. Et isse, co donnu bonu, torraitimila sa domo de
Ogothi a S[an]c[t]u Petru, cu[n] onnia p[er]tine[n]thia sua canta d'aveat lev-
108r ata, p[ro] sa a[n]i[m]a | sua et dessu fr[at]e judike Gosantine, ki la aveat appita
p[ro] pinn[us]. Test[e]s ki vi furun uve mi la torrait judike sa domo de Ogothi:
donnu Ithoccor de Navithan et donnu Comita de Serra, ki fuit armentariu
dessa domo de S[an]c[t]u Petru, et donnu Juvanne Thivita, previteru de Tula.
Test[e]s.

393. Postura. *Vingia i[n] Pulaiosa.*
Positinke a S[an]c[t]u Petru Maria Secche p[ro] sa a[n]i[m]a sua, ad ora de morte, sa binia sua dessa Pulaiosa, tottota, in co vi la aveat; et e[st] term[en] assa binia de Gosantine Reitanu. Test[e]s: donnu Ithocor Solina, p[re]viteru de Kitarone, ki la penetenthiait, et p[re]viteru donnu Juvanne Kerellu et Petru de serra et Gosantine de Lella et Juvanne Catha, su maritu. Test[e]s.

394. Kertu. *De s[er]vos.*
Kertaitili donnu Comita de Serra, in corona de judike Comita i[n] Abrio, a
Bere Ala et a Maria sa sorre, et a Furatu su frate ka 'progiteu non servites a
S[an]c[t]u Petru de Silki, ki setes servos de S[an]c[t]u Petru?' Et issos reclamar-
108v unse p[ro] kertatore ki kertaret p[ro] 'llos. Et assu postu ki lis pose[run] |
batusserun a donnu Comita Pinna, curatore de Nugor, a kertare pro 'llos. Et
do[n]nu Comita de Serra, ki fuit arm[en]tariu de S[an]c[t]u Petru, kertaitilis ca
'p[ro]gitteu bos cherites liberos, ki setes serbos de S[an]c[t]u Petru?' Et donnu
Comita Pinna torrait berbu p[ro] 'llos, plakendelis ad issos, ca 'no los inperait
S[an]c[t]u Petru p[ro] servos in co kertates.' [Et] torraitilis verbu ca 'mama
vostra Jedida Ala davat sinnata a S[an]c[t]u Petru p[ro] ankilla, et tottu sos
frates, Jorgia de Putholu et Dorgotori de Putholu et Prethiosa de Putholu. Cus-
tos furun fiios de Nivata, a[n]killa i[n]trega de S[an]c[t]u Petru de Silki.' Et issos
torrarunili verbu ca 'non bi inperastis ne in nois, ne in parentes nostros in ko
kertates.' Judicaru[n] issara in corona a bature destimonios S[an]c[t]u Petru ca
los i[m]peravat et davan sinnata p[ro] servos, et poserunilis a Pasca de maiu
a bature nois sos destimonios. Et a Pasca de maiu batussimus sos destimonios
109r et jurarun a gru.+.che ca furun[73] | servos de S[an]c[t]u Petru et ca davan sin-

73 Manuscript reads *purun.*

392. Year of the lord 1210. *The farm complex* (domo) *of Ogothi.*
I, abbess Tedora, received from iudike Comita the farm complex (*domo*) of Ogothi (Otti) that his brother, iudike Gosantine, had as a guarantee (*a ppinus*) for what he owed to the church (*domo*) of Sanctu Petru. I requested him to return it to Sanctu Petru for his soul and that of his brother. He, as a good lord, returned the farm (*domo*) of Ogothi to Sanctu Petru, with all its appurtenances, for his soul and that of his brother, iudike Gosantine, who held it as a guarantee. Witnesses who were there when iudike returned the farm of Ogothi to me: lord Ithoccor de Navithan, and lord Comita de Serra administrator (*armentariu*) of the church of Sanctu Petru, and lord Juvanne Thivita, priest of Tula. Witnesses.

393. Donation. *Vineyard in Pulaiosa.*
At the hour of her death, Maria Secche gave to Sanctu Petru, for her soul, her vineyard at Pulaiosa which she has in its entirety. The boundary is the vineyard of Gosantine Reitanu. Witnesses: lord Ithocor Solina, priest at Kitarone (Caddaroni-Sant'Eusebio) who gave the confession, and lord priest Juvanne Kerellu, and Petru de Serra, and Gosantine de Lella, and Juvanne Catha her husband. Witnesses.

394. Dispute. *Of servants.*
Lord Comita de Serra sued Bere Ala, her sister, and her brother, Furatu, at a hearing (*corona*) of iudike Comita at Abriu and asked them 'why do you not serve Sanctu Petru de Silki since you are servants (*servos*) of Sanctu Petru?' They asked for a legal representative (*kertatore*) to argue for them. When they had arranged this, lord Comita Pinna, *curatore* of Nugor (Nuoro), was brought forth to argue for them. Lord Comita de Serra, who was the administrator (*armentariu*) of Sanctu Petru, asked them 'why do you pretend to be free when you are servants of Sanctu Petru?' Lord Comita Pinna replied at their wish that 'they have not been in the service of Sanctu Petru as argued!' He replied: 'your mother, Jedida Ala, was inscribed (*sinnata*) as a servant (*ankilla*) of Sanctu Petru and all her siblings: Jorgia de Putholu, Dorgotori de Putholu, and Prethiosa de Putholu. These were children of Nivata, a female servant in full (*ankilla intrega*) of Sanctu Petru de Silki!' They replied that 'neither we, nor our parents, have been in your service as you claim!' Then they decided that Sanctu Petru bring forth witnesses to a hearing (*corona*) to attest that they were in the service of Sanctu Petru, and that they were inscribed as servants. They set Easter Day (*Pasca de Maiu*) for us to bring the witnesses. And on Easter Day we brought forth the witnesses who swore on the cross that these were servants (*servi*) of Sanctu Petru and that they were inscribed (*davan sinnata*). They

nata. Et issos reclamarunse p[ro] iscreder sos destimonios; et poserunilis ad iscreder sos destimonios a xv dies. Et assa die dessu postu andai ego a nNulabros, ad ue fuit iudike, et assu postu n[on] bennerun ne[n] issos, nen donnu Comita Pinna, ki kertavat p[ro] 'llos ad iscreder sos destimonios. Derunili iura a Petru d'Ardu servu, de S[an]c[t]u Petru, et iurait a .+. gruke ca 'in co narrun sos destimonios p[ro] custu kertu, gasi e[st] beru.' Test[e]s: su donnu meu judike Comita, in cuia corona kertai et binki, [et] donnu Barusone de Laccon, fiiu de judike de Arborea, et anbos Ithoccor de Laccon Coche, thiu [et] nepote, et issu p[re]viteru de Nulabros, donnu Jorgi Iscarpa, et donnu Comita Porcun et donnu Petru de Athen, su de Usune. Test[e]s.

395.
Ego[74] abatissa Tedora de Silki canbiai cun su p[ri]ore de Seve Paganellu: ego li dei ad isse a Iorgia Thana, [et] isse deitimi a mimi a Maria Tamuri, fiia de Ithoc-
109v cor Tamuri, dandenos | a boluntate de pare unuchis parthone issoro. T[este]s: donnu Comita de Serra, curatore de Frussia, armentariu meu [et] suo, [et] donnu Mariane Pinna, curatore de Meiulocu, [et] Ithoccor Casu, de Thathari, [et] previteros donnu Petru de Soiu [et] donnu Dorgotori de Serra, su de Cleu. T[este]s.

396. *De s[er]vis.*
Ego[75] abbatissa Tedora ki ponio in ecustu co[n]dake binkitura ki feki assu priore de Guthule. Kertait mecu su priore de Guthule do[n]nu Istefane in Kitarone, in corona de iudike Mariane, pro Ithoccor Varitho ca lu keriat pro sse, ad isse et ad ssos filios; et ego torraili verbu [et] binki pro servos pecuiares de S[an]c[t]u Petru, Ithoccor Varitho [et] issos filios. T[es]t[e]s: judike Mariane, in cuia corona binki, [et] donnu Ithoccor de Laccon, curatore d'Ulumetu, [et] donnu Ithoccor de Navithan [et] donnu Mariane Pinna, curatore de Canpulongu. T[es]t[e]s.

397. *De s[er]vis.*
Parthivimus insara a boluntate de pare, dave nanti de judike, su fetu ki avian
110r factu su servu meu Ithoccor Varitho cu[n] sa ankilla | sua; ad isse intrait Iuva[n]ne su primariu, [et] a mi[mi] intrait Victoria [et] Susanna, [et] isse appit s'atteru masclu fattu de custas, [et] remasit a cumone a mimi [et] assu priore s'assecus de totu. T[es]t[e]s: judike Mariane [et] donnu Gunnari de Maroniu [et] Gelardinu Furru. T[es]t[e]s.

74 Change of hand.
75 Change of hand.

argued to disbelieve the witnesses, and they gave them fifteen days to prove the witnesses wrong. On the appointed day, I went to Nulabros (Nulauro/Lunafras) where the iudike was, but neither they, nor lord Comita Pinna, who had been instructed to refute the witnesses, appeared. They had Petru d'Ardu, servant (*servu*) of Sanctu Petru, take an oath and he swore on the cross that 'what the witnesses said about this dispute is true!' Witnesses: my lord iudike Comita at whose hearing I made the dispute and won; lord Barusone de Laccon, son of the iudike of Arborea; the two Ithocor-s de Laccon Coche, uncle and nephew (*nipote*); the priest of Nulabros, lord Jorgi Iscarpa; lord Comita Porcu, and lord Petru de Athen from Usune (Usini). Witnesses.

395.
I, abbess Tedora de Silki, made an exchange with the prior of Seve Paganello (Santa Maria di Cea). I gave him Iorgia Thana and he gave me Maria Tamuri, daughter of Ithoccor Tamuri, giving us them by mutual agreement, each with their own share (*parthone*). Witnsses: lord Comita de Serra, *curatore* of Frussia, administrator (*armentariu*) of mine and his; lord Mariane Pinna, *curatore* of Meiulocu (Meilogu); Ithoccor Casu de Thathari (Sassari); and the priests, lord Petru de Soiu and lord Dorgotori de Serra from Cleu. Witnesses.

396. *Of servants.*
I, abbess Tedora, put in this condaghe the victory I won over the prior of Guthule (Buttule, Ozieri). The prior of Guthule, lord Istefane, sued me at Kitarone (Caddaroni-Sant'Eusebio) at a hearing (*corona*) of iudike Mariane over Ithoccor Varitho concerning both him and his sons. I replied to them and won because Ithoccor Varitho and his sons were the property (*pecuiares*) of Sanctu Petru as servants. Witnesses: iudike Mariane at whose hearing I won; lord Ithoccor Laccon, *curatore* of Ulumetu (Olmedo); lord Ithoccor de Navithan, and lord Mariane Pinna, *curatore* of Canpulongu (Campulongu).

397. *Of servants.*
In front of the iudike, we divided by mutual agreement the offspring that my servant (*servu*) Ithoccor Varitho had with his female servant (*ankilla*). He received Iuvanne, the first born, and I received Victoria and Susanna; he also had another male born from them and he remained shared between me and the prior. Witnesses: the iudike Mariane, lord Gunnari de Maroniu, and Gelardinu Furru. Witnesses.

398.
Termen dessu saltu de S[an]c[t]u Petru ki amus in Baniaria: baet dave su badu dessa cotina dessu lepporariu a derectu assu laccu de Baniaria, [et] collat a derectu assa iscla dessu cavallu, [et] girat totue sa margine a derectu assu fundu dessu kerku dessu monime[n]tu ki est supra sa via de petrade, [et] baet a derectu assa ariola, dave s'ariola falat totue sa serra de petrade a derectu assu bru[n]cu, dave su bruncu falat [et] clusat ad flumen. Custu e[st] de S[an]c[t]u Petru, ki non bi aet atter parte.

399. Abbatissa Tedora.
Conporaili a Iuva[n]ne de Thori Vardane sa parte sua dessu saltu de Sinona ki aet in Ulumetu, de VIII partes s'una, [et] si vi aet plus datu mi l'aet; [et] ego deindeli I bacha [et] missilu in servithu de S[an]c[t]u Petru ca[n]tu ad una manaca. T[es]t[e]s: Gunnari Bardane calonicu de Bosa [et] Comita de Therkillo, p[re]viteru de Bosove, [et] Petru de Varru [et] Petru de Thori de Taverra [et] Ithocor d'Ardu.

110v 400. *De s[er]vos.*
Ego[76] Comita de serra Pirella, armentariu de S[an]c[t]u Pet[ru] de Silki, parthivi homines cum boluntate de donna Tedora, abbatissa de Silki, cun donnu Comita de serra su d'Ithir, fiiu de donnikellu Mariane, ad boluntate de pare, parthinde ego, et levande isse. Levait isse p[ro] parte sua ad Comita Massilla et assos fiios, cu[n] parthone issoro. Et ego levai p[ro] S[an]c[t]u Petru de Silki, p[ro] parte sua, ad Gantine Massilla et assos fiios, cu[n] parthone issoro. Testes: Simione Carvone, su de Canpui, frate carrale de Gantine Carvone, et Janne Cocone, su de Canpui, et Petru de Save, su de Teclata, frate carrale de Jannariu de Save, et Migali Cocone Mannu, su de Canpui, et Gantine d'Iscanu su de Teclata, fiiu de Ithoc[or] de Save. Test[e]s.

401. Conporu. *Apus Biosevi.*
Ego[77] abbatissa Tedora de S[an]c[t]u Petru de Silchi ki ponio in ecustu condake co[m]poru ki feki dessu saltu de Maurelli. Conporaili ad Granuciu de Kerki et ad Gantine de Martis et ad Istefane de Martis et ad Petru de Kerki su saltu
111r de Maurelli, q[ui] est term[en] assu valliclu dessu | Cane, et est term[en] ad monticlu de Kipriane, et term[en] assu pedale d'aba de mela, et term[en] assa

76 Change of hand.
77 Change of hand.

398.
The boundary of the unworked land (*saltu*) of Sanctu Petru that we have in Baniaria goes from Badu ('the ford') of Cotina dessu Lepporariu ('rock of the hares' nests'), it passes towards Laccu de Baniaria ('the drinking trough of Baniaria'), goes towards Iscla dessu Cavallu ('the islet of the horse'), turns along the border towards Kerku dessu Monimentu ('the oak tree of the burial place'), which is above the road from Petrade. Then it goes towards s'Ariola ('the threshing floor'); from s'Ariola, it descends along Serra de Petrade ('the ridge of Petrade'), towards Bruncu ('the hilltop'), and from the hill, it descends and closes at the river (*flumen*). This belongs to Sanctu Petru, and no one can have any part of it.

399. Abbess Tedora.
I bought from Iuvanne de Thori Vardane his share (*parte*) of the unworked land (*saltu*) of Sinona which is at Ulumetu (Olmedo), [to a total] of one-eighth. If he could have given more, he would have given me it. I gave him a cow and I provide for service to Sanctu Petru as much as [is needed] for a nun. Witnesses: Gunnari Bardane, canon (*calonicu*) of Bosa; Comita de Therkillo, priest of Bosove (Latte Dolce); Petru de Varru; Petru de Thori de Taverra (Taberra), and Ithocor d'Ardu.

400. *Of servants.*
I, Comita de Serra Pirella, administrator (*armentariu*) of Sanctu Petru di Silki, with the consent of lady Tedora, abbess of Silki, made a division of men (*homines*) with lord Comita de Serra from Ithir (Ittireddu), son of *donnikellu* Mariane. I divided them by mutual agreement, and he took his share. He took Comita Massilla and her children for his share with their division; I took for Sanctu Petru de Silki Gantine Massilla and his children, with their division. Witnesses: Simione Carvone from Canpui (Campui), carnal brother (*frate carrale*) of Gantine Carvone; Janne Cocone from Canpui (Campui); Petru de Save from Teclata (Trigiada, near Romana), carnal brother of Jannariu de Save; Migali Cocone Mannu ('the elder') from Canpui (Campui); and Gantine d'Iscanu from Teclata, son of Ithocor de Save. Witnesses.

401. Purchase. *At Biosevi* (*Giusei*).
I, abbess Tedora de Sanctu Petru de Silki, put in this condaghe the purchase I made of the unworked land (*saltu*) at Maurelli. I bought from Granuciu de Kerki, Gantine de Martis, Istefane de Martis, and Petru de Kerki, the land (*saltu*) at Maurelli. The boundary is from Valliclu dessu Cane ('the vale of the dog'); one boundary is to Monticlu de Kipriane ('hill of Kipriane'); one boundary is

pathata de Favariu, et term[en] ad matta d'oriu, et term[en] ad badu Cuchesu, et term[en] assa mura de frassos, et falat tottue pus rivu ad term[en] de Silki. T[es]t[e]s: Juvanne de Nureki et Comita de serra Pirastru et Ithoccor de Varru et Gosantine de serra et Mariane de Varru et Comita de Nureki et Juva[n]ne Solina; et ego deindelis bis[antis] VI, ispiiandemi issos de donnia homine dessu mundu. Testes.

402. Term[en] de saltu. *In mo[n]tes de Lella.*

Posit su donnu meu judike Mariane ad atterminare su saltu de monte de
Lella, a ddonnu Ithoccor de Kerki, curatore de Plovake; [et] donnu Ithoccor de
Kerki andait cu[n] sos homines dessa curatoria. Andavativi Petru Sanna, su de
Plovake, dave term[en] in t[er]men, i[n] co naravat sa carta bullata, et Gantine
Plana et Comita Capra [et] do[n]nu Gu[n]nari Seta, arkip[re]te de Plovake, et
111v Gavini Seta et Dorgotori de Varru et Petru de Varru et Petru de Palmas | et Mari-
ane de Palmas et Petru Coke et Dorgotori d'Oppia et Gantine de Nurra; custos
andavan dave term[en] in term[en], i[n] co naravat sa carta bullata.

403. Adterminamentu. *Saltu de Sitale.*

Termen dessu sultu de sSitale. Dave sa via maiore de Vallinas, de co parthim[us]
de pare cu[n] judike, baet tottuve term[en] assa corona dessa funtana de
sSitale, essit tottuve sa pala, iumpatu collat ad altu assu Planu, baet tottuve
supra Latila assu bulbare de monte de clesia, de co partho cu[n] sos de Kit-
arone, et essit assa via maiore, falat tottuve sa via de balle torta, in co si 'nke
falat tottuve sa via dessos pontes, et collat tottuve flum[en] a lLauros, assu vadu
de Othikevor, et collat ivi assu fronte de nuracke Pithinnu, essit tottuve sa atha
ass'ena, collat tottuve parthindela paris s'ena derectu a binia dessos de Thori,
collat tottuve via a binia dessos Casos, girat totuve s'atha, essit tottuve su mar-
112r gine, assu margine dessu Favariu, iumpat sa via assa terra de Mariane de Varru, |
et essit assa de S[an]c[t]u Setiu, essit assa lintha de Petru de Valles, dessu planu
de Iesin, falat tottuve su margine assu de iudike, et essit tottuve su margine assa
via maiore de Vallinas.

to Aba de Mela ('water of the apple'), one boundary is to Pathata de Favariu ('bean field'), one boundary is to Matta d'Oriu (*macchia* at Oriu), one boundary is to Badu Cuchesu ('Cuchesu ford'), one boundary is to Mura de Frassos ('the brambles at the ash trees') and descends along the river to the boundary of Silki. Witnesses: Juvanne de Nureki, Comita de Serra Pirastru, Ithoccor de Varru, Gosantine de Serra, Mariano de Varru, Comita de Nureki, and Juvanne Solina. I paid them six bezants (*bisantis*), and they guaranteed me against any claim by anyone in the world. Witnesses.

402. Boundary of unworked land (*saltu*). *In the hills of Lella.*
My lord iudike Mariane asked lord Ithoccor de Kerki, *curatore* of Plovake (Ploaghe), to delimit the unworked land (*saltu*) of Monte de Lella ('hill of Lella', Monte Ledda, Ploaghe). Lord Ithoccor de Kerki went there with the men of the district (*homines dessa curatoría*). Petru Sanna from Plovake went from boundary to boundary as the charter with a seal (*carta bullata*) described. Gantine Plana; Comita Capra; lord Gunnari Seta, archpriest of Plovake; Gavini Seta; Dorgotori de Varru; Petru de Varru; Petru de Palmas; Mariane de Palmas; Petru Coke; Dorgotori d'Oppia, and Guntine de Nurra—these went from boundary to boundary as the charter with a seal described.

403. Boundary delimitation. *Unworked land* (saltu) *of Sitale.*
The boundary of the unworked land (*saltu*) of Sitale, which we share with the iudike, is from the main road (*sa via maiore*) of Vallinas; it goes along to Corona dessa Funtana de Sitale ('the hilltop at the spring of Sitale'), continues along the slope, crosses it and goes up to the plain (*su planu*), then it goes along to [a point] above Latila, to the livestock enclosure at Monte de Clesia ('church hill'), which is shared with those from Kitaronc (Caddaroni-Sant'Eusebio); then it takes the main road and goes down along the road of Balle Torta ('twisted valley'), then descends towards the road of sos Pontes ('the bridges'), passes along the river (*flumen*) to Lauros to Badu d'Uthikeor ('the ford of Uthikeor'); there, it passes in front of Pithinnu Nuraghe ('small nuraghe'), continues along the crag to the spring, passes along dividing the spring equally in the direction of the vineyard of the De Thori [family], and passes along the road to the vineyard of the Casu [family]; it turns along the crag, follows along the border, to the border of Favariu, it crosses the road to the land (*terra*) of Mariane de Varru, goes to Sanctu Setiiu, continues towards the strip of land of Petru de Valles at Planu de Iesin ('plain of Iesin'), it goes down along the border towards that of the iudike and, along the ridge, to the main road of Vallinas.

404. Adt[er]minam[en]tu dessu saltu de s'iscolca d[e] Silchy depus Cherki.
Term[en] de saltu q[ui] posit donna Maria de serra cu[n] bolu[n]tate dessu maritu ad S[an]c[t]u Petru, ki parthim[us] de pare cu[n] Bosa: sa bruke (*sic*) ki am[us] in sa via, et falat capuiosso sa via de Carru, et falat tottuve sa via a term[en] dessa bruke ki parthim[us] de pare cu[n] Gisarclu, derectu assa iscala Lansinosa, moliat cui assa gruke dessu Gisterru, dave sa gruke dessu Gisterru assas petras clopatas de monte de keias, ave mo[n]te de keias assu putha[n]caru ma[n]nu iumpatu de valle, ki e[st] i[n] sa matta ma[n]na dessa kersa, ave su puthancaru tottuve pus atha assu margine dessa ariola a destra, et benitinde a derectu assa gruke ad uve parthim[us] de pare cu[n] Bosa et cu[n] S[an]c[t]a Maria, et torrat assu bulbare dessa ficu, et affliscat, [et] clonpet assa bia de Carrucaria, assa gruke ki est in sa cotina [et] cludet.

112v 405. Parthit[ur]a. *De s[er]vos.*
Ego abbatissa Tedora ki ponio in ecustu co[n]dake parthim[en]tu d'omines ki fekit S[an]c[t]u Petru cu[n] S[an]c[t]u Nichola de Guthules. Intrait ad S[an]c[t]u Petru de Silchi Susanna, fiia de Petru Rosellu, et ad S[an]c[t]u Nichola intrait Comita, su frate; et ad S[an]c[t]u Petru intrait Janne, et ad S[an]c[t]u Nichola i[n]trait Bera; et issa fiia de Susa[n]na, Elene, remanet ad cumone.

406. Parthit[ur]a. *De s[er]vos.*
Parthivim[us] fiios de Comita Rosellu: S[an]c[t]u Petru levait ad Gantine et S[an]c[t]u Nichola levait ad Petru, S[an]c[t]u Petru levait ad Muscu et S[an]c[t]u Nicola leva[i]t ad Juva[n]ne, S[an]c[t]u Petru levait ad Mariane [et] S[an]c[t]u Nichola levait ad Bera. T[es]t[e]s: homines ki vi furun uve parthivim[us], p[re]vit[er]u Juva[n]ne Mastinu [et] Petru de serra su de Silki, et Deodatu Corsu, ispitaleri de S[an]c[t]u Blasiu, et Bonaventura, su de Guthule, et Gunnari de Varda, su de Guthule, et p[re]vit[er]u Gantine Pianu d[e] Guthule, cu[n] ken parthiamus. Testes.

407. *De s[er]vos.*
[P]arthivim[us][78] homines cu[n] su priore de S[an]c[t]u Nichola de Guthules
113r donnu Floccu, | fiios de Jacubu Batkillu, servu de S[an]c[t]u Nichola, et de Susanna Vacca, ankilla de S[an]c[t]u Petru; appit S[an]c[t]u Petru a Sardinia et a Maria et a Petru; et intrarun ad S[an]c[t]u Nichola Olisave [et] Ithoccor et

78 Change of hand.

404. Delimitation of the unworked land (*saltu*) of Iscolca de Silchy at Cherki. This is the boundary of the unworked land (*saltu*) that lady Maria de Serra gave to Sanctu Petru, with the consent of her husband, and which we have in common with [the diocese of] Bosa: [the boundary is] from the cross (*bruke*) we have in the road, then it goes steeply down the road of Carru, and descends along the road towards the boundary of Bruke—which we share with the [the diocese of] Gisarclu (Bisarcio)—then towards Iscala Lansinosa ('slippery slope'), then it turns towards Gruke dessu Gisterru ('the cross of the Gisterru'); from Gruke dessu Gisterru to Petras Clopatas ('the dolmens') of Monte de Keias ('Keias hill'), then, from Monte de Keias to where Puthancaru Mannu ('the great bog') crosses the valley, which is in Matta Manna ('the great *macchia*'), and from Puthancaru it continues along the cliff to the border of the threshing floor on the right, and goes towards the cross that marks the limit of the land of [the diocese of] Bosa and that of Sancta Maria; then it returns to Bulbare dessa Ficu ('the livestock pen of the fig tree') and ends as it reaches the road of Carrucaria at the cross that is at sa Cotina ('the rock'), and [the boundary] closes.

405. Division. *Of servants.*
I, abbess Tedora, put in this condaghe the division (*parthimentu*) of men (*omines*) that Sanctu Petru made with Sanctu Nichola de Guthules (Buttule, Ozieri). Susanna, daughter of Petru Rosellu, was conceded to Sanctu Petru, and her brother Comita was given to Sanctu Nichola. Also, Janne was given to Sanctu Petru, Bera was given to Sanctu Petru. Elene, the daughter of Susanna, remains in common.

406. Division. *Of servants.*
We divided the sons of Comita Rosellu: Sanctu Petru took Gantine; Sanctu Nichola took Petru; Sanctu Petru took Muscu; Sanctu Nichola took Juvanne; Sanctu Petru took Mariane, and Sanctu Nichola took Bera. Witnesses: the men who were there when we made the division: priest Juvanne Mastinu; Petru de Serra from Silki; Deodatu Corsu, hospitaller (*ispitaleri*) from Sanctu Blasiu (San Biagio, Sassari); Bonaventura from Guthule (Buttule, Ozieri); Gunnari de Varda from Guthule, and priest Gantine Pianu de Guthule, with whom we made the division. Witnesses.

407. *Of servants*
We made division of men (*homines*) with the prior of Sanctu Nichola di Guthules (Buttule, Ozieri), lord Floccu: the children of Iacobu Batkillu, servant (*servu*) of Sanctu Nichola, and of Susanna Vacca, female servant (*ankilla*) of Sanctu Petru. Sanctu Petru received Sardinia, Maria, and Petru; Sanctu Nichola

Furatu. T[es]t[e]s: Petru de Serra, su de Silki, et Gunnari Capitha et Barusone de Campu et Gantine de Montes et Mariane Pinna et Ithoccor Grecu et Juvanne Trampas, armentariu de Silki. T[es]t[e]s.

408.[79] *De s[er]vos.*
Ego abatissa Tedora, abatissa de Silki. Canbiai cun su priore de Seve Paganellu, cun boluntate de iudike Comita; ego li dei ad isse ad Jorgia Thana cun fiios ki ait aver factos cun su servu de Seve et ait faker dave tando inna[n]ti, et feminas et masclos cun parthone sua, et isse deitimi a mimi a Maria Tamuri, fiia de Ithoccor Tamuri et fiia de Muscu Mugra, cun fiios ki ait aver factos et ait faker dave tando innanti, et feminas et masclos cun parthone sua; et beninde ki 'nde
113v kertaret neunu donnu ki vi ait in sa domo de Seve, o acteru | homine pro Seve, pro custu kanbiu ki amus factu unpare, d'aversinde bene dessa domo d'Usune S[an]c[t]u Petru de Silki, cun onnia cantu se mandicat appus sa domo d'Usune, ki est appus Seve. Test[e]s uve fekimus custu canbiu et ecustu accordu: judike Comita et Petru d'Athen et Gos[antine] de serra et Mariane de Itil. Test[e]s.

409. *De s[er]vis.*
Ego Ogulinu dessa Rocca, p[ri]ore de Silki, ki ponio in ecustu co[n]dake. Kertaitimi su priore de Seve Marcualdu in corona de iudike Mariane in Kerki [sa die] de sinotu, et naraitimi ka 'a Maria Tamuri et assos fiios et assas fiias proitteu lo[s] levas a S[an]c[t]a Maria de Seve, ki ti los aviat postos a pinnos Paganellu pro XII bisantis? Boioti torrare sos bis[antis], et torra sos homines a S[an]c[t]a Maria de Seve.' Et ego naraili ka 'custos homines p[ro]unde mi kertas a ppecuiare furun kanbiatos;' et isse naraitimi ka 'no los havian kanbiatos a
114r pecuiare, in | co naras;' et ego naraili ka 'emmo!' Iudicarunimi a batture ego destimonios ka los kanbiarun a pecuiare, et battussi destimonios et iurarun ka los avian kanbiatos a pecuiare; et deru[ni]mi iura, et iurai et binki. Test[e]s in cuia corona binki: iudike Mariane et homines de corona, do[n]nu Pet[ru] Pinna et do[n]nu Co[mita] de Gunale et Jelardinu Furru et Ithoccor de Kerki.

410.
Ego[80] apatissa Tedora ki ponio in ecustu condake accordiu ki feki dessu fundam[en]tu depus sa domo de Cotronianu de S[an]c[t]u Pet[ru] de Silki, ki

79 Change of hand.
80 Change of hand.

received Olisave, Ithoccor, and Furatu. Witnesses: Petru de Serra from Silki, Gunnari Capitha, Barusone de Campu, Gantine de Montes, Mariane Pinna, Ithoccor Grecu, and Juvanne Trampas, administrator (*armentariu*) of Silki. Witnesses.

408. *Of servants.*
I, abbess Tedora, abbess of Silki. I made an exchange with Paganellu, the prior of Seve (Santa Maria di Cea), with the consent of iudike Comita. I gave him Jorgia Thana with the children she had had with a servant (*servu*) of Seve and any [others] she might have from then on, either females or males, with their share. He gave me Maria Tamuri, daughter of Ithoccor Tamuri and Muscu Mugra, with the children she had and those she would have thereafter, females and males, with their share. If the lord of the farm complex (*domo*) of Seve, or anyone else on behalf of Seve, intends to sue for this exchange that we have concluded, let Sanctu Petru de Silki enjoy the goods of the farmstead (*domo*) of Usune (Usini) with all that can be used at the farmstead (*domo*) of Usune (Usini) which is at Seve. Witnesses who were present when we made this exchange and this agreement (*accordu*): iudike Comita, Petru d'Athen, Gosantine de Serra, and Mariane de Itil. Witnesses.

409. *Of servants.*
I, Ogulinu dessa Rocca, prior of Silki, note in this condaghe [that] Marcualdu, the prior of Seve (Santa Maria di Cea) sued me at a hearing (*corona*) of iudike Mariane at Kerki on the day of the assembly and said to me, 'why do you take away Maria Tamuri with her sons and daughters from Sancta Maria di Seve when Paganellu had given as security (*a pinnas*) to you for twelve bezants (*bisantis*)? I want to return the bezants to you, and you return the servants (*homines*) to Sancta Maria de Seve!' I then replied that 'these servants over whom you are suing me were exchanged as our property!' He replied that 'they were not exchanged as your property (*a pecuiare*), as you say!' I then replied: 'they certainly were!' They decided that I bring forth witnesses to attest that I exchanged them as our property. I brought witnesses and they swore that they had been exchanged as our property. They had me take an oath; I swore and I won [the case]. Witnesses at whose hearing (*corona*) I won: iudike Mariane and the men of the hearing (*homines de corona*), lord Petru Pinna, lord Comita de Gunale, Ielardinu Furru, and Ithoccor de Kerki.

410.
I, abbess Tedora, register in this condaghe the agreement that I made regarding the property (*fundamentu*) at the farm complex (*domo*) of Cotronianu (Codrongianos) belonging to Sanctu Petru de Silki, which lord Saltaro de Ker-

aviat levatu donnu Saltaro de Kerchi; et nois andaimus ad corona de donnu Gant[ine] d'Ena, ki fuit curatore de Fiulinas, pro kertarendeli pro custu fundamentu de S[an]c[t]u Pet[ru], a donnu Saltaro de Kerchi, ca lu keriat isse p[ro] suo pecuiare. Et sende andatos ad Cotronianu, ad corona de donnu Gant[ine] d'Ena, ki fuit curatore de Fiulinas pro kertarendeli, plachit a donnu Saltaro de
114v Cherchi accordare | sende cun sos donnos kene kertu neunu, in custa rethone de aversi S[an]c[t]u Pe[tru] su suo, et donnu Saltaro de Cherchi su suo; ponendelu donnu Saltaro de Kerki in boluntate dessu curatore [et] dessos acteros liveros ki vi furun in corona, et cun boluntate de do[n]nu Gant[ine] Arrivacha, ki 'nde fuit do[n]nu [et] balivile dessa domo de S[an]c[t]u Pet[ru] de Silchi, pro accordarelos appare, [et] pro andare issos ave term[en] in termen, et aversi S[an]c[t]u Pet[ru] su suo, et donnu Saltaro su suo. Et issos andarun dave t[er]men in t[er]men, dessu de S[an]c[t]u Pet[ru] de Silchi, [et] andarun assu de do[n]nu Saltaro dave t[er]men in term[en], et derun ad S[an]c[t]u Petru su suo, [et] a donnu Saltaro su suo. Et plachit assos donnos dessa domo de Sanctu Petru custu adcordiu ki fakian custos ki vi furun cun su curatore, [et] a donnu Saltaro plachit at[er]u tale. Custu accordiu fuit factu anbas partes a boluntate de pare, sa die de S[an]c[t]u Bartholumeu. Et si se isgiravat do[n]nu Saltaro de
115r Kerchi de custu accordiu e 'nde | kertavat per neunu tempus, o isse, ho homine pro'sse, in pena de donnia cantu aviat. T[es]t[e]s: donnu Gant[ine] d'Ena, curatore de Figulinas, et donnu Gun[na]r[i] Seta, plovanu d'Uricke, et donnu Jenuariu, clericu dessu curatore, [et] do[n]nu Pet[ru] Coke [et] do[n]nu Pet[ru] de Kerchi et do[n]nu Manuelle de Fenu [et] donnu Mar[ia]n[e] d'Athen [et] do[n]nu Gitilesu de Varru, et servos dessa domo, Petru Unchinu ma[n]nu ki acterminavat, et Furatu Cuccu et Petru Pelle, arm[en]tariu depus sa domo de Cotronianu. T[es]t[e]s.

411.[81]

Ego[82] abbatissa P[re]thiosa qui fatho recordu dessu kertu q[ui] mi fechit Saltaro de Nuketu. Kertaitimi p[ro]ssu terraticu toctu q[ui] e[st] supta corte dessos Unchinos, in corona de messer Co[n]radu T[ri]nchis, q[ui] fuit vicariu p[ro]ssu rege in su re[n]nu de Locudore. [Et] ad kertu cale mi '[n]de fekit de lu vi[n]chi. [Et] si mi '[n]de kertavat p[er] neunu te[m]p[us] dessu mu[n]du, pacare assu re[n]nu bis[antis] c. Test[e]s: donnu Gant[ine] Pin[n]a Pisanu [et] do[n]nu Gant[ine] d'Ena et donnu Marruffu Pinna, priore de S[an]c[t]u Petru, et donnu Comita Co[r]da et do[n]nu Petru [...].[83]

81 Duplicated in entry 438.

82 Change of hand.

83 This gap of two or three words is caused by an abrasion of the parchment.

chi had taken. We went to a hearing (*corona*) of lord Gantine d'Ena, *curatore* of Figulinas, to sue lord Saltaro de Kerchi over this property (*fundamentu*) of Sanctu Petru, which he claimed to hold as his own (*pecuiare*). However, once we went to Cotronianu, to the hearing (*corona*) of lord Gantine d'Ena, *curatore* of Figulinas, to conduct the dispute, lord Saltaro de Cherchi agreed to reach a settlement (*accordare*) with the lords, without any dispute, with the condition that Sanctu Petru and he himself each had what they were entitled to, placing themselves in the hands of the *curatore* and of the other freemen (*liveros*) present at the hearing (*corona*), and with the consent of lord Gantine Arrivacha, lord and bailiff (*balivile*) of the church (*domo*) of Sanctu Petru de Silki. Thus, they agreed among themselves so that Sanctu Petru and lord Saltaro each had what they were entitled to. They went from boundary to boundary at Sanctu Petru de Silchi, and then went from boundary to boundary [on the land] of lord Saltaro, and gave Sanctu Petru and lord Saltaro what they were entitled to. This agreement, which those who went with the *curatore* made, pleased the lords of the church of Sanctu Petru, just as it pleased lord Saltaro. The agreement was made with the consent of both parties on the [feast] day of St Bartholomew, with the condition that, if one day lord Saltaro de Kerchi or others for him rejected it and sues, then he would have to give all this as a penalty. Witnesses: lord Gantine d'Ena, *curatore* de Figulinas; lord Gunnari Seta, parson (*plovanu*) of Uricke; lord Jenuariu, cleric (*clericu*) of the *curatore*; lord Petru Coke; lord Petru de Kerchi; lord Manuelle de Fenu; lord Mariane d'Athen; lord Gitilesu de Varru; and the servants (*servos*) of the farmstead (*domo*); Petru Unchinu Mannu ('the elder'), who made the delimitation; Furatu Cuccu, and Petru Pelle, administrator (*armentariu*) of the farm complex (*domo*) at Cotronianu (Codrongianos). Witnesses.

411.
I, abbess Prethiosa, make a record (*fatho recordu*) of the dispute that Saltaro de Nuketu brought against me. He sued me at a hearing (*corona*) of sir (*messer*) Conradu Trinchis, deputy of the king (*vicariu prossu rege*) in the realm (*rennu*) of Locudore (Logudoro) over the workable land (*terraticu*) that is in the farmyard (*corte*) of the Unchinos [family]. I defeated him in the dispute he brought against me, and if, at any future time, he sues me, he will have to pay the realm (*rennu*) a penalty of one hundred bezants (*bisantis*). Witnesses: lord Gantine Pinna Pisanu; lord Gantine o d'Ena; lord Marruffu Pinna, prior of Sanctu Petru; lord Comita Corda; lord Petru [de Cressente, and lord Gantine Pinna Kinfaiu. Witnesses.]

115v 412.

[...] monticlu[84] de Casula. Et collat a ddestra de matta de Plave, derettu ad su sueriu de mesa via, chi vaen sos de Vanios ad Arave, derettu ad sa petra longa. Testes: Mariane de Cannas [et] do[n]nu Petru d'Athen, cum ken aviamus su saltu, et Comita de Itin d'Arthacan et Comita Vardane. Testes.

413.

Ego Gantine Trampas chi vo[ca]i terra et tenni in sa Concha de S[an]c[t]a Maria de vulvare de Tamuri pro donnicu meu. Et est t[er]men de custa t[er]ra: dave sos forkillos dessa via ki vaen de Gutturale a destra de vulvare de Tamuri, et essit a bia de Grecos, et girat ad manka tottuve via maiore, et clompet ass'orvitu chi collat dave Torricla a destra dessa Concha assos forchillos dessa via ki venin de Gutturale; custa tenni et bocai pro donnichu meu, pro Santa Maria.

414.

Kertaitimi Dorveni de Carvia pro custa terra, ca naravat ca l'aviat tenta isse inna[n]ti meu, in corona de donnu Ithoc[or] d'Athen.[85] Et ego binkindelu ca l'avia tenta ego innanti suo. Testes in cuia corona binki: donnu Ithoc[or] d'Athen et donnu Ithoc[or] Vardane et do[n]nu Pet[ru de Thori Murclu]. Testes.

116r 415.

Kertaitimi Comita Caprinu prossa t[er]ra mia dessa conca de S[an]c[t]a Maria, et binkitindelu Comita de Campu, chi fuit kertatore meu, in corona de donnu Barusone de Murtas. Testes: donnu Comita de Carvia, su p[re]viteru dessa villa, et Comita de Thori et issu frate. Testes.

416.

Ego[86] Gavini Taras, arm[en]tariu pro S[an]c[t]u Pet[ru] de Silki in sa domo d'Ulumetu. Conporai pro donnicu meu a Pet[ru] de Mocor Pithinnu, fiiu de Furatu de Mocor, sa parte sua dessa corte in co vi l'aviat, t[er]men ad sa de S[an]c[t]u Pet[ru], cum dandemi tottu su campu dessa corte et cum sa matta dessa ficu; campaniandese Pet[ru] de Mocor cum sa sorre, pro dareli sa sorre a Pet[ru] sa parte canta vi aviat, Bittoria, in ecusta corte, chi davat Pet[ru] a S[an]c[t]u Petru de Silki; dandeli Pet[ru] a Bittoria, pro custu chi li davat,

84 Change of hand. The seven lines transcribed at the beginning of f. 115v form the final portion of entry 19, to which they have been restored.

85 The following four lines in the manuscript are largely illegible. The readings here are taken from G. Bonazzi, ed., *Condaghe di San Pietro di Silki* (Cagliari, 1900), p. 115.

86 Change of hand.

412.[87]
[…] Monticlu de Casula ('hill of Casula') and passes on the right of Matta de Plave ('*macchia* of Ploaghe'), straight towards to the cork oak half way along the road that goes from Vanios to Arave, to Petra Longa ('long rock'). Witnesses: Mariane de Cannas; lord Petru d'Athen, with whom we hold the unworked land (*saltu*); Comita de Itin d'Arthacan; and Comita Vardane. Witnesses.

413.
I, Gantine Trampas, retook and held land at Concha ('the vale') of Sancta Maria, [namely] the livestock enclosure (*vulvare*) at Tamuri as part of my domain (*donnicu*). The boundary of this land [is] from the fork in the road that goes from Gutturale to the right of the enclosure at Tamuri, then it takes Bia de Grecos ('road of the Greeks'), and turns to the left along the main road, then reaches the track that passes from Torricla (Torrija) to the right of Concha, to the fork in the road that comes from Gutturale. I held and took possession of this as part of my domain (*donnichu*) for the church of Sancta Maria.

414.
Dorveni de Carvia sued me over that land that he said he held before I did at a hearing (*corona*) of lord Ithoccor d'Athen. I defeated him because I had held it before him. Witnesses at whose hearing (*corona*) I won: lord Ithocor d'Athen, lord Ithocor Vardane, and lord Pet[ru de Thori Murclu]. Witnesses.

415.
Comita Caprinu sued me over my land at Conca de Sancta Maria; Comita de Campu, who was my legal counsel (*kertatore*), defeated him at a hearing (*corona*) of lord Barusone de Murtas. Witnesses: lord Comita de Carvia, priest of the village, and Comita de Thori, and his brother. Witnesses.

416.
I, Gavini Taras, administrator (*armentariu*) of Sanctu Petru de Silki at the farm complex (*domo*) of Ulumetu (Olmedo), bought for my domain (*pro donnicu meu*) from Petru de Mocor Pithinnu ('the young'), son of Furatu de Mocor, his part of the farmyard (*corte*), the boundary of which is that of Sanctu Petru, giving me all the field and Matta dessa Ficu ('*macchia* of the fig tree'). Petru de Mocor agreed with his sister to give him the share that she, Bittoria, held in the same farmyard which Petru gave to Sanctu Petru. In exchange, Petru gave Bitto-

87 Continuation of 19.

su latus dessa domo chi avian anbos ad cumone. Et ego deindeli unu boe [et] una bisantata d'oriu. Testes: donnu Mar[iane] de Thori, su p[re]viter[u], [et] Ithoc[or] de Mocor et Grispiiu et Ithoc[or] Morrochu et Ju[a]n[n]e Virde. Testes.

417.
Conporai a Ithoc[or] Virde Capillu, pro donnicu meu, sa parte sua dessa terra ki aviat, t[er]men ass'intratoria dessa porta de corte donnica mia, q[ui] fuit I
116v fuste de virga, cum bolu[n]tate dessu do[n]nu suo, | et ego deindeli d[ina]r[is] XII. Testes: Ithoc[or] de Mocor et donnu Mariane de Thori su previteru, et Gun[nari] de serra et Ithoc[or] Morrochu et Juan[n]e de Nurra.

418.
Ego[88] abatissa Tedora qui ponio in condake sa terra qui poserunt ad S[an]c[t]a Maria d'Usune pross'anima sua Granuciu Catha: deit sa terra dessu Muteclariu, [et] est termen de custa terra assa dessu Ispitale, et termen ad sa de Padules, et termen ad sa dessos de Martis, dessu planu dess'ariola. T[es]t[e]s: su p[re]viteru dessa villa, donnu Comita Pinna, et Comita de Campu de serra et Comita de Thori. T[es]t[e]s.

419.
Posit Comita de Martis, p[ro]ss'anima sua, ad S[an]c[t]a Maria d'Usune dessa terra sua de monticlu de Dominike su latus. T[es]t[e]s: Comita de Campu [et] Granuciu Catha et Comita de serra Pirastru. T[es]t[e]s.

420. *Cotro[n]ianu[m]*.
Ego abatissa Tedora qui ponio in ecustu condake su qui conporai ad do[n]na Gitta de Kerqui. Conporaili ad donna Gitta de Kerqui sa parthone sua canta vi aviat in Cotronianu: et domos et binias [et] cortes, et cannavarios et terras
117r et saltos, in co vi l'aviat. | Et est terra sa de Clusuras, qui est t[er]men assa de donnu Pet[ru] Coke, et assa terra qui parthiv[it] do[n]nu Petru de Kerqui cum sos nepotes. Et est term[en] ad sa de donnu Petru de Maroniu et issa lintha de Campu qui est term[en] ad sa de do[n]nu Pet[ru] Coke, et issu latus dessa terra de planu de kersas; et issa terra qui est in billa, in sas ariolas, qui est term[en] ave terra secata in terra secata; et issa parte sua de balle Gotoi, et issa parte sua dessas terras de Gurellu, et issa parte sua dessu saltu de Lecte, et de VII partes una dessu saltu d'Ala de Gunnannor; et issa parte sua dessa t[er]ra de serra de

88 Change of hand.

ria half (*latus*) the farm (*domo*) they held in common. I gave him an ox and one bezant (*bisantata*) of barley. Witnesses: lord Mariane de Thori, the priest; Ithoccor de Mocor; Grispiiu; Ithoccor Morrocchu, and Juvanne Virde. Witnesses.

417.
I bought from Ithocor Virde Capillu, for my domain (*donnicu*), his share of the land he had. The boundary [is at] the entrance (*intratoria*) at the gate (*porta*) of the farmyard (*corte*) of my domain, which was one pole-length (*fuste de virga*), with the consent of his lord. I gave him twelve coins (*dinaris*). Witnesses: Ithoccor de Mocor; lord Mariano de Thori, the priest; Gunnari de Serra; Ithoccor Morrocchu, and Juvanne de Nurra.

418.
I, abbess Tedora, note in the condaghe the land that Granuciu Catha gave to the church of Sancta Maria d'Usune (Usini) for [the salvation of] his soul. He granted the land (*terra*) at su Muteclariu. The boundary is with the land of the hospital (*ispitale*); [another] boundary is that of Padules (Santa Maria di Paulis, Ittiri), and [another] boundary is that of the land of the De Martis [family] which is in Planu dess'Ariola ('the plain of Ariola/the threshing floor'). Witnesses: the village priest (*previteru dessa villa*), lord Comita Pinna; Comita de Campu de Serra, and Comita de Thori. Witnesses.

419.
Comita de Martis donated half (*latus*) of his land on Monticlu de Dominike ('Dominike hill') to Sancta Maria d'Usune (Usini) for his soul. Witnesses: Comita de Campu, Granuciu Catha, and Comita de Serra Pirastru. Witnesses.

420. *Cotroianum*.
I, abbess Tedora, put in this condaghe that which I bought from lady Gitta de Kerqui. I bought from lady Gitta de Kerqui what she had in Cotronianu (Codrongianos): farmsteads (*domos*), vineyards, farmyards (*cortes*), hemp fields (*cannavarios*), lands and unworked lands (*saltos*), wherever she had them: the land (*terra*) of Clusuras, which borders with that of lord Petru Coke; the land that lord Petru de Kerqui shared with his nephews (*nepotes*) and with that of lord Petru de Maroniu; the strip of land (*sa lintha*) at Campu which borders with that of lord Petru Coke; half (*latus*) of the land of Planu de Kersas ('mastic trees') and the land that is in the village near sas Ariolas ('the threshing floors'), and which is between alienated lands; her part of Balle Gotoi ('Gotoi valley'); her part the lands of Gurellu; her share of the land (*saltu*) of Lecte (Lette, Codrongianos); a seventh part of the land (*saltu*) of Ala de Gunnannor;

chercos, et issa parte sua dessu cannavariu de Ponte, et issa parte sua dessa vinia de balle; et ficu, et mela, et nuke et o[mn]ia fructora canta vi aviat in Cotronianu. Et ego deindeli bis[antis] XI. T[e]st[e]s: donnu Petru de Kerqui, et donnu Petru de Maroniu et Furatu Pinna et donnu Maniuelle de Fenu et donnu Mariane d'Athen et donnu Maniuelle Coke et issu fiiu de donna Gitta. T[e]st[e]s et donnu Saltaro de Kerqui. T[e]st[e]s.

117v 421.

Ego[89] Pet[ru] de Muru, p[ri]ore de S[an]c[t]u Pet[ru] de Silchi, qui po[n]io in ecustu condake ka kertait mecu P[re]nake, su nepote de do[n]na Justa de Cleu, sendeke apatissa Tedora in Nascar, in corona de do[n]nu Com[ita] Porcu in Bosove, cum bolu[n]tate de tottu sos nepotes de do[n]na Justa de Cleu [et] dessas nectas, pone[n]devilu toctu sos ca[n]tos vi kerian parte in su de do[n]na Justa de Cleu ad kertare p[ro]'ssos, ca 'p[ro]itteu nos levas sa vinia ki aviat in Turthevi, q[ui] fuit de do[n]na Justa de Cleu, thia n[ost]ra, [et] issas domos cu[n] sa corte de Thathari?' Et ego naraili: 'do[n]na Justa de Cleu la posit, [et] domos [et] binias et corte, cando se cu[m]bersait ad S[an]c[t]u Pet[ru] de Silchi, p[ro] averla S[an]c[t]u Pet[ru] pus morte sua.' Et issos narru[n]imi, ca 'no[n] bi posit ad S[an]c[t]u Pet[ru] ne[n] domos, ne[n] corte, ne[n] bi[n]ias in co naras.' Et ego naraili ca 'e[m]mo [c]a bi la posit, [et] corte [et] domos [et] binia, p[ro] averla S[an]c[t]u Pet[ru] pus morte sua.' Judicar[un] ad mi[mi] a destimo[n]ios ca vi la posit sas domos cu[n] sa corte [et] issa vi[n]ia ki fuit sucta sa villa de T[ur]thevi, dave sa de Ga[n]t[ine] Murmusi in iosso [et] dave sa de Pet[ru] de S[er]ra in susu. Et ego battussi destimo[n]ios, [et] iuraru[n] ca aviat postu ad S[an]c[t]u Pet[ru] de Silchi sas domos cu[n] sa corte [et] cu[n] sa
118r vi[n]ia, p[ro] averla adp[us] | morte sua. Deru[ni]mi iura ad mimi factu dessos destimo[n]ios de S[an]c[t]u Pet[ru], [et] binki, ca li aviat postu pus morte sua binia [et] domos [et] corte. T[e]st[e]s in cuia corona binki: do[n]nu Com[ita] Porcu, curatore de Roma[n]ia, et ho[m]i[n]es de corona: Ith[oc]or de Thori, su d'Innoviu, [et] Pet[ru] de S[er]ra, su d'Eristala, et Alip[er]tinu Salari et Granuciu Ligaste et Bortholu de S[er]ra, su de Silchi. T[es]t[e]s.

422.

Ego abatissa Tedora. Conp[or]aili ad Nicola Mutu sa t[er]ra de Thergenianos tocta in co vi la aviat. Est t[er]men dave sa de Silchi, parthinde de pare cu[n] do[n]na Gasia, et clompet a domo de do[n]na Tedora, [et] collat toctue sa via ad S[an]c[t]u Gregori; girat toctue sa t[er]ra de S[an]c[t]u Gregori, [et]

89 Change of hand.

her part of the land of Serra de Chercos; the part of Cannavariu de Ponte ('hemp field at the bridge'); her part the vineyard of the valley; and the figs, apple trees, walnut trees and all the fruit trees that she had at Cotronianu (Codrongianos). I gave her eleven bezants (*bisantis*). Witnesses: lord Petru de Kerqui, lord Petru de Maroniu, Furatu Pinna, lord Maniuelle de Fenu, lord Mariaeo d'Athen, lord Maniuelle Coke, and the son of lady Gitta. Witness: lord Saltaro de Kerqui. Witnesses.

421.

I, Petru de Muru, prior of Sanctu Petru de Silchi, put in this condaghe that Prenake, the nephew (*nipote*) of lady Justa de Cleu, sued me at a hearing (*corona*) of lord Comita Porcu at Bosove (Latte Dolce) with the consent of all the nephews (*nepotes*) and nieces (*nectas*) of lady Justa de Cleu when the abbess Tedora was at Nascar (Asca). All of them supposed to have a share (*parte*) of [the estate of] lady Justa de Cleu and asked: 'why are you taking the vineyard in Turthevi which belonged to lady Justa de Cleu, our aunt, and the farmsteads (*domos*) with farmyard (*corte*) at Thathari (Sassari)?' I replied: 'lady Justa de Cleu donated the farmsteads, the vineyards and the farmyard when she devoted herself (*cumbersare*) to Sanctu Petru de Silki, so that Sanctu Petru would have it upon her death!' They claimed that 'she did not donate anything to Sanctu Petru, neither farmsteads, nor farmyard, nor vines as you say!' I then replied: 'Certainly she donated the farmyard, the farms, and the vineyard so that Sanctu Petru could hold them after her death!' They decided that I bring forth witnesses to attest that she had donated the farms, the yard, and the vineyard which are below the village of Turthevi, below that of Gantine Murmusi, but above that of Petru de Serra. I brought forth witnesses, and they swore that lady Iusta de Cleu had given Sanctu Petru the farms, the yard, and the vineyard to hold after her death. After the witnesses of Sanctu Petru, had me take an oath and I won because after her death there was put in place [the donation of] the vineyard, farmsteadss (*domos*) and farmyard (*corte*). Witnesses at the hearing (*corona*) in which I won: lord Comita Porcu, *curatore* of Romangia, and the men of the hearing (*corona*): Ithocor de Thori from Innoviu, Petru de Serra from Eristala (San Giovanni, Sassari), Alipertinu Salari, Granucciu Ligaste, and Bortholo de Serra from Silki. Witnesses.

422.

I, abbess Tedora, bought from Nicola Mutu all the land of Thergenianos that he had. The boundary is from that of Silchi, dividing it in equally with [the land of] lady Gasia; it reaches the farm complex (*domo*) of lady Tedora and continues along the road to Sanctu Gregori, then it turns along the land of Sanctu Gregori

clompet assa de Silchi; davi[n]de girat toctue sa via, [et] clo[m]pet assa dessos fiios de do[n]nu Com[ita] de Liios, t[er]men ad issos, [et] t[er]men assa de fiios de do[n]nu Ith[oc]or d'Ardu, [et] term[en] assa de do[n]nu Mariane de Varru, jumpat bia [et] clompet assa de Silchi, [et] cludet. Et ego deindeli III lib[ras] de dinaris jenuinos, a bolu[n]tate dessa muiere [et] de Julianu su fiiu. T[es]t[e]s: p[re]vit[er]u Mariane de S[an]c[t]u Simpliki [et] ser Vivaldu de Bartolomeu, p[ri]ore de Silchi, [et] Bonaccorsu Paiti, clericu, et Gant[ine] de Liios [et] Gant[ine] Cachis et Gunnari d'Ardu. T[es]t[e]s.

118v 423.

Posit[90] do[n]nu Bosovechesu de Navithan Ma[n]nu, su de Guthule, ad S[an]c[t]u Pet[ru] de Silchi, p[ro]ssa a[n]i[m]a sua, dessu saltu d'Othicheor et de mo[n]te de Gruke, uve aviat isse, de III partes una, su latus dessa parte ki 'nde li intravat ad isse. Est t[er]men d'ecustu saltu dave gutur d'Olidone, [et] falat toctue via, derectu ad flum[en], falat toctue flum[en], assa corona d'Inglutti-theraccos; davinde falat toctue pus flum[en] assu pedale dessa corona de balle de Cupas, collat pus atha, derectu assu bru[n]cu dessa li[n]na alba, essit toctue pus atha, derectu assa corona Iackito[r]ia de corona de Curthu, essit toctue sa bia dave corona de Curthu, derectu assa bia grechisca, girat toctue bia grekisca, fin'ad guttur d'Olidone, [et] cludet. T[es]t[e]s: su p[re]vit[er]u de S[an]c[t]u Pet[ru] d'Usune, do[n]nu Furatu Cathari, et do[n]nu Ja[n]ne Siricu ma[n]nu et do[n]nu Saltaro de Gitil Ma[n]nu et do[n]nu Ithoc[or] d'Enticlas [et] do[n]nu Ithoc[or] d'Athen Mannu, fr[at]e de custa parthone. T[es]t[e]s.

424.

119r Ego Comita de Thori Leriane, d[e] Taverra, | et muiere mea Susa[n]na de Thori, necta de Dorgotori de Cherchi, su de Taverra, cum bolu[n]tate de fiios n[ost]ros, dam[us] a S[an]c[t]u Pet[ru] de Silchi sa parte n[ost]ra dessu saltu de Tetti de VI partes una. Term[en] de custu saltu: dave sa ficu de vulvares d'oiastru, et collat su riu de balle de mo[n]te, assu puthu de Domestica, et essit assa bia ki faken sos d'Ulumetu ad Ustine, ad funtana de gutti-guttiu, et benit ad macta de Bikio, et essit ad macta de suverios, term[en] assos d'Athen; et essit toctue bia ad co[n]tra Salomone, et ruclat sas cat[ri]clas assu Titimalu, et essit assos

90 Change of hand.

and reaches that of Silchi from where it turns along the road and reaches [the land of] the sons of lord Comita de Liios as a boundary; [the next] boundary is that of the sons of lord Ithoccor d'Ardu and [the next] boundary is that of lord Mariane de Varru; it crosses the road and returns to that of Silki, and closes. I gave him three pounds (*libras*) in Genoese coins (*dinaris Jenuinos*) with the consent of his wife and Julianu, his son. Witnesses: priest Mariane di Sanctu Simpliki; sir (*ser*) Vivaldu de Bartolomeu, prior of Silki; Bonaccorso Paiti, cleric (*clericu*); Gantine de Liios; Gantine Cachis, and Gunnari d'Ardu. Witnesses.

423.
Lord Bosovekesu de Navithan Mannu ('the elder') from Guthule (Buttule, Ozieri) donated to Sanctu Petru de Silchi for his soul, a third of the unworked land (*saltu*) of Othicheor on Monte de Gruke ('cross hill') where he has it, [equal to] half (*latus*) the share (*parte*) that belonged to him. The boundary of this land (*saltu*) is from Gutur d'Olidone ('path of Olidone') and it descends along the road towards the stream (*flumen*) and descends along the river to the hilltop (*sa corona*) of Inglutti-Theraccos; from there, it descends along the stream to the foot of Corona de Balle de Cupas ('hilltop on the valley of barrels'), and passes the cliff in the direction of Bruncu dessa Linna Alba ('the hill of the white timber'), and from the cliff it goes to Corona Iackitoria ('Iackitoria hilltop') at Corona de Curthu ('hilltop of Curthu'); it goes along the road from Corona de Curthu towards Bia Grekisca ('Greek road'), turns around Bia Grekisca towards Guttur d'Olidone ('the track d'Olidone'), and closes. Witnesses: the priest of Sanctu Petru d'Usune (Usini); lord Furatu Cathari; lord Ianne Siricu Mannu ('the elder'); lord Saltaro de Gitil Mannu ('the elder'); lord Ithoccor d'Enticlas; lord Ithoccor d'Athen Mannu ('the elder'), party to this division (*frate d'ecusta parthone*). Witnesses.

424.
I, Comita de Thori Leriane of Taverra (Taberra), and my wife Susanna de Thori, niece (*necta*) of Dorgotori de Cherchi from Taverra, with the consent of our children, give to Sanctu Petru de Silchi our part of the unworked land (*saltu*) of Tecti, equal to one-sixth [of it]. The boundary of this land is from the fig tree at the animal pens of Oiastru, it passes the stream of Balle de Monte ('valley of the hill'), [goes] towards Puthu de Domestica ('the well of the farmstead'), goes to the road they take from Ulumetu (Olmedo) to Usune (Usini), to Funtana de Gutti-Guttiu ('drip-drip spring'), and reaches Macta de Bikio ('*macchia* of Bikio'), then continues to Macta de Suverios ('*macchia* of the cork oaks'), the boundary [of which] is that of the d'Athen [family], and goes along the road opposite Salomone, then crosses the furrows (*catriclas*) of Titimalu ('euphor-

vulvares de mo[n]te de palmas, et falat a bia maiore, et cludet assa ficu d[e] vulvares d'Oiastru. T[es]t[e]s: do[n]nu Belardu Carbone, ki regiat corona p[ro]ssu vicariu, et messer Babillanu Doria, [et] Bandinu Pi[n]na Pisanu et do[n]nu Barusone Fancellu et do[n]nu Ga[n]t[ine] Pi[n]na, fiiu de do[n]nu Jelardinu Pisanu, et do[n]nu Gant[ine] d'Ena. T[es]t[e]s. Et p[ro] custu bene ki feker[un] issos ad S[an]c[t]u Pet[ru] de Silchi, p[ro]ssas animas issoro, si lis fekit gra[thia]
119v abatissa Tedora et deitilis una bacha biclata, | et I boe prossu saltu de Tecti.

425.[91] *Salto d'Urchone.*

Ego Comita de Thori Leriane, de Taverra, [et] muiere mia Susa[n]na de Thori, necta de Dorgotori de Cherchi, su de Taverra, cum boluntate de fiios n[ost]ros, damus ad S[an]c[t]u Pet[ru] de Silchi sa parte n[ost]ra dessu saltu d'Urcone, de VI partes una. Term[en] de custu saltu s'iscala de Vinia Ma[n]na, toctue bia maiore ki baen ad Ulumetu, fin'assu iu[m]pato[r]iu dessu riu de Serule; falat riu, et girat su sulcu su bruncu de Do[r]beni Crispu, et essit s'orbitu ad ena te[n]nera, et benit int[er] ambos vulvares de Gemellares, assa petra cop[er]clata, et ruclat s'ena sutta sas thi[n]nigas ad mo[n]ticlu de Do[r]gotori, ad mo[n]ticlu Settitoriu, assu mo[n]ticlu Giratu, collat s'atha de Usumen, et essit a bia, et to[r]rat assos furchillos dessa petra alba, et essit toctue bia ki faken sos de Save, fin'assa iscala de bi[n]ia ma[n]na, et cludet. T[es]t[e]s: do[n]nu Com[ita] de Thori Thipircu et do[n]nu Belardu Carbone, ki regiat corona p[ro]ssu vicariu, [et] ser Babillanu Doria et Bandinu Pi[n]na Pisanu
120r et do[n]nu Barusone Fancellu et | donnu Gant[ine] Pi[n]na, fiiu de do[n]nu Jelardinu Pisanu, et do[n]nu Gant[ine] d'Ena. T[es]t[e]s. Et p[ro] custu bene ki feker[un] a S[an]c[t]u Petru, isse [et] issa muiere p[ro]ssas a[n]i[m]as issoro, si 'nde lis fekit grathia apatissa Tedora, et deitindelis in dinaris XXVI sollos.

426.

Ego Pet[ru] de Serra, ki me co[m]berso ad S[an]c[t]u Petru de Silchi et dovi assa domo, p[ro] Deu i[n]na[n]ti et p[ro]ssa anima mia, sa t[er]ra mia de petra lata, ki fui de S[an]c[t]u Petru inanti, ki e[st] t[er]men assa de do[n]nu Graneri Casu et t[er]men assa de S[an]c[t]u Pet[ru]. Et issa do[n]na sa apatissa si mi aet s[er]vire assa anima mia de kera et de tima[n]gia, et dessas casas ki vi aet esser opus, assu VII et[92] assu XXXmu, XLmu [die] et anniv[er]sariu, o[mn]i a[n]nu mitte[n]deme in parte de om[n]ia officiu issoro sa do[n]na et issas manacas

91 Cf. entry 443.

92 Manuscript reads *at*.

bia plant'), then continues to the pens on Monte de Palmas ('palms' hill'), and descends to the main road, then closes at the fig tree of the pens at Oiastru. Witnesses: lord Belardo Carbone, who presided over the hearing (*corona*) as deputy (*prossu vicariu*); sir (*messer*) Babillanu Doria, Bandino Pinna Pisanu; lord Barusone Fancellu; lord Gantine Pinna, son of lord Ielardinu Pisanu, and lord Gantine d'Ena. Witnesses. Because of the benefice that they had given to Sanctu Petru de Silchi for their souls, abbess Tedora gave them a cow with her litter and an ox as a token of her gratitude for the land (*saltu*) of Tecti.

425. *Unworked land* (salto) *at Urchone.*
I, Comita de Thori Leriane de Taverra (Taberra), and my wife Susanna de Thori, niece (*necta*) of Dorgotori de Cherchi from Taverra, with the consent of our children, give to Sanctu Petru de Silchi our share (*parte*) of one-sixth of the unworked land (*saltu*) of Urcone (Arcone). The boundary of this land (*saltu*) starts from Iscala de Vinia Manna ('the hillside of the big vineyard', Vigna Grande), [it goes] along the main road that leads to Ulumetu (Olmedo), up to the crossing of Riu de Serule ('Serule river'), goes down the river and turns towards Sulcu Bruncu ('the furrow on the hill') of Dorbeni Crispu; it continues on the path to Ena Tennera ('soft spring'), goes between the two animal pens (*vulvares*) of Gemellares, to Petra Coperclata ('the dolmen'), crosses the spring below the reeds (*sas thinnigas*), to Monticlu de Dorgotori ('hill of Dorgotori'), to Monticlu Settitoriu ('Settitoriu hill'), and to Monticlu Giratu ('the turned hill'), and passes s'Atha de Usumen ('the cliff of Usumen'), then takes the road and turns at the fork of Petra Alba ('white rock'), goes along the road they take from Save (Pala Santa Caterina) until Iscala de Binia Manna, and closes. Witnesses: lord Comita de Thori Thipircu; lord Belardu Carbone, who presided over (*regiat*) the hearing (*corona*) as his deputy (*prossu vicariu*); sir (*ser*) Babillanu Doria; Bandinu Pinna Pisanu; lord Barusone Fancellu; lord Gantine Pinna, son of lord Jelardinu Pisanu; and lord Gantine d'Ena. And for this benefice they made to Sanctu Petru, both he and his wife for their souls, abbess Tedora gave them twenty-six soldi (*sollos*) in coin (*in dinaris*).

426.
I, Petru de Serra, devote myself to (*comberso*) Sanctu Petru de Silchi, and I give to that church (*domo*) for God and for my soul, my land in Petra Lata which belonged to Sanctu Petru before, the boundary of which is that of lord Graneri Casu and that of Sanctu Petru itself. May the lady abbess offer candles and incense (*timangia*) in service of my soul, and whatever else will be needed, on the seventh, thirtieth and fortieth day from my death, and on the anniversary every year, the abbess and all the nuns will remember me at each of their func-

toctu. Et ecustu do p[ro] appatinde p[ro]de S[an]c[t]u Petru, [et] i[n] morte et in bita. T[es]t[e]s: Com[ita] Vathis et Gant[ine] de S[er]ra [et] Gun[nari] de serra [et] Gant[ine] Tha[n]ca et p[re]vit[er]u Mariane et issu p[re]vit[er]u de Silchi do[n]nu Pet[ru] Gattone, et Gun[na]r[i] de Carvia. T[es]t[e]s.

427.
Ego[93] appatissa Tedora de sSilchi qui fatho coiuvanthia dessu servu[m]
120v meu[m] Furatu Quoquone qum Elene Carta, anquilla | de S[an]c[t]u Palu, [et] ecusta quoiuvanthia fatho qu[m] bolu[n]tate de Salinbene, qui fuit biquaniu[m] de Trullas, pro parthire unpare su fetu S[an]c[t]u Petru cun S[an]c[t]u Palu, latus appare. Tes[tes]: su prev[i]teru de Quotronianu Iosso, donnu Gantine de Mularia, in cuia manu se fekit, et Mariane d'Athen et Benedicte de Liios et Comita Sanna. Tes[tes].

428. *Cotro[n]janu[m]*.
Conporaili ad Saltaro de Querqui sa terra sua de planu de vulvare, et ego deindeli unu boe in v bis[antis], et bis[antis] I in d[ina]r[is], et I berbeke. Tes[tes]: su p[re]viteru do[n]nu Gantine de Mularia et do[n]nu Petru Quoque et donnu Petru de Querqui. Tes[tes].

429.
Conporaili[94] a donnu Petru d'Erisa, su de Chelemule, sa vinea sua qui aviat in Garulatho, cu[n] fructura ca[n]ta vi aviat intro, et e[st] tenende assa de Juva[n]ne Murtinu, et hecustu mi vendit cu[n] plakim[en]tu dessos fr[ate]s dessa parthone, et ego deindeli bis[antis] VIII T[este]s: do[n]nu Clem[en]ti, p[re]viteru, et do[n]nu Com[ita] Manutha et do[n]nu Petru Falche [et] do[n]nu Petru Copiu et do[n]nu Andria Secche. T[es]t[e]s.

121r 430. *Salto d'Urey*.
Posit[95] ad S[an]c[t]u Petru donu Ith[oc]or de Thori kando se 'nke affersit, pross'anima sua, su latus dessu saltu d'Urei. Et su[n]t termenes de custu saltu: ave nurakes de Corvos falat rivu mortu ad su kercu arcatu de flum[en] minore, collat toctue pus rivu de flum[en] minore a bulvare de Petru, collat toctue valle a valle de puthu, girat toctue via de balle de locu ad su vadu desse posia, girat toctue s'atha ad s'ilike ve[n]tosa, cludet ad nurake de Corvos. T[e]st[e]s: pis-

93 Change of hand.
94 Change of hand.
95 Change of hand.

tions. I grant this so that Sanctu Petru can benefit from it in life and in death. Witnesses: Comita Vathis, Gantine de Serra, Gunnari de Serra, Gantine Thanca, priest Mariane, and the priest of Silchi, lord Petru Gattone, and Gunnari de Carvia. Witnesses.

427.
I, abbess Tedora de Silchi, marry my servant Furatu Quoquone with Elena Carta, female servant (*anquilla*) of Sanctu Palu, and I do this with the consent of Salinbene, who was vicar (*biquanium*) of Trullas, so that the churches of Sanctu Petru and Sanctu Palu can share together the offspring that will be born, taking half each. Witnesses: the priest of Quotronianu Iosso ('lower Codrongianos', Codronzanu 'e josso), and lord Gantine de Mularia, in whose hands [the marriage] was conducted, and Mariane d'Athen, Benedicte de Liios, and Comita Sanna. Witnesses.

428. *Cotronianum* (*Codrongianos*).
I bought from Sultaro de Querqui his land at Planu de Vulvare ('plain of the animal pen'). I gave him five bezants (*bisantis*) worth of an ox, one bezant in coin (*in dinaris*), and a sheep. Witnesses: lord Gantine de Mularia the priest, and lord Petru Quoque, and lord Petru de Querqui. Witnesses.

429.
I bought from lord Petru d'Erisa of Chelemule the vineyard that he has in Garulatho with the fruit orchard (*fructura*) he has there, bordering that of Juvanne Murtinu. He sold it to me with the consent of those who were party to the division (*frates dessa parthone*), and I gave him eight bezants (*bisantis*). Witnesses: lord Clementi, priest; lord Comita Manutha; lord Petru Falche; lord Petru Copiu, and lord Andria Secche. Witnesses.

430. *Unworked land* (salto) *of Urey*.
Lord Ithoccor de Thori, when he offered himself [to the church], donated half (*latus*) of the unworked land (*saltu*) of Urei to Sanctu Petru for his soul. The boundaries of this land (*saltu*) are: from the nuraghi of Corvos; it (*sic*) goes down the river bed (*rivu mortu*) towards Kercu Arcatu ('the curved oak') at Flumen Minore ('lesser river', Riu Minore, Ittiri), passes beyond the stream of Flumen Minore to Bulvare de Petru ('livestock pen of Petru'), passes along the valley towards Valle de Puthu ('valley of Puthu/the well'), and it turns towards the road of Balle de Locu ('valley of the country') up to Vadu dessa Posia ('the ford of Posia'), then turns along the cliff up to Ilike Ventosa ('the wind-swept holm oak') and closes at the nuraghe (*nurake*) of Corvos. Witnesses: bishop

copu Jorgi et Gan[tine] de Thori Murclu et Gu[n]nari de Thori Ca[m]ba-Curtha [et] Com[ita] de Itil [et] Com[ita] de Navithan. Test[e]s.

431.
Posit do[n]nu Ith[oc]or de Thori ad S[an]c[t]a Maria d'Usune [et] ad S[an]c[t]u Pet[ru] parte d'unu fiiu dessu saltu de Ca[m]pos et dessu saltu d'Arae. T[e]st[e]s: su p[re]viteru don[n]u Dericchor, qui li deit penite[n]thia, et Ja[n]ne Casula [et] Simione, su frate, et Gun[nari] de Thori. T[e]stes.

121v 432.
Conporaili ad Jorgi Tolis sa terra sua ki aveat in Uressa inter ipsas de clesia, et ego deindeli unu novellu de duos frates. T[e]st[e]s: Com[ita] de Gitil, maiore d'iscolca, [et] Ith[oc]cor de Serra. T[estes].

433.
Conporaili a Petru Natale su Thurpu sa t[er]ra de Therelis tene[n]de assa de S[an]c[t]a Maria, et ego deindeli I bacca. T[estes]: Mariane de Carbia et Ith[oc]or de Thori. T[estes].

434. *Usune.*
Conporaili a do[n]na Maria de Gunale Casta sa lintha de Therelis qui fuit inter toctas tres sas lingthas de clesia, a manca de via T[ur]resa, in co falam[us] ad Mascar, in co essit sa lintha derecta isc'a su term[en] ave ma[n]ca paris cu[n] sas adteras. Et ego deindeli II berbekes a bita [et] I ad mortu ad su serbu, ad co[m]patre Sigithellu, ca mi 'nde fecherat volu[n]tate d'a[n]daremivi assa donna sua a sSeptupalmas, ue fuit d'istare. Et osca pectitindeli volu[n]tate ad sa fiia, a do[n]na Gedida, ca mi naravat, p[us] morte dessa mama, ca 'no[n] volla deit.' Et ipsa deitimila a bolu[n]tate sua. Test[e]s: Comita Pisanu [et] do[n]nu
122r Com[ita] de Serra, qui | fuit maiore. T[e]st[e]s.

435.
Posit ad S[an]c[t]a Maria d'Usune do[n]na Jorgia de Gitil p[ro]ss'anima sua de III partes una qui aviat in su saltu de Nussu. T[e]st[e]s: do[n]nu Com[ita] de Campu Tiria [et] do[n]nu Dorg[otori] de Carvia, p[re]viteru d'Usune, q[ui] fuit in sa penite[n]thia, [et] do[n]nu Com[ita] Caprinu. T[e]st[e]s.

Jorgi, Gantine de Thori Murclu, Gunnari de Thori Camba-Curtha, Comita de Itil, and Comita de Navithan. Witnesses.

431.

Lord Ithocor de Thori donated to Sancta Maria d'Usune (Usini) and Sanctu Petru a part of the unworked land (*saltu*) of Campos and the unworked land (*saltu*) of Arae, equivalent to the part of a son. Witnesses: lord Dericchor, the priest who administered the confession, and Janne Casula, and his brother Simione, and Gunnari de Thori. Witnesses.

432.

I bought from Jorgi Tolis the land he holds at Uressa between those of the church. I gave him one of two calves from a litter. Witnesses: Comita de Gitil, head of the ward (*maiore d'iscolca*), and Ithoccor de Serra. Witnesses.

433.

I bought from Petru Natale Thurpu the land of Therelis bordering that of Sancta Maria. I gave him a cow. Witnesses: Mariane de Carbia, and Ithoccor de Thori. Witnesses.

434. *Usune* (*Usini*).

I bought from lady Maria de Gunale Casta the strip of land (*lintha*) at Therelis which was surrounded by three strips of land of the church to the left of the Turresa road, in the stretch from which we go down to Mascar (Mascari, Sassari), where a strip of land (*lintha*) goes as far as the boundary on the left along with the others. I gave her two live sheep and one killed by the servant (*serbu*), godfather (*compatre*) Sigithellu, since he had shown her goodwill (*voluntate*) by going with me to her lady in Septupalmas (Fontana Sette Palme) where she used to live. Afterwards, she sought a favour (*voluntate*) from her daughter, lady Gedida, because she told me that after the death of her mother that 'she does not want to give it away!' Thus, she gave me her consent [for the purchase]. Witnesses: Comita Pisanu, and lord Comita de Serra, who was the official (*maiore*). Witnesses.

435.

Lady Jorgia de Gitil donated to Sancta Maria d'Usune (Usini), for her soul, a third of what she held in the unworked land (*saltu*) of Nussu. Witnesses: lord Comita de Campu Tiria, and lord Dorgotori de Carvia, priest of Usune (Usini), who administered the confession, and lord Comita Caprinu.

436. *Usune.*
Posit[96] Marcusa Vardane ad S[an]c[t]a Maria d'Usune pross'anima sua, [et] i[n] vita et apus morte, sa parte canta l'intravat in su saltu de Nussu. Venit t[er]men via Turresa dessa funtana dessa ficu et t[er]men assu vadu de pithu altu, falat toctuve rivu ad s'ilike de term[en] de Patru, collat toctuve valle de iugu iunctu, lassandesi ad ma[n]ca su vigna de S[an]c[t]u Petru, collat toctue via ad sa iscala berbekile de Rivorarza, baricat toctuve s'atha et torrat ad sa via maiore. Test[e]s uve fekit custu vene ad S[an]c[t]a Maria d'Usune: do[n]nu Ju[anne] de Thori et do[n]nu Mar[iane] d[e] Itil et do[n]nu Com[ita] de Serra. T[e]st[e]s.

122v 437.
Ego[97] Petru d'Ispata, p[re]viteru de Ithir, qui fatho memoria dessu testam[en]tu qui fekit do[n]nu Com[i]t[a] de Gunale quando ve[n]nit ad ora dessa morte sua. In p[ri]mis judicait p[ro]ssa anima sua ad S[an]c[t]a T[ri]nitate de Saccaria sa vinia sua de Cotro[n]ianu. Judicavit ad S[an]c[t]u Pet[ru] de Silchy sa vinia sua tocta erema de Valle. Judicavit ad S[an]c[t]u Procopiu sa t[er]ra sua de Maroniu et issa parte sua de vi[n]ia erema de villa. Et fekit liveros sa parte q[ui] vi aviat in sos fiios de Comita de Fokile. Testes: donnu Petru d'Ispata, previteru, et donnu Gunnari Capitha, su patre, et donnu Saltaro Capitha et donnu Manuelle Fancellu et donnu Manuelle de Nurechi et donnu Bosovechesu de Gunale et donnu Juvanne de Gunale et donnu Gant[ine] Capitha et donnu Comita Locche et donnu Mariane de Thori, su de Novalia, et donnu Gunnari Locche, et ambas villas de Ithiris. Testes.

123r 438.[98]
Ego,[99] abbatissa Prethiosa, fatho recordu dessu kertu qui mi fechit Saltaro de Nuketu. Kertaitimi prossu terraticu toctu q[ui] est supta sa corte dessos Unchinos, in corona de messer Conradu Trinchis, qui fuit vicariu prossu regem in su rennu de Locudore. Et ad kertu cale mi 'nde fekit inde lu vinchy. Et si mi 'nde kertavat isse, o fiios suos, o nepotes suos, o neunu homine dessu mundu, p[er] neunu tempus dessu mundu, pacare assu rennu, in cuia corona darun kertare, bisantis c de d[ina]r[i]s junuinos minutos. Testes: donnu Gantine d'Ena, curatore de Gisarclu, et donnu Gantine Pi[n]na Pisanu et donnu Marruffu Pinna, priore de S[an]c[t]u Petru de Silchi, et donnu Comita Corda et don[nu] Petru de Cressente et donnu Gant[ine] Pi[n]na Kinfaiu. Testes.

96 Change of hand.
97 Change of hand.
98 Duplication of entry 411.
99 Change of hand.

436. *Usune* (*Usini*).
Marcusa Vardane donated to Sancta Maria d'Usune (Usini), for her soul, the share (*parte*) that belonged to her both in life and after death in the unworked land (*saltu*) of Nussu. The boundary is from Turresa road at Funtana dessa Ficu ('the spring of the fig tree'); a boundary limit is at Vadu de Pithu ('ford of Pithu'); it descends along the river to the holm oak (*s'ilke*) to the boundary of Patru, and passes along Valle de Iugu Iuntu ('valley of the joined yoke'), leaving the vineyard of Sanctu Petru on the left, it passes along the road towards Iscala Berbekile ('sheep hillside') at Rivorarza, then crosses along the cliff and returns to the main road. Witnesses when he made this benefice for Sancta Maria d'Usune (Usini): lord Juanne de Thori, lord Mariane de Itil, and lord Comita de Serra. Witnesses.

437.
I, Petru d'Ispata, priest of Ithir (Ittireddu), make a record (*fatho memoria*) of the testament lord Comita de Gunale at the hour of his death. First, he decided, for his soul, [to give] his vineyard at Cotronianu (Codrongianos) to Sancta Trinitate de Saccaria (Basilica of the Holy Trinity of Saccargia). He decided [to give] his completely derelict (*tocta erema*) vineyard at Valle to Sanctu Petru de Silchy. He also decided [to give] his land in Maroniu and his share (*parte*) of the derelict vineyard at the village to Sanctu Procopiu. Also, he made freemen (*fekit liveros*) those from among the sons of Comita de Fokile of whom he had a share. Witnesses: lord Petru d'Ispata, priest; lord Gunnari Capitha, his father; lord Saltaro Capitha; lord Manuelle Fancellu; lord Manuelle de Nurechi; lord Bosovechesu de Gunale; lord Juvanne de Gunale; lord Gantine Capitha; lord Comita Locche; lord Mariane de Thori from Novaia (Noazza); lord Gunnari Locche, and both villages of Ithiris (*ambas villas de Ithiris*). Witnesses.

438.
I, abbess Prethiosa, make a record (*fatho memoria*) of the dispute that Saltaro de Nuketu brought against me. He sued me at the hearing (*corona*) of sir (*messer*) Conradu Trinchis, the representative of the king (*vicariu prossu rege*) in the realm (*rennu*) of Locudore (Logudoro), over all the farmable land (*terraticu*) that is in the farmyard (*corte*) of the Unchinos. I defeated him, and the case was that if one day he or his children or grandchildren (*nepotes*) or any other man of this world, they would have to pay the realm (*rennu*), in whichever hearing (*corona*) they conduct the dispute, one hundred bezants (*bisantis*) in Genoese *minuti* coins (*dinaris Junuinos minutos*). Witnesses: lord Gantine d'Ena, *curatore* of Gisarclu; lord Gantine Pinna Pisanu; lord Marruffu Pinna, prior of Sanctu Petru de Silchi; lord Comita Corda; lord Petru de Cressente, and lord Gantine Pinna Kinfaiu. Witnesses.

123^v 439.
Ego[100] Agnesa, abbatissa de S[an]c[t]a Maria de Nascar et de S[an]c[t]u Petru de Silchi, fatho recordu dessu cale aet postu Armenia Pi[n]na, prossa anima sua in vita sua, ad S[an]c[t]u Petru de Silchi. In primis posit su latus dessu ortu de Cannetu, su cale conp[or]ait sa mama cun su patre Gun[nari] de sSerra[101] a Petru de Serra. Testes: do[n]nu Bonacorsu, previteru de Silchi, et Petru de Scanu, su de Thathari, et Comita de Murtas et Jorgi Pectenatu et Gantine Pala. Testes.

124^r 440.
Ego,[102] abbatissa Agnesa, qui ponio in custu condake de S[an]c[t]u Petru de Silchi de conporu q[ui] appo fattu. Conp[or]ai ad Mingarda Vassina, muiere q[ui] fuit de Comita Pithale, et Comita Corda su e[n]neru de custa Mingarda, su pastinu suo qui [est] postu in Utheri, q[ui] est t[er]m[en] assa vinia de do[n]nu Gant[ine] Pi[n]na su p[re]viteru [et] term[en] assu ortu de S[an]c[t]u Petru de Silchi, et est assa via plubica. Et ego deindelis l[i]br[as] x de d[ina]r[is] jenuinos; et issos furun de ispiaremilu de om[n]ia ho[m]i[n]e dessu mu[n]du q[ui] mi [n]d'ait baractare, in pena de l[i]br[as] L de d[ina]r[is] jan[uinos] assu re[n]nu. Testes: do[n]nu Stefane de Rosa et Çiolu not[ariu] et Ioh[ann]e Dacu et Bonifiiu Tholocu et Barusone Pirastru, arm[en]tariu. T[e]st[e]s.

124^v 441. *De s[er]vos.*
Ego[103] Agnesa, p[er] issa gra[thia] de Deum abbatissa de S[an]c[t]u Petru de Silchi, fatho recordatione d[e]ssa muiere q[ui] fuit de mastru Gant[ine] d'Etim, q[ui] fecherun servum d[e] ginithu bonu[m], q[ui] morivit et co[n]fessait sa muiere do[n]na Merelia de Derisa de Plovake, ca fuit maritu suo, et issa muiere sua leitima. Et de custu confessait dave na[n]ti dessa do[n]na s'abatissa et de toctu su cunbe[n]tu[m] et d[e]ssu p[re]viter[u] de S[an]c[t]a Julia et Andria Taras, arm[en]tariu de sigillum, [et] de Barusone Pirastru, arm[en]tariu de S[an]c[t]a Julia, et mastru Joh[ann]e Pelle et d[e] Michine de Aliprandu et de mag[ist]r[u] Gant[ine] Carbone et de mastru Antioclu Pelle et de Matheu Pelle et de Joh[ann]e Gusai, arm[en]tariu de Gennor. Et anco lassait una[m] fiia q[ui] aviat in ateru maritu,[104] a chen naravan Prethiosa d'Etim, qui est latus de S[an]c[t]u Petru et latus de S[an]c[t]u Gavignu de ginithiu bonum.

---

100 Change of hand.
101 Manuscript reads *sSarra*.
102 Change of hand.
103 Change of hand.
104 Manuscript reads *maritar*.

439.
I, Agnese, abbess of Sancta Maria de Nascar (Santa Maria di Asca) and Sanctu Petru di Silchi, make a record of what Armenia Pinna donated to Sanctu Petru de Silchi for his soul in her own lifetime. First, she donated half (*latus*) of her vegetable garden (*ortu*) of Cannetu, which her mother with her father, Gunnari de Serra, bought from Petru de Serra. Witnesses: lord Bonacorsu, priest of Silchi; Petru de Scanu from Thathari (Sassari), and Comita de Murtas, Jorgi Pectenatu, and Gantine Pala. Witnesses.

440.
I, abbess Agnesa, put in this condaghe of Sanctu Petru de Silchi the purchases that I have made. I bought from Mingarda Vassina, wife of Comita Pithale, and from Comita Corda, son-in-law (*enneru*) of this Mingarda, their new vine (*pastinu*), which is located in Utheri. The boundary is at the vineyard of lord Gantine Pinna, the priest, and the garden (*ortu*) of Sanctu Petru de Silchi, and is by the public road (*via plubica*). I gave them ten pounds (*libras*) of Genoese coins (*dinaris Jenuinos*), and they guaranteed me that no one in this world would dispute this, under penalty of fifty pounds of Genoese coins (*dinaris Januinos*) [payable] to the realm (*rennu*). Witnesses: lord Stefane de Rosa, the notary Çiolo, Iohanne Dacu, Bonfiliu Tholocu, and Barusone Pirastru [the] administrator (*armentariu*). Witnesses.

441. *Of servants.*
I, Agnesa, by the grace of God, abbess of Sanctu Petru di Silchi, make a record (*fatho recordatione*) of the wife of master (*maestru*) Gantine d'Etim whom they put into noble service (*ginithu bonum*). When he died, lady Merelia de Derisa from Plovake (Ploaghe), confessed that he was her husband and she was the legitimate wife. She confessed about this to the lady abbess and to the entire convent, and to the priest of Sancta Julia, and to Andrea Taras, keeper of the seal (*armentariu de sigillum*); to Barusone Pirastru, administrator (*armentariu*) of Sancta Julia, to master (*mastru*) Johanne Pelle; to Michine de Aliprandu; to master (*magistru*) Gantine Carbone; to master Antioclu Pelle; to Matheu Pelle; and to Johanne Gusai, administrator (*armentariu*) of Gennor (Zennos). From her previous husband, she also left a daughter they called Prethiosa d'Etim whose half (*latus*) belongs to Sanctu Petru, and the other half is in noble service (*ginithiu bonum*) at Sanctu Gavingnu (San Gavino di Torres).

125r 442. *De s[er]vos.*

Ego, abbatissa Tedora, qui fatho recordatione[m] de Victoria d'Erisa et de Maria de Erisa sa fiia, ka[105] furun anchillas de S[an]c[t]u Petru de Silchy et sun. Et fornicaitila Ithoc[or] de Martis, servu[m] de S[an]c[t]a Trinitate de Saccaria, et fekitivi custa fiia Maria d'Erisa. Et Maria fekit ad Prethiosa et a Bictoria e a Bera et a Mariane et a Ithoc[or] et a Susanna. Et Prethiosa coiuvait cum servu[m] de Sacaria Petru Seta et ativi fiios tres, innanti ad Joh[ann]e, et osca a Comita et a Susanna.

443.[106]

Ego abbatissa Tedora. Conp[or]aili a Comita de Thori Leriane, de Taverra, et assa muiere Susanna de Thori, necta de Dorgotori de Cherchi, su de Taverra, cu[m] bolu[n]tate dessos fiios, sa parte sua dessu saltu d'Urcone, et est
125v term[en] assu saltu[m] | de s'iscala de vinia manna, toctue via maiore, qui vaen ad Ulumetu ischi a su iumpatoriu dessu riu de Serule; et falat toctue riu, et girat su sulchu dessu bruncu de Dorbeni Crispu, et exit s'orbitu ad ena tennera, et benit inter ambos[107] bulbares de Gemellares assa petra coperclata, et ruclat ass'ena supta sas thinnigas ad monticlu de Dorgotori, a mmonticlu settitoriu, assu monticlu giratu, collat s'atha de Usumen, et essit a bia, et torrat assos forchillos dessa petra alba, et essit toctue via ki faken sos de Save, ischi a s'iscala de vinia manna. Testes: donnu Comita de Thori Thipirclu et do[n]nu Belardu Carvone, q[ui] regiat corona prossu vicariu, ser Babillanu Doria et Bandinu Pinna Pisanu et donnu Bar[usone] Fancellu et donnu Gantine Pinna, fiiu de donnu Gelardinu Pisanu, et donnu Guant[ine] d'Ena. T[e]stes. Et pro custu bene qui fekit ad S[an]c[t]u Pet[ru], isse et issa muiere prossas animas issoro, si 'nde lis fekit grathia apatissa Tedora, et deitindelis I vacca viclata et I boe et s[ollos] XXVI in dinaris.

105 Manuscript reads *kam*.

106 Cf. entry 425.

107 Manuscript reads *abbos*.

442. *Of servants.*
I, abbess Tedora, make a record of Victoria d'Erisa and her daughter Maria d'Erisa, who were and are female servants (*anchillas*) of Sanctu Petru de Silchy. Ithoccor de Martis, servant of Sancta Trinitate de Saccaria (Saccargia), had an illegitimate relationship and they had the said Maria d'Erisa. Then, Maria had Prethiosa, Bictoria, Bera, Mariane, Ithoccor, and Susanna. Prethiosa married a servant of Sacaria (Saccargia), Petru Seta, and had three children: first, Johanne; then Comita, and Susanna.

443. *The unworked land* (saltu) *of Urcone.*
I, abbess Tedora, bought from Comita de Thori Leriane from Taverra (Taberra) and from his wife Susanna de Thori, niece (*necta*) of Dorgotori de Cherchi from Taverra, with the consent of the children, his part of the unworked land (*saltu*) at Urcone (Arcone). The boundary of the land (*saltu*) is from Iscala de Vinia Manna ('the hillside of the large vineyard', Vigna Grande), along the main road that leads to Ulumetu (Olmedo), up to the crossing (*iumpatoriu*) of the river of Serule; then it desends along the river and turns around Sulcu Bruncu ('the furrow on the hill') of Dorbeni Crispu, goes along the path to Ena Tennera ('Tennera spring'), and comes between two livestock enclosures (*vulvares*) at Gemellares; [then] to Petra Coperclata ('the dolmen'), across the spring below sas Thinnigas ('the reeds'), to Monticlu de Dorgotori ('Dorgotori's hill'), to Monticlu Settitoriu ('hill of Settitoriu'), to Monticlu Giratu ('hill of Giratu'), it passes s'Atha de Usumen ('the cliff of Usumen'), takes the road and returns at the fork of Petra Alba ('the white rock'); it goes along the road they take from Save (Pala Santa Caterina) as far as Iscala de Vinia Manna ('hillside of the large vineyard', Vigna Grande), and closes. Witnesses: lord Comita de Thori Thipircu; lord Belardu Carvone, who presided over (*regiat*) the hearing (*coronu*) as his deputy (*prossu vicariu*); sir (*ser*) Babillanu Doria; Bandinu Pinna Pisanu; lord Barusone Fancellu; lord Gantine Pinna, son of lord Gelardinu Pisanu, and lord Guantine d'Ena. Witnesses. For this benefice both he and his wife made to Sanctu Petru for their souls, abbess Tedora gave them a cow with calf, an ox, and twenty-six soldi (*sollos*) in coin (*in dinaris*).

The Condaghe of Santa Maria di Bonárcado

 | DOI:10.1163/9789004750951_005

Introduction to the Text and Translation

The single codex of the condaghe of the basilica of Santa Maria di Bonárcado, founded in 1110, is held at the Biblioteca Universitaria di Cagliari (BUC, ms, 277). The condaghe's contents relate to the church's transactions, acquisitions, donations, concessions exchanges, and disputes from the early part of the twelfth century to the mid-thirteenth. It was published with an Italian translation by Maurizio Virdis, *Il condaghe di Santa Maria di Bonarcado* (Nuoro, 2002), prior to which there were editions by Raimondo Carta Raspi (Cagliari, 1937), and Enrico Besta and Arrigo Solmi (Milan, 1937; repr. Oristano, 1982, ed. Maurizio Virdis). The condaghe comprises 88 well conserved parchment folios, each measuring approximately 14.5 cm by 19 cm. Each folio comprises 21 lines of text in brown or black ink with some letters illuminated in red. It displays a patchwork of writing styles and hands, from Carolingian to humanistic scripts, reflecting the cultural shift of Sardinia from Italian to Iberian influence, still noticeable by the 15th century.[1] At varying times, the folios were combined into booklets which correspond to different periods of the church's activities. Thus, folios 53^{r}–68^{v} are from c. 1110 to c. 1164; 29^{r}–36^{v} relate to the years 1167–1169; 45^{r}–52^{v} are from 1171 to 1184; 37^{r}–44^{v} are from 1185 to the early thirteenth century; 86^{r}–91^{v} relate to the late twelfth century and early thirteenth century; 71^{r}–77^{v} and 78^{r}–85^{v} are both booklets from the early thirteenth century; and, finally, 1^{r}–28^{v} are from the late twelfth century and early thirteenth century. However, this booklet—the first in the codex's binding—was drafted by a fifteenth-century hand, and displays a humanist style with archaicising tendencies to make it appear gothic.[2] Overall, there are an estimated thirty-four changes of hand in the codex.

1 Olivetta Schena, 'Le scritture del condaghe di Santa Maria di Bonarcado', in *Miscellanea di studi medioevali sardo-catalani* (Cagliari, 1981), pp. 42–73 (at 69).

2 Schena, 'Le scritture del condaghe'; Ginevra Zanetti, *I Camaldolesi in Sardegna* (Cagliari, 1974).

Text

1.[3]

1r Condace S[ancte] Marie de Monarcanto. Iudex Con{stan}tini. In nomine dei
Patris et Filii et Spi[ri]tu s[an]c[t]i. Amen. E{go iudice Gostan}tine de Arborea
[...] si[mul] {c[un]} [u]xore mea d[onn]a A[nna] s[econdum] consilium [ar-
chiepiscopi] [mei] {Ho}mo {Dei} p[er] [rem]edium a[nime]} mee et pro [re-
missione] omniu[m] peccator[um] meor[um] [et] [pro] sa[lu]t[e] f{i[l]i[o-
ru]m} [meoru]m c[om]p[ono] dispono assig[no] [e]t faci[o] ist[u]d condace
[et] [ist]ud cenobi[um] ad honorem individue Trinitatis [e]t i[n]t[e]mera-
te virgi[n]is Dei genitricis Ma[rie] [et] [omn]i a[m]big[ui]tat[e] [remo]ta
{c[on]}stituo ad degendos inibi servos Dei sub regulari[4] tramite sa[nct]issimi
ac reverendi patris Benedicti, qui serviant Deo om[n]ipotenti die ac nocte
qua[m]diu hec duraverit vita. Nunc aute[m] cognitum sit om[n]ibus tam fr[at-
1v r]ibus meis qua[m] cun[ctis] affinibus, consentiente et collaudante | prelibato
archiepiscopo meo Homodei, quod ego omnino trado hoc monasterium sub
ditione et iure et potestate et regimine et disciplina abbatis sancti Zenonis
epi[scopus] sub tali conditione[m] ut abbati s[an]c[t]i Zenonis om[n]i t[em]-
p[o]r[e] mittant in hoc monasterio de suis monachis qui rega[n]t illud et
ordinent et lavore[n]t et edifice[n]t et plante[n]t ad honorem Dei et sa[n]cte
Marie et sa[n]c[t]i Benedicti et sa[n]c[t]i Zenonis et p[er] manus illoru[m]
ordinetur prepositus, que[m] ipsi eligent, cum[5] voluntate et aprobatione suc-
cessorum meoru[m], desisto atque condono:

Domo S[an]c[t]e Victorie de Mo[n]te s[an]c[t]o cum omnia cantu aet: et
terras et binias et saltus d'Orrodolazu et Oruni in quo si pesat daa ssa iaca
d'Orrodolazu et collat a nurache d'Orisezo et molliat a petra de niu de corbu
e benit assu erriu de petra de cavallu et benit assu monticlu de Utur d'Arsai et
2r benit assu castru | dessu cannisone e benit assu castru de monticlu de piscobu,
cun ho[m]i[n]es et masones d'onnia sinnu, de grussu et minudu. Et dolli asol-
tura pro custu saltu ki si llu arregant et castigent om[n]ia t[em]p[o]rale et pro
glande et pro pastu in p[er]petuu[m] in co fudi usu et est oe die de castigaresi
saltu de regnu.

Domu de sancto Augustinu de Augustis cum omnia cantu aet: et t[er]ras et binias et saltos de Gastalbennor in quo si ferit a pari cun sa semida de Digui e

3 This entry partially reproduces content found in entry 207. The opening folio is in particularly poor condition and is not legible without an ultra-violet reading lamp. Restored readings here appear between {}.

4 Change of hand from *regolari*.

5 Change of hand from *cum* to *Mo[n]te*. Previous hand continues thereafter.

1.
[Latin]: Condaghe of Sancte Marie de Monarcanto (Bonárcado). Iudex Constantini. In the name of the Father, the Son and the Holy Spirit, amen. I, iudike Gostantine de Arborea [...] together with my wife, lady Anna, according to the advice of my archbishop, for the deliverance of my soul and for the remission of all my sins and for the deliverance of my children, I draw up, dispose, affix a seal and establish this condaghe and this coenobium in honour of the indivisible Trinity and of the most pure Virgin Mary, Mother of God, and, without any ambiguity or doubt, I order that the servants of God may dwell therein under the rule of the most holy and reverend father, Benedictus, serving Almighty God day and night for as long as the world lasts. Now, therefore let it be known to all, both to my brothers and to all my kin, that, with the consent and approval of my archbishop, Homodei, I place this monastery completely under the authority, jurisdiction, power, regimen and discipline of the abbot bishop of St Zeno with this condition: that the abbots of St Zeno always send to this monastery monks of theirs to govern and to organise it, and to work, build and plant crops for the honour of God, Holy Mary, St Benedict, and St Zeno, and that by their hands a superior is appointed whom they themselves shall elect, with the will and approval of my successors. I grant as a gift and renounce [the following] assets:

The farm complex (*domo*) of Sancta Victorie de Montesancto with all that it has: lands, vineyards, and the unworked lands (*saltus*) of Orrodolazu and Oruni according to the course of the border that rises from the entrance (*iaca*) of Orrodolazu, goes up to the nuraghe of Orisezo, turns to Petra de Niu de Corbu ('the rock of the crow's nest'), comes to the river of Petra de Cavallu ('horse rock'), goes to the hill of Utur d'Arsai, reaches the nuraghe (*castru*) of Cannisone, [then] comes to the rock of Colle de Piscobu ('bishop's hill'), with men (*homines*) and livestock of every type, both large and small. I give them permission, with regard to these lands (*saltus*), to hold them and look after them in every season with regard to both acorn production and grazing for all time, as has been the custom, and still is, to use it as unworked land of the realm (*saltu de regnu*).

The farm complex (*domo*) of Sancto Augustinu de Augustis with all that pertains to it: lands and vineyards and the unworked land (*saltu*) of Gastalbennor according to the course of the boundary as it joins the boundary of the estate

cun semida de Onna, et segatsi de pare cun Zinzau, in quo girat termen et sinnas suas de tottu su saltu, et homines et masones d'onnia sinnu et de grussu et minudu. Et dolli asoltura ki si llu arregant et castigent o[mn]ia t[em]p[o]rale et pro glande et p[ro] pastu in perpetuu[m] in co fudi usu et e[st] oe a die de castigaresi saltu de regnu.

Domo de s[an]c[t]o Petru de Vidoni cun onnia cantu aet: et t[er]ras et bin-
2v ias, et saltu d'Ollimor | in quo llu girat sinnas daa iaca de Collectorio derectu a Gilispuri derettu a castru de Viola Moiu, deretu a castru de Velio, e moliat a montiglu de biscobu e molliat derettu a margine de s[an]c[t]a Victoria e molliat a castru de Stria e molliat a petra dessu cipiri derettu a castru de Ulguni derettu a erriu de Oladoriu, derettu a margine de Vice[n]du, derettu a iscalas de Ianni, derettu a aidu de Pradu de Nugedu, cu[n] serbos cum ankillas et cu[n] masones d'onnia sinnu, de grussu et minudu. Et dolli asoltura ki si llu arregant et castigent om[n]ia t[em]p[o]rale et pro glande et pro pastu in p[er]petuu[m] in co fudi usu et est oe a die de castigaresi saltu de regnu.

Et domo s[an]c[t]e Marie de Boele cun onnia cantu aet, partindo pares cun su regnu: et t[er]ras et binias et domesticas cantas ivi aviat, e issu saltu
3r d'Ilo, partindollu ladus a pare cun | clesia, cum serbos et cun anchillas et cu[n] masones d'onnia sinnu et de grussu et minudu. Et dolli asoltura ki si llu aregant et castigent om[n]ia t[em]p[o]rale et pro glande et pro pastu [et] p[ro] laore in p[er]petuu[m] in co fudi usu [et] e[st] oe a die de castigaresi saltu de regnu.

E domo s[an]c[t]i Serigi de Suei cun onnia cantu aet: cu[n] terrras, cun binias, cun servos, cun ankillas e cu[n] masones e cun sa parzone cantu aviat Tericco de Scopedu, de serbos, de ankillas et de paules e de Puzus striliges: apatsinde prode usque in fine seculi.

(*semida*) of Digui and that of Onna, and is conceded from [the territory of] Zinzau along the course of the boundary and its boundary markers of the whole land (*saltu*); it includes men (*homines*) and flocks (*masones*) of every type, both large and small. I give them permission, regarding this land (*saltu*), to hold it and exploit it perpetually for their benefit, in every season, with respect to both acorn production and the pasture, as it was and still is customary to take care of unworked land of the realm (*saltu de regnu*).

The farm complex of Sancto Petru de Vidoni (Bidonì) with all that it has: lands and vineyards, and the unworked land (*saltu*) of Ollimor along the course of the boundary, and its boundary markers from the entrance (*iaca*) of the Collectorio ('hunters' meeting place'), in the direction of Gilispuri towards the nuraghe (*castru*) of Viola Moiu, in the direction of Castru de Velio ('outcrop of Velio'); [the boundary] turns towards Colle de Biscobu ('bishop's hill'), and [then] turns towards the side (*margine*) of Santa Victoria, then turns towards Castru de Stria ('outcrop of the owl'), turns towards Petra dessu Cipiri ('rock of the rosemary'), goes in the direction of Castro de Ulguni ('outcrop of Ulguni') in the direction of Erriu de Oladoriu ('Oladoriu stream'), towards the side of Vicendu, in the direction of Iscalas de Ianni ('hillsides of Ianni'), and in the direction of the passage leading to Pradu de Nugedu ('walnut grove meadow'); [I give this] with both its male and female servants, and with flocks (*masones*) of all types, both large and small. And I give them permission, with regard to this land (*saltu*), to hold it and exploit it perpetually for their benefit, in every season, with regard to both acorn production and grazing, as has been the custom, and still is, to use to their advantage as unworked land of the realm (*saltu de regnu*).

The farm complex (*domo*) of Sancta Marie de Boele with all that pertains to it, dividing it into two equal halves with [property of] the realm (*regnu*) [and with] as many lands, vineyards and farms (*domos*) as it might have, the unworked land (*saltu*) of Ilo, dividing it in half with the property of the church, with the male and female servants, and with livestock of every type, both large and small. I give them permission, with respect to this land (*saltu*), to hold it and exploit it perpetually for their benefit, in every season, with respect to both acorn production and pasture, as it was and still is customary to use to their advantage as unworked land of the realm (*saltu de regnu*).

The farm complex (*domo*) of San Serigi de Suei with all that it has: lands, vineyards, servants (male and female), and with the share that Tericco de Scopedu owned there, of servants (*serbos*), female servants (*ankillas*), marshes (*paules*) and dry wells (*puzus striliges*), such that the monastery may have benefit for all time.

E domo de s[an]c[t]a Victoria de Serla cun onnia cantu aet: cu[n] terras, cu[n] binias, cu[n] serbos et ankillas e cun totta sa parzone ki fuit de donnu Piziellu de Sezo in co narrant cartas suas.

E domo s[an]c[t]o Iorgi de Calcaria cun onnia cantu: et terras et binias et
3v serbos et anchillas | et masones de onnia sinnu. E dolli su saltu meo peguiare de Serra de Castula in quo si segat daa saltu de Mambari et collat tuttue pus flumen de Ilbai et ergetsi in sa scala de su fruscu ue parte[n]t de pari cun saltu de S[an]c[te] Eru, e benit a pet[ra] de Scudu et falat a su bau d'Ursiarsida e falat totue pos flumen de Cannavaria e falat a bau de Sinias u'est sa figu alba et cue s'afliscat cu[n] Manbari. E dolli sa parzone ki fuit de donnu Piziellu de Sezo, ki poserat isse a S[an]c[t]u Iorgi de Calcaria cando la fegerat a nnovu, cun issa segadura de su saltu d'Aidugocippu in co llu ingirat a iaga de Drogodori de Pau, e benit a ariola de Titiriu et benit a funtana de gercu, et segatsi de pare cu[n] su saltu de Mariane d'Orruu, et giratsi a iscla de kerbu et falat post flumen a nurake d'Olixa[n]dru, et fliscatsi in Aidugocipu; et issa domestica de Cobulas
4r et sa parzone c'a- | -viat in Sezo, cum fiios d'Asinari cu[n] onnia causa issoro; e issa parzone de Sobro e de Çeçerni, cu[n] issa vinia de Rezençario cu[n] servos, cu[n] ankillas suas de iuvale et cu[n] omnia libertatos suos: poniollos et afirmolos in manu de su priore: ki ll'apat benedicta sa parzone de donnu Piziellu cantu aviat per totu logu, in co narra[n]t cartas suas.[6]

E domo s[an]c[t]i Symeonis de Vesala cun segatura dessu saltu de Vesala ki ll'est in giru dave su nuraki de Vesala e benit a nuraki picinnu e benit a masoniu de Causare e benit a masoniu de Serra de Tramaza e calat a sa mura de Mambari e afliscatsi in issu nuraki de Vesala.

E domo de S[an]c[t]u Petru de Miili Picinnu cu[n] onnia cantu aviat donna Tocoele, ki fuit donna de logu, muiere de iudige Comida de Salanis ce fegit
4v issa sa clesia illa a nnou ponendove tota sa villa de Miili Picinnu | ki[7] fuit sua peguiare, sene avere parte ne[n] lib[er]u ne[n] serbu aienu, cu[n] t[er]ras et binias et servos et a[n]cillas et lib[er]tados; et saltu ki si segat dave sa cin[n]iga d[e] figos d[e] Milianu et benit assu grisaio[n]e d[e] sa cotina suta su

6 Large cross in left-hand margin in the same hand as the text.

7 Change of hand from *ki*.

The farm complex of Santa Victoria de Serla with all that it has of lands, vineyards, of servants (serbos), female servants (*ankillas*), and with the whole share (*parzone*) that belonged to lord Piziellu de Sezo according to that which his documents (*cartas*) say.

The farm complex of San Giorgio di Calcaria with all that it has: lands, vineyards, servants (*serbos*), female servants (*ankillas*), and flocks (*masones*) of every type. I give him my own unworked land (*saltu*) of Serra de Castula as it is granted from the land (*saltu*) of Mambari; [the boundary] passes along the river of Ilbai, on the other bank, and rises up Scala de su Fruscu ('slope of butcher's broom'), where the boundary divides the land (*saltu*) of Sancte Eru (St Vero) and reaches Petra de Scudu ('rock of the shelter'), descends to Bau d'Ursiarsida ('the ford of Ursiarsida'), [then] descends along the river (*flumen*) of Cannavaria on the other bank and descends to Bau de Sinias ('ford of Sinias') where there is the white fig-tree, and there it rejoins Manbari.

I also give him the share that belonged to lord Piziellu de Sezo, which he had donated to Sanctu Iorgi de Calcaria when he renovated the church, with that which was granted from the land (*saltu*) of Aidugocippu that goes around it to the entrance (*iaga*) of Drogodori de Pau and reaches the threshing floor (*ariola*) of Titiriu and goes to Funtana de Gercu ('spring of the oak'); this is granted from the land (*saltu*) of Mariane d'Orruu which runs equally along the land (*saltu*), turns to Iscla de Kerbu ('islet of the deer') and descends beyond the river to nuraghe d'Olixandru, and rejoins Aidugocipu; [it includes] the farmhouse (*domestica*) of Cobulas and the share [of the property] he had in Sezo with the children of Asinari, with everything belonging to them; and the share of Sobro and Zezerni, with the vineyard of Rezenzario and his servants, with female servants (*ankillas*) and all his freedmen (*libertatos*). I give and confirm them into the hands of the prior. May the share of lord Piziellu be blessed, [and] all that he has throughout the land (*logu*) according to that which his documents say!

The farm complex of San Symeonis de Vesala with the grant of the unworked land (*saltu*) of Vesala that surrounds it from the nuraghe of Vesala and reaches nuraghe Picinnu ('little nuraghe'), and reaches the paddock (*masoniu*) of Causare, and reaches the paddock of Serra de Tramaza and descends to the brambles (*sa mura*) at Mambari and rejoins the nuraghe of Vesala.

The farm complex (*domo*) of Sanctu Petru de Miili Picinnu with all that was in the possession of lady Tocoele, who was first-lady of the land (*donna de logu*), the wife of iudike (*iudige*) Comida de Salanis, who renovated the church by donating it the entire village (*villa*) of Miili Picinnu, which was her own property, with no share of either freemen or the servants of others, but with lands and vineyards and [her own] male and female servants and freedmen (*libertatos*). The unworked land (*saltu*) that is granted is from Cinniga de Figos ('the

monime[n]tu de sas teso[n]es et benit assa petra de sa gruge d'[e]na de Cerkis
et benit assas petras d'ariola d[e] don[n]a et collat su t[er]m[en] de domestia
de Comida et collat a fu[n]tana de Maga[n]se et benit a ariolas de Ca[m]pu
totue via de Tune et clo[m]pet a nuraki pikin[n]u et levat sa via vetere assu
castru de muru de Comida et falat assa cin[n]iga ulpina de mata de Gausari
et ferit a sa iaca dessu pratu de Guppurriu et falat totue deretu flum[en] a
binias de muru et falat assa fu[n]tana p[ri]va d'Or[r]uinas et falat flum[en]
et afliscassi i[n] ip[s]a cin[n]iga de figos de Miliana. Et de su saltu d'Oiastru
5r parzo[n]e ca[n]tu aviat, gasi illi·lla confirmo. Et co[n]firmolli ego iudice | Petrus
darboree a icustu monasteriu toto sa parzo[n]e de don[n]a Tocoele et dessas
terras d'afiiu ki derat pro armari sa clesia et issu monum[en]tu suo. Si llis barigat
kimbe an[n]us de fagere custu serbizu, fr[ate]s suos, a ki llas derat, torre[n]t sas
t[er]ras a clesia.

Et co[n]fìrmolli sa domo de S[an]c[t]a Corona d'Errivora cu[n] o[nn]ia ca[n]tu aet: cu[n] t[er]ras, cu[n] binias, cu[n] servos et a[n]killas et cu[n] o[nn]ia maso[n]e.

Et co[n]firmolli sa domo de S[an]c[t]a Barbara de Turre cu[n] o[nn]ia ca[n]tu aet, cu[n] t[er]ras, cu[n] binias, cu[n] servos et ancillas.

2.[8]

In[9] no[m]i[n]e D[omi]ni. Am[en]. Ego Petrus p[ri]ore de Bonarcatu fazo custa
carta p[ro] kertu ki fegi p[ro] su fu[n]dam[en]tu ki poserat Mariane d'Orruu
de nuragi de vinias ad s[an]c[t]a Maria de Bona[r]catu in Billalonga. Kertei
i[n] corona de logu i[n] Aristanis, sendo i[n] kita de verruta Trogotori Seke.
Kertei cu[n] sos ho[min]es c'avia[n]t levatu custu fu[n]dam[en]tu, preideru
5v Constantine | de Bosa et Mariane de Sii et Gonstantine d'Orruu de Villalo[n]ga
et ip[s]os frades et Petru de Varca. Poseru[n]timi a mimi et apsos (*corr.* a
ipsos) a postu k'eo ben[n]e cu[n] sa carta mia. Ben[n]i ego assu postu et ipsos
n[on] ben[n]eru[n]t. Et osca poseru[n]t atteru postu a mercuris de senudu.
Ben[n]i ego et ip[s]os n[on] ben[n]eru[n]t. Et osca poseru[n]t atteru postu
a D[omi]nica de palma. Ben[n]i ego et ip[s]os n[on] ben[n]eru[n]t. Plakit
assuma[r]kesu et a totu sos lib[er]os cantos furu[n]t cussa die in corona, ki mi

8 Duplicated in entry 208.

9 An insertion mark in same hand appears in the left-hand margin.

reed-bed of fig trees') at Milianu, it reaches the hedge (*grisaione*) of the stony ground below Monimentu de sas Tesones ('the tomb of the bird-catching nets'), it reaches the rock of the cross at the spring of Cerkis, and [then] reaches the stones of the threshing floor of Donna, and passes the boundary of the rural complex (*domestia*) of Comida; it procedes to Funtana de Maganse ('the spring of Maganse') and reaches the threshing floors of Campu along the road of Tune, arrives at nuraghe Pikinnu ('little nuraghe') and takes the old road to Castru de Muru ('outcrop of Muru') at Comida; it descends to Cinniga ulpina de mata de Gausari ('fox's reed bed at Gausari's tree') and reaches the entrance (*iaca*) of the meadow of Guppurriu, [then] descends along it in the direction of the river to the vineyards of Muru, [then] descends to Funtana Priva ('the slow spring') at Orruinas and goes down the river and rejoins Cinniga de Figos at Miliana. And of the land (*saltu*) of Oiastru ('wild olive'), the share of which he held, I confirm it [to the monastery] thus. I, iudike Petrus d'Arboree, confirm to this monastery the whole share of lady Tocoele's property and affiliated lands which she donated to provide for the church and for her own tomb (*monumentu*). If they allow five years to elapse before they have performed this service, her brothers, to whom she had donated these lands, shall return them to the church.

I also confirm [to the monastery] the farm complex (*domo*) of Santa Corona di Riòla with all that it has: lands, vineyards, with male and female servants, and with all its flocks.

I also confirm [to the monastery] the farm complex of Santa Barbara de Turre with all that it has: lands, vineyards, and with male and female servants.

2.

In the name of the Lord, amen. I, Petrus, prior of Bonárcado, draw up this charter (*carta*) regarding the litigation I had over the landed property (*fundamentu*) of vineyards that Mariane d'Orruu de Nuragi donated to Sancta Maria di Bonárcado in Billalonga (Villalonga). I had recourse to a hearing of the realm (*corona de logu*) in Aristanis (Oristano), when I was serving at the summons court (*sendo in kita de verruta*) of Trogotori Seke. I argued against the men who had appropriated this land: priest Constantine de Bosa, Mariane de Sii, Gonstantine d'Orruu of Villalonga and his brothers, and Petru de Varca. They ordered me, and also them, to be present on the appointed day with my charter. I came as ordered, but they did not come. Then they appointed another day, the Wednesday of the assembly of the Assumption. I came, but they did not come. So, they appointed another day, which was Palm Sunday. I came, but they did not. The marquis (*markesu*) and all the freemen (*liberos*) who were at the hearing on that day thought it right that the land should be returned to me according to

torrare[n]t custu fu[n]dam[en]tu pro ca[n]tu narravat sa ca[r]ta mia ki no[n] mi '[n]de kertaret plus p[er]unu ho[min]e c'avia ego binkidu p[er] rasone. Et osca iuredi su ho[min]e meu i[n] factu de sa carta, et poseru[n]t a so curatore, a Trogotori Seke, pro torraremi su fu[n]dam[en]tu: custu pro ki kertei et binki.
6r Testimo[n]ios: Trogotori Seke et Mariane de Sii et Gon- | -stantine de Martis et Barusone Sportella et Petru de Nurki et Cerkis d'Orruu et Gun[n]ari de Ba[r]ca de Bauladu et Gunnari d'Uras maiore de buiakesos et Petru Paganu ca[n]celleri. Et ip[s]e Trogotori Seke ben[n]it sa p[er]sone sua a Billalo[n]ga et torredimi custu fu[n]dam[en]tu, iura[n]do[n]de custos ho[min]es pro testimonios: Gonsta[n]tine de Ba[r]ca et Petru de Ba[r]ca et Petru Littera et Furadu Casilis et Trogotori Urzaki et Gonstantine de Mogoro et Gonsta[n]tine Zukellu.

3.[10]

In[11] no[m]i[n]e D[omi]ni. Am[en]. Ego Coa[n]tine de Foge petiili bolu[n]tate assu do[n]nu meu sire Ugo de Bassa, sa die de s[an]c[t]o Ma[r]co de Si[n]nis aissora ka[n]do essia da missa, ki mi daret paravla d'offerremi a s[an]c[t]a Maria d[e] Bona[r]catu cu[n] o[nn]ia ka[n]to avia. Et isse narretimi ca 'fagellu c'a mimi bene plagit et bonu mi parit et paraula ti 'nde do.' Et ego dave go 'nd'ippi paraula daa ssu donnu meu, mi misi i[n] manu de do[n]nu Vivianu
6v p[ri]ore d[e] Bonarca[n]tu na[n]ti su donnu meu | i[n] p[re]se[n]tia sua p[ro] co[n]v[er]su, et dediili i[n] potestate sua o[nn]ia ca[n]tu avia i[n]tro de domo et de foras de domo: t[er]ras et bi[n]gnas, ca[n]tu avia de fu[n]dam[en]tu et de co[m]poru su latus et su lat[us] e[st] de mughere mia. Testes: su do[n]nu meu iudike Ugo d[e] Basso, do[n]nu B[er]na[r]du arkipiscobu da Arbaree, e do[n]nu Bonaco[r]su piscobu de s[an]c[t]a Iusta et donnu Gun[n]ari d[e] Martis curatore dessos Simagis et do[n]nu Barisone Taiabucones et do[n]nu Eissu Sakellu ma[n]nu et do[n]nu Barisone Ispanu et do[n]nu G[unn]a[ri] d[e] Ia[n]na et do[n]nu Gosa[n]tine Orrodellu et do[n]nu Iorgi de Sogos et do[n]nu Iorgi Za[n]cato[r]ta et do[n]nu Arzocu Porcu. Custos ive furu[n] ue co[n]se[n]tivit su do[n]nu meu do[n]nu Ugo de Basso s'afiiamentu ki mi fegi ad s[an]c[t]a Maria d[e] Bona[r]catu p[ro] [combersu] cu[n] totu su meu. Et ta[n]do a[n]d[e]i ad Vonarcatu cu[n] su p[ri]ore et offersimi ad D[eu]s et a s[an]c[t]a Maria et a s[an]c[t]o Zeno d[e]na[n]ti da s'altare suo, u'era[n]t totu sos monacos, p[ro] co[n]v[er]su et i[n] vita et i[n] morte. Et d[e]di totu su meu a D[eu]s et a s[an]c[t]a Maria secu[n]du co avia platicatu et iatu a su p[ri]ore davena[n]ti d[e] su do[n]nu meu Ugo de Bassa iudike d'Arbaree.

---

10 Duplicated in entry 210.

11 Change of hand from *In*. An insertion mark appears in the left-hand margin.

everything that my charter said, and that no one should make any further complaint against me because I had won according to the law (*per rasone*). Then my servant (*homine*) swore to the facts of the charter, and they ordered the *curatore*, Trogotori Seke, to restore to me the land, about which I moved legal action and won. Witnesses: Trogotori Seke, Mariane de Sii, Gonstantine de Martis, Barusone Sportella, Petru de Nurki, Cerkis d'Orruu, Gunnari de Barca from Bauladu, and Gunnari d'Uras head of the entourage (*maiore de buiakesos*), and Petru Paganu the clerk (*cancelleri*). Trogotori Seke came in person to Billalonga and returned this land to me with these men swearing as witnesses: Gonstantine de Barca, Petru de Barca, Petru Littera, Furadu Casilis, Trogotori Urzaki, Gonstantine of Mogoro, and Gonstantine Zukellu.

3.

In the name of Lord, amen. I, Coantine de Foge, asked my lord, sir Ugo de Bassa, on the day of Sancto Marco at Sinis, when he was coming out of Mass, to assure me that I could offer myself as a lay brother to Sancta Maria di Bonárcado with all my possessions. He said to me, 'Do it! For I consent to it, and it seems right to me, and I assure you of it!' And since I had assurance from my lord, I put myself into the hands of lord Viviano, prior of Bonárcado, before my lord in his presence as a lay brother, and gave him in his power all that I owned inside and outside my rustic property (*domo*): land and vineyards, what I already owned by inheritance and half of what I had acquired subsequently by purchase the other half being the property of my wife. Witnesses: my lord Ugo de Basso, lord Bernardu archbishop of Arbarea, lord Bonacorsu bishop of Santa Giusta, lord Gunnari de Martis *curatore* of Simagis, lord Barusone Taiabucones, lord Eissu Sakellu Mannu, lord Barusone Ispanu, lord Gunnari de Ianna, lord Gostantine Orrodellu, lord Iorgi de Sogos, lord Iorgi Zancatorta, and lord Arzocu Porcu. These were present when my lord, lord Ugo de Basso agreed that I should affiliate myself to Sancta Maria di Bonárcado as a lay brother, offering all my property at the same time. Then I went to Bonárcado with the prior and offered myself, in life and in death, as a lay brother to God and Sancta Maria [de Bonárcado] and St Zeno, before his altar, at which all the monks were gathered. And I gave all that I possessed to God and Sancta Maria according to what I had promised and given to the prior before my lord Ugo de Bassa, iudike of Arbarea.

4.[12]

7r Ego Iorgi Ma[r]ras petiili bolu[n]tade a su do[n]nu meu su ma[r]kesu sa die d[e] D[omi]nica d[e] palma se[n]do i[n] missa a s[an]c[t]a Iusta, ke mi daret paraula d'oferimi a s[an]c[t]a Maria d[e] Vonarcatu cu[n] totu cantu avia. Et ipse dedimi asoltura; ponendomi ipse i[n] manu d[e] su p[ri]ore do[n]nu Petru Perusino, mi ofersi a D[eu]s et a s[an]c[t]a Maria cun o[nn]ia ka[n]tu avia: domos et t[er]ras et bi[n]gnas ka[n]tu avia in pa[r]te d[e] Mili in co na[r]rant ca[r]tas mias. Da oe na[n]ti siat pecuiare d[e] s[an]c[t]a Maria de Vona[r]catu totu su meu. Testes: D[eu]s i[n]ante et su do[n]nu meu su ma[r]keso et do[n]nu B[er]na[r]du arkipiscobu d'Arbaree et do[n]nu Mazeu et do[n]nu Ub[er]tu d[e] su Grottu et donnu Saltero d[e] Se[r]ra et do[n]nu Barusone Arbarekesu et do[n]nu Gu[n]nari su frate et Gunnari d[e] Ie[n]na et totu sus ho[min]es bonos ke era[n]t i[n] missa cu[n] su do[n]nu meu, cl[er]icos et laicos.

5.

Posit Maria Cavaione una t[er]ra in Ma[r]zane tenendo a bi[n]gna d[e] Petru
7v d[e] Reu; sa t[er]ra ki posit Petru Alla i[n] Arsbilledu dave su riu | fusca a s'ariola de sa t[er]ra d[e] sos kercos de Bolosvili de Ietadu tenendo a bingna de Zancudi; una t[er]ra in Pasadoriu et atera t[er]ra in Gusnari, una t[er]ra i[n] Istakesos tene[n]do a sos d[e] Corsiga, sa parzone d[e] sa t[er]ra d[e] Ietadu d[e] sa figu d[e] Padina costas a sa t[er]ra d[e] co[m]poru d[e] Furadu Unele.

6.[13]

Posit[14] Grega de Sivi una t[er]ra a clesia i[n] capizale de patro costa a latu d[e] Gu[n]nari d[e] Maluzu capizale a t[er]ra d[e] A[n]tine Corda. Testes: do[n]nu Barasone d[e] Serra, Coa[n]tine Mu[r]tin[u] maiore d[e] scolca d'Errivora, Petro de Scanu nepote suo, do[n]nu Arzocco de Scano.

7.[15]

Conv[er]saise[16] do[n]nu Gua[n]tin[e] Mu[r]tinu a s[an]c[t]a Maria et posit una t[er]ra i[n] cruke d[e] nurake a clesia, capizale a sa domestica d[e] s[an]c[t]a Corona, da s'attera pa[r]te sa t[er]ra de s[an]c[t]a A[n]na. Testes: Gua[n]tinu Madau ma[n]datore de regno, Gua[n]tin[u] de Zori et Arzocco de Ba[r]ca.

---

12 Duplicated in entry 211.

13 Duplicated in entry 212.

14 Change of hand from *Posit*.

15 Duplicated in entry 213.

16 Change of hand from *Conversaise*.

4.
I, Iorgi Marras, asked my lord the marquis on Palm Sunday, when he was at the Mass at Santa Iusta, to give me an assurance that I could offer myself as a lay brother to Sancta Maria di Bonárcado with all my possessions. He gave me permission to do so, delivering myself into the hands of the prior, lord Petru Perusino, I offered myself as a lay brother to God and to Sancta Maria with all that I owned: farm complexes (*domos*), lands, vineyards and as much as I had in the territory (*parte*) of Mili, according to what my charters attest. From this day forth, all that I possess shall be the property of Sancta Maria di Vonarcatu. Witnesses: God in the first place and my lord the marquis, and lord Mazeu and lord Ubertu de su Grottu and lord Saltero de Serra and lord Barusone Arbarekesu and lord Gunnari his brother and Gunnari de Ienna, and all the trusted men (*homines bonos*) who were present at the Mass together with my lord, clerics and laymen.

5.
Maria Cavaione donated a [plot of] land (*terra*) in Marzane bordering on the vineyard of Petru de Reu; the land that Petru Alla had donated in Arsbilledu extending from the river to the threshing floor (*ariola*) of the land of the oaks of Bolosvili de Ietadu, and bordering on the vineyard of Zancudi; a piece of land in Pasadoriu ('resting place') and another piece of land in Gusnari, a piece of land in Istakesos bordering that of de Corsiga, the share of the land of Ietadu, located at Sa Figu ('the fig tree') at Padina, situated on the side of the land that Furadu Unele bought.

6.
Grega de Sivi donated to the church a piece of land located at the top (*capizale*) of the meadow and to the side of the land of Gunnari de Maluzu, at the top of the land of Coantine Corda. Witnesses: lord Barasone de Serra, Coantine Murtinu head of the ward (*maiore de scolca*) at Errivora, Petru de Scanu his nephew, and lord Arzocco de Scano.

7.
Lord Guantine Murtinu made himself a lay brother at Sancta Maria and donated to the church a [plot of] land in Kruke de Nurake ['cross of the nuraghe'], at the head of the farm complex (*domo*) of Santa Corona, and on the other side to the land of Sant'Anna. Witnesses: Guantine Madau representative of the realm (*mandatore de regnu*), Guantine de Zori, and Arzocco de Barca.

8.[17]

In[18] no[m]i[n]e D[omi]ni. Am[en]. Co[n]v[er]saise[19] do[n]nu Comita d[e] Çepera a D[eu]s et a s[an]c[t]a Maria d[e] Vona[r]catu i[n] manu d[e] su p[ri]ore do[n]nu Petru P[er]usino pro fakere·illi a mo[r]te sua se[r]bizu et offiçio de co[m]b[er]su et p[ro] tutare·illo i[n] sa clostra de s[an]c[t]a Maria. Et
8r d[e]dit ta[n]do | p[ro] a[n]i[m]a sua a s[an]c[t]a Maria unu cavallu et una ebba polliricata et unu iuvu et CL b[er]bekes et X mat[ri]cas d[e] po[r]cos. Et i[m]promisit et platicait a morte sua pa[r]zone ka[n]tu at avere unu de fiios suos d[e] o[nn]ia ka[n]tu at d[e] t[er]ras et d[e] bi[n]gnas et d[e] saltos et d[e] serbos et d'a[n]killas et de masciones d[e] o[nn]ia sinnu d[e] grossu et d[e] minutu et d[e] cavallos et ebbas et d[e] o[nn]ia ka[n]tu at avere i[n]tro d[e] domo et foras d[e] domo tractu sas cortes. Testes: D[eu]s e s[an]c[t]a Maria e su p[ri]ore et Irzoccor d[e] Muru ke iscripsit custa ca[r]ta et do[n]nu Mariane de Zepa[ra], do[n]nu Comita d[e] Loy, do[n]nu Gos[antine] d[e] tTori, maystru Bige[n]zu, Gont[ine] O[r]rodellu, Arzoco d[e] Ba[r]ka, Gua[n]tin[e] d[e] Muru p[re]iteru d[e] Senuski, Amira Soia, Gua[n]t[i]n[e] d[e] Fu[n]tana.

9.[20]

Co[n]v[er]sesi[21] do[n]nu Gua[n]tin[e] d'Orruu a D[eu]s et a s[an]c[t]a Maria d[e] Vona[r]catu i[n] manu d[e] su p[ri]ore Bra[n]do et dessos mo[n]acos suos et dedit ta[n]do uno boe et una vacca viglata. Et platicait a morte sua pa[r]zone d[e] uno fiio suo d[e] o[nn]ia ka[n]tu at avere a mo[r]te sua d[e] t[er]ras, de
8v bi[n]gnas et de o[nn]ia ka[n]tu at avere i[n]tro d[e] domo et foras d[e] domo: | boves III, cavallos II, ebbas II et axinus V et su cantu de sa terra cun molinu, qui servit a su conventu de sancta Maria de B[on]ar[ca]tu qui est iu[n]to sa padule de s[anct]a Ma[ri]a et Serralonga et plaza in Macumeri et, partjone pro uno

---

17 Duplicated in entry 214.

18 Change of hand from *In*.

19 Change of hand from *Conversaise*.

20 The entry, starting from the beginning of f. 8v, is written over a previous record which was later erased; the early record is scantily visible and legible. This entry is partially reproduced in 215.

21 Change of hand from *Conversesi* follows a one-line break in the text.

8.
In the name of Lord, amen. Lord Comita de Çepera gave himself to God and Sancta Maria di Bonárcado in the hands of the prior lord Petru Perusino so that the latter, when he [Comita de Çepara] died, would give him the service and the office that is given to a lay brother and would bury him in the cloister of Sancta Maria. He also gave to Sancta Maria, for his soul, a horse and a mare that had already given birth, a yoke of oxen, one hundred and fifty sheep, and ten sows. He promised that when he died he would give the share of the inheritance, which would accrue to one of his children, of all that he possessed: of lands, vineyards and unworked lands (*saltos*), male and female servants, and cattle of every size both large and small, and of horses and mares, and all that he had within and outside his farm property (*domo*), except that of farmyards (*sas cortes*). Witnesses: God and Holy Mary, and the prior, and Irzoccor de Muru who wrote this document (*carta*), and lord Mariane de Zepara, lord Comita de Loy, lord Gostantine de Tori, master (*maystru*) Bigenzu, Gontine Orrodellu, Arzoco de Barka, Guantine de Muru priest from Senuski, Amira Soia, and Guantine de Funtana.

9.
Lord Guantine d'Orruu made himself a lay brother to God and to Sancta Maria di Bonárcado in the hands of prior Brando and his monks and, on that occasion, donated an ox and a calf. He also promised that when he died, he would donate the share of the inheritance that would be due to one of his children of all that he had owned at that time, of land, vineyards, and all that he had had inside and outside his farm complex (*domo*): three oxen, two horses, two mares, and five donkeys, and as much of the land with the mill that serves the convent of Sancta Maria de Bonárcado, located near the marsh (*padule*) of Sancta Maria and Serralonga ('long ridge') and the plot of land (*plaza*) located in Macumeri, and the share of one of his children.

fiiu suo. Testes: Gunnari de Ienna, Guantine Musachi, Petru Pisanu et priore Brando in cuia manu mi ofersi.[22] Et mi lu offerin su molinu glo[ri]a.[23]

10.[24]

In[25] no[m]i[n]e D[omi]ni. Am[en]. Ego Gua[n]tine de Zori Pilardu, ke mi co[m]b[er]su a D[eu]s e a s[an]c[t]a Maria de Vona[r]catu pro remissione de sos peccatos meos in manu d[e] su p[ri]ore Gregori et dessos manacos suos. Asora kando mi confisait d[e]di a s[an]c[t]a Maria unu iuvu et kimbe mat[ri]kis d[e] po[r]cos. Et platicai a mo[r]te mia pa[r]zone d[e] unu fiio miu d[e] o[nn]ia ka[n]tu ap' avere intro de domo et foras d[e] domo, t[er]ras et bi[n]gnas et vaccas et boes, capras et b[er]bekes et po[r]cos et d[e] o[nn]ia steriu i[n]tro d[e] domo fusca a una discu. Testes: D[eu]s et s[an]c[t]a Maria, Trogodori Cocco preitero mio et do[n]na Muscu sa mugeri, Torbini Gur[olo], Gua[n]tine de Unale preitero d[e] Monte Agutu et do[n]nu Dimitri preitero.

11.

9r In nomine X[rist]i. Am[en]. Ann[o] D[omi]ni MCCXXXVIII. Ego Nicolau priore de Bono[r]catu fatio memoria d[e] ca[m]biu q[ui] feki cun Ga[n]ti[n]e Usay. Ca[m]biey sa t[er]ra de bi[n]gia i[n]suta bia d[e] locu, q[ui] e[st] costas assas t[e]rras de Po[n]te et costa a Bera de Lacon, qui est mia. Et isse mi deti sa terra sua d[e]ssas funtanas albas, capiçale assa t[er]ra de santa Elena et costas assa t[er]ra d[e] Paanu, costas a t[er]ra d[e] Stere et clo[m]pet a peale d[e]ssa funtana; ca[m]biando cun bolu[n]tate d[e] pare e bocando·[n]de d[e] si 'nd[e] kertavat neunu ho[min]e mo[r]tale o isse, d'ispiiaremila a ssa[n]ta Maria et pariare a rregnu libra I de a[r]ge[n]tu. T[e]s[te]s: do[n]nu Iu[ann]e p[re]iti de Tatasune, Coan[tine] de Gu[r]gu, Furadu de Ca[m]pu, Furatu Capay de Boele, Torbini Cappay, Terrico Cappay, Troodori de Gurgu.[26]

---

22 This is partially reproduced in entry 215. However, the latter ends at the end of f. 8r, adding the names of the witnesses who do not correspond to those of entry 9, except from Gunnari de Ienna. The list corresponds instead to the witnesses of the following entry, 216, which has no corresponding reproduction. The witnesses of n. 216 are in fact 'Gunnari de Genna et Goantine Muzaki et Pedru Pisanu et priore Brandu', and therefore are the same ones of entry 9; the witnesses of entry 215 are 'Gunnari de Ienna, Nigola de Porta et Pedru Marras et Goantine de Porta.' In entry 216, after priore Brandu we also find the phrase 'a manu mi oferi', which is not present in entry 215.

23 This sentence has no apparent connection with the details recorded in the entry.

24 Duplicated in entry 214.

25 Change of hand from *In*.

26 The next three lines of text are illegible.

10.

In the name of Lord, amen. [It is] I, Guantine de Zori Pilardu, who commit myself as a lay brother to God and Sancta Maria de Vonarcatu for remission of my sins [and put myself] into the hands of prior Gregori and his monks. When he gave me the confession, I gave to Sancta Maria a yoke of oxen and five sows. I also promised that when I died, I would give my share of the inheritance due to one of my children of all that I had at that time within and outside my farm property (*domo*): land, vineyards, cows and oxen, goats, sheep and pigs, and all the dishes (*steriu*) I had in my house, down to a single bowl. Witnesses: God and Holy Mary, Trogodori Cocco my priest (*preitero*), and lady Muscu his wife, Torbini Gurolo, Guantine de Unale priest of Monteagutu, and lord Dimitri the priest.

11.

In the name of Christ, amen. In the year of the Lord 1238, I, Nicolau prior of Bonorcatu, record the memory of an exchange I made with Gantine Usay. I exchanged the land of Bingia ('vineyard'), which is my property, situated below the main road (*via de locu*), and which is next to the lands of Ponte ('bridge') and next to the property of Bera de Lacon. He gave me his land of Funtanas Albas ('white springs') at the top of the land of Sant'Elena and next to the land of Paanu by the land of Stere coming to the foot of the spring. The exchange was made by mutual agreement and with the clause that, if any person or he himself had made a dispute about it, he would have repaid for eviction (*d'ispiiaremila*) in favour of Sancta Maria and would have paid the treasury a pound of silver. Witnesses: lord Iuanne priest of Tatasune (Tadasuni), Coantine de Gurgu, Furadu de Campu, Furatu Capay de Boele, Torbeni Cappay, Terrico Cappay, and Troodori de Gurgu.

12.[27]

In nomini D[omi]ni. Am[en]. Ego Nicolao, p[ri]ore de Bona[r]cato, reco[r]da-
tione[m] facio p[ro] sa cu[r]te ke fuit de Gua[n]tine de Po[r]ta k'aviat iata
a s[an]c[t]a Maria cu[n] totu s'ateru suo. Petivimi·illa Comita de Zuri pro
bi[n]diri·illa. Et ego dedi·illa i[n] co[m]bentu d'aberese·illa ip[s]e et sa mugieri
et fiios suos. Et ip[s]e dediminde xxx bisa[n]ti. I[n] fine se moriat ipse ken'
abere fiios, remanere a s[an]c[t]a Maria i[n] dono pro s'a[n]i[m]a sua kusta
9v co[r]te et o[nn]ia meiorame[n]tu | ka[n]tu avissi fatu ivi et o[nn]ia sua bona
remanea[n]t a s[an]c[t]a Maria de Bona[r]ca[n]to p[ro] s'a[n]i[m]a sua. Et
sa pa[r]te de sa mugiere, si obierit sine filiis, remaneat tota assa domo d[e]
s[an]c[t]a Maria p[ro] s'a[n]i[m]a sua. Et si aliq[u]and[o] co[n]ti[n]geret
q[uo]d ip[s]e Comita v[el] successor ei[us] sive heres vellet predicta[m]
curia[m] ve[n]dere n[on] habeat potestate[m] ve[n]dendi ea[m] nisi ec-
cl[es]ie beate Marie de Bona[r]ca[n]to, si p[ri]or qui t[un]c fu[er]it i[n]
eade[m] eccl[es]ia ea[m] emere volu[er]it pro eo p[re]tio quo ea[n]de[m]
curia[m] emit ip[s]e Comita a p[re]dicto p[ri]ore. Dona[n]di vero ea[m]
curia[m] potestate[m] n[on] habeat p[re]dict[us] Comita nec fili[us] ab eo
desce[n]de[n]s nec heres ei[us] aliq[ui]s v[el] successor nisi eccl[es]ie
s[an]c[t]e Marie de Bona[r]ca[n]to. T[e]s[te]s: f[rate]r Bene monac[us],
p[re]it[er]o Cocco, p[re]it[er]o Gua[n]tine Lelle, Nicola de Pane, Joh[ann]e
Zuria, Samaritan[us] clerigu, Miale de Kerchi, Gua[n]tine de Scalas, Gua[n]tine
Cauleti, Joh[ann]e Piga, Jo[r]gi Loque, Gregori Co[n]tu et alios multos.

13.

Ego[28] p[ri]ore Benedictu de Bono[r]canto fatio r[ecordacionem] dessu q[ui]
deit Co[m]i[t]a de Çori a ssantu Pet[r]u d[e] Bitoni. Deit sa domestica d[e]
Ca[m]pu de Liva q[ui] est costas a te[r]ra d[e] donna ma[n]na: et collat totue
10r bia | d[e] Campeta et clo[m]pet assa furcatura de Lenake et calat pus bia
d[e]rettu assa te[r]ra d[e] G[uantine] Colome et affliscat. T[este]s: p[re]viteru
Ma[n]ca, Gu[nna]ri de S[er]ra, Coa[ntine] d[e] Cupalla jacunu d[e] Bangeliu,
Saltaro d[e] S[er]ra, Orçoco d'O[r]ruu, Mari[an]e Ça[n]cute.

14

Deti do[n]nu Mari[an]e de Gunale, p[re]viteru a ssa[n]tu Pe[tr]u de Bitoni, sa domestica d'O[r]rea q[ui] est capiçale assa bia q[ui] collat a nNuroço et e[st] costas assu erriu de Baracconi et est capiçale assa te[r]ra d[e] do[n]nu

27 Duplicated in entry 26.

28 Change of hand from *Ego*.

12.
In the name of Lord, amen. I, Nicolao, prior of Bonarcato, make remembrance of the farm (*curte*) which was the property of Guantine de Porta, who had donated it to Sancta Maria together with the rest of his property. Comita de Zuri asked me to sell him it. I gave it to him on the condition that he and his wife and their children would have it. So, he gave me thirty bezants (*bisanti*) in payment for it with the stipulation that if he died without having any child, that farm and any improvements he had made to it should remain as a gift to Sancta Maria for his soul, as well as all his possessions. Also his wife's share, if she died childless, shall all remain with the estate of Sancta Maria for her soul. If it should happen that the said Comita, or one of his successors or heirs would wish to sell the said farm, let him not have the power to sell it except to the church of Sancta Maria de Bonarcanto, [that is to say] if the prior who governed at that time in the same church would want to buy the said farm at the same price with which the said Comita bought it from the said prior. Neither the said Comita, nor any child of his descendants nor any heir or successor of his has the power to donate this farm except to the church of Sancta Maria di Bonárcado. Witnesses: brother Bene the monk, priest Cocco, priest Guantine Lelle, Nicola de Pane, Johanne Zuria, Samaritano the cleric, Miale de Kerchi, Guantine de Scalas, Guantine Cauleti, Johanne Piga, Jorgi Loque, Gregori Contu, and many others.

13.
I, prior Benedictu of Bonorcanto, make remembrance of what Comita de Çori donated to Santu Petru de Bitoni (Bidonì). He gave the farm complex (*domestica*) of Campu de Liva ('field of Liva') with its appurtenances which is next to the land of lady Manna: the boundary of it goes up along the road of Campeda ('plateau'), it reaches the fork at Lenake and descends beyond the road in the direction of the land of Guantine Colome, and there rejoins [the starting point]. Witnesses: priest Manca, Gunnari de Serra, Coantine de Cupalla, the deacon in charge of reading the Gospel (*jacunu de bangeliu*), Saltaro de Serra, Orçoco d'Orruu, and Mariano Çancute.

14.
Lord Mariane de Gunale the priest donated to Santu Petru de Bitoni (Bidonì) the farm complex (*domestica*) of Orrea located at the top of the road that goes up to Nuroço and is situated next to the river of Baracconi at the top of the

Pisanellu et costas assa bia q[ui] collat a Bitoni. T[este]s: Orzoco d[e] Muru d[e] Monte Acutu, p[re]viteru Ma[n]ca, Baris[one] d[e] Loy, Baris[one] d[e] Gunale, Mallu[ru] d[e] Stere, Baris[one] d[e] Ma[r]tis.

15.

Anno Domini MCC.[29] [I]n Dei nomine. Ego Benedictus p[ri]or sa[n]c[t]e Marie de Bono[r]canto fatio co[m]memoratione[m] d[e]ssa c[on]ve[r]satione q[ui] si fekit a santa Maria de Bono[r]catu do[n]nu G[unnar]i de Serra su de Lokeri in manus mias. D[e]it in temp[us] meu boe unu d[e] domare, bacca una p[ro]xima et sues VII p[ro]ximas, et custu deti sende ego p[ri]ore. Et i[n] temp[us] de do[n]nu Nicolau p[ri]ore d[e]ti iugu unu a santu Sergi de Suei, et iugu unu assa co[r]te de Kiese et d[e]ti a sSuei po[r]cos XV et d[e]ti a sSuei b[er]b[e]k[es] X. Custu totu d[e]ti prossa a[n]i[m]a sua a s[an]cta Maria de Bono[r]cantu ca[n]do se acco[n]v[er]seti i[n] bita et clo[m]pit dare sendesi biu: p[rou]n[d]e su co[r]pus se devet sepellire per m[an]u dessos monacos in su monasteriu d[e] Bono[r]ca[n]tu.

16.[30]

10v Ego p[ri]ore Beneditu facio memoria d[e]ssa co[n]v[ersatione] de do[n]na Io[r]gia de S[er]ra Ocluba[r]ia de Sorratile ca be[n]nit a mo[r]te et ca c[on]firmeti et d[e]ti su ca[n]tu aviat datu in manus d[e] p[ri]ore A[r]rigu d[e]ssu cantu futi in Boele et d[e] te[r]raticu et d'abba et dessu nassariu. T[este]s: Jua[nne] Mu[r]tinu p[re]iti et issa villa de Sorratile, Gu[nna]ri Ma[n]ca p[re]iti de Bitoni.[31]

17.

11r In[32] n[om]ine trini et uni[us] Dei. Am[en]. Nos Bernardus Dei gra[tia] eccl[es]ie Arborensis archiep[i]sc[o]p[u]s dilectis in Ch[rist]o filiis Philippo abbati monasterii sa[n]c[t]i Çenonis in Pisis constituti et Petro priori monasterii s[an]c[t]i Çenonis de Bonarcanto ei[us]q[ue] fr[atr]ib[us] tam presentib[us] qua[m] futuris in perpetuum, iustis pete[n]tium desideriis prompto. Nos condecet animo assensu[m] prebere et ea que pietas exigit

29 This is followed by a two-centimetre erasure mark.

30 The entry is repeated, but with variations, in entry 31; however, because the latter records prior Arrigu instead, entry 16 appears to be a subsequent memorandum entry, made subsequently by prior Beneditu.

31 A gap of eleven ruled lines has been left before the next entry that begins at the top of folio 11r.

32 Change of hand from *In*.

land of lord Pisanellu and next to the road that goes up to Bitoni. Witnesses: Orçoco de Muru from Monte Acutu, priest Manca, Barusone de Loy, Barusone de Gunale, Malluru de Stere, and Barusone de Martis.

15.
In the year of the Lord 12[...]. In the name of God, I, Benedictus, prior of Sancta Maria de Bonorcanto, record that lord Gunnari de Serra from Lokeri committed himself as a lay brother into my hands. During the time I was prior, he donated an ox that was still to be tamed, a pregnant cow and seven pregnant sows; and this he gave when I was prior. Also in the time when lord Nicolau was prior, he gave a pair of oxen to Santu Sergi of Suei, and a pair of oxen to the farm (*corte*) of Kiese; and he also gave to Suei, fifteen swine and ten sheep. All this he gave and came to give while he was alive, for his soul, to Sancta Maria di Bonorcantu when he became a lay brother in life, for which his body must be buried by the hands of the monks at the monastery of Bonorcantu.

16.
I, prior Beneditu, record that lady Iorgia de Serra Oclubaria ('with clear eyes') from Sorradile made herself a lay sister: she came to death and confirmed the donation of all that she had already given over into the hands of prior Arrigu of all he had in Boele: arable land (*de terraticu*), water resources (*d'abba*) and the weir (*nassariu*). Witnesses: priest Juanne Murtinu and the village of Sorratile (Sorradile), [and] Gunnari Manca priest of Bitoni (Bidonì).

17. [Latin]
In the name of the Triune God (*trini e unius Dei*), amen. We, Bernardus, by the grace of God, archbishop of the church of Arborea, well disposed to the just desires of our beloved postulants in Christ, Philippo abbot of the monastery of St Zeno in Pisa and Petro, prior of the monastery of St Zeno in Bonárcado and his brethren, both present and future in perpetuity. It pleases our soul to grant our assent; and so, it is right that we grant and confirm to such pious and

et veritas non relinquit sic piis et venerabilib[us] locis concedere debemus atque firmare ut nulla in poster[um] fideliu[m] mentib[us] que et a[m]biguitas remanere. Ea p[ro]pt[er], dilecti in D[omi]no filii, v[est]ris iustis postulationib[us] inclinati, licet infrascripta ta[n]to t[em]p[o]re vos et eccl[es]ia v[est]ra quiete et pacifice possideritis cui[us] non extat memoria, ne de cetero a nobis et o[m]nib[us] successorib[us] n[ost]ris v[el] alicui ipsorum nostrum sup[er] hiis ullo modo molestemini.

Eccl[es]iam s[an]c[t]e Marie de Bonarchanto, monasteriu[m] s[an]c[t]i Çenonis ibidem positum, eccl[es]ia[m] sancti Georgii de Calcaria et eccl[es]iam sancti Simeonys de Vegela et eccl[es]ia s[an]c[t]i Petri de Milo pic-
11v chinno et | eccl[es]ia s[an]c[t]i Agustini de Agustis et eccl[es]ia s[an]c[t]e Victorie de Montesanto et eccl[es]ia s[an]c[t]e Barbare de Turre et eccl[es]ia s[an]c[t]e Corone de Rivole, in qua ius patronatus habetis, vobis et eccl[es]ie v[est]re iam dicte concedimus et prese[n]tis privilegii pagina confirmam[us], adicientes q[uo]d in predictis eccl[es]iis et parrochiis ipsar[um] decimas, primitias, oblationes, penite[n]tias sanor[um] et infirmor[um] et sepulturas tam masculor[um] quam feminar[um], parvulor[um] et adultor[um], ta[m] ibidem degentiu[m] qua[m] advenar[um], et o[m]niu[m] rer[um] et bonor[um] homin[um] parrocchianor[um] eccl[es]iar[um] predictar[um] o[mn]i[u]nq[ue] divinor[um] potestatem in eis libere et absolute habeatis, excepto q[uo]d i[n] nulla suprad[ict]ar[um] eccl[es]iaru[m] solempne batisma facietis pret[er] qua[m] in eccl[es]ia s[an]c[t]i Augustini de Agustis. Statuentes om[n]ino ut nulli p[er]sone liceat in parrochiis predictar[um] eccl[es]iar[um] oratoriu[m] aliq[uo]d erigere seu eccl[es]iam fabricare nisi de licentia v[est]ra v[el] successor[um] v[est]ror[um]. Nec alicui persone v[el] loco fas sit suprascripta o[m]nia vel aliq[uo]d eor[um] istor[um] infringere diminuere seu in aliquo violare. Si quis aute[m] clericus vel laicus hanc nostre co[n]cessionis pagina[m] infringere vel rumpere sive diminuere temtaverit, indignatione[m] Dei o[mn]ipote[n]tis et beate Marie semp[er] virginis se noverit incursurum, excommunicationis vinculo innodatu[m]. Et ad p[er]petua[m] hui[us] n[ost]ri privilegii firmitatem volumus illud n[ost]ri sigilli imp[r]essio[n]e signari atque firmari. Et ita tali ordine hec om[n]ia Bonalber-
12r gum iudicem | et notarium domni imperatoris scribe[re] rogavi. Actum Pisis in ballatorio dom[us] clastri (*corr.* castri) eccl[es]ie s[an]c[t]e Viviane, presentibus donno B[e]r[n]a[r]do monacho sancti Çenonis, Rosselmino aurifice quondam Bernardi et Guiglielmo aurifice filio Guiglielmi aurificis testib[us] ad hec rogatis.

Dominice vero incarnationis anno millesimo ducentesimo, inditione quartadecima (*corr.* quarta), tertiodecimo kalendas novembris. Ego Bernardus arborensis archiep[iscopu]s propria manu subscripsi et aliis subscribendu[m]

venerable places all that piety requires and that is befitting the truth, so that faithful minds which will come afterwards may be free of all doubt. Therefore, beloved children in the Lord, being inclined to your just requests, it is lawful for you and your church to remain, peacefully and without conflict, in possession of the things hereunder, which have been yours for so long and such a time that memory of them is lost, and furthermore that neither from us, nor from any of our successors, nor from any of us, should you suffer impediment in regard to these things.

The church of Sancta Maria de Bonárcado, the monastery of St Zeno located there, the church of Sancta Georgii at Calcaria and the church of Sancti Simeonys at Vegela and the church of Sancti Petru at Mili Pichinno, and the church of Sancti Agustini at Austis, and the church of Sancte Victorie of Montesanto, and the church of Sancte Barbare of Turre (Torres), and the church of Sancta Corone at Rivola (Riòla), in which you have the right of patronage: to you and to your above-mentioned church, we grant and confirm what is written in the present privilege, adding that in the above-mentioned churches and parishes you may collect the respective tithes, offerings, tributes, administer the penances of the healthy and the sick and the burials of both males and females, both children and adults, both residents therein and outsiders, as well as, in the aforesaid, you are granted free and absolute power over all things, over the good parishioners of the said churches and the administration of all sacred things, except that in none of the said churches may you administer solemn baptisms, with the exception of the church of Sancti Augustini at Agustis. And at the same time, we decree that no one shall be permitted to erect in the parishes of the above-mentioned churches any oratory, nor to build any church except with your permission or that of your successors. Neither shall it be lawful for any person, or realm (*loco*), to infringe, weaken, or in any way violate any of the above. And whosoever, whether cleric or layman, shall attempt to break, weaken, or annul this our grant herein written, know that he shall incur the wrath of Almighty God and of blessed and forever-Virgin Mary, and be subject to the bond of excommunication. And in perpetual confirmation of this, our privilege, we wish to secure it by imprinting our seal upon it. Thus, I have requested Bonalbergo, judge and notary to the emperor, to write all the above in this manner. Drawn up in Pisa in the loggia of the fortified house (*in ballatorio domus castri*) of Santa Bibiana, in the presence of lord Bernardo, monk of St Zeno, Rosselmino the goldsmith (*aurifice*) son of the late Bernardo, and Guiglielmo the goldsmith and son of Guiglielmo, summoned as witnesses.

Sunday of the year of the Incarnation 1204, of the fourth Indiction, on the 20th day of October. I, Bernardus archbishop of Arborea, have undersigned in

consensi. Ego Bonalbergus Ventrilii quonda[m] fili[us], domini imp[er]atoris Romanorum iudex et notarius, ha[n]c cartam, mandato s[u]p[ra]scripti domini archiep[iscop]i arborensis, scripsi, firmavi, complevi et dedi et datam complevi. Notumq[ue] sit o[mn]ibus dictos fratres habere po[testa]tem eligendi prepositum cum hac t[ame]n reserva[tion]e ut prior electus a fratribus Pisis cognoscat dominum suum iudike Constantinum successoresque suos veros et legitimos patronos sancte Marie de Bonarcanto sic ut prepositus sit de consensu et voluntate eiusdem et successorum suorum in quorum fide ego Bonalbergus Ventreli quondam filius hanc cartam subscripsi.

18.

12v Ego[33] Gregorius, p[ri]ore d[e] Bono[r]catu, facio memoria ke mi se co[n]verseti do[n]na Maria de Laco[n] de Sorratile a santa Christina de Bono[r]catu et d[e]ti do[nn]ia ca[n]tu aviat in Boele et te[r]ras et issa pa[r]te sua dessu nassariu giossu de pisq[ui]na d'Oiu, d[e] tres partes una. Custu d[e]it cu[n] volu[n]tate d'o[n]nia fiio suo. T[e]s[te]s: Goa[ntine] d'Orruvu, Saltaro preiteru de Bitoni, Gunnari de Serra de Bitoni et issu preiti suo testes.

19.

Ego[34] p[ri]ore Ioh[ann]i. Posit Terico de Scopedu a s[an]c[t]a Mar[ia] de Bona[r]cadu et a s[an]c[t]u Sergiu de Suei sa domestiga sua de Puçus Strilliges, cu[m]{mit}e[n]do intro sas terras qui apo comporadas. Inguiçadi cussa domestiga dae ssu bau dessa Mela et falat totue pus flumen i[n] co benit a bau de Ca[r]ruga deretu a pischina d'equas et falat su flumen usque ad su guturu dessa scala dessa bia qui benit ad Orruinas et collat ad su montiglu dessa terra albina derectu assu montiglu de Puçu de Forada et collat assa bia derecta qui be[n]ta cun Pedru et moliat sa bia d'Orogogo et falat sa bia d[e] Coçula deretu a Pupusone, deretu a bau dessa Mela et ibi fliscat. T[e]s[te]s: do[n]nu Com[it]a de Laco[n] archiepiscopu et Paucapalea piscopu et do[n]nigellu Orzoco.

20.[35]

13r Ego[36] Gregorius, p[ri]ore de Bona[r]cadu, fazo reco[r]datio[n]e | de II ho[min]es, ki posit iudice Petru de Serra d'Arbaree ad s[an]c[t]a Maria de Bona[r]cadu: a Bera Piana et a Ioh[ann]e su fiiu, p[ro] s'a[n]i[m]a de Iudice Barusone su patri et p[ro] s'a[n]i[m]a de mama mia et pro s'a[n]i[m]a mia et

33 Change of hand from *Ego*.
34 Change of hand from *Ego*.
35 Duplicated in entries 102 and 218.
36 Change of hand from *Ego*.

my own hand and have given consent to others to undersign. I, Bonalbergus, child of the late Ventrilio, judge and notary to the emperor of the Romans, have written this charter (*carta*) on behalf of the aforementioned lord archbishop of Arborea, signed it, fully drafted it, and dated it. Let it be known to all, that the said brothers have the power to elect a superintendent (*prepositus*), but with this reservation: that the superintendent elected by the brothers of Pisa recognises his lord, iudike Constantinus and his successors, as the true and legitimate patrons of Sancta Maria di Bonárcado and that, likewise, the superintendent rules with the consent and will of the said lord and his successors; in whose faith I, Bonalbergus, son of the late Ventreli, signed this document (*carta*).

18.
I, Gregorius, prior of Bonorcatu, record that lady Maria de Lacon of Sorratile made herself a lay sister into my hands at Santa Christina de Bonorcatu, and donated all that she possessed in Boele: the land and her share, equivalent to a quarter, of the weir situated below the pond (*pisquina*) at Oiu. She did this with the consent of all her children. Witnesses: Goantine d'Orruvu, Saltaro priest of Bidonì, Gunnari de Serra from Bitoni (Bidonì), and the priests as his witnesses.

19.
I, prior Iohanni: Terico de Scopedu donated to Sancta Maria de Bonarcadu and to Sanctu Sergiu at Suei his rustic property (*domestiga*) of Puzus Strilliges ('dry wells'), so that unity and connection within the lands I [already] bought was created. The boundary of this property begins at Bau dessa Mela ('ford of the apple') and descends along the river beyond it; there it reaches Bau de Carruga ('ford of the carriage') in the direction of Pischina d'Equas ('mares' pond') and descends the river until the track (*guturu*) of the steep road that reaches Orruinas and climbs the hill of Terra Albina ('white land'); [it then goes] in the direction of the hill of Puzu ('well') at Forada and climbs the straight stretch of the road that runs along the property of Pedru, [then] turns on the way of Orogogo and goes down the way of Coçula towards Pupusone in the direction of the Bau dessa Mela where it rejoins the starting point. Witnesses: lord Comita de Lacon, the archbishop; bishop Paulcapelea, and *donnigellu* Orzoco.

20.
I, Gregorius, prior of Bonarcadu, record the memory of two men (*homines*) whom iudike Petru de Serra of Arborea gave to Sancta Maria de Bonarcadu: Bera Piana and her son, Iohanne, for the soul of iudike Barusone his father, and for the soul of my mother, and for my soul, and for the remission of my sins.

pro remissio[n]e de sus peccados meos. T[e]s[te]s: do[n]nu Bernardu archipiscobu d'Arbaree et donnu Bonaco[r]su piscobu d[e] s[an]c[t]a Iusta et do[n]nu Gu[n]nari de Ie[n]na curadore de pa[r]te de Miili et do[n]nu Saltoro de Serra et Mariane de Barca et donnu Gu[n]nari d'Uras et Goa[n]tine de Po[r]ta et Nicola de Pane et Comida Pira et Nigola de Po[r]ta.

21.

Ego Gregori[us], p[ri]ore de Bona[r]cadu, fazo reco[r]datio[n]e de kertu, ke fegi megu Gua[n]tine Ma[r]ki. Kertai megu na[r]rando: 'ke[r]to cu[n] su priore pro XXX po[r]cos, ke p[re]stait patre miu a s[an]c[t]a Maria i[n] su te[m]p[us] de do[n]nu Domesticus, ki li me to[r]raret.' Et ego na[r]reilli: 'Patre tuo se[r]bu de s[an]c[t]a Maria de Bo[nar]cadu fuit et bi[n]diki a[n]nos stetit in Lugudore et p[er]dit su serbizu de sa domo de s[an]c[t]a Maria ke li ditava de se[r]bire; et p[ro] custu se[r]bizu ke p[er]dit, li levait kustos porcos p[ro] ke
13v k[er]tas como.' | P[re]co[n]tait do[n]nu Barusone Spanu, ki arreea sa corona sutta iudike de Gallure, potesta[n]do ip[s]e ta[n]do sa t[er]ra d'A[r]baree p[ro] iustitia, si erat i[n] potestade de su do[n]nu levare de su fatu de su serbu. Aco[r]dar[un]si sus ho[min]es de corona ka erat razone, ka[n]do plakiat a su do[n]nu, et i[n] to[r]tu et i[n] diretu, levare d[e] sa causa d[e] su serbu et usadu de sa t[er]ra d'A[r]baree erat. Rema[n]sitsinde Gua[n]tine Ma[r]ki p[ro] vi[n]kidu. Spiatu custu ke[r]tu, kerfit Gu[n]nari Ie[n]na raizone de sa gama de iudike a Gua[n]tine Ma[r]ki, k'aviat apita a maiore; mi[n]imait, ke n[on] potuit razone to[r]rare si co li kereat ip[s]e. Levar[un]illi sas causas suas cu[n] sa causa d[e] iudike et bolea[n]t te[n]ne·illu p[er] sa p[er]sona. Jetaitse Gua[n]tine Ma[r]ki a pede a su p[ri]ore et p[re]gaitimi ki ego lu basare a iudike et ego p[re]gai a iudike et a sos curatores; et ip[s]i p[ro] D[eu]s et p[ro] s[an]c[t]a
14r Maria et p[ro] amore meu li p[er]donar[un] o[nn]ia ka[n]tu | li kerea[n]t. Be[n]nit Gua[n]tine Ma[r]ki a s'altare d[e] s[an]c[t]o Zeno et iurait sup[ra] s'altare et sup[ra] sa .+. [cruke] da inde i[n]anti serbire ip[s]e et fiios suos pro serbos a s[an]c[t]a Maria de Bona[r]cadu usq[ue] i[n] se[m]pit[er]nu[m]. Et p[er]donai su ke[r]tu k'aviat fatu megu p[ro] sos porcos; si p[er]una razone ip[s]e k'aviat, p[ro] se et p[ro] kalu[n]ka p[er]sona, razone ke bolesse dima[n]dare: ip[s]e p[ro] tuti aviat ke[r]tadu et pro tuti p[er]donai. T[es]t[e]s: do[n]nu Joh[ann]e Sa[n]tesu, do[n]nu Ma[r]tinu Meo, do[n]nu Petru O[r]sa, do[n]nu Barusone Spanu curadore d[e] Nurabulia, Comita d[e] Se[r]ra Pistore ke[r]kidore maiore, Gu[n]nari Ie[n]na, curadore d[e] pa[r]te Miili, Gomita Pira, Gua[n]t[ine] de Po[r]ta, Ioh[ann]e Vulpia, Gu[n]nari d[e] Zuri d[e] s[an]c[t]u Eru d[e] Si[m]makis.

Witnesses: lord Bernardu archbishop of Arborea and lord Bonacorsu, bishop of Sancta Iusta, and lord Gunnari de Ienna *curadore* of the territory (*parte*) of Miili, and lord Saltoro de Serra, and Mariane de Barca, and lord Gunnari d'Uras, and Goantine de Porta, and Nicola de Pane, and Comida Pira, and Nigola de Porta.

21.

I, Gregorius, prior of Bonarcadu, record the memory concerning the legal action that Guantine Marki brought against me. He argued with me, saying: 'I am arguing with the prior about thirty pigs which my father lent to Sancta Maria at the time lord Domesticus [was the prior], so that he may return them to me!' I said to him: 'Your father was a servant of Sancta Maria de Bonárcado and stayed for fifteen years in Lugudore (Logudoro) and neglected the service to the house of Sancta Maria that he was due to perform; and because of the loss of this service, [lord Domestico] took away these pigs about which you are now arguing!' Lord Barusone Spanu, who presided over the hearing of the iudike of Gallura, who at that time was in charge of justice in the land (*terra*) of Arborea, asked if it was in the lord's power to requisition the property of his servant. The men at the hearing (*homines de corona*) agreed that it was right, since it pleased the lord, right or wrong, to requisition the property of his servant, and that this was also the custom (*usadu*) of the land of Arborea. So, Guantine Marki was the loser in the judgement. This quarrel resolved, Gunnari Ienna wanted Guantine Marki to account for the iudike's cattle which he had in his custody as supervisor (*maiore*); the latter was defeated since he could not account for what he [Gunnari Ienna] asked him. They confiscated his property and that of the iudike, and wanted to hold him prisoner. Guantine Marki threw himself at the prior's feet and begged me to kiss the iudike, and I begged the iudike and the *curatores*, and they, by God and Sancta Maria and for my sake, excused him all that they wanted him to account for. Guantine Marki came to the altar of St Zeno and swore on the altar and on the cross that, henceforth, he and his children, as servants, would serve Sancta Maria de Bonarcadu forever. I forgave him the fact that he had made an unfounded quarrel with me about the pigs, so that if he [Guantine Marki], on his own behalf or on behalf of other people, wanted to call the monastery to account, he [Guantine Marki] had moved legal action for all of them and for all of them I [prior Gregorius] had forgiven. Witnesses: lord Johanne Santesu, lord Martinu Meo, lord Petru Orsa, lord Barusone Spanu *curatore* of Nurabulia, Comita de Serra Pistore senior tax official (*kerkidore maiore*), Gunnari Ienna, *curadore* of the territory (*parte*) of Miili, Gomita Pira, Guantine de Porta, Iohanne Vulpia, Gunnari de Zuri of Sanctu Eru (San Vero) from Simakis (Simaxis).

22.[37]

Ego Gregori[us], p[ri]ore de Bona[r]cadu, pa[r]tivi cu[n] iudice d[e] Gallulu. Coiuvedi Goa[n]tine Mameli, serbu d[e] s[an]c[t]a Maria de Bonarcadu, cu[n] Maria de Lee, a[n]cilla de iudice d[e] Gall[ul]; feger[un] II fiios: Zipari et Justa. Clesia levait a Zipari et iudice levait a Justa. T[es]t[e]s: Nigola de Pane, Comida Pira, Goa[n]tine de Porta a[r]m[en]tariu dessu archipiscobu.

23.[38]

14ᵛ Ego Furato Birdis, ki mi co[m]mitto, ego et mugere mia Justa Kekali a bolu[n]tade d[e] pari, i[n] manu d[e] D[eu]s et d[e] s[an]c[t]a Maria d[e] Bona[r]cadu et de su p[ri]ore do[n]nu[m] Nicolau et dessus manacos suos p[ro]ssa vita et p[ro]ssa mo[r]te. Et po[n]nem[us] o[nn]ia apitu ka[n]tu am[us] et ka[n]tu am[us] potere akatare fusca assa mo[r]te n[ost]ra: dom[us] et co[r]te ki am[us] i[n] sa billa de Sinuski et t[er]ras et bi[n]nias et causa ka[n]tu am[us] aere i[n]tro d[e] domo et foras de domo. Totu lu dam[us] a s[an]c[t]a Maria d[e] Bona[r]cadu p[ro]ssas a[n]i[m]as n[ost]ras; et sus co[r]p[us] nostros et sas a[n]i[m]as offerim[us] a s[an]c[t]a Maria de Bona[r]cadu. T[es]t[e]s: p[ri]m[us] D[eu]s et s[an]c[t]a Maria et do[n]nu Nicolau su p[ri]ore, et sos manacos suos et Comita Pistore curadore d[e] Bona[r]cadu, et Nigola de Pane et Gua[n]tine d[e] Porta et Comita Pira et alios m[u]ltos. Hoc actu[m] e[st] i[n] festivitate o[m]niu[m] s[an]c[t]or[um] anno D[omi]ni MCCXXVIII i[n] claustro s[an]c[t]i Zenonis, regna[n]te iudice Mariano.

24.

Ego Nicolaus, prior de Bona[r]cadu, reco[r]datione[m] facio de ke[r]tu ki fegi cu[n] Gua[n]tine Fo[r]miga, ka be[n]nit ip[s]e assa billa de Miili Piki[n]nu et fraigai domo et ortu et bi[n]nias et arbores posuit a to[r]tu desso p[ri]ore de Bona[r]cadu. Kertai cu[n]de i[n] corona de s[an]c[t]u Nicola nar[r]a[n]doli 'kertu cu[n] Gua[n]tine Fo[r]mica ki m'ait la[r]gatu i[n] su saltu et i[n] sa
15ʳ billa | mia[39] k'apo in ca[r]ta bollata et e[st] arrennatu.' Na[r]rai ipse 'non lo skia ki fosse arrennatu et ke l'avesse in carta bollata s[an]c[t]a Maria.' Battusi sa carta bollata a corona et lessiru[n]tilla e binkilo et deru[n]timi sa domo et sa binea et s'ortu et sas arbores et o[nn]ia ka[n]tu aviat fatu. T[e]s[te]s: iudice Mariano et donnu Trogodore arkipiscobu d'A[r]baree, do[n]nu Buzakese Pinna iudike de fatu, do[n]nu Petru Murtinu curadore d[e] pa[r]te de Miili, donnu

37 Duplicated in entry 220.

38 Duplicated in entry 221.

39 Change of hand from *mia*.

22.
I, Gregorius, prior of Bonarcadu, made a division of property with the iudike of Gallulu (Gallura). Goantine Mameli, servant of Sancta Maria de Bonarcadu, married Maria de Lee, servant of the iudike of Gallura; they had two children: Zipari and Justa. The church took Zipari and the iudike took Justa. Witnesses: Nigola de Pane, Comida Pira, Goantine de Porta administrator (*armentariu*) of the archbishop.

23.
I, Furato Birdis and my wife, Justa Kekali, by common consent, commit ourselves into the hands of God and Sancta Maria di Bonarcadu and the prior lord Nicolau and his monks for life and death. We give all that we possess and have and all that we will be able to collect and acquire until the day of our death: the rustic estates (*domus*) and the farmyard (*corte*) that we have in the village (*billa*) of Sinuski, lands and vineyards and all that we will be able to have inside and outside our estates (*domus*). We give everything to Sancta Maria de Bonarcadu for our souls; and our bodies and souls we offer to Sancta Maria de Bonárcado. Witnesses: first of all, God, and Sancta Maria, and lord Nicolau the prior and his monks, and Comita Pistore *curadore* of Bonarcadu, and Nigola de Pane, Guantine de Porta, Comita Pira, and many others. This was done on the feast of All Saints in the year 1228 in the cloister of St Zeno while iudike Mariano was in power.

24.
I, Nicolaus, prior of Bonarcadu, record the dispute that Guantine Formiga brought against me. He came to the village (*billa*) of Miili Pikinnu ('Little Milis') built a house (*domo*) and planted a vegetable garden (*ortu*), vineyards and trees against the will of the prior of Bonarcadu. I summoned him to a hearing (*corona*) of Sanctu Nicola saying: 'I am suing Guantine Formica who has misappropriated that which is my property in the unworked land (*saltu*) and in my village (*billa*) which I have registered in a charter with a seal (*carta bollata*) and is part of the realm (*arrenatu*)!' He said: 'I did not know that it was part of the realm and that Sancta Maria had a sealed charter!' I brought the sealed charter to the hearing; they read it and I won, so they gave me back the house, the vineyard, the garden, the trees, and everything he had done there. Witnesses: iudike Mariano and lord Trogodore archbishop of Arborea, lord Buzakese Pinna the iudike at the time, lord Petru Murtinu *curadore* of the territory (*parte*) of

Arzocco d[e] Martis curadore dessus Simakis, Comita Seke maiore de cavallos, Gu[n]nari Arburakesu et Petru su nebode, donnu Marianu Sabiu et Comida Pistore curadore d[e] Bona[r]cadu et Furadu Zo[r]ru[m]pi et Gua[n]t[ine] Ie[n]na et tota sa corona, in quo erat p[ro] s[an]c[t]u Nicola.

25.

Ego Nicolaus, priore d[e] Bonarcatu, cu[n] do[n]nu Petru Murtinu, armentariu meu adpus sa domo de s[an]c[t]a Maria de Bonorcadu, fagemus recordatione p[ro] kertu ki fegerus in corona de donnu Petru de Figus armentariu de logu. Kerterus p[ro]ssos fiios de Erradore Pisanu, ki fudi serbu de s[an]c[t]u Jorgi de Calcaria, c'aviat fattus dave Bera de Zori et no llus boliat dare a sserbire. Et pedivitse kertadore suo in corona a donnu Furadu de Çori Zorrompis ki fudi
15v parente suo et arresposit p[ro] eu: | 'Custus serbos, ki kertadis, fiios de libera sunt et impare non furunt coiuados.' Et naredi donnu Petru Murtinu ca 'fiios dessu serbu de s[an]c[t]u Iorgi sunt et impare su[n]t istetidus dessus annos xx.' Et donnu Furadu de Çori Zorrompis resposit et tramudessi, ca viiat ca llu podestava, et naredi: 'fiios de ankilla de juigi sunt.' Et donnu Petru Murtinu naredi ca 'custa Bera de Çori fiia de liberu et de libera est et issos fiios c'at fattus sunt fiios de serbu de s[an]c[t]u Jorgi et de custa libera.' Iuigaru[n]timi ad bature destimonios ca fudi Bera de Çori libera et de mama et de patre et ca fudi stetida cu[n] su serbu de s[an]c[t]u Jorgi d[e]ssos annos xx. Et batusi destimonios, ki iurarunt in bangeleu de Deu ca 'custa Bera de Zori fiia de Alene de Zori est, k'est libera'.

Honori de Figu et Goantini de Lacon et Gunnari Zukellu et Jorgi Mamelli de villa d[e] Tremaza et Mariani d[e] Lacon, Cannau d[e] Bauladu et Orzoco de Varca de Baratiri, fradili p[ri]mariu de Alene d[e] Zori. Custos narrunt, dave co iuraru[n]t, ca 'custa Bera de Zori fiia d[e] Alene de Zori est, k'est libera maiorali.' Et p[ro] Petru Seke su padre batusi destimonios ad Tractasu de Unali et ad Torbini Marçias et ad Comida Paanu et ad Petru d'Orruu de villa de Ziorfaliu
16r et Furatu de Nuri de Solarussa | et Furadu de Lacon de Villalonga et Petru de Martis de Sii maiore.

Custos iuraru[n]t in bangeleu de Deu et narru[n]t, dave co iuraru[n]t, ca 'custa Bera de Çori est fiia de Petru Seke ki fudi liberu maiorali et de mama et de patre.' Parsit resone assa iustitia ca ll'avia binkidu. Poserunt et torraru[n]timi

Miili (Milis), lord Arzocco de Martis *curadore* of Simakis (Simaxis), Comita Seke head of the horses (*maiore de cavallos*), Gunnari Arburakesu and Petru his nephew, lord Marianu Sabiu, Comida Pistore *curadore* of Bonarcadu; Furadu Zorrumpi, Guantine Ienna, and the whole hearing as [present] on [the feast day of] Sanctu Nicola.

25.

I, Nicolaus, prior of Bonarcatu, together with lord Petru Murtinu, my administrator (*armentariu*) at the house of Sancta Maria de Bonorcadu, record memory of the legal dispute we had at a hearing (*corona*) presided over by lord Petru de Figus, administrator of the realm (*armentariu de logu*). We quarrelled over the children of Erradore Pisanu, who was a servant of Sanctu Iorgi of Calcaria, whom he had with Bera de Zori and did not want to give them to serve. He [Erradore Pisanu] demanded that lord Furadu de Çori Zorrompis, who was a relative of his, answer for him in court, and he said: 'These servants over whom you are disputing are the children of a free woman, and the two of them were not married!' Lord Petru Murtinu said: 'They are the children of the servant of Sanctu Iorgi and they have been living together for twenty years!' Lord Furadu de Çori Zorrompis answered changing his line and strategy of defence because he realised that the other [Petru Murtinu] was taking the upper hand, and said: 'They are the children of the servant of the iudike (*juigi*)!' Lord Petro Murtinu said: 'this Bera de Çori is the daughter of a freeman and a free woman, and the children she has had are the children of the servant of Sanctu Iorgi and of this free woman!' They demanded that I produce witnesses to prove that Bera de Zori was a free woman on both her mother's and father's side, and that she had been living with the servant of Sanctu Iorgi for twenty years. I brought the witnesses, who swore by the gospel of God: 'This Bera de Çori is the daughter of Alena de Zori, who is free and of the upper social class (*liber maiorali*)'.

They—Honori de Figu and Goantini de Lacon and Gunnari Zukellu and Jorgi Mamelli of the village (*villa*) of Tramaza and Mariani de Lacon, Cannau de Bauladu and Orzoco de Varca from Baratili, first cousin of Alena de Zori—said, after having sworn that: 'This Bera de Zori is the daughter of Alene de Zori, who is a free *maior* (from upper social class of *maiorali*)!' And as for her father, Petru Seke, I produced as witnesses Tractasu de Unali, Torbeni Marçias, Comida Paanu and Petru d'Orruu of the village (*villa*) de Ziorfaliu (Zerfaliu), and Furatu de Nuri of Solarussa, Furadu de Lacon from Villalonga, and Petru de Martis from Sii Maiore (Siamaggiore).

These swore on the gospel of God and said, after they had sworn, 'this Bera de Çori is the daughter of Petru Seke who was a free *maior* on both the mother's and the father's side'. It seemed right to the hearing that I had defeated him.

sos serbos: ad Petru de Çori et ad Mariane de Zori su frade. Narei in corona ad Bera de Çori; 'No[n] boio k'istis plus cum su serbu de s[an]c[t]u Jorgi de Calcaria.' Et Bera de Çori naredi: 'Pusco perdo ad fiios m[e]os, non mi bolio bogare de·llu.' Et adcordarus·nos impare i[n] sa corona ad plakimentu bonu de pare de staresi impare Bera de Zori cun su serbu d[e] s[an]c[t]u Jorgi p[ro] maridu et p[ro] mugere et fiios cantos enti fagere essere serbos d[e] s[an]c[t]u Jorgi de Calcaria. T[e]s[te]s: donnu Petru de Figus, armentariu de logu c'arreiat corona, et do[n]nu Petru Murtinu curadore de parti de Miili, et do[n]nu Furadu de Çori Zorrompis curadore de Nurabulia, et do[n]nu Baldufinu et Comida d'Orruu su fiiu, et Orçoco d'Açene et Petru d'Açene su frade, et Goa[ntine] de Varca et Andria de Varca su frade, et Sueione Manca et Goa[ntine] Manca Mauru et Petru de Serra Cariga et Bellomini de Serra d'Urasanna.

26.[40]

16ᵛ In nomine D[omi]ni. Am[en]. Ego Nicolao p[ri]ore d[e] Bonarcato | recordationem facio p[ro] sa curte ke fuit de Guantine de Porta, k'aviat iata a s[an]c[t]a Maria cu[n] totu s'attru suo. Petivimi·illa Comita de Zuri p[ro] bindiri·illa; et ego dedi·illa in conbentu d'aberese·illa ip[s]e et sa mugiere et fiios suos. Et ip[s]e dediminde XXX bisanti. In fine, se moriat ip[s]e kene abere fiios, remanere a s[an]c[t]a Maria, in dono p[ro] s'a[n]i[m]a sua, custa curte et o[nn]ia melioram[en]tu, kantu avissi fatu ibi. Et o[nn]ia sua bona remaneant a s[an]c[t]a Maria de Bonorcato p[ro] s'a[n]i[m]a sua. Et sa parte de sa mugiere, si obierit sine filiis, remaneat tota assa domo d[e] s[an]c[t]a Maria p[ro] s'a[n]i[m]a sua. Et si aliq[u]and[o] co[n]ti[n]geret q[uo]d ip[s]e Comita v[el] successor ei[us] sive heres vellet p[re]dicta[m] curia[m] vendere, n[on] habeat potestate[m] vende[n]di ea[m] nisi eccl[es]ie beate Marie d[e] Bonarcato si prior q[ui] t[un]c fuerit in eade[m] eccl[es]ia ea[m] emere voluerit p[ro] eo p[re]tio quo ea[m] emit ip[s]e Comita. Dona[n]di vero ea[m] curia[m] potestate[m] n[on] habeat predict[us] Comita nec filius ab eo descende[n]s nec heres ei[us] aliquis v[e]l successor nisi eccl[es]ie s[an]c[t]e Maria de Bonar-
17ʳ cato, {pro eo p[re]tio quo eandem curia[m] emit ip[s]e Comita a p[re]dicto | priore}. Testes: fr[ater] Bene monac[us], p[re]it[er]o Cocco, p[re]it[er]o Gua[n]tine Lelle, Nicola de Pane, Ioh[ann]e Zuria, Samaritan[us] clerigu, Miale de Kerchi, Gua[n]tine de Scalas, Gua[n]tine Cauleti, Ioh[ann]e Piga, Iorgi Loke, Gregori Co[n]tu, et alios multos.

---

40 Duplicated in entry 12.

They decided that my servants should be returned to me: Petru de Çori and Mariani de Zori, his brother. I said to Bera de Çori at the hearing, 'I do not want you to live with the servant of Sanctu Iorgi de Calcaria any longer!' Thereupon, Bera de Çori said, 'since I am losing my children, I do not want to be separated from him!' We agreed with one accord at the hearing that Bera de Zori and the servant of Sanctu Iorgi de Calcaria should live together. Witnesses: lord Petru de Figus, state administrator (*armentariu de logu*), who presided over the hearing, and lord Petro Murtinu *curadore* of the territory (*parte*) of Miili (Milis), and lord Furadu de Çori Zorrompis *curadore* of Nurabulia, and lord Baldufinu and Comida d'Orruu his child, and Orçoco d'Acene and Petru d'Açene his brother, Goantine de Varca, Andria de Varca his brother, Sueione Manca, Goantine Manca Mauru, Petru de Serra Cariga, and Bellomini de Serra from Urasanna.

26.

In the name of Lord, amen. I, Nicolao, prior of Bonarcato, make a record of the farm (*curte*) that was owned by Guantine de Porta, who donated it to Sancta Maria together with the rest of his property. Comita de Zuri asked me to sell it to him. So, I gave it to him on the condition that he, his wife and children would have it. He gave me thirty bezants (*bisanti*) for it, with the stipulation that if he died without any children, that farm (*curte*) and any improvements he had made to it should remain as a gift to Sancta Maria for his soul, as well as all his possessions. And the portion belonging to his wife, if she died without children, shall all remain as [part of] the rural estate (*domo*) of Sancta Maria for her soul. And if it should happen that the said Comita, or one of his successors or his heirs would want to sell the said farm (*curia*), let him not have the power to sell it except to the church of the Sancta Maria at Bonarcato, if the prior who governed at that time in the same church would want to buy the said farm at the same price Comita bought it from the prior. Neither the said Comita, nor any child of his descended from him nor any heir or successor of his who has the power to give away this farm except to the church of Sancta Maria de Bonarcato. Witnesses: friar Bene the monk, priest Cocco, priest Guantine Lelle, Nicola de Pane, Iohanne Zuria, Samaritanus the cleric, Miale de Kerchi, Guantine de Scalas, Guantine Cauleti, Iohanne Piga, Iorgi Loke, Gregori Contu, and many others.

27.

Ego priore Nicolau façu recordatione de ca[m]biu ki fegi cun juigi Guiielemu in su palatiu de corte de Fununi. Deilli ego ad juigi parzone ca[n]tu avia in Iorgi Lardu fiiu de Susanna Oscheri ki fudi ankilla d[e] s[an]c[t]u Jorgi d[e] Calcaria, su ladus, et d[e] Comida Lardu serbu d[e] juigi depus sa domo de Piscobiu. Et juigi Guiielemu dedimi in ca[m]biu ad Maria Lada fiia de Alene Lada, et Petru Ladu fiiu d[e] Alene Lada. Arramasit ad iuigi su ladus et pee et iss'ateru pee a s[an]c[t]u Paulu. Custu ca[m]biu fegerus ad plakimentu bonu de pare. Testes: do[n]nu Petru d[e] Figus armentariu de logu, et donnu Comida Spanu, maiore de cavallus, et do[n]nu Furadu de Çori Çorrompis et Gunnari Madau, armentariu dessa domo de Piscobiu, et Saltaro de Martis et Comida Mauronti et Basilli Pinna et Ioh[ann]e Leo scriptore.

28.

17v Ego Arrigu, priore de s[an]c[t]a Maria de Bonorcadu, et Samaridanu, servidore de s[an]c[t]u Georgii d[e] Calcaria, fagem[us] recordatione d[e] serbos et ankillas c'aviat s[an]c[t]u Georgii d[e] Calcaria cun s[an]c[t]u Gregorii d[e] Bauladu. Partirus cu[n] priore Ioh[ann]e ad Ioh[ann]e de Urri, ubi aviat s[an]c[t]u Georgii III pees et s[an]c[t]u Gregorii unu pee, et ad Maria de Urri sa sorre, ubi aviat s[an]c[t]u Georgii III pees et s[an]c[t]u Gregorii unu pee. Girarus manu et cambiarus a plakimentu bonu d[e] pare. Levait p[ri]ore Ioh[ann]e p[ro] s[an]c[t]u G[re]g[orii] su pee d[e] Maria d[e] Urri et s[an]c[t]u Georgii levait su pee d[e] Ioh[ann]e d[e] Urri su frade. Arramasit Maria de Urri a s[an]c[t]u G[re]g[orii] su ladus et Ioh[ann]e d[e] Urri ramasit a s[an]c[t]u Georgii totu intreu. T[e]s[te]s ubi fegerus custus cambius a plakime[n]tu bonu d[e] pari: donnu Trogodori Corsu curadore d[e] factu d[e] Bonorcadu, et Torbini d[e] Piras, maiore d[e] scolca, et Goa[n]t[ine] de Baniu cl[er]igu et Petru Marki, cl[er]igu d[e] Solagrussa, et P[etru] d'Ardaule cl[er]igu, et P[etru] Co[n]tu et Goa[n]t[ine] Rue et Tericu Maiu et Taniel Kerssa
18r et P[etru] Coco et Benzivenni et P[etru] | Manis.

Girerus anco manu et partirus Arçoco Ladu, fudi filiu de Bera Casa, ki fudi ladus de s[an]c[t]u Georgii et ladus de sanctu G[re]g[orii] et fegit a Orçoco in forrizu, de ki gitavat ad s[an]c[t]u G[re]g[orii] su ladus et ladus ad s[an]c[t]u Georgii.

Coiuvait custa Bera Casa cu[n] Trog[otori] Gaça, serbu d[e] juigi, et fegerunt unu filiu, a ki narava[n]t Gaini, d[e] ki gitavat ad juigi su ladus, et daitillu juigi a s[an]c[t]a Maria de Bonorcadu, et issu ateru ladus pee a sanctu Georgii et pee a s[anct]u G[re]g[orii].

27.
I, prior Nicolau, record the exchange that I made with iudike (*juigi*) Guiielemu in the palace (*palatiu*) of the court (*corte*) at Fununi. I gave to the iudike (*juigi*) my share of Iorgi Lardu, son of Susanna Oscheri, who was a half servant of Sanctu Jorgi de Calcaria, and of Comida Lardu, servant of the iudike at the household (*domo*) of Piscobiu. In exchange, the iudike Guiielemu gave me Maria Lada, daughter of Alene Lada, and Petru Ladu, the son of Alene Lada. Half and a quarter [of their services] remained with the iudike, and the other quarter with Sanctu Paulu. This exchange we made by mutual agreement. Witnesses: lord Petru de Figus, state administrator (*armentariu de logu*), and lord Comida Spanu, head of the horses (*maiore de cavallus*), lord Furadu de Çori Çorrompis, Gunnari Madau administrator of the household (*armentariu de sa domo*) at Piscobiu, and Saltaro de Martis, Comida Mauronti, Basili Pinna, and Iohanne Leo the scribe (*scriptore*).

28.
I, Arrigu, prior of Sancta Maria de Bonorcadu, and Samaridanu, servant (*servidore*) of Sanctu Georgii de Calcaria, record the male and female servants (*serbos et ankillas*) that Sanctu Georgii de Calcaria had in common with Sanctu Gregorii de Bauladu. We made a division [of their services] with prior Iohanne de Urri, of whom Sanctu Georgii possessed three quarters and Sanctu Gregorii a quarter; and Maria de Urri his sister, of whom Sanctu Georgii possessed three quarters and Sanctu Gregorii a quarter. We took turns in choosing and exchanging by mutual agreement. The prior Iohanne took for Sanctu Gregorii the quarter of Maria de Urri, and Sanctu Georgii the quarter of Iohanne de Urri his brother. The half of Maria de Urri remained at Sanctu Gregorii, and the whole of Iohanne de Urri remained at Sanctu Georgii. Witnesses to this exchange, made by good and common consent: lord Trogodori Corsu *curadore* of Bonarcadu at the time, and Torbini de Piras, head of the ward (*maiore de scolca*), and Goantine de Baniu cleric and Petru Marki, cleric of Solagrussa, and Petru d'Ardaule the cleric, Petru Contu, Goantine Rue, Tericu Maiu, Taniel Kerssa, Petru Coco, Benzivenni, and Petru Manis.

We again changed the rota and divided Arçoco Ladu, who was the son of Bera Casa, who was half the property of Sanctu Georgii and half of Sanctu Gregorii, and who had had Orçoco as an illegitimate child, of whom half was due to Sanctu Gregorii and the other half to Sanctu Georgii.

This Bera Casa married Trogodori Gaça, a servant of the iudike (*juigi*), and they had a child named Gaini, of whom half was due to the iudike, but the iudike gave him to Sancta Maria de Bonorcadu; and of the other half, a quarter went to Sanctu Georgii and the other quarter to Sanctu Gregorii.

Coiuvait Iuxta [...] ankilla d[e] s[anct]u Gregorii cu[n] Petru Pisanu, ki fudi lad[us] de s[an]c[t]a Maria de Bonorcadu et ladus d[e] Petru d[e] Serra Cariga et fegerunt unu filiu a ki narava[n]t Trog[o]d[ori], d[e] ki gitavat lad[us] a s[an]c[t]u Gregorii et pee a s[an]c[t]a Maria et pee ad Petru d[e] Serra Cariga. Et icustu pee de Trogodori, ki lli gitavat ad Petru de Serra Cariga, illu co[m]p[ore]i ego Samaridanu p[ro] s[an]c[t]u Georgii et d[e]indelli in dinaris s[ollos] XXX et cl[omplilli] p[re]zu. T[e]s[te]s: donnu Petru d[e] Figus arm[en]tariu de logu, et Joh[ann]i Leo scriptore, et Mari[ane] de Çori cl[er]igu, et Baruso[n]e Uras et Petru Pintore et Bellomini de Serra d'Urasanna.

29.

18v Cambiarus custos serbos in pare cu[n] donnu Ioh[ann]e, p[ri]ore de Bauladu. Ego levai p[ro] s[an]c[t]u Georgii su ladus de Arçocco Ladu et ip[s]e levait p[ro] s[an]c[t]u Gregorii su ladus d[e] Trog[o]d[ori] Porcu. Levai ego p[ro] s[an]c[t]u Georgii su pee d[e] Gavini et ip[s]e levait pro s[an]c[t]u Gregorii unu pee d[e] Maria d[e] Urri et at como s[an]c[t]u Gregorii in Maria de Urri III pees et s[an]c[t]u Georgii unu pee. Et arramanint a comuni filios de custos, ki furunt fatos in ankillas de s[an]c[t]u Georgii innanti d[e] partire: Goa[n]t[ine] et Iuxta et Bera, filios de Gavini et de Alene Pisana (est a[n]killa d[e] s[an]c[t]u Georgii intrea), et Goa[n]t[ine] et Maria, filios de Arzoco Ladu et d[e] Justa Coco, ankilla de s[an]c[t]u Greorgii intrea: d[e] custos V serbos gitat a s[an]c[t]u Gregorii ladus et pee, et Barbariske et totu s'ateru ramanet a sanctu Georgii. Et icusta partitione fegerus a bene fagiri. Et filios, cantos enti fagire dava sa die, sos ki levava ego, ra[m]manent a s[an]c[t]u Georgii et issos ki levait ip[s]e ramanni[n]t a s[an]c[t]u Gregorii. T[e]s[te]s: Simio[n]e iagunu d[e] s[anct]u
19r Gregorii, et Com[ita] d[e] Çori et | Petru d[e] Serra et Gun[nar]i de Serra et Ioh[annn]e Peza et Goa[n]t[ine] Marras et Orçoco d[e] Scanu et Gunnari d[e] Scanu et Çipari Murtinu et Petru Carru et Pet[ru] Casa et Goa[n]t[ine] Casa et Jorgi Cogone et Com[ita] Marki et Goa[n]t[ine] Lollo et Trogodori Corssu. Custa partitione fut facta, davana[n]ti de custos, in corte de s[an]c[t]u Gregorii in Bauladu.

30.

Anni[41] D[omi]ni MCCLI. Ego Arrigu, p[ri]ore de Bonorcatu, fatio memoria[m] ca deti a ssanta Maria de Bono[r]catu p[ro]ssa a[n]i[m]a sua i[n] manus mias Ga[n]t[ine] d[e] Lacon, su de Nuroço, do[n]nia cantu aviat in Boele de te[r]ra, et parte sua d[e] nassa[r]iu de Pisq[ui]na d'Oiu; et assa fine d[e] co[n]ve[r]sare-

41 Change of hand from *Anni*.

Iuxta [...] female servant (*ankilla*) of Sanctu Gregorii married Petru Pisanu, half of whom was owned by Sancta Maria de Bonorcadu and half by Petru de Serra Cariga; they had a child named Trogodori of whom half went to Sanctu Gregorii, a quarter to Sancta Maria, and the other quarter to Petru de Serra Cariga. I bought this quarter of Trogodori, which belonged to Petru de Serra Cariga for Sanctu Georgii, and I gave him thirty soldi (*sollos*) in money (*in dinaris*) and settled the payment. Witnesses: lord Petru de Figus state administrator (*armentariu de logu*), and Johanni Leo scribe (*scriptore*), and Mariane de Çori cleric, and Barusone Uras, Petru Pintore, and Bellomini de Serra from Urasanna.

29.
I with lord Iohanne, prior of Bauladu, exchanged these servants together. I took for Sanctu Georgii half of Arçocco Ladu and he took for Sanctu Gregorii half of Trogodori Porcu. I took for Sanctu Georgii quarter of Gavini and he took for Sanctu Gregorii a quarter of Maria de Urri, and so now Sanctu Gregorii has three quarters of Maria de Urri and Sanctu Georgii a quarter. There remain in common the children of these, which were born of the servants of Sanctu Georgii before the division: Goantine and Iuxta and Bera, the children of Gavini and Alene Pisana (who is the servant of Sanctu Georgii in her entirety), and Goantine and Maria, the children of Arzoco Ladu and Justa Coco, who is the servant of Sanctu Gregorii in her entirety. Of these five servants, half and a quarter belong to Sanctu Gregorii and Barbariske and all the rest remain to Sanctu Georgii. This division we made for the best. And as many children as were born from that day forth, of those who were due to me after the division, shall remain at Sanctu Georgii; and the children of those whom he took shall remain to Sanctu Gregorii. Witnesses: Simione deacon of Sanctu Gregorii, and Comita de Çori, Petru de Serra, Gunnari de Serra, Iohanne Peza, Goantine Marras, Orçoco de Scanu, Gonario de Scanu, Çipari Murtinu, Petru Carru, Petru Casa, Goantine Casa, Jorgi Cogone, Comita Marki, Goantine Lollo, and Trogodori Corssu. This division was made in front of them in the court (*corte*) of Sanctu Gregorii in Bauladu.

30.
In the year of the Lord 1251, I, Arrigu, prior of Bonorcatu, record the memory that Gantine de Lacon from Nuroço gave to Sacta Maria of Bonorcatu for his soul in my hands, all his landed property that he had in Boele, and his part of the weir (*nassariu*) of Pisquina ('pool') d'Oiu; and said that he would finally be a lay

si assa co[r]te. T[e]s[te]s: su piscopu de sa[n]ta Iusta et issu a[r]q[ui]p[re]te suo, donnu Gu[nna]ri de Maro[n]ju, Ga[n]ti[n]e d[e] Serra d'Urogogo, Goantine d'O[r]ruu d[e] Bidoni, Saltaro d[e] Serra, Torbeni Urrolo, Gu[nna]ri Ma[n]ca p[re]iti. Custos furu[n]t ue posit et d[e]ti cu[n] lassando pa[r]te a ffiios e a do[n]nia frate suo. Et, si p[er]unu ho[m]i[n]e suo deit molestare sa clesia, d'ispiciarelu et pacare a [r]regnu lib[ra] una d'a[r]ge[n]tu.

31.

19v Ego p[ri]ore Arrigu fatio memoria[m] d[e]ssa co[n]ve[r]ssatione q[ui] feq[u]it
a santa Maria de Bono[r]catu in manus mias do[n]na Io[r]gia de Serra Ocluba[r]ia de Sorratile. D[e]ti a ssanta Maria su ca[n]tu aviat i[n] Boele de te[r]raticu et issu nassa[r]iu de Pisquina d'Oiu cu[n] bolu[n]tate bona dessu maritu et d[e] onnia fiiu suo. Et posit, si assa mo[r]te no[n] pariat bonu assos fiios, dare sos fiios pa[r]zo[n]e d'unu fiiu de o[n]nia ca[n]tu eti lassare et d[e] te[r]ras et de bi[n]gias et d[e] saltos et d[e] domos. T[e]s[te]s: su piscopu d[e] sa[n]ta Iusta, Gu[nna]ri Ma[n]ca p[re]iti d[e] Bitoni, su p[re]iti d[e] So[r]ratili, Saltaro d[e] Serra, Torbeni Urrolo, p[re]itoru Coco.

31.bis

Ego[42] Nicolaus prioris santa Maria de Bonarcadu req.

32.

20r Anno[43] Domini MCCXLII merc[uri]s a di[e] XXV de s[an]c[t]o Sadur[ru]. Ego
p[ri]ore Arrigu faço memoria dessa conversacione qui si feguit donn[u] Petru Mu[r]tinu a s[an]c[t]a Maria de Bonarcadu a oram dessa morte sua[m]. Confesedi su corpus suu a suterrari in s[an]c[t]a Mar[ia] de Bonarcadu. Dedi p[ro] spendere i[n] su morime[n]tu, qua[n]do s'edi suterrari, lib[ra]s V. Dedi a sancta Mar[ia] de Bona[r]cadu madrassas IIII et banita I de bombagiu et paiu I de lençolos novos et cabiçalis II et bestiri I et isca[n]iali I d'arguentu et b[e]br[eces] DCCC et bacas XXX et ebbas X et capras CC et suis mat[ri]k[e]s C et maialis L. Et dedit anc[u] a s[an]c[t]a Mar[ia] d[e] Bonarcadu sa cl[es]ia de s[an]c[t]a Mar[ia] d[e] Sorrachesos cum su saltu de Sorrachesos totu[m] s[e]c[un]d[u]m in co si segat dae bau d[e] coroniu; et collat totue sa via q[ui] faguint dae T[r]amaça a Solarusa derectu assu crastu ma[n]nu ck'e[st] oru sa via d[e] Solarusa, derectu assu crastu ma[n]nu ck'e[st] i[n] mesu de su montiglu ck'est
20v inter Alisandro | et Sorrachesos, derectu assu crastu ma[n]nu ck'e[st] cabiça

42 Change of hand from *Ego*, followed by a gap of six ruled lines.

43 Change of hand from *Anno*.

brother of the monastery [of Bonárcado]. Witnesses: the bishop of Santa Iusta, and his archpriest, lord Gunnari de Maronju; Gantine de Serra from Urogogo, Goantine d'Orruu from Bidoni, Saltaro de Serra, Torbeni Urrolo, and the priest Gunnari Manca. These were present at the place where he made this donation, leaving his share to his children and to each of his brothers. If any of his servants should complain to the church, he was to answer for eviction (*d'ispiciarelu*) and pay the realm a pound of silver.

31.
I, prior Arrigu, record the conversion that lady Iorgia de Serra Oclubaria ('with clear eyes') from Sorratile made in my hands to Santa Maria di Bonarcatu. She donated to Santa Maria all the workable land she owned in Boele and the weir (*nassariu*) at Pisquina d'Oiu with the consent of her husband and all her children, with the proviso that if, on her death, her children did not think this was right, they would donate the share that would be due to one of her children of all that she had left of land, vineyards, unworked lands (*saltos*), and farm complexes (*domos*). Witnesses: the bishop of Santa Iusta, Gunnari Manca priest of Bitonì, the priest of Sorratili (Sorradile), Saltaro de Serra, Torbeni Urrolo, and the priest Coco.

31.bis
I, Nicolaus, prior of Santa Maria de Bonarcadu req.

32.
In the name of the Lord 1242, on Wednesday the 25th October, I, Arrigu, the prior, record the conversion of lord Petru Murtinu in Sancta Maria di Bonarcadu at the hour of his death. He asked in confession that his body be buried in the monastery of Sancta Maria de Bonarcadu. He gave five (*libras*) to be spent on his grave when he was buried. He gave to Sancta Maria de Bonarcadu four mattresses, a cotton blanket, a pair of new sheets, two pillows, a dress, a silver vessel and eight hundred sheep, thirty cows, ten mares, two hundred goats, a hundred sows, and fifty pigs. He also gave to Sancta Maria de Bonarcadu the church of Sancta Maria de Sorrachesos with the unworked land (*saltu*) of Sorrachesos all according to how it is defined: from the ford of Coroniu, [the boundary] goes up along the road from Tramazza to Solarussa in the direction of the large boulder that stands at the edge of the road to Solarussa; towards the large boulder that stands in the middle of the hill between Alisandro and Sorrachesos, towards the large boulder that stands at the head of the spring of

assa ena de su fraxinu derectu assa petra pickina, ck'est in mesu s'ena, derectu assu urbidu de Selaki ck'est palas assu masognu hue iaguiat donnu Barbaru, et collat totue sa via qui fagint sos de Celleani cun carru qui baet sutu nuracki da Uras e lonpet derectu pus via assu capiçali d[e] sa te[r]ra d[e] sos d'Uras et collat derectu assa mata ma[n]na d[e] sa molici d[e]ssu cucuru de {...} de covallus et barigat pus capizale a sa te[r]ra d[e] sos d'Uras derectu assu crastu cki es[t] in su mesu, cabiçali de sa terra de sos d'Uras cki est oru sa via qui fagint sos de parte de Guelcivere ad Aristanis et boltat totuve cussa via deretu assu crastu ck'est in sa terra d'Arçoccu Çuckellu ck'est oru sa via suprascrita et incurbassi dae su crastu in ioso a sa ena derectu assu crastu mannu ki est probe e de sa terra
21r c'aradeit | donn[u] Petru Betera, et falat derectu a corognu de Pibera et boltat totue sa via de ariolas de Guilarci qui faguint sos de Tramatza ad Aristanis cun ca[r]ru qua[n]do est te[m]p[us] malu[m], et clompet assu fosadu q[ui] fudi in bau de berbegues cabiça assa te[r]ra d[e] donnu Ma[n]nu de Figu et clompet assu flumen derectu assu nasariu d[e] bau de b[er]b[e]ges q[ui] fudi de Dominigui Maniu, et collat totue depus flumen derectu a bau d'Ogiu derectu a bau de cannas derectu pus flumen et boltat assu crastu mannu de su giradoriu derectu assu iumpadoriu de su erriu et dae via qui fagint sos de Solarussa a Tramazza et afliscatsi a pari. Et dedi ancu a s[an]c[t]a Mar[ia] de Bonarcadu serbos xvi, masc[ulo]s viii et feminas viii, et covallos iii (unu covallu albu et sella sua et ateros duos), et boes x domados et servos ii; et in dinaris l[i]b[ra]s l et triticu
21v cantares cc et oriu cantares s. cc, et fundamentu | suu totu c'aviat in Calcaria d[e] Com[ita] d[e] Muru. Et dedi anc[u] a s[an]c[t]a Mar[ia] de Bonarcadu sa cl[es]ia d[e] s[an]c[to] Antoni de Serra Çullas cu[n] saltus et cu[n] t[er]ras et cu[n] ortos et cu[n] vinias, cu[n] s[er]vos et cu[n] anchillas et cu[n] o[nn]ia quanto si loe ap[ar]teniat a icussa cl[es]ia de s[an]c[t]o Antoni de S[er]ra Çullas.

33.

In[44] no[min]e D[omi]ni. Ame[n]. Ego Petrus de Lacone iudice de Arborea et visconte de Basso ad honore de Deus et de sancta Maria et de totos sos sa[n]tos et cum voluntade bona de do[n]na Diana mugere mia do[n]na de Arborea fato custa carta et renovola a sancta Maria de Bonarcado pro dona[tio]ne qui fecit

44 Change of hand from *In*.

su Fraxinu ('the ash tree'), towards the small stone which stands in the middle of the well, towards the Selaki lane behind the shelter where lord Barbaru used to bring his cattle, and [then the boundary] goes up along the road that the inhabitants of Zeddiani take with their carts and that goes below the nuraghe of Uras and comes out directly beyond the road to the boundary of the land of those of Uras, and comes out directly at the large mastic tree of the top of [...] de Covallus ('of horses'); it passes beyond the boundary to the land of those at Uras, [then] towards the nuraghe that is placed in the middle, [then] to the end of the land of those of Uras that is at the edge of the road that the inhabitants of the territory (*parte*) of Ghilziber travel, [then] in the direction of Oristano and turns along that road in the direction of the stone that is in the land of Arzoccu Zuckellu that is at the edge of the aforementioned road, and [it then] descends from the boulder down towards the well in the direction of the large boulder that stands next to it and next to the land that was worked by lord Petru Betera, and [then it] descends towards the peak of Pibera ('grass snake'), and turns along the Ghilarza farmyard road that the inhabitants of Tramazza take towards Oristano with the cart when the weather is bad, and [then it] comes to the ditch that was near Bau de Berbegues ('ford of sheep'), [then] to the head of the land of lord Mannu de Figu, it comes to the river in the direction of the weir of Bau de Berbeges that belonged to Dominigui Maniu, and, thus following, it reaches the other side of the river in the direction of the ford of Ogiu towards Bau de Cannas ('ford of reeds') directly beyond the river and turns to the large boulder of the drainage ditch in the direction of the crossing ford (*iumpadoriu*) of the stream; and from the road that the inhabitants of Solarussa take towards Tramazza where it rejoins the starting point. He also gave to Sancta Maria di Bonárcado sixteen servants, eight male and eight female, three horses (one white horse with its saddle and two others), and ten tame oxen and two servants; and in money fifty pounds, and two hundred measures (*cantaros*) of wheat and two hundred *cantaros* of barley, as well as his landed property that he had in Calcaria of Comita de Muru. He also gave to Sancta Maria di Bonárcado the church of Sancto Antoni of Serra Çullas with the unworked land (*saltus*), land, vegetable gardens and vineyards, and with male and female servants, and all that was pertaining to that church of Sancto Antoni de Serra Çullas.

33.

In the name of Lord, amen. I, Petrus de Lacone, iudike of Arborea and viscount (*visconte*) of Basso, in the honour of God, Holy Mary and all the saints, and with the consent of my wife, Diana, the [leading] lady (*donna*) of Arborea, do make and renew this charter (*carta*) in favour of Sancta Maria de Bonárcado

donnu Ugo de Basso padre meu et donna Preciosa de Lacono mama mia: et ego la confirmo p[ro] sa a[n]i[m]a de babu meu et de mama mia a su monasteriu de s[anct]a M[ar]ia de Bonarcadu p[ro] piscare in mare de Ponte cu[n] duas barcas et in mare vivu. Et siant liberos que no lis levent paga et non li levent pisq[ue] de p[er]unu tempus; et fatolis libera sa baina qu'i hat in ponte de Sinis qui bogarat Nigoli de Bangi, et p[ro] hierru et p[ro] istade, q[ui] no lis levent paga et no lis partant pisque ni anbilla. Et bogolis de o[mn]ia serbizu de curadores et de armentarios et de ma[n]dadores et de maiores de scolca et de o[mn]ia q[u]antu nd'at p[er] totu regnu: q[ui] no lis tollia[n]t donam[en]tu nixun fatu insoru. Nen p[ro]curadore, nen p[er]unu homine mortale ad ester-
22r minare custu donu qui apo eo fatu a s[anct]a Ma[ri]a | de Bonarcando prossa anima de padre meu et de mama mia et p[ro] remiss[ion]e de sos pecadus mios.

Et fatoli donatione iuntamente de su riu monte, q[ui] est iuntu a sa pisquera de mare Ponte, q[ui] lu narran riu Zenu, qui siat de S[anct]a Maria de Bonarcadu in p[er]petu[um]. Et no[n] siat ausu ne[n] iudice, qui hat a esser de post me, nen donnicellu nen donna nen donnicella, no[n] curadore, no[n] maiore, no[n] arme[n]tario et no[n] p[er]unu homine mortale q[ui] istrumet custu bene q[ui] apo ordinadu et factu ego Petru de Lacono iudice de Arborea et visconte de Basso. Et sunt testes: p[rimus] Deus, s[anct]a Ma[ri]a, et o[mn]es s[an]tus et santas Dei, donnu Trodori de Muru arch[ipisco]pu de Arbarea et don[n]u Gunari de Scuru ep[iscop]u de Terralba et don[n]u Petru de Martis ep[iscop]u de sancta Iusta et Larenzu de Çori curadore de donnu Pedru Erili, et Pedru Martini et Gontini de Martis, cur[ador]es de Campidanu, e Furadu de Çori cur[ador]e de Narabolia, Arçocco Prede, Gunari d'Onu, Barusone Diana cur[ador]es de parte Valenza, et Gantine de Tori castellanu de Marmilla et cur[ador]e de Barumini et Gantini de Serra preideru maiore de Manis, et Comida Spanu quirquidore maiore de Sinis, Cespuli maiore de buiaq[ue]sos cun golleanes suos. Et q[ui] h[ab]et di[ce]re q[ui]a bene est custu donu et dota[ti]one q[ui] fato ego Petru de Lacono iudice de Arborea a su monasteriu de s[anct]a Ma[ri]a de Bonarcantu habeat bendic[tio]ni de De[us] et de s[anct]a Ma[ri]a et de o[mn]es sa[n]tos et sa[n]tas Dei. Amen. Et qui hat dicere quia male est h[ab]eat maledic[tion]em de Deus et de santa Maria et de omnes santos et santas Dei. Amen. Et h[ab]eat partem cu[n] iniquo Herode et cun Iuda traditore et cun diabolo in infernu[m]. Fiat, fiat. Amen.

34.

22v In[45] nomine D[omi]ni. Amen. Ego Petr[us] de L[acon] iudex et rex arborensis et visconte de Basso, cu[n] volu[n]tade de D[eu]s et de s[an]c[t]a Maria et de

45 Change of hand from *In*.

in relation to the donation made by lord Ugo de Basso, my father, and by lady Preziosa de Lacono, my mother, that [the monks at] the monastery of Bonárcado be allowed to fish in the lagoon (*mare*) of Ponte with two boats, and also in the open sea (*mare vivu*). And they shall be free and exempt from any taxation that they may have to pay in money or in catch, in any season; and I grant them freedom from the lagoon at Ponte de Sinis which was obtained from Nigoli de Bangi, both in winter and in summer, so that nobody may demand payment from them for their catch: neither for fish nor eels. I also exempt them from any service to be rendered to the *curadores* and administrators (*armentarios*), representative (*mandatores*) and the heads of the ward (*maiores de scolca*), and to any official of the realm, that they do not take away any donation that has been made to them, neither procurator nor any other person, in order to annul this donation which I have made to Sancta Maria di Bonárcado for the soul of my father, of my mother, and in remission of my sins.

And, at the same time, I give to them the river Monte, which is joined to the fish farm of the lagoon of Ponte, which is named Zenu river (*riu Zenu*), to belong to Sancta Maria di Bonárcado in perpetuity. And let neither any iudike who shall be after me, nor lord, nor child of the *donnicellu*, nor leading lady (*donna*) nor *donnicella*, nor *curadore*, nor any lord (*maiore*), nor administrator (*armentariu*), nor any other person dare to nullify this donation which I, Petru de Lacono the iudike of Arborea and viscount of Basso, have ordered and made. The witnesses are: God in the first place; Holy Mary; all the saints of God; lord Trodori de Muru, archbishop of Arbarea; lord Gunari de Scuru, bishop of Terralba; lord Petru de Martis, bishop of Santa Iusta; Larenzu de Çori, *curadore* of lord Pedru Erili; Pedru Martini and Gontini de Martis, *curadores* of Campidanu; Furadu de Çori, *curadore* of Narabolia (Narbolia); Arçocco Prede; Gunari d'Onu; Barusone Diana, *curadores* of the territory (*parte*) of Valenza; Gantine de Tori, castellan of Marmilla; *curadore* of Barumini; Gantini de Serra, senior priest of Manis; Comida Spanu head revenue-collector (*quirquidore maiore*) from Sinis; Cespuli, the head of the entourage (*buiakesos*) with his followers (*golleanes suos*). And whoever says that this donation and endowment that I, Petru de Lacono, iudike of Arborea, have made to the monastery of Sancta Maria di Bonárcado is good, may God bless him and Holy Maria and all the saints of God! Amen. And whoever says that it is evil, may he receive a curse from God and Holy Mary and from all the saints of God! Amen. And let him share his fate with wicked Herod, Judas the traitor, and with the Devil in Hell! Let it be! Let it be! Amen.

34.

In the name of Lord, amen. I, Petrus de Lacon, iudike and king (*iudex et rex*) of Arborea and viscount of Basso, by the will of God and of Holy Mary and all

totu sos s[an]c[t]os, et cu[n] bolu[n]tade de do[n]na Diana uxor mea regina de loghu, et p[ro] anima de iudice Goa[n]tine d'Arbare et p[ro] a[n]i[m]a de iudice Comita et pro a[n]i[m]a de iudice Baruso[n]e et p[ro] a[n]i[m]a de Ugo de Bassu, padri meu, et p[ro] remissio[n]e dessos peccados meus, ffaço carta ad s[an]c[t]a Ma[r]ia de Bona[r]cadu p[ro] s[an]c[t]a Victoria de Montes[an]c[t]u cu[n] servos et ankillas. Et confirmoli saltu de Chanas de su Iehsu p[ro] la[n]de et p[ro] pastu et q[ui] lu depiat salitar[e] et guardar[e] de o[n]nia t[em]p[or]ali. Incomi[n]çat dae su redangiu de Nordae in Co[r]tade et eo totu No[r]dae derectu ad piras sfe[r]tas et adfliscat ad suergiu co[r]siu et da i[n]de ad ma[r]ghin[e] d'Urosolo deretu ad hena de tidu, deretu ad mo[n]te de Çuris, deretu ad su sue[r]giu de sa Çacigha, deretu ad pedra de Rosa, deretu ad pedra de curador[e] [...].[46]

35.

24r Maria et om[n]ib[u]s s[an]c[t]is et s[an]c[t]e Dei. Amen amen fiat fiat. Anno Domini Mille CCXXXIIII [...].[47]

36.

25r Condague[48] s[an]c[te] Marie Monarcanto fato pro sus res de Arborea biscondes de Barusau et de su iudice Constantino. In nomiine Dei, Patris et Filii et Spi[rit]u S[an]c[t]u. Amen. Ego iudice Constantino de Arborea et[ia]n cu[m] uxore donna Anna ex consilium archi[e]pisc[o]pi mei Homodei pro remedium a[n]i[m]e mee et pro remissione omnium peccator[um] regu[m] arborensi[um] qui hanc eccl[es]iam s[an]c[te] Marie Monarcanto fundaverunt et donationes territorior[um] donaverunt, cum domna Diana regina de logu, que, pro remissione peccator[um] regis Arbor[ee], mariti sui, donavit eccl[es]iam s[an]c[te] Marie de Montesanto cum saltu de canale de figu cum terminis et iurisdictionib[us] que don[n]a Diana regina fuit patrona: et ita volo, et[ia]m pro remissione peccator[um] illius et salutis anime mee et meor[um] filiorum, compono, asigno et dispono et istud condace regu[m] arb[oren]si[um] acresco et facio ad honorem s[anct]ìssime Trinitatis et intemerate virginis

26r Dei genitricis Marie, et facio istud [25v is missing] | caenobium mihi et sucesso-

46 The text ends abruptly at the final line of f. 22v, before completing the boundary description. Folio 23 is missing.

47 The remainder of this folio has been left blank after the first two lines of text. An irregular section, approximately four centimeters high and five centimeters long has been excised from the folio which is filled with rough sketches of two faces, a horse(?), a large erasure mark and four scribbled names, not apparently related to the main text and in a different hand to the preceding text.

48 Change of hand from *Condague*.

the saints, and with the consent of my wife Diana, queen of the realm (*regina de loghu*), and for the soul of iudike Goantine of Arbare and for the soul of iudike Comita, and for the soul of iudike Barusone, and for the soul of Ugo de Basso, my father, and for the remission of my sins, I issue this charter (*carta*) in favour of Sancta Maria di Bonárcado in what concerns Sancta Victoria de Montesanctu with the male and female servants pertaining thereto. I confirm to it the unworked land (*saltu*) of Chanas de su Iehsu as regards both acorn production and pasture, so that Sancta Victoria de Montesanctu may safeguard it and take care of it for all time. It begins at the property of Nordae in Cortade and, from there, it follows the territory of Nordae in the direction of the grafted pear trees and ends at the oak; and from there, it goes to the edge of Urosolo towards Fonte de Tidu ('spring of the pigeon') and Monte de Zuris in the direction of the oak of Çacigha, [then] towards the rock (*pedra*) de Rosa, and the rock (*pedra*) de *curatore* [...].

35.
Maria and all the saints and Holy God. Amen. Amen. Let it be! Let it Be! In the year of the Lord 1234.

36.
Condaghe of Sancta Maria Monarcanto (Bonárcado) made by the kings (*res*) of Arborea, viscounts (*biscondes*) of Barusau, and the iudike Constantino. In the name of God the Father, the Son and Holy Spirit, amen. I, Iudike Constantino of Arborea, together with my wife, lady Anna, on the advice of my archbishop, Homodei, for [the salvation of] my soul and the remission of the sins of the kings (*regis*) of Arborea, who founded this church of Sancta Maria Monarcanto and made donations to it, with lady Diana queen of the realm (*regina de logu*), who, for the remission of the sins of the king of Arborea, her husband, donated the church of Sancta Maria de Montesanto with the unworked land (*saltu*) of Canale de Figu ('narrow valley of the Fig') within the boundaries and jurisdictions of which lady Diana was patron. Therefore, I will, also for the remission of her sins and [the salvation of] my soul and of my children, draw up, affix the seal and dispose, and increase and constitute this condaghe of the kings of Arborea for the honour of the most Holy Trinity and of the most pure Virgin Mary, mother of God, and I constitute this monastery for myself and for

rib[us] meis usque in sempiternum. Et ita volo, omni ambiguitate remota, fundare hoc cenobium ut in illo vivant fratres religiosi sub regulari tramite r[e]v[erendissi]mi p[atr]is Benedicti, qui die ac nocte serviant Deo omnipotenti. Nunc aut[em] cognitum sit o[mn]ib[us] qua[m] et[ia]m fr[atr]ib[us] meis et omnib[us] affinibus, consentiente prelibato archi[e]pisc[o]po meo Homodeo, trado hoc monasteriu[m] sub regimine et pote[state] abatis Pise cum hac conditione ut dictus Abas sancti Zenonis mittat de suis fratrib[us] qui regant illud, laborent et plantent et die et nocte orent p[ro] remissione [peccatorum] regu[m] arborensi[um] et pecca[to]r[um] Diane regine, que et[ia]m hanc fundationem erexit sibi et successorib[us] suis et illi ex illis nomine[n]t prepositu[m] idoneu[m] ad bonu[m] regimen cu[m] complacen[ci]a et consensu meo et filiorum et successorum meorum. Et ita confirmo et ap[ro]bo donationes supradic[t]as regu[m] arborensi[um] et domne Diane regine. Et ita
27r ad degendos [26v is missing] | fratres qui in cenobio vivant do illis pote[state]m ut laborent et plantent, edificent ad honorem s[an]c[te] Marie et s[anct]i Benedicti et s[anct]i Zenonis et per man[us] illor[um] ordinetur prepositus idoneus ad recte gubernandum cenobium et ita sub hac conditione ut preposit[us] nominat[us] a dictis fr[atr]ib[us] sit cum voluntate et complacentia tam mea quam successor[um] meor[um] et ita illis trado et delivero:

Domo sancte Victorie de Montesanto cum o[mn]ia cantu aet et terras et binias et salt[us] d'Orrodolazu et collat a nuracke d'Orisezo et moliat a petra de niu de corbu et benit a sueriu de petra de cavallu et benit a su monticlu de Utur d'Arsai et benit assu castru dessu cannissone et benit a su castru de monticlu de piscobu, cun ho[min]es et masones d'onnia sinnu, de grussu et minudu. Et
27v dolli pro custu saltu qui si lu arregant, castigent omnia | te[mpo]rale et pro glande et pro pastu in p[er]petuu[m] in co fudi usu et est oi in usu in saltu de regnu.

E domo s[an]c[t]e Marie de Boele cum omnia cantu at, partindo paris cun su regnu et terras et binias et domesticas si vi aviat, e issu saltu d'Ilo, partindolo de ladus a pare cu[n] clesia cum serbos et cu[n] anchillas et cu[n] masones de omnia sinnu et de grussu et minudu. E de omni apat fine a su fine in seculum.

E domo de s[anct]a Victoria et cantu aet. E dolli su saltu meu cum cantu aet. E dolli sa parzone ki fuit de donnu Piziellu de Sezo cu[n] o[mn]i cantu at.

my successors in perpetuity. And therefore, I wish, in full clarity and beyond any doubt, to establish this monastery so that in it the religious brothers may live in observance of the rule of the most reverend Father Benedict, so that day and night they may serve Almighty God. Now, therefore let it be known to all, both to my brothers and to all my kindred, that, with the consent and approval of my archbishop Homodeo mentioned above, I put this monastery under the government and power of the abbot of Pisa on the condition that the said abbot of St Zeno send some of his brothers to govern it, to work and to plant crops, and day and night to pray for the remission of the sins of the kings of Arborea and the sins of queen (*regine*) Diana, who also established this foundation for herself and her successors. They shall appoint from among their number a suitable superintendent who shall rule well to my satisfaction and consent and that of my children and successors. And therefore, I confirm and approve the aforesaid donations of the kings of Arborea and of the queen, Diana. And so that the brothers may reside and live in this monastery, I grant them the power to work and to plant crops, to build in honour of Holy Mary, St Benedict and St Zeno, and by their hands be ordained a suitable superintendent who will govern the monastery properly, but under the condition that the said superintendent be appointed by the said brothers with the consent and satisfaction of myself and my successors, and therefore I entrust and hand over to them:

The farm complex (*domo*) of Sancta Victorie di Montesanto with all that pertains to it: lands and vineyards and the unworked land (*saltus*) of Orisezo (Orrodolazu); [the boundary] goes up to the nuraghe of Orisezo and turns to Sasso de Niu de Corbu ('crow's nest rock') and reaches the oak of the Sasso de Cavallu ('horse's rock') and reaches the hill of Utur d'Arsai and reaches the boulder of the Colle de Piscobu ('bishop's hill'), with servants and cattle of every size, large and small. And I give them licence, with regard to this land (*saltu*) to hold it and make use of it perpetually for their benefit, in every season, with regard to both acorn production and pasture in perpetuity, as has been the custom and still is for unworked land of the realm (*saltu de regnu*).

[I also give them] the farm complex (*domo*) of Sancte Marie de Boele with all that pertains to it, dividing it in two equal halves with the state property: land and vineyards and the farm complexes that are therein, and the country of Ilo, dividing it in half with the property of the church, with the servants and with the servants, and with the cattle of all sizes, both large and small. And all this in perpetuity.

And the farm of Sancta Victoria with all that pertains thereto. And I also give my country with all that pertains thereto. And I add my share of the property that belonged to lord Piziellu de Sezo with all that pertains thereto.

E domo s[anct]i Simeonis de Vessalla cum omni cantu at.

E domo de santu Petru de Mili Picinu cun onnia cantu aviat donna Tocode (*corr.* Tocoele),[49] ki fuit donna de logu, muiere de iudige Comida, e fegit issa sa clesia illa a nnou ponendove tota sa villa de Mili piccinu ki[50] fuit sua peguiare, sene avere parte ne[n] lib[er]u ne[n] serbu aienu, cun terras et binias et servos et a[n]cillas, libertados; et saltu ki si segat dave sa cinniga de figos de Milianu.

28r E confirmola sa domo de sancta Barbara | de Turre cum omnia cantu aet et cum terras cum binias et cum omnia masone.

Et confirmolli sa domo de sancta Barbara de Turre cum omnia cantu aet cun terras cum binias cum servos et ancillas; et apala comente est a biere in su primu foliu et in sus ateros autus et donationes in fide de totus sus veriderus.

Cum boluntade de su archiepiscopu meu Homodei apo fundadu custo monasteriu pro remissione de sus peccados meos e de sus res de Arborea et de sa regina Diana et de sos figios: in fide e pius testimonius resta su p[rese]nte fato et firmado da testimonzus et de su not[ario] ap[ostoli]co Bernardu Ventrelij et de sus testimonzus p[rese]ntes; et ad perpetua[m] firmitatem privilegii volumus illud n[ost]ri sigilli impressione signari. Et signatu[m] fuit Pisis in balla[tori]o dom[us] castri ecc[lesi]e s[an]c[te] Viviane an[n]o mil[lesimo] duc[entesi]mo, XIII kal. novembris. Guilelm[u]s aurifex et Roselinus aurifex testes fuerunt in p[rese]ntia D[omi]ni Bernardi monachi. Ego Bernardus arborensis propria manu subscripsi et aliis subscribendu[m] sensi. Ego Bernardus Ventrelii D[omi]ni imperatoris Romanorum iudex mea manu fìrmavi.

37.

28v Ego[51] Thomas de Madrona ki mi conberso ad D[eu]s et a s[an]c[t]a Maria de Bonarcadu in man[us] de priore Pedru Perosinu et dessos monagos suos p[ro] co[n]versu: et de om[n]ia ca[n]tu appo intro d[e] domo et foras d[e] domo et issa co[r]te mia d[e] Barigadu, liberos, et binias et ortos et t[er]ras cantu appo in pa[r]te de Miile et I binia mia k'appo in Senege et I binia k'appo in Buriedu et I binia in bau de Barbara (custas III binias appo ad ispiiatu d[e] do[n]nia fr[at]e meu), et parçone d[e] s[er]bos c'appo cu[n] sus liberos d[e] Bauladu

49 Corrected following the reading in entry 1.

50 Change of hand from *ki fuit.*

51 Change of hand from *Ego.*

The farm complex (*domo*) of Sancti Simeonis de Vessalla with all that pertains thereto.

And the rural complex (*domo*) of Santu Petru de Mili Picinu ('Little Mili') together with all that was owned by lady (*donna*) Tocoele, who was the first lady of the land (*donna de logu*) and wife of iudike Comita, and who renovated the church, adding to it the entire village (*villa*) of Milis Picinnu, which was her own property (*sua peguiare*), without having any share [that belonged to others] in it, neither free nor servant of others, with lands and vineyards and servants and freedmen; and the land (*saltu*) that is granted from Cinniga de Figos ('rushes of figs') at Milianu.

And I confirm the farm complex (*domo*) of Sancta Barbara de Turre with all that pertains to it and with the lands, with the vineyards and with all the livestock.

I also confirm the farm complex (*domo*) of Sancta Barbara de Turre with all that pertains to it with the lands, with the vineyards, with both male and female servants; and I have possession of it as it can be seen in the first sheet (*foliu*) and in the other documents (*autus*) and donations in faith of all those who are true.

With the consent of my archbishop Homodei, I founded this monastery for the remission of my sins and those of the kings (*res*) of Arborea and queen (*regina*) Diana and their children. The present document, made and signed by witnesses and by the apostolic notary Bernardu Ventrelij and by the witnesses present, is authentic; and we wish to imprint our seal on it as a perpetual confirmation of this privilege. And it was sealed in Pisa in the loggia of the fortified house (*domus castri*) of the church of Sancte Viviane, in the year 1200, on the 20th day of the month of October. Guilelmus the goldsmith (*aurifex*) and Roselinus the goldsmith were witnesses in the presence of lord Bernardus the monk. I, Bernardus Arborense, in my own hand, signed and gave consent to others to sign. I, Bernardis Ventrelij, iudex of the lord Emperor of the Romans (*domini imperatoris Rofarm complexum*), signed in my own hand.

37.

[It is] I, Thomas de Madrona, who render myself to God and Sancta Maria de Bonárcado into the hands of prior Pedru Perosinu and his monks with all I own within and outside my farm complex (*domo*): may the farm (*corte*) in Barigadu, freemen (*liberos*), and vineyards, gardens, lands as much as I own in the territory (*parte*) of Milis, as well as a vineyard of mine that I own in Senege (Seneghe) and a vineyard I own in Barigadu (Buriedu), and a vineyard near the ford (*bau*) of Barbara—I own these vineyards free from any claims of my brothers and the share due to me of servants that I share with the freemen of Bauladu

et om[n]ia canto ant proare qui si ap[ar]teniat a mimi, siat d[e] s[an]c[t]a Maria. Custa co[m]bersio[n]e fegi dominiga de palma in s[an]c[t]a Iusta, dandomi adsoltura su do[n]nu m[e]u su markesu. Et sunt t[e]st[e]s donnu Bernardu arkipiscobu d'Arbaree et donnu Bonacorsu piscobu de sancta Iusta et donnu Baruso[n]e Taiabucones curadore d[e] parte d[e] Miili et donnu Barusone Spanu et donnu Com[ita] Pistore et donnu P[etru] de S[er]ra Spe[n]tumadu et G[u]n[na]ri de Je[n]na.[52]

38.[53]

29r Ma[n]ca et Orçoco ciu meu. Posi I boe et I cuba et II parzones de vi[n]ia: una e[st] tene[n]do assa de Iorgi Ma[n]ca et iss'atra tene[n]do assa de Troodori Vidri[n]kis. Et ego Comita de Lac[on] Ludru pono p[ro] a[n]i[m]a mea ad s[an]c[t]a Maria de Bonarcatu cuba I et II parçones de vi[n]ia: una e[st] tene[n]do assa de s[an]c[t]a Maria de Senege et iss'atera parçone tene[n]do assa de Petru Latu.

39.

Cartula de Suei. In no[min]e D[omi]ni. Am[en]. Ego p[ri]ore Ioh[ann]e de Bonarcato facio recordatio[n]e cu[n] volu[n]tate de D[eu]s et de iudice Barusone. Petivilli t[er]ra a iudice Barusone i[n] piscina de ebbas, ki si segat dava su flum[en] p[ro]pe de saltu[m] meu[m], et isse dedimilla. Testes: donnu Comita de Lac[on] archiepisc[o]pu et Paucapalea ep[iscop]u de s[an]c[t]a Justa, Troodori Paganu et Troodori de Foge buiakesu, donnigellu Orçoco curatore de Gilciver, Jorgi Capai, curatore de factu, et Goa[n]tine Rubiu, ma[n]datore de regnu[m].

40.

Posit Iorgi Capai t[er]ra de Gavini Cap[ra] a c[le]sia. T[este]s Joh[ann]e Capai e Goa[n]tine Cọgone et Gavine Capai.

41.

29v Co[m]porei assa villa de Orogogo su comunariu | issoro et deilis vacca in sollu et sollu de peculiu. T[este]s: Comida de Solas maiore de scolca et Gosa[n]tine Pollige p[or]cariu et Gu[n]nari de Solas, nu[n]zadore.

42.

Comporeilli a Goa[n]tine Pasi et a fr[ate]s suos sa terra dess'iscla te[n]endo assu com[m]unariu; et deillis sollu de laore et peza porcina in II tremisses et

---

52 End of Booklet H.

53 Booklet B (1167–1169) begins here.

and all that can be proved to belong to me, be in the ownership of Sancta Maria. I made this conversion on Palm Sunday in Sancta Iusta, giving me, my lord the marquis (*markesu*), permission (*assoltura*). The witnesses are: lord Bernardu, archbishop of Arbarea; lord Bonacorso, bishop of Sancta Iusta; lord Barusone Taiabucones, *curadore* of the territory (*part*) of Miili; lord Barusone Spanu; lord Comita Pistore; lord Petru de Serra Spentumadu, and Gunnari de Jenna.

38.
Manca and Orçoco my uncle: I donated an ox, a barrel (*cuba*) and two shares of the vineyard; one bordering on that of Iorgi Manca, and the other on that of Troodori Vidrinkis. And I, Comita de Lacon Ludru, give for my soul to Sancta Maria di Bonárcado a barrel and two shares of the vineyard; one bordering on that of Sancta Maria de Senege, and the other on that of Petru Latu.

39. Charter (*cartula*) of Suei
In the name of God, amen. I, prior Iohanne of Bonarcato, record my memory by the will of God and with the consent of iudike Barusone. I asked from iudike Barusone for a plot of land near Pischina de Ebbas ('pond of the mares'), which is taken from the river near my unworked land (*saltu*); and he gave it to me. Witnesses: lord Comita de Lacon archbishop; and Paucapalea, bishop of Sancta Justa; Troodori Paganu; and Troodori de Foge of the iudike's guard (*buiakesu*); *donnicello* Orçoco, *curatore* of Gilciver (Ghilarza), Jorgi Capai, the *curatore* at the time; and Goantine Rubiu, representative of the realm (*mandatore de rengum*).

40.
Iorgi Capai donated the land of Gavini Capra to the church. Witnesses: Johanne Capai, Goantine Cogone, and Gavine Capai.

41.
I bought from the village (*villa*) of Orogogo its common land (*su communariu*) and gave them a cow worth a soldu (*sollu*), and cattle worth a soldo in money. Witnesses: Comida de Solas head of ward (*maiore de scolca*), and Gostantine Pollige the swineherd, and Gonario de Solas the bailiff (*nunzatore*).

42.
I bought from Gosantine Pasi and his brothers the islet (*iscla*) bordering on the common land (*su communariu*); and I gave him wheat worth one soldo (*sollo*) and pork meat worth two tremisses (*tremisse*), and two rams worth a tremissis

II masclos in tremisse et co[m]plilli p[re]çu. T[este]s: Iorgi Capai, curatore de factu cu[n] tota curatoria.

43.
Co[m]poreilli a Iorgi Martalu t[er]ra in t[er]ra de Gavini Cap[ra] et deilli ebba i[n] sollu et matrige de porcu i[n] tremisse de pecuiu et co[m]plilli. T[este]s: Trobini Gaciella, maiore de scolca de Domos novas cun iscolca sua.

44.
Comporeilli a Terico Pasi et ad Petru de Figu t[er]ra i[n] piscina d'ebbas et deilli matrige de porcu i[n] tremisse et II masclos [i]n tremisse et I ligone i[n] II ob[er]as. Et co[m]plilli. T[este]s: Troodori Gaciella et Iorgi Martalu.

45.
Comporeilli a Cipari Çote t[er]ra i[n] ariola de Pubusone et deilli vacca i[n] sollu et co[m]plilli. T[este]s: Goa[n]tine de Muru et Mariane Devotu.

46.
Co[m]poreilli a Niellu Peccatu et ad fr[ate]s suos t[er]ra i[n] ariola de Pub-
30r usone et deilli peza porcina i[n] VIII op[er]as | et II masclos i[n] tremisse et II ob[er]as de laore. Testes: Janni Piga et Mailade fabru.

47.
Co[m]poreilli a Petru Pilieri t[er]ra i[n] ariola de Bubusone et fegilli II oberas et co[m]plilli. T[este]s: Petru Cogu.

48.
Co[m]poreilli a Petru Çote t[er]ra i[n] Pubusone et fegi[n]delli sollu et co[m]plilli]. T[este]s: Iorgi Martalu.

49.
Comporeilli a Petru Pio t[er]ra et deilli sollu et co[mplilli]. Testes: Troodori d'Uras.

(*tremisse*), and settled the payment. Witnesses: Iorgi Capai, *curatore* at the time with his whole district (*tota curatoria*).

43.
I bought from Iorgi Martalu a piece of land situated on the land of Gavini Capra and I gave him a mare worth one soldo (*sollu*) and a sow worth a tremissis (*tremisse*) and I settled the payment. Witnesses: Trobeno Gaciella, head of the ward (*maiore de scolca*) of Domos Novas ('new houses') with his guard (*cun iscolca sua*).

44.
I bought from Terico Pasi and Petru de Figu a piece of land near Pischina de Ebbas ('mares' pond') and gave him a sow worth a tremissis (*tremisse*), and two rams worth a tremissis, and a hoe (*ligone*) worth two days' work. And I settled the payment. Witnesses: Troodori Gaciella and Iorgi Martalu.

45.
I bought from Cipari Çote some land near the threshing floor (*ariola*) of Pubusone and I gave him a cow worth a bezant, and settled the payment. Witnesses: Goantine de Muru and Mariane Devotu.

46.
I bought from Niellu Peccatu and his brothers land near the threshing floor (*ariola*) of Pubusone, and I gave them some pork meat worth eight days' work (*in VIII oberas*), two rams worth a tremissis, and some wheat worth two days of labour (*in II oberas de laore*). Witnesses: Janni Piga and Mailada Fabru.

47.
I bought from Petru Pilieri land near the threshing floor of Pubusone and I appraised it as being worth two days' work, and I settled the payment. Witnesses: Petru Cogu.

48.
I bought from Petru Çote land in Pubusone and I appraised it at the value of a soldo to settle the account. Witnesses: Iorgi Martalu.

49.
I bought from Petru Pio some land; I gave him a bezant and settled the payment. Witnesses: Troodori d'Uras.

50.
Comporeillis a Torbini Vulpia et a fr[ate]s suos t[er]ra i[n] Pubusone et fegillis sollu et co[m]plill[is]. T[este]s: Gostantine Fro[n]ia.

51.
Comporeilli a Iorgi Martalu t[er]ra tene[n]do a saltu meu et deilli sollu et co[m]plill[i]. T[este]s: Trodori Gaciella cu[n] iscolca sua.

52.
Co[m]poreilli a Basile Milia t[er]ra i[n] Pubusone et fegilli tremisse et co[m]plilli. T[esti]s: Gostantine de Muru.

53.
Tramutar[us] t[er]ras cu[n] Ia[n]ni Milia et deilli ca[m]biu in mura de Carvias. T[esti]s: Iorgi Gusai.

54.
Comporeillis a Salamo Milia et a Salui, su c[on]nadu, parçone issoro i[n] Pubusone et deillis IIII op[er]as. T[esti]s: Ia[n]ni Piga.

55.
Comporeilli a Mariane Çokella et assu ciu t[er]ra te[n]endo a saltu meu et fegilli tremisse e c[o]mplill[i]. Testes: Troodori C[un]iale.

56.
30v Co[m]poreli | t[er]ra a Mariane Carau i[n] via d'Orogogo e deilli sollu. T[esti]s: Ia[n]ni Piga.

57.
Co[m]poreilli a Petru Coa t[er]ra i[n] via d'Orogogo et fegilli tremisse. T[esti]s: Ia[n]ni Guperi.

58.
Co[m]poreilli a Gavine Kerbio t[er]ra i[n] via d'Orogogo et fegilli II tremises et co[mplilli]. T[este]s: Gavine Corria et Petru de Figu.

50.
I bought from Torbini Vulpia and his brothers land at Pubusone and I appraised it at the value of a soldo and settled the payment. Witnesses: Gostantine Fronia.

51.
I bought from Iorgi Martalu land bordering on unworked land (*saltu*); I gave him a soldo and settled the payment. Witnesses: Torchitorio Gaciella with his guard.

52.
I bought from Basilius Milia land at Pubusone; I appraised it [as worth] a tremissis and settled the payment. Witness: Gostantino de Muru.

53.
We exchanged lands with Ianni Milia and I gave in exchange some land near the blackberries at Carvias. Witness: Iorgi Gusai.

54.
I bought from Salamo Milia and Salui, his brother-in-law, the share that they owned at Pubusone, and I payed them the worth of four days' work (*IIII operas*). Witness: Ianni Piga.

55.
I bought from Mariane Çokello and his uncle a land bordering my unworked land (*saltu*) and I appraised it as being worth a tremissis and I made an agreement with him settling the account. Witness: Torchitorio Cuniale.

56.
I bought a land from Marian Carau in the way of Orogogo and I gave him a bezant (*sollu*). Witness: Ianni Piga.

57.
I bought from Petru Coa land in the way of Orogogo and I made [an agreement about payment] with him a tremissis. Witness: Ianni Guperi.

58.
I bought from Gavine Kerbio some land on the road at Orogogo and I evaluated it as worth a tremissis, and settled the payment. Witnesses: Gavino Corria and Petru de Figu.

59.
Co[m]poreilli a Gavini Coda et assu fr[at]e t[er]ra i[n] via d'Orogogo et fegillis II tremisses et co[m]plillis. Testes: Jorgi Capai et Iorgi Loriagi.

60.
Co[m]porai a Comida Kellarida t[er]ra tenendo a saltu meu et fegi[n]delli sollu et co[m]plilli p[re]z[u]. T[este]s: Trogotori Pasi et Gosta[n]tine Nonne.

61.
Co[m]poreilli a Mariane Arte et a fr[ate]s suos t[er]ra in Puçu de Forada et fegi[n]delli sollu. Te[ste]s: Orzocor Pellis et Cristi[n]kine Sale.

62.
Co[m]poreilli a Petru Pollige t[er]ra i[n] Puzu de Forada et deilli VI ob[era]s et co[m]plill[i]. Testes: Comita de Solas et Iorgi Pasi.

63.
C[art]a de cap[ri]les
In n[omin]e Patris et filii et Sp[iritu]s S[ancti]. Am[en]. Ego p[ri]ore Ugo de s[an]c[t]a Maria de Bonarcato cu[n] volu[n]tate de D[eu]s et de iudice
31r Gostantine | de Lac[on] et uxore sua donna Anna de Çori facio custa recordatio[n]e. Co[m]poreilli a Gostantine d'Orruinas t[er]ra torta in Cap[ri]les et deindelli boe de sollu. T[este]s: Petru Loce maiore de scolca, cu[n] fr[ate]s suos.

64.
Furedi sas apes Troodori Paranna. Tenni corona cu·llu et vincillu et leveindelli una t[er]ra in T[er]ra maiore. T[este]s: Petru Loke, maiore de scolca, cu[n] fr[ate]s suos.

65.
Furedimi Mariane Catellu sa masone et vi[n]cillu et leveindelli I t[er]ra a costa dessa de cl[esi]a. T[este]s: Petru Loke maiore de scolca cu[n] tota scolca sua.

59.
I bought from Gavini Coda and his brother land in the way of Orogogo and I evaluated it as the price of two tremisses settling the account. Witnesses: Iorgi Capai and Iorgi Loriagi.

60.
I bought from Comida Kellarida a land bordering on my unworked land (*saltu*) and I evaluated it as worth two tremisses settling the account. Witnesses: Trogotori Pasi and Gosantine Nonne.

61.
I bought from Marian Arte and his brothers land (*terra*) near Puçu de Forda ('hollow well') and I evaluated it as worth one soldo. Witnesses: Orzocor Pellis and Cristinkine Sale.

62.
I bought from Petru Pollige land (*terra*) near Puçu de Forda and I gave him the value of six days' work (*VI oberas*), and I appraised it with him settling the account. Witnesses: Comita de Solas and Iorgi Pasi.

63.
Charter (*carta*) of Capriles

In the name of the Father, the Son, and the Holy Spirit, amen. I prior Ugo of Sancta Maria de Bonarcato, by the will of God and with the consent of iudike Gostantine de Lacon and his lady wife Anna de Çori record this memory. I bought from Gostantine d'Orruinas the curved [stretch of] land situated in Capriles and I gave him an ox worth a soldo. Witnesses: Petru Loce, head of the ward (*maiore de scolca*), and his brothers.

64.
Troodori Paranna stole my bees. I took legal action against him and won, and took from him a piece of land in Terra Maiore ('main land'). Witnesses: Petru Loke, head of the ward (*maiore de scolca*), and his brothers.

65.
Mariane Catellu stole my livestock and I defeated him in legal action, and so I took from him a piece of land located next to the property of the church. Witnesses: Petru Loke, head of the ward (*maiore de scolca*) with all his guard (*cun tota scolca sua*).

66.

Ca[rta] de Gilcare

In no[min]e D[omi]ni. Am[en]. In gra[tia] de D[eu]s et de s[an]c[t]u Agustinu et de donnu meu iudice Dorgotori, ego p[re]b[ite]ru Petru de Pau faço recordatione pro saltu de Gilcare. Abiat ibe regnu[m] q[ui]ndeci sollos. Benni iudice Cerkis ad Agustis: sos dege sollos dedillos a s[an]c[t]u Augustinu et issos v dedillos a sanctu Iorgi de Azara. Abiat ibi Comita Zancuti x sollos: co[m]poraivelli VIIII sollos, et issu de dece positivillu a s[an]c[t]u Augustinu
31v pro a[n]i[m]a sua. | Abiat ive in icussu saltu v sollos Zipari de Ruinas, ki fuit curatore, et teniat i[n] Agustis. Abiatillu ad Artace porcariu su curatore; furedi Artace porcos de sanctu Augustinu. Bennit iudice Dorgotori ad Augustis, tenni corona de logu et vi[n]killu assu curadore, et dedimi sos v sollos ki aviat in icussu saltu p[ro]ssu servu ki furarat sos porcos de cl[es]ia cu[n] iura[n]donde Stephane su porcariu de cl[es]ia. Et e[st] su saltu dava su riu de sos alinos, ubi e[st] su kerku maore; et e[st] totu puspare XXX sollos; et alteru homine non i at bias in icussu p[er] ista .+. [cruke].

67.

In N[omin]e D[omi]ni. Am[en]. Ego Cipari de Lac[on] avia saltu cu[n] s[an]c[t]u Augustinu et cu[n] donnigella Maria, cia mea, cada VII sollos. Sa parçone mea ve[n]dilla a s[an]c[t]u Augustinu cun iski de iudice Trogotori donnu meu et cun asoltura de donnigella Maria, cia mia. Levainde primariu iugu iu[n]ctu
32r de domatos et iugu dave vaccas et sollu de verbeges | et sollu de porcos, et clo[m]peruntimi p[re]zu et benedixerus·nos de pare. Et sunt t[este]s: primus D[eu]s et s[an]c[t]a Maria, Gu[n]nari d'Orruinas maiore de cavallos, Presnage de Lella maiore de canes, et Pilosu d'Orruinas; de poriglos de angaria: Orzoco de Opo e tota kita sua. Et ki at pu[n]nare ad isturminare istu negotiu[m] ki arminai ego Cipari de Lac[on] isbertinetillu D[eu]s de magine sua et de via de paradisu. Et appat anathema de XII ap[osto]los, de XVI p[ro]phetas, de XXIIII seniores, de CCCXVIII patres s[anct]os q[ui] canones disposuer[un]t; et apat parçone cu[n] Herode et cu[n] Iudas traditore et cu[n] diabolus in infernu[m]. Am[en], Am[en], Amen. Fiat, Fiat, Fiat.

66.
Charter (*carta*) of Gilcare.

In the name of the Lord, amen. By the grace of God and of Sanctu Agustinu and of my lord iudike Dorgotori, I, the priest Petru de Pau, record the memory of the unworked land (*saltu*) at Gilcare. The realm owned there a share worth fifteen soldi (*sollos*). The iudike Cerkis came to Agustis and donated a share of this land (*saltu*), equal to ten soldi, to Sanctu Augustinu and donated the remaining share, worth five bezants, to Sanctu Iorgi at Atzara. Comida Zancuti owned a share of the said land (*saltu*), worth ten soldi, I bought a share, equal to nine soldi, and he donated the remaining share, worth a bezant, to Sanctu Augustinu for his soul. Zipari de Ruinas, who was *curatore* and had properties at Agustis, owned in this land (*saltu*) a share worth five soldi. He had Artace as a swineherd; Artace stole the pigs of Sanctu Augustinu. The iudike Dorgotori came to Augustis; I appealed to the hearing (*corona*) presided over by him and I defeated the *curatore*, and this gave me the share equal to the value in that land (*saltu*) in compensation for the theft of the church pigs by his servant about which Stephane the church swineherd swore an oath. The boundaries of the land (*saltu*) go from Rio de sos Alinos ('river of the alders'), where the great oak stands. All of it comes to thirty soldi; and no one else has any right to this land (*saltu*) by this cross.

67.
In the name of the Lord, amen. I, Cipari de Lacon, held some unworked land (*saltu*) along with Sanctu Augustinu and the *donnicella* Maria, my aunt, each worth seven bezants (*sollos*). I sold my share to Sanctu Augustinu, making iudike Trogotori, my lord, aware of it and having received permission [to do so] from *donnicella* Maria, my aunt. I received in exchange first of all a pair of oxen and a pair of cows, and sheep worth one soldo (*sollu*), and pigs worth one soldo. They settled the payment with me and we exchanged a blessing. These are witnesses: God first, and Holy Mary, Gunnari d'Orruinas the head of the stables (*maiore de cavallos*), Presnage de Lella the head of the dogs (*maiore de canes*), and Pilosu d'Orruinas; from those who provide mounts (*poriglos de angaria*) [there was] Orzoco de Opo with all his guard (*kita*). Whosoever shall attempt to frustrate this business which I Cipari de Lacon have arranged, may God destroy him from his physical integrity and remove him from the way of Paradise! And may he receive a curse from God, the Twelve Apostles, the sixteen Prophets, the twenty-four Elders, and the 318 Holy Fathers who disposed the canons; and let him have the same fate as Herod and Judas the traitor with the Devil in Hell! Amen, amen, amen. Let it be, let it be, let it be!

68.
Tramudarus cum donnu Petru de Bonanu p[re]sb[ite]r de Solagrussa homines: isse levedi a Bera Forma et Bonarcadu levedi a Iorgi Cucu. T[este]s: sos monagos et Iorgi Cap[ra], ma[n]datore de Bonarcatu, et Justu Bakia.

69.
32ᵛ Coiuvedi Iorgi Cazula servu de s[an]c[t]a Victoria cun Iusta Turui ancilla de regnu[m] et feger[un]t III fiios: Maria primaria et Goa[n]tine post illa et Mindala. Maria a ssi morivit senza llos partire. Postea partirus cu[n] Frevare Coco, mandatore de regnu[m]: iudice levedi a Goa[n]tine e clesia a Mindala. Teste[s]: donnu Armannu camarlingu et presbiteru Nigola de Bitoni et Petru de Riu.

70.
Ego Armann[us], p[ri]or de Bonarcato, co[m]poreilli ad Abisatu et a Corsa Ca[n]kella, soc[ra] sua et a muliere sua Vera, plaza i[n] Celleva[n]e tene[n]do assa de Furadu Corria servu de s[an]c[t]a Maria de Bonarcato; et deindelli boe i[n] IIII tremisses et fargala i[n] VIII op[er]as et XI cubita de pannu i[n] IIII ob[er]as et II ferros in o[ber]a et co[m]plilli p[re]zu. T[este]s dessa p[re]zatura et dessu p[re]çu: donnu Comida de Çori de Cellevane et Goantine Mafro[n]ti et Petru Mafro[n]ti et Ioh[ann]e Tri[n]ti et Petru de Çori et Troodori Seke
33ʳ et Comita de Cerkillo et Dominige Nanu et Iorgi de Corte | et Furadu Corria ma[n]datore de cl[es]ia et Iorgi Pasi et Iustu Cankella et Ioh[ann]e Musca et Ioh[ann]e Pistore t[er]rale de fictu de Bonarcatu.

71.
Dom[i]na Algaburs regina.[54] Ego donna Algaburs regina de logu d'Arbore, ki lli do a s[an]c[t]a Maria de Bonarcatu su lat[us] ki avia i[n] Lugia, sa fiia de Egizu Figos, et lat[us] de Maria, fiia de Lugia. Lat[us] de sa matre et lat[us] dessa fiia li dei a ss[an]c[t]a Maria p[ro]ssa anima de Berri[n]geri de Scol. Bennit Comida de Corte ma[n]datore de s[an]c[t]e Eru a Bonarcatu p[er] coma[n]dame[n]tu dessa donna et positilla i[n] sa manu dessu p[ri]ore Armannu, ki erat ta[n]do camarli[n]gu. T[este]s: Petru de Cogos, et Petru de Coro[n]iu et Iunellu, Iustu Bakia et Petru Figos et Iohanne Loke.

72.
In no[min]e D[omi]ni. Am[en]. Ego Ioh[anne]s, p[ri]or de Bonarcato, facio ista recordatione p[ro] sas mulieres que t[ra]mutavim[us] cu[n] iudice. Ded-

54 Algaburs was the second wife of Barusone I of Arborea whom he married in 1157 after his divorce from Pellegrina de Lacon. She ruled in the absence of her husband who was held captive in Genoa between 1164 and 1172.

68.
I exchanged servants with lord Petru de Bonanu, priest of Solagrussa: he took Bera Forma and Bonárcado took Iorgi Cucu. Witnesses: the monks and Iorgi Capra, representative of Bonarcatu and Justu Bakia.

69.
Iorgi Cazula, a servant (*servu*) of Sancta Victoria was married with Iusta Turui, a servant of the realm (*regnum*) and they had three children: Maria the first and after her, Goantine and Mindala. Maria died before these children were divided. We later made a division with Frevare Coco, representative of the realm (*mandatore de regnum*): iudike took Goantine and the church took Mindala.

70.
I, Armannus, prior of Bonarcato, bought from Abisatu and from Corsa Cankella, his in-law (*socra*), and from his wife, Vera, a plot of land (*plaza*) located in Zeddiani, bordering on that of Furadu Corria servant of Sancta Maria de Bonarcato. I gave him an ox worth four tremisses and a grindstone (*fargala*) worth eight day's work, and eleven cubits of cloth worth four day's work and two iron tools (*II ferros*) worth one day's work (*in obera*) and I settled the payment. Witnesses of the evaluation and the payment: lord Comita de Çori of Zeddiani, Goantine Mafronti, Petru Mafronti, Iohanne Trinti, Petru de Zori, Troodori Seke, Comita de Cerkillo, Dominige Nanu, Iorgi de Corte, Furadu Corria representative of the church (*mandatore de clesia*), Iorgi Pasi, Iustu Cankella, Iohanne Musca, and Iohanne Pistore a tenant farmer (*terrale de fictu*) of Bonarcatu.

71.
Lady (*domina*) Algaburs, the queen (*regina*): [it is] I, lady (*donna*) Algaburs, queen of the realm (*regina de logu*) of Arbore, who donate to Sancta Maria de Bonarcatu the half that I have of Lugia, the daughter of Egizu Figos, and the half of Maria, Lugia's daughter. Half of the mother and half of the daughter I gave to Sancta Maria for the soul of Berringeri de Scol. The representative (*mandatore*) of Sancte Ero (St Vero), Comida de Corte, by order of the said lady, came to Bonarcato and donated her into the hands of prior Armannu, who was then chamberlain (*camerlingu*). Witnesses: Petru de Cogos, Petru de Coroniu, Iunellu, Iustu Bakia, Petru Figos, and Iohanne Loke.

72.
In the name of the Lord, amen. I, Iohannes, prior of Bonarcato, make this record about female servants we exchanged with the iudike. The iudike gave to Goan-

illi iudice a Goa[n]tine Spanu una a[n]cilla, Vera Carru, q[ui] erat latus de s[an]c[t]a Maria et lat[us] de iudice. Et dedimi iudice, p[ro]ssu lat[us] de
33v cl[es]ia, lat[us] de Vera Pisana | q[ui]a su aturu latus de clesia erat. Testes: Goa[n]tine M[ur]tinu armentariu de Sollie et Iorgi Cap[ra] ma[n]datore de cl[es]ia et Troodori Tolu.

73.
Ego Maria Keuge, muliere de Migale Spanu fabru, ki lli do a s[an]c[t]a Maria de Bonarcato t[er]ra de Petru Cacabu. Dollila a s[an]c[t]a Maria de Bonarcatu p[ro] a[n]i[m]a de Migale Spanu, maridu meu. Apatsinde p[ro]de s[an]c[t]a Maria de Bonarcato. T[este]s: donnu Petru Raskis su pr[es]b[ite]ru meu, et Miale ma[n]datore de cl[es]ia, Iorgi Coco et tota villa de Suei.

74.
In No[min]e D[omi]ni. Am[en]. Ego Armannus p[ri]or de Bonarcato cu[n] s'arme[n]tariu meu donnu Petru de Serra de T[ra]maza fagem[us] custa recordatione p[ro] fiios de Dominige de Pane, ki se fur[un]t lib[er]tatos. Kertei pro·llos donnu Petru de Serra de T[ra]maza, arme[n]tariu de s[an]c[t]a Maria de Bonarcatu i[n] corona dessu donnu n[ost]ru iudice Barusone ubi fur[un]t curatores de locu. Torrar[un]t verbu p[ro]·llos Mariane d'Orruinas et Goantine de Sivi et
34r Orzoco Pinna de Poriose, ki aviat una fiia de Dominige de Pane daunde | aviat duos fiios, narando ca 'lib[e]ros sunt et fr[ate]s n[ost]ros s[un]t.' Et iudicarunt de batuere testimonios ca furunt servos et serviant a cl[es]ia. Et ego batusi testimonios bonos, q[ui] iurarunt q[ui]a 'nos illos cognovim[us] servos et servindo ad clesia.' Iurait pro·llos Goa[n]tine Mellone servu de iudice et Trogotori de Napoli et Troodori de Çori Rarda et Ioh[ann]e Fladone, pr[es]b[ite]ru de s[an]c[t]u Iorgi de Calcaria et vi[n]killos p[ro] esser servos et a[m]bos fiios d'Orçoco Pinna de Puriose. T[este]s: donnu Barusone de Senuski curatore de Bunurçule ki regiat sa corona et donnu Barusone de Serra mannu et donnu Orçoco de Lac[on] saviu et donnu Comita de Serra de donnigellu et donnigellu Orçoco de Lac[on], fiiu de donnigellu Cerkis, et donnu Mariane de Lac[on] de Sedilo.

75.
Coiuvedi Furadu de Ienna cu[n] Alab[er]ta Carru; fegerunt II fiios: Luxuria a
34v Genua e Ianne a clesia. Argentata | a clesia et Olisae a iudice. T[este]s: Petru

tine Spanu a female servant, Vera Carru, half of whom belonged to Sancta Maria and half to the iudike. And the iudike, for the half that belonged to the church, gave me Vera Pisana because the other half already belonged to the church. Witnesses: Goantine Murtinu administrator (*armentariu*) of Sollie, Iorgi Capra representative (*mandatore*) of the church, and Troodori Tolu.

73.
I, Maria Keuge, wife of Migale Spanu the smith (*fabru*), donated the land of Petru Cacabu to Sancta Maria at Bonarcatu. I donate it to Sancta Maria de Bonarcatu for the soul of Migale Spanu, my husband. May Sancta Maria de Bonarcato benefit and profit from it! Witnesses: lord Petru Raskis my priest, and Miale representative (*mandatore*) of the church, Iorgi Coco, and the whole village (*villa*) of Suei.

74.
In the name of the Lord, amen. I, Armannus, prior of Bonarcato, with my administrator (*armentariu*), lord Petru de Serra of Tramaza (Tramatza), make this record concerning the children of Dominige de Pane, who had set themselves free. Lord Petru de Serra of Tramaza, administrator (*armentariu*) of Sancta Maria de Bonarcatu, raised a legal action at the hearing of our lord iudike Barusone, of which the *curatores* of the realm (*de logu*) were present. Mariane d'Orruinas, Goantine de Sivi, and Orzoco Pinna de Poriose, who had a daughter of Dominige de Pane by whom he had two children, answered for them, saying, 'They are free and they are our brothers!' They decided they should produce witnesses who could prove they were servants and that they served the church. So I produced reliable witnesses who swore, 'We have always known them to be servants in the service of the church!' The [following] swore about them: Goantine Mellone, servant of the iudike; Trogotori de Napoli; Troodori de Zori Rarda, and Iohanne Fladone, priest of Sanctu Iorgi de Calcaria. I defeated them by proving that they were servants and both children of Orçoco Pinna de Puriose. Witnesses: lord Barusone de Senuski *curatore* of Bunurçule (Bonorzuli), who presided over the hearing; and lord Barusone de Serra Mannu; lord Orçoco de Lacon Saviu; lord Comita de Serra *donnigellu*; and *donnicello* Orçoco de Lacon, the son of *donnicello* Cerkis, and lord Mariane de Lacon from Sedilo.

75.
Furadu de Ienna was married to Alaberta Carru; they had two children: Luxoria went [as a servant] to Genua (Genoa) and Ianne to the church; Argentata [went] to the church and Olisae to the iudike. Witnesses: Petru de Serra *cura-*

de Serra curadore de factu et Goantine de Sivi, maiore de scolca cu[n] tota scolca sua.

76.
Ego Armann[us], p[ri]or de Bonarcatu, partivi fiios de Ioh[ann]e Titu et de Margarita Galare cu[n] su c[on]te: clesia levavit a Iorgia et issu c[on]te a Bera. Testes: Ianne Corsu et Golorki Gusai arm[en]tariu dessu c[on]te et Petru P[er]ra, mandatore dessu c[on]te de Sollie.

77.
Quando morivit Pascasi de Corte, in iostra lu tutar[us], et posuit p[ro] anima sua ad s[an]c[t]a Maria de Bonarcatu I t[er]ra i[n] Cellevane i[n] Masone maiore, t[en]endo assa t[er]ra de Mariane M[ur]tinu, et III ordines de vi[n]ia i[n] Patru tene[n]do assos d'Orruvu. T[este]s: Mariane M[ur]tinu et Gunnari Piga et Goantine Arte su de T[ra]maza.

78.
Posuit Furadu Piga p[ro] anima dessu fr[at]e ad s[an]c[t]a Maria de Bonarcatu t[er]ra i[n] Gergun Picinnu tene[n]do assa de donnu Egizu de Scanu
35v [folio 35r is missing] | et Goa[n]tine Melone servu de Egizu de Scanu et Gunnari Piga.

79.
Ego Bera Lauri, ki mi c[on]verto i[n] manu de D[eu]s et de s[an]c[t]a Maria de Bonarcatu et i[n] manu de donnu Armannu su p[ri]ore et in manu de sos monagos suos. Et pos morte mia apatsinde p[ro]de s[an]c[t]a Maria dessa plaza mia cu[n] sas domos et issas bi[n]ias et omnia quantu appo. Testes: Gunnari de Pau et Ioh[ann]i de Cappai et Iustu Bakia.

80.
Ego Armann[us], p[ri]or de Bonarcatu, facio recordatione p[ro] sos homines ki partirus cu[n] su c[on]te. Coiugait Migale Mancosu servu de s[an]c[t]u Serigi de Suei cu[n] a[n]cilla de iudice; feger[un]t IIII fiios: custos partim[us] cu[n] su c[on]te. Su c[on]te levait a Natalia, sa primaria; et clesia levait a Petru; Goa[n]tine a clesia et a issu c[on]te Iorgi. T[este]s de custa partitione: Ja[n]ne Corsu, su de Gilarce arm[en]tariu de Suei, Golorki Gusai arm[en]tariu dessu
35v c[on]te, Petru P[er]ra | mandatore dessu c[on]te de Sollie.

tore at the time, and Goantino de Sivi, head of the ward (*maiore de scolca*) with all his guard (*scolca*).

76.
I, Armannus, prior of Bonarcatu, divided the children of Iohanne Titu and Margarita Galare with the count (*conte*): the church took Iorgia and the count took Bera. Witnesses: Ianne Corsu, Golorki Gusai administrator (*armentariu*) of the count, and Petru Perra representative (*mandatore*) of the count from Sollie.

77.
When Pascasi de Corte died, we buried him in the cloister, and he donated for his soul to Sancta Maria di Bonárcado a piece of land in Zeddiani in Masone Maiore ('the great herd'), bordering on the land of Mariane Murtinu, and three rows (*ordines*) of vineyard in Patru ('meadow') bordering on the property of the Orruvu family. Witnesses: Mariane Murtinu, Gunnari Piga, and Goantine Arte from Tramazaa.

78.
Furadu Piga donated for the soul of his brother to Sancta Maria di Bonarcato a piece of land (*terra*) in Gergun Picinnu bordering with that of lord Egizu de Scanu and Goantine Melone, servant of Egizu de Scanu and Gunnari Piga.

79.
[It is] I, Bera Lauri, who commit myself (*converto*) into the hands of God and Sancta Maria di Bonárcado and into the hands of lord Armannu the prior and into the hands of his monks. After my death, may Sancta Maria have the benefit and profit of my small plot of land together with the rural complexes (*domos*) and the vineyards, and all that I possess! Witnesses: Gunnari de Pau, Iohanni de Cappai, and Iusto Bakia.

80.
I, Armannus, prior of Bonarcatu, register my memory regarding the servants (*homines*) we divided with the count (*conte*). Migale Mancosu, servant (*servu*) of Sanctu Serigi (Sergius) of Suei, was married to the iudike's servant; they had four children, and these we divided with the count. The count took Natalia, the eldest; and the church took Petru; Goatine [went] to the church, and Iorgi to the count. Witnesses to this division: Janne Corsu of Gilace (Ghilarza) the administrator (*armentariu*) of Suei, Golorki Gusai administrator (*armentariu*) of the count, [and] Petru Perra representative (*mandatore*) of the count from Sollie.

81.
Co[m]poreilli assu c[on]te custa a[n]cilla sua Natalia, fiia de Miale Ma[n]cosu, et deilli vaccas x et media libra de arge[n]to. T[este]s pro custu c[om]poru: Ponzu d'Albarete curatore de Gilciver, Ianne Corsu et Ia[n]ne de Bosa et Cerkis de Muru, Golorki Gusai, Petru P[er]ra et Troodori d'Uras ma[n]datore de clesia, et p[re]b[ite]ru Ioh[ann]e Corbu.

82.
Ego Girardo, prior de Bonarcato, facio partione cu[n] iudice: homines ki am[us] i[n] pare i[n] Augustis. Fiios de Petru Mula Debonada: Goa[n]tine a cl[es]ia et Orçoco ad iudice. Filios de Mariane Lassu: Iusta a cl[es]ia et Barbara ad iudice. Fiios de Petru de Canio: Furadu a cl[es]ia et Iorgi a iudice. Et fiios de Petru Mula: Ia[n]ni a clesia et Nastasia a iudice; et Furadu lat[us] lat[us] fuit et Targe[n]ti (*corr.* Argenti) Zipulas lat[us] lat[us] fuit: Arge[n]ti a cl[es]ia et Furadu Lassu ad iudice. Dorgotori Musca IIII fiios appit: Terico et Iorgia a clesia
36r e Gunnari et Maria a iudice. De fiios | de Gosantini Samudi: Iusta Talu a iudice et Iorgi Samudi a clesia; Orabona Talu, fiia de Goantine Samudi, a cl[es]ia. Fiios de Furadu Saraginu: Goa[n]tine e Torbini a cl[es]ia et Iorgi et Orçoco ad iudice. In ca[m]biu de Orabona, muliere de Torbini de Prunedu, Iusta Pissi, fiia de Golorki Pissi, a iudice. Fiios de Torbini Marke: Iusta et Goa[n]tine a clesia et Iorgi et Furadu a iudice. De villa de Teti: fiios de Petru Tuturu: Goa[n]ti a clesia et Torbini su fr[at]e a iudice. Fiios de Troodori Samudi: Iorgi et Iusta a clesia, Torbini et Ianne ad iudice. Fiios de Torbini Ucoli: Iane a cl[es]ia et Iusta a iudice. Testes: donnu Orçoco de Lac[on] ki fuit curadore de Ma[n]dra Olisai, ki fegit cu[n] su p[ri]ore sa partione, et ma[n]datore de regnu Peruki et Gai[n]tine Puliga maiore de scolca et p[re]b[ite]ru Mariane Ca[n]cella et p[re]b[ite]ru Cassianu et Goantine Cipulas mandatore de cl[es]ia et Furadu Gupadu et Goa[n]tine Misilade. Custa partitione fuit facta sa die dessu natale de s[an]c[t]u Augustinu.

83.
36v Ego Domesticus, p[ri]or de Bonarcato, facio particio[n]e cun iudice: homines ki amus i[n] pare i[n] Barbaria. Eccl[es]ia levait a Gunnari Cosi et Saraginu Mula et Goa[n]line su fr[at]e, Troodori Sporçoro, Maria Markella, Pisana Lassa, Troodori Marki et Ia[n]ne su fr[at]e, Orçoco Lassu et Orabona, Furada Çipula, et Erradore su fiiu, Gosta[n]tine Marki et Orçoco su fiiu, Petru Çip-

81.
I bought from the count this servant of his, Natalia, daughter of Miale Mancosu, and gave him ten cows and half a pound of silver. Witnesses to this purchase: Ponzu d'Albarete *curatore* of Gilciver (Ghilziber), Ianne Corsu, Ianne de Bosa, Cerkis de Muru, Golorki Gusai, Petru Perra, Troodori d'Uras representative (*mandatore*) of the church, and priest Iohanne Corbu.

82.
I, Girardo, prior of Bonarcato, make this division with the iudike. Servants (*homines*) we hold in common in Augustis. Of the children of Petru Mula Debonada, Goantine [belongs] to the church and Orçoco to the iudike. The children of Mariane Lassu: Iusta to the church and Barbara to the iudike. The sons of Petru de Canio: Furadu to the church and Iorgi to the iudike. The children of Petru Mula: Ianni to the church and Nastasia to the iudike; Furadu was [divided] half and half; Argenti Zipulas was half and half: Argenti [went] to the church and Furadu Lassu to the iudike. Dorgotori Musca had four children: Terico and Iorgia to the church; Gunnari and Maria to the iudike. Of the children of Gosantini Samudi: Iusta Talu to the iudike; Iorgi Samudi to the church. Orabona Talu, daughter of Goantine Samudi, to the church. The sons of Furadu Saraginu: Goantine and Torbini to the church; Iorgi and Orçoco to the iudike. In exchange for Orabona, wife of Torbini de Prunedu, Iusta Pissi daughter of Golorki Pissi [went] to the iudike. The children of Torbini Marke: Iusta and Goantine to the church; Iorgi and Furadu to the iudike. From the village (*villa*) of Teti—the sons of Petru Tuturu: Goantine to the church, and Torbini his brother to the iudike. The children of Troodori Samudi: Iorgi and Iusta to the church, and Torbini and Ianne to the iudike. The children of Torbini Ucoli: Ianne to the church; Iusta to the iudike. Witnesses: lord Orçoco de Lacon who was *curadore* of Mandra Olisai and who made this division with the prior; the representative (*mandatore*) of the realm, Peruki; Gaintine Puliga head of the ward (*maiore de scolca*); the priest Mariane Cancella; the priest Cassianu; Goantine Cipulas, representative (*mandatore*) of the church; Furadu Gupadu, and Goantine Misilade. This division was made on the [anniversary] day of St Augustine's birth.

83.
I, Domesticus, prior of Bonarcato, make this division with the iudike. Servants (*homines*) we share in Barbaria: the church took Gunnari Cosi, Saraginu Mula, and Goantine his brother, Troodori Sporçoro, Maria Markella, Pisana Lassa, Troodori Marki and Ianne his brother, Orçoco Lassu, Orabona, Furada Çipula, and Erradore his son, Gosantine Marki and Orçoco his son, Petru Zipula,

ula, Sarigina Copatu, Iusta Zu[n]cla, Vera Çolu[m]ba, Maria Sigale, cu[n] III fiios suos, Orçoco Sigale et Ioh[ann]e su fiiu, Maria Camisa, Vera Markella et Sissi su fr[at]e, Sinnada fiia de Gavine Capigla, Gosta[n]tine Osai, Vera Calle cu[n] II fiias suas, Orçoco Bateri, Iorgi Talu, Nastasia Urcake, et fiia de Ianne Saltore, Goantine de Puzu, Furadu Sadeli, fiiu de Mariane Sadeli, a cl[esi]a; Gavine Capigla et issa neta a iuige i[n] ca[m]biu dessu fiiu de Mariane Sadeli. Testes: Orçoco de Lac[on] arbarakesu et Orçoco de Lac[on] Sakellu et Peruki et Goantine Puliga, Goantine Musca.

84.[55]

37r Ego Benedictu, p[ri]ore de Bonarcadu, faço recordatione dessos ho[m]i[n]es ki partivi cu[n] iudice: fiios de Goantine Cariga, serbu de s[an]c[t]u Serige et Caterina Corsu, fuit ankilla dessa domo de Gilarce. Iudice levait a Petru su p[ri]mariu et clesia levedi ad Barbara. T[este]s: Iorgi Capay et Iorgi Loriage et Petru Capay et Petru Usay ma[n]dadore dessa domo de Gilarce.

85.

Ego Ormannu p[ri]ore de Bonarcadu, faço recordatione p[ro] sus fiius de Luxuri Melone, i[n] ki mi kertavat iudice Barusone d'Arbaree. Kertavatimi Comida Bais ki fuit arm[en]tariu suo. Et ego bingi i[n] corona de iudice i[n] su colletoriu de Gerkedu. T[este]s: Comida de Serra fiiu de do[n]nigellu, curadore de Miili, et Gu[n]nari de Lac[on] de Lella et Comida Fronteacuça et Orçoco Sakellu et Mariane de Barca maiore de portu. Custos bi furu[n]t kerra binki in corona sua.

86.

37v Posit Terico de Scobedu | ad s[anct]u Serige a Mascuri et a Zura et a s[an]c[t]a Maria de Boele a Cipari su fiiu, et II fiias suas: Bera et Maria. Partivi homines cu[n] donnu Petru Capai: iudice levait a Cipari et a Gavini et a Janne; et levait clesia a Maria et a Jorgia et a Nastasia, plagendo·nos a pare, pedindomi ipse merkee p[ro] dareli sos barones, et ego fegindelli boluntade. T[este]s: Iorgi Capay curadore de parte de Gilciver et Troodori Capai ma[n]dadore de regnu de Boele, et Iorgi Loriage.

87.

In n[om]i[n]e D[omi]ni. Am[en]. In grat[tia] de D[eu]s et dessu do[n]nu meu iudice Petru d'Arbaree. Ego Goa[n]tine Spanu faço recordatio[n]e, asol-

55 Booklet D (1185–c. 1210) begins here.

Sarigina Copatu, Iusta Zuncla, Vera Çolumba, Maria Sigale with her three sons, Orçoco Sigale and Iohanne his son, Maria Camisa, Vera Markella and Sissi her brother, Sinnada daughter of Gavine Capigla, Gosantine Osai, Vera Calle with her two daughters, Orçoco Bateri, Iorgi Talu, Nastasia Urcake, and the daughter of Ianne Saltore, Goantine de Puzu, Furadu Sadeli, child of Mariane Sadeli—[all of them] to the church; to the iudike, Gavino Capigla and his niece in exchange for Mariane Sadeli's child. Witnesses: Orçoco de Lacon the Arborean (*Arbarakesu*), Orçoco de Lacon Sakellu, and Peruki, and Goantine Puliga, and Goantine Musca.

84.
I, Benedictu prior of Bonarcadu, record the memory regarding servants (*homines*) whom I divided with the iudike: the children of Goantine Cariga, servant of Sanctu Serige (Sergius) and Caterina Corsu, who was a servant of the church (*domo*) of Gilarce (Ghilarza). The iudike took Petru, the eldest, and the church took Barbara. Witnesses: Iorgi Capay, Iorgi Loriage, Petru Capay, and Petru Usay representative (*mandatore*) of the church at Gilarce.

85.
I, Ormannu, prior of Bonarcadu, record my memory concerning the children of Luxuri Melone, for whom I was being sued by iudike Barusone of Arborea. Comida Bais, who was his administrator (*armentariu*), summoned me, but I won the dispute at the hearing of the iudike (*corona de iudike*) at the meeting place (*colletoriu*) of Gerkedu ('oak wood'). Witnesses: Comida de Serra son of the *donnigellu* [and] *curadore* of Milis, Gunnari de Lacon de Lella, Comida Fronteacuça, Orçoco Sakellu, and Mariane de Barca head of the port (*maiore de portu*). These were present when I won at the hearing over which he presided.

86.
Terico de Scobedu gave to Sanctu Serige, Mascuri and Zura, and to Sancta Maria de Boele, Cipari his child, and two of his daughters, Bera and Maria. I shared out the servants (*homines*) with lord Petru Capai: the iudike took Cipari, Gavini and Janne; the church took Maria, Jorgia and Nastasia by mutual agreement. At the same time, he asked me for the grace to give him the male servants (*barones*), and I granted his request. Witnesses: Iorgi Capay, *curadore* of the territory of Gilziver (*parte de Gilciver*) and Troodori Capai representative of the realm (*mandadore de regnu*) from Boele, and Iorgi Loriage.

87.
In the name of the Lord, amen. By the grace of God and of my lord iudike, Petru of Arbarea, I, Goantine Spanu record my memory, having received permission

bendomi su do[n]nu meu, iudice Petru d'Arbaree, p[ro] homines ki lli do ad
s[an]c[t]a Maria de Bonarcadu p[ro] s'a[n]i[m]a mea et de muiere mea donna
Susa[n]na d[e] Lac[on], fiia de iudice d'Arboree. Dolli tres pedes de Barusone
Puliga fiiu de Troodori Puliga et Gu[n]nari Macis intreu et assu fiiu et a Troodori
Galare. Et su[n]t testes: prim[us] D[eu]s et s[an]c[t]a Maria et issu do[n]nu
38r meu iudice Petru d'Arboree | et do[n]nu Comida Bais piscobu d'Usellos et
do[n]nu Mariane d'Uda, arm[en]tariu de s[an]c[t]a Maria, et do[n]nu Gun-
nari de Lac[on] curadore d'Aristanis et donnu Baruso[n]e de Serra de Senuski
et Comida de Lac[on] Pees et Barusone d[e] Serra fiiu de donna Bona.

88.
In no[m]i[n]e D[omi]ni. Am[en]. Ego do[n]nu Costantine rege et muliere mia
do[n]na Anna et fiiu meu[m] do[n]nu Comida de Gilciver. Et ego tramudu
cu[n] monagu Petru de Bonarcadu. Dedimi a mimi IIII serbos: ad Barbara
Lisice[n] et III fiios suos, et ego dolli p[ro]·ssos a Maria Tufuti et fiios suos a
s[an]c[t]u Petru de Bidonii, ki fuit ankilla mea de Canpeda. T[este]s: do[n]nu
Comida, fiiu meu, curadore de Gilcivere et Comida de Lac[on] et Petru de Sivi
et Comida de Sogos et Mariane de Uta et Comida Norio et Troodori Cacau et
Petru de Matrona et Mariane de Barca et Petru de Canpeda, Furadu Lisione,
ma[n]dadore de re[n]gnu, Petru Orruiu, Iorgi Usay, Torbini Çurio, ma[n]dadore
de Bidoni. Et si quis ista carta audire ea[m] voluerit et n[ost]ra ordinatione
co[n]fortaverit habeat benedictio[n]e de D[eu]s et de s[an]c[t]a Maria et de
38v s[an]c[t]u Petru de Bidoni. | Et si quis ista carta destruere ea[m] voluerit aut
iudice aut curatore sive ma[n]datore, habeat maledictio[n]e de D[eu]s et de
s[an]c[t]a Maria et de XII apo[sto]los et de XVI p[ro]ph[et]as et de XXIIIIor
seniores et de CCCXVIII patres s[an]c[t]os et ma[n]sione[m] sua[m] siat in
i[n]ferno. Am[en]. Fiat, fiat.

89.
Coniuedi Miale Pasi, serbu de s[an]c[t]a Maria de Bonarcadu cu[n] Castula Novagla ancilla de iudice apus binarios. Fegeru[n]t VI fiios: Torbini p[ri]mariu et i[n] factu suo Goa[n]tine et Jorgia et Ciçella et Istephane et Bera. Custos partivi cu[n] iudice, levando Troodori Paganu, maiore de vino: levait iudice a Torbini et a Bera et clesia levait a Goa[n]tine et a Iorgia; judice levedi a Ciçella et clesia ad Stephane. Testes: Petru de Serra et Goa[n]tine Mafro[n]ti et Petru Mafro[n]ti.

90.
Ego Remundu, priore de Bonarcadu, faço recordatio[n]e p[ro] fiios de Ioh-[ann]e Bulla, ki partivi cu[n] p[res]b[ite]ru Orçoco de Luketas. Ipse levedi a

from my lord iudike Petru d'Arbarea, regarding the servants I donate to Sancta Maria de Bonarcadu for the soul of myself and my wife, lady Susanna de Lacon, daughter of the iudike of Arborea. I donate three quarters (*tres pedes*) of Barusone Puliga, child of Troodori Puliga, and whole of Gunnari Macis and his child, and Troodori Galare too. The witnesses are: God first, and Holy Mary, and my lord iudike Petru d'Arborea and lord Comida Bais bishop of Usellos and lord Mariane di Uda, administrator (*armentariu*) of Sancta Maria, and lord Gunnari de Lacon *curadore* of Aristanis (Oristano), and lord Barusone de Serra from Senuski, and Comita de Lacon Pees, and Barusone de Serra the son of lady Bona.

88.

In the name of the Lord, amen. I, lord Costantine the king (*rege*), my wife lady Anna and my son, lord Comida of Gilciver. I make an exchange with the monk Petru of Bonarcadu. He gave me four servants, Barbara Lisicen and three of her children, and I gave him, in exchange for them, Maria Tufuti, who was my servant at Canpeda, and her children at Sanctu Petru de Bidoni. Witnesses: lord Comida, my son, and *curadore* of Gilciver; Comida de Lacon, Petru de Sivi, Comida de Sogos, Mariane de Uta, Comida Norio, Troodori Cacau, Petru de Matrona, Mariane de Barca, and Petru de Canpeda; Furadu Lisione, representative of the realm (*mandadore de rengnu*); Petru Orruiu, Iorgi Usay, and Torbini Çurio, representative (*mandadore*) of Bidonì. Whoever wishes to obey this order and give strength to what we have ordered, may God bless him and Sancta Maria and Sanctu Petru at Bidonì! Whosoever disregards this commandment, whether iudike, *curatore* or a representative (*mandatore*), may he receive a curse from God and from Holy Mary, from the Twelve Apostles, the sixteen Prophets, the twenty-four Elders, and the 318 Holy Fathers, and may his dwelling place be in Hell! Amen. Let it be, let it be!

89.

Miale Pasi, a servant of Sancta Maria de Bonarcadu, was married to Castula Novagla, the iudike's servant (*ankilla*) to the vintners (*apus binarios*). They had six children, Torbini the eldest, then after him Goantine, Jorgia, Ciçella, Istephane, and Bera. These I shared with the iudike since Troodori Paganu, who was in charge of the vintners, made the division for the iudike: the iudike took Torbini and Bera, the church took Goantine and Iorgia; the iudike took Ciçella and the church took Stephane. Witnesses: Petru de Serra, Goantine Mafronti, and Petru Mafronti.

90.

I, Remundu, prior of Bonarcadu, record the memory of the children of Iohanne Bulla whom I shared with priest Orçoco de Luketas. He took Iorgi son of Maria

Iorgi fiiu de Maria de Petra et ego levei a Petru fiiu de Maria Ca[m]pana; et
39r Gregori lad[us] ad lad[us]. T[este]s: Do[n]nu | Iustu archipiscobu et Comida Norio et Altumonte.

91.

Partivi ho[m]i[n]es cu[n] s'archiepisc[o]pus Justu i[n] Tadasune. Ego levei ad Orçoco et issu archipiscobu a Tericu. T[este]s: Janni Corsu et issos fiios et do[n]nu Orçoco de Luketas.

92.[56]

Ego Albertu Ginivesu, p[ri]ore de Bonarcadu, facio recordatio[n]e p[ro] su padru de s[an]c[tu]m Symione. Bennit Orçoco de Martis, ki fudi maiore de scolca de Miili, a levari su padru a força. Andaru[n]t sos ho[m]i[n]es meos et largarunt in pare i[n] su padru de clesia. Andaru[n]t ad corona de logu ad Nuraginiellu ubi fuit iudice Barusone. Kertarunt in pare Terico Pisanu ma[n]dadore de clesia et Orçoco de Martis. Iudicarunt assu ma[n]dadore de clesia a batuere destimonios homines maiores de parte de Miili. Bennit Iorgi Tamaglu serbu de regnu[m] et Teore su fr[at]e et Goa[n]tine Cucu et Mariane d'Orruinas et
39v Terico | Barbarakinu. Custos v iuraru[n]t in s[an]c[tu]m Evang[e]lium p[ro] custu padru de s[an]c[tu]m Symione. Parsit iustitia ad iudice et a tottu logu qua fuit binkidu et torraru[n]t su saltu ad clesia.

93.

Ego Petru Florentinu, priore de Bonarcadu, facio recordatio[n]e p[ro] kertu ki fegit mecu[m] Goa[n]tine de Sivi p[ro] Sufia de Urri, fiia de Bera de Urri, ancilla de s[an]c[tu]m Iorgi. Kertedi in corona de curadoria, et narait: 'livera sorre mia e[st] et ankilla no[n] est.' Et ego narai: 'fiia d'ankilla de clesia est et in condage l'apo.' Et poseru[n]t·nos ad corona de logu ad duger su condage meu[m] et ipse su suo. Ismendaru[n]t su condage suo in corona de logu, ki aviat factu ad ingeniu[m] et segaru[n]tillu[m] et torraru[n]t sos serbos ad s[an]c[tu]m Iorgi de Calcaria, a sSufia et assos fiios, in ki nos kertavat. T[este]s: donnu Justu archiep[iscop]us et do[n]nu Stephone piscobu de s[an]c[t]a Iusta et do[n]nu
40r Comida Bais piscobu d'Usellos | et do[n]nu Mariane Çorraki, piscobu de Terralba, et do[n]nu Barusone de Serra de Senuski et do[n]nu Baruso[n]e d[e] Serra fiiu de do[n]na Bera et do[n]nu Mariane de Sivi et do[n]nu Troodori

56 Duplicated in entry 161, although the latter records additional information.

de Petra, and I took Petru son of Maria Campana; and Gregori was half and half. Witnesses: lord Iustu the archbishop, Comida Norio, and Altumonte.

91.
I made a division of servants (*homines*) with archbishop Justu at Tadasune. I took Orçoco and archbishop [took] Tericu. Witnesses: Janni Corsu and his children, and lord Orçoco de Luketas.

92.
I, Albertu Ginivesu ('from Genoa'), prior of Bonarcadu, make this record concerning the meadow (*padru*) of Sanctum Symione. It came to pass that Orçoco de Martis, who was head of the ward (*maiore de scolca*) at Milis, illegally occupied and used the meadow. My servants went together to the said meadow of the church to retake it by force. They went to the hearing of the realm (*corona de logu*) in Nuraginieddu where Barusone the iudike was. Terico Pisanu, representative (*mandadore*) of the church, and Orçoco de Martis argued in court. They made the representative of the church produce as witnesses senior men (*homines maiores*) from the territory of Miili (*de parte de Miili*). There came forward Iorgi Tamaglu, servant of the realm (*serbu de regnum*), Teore his brother, Goantine Cucu, Mariane d'Orruinas, and Terico Barbarakinu. These five swore by the Holy Gospel concerning this pasture of Sanctu Symione. It seemed right to the iudike and to all the members of the court that he [Orçoco de Martis] had been defeated [in judgment] and they returned the unworked land (*saltu*) to the church.

93.
I, Petru Florentinu, prior of Bonarcadu, record the memory of the legal action that Goantine de Sivi moved against me regarding Sufia de Urri, daughter of Bera de Urri, servant (*ankilla*) of Sanctu Iorgi. He argued with me in the hearing of the *curadore*'s district (*corona de curadoria*) and said: 'My sister is free (*livera*) and not a servant (*ankilla*)!' Then I said, 'She is the daughter of a servant of the church, and this is recorded in the condaghe!' So they bid that we should produce our respective condaghes for the hearing of the realm (*corona de logu*). They proved his condaghe false at the hearing as it was made with artifice and deception, so they returned the servants (*serbos*) to Sancti Iorgi of Calcaria: Sufia and her children, about whom he was arguing with us. Witnesses: lord Justu the archbishop, lord Stephone bishop of Sancta Iusta, and lord Comida Bais bishop of Usellos, lord Mariane Çorraki bishop of Terralba, lord Barusone de Serra from Senuski, lord Barusone de Serra son of lady Bera, lord Mariane de Sivi, lord Troodori d'Orruu Seke, lord Mariane de Lacon from

d'Orruu Seke et do[n]nu Mariane de Lac[on] de Sedilo et totu logu in co 'e furunt dominica de palma.

94.
Posit Janne de Mo[n]te t[er]ra ad clesia in Guraeda, cabiçale assa binia vedere de do[n]nu Goa[n]tine de Laco[n], tenendo assas cinnigas, p[ro] s'a[n]i[m]a sua cu[n] bolu[n]tade bona de Ioh[ann]e Cadalanu et de do[n]na Preciosa. T[este]s: do[n]nu Comida de Sivi, su p[re]b[ite]ru ki llu penedentiedi et Goa[n]tine de Unale, curadore d[e] factu de parti de Miili, et Iuanne de Stavara et Altimo[n]te Madau et Gu[n]nari Cece.

95.
Posit Elene de Villa t[er]ra ad clesia cabiçale assa t[er]ra alba. T[este]s: p[re]b[ite]ru Comida de Sivi ki lla penedentiedi et issu maridu Bidoni et Goa[n]tine Marras, su co[n]nadu, et Goa[n]tine de Turri, nebode suo.

96.
40v Ego Viviano p[ri]ore de Bonarcadu | facio recordatione de ca[m]biu ki fegi cu[n] Petru Pisanu: sa binia de Petrogna et figu et o[nn]ia quantu i at intro tenendo cu[n] sa binia do[n]niga, cu[n] su cantu advia[t intro de] [...] cu[n] levandosi ipse in pala de spiarella da om[n]ia homini. Et su[n]t t[este]s: do[n]nu Comida de Sivi et Furadu Esuri et do[n]nu Tomas, ma[n]dadores de regnu, Eizo Galaça, maiore de Suli, et Torbini de Uri et Creskentino. Et fecisi custa ca[m]bia in temp[us] de do[n]nu Joha[nn]e Castana.

97.
Co[m]p[ere]i a Petru d'Ardu, fiiu de Comida Sepis et d'Elene d'Ardu, a Comida de Kerchi et a Goa[n]tine su fr[at]e et Elene sa sorre et deillis a resone de XV bisantes inter berbeges et capras et bacca et bisantes, leva[n]dosimi i[n] pala, de p[er]unu ho[m]i[n]e ki mi '[n]de chertare, de spiiaremilu ipsos. T[este]s: do[n]nu Samaridanu Veccla ki fudi maiore de scolca de Bonarcadu et Goa[n]tine Ladu, maiore de scolca de Iporrui, et Comida Pira et Petru Spada
41r et Furadu Pira et Terico Coniale et Samaridanu Madau | et Miale de Kerchi et Petru de Iala et Petru Lafra su clerigu et Goa[n]tine de Ienna et Joh[ann]e Kigali et Samaridanu Co[n]iali et Terico de Unali et Goa[n]tine Madau et Joh[ann]e Laura.

Sedilo, and [others from] the whole land (*e totu logu*) who were there on Palm Sunday (*Dominica de Palma*).

94.
Janne de Monte donated to the church a piece of land in Guraeda, at the head of the old vineyard of lord Goantine de Lacon, bordering on the reed bed (*cinnigas*), for his soul and with the consent of Iohanne Cadalanu and lady Preciosa. Witnesses: lord Comida de Sivi the priest who took his confession, and Goantine de Unale the *curadore* at the time (*curadore de factu*) of the territory of Miili (*de parte de Miili*), and Iuanne de Stavara, Altimonte Madau, and Gunnari Cece.

95.
Elene de Villa donated a piece of land to the church, [located at] the top of Terra Alba ('white land'). Witnesses: priest Comida de Sivi who took his confession, and her husband Bidoni, Goantine Marras her brother-in-law, and Goantine de Turri her nephew.

96.
I, Viviano, prior of Bonarcadu, record the memory concerning the exchange that I made with Petru Pisanu: the vineyard of Petrogna with the fig trees and with everything in it, bordering on the vineyard of the iudike (*binia donniga*) with everything there [...] taking upon himself the burden of answering for eviction. And the witnesses are: lord Comida de Sivi, Furadu Esuri and lord Tomas representatives of the realm (*mandadores de regnu*), Eizo Galaça mayor (*maiore*) of Suli, Torbini de Uri, and Creskentino. This exchange was made in the time of lord Johanne Castana.

97.
I bought from Petru d'Ardu, son of Comida Sepis and Elene d'Ardu, [the servants] Comida de Kerchi, Goantine his brother and Elene his sister, and gave them at a price of fifteen bezants in sheep, goats, cows and cash (*bisantes*), and he assumed the burden of freeing what I bought from the claims of anyone. Witnesses: lord Samaridanu Veccla who was head of the ward (*maiore de scolca*) of Bonarcadu, Goantine Ladu, head of the ward (*maiore de scolca*) of Iporrui, Comida Pira, Petru Spada, Furadu Pira, Terico Coniale, Samaridanu Madau, Miale de Kerchi, Petru de Iala and Petru Lafra the cleric, and Goantine de Ienna, Johanne Kigali, Samaridanu Coniali, Terico de Unali, Goantine Madau, and Johanne Laura.

98.
Ego Gordianus, vicarius de Bonarcadu, facio recordatio[n]e p[ro] homines c'aviam[us] i[n] pari cu[n] s'archipiscobu Bernardu d'Arbaree. Zuigirido fuit serbu de s[an]c[t]u Agustino d'Austis: coiuvedi cun Maseda, ancilla d[e] s[an]c[t]u Iorgi d'Açara. Fegeru[n]t IIII fiios. S[an]c[t]a Maria de Bonarcadu levedi ad Jedida et a Furadu cu[n] fiios cantos aviant et furu[n]t de fager. Et s[an]c[t]a Maria d'Aristanis levedi a Torbini et a Furada cu[n] fiios ca[n]tos adviant et cantos furu[n]t de fager in se[m]pit[er]nu[m]. Et s[un]t testimonios: p[ri]mus D[eu]s et s[an]c[t]a Maria et issu arm[en]tariu do[n]nu Salusi et do[n]nu Barusone arbarigesu curadore de Mandra Olisay, et do[n]nu Goa[n]tine p[re]bi[t]eru d'Austis et do[n]nu Petru Cabru p[re]bi[t]eru de Leonissa et do[n]nu Leonardu, ma[n]dadore de Tonara, et Samaridanu ma[n]dadore de Bonarcadu, et Goantine Marki clerigu et totu sa gorona.

99.
41ᵛ Ego Petrus Perosino, p[ri]ore de Bonarcadu, facio recordatione de binkidura c'apo facta in corona de do[n]nu Hugo de Bassu iudice d'Arboree, c'aviat tandu su mesu dessu logu et ipsu ateru mesu fuit de do[n]nu Guigelmu marchesu, iudice de Plomin[us]. Kertei in corona sua in Fununi in corte ki fuit de Mariane Guçeri cu[n] Marcu d'Abas p[ro] o[nn]ia f[rat]i suo ca 'furu[n]t serbos de s[an]c[t]a Maria de Bonarcadu' et ca: 'lus avia i[n] condagi sus parentes suos'; et ip[s]e torredimi verbu ca 'fudi lib[er]u et ipse et issus fr[at]es.' Positimi iudice a batuere su condagi a corona in co mi posit iudice. Et iudice dedillu su condagi a leere ad Caminu, su scriptore suo. Lesit su co[n]dagi de iudice Goantine, ki fegit sa badia de Bonarcadu et ipsu co[n]dagi de iudice Comida, su fiiu, cum[en]te lus deru[n]t assus parentes de cusse ad Bonarcadu et a totu sa generatione k'edi nasciri de·llos. P[er]co[n]tedi iudice a sa corona kiteu 'nde llis pariat. Adcordaru[n]tsi totos sus ki furunt i[n] corona a torrari sos ho[min]es a
42ʳ serbiçu de s[anct]a Maria de Bonarcadu in co naravant sus co[n]dagis | et iudice torredimi sus ho[min]es a serbiçu de s[an]c[t]a Maria de Bonarcadu et bingillus. T[e]s[te]s: do[n]nu Comida d'Açene d'Urasara et Barusone su fiiu, Comida Pistore curadore de Nurabulia, Petru de Serra spentumadu et Eissu Sakellu Burigu curadore d'Austis, et Iorgi Çancatorta maiore de cavallos et Baruso[n]e Lafri, ma[n]dadore de Fununi, et Comida d[e] Villa maiore de scolca de Nurabilia, Comida de Çepera, curadore de Gilarci, et Mariane de Laco[n] d'Uras,

98.
I, Gordianus, vicar (*vicarius*) of Bonarcadu, record the memory concerning the servants (*homines*) we had in common (*in pari*) with archbishop Bernardu of Arbarea. Zuigirido was servant (*serbu*) of Sanctu Agustino at Austis—he married Maseda, servant of Sanctu Iorgi at Açara. They had four children. Sancta Maria de Bonarcadu took Jedida and Furadu with all the children they had and as many as they would have [in future]. Sancta Maria de Aristanis ('Oristano') took Torbini and Furada with all the children they had and as many as they would have at any time in the future. The witnesses are: God first, and Holy Mary, and the administrator (*armentariu*) lord Salusio, lord Barusone Arbarigesu *curadore* of Mandra Olisai (Mandrolisai), lord Goantine priest of Austis, lord Petru Cabru priest of Leonissa, lord Leonardu representative (*mandadore*) of Tonara, and Samaridanu representative (*mandadore*) of Bonarcadu, Goantine Marki the cleric, and the whole hearing (*totu sa gorona*).

99.
I, Petru Perosino, prior of Bonarcadu, record the memory concerning victory I obtained in the hearing (*corona*) of lord Hugo de Bassu, iudike of Arborea, who at that time ruled half of the realm while the other half was ruled by lord Guigelmu Markesu ('the marquis'), iudike of Plominus (Cagliari). In the hearing presided over by him [Hugo de Bassu] at Fununi, in the court (*corte*) of Mariane Guçeri, I argued against Marcu d'Abas in relation to all his brothers stating: 'They were servants of Sancta Maria di Bonarcadu, and their parents were registered in my condaghe!' He replied, 'Both he and his brothers were free!' The iudike bid me in court to produce my condaghe at the sitting appointed by him. The iudike delivered the condaghe to Caminu his scribe (*scriptore*) so that he might read it. He read the condaghe drawn up by the iudike Goantine, who had founded the abbey of Bonarcadu, and the condaghe drawn up by the iudike Comida, his son, in which it was recorded that the two iudikes had given to Bonarcadu, as servants, the parents of that man [Marcus d'Abas] and all the descendants who were born to them forever. The iudike asked for the opinion of the hearing (*corona*). They all agreed that the servants should be returned to the service of Sancta Maria de Bonarcadu, in accordance with the condaghes, so the iudike returned the servants to the service of Sancta Maria de Bonarcadu and I defeated them [at the hearing]. Witnesses: lord Comida d'Açene from Urasara, and Barusone his son, Comita Pistore *curadore* of Nurabulia, Petru de Serra Spentumadu, Eissu Sakellu Burigu *curadore* of Austis, Iorgi Çancatorta head (*maiore*) of horses, Barusone Lafri representative (*mandadore*) of Fununi, Comida de Villa head of the ward (*maiore de scolca*) of Nurabulia, Comita de Zepera *curadore* of Gilarci, Mariane de Lacon from Uras the coun-

kergidore de Sinnis, et Goa[n]tine Orrodellu, ma[n]dadore de regnu de Piscobiu, et toctos cantos furu[n]t sa die i[n] corona i[n] Fununi dava co exivit de silva iudice, dava bau ludosu. Et icusta binkidura fuit facta secu[n]do die intra[n]te agusti Anno D[omi]ni Mill [es]i[mo] CCV.

100.
Ego Thomas, conbersu de Bonarcadu, facio recordatione d[e] sas particio[n]es dessa domo d'Austis, ka mi ma[n]dait iudice sere Ugo de Bassu cu[n] su curadore do[n]nu Bonacorsu a partire sos ho[min]es ki aviam[us] i[n] comune in
42v Agustis. Et nos fegerus ca[n]tu nos co[m]ma[n]dait iudice. Poserus ad iurari | ho[min]es VIII de sa villa ki furu[n]t senekes, ki 'nde narre[n]t sa meius beridadi k'enti iskire kerra de los pregontare. Et dave co narru[n]t ipsos, ingiçarus a partire:

Fiios de Furadu Mula et de Iorgia Tidu. Levarus kis suo: levait clesia a Iorgi et iudice levait a Orçoco.

Fiios de Goa[n]tine Camisa et de Ravona Sisoy, fuit ankilla de iudice. Levait iudice a Bera cu[n] II fiios suos et levait clesia a Maria cun II fìios suos et a Terico Sisoy, fr[at]e de cussas; et i[n] ca[m]biu de custu levait iudice a Goa[n]tine Tidu, fiiu d[e] Iorgia Tidu.

Partirus fiios d[e] Justa de Scala et de Eizu de Esule: et levarus fiios de cussos cana II. Appit clesia a Goa[n]tine et a Maria, et iudice levait a Nastasia et a Troodori; et dessu atteru maridu apperus kis suo: iudice levait a Torbini et appit cl[esi]a a Janne, ca fuit ankilla d[e] cl[esi]a Justa de Scalas.

Partirus fiios d[e] Goa[n]tine Marki: levait iudice a Jorgi cu[n] III fiios suos et a Troodori cu[n] I fiia sua, et levait cl[esi]a Arzoco cu[n] I fiia sua et a Torb-
43r ini d[e] Rurunkis, no[n] | aviat fiiu, et mama de cussos fuit Barbara Misi ankilla d[e] iudice.

De fiios de Maria Calva apit cl[esi]a VI: a Ravona et a Justa cu[n] fiios cana II et appit iudice atteros VI: a Bictoria et a Nastasia cu[n] cana II fiios suos.

Partir[us] fiios d[e] Torbini d[e] Prunedu. Levait iudice ad Maria et a Nastasia cu[n] kis fiiu ipsoro. Et levait cl[esi]a a Muscu cu[n] II fios suos et assu fr[at]e Jorgi: levait iudice sa muiere de Mariane Usay cu[n] II fiios suos, et levait cl[esi]a sa sorre d[e] cussa cu[n] II fiios suos.

Partir[us] fiios d[e] Justa Pisi: levait iudice a Barbara cu[n] I fiia sua et levait cl[esi]a a Goa[n]tine Gari cu[n] ladus de I fiia sua.

sellor (*kergidore*) of Sinnis, and Goantine Orrodellu representative of the realm (*mandadore de regnu*) from Piscobiu, and all those who were present that day at the hearing in Fununi after the iudike had concluded the hunt at Bau Ludosu ('muddy ford'). This victory took place on the second day of August in the year of the Lord 1205.

100.

I, Thomas, lay brother (*conbersu*) of Bonárcado, record the memory concerning divisions made in the farm complex (*domo*) of Austis, because the iudike, sir (*sere*) Ugo de Bassu, asked me, together with the *curadore*, lord Bonacorso, to divide the servants (*homines*) we held in common at Austis. So we did as the iudike ordered. They had eight men (*homines*) of the village (*villa*) who were senior (*senekes*) swear to tell the best truth that they knew when they were questioned. Then, we began to divide them up according to what they said:

The children of Furadu Mula and Iorgia Tidu: each took what was due to him. The church took Iorgi, and the iudike took Orçoco.

The children of Goatine Camisa and Ravona Sisoy, who was the iudike's servant. The iudike took Bera with her two children, and the church took Maria with her two children, and Tericho Sisoy their brother; and for this the iudike took Goatine Tidu, the son of Iorgia Tidu.

We divided the children of Justa de Scala and Eizu de Esule: and we took two children each. The church took Goantine and Maria, and the iudike took Nastasia and Troodori; and on the other husband's side we took one child each: the iudike took Torbini, and the church took Janne since Justa de Scalas was a servant of the church.

We divided the children of Goantine Marki: the iudike took Jorgi with three of his children, and Troodori with one of his daughters, and the church took Arzoco with her daughter and Torbini de Rurunkis, who had no children, their mother being Barbara Misi, the iudike's servant (*ankilla*).

Of the children of Maria Calva, the church took six, Ravona and Justa, with two children of each; and the iudike took six more, Bictoria and Nastasia with two children of each.

We divided the children of Torbini de Prunedu. The iudike took Maria and Nastasia with the children of each of them. And the church took Muscu with her two children, and her brother Jorgi: and the iudike took Mariane Usay's wife with her two children, and the church took her sister with two of her children.

We divided the children of Justa Pisi: the iudike took Barbara with her daughter, and the church took Goatine Gari with half of one of her daughters.

Partirus fiios de Maria Lassu: iudice levait a Gutoni et cl[esi]a levait a Goa[n]tine et II mi levaru[n]t p[us] su maridu, ki fuit liveru mu[n]iariu, cun clama[n]dominde ca mi fakiant tortu.

Partirus fiias de Nastasia Gurberi: levait iudice a Justa et cl[esi]a levait a Maria cu[n] II fiios suos.

Partir[us] fiios d[e] Justa Maninu: levait iudice a Goa[n]tine et cl[esi]a levait a Torbini. Et fuit su maridu d[e] Justa liveru mu[n]iariu et levaru[n]t s'unu p[ro]
43ᵛ iudice | clama[n]domi ca mi fakiant tortu.

Partir[us] fiios de Zipari Polla c'aviat dave s'ankilla de clesia: levait cl[esi]a ad Elene et a Jorgi levait su patre, ca lilu fegit iudice liveru, et Orçoco rema[n]sit ad accomuni ca fuit semu.

Dave kunde andai ad Mo[n]tes[an]c[t]o et deru[n]timi ad Araona Cucuda cu[n] II fiios suos, et ego dei a Maria Çuru[m]ba cun II fiios suos. Adcatarus IIII in Mo[n]tes[an]c[t]u, ladus de II terrales: et ego deinde sa fiia de Joh[ann]e Corsu i[n] Masone d[e] Cabras, plakendeli assu curadore et assos maiores de iudice; et dei su ladus de Petru p[ro] su ladus de Torbeni Macirida su de Noçolensa, et dei p[ro] Goa[n]tine Marke, ki fuit in Mo[n]tes[an]c[t]u, a Miale Piccu cu[n] II fiios suos. Et deru[n]timi a Kalenda ki est i[n] Noçolensa, ki est i[n] Masone de Cabras. Deru[n]timi a Petru Derise in Montes[an]c[t]u et ego dei a Goa[n]tine, su fradile, in Austis. Ispiiarus·nos de pare dave Montes[an]c[t]u ki no[n] bi arramasit serbu apus iudice. Custa partidura fegerus plagende assu curadore et assos maiores ki levaant sa parti p[ro] iudice.

101.

44ʳ Ego Brandus, priore de Bonarcadu, facio recordatio[n]e p[ro] serbos c'aviam[us] in pari cu[n] do[n]nu Barusone d[e] Serra Taliabucco[n]e. Fiios d'Orçoco de [...] levet isse et clesia levait su ladus de Manina. Custa particio[n]e fuit facta in Masone d[e] Cabras davenanti Ugo de Bassu iudice d'Arboree ubi erat do[n]nu Parusone et Gu[n]nari Fronia, maiore suo, et Mariane d[e] Funtana, arm[en]tariu suo, et Petru d[e] Serra, su fiiu.

102.

Ego Gregorius, p[ri]ore de Bonarcadu, facio recordatio[n]e de II ho[m]in[e]s ki posit iudice Petru d[e] Serra d'Arbaree ad s[an]c[t]a Maria d[e] Bonarcadu: a Bera Piana et a Ioh[ann]e su fiiu, p[ro] s'a[n]i[m]a d[e] iudice Barusone su patri

We divided the children of Maria Lassu: the iudike took Gutoni and the church took Goantine and her two children were taken away from me by her husband who was a freeman with certain duties (*liveru muniariu*), and I, at the same time, appealed claiming that they were doing me wrong.

We divded the daughters of Nastasia Gurberi: the iudike took Justa and the church took Maria with two of her children.

We shared the children of Justa Maninu: the iudike took Goatine, and the church took Torbini. Now, Justa's husband was a freeman with certain duties (*liveru muniariu*), so they took one of them for the iudike, and I appealed at the same time, claiming that they were doing me wrong.

We shared the children of Zipari Polla, whom he had by the servant of the church: the church took Helen, and Iorgi was taken by his father because the iudike had made him free; Orçoco remained in common, because he remained odd in the count.

After that, I went to Montesanto and they gave me Araona Cucuda with two of her children, and I gave Maria Çurumba with two of her children. There were four in Montesanctu, half of two tenant farmers (*terrales*): and I gave the daughter of Johanne Corsu in Masone de Cabras, with the consent of the *curadore* and the representatives (*maiores*) of the iudike; and I gave the half of Petru in exchange for the half of Torbini Macirida from Noçolensa, and I gave in exchange for Goantine Marke, who was in Montesanctu, Miale Piccu with two of his children. And they gave me Kalenda, who is in Noçolensa, who is in Masone de Cabras (*sic*). They gave me Petru Derise in Montesanctu, and I gave Goantine, his cousin (*fradile*) in Austis. We settled the matter at Montesanctu because no servant was left there on the side of the iudike. This division we made with the consent of the *curadore* and the officials (*maiores*), who acquired what was due to the iudike on his behalf.

101.

I, Brandus, prior of Bonarcadu, record the memory concerning the servants we had in common with lord Barusone de Serra Taliabuccone. He took the children of Orçoco de [...] and the church took half of Manina. This division was made at Masone de Cabras before Ugo de Bassu iudike of Arborea in the presence of lord Barusone and Gunnari Fronia, his official (*maiore*); Mariane de Funtana, his administrator (*armentariu*), and Petru de Serra, his son.

102.

I, Gregorius, prior of Bonarcadu, record the memory concerning two servants whom iudike Petru de Serra of Arbarea had given to Sancta Maria of Bonarcadu: Bera Piana and Iohanne her son, for the soul of iudike Barusone his father

et p[ro] s'a[n]i[m]a d[e] mama mia et de (*corr.* pro)[57] sa[n]i[m]a mia et p[ro] remissio[n]e d[e] sus peccados meos. T[e]s[te]s: do[n]nu Bernardu archipiscobu d'Arbaree et do[n]nu Bonacorsu, piscobu de s[an]c[t]a Justa, et do[n]nu Gu[n]nari d[e] Ienna, curadore de parte de Miili, et do[n]nu Saltoro de Serra et Mariane d[e] Barca et do[n]nu Gu[n]nari d'Uras de Simagis et Goa[n]tine d[e] Porta et Nigola de Pane et Comida Pira et Çipari de Ienna et Petru Ispada et Nigola de Porta.

103.

44v Partivi cu[n] iudice de Gallulu. Coiuvedi Goa[n]tine Mameli, serbu d[e] s[an]c[t]a Maria de Bonarcadu, cu[n] Maria de Lee, ancilla de iudice de Gallul; fegeru[n]t II fiios: Çipari et Justa. Clesia levait a Çipari et iudice levait a Justa. T[e]s[te]s: Nigola d[e] Pani, Comida Pira, Goa[n]tine d[e] Porta armentariu dessu archipiscobu.

104.

Ego Nicolaus, p[ri]ore de s[an]c[t]a Maria de Bonarcadu, facio recordatio[n]e de kertu q[ui] fegit megu Orçoco Cucurra in corona de logu d[e] s[anct]u Petru arreendo corona ser Arrimu[n]du suta do[n]nu Ogu d[e] Torroia. Kerteit megu p[ro] Jorgi Parana, ca 'fuit serbu dessa domo d'Oiastra'; et deo nareilli ca 'no[n] e[st] fiiu de custu p[ro] ki mi naras.' Iuigaru[n]tilli ad Orçoco Cucurra a batuere destimo[n]ios, ca fu fiiu de custu serbu p[ro] ki mi naravat. Clamedi destimoniu a Goa[n]tine d[e] Porta et a Nigola d[e] Pani et a Comida d[e] Pira. Et icustus iuraru[n]t ca 'no[n] cognoskem[us] q[ui] fudi patri suo.' Parsit iustitia a totu corona de logu c'aviat binkidu s[an]c[t]a Maria.

105.[58]

45r In Dei no[min]e. Am[en]. Ego Domesticus, priore de Bonarcadu, facio recordatio[n]e[m] de comp[or]u c'apo factu. Conp[ere]i ad Sissi Cabru sa parçone sua dessu cuniadu, cu[n] binia et cu[n] pomu, in fu[n]tana de listincu et deilli sollu int[er] peça et casu et clompilli p[re]zu. T[e]s[te]s: Justu Bakia et Samaritanu Capay et Samaritanu Vegla et Furadu de Ca[m]pu et tota villa.

106.

Posit Goa[n]tine Mellone ad s[an]c[t]a Maria p[ro] s'a[n]i[m]a sua sa parçone de sa binia c'aviat cu[n] Sissi Cabru i[n] funtana de Listincu. Sissi sa barto[n]e sua a clesia la vendit. T[este]s: tota villa.

57 This entry is a reproduction of entry 20, which is also duplicated in entry 218; in all three there is the same variant of *de s'anima* instead of *pro s'anima*.

58 Booklet C (1171–1184) begins here.

and for the soul of my mother and for the remission of my sins. Witnesses: lord Bernardu archbishop of Arbarea and lord Bonacorso, bishop of Sancta Justa, and lord Gunnari de Ienna, *curadore* of the territory (*parte*) of Miili, lord Saltoro de Serra, Mariane de Barca, lord Gunnari d'Uras from Simagis (Simaxis), Goantine de Porta, Nigola de Pane, Comida Pira Çipari de Ienna, Petru Ispada, and Nigola de Porta.

103.
I made a division with the iudike of Gallura. Goantine Mameli, a servant of Sancta Maria de Bonarcadu, was married to Maria de Lee, a servant of the iudike of Gallul (Gallura). They had two children: Çipari and Justa. The church took Çipari and the iudike took Justa. Witnesses: Nigola de Pani, Comida Pira, and Goatine de Porta administrator (*armentariu*) of the archbishop.

104.
I, Nicolaus, prior of Sancta Maria de Bonarcadu, record the memory of the dispute that Orçoco Cucurra brought against me at a hearing of the realm (*corona de logu*) held on the day of St Peter's and presided over by sir (*ser*) Arrimundu under lord Ogu de Torroia. He moved legal action against me concerning Jorgi Parana, saying, 'He was a servant at the farm complex (*domo*) of Oiastra,' and I said to him, 'He is not the child about whom you are telling me!' They commanded Orçoco Cucurra to produce witnesses to prove that he [Jorgi Parana] was the child of this servant of whom he told me. So, he called as witnesses Goantine de Porta, Nigola de Pani, and Comida de Pira. These swore: 'We do not know who his father was!' It seemed right to all the hearing that Sancta Maria had won.

105.
In the name of God, amen. I, Domesticus, prior of Bonarcadu, record the purchase that I have made. I bought from Sissi Cabru her share of enclosed land (*cuniadu*), with vineyard and orchard, near Funtana de Listincu ('the spring of the lentisk tree') and I gave him meat and cheese worth a soldo, and settled the payment. Witnesses: Justu Bakia, Samaritanu Capay, Samaritanu Vegla, Furadu de Campu, and the whole village (*tota villa*).

106.
Goatine Mellone donated to Sancta Maria for his soul, his share of the vineyard he shared with Sissi Cabru at Funtana de Listincu ('the spring of the lentisk tree'). Sissi sold her share to the church. Witnesses: the whole village (*villa*).

107.
Co[m]p[ere]i a Comida Capay binia c'aviat in sa binia mea d[e] Calcaria cu[n] parço[n]e de figu ki ma[n]digavat p[ro] sa mama et ladus dessa sugaria c'aviat cu[n] su p[re]b[ite]ru, ave[n]dolla ipse ad ispiiada de om[n]ia fr[at]e suo. Et deilli I ebba capud a pare et clo[mplilli] p[re]zu. T[este]s: Torbini de Serra,
45v maiore de scolca et Goa[n]tine de Sivi | et Jorgi Marras mandadore de regnu et Goa[n]tine Peça.

108.
Coiuedi Goantine de Riu cu[n] ankilla de clesia de s[an]c[t]a Victoria et iuredi in s[an]c[t]u Petru d'Arsuneli i[n] s[an]c[t]u deva[n]g[e]liu[m] d'esser servu[m] de s[an]c[t]a Victoria et de fager su ca[n]tu l'ei co[m]ma[n]dare de serbire, cantu totu sos ateros servos. T[este]s: Torbini de Liia p[re]b[ite]ru et Torbini de Scanu maiore de scolca d'Arsuneli, et Comida de Paule de Sumugleo et Trogodori de Sivi et Gavine Cabru.

109.
Adviamus ad comune cu[n] iudice ad Petru Cogu ladus ad ladus; et ipse p[ro] honore de D[eu]s et de s[an]c[t]a Maria et p[ro] s'a[n]i[m]a sua dedillu su ladus suo ad s[an]c[t]a Maria.

110.
Terico Melo[n]e fuit servu[m] de iudice et ego petivillu; et ipse p[ro] honore sua dedimillu. Et ego deilli ad Pa[n]dulfinu, maiore de portu, C masclos et II baccas, p[ro] iudice. T[este]s: do[n]nu Comida de Martis, archipiscobu d'Arboree,
46r et donnu Comida Bais piscobu d'Usellos, do[n]nu Mariane Çorraki piscobu | de T[er]ralba. Dessos lib[er]os: do[n]nu Barusone de Serra de Senuski et Comida de Lac[on] Fro[n]teacuza et Comida de Laco[n] Pees et Orçoco Sabiu et Barusone Sportella et Barusone de Serra fiiu de do[n]na Bera et Comida de Laco[n] de Iana et Goa[n]tine de Martis et Troodori Seke et Pa[n]dulfinu maiore de portu. Custos sunt testimonios et totu logu, in co furunt cu[n] iudice i[n] Bonarcadu in su biidoriu.

111.
Coiuedi Iorgi Picu, servu[m] dess'archipiscobu, cu[n] Maria Pasi, ankilla de s[an]c[t]a Maria de Bonarcadu. Fegeru[n]t V fiios: a Iorgia et a Miale et a Goa[n]tine et Petru et a Terico. Partirus cu[n] s'archipiscobu: ego levei a Miale et a Goa[n]tine; et issu archipiscobu levedi a Petru et a Terico: hecco sos

107.
I bought from Comita Capay a vineyard that he owned within my vineyard in Calcaria with part of a fig-tree plantation for which he had the usufruct from his mother, and half of the cork-oak plantation of which he held with the priest, holding it free of all claims and rights of his brothers. I gave him a mare to the same value, and settled the payment. Witnesses: Torbini de Serra, head of the ward (*maiore de scolca*) and Goantine de Sivi, Jorgi Marras representative of the realm (*mandadore de regnu*), and Goantine Peça.

108.
Goantine de Riu was married to the servant (*ankilla*) of the church of Sancta Victoria and swore to Santu Petru of Arsuneli on the Holy Gospels to be a servant (*servum*) of Sancta Victoria and to perform any service I ordered him, just as all the other servants. Witnesses: Torbini de Liia the priest, Torbini de Scanu head of the ward (*maiore de scolca*) at Arsuneli, Comida de Paule from Sumugleo, Trogodori de Sivi, and Gavine Cabru.

109.
We hold [property] in common (*ad comune*) with iudike Petru Cogu, half and half; and he, in honour of God and Sancta Maria [of Bonarcado] and for his soul, gave his half to Sancta Maria.

110.
Terico Melone was a servant of the iudike, and I sought to request him, so he [the iudike] granted him to me for his honour (*honore*). I gave him in exchange, Pandulfinu, who was in charge of the port (*maiore de portu*), a hundred rams and two cows for the iudike. Witnesses: lord Comida de Martis, archbishop of Arborea, lord Comida Bais bishop of Usellos, lord Mariane Çorraki bishop of Terralba. Of the freemen (*liberos*): lord Barusone de Serra de Senuski, Comida de Lacon Fronteacuza, Comida de Lacon Pees and Orçoco Sabiu, Barusone Sportella, Barusone de Serra son of lady Bera, Comida de Lacon from Iana, Goatine de Martis, Troodori Seke, and Pandulfinu head of the port (*maiore de portu*). These are witnesses together with the whole land (*totu logu*), and with the iudike at Bonarcadu at su Biidoriu ('the watering place').

111.
Iorgi Picu, servant of the archbishop, was married to Maria Pasi, servant of Sancta Maria de Bonarcadu. They had five children: Iorgia, Miale, Goantine, Petru, and Terico. We made a division with the archbishop: I took Miale and Goantine, and the archbishop took Petru and Tericho. We took turns and

masclos. Girarus manu et partirus sas feminas: levedi isse a Iorgia sa fiia de Petru Picu, et ego levei a Iorgia, sa fiia de Iorgi Picu, su fr[at]e.

112.

46v Tramudarus ho[m]i[n]es cu[n] s'archipiscobu Comida de Laco[n]: successor archiep[i]s[copu]s Petrus. Isse levedi a Petru Musca ki stavat in Ortueri, servu[m] de s[an]c[t]u Augustinu d'Agustis: et s[an]c[t]a Maria de Bonarcadu levedi a Gavine de Iagunu. T[este]s: Troodori Çukellu, ma[n]dadore de Gilarce, et Cipare Piludu et Orçoco de Varca de Scudu. Et icustu tramudu fegit in Gilarce cun bolu[n]tade sua bona.

113.

Barbara Pisana fuit ankilla de s[an]c[t]a Maria de Bonarcadu apus sa domo de Suei. Et coiuedi cu[n] Gavine Zabarruskis servu[m] de s[an]c[t]u Paraminu de Gilarce, et fegeru[n]t III fiios. Partir[us]illos cun su archipiscobu i[n] Gilarce. Isse levedi ad Margarida et levait s[an]c[t]a Maria de Bonarcadu a Maria, et a Petru lad[us] ladus. Et Terico fuit fiiu d'ateru patre, ki fuit lib[er]u, factu in ankilla mia: in icustu Terico Pio no[n] i aviat parte s'archipiscobu. T[este]s: Ianne
47r Corsu et Goa[n]tine su fiiu et Petru | Aspru et Troodori Zukellu ma[n]dadore de Gilarce et donnu Ioh[ann]i Corri p[re]b[ite]ru de Gilarce k'ie furu[n]t ca la partiat s'archipiscobu.

114.

Iorgi Çukellu misisi i[n] manu de D[eu]s et de s[an]c[t]a Maria de Bonarcadu et dessa mia, in vita et i[n] morte. Posit ad s[an]c[t]a Maria pro s'a[n]i[m]a sua parçone quant'aviat in Cellevane: sa plaça c'aviad cu[n] sos Ma[n]dris tenendo ad Mariane Murtinu et atera t[er]ra c'aviad cun sos de Vegla tene[n]do assa binia ki fuit de Goa[n]tine d'Uras et issa t[er]ra c'aviat i[n] Murginilis tene[n]do assos Ma[n]dris, et issa parçone c'aviad cu[n] sos Ma[n]dris i[n] Gergone et issa t[er]ra c'aviad i[n] Gergone, co[m]poru de su patre et dessa mama, et issa plaça de Foge tenendo ad Joh[ann]i Gespa et issa t[er]ra tene[n]do assa binia de Ioh[ann]i Gespa, et I t[er]ra in ena de Grega tene[n]do ad Ioh[ann]e Trinti, et
47v atera t[er]ra i[n] Pirastru tene[n]do assa de Petru Madau; | sa t[er]ra longa dessas petras in co 'nke vamus a sSepoy et issa terra rodunda dessas petras a dextra de via, et terra i[n] Masone tenendo assos de Vegla et t[er]ra in ena de Sepoy sa

divided the daughters: he took Iorgia, the daughter of Petru Picu, and I took Iorgia, the daughter of Iorgi Picu, her brother.

112.

We exchanged servants with archbishop Comida de Lacon, the successor of Petrus the archbishop. He took Petru Musca, who lived in Ortueri, [but was a] servant of Sanctu Augustinu at Agustis; Sancta Maria de Bonárcado took Gavino de Iagunu. Witnesses: Troodori Çukellu representative (*mandadore*) of Gilarce (Ghilarza), Cipare Piludu, and Orçoco de Varca from Scudu. And this exchange he made at Gilarce with his good will.

113.

Barbara Pisana was a servant of Sancta Maria de Bonárcado at the farm complex (*domo*) of Suei. She married Gavine Zabarruskis, servant of Sanctu Paraminu of Gilarce (Ghilarza), and they had four children. We divided them with the archbishop at Gilarce. He took Margarida, and Sancta Maria de Bonárcado took Maria; Petru [was divided] half and half. Terico was the son of another father, who was a freeman (*liberu*), born from my servant. The archbishop had no right to this Terico Pio. Witnesses: Ianne Corsu and Goantine his son, and Petru Aspru, and Troodori Zukellu, representative (*mandatore*) of Gilarce, and lord Iohanni Corri, priest of Gilarce, who were present at the division on the part of the archbishop.

114.

Iorgi Çukellu put himself into the hands of God and Sancta Maria di Bonárcado and into mine, for life and for death. He donated to Sancta Maria for his soul the share of property he had in Cellevane: the plot of land (*plaça*) that he shared with the Mandris [family] bordering on [the property of] Mariane Murtinu, and another piece of land that he shared with the Veglas [family] bordering on the vineyard that belonged to Goantine d'Uras, and the land (*parçone*) that he owned in Murginilis bordering on that of the Mandris [family], and the share of property that he held with the Mandris [family] in Gergone and the land (*terra*) that he owned in Gergone, which was the result of an acquisition by his father and mother, and the small plot of land in Foge ('river mouth') bordering on the property of Iohanni Gespa and the land bordering on the vineyard of Iohanni Gespa, and a piece of land near the well of Grega bordering on the property of Iohanne Trinti, and another piece of land in Pirastru ('pear orchard') bordering on the property of Petru Madau; the long land 'of the stones' (*dessas petras*) through which one passes on the way to Sepoy and the round land 'of the stones' to the right of the road, and the land situated at Masone bordering

orrudunda et terra i[n] cinnigas de donnigellu tene[n]do assos Beglas et t[er]ra i[n] Iaca tene[n]do assos de Frau et II t[er]ras i[n] Serras d'Oriu tene[n]do assos de Vegla. Et do sa binia de patru de Truiscu k'appo de patre meu: inter plaças et t[er]ras aradorias su[n]t XVI. Testes: Goa[n]tine Mafro[n]ti et Petru Madau et Comida Norio et Dominigi Nanu et Goa[n]tine de Unali.

115.

In nomine D[omi]ni. Am[en]. Ego iudice Orçoco de Çori potestando logu d'Arboree faço recordatione p[ro] fiios de Jorgi Longu: ki siant serbos de s[an-ct]a Corona totos tres: Eiçu et Mariane et Petru. Et no[n] apat ausu nen comiadu, no[n] iudice de post me et no[n] donnigellos et no[n] arm[en]tariu et no[n] mandadore a levarindellos de servizu de s[an]c[t]a Corona. Et sia[n]t in
48r manu de sacerdote | ki at serbire in te[m]plu de s[an]c[t]a Corona, ipsos et fiios
ipsoro et nepotes et nepotes nebodor[um] suor[um] usque in sempiternu[m]. Amen. Et sunt testes: prim[us] D[eu]s et s[an]c[t]a Maria mat[er] D[omi]ni et s[an]c[t]a Corona ad ube llos ponio et do[n]na Fiorença regina et Gu[n]nari de Bauladu nebode meu, ki mi fuit arm[en]tariu i[n] Gipacipirio, sendo ma[n]dadore Melleos Cugurra et p[re]b[ite]ru Terico Arrasca pr[e]idaru de s[an]c[t]a Corona.

116.

Petru Pianu fuit serbu de s[an]c[t]a Maria de Bonarcadu. Coiuvedi cu[n] Paulesa ki fuit lib[er]a. Fegeru[n]t IIII fiios. Giraru[n]tsime ka si teniant lib[er]os: no[n] boliant serbire a cl[esi]a. Kertei p[ro] Elene Marras et p[ro] Bera, sa sorre, in corona de iudice Petru et binki. T[este]s: Barusone de Serra de Senuski et Barusone Sportella et Iorgi de Stavara et Troodori de Stavara.

117.

Partivi cu[n] iudice fiios da Gavine de Porta. Iudice levait ad Nigola et a Maria
48v et a Petru: et cl[esi]a levedi a Goa[n]tine et | a Iorgia et a Bera.

118.

Posit iudice Petrus homines ad s[an]c[t]a Maria de Bonarcadu: ad Elene Tolu et assu fiiu et a Furadu Mameli et ad Paganellu cu[n] su fiiu. T[este]s: Troodori

on the Veglas [family] property and the land situated near the spring (*ena*) at Sepoy, Sa Orrudunda ('the round one'), and the land near the reed bed of the *donnicello* bordering on the Beglas [family] property, and the land situated near Iaca bordering on the Frau [family] property and two lands in Serras d'Oriu ('ridges of barley') bordering on the Veglas [family] property. I give the vineyard in the meadow of Truiscu, which I own on my father's side. Between small plots of land and ploughlands (*aradorias*) there are sixteen. Witnesses: Goantine Mafronti, Petru Madau, Comida Norio, Dominigi Nanu, and Goantine de Unali.

115.
In the name of the Lord, amen. I iudike, I Orçoco de Çori, ruling the realm (*logu*) of Arborea, record the memory concerning the sons of Jorgi Longu: all three of them were servants of Sancta Corona: Eiçu, Mariane and Petru. Let nobody dare nor have licence, neither any iudike that will succeed me, nor any administrator (*armentariu*), nor any representative (*mandadore*) of mine to remove them from the service of Sancta Corona! Let them and their children and their grandchildren and their grandchildren's grandchildren be in the power of the priest who will serve in the church (*templum*) of Sancta Corona forever! Amen. The witnesses are: God, in the first instance; and Holy Mary, Mother of the Lord; and Sancta Corona, where I place them to serve; and lady Fiorença, the queen (*regina*); and Gunnari de Bauladu, my nephew, who was my administrator (*armentariu*) at Gipacipirio; [and] Melleos Cugurra, being the representative (*mandadore*), and Terico Arrasca, priest of Sancta Corona.

116.
Petru Pianu was a servant (*serbu*) of Sancta Maria de Bonarcadu. He married Paulesa who was free (*libera*). They had four children. These four children left [their service] because they considered themselves free: they did not want to serve the church. I made a case for Elene Marras and Bera, her sister, at the hearing (*corona*) of iudike Petru, and I won. Witnesses: Barusone de Serra, from Senuski; Barusone Sportella, Iorgi de Stavara; and Troodori de Stavara.

117.
I divded with the iudike the children of Gavine de Porta. The iudike took Nigola, Maria, and Petru: the church took Goantine, Iorgia, and Bera.

118.
The iudike Petrus gave servants (*homines*) to Sancta Maria de Bonarcadu: Elene Tolu and her child, Furadu Mameli, and Paganellu with his child. Witnesses:

de Stavara et Orçoco Manigas et Comida Norio et Samaritanu Capay et Samaritanu Vegla et Gu[n]nari de Ienna.

119.

Pedivilli t[er]ra assu do[n]nu meu iudice Petru d'Arboree, et isse dedimi t[er]ra i[n] Patru maiore: sa domestiga de Figos de do[n]nigellu, cabizali ass'ortu de s[an]c[t]e Eru et costas ass'ortu meu de nante: et falat totue s'orroia fusca assas petras fictas et clonpet ass'ortu de iudice de Gallulu. Testes: Troodori de Stavara, ki mi dedi sa t[er]ra i[n] co lli posit iudice, et do[n]nu Barusone de Serra Sportella et Comida Capay ma[n]dadore de regnu et Iorgi Marras et Thomas et Orçoco Milia et Goa[n]tine Ladu.

120.

49r Posit Goantine Mellone sa binia ki lli derant dave clesia ad s[an]c[t]a Maria de | Bonarcadu pro s'anima sua et issa c'apit de fundam[en]tu, et adiunsit sa c'appit de conp[or]u cu[n] sa muiere Caderina ad boluntade bona de bare in Pedronia. Testes: Petru Pisanu ma[n]dadore de clesia, et Goa[n]tine Zukellu et Troodori Pulla et Petru de Iala.

121.

Petru Pianu fuit serbu de s[an]c[t]a Maria de Bonarcadu. Coiuvedi cu[n] Paulesa ki fuit lib[er]a ad boluntad[e] bona de bari: in domo de su serbu fegerunt IIII fiios: Elene e Miali e Bera e Iusta. Kiraru[n]tsi de serbire. Kertei pro·llos in corona de iudice Petru. Et torredi verbu pro·llos donnu Orçoco Sakellu et Orçoco de Laco[n] fiiu de iudice et Goa[n]tine de Loy, su de S[an]c[t]e Eru, et binkillos pro serbos, ca parsit arresone ad iudice et a tota sa corona ca fuit lib[er]a sa mama Paulesa. T[este]s: do[n]nu Orçoco de Laco[n] sabiu, do[n]nu Barusone de Serra de Senuski et do[n]nu Barusone Sportella et Troodori Seke et do[n]nu Goa[n]tine de Martis et do[n]nu Troodori de Stavara et do[n]nu Jorgi de Stavara.

122.

49v In nom[ine] Patris et Filii et Spi[ritus] Sanc[t]i. Am[en]. Ego rege Barusone d'Arbaree, ki faço custa carta pro su saltu ki tramudarus cu[n] Bonarcadu. Bennitimi donnu Domestigu, priore de Bonarcadu, et pedivitimi misericordia pro tramudarelli saltu in Barbaria. Et ego deilli su saltu meu de Udullu, ki si ingiçat

Troodori de Stavara, Orçoco Manigas, Comida Norio, Samaritanu Capay, Samaritanu Vegla, and Gunnari de Ienna.

119.

I asked my lord iudike Petru of Arborea for some land (*terra*), and he gave me a piece of land in Patru Maiore ('main meadow'): the farm complex (*domestiga*) of Figos de Donnigellu ('the *donnigellu's* figs'), at the top of the vegetable garden (*ortu*) of Sancte Eru [San Vero], and on the side of my garden which is in front of it: and [its boundary] goes down along the flow of the stream (*s'orroia*) as far as the dense stones (*petras fictas*) and reaches the garden of the iudike of Gallulu [Gallura]. Witnesses: Troodori de Stavara, who gave me the land as the iudike ordered him to; lord Barusone de Serra Sportella; Comida Capay. representative of the realm (*mandadore de regnu*); Iorgi Marras; Thomas and Orçoco Milia, and Goantine Ladu.

120.

Goantine Mellone donated to Sancta Maria de Bonarcadu, for his soul, the vineyard he had received as a gift from the church and the one that was already part of his patrimony; he added the one that he had acquired by purchase with his wife Caderina, in Pedronia, by mutual agreement with her. Witnesses: Petru Pisanu; representative (*mandadore*) of the church; Goantine Zukellu; Troodori Pulla, and Petru de Iala.

121.

Petru Pianu was a servant of Sancta Maria de Bonarcadu. He married Paulesa, a free woman (*libera*), by mutual consent. In the house (*domo*) of the servant (*serbu*) they had four children: Elene, Miali, Bera, and Iusta. They ceased serving. I had a dispute over them at the hearing (*corona*) of iudike Petru. Lord Orçoco Sakellu, Orçoco de Lacon son of the iudike, and Goantine de Loy from San Vero, replied for them; I defeated them regarding the servants (*serbos*), for it seemed right to the iudike and the entire hearing (*corona*) that the [only] free one was the mother, Paulesa. Witnesses: lord Orçoco de Lacon Sabiu, lord Barusone de Serra de Senuski, lord Barusone Sportella, Troodori Seke, lord Goantine de Martis, lord Troodori de Stavara, and lord Jorgi de Stavara.

122.

In the name of the Father, the Son, and the Holy Spirit, amen. I, king (*rege*) Barusone d'Arbaree, draw up this charter relating to the unworked land (*saltu*) that we exchanged with Bonarcadu. Lord Domestigu, prior of Bonarcadu, came to me and asked me to grant him land (*saltu*) in Barbaria (Barbagia). I gave him

assu monim[en]tu d'Orçoco de Curcu et benit assa margine de su Retangio et
benit assu coroniu de Maçigane et benit assu sueriu curbu et benit a s[an]c[t]a
Maria de Urossulo et ergetsi assu nurachi de Nole et benit derectu ad su narado
de Gerkiiu et benit assa codina de niu de corbu et moliasi assu sueriu de Furadu
Marchi et benit derectu ad ssu cannisone et benit at castro de Stria et benit
ad petra de Çippiri et ferits' a pare cu[n] su monim[en]to. Et ipse mi dedi su
saltu de Çerkitana et adiunsitimi sa domestia sua de binias c'apo postu ad ortu.
50r Et su[n]t testimonios | prim[us] D[eu]s et s[an]c[t]a Maria et donnu Ugo pis-
cobu de s[an]c[t]a Iusta et do[n]nu Mariane Çorraki piscobu de T[er]ralba
et do[n]nu Comida Bays piscobu d'Usellos et Punçu nebode meu, curadore
de parte de Bonurçuli et Berrigeri conte, curadore de parte de Gilciber et de
Fotoriani et iudice Barusone de Gallulu curadore de parte de Miili, et Com-
ida de Laco[n] Pees, curadore de parte de Valença et Comida de Laco[n] sabiu,
curadore de parte Usellos, et Comida de Laco[n] Fronteacuça curadore de Can-
pitano, et Orçoco Sakellu maiore de buiakesos cu[n] golleanes suos.

Anno D[omi]ni MCLXXXIIII indictio[n]e XV mense Feb[ruari]i. Et si q[ui]s dixerit q[ui]a male e[st] habeat maledictio[n]e de D[eu]s et de s[an]c[t]a Maria et de IIIIor eva[n]gelistas et de XIIci[m] ap[osto]los et de XXIIIIor seniores et de XVI p[ro]ph[et]as et de CCCXVIII patres s[an]c[t]os et apat parço[n]e cu[n] Dathan et Abiron et cu[n] Herode et Iudas traditore et cu[n] diabolus in inferno. Fiat, fiat. Amen.

123.

50v Ego Ioh[ann]e Mellone, priore de Bonarcadu, faço recordatione pro ho[m]i-
[n]es ki partirus cu[n] Comida de Serra in Gilarce in sa corte dessu archipis-
cobu: fiios de Troori Piçu, serbu de do[n]niçellu depus sa domo d[e] Gilarce, et
issa muiere Colu[m]ba Ulpia, ançilla de s[an]c[t]u Serige de Suei: fegeru[n]t
III fiios II masclos et I femina. S[an]c[t]u Serige levedi a Gavine, et Com-
ida de Serra ad Ianne. Et issa femina coiuvedi cu[n] Eiçu Co[n]iale serbu de
s[an]c[t]u Paraminu; fegeru[n]t VI fiios. Su archipiscobu levedi a Gavine et
a Colu[m]ba et ad Argenti, et s[an]c[t]u Serige levait a Maria et a Terico et
a Janne cu[n] Comida de Serra. Girarus manu et partirus cu[n] Comida de
Serra. S[an]c[t]u Serige levedi a Maria, et Comida d[e] Serra a Terico; et a
Janne ladus a lad[us]. T[este]s: Judice Petru et Goa[n]tine de Serra, i[n] cuia
corona partirus sendo iudice maiore i[n] Genua, Troodori Çukellu et Mari-
51r ane Mameli | et Mariane de Laco[n] de Sedilo et Troodori de Foge et tota
curadoria.

my land (*saltu*) at Udullu, which begins at the tomb (*monimentu*) of Orçoco de Curcu then comes to the edge of Retangio, reaches the peak of Maçigane, reaches Sueriu Curbu ('curved oak') then reaches Sancta Maria de Urossulo and climbs to the nuraghe of Nole; it goes directly to the place called Gerkiiu and comes to the hill (*codina*) of Niu de Corbu ('crow's nest') then turns to the oak of Furadu Marchi and comes directly to the marshy reed thicket and comes to the outcrop (*castro*) of Stria ('barn owl'), then comes to the rock (*petra*) of Çippiri and rejoins the tomb [of Orçoco de Curcu]. Then, he gave me the land (*saltu*) of Çerkitana and added his farmstead (*domestia*) of vineyards (*binias*) which I planted as a vegetable garden (*ortu*). The witnesses are, first, God and Holy Mary; lord Ugo bishop of Sancta Iusta; lord Mariano Zorraki bishop of Terralba; lord Comita Bays, bishop of Usellos (Usellus); Punçu, my nephew, *curadore* of the territory (*parte*) of Bonurçuli (Bonorzuli); Berrigeri Conte, *curadore* of the territory of Ghilziber and Frotoriani; iudike Barisone of Gallura, *curadore* of the territory of Milis, and Comita de Lacon Pees, *curadore* of the territory of Valenza and Comita de Lacon Sabiu, *curadore* of the territory of Usellus; Comita de Lacon Fronteacuza *curadore* of the territory of Campitano, and Orçoco Sakellu head of the iudike's entourage (*buiakesos*) with his college (*golleanes suos*).

In the year of the Lord 1184, of the 15th Indiction, in the month of February. May whoever says that this is wrong receive a curse from God and Holy Mary, and from the four Evangelists, the Twelve Apostles as well as the twenty-four Elders, the sixteen Prophets, and the 318 eighteen Holy Fathers! And let him share the fate of Dathan, Abiron, Herod, Judas the traitor, and the Devil in Hell! Let it be done, let it be done! Amen.

123.

I, Iohanne Mellone, prior of Bonarcadu, record the memory concerning the servants (*homines*) whom we shared with Comida de Serra in Gilarce (Ghilarza) at the court of the archbishop: We shared the children of Troori Piçu, servant (*serbu*) of the *donniçellu* at the farm complex (*domo*) at Gilarce (Ghilarza), and of his wife Columba Ulpia, servant (*ançilla*) of Sanctu Serige de Suei; they had three children, two male and a female. Sanctu Serige took Gavine, and Comida de Serra took Ianne. As for the girl, she married Eiçu Coniale, servant (*serbu*) of Sanctu Paraminu, and they had six children. The archbishop took Gavine and Columba and Argenti, and Sanctu Serige took Maria and Terico and Janne with Comida de Serra. We took turns and made a division with Comida de Serra. Sanctu Serige took Maria, and Comida de Serra took Terico, and Janne [was divided] half each. Witnesses: iudike Petru and Goantine de Serra, in whose hearing (*corona*) we carried out the division while the main iudike (*iudice maiore*) was in Genua (Genoa); Troodori Çukellu; Mariane Mameli; Mariane de Lacon of Sedilo; Troodori de Foge, and all the *curatore*'s district (*curatoria*).

124.
Partivi cu[n] do[n]nu Petru Skintu p[re]b[ite]ru de s[an]c[t]u Sat[ur]ru de Tramaça fiios de Petru Casa serbu de s[an]c[t]u Saturru et Maria sa mui[er]e, fudi ankilla de s[an]c[t]u Iorgi de Calcaria. Fegeru[n]t IIII fiios: II masclos et II feminas. In primariu levedi ad s[an]c[t]u Iorgi ad Sufia et s[an]c[t]u Saturru levedi ad Miale. Girarus manu et levait s[an]c[t]u Saturru ad Bera et s[an]c[t]u Iorgi ad Terico. Et icusta particione feger[us] in sa corte de s[an]c[t]u Iorgi. T[este]s: do[n]nu Iohanne Beglu p[re]b[ite]ru dessa clesia de Mura et Ioh[ann]i Beligicta preideru de Miili et Comida Lorio et Gu[n]nari de Stere et Comida su fr[at]e et Goa[n]tini Çukellu et Troodori d'Uras et Nigola de Porta.

125.
Kertait megu Bernardu Maluvidere, genneru de Goa[n]tine Lauri, p[ro] sa corte d[e] Petru Lauri et d[e] Bera sa necta. Et ego bingi[n]dellu in corona d[e] logu sa die de s[an]c[t]u Miali, sendoe i[n] sa corona do[n]nu Comida de Martis
51v archipiscobu | d'Arbaree et do[n]nu Comida Bais piscobu d'Usellos et do[n]nu Mariane Çorraki piscobu de T[er]ralba et liberos: Baruso[n]e Sportella ki kertavat pro s[an]c[t]a Maria et Baruso[n]e de Senuski et Barusone d[e] Serra fiiu d[e] do[n]na Bera et Goa[n]tine de Serra fiiu d[e] do[n]nigellu et Goa[n]tine de Martis et Troodori Seke et Orçoco de Laco[n] arbarikesu et Troodori Cacau et Petru d[e] Matrona. Custos su[n]t testimonios meos; et Janni Corsu, ki iuredi et binki su kertu in Aristanis, et tota sa gorona.

126.
Coiuvedi Grega Pasi, ankilla de sanctu Iorgi de Calcaria, cu[n] Terico de Paule serbu de s[an]c[t]a Maria de Norgillo. Fegeru[n]t II fiios: Goa[n]tine et Maria. Levedi s[an]c[t]a Maria de Norgillo ad Goa[n]tine et levedi s[an]c[t]u Iorgi de Calcaria ad Maria, plagendolli ad do[n]nu Iorgi Carru, p[re]b[ite]ru de Norgillo. T[este]s: do[n]nu Iorgi Capay et do[n]nu Petru su fradi, et do[n]nu Terico Pala et do[n]nu Zerkis Capai.

127.
Partivi ho[m]i[n]es c'avia cu[n] iudice: Bera Mascaganna, fuit ankilla de s[an]c-
52r [t]u Iorgi de Calcaria. | Coiuvedi cu[n] Goa[n]tine Melone. Fegeru[n]t II fiios: a Gregori et a Iusta. Levait iudice a Gregori et Iusta ad clesia. T[este]s: Petru d[e] Serra de do[n]nigellu, ki fudi curadore de parti de Miili, et Ioh[ann]e Madau, ki levava[n]t parçone p[ro] iudice plagendo·nos a pare, et Ioh[ann]e Te[n]neru manno et Goa[n]tine Mafronti et Petru su fradi et Petru de Laco[n] Cannau, k'ie furu[n]t in sa particione.

124.
I shared with lord Petru Skintu, priest of Sanctu Saturru de Tramaça, the children of Petru Casa, servant (*serbu*) of Sanctu Saturru, and Maria his wife, who was a servant (*ankilla*) of Sanctu Iorgi de Calcaria. They had four children, two men and two women. Sanctu Iorgi took the first and took Sufia, and Sanctu Saturru took Miale. And we changed the turn, and Sanctu Saturru took Bera, and Sanctu Iorgi took Terico. This division we made in the court (*corte*) of Sanctu Iorgi. Witnesses: lord (*donno*) Iohanne Beglu, priest of the church of Mura; Iohanni Beligicta, priest of Miili (Milis); Comida Lorio; Gunnari de Stere, and Comida his brother; Goantini Çukellu, Troodori d'Uras, and Nigola de Porta.

125.
Bernardu Maluvidere, Goantine Lauri's son-in-law, sued me over the farmyard (*corte*) of Petru Lauri and his niece, Bera. I defeated him in a hearing of the realm (*corona de logu*) held on St Michael's day (Sanctu Miali). At the hearing (*corona*) there was lord Comida de Martis, archbishop of Arbaree (Arborea); lord Comida Bais, bishop of Usellos (Usellus); lord Mariane Çorraki, bishop of Terralba; and the following freemen: Barusone Sportella, who argued the dispute on behalf of Sancta Maria; Barusone de Senuski; Barusone de Serra, son of lady Bera; Goantine de Serra, son of the *donnigellu*; Goantine de Martis; Troodori Seke; Orçoco de Lacon Arbarikesu; Troodori Cacaua, and Petru de Matrona. These are my witnesses: Janni Corsu, by whose sworn testimony I won the case in Aristanis (Oristano), and the entire hearing (*gorona*).

126.
[Concerning] Grega Pasi, servant (*ankilla*) of Sanctu Iorgi di Calcaria, with Terico de Paule, servant (*serbu*) of Sancta Maria de Norgillo (Norbello). They had two children: Goantine and Maria. Sancta Maria de Norgillo took Goantine and Sanctu Iorgi de Calcaria took Maria, with the consent of Iorgi Carru, priest of Norgillo (Norbello). Witnesses: lord Iorgi Capay; lord Petru, his brother; lord Terico Pala, and lord Zerkis Capai.

127.
I shared the servants (*homines*) I had in common with the iudike. Bera Mascaganna, who was a servant (*ankilla*) of Sanctu Iorgi of Calcaria, married Goantine Melon; they had two children: Gregori and Iusta. The iudike took Gregori and the church took Iusta. Witnesses: Petru de Serra de *donnigellu*, who was *curadore* of the territory (*parte*) of Miili (Milis); Iohanne Madau, to whom was given, on behalf of the iudike, the share due to him by our mutual consent; Iohanne Tenneru Manno; Goantine Mafronti; Petru, his brother, and Petru de Lacon Cannau, who was present at the division.

128.

Morivit enea Limpida Trogu et posit s'ortu de Miili piccinnu suo ad ispiiadu ad s[an]c[t]u Petru de Miili piccinnu pro s'a[n]i[m]a sua kena aer parte p[er]unu fr[at]e suo. T[este]s: Petru Seke, Torbini Cara, Furadu Ma[n]ca.

129.

Partivi cu[n] iudice Petru d'Arbaree, sendo su patri in Ienua, serbos c'aviam[us] in pari. Petru Tamaglu, fuit serbu d[e] s[an]c[t]u Iorgi, coniuvedi cu[n] Iorgia d'Eregu, angilla de siillu. Fegeru[n]t IIII fiios: a Maria et Luxuria, Elena et Bera. Partirus i[n] pari sos fiios: iudice levait ad Maria: ecclesia levedi ad Luxuria et a Elena et iudice levedi ad Bera. T[este]s: do[n]nu Goa[n]tine d[e] Serra et Petru
52v d[e] Serra d[e] Tremaça curadore d[e] Miili, | Elias Contu, Mariane de Linna d[e] sa turma de rennu, Furadu Moiu maiore de siillu et Comida de Çori d[e] Bauladu.

130.

Posit do[n]na Bera d'Uda parçone sua ad ispiiadu ad s[an]c[t]a Maria de Bonarcadu ad ora de morte sua, mugere d[e] do[n]nu Mariane d[e] Laco[n] Ca[n]tarellu. Posit sa t[er]ra de Puçu d[e] Sergi, i[n]tr' a terra de fuste albu, costas assa figu de Ma[n]nale et cabiça a sa t[er]ra de Salusi Bacca, et atera t[er]ra capud ad billa, pees a s 'ortu d[e] Puriose de Lella et cabiçale a corte de Troodori d'Ardu et ipsa t[er]ra de fr[at]es, pees ass'erriu et cabiçali ad orriola de Bera et issa t[er]ra d[e] Planu d[e] Mo[n]te et issa binia de Canale, pees a s'erriu et cabizali ad mo[n]tem. Totu dedi a s[an]c[t]a Maria cu[n] bolu[n]tade bona dessos fr[at]es cun lassandollis ad issos p[ro] levari aterue i[n] ca[m]biu de custas q[ui] poniat ad s[an]c[t]a Maria d[e] Bonarcadu. T[e]s[te]s: Goa[n]tine de Po[n]te et Troodori Capai et Troodori Berre et Comida de Sii p[re]b[ite]ru et p[re]b[ite]ru Petru Coco et issu p[re]b[ite]ru de s[an]c[t]a Lucia et Puriose d[e] Lella et Furadu d[e] Barca et Salusi Barca, et Salusi Sias.

131.[59]

53r Costa[n]tin[us] iudex. In[60] no[min]e Patris et Filii et Sp[iritu]s S[an]c[t]i. Amen et in gra[tia] de D[eu]s et de s[an]c[t]a Maria. Ego iudice Gostantine de Lac[on] faço custu condage p[ro] homines de Bonarcatu. Q[u]ando andei a Bonarcatu, acateillos sos homines totos sena acabidu ketra (*corr.* kena) serbire

---

59 Booklet A, section 1, (c. 1110–1146) begins here.

60 Change of hand from *In*.

128.
Limpida Trogu died without leaving heirs and donated her vegetable garden (*ortu*) of Miili Piccinnu ('Little Milis') free of burdens (*ad ispiiadu*) to Sanctu Petru de Miili Piccinnu for the salvation of her soul, without any of her brothers having a share of it. Witnesses: Petru Seke, Torbini Cara, and Furadu Manca.

129.
I made a division with iudike Petru of Arbaree (Arborea) when his father was in Ienua (Genoa), between the servants (*serbos*) we had in common. Petru Tamaglu, who was servant of Sanctu Iorgi, married Iorgia d'Eregu, servant [keeper] of the [document] seal (*angilla de siillu*). They had four children: Maria, Luxuria, Elena, and Bera. We divided up their children: the iudike took Maria, the church took Luxuria and Elena, and the iudike took Bera. Witnesses: lord Goantine de Serra; Petru de Serra from Tramaça, *curadore* of Miili (Milis); Elias Contu; Mariane de Linna, from the regiment of the realm (*turma de rennu*); Furadu Moiu, keeper of the seal (*maiore de siilu*), and Comida de Çori from Bauladu.

130.
At the time of her death, Lady Bera of Uda, wife of lord Marian de Lacon Cantarellu, donated to Sancta Maria de Bonarcadu her share (*parçone*), free of burdens (*ad ispiiadu*). She donated the land of Puçu de Sergi, located within the land of Fuste Albu ('poplar trees'), at the side of the fig tree of Mannale and at the head of the land of Salusio Bacca; and another land at the top of the village (*villa*), at the foot of the garden of Puriose de Lella and at the top end of the farmyard (*corte*) of Troodori d'Ardu, as well as the land of her brother located at the foot of the river and at the head of the threshing floor (*orriola*) of Bera, and the land of Planu de Monte, and the vineyard of Canale located between the lower end of the river and the top of the hill. All this she gave to Sancta Maria with the consent of her brothers, leaving them the possibility and the right to have their just compensation by acquiring other properties in exchange for these lands that she gave to Sancta Maria de Bonarcadu. Witnesses: Goantine de Ponte; Troodori Capai; Troodori Berre; priest Comida de Sii (Sivi); priest Petru Coco; the priest of Sancta Lucia; and Puriose de Lella; Furadu de Barca; Salusi Barca, and Salusi Sias.

131.
Costantinus iudex: in the name of the Father, the Son and the Holy Spirit, amen, and by the grace of God and Holy Mary. I, iudike (iudike) Gostantine de Lacon make this condaghe regarding the men (*homines*) of Bonarcatu. When I went to Bonarcatu, I found that none of the men was subjected to any order and that

force pagu. Parsitiminde male et posillos a iurare a servire a iuale IIII dies i[n] setimana: et issos apiaresos et issos agasones et canarios cantu aent fagere i[n] cita de domo serviant a clesia om[n]ia lunis i[n] om[n]ia op[us] qua[n]tu aent fagere sos ateros colivertos.

Costantine Stapu qua[n]do okisit s'omine in s[an]c[t]e Eru venit ad Bonarcatu et fegit sibi domu[m] et pla[n]tavit vinea. Narruntiminde ca fuit benidu, pregonteillu: 'voles torrare a s[an]c[t]e Eru?' Et naredimi ipse: 'servu volo essere
53v a s[an]c[t]a Maria de Bonarcatu, et ego et fiios meos.' Et ego posillu | a iurare de servire a iuale et ipse et fiios suos a clesia: ad Orçoco et a Comida et a Ioh[ann]i, co et ipsos at[er]os servos. Et mulieres moiant et cogant et purgent et sabunent et filent et tessant et, in temp[us] de mersare, mersent o[nn]ia lunis, sas ki no[n] ant aere genezu donnigu. Custu fegi ego iudice Gosta[n]tine i[n] collatura ki fegi a silva de Cercetu, sendo ibi mecu[m] o[nn]ia fr[at]e meu[m].

Et n[on] fuit tale homine ki 'nde pro·llos naredi: 'custos ho[min]es meos s[un]t', borce narandomi totos 'bostros s[un]t de regnu[m].' Et ego, ca iskivi bene ca furunt meos, poniollos ut servia[n]t a s[an]c[t]a Maria de Bonarcatu et ipsos et fiios suos et nepotes nepotor[um] suor[um] usq[ue] i[n] se[m]pit[er]nu[m]. Et issu ki si 'nd'a bolere levare dava su servitiu de s[an]c[t]a Maria de Bonarcatu dentillis disciplina issoro p[ri]ore ki at essere. Et torrent a servitiu de clesia ad ue los delego ego iudice Gosta[n]tine q[ui] faço custa abba-
54r dia. Et non | appat ausu[m] nullu[m] homine[m] n[on] iudice et non pauperu[m] a tollere[n]de custos h[omin]es dave servitiu de s[an]c[t]a Maria de Bonarcatu. Ive servia[n]t usq[ue] i[n] se[m]pit[er]nu[m] et siant in manu de D[eu]s et de iudice de logu et de monagos ki ant servire ad sancta Maria de Bonarcatu. N'a ateru serviçu de logu n[on] si levent n[on] p[er] curadore et n[on] per maiore de scolca p[ro] nulla presse d'op[us] de logu. Se[m]p[er] siant a volu[n]tate dessos monagos, a ki llos delegai et serviantillis i[n] fide bona.

Et dollis assos monagos asoltura de pegos ki ant occidere servos dessos monagos i[n] silva de Kerketu au a digitu au a casside aut a cavallu. N[on] appat ausu no[n] curatore et no[n] maiore de canes et no[n] canariu et no[n] kerkitore et non ma[n]datore de regnu[m] a tollerellis no[n] peza, no[n] pelles, no[n] d'iverru et no[n] de veranu: force assos monagos si dent a se[m]pit[er]nu[m].

they did not give service except in a small part. It seemed wrong to me, and I ordered them to swear that they would give farm-labour services (*a iuale* 'of the yoke'), four days a week. Also, the beekeepers (*apiaresos*), horse-keepers (*agasones*), and dog-keepers (*canarios*) must provide the same service to the church that they had to perform for our [iudike's] house every Monday, as their work is needed, and to the same extent as the other unbound servants (*coliver-tos*).

Costantine Stapu, after killing a man at Sancte Eru (St Vero), came to Bonarcatu, built a house and planted a vineyard. They informed me of his arrival, and I asked him: 'Do you want to go back to Sancte Eru?' He replied, 'I want to be a servant (*servu*) at Sancta Maria de Bonarcatu—me and my children!' So, I made him swear that he would serve at the church with his children: Orçoco, Comida, and Iohanni, like the other servants. The women shall grind the grain and bake, and sift the grain, do the laundry, spin and weave and, in harvest season, reap every Monday—the women who were [formerly] free from compulsory service to the iudike (*genezu donnigu*). All this I, iudike Gostantine, did when I went to the wood (*silva*) of Cercetu (Cherchedu), accompanied by all my brethren.

And there was no one who said to me concerning them [the servants], 'These men are mine,' which indeed they all affirmed: 'They are yours, of the realm (*regnum*)!' And I, who knew well that they were mine, put them to serve Sancta Maria de Bonarcatu, they and their children, and the grandchildren of their grandchildren—in perpetuity. Whoever wishes to abandon the service due to Sancta Maria de Bonarcatu let them be subject to the discipline of the prior, whoever he may be! And let them return to the service of the church to which I, iudike Gostantine, who is the founder of this abbey, delegate them to! And let no one, no men nor iudike nor minor lord (*pauperum*), dare to take these men away from the service of Sancta Maria de Bonarcatu! They serve there in perpetuity and are subjected to God, to the iudike of the realm (*logu*) and to the monks who will serve at Sancta Maria de Bonarcatu. Nor are they assigned to any other service in the realm (*logu*), either by *curadore* or head of the ward (*maiore de scolca*) for any urgency or labour requirement of the realm, but [instead] always be subject to the will of the monks to whom I have assigned them, and to serve them in good faith.

I also give the monks a hunting permit (*asoltura*) with respect to the beasts that the servants of those monks might kill in the wood of Keketu (Cherchedu) bare-handed, or with a net, or on horseback. And let no *curatore* nor head dog-keeper (*maiore de canes*), nor tax official (*kerkitore*), nor representative of the realm (*mandatore de regnum*) dare to demand from them either meat or skin, either in winter or in summer. Everything is instead due to the monks in perpetuity.

Et ki at co[n]forzare ista armi[n]antia q[ui] arminavi ego iudice Gosta[n]-
54v tine et dixerit | quia bene e[st] habeat benedictione de D[eu]s et de s[an]c[t]a
Maria virgo et de o[mne]s s[an]c[t]os et s[an]c[t]as D[e]i. Am[en]. Et q[ui] aet
punnare et dicere aet et sterminare ca non siat, siat ille exterminatu de magine
sua in isto s[e]c[u]lo et post morte sua no[n] appat paradisu et appat par-
çone cu[n] Herode et cu[n] Iuda traditore et cu[n] diabolu[m] in infernu[m]
i[n]feriore. Am[en] Am[en]. Fiat, fiat.

132.
In nomine D[omi]ni. Am[en]. Ego Petru kerigu p[ri]ore de Bonarcatu cu[n]
s'arm[en]tariu meu p[re]vid[er]u Calafrede scribem[us] ista recorda[n]tia.
Gavini Formiga et Bera de Porta furunt coiuvados in pare et positi[n]kellos a
servos ad s[an]c[t]a Maria iudice C[on]stantini quando fegit s'abbadia. Servin-
do bene a[m]bos, maridu et muiere, a clesia, feger[un]t VII fiios: Petru de
Porta et Zipari et Torbini et Ioanni et Maria et Margarita et Saina. Servindo
55r bene a cl[esi]a custos cun pare[n]tes ipsoro, | morrunt sos pare[n]tes; steterunt
totos VII fiios, servindo ue los poniam[us]. Fegerunt c[un]siiu cu[n] Saina
Tussia, cia ipsoro, buiaria dessu regnu de iudice C[on]sta[n]tini et postea de
iudice Comita. Feger[un]t sibi carta de lib[er]os et bullar[un]t cu[n] bullat-
oriu de iudice Comita. Rege[n]dosilla custa carta a cua, si girarunt de servire.
Bolbillos ego i[m]p[re]ssare i[n] s'op[us] et narruntimi 'lib[er]os sum[us] et
ave stara n[on] ti servim[us].' Andainke ego a iudice Comita et torreindelli
verbu: 'ma[n]det p[ro]·llos iudice;' et andar[un]ti[n]ke totos septe fr[at]es ad
Nurageniellu. Certei cu·llos i[n] corona de iudice: 'Custos fiios de Gavini For-
miga, ki posit iuige Gosta[n]tine, patre vostru, a cl[esi]a, p[ro]giteu n[on] mi
servint?' Torraru[n]timi ipsos verbu[m]: 'Nos lib[er]os sum[us] et carta nos-
tra nos am[us].' Iudigedi iuige de batuere carta et beridade daunde furu[n]t
lib[er]os custos. Batuserunt carta bullata cu[n] bullatoriu de iudice Comita,
55v ki aviant armada a iscusi suo. Vidit | iuige custa carta et connoscit ca ll'aviant
facta a fura sua. Strixit corona, et bennit sa buiaria et bingitilla sara, ad ipsa et
ad ipsos. Ad ipsa volvitilla occidere i[n] corona et assos fr[at]es iscodoglare et
afurcare. Sendo sos ferros cagentes et issas furcas pesadas, bennit donna Anna,
sa mama, et isculpitillos de no llos okier p[ro] fide de s[an]c[t]a Maria de Bon-

Whoever will observe this order which I, iudike Gostantine, commanded, will say that it is good to be blessed by God and by the Holy Virgin Mary and by all the saints of God! Amen. But he who will not do so or will ensure that this order is not put into effect, whether it is destroyed in the integrity of his person in this life or after death, let him not enter Heaven, but share the fate of Herod, Judas the traitor, and the Devil in the deepest part of Hell! Amen, amen. Let it be, let it be!

132.

In the name of the Lord, amen. I, Petru, cleric and prior of Bonarcatu, together with my administrator (*armentariu*), priest Calafrede, write this record. Gavini Formiga and Bera de Porta were married to one another, and iudike Constantini had given them as servants (*servos*) to Sancta Maria when he founded the abbey. During their service, which both husband and wife gave to the church, they had seven children: Petru de Porta, Zipari, Torbini, Ioanni, Maria, Margarita, and Saina. These children willingly gave their service to the church along with their parents, until their parents came to their death. The seven offspring [then] remained to serve as we had commanded them. They took advice (*cunsiiu*) from Saina Tussia, their aunt, who kept the seal-press of the realm (*buiaria dessu regnu*) under iudike Constantini, and afterwards of iudike Comita. They made for themselves a freeman's charter (*carta de liberos*) and sealed it with [a seal from] the seal-press (*bullatoriu*) of iudike Comita. With this document of theirs as evidence, they moved away from service. I wanted to compel them to work, but they told me, 'We are free (*liberos*) and, from now, we do not serve you!' I then went to iudike Comita and told him, 'Let the iudike summon them!' The seven siblings all went to Nurageniellu (Nuraxinieddu, 'black nuraghe'). I argued with them at the hearing (*corona*), saying, 'Why do these offspring of Gavini Formiga, whom your father, iudike Gostantine, gave to the church, not serve me?' They argued, replying, 'We are free, and we have our document (*carta*)!' The iudike decreed that they should produce the document that they really were freemen. They brought the document fitted with a seal made with the seal-press (*carta bullata cun bullatoriu*) of iudike Comita, which they had fraudulently made and without his knowledge. The iudike looked at the document and realised that they had made it fraudulently and without his knowledge. He convened the hearing (*corona*) and the seal-press keeper (*sa buiaria*) [Saina Tussia] came. They defeated both her and them [the seven siblings]. He wanted to execute her on the spot and that the siblings be tortured so that they might confess, and then to kill them by hanging. The irons were already hot (*ferros cagantes*) and the gallows raised (*furcas pesadas*) when lady Anna, the mother [of iudike Comita], arrived and begged that they should not be killed

arcatu. Et iudice narait i[n] sa corona: 'levade·bos·inke sos servos de s[an]c[t]a Maria.' Et ego batusindellos pone[n]dollos iudice a iurare d'esser servos de s[an]c[t]a Maria de Bonarcadu et ipsos et fiios issoro et nepotes nepotor[um] suor[um] qua[nt]'aet esser ipsa generatione. Testimonios: Petru de Lac[on] curadore maiore, Petru de Lacon de Iana curatore de Vale[n]za, Costa[n]tini d'Orruvu Forte a pilu, curatore de Migil, Orçoco de Urgu curatore de Usellos, Petru de Sivi curatore de Gilciver, Puriose curadore de Frotoriane et Gunnare
56r d'Orruvu Dentes | curatore de Bunurçuli et totu logu. T[este]s.

133.

Comida iudex. In nomine Patris et Filii et Spi[ritu]s S[an]c[t]i. Am[en]. Ego iudice Comida de Lac[on] facio recordatione. Sa die ki andei a Bonarcatu a ponneve su saltu de Petra p[er]tusa a s[an]c[t]a Maria, sa die mi torredi verbu p[ri]ore Boniçu p[ro] sos fiios de Gosta[n]tine Stapu, ki poserat patre meu iudice Gosta[n]tine ad s[an]c[t]a Maria ca 'n[on] mi servint bene et issu servizu ki llis poserat patre vostru p[ro] fagere a clesia a llu lassant.' Mandei pro·llos et benneruntimi totos tres fr[at]es fiios de Gostantine Stapu: Orçoco et Comida et Ioh[ann]e. Bolbillos fustigare ca lassavant s'op[us] de clesia ki llis poserat patre meu. Et basaruntimi·llos et no llos fustigei. Et ego posillos ad iurare d'essere servos de iuvale ad s[an]c[t]a Maria de Bonarcatu, ad ube los poserat patre meu, issos et mulieres issoro: Pascasia d'Abbas muiere d'Orçoco Stapu, et Luxuria de Casta[n]ias muliere de Comita Stapu. Et Ioh[ann]e fr[at]e issoro
56v coiuvadu | fuit cu[n] Saina de Porta, ancilla i[n]trega de cl[esi]a; appatsinde p[ro]de s[an]c[t]a Maria de Bonarcadu de·ssos et de fiios issoro et de nepotes nepotor[um] suor[um] quantu aet essere ipsa generatio[n]e usq[ue] in se[m]pit[er]nu[m]. Et n[on] appat ausu nullu[m] homine[m] a ttollere[n]dellos aliga[n]do de servitiu de s[an]c[t]a Maria, ad ube llos delegarat patre meu et ego: n[on] iudices, n[on] curatores, n[on] servos meos, n[on] armentarios et n[on] ma[n]datores de post sa domo de s[an]c[t]e Eru, daunde vennerant pross'homine ki ociserat Gosta[n]tine Stapu, patre issoro. Et s[un]t testimonios: prim[us] D[eu]s et s[an]c[t]a Maria et Gosta[n]tine d'Orruvu, fradile meu, curadore de Miili, Petru de Sivi curatore de Bonurçule, Orçoco de Urgu curatore de Usellos, Petru de Iana curatore de Vale[n]za, Petru de Lac[on] curatore maiore. Custos furunt sa die mecu de co fegi custa carta i[n] Bonarcatu. Si
57r q[ui]s dixerit q[ui]a bene e[st] quo ordinavi ego iudice Comita | et narr'aet ca veritate e[st], habeat benedictione de d[eu]m patre[m] om[n]ip[o]t[en]te[m] et de s[an]c[t]a Maria et de o[mne]s s[an]c[to]s et s[an]c[t]as D[e]i. Amen, Am[en], fiat, fiat. Et si q[ui]s dixerit q[ui]a male e[st] et destruere ea voluerit

for the dignity of (*pro fede*) Sancta Maria de Bonarcatu. Then the iudike said to the hearing, 'Take them yourselves as servants of Sancta Maria!' So, I took them, and the iudike made them swear to be the servants of Sancta Maria de Bonarcadu as well as their children and the grandchildren of their grandchildren, forever, as long as their line lasts. Witnesses: Petru de Lacon, head *curadore* (*maiore*); Petru de Lacon from Iana, *curatore* of Valenza; Costantini d'Orruvu 'Forte a Pilu,' *curatore* of Migil (Milis); Orçoco de Urgu, *curatore* of Usellos (Usellus); Petru de Sivi, *curatore* of Gilciver (Gilziver); Puriose, *curatore* of Frotoriane (Fordongianus); Gunnarie d'Orruvu Dentes, *curatore* of Bunurçuli (Bunurzuli), and the whole country (*et totu logu*). Witnesses.

133. Comida iudex
In the name of the Father, the Son, and the Holy Spirit, amen. I, iudike Comida de Lacon, record this memory: on the day that I went to Bonarcatu to donate the unworked land (*saltu*) of Petra Pertusa ('pierced stone') to Sancta Maria, that day prior Boniçu complained to me about the children of Gostantine Stapu, whom my father iudike Gostantine had donated to Sancta Maria, saying, 'They do not serve me well and they neglect the service that your father obliged them to give to the church'. I summoned them to court, and all three brothers, the children of Gostantine Stapu, came: Orçoco, Comida, and Iohanne. I wanted to flog them because they neglected the work they were to do for the church as my father had commanded them. They kissed me, so I did not flog them; I made them swear to be servants 'of the yoke' (*servos de iuvale*) at Sancta Maria de Bonarcatu, to whom my father had given them and their wives: Pascasia d'Abbas, wife of Orçoco Stapu, and Luxuria de Castanias, wife of Comita Stapu. Iohanne, their brother, was married to Saina de Porta, a servant (*ancilla*) of the church. May Sancta Maria de Bonarcadu benefit from them and their children and their grandchildren's granchildren for as long as the lineage lasts! And let no one dare to take them away from the service of Sancta Maria, to which my father and I had assigned them: neither iudikes, nor *curatores*, nor any of my servants, nor administrators (*armentarios*), nor representatives (*mandatores*) in the house of Sancte Eru, whence they had come because of the murder (*pross'homine ki ociserat*) committed by Gostantine Stapu, their father! The witnesses are: God, first before all else, and Holy Mary; Gostantine d'Orruvu, my cousin, *curatore* of Miili (Milis); Petru de Sivi, *curatore* of Bonurçule (Bonorzuli); Orçoco de Urgu, *curatore* of Usellos (Usellus); Pettru de Iana, *curatore* of Valenza; Petru de Lacon, head *curatore* (*maiore*). These were with me when I made this charter in Bonarcatu. Whoever will say that which I, iudike Comita, ordered is good and will say that it is true, may he be blessed by God the Father Almighty and by Holy Mary and by all the saints of God! Amen, amen. Let it be done! And whoever says that it is

fiat excomunicatu et maledictu de D[eu]s et de s[an]c[t]a Maria et de o[mne]s s[an]c[t]os et s[an]c[t]as D[e]i et appat anathema sicut Dathan et Abiron, q[ui] deglutivit t[er]ra et appat parçone cu[n] Iuda traditore et cu[n] Herode et Pilat[us] et cun diabol[us] i[n] infernu[m]. Am[en], Am[en]. Fiat, fiat.

134.

In no[min]e D[omi]ni. Am[en]. Ego Boniço peccator, monach[us] et priore s[anct]e Marie de Bonarcatu ki faço custa carta, cu[n] volu[n]tate de D[eu]s et dessu donnu meu iudice Comita, de co[m]poru et de t[ra]mutu quantu fegi i[n] te[m]pus meu. Comporei fundam[en]tu i[n] s[an]c[t]u Iorgi de Calcaria et posi ad ortu de cedru et de om[n]ia pomu. Co[m]poreilli a Cipari Capai t[er]ra de ortu tene[n]do assa de cl[esi]a post monasterio et ad Iorgi su fr[at]e i[n] co
57v partiant | i[n] pare. Et fegindellis kis tremisse issoro i[n]t[er] peza cap[ri]na et laore, et co[m]plillis. Tramudeilli a Mele de Foge parçone sua qua[n]tu aviat i[n] icussu ortu et dei[n]delli i[n]tesiga vi[n]ia in Istra[m]padoriu. T[este]s: Luxuri Picu ma[n]datore de regnu[m] et Torbini d'Ardu, maiore de scolca, cu[n] tota scolca sua et Gervasi Vilidu[n] ma[n]datore de cl[esi]a. Co[m]poreilli a Iorgia Molligine et a Marra, sa muiere de Malusone, parçone issoro quanta aviant in icussu ortu depost monasteriu. Et fegindellis tremisse de peza cap[ri]na i[n]t[er] pare et co[m]plillis p[re]zu. Testes: Luxuri Picu mandatore de regnu[m] et tota villa. Et i[n]dulsit·nos Torbini d'Orruinas sa parçone sua quanta aviat in icussu ortu. Et posuit p[ro] anima sua Iorgi de Corrariu parçone sua quanta aviat in icussu ortu de post monasteriu[m]. Testes: Luxuri Picu ma[n]datore de regnu[m] et Gervasi Vilidu cu[n] colivertos suos.

135.

58r Furet·nos Flacone d'Orruinas su | monasteriu et binker[us]illu i[n] corona de Gostantine d'Orruvu[m], sendo isse curadore. Et det·nos i[n]de sa parçone sua de cussu ortu. T[este]s: su curatore cu[n] tota curatoria.

136.

Et ego monagu Benedictu, rege[n]do sa domo de Bonarcatu, co[m]porei ad Maria Caydana et assu maridu, Furadu Cugurra, vinia tene[n]do assa de s[an]c-

evil and wishes to destroy it [this ordinance], let him be excommunicated and be cursed by God and Holy Mary, and by all the saints and holy women of God, and be cursed like Dathan and Abiron who were swallowed up by the earth, and let them share the fate of Judas the traitor and Herod, Pilate and the Devil in the depths of Hell! Amen, amen. Let it be done, let it be done!

134.
In the name of the Lord, amen. I, Boniço the sinner, monk and prior Sancte Marie de Bonarcatu make this charter by the will of God and my lord iudike Comita concerning the purchases and exchanges made by me during my priory. I bought a landed property (*fundamentu*) near Sanctu Iorgi de Calcari and planted cedar trees and various kinds of fruit. I bought from Cipari Capai a piece of land planted with a vegetable garden (*ortu*) bordering on the land of the church near the monastery, and from Iorgi, his brother, another piece of land, the two properties being adjacent to each other. And I gave to each of them the value of a tremissis (*tremisse*) of goat meat and grain; I settled the account with them. I exchanged with Mele de Foge the share of his property within that orchard and gave him in exchange the vineyard located in Istrampadoriu ('the cliff'). Witnesses: Luxuri Picu, representative of the realm (*mandatore de regnum*); Torbini d'Ardu, head of the ward (*maiore de scolca*), together with his guard (*scolca*); and Gervasi Vilidun, representative of the church (*mandatore de clesia*). I bought from Iorgia Molligine and from Marra, wife of Malusone, their due share (*parçone*) that they held in that orchard near the monastery. I gave them a tremissis of goat meat between the two of them, and settled the account. Witnesses: Luxuri Picu, representative of the realm (*mandatore de regnum*), and the entire village (*villa*). Torbeni d'Orruinas gave us the share to which he was entitled that he held in that garden (*ortu*). Iorgi Corrariu donated, for [the salvation of] his soul, the share to which he was entitled that he held in that garden near the monastery. Witnesses: Luxuri Picu, representative of the realm (*mandatore de regnum*), and Gervasi Vilidu with his unbound servants (*colivertos*).

135.
Flacone d'Orruinas stole from us at the monastery and I defeated him at the hearing (*corona*) of Gostantine d'Orruvum, while he was *curadore*. He gave us, in compensation, the part of his property within that vegetable garden (*ortu*). Witnesses: the *curatore* with his entire district (*curatoria*).

136.
I, Benedictu the monk, ruling the house of Bonarcatu, bought from Maria Caydana and her husband, Furadu Cugurra, a vineyard bordering on that of Sanctu

[t]u Symio[n]e: deindelli una ebba i[n] sollu e tremisse de laore. Et co[m]plillis. T[este]s: Petru Te[m]pla, ma[n]datore de regnu[m] et Mugedi de Seço, maiore de scolca, cu[n] tota scolca sua.

137.
Tramudar[us] vineas cu[n] p[re]bi[ter]u Mellose de Segaços. Ego deilli una vi[n]ia in iscla de Ciçopu, pares cu[n] s[an]c[t]u Petru de Serras, et isse dedimi vi[n]ia i[n] ortu de lacu plage[n]do·nos a pare. T[este]s: Gosta[n]tine d'Orruvu curatore de Migil et iudice Comita ante ki llu fegerus su t[ra]mudu.

138.
Bennitimi ad penite[n]tia[m] Zipari Cappay p[ro]ssu fiiu ki lanzedi de virga a
58v manu sua; et ego deil | li penitentia. Et ipse posuit p[ro] anima sua ad s[an]c[t]o Georgi vinea in vinea de lacu. T[este]s: Petru Te[m]pla et P[re]s[n]age Marras et Mele de Foge cu[n] totos ca[n]tu 'e furunt i[n] clesia.

139.
Posit a cl[esi]a Petru Te[m]pla vi[n]ia p[ro] a[n]i[m]a sua in Istrampadoriu in morte sua. T[este]s: Orçoco d'Astere et Iorgi Manca et Pellio su frate.

140.
Posuit Granuzu in morte p[ro] a[n]i[m]a sua vinea i[n] Petronia a cl[esi]a. T[este]s: Iorgi Ma[n]ca et Trodori Milia et Torbini su fradile.

141.
Ego Comida de Varca ki llu vi[n]ki a Dominige de Pane i[n] corona de curadoria p[ro] vacca ki mi furait; et isse dedimi vi[n]ia in Petronia et ego deilla a clesia pro a[n]i[m]a de muliere mea. Cu[n] testimonios tota passassione de clesia et cu[n] colivertos quantos ie fur[un]t.

142.
Posit Cipari Arrasca vinea a clesia p[ro] a[n]i[m]a sua in erriu de Alat[er]ru. Testes: Fra[n]cu Iorca et iacunu Paule et p[re]b[ite]ru Trogotori.

Symione: I gave them a mare, cash (*sollu*) and a tremissis (*tremisse*) of grain, and settled the account with them. Witnesses: Petru Templa, representative of the realm (*mandatore de regnum*); and Mugedi de Sezo, head of the ward (*maiore de scolca*), with his entire guard (*scolca*).

137.
I exchanged vineyards with the priest Mellose de Segaços. I gave him a vineyard in the valley of Ciçopu (Cizopu), contiguous to Sanctu Petru de Serras, and he gave me a vineyard within the garden (*ortu*) of Lacu ('lake') by mutual agreement. Witnesses: Gostantine d'Orruvu, *curatore* of Migil (Milis), and the iudike Comita, before whom we made the exchange.

138.
Zipari Cappay came to me as a penitent because he had stabbed his own child with a rod (*virga*) by his own hand, so I imposed penance on him. And he gave, for the salvation of his soul, to Sancto Georgi a vineyard near the vineyard of Lacu ('lake'). Witnesses: Petru Templa, Presnage Marras, and Mele de Foge, with all those who were present in the church.

139.
Petru Templa donated to the church a vineyard in Istrampadoriu ('cliff') for [the salvation of] his soul when he died. Witnesses: Orçoco d'Astere, Iorgi Manca, and Pellio his brother.

140.
Granuzu, on his deathbed, donated to the church, for his soul, a vineyard in Petronia. Witnesses: Iorgi Manca, Trodori Millia, and Torbini, his cousin.

141.
I, Comita de Varca, defeated Dominige de Pane at a *curatore*'s district hearing (*corona de curatoria*) concerning the theft of a cow which he had stolen from me. He gave me a vineyard in Petronia and I gave it to the church for my wife's soul. Witnesses were all those held by the church (*passassione de clesia*), together with the unbound servants (*colivertos*) who were there.

142.
Cipari Arrasca donated to the church a vineyard located near the river of Alaterru ('buckthorn'), for his soul. Witnesses: Francu Iorca, the deacon Paule, and the priest Trogotori.

143.

Et iteru[m] revertam[us] ad s'ortu depos monasteriu. Comporeilli a Terico
59r Puliga parzone sua quanta aviat in icussu ortu. | Et fegindelli VI oberas i[n]t[er]
peza et casu et co[m]plilli. T[este]s: Presnage Marras et Petru Te[m]pla ma[n]datore de regnu[m].

Co[m]poreilli a Gosa[n]tine Marras sa parçone sua quanta aviat in icussu ortu. Et deindelli VI oberas i[n]t[er] peza et casu et co[m]pli[ll]i. T[este]s: Petru Te[m]pla ma[n]datore de regnu[m] cu[n] tota scolca sua et Gervasi Vilidu mandatore de clesia.

Co[m]poreilli a Troodori de Puzu sa parçone sua dess'ortu de post monasteriu et deilli II op[er]as de laore et co[m]plilli p[re]çu. T[este]s: Petru Te[m]pla cu[n] tota scolca.

Co[m]poreilli ad Alaverru sa parçone sua de cussu ortu: et deilli II op[er]as de laore. Et co[m]plil[l]i. T[este]s: Petru Te[m]pla cu[n] tota scolca sua.

Co[m]poreilli a Torbini de Puzu sa parçone sua de cussu ortu quantu ibi aviat de co[m]por[u], et deindelli II ob[er]as de sale. T[este]s: Nunnusi de Moore maiore de scolca cu[n] tota scolca sua.

144.

59v Barusone iudex. In no[min]e D[omi]ni n[ost]ri Ih[es]u Chr[ist]i. Am[en]. |
Ego iudice Barusone de Serra potestando locu de Arborea faço custa carta p[ro] saltu q[ui] do a s[an]c[t]a Maria de Bonarcatu i[n] sa sacratio[n]e dessa clesia nova, p[ro] a[n]i[m]a mea et de pare[n]tes meos daunde lo cognosco su regnu de Arbore; et p[ro] dedimi D[eu]s et s[an]c[t]a Maria vita et sanitate et fiios bonos, ki potestent su regnu[m] post varicatione mea. Dolli su saltu de A[n]glone, q[ui] levo dave su regnu de Piscopio cu[n] volu[n]tate mea bona et de o[nn]ia fratre meu[m]. Dollilu dave i[n] co si segat dave s'ariola de cl[esi]a et falat via deretu assa .+. [cruke] ki e[st] facta in issa pet[ra] suta su sueriu pares cun issu quercu de Mariane de Scanu et ergesi assu castru de Serra de Copios ubi e[st] facta sa .+. [cruke] in issa petra. Et falat assu flum[en] a bau de b[er]beges ube si amesturant appare sos flumenes. Cue si ferint a pare cun issu saltu de cl[esi]a de Pet[ra] P[er]tusa. Eco custu datu li faço ego iudice Barusone a s[an]c[t]a Maria de Bonarcatu. Appa[n]ti[n]de
60r prode usq[ue] in sec[u]l[u]m monagos q[ui] ant s[er]vire in iss' | abbadia
p[ro] a[n]i[m]a mea et de pare[n]tes meos: et de pastu et de aqua et de

143.
And now we return to the vegetable garden (*ortu*) near the monastery. I bought from Terico Puliga his share (*parzone*) of the garden. I also paid him the value of six working days (*oberas*) in meat and cheese; I settled the account. Witnesses: Presnage Marras, and Petru Templa, representative of the realm (*mandatore de regnum*).

I bought from Gosantine Marras his share (*parçone*) of that garden. I also gave him the value of six working days in meat and cheese; I settled the account. Witnesses: Petru Templa, representative of the realm, with his entire guard (*scolca*), and Gervasi Vilidu, representative of the church (*mandatore de clesia*).

I bought from Troodori de Puzu his share of the garden near the monastery, and I gave him the value of two working days in grain; I settled the account. Witnesses: Petru Templa, with his entire guard.

I bought from Alaverru his share of the garden and gave him the value of two working days in grain; I settled the account. Witnesses: Petru Templa, with his entire guard.

I bought from Torbini de Puzu his share of the garden, as much as he had acquired there because of the purchase, and I gave him the value of two working days in salt. Witnesses: Nunnusi de Moore, head of the ward (*maiore de scolca*), together with his entire guard (*scolca*).

144.
Barusone iudex. In the name of the Lord Jesus Christ, amen. I, iudike Barusone de Serra, ruling the country (*locu*) of Arborea, make this charter concerning to the unworked land (*saltu*) that I donate to Sancta Maria de Bonarcatu on the occasion of the consecration of the new church, for [the salvation of] my soul and that of my relatives from whom I inherited the realm (*regnu*) of Arborea; and because God and Holy Mary have granted me life and health and good children, who may then have power over the realm after my death. I donate the land (*saltu*) of Anglone, taking it out from the realm owned Piscopio with the consent of myself and all my brothers. I give it as it is alienated, following the boundary from the church yard and descends along the road in the direction of the cross which is placed on the stone under the oak tree next to the oak tree of Mariane de Scanu and goes up to the rock of Serra de Copios where the cross is placed on the stone. And it descends to the river toward Bau de Berbeges ('ford of sheep') at the confluence of the rivers. That there joins with the land (*saltu*) of the church of Petra Pertusa ('pierced stone'). This donation that I, iudike Barusone, make to Sancta Maria de Bonarcatu. The monks who will serve at the abbey for my soul and that of my parents will have an everlasting benefit from it: and regarding the pasture and the water and the acorn production and

gla[n]de et de aratoriu[m] castiga[n]dollu co et ateros saltos de regnu[m]. Et n[on] apat ausu n[on] iudice, n[on] curatore, n[on] ma[n]datore, n[on] nullu maiore de regnu[m] depus sa domo de Piscopio a kertarende et ne ad int[ra]reve in icussu saltu a tuturu dessos monagos. T[este]s: donnu Comita de Lac[on] archipiscobu d'Aristanes, donnu Paucapalea piscobu de s[an]c[t]a Iusta, donnu Alibra[n]dinu piscobu de T[er]ra alba, donnu M[ur]rellu piscobu d'Usellos, donnu Azu archiep[iscop]u de Turres, donnu Mariane Thelle ep[iscop]u de Gisarclu i[n] co 'e fur[un]t a sacr[ar]e sa clesia; et issos et populu[m] quantu ibi fuit a sa sac[ra]tio[n]e s[un]t testes.

145.[61]

Barusone iudex. Et ego iudice Barusone ki faço ateru bene ad s[an]c[t]a Maria de Bonarcatu p[ro] lucr[ar]ellu su regnu[m] d'Arbore et p[ro] dedimi D[eu]s fiios et pace i[n] su regnu[m]. Atungolli a su saltu de cl[esi]a de Petra p[er]tusa,
60v ki ant a pradu de cavallos: dolli dave su vadu dessu giradoriu dessu | molinu i[n] co collat su flum[en] usq[ue] a bau de canales; et ergesi sa via de Serra lo[n]ga usque assa Torrigla, et falat a nnurake rubiu et ferissi assu pratu dessos cavallos de cl[esi]a. Custa atuntura ki lli faço ad s[an]c[t]a Maria la sego dave su regnu de Migil: apatsinde i[n] se[m]pit[er]nu[m]. Et n[on] siat ausu n[on] iudice, n[on] curatore, n[on] ma[n]datore, n[on] nullu servu[m] meu[m] a kertare[n]de et ne ad int[ra]reve a tuturu dessos monagos. Et s[un]t testes: donnu Villanu archiep[iscop]u de Pisas, ki fuit benidu p[ro] cardinale de Roma cu[n] o[nn]ia clericatu suo; et iudice Costa[n]tine de Plominos, iudice Gunnari de Logudore, iudice Gosta[n]tine gallulesu, c[on]natu meu, cum o[nn]ia curatore et cun o[nn]ia lib[er]u de capudu de Sardigna quantos ibi fur[un]t in icusta collecta, quando fagiam[us] sa corona i[n] Bonarcato i[n]ter iudice Gosta[n]tine gallulesu et fiios de Comita Spanu p[ro]ssu castellu de Balaianu:
61r sa die l'aiu[n]xi custu saltu a s[an]c[t]a | Maria de Bonarcato. Et s[un]t testes d'a[m]bas daturas donnigellu Izocor curatore de Gilciver, Costa[n]tine de Çori curatore de Migil, Orçoco de Lac[on] curatore maiore, Petru de Lacon curatore de Fro[n]toriane, Orçoco de Lac[on] curatore de Barbaria, Gunnari de Lac[on] curatore de Vale[n]za, Gunnari d'Orruvu[m] curatore de Bonurçule, Costantine de Lac[on] curatore d'Usellos. De buiakesos: Terico de Ca[m]pu et golleanes

61 Booklet A, section 2, (1146–c. 1164) begins here.

the ploughing land, taking care of it for their own benefit, as is done with every land (*saltu*) of the realm. And dare not iudike, nor *curatore*, nor representative (*mandatore*), nor any senior person of the realm (*maiore de regnum*) at the house of Piscopio make a dispute about it, nor enter that land (*saltu*) against the will of the monks. Witnesses: lord Comita de Lacon, archbishop of Aristanes (Oristano); lord Paucapalea, bishop of Sancta Iusta (Santa Giusta); lord Alibrandinu, bishop of Terra Alba (Terralba); lord Murrellu, bishop of Usellos (Usellus); lord Azu, archbishop of Turres (Torres); lord Mariane Thelle, bishop of Gisarclu, who is present at the consecration of the church; they and the people who were present at the consecration are witnesses.

145.
Barusone iudex. [It is] I, iudike Barusone, who makes another donation to Sancta Maria de Bonarcatu to merit the realm (*regnum*) of Arbore (Arborea) and because God has granted me children and peace in the realm. I make an addition to the unworked land (*saltu*) of the church of Petra Pertusa ('pierced stone'), which they keep as a meadow for horses: I donate it [with the boundary that goes] from the ford of Giradoriu dessu Molinu ('drainage ditch of the mill') up the river until Bau de canales ('the ford of narrow valley') and goes up the road of Serra Longa ('long ridge') until the Torrigla, goes down to Nuraghe Rubiu ('red nuraghe') then comes to the meadow of the horses of the church. This territorial addition that I am making as a gift to Sancta Maria; I am taking it out from the realm (*regnu*) under Migil: let [the church] hold it forever! And let no iudike, nor *curatore*, nor representative (*mandatore*), nor any of my servants dare to make any dispute, nor enter it against the will of the monks. And the witnesses are: lord Villanu, archbishop of Pisas (Pisa)—who had come as cardinal of Rome with all his clerical staff; iudike Costantine de Plominos (Cagliari); iudike Gunnari of Logudore (Torres); iudike Gostantine Gallulesu (of Gallura), my brother-in-law; together with all the *curatores* and every freeman of the important men of Sardinia (*onnia liberu de capudu de Sardigna*), as many as were present in this assembly (*collecta*) when we summoned the hearing (*corona*) at Bonarcato for iudike Gostantine Gallulesu and the children of Comita Spanu regarding the castle (*castellu*) of Balaianu. That day, I added as a gift this land (*saltu*) to Sancta Maria de Bonarcato. Witnesses of both donations are: *donnigellu* Izocor, *curatore* of Gilciver (Gilziber); Costantine de Çori, *curatore* of Migil (Milis); Orçoco de Lacon, head *curatore* (*maiore*); Petru de Lacon, *curatore* of Frontoriane (Fordongianus); Orçoco de Lacon, *curatore* of Barbaria (Barbagia); Gunnari de Lacon, *curatore* of Valenza; Gunnari d'Orruvum, *curatore* of Bonurçule (Bonorzuli), and Costantine de Lacon, *curatore* of Usellos (Usellus). Of the iudike's entourage (*buiakesis*): Terico de Campu

suos. De poriglos de angarias: Mariane d'Orruvu et colleanes suos. Et si q[ui]s dixerit q[ui]a bene e[st], habeat benedictione de D[eu]s et de s[an]c[t]a Maria. Et cui n[on] placuerit et c[on]de[m]pnaverit hec ordinatio, habeat maledictio[n]e de D[eu]s et de s[an]c[t]a Maria et de IIIIor eva[n]g[e]listas et de XII ap[ost]olos, de XVI p[ro]ph[et]as, de XXIV seniores, de CCCXVIII patres s[an]c[t]os, de CXLIVor i[n]noce[n]tes ma[rt]i[re]s. Et apat parçone cu[n] Iuda traditore et cu[n] Herode et cu[n] diabol[us] in i[n]fernu[m]. Am[en]. Am[en]. Fiat, fiat.

146.

61v Donnigellu Orzoco. In no[min]e D[omi]ni. Am[en]. Ego donnigellu Orçoco | de Lac[on] simul cu[n] uxore mea Maria de Çori fagem[us] recordatio[n]e cu[n] volu[n]tate de D[eu]s et de iudice Barusone nepote meu. Ponem[us]illu a Gavine Gulpia, fiiu de Ithocor Gulpia [et de ...], servos n[ost]ros depost sa domo n[ost]ra de Gilarci, ad s[anct]a Maria de Bonarcato a servu de iugale: a Gavini et fiios suos et nepotes nepotor[um] suor[um] quantu aet esser sa gen[er]atio[n]e usq[ue] i[n] se[m]pit[er]nu[m], p[ro] a[n]i[m]a n[ost]ra et de parentes n[ost]ros et p[ro] sanitate de fiios n[ostr]os; sa die de s[an]c[t]u Antiochu[m] et de s[an]c[t]u Evesu[m], audiendu[m] missa i[n] s[an]c[t]u Symeone de Senuski, li posi i[n] manu de su p[ri]ore Ioh[ann]e a Gavini Gulpia: apatsinde p[ro]de s[an]c[t]a Maria de Bonarcatu. Et non apat ausu nullu fiiu nostru nec nepotes n[ostr]os a tollere[n]dellu dessu servitiu[m] de sancta Maria. Et s[un]t testes: primus D[eu]s et s[an]c[t]a Maria, deinde Petru de Serra fiiu[m] meu[m], Comita de Gothula et Ithocor de Pira t[er]rales meos de fictu k'ie furunt mecu kerra lu posi ad eccl[es]ia. Testes: Orçoco
62r de Lac[on] de Lella, Gostantine de Lac[on] d'Uda, | Petru de Lac[on] curatore de Migil, p[re]b[ite]ru Paule Forma, capellanu[m] meu[m] de Senuski, et Ia[n]ni Novagla diaconu[m]. Et si q[ui]s dixerit q[ui]a bene e[st], habeat benedictione de D[eu]s et de s[an]c[t]a Maria mater D[omi]ni n[ost]ri I[e]hsu Chri[st]i et de o[mne]s s[an]c[t]os et s[an]c[t]as D[e]i. Am[en], Am[en]. Fiat, fiat, fiat. Et si q[ui]s ext[er]minare et c[on]de[m]nare ea[m] voluerit fiat ille c[on]de[m]pnat[us] et ext[er]minat[us] de ymagine sua et de via de paradisu[m]; et apat parçone cu[n] Herode et cu[n] Iuda t[ra]ditore et cu[n] diabolo i[n] i[n]fernu[m]. Am[en]. Fiat.

147.

In no[min]e D[omi]ni n[ost]ri I[e]h[s]u Chr[isti]. Am[en]. In gra[tia] de D[eu]s et de donnu meu iudice Comita de Serra et de d[on]na regina Vera de Gunale. Ego Costa[n]tine Ferrare q[ui] me offersi a s[an]c[t]um Symeo[n]e ad essereve servu sendo in infirmitate magna et postea sanavi; et andei assu donnu

and his colleagues. From those who provide mounts (*poriglos de angarias*), there was Mariane d'Orruvu with his colleagues. And whoever will say that it is good, may he have a blessing from God and from Holy Mary. And may whoever opposes and does not observe this ordinance, receive a curse from God and Holy Mary, and from the four Evangelists, the Twelve Apostles, the sixteen Prophets, the twenty-four Elders, the 318 Holy Fathers, and the 144 innocent martyrs, and let them share their fate with Judas the traitor, Herod, and with the Devil in Hell! Amen. Amen. Let it be, let it be!

146.
Donnigellu Orzoco. In the name of the Lord, amen. I, *donnigellu* Orçoco de Lacon together with my wife Maria de Çori, make this record by the will of God and the consent of iudike Barusone, my nephew. We donate Gavine Gulpia, child of Ithocor Gulpia [and of ...], our servants (*servos*) at our farm complex (*domo*) in Gilarci, to Sancta Maria de Bonarcato as a servant 'of the yoke' (*de iugale*): Gavini and his children and the grandchildren of his grandchildren as long as the lineage lasts in perpetuity, for the salvation our souls and those of our parents and for the salvation of our children; on the day of St Antiochus and St Ephisius, while listening to Mass at Sanctu Symeone de Senuski, I placed Gavino Gulpia in the hands of prior Iohanne—may Sancta Maria de Bonarcatu profit from that! And let no son nor grandchildren of ours dare to take him away from the service of Sancta Maria! Witnesses are God, first before all else, and Holy Mary; then, Petru de Serra, my son; Comita de Gothula and Ithocor de Pira, my tenant farmers (*terrales*) who were with me when I made this donation to the church. Witnesses: Orçoco de Lacon de Lella; Gostantine de Lacon from Uda; Petru de Lacon, *curatore* of Migil (Milis); priest Paule Forma, my chaplain of Senuski, and Ianni Novagla the deacon. And whosoever will say that this is good, may he have a blessing from God and from Holy Mary the mother of our Lord Jesus Christ, and from all the saints of God! Amen, amen. Let it be done, let it be done! And whosoever will nullify [this ordinance] and not observe it, let him be condemned and be destroyed in his physical integrity and turned away from the way of Paradise, and let him have his fate with Herod, Judas the traitor and with the Devil in Hell! Amen. Let it be!

147.
In the name of our Lord, amen. By the grace of God and of my lord iudike Comita de Serra and of lady queen Vera de Gunale. I, Costantine Ferrare, offered myself as a servant (*servu*) to Sanctu Symeone because I was in a [state of] great weakness, but then I recovered. I went to my lord iudike Comita de Serra

meu iudice Comita de Serra, et petivilli mercede p[ro] asolberemi a fagemi carta de servu a s[an]c[t]o Symeone et ipse absolvitime cu[n] bona volu[n]tate sua et de fr[at]es suos. Et ego la scribo et c[on]firmo custa recordatione ad
62v esser servu a s[an]c[t]o Symeone et ego et fiios meos et nepotes nepotoru[m] | meor[um] usq[ue] in sempiternum. Et sunt testimonios Costa[n]tine d'Orruu, curatore de Migil, et Orçoco de Lac[on] et Cerkis de Sivi et Gidimel de Serra Orikesu simul cu[n] o[mn]es q[ui] erant cu[m] eo in domestica de Patru de Geas. Et si q[ui]s dixerit q[ui]a bene e[st] habeat benedictione de D[eu]s et de s[an]c[t]a Maria mat[er] D[omi]ni et de o[mne]s s[an]c[t]os et s[an]c[t]as D[e]i. Am[en]. Am[en]. Fiat, fiat.

148.
De Suei. In no[min]e D[omi]ni. Am[en]. Ego monacu Ugo facio recordatio[n]e p[ro] homines ki acatei levados dava s[an]c[t]u[m] Serige de Suei. Narru[n]-timinde p[ro]·llos ca '[n]de llos aviat levatos Mariane Correli et fr[at]es suos. Nareinde ad iudice Costa[n]tine et isse naraitimi p[ro] tenne corona. Tenni corona i[n] Gilarce i[n] s[an]c[t]u Paraminu, ubi fuit totu logu et issu archiep-[iscop]u, cun Mariane Correli et vi[n]killu dave testimonios ki '[n]de iskia[n]t bene ca n[on] ibi aviat bias Mariane ne frates suos. Et kertait cu·llu iudice ca llos cuavat sos servos de cl[esi]a de regnu[m]. Et fur[un]t ipsos ho[min]es
63r dece[m] et octo | inter intreos et latus et pedes, i[n]t[er] barones et mulieres, i[n]t[er] maiores et zaracos: Orikesu Ca[m]pana et fiios suos et Picinnu Campana et fiios suos et Cassia, sa sorre, cun fiios suos et lat[us] de Petru Ca[m]pana et Maria Ca[m]pana cun fiios suos, Miale Mancosu et fiios suos, Janne Çunku et fiios suos; Torbini Coco et fiios suos. Et s[un]t testimonios: prim[us] D[eu]s et s[an]c[t]a Maria et s[an]c[t]u Serigi et donnu Gostantine de Zori et issu archiepiscopu[m] et Mariane d'Orruvu k'ie fuit curatore de Gilciver cum totu locum, ki andavant cum iudice. Et ki aet confortare ista arminantia, q[ui] arminavi ego monacu Ugo, sendo priore in s'abbatia ki armait iudice Costantine et frates suos, et dicere aent q[ui]a bene est, habeant benedictione de Deus omnipotens. Et q[ui] at pugnare ad isterminare et dicere aet quod n[on] sit, siat ille exterminatu de magine sua in istu seculum et de via de paradisu. Et apat anathema de XII apostoli et de XVI p[ro]ph[et]as
63v et de XXIIII | seniores et de CCCXVIII patres sanctos; et apat parzone cum Herode et cun Iudas traditore et cun diabolus in infernum. Amen, Amen. Fiat, fiat.

and asked him mercifully to allow me to draw up a document by which I would make myself a servant to Sanctu Symeone and he granted it to me with his agreement and that of his brothers. And I write and confirm this memorial, whereby I make myself a servant unto Sanctu Symeone, and my children, and my grandchildren's grandchildren forever. The witnesses are: Costantine of Orruu, *curatore* of Migil (Milis); Orçoco of Lacon; Cerkis of Sivi; and Gidimel de Serra Orikesu, together with all those who were with him in the farmhouse (*domestica*) of Patru de Geas ('meadow of hollow plane'). Whoever says that this is good, may he have a blessing from God and from Holy Mary, mother of the Lord, and from all the saints of God! Amen, amen. Let it be, let it be!

148.
Of Suei. In the name of the Lord, amen. I, monk Ugo, make this record concerning the servants whom I found removed from the service of Sanctu Serige de Suei. Of them, they told me that Mariane Correli and his brothers had taken them away. I reported this to the iudike Constantine, and he told me to appeal to a hearing (*corona*). I sued Mariane Correli at a hearing in Gilarce, at Sanctu Paraminu, where the entire country (*totu logu*) and the archbishop were; I defeated him by producing witnesses who knew that neither he, nor his brothers, had any right to it. Then he argued in front of the iudike that he hid the servants of the church who were already of the realm (*regnum*). And the said servants were eighteen in number, both men and women, adults and children, either as his entire property or for half, or for a quarter: Orikesu Campana and his children, and Picinnu Campana and his children, and Cassia his sister, and her children, and half of the property of Petru Campana, and Maria Campana and her children, Mlale Mancosu and his children, Janne Çunku and his children, and Torbini Coco and his children. The witnesses are God, first before anything else, and Holy Mary and St Sergius; lord Gostantine de Zori; the archbishop; Mariane d'Orruvu, who was *curatore* of Gilciver (Ghilarza), together with the entire country who accompanied the iudike. And whoever will enforce this ordinance, which I, the monk Ugo, as prior of the abbey that was established by iudike Costantine and his brothers, and will say that it is good, may he have blessing from Almighty God. And whoever tries to nullify it by saying that it should not be applied, let him be destroyed in his bodily integrity in this life and turned away from the way of Paradise! And may he receive a curse from the Twelve Apostles, the sixteen Prophets, the twenty-four Elders, and the 318 Holy Fathers, and have his fate with Herod, Judas the traitor, and the Devil in Hell! Amen, amen. Let it be, let it be!

149.
In no[min]e D[omi]ni. Am[en]. Ego Albert[us], p[ri]or de Bonarcato, facio recordatio[n]e, p[ro] ho[min]es ki partivi cu[n] fiios de donnigellu. De fiios d'Orçoco Zu[n]cu clesia levait ad Ia[n]ni et ad Furadu, et fiios de donnigellu levar[un]t ad Fortis et ad Gavini. De fiios de Vera Ca[m]pana clesia levait a Petru et a Troodori, su minore, et donnigellu levait unu masclu et una femina. T[este]s: iudice Barusone ki partiat: se[n]do curatore Barusone de Serra et Gu[n]nari de Lac[on] curatore de Vale[n]za, et Goa[n]tine de Lac[on] curatore d'Usellos, et Petru de Lac[on] curatore maiore.

150.
In no[min]e D[omi]ni. Am[en]. In gra[tia] de D[eu]s et dessu donnu meu[m] iudice Barusone de Serra. Ego Ioh[ann]e Melone facio recordatio[n]e pro ho[min]es de s[an]c[t]u Augustinu de Augustis ki vi[n]ki i[n] corona de tota cur-
64ʳ atoria se[n]do curatore de factu Torbini Maninu, | avendomi lassadu i[n]tesiga sua priore Ioh[ann]e quando ke andarat a t[er]ra manna. Kertei i[n] corona de tota curatoria sa die de s[an]c[t]u Augustinu. Bi[n]ki p[ro] Furadu Zu[n]cla ki '[n]de fuit fugitu et adonnigadu i[n]tro i[n] Alasla et positillu a iurare su curatore d'esser servu de s[an]c[t]u Austinu isse et fiios suos et nepotes nepotorum suorum. Kertei p[ro] Golorki Madau et p[ro] su fiiu Torbini et binki p[ro]·llos. Kertei p[ro] Vera Porkellu et bi[n]ki pro·lla et partir[us] sos fiios: levei ego ad Orçoco e iudice a Torbeni e a Gosta[n]tine latus latus. Kertei p[ro] Terico Markelle et bi[n]ki p[ro]·llu. Kertei p[ro] Vera Titu et bi[n]ki p[ro]·lla et partir[us] sos fiios: ego levei a Mariane et a Iorgi et iudice a Peruki et assu fiiu de Iusta Gosta[n]tine Corbe. Kertei p[ro] Nastasia Manina et bi[n]ki p[ro]·lla: ego levei a Getadu et iudice assu fr[at]e. Kertei p[ro] Maria Lassa et bi[n]ki p[ro]·lla: et partirus sos fiios. Et sunt testimonios de kerra vi[n]ki et partirus custos homines: Torbini Maninu, ki fuit curatore de factu, et Peruki ma[n]datore
64ᵛ de regnu[m], Jorgi Ma[n]ca, su fiiu, canariu de re | gnu[m], Ianni Puliga agasone de regnu, Terico Puliga porcariu de regnu, Golorki Ma[n]ca et Caidanu et tota curatoria cu[n] ho[min]es quantos ie fur[un]t i[n] sa festa de s[an]c[t]u Austinu.

151.
In no[min]e D[omi]ni. Am[en]. Ego Ia[n]ne Mellone, p[ri]ore de Bonarcatu, q[ui] scribo custa recordaria. Poseruntillu a Gosa[n]tine de Lac[on] Lauri arm-

149.
In the name of the Lord, amen. I, Albertus, prior of Bonarcato, make a record concerning the servants (*homines*) I shared with the children of the *donnigellu*. Of the children of Orçoco Zuncu the church took Ianni and Furadu, and the children of the *donnigellu* took Fortis and Gavini. Of the children of Vera Campana, the church took Petru and Troodori, the youngest, and the *donnigellu* took a man and a woman. Witnesses: iudike Barusone, who carried out the division while being *curatore*; Barusone de Serra, Gunnari de Lacon, *curatore* of Valenza; Goantine de Lacon, *curatore* of Usellos (Usellus), and Petru de Lacon, the senior *curatore* (*maiore*).

150.
In the name of the Lord, amen. In the name of God and of my lord iudike Barusone de Serra. I, Iohanne Melone, make a record concerning the servants (*homines*) of Sanctu Augustinu de Augustis, whom I won from a dispute heard at the hearing (*corona*) of the entire *curatore*'s district (*curatoria*) while Torbini Maninu was the *curatore* at the time, and when prior Iohanne left me in his stead as he went to the mainland (*terra manna*). I brought the dispute to the hearing of the entire district on St Augustine's Day. I defeated Furadu Zuncla who had fled and had placed himself in the service of another lord in Alasla; the *curatore* made him swear that he and his children and his grandchildren's grandchildren would be servants of Sanctu Austinu. I sued Golorki Madau and his son Torbini, and I defeated them. I sued Vera Porkellu and defeated her, and we divided the children: I took Orçoco, the iudike took Torbeni, and Gostantine remained half for each. I sued Terico Markelle and defeated him. I sued Vera Titu, and defeated her, and we shared the children: I took Mariane and Iorgi, and the iudike took Peruki and the son of Iusta, Gostantine Corbe. I sued Nastasia Manina, and defeated her: I took Getadu, and the iudike took his brother. I sued Maria Lassa, and I defeated her: and we shared her children. The witnesses of this victory and of the division of these servants are: Torbini Maninu, who was *curatore* at the time; Peruki, representative of the realm (*mandatore de regnum*); Jorgi Manca, his child, dog-keeper of the realm (*canariu de regnum*) of the realm; Ianni Puliga, realm's horse-keeper (*agasone de regnu*); Terico Puliga realm's swine-keeper (*porcariu de regnu*); Golorki Manca; Caidanu; and the entire *curatore*'s district (*curatoria*) together with all the men who were present at the feast of St Augustine.

151.
In the name of the Lord, amen. I, Ianne Mellone, prior of Bonarcatu, make this record. Gosantine de Lacon Lauri was appointed administrator (*armentariu*)

[en]tariu de Sollie. Kertait mecu[m], rege[n]de isse corona, p[ro] Maria de Porta et pro Nivada, sa fiia: 'Ancillas de iudice s[un]t.' Et ego kertai: 'et mama et fiia et pare[n]tes issoro a[n]cillas de s[an]c[t]a Maria de Bonarcatu fur[un]t.' Iudicait isse a bature ego testimonios ca servir[un]t a cl[esi]a, ipsas et par[e]ntes issoro. Et ego batusi testimonios bonos ki lli plakerunt ad isse et ad tota corona: a Gu[n]nari de Pau et a Ioh[ann]e Capai: et iurarunt a .+. [cruke] a[m]bos cu[n] Iorgi Cap[ra] ma[n]datore de clesia: 'Custas et pare[n]tes issoro
65r a[n]killas de s[an]c[t]a | Maria de Bonarcadu fur[un]t' et ki: 'c[on]gnoscer[us] nos servi[n]do a ccl[es]ia.' Testes: tota sa villa, Gu[n]nari de Pau, Ioh[ann]e Capai, Goa[n]tine Mello[n]e, Justu Bakia.

152.
Partirus fiios de Iorgi Capra cu[n] Gosa[n]tine de Lac[on] Lauri, arm[en]tariu de Sollie. Clesia levait a Gosa[n]tine et a Samaridanu, et iuige levait a Gu[n]nari et ad Elene. T[este]s: Evisu su ma[n]datore suo, et Iustu Bakia et Ioh[ann]e Capai et Goa[n]tine Mellone.

153.
Ego, priore Alb[er]tu de Bonarcatu, kertai p[ro] sos fr[at]es Samudes, ki si mi fur[un]t adonnigados se[n]do servos de s[an]c[t]a Victoria de Mo[nt]es[an]c[t]u. Kertai p[ro]·llos i[n] corona de iudice Barusone: 'Iorgi Samude servu i[n]tregu de s[an]c[t]a Victoria de Mo[n]tes[an]c[t]u fuit; coiuvedi cu[n] Maria Amisi ancilla de iudice de regnu d'Agustis. Feger[un]t duos fiios: Bitoria p[ri]maria: levar[un]t apus mama, et Petru post illa: levar[un]t ap[us]
65v patre. Petru | coiuvedi cun Bera Marki, a[n]killa de iudige de regnu d'Agustis. Fegeru[n]t IIII fiios: Furadu p[ri]mariu et Torbini post illu et osca Iorgi et Troodori a seg[us].' Gasi kertai i[n] corona de iudice Barusone, cu[n] Torbini Maninu, curadore de factu et cu[n] Peruki ma[n]datore de regnu[m]: kertai et bi[n]ki p[ro]·llos. T[este]s p[ro] sa vi[n]citura: Petru de Lac[on] de Sivi et Gunari d'Orruvu Muria.

154.
Positillu iudice a su curatore de Barbaria Petru de Serra Passa[n]te a partire custos ho[min]es cu[n] cl[esi]a i[n] co fur[un]t a nnatias. Fiios de Iorgi Samude: Bitoria fuit p[ri]maria, levar[un]t ap[us] mama; et Petrus fuit post illa, levar[un]t a cl[esi]a ap[us] patre. Fiios de Petru: Furadu fuit p[ri]mariu, levar[un]t

of Sollie. He sued me, he himself presiding over the hearing (*corona*), concerning Maria de Porta and Nivada, her daughter, arguing that: 'They are servants (*ancillas*) of the iudike!' I argued: 'Both the mother and the daughter and their parents were servants of Sancta Maria de Bonarcatu!' Then he ordered me to bring forth witnesses that they and their parents had served the church. So I brought forth reliable witnesses with his approval and that of the entire hearing: Gunnari de Pau and Iohanne Capai who swore on the cross, both together with Iorgi Capra, the representative (*mandatore*) of the church, that: 'These servants and their parents were servants of Sancta Maria de Bonarcadu,' adding, 'we have always known that they served the church!' Witnesses: the entire village (*villa*), Gunnari de Pau, Iohanne Capai, Goantine Mellone, and Justu Bakia.

152.
The children of Iorgi Capra shared with Gosantine de Lacon Lauri, administrator (*armentariu*) of Sollie. The church took Gosantine and Samaridanu, and the iudike took Gunnari and Elene. Witnesses: Evisu, his representative (*mandatore*); Iustu Bakia; Iohanne Capai, and Goantine Mellone.

153.
I, prior Alberte of Bonarcatu, sued the Samudes brothers, who had placed themselves in the service of another lord while they were servants (*servos*) of Sancta Victoria of Montesanctu. I sued them at the hearing (*corona*) of iudike Barusone, saying, 'Iorgi Samude was a full servant (*intregu*) of Sancta Victoria de Montesanctu; he married Maria Amisi, who had already been a iudike's servant (*ancilla*) of the realm (*regnu*) at Agustis. They had two children: Bitoria first, on the mother's side, and Petru [born] after her, on the father's side! Petru married Bera Marki, a iudike's servant of the realm at Agustis. They had four children: Furadu the eldest and Torbini after him, then Iorgi and Troodori!' In this way, I sued [them] at the hearing of iudike Barusone, with Torbini Maninu, the *curatore* at the time, and Peruki, representative of the realm (*mandatore de regnum*). I sued and won concerning these servants. Witnesses to this victory: Petru de Lacon de Sivi and Gunari d'Orruvu Muria.

154.
The iudike had the *curatore* of Barbaria (Barbagia), Petru de Serra Passante, share these servants (*homines*) with the church according to their order of their birth (*nnatias*). [Of] the children of Iorgi Samude, Bitoria was the eldest and they took her on account of her mother; Petru was born after her, and the church took him on account of his father. [Of] the children of Petru, Furadu

ap[us] mama: hecco a iudice; et Torbini levar[un]t ap[us] patre: ecco a cclesia. Et Iorgi levar[un]t apus mama: ecco a iudice; e Troodori andedi a patre: ecco a clesia.

155.

Ego Ia[n]ni Mellone, p[ri]ore de Bonarcato ki partim[us] homines cu[m] iud-
66r ice | Petru d'A[r]bore, sendo su patre i[n] Genua. Maria Ca[n]gella, a[n]cilla
de s[an]c[t]u Iorgi de Calcaria, coiuedi cum Dominige de Casas; fegeru[n]t VI fiios. Iusta p[ri]maria: ecco a ccl[es]ia et Furadu et Gosa[n]tine; et iudice a Bera et a nNivada et a Sadurre. Fiios de Ia[n]ni Moiu: levait cl[esi]a a sSat[ur]re su p[ri]mariu et a Iusta; et iudice levait a Iorgia et a Maria. Fiios d'Elene Moiu: levait cl[esi]a ad Laure[n]tiu et a Maria; et iudice levait a Ioh[ann]e et a Lugia, partindollos a nnatias.

156.

Ego Janne Mellone, priore de Bonarcato, facio recordatione pro Iusta Ulbara, ki fuit a[n]cilla de s[an]c[t]u Iorgi de Calcaria, et coiuvedi i[n] T[ra]maza cu[n] Ia[n]ne Siris, servu dep[us] Tune. Fegerunt V fiios: III masclos et II feminas. Et partivim[us]illos cu[n] iudice Petru et cu[n] sa mama donna Pelerina de Lac[on], ki regiant su logu p[ro] iudice Barusone, ki stavat i[n] Genua. Deruntimi p[ro] cl[esi]a a Goa[n]tine Syris i[n]tregu cu[n] su fiiu Petru, zaracu
66v de VII annos, p[ro] su lat[us] ki mi i[n]travat | in Comita, su frate de Goantine,
et ad Elene, sa sorre, i[n]trega. Et p[ro] iudice levaru[n]t ad Furadu et Comita et D[omi]nica. T[este]s: Comita de Varca, ki fuit arm[en]tariu dep[us] Tune, cu[n] ki partiam[us], et Ioh[ann]e de Sorrai et Gunnari de Lac[on] et Mariane de Varca.

Coiuvedi Egizu C[un]iale, servu de s[an]c[t]u Paraminu cu[n] Bera Gulpia, a[n]killa lat[us] de s[an]c[t]u Serigi et lat[us] de Comita de Serra. Fegerunt VI fiios: leveit su archiep[iscop]u a Gavini et a Colu[m]ba et ad Arge[n]ti; et ego levo cu[n] Comita de Serra a Maria et a Terico; et ad Ianne ad in comune, parti[n]do ad natias. Et posca partir[us] cu[n] Comita de Serra: ego levei a Maria et lat[us] de Ia[n]ne, leva[n]do parzçone de Comita de Serra Ianni de Orroolo ki lli fuit arm[en]tariu depus Gilarce. T[este]s: Troodori Zukellu et Mariane Mamile, k'ie fur[un]t ube partiam[us].

Coiuvedi Luxuria Mellone a[n]killa de s[an]c[t]u Iorgi de Calcaria i[n] Fun-
67r uni cu[n] Furatu | Agedu servu de donnigellu Orçoco et feger[un]t IIII fiios: a
Miale et a Ianni et a Pelerina. Kertait mecu Petru de Serra, fiiu de donnigellu, pro custos ho[min]es ca 'fur[un]t partitos.' Campaniar[us]·nos in pare et partirus su fedu de cussos.

was the eldest, and so was for the iudike on account of his mother; Torbini was for the church on account of his father. They also took Iorgi for the iudike on account of his mother, and so Troodori was for the church on account of his father.

155.
I, Ianni Mellone, prior of Bonarcato, shared the servants (*homines*) with iudike Petru d'Arbore (Arborea) while his father was in Genua (Genoa). Maria Cangella, servant (*ancilla*) of Sanctu Iorgi de Calcaria, was married to Dominige de Casas; they had six children. First came Iusta: she was for church with Furadu and Gosantine; the iudike had Bera, Nivada and Sadurre. The children of Ianni Moiu: the church took Saturre the eldest and Iusta, while the iudike took Iorgia and Maria. The children of Elene Moiu: the church took Laurentiu and Maria; and the iudike took Iohanne and Lugia, and the division was according to their order of their birth (*a nnatias*).

156.
I, Janne Mellone, prior of Bonarcato, made a record concerning Iusta Ulbara, who was a servant (*ancilla*) of Sanctu Iorgi de Calcaria, and was married at Tramaza (Tramatza) to Ianne Siris, a servant (*servu*) at Tune. They had five children, three men and two women. We shared them with iudike Petru and his mother, Pelerina de Lacon, who ruled the country (*logu*) instead of iudike Barusone, who was in Genua (Genoa). They gave me in full (*intregu*) for the church, Goantine Syris, with his child Petru, a boy of seven years old, as I was entitled to half of Comita, Goantine's brother, and Elene, his sister, in full. And on the iudike's side, they took Furadu, Comita and Domenica. Witnesses: Comita de Varca, who was administrator (*armentariu*) at Tune (with whom we made the partition), Iohanne de Sorrai; Gunnari de Lacon; and Mariane de Varca.

Egizu Cuniale, servant of Sanctu Paraminu, was married to Bera Gulpia, half servant (*ankilla*) of Sanctu Serigi and half servant of Comita de Serra. They had six children: the archbishop took Gavini, Columba and Argenti; and I took, with Comita de Serra, Maria and Terico; Ianne remained in common, and the division was made according to their order of their birth (*ad natias*). Then we made a division with Comita de Serra: I took Maria and half of Ianni, and Comita de Serra, who was his administrator (*armentariu*) at Gilarce, took his share of Ianni de Orroolo. Witnesses: Troodori Zukellu and Mariane Mamile, present at the partition.

Luxuria Mellone, servant of Sanctu Iorgi de Calcaria, married Furatu Agedu, servant of Orçoco, in Fununi and they had four children: Miale, Ianni, and Pelerina. Petru de Serra, son of the *donnigellu*, sued me concerning these servants, claiming that they had been shared out. We agreed to divide their offspring.

157.
In gra[tia] de D[eu]s et dessu donnu meu iudice Gosta[n]tine d'Orruvu. Ego Petru, p[ri]ore de Bonarcato, facio recordatio[n]e pro ortu ki c[om]porei apud s[an]c[t]u Georgio de Calcaria i[n] Sollie. Co[m]poreilli a Petru Carelle et a fr[ate]s suos sa parçone issoro de cussu ortu et fegi[n]dellis sollu inter laore et peza et co[m]plillis p[re]çu. Co[m]poreilli a Iorgi Muravegla in icussu ortu et fegilli II tremisses i[n]t[er] laore et peza et complilli. Co[m]poreilli ad Eizu Çoris in icustu ortu et deilli tremisse de laore et II masclos et co[mplilli]. Co[m]poreilli a Luxuri Carru in icussu ortu parçone sua et deilli boe i[n]
67v soll[u] | et co[m]plilli p[re]çu. Co[m]poreilli a Golorki de Sueriu in icussu ortu et deilli vinea i[n] III sollos et co[m]plilli p[re]zu. Co[m]poreilli a Iorgia Marras in icussu ortu parçone sua ki aviat et deilli IIII moios d'oriu et co[m]plilli p[re]zu. T[este]s p[ro] totu custu co[m]por[u]: Gosta[n]tine d'Uta, curatore de Migil et P[re]snagi Urru, maiore de scolca cu[n] tota scolca sua, et Golorki Ferrari ortulanu de iudice. Testes.

158.
In no[min]e D[omi]ni. Am[en]. Ego Mariane d'Uta ki po[n]io ad s[an]c[t]a Maria de Bonarcatu p[ro] a[n]i[m]a mea t[er]ras quantas apo i[n] Erriora et i[n] Baratiri et i[n]tro de saltu et foras de saltu, foras de una terra ki '[n]de voco. Et do sa plaza de Cellevane ki tenet a sa plaza de Furadu Corria, et parçone de Cucusa, sorrastra mia ki morivit enea, sa ca[n]tu mi '[n]de p[er]tinet a mimi, semute dessa t[er]ra sua de Vestarda ki posit a ccl[es]ia quando infirmavit in Senusci. T[este]s: domnu Ioh[ann]e ep[iscop]u de Usellos et Goa[n]tine de
68r Plana arm[en]tariu suo et Orçoco de Corona e Symione de Pira | et Troodori de Lac[on] d'Uras et Fatosu su kellaridu suo. Custas t[er]ras s[un]t una i[n] Ariolas, alt[er]a capizale assa via de nurake, alt[er]a in Pe[tr]a de s[an]c[t]a Maria, alt[er]a sup[ra] paule de Marcu, alt[er]a i[n] ena de Cogoti, altera i[n] serra de Siliquas, alt[er]a i[n] padule de Golorki, alt[er]a i[n] padule de Gonu et susu et iosso, alt[er]a ante sa vi[n]ia de Goa[n]tine de Lac[on], alt[er]a ante ariola de Musellu, alt[er]a i[n] sa via ki vat dava Baratile ad nurake, alt[er]as duas i[n] Albucedu in plaza de Baratiri, II in t[er]ras de corte, una parzçone de a[m]bos fr[ate]s in Poiolu de Ma[n]dra, II al[te]ras i[n] Masone de pet[ra]s ante sa vi[n]ia de sos d'Orruvu; alt[er]a in serras de Gregori; alt[er]a sup[ra]

157.
By the grace of God and of my lord iudike Gostantine d'Orruvu. I, Petru, prior of Bonarcato, made the record of the vegetable garden (*ortu*) that I bought near Sanctu Georgio de Calcaria in Sollie. I bought from Petru Carelle and his brothers their share of the orchard and paid them a soldo (*sollu*) worth of grain and meat; I settled the account. I bought from Iorgi Muravegla his share (*parçone*) of the orchard and paid them a tremisses (*tremisse*) of corn and meat; I settled the account. I made a purchase from Eizu Çoris in that orchard and gave him a tremissis of corn, two rams, and I settled the account. I bought from Luxuri Carru his portion in the orchard and gave him an ox in coin (*in sollu*); I settled the balance. I bought from Golorki de Sueriu [his share] in that orchard and I gave him a vineyard worth three soldi (*sollos*); I settled the account. I bought from Iorgia Marras in that garden the share due to her in that orchard and gave her four bushels of barley; I settled the account. Witnesses to this sale: Gostantine d'Uta, *curatore* of Migil (Milis); Presnagi Urru, head of the guard (*maiore de scolca*), together with all his guard; and Golorki Ferrari, gardener (*ortulanu*) of the iudike. Witnesses.

158.
In the name of the Lord, amen. I, Mariane d'Uta, donate to Sancta Maria de Bonarcatu, for [the salvation of] my soul, all the land that I own at Erriora and Baratiri, both inside and outside the unworked land (*saltu*), apart from one piece of land which I leave excluded. I also donate the plot of land (*plaza*) at Cellevani bordering on the land of Furadu Corria, and my share (*parçone*) of the land formerly belonging to Cucusa, my cousin, who died without heirs (*enea*), except for her land in Vestarda which she donated to the church when she fell ill in Senusci. Witnesses: lord Iohanne, bishop of Usellos (Usellus) and Goantine de Plana, his administrator (*armentariu*); Orçoco de Corona; Symione de Pira; Troodori de Lacon from Uras; and Fatosu, his watchman (*kellaridu*). These lands are one in Ariolas, another at the top of Nurake ('nuraghe') road, another in Petra de Sancta Maria ('rock of Holy Mary'), another over the marsh of Marcu, another by the well of Cogoti, another in Serra de Siliquas ('ridge of the carob trees'), another by the marsh of Golorki, another by the marsh of Gonu, above and below it, another in front of the vineyard of Goantine de Lacon, another in front of the threshing floor (*ariola*) of Musellu, another near the road from Baratile to Nurake, another two in Albucedu near the plot of land (*plaza*) at Baratiri, two in Terras de Corte, one share of both brothers in Poiolu de Mandra ('ditch of enclosed meadow'), two others in Masone de Petras ('corral of rocks') in front of the vineyard of the d'Orruvu; another in Serras de Gregori ('ridge of sandy land'), another above Lorissa and above the parcel in

Lorissa et issa plaza ante Comida de Urri et t[er]ra et pet[ra] et issa plaza de Cellevane et issa mia et issa de fr[at]e meu.

159.

In no[min]e D[omi]ni. Am[en]. Ego p[re]b[ite]ru Remu[n]dinu de Varca, ki mi faço manago ad hora dessa morte i[n] s[an]c[t]a Maria de Bonarcatu i[n] manu dessu p[ri]ore donnu Ia[n]ne Melone et dessos monagos suos et cu[n]
68v volu[n]tate dessu donnu | meu donnu Ugo archiep[iscop]u de Arbore. Et poniove ad s[an]c[t]a Maria de Bonarcatu una libra de arge[n]tu laborata et duas mantaduras de vulpe coop[er]tas de mustarolu et issu letu meu armatu bene et issa parçone mia dessa vi[n]ia de Cinniga, porkile ki parço cu[n] sorre mia Saragina tene[n]do assa vinia de Iorgi Corda. T[est]es: su p[ri]ore cun sos monagos suos et homines dessa villa, Ioh[ann]i Capai et Iustu Bakia et Gregori C[on]tu.

160.

In no[min]e D[omi]ni. Am[en]. Ego Petru Milia, ki mi c[on]verso i[n] s[anct]a Maria de Bonarcatu i[n] manu dessu p[ri]ore donnu Ia[n]ne Mellone et dessos monagos suos. Post c'ant ispiiare et partire sa causa i[n]t[er] me et muliere mea, su lat[us] dessa causa de muliere mea fazatinde sa volu[n]tate sua, et dessu lat[us] meu parzantillu pares. S'una parte apant fr[ate]s meos et iss'at[er]a parte poniolla a s[an]c[t]a Maria de Bonarcatu et tudentimi i[n] iostra. T[este]s: donnu G[ra]nuzu p[re]b[ite]ru, ciu meu et Goa[n]tine.[62]

161.[63]

69r [64] Ego Albertu Ginivesu priore de Bonorcadu facio recordatio[n]e p[ro]ssu padru de s[anct]u[m] Symione. Bennit Orçoco de Martis ki fudi maiore de scolca de Miili a levari su padru a força. Andar[un]t sos h[omin]es meos et largar[un]t in pare in su padru de clesia de s[an]c[t]u Symione d[e] Vesala, ki fuit billa isfata. Andaru[n]t a corona de logu ad Nuraginiellu, ubi fuit iudice Baruso[n]e. Kertaru[n]t in pare Terico Pisanu ma[n]dadore de clesia et Orçoco d[e] Martis. Iuigaru[n]t assu ma[n]dadore de cl[esi]a a batuere d[e]stimonios ho[m]i[n]es maiores d[e] parte d[e] Miili. Bennit Iorgi Tamaglu, serbu

62 Booklet A ends here. The next folios of the manuscript—i.e. 69 and 70—appear to have been removed at some point and then sewn back into the codex after folio 85.

63 Entry 161 is abridged in entry 92, as the latter omits certain details provided here, such as the description of the boundaries of the unworked land (*saltu*) and the confirmation of the donation by iudike Barusone.

64 Folios 69 and 70 constitute a separate folded parchment sheet. Based on the numbering of the folios, this sheet seems to have been taken out of the codex, and later sewn back into the current binding between booklets G and E.

front of the property of Comida de Urri, and the land and stony ground and the parcel [of land] at Cellevane as well as mine and that of my brother.

159.
In the name of the Lord, amen. I, priest Remundinu de Varca, who on my deathbed become a monk at Sancta Maria de Bonarcatu, in the hands of the prior lord Ianne Melone and his monks, and with the consent of my lord Ugo archbishop of Arbore (Arborea). And I donate to Sancta Maria de Bonarcatu a pound of wrought silver (*argentu laborata*) and two fox furs (*mantaduras de vulpe*) lined with cloth, my well furnished bed, and my due share of the vineyard of Cinniga ('reed'), and the pig-pen I share with my sister Saragina bordering on the vineyard of Iorgi Corda. Witnesses: the prior with his monks and the men of the village (*villa*), Iohanni Capai, Iustu Bakia, and Gregori Contu.

160.
In the name of the Lord, amen. I, Petru Milia, hereby make myself a lay brother in Sancta Maria de Bonarcatu, in the hands of the prior, lord Ianne Mellone, and his monks. After they have settled all just claims and demands about that whicht belongs to me and have divided it between my wife and me, let my wife dispose of the half that belongs to her according to her own will; and let the half that belongs to me be divided into two parts. Let one part be given to my brothers, and the other part to Sancta Maria de Bonarcatu, where they may bury me in the cloister! Witnesses: lord Granuzu priest, my uncle, and Goantine.

161.
I, Albertu Ginivesu, prior of Bonorcadu, make a record concerning the pasture of Sanctum Symione. Orçoco de Martis, who was head of the ward (*maiore de scolca*) at Miili (Milis), came and illegally took possession of the meadow. My men went in turn to forcibly repossess the meadow of Sanctu Symione de Vesala, which was a ruined village (*villa isfata*) belonging to the church. They went to a hearing of the realm (*corona de logu*) at Nuraginiellu (Nuraxinieddu), where iudike Barusone was. They sued together with Terico Pisanu, counsellor (*mandadore*) of the church, and Orçoco de Martis. They ordered the representative (*mandadore*) of the church to bring forth as witnesses the elderly men of the territory (*parte*) of Miili (Milis): Iorgi Tamaglu, a realm's (*regnu*) servant

d[e] regnu, et Teore su fr[at]e et Goantine Cucu et Mariane d'Orruinas et Terico Barbariginu et Goa[n]tine Formiga. Poser[un]tillos ad iurare custos VI d[e] nar[r]e[n]de sa mei[us] beridad[e] ki'nd'enti iskire p[ro] custu padru de s[an]c[t]u Symione com[en]te fudi et daund[e] fur[un]t limides suas et
69ᵛ narr[un]t ka 'fuit villa isfata, | et clabavassi ad sanctu Symeone; et iudice Comida la d[e]it a donnu Piciellu de Seço cu[n] tota sa p[er]tene[n]cia sua et ip[s]e la posit ad s[an]c[t]u Iorgi d[e] Calcaria cando fraigait sa cl[es]ia ad novu. Et ingiçasi dae su nuraki d[e] Besala et calat oru margine segando de pare cu[n] Mambari d[e] s[an]c[t]a Iusta et clo[m]pet usq[ue] assa bia d[e]ssu bau d[e]ssu carru et bat cu[n] sa bia maiore usq[ue] ad pedras colbadas d[e] Murtas et bat cu[n] bia usq[ue] ad bau cavallare et collat totue cu[n] flum[en] usq[ue] ad bau d'ebbas et collat d[e]retu assa ci[n]niga ad ue ferit su saltu d[e] s[er]ra de Tremaça et collat d[e]rectu assa bia d[e] logu d[e] colletoriu ue su[n] sas pedras et calat cu[n] bia d[e] logu usq[ue] ad co si faget pares cu[n] nuraki albu et da ind[e] essit deretu assu muru d[e] segus d[e] s[an]c[t]u Symione et essit d[e]rectu assu nuraki d[e] Besala et ive si afliscat appare cu[n] su saltu de nuraki pikinnu et cu[n] saltu de s[an]c[t]a Iusta.
70ʳ Custu co[n]gnovim[us] et iskimus.' Parsit iusticia a iudice et a totu logu | ka fuit binkidu et torrar[un]t su saltu ad cl[es]ia et posit iudice d[e]ssas binias k'ie fur[un]t, dae co s'ar[en]t isfagere, torrare ad cl[es]ia. Et ego iudice Barusone gasi lu co[n]firmo ad s[an]c[t]a Maria de Bonarcadu et ad s[an]c[t]u Iorgi de Calcaria custu saltu, ki llu rega[n]t et castige[n]t in co si castigat saltu d[e] regnu d[e] donnia t[em]p[or]ale dessu annu.

T[este]s: donnigellu Ithocor curadore d[e] Guilciver, Goa[n]t[ine] de Çori curadore d[e] Miili, Orzoco de Lacon curadore maiore, Pedru de Lacon curadore de Frodoriane, Orçoco de Lac[on] curadore d[e] Ba[r]baria, Gun[na]ri de Lac[on] curadore d[e] Bale[n]ça, Gun[na]ri d'Orruu curadore de Bono[r]çuli, Goa[n]t[ine] de Lac[on] curadore d'Usellos. D[e] buiakesos: Terico d[e] Ganpu et golleanes suos. D[e] porigl[us] de angarias: Mariane de O[r]ruu et golleanes suos. Et si q[ui]s dixerit qu[ia] b[e]n[e] est abeat b[e]n[e]dictio[n]e d[e] D[eu]s et de s[an]c[t]a Maria et d[e] om[n]ib[us] s[an]c[t]is. Et cui n[on] placue[ri]t et co[n]demnav[er]it hec ordinatio, habeat maleditio[n]e d[e] D[eu]s et de s[an]c[t]a Maria et d[e] om[n]ib[us] s[an]c[t]is D[e]i. Am[en].

162.

70ᵛ Pedivili[65] assu donnu m[e]u iudice Barusone sa die ki mi daret asoltura d[e] fager molinos in Bono[r]cadu et in Calcaria et in Miile Pikinnu; et ip[s]e daitimi

65 Change of hand from *Pedivili*.

(*serbu*). Teore his brother, Goantine Cucu, Mariane d'Orruinas, Terico Barbariginu, and Goantine Formiga came forward. They made these six swear to expose, in the most exact way, the truth that they knew about this meadow of Sanctu Symione, in what condition it was and what the boundaries of it were and they said 'it was a ruined village, and it was included in the territory of Sanctu Symeone!' Iudike Comida gave it to lord Piciellu de Seço with all that pertained to it, and he gave it to Sanctu Iorgi de Calcaria when he rebuilt the church. It begins at the nuraghe of Besala and descends along the mountainous edge and cuts itself off, separating itself from Mambari di Sancta Iusta, and comes up to Bau dessu Carru ('ford of the cart') and follows the main road up to the paired rocks of Murtas and follows along the road up to the Bau Cavallare ('knight's ford') and goes up along the course of the river up to the Bau d'Ebbas ('ford of the mares') and goes up in the direction of the reed bed where it arrives at the unworked land (*saltu*) of Serra de Tremaça and goes up along the main road leading to the gathering place (*colletoriu*) and descends along the main road (*via de logu*) until it joins Nuraghe Albu ('white nuraghe') and from there heads to the wall behind Sanctu Symione and comes out at Nuraghe Besala and there returns to the land (*saltu*) of Nuraki Pikinnu ('little nuraghe') with the land (*saltu*) of Sancta Iusta. This we have known, and we know. It seemed just to the iudike and to the whole country (*totu logu*) that he had been defeated and they returned the woodland to the church, and the iudike ordered that the vineyards that were near there be returned to the church, since they would have been lost. And I, iudike Barusone, hereby confirm this land (*saltu*) to be of Sancta Maria de Bonarcadu and Sanctu Iorgi de Calcaria, that they may hold it and take care of it as one would take care of a state land (*saltu de regnu*) in every season of the year.

Witnesses: *donnicello* Ithocor, *curadore* of Guilciver; Goantine de Çori, *curadore* of Miili (Milis); Orzoco de Lacon, head *curadore* (*maiore*); Petru de Lacon, *curadore* of Frodoriane (Fordongianus); Orçoco de Lacon, *curadore* of Barbaria (Barbagia); Gunnari de Lacon, *curadore* of Valenza, Gunnari d'Orruu, *curadore* di Bonurçuli (Bonorzuli), and Goantine de Lacon, *curadore* of Usellos (Usellus). Of the iudike's entourage (*buiakesos*): Terico de Ganpu and his colleagues. From those who provide mounts (*poriglos de angarias*), there was Mariane d'Orruu with his colleagues. And whoever will say that it is good, may he have blessing from God and from Holy Mary and from all the saints! And whoever opposes and does not observe this order, may he receive a curse from God and Holy Mary, and from all the saints of God! Amen.

162.

On that day, I asked my lord iudike Barusone to grant me permission (asoltura) to make mills for my use in Bonorcadu and Calcaria and Miile Pikinnu ('Lit-

adsoltura de levare s'abba et de fager girado[r]iu et p[ro] molinos et p[ro] ortos et p[ro] binias et de no mi·lla levare s'abba ne[n] a de die nen d[e] nocte, no[n] p[ro] iudice, no[n] p[ro] curadore, non pro liberu, no[n] pro s[er]bu. Et daitimi adsoltura de bardare su girado[r]iu in co si bardat saltu de regnu, getadura d[e] birga p[er] parte. Et dait at[er]a adsoltura d[e] fager nassarios in om[n]ia flum[en] et ess[er] liberos et fra[n]cos in co e[st] lib[er]u su factu d[e]ssu regnu. Custu b[e]n[e] li faço ego iudice Barusone ad s[an]c[t]a Maria d[e] Bonarcadu p[ro] amore d[e] D[eu]s et de s[an]c[t]a Maria et d[e] om[n]ib[us] s[an]c[t]is et pro remissio[n]e dessos pecados meos et de om[n]ia pare[n]te m[e]u. Et sunt t[e]s[te]s: p[ri]mus D[eu]s et s[an]c[t]a Maria et do[n]nigellu Ithocor curadore de Bilciver, Goa[n]t[ine] d[e] Çori curadore d[e] Miili, Orçoco de Lacon curadore maiore, Pedru d[e] Lac[on] curadore de Frodoriane, Orçoco d[e] Laco[n] curadore d[e] Barbaria et Gun[na]ri de Laco[n] curadore d[e] Bale[n]ça, Gun[na]ri d'Orruvu curadore de Bono[r]çuli, Gan[tine] de Lac[on] curadore de Usellos.

163.[66]

71r […][67] | T[e]s[te]s: ser Remu[n]du c'arreiat corona et Trog[odori] d[e] Sogu curado[r]e de parte de Ilciver et Barusone Spanu, curado[r]e de Miili, et Comida Pistore, kerkidore maiore, et Busakesu Pinna, curado[r]e de Sedelu.

164.

Ego p[ri]ore Ioh[ann]i q[ui] faço r[ecordacione] ca posuit do[n]nu Tericu d[e] Scopedu a santa Maria de Bona[r]cadu sa domestica sua de padru de domo et ip[s]a domestica de Mura d'Ulumos cu[n] sas palas de Tu[r]re et cu[n] s'ortu suo d[e]ssas benas de Tu[r]re et ip[s]as te[r]ras suas d'Abbaviva et de Tave[r]ra et d'Oia d[e] Fustes q[ui] fia[n]t peguiares de s[an]c[t]a Maria de Bona[r]cadu et d[e] s[an]c[t]a Victoria de Sella p[ro] pastu et p[ro] lao[r]iu. T[este]s: iudike Parasone et do[n]nu Comida de Lacon arkipiscopu, Paucapalea piscopu de s[an]c[t]a Iusta et do[n]nigellu Orçoco, curado[r]e de Gelciver et tota corona.

165.

Campaniemi cu[n] do[n]nu Comida d[e] S[er]ra Pirella. Coiuar[us] I serbu d[e] s[an]c[t]a Maria, Goa[n]t[ine] Celle cum Speciosa Ma[r]q[ui] ankilla de

66 Booklet F (early 13th century) begins here.

67 It appears that an entry which should have followed is in fact missing. As a result, the subsequent surviving entry has no immediate connection to the previous one. For instance, the *curadore* of Bilciver—alternatively spelled Illciver, Gilciver, or Guilcier—mentioned in entry 162 was *donnigellu* Ithocor; however, here, Trogodori de Sogu is recorded instead.

tle Milis'). He granted me permission to draw water and to make a drainage channel for the mills and for the gardens and vineyards, and he said that no water would be taken from me by day or by night, neither by the iudike nor by any *curadore* nor by a free person nor a servant (*serbu*). And he granted me that I might have the care and use of the drain in the same manner as with unworked land of the realm (*saltu de regnu*), for the space of a thrown rod (*getadura de birga*) [as a measure of extension] on both sides [of the drain]. And he also granted me that I might make fishponds in every river, and that they should be free and exempt from all rights, just as all royal property is free and exempt. This donation I, iudike Barusone, make to Sancta Maria de Bonarcadu for the love of God and Holy Mary and all the saints, for the remission of sins, mine and of all my relatives. The witnesses are: God, first before anythings else, and Holy Mary; *donnicello* Ithocor, *curadore* of Bilciver; Goantine de Çori, *curadore* of Miili (Milis); Orçoco de Lacon, head *curadore* (*maiore*); Pedru de Lacon, *curadore* of Frodoriane (Fordongianus); Orçoco de Lacon, *curadore* of Barbaria (Barbagia); Gunnari de Lacon, *curadore* of Balença (Valenza); Gunnari d'Orruvu, *curadore* of Bonurçuli (Bonorzuli), Gantine de Lacon, *curadore* of Usellos (Usellus).

163.
[...] Witnesses: sir Remundu, who presided over the hearing (*corona*); Trogodori de Sogu, *curadore* of the territory (*parte*) of Ilciver; Barisone Spanu, *curadore* of Miili; Comida Pistore, senior tax official (*kerkidore maiore*); and Busakesu Pinna, *curadore* of Sedelu (Sedele).

164.
[It is] I, prior Iohanni, who make a record concerning the fact that lord Tericu de Scopedu donated to Sancta Maria de Bonarcadu his own farmhouse (*domestica*) of Padru de Gomo ('house meadow') and the farmhouse (*domestica*) of Mura d'Ulumos ('blackberry of elms') with the slopes of Turre ('tower') and with the vegetable garden (*ortu*) of Sas Benas de Turre ('the tower wells'), his lands of Abbaviva ('living water') and Taverra and Oia de Fustes, which were properties (*peguiares*) of Sancta Maria de Bonarcadu and Sancta Victoria de Sella, used for grazing and cultivation. Witnesses: iudike Parasone; lord Comida de Lacon, archbishop; Paucapalea, bishop of Sancta Iusta; *donnigellu* Orçoco, *curadore* of Gelziver, and all the hearing (*corona*).

165.
I made an agreement with lord Comida de Serra Pirella. A servant (*serbu*) of Sancta Maria, Goantine Celle, was married to Speciosa Marqui, servant

Com[ida] Pirella. Levavatsinde do[n]nu Comida Pirella fiios cantu fagiat: ietait sa muiere dave domo d[e]ssu s[er]bu meu. Bennit do[n]nu Comida d[e] S[er]ra Pirella a Bona[r]cadu et d[e]dimi una d[e]ssas fiias c'avia[n]t facta in pare su s[er]bu meu cu[n] s'ankilla sua, a q[ui] narava[n]t Bera, et ip[s]os lados de Pedru su frade et posit megu dav'i[n]d[e] inna[n]te, de, si faguia[n]t fiios, d[e] pa[r]tire ladus a pare. T[este]s: Pedru Pirella et Goa[n]t[ine] de Po[r]ta et do[nnu] Ioh[ann]e Santesu et Trogodori Coco preid[e]ru de Bitoni.

166.

71v Partivi cu[n] su piscop[u] d[e] s[an]c[t]a Iusta fiios de Goa[n]t[ine] d[e] Figus et d[e] Iusta Barbis. Ego levei a Maria et a Bera, su piscopu levedi a Io[r]gi et a Muscu. Custu pa[r]timentu am[us] factu, sos do[n]nos, a bene. T[este]s: Freare Coco et Goa[n]t[ine] d[e] Po[r]ta et Nicola d[e] Pane et Trog[o]d[ori] Ma[r]talu et Miale Ma[r]ras et Pedru de Baniu.

167.

Partivi cum do[n]nu Troodori Coco arkipiscopu:

Coiuedi Goa[n]t[ine] Anione s[er]bu d[e] s[an]c[t]a Maria de Bona[r]cad[u] cu[n] Furada Cambuli, ankilla d[e] s[an]c[t]a Maria d'Aristanes; feguerunt IIII fiios. S[an]c[t]a Maria d'Aristanis levedi ad Samaridanu et a Iorgi et s[an]c[t]a Maria de Bonarcadu levedi a Ianni et ad Ioh[ann]e.

Terico Maçis, serbu d[e] s[an]c[t]a Maria de Bonarcadu coiuedi cum Maria Murra ankilla de santa Maria d'Aristanes. Fegerunt III fiios: Iorgia et Bera et Pedru. Santa Maria levedi ad Iusta Mameli cu[n] sos fiios, fiia de Pedru Formiga serbu de santa Maria de Bonarcadu et de Barbara Mameli ankilla de santa Maria de Aristanis. Santa Maria de Bonarcadu levedi a Iorgia Murra cum toto sos fiios suos.

Sas fiias de Terico Macis, serbu de sancta Maria de Bonarcadu fuid et Maria
72r Murra fuit ankilla de sancta Maria | d'Aristanis:[68] s[an]c[t]a Maria d[e] Bonar-
cadu levedi ad Elene et ad Caderina et ad Furadu.

Fiios de Comida Murra, serbu de s[an]c[t]a Maria d[e] Bonarcadu et Maria Orruia ankilla de s[an]c[t]u Paraminu. S[an]c[t]a Maria d'Aristanis levedi ad Bera et ad Petru.

Fiios d[e] Terico Macis serbu d[e] s[an]c[t]a Maria de Bonarcadu et d[e] Maria Murra ankilla d[e] s[an]c[t]a Maria d'Aristanis, et de Muscu fiia d[e] Ioh[ann]e Tigas serbu de s[an]c[t]a Maria de Bonarcadu et de Siilla Moiolu ankilla d[e] s[an]c[t]a Maria d'Aristanis. Levedi s[an]c[t]a Maria d'Aristanis ad

68 Change of hand from *d'Aristanis*.

(*ankilla*) of Comida Pirella. Lord Comida Pirella took for himself the children whom she gave birth to in time: in the end, he drove the woman out of my servant's house. Lord Comida de Serra Pirella came to Bonarcadu and gave me one of the daughters, named Bera, whom my servant and his servant had fathered together, and both halves of the share of Pedru his brother, and proposed that from then on, if the two aforementioned servants had fathered more children, we should divide them half each. Witnesses: Pedru Pirella; Goantine de Porta; lord Iohanne Santesu, and Trogodori Coco, priest of Bitoni.

166.
I divided with the bishop of Sancta Iusta the children of Goantine de Figus and Iusta Barbis. I took Maria and Bera, the bishop took Iorgi and Muscu. We, the lords, did this division for good. Witnesses: Freare Coco; Goantine de Porta; Nicola de Pane; Trogodori Martalu; Miale Marras, and Pedru de Baniu.

167.
I divided with lord Troodori Coco, the archbishop:

Goantine Anione, servant (*serbu*) of Sancta Maria de Bonarcadu, married to Furada Cambuli, servant (*ankilla*) of Sancta Maria d'Aristanes (Oristano); they had four children. Sancta Maria d'Aristanes took Samaridanu and Iorgi, and Sancta Maria de Bonarcadu took Ianni and Iohanni.

Terico Maçis, servant (*serbu*) of Sancta Maria de Bonarcadu, married to Maria Murra, servant of Sancta Maria d'Aristanes. They had three children: Iorgia, Bera, and Pedru. Sancta Maria took Iusta Mameli with her children, daughter of Pedru Formiga, servant of Santa Maria de Bonarcadu, and Barbara Mameli, servant of Sancta Maria d'Aristanes. Sancta Maria de Bonarcadu took Iorgia Murra with all her children.

The daughters of Terico Macis, who was servant of Sancta Maria de Bonarcadu and Maria Murra who was servant (*ankilla*) of Sancta Maria d'Aristanes: Sancta Maria de Bonarcadu took Elene, Caderina and Furadu.

The children of Comida Murra, servant of Sancta Maria de Bonarcadu and Maria Orruia, servant of Sanctu Paraminu. Sancta Maria d'Aristanes took Bera and Petru.

The children of Terico Macis, servant of Sancta Maria de Bonarcadu, and Maria Murra, servant of Sancta Maria d'Aristanes, and Muscu, daughter of Iohanne Tigas, servant of Sancta Maria de Bonarcadu, and Sybil Moiolu, servant of Sancta Maria d'Aristanes. Sancta Maria d'Aristanes took Maria Code,

Maria Code, fiia de Iorgi Parana, serbu de s[an]c[t]a Maria de Bonarcadu et d[e] Bera Çote, ankilla de s[an]c[t]u Paraminu.

Et s[an]c[t]a Maria de Bonarcadu levedi a Furada Buriga, fiia de Ia[n]ni Ca[m]buli serbu de s[an]c[t]u Pararminu et de Maria Ca[m]pana, ankilla de s[an]c[t]a Maria de Bonarcadu. Et am[us] I pede i[n] Samaridanu, fiiu d[e] Iusta.

Furada Buriga, mugere d[e] Torbini de Puçu: levedi s[an]c[t]a Maria d'Aristanis ad Pe[tru] Cacaus et ad Grega et ad Frassia cu[n] fiios ip[s]oro, fiios d[e] 72v Ioh[ann]e Cacaus, serbu de s[an]c[t]u Paulu d[e] Miili | et d[e] s[an]c[t]u Iorgi d[e] Calcaria, ladus ad ladus, et de Maria d[e] Cogos, ankilla d[e] s[an]c[t]a Maria d'Aristanis; et s[an]c[t]a Maria de Bonarcatu levedi ad Ianni Saba, fiiu d[e] Iorgi Murru, serbu de s[an]c[t]u Paraminu et de Bonaci d'Urrolo, ankilla d[e] s[an]c[t]u Sergi de Suei.

Et remaseru[n]t d[e]pus custa particio[n]e ad comuni Ioh[ann]e et Torbini fiios d[e] Comida Murra et d[e] Maria Orruia et Iorgi Frau, fiiu de Gavini Frau et de Maria de Cicuri, et Petru fiiu de Goa[n]t[ine] Muscas et de Susa[n]na de Cicuri et Barbara fiia d[e] Petru Corbu et de Iorgia Martalu.

T[e]s[te]s: Ioh[ann]e d[e] Martis maiore de scolca, et Orçoco Ca[m]ba p[re]b[ite]ru de Segaçus, Goa[n]tine de Porta, arm[en]tariu d[e] s[an]c[t]a Maria d[e] Bonarcadu, Arçoco de Muru diacon[us], Freari Coco maiore de s[an]c[t]u Paraminu de Gilarci, Nigolla de Pani, Comida d[e] Çori, Gu[n]nari de Kerki, Miali Marras, Gavini Celle ma[n]dadore de Bonarcadu, Terico Co[n]gnali, Trogodori de Pau abiaresu.

168.

Kertait megu do[n]nu Gu[n]nari de Stavara p[re]b[ite]ru de Tremaça p[ro] 73r Suia Pasci et p[ro] sos fiios et p[ro] Terico su fr[at]e. Kertait megu i[n] kida | de verruda. Poseru[n]timi ad p[re]gontaremi et benni ad su postu p[re]gontadu, arreendo corona do[n]nu Comida de Martis, fiiu d[e] Gu[n]nari de Martis. Ma[n]dait iudice p[ro] custu kertu ki no[n] si kertaret fisca a do[n]nu Petru d[e] Çori, ki llu posit ad su curadore ad corona de logu ad s[an]c[t]u Petru, ki fudi s'atera kida, p[ro]iteu ca fudi iudice arm[en]tariu de s[an]c[t]a Maria. Ad corona de s[an]c[t]u Petru benni ad su postu. Pesesi Gu[n]nari de Stavara ad kertari p[ro] sa clesia sua; et pesaise do[n]nu Comida de Cep[er]a ad torrari verbu ca 'furu[n]t partidus' et ca 'fudi sa particio[n]e in su condage de s[an]c[t]a Maria.' Remasisinde su p[re]b[ite]ru et no[n] bolbit kertare. Et ego binkindellu, ca s'aviat appida sa parte sua. Testes: do[n]nu Busakesu et ser Arremu[n]du iudices d[e] factu, k'arreiant corona et do[n]nu Comida de Cep[er]a curadore d[e] Ca[m]pidanu, do[n]nu Comida de Martis curadore de Simagis et tota sa corona.

daughter of Iorgi Parana, servant of Sancta Maria de Bonarcadu, and of Bera Çote, servant of Sanctu Paraminu.

Sancta Maria de Bonarcadu took Furada Buriga, daughter of Ianni Cambuli, servant of Sanctu Paraminu, and Maria Campana, servant of Sancta Maria de Bonarcadu. And we have a quarter share of Samaridanu, child of Iusta.

Furada Buriga, wife of Torbini de Puçu: Sancta Maria d'Aristanes took Petru Cacaus, Grega and Frassia, with their children, children of Iohanne Cacaus, half servant of Sanctu Paulu de Miili (Milis) and half of Sanctu Iorgi de Calcaria, and of Maria de Cogos, servant of Sancta Maria d'Aristanes; and Sancta Maria de Bonarcadu took Ianni Saba, child of Iorgi Murru, servant of Sanctu Paraminu and of Bonaci d'Urrolo, servant of Sanctu Sergi de Suei.

They remained in common, after this division, Iohanne and Torbini, children of Comida Murra and Maria Orruia, and Iorgi Frau, child of Gavini Frau and Maria de Cicuri, and Petru, son of Goantine Muscas and Susanna de Cicuri and Barbara, daughter of Petru Corbu and Iorgia Martalu.

Witnesses: Iohanni de Martis, head of the ward (*maiore de scolca*); Orçoco Camba, priest of Segaçus; Goantine de Porta, administrator (*armentariu*) of Sancta Maria de Bonarcadu; Arzoco de Muru, deacon; Freari Coco, head (*maiore*) of Sanctu Paraminu de Gilarci; Nigolla de Pani; Comida de Çori; Gunnari de Kerki; Miali Marras; Gavini Celle, representative (*mandadore*) of Bonarcadu; Terico Congnali, and Trogodori de Pau, beekeeper (*abiaresu*).

168.

Lord Gunnari de Stavara, priest of Tremaça, sued me over Suia Pasci, her children and Terico, her brother. He sued me in a summoning tribunal [of (arms-bearing) men] (*kida de verruda*). They fixed an appointed day for my interrogation; I appeared as requested on the agreed at the hearing (*corona*) [of] Comida de Martis, son of Gunnari de Martis. The iudike ordered that the dispute should not be argued until Petru de Çori's [arrived] and ordered that the *curadore* [Pietro de Çori] should attend the hearing of the realm (*corona de logu*) to be held on St Peter['s day], which was another summoning tribunal (*kida*); this because the iudike was administrator (*armentariu*) of Sancta Maria. I appeared at the hearing [on the feast day] of St Peter. Gunnari de Stavara stood up to argue on behalf of his church, and lord Comida de Cepera stood up, saying and objecting: 'they had been already divided up,' and 'this division had been recorded in the condage of Sancta Maria!' The priest did not add anything else and gave up the argument. I defeated him, proving that he had received his due share. Witnesses: lord Busakesu and sir Arremundu, iudikes at the time who presided over the hearing; and lord Comida de Cepera, *curadore* of Campidanu (Campidano); lord Comida de Martis, *curadore* of Simagis (Simaxis), and the entire hearing.

169.
73v Kertait Orçoco d'Uda cu[n] Muiedi Ma[n]nale p[ro] custa parçone ki posit
do[n]na Bera d'Uda ad s[an]c[t]a Maria de Bonarcadu. Et ego andai assa cor-
ona, et ip[s]e bii ca fuit fallidu. Clamait sua culpa et torraitilla custa parço[n]e
ad s[an]c[t]a Maria de Bonarcadu cuia fudi, cu[n] ateru de su suo p[ro] ca si
adfiiedi sa die ad s[an]c[t]a Maria de Bonarcadu. Posit I boe et L b[er]b[e]k[es]
et issa t[er]ra de s'ena, cabiçali ad corte de Puriose et costas assa t[er]ra de
Troodori de Stere. Custu posit ad s[an]c[t]a Maria de Bonarcadu cun bolu[n]-
tade bona de sa mugere Iusta Pi[n]na et de dotu sus fr[at]es. T[e]s[te]s: Comida
Bacca maiore de scolca, et p[re]b[ite]ru Comida Tolu et Orçoco de Medada et
Goa[n]t[ine] Gatu et Goa[n]tine Zacasi et Troodori de Muru nunçadore. Ante
totu custos fegit custu bene ad s[an]c[t]a Maria de Bonarcadu p[ro] D[eu]s
i[n]nanti et p[ro] s[an]c[t]a Maria et p[ro] sa anima sua.

170.
Bennitimi Nicola de Pane et Goa[n]tine Loke, su nepode, et pedivitimi sa
74r terra k'est tenendo ad sa domo de Ioh[ann]e Pirella fusc'a sa corte | de Petru
Spada p[ro] Goa[n]tine Loke, su nebode, p[ro] fraigaresi ive su fraile, naran-
domi Nigola de Pane et Goa[n]tine Loke, ambos i[n] pare, c'aviat tandu mortu
I fradile suo in Gilarçe et no[n] podiat stare ivi p[ro]ss'arrivalia. Et ego p[ro]
D[eu]s i[n]nanti et p[ro] amore de Nigola de Pane et p[ro] ip[s]e ki mi 'nde
p[ro]mitiat de serviremi[n]de de s'arte sua p[er] te[m]porale i[n] vita sua,
deilli sa t[er]ra et issa petra, k'est ive, p[ro] fraigare et p[ro] godiresilla i[n]
vita sua, et ad morte sua o[mn]ia cantu ad aer factu remagnat ad s[an]c[t]a
Maria i[n] pake et i[n] ketu (*corr.* kertu). Et casi mi pladigaru[n]t Goa[n]tine
Loke et Nigola de Pane, basandomi[n]de ipsos a[m]bos et totu sos ho[m]i[n]es
de sa domo de Nigola de Pane. Testes: do[n]nu Benedictu p[ri]ore d'Oiastra et
do[n]nu Ioh[ann]e Santesu et do[n]nu Petru Ursa p[re]b[ite]ru, ki mi '[n]de
p[re]gavant p[ro] darelilla, et Nigola de Pane et Petru Spada et Petru Coco et
ateros ho[m]i[n]es ki furu[n]t ibi. Custu co[m]bentu fuit factu i[n] sa via k'est
inter cl[esi]a et s[an]c[t]i Çenonis, anni D[omi]ni MCCXXIII.

171.
Nunçailla ad corona d[e] kida de verruda d'Aristanis a Bera d'Acene, fiia de
74v Ioh[ann]e Çukellu, serbu de s[an]c[t]a Maria | p[ro] kertare cu·lla p[ro] ank-
illa de s[an]c[t]a Maria de Bonarcadu. Ma[n]dait nu[n]ça p[er] carta do[n]nu

169.
Orçoco d'Uda sued Muiedi Mannale concerning the share (*parçone*) that lady Bera d'Uda had donated to Sancta Maria de Bonarcadu. I went to the hearing (*corona*), and he realised that he was wrong. He declared his guilt and returned the above to Sancta Maria de Bonarcadu, to whom it belonged, with more of his own as he affiliated himself that day Sancta Maria de Bonarcadu. He donated an ox and fifty sheep and the land of S'Ena ('the spring'), located at the head of the farmyard (*corte*) of Puriose and at the side of the land of Troodori de Stere. All this he donated to Sancta Maria de Bonarcadu with the consent of his wife Iusta Pinna and all his brothers. Witnesses: Comida Bacca, head of the ward (*maiore de scolca*); priest Comida Tolu; Orçoco de Medada; Goantine Gatu; Goantine Zacasi; Troodori de Muru, bailiff (*nunçadore*). In the presence of all these, he made this donation to Sancta Maria de Bonarcadu for God, above all, Holy Mary, and for the salvation of his soul.

170.
There came to me Nicola de Pane and Goantine Loke, his nephew, and asked me for the land bordering on the farm complex (*domo*) of Iohanne Pirella up to the farmyard (*corte*) of Petru Spada in favour of Goantine Loke, his nephew, in order to build there his blacksmith's workshop, telling me Nigola de Pane and Goantine Loke, both together, that, some time before, he had killed a cousin in Gilarçe (Ghilarza) so he could not stay there because of the animosity. For God's sake and for the sake of Nigola de Pane, who promised me that he would serve me in his art as long as he lived, I gave him the land and the possibility of using the stone, which is there, so that he could make [what he wished] and benefit from it for the rest of his life; and at his death everything he had made should remain the property of Sancta Maria without any claims or demands from anyone. And so, Goantine Loke and Nigola de Pane made me this promise, both kissing me, together with all the servants (*homines*) of the house of Nigola de Pane. Witnesses: lord Benedictu, prior of Oiastra (Ollastra); lord Iohanne Santesu; lord Petru Ursa, priest, who begged me to give him what he requested; Nigola de Pane; Petru Spada; Petru Coco; and other men present there. This agreement was made on the way between the church and Sancti Çenonis (St Zeno) in the year 1223.

171.
I sued Bera d'Acene, daughter of Iohanne Çukellu, servant (*serbu*) of Sancta Maria, at the summoning tribunal [of (arms-bearing) men] (*kida de verruda*) at Aristanis (Oristano), because I intended to sue her [first] over [her condition as] servant (*ankilla*) of Sancta Maria de Bonarcadu. Lord Goantine de Mar-

Goa[n]tine de Martis, curadore de kida de verruda, ad Bera d'Acene q[ui] vennet a torrari verbu, ca kertavat cu[n]da su priore p[ro] ankilla d[e] s[an]c[t]a Maria. Adcatedilli nu[n]ça et minimedi de venne, ne ipsa ne ho[m]i[n]e pro·ssa: binkilla ad minima[n]ça. Testes: do[n]nu Goa[n]tine de Martis, curadore de Sia, et do[n]nu Comida, su fr[at]e, et do[n]nu Gu[n]nari de Çori et Ioh[ann]e de Çori et Ioh[ann]e Ulpia et Miali Kico[n]ia et Orçoco d[e] Scanu et Petru de Çori et do[n]nu Goa[n]tine d'Uda d[e] Palmas et Comida de Çori et Petru d[e] Çori et Petru d'Açene et Ioh[ann]e de Çori (custos bator su[n]t de s[an]c[t]u Miali) et do[n]nu Orçoco d'Acene, curadore de factu de Ca[m]pitano, ki ma[n]dedi sa carta a do[n]nu Comida de Serra Pistore, curadore de Bonarcadu, ki ponnet in manu ad Bera d'Açene assu p[ri]ore p[ro] s[an]c[t]a Maria pr'ankilla sua pecuiare.

172.

Ego Nicolaus, prior de Bonarcha[n]to, faço recordatione[m] p[ro] kertu ke
75r feki pro Maria Pisana | et[69] pro I fiiu suo i[n] corona de sinodo in Aristanis, arregendo corona do[n]nu Laurençu. Kertait su p[ri]ore de Baulatu, do[n]nu Francardu, narrande 'kerto cu[n] Maria Pisana ka est fiia de serbu et d'ankilla de s[an]c[t]a Maria de Bonarkanto.' Torraimi verbu Bellomo, su fiiastru de Comita Manika, narrando: 'pro custa muiere ki kertas, livera est et ankilla n[on] est.' Iuicaru[n]t a mimi a battuere testimonios ka fuit fiia de serbu et d'ankilla de s[an]c[t]a Maria. Et ego battussi testimonios bonos: a donnu Petru de Çori de Baulata et donnu Go[n]nari Papis de Sant'Eru et a donnu Coantine de Ienna, curatore de factu de parte de Mili. Custos III iuraru[n]t ad vangeliu de Deu narrando: 'Custa muiere pro ke kerta su priore nos la co[n]noskimus ka fuit fiia de Petru Pisanu cki fur[un]t serbus ambos de s[an]c[t]a Maria de Bonarkanto, et nos los conoskimus servire p[ro] serbos a s[an]c[t]a Maria de Bonarckanto.' Parsit iustitia a totta sa corona ka avea vi[n]kito et ka furunt testimonios. Donnu Laure[n]çu ke arreiat sa corona tennit custa muiere et positimila in manus pro ankilla et issa et su fiiu coram testibus Arçocco Secke
75v curatore de Cebera grussa, Guantine de Martis curadore de | Campitano, su piscopu de Terralba Gonnari Savio, donnu Comita Pee curatore de Jenone, Arçocco de Martis curadore de Ortueri, Guantine Jana, Petru de Laccon, Furato Karras curadore de Arestanis, Sogillione Manca, Iovanne Sarakino, Iovanni de Casta, Comita Seckie maiore de cavallos, Gantine Mameli, Iovanni Papis, Mariane Cannavu, Arge[n]ti Zuckellu et totta sa corona como est adunata ad sinodu.

---

69 Change of hand from *et*.

tis, *curadore* of the summoning tribunal, sent written word (*per carta*) to Bera d'Acene so that she should come and answer, because the prior was suing her concerning the fact that she was a servant of Sancta Maria. He gave her the summons, but she refused to appear—neither she nor anyone else on her behalf and for her benefit. I defeated her in absentia (*ad minimança*). Witnesses: lord Goantine de Martis, *curadore* de Sia; lord Comida, his brother; lord Gunnari de Çori; Iohanne de Çori; Iohanne Ulpia; Miale Kiconia; Orçoco de Scanu; Petru de Çori; lord Goantine d'Uda from Palmas; Comida de Çori; Petru de Çori; Petru d'Acene; Iohanne de Çori—these four are from Sanctu Miali—and lord Orçoco d'Açene, *curadore* at the time of Campitano (Campidano)—who delivered to lord Comida de Serra Pistore, *curadore* of Bonarcadu, the charter that brought Bera d'Açene into the hands of the prior because she belonged to (*pecuiare*) of Sancta Maria as a servant.

172.

I, Nicolaus, prior of Bonarchanto, make a record concerning the dispute I had concerning Maria Pisana and one of her children in hearing of the assembly (*corona de sinodo*) in Aristanis (Oristano), hearing presided over by lord Laurençu. The prior of Baulatu (Bauladu), lord Francardu, argued that 'I sued over Maria Pisana because she is the daughter of a father and a mother who are both servants (*serbu et ankilla*) of Sancta Maria de Bonarkanto!' I was opposed by Bellomo, the stepson of Comita Manika, saying that 'regarding this woman over whom you are suing, she is free and not a servant!' They demanded that I bring forth witnesses to testify that she was the daughter of parents who were both servants of Sancta Maria. I brought forth reliable witnesses: lord Petru de Çori of (Baulata) Bauladu; lord Gonnari Papis of Sant'Eru; and lord Coantine de Ienna, *curatore* at the time of the territory (*parte*) of Mili (Milis). These three swore on the gospel of God, saying: 'this woman, over whom the prior is suing, we know to be the daughter of Petru Pisanu, and we know that both were servants of Sancta Maria de Bonarkanto, and we know that they have always served as servants of Sancta Maria de Bonarckanto!' It seemed just to the entire hearing that I had won and that there had been sufficient testimony. Lord Laurençu, who presided over the hearing, took this woman and handed her over to me as a servant, and her and her child in the presence of the witnesses Arçocco Secke, *curatore* of Cebera Grussa (Solarussa); Guantine de Martis, *curatore* of Campitano (Campidano); the bishop of Terralba, Gonari Savio; lord Comita Pee, *curatore* of Jenone (Genoni), Arçocco de Martis, *curatore* of Ortueri; Guantine Jana; Petru de Laccon; Furato Karras, *curatore* of Aristanis (Oristano); Sogillione Manca; Iovanne Sarakino, Iovanni de Casta; Comita Seckie, head of the horses (*maiore de cavallos*); Gantine Mameli; Iovanne Papis; Mariane Cannavu; Argenti Zuckellu, and the entire hearing gathered at the assembly.

173.
In no[m]i[n]e D[omi]ni. Am[en]. Recordatione[m] facio p[ro] Maria Capra ka sse rebellait dessu serbithu de s[an]c[t]a Maria et addonnicaitse a Petru Çuckellu, arm[en]tariu de Mandra Ulisay. Andainde a reclamo assu donnu meu iudicke Mariane, ke erat tando donnu dessa terra d'Arbaree. Posimi a kertarende in corona de ser Bruno, ke erat iudike de factu in Arbaree. Kertai in Arestanes i[n] corona sua: 'Kertu p[ro] Maria Capra ke est fiia de serbu et d'ankilla de s[an]c[t]a Maria de Bonarcka[n]to et est andata dassu serbithiu de s[an]c[t]a Maria.' Torraimi verbu Petru Çuckellu ka 'no[n] est ankilla de s[an]c[t]a Maria et da serbithu suo no[n] est andata.' Iudicaruntimi a batuer testimonios ka fuit fiia de serbu et d'ankilla de s[an]c[t]a Maria et ka erat andata
76r dessu serbiçu | de s[an]c[t]a Maria. Et ego battusi testimonios bonos: a Nicola de Pane et Gantine de Porta et Comita Pira et Janne de Vaias, Iorgi Virrake et Gonnari de Muro. Custos kinbe iuraru[n]t ad bangheliu de Deus ka: 'Maria Capra fuit fiia de serbu et d'ankilla de s[an]c[t]a Maria de Bonarca[n]to et nos los conoskimus servire su patre et sa mama et sa fiia Maria Capra a s[an]c[t]a Maria de Bonarka[n]to p[ro] serbos.' Parsit iustitia assu iudike de factu et a tottu sa corona ka aveat vi[n]kitu s[an]c[t]a Maria. Torraruntimi s'a[n]killa cu[n] VI fiios suos. Testes: p[ri]mo Deus et s[an]c[t]a Maria et ser Bruno, i[n] cuia corona kertava, Petru Çuckello, do[n]nu Muiedi de Laccon, Comita de Theppar curatore de Campitano, Mariane de Theppar su frate, Mariane de Serra curatore de Nuckedu, Comita su frate, Gon[tine] Piga, donnu Francardellu su p[ri]ore de Baulata, Petro de Martis de Nurghillo, Torbeni Melone, Frevari Cocco, Torbeni Gurolo, Petru d 'Orruu de Terralba, Gonnari Karruca p[ri]ore de s[an]c[t]o Paule de Sinnas, Comita Çori Trombas, Gavine Murghia, et alios multos q[ui] erant ibi.

174.
Coniugait Lughia Cuperi ankilla de s[an]c[t]u Serghi de Suei cu[n] Trogodori Nechi et fekerunt kimbe fiios. Rebellasimi s'ankilla et fuivit cun sos fiios ka si teniat parente de iuike Mariane. Andainde a reclamo a Silano a iuicke et nar-
76v raili: | 'A vos, do[n]nu meu, ve[n]ghio a merkede p[ro] una ankilla cu[n] kinbe fiios suos, ka mi sunt fuitos.' Mandait iudike prollos ki los obviasseru[n]t assa fontana de Bolorki et aivi venneru[n]t et battuseru[n]t I carta come erat liveru su patre. Narrai iuike: 'da ke est liveru su patre et sa mama e[st] ankilla, fiios k'anta fattos siant serbos de s[an]c[t]a Maria da oe innanti et serviant a

173.
In the name of the Lord, amen. I make this record concerning Maria Capra, who rebelled against the service she was to perform at Sancta Maria and entered the service of Peru Çuckellu, administrator (*armentariu*) of Mandra Ulisay. I complained to my lord iudicke Mariane, who was then lord of the land of Arbaree (Arborea). I sued at the hearing (*corona*) of sir Bruno, who was the de facto iudike of Arbaree at the time. In Aristanis (Oristano), in his hearing, I argued that 'I am suing over Maria Capra, who is the daughter of a servant (*serbu*) and female servant (*ankilla*) of Sancta Maria de Bonarckanto and has left the service of Sancta Maria!' Petru Zuckellu countered that 'she is not a servant of Sancta Maria and therefore has not left her service!' They required me to bring forth witnesses to testify that she was the daughter of servants of Sancta Maria, and that she had left the service she was to provide to Sancta Maria. I brought forth reliable witnesses: Nicola de Pane, Gantine de Porta, Comita Pira, Janne de Vaias, Iorgi Virrake, and Gonnari de Muro. These five swore on the Gospel of God: 'Maria Capra was the daughter of servants of Sancta Maria de Bonarcanto and we have known them to serve, the father and mother and the daughter Maria Capra at Sancta Maria de Bonarkanto as servants!' It seemed just to the iudike at the time and to all the hearing that Sancta Maria had won. The female servant was returned to me with six of her children. Witnesses: God, first before anything else, and Holy Mary; sir Bruno, in whose hearing I was suing; Petru Çuckello; lord Muiedi de Laccon; Comita de Theppar, *curatore* of Campitano (Campidano); Mariane de Theppar, his brother; Mariane de Serra, *curatore* of Nuckedu (Nuketu), Comita, his brother; Gontine Piga; lord Francardellu, the prior of Bauladu; Petro de Martis from Norghillo; Torbeni Melone; Frevari Cocco; Torbeni Gurolo; Petru d'Orruu from Terralba; Gonnari Karruca, prior of Sancto Paule de Sinnas; Comita Çori Trombas; Gavine Murghia, and many others who were there.

174.
Lughia Cuperi, servant (*ankilla*) of Sanctu Serghi de Suei, was married to Trogodori Nechi and they had five children. This female servant rebelled against the service and fled with her children because she thought she was related to iudike Mariane. I complained to the iudike in Silano, and said to him: 'my lord, I come to you to seek your mercy concerning a servant and her five children who have fled from me!' The iudike summoned them and commanded them to come to a meeting with him at the fountain of Bolorki, and there they came and brought a charter which showed that their father was free. The iudike said that 'since the father is free and the mother is a servant, let the children they may have from this day forward be servants of Sancta Maria and serve

s[an]c[t]a Maria p[ro] serbos.' Testes: Manuele Pi[n]na, Comita Theppar, Petru de Ficos, Barusone Pinna et Petru su frate, et Petru de Sogas et Dorgodori su frate, Petru de Martis, Torbine Melone et ivi erat cu[n] iuike do[n]nikellu Petru et do[n]nu Ramu[n]do su fratile. Et osca posit iuike Mariane a Dorgodori de Sogos et a Iorgi Pala a daremi s'ankilla con sos fiios ke era[n]t i[n] domo di Dorgodori de Sogos, curatore de Norghillos. Ann[o] D[omi]ni MCCXXVIIII.

175.
In no[m]i[n]e D[omi]ni. Am[en]. Ego Nicolaus p[ri]or fazo reco[r]datione[m] d[e] kertu ke feki. Kertai i[n] Bidoni i[n] corona d[e] do[n]nu Pismake, curatore di factu, p[ro] sa pa[r]zone ki aviat posta a s[an]c[t]a Maria Gua[n]tine de Zori. Giraru[n]timi sos fiios et n[on] mi la bolea[n]t dare. Kertei cu[n]dos et bi[n]chi[n]delos ue erat tota curadoria na[n]ti santo Petru d[e] Bidoni. Testes:
77^{r} Guantine Unale preitero | de s[an]c[t]o Petru, donnu Iorgi Pala ki kertavat su kertu pro me, donnu Ma[r]ian[e] d[e] S[er]ra de Sorratile, Torbini Gu[r]rolo, Comida d[e] Çori, Pedru de Çori.

176.
Ego Domestigu, p[ri]ore de Bona[r]cadu. Posuit Terico d[e] Scopedu a santa Maria de Bonarcadu et a santu Sergiu d[e] Suei su saltu de Sourre, in co si inguiçat daessa mura d[e] Carvias et benit ad sas ariolas floradas de figos de Ciperi et benit assu gutturu dess'oiastru d'Aiga et benit ad sa mura d[e]ssa soga[r]ia d[e] Pedra lada et falat a nurake o[r]rubiu et falat a bia de strada et ibi fliscat. Apatsinde proe usque in finem sec[ul]i et pro laoriu et pro pastu. T[este]s: donnu Ugo piscopu d[e] s[an]c[t]a Iusta et donnu Ma[r]iani Çorrake piscopu de T[er]ralba et do[n]nu Com[ita] Pais piscopu d'Usellos et Punçu, curado[r]e de pa[r]te de Bonorçuli et Berringeri co[n]te de pa[r]te d[e] Gelcier et d[e] Fodoriane et tota curatoria.

177.
Ego N[icol]a[u], p[ri]ore de Bona[r]cadu, et Pedru d[e] Figos arm[en]tariu de logu, pa[r]tirus sos serbos c'amus in Agustis p[er] paraula de iuike. Levait iudice a Goa[n]t[ine] Macirida et clesia levait a Goa[n]t[ine] d[e] Puçu; levedi iudice a Ianni Frunda et clesia levedi a Torbini Marki; levedi iudice ad Arçoco Marki et
77^{v} clesia levait a Goa[n]t[ine] | Marki;[70] levedi iudice a Goantini Musca et clesia

70 Change of hand from *Marki*.

Sancta Maria as servants!' Witnesses: Manuele Pinna, Comita Theppar, Petru de Ficos, Barusone Pinna, his brother Petru, Petru de Sogas, his brother Dorgodori, Petru de Martis, Torbine Melone, and with the iudike there was also *donnikellu* Petru and his cousin, lord Ramundu. Then iudike Mariane ordered Dorgodori de Sogos and Iorgi Pala to hand over the servant and her children who were staying at the house of Dorgodori de Sogos, *curatore* of Norghillos (Norghillo). Year of the Lord, 1229.

175.

In the name of the Lord, amen. I, Nicolaus, prior, make a record concerning the suit I filed. I sued in Bidoni, in a hearing (*corona*) of lord Pismake, *curadore* at the time, over the share (*parzone*) that Guantine de Zori had donated to Sancta Maria. His children changed their opinion and conviction and did not want to give it to me. I sued and defeated them before the entire *curadore*'s district (*curadoría*), in front of Santo Petru de Bidoni. Witnesses: Guantine Unale, priest of Sancto Petru; lord Iorgi Pala, who argued in my stead and to my advantage; lord Mariane de Serra from Sorratile; Torbini Gurrolo; Comida de Çori, and Pedru de Çori.

176.

I, Domestigu, prior of Bonarcadu. Terico de Scopedu donated to Santa Maria de Bonarcadu and Santu Sergiu of Suei the unworked land (*saltu*) of Sourre, according to this course of the boundary: it begins at Sa Mura de Carvias ('the blackberry of Carvias') and reaches Sas Ariolas Floradas ('the flowering threshing floors') of Figos de Ciperi ('figs of Ciperi') and joins the gorge of the wild olive d'Aiga and reaches the blackberry near the hackberry of Pedra Lada ('flat stone') and descends to Nurake Crrubiu ('red nuraghe') and reaches the paved road and there returns to the point of departure. He will benefit from it in perpetuity as arable land and pastureland (*pastu*). Witnesses: lord Ugo, bishop of Sancta Iusta; lord Mariani Çorrake, bishop of Terralba; lord Comita Pais, bishop of Usellos (Usellus); Punçu, *curadore* of the territory (*parte*) of Bonurçuli (Bonorzuli); Berringeri, count of the territory (*parte*) of Gelcier and of Fodoriane, and the entire *curatore*'s district (*curatoría*).

177.

I, Nicolau, prior of Bonarcadu, and Pedru de Figos, state administrator (*armentariu de logu*), shared the servants (*serbos*) we have in Agustis on behalf of the iudike. The iudike took Goantine Macirida and the church took Goantine de Puçu; the iudike took Ianni Frunda and the church took Torbini Marki; the iudike took Arçoco Marki and the church took Goantine Marki; the iudike took

levait a Goantine Muçullu; levedi iudice a Georgi Totolle et clesia levait a Gunnari Pelles; levedi iudice a Goantini de Scala et a Iorgia, sa sorre, et clesia levedi a Maria Totu et issu fiiu et a fFurada de Puçu; levedi iudice ad Elene Pistore et clesia levedi a Bera Totolle; levedi iudice a Petro Canie et clesia levait assa sorre, k'este amanti de Petru de Çori de Ortelli, et ipsa attera sorre arramasit a cumoni.

178.[71]

Ego N[icol]a[u], p[ri]o[r]e d[e] Bona[r]cadu, faço r[ecordacione]. Ke[r]tei cu[n] Goa[n]t[ine] d[e] Sogos d'O[r]ruinas p[ro] E[r]rado[r]e Paanu fiiu d'A[r]çocu Paanu, s[er]bu d[e] s[an]c[t]a Maria. Posit ad su p[r]ideru d'A[r]riora a kerta[r]e, do[n]nu T[ro]g[o]d[ori] Coco, i[n] co[ro]na de sinodu et naredi: 'Kerto cu[n] Goa[n]t[ine] de Sogos p[ro] E[r]rado[re] Paan[u], fiiu d'Arçoco Paan[u], c'at ip[s]e a s[er]biçu suo; ke[r]re l'epi a s[er]biçu de s[an]c[t]a Maria.' Et Goa[n]t[ine] de Sogos naredi: 'E[r]rato[r]e, p[ro] ki mi ke[r]tas, fiiu de lib[er]a est et do[n]nu Grego[r]i, q[ui] fudi i[n]na[n]ti de custu p[ri]o[r]e, i[n]d[e] kertedi cu[n] padre meu et binkit assu p[ri]o[r]e.' Positilli iudice et totu sa corona a do[n]nu Goa[n]t[ine] d[e] Sogos ad batiere beridade et donnu Goantini de Sogos batusit co[n]dake d[e]ssu padre cu[n] o[nn]ia d[e]stimo[n]iu mor[tu] […].

179.[72]

78r [a]sendo biu su s[er]bu a ki kertava. Parsit rasone ad totu sus liberos ki furu[n] in coro[n]a, ka non fuit su condage de creer et ca fudi fatu in falsidade. Posit donnu P[etru] M[ur]tin[u] c'arreiat corona dae pa[r]te de iudice ki to[r]raret su s[er]bu ad sancta Mar[ia] et p[er]contait assos liberos ki furu[n] in coro[n]a 'kiteu ve parit de f[ager/ dessu condage ki fuit falsu?' Et ipsos narrunt: 'Iudex inde faciat su k'illi ad plagere: ad nos bene parit rasone de haberellu et gittarellu in fogu.' Testes: donnu P(etru] Murtinu c'arreiat corona dae parte de judice et donnu P[etru) de Martis piscobu de sancta Iusta et donnu Goa[n]t[ine] de Fioru, piscobu de T[er]ralba et donnu P[etru] de Figos, arm[en]tariu de logu, et donnu Ar[zoco] Pees et donnu Goantine de Martis, donnu Ar[zoco] de Mar-

71 In Besta's edition this entry was merged with 179 as the text of both is located between two folios: one that ends at 77^{v} and one starting at 78^{r}. In passing from one folio to another, the hands change. Even if it appears that there is some continuity of argument and narration in entry 179, the syntactic and textual structure differs between 178 and 179. Hence, it is likely that in the succession of scribes, the second omitted some portion of the text with respect to the point where the first of the two had stopped.

72 Booklet G (early 13th century) begins here.

Goantini Musca and the church took Goantine Muçullu; the iudike took Georgi Totolle and the church took Gunnari Pelles; the iudike took Goantini de Scala and Iorgia, his sister, and the church took Maria Totu and her child and Furada de Puçu; the iudike took Elene Pistore and the church took Bera Totolle; the iudike took Petro Canie and the church took his sister, who is the lover (*amanti*) of Petru de Çori from Ortelli.

178.
I, Nicolau, prior of Bonarcadu, record this memory. I sued Goantine de Sogos from Orruinas (Ruinas) over Erradore Paanu, son of Arçocu Paanu, servant (*serbu*) of Sancta Maria. He had the litigation conducted, on his behalf and for his benefit, by the priest of Arriora, lord Trogodori Coco, at the hearing (*corona*) of assembly and said: 'I am in dispute with Goantine de Sogos over Erradore Paanu, son of Arçoco Paanu, whom he keeps in his service; I would like him to serve at Sancta Maria!' Goantine de Sogos said: 'Erratore, about whom you are suing me, is the son of a free woman (*libera*), and lord Gregori, who was prior before the current one, had a dispute with my father about him, and he won the case against the prior!' The iudike and the entire hearing bid lord Goantini de Sogos to produce evidence of what he claimed to be true, and lord Goantini de Sogos produced the condaghe (*condake*) of his father with every dead witness [...].

179.
[...] as long as the servant (*serbu*) to whom he was complaining was alive. It seemed right to all the free men who were present at the hearing (*corona*), that the condaghe (*condage*) was not credible and that it had been written in falsehood. Lord Petru Murtinu, who presided over the assize on the iudike's behalf, demanded in court that the servant be returned to Sancta Maria and asked the freemen present at the hearing: 'what do you think you should do with the forged condaghe?' They said: 'let the iudike (*iudex*) do what he wills with it, but we think it is right to take it and throw it into the fire!' Witnesses: lord Petru Murtinu, who presided over the hearing on iudike's behalf; Petru de Martis, bishop of Sancta Iusta; lord Goantine de Fioru, bishop of Terralba; lord Petru de Figos, state administrator (*armentariu de logu*); lord Arçoco Pees; lord Goantine

tis et donnu Gunnari d'Orruu d'Orruinas et donnu Baris[one] de Ie[n]na et donnu Goa[n]t[ine] de Iana et donnu Goa[n]t[ine] de Zori de Jenone et donnu Gunnari de S[er]ra arbarikesu et donnu Fur[atu] Çorrompis, donnu Franku de Sivi, donnu Ar[zoco] Soto, donnu Gunnari Pees et donnu Mari[ane] de Kerki et donnu Com[ita] de Urgu et donnu de Martis et donnu Baldufinu de Senuske et Suejo[n]e Ma[n]ca.

180.

78v Ego[73] Furadu de Çori Çorro[m]pis, ki mi co[n]v[er]so ad D[eu]s et a s[an]c[t]a Maria d[e] Bonorcadu in manu d[e] donnu Arrigu p[ri]ore, et do parçone de I fiiu miu d[e] quadrupedia et issa parçone mia d[e]ssu saltu d[e] Fliscales et parçone ca[n]tu appo in So[r]radile. Et sunt t[e]s[te]s: p[r]im[us] D[eu]s et s[an]c[t]a Maria et do[n]nu Iua[n]nitu canonigu d[e] s[an]c[t]a Mar[ia] d[e] Aristanis et do[n]nu Arçoco Moiu p[re]b[ite]ru miu, et donnu P[etru] Coco p[re]b[ite]ru de Miili Pikinnu et donnu Samaridanu p[re]b[ite]ru de Calcaria et do[n]nu Arç[oco] de Martis et Com[ita] Moiu clerigu et Gunnari d[e] Kerki, ge[n]neru miu et Fura[tu] d[e] S[er]ra, nebod[e] miu et Comida d[e] Lella et Mari[ane] Corbu.

181.

Conversaitsi do[n]nu Samaridan[u] de Enna ad s[an]c[t]a Maria d[e] Bonarcadu et dait sa parçone sua d[e]ssu saltu d[e] s'Alama c'aviat cu[n] Goa[n]t[ine], su fr[at]e, et cu[n] Maria sa sorre, et issa parçone sua d[e]ssu bestare de Bono[r]cadu, ki binkera[n]t ad Maria de Ie[n]na. T[e]s[te]s: donnu Mari[ane] Neos p[re]b[ite]ru de Spinalba et do[n]nu P[etru] Coco p[re]b[ite]ru de Miile
79r Piki[n]nu et donnu Samaridanu | p[re]b[ite]ru de Calcaria et do[n]nu Goa[n]t[ine] d[e] Enna su f[ra]te, et Busakesu su fiiu d[e] Goa[n]t[ine] d[e] Enna et P[etru] Celle et Sisi[n]ni Capay.

182.

C[on]v[er]saitsi donna Bera de Çene, muiere d[e] do[n]nu Goa[n]t[ine] Madau, ad s[an]c[t]a Maria d[e] Bonarcadu. Et posit parçone de I fiiu suu d[e] om[n]ia cantu aviat intru d[e] domo et foras d[e] domo et parzone cantu aviat intru d'Arbaree et de Polmin[us], de co[r]tes, de bi[n]ias et ortos et de domestigas et d[e] saltos et d[e] om[n]ia cantu si li ap[ar]teniat ad ip[s]a, tratu de s[er]bu et ankilla, ki no[n] dait. T[e]s[te]s: do[n]nu Ioh[ann]i Co[r]bu p[re]b[ite]ru d'[E]rriora, ki lla penedentiait et in cuia manu si ac[on]versait,

73 Change of hand from *Ego*.

de Martis; lord Arzoco de Martis; lord Gunnari d'Orruu from Orruinas (Ruinas); lord Barisone de Ienna; Goantine de Iana; Goantine de Zori; Jenone; lord Gonnari de Serra Arbarikesu; lord Furatu Çorrompis; lord Franku de Sivi; lord Arzoco Soto; lord Gunnari Pees; lord Mariane de Kerki; lord Comita de Urgu; lord de Martis; lord Baldufinu de Senuske, and Suejone Manca.

180.
I, Furadu de Çori Çorrompis, I render myself lay brother to God and to Sancta Maria de Bonorcadu in the hands of lord Arrigu, prior, and I donate my child's share (*parçone*) of the inheritance of the cattle (*quadrupedia*) and my share of the unworked land (*saltu*) of Fliscales and my share of what I have at Sorradile. And the witnesses are: God, first before anything else, and Holy Mary; lord Iuannitu, canonical of Sancta Maria de Aristanis (Oristano); lord Arçoco Moiu, my priest; lord Petru Coco, priest of Miili Pikinnu ('Little Milis'); lord Samaridanu, priest of Calcaria; lord Arçoco de Martis; Comita Moiu, cleric; Gunnari de Kerki, my son-in-law; Furatu de Serra, my nephew; Comida de Lella, and Mariane Corbu.

181.
Lord Samaridanu de Enna made himself a lay brother of Sancta Maria de Bonarcadu and donated his share (*parçone*) of the unworked land (*saltu*) of Alama that he shared with Goantine his brother and Maria his sister, and his share of the dwelling (bestare) of Bonorcadu, which he won from Maria de Ienna. Witnesses: lord Mariane Neos, priest of Spinalba; lord Petru Coco, priest of Miile Pikinnu ('Little Milis'); lord Samaridanu, priest of Calcaria; lord Goantine de Enna, his brother; Busakesu, the son of Goantine de Enna; Petru Celle, and Sisinni Capay.

182.
Lady Bera de Çene, wife of lord Goantine Madau, became a lay sister of Sancta Maria de Bonarcadu. And she donated her share (*parçone*) of the inheritance that would have been due to one of her children of all that she owned inside and outside of her farm complex (*domo*) and her share of all that she possessed in Arbaree (Arborea) and in Polminus (Pluminos, Cagliari), of farmyards (*cortes*), vineyards, vegetable plots (*ortos*), farmhouses (*domestigas*), lands (*saltos*), and of all that belonged to her, except for the servant (*serbu*) and female servant (*ankilla*) that were not donated by her. Witnesses: lord Iohanni Corbu, priest of Erriora, who confessed her and into whose hands she was made a lay sis-

do[n]nu Arç[oco] Muria, p[re]b[ite]ru et Goa[n]t[ine] Madau, su maridu, et Gun[n]ari Madau et Teric[o] d[e] Ca[m]pu et Gu[nna]ri de S[er]ra et Arç[oco] d'O[r]ruu.

183.
Ego[74] p[ri]ore Nicolau fatio r[ecordatione] dessu bene q[ui] fekit a s[an]c[t]a Maria de Bo[nar]catu Iuike P[etr]u de Bassu. Ditili in Agustis de stare cund onnia causa sua p[ro] iaker et p[ro] pasker i[n] sas mandras d'Aloy et i[n] sos cast[r]os et i[n] totu s'aperile ca[n]tu si p[er]tenet assa villa d'Agustis, un[d]e cuma[n]dait assos ho[m]i[n]es dessa villa q[ui] no[n] avere[n] a ffakeremi isto[r]piu, et issos go[n]nesseru[n] sa casa p[ro] totu te[m]pus in co sem[us] et bikinos de pare p[ro]ssa domo d'Agustis q[ui] est n[ost]ra.

184.
79v Ego Samaridanu, p[re]b[ite]ru de Calcaria, faço r[ecordatione] de paru et de comp[or]u canto appo fatu assa domo d[e] s[an]c[t]u Iorgi de Calcaria. Comp[ore]i a Trood[ori] Gaça I co[r]ria d[e] t[er]ra in bi[n]ia de Pedro[n]ia, et pubuliainas II cum bid[e], k'est tenendo ad s'una parte assa semida d[e]ssa figu d[e] s[an]c[t]u Symio[n]e et clo[m]pet usq[ue] ad flum[en] et ad s'at[er]a parte ferit assa parçone de Barbara de Urri; et dailli s[ollos] II de d[i]n[a]r[i]s et clo[mplilli] p[re]çu. T[e]s[te]s: Goa[n]t[ine] Capay clerigu, Ianni d'U[r]rolo, Goa[n]t[ine] Coco, P[etru] d'Urrolo.

185.
Donaitimi Barbara d[e] Urri et ip[s]as so[r]res, ki staa[n]t in Do[n]nigaia noa et in s[an]c[t]e Eru, sa parzo[n]e ip[s]oro k'avia[n]t tene[n]do assa d[e] Trood[ori] Gaça et a es'atera parte ad P[etru] d[e] Syi. T[e]s[te]s: Ga[n]t[ine] Coco et Cipari Murtinu et Ga[n]t[ine] Co[r]su.

186.
Donaitimi P[etru] d[e] Siy puru cue sa parço[n]e ki vi aviat tenendo ad Barbara d[e] Urri et tene[n]do ad Baruso[n]e Mellone. T[e]s[te]s: Nigola Pardis et Ga[n]t[ine] Begla et P[etru] de Piras et Com[ita] de Porta et Mar[iane] Corbu.

187.
Donaitimi Barusone Mello[n]e puru cue sa parço[n]e sua et d[e]ssos fr[at]es: et ego donailli duos s[ollos] d[e] d[i]n[a]r[i]s. T[e]s[te]s: donnu Nigola p[ri]ore

---

74 Change of hand from *Ego*.

ter; lord Arçoco Muria, priest; Goantine Madau, her husband; Gunnari Madau; Terico de Campu; Gunnari de Serra, and Arçoco d'Orruu.

183.
I, prior Nicolau, make a record of the donation made by iudike Petru de Bas to Sancta Maria de Bonarcatu. He granted that we could stay in Agustis with all our cattle and that we could keep them there and graze them in the enclosures (*mandras*) of Aloy, in the sheltered grounds (*castros*), and in all the open land that pertains to the village (*villa*) of Agustis for which he ordered the men of the village not to damage me, and they acknowledged this for as long as we are ourselves neighbours with regard to the farm complex (*domo*) of Agustis, which is ours.

184.
I, Samaridanu, priest of Calcaria, make a record of the acquisition and purchase that I made in favour of the farm complex (*domo*) of Sanctu Iorgi de Calcaria. I bought from Troodori Gaça a strip of land within the vineyard of Pedronia, and two poplar groves with vines, bordering on one side with the land of the fig orchard (*figu*) of Sanctu Symione, and reaching as far as the river (*flumen*), and on the other side reaching the portion of the property of Barbara de Urri; and I gave him soldi in coin (*sollos de dinaris*); I settled the account. Witnesses: cleric Goantine Capay, Ianni d'Urrolo, Goantine Coco, and Petru d'Urrolo.

185.
Barbara de Urri and her sisters, who live in Donnigaia and Sacte Eru, gave me their share (*parzone*) of the property bordering on that of Troodori Gaça and, on the other side, on that of Petru de Syi. Witnesses: Gantine Coco, Cipari Murtinu, and Gantine Corsu.

186.
Petru de Siy donated to me, still on that site [mentioned in the previous record], his share (*parçone*) of the property bordering on that of Barbara de Urri and that of Barusone Mellone. Witnesses: Nigola Pardis, Gantine Begla, Petru de Piras, Comita de Porta, and Mariane Corbu.

187.
Barusone Mellone gave me his and his brothers' share (*parçone*) on that place: and I gave him two soldi (*sollos*) in coins (*de dinaris*). Witnesses: lord Nigola,

d[e] Bo[n]arcadu et donnu P[etru] Coco p[re]id[e]ru de Miili Piki[n]nu et Ga[n]t[ine] Mele et Goa[n]t[ine] Coco et Ga[n]tine d[e] Kerki, maiore d[e] coallos d[e] stalla de iud[ice].

188.

80r Donaitimi Arz[oco] Capai sa parçone d[e]ssa figu d[e] Pedro[n]ia et issa t[er]ra ki fuit d[e] Iuanni d[e] Prunedu pr[e]id[e]ru; et ego donailli s[ollos] III et m[esu] d[e] d[i]n[a]r[i]s. T[e]s[te]s: P[etru] Ca[r]ru clerigu, et Ga[n]t[ine] Coco et P[etru] de d'Urrolo et Ga[n]t[ine] Ma[n]ca et P[etru] Coco et Com[ita] Tokeri.

189.

Donaitimi P[etru] Capai sa parçone sua et de fr[at]es suos d[e]ssa figu canasturça et ip[s]a t[er]ra k'est tene[n]do ad bi[n]ia d[e] s[an]c[t]u Iorgi et a is'atera parte assa binia d[e] sos d[e] T[re]maza; et levaitsi in pala p[ro] se et p[ro] fr[at]es suos d[e] darellis ca[m]biu. Et ego donailli masclu I p[ro] s[ollos] II et t[ri]t[icu] c[anta]r[e] I p[ro] d[i]n[a]r[i]s XV. T[e]s[te]s: Goa[n]t[ine] clerigu et Goa[n]t[ine] Coco et Cipari M[ur]tinu, Goa[n]t[ine] Corsu, Goa[n]t[ine] Ma[n]ca.

190.

Donait Honori d[e] Figu d[e] Tremaça et Iorgi Merkis et Iorgi Mameli et P[etru] Mameli et Furada Mamelli et do[n]nia fr[at]e ip[s]oro sa parçone k'aviant int[ro] d[e] bi[n]ia d[e] s[an]c[t]u Iorgi de sa figu canasturça: et t[er]ra et frutu et bid[e] donaru[n]t ad s[an]c[t]u Iorgi et a s[an]c[t]u Simione p[ro] amore de D[eu]s et de s[an]c[t]a Maria et p[ro] a[n]i[m]a ip[s]oro et d[e]ssos parentes et p[ro] p[re]gu ki 'nd[e] fegit do[n]nu P[etru] d[e] Figos arm[en]tariu d[e] logu. T[e]s[te]s: donnu P[etru] de Figos, arm[en]tariu d[e] logu et ip[s]u fiiu Leonardu et Busakesu d'Ula et Goa[n]t[ine] d[e] Laco[n] et Com[ita] d[e] Çori et Marcu Çukellu et Busakesu d[e] Enna et Ga[n]t[ine] Capai clerigu et Com[ita] Kersa cl[er]igu et Troo[dori] Cosu.

191.

80v Donaitimi Altrumare sa parçone sua k'aviat int[ro] d[e] bi[n]ia d[e] s[an]c[t]o Iorgi tene[n]do a s'una parte a ortu d[e] Fraos et t[er]ra et figu et bid[e] et sogaria et o[r]medu et levaitsi supra pala p[ro] se et p[ro] fr[at]es suos d[e] spiiaremilla et darend[e] canbiu et ego donailli s[ollos] II d[e] d[i]n[a]r[i]s. T[e]s[te]s: Goa[n]t[ine] Capay clerigu et Ianni d'U[r]rolo et P[etru] su fiiu et Goa[n]t[ine] Coco.

prior of Bonarcadu; lord Petru Coco, priest of Miili Pikinnu ('Little Milis'); Gantine Mele; Goantine Coco; Gantine de Kerki, head of the iudike's horse stables (*maiore de coallos de stalla de iudike*).

188.
Arzoco Capai gave me his share (*parçone*) of the fig orchard (*figu*) in Pedronia and the land that was of Iuanni de Prunedu, priest; I gave him three and a half soldi in coin (*sollos de dinaris*). Witnesses: cleric Petru Carru, Gantine Coco, Petru de d'Urrolo, Gantine Manca, Petru Coco, and Comita Tokeri.

189.
Petru Capai gave me his share (*parçone*) and that of his brothers of the orchard of 'canasturza' figs (*figu canasturça*) and the land bordering on the vineyard of Sanctu Iorgi and on the other side with the vineyard of those from Tremaza; and he took upon himself and his brothers to make an exchange. And I gave him a ram for [the value of] two soldi (*sollos*) and one measure (*cantaro*) of wheat for [the value of] fifteen coins (*dinaris*). Witnesses: Goantine cleric, Goantine Coco, Cipari Murtinu, Goantine Corsu, and Goantine Manca.

190.
Honori de Figu from Tremaça, Iorgi Merkis, Iorgi Mameli, Petrr Mameli, Furada Mamelli, and all their brothers donated to me their share of the property they held in the vineyard of Sanctu Iorgi of the plantation of 'canasturza' figs (*figu canasturça*), and land, fruit orchard (*frutu*), and vineyard they donated to Sanctu Iorgi and Sanctu Simione for the love of God and Holy Mary, and for the salvation of their souls and those of their parents and because it was prayed for by lord Petru de Figos, state administrator (*armentariu de logu*). Witnesses: lord Petru de Figos, state administrator, and his son Leonardu; Busakesu d'Ula; Goantine de Lacon; Comita de Çori; Marcu Çukellu; Busakesu de Enna; Gantine Capai, cleric; Comita Kersa, cleric, and Troodori Cosu.

191.
Altrumare gave me his share (*parçone*) that he held in the vineyard of Sancto Iorgi, bordering, on the one hand, on the vegetable garden (*ortu*) of Fraos, and the land, the fig trees, the vines, the hackberry, and the elms; and he took upon himself and his brothers the burden of freeing it from the claims of others and of making an exchange for it, and I gave him two soldi in coins (*sollos de dinaris*). Witnesses: Goantine Capay, cleric; Ianni d'Urrolo; Petru, his child, and Goantine Coco.

192.
Posit a cl[esi]a Saragina Capai, muiere d[e] Ia[n]ni d'Urrolo, II ordines de bi[n]ia in Pedro[n]ia, costas ad bi[n]ia de s[an]c[t]u Iorgi. T[e]s[te]s: do[n]nu P[etru] d[e] Kerki, p[re]id[e]ru de Suei, et do[n]nu P[etru] Coco, p[re]id[e]ru de Miili Piki[n]nu, et do[n]nu Arç[oco] Co[r]su, pr[e]id[e]ru de Tremaça, et Ga[n]t[ine] Coco et P[etru] d'Urroolo ma[n]nu et Torb[en]i su fr[at]e.

193.
Donaitimi Barbara d[e] Urri et issas sorres de Donnigaia noa et de S[an]c[t]e Eru II co[r]rias d[e] t[er]ra in Pirastru de Çi[n]çalu. T[e]s[te]s: Goa[n]t[ine] Coco et Cipari Mu[r]tinu et Goa[n]t[ine] Corsu.

194.
Comporai a Teric[o] No[n]ne e a Eissu d[e] M[ur]tas et assas so[r]res t[er]ra et figu et o[nn]ia cantu avia[n]t in Pirastru de Çi[nç]alu et I t[er]ra dae seg[us] d[e] domo de Iua[n]ni d[e] Urri et clo[m]pet usq[ue] assos ortos d[e]ssu erriu. Deilli in prezu sollos XII de dinaris et clomplilli. T[e]s[te]s: Eissu Ma[r]ras et Iorgi Ma[r]ras, Goa[n]t[ine] Coco. Ianni d'Urrolo et P[etru] d'Urrolo et P[etru] Saba muraiolu.

195.
81r Cambiei cu[n] P[etru] Ladu et cu[n] Furadiça sa so[r]re. Daru[n]t ipsos ad mimi p[ro] s[an]c[t]u Iorgi sa parço[n]e ip[s]oro d[e]ssu ortu d[e]ssu molinu; et ego daillis in ca[m]biu sa parçone d[e] Helene sa sorre, ki moriit enea, in binia d[e] su herriu. Et co[m]p[or]ai sa parçone d[e] cussu ortu ad Iusta Ladu et dailli in p[re]çu d[i]n[a]r[i]s XII et ca[nt]ar[es] II de or[iu].

196.
Cambiai cu[n] Furad[u] Ladu int[ro] d[e] cussu ortu: eo levai sa parço[n]e sua et dailli in ca[m]biu sa parço[n]e de Helen[e] sa sorre, ki moriit enea, in s'o[r]tu d[e]ssa casta[n]ia et in bi[n]ia d[e] do[n]nu Paule et ca[m]pan-iar[us]·nos appare. Ip[s]os apper[un]t custu et eo appi p[ro] s[an]c[t]u Iorgi s'ortu d[e]ssu molinu cu[n] o[nn]ia cantu at, t[er]ra et frutu et arbores. Et Goa[n]t[ine] Ladu, padre ip[s]oro, posit sa parço[n]e sua ad s[an]c[t]u Iorgi. T[e]s[te]s: do[n]nu Gun[na]ri Leras p[re]b[ite]ru et do[n]nu P[etru] de Kerki p[re]id[e]ru d[e] Suei et Goa[n]t[ine] mo[n]igu et P[etru] d'Ardaule cl[er]igos, Goa[n]t[ine] Coco et Com[ita] Capai, Ioh[ann]i de Urri, Ioh[ann]i Pysanu, Iorg[i] Capra, P[etru] d[e] Urri et Goa[n]t[ine] Manca.

192.
Saragina Capai, wife of Ianni d'Urrolo, donated to the church two orders of a vineyard in Pedronia, next to the vineyard of Sanctu Iorgi. Witnesses: lord Petru de Kerki, priest of Suei; lord Petru Coco, priest of Miili Pikinnu ('Little Milis'); lord Arçoco Corsu, priest of Tremaça (Tremaza); Gantine Coco; Petru d'Urroolo, the elder (*mannu*), and Torbeni, his brother.

193.
Barbara de Urri and her sisters from Donnigaia Noa and Sancte Eru gave me two strips of land in Pirastru de Çinçalu. Witnesses: Goantine Coco, Cipari Murtinu, and Goantine Corsu.

194.
I bought from Terico Nonne and Eissu de Murtas and his sisters land and a fig orchard (*figu*) and all that they owned in Pirastru de Çinçalu ('wild pear of the jujube') and land behind the farm complex (*domo*) of Iuanni de Urri, the boundary of which reaches as far as the vegetable gardens (*ortos*) by the river (erriu). I paid him twelve soldi in coin (*sollos de dinaris*); I settled the account. Witnesses: Eissu Marras, Iorgi Marras, Goantine Coco, Ianni d'Urrolo, Petru d'Urrolo, and Petru Saba, the builder (*muraiolu*).

195.
I made an exchange with Petru Ladu and Furadiza, his sister. They gave me, in favour of Sanctu Iorgi, their share (*parçone*) of the vegetable garden (*ortu*) near the mill; and I gave them in exchange the share of their sister Helene, who died without an heir, that she had near the river (*herriu*). And I bought the share of that orchard from Iusta Ladu, and paid her twelve coins (*dinaris*) and two large measures (*cantares*) of barley.

196.
I made an exchange with Furadu Ladu in that vegetable garden (*ortu*). I took his share and gave him in exchange the share of Helene, his sister, who died without an heir, in the chestnut orchard (*castania*) and the vineyard of lord Paule, and so we agreed: they had this and I had for Sanctu Iorgi the orchard near the mill with all what pertains to it, land and orchard (*frutu*) and trees. Goantine Ladu, their father, donated his share to Sanctu Iorgi. Witnesses: lord Gunnari Leras, priest; lord Petru de Kerki, priest of Suei; the monk Goantine and Petru d'Ardaule, clerics; Goantine Coco; Comita Capai; Iohanni de Urri; Iohanni Pysanu; Iorgi Capra; Petru de Urri, and Goantine Manca.

197.

Comp[or]ai a lladus d[e] cussu ortu ad Goa[n]t[ine] d[e] Porta et a Bera sa sorre, sa parçone ip[s]oro d[e]ssu ortu k'est costas a s'ortu dessa castania et daillis s[ollos] VIII et clo[mplilli] p[re]çu. T[e]s[te]s: P[etru] Capai, Com[ita] de
81v Ma[r]tis, Goa[n]t[ine] clerigu, Goa[n]t[ine] | Coco, Ianni d'Urrolo et Torb[en]i su nebode, et Cipari M[ur]tinu.

198.

Posit ad s[an]c[t]u Iorg[i] Marcusa Pardis parço[n]e sua ca[n]tu aviat in Calcaria et in Miile: plaça et t[er]ra et figu et bid[e] et om[n]ia cantu si li ap[ar]teniat. T[e]s[te]s: do[n]nu P[etru] Coco p[re]id[e]ru de Miili Pikinnu, do[n]nu Trood[ori] Annoesu, p[re]b[ite]ru de Tune, do[n]nu Com[ita] Ma[n]ca, pr[ei]d[e]ru de Basylai, do[n]nu Mari[ane] d'Uras, p[re]b[ite]ru de Tremaça, donnu Goa[n]t[ine] cl[er]igu, Goa[n]tine monagu cl[er]igu.

199.

Kertai cu[n] Ia[n]ni d'Urrolo p[ro]ssa pa[r]ço[n]e de Ter[i]c[o] Melo[n]e, ki fuit s[er]bu de s[an]c[t]u Iorg[i] et moriit eneu et ma[n]digaatilla ip[s]e sa parço[n]e et binkilu reendo coro[n]a Goa[n]t[ine] d[e] Enna et Honori d[e] Figu, sa die d[e] s[an]c[t]u Simio[n]e. Et binki plaças et t[er]ras et issa figu calaridana et ip[s]a t[er]ra in pirastru d[e] Çinçalu et in bi[n]ias de Mo[n]te et t[er]ra de po[n]ne ad ortu de gibulla in su riu d[e] Calcaria. T[e]s[te]s: Goa[n]t[ine] d[e] Enna et Honori d[e] Figu, curadores de fatu, Com[ita] d[e] Çori, Troo[dori] Co[r]su, curadores de factu de Bonarcadu, Mari[ane] d[e] Laco[n] et Com[ida] d[e] Çori d[e] Bauladu.

200.

82r Posit Goa[n]t[ine] Tamaglu ad s[an]c[t]u Iorgi sa parzo[n]e sua cantu aviat in parte d[e] Miile in binia d[e] Tamaglus et in binia d'Arrascas, t[er]ra et flgu et bid[e] et de onnia pumu et bi[n]ia de Gaini. T[e]s[te]s: donnu P[etru] d[e] Figos arm[en]tariu d[e] logu et Leonardu su fiiu et Goa[n]t[ine] de Enna et Mari[ane] de Iala et Leonardu Porkellu et Ar[zocco] de Muru de Bo[n]arcadu.

201.

Dait Iorgi Tamaglu su fr[at]e tota sa parço[n]e sua puru cue; et ego daili p[ro] amore d[e] D[eu]s s[ollos] III de d[i]n[a]r[i]s. T[e]s[te]s: Goa[n]t[ine] monagu cl[er]igu et Com[ita] Tokeri et Goa[n]tine Coco et Ja[n]ni d'U[r]rolo.

197.
I bought from Goantine de Porta and Bera his sister their share (*parçone*) of the vegetable garden (*ortu*) next to the chestnut orchard (*castania*), and I gave them eight soldi (*sollos*); I settled the account. Witnesses: Petru Capai, Comita de Martis, Goantine cleric, Goantine Coco, Ianni d'Urrolo, Torbeni his nephew, and Cipari Murtinu.

198.
Marcusa Pardis donated to Sanctu Iorgi her share (*parçone*) she held in Calcaria and in Miile (Milis): parcel (*plaça*), land, fig orchard (*figu*), vines, and all that belonged to her. Witnesses: lord Petru Coco, priest of Miili Pikinnu ('Little Milis'); lord Troodori Annoesu, priest of Tune; lord Comita Manca, priest of Basylai; lord Mariane d'Uras, priest of Tremaça (Tremaza), lord Goantine, cleric, and Goantine the cleric-monk.

199.
I sued Ianni d'Urrolo over his share (*parçone*) of Terico Melone, who was a servant of Sanctu Iorgi and who died without an heir, because he was profiting from it, and I defeated him at the hearing (*corona*) of Goantine de Enna and Honori de Figu, on St Simeon's day. I won the plots (*plaças*), the lands, the Calaritan fig orchard ('figu Calaridana'), the land in Pirastru de Zinzalu ('wild pear of jujube') and in the vineyards of Monte ('hill'), and the land to be planted as an onion patch (*ortu de gibulla*) by the river of Calcaria. Witnesses: Goantine de Enna and Honori de Figu, *curadores* at the time; Comita de Çori; Troodori Corsu, *curadores* of Bonarcadu at the time; Mariane de Lacon, and Comida de Çori of Bauladu.

200.
Goantine Tamaglu donated to Sanctu Iorgi his share (*parçone*) he held in the territory (*parte*) of Miile (Milis) within the vineyard of Tamaglus and the vineyard of Arrascas, with land, fig trees (*figu*), vines, all the fruit orchards (*pumu*), and vineyard of Gaini. Witnesses: lord Petru de Figos, state administrator (*armentariu de logu*); Leonardu, his son; Goantine de Enna; Mariane de Iala; Leonardu Porkellu, and Arzocco de Muru of Bonarcadu.

201.
Iorgi Tamaglu his brother gave all his share (*parçone*), also in the said place; and for the love of God I gave him three soldi in coin (*sollos de dinaris*). Witnesses: Goantine, cleric monk; Comita Tokeri; Goantine Coco, and Janni d'Urrolo.

202.
Conversaitsi Goa[n]t[ine] Tamaglu ad s[an]c[t]u Iorgi d[e] Calcaria et posit p[ro]ssa a[n]i[m]a sua sa parço[n]e sua d[e]ssa domo d[e] Bo[n]arcadu et ip[s]a binia sua tota de Tommanu k'est costas assa d[e] Ar[zoco] d[e] Muru. T[e]s[te]s: Basili Pi[n]na et Iorgi Mameli binarios de iudice, et do[n]nu P[etru] de Kerki p[re]id[e]ru d[e] Suei et Arzoco d[e] Muru, diaconus et Troo[dori] Co[r]su curadore d[e] fatu et Nigola Pa[r]dis maiore et Iuanni d[e] Enna et do[n]nu Gu[n]n[a]r[i] Leras p[re]id[e]ru et do[n]nu Goa[n]t[ine] de Lellu p[re]b[ite]ru.

203.
82v Donait Aketore Saba et ip[s]os fr[at]es sa parço[n]e ip[s]oro d[e] s'ortu k'avia[n]t cu[n] Goa[n]t[ine] d[e] Porta et cu[n] Maria Soru a llad[us] d[e] s'ortu d[e] issa casta[n]ia et dave s'at[er]a parte a s'ortu de Fur[adu] Ladu et dessos fr[ate]s, k'aviat co[m]p[or]adu; et donailli in ca[m]biu ad ip[s]e et assos fr[at]es s[ollos] II de d[i]n[a]r[i]s et ca[nta]r[e] I de t[ri]t[icu] et ca[nta]r[e] I d'or[iu]. Et Maria Soru donait sa parte sua ad s[an]c[t]u Iorgi de cussu ortu et remasit totu s'ortu ad cl[es]ia dave su molinu usq[ue] assu ortu d[e]ssa castania cu[n] parço[n]e ki dait Iusta Marki ad cl[es]ia ad ora d[e]ssa mo[r]te d[e] s'ortu ki partiat cun Furadiçu. T[e]s[te]s: do[n]nu P[etru] de Kerki p[re]b[ite]ru de Suei, Goa[n]t[ine] mo[n]agu cl[er]igu et P[etru] Ladu et Goa[n]tine cl[er]igu et Goa[n]t[ine] Coco et Goa[n]t[ine] Manka.

204.
Donait iudice P[etru] ad Gaini Gaza, fiiu d[e] Troo[dori] Gaça, s[er]bu suo, et d[e] Bera Casa, ki fuit ankilla de s[an]c[t]u Iorg[i], su lad[us] et lad[us] d[e] s[an]c[t]u Gregori d[e] Bauladu, ad s[an]c[t]a Mar[ia] d[e] Bo[n]arcadu. Mortu iuige P[etru], bennit Iorg[i] Mameli a llevarellu p[ro] minore suo; et ego andaind[e] a do[n]nu P[etru] de Figos arm[en]tariu d[e] logu et narai [...].[75]

205.
84r In[76] no[min]e Pat[ri]s et Filii et Sp[iritu]s Sancti. Amen. Ego Arrigu, p[ri]ore de s[an]c[t]a Mar[ia] d[e] Bonarcadu, partivi serbos cu[n] s'arcipiscopu Tro[odori] de Muru arciep[iscopu]s de sancta Maria d'Aristanis.

In p[ri]mis levedi s[an]c[t]a Maria d'Aristanis ad Goa[n]t[ine] Tail[e], fiiu de Farastia Porcu, a[n]cilla d[e] s[an]c[t]u Petru d[e] Kersos et d[e] Tro[odori]

75 Folio 83 is missing.
76 Change of hand from *In*.

202.
Goantine Tamaglu made himself a lay brother of Sanctu Iorgi de Calcaria and donated for his soul his share (*parçone*) of the farm complex (*domo*) of Bonarcadu and his entire vineyard of Tommanu, located on the side of that of Arzoco de Muru. Witnesses: Basili Pinna and Iorgi Mameli, vintners of the iudike; lord Petru de Kerki, priest of Suei; Arzoco de Muru, deacon; Troodori Corsu, *curadore* at the time; Nigola Pardis, head (*maiore*); Ivanni de Enna; lord Gunnari Leras, priest, and lord Goantine de Lellu, priest.

203.
Achetore Saba and his brothers donated their share (*parçone*) of the vegetable garden (*ortu*) that they had together with Goantine de Porta and Maria Soru, located next to the chestnut orchard (*castania*) and on the other side next to the garden of Furadu Ladu and his brothers, a garden that he had acquired by purchase. I gave him and his brothers two soldi in coin (*sollos de dinaris*) and one large measure (*cantare*) of wheat and one large measure of barley in exchange. Maria Soru gave to Sanctu Iorgi her part of the garden (*ortu*). All the garden was thus acquired by the church, from the mill to the chestnut orchard, including the share in the garden which she shared with Furadiçu, that Iusta Marki had given to the church at the time of her death. Witnesses: lord Petru de Kerki, priest de Suei; Costantine, monk cleric; Petru Ladu; Goantine, cleric; Goantine Coco, and Goantine Manka.

204.
Iudike Petru donated half of Gaini Gaça, son of Troodori Gaça, his servant (*serbu*), and Bera Casa, who was servant (*ankilla*) of Sanctu Iorgi; [he gave] the half of Sanctu Gregori de Bauladu to Sancta Maria de Bonarcadu. Once iudike Petru died, Iorgi Mameli came and took him away as his servant while still a minor, and I went to lord Petru de Figos, state administrator (*armentariu de logu*) and said [...]

205.
In the name of the Father, the Son, and the Holy Spirit, amen. I, Arrigu, prior of Sancta Maria de Bonarcadu, shared servants (*serbos*) with archbishop Troodori de Muru, the archbishop of Sancta Maria d'Aristanis (Oristano).

Sancta Maria d'Aristanis took first Goantine Taile, child of Farastia Porcu, servant (*ancilla*) of Sanctu Petru de Kersos and of Troodori Taile, servant (*serbu*)

Tail[e], s[er]bu de s[an]c[t]u Iustu d[e] Cap[ri]les. Et s[an]c[t]a Maria d[e] Bonarcadu levedi ad Iorgi Camisa, fiiu d[e] Maria Camisa, ancilla de s[an]c[t]u Ag[us]tinu d'Ag[us]tis et d[e] Paule Mudu, s[er]bu d[e] s[an]c[t]a Maria d'Ortueri.

It[em] levedi s[an]c[t]a Maria d[e] Bonarcad[u] ad Bera Lollo cu[n] sos fiios e s[an]c[t]a Maria d'Aristanis levedi ad Maria et ad Com[ita] Niellu, fiios d[e] Maria Lollo, a[n]cilla d[e] Bonarcad[u] d[e] sa domo d[e] Baromella et d[e] Petru Niellu, s[er]bu de s[an]c[t]a Maria de Aristanis.

It[em] Miale Çukell[u], s[er]bu d[e] s[an]c[t]a Maria de Bonarcadu, et Bera Polligi, a[n]cilla d[e] s[an]c[t]a Maria d'Aristanis, furu[n]t maridu et mugere: fegeru[n]t fiios IIII: Iorgia et Lucia et Gavino et Tro[o]d[ori]. Levedi s[an]c[t]a Maria d'Aristanis ad Lucia et ad Tro[o]d[ori] et santa Maria de Bonarcadu api[t] ad Iorgia et ad Gavino.

It[em] levedi s[an]c[t]a Maria d[e] Bonarcadu ad Petru Gulpia, fiio de Bera
84v Gulpia et d[e] Goa[n]t[ine] | Usay et s[an]c[t]a Maria d'Aristan[is] levedi ad Petru Muscas, fiiu de Gu[nn]ar[i] Muscas et de Bera Pasy.

It[em] levedi s[an]c[t]a Maria d'Aristan[is] ad Petru Mascas, fiiu de Goa[n]t[ine] Mascas et de Susa[n]na Cicuri et s[an]c[t]a Maria d[e] Bonarcadu levedi ad Argenti Gulpia, fiiu d[e] Bera Gulpia et de Goa[n]t[ine] Usay.

It[em] levedi s[an]c[t]a Maria de Bonarcadu ad Maria Pasy, et s[an]c[t]a Maria d'Aristano levedi ad Bera Pasy sa sorre; fiias de Gunari Mascas et de Barbara Pasy.

Item levedi s[an]c[t]a Maria d'Arista[n]es ad Iusta, fiia d[e] Gunari Mascas et d[e] Barbara Pasy, et s[an]c[t]a Maria d[e] Bonarcadu ad P[re]ciosa fiia de Goa[n]t[ine] Mascas et d[e] Susanna Çicuri.

It[em] levedi s[an]c[t]a Maria d[e] Bonarcadu ad Bera Çukella fiia d[e] Gavino Çukello et de Iusta Loq[ue]: et s[an]c[t]a Maria d'Aristano levedi ad Iusta fiia d[e] Goa[n]t[ine] Muscas et d[e] Susanna Cicuri.

It[em] levedi s[an]c[t]a Maria d'Aristano ad P[re]ciosa, fiia d[e] Iusta Loq-
85r [ue] et d[e] Gavino Çukellu et s[an]c[t]a Maria d[e] Bonarcatu, | levedi ad Elene fiia de Goa[n]t[ine] Muscas et de Susanna Çicuri.

It[em] levedi s[an]c[t]a Maria d[e] Bonarcadu ad Furadu Lera, fiiu d[e] Iorgi Usalla et d[e] Iorgia Lera, et s[an]c[t]a Maria d'Aristanes levedi ad Ioh[ann]i Burigu, fiiu d[e] Samaridanu Anione et serbu d[e] s[an]c[t]a Maria d'Aristanes et d[e] Bera Usai ançilla d[e] Bonarcadu.

It[em] levedi s[an]c[t]a Maria d'Aristano ad Ioh[ann]i Orruiu, fiiu d[e] Maria Orruia, ançilla d'Aristano et de Com[ita] Mu[r]ru, s[er]bu d[e] Bonarca[n]du; et s[an]c[t]a Maria de Bonarcadu levedi a Goa[n]t[ine] Lera, fiiu d[e] Iorgia Lera, ançilla d[e] Bonarcadu, et d[e] Iorgi Usalla, serbu d[e] s[an]c[t]a Maria d'Aristan[es].

of Sanctu Iustu de Capriles. Sancta Maria de Bonarcadu took Iorgi Camisa, son of Maria Camisa, servant of Sanctu Agustinu of Agustis and of Paule Mudu, servant of Sancta Maria d'Ortueri.

Sancta Maria de Bonarcadu took Bera Lollo with her children and Sancta Maria d'Aristanis took Maria and Comita Niellu, children of Maria Lollo, servant of Bonarcadu at the farm complex (*domo*) of Baromella and Petru Niellu, servant of Sancta Maria d'Aristanis.

Miale Çukellu, servant of Sancta Maria de Bonarcadu, and Bera Polligi, servant of Sancta Maria d'Aristanis, were husband and wife: they had four children: Iorgia, Lucia, Gavino, and Troodori. Sancta Maria d'Aristanis took Lucia and Troodori, and Sancta Maria de Bonarcadu Iorgia and Gavino.

Sancta Maria de Bonarcadu took Petru Gulpia, son of Bera Gulpia and Goantine Usay, and Sancta Maria d'Aristanis took Petru Muscas, son of Gunnari Muscas and Bera Pasy.

Sancta Maria d'Aristanis took Petru Mascas, son of Goantine Mascas and Susanna Cicuri, and Sancta Maria de Bonarcadu took Argenti Gulpia, son of Bera Gulpia and Goantine Usay.

Sancta Maria de Bonarcadu took Mari Pasy, and Sancta Maria d'Aristanis took Bera Pasy, her sister; daughters of Gunari Mascas and Barbara Pasy.

Sancta Maria d'Aristanis took Iusta, daughter of Gunari Mascas and of Barbara Pasy, and Sancta Maria de Bonarcadu took Preciosa, daughter of Goantine Mascas and Susanna Çicuri.

Sancta Maria de Bonarcadu took Bera Çukella, daughter of Gavino Çukello and Iusta Loque; and Sancta Maria d'Aristanis took Iusta, daughter of Goantine Muscas and Susanna Cicuri.

Sancta Maria d'Aristanis took Preciosa, daughter of Iusta Loque and Gavino Çukellu; and St Sancta Maria de Bonarcatu took Elene, daughter of Goantine Muscas and Susanna Çicuri.

Sancta Maria de Bonarcadu took Furadu Lera, son of Iorgi Usalla and Iorgi Lera, and Sancta Maria d'Aristanis took Iohanni Burigu, son of Samaridanu Anione, servant of Sancta Maria d'Aristanis, and Bera Usai, servant of Bonarcadu.

Sancta Maria d'Aristanis took Iohanni Orruiu, son of Maria Orruia, servant of Aristano and Comita Murru, servant of Bonarcandu; and Sancta Maria de Bonarcadu took Goantine Lera, son of Iorgia Lera, servant of Bonarcadu, and Iorgi Usalla, servant of Sancta Maria d'Aristanis.

It[em] levedi s[an]c[t]a Maria d[e] Bonarcadu ad Bera Marras, fiia de Maria Marras, ançilla d[e] Bonarcadu et d[e] Goa[n]t[ine] Bardane, s[er]bu d[e] s[an]c[t]a Maria d'Aristanes, et s[an]c[t]a Maria d'Aristanes levedi ad Iusta Saba, fiia d[e] Muscu Tigas, ançilla d'Aristano et de Petru Saba, s[er]bu d[e] Bonarcadu.

Item levedi s[an]c[t]a Maria d'Aristanes ad Torb[enu] Mu[r]ra fiiu de Com-
85v [ita] Murra s[er]bu de s[an]c[t]a Maria de Bona[r]ca[n]tu | et de Maria Orruia, ançilla d'Aristano, et Bonarcatu levedi ad Iorgi Frau, fiiu d[e] Maria d[e] Cicuri, ancilla d[e] Bonarca[n]tu, et de Gavino Fraus, s[er]bu d[e] s[an]c[t]a Maria d'Aristanes.

T[e]s[te]s, q[ui] fur[unt] in icustu co[n]ventu: Tro[o]d[ori] Coco calonigu de s[an]c[t]a Maria et do[n]nu Gu[nna]ri Leras p[re]b[ite]r et Arzoqo d[e] Muru jagunu, et Mari[ane] de Scanu, jagunu de bangeleu d'Aristanes, et Tro[odori] Corsu, curadore de Bonarca[n]tu et Petru d'Ardaule cl[er]igu et Furad[u] Ladu, mandadore d[e] Bonarca[n]tu, et Goa[n]t[ine] Mascas, ma[n]dadore d[e] s[an]c[t]a Maria d'Aristanes et D[omi]nige Pistore.

206.

Anni[77] D[omi]ni MCCLXI a dies XI de Frevariu. Ego donnu Benedictu, p[ri]ore d[e] Bonorca[n]to, partivi serbos cu[n] s'arkipiscopu d'Arbare do[n]nu Trogodori Cocco. Nois levam[us] a Barusone fiiu de Petru Sapa et de Muscu Ticas ankilla d[e] s[an]c[t]a Maria d'Aristanis et issu arkipiscopu levait a Iu[ann]e Po[r]ru, fiiu de P[etr]u Porru serbu de santa Corona d'Erri{ora ...}[78]

207.[79]

86r [...][80] | ri[81] e collat totue pus flumen de Ilbai et ergetsi in issa scala dessu fruscu ue parte[n]t de pare cu[n] su saltu de s[an]c[t]'Eru e benit a Petra de scudu e falat assu bau d'Ursiarsida e falat totue pos flumen de Cannavaria e falat a bau de Sinias u'est sa figu alba et cue s'afliscat cu[n] Mambari. E dolli sa parçone ki fuit de do[n]nu Piçiellu de Sezo ki poserat isse a s[an]c[t]u Iorgi de Calcaria cando la fegerat a nnou, cun issa segadura de su saltu d'Aidugocippu in co llu ingirat a iaga de Troodori de Pau: e benit a ariola de Titiriu e benit a funtana

77 Change of hand from *Anni*.

78 The entry is incomplete, ending abruptly at the bottom of folio 85v. It seems that some folios are missing from the current codex. The next two folios, originally numbered 69 and 70, constitute a separate sheet that was later sewn back here, between this booklet and booklet E, which begins on folio 86r.

79 Booklet E (late 12th–13th century) begins here.

80 The surviving part of this entry replicates entry 1.

81 Change of hand from *ri*.

Sancta Maria de Bonarcadu took Bera Marras, daughter of Maria Marras, servant of Bonarcadu, and of Goantine Bardane, servant of Sancta Maria d'Aristanis; Sancta Maria d'Aristanis took Iusta Saba, daughter of Muscu Tigas, servant of Aristano, and of Petru Saba, servant of Bonarcadu.

Sancta Maria d'Aristanis took Torbenu Murra, son of Comita Murra, servant of Sancta Maria de Bonarcantu and of Maria Orruia, servant of Aristano; Bonarcatu took Iorgi Frau, son of Maria de Cicuri, servant of Bonarcantu and of Gavino Fraus, servant of Sancta Maria d'Aristanis.

Witnesses, who were present at this agreement: Troodori Coco, canon of Sancta Maria; lord Gunnari Leras, priest; Arzoqo de Muru, deacon; Mariane de Scanu, deacon of Aristanes in charge of reading the Gospel; Troodori Corsu, *curadore* of Bonarcantu; Petru d'Ardaule, cleric; Furadu Ladu, representative (*mandadore*) of Bonarcantu; Goantine Mascas, representative of Sancta Maria d'Aristanis, and Dominige Pistore.

206.

Year of the Lord 1261, on 11 February. I, lord Benedictu, prior of Bonorcanto, shared out the servants (*serbos*) with the archbishop of Arbare (Arborea), lord Trogodori Cocco. We took Barusone, son of Petru Sapa and Muscu Ticas, female servant (*ankilla*) of Sancta Maria d'Aristanis; the archbishop took Iuanne Porru, son of Petru Porru, servant of Santa Corona de'Erri[ora] (Riola) [...]

207.

[...] and [the boundary] goes up along the river (*flumen*) of Ilbai, on the other bank, and rises up the slope of su Fruscu '(butcher's broom'), where the boundary divides the unworked land (*saltu*) of Sanctu Eru, and reaches Petra de Scudu ('notched rock') and descends to the ford of Ursiarsida and descends along the river of Cannavaria ('rushes'), on the other bank and descends to the ford of Sinias ('reeds') there where the Figu Alba ('the white fig') is and there returns to Mambari. I give him the share (*parçone*) that belonged to lord Piçiellu de Sezo, which he had donated to Sanctu Iorgi de Calcaria when he renovated the church, with the alienated part (*segadura*) of the land (*saltu*) of Aidugocippu according to the course of the boundary that goes around it near the entrance (*iaga*) of Troodori de Pau, and comes to the threshing floor (*ariola*) of Titiriu and comes to Funtana de Kercu ('well of the oak'), and granted from

de kercu et segatsi de pare cu[n] su saltu de Mariane d'Orruu et getatsi a iscla de kerbu et falat post flumen a nurake d'Olyxandru et fliscatsi in Aidugocippu; et issa domestiga de Cobulas e issa parçone c'aviat in Seço cu[n] fiios d'Asinari cun onnia causa issoro e issa parçone de Sobro e de Çeçerni cun issa binia de Recenzario cu[n] serbos, cun ankillas suas de iuale et cun om[n]ia libertados suos. Poniollos et afirmollos in manu dessu priore ki ll'appat benedicta sa
86v parçone de donnu Piciellu cantu aviat p[er] totu logu in co narant cartas suas. |

E domo de Vesala cu[n] segadura dessu saltu de Vesala ki ll'est in giru dave su nurake de Vesala e benit a nuraki pikinnu et benit a masoniu de Causare e benit a masoniu de Serra de Tremaza e calat assa mura de Mambari e afliscatsi in issu nuraki de Vesala.

E domo de Miili Pikinnu cun om[n]ia cantu aet donna Tocoele ki fuit donna de logu, mugere de iudice Comida de Salanis et fegit issa sa clesia illa a nou ponendove tota sa villa de Miili Pikinnu ki fuit sua peguiare senae avere parte ne[n] liveru ne[n] serbu aienu, cu[n] t[er]ras et binias et servos et ankillas et libertados et saltu ki si segat dave sa cinniga de figos de Milianu et benit assu grisaio[n]e dessa cotina sutta su munim[en]tu dessas tesones, et benit assa pedra dessa grugi d'ena de Cerkis et benit assas pedras d'ariola de do[n]na et collat su term[en] de domestia de Comida et collat a funtana de Maga[n]se, et benit a ariolas de Ca[m]pu totue via de Tune et clo[m]pet a nuraki pikinnu et levat sa via vetere assu castru de muru de Comida et falat assa ci[n]niga ulpina
87r de mata de Gausari | et ferit assa iaca dessu padru de Guppurriu et falat totue deretu flum[en] a binias de muru et falat assa funtana priva d'Orruinas et falat flum[en] et aflisca[t]si in ip[s]a ci[n]niga de figos de Miliana; et dessu saltu d'Oiastru parçone cantu aviat, gasi illi·lla co[n]firmo.

Et co[n]firmolli ego iudice Petrus d'Arboree a icustu monasteriu toto sa parçone de do[n]na Tocoele et dessas t[er]ras d'afiiu, ki derat p[ro] armari sa

the main estate (*segatsi*) with the land (*saltu*) of Mariane d'Orruu, according to the course of the border, and turns at Iscla de Kerbu ('islet of the deer'), and descends across the river (*flumen*) to Nurake of Olixandru ('nuraghe of Alixanders'), and returns to Aidugocipu; the farmhouse (*domestiga*) of Cobulas and the share which he shared in Seço with the children of Asinari, with everything belonging to them; and the share of Sobro and Çeçerni, with the vineyard of Rezenzario with his male and female farm servants (*de iuale* 'of the yoke'), and with all his freedmen (*libertados*). I give and confirm them in the hand of the prior: that he may have blessed the share of lord Piciellu, as much as he possessed for the entire territory of the country (*logu*), according to what his charters say.

And the farm complex (*domo*) of Vesala with the alienated part of the unworked land (*saltu*) de Vesala that surrounds it from the nuraghe of Vesala and reaches Nuraki Pikinnu ('little nuraghe') and reaches the enclosure (*masoniu*) of Causare and reaches the enclosure of Serra de Tremaza ('ridge of Tremazza') and descends to the wall of Mambari and returns to the nuraghe of Vesala.

And the farm complex of Sanctu Petru de Miili Pikinnu ('Little Milis') with all that was in the possession of lady Tocoele, who was the [first] lady of the land (*donna de logu*), wife of iudike Comida de Salanis, who renovated the church by donating to it the whole village (*villa*) of Milis Pikinnu, which was her property (*peguiare*), without having any share in it, neither freeman nor servant of others, with lands and vineyards and servants and freedmen; and the unworked land (*saltu*) from the rushes of the figs at Milianu, to the boundary hedge (*grisaione*) of the stony ground under su Monimentu de Sas Tesones ('sepulchre at the trapping nets for birds'), and arrives to the boulder of the cross of s'Ena de Cerkis ('the spring of Cerkis') and reaches the stones of Ariola de Donna ('threshing floor of the lady') and climbs along the border of the farmhouse (*domestia*) of Comida and climbs to the well of Maganse and reaches the threshing floors at Campu ('field') along the Tune road and arrives to Nuraki Pikinnu; it then takes the old road in the direction of Castru de Muru ('the walled stronghold') of Comida and descends to Sa Cinniga Ulpina de Mata of Gausari and reaches the entrance (*iaca*) of the meadow (*padru*) of Guppurriu and descends along it in the direction of the river to vineyards of Muru ('wall') and descends to Funtana Priva ('spring giving little water') at Orruinas, and descends the river and returns to the fig rushes of Miliana. And of the unworked land (*saltu*) of Oiastru ('wild pear'), I confirm to him the share that he held in this way.

I, iudike Petrus d'Arboree (Arborea), confirm to this monastery the entire share of lady Tocoele and the lands affiliated to her, and which she had

cl[es]ia et issu monum[en]tu suo. Si llis barigat kimbe a[n]nus de fagere custu serbizu, fr[at]es suos, a ki llas derat, torrent sas t[er]ras a cl[es]ia.

Et co[n]firmolli sa domo d'Erriora cun o[nn]ia cantu aet cu[n] terras, cu[n] binias, cu[n] serbos et a[n]killas et cu[n] o[nn]ia maso[n]e. Et co[n]firmolli sa domo de s[an]c[t]a Barbara de Turre cu[n] o[nn]ia cantu aet, cu[n] t[er]ras, cu[n] binias cu[n] serbos et ankillas.

208.[82]

In no[m]i[n]e D[omi]ni. Am[en]. Ego Pedru p[ri]ore de Bonarcadu faço regordatio[n]e p[ro] kertu ki fegi p[ro] su fundam[en]tu ki poserat Mariane d'Orruu de nuragi de vinias ad s[an]c[t]a Maria de Bonarcadu in Villalonga. Kertei in corona de logu in Aristanis, sendo in kida de berruda Troodori Seke. Ker-
87v tei cu[n] sos ho[m]i[n]es c'avia[n]t levadu | custu fundam[en]tu: p[re]ideru Co[n]stantine de Bosa et Mariane de Sivi et Co[n]sta[n]tine d'Orruu de Villalonga et ipsos frades et Pedru de Varca. Poser[unt]imi a mimi et ad ip[s]os a postu k'eo benne cu[n] sa carta mia. Be[n]ni ego assu postu et ip[s]os n[on] be[n]ner[unt]. Et osca poser[un] ateru postu a mercuris de senudu. Be[n]ni ego et ip[s]os n[on] be[n]ner[unt]. Et osca poserun atteru postu a D[omi]niga de palma. Be[n]ni ego et ip[s]os n[on] be[n]ner[unt]. Plakit assu markesu et a totu sos liveros cantos furu[n]t cussa die i[n] corona ki mi torrari[n]t custu fundam[en]tu p[ro] gantu naravat sa carta mia ki non mi 'nde kertaret plus p[er]unu ho[m]i[n]e, c'avia ego binkidu p[er] rasone. Et osca iuredi s'omine meu i[n] fatu de sa carta. Et poser[unt] assu curadore, a Troodori Seke, p[ro] torraremi su fu[n]dam[en]tu, custu p[ro] ki kertei et binki. Testimonios: Troodori Seke et Mariane de Sii et Gostantine de Martis et Baruso[n]e Sportella et Pedru de Nurki et Cerkis d'Orruu et Gunari de Barca de Bauladu et Gu[n]nari d'Uras maiore de buiakesos, et Pedru Paganu ca[n]celleri. Et ip[s]e Troodo[r]i Seke be[n]nit, sa persone sua, a Billalonga et torredimi custu fundam[en]tu iurandonde custos ho[m]i[n]es p[ro] testimo[n]ios: Goa[n]t[ine] de Varca
88r et Pedru de Varca et Petru Littera et Furadu | Casilis et Troodori Urçaki et Goa[n]t[ine] de Mogoro et Goa[n]t[ine] Zukellu.

209.[83]

In no[m]i[n]e D[omi]ni. Am[en]. Ego Goa[n]t[ine] de Foge petivilli boluntade assu do[n]nu meu ser Ugo de Bassa sa die de s[an]c[t]u Marcu de Si[n]nis

82 Duplicated in entry 2.

83 Duplicated in entry 3.

donated to endow the church with assets and to build her own sepulchre. If they allow five years to elapse before they have performed this service, her brothers, to whom she had given them, shall return them to the church.

I confirm the farm complex of Erriora, with all that pertains thereto, with the lands, and with the vineyards, and with the servants, and with all the cattle. I confirm to him the farm complex of Sancta Barbara de Turre (Torres) with all that pertains to it, with the lands, with the vineyards, with the male and female servants.

208.

In the name of the Lord, amen. I, Petru, prior of Bonarcadu, make this record concerning the dispute I had regarding the estate (*fundamentu*) of vineyards that Mariane d'Orruu de Nuragi had donated Sancta Maria de Bonarcadu in Villalonga. I sued him in the hearing of the realm (*corona de logu*) in Aristanis (Oristano), being Troodori Seke on the summons court of freemen (*kida de berruda*). I sued the men who had illegally appropriated this estate, priest Constantine de Bosa and Mariane de Sivi and Constantine d'Orruu of Villalonga and his brothers and Pedru de Varca. They ordered me and them to appear on the appointed and agreed day with my charter. I appeared on the said appointed day, and they did not appear. Then they fixed another date, the Wednesday of the assembly. I came, but they did not. Then they fixed another date, which was fixed on Palm Sunday. I came, but they did not come. The marquis and all the freemen who were assembled in the assembly on that day thought it right that this land property (*fundamentu*) should be returned to me according to the terms of my charter, and that no one should make any further claims against me, for I had won according to my reason. Then my servant swore in accordance with my charter. They made the curator (*curadore*), Troodori Seke, restore to me the estate (*fundamentu*), over which I sued and won. Witnesses: Troodori Seke; Mariane de Sii (Sivi); Gostantine de Martis; Barusone Sportella; Pedru de Nurki; Cerkis d'Orruu; Gunnaro de Barca from Bauladu; Gunnario d'Uras, head of the iudike's entourage (*maiore de buiakesos*); and Pedru Paganu, chancellor (*cancelleri*). The aforesaid Troodori Seke came in person to Billalonga (Villalonga) and returned the said estate (*fundamentu*) to me, with the testimony under oath of the following men as witnesses: Goantine de Varca, Pedru de Varca, Petru Littera, Furadu Casilis, Troodori Urçaki, Goantine de Mogoro, and Goantine Zukellu.

209.

In the name of Lord, amen. I, Goantine de Foge, asked my lord, sir Ugo de Bassa, on the day of St Mark of Sinnis (Sinis), when he was coming out of Mass, to

aissora kandu essiat de missa ki mi darit paraula de offerremi a s[an]c[t]a Maria de Bonarcadu cu[n] o[nn]ia cantu avia; et ip[s]e naredimi ca 'faguellu c'a mimi b[e]n[e] mi plaguit et bonu mi parit et paraula ti 'nde do.' Et ego dave co '[n]d'appi p[ar]aula dava su do[n]nu meu mi misi in manu de do[n]nu Vivianu p[ri]ore de Bonarcadu davenanti dessu do[n]nu m[e]u in p[re]sentia sua p[ro] co[m]bersu et deilli i[n] potestate sua o[nn]ia cantu avia i[n]tro de domo et de foras de domo, t[er]ras et binias ca[n]tu avia de fundam[en]tu meu et de co[m]poru su ladus et iss'at[er]u ladus e[st] de mugere mia. Testes: su do[n]nu meu iudice Ugo de Basso et do[n]nu Bonacorsu, piscobu de s[an]c[t]a Iusta, et do[n]nu Gu[n]na[r]i de Martis, curadore dessos Simaguis, et do[n]nu Baruso[n]e Taiabuco[n]es et do[n]nu Eissu Sakellu ma[n]nu et do[n]nu Baruso[n]e Spanu et do[n]nu Gu[n]nari de Iana et donnu Goantine Orrodelle et do[n]nu,
88v Jorgi de Sogos et donnu | Iorgi Zancatorta et donnu Arçoco Porcu. Custos ive fur[un] ue co[n]sentiit su do[n]nu meu do[n]nu Ugo de Basso s'afiiam[en]tu ki mi fegi a s[an]c[t]a Maria de Bonarcadu p[ro] co[m]bersu cu[n] totu su meu. Et ta[n]du andei a Bonarcadu cu[n] su p[ri]ore et offersimi a D[eu]s et a s[an]c[t]a Maria et a s[an]c[t]o Zeno denanti dess'altari suo, ue era[n]t totu sos monagos, pro co[m]bersu et in bida et i[n] morte. Et dedi totu su m[e]u a D[eu]s et a s[an]c[t]a Maria segu[n]du co avia platigadu et iadu assu p[ri]ore daena[n]ti dessu do[n]nu meu Ugo de Bassa iudice d'Arbaree.

210.[84]

Ego Iorgi Ma[r]ras petilli boluntade assu do[n]nu m[e]u su markesu sa die de D[omi]niga de palma, sendo i[n] missa a s[an]c[t]a Iusta ke mi daret paraula d'offeremi a s[an]c[t]a Maria de Bonarcadu cu[n] totu ca[n]tu avia. Et ip[s]e dedimi assoltura; pone[n]domi ip[s]e i[n] manu dessu p[ri]ore do[n]nu Pedru P[er]usinu, mi offersi a D[eu]s et a s[an]c[t]a Maria cu[n] o[nn]ia ca[n]tu avea: domos, t[er]ras et binias, ca[n]tu avia i[n] parte de Miili i[n] co nara[n]t ca[r]tas mias. Da oe na[n]ti siat peguiare de s[an]c[t]a Maria de Bona[r]cadu totu su meu. T[e]s[te]s: D[eu]s i[n]nante et issu do[n]nu meu su ma[r]kesu, do[n]nu Bernardu a[r]kipiscobu d'Arba[r]ee et do[n]nu Maceu et do[n]nu
89r Ubertu dessu Grotto et do[n]nu | Saltoro de Se[r]ra et do[n]nu Baruso[n]e de Se[r]ra arbarikesu et do[n]nu Gu[n]nari su frade et Gu[n]nari de Iena et totu sos ho[m]i[n]es bonos ke era[n]t in missa cu[n] su do[n]nu m[e]u, cl[er]igos et laigos.

84 Duplicated in entry 4.

assure me that I could offer myself as a lay brother of Sancta Maria de Bonarcadu with all my possessions. And he said to me: 'do it, for I consent to it, and it seems right to me, and I assure you of it!' Since I got the approval (*paraula*) from my lord, I placed myself into the hands of lord Vivianu, prior of Bonarcadu, before my lord in his presence as a lay brother and gave him in his power all that I owned inside and outside my farm complex (*domo*): land and vineyards, the half that I already had as estate and by purchase; the other half is my wife's. Witnesses: my lord iudike Ugo de Basso; lord Bonacorsu, bishop of Sancta Iusta; lord Gunnari de Martis, *curatore* of the Simaguis (Simagis); lord Barusone Taiabucones; lord Eissu Sakellu the elder (*mannu*); lord Barusone Ispanu; lord Gunnari de Ianna; lord Goantine Orrodelle; lord Jorgi de Sogos; lord Iorgi Zancatorta, and lord Arçocu Porcu. These were present when the lord, my lord, Ugo de Basso, agreed that I should dedicate myself to Sancta Maria de Bonarcadu as a lay brother, offering all my property at the same time. Then I went to Bonarcadu with the prior and offered myself, in life and in death, as a lay brother to God, Sancta Maria [of Bonárcado] and St Zeno, before his altar, at which all the monks were gathered. I gave all that I possessed to God and Sancta Maria according to what I had promised and given to the prior before my lord Ugo de Bassa, iudike of Arbaree (Arborea).

210.

I, Iorgi Marras, asked my lord the marquis on Palm Sunday, when he was at the Mass at Sancta Iusta, to give me the approval (*paraula*) to offer myself as a lay brother of Sancta Maria de Bonarcadu with all my possessions. He gave me permission (*assoltura*) to do so, delivering myself into the hands of the prior, lord Pedru Perusino, I offered myself as a lay brother to God and to Holy Mary with all that I owned: farm complexes (*domos*), lands and as much land and vineyards I owned in the territory (*parte*) of Miili (Milis), in accordance with what my charters attest. From this day forth, all that I possess shall be the property of Sancta Maria de Bonarcadu. Witnesses: God, first before anything else; my lord the marquis; lord Maceu; lord Ubertu of the Grotto; lord Saltoro de Serra; lord Barusone Arbarikesu; lord Gunnari, his brother; Gunnari de Iena, and all the trusted men (*homines bonos*) who were present at the Mass (*in missa*) with my lord, clerics, and laymen.

211.[85]
Posit Maria Cavaio[n]e una t[er]ra i[n] Ma[r]zane tene[n]do a binia de Petru de Reu; sa t[er]ra ki posit Pedru Alla in Arsbilledu dave s'e[r]riu fusca ass'ariola dessa t[er]ra dessos kercos de Bolosvili de Ietadu tene[n]do a binia de Zancudi; una t[er]ra in Passadoriu et atera t[er]ra i[n] Gusnari, una t[er]ra in Istakesos, tene[n]do assos de Corsiga sa parço[n]e dessa t[er]ra de Getadu daessa figu de Padina, costas a sa t[er]ra de co[m]poru de Furadu Unele.

212.[86]
Posit Grega de Sii una t[er]ra a cl[es]ia in capizale de padro, costa a latu de Gu[n]na[r]i de Maluzu, cabiçale a t[er]ra de Goa[n]t[ine] Co[r]da. T[e]s[te]s: donnu Baruso[n]e de Se[r]ra et Goa[n]t[ine] Murtinu, maiore de scolca d'Erriora, et Pedru de Scanu nepode suu, et do[n]nu Arçoco de Scanu.

213.[87]
Conv[er]saisse do[n]nu Goa[n]t[ine] Murtinu a s[an]c[t]a Maria et posit una t[er]ra in G[r]ugue de nurake a cl[es]ia, capizale a sa domestia de s[an]c[t]a Corona, dae s'atera parte sa t[er]ra de s[an]c[t]a Anna. T[e]s[te]s: Goa[n]t[ine] Madau ma[n]dado[r]e de regnu et Goa[n]t[ine] de Zori et Arçoco de Barca.

214.[88]
89v In no[m]i[n]e D[omi]ni. Am[en]. Co[n]v[er]saisse do[n]nu Comida de Cepara a D[eu]s et a s[an]c[t]a Maria de Bona[r]cadu i[n] manu de su p[ri]ore donnu Pedru P[er]usinu p[ro] faguerelli, a morte sua, serbiciu et officiu de co[n]v[er]su et p[ro] tutarellu i[n] sa clostra de s[an]c[t]a Maria. Dedi ta[n]du pro a[n]i[m]a sua a s[an]c[t]a Maria unu cavallu et una ebba pullerigada et unu iuvu et C·L· berbegues et X madrigues de porcu. Et i[m]p[ro]misit et pladigait a morte sua pa[r]zo[n]e cantu at avere unu de fiios suos de o[nn]ia cantu at de t[er]ras et de binias et de saltos et de serbos et d'a[n]killas et de maso[n]es de o[nn]ia si[n]nu de grossu et de minudu et cavallos et ebbas et de o[nn]ia ca[n]tu at avere i[n]tro de domo et foras de domo, tratu sas co[r]tes. T[e]s[te]s: D[eu]s et s[an]c[t]a Maria et issu p[ri]ore et Arçoco de Muru et do[n]nu Mariani de Cep[er]a et do[n]nu Comida de Loy et do[n]nu Goa[n]t[ine] de Çori et maistru Bigenzu et Goa[n]t[ine] O[r]rodellu et Arçoco de Barca et Goa[n]t[ine] de Muru p[re]ideru de Senuski, et Amira Soia et Goa[n]t[ine] de Fu[n]tana.

85 Duplicated in entry 5.
86 Duplicated in entry 6.
87 Duplicated in entry 7.
88 Duplicated in entry 8.

211.
Maria Cavaione donated a land in Marzane bordering on the vineyard of Petru of Reu; the land that Pedru Alla had donated in Arsbilledu ('onion field'), extending from the river (*erriu*) to the threshing floor (*ariola*) of the oaks of Bolosvili de Ietadu, and bordering on the vineyard of Zancudi; a piece of land in Passadoriu ('resting place') and another piece of land in Gusnari, a piece of land in Istakesos bordering that of Corsiga, the share (*parçone*) of Getadu, situated in the locality of sa Figu de Padina ('the fig tree atddd Padina'), located on the side of the land that Furadu Unele had purchased.

212.
Grega de Sii (Sivi) donated to the church a piece of land located at the top end (*capizale*) of the meadow (*padro*) and at the side of the land of Gunnari de Maluzu, at the end of the land of Goantine Corda. Witnesses: lord Barusone de Serra; Goantine Murtinu, head of the ward at Erriora (*maiore de scolca d'Erriora*); Pedru de Scanu, his nephew, and lord Arçoco de Scanu.

213.
Lord Goantine Murtinu made himself lay brother of Sancta Maria and donated to the church a land in Grugue de Nurake ('cross of the nuraghe'), at the top end (*capizale*) of the farm complex (*domo*) of Sancta Corona, and on the other side to the land of Sancta Anna. Witnesses: Goantine Madau, representative of the realm (*mandadore de regnu*); Goantine de Zori, and Arçoco de Barca.

214.
In the name of Lord, amen. Lord Comida de Cepera offered himself to God and Sancta Maria de Bonarcadu, [placing himself] in the hands of the prior, lord Pedru Perusinu, so that the latter, when he former died, would give him the service and the office that is given to a lay brother and would bury him in the cloister of Sancta Maria. For the salvation of his soul, he gave Sancta Maria a horse and a mare that had already given birth, a yoke of oxen, 150 sheep, and ten sows. He promised that, when he died, he will give the share (*parçone*) of one of his children, of all that he possessed: of lands vineyards and unworked lands (*saltos*), of male and female servants (*serbos et ankillas*), cattle of every size both large and small, and of horses and mares, and all that he had inside and outside his farm complex (*domo*), except for the yards (*cortes*). Witnesses: God and Holy Mary; the prior; Arçoco de Muru; lord Mariani de Cepara; lord Comida de Loy; lord Goantine de Çori; master (*maistru*) Bigenzu; Goantine Orrodellu; Arçoco de Barka; Goantine de Muru, priest of Senuski; Amira Soia, and Goantine de Funtana.

215.[89]

Conv[er]sessi do[n]nu Goa[n]tine d'O[r]ruu a D[eu]s et a s[an]c[t]a Maria de Bona[r]cadu i[n] manu dessu p[ri]ore Du[m] Brando et dessos monagos suos et dedi ta[n]do unu boe et una vacca biglada et platigait a mo[r]te sua
90r parço[n]e de unu fiiu suo de o[nn]ia cantu at avere a mo[r]te | sua de t[er]ras de binias et de o[nn]ia cantu at avere i[n]tro de domo et de foras de domo. T[e]s[te]s: Gu[n]na[r]i de Ienna, Nigola de Porta et Pedru Ma[r]ras et Goa[n]-t[ine] d[e] Po[r]ta.

216.

Co[n]v[er]saisse Goa[n]t[ine] Ladu a s[an]c[t]a Ma[r]ia de Bona[r]cadu. Gedi tando xx b[er]begues et unu boe et platigait a mo[r]te sua parzone de uno fiiu suo. T[e]s[te]s: Gu[n]nari de Ge[n]na et Goa[n]t[ine] Muzaki et Pedru Pisanu et p[ri]ore Brandu, in cuia manu mi offersi.[90]

217.[91]

In no[m]i[n]e D[omi]ni. Am[en]. Ego Goa[n]t[ine] de Çori Pilarda ke mi c[om]b[er]so a D[eu]s et a s[an]c[t]a Ma[r]ia de Bona[r]cadu p[ro] remissione dessos peccados meos i[n] manu dessu p[ri]ore Gregoriu et dessos monagos suos: assora cando mi c[om]b[er]sai dei a s[an]c[t]a Maria unu iuvu et v madrigues de porcu et platigai a morte mia parço[n]e de unu fiiu meu de o[nn]ia ca[n]tu apu avere i[n]tru de domo et foras de domo, t[er]ras et bi[n]ias, baccas et boves, capras et b[er]begues et po[r]cos et de o[nn]ia steriu i[n]tru de domo fusca a una discu. T[e]s[te]s: D[eu]s et s[an]c[t]a Maria et Trogodo[r]i Cocco, p[re]it[er]o meo et do[n]na Muscu, sa mug[er]e, et Torb[en]i U[r]rolo et Goa[n]t[ine] de Unali p[re]it[er]o de Mo[n]te acudu.

218.[92]

90v Ego Grego[r]i[us], p[ri]ore de Bonarcadu, faço regordatio[n]e | de duos ho[m]-i[n]es, ki posit iudice Pedru de Se[r]ra d'Arbaree a s[an]c[t]a Ma[r]ia de Bonarcadu, a Bera Piana et a Ioh[ann]e su fiiu, p[ro] s'a[n]i[m]a de iudice Baruso[n]e su padri et p[ro] s'a[n]i[m]a de mama mia et pro s'a[n]i[m]a mia et pro remissio[n]e dessos pecactos meos. T[e]s[te]s: do[n]nu Berna[r]du archipiscobu

89 Duplicated in entry 9.

90 This list of witnesses corresponds to that of entry 9 which, in turn, coincides partially with entry 215.

91 Duplicated in entry 10.

92 Duplicated in entries 20 and 102.

215.
Lord Goantine d'Orruu offered himself as a lay brother to God and to Sancta Maria de Bonarcadu, [placing himself] in the hands of prior Brando and his monks, and on that occasion, he donated an ox and a calf. He promised that, when he died, he will donate the share (*parçone*) of one of his children, of all that he had owned at the time of his death, of land, vineyards, and all that he had owned inside and outside of his farm (*domo*): Witnesses: Gunnari de Ienna, Nigola de Porta, Pedru Marras, and Goantine de Porta.

216.
Goantine Ladu offered himself to Sancta Maria de Bonarcadu. On that occasion, he donated twenty sheep and an ox and promised that, when he died, he will donate the share (*parçone*) of one of his children. Witnesses: Gunnari de Genna, Goantine Muzaki, Pedru Pisanu, and prior Brandu, into whose hands I place myself as a lay brother.

217.
In the name of Lord, amen. It is I, Goantine de Çori Pilarda, who offer myself to God and Sancta Maria de Bonarcadu for the remission of my sins, [placing myself] in the hands of prior Gregoriu and his monks. When he took my confession, I gave to Sancta Maria a yoke of oxen and five sows. I promised that, when I died, I will give my share (*parçone*) of one of my children, of all that I possessed at that time, inside and outside of my farm complex (*domo*): land, vineyards, cows and oxen, goats, sheep and pigs, and all the pots I had in my house, down to single bowl. Witnesses: God and Holy Mary; Trogodori Cocco, my priest; lady Muscu, his wife; Torbeni Urrolo; and Goantine de Unale, priest of Monte Acudu ('sharp hill').

218.
I, Gregorius, prior of Bonarcadu, make a record of two men whom iudike Pedru de Serra of Arbaree (Arborea) gave to Sancta Maria de Bonarcadu: Bera Piana and his son Iohanne, for the salvation of the soul of iudike Barusone, his father, and the soul of my mother, and my soul, and for the remission of my sins.

d'Arbaree, et do[n]nu Bonaco[r]su piscobu de s[an]c[t]a Iusta et do[n]nu Gu[n]na[r]i de Ie[n]na curado[r]e de pa[r]te de Miili et d[onnu] Salto[r]o de Se[r]ra et Ma[r]iani de Ba[r]ca et do[n]nu Gunari d'Uras et Goa[ntine] de Porta et Nigola de Pane et Comida Pira et Nigola de Porta.

219.[93]

Ego Gregori[us], p[ri]ore de Bona[r]cadu, faço regordatio[n]e de kertu ki fegit megu Goa[n]t[ine] Marki. Kertait megu nara[n]do: 'Kerto cu[n] su priore pro XXX porcos ke p[re]stait padre meu a s[an]c[t]a Maria i[n] su te[m]p[u]s de do[n]nu Domestigu ki mi·llos to[r]raret.' Et ego nareilli: 'padre tuo serbu de sancta Maria de Bona[r]cadu fuit et XV a[n]nos stetit in Logudore et p[er]dit su serbizu dessa domo de s[an]c[t]a Maria ki lli gitavat de serbire et pro custu serbizu ki p[er]dit li llevait custos porcos p[ro] ki kertas como.' P[er]contait do[n]nu Baruso[n]e Spanu, k'a[r]reiat corona sutta iudice de Gallure, pot-
91r esta[n]do ip[s]e ta[n]do sa te[r]ra | d'Arbaree p[ro] iustitia, si erat i[n] podestade dessu do[n]nu levare dessu fatu dessu serbu. Acordaru[n]tsi sos ho[m]i[n]es de gorona ka erat razo[n]e, ca[n]do plaguiat assu do[n]nu et in tortu et in deretu, levare dessa causa dessu serbu et usadu dessa te[r]ra d'Arbaree erat. Remasitsinde Goa[n]t[ine] Ma[r]ki pro binkidu.

Spiiadu custu kertu, kerfit Gu[n]nari de Ienna razone dessa gama de iudice a Goa[ntine] Ma[r]ki c'aviat apida a maiore. Minimait, ke no[n] potuit razo[n]e torrare si co lli kereat ip[s]e. Levar[unt]illi sas causas suas, cu[n] sa causa de iudice et bolia[n]t te[n]nellu p[er] sa p[er]sone. Getaitse Goa[n]tine Ma[r]ki a pedes dessu priore et p[re]gaitimi ki ego lu basare a iudice. Et ego p[re]gai a iudice et assos curadores, et i[ps]i p[ro] D[eu]s et p[ro] s'a[n]i[m]a sua et pro s[an]c[t]a Maria et p[ro] amore mia li p[er]donar[unt] o[nn]ia ca[n]tu li kerea[n]t. Be[n]nit Goa[ntine] Ma[r]ki a s'alta[r]i de s[an]c[t]o Zeno et iurait sup[ra] s'altare et sup[ra] sa ruge da inde in[n]anti serbire, ip[s]e et fiios suos, p[ro] serbos a s[an]c[t]a Maria de Bonarcadu usq[ue] i[n] sempit[er]nu[m]. Et p[er]donai su kertu c'aviat fatu megu p[ro] sos porcos; si p[er]una razo[n]e ipse c'aviat, p[ro] se et p[ro] calunca p[er]sona, razo[n]e ke bolisset dema[n]dari,
91v ip[s]e p[ro] tuti aviat kertadu et p[ro] tuti perdonai. | Testes: Iuanne Santesu, donnu Martinu Ze[no], donnu Petru Orsa, donnu Barusone Spanu curadore de Nurapulia, Comita de Serra Pisiore kerq[ui]dore maiore et Gu[n]na[r]i de Serra, curadore de parte de Miili, Comita de Pira, Gantine de Porta, Juanni Vulpia, Gu[n]nari de Zori de sant'Eru de Simagis.

93 Duplicated in entry 21.

Witnesses: lord Bernardu, archbishop of Arbaree (Arborea); lord Bonacorsu, bishop of Sancta Iusta; lord Gunnari de Ienna, *curadore* of the territory (*parte*) of Miili (Milis); lord Saltoro de Serra; Mariani de Barca; lord Gunari d'Uras; Goantine de Porta; Nigola de Pane; Comida Pira; and Nigola de Porta.

219.

I, Gregorius, prior of Bonarcadu, make the record of the dispute that Goantine Marki had against me. He sued me, saying: 'I am suing the prior over thirty pigs which my father lent to Sancta Maria at the time of lord Domestigu, so that he may return them to me!' And I said to him: 'your father was a servant (*serbu*) of Sancta Maria de Bonarcadu, stayed for fifteen years in Logudore (Torres), and fleeced the house of Sancta Maria of the service that he was due to perform; and because of the loss of this service, he [the prior] took away these pigs for which you are now suing!' Lord Barusone Spanu, who presided over the hearing (*corona*) under the iudike of Gallure (Gallura)—who at that time ruled the land of Arbaree (Arborea)—made justice [by determining that] it was indeed in the lord's power to take the goods of his servant. The men of the hearing agreed that it was right, because the lord required, for better or worse, to take the goods of his servant, and that this was also custom of the land of Arbaree. Goantine Marki then lost.

Once this dispute was resolved, Gunnari de Ienna wanted Goantine Marki to account for the iudike's cattle, which he had in custody as an official (*maiore*); the latter was defeated, since he could not account for what he [Gunnari] asked him. They confiscated his belongings and the belongings of the iudike, and wanted to imprison him. Goantine Marki threw himself at the prior's feet and begged me to kiss the iudike for him, and I begged the iudike and the *curadores*, and they, by God and Holy Mary, and for my sake, pardoned him for all that they wanted him to account. Goantine Marki came to the altar of St Zeno and swore over the altar and over the cross that from that moment on, he and his children, as servants, would serve Sancta Maria de Bonarcadu forever. I forgave him for suing me over the pigs; he indeed on his own behalf or on behalf of other people wanted, for whatever reason, to sue the monastery over all those things, but I still forgave him. Witnesses: Iuanne Santesu; lord Martinu Zeno; lord Petru Orsa; lord Barusone Spanu, *curadore* of Nurapulia; Comita de Serra Pisiore, head counsellor (*kerquidore maiore*); Gunnari de Serra, *curadore* of the territory (*parte*) of Miili (Milis); Comita de Pira; Gantine de Porta; Juanni Vulpia, and Gunnari de Zori from Sant'Eru at Simagis (Simaxis).

220.[94]

Ego Gregorius, p[ri]ore de Bona[r]cadu. Pa[r]tivi cu[n] iudice de Gallulu. C[on]iuvedi Goa[n]t[ine] Mameli, serbu de s[an]c[t]a Maria de Bonarcadu cun Maria de Lee, ankilla de iudice de Gall[ulu]. Feger[unt] duos fiios: Cipari et Iusta. Clesia levait a Cipari et iudice levait a Iusta. Testes: Nigola de Pani et Comida Pira et Goantine de Porta a[r]m[en]ta[r]iu dessu archipiscobu.

221.[95]

Ego Furadu Birdis, ki mi converso ego et mug[ere] mia Iusta Kecalis, a boluntade de pari, in manu de D[eu]s et de s[an]c[t]a Maria de Bonarcadu et dessu [priore] donnu N[icolau et dessos] managos suos pro sa vita et p[ro] sa morte. Ponimus omnia appidu cantu amus et cantu amus poter acatare fina assa morte nostra: domos et corte ki am[us] in sa villa de Senuski, t[er]ras et binias et causa ca[n]ta am[us] avere i[n]tro de domo et foras de domo, totu lu damus a s[an]c[t]a Maria de Bonarcadu.

94 Duplicated in entry 22.

95 Duplicated in entry 23.

220.

I, Gregorius, prior of Bonarcadu, made a division [of servants] with the iudike of Gallulu (Gallura). Goantine Mameli, servant (*serbu*) of Sancta Maria de Bonarcadu, married Maria de Lee, servant (*ankilla*) of the iudike of Gallulu; they had two children: Cipari and Iusta. The church took Cipari and the iudike took Iusta. Witnesses: Nigola de Pane, Comida Pira, and Goantine de Porta, administrator (*armentariu*) of the archbishop.

221.

I, Furadu Birdis, with my wife Iusta Kekali, by mutual consent, make myself a lay brother, [committing myself] in the hands of God and Sancta Maria de Bonarcadu, and of the prior lord Nicolau and his monks for life and death. We give all that we possess and have and all that we will be able to collect and acquire until the day of our death: the farm complexes (*domos*) and farmyard (*corte*) that we have in the village (*billa*) of Senuski (Sinuski), lands and vineyards and all that we will be able to have inside and outside the farm. We give it all to Sancta Maria de Bonarcadu.

The Carta de Logu *of Arborea*

 | DOI:10.1163/9789004750951_006

Introduction to the Text and Translation

The *incunabulum* of the *Carta de Logu* of Arborea is held at Biblioteca Universitaria di Cagliari (BUC Inc. 230). It comprises fifty-four parchment folios written in a clear bookhand dating from the final two decades of the fifteenth century. A facsimile version of the *incunabulum* was produced as *Carta de Logu* by Antonina Scanu, and an edition was published by Giulia Murgia, *Carta de Logu d'Arborea secondo l'editio princeps*. The lines on each folio are here indicated by a superscript numeral.

Text

Proemio di Eleonora.

1r (1)Cum sciò siat causa qui su acrescimentu et exaltamentu dessas provincias, rexio[n]es et terras desce[n]dant et bengiant dae sa iusticia et qui per issos bonos capidulos sa superbia dessos reos et malvagios hominis si affrenent et constringhant, ad ciò qui sos bonos et puros et innocentes pozant viver et istare i[n]ter issos reos ad seguritades pro paura dessas penas e issos bonos prossa vertudi dessu amore siant tottu hobedie[n]tes assos capidulos et ordi[n]ame[n]tos de custa Carta de Loghu, imperò nos Elionora, pro issa gracia de De[us] iuyghissa de Arbaree, contissa de Ghociani et bisco[n]tissa de Baso, desiderando qui sos fideles et subdictos nostros dessu rennu nostru de Arbaree siant informados de capidulos et ordiname[n]tos prossos quales pozant vivere et si pozant conservare in sa via dessa viridadi et dessa iusticia et in bono, pacifichu et tranquillu istadu ad honore de Deus omnipotente et dessa gloriosa Virgini Madonna sancta Maria mama sua et pro co[n]servare sa iusticia et pacifichu, tranquillu et bonu istadu dessu pobulu dessu rennu nostru p[re]dicto et dessas ecclesias, regiones echesiastighas et dessos lieros et bonos ho[min]is et pobulu tottu dessa dicta terra nostra et dessu rennu de Arbaree, fachim[us] sas ordi[n]atio[n]es et capidulos infrascriptos, sos qualis bolem[us] et comandamus exp[re]samenti qui si deppiant attenne et oservare pro legie per ciaschaduno dessu Iuyghadu nostru de Arbaree perdittu in iudiciu et exstra.

(2)Sa Cartha de Loghu, sa quali cum grandissimo [sinnu] et providime[n]to fudi facta per issa bo[n]a memoria de iuighi Margiani padre nostru, in qua directu iuyghi de Arbaree, no[n] essendo correcta per ispaciu de .XVI. annos passados, commo, per multas varietadis de te[m]pus bissognando de necessitadi corrigere·la et me[n]dari, considerando sa variedadi et mutacio[n]e dessos te[m]pos qui suntu istadus seghidus poscha et issa conditione dessos ho[min]is qui est istadu dae tandu i[n]noghi multu permutada, et plus per qui ciaschuno est plus inquenivili assu ma-
1v | lu fageri qui no[n] assu benedessa replubigha sardischa, cum deliberadu consigiu illa corrigem[us] et fagem[us] et mutam[us] dae bene in megius et comandam[us] qui si deppiant observare integrame[n]te dae ssa suprascripta die innantes per issu modo infrascripto, ciò est:

Ca[pidulu] I. De qui offenderet sa sengoria.

(1)Ordinamus qui [si] alcuna persona tratarit et consenterit qui nos over alcuno figiu nostru over donna nostra o figios [de figios] no[st]ros o donna issoro esseremus offesidos o faghirint offender et consentire[n]t qui esserem[us]

Preface of Eleanor

(1)Since the prosperity and increase of provinces, regions, and lands are the effect and outcome of justice, and since, through good dispositions, the pride of the guilty and of evil-doers is curbed and suppressed so that the fear of punishment may allow the righteous, honest, and innocent to live and be among the guilty with security, and that the righteous, by virtue of love, may all then be obedient to the articles and ordinances of this *Carta de Logu*. For all this we, Eleanor, by the grace of God, iudikessa (*iuyghissa*) of Arborea, countess (*contissa*) of Ghociani (Goceano) and viscountess (*biscontissa*) of Baso (Bas), desiring that our vassals and subjects of our realm of Arborea may have notion and knowledge of the articles and ordinances by which they live and are kept in the way of truth and justice, and in a fine, peaceful and tranquil state, to the honour of Almighty God and of the glorious Virgin Holy Mary, His Mother, to maintain justice and a peaceful, tranquil and good condition of the people of our aforesaid realm; and also for the churches, ecclesiastical dioceses and of free and upright men, and of all the people of our said land and of the realm of Arborea, we make the ordinances and following articles, which we will expressly order to be observed, adhering to them as valid law in force for every person of the our said realm of Arborea, in judgement and extrajudicially.

(2)The *Carta de Logu* which, with great discernment and provision, was made by the good memory of iudike (*iuyghi*) Mariano our father as the rightful iudike of Arborea, not having been amended for a lapse of time of sixteen years, now, because of the change of times necessarily needing amendment and modification, taking into account the diversity and change of the times that have much altered since then until now, and still more because of the fact that everyone is more inclined to do evil than good for Sardinian public affairs (*replubigha*), with deliberate counsel we amend and factually update and improve it and order that it should be observed in full, from the said day forward, in the manner hereafter written, namely:

Article 1. About those who shall cause offence to the lordship.(1)

We order that if any person shall conspire and allow us or any of our sons or a woman, or a child of our children or their wives to be the subject of an offence, or shall cause them to be offended and permit us to be offended, he is to be

offesidos, deppiant esser postu supra uno carro et attanagiadu per totu sa terra n[ost]ra d'Aristanis et poscha si deppiat dughiri attanagando·lu infini assa furcha et innie si furchit qui 'ndi morgiat. (2)Et issos benes suos totu deppiant esser appropiadus assa corte nostra dummodo qui ssa donna sua coyada assa sardischa over a dodas no[n]perdat sa parti sua in casu qui non si achaptarit culpabili in alcunu attu. (3)Et si alcuna persone qui esseret in su dictu trattadu lu fagere[n]t ad inte[n]der a nnos inantes qui nos illu ischirem[us], siat·illi perdonadu sa dicta pena et no 'ndi siat ponidu et depiat aviri p[re]miu et gracia dessu espalesari qui at aver fattu dessu dictu trattadu.

II. De qui tractarit traycioni o desonore.

(1)Item ordinam[us] qui si alcuna persona tractarit o consenterit causas alcunas prossa quali nos perdirem[us] honore, terra over castellu de cussos qui am[us] hoe ho de cussos qui aquistarem[us] dae como inantes deppiant esser istraxinad[us] a coha de cavallo per totu sa terra nostra d'Aristanis et poscha i[n]fini assa furcha et inie si i[n]furchet qui '[n]di morgiat et issos benes suos tottu approp[ri]ad[us] assu re[n]no, (2)si verame[n]te qui in casu su dictu traditore avirit mugere et esseret coyada assu modu sardischu, que sa dicta mugere appat sa parti sua senza ma[n]came[n]tu alcuno, secundu qui i[n] su dictu capidulo si co[n]tenet. (3)Et si avirit appidu mughere per inantes assa sardischa dessa quali avirit alcuno figio o ffigios, cussu figiu o ffigios come[n]te et heredes de cussa mama issoro appant et aver deppiant sa parti issoro dessos 2r benes p[re]dictos secundu ussanza sardisca | senza mancame[n]tu alcuno, secu[n]du qu'est naradu de supra prossos atteros. (4)Et si esseret coyada a dodas a modo pisanischu su simili sas dodas suas senza alcuno manchame[n]tu, pro qui no[n] est ragione qui issos perdant per culpa et defectu dessu padre et dessu maridu. (5)Et semper si inte[n]dat qui ciaschuno creditore qui avirit at riciver i[n]antes que su dictu maleficiu esseret perpetradu et factu, qui siat paghadu de tottu que iustamente at mostrare qui appat a reciver.

III. Qui ochirit homini.

(1)Volem[us] et ordinam[us] que si alcuna persona ochirit ho[min]i et est·indi co[n]fesso in su iudiciu over co[n]vinto secundu que ssu ordini dessa ragoni coma[n]dat, siat·illi segada sa testa in su loghu dessa iusticia per modu qui 'ndi morgiat et pro di[n]ari alcuno no[n] campit, (2)salvu si su dictu ho[min]i hochirit deffende[n]do a si, sa quali deffensa deppiat provari et mostrare legit

placed on a cart and, bound, led through all our land of Oristano (*d'Aristanis*), and is then to be led, still bound, to the gallows and there to be hanged in such a manner that he dies. (2)And his property is to be acquired by our court in such a manner that the wife [of the offender] who is married to him according to Sardinian jurisdiction or by marriage contract according to the dotal regime shall not, providing that she is not found to be implicated in any action, lose her share. (3)And if any person who was implicated in such a conspiracy should make it known to us before we learn of it, let the said punishment be condoned and let him not be punished, and let him be granted reward and pardoned for the damage she shall have caused by the said slander (*trattatu*).

Article 2. About those who shall plot treason or dishonour.
(1)Item: we order that if any person conspires or allows there to be some cause for which we should lose honour, land or a castle among those which we now possess or which we shall acquire from now, he is to be dragged by the tail of a horse through all our land of Oristano and then to the gallows where he is to be hanged so that he dies, and all his property is acquired by the realm. (2)If indeed it be the case that the said traitor has a wife with whom he has contracted a marriage according to Sardinian custom, let the said wife retain her due share without anything being taken from her according to what is contained in the said article.(3) If he has previously had a wife according to Sardinian law, by whom he has had one or more children, that child or those children, as heirs of that mother of theirs, have and should have their due share of the aforesaid property, according to Sardinian legal usage without anything being taken from them, in line with what is said above for similar cases.(4) And if she had contracted a marriage in the Pisan dowry tradition, let it proceed similarly with respect to her dowry, without anything being taken from her, since it is not right that they should suffer any loss through the fault or defect of their father and husband. (5)And it shall always be understood that each creditor, who has to receive that which is due to him, shall be paid whatever according to justice, and shall prove that which he is entitled to receive, relative to the time before the said crime was perpetrated and committed.

Article 3. Who kills a man.(1)
We wish and we order that if any person shall kill a man and either confesses himself guilty of it in court (*in su loghu dessa iusticia*) or is convicted of it according to the principles that the law (*sa ragioni*) requires, he shall be beheaded at the place of justice in such manner that he dies, and that he cannot escape such punishment by payment of money (2)except if the said man has killed in self-defence, which he must prove legitimately through [the testi-

timame[n]te per bonos ho[min]is infra dies .xv. dae ssa die qui l'at esser comandado per issu arme[n]targiu nostru de Loghu over per atero officiali nostru at qui sa dicta causa esseret comissida. (3)Et in casu qui provarit aver mortu su dictu ho[min]i deffende[n]do a ssi come[n]te est naradu de supra no[n] siat mortu et pena alcuna no[n] patischat et no[n] paghit. (4)Et si per ve[n]tura avenerit qui pl[us] ho[min]is essere[n]t in co[m]pagnia de pari et unu de cussos hochirit alcuno artero ho[min]i et issos ateros qui no[n] essere[n]t in culpa assa dicta morte no[n] benere[n]t assa corte et no[n] si ischulparint legittimame[n]te que issus no[n] furunt culpabilis ne[n] co[n]sentivilis assa morte de cussu tali ho[min]i infra tres dies, qui issos siant ponid[us] et co[n]de[m]pnad[us] a morte come[n]te et issu qui avirit mortu su dictu ho[min]i pro qui nara[n]t sas leges 'age[n]tes et co[n]sentie[n]tes pari pe[n]a puniuntu'. (5)Et in casu qui alcuno homi[n]i hochirit alcuno attero ho[min]i inprovisame[n]te et no[n] cum animu deliberadu et no[n] pe[n]sadame[n]te ma pro causa fortunabili secundu qui solint avenne multos desastros, volem[us] qui in tali casu istet et istari depiat at arbitriu et correctione nostra.

IV. Idem.

(1)Constituim[us] et ordinam[us] qui si alcuno ho[min]i hochirit at alcuno atteru ho[min]i minando over corre[n]do cavallo i[n] plaza o in bia o in campu
2v o in silva o i[n] attero modu, qui | cussu ho[min]i qui avirit mortu su dittu ho[min]i siat mortu, si parit ver et simili assus bonus hom[i]nis et iuhigantis de sa corona qui sientimente et cum animo deliberado illu appat mortu. (2)Et si cussu homini qui adi aviri mortu su dictu homini gasi minandu cavallu come[n]ti est naradu de supra no[n] l'averit mortu a voluntadi sua et siat istadu disastro, siat tentu et missidu im p[re]gioni et siat in ambitrio nostru de illu conde[m]pnari pro sa dita morti.

V. De venenu.

(1)Item ordinam[us] qui si alcuna persona maschiu o femina darit ad mandigare over a biere alcuno venenu malu o tosighu dessu quali poderet morri su homini over sa femi[n]a a qui esseret dadu, si 'ndi esseret confessu over qui illi esseret provadu legittimame[n]ti, et morret·inde su homini over sa femina ad qui esseret dadu, si est homi[n]i cussu qui adi fattu su dictu mali, siat infurcadu qui 'ndi morgiat. (2)Et si esseret femi[n]a, siat arsida et non campit pro dinari alcuno. (3)Et si cussu ad qui si lu darit su dito toscho over venenu no 'ndi morrit ni avirit mancame[n]tu dessa persona, siat·illi segada sa manu destra et pro dinari alcuno non campit qui non li siat segada. (4)Et issu simili siat conde[m]pnadu cussu qui si accatarit in culpa et in co[n]sentime[n]tu de tali casu. (5)Et inte[n]dat·si qui cussu qui at aviri comissidu su dictu maleficiu

mony of] trusted men (*bonos hominis*) within fifteen days from the day when it shall be communicated to him by our senior judicial official (*armentargiu de Loghu*) or by another official of ours to whom such a case has been assigned. (3)And in the event that he can prove he killed the said man in self-defence, as aforesaid, he shall incur neither capital nor financial punishment. (4)And if by chance it happens that several men act in company with each other, and one of them kills someone, and the others who are not at fault in the alleged death do not come to the court and legitimately exonerate themselves within three days, and do not affirm that they were not consenting in regard to the death of the said man, let them be punished and sentenced to death as well as he who killed the said man; for the laws say that 'perpetrators and assistants suffer equal punishment.' (5)In the case that a man kills any other man without premeditation and not with a deliberate mind nor intentionally but by fortuitous cause, so as many events often occur unexpectedly, we wish that in such a case the fact and the punishment relating thereto remain and should remain at our discretion.

Article 4. Idem.
(1)We decree and order that if any man kills any other man by leading a horse or by riding it in the square or in the street or in the country or in the woods or in any other way, then the man who shall have killed the said man shall be put to death, if it seems likely to the trusted men (*bonos hominis*) and jurors of the court (*sa corona*) that he knowingly and deliberately killed him. (2)And if that man who shall have killed the aforesaid man by leading the horse as said and shall not have killed him wilfully and the matter was accidental, let him be arrested and brought to prison (*pregioni*), and let it be in our discretion to condemn him for the said death.

Article 5. On poison.
(1)Item: we order that if any person, male or female, gives to eat or drink any malefic or toxic poison of which the man or woman to whom it is administered may die, if he shall have made confession of it or if it shall be legitimately proved to him, and the man or woman to whom it has been administered shall die of it, if he who has committed the said evil deed is a man let him be hanged so that he may die. (2)And if she is a woman, let her be burned and not escape punishment by any financial payment. (3)And if he to whom the said venom or poison is administered shall not come to death nor have any maiming in his person, let his [the offender's] right hand be amputated and he shall not escape for any financial payment the mutilation of his hand. (4)And, in like manner, let he who was in guilt and complicitly in connection with such a case be condemned. (5)And it is understood that he who shall have done the said misdeed

paghet et pagare deppiat sas dispesas, manchamentos, dampnos et interesses qui at aviri appidu et i[n]cursu chussu a quini esseret dadu su ditu venenu, gasi de mehigos come[n]ti et de meighinas et ateras causas necessarias, a provigione de duos o tres bonus hominis electos pro issa corti.

VI. De tenne su malefactore.
(1)Volem[us] et ordinam[us] qui si alcuna persona esseret morta in alcuna villa de foras o in confines et habitationes de sa villa, siant tenudus sus iuradus dessa dita villa de provare et de tenne su malufactore et de 'llu batire tentu assa corti nostra infra unu mese pro faghire·nde sa iusticia. (2)Et in casu que su malufactore non tenere[n]t et no lu batire[n]t assa corti nostra infra su dictu
3r te[m]pus, paghint sos iurad[us] totu et issos ho- | minis dessa dita villa pro sa maquicia et pro sa neglige[n]tia issoro, pro que non te[n]sierunt su ho[min]i, l[ib]r[a]s ducentas si est sa villa manna et issa villa pixia paghit l[ib]r[a]s .C. (3)Et si cussu ho[min]i qui avirit mortu su ho[min]i fuirit et no[n] si poderet aviri infra su dito te[m]pus de uno mese, siat isbandidu dae sas terras nostras et issos benes suos totu siant confiscad[us]assa corte nostra, reservando p[e]rò sas ragiones de sas mugeres et de sos figios que avirint dae atera mugere qui non avirint appidu sa parti pertinenti ad issos pro parti de sa prima mugheri. (4)Et similime[n]ti si inte[n]dat salvas sas ragio[n]es de sos creditores qui avire[n]t ad ricivir supra sos benes de cussos. (5)Et si per alcuno te[m]pus cussu ho[min]i qui avirit mortu su ho[min]i beneret in forza nostra non esendo fidado, siat·illi tagiada sa testa per modu qui '[n]di morgiat et nie[n]te de min[us] ogne persona illu pozat offendere in persone et dare·li morte senza incurrere pe[n]a ne maquicia alcuna duranti su dictu te[m]p[us] de su isbandime[n]tu suo.

VII. Qui esseret isbandidu.
(1)Constituim[us] et ordinam[us] qui si alcuno esseret isbandidu dae sas terras nostras pro homicidiu over per alcuna atera occasio[n]e pro sa quale deberet morre et beneret ad alcuna dessas villas nostras senza essere fidadu et basadu per nos, siant tenudos sos iurados et ho[min]is de cussa villa de te[n]nere·llu et batiri·lu a sa corte nostra. (2)Et si non lu te[n]nere[n]t et batirint secundu que est naradu de supra, paghint sa villa manna assa corte nostra pro sa neglige[n]sia issoro l[ib]r[a]s .XXV. et ipsa villa pizina l[ib]r[a]s .XV., et iso maiore de cussa villa de per se libras .X. et ciascuno iurado l[ib]r[a]s .V. (3)Et ciò s'inte[n]dat si sus ho[min]is de cussa tali villa illu ischiri[n]t et alc[u]no ho[min]i de sa dita villa illu recivirit et receptarit cussus talis isbandid[us] pal-

shall pay and must pay the expenses, losses, damages, and interest which the person who had taken the poison would have had or paid: both in relation to physicians and to medicines and other necessary things, according to the decision of two or three trusted men (*bonos hominis*) elected by the court (*issa corti*).

Article 6. On the capture of the wrongdoer.
(1)We wish and order that if any person shall be killed in any village, outside or within the boundaries of the areas set apart for the cultivation of the said village itself, those under oath (*sos iurados*) of the said village shall be required to prove the guilt of the wrongdoer and to arrest him and bring him captive to our court within one month so that justice may be done. (2)And in the event that they do not keep the wrongdoer under arrest and do not bring him to our court within the said time, let all those under oath and the men of the said village pay the financial penalty due and for their negligence, inasmuch as they have not caught the man: two hundred lire (*libras*) if it is a large village, and if it is a small village they shall pay one hundred lire. (3)And if that man who committed the homicide should escape and could not be captured within the time of one month, let him be banished from our lands, and all his property be forfeited to our court, safeguarding, however, the rights of the wives and children whom he had from his previous wife [to the present one], if the latter have not had their due share from the first wife [their mother]. (4)And similarly it is to be understood as without prejudice to the rights of creditors who have to collect [dues] on their property. (5)And if at any time that man who has committed the homicide should come into our power without being endowed with entrusted leave, let him be beheaded so that he may die. Nonetheless, any person may aggrieve him in person and put him to death without incurring the penalty, even financial, of punishment during the said period of his absconding.

Article 7. Those who are banished.
(1)We decree and order that if any person be banished from our lands for homicide or for some other reason for which he is to be sentenced to death, and should come to any of our villages without our trust and without being kissed [as a greeting], those under oath (*sos iurados*) and men of that village shall be bound to arrest him and bring him to our court. (2)If they do not arrest him and bring him in accordance with the aforesaid, let a large village pay to our court for their negligence twenty-five lire, and a small village fifteen lire, and the mayor (*maiore*) of that village ten lire for himself, and for each juror five lire. (3)And this is to be understood if the men of such a village have knowledge of it, and if any man of the said village received and gave shelter to those

isime[n]ti et at fura et darit·illi aiuda, co[n]sigiu o ffavore, si 'lli est provadu, paghit assu rennu l[ib]r[a]s .c. (4)Et si no[n] paghat isso o atero ho[min]i pro se istet in presone ad voluntadi nostra, salvu si cussu isbandidu beneret a domo de sa mogere over dessu padri o de sa mamma o dessu avio et avia o dessu figio o ffigia o dessu fradi o dessa sorre carrali. (5)Que cussas persones non siant tenudos assa maquicia dessas p[re]ditas liras chentu in tottu ne in parti.

3v VIII. Qui si ochiret.

(1)Item ordinamus qui si alcuna persona si hochieret isu istesu ape[n]sadame[n]ti in alcuno modo, si deppiat istrasinare et infurchare in alcuna furcha que si deppiat faghere a prope dessa villa hui s'at ochier. (2)Et issu officiali de cussa villa deppiat fagheri iscriviri totus sus benes suos infini ad atero comandame[n]tu nostru, et simigantemente a i[n]vestigare et p[re]ghontare assos iurad[us] et bonus ho[min]is de cussa villa dessa occagione pro iteu cussu ho[min]i s'at esser mortu et icussu p[re]gontu ad fagheri scriviri, su quale pregontu deppiat batiri a nnos de p[re]sente ad ciò qui nos illu pozamus mostrare assos savios nostros pro co[n]sigiare·nos·inde cussu qui '[n]d'am[us] aviri a ffagheri dessos dittos benes.

IX. De feridas.

(1)Volem[us] et ordinam[us] qui si alcuno homini at ferre s'unu at s'ateru de fferro o de fusti o de pedra o de manu over de atera causa dundi essirit sambini et no '[n]di perderet me[m]bru, si 'nd'est binchidu paghit assu rennu prossa ferida de ferro infra dies .xv. de c'at esser iuyghadu l[ib]r[a]s .xxv., et si no[n]paghat siat ischovado per issa terra. (2)Et pro sa ferida de fusti over de pedra o de atera ca[us][a] dundi esserit sanbani, paghit l[ib]r[a]s .xv. (3)Et si no[n] paghat infra dies .xv. de c'at esser iuigadu, siat afrustadu over iscovadu per issa terra sec[u]ndu qu'est narrado de subra, salvu si sa ferida si fagherit i[n] sa faghi et romannet illoy alcuno signu notabili et de creder. (4)Qui paghit in cussu casu l[ib]r[a]s .L. i[n]fra dies .xv. de c'at esser iuyghadu, et si no[n] paghat fazat·si·lli su simili signu c'at aviri factu i[n] su simili loghu. (5)Et si sambini no '[n]di esserit in sas dittas feridas de ferro o de fusti o de pedra over de atera causa, paghit dae l[ib]r[a]s .v. infini in l[ib]r[a]s .x., co[n]sideradu sa qualidadi dessa persona qu'est offensida et qui offendet et issu modu dessu ecessu

such men who were banished, overtly or covertly, and gave them aid, advice, or favour, if it be proved to him, then he shall pay to the realm one hundred lire. (4)And if he, or others for him, does not pay, he shall remain in prison at our will unless the said banished man comes to the house of his wife or father or mother or grandfather or grandmother or son or daughter or brother or sister, (5)so that in a case as this, such persons shall not incur, in whole or in part, the financial penalty of the aforesaid one hundred lire.

Article 8. Those who kill themselves.
(1)Item: we order that if any person shall deliberately procure death for himself, his body shall be dragged and hanged in some gallows which shall be erected near the village where he had killed himself. (2)And the official of the said village shall record all his property until otherwise ordered by us, and similarly he shall hold an inquiry and submit to question those under oath (*sos iurados*) and trusted men (*bonus hominis*) of that village about the reason why that man killed himself; and that question he shall cause to be recorded in writing, and he shall then bring it to us immediately so that we may show it to our experts (*assos savios nostros*) for advice about what we shall do with the said property.

Article 9. Concerning wounds.
(1)We wish and we order that if any man shall wound another either with an iron weapon or with a stick or a stone or with his hands or in any other way such that it draws blood without, however, losing any member of the body, if he shall be defeated [in court], then he shall pay to the realm, for the wound of an iron weapon, within fifteen days from the time when he is judged, twenty-five lire. If he does not pay, he shall be taken publicly around the country and whipped with the strokes of a broom scourge. (2)And for a wound caused by a stick, or by a stone, or by anything which draws blood, then he shall pay fifteen lire. (3)And if he does not pay within fifteen days from the time he shall be judged, let him be whipped or flogged with a broom by taking him publicly about the country according to the foresaid, except in the case where the wound is made on the face and there remains any visible mark thereon which may be believed [to be caused by the said wound], (4)he shall pay in that case fifty lire within fifteen days from the time that he shall be judged. And if he does not pay, a scar similar to that which he has caused to the other shall be made on him, in the corresponding place [of the body]. (5)And if from the said wounds, from an iron weapon or stick or stone or any other weapon, there was no spilling of blood, he shall pay a sum from five to ten lire, in relation to the condition of the person who is aggrieved and of the person who takes offence, and to the manner in which the offence was committed. (6)And if he does not

comissu. (6)Et si no[n] paghat i[n]fra dies .xv., afruste[n]t·illu per issa terra. (7)Et si alcunu delictu ave[n]net per dixastro et qui no[n] esseret fatu ape[n]sadame[n]te, bolem[us] qui siat in arbitriu nostru et de bonos ho[min]es per nos depudados, come[n]te e[st] narradu de subra. (8)Et si [pro] alc[u]na dessas ditas feridas si 'ndi perderet me[m]bro per modu qui su me[m]bro indi andarit
4r a tter[r]a over qui '[n]di esseret semmu, perdat su simiga[n]te me[m]-|bro et pro dinari nexuno no[n] campit. (9)Et si esseret me[m]bro p[ri]ncipali debilitadu, paghit l[ib]r[a]s .c. senza misericordia alc[u]na, et prossu me[m]bru particulari [qui] esseret debilitadu paghit dae l[ib]r[a]s .c. in giosso at arbitriu no[st]ru over de bonos ho[min]is pro nos deputados. (10)Et semper si inte[n]dat si 'llu faghit defende[n]do a ssi et provarit·illu legitti[m]ame[n]te qui no '[n]di siat tenudo a ppe[n]a alc[u]na. (11)Et si alc[u]na persona ferret dessa manu in sa faghi over tirarit at alc[u]no sos pilos over qui po[n]net at attiri sas man[us] in su pect[us]over qui 'lli istrazarit sos pannos over qui 'llu getarit a tter[r]a over qui fagherit a chalchis et non lu fagherit defende[n]do a ssi et sanbani de ciò no[n] essirit paghit assu re[n]nu l[ib]r[a]s tres infini in l[ib]r[a]s ses, co[n]siderandu sa qualidadi dessa persona offesida o qui ofe[n]det. (12)Et si no[n] paghat, istet in p[re]gioni a voluntadi nostra, salvu si sa persona ferida esseret mugeri o ffigiu o ffigiu de figiu o fradri carrali o sorre o nebodi de fradi over de sorri over famigiali suo [qui istarit a pani et a vinu suo over discipulu] qui istarit at i[m]parare, qui cussu qui 'll'at ferre, essendo per issu fatu modu qu'est naradu de subra, illu pozat batiri et castigare aco[n]zadame[n]ti et i[n] cussu actu no '[n]di paghit pe[n]a alc[u]na. (13)Et i[n]te[n]dat·si qui pe[n]a alcuna no[n] paghit si 'lli bogharit sambini dae ssa bucha over dae ssu nassu over qui 'llu ischarrafiarit in sa fachi o i[n] atera parti dessa persona sua qui danno no '[n]di avirit. (14)Et simili si inte[n]dat dessus tudores et curadores de alcunos mi[n]ores qui castigharint et batirint cussos qui instant supta cura et tudoria issoro. (15)Qui no '[n]di paghint pe[n]a alcuna castigando·l[us] per issu ditu modu. (16)Et si alc[u]na persona fagerit dessas ditas maquicias qui suntu naradas de subra et si paghi indi podere[n]t et bolere[n]t fagueri chun icussa persona at qui avirit offesidu deppiat be[n]ne daenante dessu officiali maiore de cussa terra over co[n]trada infra dies .xv. c'at esser facta sa dicta maquicia et in presentia dessu dictu officiali si fazat sa paghi. (17)Et nos, pro amore de Deus, perdonam[us] prossa dicta paghi fata sa quarta parti de cussa maquicia qui at deber paghare.

x. De feridas.

(1)Constituim[us] et ordinam[us] subra sos maleficios et feridas i[n]certas q[u]i si alc[u]na persona esseret ferida de nocte te[m]p[us] over ancu ad de die
4v et no[n] loy averit testi[m]ongios, no[n] siat cretidu. | (2)Et ciascuna persona

pay within fifteen days, he shall be whipped while being publicly taken about the country. (7)And if any offence occurs unintentionally and is not deliberately committed, we wish it to be at our discretion and that of trusted men (*bonos hominis*) chosen by us, as aforesaid. (8)And if, by any of the said wounds, the offended should lose a member in such a manner that such a member falls to the ground, or he is maimed by it, then he who has caused the offence shall lose the corresponding member and shall not be able to escape by payment of money. (9)And if it be a principal limb that of which the offended is maimed, let him pay one hundred lire without mercy of any kind; if it be a secondary member, let him pay from one hundred lire or less at our discretion or at the discretion of the trusted men (*bonos hominis*) deputed by us. (10)And it is always understood that if the wounding is done in self-defence and he can legitimately prove it, then he should pay no penalty. (11)And if any person wounds with his hands in the face or pulls at a person's hair or brings his hands to his chest or tears his clothes or throws him to the ground or kicks him, and this he has not done in self-defence, and there is no spillage of blood, then he shall pay to the realm from three to six lire in relation to the condition of the one who remains aggrieved and the one who offends. (12)And if he does not pay he shall remain in prison at our discretion, except if the person offended be his wife, or child, or grandchild, or brother, or sister, or nephew on his brother's or sister's side, or family member of his who is fed and maintained by him, or an apprentice, for he who shall have inflicted injury in the aforementioned way may beat and chastise him freely, and for such action he shall pay no penalty. (13)And it is to be understood that he shall not pay any penalty if he should produce a spilling of blood from his mouth or nose, or if he should scratch him in the face or other part of his body without doing him harm. (14)And similarly let it be understood of the guardians and curators of minors who chastise and beat those under their guardianship and care (15)that they shall not pay any penalty if it is thereby done for [just] chastisement. (16)And if any person commits any of the above offences, and if he can or will make peace with that person whom he has aggrieved, then he must come before the senior official of that land or district (*dessu officiali maiore de cussa terra over contrada*) within fifteen days from the time such an offence is committed and make peace before the official. (17)And we, for the love of God, condone, by virtue of the said peace which shall be made, the fourth part of the said fine which he shall have to pay.

Article 10. Concerning wounds.

(1)We decree and order concerning misdeeds and uncertain wounds [that is, whose responsibility remains undetermined] that if any person be injured at night, or even by day, and does not have witnesses, then he shall not be believed.

qui siat de bona famma et siat feridu siat cretidu a sagrame[n]tu suo hui non avirit testimongios ecceptuadas issas p[re]dictas causas et a provisioni dessu officiali et dessu consigiu suo. (3)Et si sa persona achusanti o ppacie[n]te no esseret de bona famma et achusarit persona qui esseret de bona fama, istet a provigione dessu officiali et consigiu suo p[re]dictu. (4)Et si aveneret una brigha i[n]ter duos over pl[us] personas qui feridas o percussiones illoy inchurrere[n]t et non si podere[n]t provare discretame[n]te quales de cussos averit factu sa brigha, sa conde[m]pnagione qui si avenit assa corte paghi[n]t totu, ciò est cussas personas qui essere[n]t istadas assa dita brigha participantes, pro quantas feridas s'anti acaptare. (5)Et i[n] cussas causas si intendat in feridas qui non bie siat morte ne[n]perdime[n]tu de me[m]bro. (6)Et a ciò qui, secundu sos colp[us] sas laxas, cussos assos quales at esser comissidu per nos las pozant atazari secundu su colpu over colp[us] qui ant esser fact[us], su officiale qui at mandare sas maquicias las deppiat ordi[n]a[da]me[n]te mandari scriptas, declarando su colpu qui at esser mannu et issu colpu qui at esser pizinu.

xi. Asaltegu.

(1)Item ordinam[us] qui si alcuna persona asaghirit ad alcuna persona atera cum arma assa domo hui istarit o in terra o in vigna sua hui esseret pro faguiri factos suos, paghit pl[us] de cussu qui est ordi[n]adu de supra dessas maquicias, ciò est si lu offendet i[n] persona s[oldo]s .c., et si no lu offendet paghit s[oldo]s .l. (2)Et si lu assaghirit senza arma ad alc[u]no dessus ditos loghus et offenderet·illu, paghit l[ib]r[a]s .iii.; et si non lu offenderet, paghit pro sa asaghida s[oldo]s .xxx. (3)Et si in atero loghu chi de cussus qui sunt naradus de supra illu assaghirit et offe[n]deret·illu, paghit s[oldo]s .xl.; et si non lu offenderet, paghit s[oldo]s xx. (4)Et ciò s'inte[n]dat si dessas dittas causas o alcuna de cussas indi esseret binchidu.

xii. Feridas.

(1)Volem[us] et ordinam[us] qui si alcuna persona esseret ferida et qui sa ferida esseret perigulosa qui si dubitarit de morti, cussu ho[min]i qui avirit factu sa dicta ferida depiat istari in p[re]gione, infini a tantu qui su meyghu over
5r meyghos ant | narre per sagramentu issoru qui cussu ho[min]i feridu siat foras de perigulu de morti pro cussa ferida, tanti cum liberatione de bonos ho[min]es. (2)Et si si dubitarit de cussa ferida, istet in p[re]gione infini .lx. dies, et passadu su dictu te[m]pus de .lx. dies, et i[n]fra su dictu temp[us] su feridu non esseret mortu, siat liberadu su delinchente dessa morti et paghit sa

(2)Anyone who is of good repute and is wounded shall be believed on swearing, if there are no witnesses, except for the above cases and at the discretion of the official and his council. (3)And if the person accusing or injured be not of good repute and the accused is a person who is of good repute, then let the matter remain at the discretion of the official and his aforesaid council. (4)And if there should happen to be a brawl between two or more persons in which injuries or beatings occurred, and they cannot be accurately proved which of these participants in the brawl initiated it, the punishment determined by the court shall be paid by all; that is, by all those who participated in the brawl, however many injuries are found. (5)And this shall remain limited in those cases in which death or loss of limb is not caused. (6)And in this regard, in accordance with the principle that the punishment should be proportional to the blows inflicted, those who are delegated by us to do so may determine the amount of the fine in relation to the blow or blows that have been inflicted. The official who is then to serve the fine shall deliver accurately written reports (*scriptas*) pertaining thereto, specifying the greater or lesser blow.

Article 11. Assault.

(1)Item: we order that if any person assaults another person with a weapon in the house where he lives, or in his land or vineyard where he is in order to attend to his business, he shall pay to a greater extent than ordered above with regard to financial penalties; that is, if he offends him in person he shall pay one hundred soldi, but if he does not offend him bodily he shall pay fifty soldi. (2)If the assault takes place without the use of a weapon in the aforementioned places and he commits an offence against the body: pay three lire; if he does not aggrieve him: pay thirty soldi for the assault. (3)And if he assaults another in places except those above mentioned and he causes an offence, he shall pay forty soldi; and if he does not cause a grievance he shall pay twenty soldi. (4)And this is to be understood if he has won [at a hearing] concerning the said cases or some of them.

Article 12. Wounds.

(1)We wish and order that if any person remains wounded and the wound endangers his life, that man who shall have inflicted such a wound shall remain in prison until the physician or physicians shall affirm under oath that such person is out of danger of death with respect to such a wound, and only by resolution of the probationers (*bonos homines*). (2)And if any doubt remains with respect to such a wound, he shall remain in prison for up to sixty days; and if, after the said time of sixty days has elapsed, the wounded person has not died, then the offender shall not incur the death penalty, but shall pay to the court a

maquicia de sa ferida assa corte. (3)Et in casu que su ferido pro ave[n]tura morret infra su dictu temp[us] de .lx. dies per mala cura et guardia et per culpa sua, et ave[n]do lassado su meychu foras de dubitu, qui cussu delinque[n]te no '[n]di morgiat, ma paghit sa maquicia de sa ferida secundu qui est naradu de supra.

xiii. Strada.

(1)Constituim[us] et ordinam[us] qui si alc[u]na persona esseret te[n]tu per robaria de strada publica et est·inde binchidu, siat inpicadu qui 'ndi morgiat in cussu loghu hoe ad avere fatu sa dicta robaria et non campit pro dinari alcuno. (2)Et in casu qui fagheret sa dita robaria foras de strada publica, zò est in villa o in campu o in saltu, sos ho[min]is de sa dicta villa hui ad fagher sa ditta robaria siant tenudos de te[n]ni cussu tali robadore et batiri·llu assa corte. (3)Et si 'nd'est binchidu, paghit assa corte l[ib]r[a]s .cc. dae sa die qui adi essere iuygadu a dies bindighi. (4)Et si no[n] paghat issu over atero ho[min]i pro se, infurche[n]t·illu qui 'ndi morgiat. (5)Et si no[n] lu tenere[n]t sos ho[min]is de cussa villa, paghit sa villa manna l[ib]r[a]s .l. et issa villa pizina l[ib]r[a]s .xxv. et isso dampno a qui ad essere factu, et nie[n]te de min[us]deppiat·illu denunciare assa corte infra dies .xv. et siat isbandidu dae sas terras nostras. (6)Et si per alc[u]no te[m]p[us] benneret in forza nostra, paghit sa suprascripta pena si sa dita robaria avirit fatu foras de strada publicha. (7)Et si no[n] paghat siat iusticiadu in persona secundu qui est ordinadu in su p[re]senti capidulu et issos benes suos si co[n]fischint assa corte, reservando sas ragio[n]es de sas mugeres secundu qui per inantis est narradu in casu qui esseret iusticiadu in persona.

xiiii. De inquisitione.

(1)Item ordinam[us] qui si no[n] illoe avirit testimongios, qui su officiali procedat supra sa dicta causa per via de i[n]quisitione, secundu que in su supras-
5v cripto capidulu de qui ferit si | contennet.

xv. De deli[n]quentes.

(1)Volemus et ordinam[us] qui si su dili[n]que[n]te esseret tentu per issu officiali over ho[min]is dessa co[n]trada hui esseret factu su delittu in aliguno loghu qui no[n] esseret franchu infra unu mese, qui sa co[n]trada over sa villa esseret libera dessa suprascripta maquicia. (2)Et si su officiali in hui esseret sa persona qui avirit factu su maleficio non daret su brasu suo e favore ad icussu officiali over persones qui lu requedere[n]t, siat condempnadu in sa dita maquicia.

fine relating to the wounds. (3)In the event that the wounded person should die within the said period of sixty days through lack of proper care and assistance or through his own fault, the physician (*su meychu*) having declared him out of danger, the offender shall not incur the death penalty, but shall pay a financial penalty concerning the wound in accordance with the aforesaid.

Article 13. [Robberies in the] Street.
(1)We decree and order that if any person be arrested for robbery on a public street and loses the case at court, he shall be hanged so that he shall die in the very place where he had committed the said robbery and shall not escape by payment of any money. (2)And in a case where he has committed an alleged robbery away from a public street, that is, within a village, or in a field, or in the countryside (*saltu*), the men of the said village where he had committed the said robbery shall be bound to arrest the alleged robber and to bring him to court. (3)And if he loses the case in court, let him pay to the court two hundred lire within fifteen days from the day he is tried. (4)And if he himself does not pay, nor another person for him, let him be hanged so that he dies. (5)And if the men (*sos hominis*) of that village do not arrest him, then they have to pay fifty lire for a large village and twenty-five lire for a small village; and let [the village] make reparation for the damage to those who have suffered it, and in any case, let the village report him [the robber] to the court within fifteen days. And let him be banished from our lands. (6)And if at any time he should come into our power, let him pay the above penalty if the robbery has been done away from a public road. (7)And if he does not pay, he shall be executed in person according to that which is ordained in this article, and his property shall be confiscated by the court, reserving the rights of his wives according to what is said before should he be convicted and executed.

Article 14. Of inquisitions.
(1)Item: we order that if there were no witnesses, then the official proceed with the alleged case with an inquisition, according to that which is contained in the above article on wounds.

Article 15. On criminals.
(1)We wish and order that if the criminal be arrested within a month by the official or man of the district (*contrada*) where the crime has been committed, if it be any place which is not free (*franchu*), that the district or village be free from the above penalty. (2)And if the official of the place where the person who committed the crime was, does not co-operate and does not give his assistance to that officer or to those persons who look for him, let him be sentenced to the said fine.

xvi. Jurados de Loghu.

(1)Constituim[us] et ordinam[us] qui in ciaschuna villa si depiat ponne a iurare pro iurados de Loghu in sa villa manna ho[min]is .x., in sa pizina ho[min]is .v., sus megios ho[min]is qui illoi an[t] esser a voluntadi dessu officiali. (2)Et isso scripto de sos iurados villa ad villa, ho[min]i ad ho[min]i torre[n]t a sa camera sus curadores dae cussa die ad corona de Loghu de sanctu Pedru de lampadas ad pe[n]a de pagare l[ib]r[a]s .viii. assa corte, sos qualis depiant provari sas largas e furas qui si faghint i[n] sa villa o in sa aydatione de sa villa et de te[n]ne sos malosfactores et batiri·lus a sa corte. (3)Et si no los tene[n]t, paghi[n]t sus iurados s[oldo]s .xx. per ciaschaduno et paghint comoname[n]ti sus ho[min]is de sa villa et issos iurados su dannu ad cuy at essere et issa maquicia assu re[n]nu. (4)Et siant cretidos sus iurad[us] assu narre issoro; (5)si totu o sa maiore parte non essere[n]t in concordia no siant credidos et paghint sa maquicia secundu qui de supra narat. (6)Et si cussa persona ch'eseret dada de iurados boleret provare legitimame[n]ti qui atera persona et non issu avirit factu sa dita fura over accessu, qui i[n] cussu casu issu siat liberu et cussa persona a qui contra esseret provadu siat constritu a pagari sa maquicia. (7)Et issu maiore et iurados non siant però conde[m]pnados pro qui avirint dada sa maquicia ad icussu qui esseret defesu, ma paghit sa maquicia cussu ad qui at contra esser legitimame[n]ti provado e supra sa quali prova chusu ch'eseret dada de iurados deppiat mostrare infra uno mese. (8)Et similimente siant tenudos de faghire scrivire et colliri totu sas ragio[n]es dessu re[n]nu
6r cantu si det colliri et pagari i[n] sa villa q[ua]n[do] essere[n]t requestos per |
ipso officiali issoro o maiore. (9)Et icusa persona q[u]i no[n] bolirit iurari pro iuradu de crede[n]tia o per andari a chircari sas domos et logh[us] pro sas furas paghit assu re[n]nu pro dognia bolta qui '[n]di adi essere req[u]esto dae su officiali de sa co[n]trada l[ib]r[a]s .viii. a sa corte et a su curadore boe uno. (10)Et isso officiali o curadore qui adi essere siat tenudo per sagrame[n]to de provare·lu et denunciare·lu assa corte q[ua]n[do] at benne pro faghere raxone assa camera. (11)Et cussu capidulu no si i[n]te[n]dat per morte de ho[min]i, ma de cussu si observet secundu qui in su capidulu de q[u]i ochirit ho[min]i si co[n]tenit.

xvii. De maleficios [qui] sus iurados de Logu hant a chircare.

(1)Item ordinam[us] qui sos curadores cum sus ateros iurados de Loghu siant tenudos de chircare sos dannos dessos ho[min]is de sa villa et issos loghos hui

Article 16. Jurors (*jurados*) of the realm.
(1)We establish and order that in each village of the realm (*de Loghu*), jurors (*iurados*) shall be appointed on oath: in a large village, ten men; in a small village, five, such as they shall be chosen by the official as being of integrity, from among those who are in each village. (2)And the written list of those under oath (*sos iurados*), village by village, man by man, shall be delivered by the curators (*curadores*) to the Chamber (*sa Camera*), from the said day until the royal Court (*corona de loghu*) of St Peter's meets in June, under penalty of paying to the Court eight lire. Those who shall ascertain robberies and thefts occurring in a village or in cultivations pertaining to it, may arrest the malefactors and bring them to the Court. (3)And if they do not arrest them, those under oath shall each pay twenty soldi, and collectively the men of the village and those under oath shall indemnify the corresponding damage to those who have suffered it, and the fine to the realm. (4)And let those under oath be believed in their declarations; (5)if their declarations are not unanimous, or they do not agree by a majority, let them not be believed, and let them pay the financial penalty according to the foregoing. (6)And if that person who has been referred to the court by those under oath wishes to prove in lawful terms that another person, and not he, has committed the alleged theft or crime, in that case let him go free and let the person who will be proved to be responsible be compelled to pay the fine. (7)And the senior official (*maiore*) and those under oath shall not, however, be convicted of imposing the financial penalty on him who defended himself [from the accusation], but such penalty shall be paid by him whose guilt shall be proved; and such proof, he on whom the penalty had been imposed by those under oath shall produce it within the period of one month. (8)And similarly let those under oath be bound to have the taxes due to the realm recorded and collected in respect of what is to be collected and paid by the villages when their official or *maiore* shall demand them. (9)And that person who will not swear as under faithful oath, being remanded to inquire for dwellings or extra-domestic places, shall pay to the realm, for each time it shall be demanded by the official of the district (*sa contrada*), eight lire to the court and one ox to the curator. (10)And the official or curator (*curadore*) who shall be in office is required under oath to prove and report this to the court when he goes there to make an account to the Chamber (*Sa Camera*). (11)And that article shall not apply in the case of the killing of a man, but in this respect the provisions of the article relating to homicides shall be observed.

Article 17. About crimes that those under oath of the realm will have to hold an inquisition.
(1)Item: we order that the curators (*curadores*), together with the other jurors of the realm (*iurados de Loghu*), be required to inquire and identify, once a month,

ant avire suspectu dogna mese una volta et siant te[n]udos de chirchare sas domos dessos merchedantis et negosantis c'ant essere i[n] sa villa duas boltas su mese. (2)Ichusu deppiant faghire ciaschuno mese sos curadores e iurados qui illoy ant essere in sa villa, salvu qui alc[u]no curadore over iuradu no[n] esseret in sa villa et siat andado in alcuno loghu legitimame[n]ti e senza fraudi pro fagheri alcuno factu no[st]ro o suo no '[n]di siat tenudo. (3)Ma cussos iurad[us] qui illoy ant essere i[n] sa villa illu deppiant fagheri no[n] lassando et no[n] romanendo per cussu o per cussos qui '[n]d'ant manchare. (4)Et inte[n]dat·si que si assa domo intrant .III. iurad[us] o pl[us] et chirchant·illa bene sensa fraude qui siat tantu quantu et que si loy intrari[n]t totu sus iurados. (5)Et i[n]casu qui i[n] zò esseret su curadore neglige[n]te paghit assa corte s[oldo]s .C. et isso maiore de sa villa s[oldo]s .XL. et ciasch[u]no iurado s[oldo]s .XX.

XVIII. Furas.

(1)Volem[us] et ordinam[us] qui q[ua]n[do] su curadore et issos iurados de Loghu ant andare chircando sas domos et issos loghos pro sas furas et achatarit illoe algunu corgio de boe, de vacha o de cavallu o d'ebba, mostret su qui lu adi aviri a qui lo at achatari come[n]ti siat suo pegogiari o de domo sua o de ateri qui si l'edi avire acomandado. (2)Et si cussu no[n] mostrat, siat te[n]tu su ho[min]i et batidu assa corte et paghit secundu qui narat sa Carta de Loghu pro su furoni.

XIX. De pregontari.

6v (1)Constituim[us] et ordinam[us] qui sos officialis de regnu over curadores c'ant esser in sas contradas siant tenudos de p[re]gontare sos iurados de ciaschuna villa tres voltas s'annu et non plus pro sas furas et pro sas largas qui s'ant faghere in sa villa o in sa aditioni de sa villa et pro sos corgios qui ant esser acatados in sas domos. (2)Qui cussos officialis de re[n]nu o curadores c'ant essere in sas co[n]tradas pozant batire per iscritu su p[re]gontu et issu c'ant avire naradu sos iurados et ipsu c'ant avire factu secundo ragio[n]e de sas furas et de sas largas et de sas maquicias, si qui sus dictos officiales [o] curadores c'ant essere in sas contradas i[n]di pozant faghere ragione a sa camera tres voltas s'annu, zò e[st] pro corona de Loghu de S[a][n]cto Marcho et pro corona de Sancto Nicola et pro corona de Plama.

the harms committed by men of the village and the places where they are suspected of occurring, and to be required to search the houses of merchants and traders who are present in the village twice a month. (2)These curators and jurors in the village shall be required to do this every month, except if any curator or juror shall be absent from the village for having gone, lawfully and without deception, elsewhere to attend to some duty entrusted to him by us or his own; for in that case he shall not be bound thereby. (3)But those jurors who will be present in the village are bound by this obligation without ignoring it or shirking it because of one or more who will be absent. (4)And it is to be understood that if three jurors or more enter a house and search therein adequately without deception, then this shall be as much as if all those under oath (*sos iurados*) had entered therein. (5)And in the event that in such an action the curator behaves negligently, let him pay to the court one hundred soldi, and the mayor (*maiore*) of the village forty soldi and each juror twenty soldi.

Article 18. Thefts.
(1)We wish and we order that when the curator (*curadore*) and those under oath (*sos iurados*) of the realm shall go searching through houses and different places in regard to thefts, and they find therein any hide of ox, cow, horse or mare, it shall be the duty of the one who possesses it to prove to the one who shall have found it the manner in which he himself came into possession of it, or others in his house cohabiting with him, or others who entrusted it to him. (2)And if he is unable to prove this, let him be arrested and brought to court and pay according to that which the *Carta de Logu* says about thieves.

Article 19. Of interrogation.
(1)We direct and order that the officials of the realm or curators (*curadores*) who have jurisdiction in the districts (*contradas*) shall be obliged to interrogate those under oath (*sos iurados*) of each village three times a year and no more, in regard to thefts and robberies that have taken place in the village or in pertinent cultivations, and in regard to hides that shall be found inside houses. (2)Officials of the realm or curators (*curadores*) who shall have jurisdiction over the district may bring in writing the report of an interrogation and of what those under oath shall have said and what they shall have lawfully done in relation to the thefts, robberies and offences, and the fines imposed, so that the said officials or curators who shall have jurisdiction in the district may render an account of it to the Chamber (*Sa camera*) three times a year, namely, for the Royal Tribunal (*Corona de Loghu*) on St Mark's Day and for the judicial assembly (*corona*) held on St Nicholas' Day, and for judicial assembly (*corona*) held on Palm Sunday.

xx. De sus pregontus.
(1)Item ordinam[us] qui sus officialis nostros tottu de Arbaree siant tenudos ciaschaduno i[n] sa coradoria sua de provare et de investigare sas furas et largas et issas maquicias qui si loy ant faghere in sas dictas co[n]tradas et batiri iscritu tres voltas s'annu in sa camera nostra, zò est pro corona de Loghu de Sanctu Marcho et pro corona de Sanctu Nichola et pro corona de Plama. (2)Pro ciò bolem[us] creder et dari fidi assu officiali de cussu qui 'nd'at provare et narri, come[n]te et assos iurados de Loghu totu. (3)Et similime[n]ti bolem[us] qui su officiali nostru p[re]gontit sos iurados dessas villas afeadas pro sas maquicias qui si 'lloe ant faghere et batiant·inde su iscritu a sa camera nostra, zò est de cussas maquicias de sanben qui si loy ant faghere et qui si loy apertene[n]t a sa ragione nostra.

xxi. Qui levarit mulieri.
(1)Volem[us] et ordinam[us] qui si alcuno ho[min]i levarit per forza muleri coyada over alcuna atera femi[n]a q[u]i esseret iurada o ispo[n]xelarit alc[u]na virgini per forza et dessas suprascriptas causas esseret legitimame[n]ti bi[n]quido, siat iuygado qui paghit pro sa coyada l[ib]r[a]s .D. (2)Et si no[n] paghat i[n]fra dies .xv. de c'at esser iuygadu, siat·illi segadu s'uno pee, pro modu q[u]i 'llu perdat. (3)Et pro sa bagadia siat iuygadu q[u]i paghit l[ib]r[a]s .cc., et
7r siat anchu tenudo pro levare·la pro mugere si e[st] senza ma- | rido et plaquiat a sa femina. (4)Et si non la levat pro mugere, siat anchu te[n]tu pro coyare·la secundu sa conditioni de sa femi[n]a et issa qualidadi dessu homini. (5)Et si cussas causas issu non podet faghire a dies .xv. de c'at essere iuygadu, siat·illi segado s'uno pee per modu que lu perdat. (6)Et pro sa virgini paguit sa simili pena, et si non adi dae hui pagare seguint·illi uno pee ut supra.

xxii. Qui intrarit in domo.
(1)Item ordinamus qui si alcuno homini intrarit per forza a domu d'alcuna femina coyada et tene[n]t·bie·llu et non l'apat apida carnalime[n]ti et est·inde binchido legitti[m]ame[n]te, siat iuigadu a pagare liras .c. (2)Et si non pagat a dies .xv. de c'at esser iuygadu, segue[n]t·illi una origa tota. (3)Et si alcuno homini esseret te[n]tu cu[m] alcuna femi[n]a coyada in domo dessa femina et esseret voluntadi de sa femina, cussa codali femina siat afrustada et fostigada et ispossedida dessos benes suos totu et de sas raxones suas gasi de dodas

Article 20. Of interrogations.
(1)Item: we order that all our officials of Arborea shall be required, each in his own district (*curadoria*), to ascertain and hold an inquiry into robberies, thefts and crimes punishable by fine that shall be perpetrated there, and to bring a written report of them three times a year to our Chamber, namely, for the Royal Tribunal (*Corona de Loghu*) of St Mark and for the judicial assembly (*corona*) of St Nicholas and for the assembly (*corona*) of Palm Sunday. (2)Therefore, we are desirous to credit and to give faith to the official concerning that on which he will declare and produce evidence, as well as to all royal (*de Loghu*) jurors. (3)And similarly we want our official to question those under oath (*sos iurados*) of enfeoffed villages (*villas afeadas*) concerning crimes punishable by fine which will be committed there, and to bring a written report of them to our Chamber (*sa Camera*); that is to say, concerning those crimes of blood, punishable by fine, which will be committed there and which fall under our jurisdiction.

Article 21. Who shall use violence against a woman.
(1)We wish and order that if any man shall do violence to any married woman or to any woman who is betrothed, or shall deflower any virgin against her will, and with regard to the above charges he shall be lawfully defeated in court, he shall be sentenced to pay, if it be a married woman, five hundred lire. (2)And if he does not pay within fifteen days after he is condemned, let one foot be amputated so that he loses it. (3)And if it be an unmarried woman, let him be condemned to pay two hundred lire, and let him be bound to take her as wife if the woman is without a husband and if she consents to it. (4)And if he does not take her to be wife, let him then be bound to arrange to give her as wife according to the condition of the woman and the rank of the man. (5)And if all this he cannot do within fifteen days after judgement is rendered, let one of his feet be cut off so that he loses it. (6)And with regard to [the crime committed against] the virgin, let the same punishment be imposed on him, and if he has not enough to pay for it let a foot be amputated from him, as above.

Article 22. Whoever enters another's house.
(1)Item: we order that if any man forcibly enters the house of a married woman and is arrested, and the woman had no carnal relations with him and this is lawfully established in court, he shall be sentenced to pay one hundred lire. (2)And if he does not pay within fifteen days after he is tried, let him have one whole ear amputated. (3)And if any man shall be arrested in the house of any married woman in the company of her consenting, that such woman shall be whipped, flogged and dispossessed of all her property and of all her rights, both

come[n]ti de ateros benis et romangat a su marido et non a ffigios qui avirit cum cussu marido et ne cum atero marido ch'averet apidu per innantis et ne ad atero pare[n]te suo, exceptu ad plaghere de cussu marido cu[m] su quali avirit factu sa dita fallanza. (4)Et issu homini cun su quali esseret acaptada non siat frustadu, ma deppiat pagare i[n]fra dies .xv. de c'at essere iuygadu l[ib]r[a]s .c. (5)Et si non pagarit infra su dictu te[m]pus, siat·illi segada una origa in totu. (6)Et zò non si inte[n]dat pro femi[n]as qui siant publicas meretrices nen anchu in casu qui sa femina andarit a domo de su homini over de atera persona qui non esseret habitatione dessa dita femi[n]a. (7)Qui in cussu casu su homini paguit l[ib]r[a]s .xxv., ma sa femina siat afrustada ut supra.

XXIII. De femina coyada.

(1)Volemus et ordinam[us] qui si alcuno homini reeret over teneret femina alcuna coyada palesame[n]ti cu[m] sa cali averet ad faghere carnalime[n]te contra assa voluntadi dessu marido, et dimandando·si·la cussu marido si la denegarit, siat conde[m]pnado in l[ib]r[a]s .c., sas qualis deppiat pagare infra
7v dies .xv. de c'at essere iuygadu. (2)Et si non pagat, siat·illi se- | gada una origa in totu et issa femina siat conde[m]pnada secundu in su capidulu si contenit.

XXIV: Qui andarit a festa.

(1)Constituimus et ordinamus qui alcuno homini qui andarit a festa o a sagra de clesia non bie deppiant portare arma peruna a ppena de l[ib]r[a]s .xxv. et de perdere s'arma. (2)Et sunt tenudos sus curadores et issos ho[min]is dessas villas de ciascuna curadoria hue s'at faghere sa sagra o festa de tenne cusso homini qui adi benne armado et bature·llu tentu assa corte cum s'arma qui l'adi acatari, ad pena de pagare, sus curadores cum sus hominis dessa curodoria, l[ib]ra[s] deghe.

XXV. De carthas bulladas.

(1)Item ordinamus qui [a] ciaschuna persona siat licidu de batiri et inp[re]sentari assa corte ad omni bisungio carta bullada o non bullada, co[n]daghi over ateras scripturas aute[n]ticas registradas o non registradas qui siant in sa corte. (2)Et si alcuna persona batiret carta de notaiu ad corona qui esseret falsa et usaret·illa malesiosame[n]te, co[n]noxe[n]do cusu qui l'edi batiri ch'edi essere falza, siat te[n]tu et missidu in p[re]gioni et co[n]de[n]nado in arbitrio nostro. (3)Et isso nodaiu over scrivanu qui sa ditta carta avirit iscrita, siat conde[m]pnadu et paghit l[ib]r[a]s che[n]tu. (4)Et si no[n] pagat infra unu mese, tagit·si·la sa manu destra. (5)Et icussas causas over posessiones pro qui chertarit over qui defenderet per issu vigore de custa carta falza, siat las-

of her dowry and of other property, which shall remain with her husband and not with the children whom she shall have had by such husband or with any other husband whom she shall have had before, nor with any other relative of hers, unless the husband, with respect to whom she has committed adultery, consents. (4)And the man with whom she was found shall not be whipped, but shall be required to pay, within fifteen days after he shall be tried, one hundred lire. (5)And if he does not pay within that period, let one whole ear be cut off. (6)And this is not to be intended for women who are public prostitutes, even in the case that such a woman goes to the man's house or to another person's house, in a house that is not her own. (7) In such a case, the man shall pay twenty-five lire, but the woman shall be whipped as above.

Article 23. Of married women.
(1)We wish and order that if any man retains or keeps with him, and this being a manifest fact, any married woman with whom he has carnal intercourse against the will of her husband, in case the husband demands it, if he denies it to him, let him be condemned to pay one hundred lire, which he shall pay within fifteen days from the time he is judged. (2)And if he does not pay, let one whole ear be amputated, and the woman be condemned according to what is said in the appropriate article.

Article 24. Who would go to the feast.
(1)We direct and order that if any man goes to a feast or religious festival, he shall not carry any weapon with him under penalty of payment of twenty-five lire and seizure of the weapon. (2)And the curators (*curadores*) and the men of the villages of each district in which the feast or festival is to be held are bound to arrest any man who shall have come armed, and to bring him under arrest to the court with the weapon which shall be found with him, under penalty of paying, both the curators and the men of the district, ten lire.

Article 25. On charters with seals.
(1)Item: we order that it shall be lawful for any person to bring and present to the court for any need, a charter with or without a seal, a *condaghe*, or any other authentic writing, registered or unregistered at the court. (2)And if any person brings to the court a notarial document that is false and uses it fraudulently, and if the one who produced it is aware of its falseness, he shall be arrested and taken to prison and sentenced at our discretion. (3)As for the notary or scribe who wrote this document, let him be condemned to pay one hundred lire. (4)If he does not pay within a month, let his right hand be amputated. (5)And those things or possessions for which he has litigated or whose possession he wishes

ada pasificamenti ad icussa persona de qui deberet essere ragionibilimente et ichusu dictu nodaiu plus non deppiat usare su officiu dessa nodaria.

Ordinamentos de furas.
XXVI. (1)Volemus et ordinam[us] qui si alcuna persona furarit alcuna causa sagrada dae alcuna ecclesia o de domo de clesia, ciò est parame[n]tus, libros et chalighis o attera causa sagrada, et est·indi binchidu per testimo[n]gios over qui 'llu confessarit, paghit prossa fura primarga assa ecclesia pross'unu .V. et assu rennu prossa maquicia l[ib]r[a]s .L. (2)Et si no[n] paghat sas l[ib]r[a]s .L. et pro s'unu .V. secundu qu'est naradu de subra, boghet·si·lli s'unu ogui. (3)Et dae ssa fura primargia i[n]antes siat i[m]picadu qui '[n]di morgiat et no[n] campit pro di[n]ari.

XXVII. De cavallu e boy.
8r (1)Constituim[us] et ordinam[us] que si alcuna persona furarit covallu domadu, ebba domada o boe domado et est fura primargia, si est dessu rennu paghit pross'uno deghe et de maquicia l[ib]r[a]s .XXV., et si est de clesia over de attera persona paghit pross'unu quinbi et de maquicia l[ib]r[a]s .XV. (2)Et si non paghat isso over atero ho[min]i pro see, segue[n]t·illi una origla prossa fura primargia, et dae cussa fura primargia inanti affurche[n]t·illu qui 'ndi morgiat.

XXVIII. De cavallu rude.
(1)Item ordinam[us] que si alcuna persona furarit covallu rude, ebba, vaca, boe over mole[n]te dessu rennu, paghit pross'unu deghe. (2)Et si e[st] de clesia o de atera persona paghit pross'unu quimbi et de maquicia l[ib]r[a]s .XV. prossa fura primargia, secundu qu'est naradu de subra. (3)Et si no[n] paghat i[n]fra dies .XV., siat segada una origla. (4)Et pro sa secunda fura paghit l[ib]r[a]s .XXV. infra dies .XV. de c'at esser iuygadu et si non paghat isso over atero ho[min]i pro see tagint·illi s'attera origla. (5)Et dae ssas duas furas in susu affurchent·illu.

XXIX. De berbegues.
(1)Volem[us] et ordinam[us] que si alcuna persona furarit berbeghues o porcho over cabra et est·indi binchidu et est dessu rennu paghit pross'unu deghi. (2)Et

to defend by virtue of such false document, be remitted without opposition to that person to whom by right they belong, and the said notary be dismissed from his notarial office.

Article 26. Orders about thefts.
(1)We wish and order that if any person steals any sacred furnishings from a church or ecclesiastical building, that is vestments, books, chalices or some other sacred thing, and if he loses [his case] through witnesses or by his confession, he shall pay to the church, if it is for the first time that he commits the theft, five times as much [as the value of what was stolen], and to the realm, as a financial penalty, fifty lire. (2)And if he does not pay the fifty lire and the amount of five times as much, according to the above, let him lose one eye. (3)And if a [known] criminal, let him be hanged so that he dies and does not escape by payment in money.

Article 27. Of horses and oxen.
(1)We direct and order that if any person shall have stolen a tamed horse, a tamed mare, or a tamed ox, and it is a theft committed for the first time, if it is a head of cattle belonging to the realm he shall pay the amount of ten times the value of that which was stolen and twenty-five lire as a fine. If it is of the Church or of another person, he shall pay five times the value of what was stolen and fifteen lire as a fine. (2)And if he does not pay himself, or others for him, let an ear be amputated for the theft committed for the first time; if a criminal, let him be hanged so that he dies.

Article 28. Of wild horses.
(1)Item: we order that if any person steals a wild horse, mare, cow, ox, or donkey belonging to the realm, he shall pay an amount ten times the value. (2)And if it belongs to the Church or to some other person, he shall pay five times the value, and fifteen lire as a fine, if it is theft committed for the first time, according to the above. (3)And if he does not pay within fifteen days, let one ear be amputated. (4)And for the theft committed for the second time, let him pay twenty-five lire within fifteen days from the time he is tried, and if he does not pay himself, or others for him, let his other ear be amputated. (5)And after two thefts let him be hanged.

Article 29. Of sheep.
(1)We wish and order that if any person steals sheep, pigs or goats and has lost [his legal case], and the stolen goods are the property of the realm, he shall pay an amount ten times the value of what was stolen. (2)And if it belongs to the

si esseret de ecclesia over de attera persona paghit pross'unu qui[m]bi. (3)Et paghit prossa fura primargia de maquicia l[ib]r[a]s .xv. (4)Et si non paghat issu over atero ho[min]i pro se infra dies .xv. de c'at essere iuygadu, seghe[n]t·illi una origla. (5)Et prossa secunda fura paghit prossa maquicia l[ib]r[a]s .xxv. (6)Et si no paghat isso o attero ho[min]i pro sse seghet·si·lli s'atera origla. (7)Et dae ssas duas furas in susu affurche[n]t·illu qui 'ndi morgiat. (8)Et bolem[us]qui si pl[us] persones essere[n]t a ffaguiri dessas ditas furas et essere[n]t·illi[s] legitimame[n]te provadu qui ciascuno deppiat i[n]currere i[n] sas suprascriptas pe[n]as come[n]ti et participes et consent[i]e[n]tes et come[n]ti et issu principali se esseret solu. (9)Et inte[n]dat·si de impicari dae .v. pegus in susu et dae .v. pegos in giosso paghit secundo de supra.

XXX. De cani.
(1)Constituim[us] et ordinam[us] qui si alcuna persona furarit alcuno cani de loru o giagaru et esseret dessu re[n]nu et ind'est bi[n]chidu, pagit i[n]fra dies
8v .xv. de c'at esser iuigadu | pro s'uno deghe. (2)Et si esseret de ecclesia over de atera persona, paghit pross'unnu quinbi et de maquicia libras quimbi.

XXXI. De ortu d'abis.
(1)Item ordinamus que si alcuna persona furarit hortu d'abis et esseret dessu rennu paghit infra dies .xv. de c'at esser iuygadu pross'unu deghe. (2)Et si esseret de clesia over de atera persona, paghit dess'unnu quinbi et niente de minus paghit de maquicia assa corte s[oldo]s che[n]tu et eme[n]det su damnu at chui at esser. (3)Et si non pagat issu over attero homini pro se infra dies .xv. de c'at esser iuigada, tagint·illi una origla.

XXXII. Fura de lavore.
(1)Volemus et ordinam[us] qui [si] alcuna persona furarit lavore messadu over senza messare et esseret dessu rennu, paghit pross'unnu deghe. (2)Et si esseret de clesia over de atera persona, paghit pross'unnu qui[m]bi si 'ndi est binchidu et pro maquicia paguit l[ib]r[a]s .xv. (3)Et si non paghat issu over atteru homini pro see, seghit·si·lli una origla.

XXXIII. Fura de domo.
(1)Constituimus et ordinamus qui si alcuna persona furarit domu agiena et illa pertungherit a ffura in muro o in gie[n]na o in fenestra o in cobertura, si 'lli est provado et indi est binchidu, siat inpicado per issa ghula qui 'ndi morgiat et dae

Church or to another person, he is to pay five times the value. (3)He shall also pay, if it is theft committed for the first time, fifteen lire. (4)And if he does not pay himself or others for him within fifteen days from the time he is judged, let one ear be amputated. (5)And if it is theft committed for the second time, let him pay as a fine twenty-five lire. (6)And if he does not pay himself or others for him, let his other ear be amputated. (7)And after two thefts let him be hanged so that he dies. (8)And we wish that, if the theft is committed by several persons together and it will be legitimately proved to be them, each one should incur the above punishments as a consenting accomplice, just as if he had committed the crime alone. (9)And it is to be understood that he should be hanged for theft for five heads of cattle or more, and for five heads of cattle or less, he should pay according to the above.

Article 30. Of dogs.

(1)We direct and order that if any person steals any watching or hunting dog and it belongs to the realm and is defeated [in a legal case], he shall pay within fifteen days from the time he is judged an amount equal to ten times the value. (2)And if it belongs to the Church or other person, he shall pay in the amount of five times the value, and a five-lire fine.

Article 31. On beehives.

(1)Item: we order that if any person steals a beehive and it belongs to the realm, he shall pay, within fifteen days from the time it is judged, an amount ten times the value. (2)And if it belongs to the Church or to some other person, he shall pay five times the value; nonetheless, he shall pay as a fine to the court one hundred soldi and shall pay compensation to the person who has suffered it. (3)And if he does not pay himself, or others for him, within fifteen days after he shall be tried, let him have an ear amputated.

Article 32. Theft of wheat (*lavore*).

(1)We wish and command that if any person steals harvested or unharvested grain and it belongs to the realm, he shall pay ten times the value. (2)And if it belonged to the Church or to any other person, he shall pay five times the value if he is a loser in court, and a fine of fifteen lire. (3)And if he does not pay himself, or others for him, let an ear be amputated.

Article 33. Theft from a home.

(1)We decree and order that if any person shall steal from another's house and shall furtively make an opening in the wall or door or window or roof, if it shall be proved to him in court and therein he shall be a loser, he shall be hanged by

sos benes suos si paghit su dampnu at qui at esser fattu. (2)Et nie[n]te de minus sus iuradus dessa villa siant tenudus de provari et de 'llu batire a diclarare et de te[n]ne su homini in pressona qui at aviri factu su mali. (3)Et si non tene[n]t et provant, paghint sos iuradus comunalime[n]ti cun ssu maiore et cun sus ateros homi[n]es dessa villa su dampnu at chui at esser. (4)Et assu rennu paghint sa villa manna l[ib]r[a]s .c. et issa villa pizina l[ib]r[a]s .l. (5)Et issos benes de cussu homini qui ad avere fattu su mali siat in su pagamentu dessus dittos dinaris.

xxxiiii. Lamentu de fura in domo.

(1)Item ordinamus qui si alcuna persona si lamentarit de fura de domo qui
9r 'lli at esser facta, si non est facta | in muro segadu o in gienna seghada o in fenestra seghada over in cobertura seghada, deppiant andare assu curadore a lamentari·si et issu curadore siat tenudo de andari cun ssos iurados dessa villa chircandu et i[n]vestigando cussa fura. (2)Et si achaptant su cabudu de sa fura, cussu in domo de qui 'll'ant acaptare sa cosa furada mostret come[n]te siat sua propria o de alcuna persona qui si 'll'averit acomandada et dae qui 'll'at aver comporada. (3)Et si cussa prova non mostrat, paghit cussa fura ad icussu at qui esseret facta a sagrame[n]to suo qui 'ndi ad fagheri i[n] manu dessu officiali. (4)Et paghit de maquicia assa corte l[ib]r[a]s .l. i[n]fra dies .xv. de c'at essere iuygadu. (5)Et si non paghat isso over atero ho[min]i pro ssee, segue[n]t·illi una origla prossa fura p[ri]margia et dae ssa primargia infurche[n]t·illu qui 'ndi morgiat. (6)Et si no[n] si acaptarit su chabudu dessa fura, cherte[n]t·indi cussu qui ad aviri recivido su dampno cum quimbi ho[min]is de sa villa ad qui 'ndi ad aviri suspectu in cussu modo, ciò est qui cullu qui dimandat sa causa et narat qui siat sua et qui si 'lli siat furada mostret et provet qui cussa causa sia sua peghugiare. (7)Et si no[n] mostrat, deppiat iurare culle a qui s'at acaptare qui non si 'll'at furada nen levada issu nen atere pro see. (8)Et iuradu qui at averi siat libero et no[n] siat tenudo a pena nen co[n]de[m]naptio[n]e peruna.

xxxv. De tenne su furone.

(1)Volemus et ordinam[us] que si sa fura qui s'at fagheri si iugheret et lavarit dae ss'una curadoria a sa atera, sia tenudo su curadore de cussa villa ad hui s'at iughere de reer sa fura et de te[n]ni su furoni, si 'll'at isquire, infini ad qui ad

the throat so that he shall die, and from his property there shall be paid for the damage done to him who shall have suffered it. (2)And nonetheless let those of the village under oath be required to prove the crime and may call on the one who shall have committed the crime to admit it and may arrest him. (3)And if they do not arrest him or do not prove the crime, let those under oath (*sos iurados*), all together and along with the mayor (*maiore*) and the other men of the village, pay the damage to him who has suffered it. (4)And let them pay to the realm, for a large village one hundred lire, and a small village fifty lire. (5)And let the property of him who shall have committed the crime be used for the payment of the said financial sum.

Article 34. Complaint of theft in a home.
(1)Item: we order that if any person complains of a theft carried out in a home, if the deed was not perpetrated by means of an opening made in the wall or on the door, window, roof, he shall go to the curator and to complain. The curator (*curadore*) shall be required to inquire and investigate into such theft together with those under oath of the village. (2)And if they find the stolen item, then the one in whose dwelling the stolen good is found shall be required to prove in what manner it is his property or the property of another person who entrusted it to him or from whom he had bought it. (3)And if he will not be able to prove it, he shall pay the value of the stolen property to the person who suffered the theft after the latter has sworn before the official. (4)And he shall pay by fine to the court fifty lire within fifteen days after the judgement is rendered. (5)And if he does not pay himself or others for him, let an ear be amputated if it is theft committed for the first time, and if he is a criminal let him be hanged so that he dies. (6)And if the stolen item is not found, let the one who has suffered the damage bring a dispute, together with five men of the village, against him whom he suspects of the crime, so that he who claims what has been stolen from him declares it to be his property and that it has been stolen from him, shall demonstrate and prove that all this is his own property. (7)And if he cannot prove it, the person who was apprehended shall swear that he has not taken or stolen it, neither he nor anyone else on his behalf. (8)And after swearing that it is as he said, let him be free, and be under no penalty or condemnation whatsoever.

Article 35. On the arrest (*de tenne*) of a thief (*su furone*).
(1)We wish and command that if the stolen goods of an actual theft shall be taken away and transferred from one village to another, the curator of that village to which it has been transferred shall be obliged to requisition the stolen goods, and to detain the thief, if he comes to discover it before the owner of that

be[n]ne su pubillu dessa causa furada. (2)Et si non lu tennet et no[n] arreeret sa fura, cussu curadore paghit assu rennu, si 'nd'est binchidu, l[ib]r[a]s .xxv. prossa neglige[n]tia sua et issa valsuda dessa fura ad cuy at esser.

XXXVI. De denunciare sas largas.
(1)Constituim[us] et ordinam[us] qui siant tenudos sus curadores, ciascuno in sa curadoria sua, de denunciare sas largas et issas furas qui si 'lloy ant fagueri a
9v su arme[n]targiu nostru de Loghu over officiali maiore dae ssa die qui at | esser facta sa maquicia a dies .xv. (2)Et issu curadore qui non las at denunciare assu termen paghit de maquicia assu re[n]nu l[ib]r[a]s .defusc xxv.

XXXVII. De tenne sus furones.
(1)Item ordinam[us] que sus curadores siant tenudos, ciaschunu in sa curadoria sua, de te[n]ne et fagheri te[n]ne sos furones et mal[us]factores et de mandare·los assa corte nostra cussos qui ant aviri factu sa maquicia dae s[oldo]s .C. in susu. (2)Et icussus qui ant aviri factu maquicia dae s[oldo]s .C. in giosso, de cussos si fazat paghare su curadore et non los mandit assa corte.

XXXVIII. De proare sos cavallos.
(1)Volem[us] et ordinam[us] qui sos iurad[us] siant tenudos, ciaschuno in sa curadoria sua, de provare sos cavallos domados et issas ebbas domadas et issos boes domados et mole[n]tes qui s'ant hochier a ffura o qui s'ant furare in sa villa o in habitat[i]o[n]e dessa villa. (2)Et si non lu provarint, paghint sa fura a sos pubillos comunalime[n]te sos iurad[us] cun sos ho[min]is tottu de sa villa. (3)Et icussu bestiame[n] c'ant achaptare sos iurad[us] de pardu ispeciadu a de nocte, ciò e[st] covallu domado, ebba domada, boe domadu et mole[n]te, siant tenud[us] de 'llu te[n]ne et bature·llu assa corte et issos iurad[us] indi appant de cussu qui ant batire a sa corte sa terza parte dessas te[n]turas. (4)Et ciò si intendat pro boes domad[us], qui in cussu te[m]pus si paschit a muda, si tenerent, pro qui debe[n]t giaghere in sa corte et appant·i[n]di su tersu, secundu qu'est naradu de supra. (5)Et si alcuno maiore de pardu over atera persona miteret alcuno bestiame[n] d'issu qu'est naradu de supra dae foras at intro paghit s[oldo]s binti pro ciaschuna bolta et per ciaschuna bestia si 'ndi est convinto.

which has been stolen has arrived. (2)And if he does not arrest him and requisition the stolen goods, let the said curator (*curadore*), if he wins [in court], pay to the realm twenty-five lire for his negligence, and pay to the rightful owner the value of the stolen goods.

Article 36. On reporting thefts.

(1)We direct and order that the curators (*curadores*) shall be obliged, each in his own curatorial district, to report to our State administrator (*armentargiu de Loghu*), or to the high-ranking officials (*officiali maiore*), any thefts and robberies that may be perpetrated there within fifteen days from the day on which the crime punishable by fine is committed. (2)The curator who fails to report them shall pay by fine to the realm twenty-five lire.

Article 37. On the arrest of robbers.

(1)Item: we order that the curators (*curadores*) shall be bound, each in his own curatorial district (*in sa curadoria sua*), to arrest and cause to be arrested thieves and malefactors, and to bring to our court those who have committed the offence punishable by one hundred soldi and upward. (2)And those who shall have committed an offence punishable [with a fine] of one hundred soldi or less, of them let the curator receive payment without taking them to court.

Article 38. Of gathering evidence concerning horses.

(1)We wish and order that those under oath (*sos iurados*) shall be required, each in his own curatorial district, to collect evidence concerning tamed horses, tamed mares, tamed oxen, and donkeys that will be killed secretly or that will be stolen in the village or in the cultivated fields adjacent. (2)If they fail to acquire the evidence, those under oath shall pay collectively, together with the men of the village, the value of all this to the owners. (3)And the livestock left wandering at night which the officials of the pasture (*iuradus de pardu*) control will requisition: that is, tamed horses, tamed mares, tamed oxen, and donkeys, let the latter be required to retain them and to bring them to the court, and let those under oath retain of what they bring to the court after requisitioning them: one-third part of the penalty due for the capture. (4)And this is to be understood [also] for the tamed oxen, at the time when they are put to graze under supervision performed according to a rotation (*a muda*): if they requisition them for the purpose of bringing them to court, let them retain for themselves one-third part of [of the penalty] according to what has been said above. (5)And if any official in charge of pastures (*maiore de pardu*) or other person shall move any head of cattle of those specified above, from outside to inside [the pasture], let him pay twenty soldi for each time and for each animal, if this shall be proved against him.

XXXIX. Qui non tennint su furone.

(1)Item ordinam[us] qui sos iuradus qui at comandare su curadore pro te[n]ne su furoni et no[n] l'ant te[n]ne su furone, paghint assu re[n]nu s[oldo]s .xx. per iuradu, et issu damnu q[u]i at aviri factu et issos iurad[us] pagint sa maquicia cominalime[n]te cun sa villa. (2)Et si cussu ho[min]i c'at aviri fatu custa fura
10r at esser fuidu et avirit alc[u]na causa de su suo, levet·si·lli et co[n]vertischat· | si in cussu qui ant paghari sos iuradus cun sa villa pro pagame[n]tu de cussu damnu c'at aviri factu et dessa maquicia.

XL. Qui compararit cavallu.

(1)Volemus et ordinam[us] qui si alcuno ho[min]i at co[m]porare covallu, ebba, boe, vacha, porcho, capra over berbegue de su rennu dae alcuno officiali maiore o pastore de rennu senza paraula dessu sengore iuigi o de clesia o de atera persona senza paraula de su do[n]no suo, paghit su co[m]poradore secundu qui issu furoni et assu re[n]nu per unu deghe et s'atera persona pro unu .v. (2)Et icussu qui at fagheri cussas co[m]poras et no[n] pagharit, istit in p[re]gioni infini a qui at aviri paghadu ad icussu a qui at esser fata sa fura et paghit de maquicia l[ib]r[a]s .xv.

XLI. Qui isfundarit vigna agiene.

(1)Item ordi[n]am[us] qui si alcuna persona isfundarit vigna agiena o pumura a ffura et issa vigna o pumura e[st] dessu rennu, paghit de maquicia l[ib]r[a]s .L. et issu damno c'at aviri factu. (2)Et si est sa vigna o pumura de clesia over de attera per[s]ona, paghit de maquicia l[ib]r[a]s .xxv. et issu damnu. (3)Et si non paghat i[n]fra dies .xv. de c'at esser iuigadu, seghit·si·lli sa manu destra et mendet su dampnu at chui at esser factu inantes qui essat dae p[re]gioni. (4)Et de custos siant tenudos sos iurad[us] de tenni su ho[min]i qui at aviri factu su mali et rep[re]sentari·lu assa corte infra dies .xv. (5)Et si no[n] lu p[re]sentarint infra su dictu terme[n], paghint sos iurad[us] su dampnu at chui at esser factu et a sa camera nostra s[oldo]s .x. per iuradu.

XLII. De qui lavarit prestanza.

(1)Volemus et ordinamus qui caluncha persona, de chalunca gradu over stadu siat, at levare alc[u]na p[re]stanza, acomandicia over deppidu alc[u]no i[n] crede[n]za over in atero mo[do], cu[m] carta o ssenza carta, et no[n] at paghare

Article 39. Those who do not arrest thieves.
(1)Item: we order that those under oath (*sos iurados*) to whom the curator shall give a command for a thief to be arrested, but who do not carry out the order, shall pay to the realm twenty soldi each, and shall pay compensation for the damage which he [he thief] shall have done; and those under oath, together with the village, shall pay the fine. (2)And if that man who has committed this theft shall have escaped and shall be in possession of anything belonging to him, let it be requisitioned from him, and let it be converted and used by those under oath, together with the village, for the payment of the damage done and the penalty.

Article 40. Who shall buy a horse.
(1)We wish and order that if any man shall buy a horse, mare, ox, cow, pig, goat or sheep belonging to the realm from any senior official or shepherd of the realm without the consent of the lord iudike, or if it belongs to the Church or other person, without the consent of his lord, then the purchaser is as a thief and shall pay to the realm ten times the value [of the animal], and to other person five times the value. (2)And he who has made such purchases and does not pay, let him remain in prison until he has paid the man from whom he has stolen, and let him also pay a penalty of fifteen lire.

Article 41. Whoever shall break down the fence of another's vineyard.
(1)Item: we order that if any person shall break down the fence of another's vineyard or orchard, and the vineyard or orchard belongs to the realm, he shall pay as a fine fifty lire for the damage he shall have done. (2)And if the vineyard or orchard belongs to the Church or to another person, he shall pay as a fine twenty-five lire for the damage. (3)And if he does not pay within fifteen days after he shall be tried, let his right hand be amputated and let him make reparation for the damage to the person who has suffered it before he comes out of prison. (4)And with respect thereto, let those under oath (*sos iurados*) be required to arrest the one who committed the offence and bring him, and present him, to the court within fifteen days. (5)And if they do not present him within the said time, those under oath shall pay for the damage to the one who shall have suffered it and to our Chamber ten soldi per juror.

Article 42. Of those who take out loans.
(1)We wish and order that any person, of whatever rank or status he may be, who shall borrow or have as a secured deposit or contract any debt by credit (*prestanza, acomandicia over deppidu alcuno in credenza*) or otherwise, whether there be a written record thereof or not, and shall not pay back the

ad icussu qui 'll'at aviri p[re]stadu, acomandadu over fatu crede[n]za i[n]fra su ditu te[m]p[us] qui i[n]tra issos at esser postu, et ciò ad esser legitti[m]ame-
10v [n]te co[n]vi[n]tu, su officiali de cussu loghu, at requesta dessu creditore qui | at avire sa restitutioni, deppiant fagheri tenni et miter in pregione a su ditu debitore dae l[ib]r[a]s .V. in susu, exceptu qui su dictu debitore darit paghadores a su dictu creditore de 'llu paghare infra dies .VIII. (2)Qui in custu casu non lu deppiant miter in p[re]gione. (3)Et si non dat sos dictos pagadores, qui istit in p[re]gione infini qui at aviri satisfactu su dictu depidu, supta pe[n]a ad icussu officiali qui co[n]tra faghirit de l[ib]r[a]s .X. et de paghari su dictu deppidu dae sse over dae ssos benes suos.

XLIII. Qui levarit raygua.

(1)Constituim[us] et ordinam[us] qui si alcuna persona si provarit qui avirit levadu raigha o clesura over iscungiarit fossadu de alcuna vigna agiena over orto over de corte de boes o de atero bestiamen, a ffura o palesi, paghit s[oldo]s .XX. et mendet su dampnu per dogna volta, dae sos quales dinaris appat su rennu su mesu et iss'aturu mesu su curadore cun sos iuradus. (2)Et issos officiales siant tenudus de p[re]gontari·ndi assos iurad[us] pro dogna volta qui 'llos debe[n]t pregontare.

XLIIII. De qui accusarit.

(1)Item ordinam[us] qui si alcuna persona at accusare over denunciare at alcuna atera persona de alcuno crimen, delictu over malificio et si 'll'at provare, no 'ndi siat condempnadu. (2)Et qualuncha persona narrit at qualuncha atera persona traitore o furoni, siat conde[m]pnadu in l[ib]r[a]s .XXV. si non lu provarit qui legittimame[n]ti esseret traitore ho furoni.

Ordinamentos de foghus.

XLV. (1)Volemus et ordinamus qui nexuna persona deppiat ne pozat ponne foghu i[n]fini ad passadu sa festa de sancta Maria qui est a dies .VIII. de capudanni. (2)Et qui contra fagherit paghit de maquicia l[ib]r[a]s .XXV. et ultra sò paghit su dampnu c'at fagher a cuy ad esser. (3)Et dae cussa die inantes ciaschaduna persona pozat ponne foghu a voluntadi sua, guardando·si però non fazat damnu ad atere. (4)Et si fagheret damno, paghit per maquicia l[ib]r[a]s .X. et issu dampnu ad cui l'at aver factu. (5)Et si non ad dae chiteu pagare
11r cussu qui ad esser condem- | nadu in l[ib]r[a]s .X. istit in pregione ad voluntadi nostra. (6)Et issus iurados de sa villa hue s'at ponne su foghu siant tenudus de provare et tenne sos malefactores p[re]dictos et de rep[re]sentare·llos assa corte nostra infra .XV. dies. (7)Et si no[n] los tenint in su dictu te[m]pus, sus

man who had lent to him or had given him in trust, or had given him credit within the terms agreed upon between the parties, and lawful evidence thereof shall be given to him, [then] the official of that place, at the request of the creditor demanding restitution, shall arrest and take the alleged debtor to prison in respect of a sum of five lire and upward, unless the alleged debtor offers the creditor guarantors to assure payment within eight days. (2)In such a case, he shall not be kept in prison. (3)But if he does not provide such guarantors, let him remain in prison until he has satisfied the alleged debt. The official who shall act contrary to that which is herein stipulated, is under penalty of paying ten lire and of paying the alleged debt from his own resources or property.

Article 43. Who shall remove fence posts.
(1)We decree and order that if any person against whom it shall be proved that he has pulled out fence posts or a hedge, or removed [by levelling] a ditch of demarcation of some other person's vineyard, vegetable garden or oxen enclosure, or that of other livestock, secretly or openly, [then] he shall pay twenty soldi and shall refund the damage for each time; and from this sum of money, the realm shall acquire half and the other half the curator and jurors. (2)The officials will be required to make inquiries to those under oath every time they must be asked.

Article 44. Of the one who makes accusations.
(1)Item: we order that if any person shall accuse or denounce any other person of any crime, felony, or misdemeanour, if all this be proved, he shall not be convicted. (2)And let any person who shall claim that any other person is a liar (*traitore*) or thief, be condemned at the rate of twenty-five lire if he cannot prove that such person is according to law a liar or thief.

Article 45. Ordinances on fires.
(1)We wish and order that no person shall or may light a fire before the feast of Holy Mary on 8th September has passed. (2)And whoever shall do otherwise shall pay a twenty-five lire fine, and in addition to this he shall pay for damage to those who should suffer it. (3)And from that day forward anyone may light a fire at his own will, taking care, however, not to cause harm to others. (4)And if he shall do harm, he shall pay a fine of ten lire and [also pay for] damages to the man against whom he shall have done it. (5)And if he who shall be sentenced to pay ten lire shall have no [money] to pay, let him remain in prison at our will. (6)And let those under oath (*sos iurados*) of the village where the fire will be ignited be required to collect the evidence and to arrest the alleged wrongdoers and bring and present them to our court within fifteen days. (7)And

dictos iurados cum sos ho[min]is dessa villa paghi[n]t de maquicia, ciò est sa villa manna l[ib]r[a]s .xxx. et issa villa pizina l[ib]r[a]s .xv. (8)Et issu curadore de ciasc[u]na de cussas villas paghit s[oldo]s .c. (9)Et de sos benes c'ant lassari, ciò est sos c'ant essere fuidos et inculpad[us], si deppiant paghare su damnu ad cuy ad esser et issu remane[n]te de cussus benes si deppiant contari in su pagamentu qui ant fagher sos hominis dessa villa.

XLVI. Qui ponne fogu in domo.
(1)Constituimus et ordinam[us] qui si alcuna persona po[n]neret foghu ad domo de persona alcuna istodiosame[n]te et fagherit damnu o non, et est·inde binchidu, siant tenudos sos iuradus et ho[min]is de sa villa de provare et de tenne su ho[min]i qui ad aviri postu su dictu foghu et de 'llu battiri tentu assa corte nostra. (2)Et siat iuighadu de 'llu ligare ad unu palu et faghere·llu arder. (3)Et si issos iurados et ho[min]is de sa villa no[n] tennere[n]t su ho[min]i qui ad aver factu su male, paghint comonalime[n]ti sa villa manna l[ib]r[a]s .c. et issa villa pizina l[ib]r[a]s .l. (4)Et de sos benes de cussos ho[min]is qui ad aviri postu su foghu, si depiat pagare su damnu qui ad aviri factu.

XLVII. De foghu in lavore.
(1)Item ordinam[us] qui si alcuna persona ponneret foghu istudiosame[n]ti a lavore messadu over ad messare o a vigna o at ortu et est·indi binchidu, paghit pro maquicia l[ib]r[a]s .l. et issu damnu a qui 'll'at avire factu. (2)Et si no[n] paghat ipso over atero pro se, seghit·si·lli sa manu destra. (3)Et issos iurados siant tenudos de provare et de tenne sus mal[us]factores ad icussa pena qui narat su suprascriptu capidulu.

XLVIII. De foghu.
(1)Volemus et ordinam[us] qui de su foghu qui s'adi po[n]ni in sa villa over in sa
habitationi dessa dita villa qui fazat perdime[n]tu siant tenudos sus curadores,
11v ciascadunu in sa curadoria sua, et issus officialis qui ant sas villas a | feu et issos
officialis o arme[n]targios dessas villas issoro depiant a[n]dare ad p[re]zare su
damnu q[u]i ad aviri fatu su foghu cu[m] sus megios ho[min]is dessa villa et
de benne assa corte, da inde a dies .xv., ad denunciare·llu assa corte nostra, a
pena de pagare su curadore assa corte libras .xxv.

if they do not arrest them within the said time, the said jurors with the men of the village shall pay the fine: for a large village, thirty lire; and a small village, fifteen lire. (8)And the curator of each of those villages shall pay one hundred soldi. (9)And out of the property that those who are accused and then flee, may have left, [then] the damage shall be paid to those who have suffered it, and the remainder of that property shall be put into account for the payment to be made by the men of the village.

Article 46. Who shall set fire to the house.
(1)We decree and order that if any person shall intentionally set fire to someone's house, whether he causes harm or not, and if he has lost his [legal] case, then those under oath (*sos iurados*) and the men of the village shall be required to prove the fact, and to arrest the man who shall have set the alleged fire and to take him prisoner to our court. (2)And let him be sentenced on trial to be tied to a stake and to be burned. (3)And if those under oath and the men of the village do not arrest the man who committed the misdeed, let them all pay together: for a large village, one hundred lire, and a small village, fifty lire. (4)And from the property of that man who shall have set the fire, there shall be paid the damage which he shall have caused.

Article 47. Concerning fire among the harvest (*in lavore*).
(1)Item: we order that if any person shall intentionally set fire to the farming yield to be reaped or already reaped, or to a vineyard or vegetable garden and loses their case, he shall pay as a fine fifty lire and refund the damage to those who have suffered it. (2)And if he or others for him do not pay, let his right hand be amputated. (3)And let those under oath (*sos iurados*) be required to take evidence and arrest the wrongdoers, according to what is prescribed on punishment by the above article.

Article 48. Of fires.
(1)We wish and order that in regard to a fire that shall be set in a village or in neighbouring farmlands a particular village, and that shall cause a loss, then the curators, each in his own curatorial district (*curadoria*) as well as the officials (*officialis*) who hold villages in fief (*a feu*), and the officials and administrators (*armentargios*) of their respective villages, are required to go to assess, with the best men (*sus megios hominis*) of the village, the damage that the fire will have caused, and they must then go to the court within fifteen days to report it to our court under penalty of the curator paying twenty-five lire to the court.

XLIX. De foghu.
(1)Constituimus et ordinam[us] qui sas villas qui sunt usadas de faghere sa doha pro guardia dessu foghu, deppiant·illa fagher sa doha secundu qui fudi usadu per te[m]porale ciaschaduna villa in sa habitationi sua. (2)Et qui no l'at aviri fata per sanctu Pedru de lampadas, paghit s[oldo]s .x. per ho[min]i. (3)Et issa villa qui l'at faghire, fazat·illa qui foghu no[n] la barighit, sa doha. (4)Et si foghu illa barighat et faghit perdime[n]tu, paghit sa villa s[oldo]s .x. per ho[min]i, sec[u]ndu qu'est usadu, et issu curadore l[ib]r[a]s .x. assa corte. (5)Et si su curadore comandarit assus iurad[us] over a sus ateros ho[min]is dessa villa de faghere sa dicta doha et no[n] la faghere[n]t, paghi[n]t comonalime[n]ti sa pe[n]a qui deviat paghare su officiali et icussu officiali siat liberu.

Ordinamentos de chertos e de nunzas.
L. (1)Item ordinam[us] qui nexuna femi[n]a qui siat over at esser fanti de lectu agiena o qui no[n] siat mughere legiti[m]a usit nen deppiat levare dae ssa domo dessa habitatio[n]i qui fagheri[n]t i[m]pari cun su amighu causa alcuna dessu ho[min]i suo contra sa voluntadi de cussu, suta pe[n]a de esser co[n]dempnada et punida per fura et seghundo qui in su capidulu dessas furas si co[n]tenet. (2)Et siat tenuda de restituiri sas causas furadas et levadas. (3)Et simili pena si inte[n]dat assu amighu qui levarit co[n]tra sa voluntadi dessa amigha causas proprias.

LI. Testamentos.
(1)Volemus et ordinam[us], co[n]siderando su grandu defectu et ma[n]chame[n]tu qu'est de notare i[n] sa isula de Sardigna, non solame[n]te i[n] sas citadis, terras et loghos murados, ma etiam de[us] via plus in sas villas de foras, et qui pro cussu defectu ent poder manchare multas bo[n]as et pietosas ca[us][a]s qui si lassant et faghint pro issos testadores in sa fine issoro, volemus et ordi-
12r nam[us], qui tantas bonas et pias causas no[n] roman- | giant senza mandare·si ad executioni, qui sos testame[n]tos qui s'ant faghire per alcunas personas in sa fine issoro bagiat et tenghat et appat valore et efectu, come[n]ti et qui essere[n]t factos per manus de noday[u], dummodo qui sos dictos testame[n]tos siant factos in forma debita et per man[us] dessu capellanu dessa villa over dessu scrivanu publichu dessu officiale dessa contrada, si aver si podet. (2)Et in casu qui su dictu capellanu over scrivano non si poderit aviri assu bisognu, bolem[us] qui si pozat fagheri per manus de alcunu scrivanu dessu Loghu in presentia de .VII. over de .V. testi[m]onios prossu min[us].

Article 49. Of fires.
(1)We decree and order that the villages that have the custom of making *sa doha* [a dug firebreak strip] in defence of fire, shall make it in the manner used seasonally for each village in its own neighbouring farmland. (2)The village that will not have done it by St Peter's [feast] in June shall pay ten soldi per person. (3)And the village that will do it, let it do it in such a way that the fire will not overrun it. (4)And if the fire overruns it and causes damage, let the village pay ten soldi per person, according to custom; also the curator [will pay] ten lire to the court. (5)And if the curator commands those under oath (*sos iurados*) or other men of the village to make the said firebreak and they have not done it, let them all pay together the penalty that the official should have paid, and let that official go free.

Ordinances concerning disputes and summons (*nunzas*).
Article 50. (1)Item: we order that no woman who is or will be a concubine (*fante de lectu*), a stranger to the family or not a lawful wife, shall dare to steal anything belonging to the man against his will from the home in which she has gone to dwell with her 'friend' (*amighu*), under penalty of being condemned and punished for theft according to what is contained in the article on theft. (2)And she shall be obliged to return any stolen and removed items. (3)A similar penalty shall be set for her 'friend' who would take from her 'friend' anything belonging to her.

Article 51. Wills.
(1)We wish and order, considering the great deficiency and scarcity of notaries that there is in the island of Sardinia, not only in the cities (*citadis*), lands (*terras*) and walled settlements (*loghos murados*), but all the more in outlying villages (*villas de foras*) too. Due to that deficiency, many good and charitable dispositions that are made and give rise to bequests by testators at the end of their lives might fail, we wish and order that so many good and pious dispositions shall not remain without going into effect, and therefore that the wills which shall be made by certain persons at the end of their lives shall have worth, be counted, and have value and effect, as if they were made by notaries, provided that such wills shall be made in due form and by the hand of the chaplain (*capellanu*) of the village or the public scribe (*scrivanu publichu*) of the official of the district (*contrada*), if there be any. (2)In the event that there is no need for a said chaplain or scribe, we desire that the will be made by the hand of some scribe of the realm (*de Loghu*) in the presence of seven, or at least, five witnesses.

LII. De corona.

(1)Constituim[us] et ordi[n]am[us] qui cussa persona c'at esser mandada cum nunza dae corona de Loghu o de corona de quide de berruda per domo o per fundame[n]tu o per alc[u]na atera possessione, siat postu ad iurare, per issu curadore c'at arreire corona, qui de sa nunza bene et lealime[n]te at faghiri. (2)Et poscha bayat et det sa nunza in p[re]sentia de tres bon[us] ho[min]is dessa villa. (3)Et icussu ho[min]i at que si mandat, si 'llu acatat in persona, et si sa dicta nunza si li dat in persona, deppiat be[n]nere assa coro[n]a ad icussu terme[n] qui si loy ad co[n]tenni. (4)Et si per adve[n]tura no[n] lu acatat in persona, det sa nunza in sa domo hui at torrari, si loy acatat alc[u]na persona habitanti, i[n] p[re]sentia de tres bonos ho[min]is dessa villa over de .II. (5)Et deppiant be[n]ni ad corona dae ssas .VIII. dies a su bindichi per respo[n]deri ad icussa p[erso]na qui illi adi aviri mandadu sa nunza. (6)Et isso ho[min]i qui adi portare sa nunza deppiat torrari ad corona ad fagher iscrivere in iteu modu ad aviri dada sa nunza. (7)Et si non torrat, siat condempnadu de paghare s[oldo]s .XX. assa corte et no 'ndi siat in periudiciu de sas partis. (8)Et torrit et mandit·illi nunza dae nou sa terza bolta per isso modu que est narradu de supra. (9)Et si cussu ho[min]i [a] qui ad aviri mandadu sa nunza .III. boltas no[n] be[n]nerit a corona a sus termi[n]is qui suntu narrados de supra, deppiat·si mitire i[n] possessio[n]e de cussa ca[us][a] over possessio[n]e pro q[u]i l'at avire mandadu
12v nunza et reat et servat·si·lla unu annu cussu q[u]i at aviri mandadu sa nunza. | (10)Et si in cussu annu non beneret ad respondere et defendere·si de sa nunza qui l'at esser mandada, appat bintu cussa causa over possessioni cussu pro c'at avire mandadu sa nunza et siat sua propria. (11)Et si cussu ho[min]i ad qu'eseret mandada sa nunza si beneret intro de cussu annu et bogiat·illa paghare cum totu su ispendiu c'at aviri factu in su dictu certu, siat tenudo su curadore de fagheri·llu torrare sa possessioni qui li fudi levada et inte[n]dere ad ragioni at ambas partis et dae ca ad esser deffinidu su chertu cussa possessioni deppiat dari ad icussa persona qui l'adi avire binchidu de raxioni. (12)Et issas ispe[n]dias qui ant esser factas per issas partis, cussu c'at perdere deppiat satisfahiri assu c'at binchire secundu qui at parri da taxari assu armentargiu nostru de Loghu over officiali qui '[n]de reeret rexioni cu[m] su sagrame[n]tu de cussu qui ad aviri factu sas ispe[n]dias. (13)Et de fructu qui ad avire apidu dae ssa die qui

Article 52. Of the judicial assembly (*corona*).

(1)We decree and order that the person who shall be appointed to deliver a summons (*nunza*) from the Royal Tribunal (*Corona de Loghu*) or from the *Corona de Chida de Berruda* ('Court of Trusted Men') concerning a house or estate or any other possession, shall be made to swear, by the curator (*curadore*) who shall preside over the assize court (*corona*), that in regard to the summons he shall communicate it correctly and faithfully. (2)Thereafter, he must go and deliver the summons in the presence of three trusted men (*bonus homines*) of the village. (3)And that man to whom it is delivered, if he finds him in person, and delivers to him the summons, he shall go to the court within the time that shall be specified. (4)And if he does not find him in person, he shall deposit the summons at his usual dwelling, if he finds any person living therein, in the presence of two or three trusted men (*bonos hominis*) of the village. (5)And [those who received the summons] shall come to the court within a period of between eight and fifteen days to respond to the person who shall have served the summons to them. (6)And the person who shall have served the summons shall return to the court and have it recorded in writing in what manner he delivered the summons notice. (7)And if he does not return, he shall be ordered to pay twenty soldi to the court. Such failure shall not be prejudicial to the parties. (8)And let him return and serve the notice for the third time in the manner said above. (9)And if that person to whom notice shall be given three times fails to appear at the assize within the aforesaid time, he who shall have asked for service of the summons shall be put in possession of the goods or property of that for which he shall have asked for service to be delivered, and that he shall hold [that property] by administering it and making use of it for one year. (10)And if the person sued shall not appear within one year to answer and defend himself concerning that to which the summons delivered to him relates, he who shall have requested the summons shall be deemed to have won the law case or [just] possession, and shall hold it as his own. (11)And if that person to whom the summons shall be delivered shall appear within the year and shall wish to pay all the expenses which [the other party] shall have incurred in the said law case, the curator (*curadore*) shall be bound to restore to him the possession which had been taken from him, and to hear the reasons of both parties according to right. After the case shall be concluded and settled, he shall assign possession to him who shall have won the case according to justice. (12)And with regard to the expenses incurred by the parties, he who shall have lost the case shall satisfy the victor according to the amount which it shall seem proper to determine to our State administrator (*armentargiu de Loghu*), that is, to the official having judicial functions by the oath taken by him who shall have incurred the expenses. (13)And of the profit which he shall have enjoyed from

ad aviri apidu sa possessione infini ad icussa die qui l'at aviri torrada non siat tenudu de indi fagher restitucione alcuna.

LIII. De nunza de corona.

(1)Item ordinam[us] qui si alcuna persona [a] c'at esser mandada nunza dae corona de Loghu et dae corona de quida de berruda o dae corona de portu o dae alcuna atera corona qui de cussas qui sunt naradas de supra pro alchuna causa et non at benne ad corona assu termen qui s'at conte[n]ne in sa nunza no[n] deppiat perdere su certu a minimanza ne[n] pro sa prima nunza ne[n] pro sa secunda, ma satisfazat su ispendiu c'at avire factu cussa persona c'at avire mandadu sa nunza. (2)Et siat conde[m]pnadu et paghit a sa camera nostra per ciaschaduna bolta qui li at esser mandada sa nunza dinaris .VI. per lira pro sa p[ri]marga et torrint·illu a mandari nunza. (3)Et pro sa secunda nunza [qui] l'at esser mandado et no[n] at benne, paghit dinaris .XX. per lira et satisfacat su spe[n]diu simigiantime[n]ti. (4)Et anchu si li mandi[n]t nunza, et si ad sa terza bolta non benit de qui l'at esser mandadu nunza, perdat cussu chertu a minimanza secu[n]du sa usanza antiga. (5)Et simigiantime[n]ti si inte[n]dat pro su terramangieso a c'at ma[n]dari nunza sardu e gosi pro
13r su sardu a c'at | mandari nunza su terramangeso. (6)Et si cussa persona qui non ad benne assas dictas nunzas boleret fagher defensa sua pro qui non pozint benne assu te[m]pus, siat intesidu a ragione. (7)Et si mostrat legitimame[n]ti occasione pro sa quali non poderit be[n]ne non li siat periudiciu, si non satisfaghere su ispendiu ad icussa persona qui l'at aviri mandadu sa nunza.

LIV. Corona.

(1)Volemus et ordinam[us] qui si alcuna persona mandarit nunza dae corona de curadore pro larga o per alcuno mali qui avirit factu, si 'lli acatat nunza e no[n] be[n]nit assa nunza p[ri]margia et partit·si per pahura qui '[n]d'averit, torrit et mandit·illi nunza. (2)Et si no[n] lu acatat a dari·li sa nunza, det sa nunza assa domo in p[re]sentia de tres ho[min]is de sa villa, si 'lloy acatat alcuno habitanti. (3)Et si non bennint assu bindighi, siat binchidu.

the day that he was placed in possession until the day that he returns it, he shall not be bound to account for it.

Article 53. Of the summons of the judicial court (*corona*).
(1)Item: we order that if any person to whom notice of summons shall be served by the Royal Tribunal (*Corona de Loghu*) or the *Corona de Chida de Berruda* (Court of Trusted Men) or the Harbour Court (*Corona de Portu*) or any other court (*corona*), such as those aforesaid, for any cause whatsoever, and does not appear at the assize within the time which shall be stated in the notice of summons, he shall lose the case by default either for the first or the second notice, but he shall be obliged to pay compensation for the expenses which shall have been incurred by that person who caused the summons to be delivered to him. (2)And he shall be ordered to pay to our Chamber (*camera*), for each time he shall have received the summons, six coins (*dinaris*) per lira the first time, and he shall be sent the summons another time. (3)And for the second summons which shall be served on him without his appearing, let him pay twenty denari per lira, and let him pay expenses in like manner. (4)And again let him be served notice, and if even the third time he is served he does not appear, let him lose the case by default according to ancient custom (*uzanza antiga*). (5)Likewise, let it be understood for a mainlander (*terramangieso*) to whom he shall cause a summons to be delivered by a Sardinian, and likewise for a Sardinian to whom he shall cause a summons to be delivered by someone from the mainland. (6)If that person who fails to appear [in court] with respect to the above-mentioned summonses wishes to defend himself with respect to the fact that he failed to appear within the time limit set, let him be heard according to law. (7)And if he shows legitimate reason why he could not appear, this shall not be prejudicial to him, except that he shall have to reimburse the expenses to that person who sent him the summons.

Article 54. Court (*Corona*).
(1)We wish and order that if any person shall have summons delivered by the court presided over by the curator (*Corona de Curadore*) for theft or other misdemeanour that has been committed, if the addressee shall be delivered the summons, but he does not show up after the first notification and goes away for fear that this prejudices him, [then the messenger] shall return and another time deliver it to him. (2)And if he does not find him to deliver him the summons, he shall deliver the summons to whomever he shall find at the home in the presence of three men of the village, if he shall find anyone there. (3)And if he does not show up within fifteen days, let him be considered as having lost in court.

LV. Nunzas.
(1)Constituim[us] et ordinam[us] qui sas dictas nunzas qui s'ant mandari dae corona de Loghu o dae coro[n]a de berrude o dae corona de alcuno atero officiali si deppiat fagheri iscrivire in su cartolayo et leer assos lieros c'ant esser in sa corona et, factu ciò, exe[m]plare sas dictas nunzas dae su cartolaiu et dare·llu in sa corona ad icussa persona qui l'at deber portare et faghendo·li fagher cussa sole[n]nidadi qui si co[n]tennit in su primu capitulu dessas nunzas.

LVI. De iscrianos.
(1)Item ordinam[us] qui sos scrivan[us] c'ant esser in sas coronas deputados ad scrivire sos chertos qui s'ant fagher deppiant esser conscritos et scrivant ordinadame[n]ti su narri dessas partis. (2)Et poscha c'at aviri factu sas ditas scripturas illu deppiant leer sentendo sas partes et issos lieros c'ant esser i[n] sas coronas pro iuighari. (3)Et factu ciò, su arme[n]tagiu no[st]ro de Loghu over alcuno officiali nostru qui reeret corona deppiat pesari sos lieros dessa corona ad iuigare secundu ch'est usadu et faghere·[n]de ad cusu qui '[n]d'at achatare de raxone qui faghire·si·ndi deppiant.

LVII. De possessione.
(1)Volem[us] et ordi[n]am[us] qui si alcuna persona avirit et possederit domo
13v o fundame[n]tu alcuno pacificame[n]ti et al- | cuna persona si lu levarit senza sa iusticia et icussu homini a ch'eseret levadu indi faghirit lame[n]tu a su officiali, cussu officiali a chi su ditu lame[n]tu s'at fagher siat tenudo de 'lli faghire restituire et torrari a dari cussa causa de chi loy ad esser dimandada chi l'edi esser leada senza iusticia, si acatat qui siat gasi et conde[m]pnari·llu a paghare assa camera nostra l[ib]r[a]s .x. (2)Et poscha inte[n]dat ragione [ad] ambas partis.

LVIII. De mandare nunza.
(1)Constituim[us] et ordinam[us] qui sciat licitu a chaluncha persona ad boler mandare nunza qui 'lla mandit dae corona de Loghu over dae corona de berruda in qualuncha parte ad boler, paghandu issu missu qui 'll'at portare ad arbitriu dessu arme[n]tagiu nostru de Loghu et dessos ateros officiales in sos officios issoro. (2)Et o[m][n]ia atera ispendia qui s'ant faghiri in sos chertos si deppiant satisfaghere dae cussa parti qui at perder assa parti qui at bincher, ataxando sos ditos ispendios su arme[n]targiu nostru de Loghu c'at esser over

Article 55. Summons

(1)We decree and order that said summons, which shall be conveyed by the Royal Tribunal (*Corona de Loghu*) or the *Corona de Chida de Berruda* (Court of Trusted Men) or the court of any other official, shall be caused to be recorded in the cartulary (*su cartolayu*) and shall be read by the freemen (*lieros*) who shall be present in the court (*corona*). Having done so, the said summons shall be copied from the cartulary and delivered in the court to that person who shall deliver them, in notification, following the same formal practice as is contained in the first article about summons [no. 53].

Article 56. Of scribes (*iscrainos*).

(1)Item: we order that the scribes who shall be at assize courts (*coronas*) deputed to record the judicial disputes that shall be dealt with, shall be bound to record, in writing and in order, the depositions of the parties. (2)And having made such records, they shall read them, having them heard by the parties and by the freemen who shall be present in the court to judge. (3)And having done this, our State administrator (*armentargiu de Loghu*) or some of our officials presiding over the court shall call the freemen of the court to judgement according to custom, adhering to what, in accordance with law (*raxone*), ought to be done.

Article 57. Of ownership (*possessione*).

(1)We wish and order that if any person has any house or rustic estate (*fundamentu*) in his possession without any dispute, and any person takes it from him without any right, and that man from whom it shall be taken shall file a complaint concerning it with the official, let that official to whom the complaint shall be addressed be obliged to make him return and redeliver the property which is claimed as being unlawfully taken. If he finds that it is so, he shall order him to pay to our Chamber ten lire. (2)Thereafter he must hear the arguments of both parties.

Article 58. Of delivering summons.

(1)We decree and order that it shall be lawful for each person who wishes to have a summons delivered in court that he shall have it delivered by the Royal Tribunal (*Corona de Loghu*) or the *Corona de Berruda* (Court of Trusted Men) against whichever party he wishes, paying the messenger who shall have it delivered according to that which our State administrator (*armentargiu de Loghu*) and the other officials employed in their respective offices shall determine. (2)And any other expenses which shall be incurred in the proceedings of the judicial case shall be borne by the party who shall lose the case against the party who shall have won it; our State administrator establishing the amount

attero officiali qui at te[n]ne sa iusticia pro nos et faghe[n]do iurare sa parti c'at deber recivere su satisfaghume[n]tu dessu ispendiu.

LIX. De inprestanza.
(1)Item ordinam[us] que dessu imp[re]stidu over dessa acomandicia qui faghint s'unu ho[min]i ass'atero et co[m]pellit·inde·llu a chertu et bi[n]chidi·inde·llu, paghit·illu ad ecussu qui 'll'at aviri binchidu. (2)Et anchu paghit assa corte nostra de cussu qui at mo[n]tare su chertu, ciò est dessa acomandicia de baturo una et de su imp[re]stidu de quimbi unu.

LX. De qui esseret binchidu.
(1)Volemus et ordinam[us] qui su chertu c'at esser binchidu in corona dessu curadore et issu ho[min]i c'at esser bintu si 'ndi andarit ad atera curadoria, benghat su ho[min]i c'at aviri binchidu su chertu daenante dessu curadore hui ad aver chertadu et fazat·illi fagheri su dictu curadore litera dae corona et baiat cun issa daenante dessu curadore hui at istare cussu binchidu et fazat·illu paghare de su suo si 'llu achaptat. (2)Et si su curadore non lu faghiret paghare
14r achaptando·li dessu suo, fazat·illu paghare su arme[n]targiu no- | stru de Loghu de cussus benes de cussu curadore qui at esser istadu neglige[n]te, et etiam de[us] illi fazat pagare per maquicia assa corte nostra l[ib]r[a]s .x. si su chertu est dae l[ib]r[a]s .c. in giosso, et si esseret dae l[ib]r[a]s .c. in susu pagit cussu tali curadore pro maquicia libras .xv.

LXI. De iurari.
(1)Constituim[us] et ordinam[us] qui si alc[u]no ho[min]i cum qui ant certare et ponne ill'ant a [iurare in] grughi de credenza, bengiat a iurare in man[us] dessu officiali qui at reere corona et non deppiant iurare in grughi de crede[n]tia. (2)Et icussos litigantis no[n] deppiant canpaniari·si unpare senza sa iusticia, si no[n] daenanti dessu officiali. (3)Et si si campaniant, paghit su chertadore assa corte nostra l[ib]r[a]s .x. et boe unu assu curadore. (4)Et si de su chertu portat de paghare maquicia assu rennu, paghit cullu qui debet iurare quali e qui esseret binchidu. (5)Et ciò si inte[n]dat in cosas criminales.

of the expense, or other official who shall administer justice on our behalf, and making the party who is to receive the compensation for the expenses swear an oath.

Article 59. Of loans.
(1)Item: we order that in regard to loans or secured loans (*acomandicia*) which shall be contracted between two men and which shall give rise to a judicial dispute with either party winning, it shall be the losing party who shall pay. (2)And the latter shall also pay to our court in relation to the extent of the litigation over which it is contested: for the secured loan (*acomandicia*) one-fourth, and for the loan one-fifth.

Article 60. On those who lose a legal case.
(1)We desire and command that, in regard to the dispute (*chertu*) which shall be decided in the curator's judicial court (*corona*), if he who shall have lost move to another curatorial district (*curadoria*), the person who shall have won the case shall appear before the curator at whose curatorial district he has brought the case; and the curator shall have a letter drawn up by the court for the winner, and he shall go, bearing this letter with him, before the curator in which he who lost the case resides, and, if he [the curator] finds him, he shall cause him to pay from his own [resources]. (2)But if the curator, having found him, does not make him pay from his own resources, let our State administrator (*armentargiu de Loghu*) make the negligent curator pay from his own property; and furthermore let him pay a fine for the benefit of our court: ten lire if the case concerns an amount from one hundred lire or less; and if the amount exceeds one hundred lire, let the curator pay fifteen lire by fine.

Article 61. On swearing an oath.
(1)We establish and order that if any man with whom a case is to be argued and who has been required to swear on the cross of [true] faith, he shall come and swear before the official who shall preside over the court (*corona*) without his having to swear on the cross of faith. (2)The two disputants must not agree with each other outside the court proceedings, but only before the official. (3)And if they agree, let the one who brings the dispute (*chertadore*) pay to our court ten lire and an ox to the curator. (4)If the case involves the payment of a penalty for the benefit of the realm, let him who is required to swear pay it in the same manner as he who has lost the case. (5)This is to be understood [as the process] in criminal cases too.

LXII. De chertadore.

(1)Item ordinam[us] qui su ho[min]i c'at dimandare chertadore non sciat tenudo sa corona de inde 'lli dare, salvu si su ho[min]i boleret esser chertadore a voluntade et plaguere suo. (2)Et nie[n]te de min[us] bolem[us] qui si depiat dare chertadore a clesias et a logos religiosos qui no[n] ant aviri arme[n]tarios issoro et simili a viduas et a orfanos et a ppoveros, istranieris et mercantes qui 'ndi adimandari[n]t et no[n] avirint arme[n]targios issoro.

LXIII. De chertu.

(1)Volem[us] et ordinam[us] qui assu ho[min]i c'at chertare o qui ant boler chertare in corona non li dent pro co[n]sigiu plus de unu homini. (2)Et icussu qui 'll'at consigiare et dari non siat et non deppiat esser iuighante pl[us] in cussu chertu.

LXIIII. De turmentu.

(1)Co[n]stituimus et ordinamus qui alcuno homini de su rennu de Arbaree qui siat de bona famma no[n] depiat esser posto a trume[n]tu pro alcuno chertu qui 'lli esseret factu de fura. (2)Ma bolem[us] et comitemus assu armentargiu nostru de Loghu et assos officiales no[st]ros qui de ciò et supra ciò reere[n]t corona, cu[n] sos lieros qui ant esser in sa corona, qui si cussu homini ad qui
14v ant fagher su chertu de fura est ho[min]i de | mala fama, qui si pozat mittere a trumentu et non in attero modo. (3)Ma bolem[us], si est de bona fama et si non [est] binchidu a testimongios, qui siat postu a iurare dae cussu officiale et siat libere dessa dicta causa o cchertu.

LXV. Quida de berruda.

(1)Item ordinam[us] qui sos curadores et officiales dessas co[n]tradas siant tenudos de fagueri sa quida de berruda im p[re]ssones issoro et de reere sa dita corona assu minus cum .v. ho[min]is dessu officiu suo. (2)Et si venere[n]t de minus, paghit su curadore pro sa neglige[n]cia sua assa corte nostra s[oldo]s .C. et ciaschuno de cussus ho[min]is qui 'lloy ant esser et ant manchari s[oldo]s .XX. per ho[min]i.

LXVI. De qui s'at a clamari pro fradis ultramare.

(1)Volem[us] et ordinam[us] que su ho[min]i a ch'ant chertare et clamari s'at pro fradis d'ultramari, po[n]giat a nnoe meses et si mostrat beridadi infra .VIII. dies, si suntu in Arbaree over in corona, qui 'lloy at aviri i[n] ultramari fradi over

Article 62. Of the legal disputant (*chertadore*).
(1)Item: we order that if a person shall apply for a legal disputant (*chertadore*), the court (*corona*) shall not be bound to assign him one, unless someone, by his own will and desire, wishes to take upon himself the burden of being a disputant. (2)In any case, we wish that a disputant should be assigned to churches and religious institutions that do not have their own representative (*armentargiu*); similarly for widows, orphans, the poor, foreigners, and merchants who would apply for one and who do not have their own representative.

Article 63. Of the judicial dispute (*chertu*).
(1)We desire and order that the man who shall move litigation or against whom disputes are to be conducted in court (*corona*), shall not be assigned to him for defence counsel more than one man. (2)And he who shall be assigned to him for counsel shall not be allowed or required to be a member of the panel of judges in that trial.

Article 64. Of torture.
(1)We decree and order that no man of the realm of Arborea who is of good repute shall be subjected to torture for any proceedings brought against him for theft. (2)However, we wish and order our State administrator (*armentargiu de Loghu*) and our officials, who in relation thereto hold the court (*corona*), together with the freemen present in the court, that if that man against whom the case for theft shall be brought is a man of ill repute, he may be subjected to torture and not otherwise proceeded against. (3)But we wish that, if he is of good repute and if he will not lose at trial by testimony, that he be made to swear by the official and be acquitted concerning the said case or dispute.

Article 65. *Quida de Berruda* ('Court of Trusted Men').
(1)Item: we order that the curators (*curadores*) and officials (*officiales*) of the districts (*contradas*) be required to hold the *Chida de Berruda* in person and to hold the judicial assizes (*corona*) with at least five men of their office. (2)And if fewer show up, the curator shall pay to our court for his negligence one hundred soldi, and the men who are supposed to be present, but miss their commitment, shall pay twenty soldi each.

Article 66. Of those who shall claim to have brethren overseas.
(1)We wish and order that the man against whom a law case is brought and who will claim that he has brothers overseas, shall be granted nine months [to have his brothers presented in court], provided that within eight days he proves the truth; namely, that there is a brother or brothers of his own overseas who

fradis suos qui appant parti in cussu pro qui 'llu chertant sos testimongios inter de Arbaree, et si suntu i[n] atero loghu dessa isula de Sardigna infra dies .XV. (2)Et si non mostrat cussa veridadi, respondat e si non respondet, siat binchidu. (3)Et icussu istessu siat prossu ho[min]i at qui at chertari et pretender s'at pro fradis c'ant esser i[n] terrafirma et siat postu a bactore meses a batiri·nde su fradi o fradis de terrafirma, adiunghendo qui cussu a qui ad esser chertadu deppiat respondere prossa parti sua. (4)Et pro s'atera parte qui at allegare qui 'lloy appat parte alcuno frade suo qui siat in cussos ditos loghos o in alcuno de cussos, cussa parti istet pendenti infini at ispirari su tenpus supra ordinadu.

Ordinamentos de prescriptiones e de possessiones.

LXVII. (1)Constituim[us] et ordinamus qui si alcuna persona o personas avirit tenuda e possedida cum iustu titulo alcuna possessione dessu rennu pro ispacio de .L. annos et possessio[n]es de clesia per ispaciu de .XXXX. annos et possessio[n]e de atera persona per ispaciu de .XXX. annos et non illi esserent dimandadas infra su dictu tempus, siant peghugiare issoro. (2)Et icussos
15r qui si faghia[n]t et crediant esser pobil[us] de cussas talis | causas possessiones, qui non las avirit dimandadas infra sos dictos terminos, indi siant in totu privad[us] et romangiant liberos et ispeditas ad cussas qui 'llas ant aver possedidas pacificame[n]ti per totu sos dictos te[m]pus. (3)Et icussa p[re]scriptioni de te[m]pus non si inte[n]dat et non periudischat a sos orfanus et minores qui non achaptarint tempus de dimandari sas raxiones issoro.

LXVIII. De qui possiderit.

(1)Item ordinam[us] qui si alcuna persona cum iustu titulu possederit alcuna causa mobili per ispaciu de annos tres senza inde 'lli esser factu questioni, qui passadu su dictu temp[us] non inde 'lli pozat esser factu pl[us] questioni. (2)Et icustu capidulu non periudichit assu capidulu de supra.

LXIX. De testimongius.

(1)Volemus et ordinam[us] qui si alcuna persona chertarit ad atera persona pro alcuna causa et provarit per carta over per testimongios cussa causa per qui chertarit, over qui 'nde esseret confessu, deppiat esser pagadu intergame[n]ti de cussu pro c'at avire chertadu et bi[n]chidu per carta o per testimongios [o] per confessione et non deppiat isse iurare afactu dessus testimongios. (2)Et si causa esseret que cussus testimongios qui avirit clamadu non binchere[n]t

are involved in the case brought against him, if the witnesses are in Arborea or near the place of the assizes (*corona*). If they are instead in another realm of Sardinia, he shall have fifteen days to prove this. (2)And if he cannot prove such truth, let him answer in court; and if he does not answer, he will have lost [the case]. (3)And the same thing shall apply to the man against whom a case is brought and who shall allege that he has brothers on the continent: let him be given four months to bring in his brother or brothers who are on the continent; and let it be further added that he to whom case is brought shall answer only in regard to that which pertains to him. (4)And if he produces any of his brothers who are in the aforesaid places or in such like, that part [of the case] shall remain pending until the end of the appointed time.

Orders of prescriptions and possessions.
Article 67. (1)We prescribe and order that if any person or persons have held and rightfully hold any possession of the realm for a period of fifty years, or ecclesiastical possessions for a period of forty years, or possession of another person for a period of thirty years, and no claim is made to possession of them within the aforesaid time, [then] the said possessions shall be their property. (2)And those who made themselves and held themselves to be the owners of those said possessions and did not claim them within the aforesaid time, let them be totally deprived of aforesaid possessions, and to remain free from encumbrance and impediment in the ownership of those who shall have possessed them peacefully throughout the said time. (3)And that prescription of time shall not be applied nor be prejudicial to orphans and minors of age inasmuch as they will be too young to claim their rights.

Article 68. Of those who possess [movable property].
(1)Item: we order that if any person rightfully possesses any movable property (*causa mobili*) for a period of time of three years without any objection being made to him, after the said time has elapsed nothing shall be disputed against him. (2)And this article shall not invalidate the article above.

Article 69. Of witnesses.
(1)We desire and order that if any person moves litigation against another person for any cause whatsoever and proves by written document or by witnesses that argue for which he has moved litigation, or that he [the opposing party] confesses, he is to be paid in full by the one who has moved litigation and who shall have lost the case by [reason of a] document, witness or confession, and he shall not have to swear after the witnesses. (2)And if it should happen that the witnesses he has produced do not win the dispute, the person against

cussu chertu, ad icussu ho[min]i a c'at aviri chertadu non siat dadu [sagramentu et satisfazat s'ispendiu sa parti qui at perdere a sa qui at binchire, secundu qui est ordinadu exceptu] sagramentu de calumpnia, que si pozat [dari] a ciaschuna dessas partis quando siat requestu in su principiu dessa questione et co[n]testada sa lite.

LXX. De chertus.

(1)Constituim[us] et ordinam[us] qui si alcunu ho[min]i c'at chertari s'unu cum s'atero et ponni l'at a sagramentu, si si pesat alcunu ho[min]i a chertari in corona dae parti de cussu c'at esser postu a sagrame[n]tu, non siat tenudu de 'lli respondere infini c'at esser ispidiadu de cussu chertu que l'at avire fatu, eccepto per via de reconve[n]tione, sa cali reconve[n]tione si fazat inanti qui sa lite siat contestada.

LXXI. Forma de corona.

(1)Item qui sos officiales nostros et curadores et maiores, ciaschunu i[n] sa
15v curadoria, maioria, et officiu suo, no[n] | deppiant reer corona cum minus de .v. ho[min]is. (2)Et cussa persona c'at chertare et clamare at testimongios clamet·inde a voluntade sua infine in .x. et no[n] pl[us], et facat·ill[us] scrivere a su iscrianu de corona inanti qui sa corona hui ant chertare si leit, salvu si no[n] si recordarit dessus no[min]es dessus testimo[n]gios et at dimandari te[m]p[us] a recordari·si·ndi, qui tando su officiali il[l]i dedi te[m]p[us] de clamare·los et denunciare·llus, et in aterame[n]te no[n] si 'ndi ricivat alcuno. (3)Et bolem[us]qui no[n] clamit ne[n] pozat clamare ho[min]i perunu pro testi[m]ongio qui non at avire .XVIII. annos co[m]plidos. (4)Et si lu clamat, no[n] li siat dada ne[n] chertitu pro testi[m]onio. (5)Et chaluncha persona clamarit pro testi[m]onio qualic[u]na sorasta q[u]i no[n] esseret i[n] Sardigna per via de cavillat[i]o[n]e et fugime[n]tu de te[m]p[us] et i[n] ssu te[m]p[us] qui 'lli ad esser assignadu dae su officiali qui teneret rexone non provarit per icussus paghit de pe[n]a l[ib]r[a]s .XXV., et issas ispesas, dannos et interessos paghit assa parti cu[m] qui avirit sa questioni. (6)Et issos testi[m]o[n]gios qui ad clamare pongiat at iurare su curadore over ateru officiali qui at reer corona bene et dilige[n]teme[n]te in p[re]sentia de ambas partis, si 'lloy pode[n]t et bole[n]t esser. (7)Et poscha su curadore over ateru officiali et issu iscrianu de corona cum ateros tres ho[min]is illos deppiant exami[n]are et p[re]go[n]tari secretame[n]te ad unu ad unu, qui no[n]ischiat s'unu de s'atero et qui non lus inte[n]dat alcunos dessas partes, et fagheri iscriviri su narri issoro. (8)Et p[re]gontad[us] c'ant esser, su iscrianu de corona leat et publichit su qui ant

whom he has litigated shall not be required to take the oath, and the losing party shall meet the costs of the man who shall have won, according to what has been established; with the exception of the oath of slander [an oath by which it is sworn that one party has slandered the other], which may, however, be enjoined on either party when it is required at the beginning of the proceedings and after the litigation has been contested.

Article 70. Of disputes (*chertus*).
(1)We direct and order that if any man shall move litigation against another, and the latter shall enjoin the oath, if any person rises in the court (*corona*) conducting the litigation in defence of the one to whom the oath shall be enjoined, the latter shall not be bound to answer him until the case brought against him is settled, unless there is reconvention, which must in any case be brought before the litigation is disputed.

Article 71. Operation of the assize court (*corona*).
(1)Item: that our senior functionaries (*officiales*), curators (*curadores*) and officials (*maiores*), each in his own curatorial district, jurisdiction, and office shall not preside over judicial assizes (*corona*) with less than five men. (2)And that person who shall litigate in court and require witnesses shall call up to ten and no more at his discretion, and shall have their names recorded by the scribe (*iscrianu*) of the assizes (*corona*) before the court (*corona*) where the hearing shall take place is convened, unless he has forgotten the names of the witnesses. In which case, he shall ask for time to recall them, and then the official shall allow him time to summon them and have them recorded by name, otherwise not even one shall be admitted. (3)And we wish that no man under the age of eighteen years shall be called nor be allowed to be called to testify. (4)And if he is called to testify, no credence shall be given to his testimony. (5)And if, in calling him to testify, speciously and for the sake of wasting time, any cousin who is not in Sardinia, and within the time allotted him by the official, failing to prove himself right through the said witnesses, shall pay as a penalty twenty-five lire, and expenses, in damages and interest to the party against whom he is suing. (6)And to the witnesses whom the curator (*curadore*), or other official who shall preside at the assize (*corona*), shall call, be enjoined to swear properly and diligently in the presence of both parties if they can and will be present. (7)And thereafter the curator (*curadore*) or other official and the scribe of the assize, together with three other men, shall examine and question them confidentially one by one, that no one may know what the others have deposed, and that neither party may hear them, and he shall have their testimony recorded. (8)And when they have been questioned, let the scribe of

aviri narradu sos testi[m]o[n]gios in presentia dessu curadore et dessus ho[min]is qui ant esser in corona, essendo·loe ambas partis, si esser illoy pode[n][t] et bole[n]t. (9)Et ligidu qui ant aviri su iscrianu su narri qui at aviri factu sos testi[m]ongios, su curadore et officiale qui at reer sa corona depiat p[re]gontari cussa parti incontra a qui ant esser clamad[us] sos dictos testi[m]ongios si bole[n]t oppone o narri alcuna causa contra sas personas issoro et contra assu qui ant averi narradu et testificadu. (10)Et si bole[n]t oppone o narri alcuna causa qui pargiat raxonivili et iusta, siat intesidu et dadu·li terme[n] de .VIII. dies at oppone et provare cussu qui at boler narre et
16r opponnere. (11)Et si custas qui at | averi oppostu provat, custu testimongio, contra a qui ad aviri oppostu, over su ditu suo non siat cretidu. (12)Et issu curadore c'at reer sa dita corona peset a iuygare sos li[e]ros dessa corona pro sa dicta testificat[i]o[n]e dessos ateros testi[m]ongios. (13)Et icussu qui ant iuygare sa maiore parti dessos lieros fazat scrivire assu iscrianu dessa corona et mandit·illa ad executioni. (14)Et issos lieros et iuigantes c'ant esser in sas coronas siant tenud[us] de iuyghare et dare legittimame[n]te in concie[n]tia dessas a[n]i[m]as issoro sa megi[us]ragione et iusticia qui 'nde 'll[us] at parre, non iuighandu però co[n]tra sa Carta de Loghu. (15)Et si iuigharint co[n]tra su capidulu de Carta de Loghu scientimenti, non bagiat nen te[n]ghat su iuigamentu issoro et siant conde[m]pnad[us] cussos qui contra iuigharint in l[ib]r[a]s .V. per ho[min]i pro chascaduna bolta.

LXXII. De sos iuighantes.

(1)Volemus et ordinamus qui nixunu procuratore nen avochadu qui usat publicame[n]te su officiu dessa procurationi overo avocachione usit nen deppiat, in neuna dessas cortis qui ant tenne sos officiales no[st]ros, iuighantis essere, a pe[n]a de l[ib]r[a]s .XXV. per ciaschaduna bolta qui iuigharit. (2)Et issu officiali qui lu clamarit o laxarit iuigare, isquie[n]do·lu qui esseret procuradore et avocadu, paghit et siat condempnadu et icussu in sa simili pena de l[ib]r[a]s .XXV. per ciaschuna bolta. (3)Et issu iuigamentu o nnarre qui alcuno dessos suprascriptos fagherint over avirint factu siat nulla et de nexunu valore. (4)Et ciò non si intendat in compromissos [ne] in questiones qui si comitteri[n]t per via de compromissione de voluntadi dessas partis.

LXXIII. De qui ant advocare.

(1)Constituimus et ordinamus qui nexuno auditore dessa Audencia nostra et nexuno atero officiali maiore nen mi[n]ore, mentre qui at istare in su officiu, et simili nexuno nodaiu dessa corte nostra et nen dessu potestade durante in su officiu issoro, in sa corte issoro, usint nen deppiant esser procuradore alcuno nen advocadu.

the assize take charge of, and publish, the depositions of the witnesses in the presence of the curator and the men present in the assize, both parties being present there, if they can or will. (9)And after the scribe has read the testimonies, the curator and the official who shall preside at the assize shall ask the party against whom the witnesses have been called, whether they wish to oppose or state anything against their persons and against their depositions and testimonies. (10)And if they want to oppose or say anything that seems reasonable and just, let them be heard and given eight days to oppose and prove what they want to say and oppose. (11)And if he succeeds in proving what he has opposed, the witness against whom he has opposed or what he has deposed shall not be believed. (12)And the curator who shall preside over the said assize shall call to judgement the freemen (*lieros*) of the assizes concerning the said deposition of the other witnesses. (13)And what shall be judged by the majority of the freemen shall be recorded by the scribe of the assize who shall give instructions to execute the judgement. (14)And let the freemen who shall be judges (*iugantes*) in the assizes be bound to judge and give, according to law and according to the conscience of their souls, the best reason and justice that shall seem to them, but without making judgements that are contrary to the *Carta de Logu*. (15)And if they knowingly judge against the article of the *Carta de Logu*, their judgements shall be of no value or importance whatsoever, and let those who have judged contrary to what it establishes be condemned, at the rate of five lire each and for each time.

Article 72. Of judges (*iuighantes*).

(1)We wish and order that no prosecutor or lawyer who publicly operates in the office of prosecutor or counsel, dare be permitted, in any of the courts that our officials shall hold, to be part of the panel of judges, under penalty of payment of twenty-five lire for each time that this should happen to him. (2)And the official who would call or permit him to judge, being cognisant that he is a prosecutor (*procuradore*) or lawyer (*avocadu*), shall pay and be sentenced likewise to the same penalty of twenty-five lire for each time. (3)And let the judgement or opinion rendered, or that which has been given by the above, be void and of no value. (4)And this shall not be intended in conciliations (*compromessos*) or in matters in which compromises are made by the will of the parties.

Article 73. Of those who shall act as counsels.

(1)We direct and order that no auditor at a hearing (*audencia*) of ours, and no other senior or minor official, so long as he shall remain in his office (*officiu*)—and similarly no notary (*nodaiu*) of our court (*corte*) or of the authorities (*podestà*) while in office in their respective courts—shall dare to be a prosecutor or lawyer, nor it is lawful for him.

LXXIIII. De qui ant esser clamados pro testimongios.

16v (1)Item ordinamus qui tottu cussas personas sardas et terrame[n]giesos c'ant esser clamados pro testimo[n]gios siant tenudos de iurare i[n] man[us] de su officiale c'at reer sa corona et de render testi[m]onianza de cussu qui at esser clamadu et domandadu non obstanti alcuno capidulu de breve over usanza qui esseret facta et observada per te[m]pus passadu.

LXXV. De faguere procuradore.

(1)Volemus et ordinam[us] qui si alcuno ho[min]i esseret chertadu o qui lu chertari[n]t pro largha o pro fura over pro alcuno altero maleficiu qui aviri[n]t factu, deppiat responder i[n] presona sua et non deppiat responder procuradore ne[n] atera persona pro see, eceptu qui pozat ponne procuradore, ista[n]du su q[u]i est principali in persona sua in sa corona. (2)Et depiat dare paghadores ad istare a sa raxioni at rechonoschime[n]tu dessu officiali et iuighantes suos.

LXXVI. Qui iurat pro testimonio.

(1)Item ordinam[us] qui alcuno ho[min]i c'at iurare pro testimo[n]gio falzu, si 'ndi est binchidu, paghit l[ib]r[a]s qui[m]banta i[n]fra dies .xv. de c'at esser iuyghadu. (2)Et si no[n] paghat, siat·illi missidu unu ammu in sa limba et iughat·si affrustandu per totu sa terra infini assu mo[n]tonargiu. (3)Et inie si 'lli tagit sa limba et lassint·illu andare et pl[us] no[n] si siat dadu fidi pro testimongiu.

LXXVII. De chertos dubitosos.

(1)Volemus et ordinam[us], cum ciò siat causa qui in sas coronas nostras de Loghu et ateras qui se tene[n]t per nos [o] per issu arme[n]tagiu nostru multas boltas advenit que inter issos lieros que sunt in sas ditas coronas est adivisioni, discordia over differe[n]tia in su iuygare que faghint supra alcuno chertu, et desiderando nos qui ciascuna dessas terras nostras siant mantesidas et conservadas in iusticia et in r[a]xone et pro efectu dessa dita divisione over discordia no[n] perdat ne[n] manquit alcuna raxone sua, ordinamus et bolem[us] qui, si in alcuna dessas ditas coronas pervengiat alcunu chertu qu'esseret grosso et dubitosu, de su quali sos lieros dessa dita corona essere[n]t partidos et
17r divisidos | in su iuigari issoro, qui in cusso casu su armentargiu nostru de Loghu over atero officiali nostru, qu'est assu presenti o ch'at essere per inantes, sia tenudo, dessu chertu et dessu iuighame[n]tu c'ant faghire sos ditos lieros supra su dictu chertu, de avire·[n]de consigiu cum sos savios dessa corte nos-

Article 74. Of whom shall be called to testify.
(1)Item: we order that all those Sardinian and mainland persons who shall be called to testify shall be required to swear in the hands of the official who shall preside at the assizes (*corona*) and to give testimony concerning that for which they shall be called. The questioning shall be carried out without any article of brief or of the custom that was established and observed in time past being an obstacle to this.

Article 75. Of the functions of the prosecutor.
(1)We wish and order that if any man shall be sued or be put under indictment for robbery or theft, or for any other crime which he has committed, he shall answer for himself, and neither procurator nor any other person shall answer for him, except that he may propose a counsel (*procuradore*); with the exception that a counsel of his own may answer for him if he himself [the accused] is present in the assizes (*corona*). (2)And he shall provide guarantors (*paghadores*) who shall pledge that he will defer to the judicial outcome of his officials and judges, and that they shall be acknowledged by them.

Article 76. Who swears in testimony.
(1)Item: we order that any man who shall give false testimony, if he loses his case, shall pay fifty lire within fifteen days from the time he shall be judged. (2)And if he does not pay, let a hook be put through his tongue, and let him be led [and] whipped through the whole country up to [every] rubbish tip (*montonargiu*). (3)And there let his tongue be cut off and let him go, and no more shall his testimony be believed.

Article 77. Of contentious disputes.
(1)We desire and order, since in our Royal Tribunals (*coronas de Loghu*) or others held on our behalf or by our administrator (*armentagiu*), it happens many times that among the freemen (*lieros*) present in the said assizes (*coronas*) there is a disagreement, a discord or a divergence in the judgement to be rendered about certain disputes, but desiring that all our lands shall be maintained and preserved according to justice and what is right, and that, by reason of dissension or discord, no right shall be lost or diminished, we order and desire that, if in any of the said assizes a contentious and difficult dispute comes up concerning which the freemen of the assizes were divided and of different opinion among themselves in their judgement, that in such a case our State administrator (*armentargiu de Loghu*) or other of our officials, now or in office in future, be held, with regard to the judgement which the aforesaid freemen shall make on the said litigation, to take council with the wise men of our court (*savios*

tra et cum alc[u]nos dessos lieros de sa corona qui pargiant sufficie[n]tes ad elect[i]o[n]e dessu ditu arme[n]targiu over officiali c'at reer sa corona. (2)Et icussu qui pro issos o per ipsa maiore parti dessos s'at deliberari de raxione siat de faghire dessu dito chertu, su arme[n]targiu over officiali nostru fazat leer et publicare in sa p[re]dicta corona in presentia de ambas partis pro sente[n]cia diffinitiva et mandit ad executione, si appellado no[n] est infra te[m]pus legittim[us] de dies deghi come[n]ti comandat sa lege, no[n] infirmando però sa Carta de Loghu.

LXXVIII. De appellationibus.
(1)Constituimus et ordinam[us] qui ciascuna persona qui si sentirit agravada de alc[u]na sente[n]tia qui 'lli esseret dada inco[n]tra, subra alcuno chertu de alc[u]na questio[n]e qui avirit daenante de qualuncha officiali, si pozat, si bolet, appellare·si, infra su te[m]pus ordinadu dae ssa ragione, duas boltas, secundu qu'est naradu de subra, ciò est de una questione non usit et non si pozat appellari pl[us]. (2)Et in casu qui pl[us] boltas si appellarit, ultra sas suprascriptas duas, non si 'lli deppiant amittere nen acceptare.

LXXIX De appellationibus.
(1)Item ordinam[us] [qui] ciascuna persona qui s'at sentiri agravadu de alcuna sente[n]cia qui 'lli esseret dada inco[n]tra si pozat appellari, si bolet, inco[n]tinente viva voce, o per iscriptu infra dies .X. de qui ad esser dada sa sente[n]tia, et qui cussa appellatione et icussu processu dessa questione deppiant levare et p[re]sentare assa corte infra ad ateras dies .XV., et si ya no[n] romaneret pro culpa et negligencia dessu nodaiu over scrivanu qui no[n] lu daret su processu infra su dictu tempus.

LXXX. De appellare·si.
(1)Volemus et ordinam[us], pro cessare ispesas a sos subditos no[st]ros et lit-
17v igantes nostros, qui de alcuna sente[n]tia et iuighamentu c'at esser | factu per armentargiu nostru de Loghu o per chaluncha atero officiali nostru subra alcuna questione nostra o chertu qui esseret dae .C. s[oldo]s in giosso non usit nen deppiat appellari a nnos nen ad atter officiali nen etiam de[us] assos auditores no[st]ros. (2)In casu qui si appellarit, bolem[us] que ssa dicta appellatio[n]e non bagiat nen tenyat pro qui bolem[us] qui [sa] sente[n]cia qui sos officialis no[st]ros in tali causa ant dari et liberari bagiat et tenghat et mandit a executio[n]e, secundu qui per issos iuighantes issoro at essere determinadu.

Ordinamentos de silvas.
LXXXI. (1)Constituim[us] et ordinam[us] qui cussas villas et curadorias qui suntu usadas de faghere silvas de curadore, siant tenudos sos homi[n]is totu

dessa corte nostra) and with some of the freemen (*lieros*) of the assizes who, at the discretion of the said administrator or official who shall preside over the assizes, appear capable and up to the task. (2)And what shall be deliberated by them or by the majority of them according to the deliberations of the law, shall be applied to the said litigation; and our administrator or official shall cause this to be read and published in the said assizes in the presence of both parties, as a final judgement, and shall make it enforceable, if no appeal is made within the period of ten days prescribed by law and without this being contrary to the *Carta de Logu*.

Article 78. Of appeals.
(1)We direct and order that any person who feels aggrieved by any judgement rendered against him, concerning a dispute about a matter which he will raise before some official, may, if he wishes, appeal twice, within the time prescribed by law, according to what has been said above; namely, twice, then his claims shall not be admitted or accepted.

Article 79. Of appeals.
(1)Item: we order that each person who feels aggrieved by any judgement rendered against him may appeal, if he pleases, immediately *viva voce*, or in writing within ten days after the judgement has been passed, and that the said appeal and the records of the proceedings must be presented to the court within a further fifteen days, provided that, through the negligence of the notary or scribe, it turns out not to have been delivered within the said time.

Article 80. Of making an appeal.
(1)We wish and order, so that no expense may be incurred by our subjects who are in litigation, that in regard to any judgement or verdict to be rendered by our State administrator (*armentargiu de Loghu*) or by any other official of ours about any of our disputes or litigations involving matters under one hundred soldi, let no one dare to make an appeal (*appellari*) either from us or from any other official or from any of our auditors (*auditores*). (2)In the event that an appeal should be requested, we wish that the said request be of no value whatsoever, as we wish the judgement that our officials shall render, with regard to said case, to have value and to be sent for completion, as determined by the judges thereof.

Orders about collective hunting parties (*de silvas*).
Article 81. (1)We decree and order that the men of those villages and curatorial districts (*curadorias*) who by custom hold collective hunting parties called by

de cussas villas et curadorias de 'lloy andare una bolta s'annu, et qui su liere de covallu qui at esser nunzadu et no[n] loy andarit paghit [at su regnu soldos .x., et issu homini qui at esser nunzadu et no[n] loy andarit paghit] assu curadore s[oldo]s duos, si verame[n]te no[n] averit excusa legiti[m]a.

LXXXII. Silva.
(1)Item ordinam[us] qui alcuno homini c'at benne a silva nostra ho de curadore et non at benne a gholetorgiu cun su pegus qui at aviri mortu, leve[n]t·illi pro su re[n]nu boe unu et pro su curadore s[oldo]s .x.

LXXXIII. Armadu a silva.
(1)Volemus et ordinam[us] qui su ho[min]i qui at benne armadu a silva nostra o de curadore, levent·illi prossa silva nostra berbeghes deghi et pro sa silva dessu curadore boe unu et perdat s'arma. (2)Et siò no[n] si inte[n]dat pro virgas, ghortellu et ispada.

LXXXIIII. Qui levarit su servu.
(1)Constituimus et ordinam[us] qui su ho[min]i c'at levari su servu dae ssu yagharu et lo[m]pet illoy canargiu et non torrant su peghus, paghit boe unu, assu canargiu det s[oldo]s .xx. et appat·inde su curadore de tres unu, si 'nde 'llu binchit.

LXXXV. Qui alluarit abba.
(1)Item ordinamus qui su homini c'at chundire inantes de sanctu Miali, paghit a su rennu s[oldo]s .xx. et a su curadore s[oldo]s .x. (2)Et issos officiales inde preghontent sos iurados per om[n]i bolta qui los debent pregontare.

LXXXVI. De mesura falsa.
18r (1)Volemus et ordinam[us] qui a cussas personas a qui s'ant achatare per issos officialis nostros mesura falsa o stadea falsa, qui siat condempnadu de paghare a sa camera nostra libras .xxv. dae cussa die qui 'll'at esser achatada a .xv. dies. (2)Et si no[n] paghat assu dictu termen, siat affrustadu per totu su loghu hui at aviri comissidu su delittu.

LXXXVII. De astores.
(1)Constituimus et ordinam[us] qui alcuno homini no[n] deppiat boghare astore ne flacone dae niu. (2)Et icussu qui l'at boghare, siat tenudu su curadore

the curator shall be required to go there once a year, and that the *liere de covallu* [a freeman who has a horse, required to bear arms] who shall be summoned, but fails to attend, shall pay to the realm ten soldi, and the man who shall be summoned and fails to attend shall pay to the curator two soldi, unless he has legitimate and proven justification.

Article 82. Collective hunting (*silva*).
(1)Item: we order that the person who shall participate in the collective hunt summoned by us or by the curator (*curadore*) and does not present himself at the place of gathering with the game he has killed, shall have an ox requisitioned from him in favour of the realm, and pay to the curator ten soldi.

Article 83. The armed man at the collective hunt.
(1)We wish and order that the person who shall take part armed in a collective hunt called by us or by curator shall be requisitioned, if a hunt called by us, for fifteen sheep; if called by the curator, an ox, and his weapon shall be seized. (2)And this does not count for throwing weapons, knives or swords.

Article 84. Who steals the deer.
(1)We decree and order that the person who shall steal deer from a hound, if the keeper of the dogs (*canargiu*) arrives there, and he shall not return the game to him, he shall pay an ox to the keeper of the dogs, and give twenty soldi, of which the keeper of the dogs (*canargiu*) shall have a third, if he wins the case [in court].

Article 85. Who uses poison in water.
(1)Item: we order that the person who shall contaminate the water [that is, to poison with euphorbia (*lua*) for fishing] before Michaelmas Day shall pay to the realm twenty soldi, and to the curator ten soldi. (2)And the officials shall hold an inquiry with those under oath (*sos iurados*) whenever necessary.

Article 86. Of false measures.
(1)We desire and order that persons using a false measure or rigged balance (*stadea*) who shall be found by our officials, shall be ordered to pay to our Chamber twenty-five lire within fifteen days from the time it shall be found for them. (2)And if he does not pay within the said term, let him be whipped around the place where they will have committed the crime.

Article 87. Of goshawks (*astores*).
(1)We direct and command that no person shall remove from the nest, appropriating it, either a goshawk or falcon (*flacone*). (2)And with regard to anyone

dessa curadoria dundi at esser su homini de tenne·llu et bature·llu ad nos ad pena de pagare su curadore l[ib]r[a]s quimbi.

LXXXVIII. De vendere cavallos.
(1)Item ordinamus qui sos hominis totu dessa terra nostra de Arbaree c'ant avire cavallus issoro, illus posant bendere a voluntadi issoro intro Arbaree a ssardos et no[n] a terramangessos senza paraula nostra, at pena de paghare assa corte l[ib]r[a]s .L. (2)Et i[n] ssos terramangessos non si intendant alcunu parladu over abbadi o atero clerigo dessa terra nostra de Arbaree o burghesi de terra nostra.

LXXXIX. De sus lieros.
(1)Volemus et ordinamus qui sos lieros tottu dessas terras de Arbaree, sos calis sunt tenudos de servire sa corte cum cavallos et cum armas, non pozant nen deppiant bendere nen donari nen cambiare su cavallu qui 'lli at esser scriptu in su cadernu de sa mostra senza voluntadi nostra. (2)Et qui co[n]tra de ciò fagherit et est·illi provadu, pagit de maquicia l[ib]r[a]s .XXV. et remittat in iscambiu de cussu qui ad aviri baratadu bono o sufficie[n]te cavallo.

XC. De sus lieros.
1Item ordinamus qui negunu liero de cavallu et nen soldadu non si deppiat representari ad monstra et nen compare cun cavallu de atera persona assa mostra, subta pena de libras ceppari.

XCI. Lieros.
18v (1)Volemus et ordinamus qui sus lieros homines dessa terra nostra de Arbare, sos qualis sunt tenudos de servire cum cavall[us] et armas et sunt·indi de ciò colados, deppiant aviri cavall[us] masch[us]qui bagiant dae l[ib]r[a]s .X. in susu et tota arma chi bisognant ad ho[min]i de covallu assa sardisca et siant semper aparigiad[us] cu[m] suos ditos cavallos et armas pro faghere sa mostra et pro cavalcare q[ua]n[do]nos illos faghiremus requeder. (2)Et qui ciò non at fagheri, torret assa mungia.

XCII. Lieros.
(1)Constituimus et ordinam[us] qui sos lieros qui non sunt appusti fideles o terrali de fictu o ho[min]i dessa corti qui istit in sa villa affeada no[n] deppiat paghare nen dari trabuda assu fidele c'at aviri sa villa. (2)Et icussu qui a deber

who commits this, let the curator (*curadore*) of the district (*curadoria*) to which such persons belong, under penalty of paying five lire, be required to arrest him and bring him to us.

Article 88. Of selling horses.
(1)Item: we order that all men of our land of Arborea who shall be in possession of their own horses may sell them at their will within the territory of Arborea to Sardinians, but not to those from the mainland without our permission, under penalty of paying to our court fifty lire. (2)Mainlanders do not include prelates, abbots or others belonging to the clergy, nor burgesses (*burghesi*) of our land.

Article 89. Of freemen (*lieros*).
(1)We will and command that all the freemen (*lieros*) of the lands of Arborea, who are bound to serve the court with horses (*cavallos*) and in arms (*cum armas*), may not and shall not sell, nor give or change the horse which shall written against them and recorded in writing in the inventory (*cadernu*) of the review (*sa mostra*), without our will. (2)And whosoever shall act against this and it shall be proved in court, let him pay a penalty of twenty-five lire, and compensate, in exchange for that which he shall have changed, a horse of good and sufficient quality.

Article 90. Of freemen.
(1)Item: we order that no free person who owns a horse nor soldier (*soldadu*) shall present himself at the [cadastral] survey (*sa mostra*) nor appear with another person's horse at the survey, under penalty of ten lire.

Article 91. Freemen.
(1)We wish and order that the freemen of our land of Arborea, who are bound to serve with horses and arms and are for that purpose enlisted, shall have male horses of the value of ten lire and upwards, and [also] any weapon necessary to men bound to serve on horseback according to the Sardinian way (*covallu assa Sardisca*). They shall always be ready with their said horses and arms to submit themselves to the survey and to ride when requested by us. (2)And those who will not do all this, should return to lower public service.

Article 92. Freemen.
(1)We decree and order that freemen who do not serve vassals (*fideles*) or tenant farmers (*terrali de fictu*) or men of the court (*homini dessa corti*) residing in an enfeoffed village (*villa affeada*) shall not pay or give tribute to the vassal (*fidele*) who holds the village. (2)And he who shall be liable to pay or give trib-

paghare o dari pro raxione de iurad[us] o pro atera raxione paghit assa corte et non assu fidele.

XCIII. De sus iurados.

(1)Item ordinam[us] qui sos fideles c'ant villas in feu siant tenudos ciaschunu de pponni a iurare su maiore dessa villa pro iuradu de Loghu et issos megios dessa villa, (2)sos quales iuradus deppiant su fidele qui chue at esser in persona battire·llos per iscriptu assa camera dae 'noghi a corona de sanctu Pedru de lampadas. (3)Et pro su fidele qui no 'nchi at esser in persona siat tenudu su officiali suo et maiore suo su qui at esser pro issu i[n] ssa villa de batire·llus a sa camera per iscriptu sos iurad[us]. (4)E si no[n] los batirit a su dictu terme[n], paghit su fidele o maiore o faghidore dessu fidele qui contra fagherit et qui no[n] ad esser l[ib]r[a]s .x.

XCIIII. De sotzus.

(1)Volem[us] et ordinamus qui alcuno terramangiesu c'at dare iuo suo a ssardu, pro iuargiu o pro soci[u], non appat ad cherre at perunu homi[n]i, salvu a qui 'llu ad aviri dadu. (2)Et issu iuargiu istit assa usansa dessa terra.

XCV. De cavallus.

(1)Constituim[us] et ordinam[us] qui si alcuno cavallu nostru morret in silba over qui si semet, qui no siat secidu per paraula nostra, su maiore de cavall[us] paghit prossu dictu cavallu a nnos pro s'unu deghe, secundu qui narat sa Carta
19r de Loghu pro causas dessu rennu furada. (2)Et icussu ho[min]i qui 'll'at | seer, siat condempnadu de pagare assa corte s[oldo]s chentu.

XCVI. De qui si 'ndi andarit.

(1)Item ordinam[us] qui si alcuno ho[min]i de sa terra nostra de Arbaree si partirit pro andare at istare dae ss'una curadoria a s'atera, cussu officiale de cussa curadoria ad hui at esser andadu ad istare siat tenudo de fagheri paghare ass'atero officiali pari suo, q[ua]n[do] illu adimandarit, cussas raxio[n]es qui debent pagare a nnos prossu officiu suo. (2)Et icussas raxiones c'at aver a dimandare s'unu officiali ass'atero prossos homi[n]is c'ant esser partidos dae ss'una curadoria ass'atera, siat tenudo ciasc[u]no c'at aviri a rreciviri de dimandare sas raxio[n]es suprascriptas duas boltas s'annu, ciò est pro corona de Loghu

ute because he is a juror (*de iurados*) or is otherwise required by law, let him pay to the court and not to the vassal.

Article 93. Of those under oath (*sos iurados*).
(1)Item: we order that vassals (*fideles*) who hold villages in fief (*in feu*) shall all be required to have the mayor of the village (*maiore dessa villa*) sworn in as a State juror (*iuradu de Loghu*), and likewise the best men (*issos megios*) of the villa; (2)the vassal (*su fidele*) who shall be present there in person shall bring in writing to the Chamber (*sa camera*) the names of those under oath (*sos iurados*) by the assizes (*corona*) of St Peter in June. (3)And as for the vassal who will not be present there in person, let his official or mayor (*maiore*) who acts as his deputy in the village be required to deliver to the Chamber the names of those under oath in writing. (4)And if the vassal or the mayor or the one acting in the vassal's stead do not deliver within the prescribed time and do what is prescribed, they shall pay ten lire.

Article 94. Of partnerships (*sotzus*).
(1)We wish and order that if anyone from the continent shall give a yoke of oxen of his own to a Sardinian, either as a drover or as a partner, he shall not require any other man but he to whom he has given it. (2)And the drover shall abide by the customs of the land (*sa terra*).

Article 95. Of horses.
(1)We direct and order that if any horse of ours, which is mounted against our permission, dies or remains maimed during a collective hunt, the official overseeing horses (*maiore de cavallus*) shall pay to us for the said horse ten times its value, according to what the *Carta de Logu* prescribes in regard to stolen things of the realm. (2)And let that man who mounts him be sentenced to pay to the court one hundred soldi.

Article 96. Of those who move.
(1)Item: we order that if any man (*homini*) of our land of Arborea shall move to go and reside from one curatorial district (*curadoria*) to another, the official of that curatorial district to which he shall have moved shall be bound, so far as his office is concerned, to require him to pay to the other official his equal, should the latter require it, the tributes which are to be paid to us according to what is due. (2)And in regard to those tributes, which he shall exact from one official to the other in regard to the men who shall have moved from one curatorial district to another, let each of those who shall collect them be obliged to exact the aforesaid tributes twice a year, that is, for the Royal Tribunal (*Corona de Loghu*)

de sanctu Nichola et pro corona de Loghu de s[a][n]cto Pedro de lampadas. (3)Et de ciò su officiali non constringhirit nen deppiat agravare su maiore over alcuno iuradu pro mandare·llas a gholliri alcunas raxio[n]es foras dessa curadoria issoro. (4)Et icussu curadore over officiali q[u]i at fagheri secundu qui narat de supra, per ogna volta qui 'll'at esser provadu qui contra faghirit, siat condemnadu de paghare assa camera nostra s[oldo]s che[n]tu. (5)Et siat cretidu su officiali over curadore c'at aviri adimandadu sas raxiones c'at aviri a rrecivire dae s'atero officiali pari suo a sagramentu suo.

XCVII. De deseredari.
(1)Volemus et ordinamus qui nexuna persona de su rennu nostru de Arbaree usit nen deppiat deseredare sos figios over nebodes suos nados dessos figios dessas rexones qui si 'llis at apertenne pro sa hereditadi de su padre over de sa mamma issoro, salvo si su padre over sa mamma a sa morte issoro bolerent narri et apponere[n]t contra issos figios over nebodes iusta ochaxione prossa quale issos deberent diseredare. (2)Et issa dita ocaxione si deppiat provare legittimamente [per icusos a qui ant] aviri lexadu sos benes issoro infra unu mese dae ssa die de sa morte de su testadore.

XCVIII. De coyamentos.
(1)Constituimus et ordinamus qui si alcuna persona coiarit figia sua a dodas,
19v qui non siat tenudu de lassare·li | nen dare·lli in vida nen in morte sua, si non cussu qui 'll'at aviri dadu in dodas si non a voluntadi sua. (2)Salvu qui si isse no[n] avirit ateru figiu, qui 'lli deppiat laxare sa parti sua, secundu raxione, contadu illoy in cussa parte c'at deber avire sas dodas c'at aviri appidu daenante. (3)Et simigiante si inte[n]dat pro tottu sos dixendentes suos. (4)Et totu s'atero qui 'll'at romanne inde possat faguere cussu qui 'll'at plaghere. (5)Et in casu qui morret ab intestadu, sussedat sa figia femina coiada cu[m] sus ateros fradis et sorris suas, isco[n]tandu dae ssa parti sua cun ssa doda qui at aviri appidu.

XCIX. De coyanza et heretamentu.
(1)Item ordinamus qui si alcuna femina si coiarit a mmodo sardischo over a dodas et morret et lassarit alcunu figiu piciu, si cussu figiu piciu morret poscha senza legitima aedadi de annos .XVIII., qui su padri dessu ditu ceracho succedat et appat sa heredidadi dessu dictu figiu suo. (2)Et simigia[n]teme[n]te sussedat sa mamma assu figiu pixinu in cussus benes qui 'lli furuntu romasidos de su padre, exceptu qui ssu padre over sa mamma avirint factu testamentu.

of St Nicholas and for the Royal Tribunal (*Corona de Loghu*) of St Peter in June. (3)And in this regard the official shall neither compel nor charge the senior official (*maiore*), nor any juror to go and exact tribute outside his own curatorial district (*curadoria*). (4)And that curator (*curadore*) or official who shall not act as aforesaid [i.e., who shall depart from the above provisions], for each time he shall be proved to have acted otherwise, let him be condemned to pay to our Chamber one hundred soldi. (5)And on oath, let the official or curator, who shall have demanded the tributes which he shall receive from the other official equal to himself, be trusted.

Article 97. Of disinheritance.
(1)We will and command that no person in our realm of Arborea shall dare to disinherit his children or grandchildren born of his children of the rights which belong to them by inheritance from their father or mother, unless the father or mother, at the time of their death, wishes to oppose any just cause for which they should disinherit their sons. (2)Such cause shall be proved according to law by those to whom they have left their property, within one month from the day of the testator's death.

Article 98. Of marriages (*coyamentos*).
(1)We decree and order that if any person marries his daughter under a dowry arrangement, he shall not be bound to leave her or to give her, either during his lifetime or after his death, anything other than what he shall have given her in the dowry, unless he wishes otherwise. (2)An exception is the case where he has no other children: in which case he is to leave, according to right, a part of the inheritance, counting therein, in that part which she is to have as her inheritance, the dowry which she will have previously had. (3)And similarly it will be intended for all his descendants. (4)And of all that remains to him, he may do with it what he pleases. (5)And in the event that he dies without a will (*ab intestato*), let his married daughter succeed him, together with her other brothers and sisters, discounting, from the latter's share of the inheritance, the dowry she will have had.

Article 99. Of marriage and inheritance.
(1)Item: we order that if any woman marry 'in the Sardinian way' (*a sa Sardisca*) or according to the dowry arrangement and dies leaving a minor child, if such child subsequently dies before the legal age of eighteen years or more, then the father of the said minor shall succeed him in the inheritance. (2)And similarly the mother shall succeed the minor child in those properties left to her by the father, except in the case where either the father or the mother has made a will.

(3)Qui in cussu casu si deppiat observare su ordini de cussu testame[n]tu et issa voluntadi dessu testadore.

C. De donatione.
(1)Volemus et ordinam[us] qui alcuna femina no[n] usit nen deppiat dari in alcuno modo assu maridu nen in vida nen in morte sua pl[us] de l[ib]r[a]s .x. et issu maridu assa mughere atero e tantu dessu issoro peghugiare. (2)Et icussu det cussu c'at aviri valsente de l[ib]r[a]s .xx. in susu, et icussu qui at aviri valsenti dae l[ib]r[a]s .xx. in giosso det s[oldo]s .xx. (3)Et icustu det s'unu ass'atero si 'll'at plagher, et si non li plagheret no 'ndi siat tenudu nen assu marido nen assa mughere. (4)Et icustu capidulo appat legitime loghu in casu qui su marido over mughere avirint dexendentes over ascende[n]tes. (5)Et si no 'ndi avirit, siat·illis
20r licitu de llassare·si s'unu ass'atero pro testamentu over per donatio[n]e | causa mortis tottu ciò qui ad boler dessos benes issoro.

CI. De inventario.
(1)Constituimus et ordinamus qui sos curadores et officiales nostros de corte de Arbaree, ciaschuno in ssa curadoria et officiu suo c'ant aviri in manu, deppiant esser tenudus, quandu alcuno homini morreret senza faghere testamentu et lassarit figiu o figias pixinas et non las acoma[n]darit per testamentu, qui sus benes suos proprios qui romanint dintro de domo et foras qui si deppiant totu fagheri iscrivere ordinadamenti, avendo su officiali at compangia sua dessos bonos hominis dessa contrada over dessa villa. (2)Et unu scriptu de cussos benis qui 'ndi deppiat batiri assa corte nostra et uno atero iscriptu indi depiat [dari] ad icussa personi a qui ad avire acomandado sos figius. (3)Et si acomandados non los avirit, su officiali over curadore los deppiant acomandare per vigore dessu officiu suo ad alcuno parente destrittu dessos serachos et qui siant sufficientes. (4)Et si parente qui esseret sufficiente non avirint sos cerachos, deppiant·illos acomandari ad una atera persona qui siat sufficienti et que ad parre assu officiali qui siat bonu homini et qui fazat bene fatos dessos cerachos [infini a] .XVIII. annos, qui li ant dari su issoro cussu o cusas a qui at acomandari su officiali sos dictos benes. (5)Et illu deppiant ponne a iurare de faghere bene et lealimente sos factos de cussos cerachos. (6)Et si cussos gotalis parentis over ateros hominis ad qui su officiali acomandarit sos dictos benes non los bollirint recivir, deppiat·illus co[n]stringere su officiali e ponne pena. (7)Et simigiantemente ordinamus qui cussas personas qui at clamare cusu homi[n]i qui fagherit testame[n]tu pro curadores de cussos cerachos dessos benes issoro, e siant presentes a su faghire su testamentu o non, deppiant·indi esser constric-

(3)In that case, the provisions of that will and the will of the testator shall be observed.

Article 100. Of donations.
(1)We wish and order that no woman dare nor shall give in any way to her husband, either during his lifetime or at her death, more than ten lire, and likewise the husband to his wife, from their personal estate. (2)And this amount may be given by those who have wealth from twenty lire upward; those who possess twenty lire or less may give twenty soldi. (3)And one spouse may give this amount to the other spouse if they please, and if it is not their wish, there is no mutual obligation. (4)And this article shall have legal force in case the husband or wife has descendants or ancestors. (5)And if they have none, let it be lawful for them to give one to the other, by will or *causa mortis* donation, all that he or she wills of his or her property.

Article 101. Of the inventory (*inventario*).
(1)We decree and order that our curators (*curadores*) and officials of the court of Arborea, each in a curatorial district (*curadoria*) and office to which they are appointed and of which they are in charge, should be required, when any man dies without making a will and leaves minor children or daughters and will not have considered them in the will, that his own property which remains in or out of the house should be precisely inventoried, the official having the assistance of trusted men (*bonos hominis*) of the country or village. (2)And a copy of this inventory of property shall be delivered to our court, and another copy shall be delivered to the person to whom the guardianship of the children has been entrusted. (3)And if he shall not have placed them under guardianship, the official or curator shall, by virtue of his office, place them under the guardianship of some close relative of the said minors who has sufficient capacity. (4)And if the said minors have no relative of sufficient capacity, they shall be placed under the guardianship of some other person who has such capacity, and who, in the judgement of the official, is a person of such good qualities as can provide for the good of the minors until the age of eighteen years, when to such persons the guardians shall remit what is due to them. (5)And they shall take an oath that they shall look after the interests of those minors well and lawfully. (6)And if such relatives or other persons to whom the official shall have entrusted the guardianship of the said property do not wish to accept, the official shall oblige them by force of law and under intimidation of penalty. (7)And we similarly order that those persons whom the testator shall designate in the will as guardians of the property of minors, whether or not they were present at the time of the making of the will, shall be obliged to assume the guardian-

tus de lus recivire et de esser tudores issoro, salvu si monstrarit legittimamente
excusa pro sa quali non los podere[n]t recivire et no[n] podere[n]t esser in sa
20v dita tutela o curadoria. | (8)Et icusso officiali over curadore qui cussas causas
non ad fagheri, per do[n]nia bolta que li at esser provadu paghit a sa corte nos-
tra l[ib]r[a]s .x. et poscha su arme[n]targiu no[st]ro de Loghu fassat faghere, et
nie[n]te de minus tottu su damnu c'ant aviri recivido sos cerachos per culpa et
negligentia dessos ditos tudores et curadores et siant tenudos de me[n]dari et
satisfagheri a sos ditos pixinus.

CII. De tutores e curadores.

(1)Item ordinam[us] qui si alcuna persona, depusti morti sua, lasarit figios pixin[us] et in su testame[n]tu suo illis lassarit tudore over curadore, over qui 'llis esseret dada per issos officialis no[st]ros, q[u]i cussus tudores o curadores no[n] siant tenud[us] respo[n]der a chertu alcunu qui 'llis esseret factu pro cussos pixinus de caluncha causa, si no[n] in sa corte nostra over corona de Loghu. (2)Siant tenudos de responder in sa dicta corte et corona a ciascuna persona qui 'llis at chertare pro cussos pixinos. (3)Et si sos ditos tudores no[n] parere[n]t a su arme[n]targiu nostru de Loghu c'at reer corona over ad icussos qui 'llas inte[n]dat in sa corte nostra qui essere[n]t sufficie[n]tes a ppoder demandare over defendere cussos chert[us] qui 'llis essere[n]t fact[us] over qui faghirint prossos ditos pixinos, siat tenudo su dictu armentargiu nostru de Loghu c'at reer corona over cussu a qui esseret comissidu per nos de dare et co[n]stringere unu dessos bonos dessa coro[n]a over alcuno atero pro issu, quali si possat adimandare over defendere cussu chertu qui at esser factu assos tudores over curadores pro sos dictos pixinos.

CIII. De prea.

(1)Volemus et ordinam[us] qui alcuno curadore over officiali nostru de Arbaree non possat reer pro se prea alcuna c'at fagheri pro raxione dessu rennu et [a] qui at esser provadu paghit per dogna volta l[ib]ra[s] .xxv.

CIIII. De mantenni iusticia.

(1)Constituimus et ordinamus qui si alcuno homini dessa terra nostra de Arba-
ree offenderet o qui avirit a ffagueri pro alcuna causa cu[m] alcuno atero hom-
21r ini de Sardigna que non esseret de sas terras nostras, qui cussa persona | siat
intessida a raxione pro icussu modu qui in sa terra dundi esseret issu si fagherit
raxio[n]i assos ho[min]is dessas terras nostras.

ship and thus be guardians thereof, except where they can show legitimate exemption for which they cannot be entrusted with guardianship or advocacy. (8)And that official or curator who shall fail to perform these prescribed duties shall pay to our court ten lire for each time the failure shall be proved against him; and thereafter our State administrator (*armentargiu nostro de Loghu*) shall enforce these provisions. Nonetheless, for all the harm which the minors shall have received through the fault and negligence of the said guardians and curators, the latter shall be bound to compensate the said minors to full satisfaction.

Article 102. Of guardians and curators.
(1)Item: we order that if any person, after his death, leaves any minor children (*figios pixinus*), and if in his will he designates a guardian or curator, or if the said guardianship is assigned to them by our officials, that those guardians or curators shall not be bound to answer to any litigation that may be brought against them for any cause whatsoever on behalf of those minors, except in our court or in the Royal Tribunal (*Corona de Loghu*). (2)They shall be bound to answer in the said court or assizes (*corona*) to each person who shall bring any case against them concerning said minors. (3)And if the said guardians shall not be deemed, by our State administrator (*armentargiu de Loghu*) who shall preside over the assizes or by the auditors at our court, capable and able to support the interests and claims of the said minors or to assume their defence in connection with those disputes which shall be brought against them or which they shall move on their behalf, be it incumbent upon our State administrator (*armentargiu de Loghu*) who shall preside over the assizes, or upon him who shall be designated by us for this purpose, to procure by force of obligation one of the good men of the assizes or some other for him, who shall be capable of supporting the defence in the cause of litigation which shall be brought against the guardians on behalf of the said minors [for their alleged deeds].

Article 103. Of seized property (*prea*).
(1)We wish and order that no curator or official of ours in Arborea may keep for himself any property which he shall have seized for rights of the realm. He, against whom this shall be proved, shall pay for each time twenty-five lire.

Article 104. Of the maintenance of justice.
(1)We decree and order that if any man of our land (*terra*) of Arborea causes offence or will have some legal case for some reason with another man of Sardinia who does not belong to our lands (*terras*), then that person shall be heard according to law (*raxione*) in the same manner as justice (*raxioni*) is done in the land (*terra*) of his origin to the persons of our lands (*terras*).

CV. De tavernayos.

(1)Item ordinamus qui sos curadores nostros qui ant essere in ciascuna curadoria deppiant dari comandame[n]tu assos tavernaios, ciaschuno in sas villas qui ant aviri in manu, qui non deppiant bendere vinu at attera mesura si non assa mesura d'Aristanis et sinnada de su sinnu nostru, et fassat bonas mesuras dintro et de foras, dando·lis terme[n] de benne in Aristanis assu maiore de portu pro levari ciaschunu tavernaiu mesura et mesa mesura et derredali. (2)Et icussas mesuras siat tenudu ciascunu qui bendit vinu de aviri a corona de Loghu de sanctu Marchu proximu qui nos be[n]nit. (3)Et dae cussa corona inantes cussu tavernaiu a qui ad esser provadu c'at bender cum atera mesura qui de cussas qui suntu naradas de supra paghit per dogna volta s[oldo]s .VI., dessos quales dinares apat cussa persona qui 'llus at acusare sa mesidadi et iss'atera mesidadi apat su officiali prossu rennu. (4)Et siat chertida cussa persona qui 'llos at achusare assu sagramentu suo.

Ordinamentos de corgios et de mercantes.

CVI. (1)Volemus et ordinamus qui sos corgios tottu de boes et de vachas et de cavallu et de ebbas c'ant morre dessa terra nostra de Arbaree et batire a sa terra nostra d'Aristanis per issos pubillos over missos issoro si deppiant batiri daenanti de cussos hominis qui sunt ordinadus in sa corte a sinare·llos, sos qualis hominis cussos corgios deppiant iscriviri cui ant esser per nome[n] et qui 'llos at batiri per nome[n] et de quale villa, conoschendo cussu homini qui at batiri su corgiu over corgios. (2)Et s'est homini qui non siat conoschente o parixente, cussos homines qui debent sinnari sos corgios indi adimandi[n]t homini qui 'llu conoschat, qui no 'ndi siant inghannad[us]. (3)Et deppiant·illos sinnare sos corgios a fferro caldu de cussu sinnu qui est ordinadu et [si] poscha qui sos cor-

21v gios ant esser sinnadus, su pubillu cui ant esser, o missu suo qui 'll'at ba- | tiri, illu bogiat bender, deppiat·illu bender in presentia de cussos hominis qui 'll'ant avir sinnado assu mercanti, iscrivendo sus ho[min]is c'ant sinnare sos corgios su mercante qui 'llos at comporare per nome[n] et pronomen e su bendidore. (4)Et si su pubillu chui at essere su corgiu, o missu suo qui 'll'at batiri, non lu boleret bender et indi boleret fagheri alcuno factu suo o suegher o atero dae c'at esser sinnadu su corgiu, pozat·i[n]che·llu boghare senza indi paghare alcuno diritu et faghiri·ndi alcuno factu issoro. (5)Et de custu siant tenudus sos clerigos et totu sos ho[min]es de ciascuna villa de Arbaree, qui sos corgios totu, secundo qu'est narradu de supra, deppiant batiri at Aristanis a sinnari·si de cussu sinnu

Article 105. Of tavern keepers.
(1)Item: we order that our curators who shall be in office in each curatorial district (*curadoria*), each [curator being] in villages under his jurisdiction, must order tavern keepers not to sell wine at any other measure than that of Oristano, and identified (*sinnada*) with our mark (*sinna*), and that such measurements must be accurate inside and outside [the tavern], and [the curators] must give the tavern keepers a time limit to present themselves in Oristano with the port official (*maiore de portu*) to test the measure, the half measure, and the *derradali* [a lower capacity liquid measure]. (2)And whoever sells wine is required to hold those measures by the day of the Royal Tribunal (*Corona de Loghu*) of the next coming [feast day of] St Mark (25 April). (3)And from the day of the said court (*corona*) onward, the tavern keeper against whom the selling [of wine] with a different measure than those said above shall be proved, shall pay for each time six soldi, of which half the sum of money (*dinares*) shall go to that person who shall accuse them, and the other half shall be collected by the official in favour of the realm. (4)And let that person who shall accuse them be believed on oath.

Orders about hides and merchants.
Article 106. (1)We wish and order that all the hides of oxen, cows, horses, and mares of our land of Arborea, which shall die and be brought into the land of Oristano by the owners or their trustees, shall be brought before the men who are appointed at our court to affix the [identification] mark upon them, which men shall record the name of their respective owners, and also the name of the person who shall have delivered them, and of the village whence they came, if the one who shall have brought the hide or hides is an identifiable person. (2)And if it is an unknown or unidentifiable person, those who are in charge of marking the hides shall seek out persons whom they may know without possibility of doubt or deception. (3)And they shall brand the hides by a red-hot iron with the prescribed mark, and if, after branding, the owners of the leather or their proxies who have brought it, wish to sell it to a merchant, they may do so only in the presence of the persons who have branded the hides, and they shall record the name and surname of the merchant who will buy it and of the one who sells it. (4)And if the owner of the leather or his proxy who shall have delivered [the hides], but does not wish to sell them and wishes to make personal use of them, or to tan them, or anything else after the leather has been branded, he may take them away freely without having to pay any fee, and dispose of them at his will. (5)And to this the clerics and all the men of each of the villages of Arborea are bound; namely, that they shall bring the hides, all of them, to Oristano to be branded, according to what has been said above, with

qu'est ordinadu. (6)Et qui alcuno homini alcuno corgiu de boe o de bacha o de cavallu o de ebba no[n] deppiat boghare foras dessa terra de Arbaree, ni bender at alcuna attera persona, nen comporare in Arbaree, si non Aristanis, dae c'at esser sinnadu, nen in peruno factu suo, si non est sinnadu in Aristanis. (7)Et dae c'at esser provadu, paghit secundu qui narat su capidulu de Carta de Loghu: s'est boe pro boe, s'est vacha pro vacha, [s'est cavallu pro cavallu], s'est ebba pro ebba. (8)Et in ciaschuna villa si te[n]ghat per issu maiore et iuradus unu ferro cu[n] ssu quali si marchint sos corgios et qui 'llos deppiant fagheri iscriviri et dae mese in mese mandit su iscripto assu officiali maiore et infra su dictu temp[us] cussu officiali maiore illu mandit per iscriptu assa camera. (9)Et niente de minus omni simana si deppiant chirquare sas dommos pro sas furas assu minus una bolta per simana, supta pena, assu officiali maiore, si in ciò esseret negligente, de s[oldo]s che[n]tu et assu maiore de s[oldo]s qui[m]banta et de s[oldo]s .xx. per iurado senza misericordia alcuna.

CVII. De negociantes.

(1)Constituimus et ordinam[us] qui [si] assos negociantes c'ant fagheri mercantia in sas villas acatant causa furada, o batiat qui si 'lla dedi o paghit sa fura, secundu qui si co[n]tenit in sa Carta de Loghu pro causa furadissa. (2)Et issos
22r negociantes c'ant fagheri mercantia in sas villas non posant com- | porare corgiu de boe, nen de vacha, nen de covallu, et nen d'ebba, nen d'asino. (3)Et si 'ndi comporarit, paghit secundu qui narat su capidulu de Cartha de Loghu pro covallu, pro ebba, pro boe et de vacha. (4)Bolem[us] però qui ciaschuno negociante pozat comporare corgiu de boe et de vacha et de ebba et de covallu et de asinu, puro qui siat marchadu de su marchu de sa corte et qui lu comporit daenante dessu officiali over maiore de sa villa. (5)Et qui contra fagheret paghit secundo qui in supra[scripto] capidulu si contenet. (6)Et bolem[us] ancho qui ciaschuno officiali over maiore deppiat sinnari o fagheri sinnari tottu sos dictos corgios et ciaschuno de cussos cun su marchu dessa corte qui 'lli at essere mandadu. (7)Et qualuncha atera persona teneret marcho siat condempnado in l[ib]r[a]s .x.

CVIII. De is suetoris.

(1)Item ordinamus qui alcuno suetore over conzadore de coiamen non deppiat suegher nen conzare alcuno corgiu de boe nen [de] vacha nen de covallu nen de ebba nen de asinu, si non est sinnadu in Aristanis dessu sinnu qu'est ordinado. (2)Et a c'at esser provadu, paghit secundu[m] qui narat sa Carta de Loghu prossa

the set mark. (6)And that no man shall bring out of the land of Arborea any ox, cow, horse or mare's hide; nor, since it shall be branded, [shall he] sell it to any other person, nor buy it in Arborea except in Oristano, nor use it for his own private purposes, unless it is branded in Oristano. (7)And if it shall be proved against him that he has contravened all these things, he shall pay according to that which the article of the *Carta de Logu* says: if it be leather of ox for [theft of] an ox, if of cow for [theft of] a cow, if of horse for [theft of] a horse, if of a mare for [theft of] a mare. (8)And in each village let there be at the disposal for the mayor (*maiore*) and those under oath (*sos iurados*), an iron with which to brand the hides, and let them have it registered and, month by month, let he [the mayor] send the registration to the senior official (*officiali maiore*) and, within the said time, let such senior official deliver it in writing to the Chamber (*sa Camera*). (9)And nonetheless every week, for once at least, they shall make in inquiry at the houses in connection with thefts, imposing punishment: if it be the senior official (*officiali maiore*) who shall be negligent in this, to pay one hundred soldi; if it be the mayor (*maiore*), fifty soldi, and if it be the juror, twenty soldi without leniency of any kind.

Article 107. Of merchants (*negociantes*).
(1)We direct and order that if merchants who practise trade in the villages find stolen goods, they shall either hand over the one from whom they got them, or they shall pay for the theft according to that which is contained in the *Carta de Logu* concerning theft. (2)And the merchants who shall practise trade in the villages shall not buy ox leather, nor cow leather, nor horse leather, nor mare leather, nor donkey leather. (3)And if they shall buy any, let them pay according to that which the article of the *Carta de Logu* says concerning horses, mares, oxen or cows. (4)We grant, however, that each merchant may buy leather of an ox, cow, mare, horse, and donkey, provided it is branded with the mark of the court and that he buys it in the presence of the official or mayor of the village. (5)And whoever shall contravene this, shall pay according to what is contained in the above article. (6)And we further direct that each official or mayor shall brand, or cause to be branded, all the said hides, each of them with the mark of the court which shall be delivered to him. (7)And any other person who removes the mark shall be sentenced to the penalty of ten lire.

Article 108. Of those who macerate [hides].
(1)Item: we order that no macerator or tanner of hides shall either macerate or tan any leather of ox, nor of cow, nor of horse, nor of mare, nor of donkey if [the leather] has not been branded in Oristano with the requisite mark. (2)And if it shall be proved against him, he shall pay according to that which the *Carta*

fura s'est boe pro boe et vacha pro vacha, covallu pro covallu, si est ebba pro ebba, s'est asinu pro asinu, secundu qui in su suprascripto capidulu si contenet.

CIX. De sus mercantis.
(1)Volemus et ordinam[us] qui alcuno mercante d'Aristanis nen alcuna atera persona no[n] deppiat co[m]porare alc[u]no corgiu de boe nen de vacha nen de cavallu nen de ebba ne[n] de molente, si non sinnado dessu sinnu qu'est ordinadu. (2)Ad icussa qui esseret provadu qui 'll'at co[m]porare senza esser sinnado secundo qu'est ordinado et est·illi acaptado su corgiu, si 'ndi esti binchidu, paghit su dampnu a chui at esser factu et s[oldo]s .c. assa corte pro ciasch[u]no corgiu, secundu qui in ssos suprascriptos capidulos si contenet.

CX. De corgius.
(1)Constituimus et ordinamus qui nexuna persona no[n] deppiat co[m]parare
nen bender corgiu perunu de boe nen de vacha nen de cavallu nen de ebba nen
22v de mo- | lente, [qui non] siat cottu, si non im plassa publicame[n]te daenante
de tottu supta pe[n]a de l[ib]r[a]s .v. (2)Et ciò si inte[n]dat pro cussos qui ant
comporare in Aristanis.

CXI. Idem de ligadores.
(1)Item ordinam[us] qui cussos ligadores totu qui lighant corgios in Aristanis siant tenudus de no[n] lighare corgiu peruno in faschi si no[n] est sinnadu de cussu sinnu qu'est ordinado. (2)Et qui co[n]tra faghirit siat postu in su panghuliere cum uno corgiu a guturu et poscha istit in p[re]xione infini at qui at aviri paghado s[oldo]s .xx.

Ordiname[n]tos de sa guardia de sus laores, vingnas et ortos.
CXII. (1)Volemus et ordinam[us] qui siant tenud[us] sus homi[n]is qui ant vingnas issoro et ortos de cungare·llos bene et cungiadas qui illas ant aviri bene, dughant·loy su officiali et issos maiores et iurados .v. dae sa villa pixina et dae ssa villa manna iuradus .x. pro videre et ischire si ant esser benecuniadas. (2)Et si ad issos at parri qui siant bene co[n]iadas et intrat illoy bestiamen, cussu pubillo istesu dessas vignas et dessos ortos, armentargiu o ho[min]i o famegiare suo c'apat, qui l'adi aviri acomandadu cu[m] ateros ho[min]is de credere o pone[n]do boghi, illu possat maxedari et te[n]ni et dare·llu in manu dessu officiali qui ad esser pro nos in sa contrada, sò est boe domado, cavallu domado,

de Logu says about theft: if [it is leather of] ox for [theft of] an ox, if of cow for [theft of] a cow, if of horse for [theft of] a horse, if of mare for [theft of] a mare, if of donkey for [theft of] a donkey, according to what is contained in the above article.

Article 109. Of merchants (*merchantis*).
(1)We wish and order that no merchant of Oristano, nor any other person, shall buy any leather of ox or cow or horse or mare or donkey unless it bears the mark of ordinance. (2)That person who shall be proved to have purchased it without it having been previously branded according to the ordinance and to whom such leather shall be found, if he is won of it in court, shall pay damages to him who shall have caused it, and [give] one hundred soldi to the court for each leather, according to what is contained in the above articles.

Article 110. Of animal hides (*corgius*).
(1)We establish and order that no person shall buy or sell any leather of ox, cow, horse, mare or donkey that is not cooked in boiling water, if not publicly in the square and in the public presence, under penalty of five lire. (2)And this is intended for those who will buy in Oristano.

Article 111. Idem of hide binders (*ligadores*).
(1)Item: we order that all those hide binders who bind hides in Oristano be bound not to bind any leather in bundles unless it bears the mark of ordinance. (2)And whoever shall do otherwise shall be put to the pillory (*in su panghuliere*) with a hide at his throat and thereafter remain in prison until he has paid twenty soldi.

Ordinances on the supervision of cultivations (*laores*), vineyards (*vingnas*), and vegetable gardens (*ortos*).
Article 112. (1)We wish and order that men who possess vineyards and gardens be required to enclose them properly with fencing and, once they have them well fenced, let them bring the official and senior officials (*maiores*) and jurors (*iuradoes*) there, five from a small village and ten jurors from a large village, so that they may check whether the fencing has been well set up. (2)And if it shall appear to these that they have been properly fenced, and livestock then penetrate them, the owner of the vineyards and gardens himself, or the senior official (*armentargiu*), or man or employee of his to whom he has given delegated authority, may, giving [prior] notice through other men of good faith or by public notice, slaughter and capture it and deliver it to the official appointed by us in the district; this he may do if it be tame ox, tame horse, tame cow or

bacha domada et mole[n]te. (3)Et issu officiali, [per] ciaschuna de cussas causas qui sunt scriptas de supra, deppiat levare a su ho[min]i c'at paschiri cussu bestiami[n]i s[oldo]s .VI. per ciascuno pegh[us] per o[m][n]ia bolta qui 'lloy ant esser te[n]tus. (4)Et si cussu bestiamini no[n] at pastore, deppiat·si pagare dae ssu pubillu dessu bestiame[n], dessus callis denaris appat su rennu s[oldo]s .IIII. et issu qui 'llo at te[n]ne s[oldo]s .II. (5)[De] su armentu dessas bachas et dessas trumas dessas ebbas bie 'nde possant ochire una et dessa gamma dessas berbeghis et dessa gamma dessas cabras et dessa gamma dessos porchos bie 'nde possant ochire o levare a biu duos et paghare su dampnu at cuy at esser.
23r (6)Su porcho magnale ochiant·bie·llu. | (7)Et issu damnu qui at faghere cussu bestiamen sus iuradus siant tenudos de apressare·llos bene et lealeme[n]te et de faghere paghare su damnu a sus pobill[us] qui 'll'ant aviri recivido. (8)Et gasi si i[n]te[n]dat pro sos laores, come[n]te narat de supra pro sas vignas et pro sos ortos. (9)Et q[ua]n[do] pro isso maiore de pardu over pardassus co[m]pangius suos non si fagherint paghare su damno, et issu arme[n]targiu nostru de Loghu over officiali dessa curadoria indi avirit lame[n]tu, per dogna bolta qui 'llis at esser provadu, indi siat conde[m]pnado a pagare assa camera nostra s[oldo]s .XX. per iurado. (10)Et q[ua]n[do] bestiame[n] de una villa faghirit de cussos damnos [in attera villa, cusus dannos] c'ant esser fact[us] et ap[re]ssad[us], siat tenudo su officiali de cussa villa de undi at esser su bestiame[n] q[u]i at aviri fatu su da[m]no de illa faghiri pagari i[n] manu de su maiore de pardo over dessus iurados qui 'lloy ant benne. (11)Et q[ua]n[do] zò non faghirit, cussu officiali over curadore, per dogna bolta qui l'at esser provado, siat condempnado a paghare assa camera nostra s[oldo]s .C. (12)Et si aveneret per alcuna persona over personas qui avere[n]t boy over boes over cavallos domados qui essere[n]t delead[us] et issos dessa villa illos avire[n]t dadus pro delead[us], illus deppiant ochire in sos lavores et in sas vignas et ortos ad clesura qu'ant aviri senza clamu alcuno. (13)Et si aveneret per alcuna persona over personas qui iscuniarit alc[u]na cuniadura agie[n]a et illu ad esser provadu, deppiat paghare per dogna bolta l[ib]r[a]s quimbi. (14)Su porcho manale qui non at portare furchida palm[us] noe si deppiat ochire in sas vignas et ortus et lavores qui sunt usades de reer cuniadura. (15)Et si la portat secundu de supra non bie 'llu depiant ochire. (16)Et in sus ateros loghus qui non si reeret cuniadura, bie 'llu deppiat ochire cum fruchida o senza fruchida.

CXIII. De qui portarit boes in viagiu.

(1)Constituim[us] et ordinam[us] qui sos carradores et ogna atera persona c'at andari et dugher bois in biagiu siant tenudos de los torrare assas iuas et dari·ll[us] in manu dessos boynargi[us] c'ant gardare et paschire cussa iua, a dognia hora c'ant torrare dae biagiu, o de die o de nocte qui torrarint.

donkey. (3)And the official, for each of the above written, shall take from the man who shall pasture that livestock six soldi for each head of livestock, and for each time thereafter [livestock] shall be caught therein. (4)And if those livestock are not fed and tended by a shepherd, the owner of them shall pay, and of that money the realm shall have four soldi, and he who shall have captured them, two soldi. (5)Of herds of cows and of mares, may one be killed, and for the herd of sheep or goats or from the herd of pigs may two be killed or taken alive, and there shall be paid the loss to him who has suffered it. (6)The swine reared shall be killed. (7)The jurors are bound to assess the damage done by that livestock, for good and fair, and to oversee payment for the damages suffered by the owner. (8)And so be it with crops and, as stated above, with vineyards and gardens. (9)And when the damage is not paid by the official in charge of the control of pastures (*maiores de pardu*) or his assistant officials, and our State administrator (*armentargiu de Loghu*) or the official of the curatorial district (*curadoria*) receives a report of it, let him be condemned to pay twenty soldi for each juror, for each time it is proved against him. (10)And when the livestock of one village shall do similar damage in another village, once that the said damage caused has been assessed, let the official of the village from where the livestock that caused the damage came, be obliged to have it made good by the hands of the officials in charge of the control of pastures (*maiores de pardo*) or by those under oath (*sos iurados*) who shall appear there. (11)And where he does not do so, let that official or curator be condemned to pay to our Chamber one hundred soldi for each time it shall be proved against him. (12)And if it shall happen that any person having an ox or tame oxen or horses that are restless, and the men of the village shall have reported them as such, they shall kill them in the cultivations (*laores*), vineyards, and fenced gardens (*ortos ad clesura*) without need of any notice. (13)And if any person happens to break down any of the fences of others, and this shall be proved against him, he shall pay for each time five lire. (14)The reared swine that does not carry a collar (*furchidda*) of nine spans shall be killed [if found] in the vineyards, gardens and cultivations where it is customary to keep fenced. (15)And if it wears it as described above, it is not to be killed. (16)And in other places where there is no fence, let it be killed with or without a collar.

Article 113. Of those who drive oxen.

(1)We direct and order that cart drivers (*carradores*) and any other person who shall go on a journey using oxen for draught and transport, shall be bound to reunite them to herds and deliver them into the hands of the drover (*boynargius*) who shall guard and watch over the pasture of that herd at whatever time they shall return from their journey, whether it be day or night that they

23v (2)Et | si cussos carradores et persones c'ant torrare dae biagiu ispaciant sus boes c'ant iughere, senza illos iungere assa iua secundu qu'est narrado de supra, et acaptarint·si·ndi alcunos de cussos boes spaciados in vignas over in ortos ch'esere[n]t bene coniadus, secundu ch'est ordinado, sos pobillos de custas vignas, ort[us] o arme[n]targios o famigialis issoro illos deppiant te[n]ne et dari·llos in manu dessu curadore dessa villa. (3)Et issu curadore siat tenudu de los retinere pro su rennu et mandare·llos inco[n]tinenti assa corte nostra. (4)Et si incontinenti ciò non fagherit su curadore, et isso officiali maiore inde avirit clamu et provarit·si·llu, siat·inde condempnadu su curadore et paghit per ogna bolta qui l'at esser provadu s[oldo]s .c. (5)Et si per ave[n]tura cussos boes qui sunt narados de supra non si 'llos podere[n]t tenne in sas vignas et in sus ortos, sos pobillos de cussas vignas et ortos inde deppiant lame[n]tari assos pobillos de cussos boes, daenanti de cussos hominis dessa villa duas boltas, dando·lis at inte[n]dere assos pobillos de cussos boes, in p[re]sentia de cussos hominis dessa villa, de chiteu pilu et chiteu boes ant avire achatadu in sas vignas et in sos ortos issoro. (6)Et dae c'ant avire factu cussos duos clamos, si bie 'ndi achatant pl[us] de cussos boes qui s'ant esser lame[n]tados, ochiant·bie·llu. (7)Et simigiantime[n]ti si inte[n]dat et deppiat·si faghire q[ua]n[do] de cussos boes qui sunt narados de supra s'ant agatare in sos lavores dae ssa prima die de marzu inanti. (8)Et de atero ap[re]ssu de damnu qui fagheri[n]t cussos suprascriptos boes in vignas et in ortos et in lavores no[n] si 'ndi deppiat faghere nen inte[n]dere·llu a chertu qui 'nde bolere[n]t mover.

CXIIII. De su molenti in lavores.

(1)Item ordinam[us] qui su molente qui si adi acatare in su lavore seguit·si·lli una origla sa prima bolta qui loy at esser acatadu et iss'atera secunda bolta illi seguit s'atera origla. (2)Et dae cussas duas boltas inanti, q[ua]n[do] illoy at esser acatado in sos lavores, sus pubillos dessos lavores, famigiales o armentargio issoro bie 'llo posant tenni et mandare·llo i[n] manu dessu curadore dessa
24r villa. (3)Et isso curadore siat tenudo de 'l- | lu recivire pro su rennu et de mandare·llos incontinenti a sa corte nostra. (4)Et si co[n]tra a zò faguirit, su curadore paghit a sa corte nostra s[oldo]s .c., secundu qui si co[n]tenit de supra. (5)Et isso damno siat imendadu a su pubillu de su lavore pro isso pubillo de su molente.

CXV. Bestiamen in bingnas.

(1)Volem[us] et ordinam[us] qui su bestiame[n] domado qui s'at acatare in bingnas, in ortos o in lavores andando cum bestiame[n] rude, si sos pubillos dessas vignas et dessos ortos et de sos lavores, servidores o arme[n]targios

return. (2)And if those cart drivers and persons who return from the journey let loose the oxen which they will bring by letting them wander about, without reuniting them with a herd according to what has been said above, and if some of those oxen are found wandering in the vineyards or gardens which are well fenced according to what has been provided, the owners of those vineyards and gardens, or their representatives (*armentargios*), or their employees shall capture them and deliver them into the hands of the curator of the village. (3)And let the curator be bound to requisition them on behalf of the realm and to conduct them immediately to our court. (4)And if the curator does not do this immediately and the senior official receives report of it and it is proved, let him be condemned and pay for each time it is proved against him, one hundred soldi. (5)And if by any chance those oxen mentioned above shall not be caught in the vineyards or gardens, the owners of those vineyards and gardens shall twice direct a complaint against the owners of those oxen, before the men of the village, making to the owners of those oxen known, in the presence of the said men of the village, what kind of oxen and what coat they shall have found in their vineyards and gardens. (6)And after they have made such a report twice, if they still find those oxen about which they have complained, let them kill them. (7)And, similarly, it is intended and ought to be done when some of the above oxen are found in the crops from the first day of March onward. (8)And with regard to further assessment of the damage that the aforementioned oxen have done in the vineyards, gardens and cultivations, no judicial dispute should be moved or entertained.

Article 114. Of donkeys in cultivations (*lavores*).
(1)Item: we order that a donkey which shall be found in the cultivations shall have one ear cut off the first time it is found there, and the second time its other ear shall be cut off. (2)And after those two times forward, when it is found in the cultivations, the owners of the cultivations, their employees or their representative (*armentargio*) therein may catch it and put it back into the hands of the curator of the village. (3)And let the curator be bound to receive it [the donkey] on behalf of the realm and to transmit it immediately to our court. (4)And if he acts otherwise, let the curator pay to our court one hundred soldi according to what is contained above. (5)And the damage is to be compensated to the owner of the crop by the owner of the donkey.

Article 115. Livestock in the vineyards.
(1)We wish and order that, in regard to tame livestock that shall be found in vineyards, vegetable gardens, or cultivations beside untamed livestock, if the owners of the vineyards, gardens, and cultivations, or the employees or repre-

issoro bie '[n]de lensare[n]t ietando a su bestiame[n] rude e morrit·inde de su bestiamen domado, qui no 'ndi appat carrigu nen damnu cusso qui bie 'llo at ochire o lenzare co[n]tra voluntadi sua. (2)Et caluncha persona qui adi levorare in su mo[n]te in su quale non est usadu de lavorare et ad esser travigho de bestiame[n] rude, illu depiant rere bene cuniadu. (3)Et si no[n] lu cuniat bene, su damnu qui si lo[y] at faghir no[n] si deppiat ap[re]ssare et no '[n]di deppiat pagare te[n]turas. (4)Et si est benecuniado, si deppiat maghellare, secundu qui si contenit in sus capidulus dessu bestiamen rude.

CXVI. De is pastores.
(1)Constituimus et ordinam[us] qui sos maghellos et ap[re]ssos qui s'ant fagheri deppiant pagare sos pastores. (2)Et si non ant de ghiteu pagare sos pastores, paghit su pubillu de su bestiame[n] et posca si fazat pagare dae ssu salariu dessos ditos pastores.

CXVII. De is pastores.
(1)Item ordinamus qui sas ghammas qui s'ant perdere de s'abba fera paghint·illas sos pastores, reservandu qui non esseret culpa dessos pastores.

CXVIII. De pastores.
(1)Volemus et ordinamus qui siant tenudos sos pastores de paghare su perdime[n]tu c'ant fagheri su bestiame[n] c'at paschire, su de noti chali et issu de di', si no[n] boghant ad claru in cuia chida si at faguere su perdimentu.

CXIX. De is paximentos.
24v (1)Constituimus et ordinam[us] qui sos qui ant paschire ad alcuna persona pro sa raxione issoro siant tenudos de guardare cussu bestiamen qui 'llis at esser acomandados. (2)Et si su pubillu de cussu bestiame[n] inde reciveret alcuno damno per culpa sua et esseret·indi bi[n]chidu, pagit cussu damnu ad icussa persona qui 'll'at aviri acommandadu cussu bestiamen. (3)Et si non ad de ghiteu paghare, instet in prexione i[n]fini a tantu q[u]i siat aconziu cun issu pubillu de su bestiame[n].

CXX. Qui maxellaret a tortu.
(1)Item ordinamus qui alcuno ho[min]i qui at magellare a tortu causas de rennu, paghit pross'uno .v., si 'nd'est binchidu. (2)Et si est de clesia o de atera persona,

sentative (*armentargio*) of them should strike the said untamed livestock with a throwing weapon or hurled object, and any head of tame livestock shall be struck dead, this shall not be imputed to the charge or damage against him who unintentionally killed or made the strike. (2)And any person who shall work the land in a mountainous place in which it is not customary to work, and there is a transit of untamed livestock there, he shall always keep [the land] well fenced. (3)And if he does not fence it well, the damage that shall be done thereon shall not be assessed, and the capture of the animal shall not be paid for. (4)But if it is well fenced, the animal shall be slaughtered, according to that which is contained in the articles on untamed livestock.

Article 116. Of shepherds (*pastores*).
(1)We direct and order that slaughter and assessments [of value] to be made shall be paid for by shepherds. (2)And if the shepherds have not enough to pay, let the owner of the livestock pay, and thereafter he shall make up the expenses out of the shepherds' wages (*su salariu*).

Article 117. Of shepherds.
(1)Item: we order that the flocks that will be lost because of poisoned water shall be compensated by the shepherds, unless they are not responsible for it.

Article 118. Of shepherds.
(1)We wish and order that all the shepherds be obliged to compensate for the loss of livestock which they put to pasture both by night and day, unless they prove on whose watch the loss will have been caused.

Article 119. Of pastures (*paximentos*).
(1)We direct and order that those who shall put to pasture livestock on behalf of another person and receive compensation from him shall be bound to watch over the said livestock that are entrusted to them. (2)And if the owner of such livestock suffers any damage through their fault and they are defeated by them in court, let them pay the damage to the person who entrusted that livestock to them. (3)And if he has nothing with which to pay, let him remain in prison until he settles with the owner of the livestock.

Article 120. Whoever slaughters [livestock] without having the right to do so.
(1)Item: we order that any man who slaughters livestock in the realm without having the right to do so, shall pay, if he is defeated in court, five times as much [as the value of the livestock slaughtered]. (2)And if the livestock belong to the

paghit pross'uno tres, pro quale at esser sa causa c'at aver maxelladu et s[oldo]s .c. de maquicia et boe unu assu curadore.

CXXI. De feriis.
(1)Volemus et ordinamus qui si inte[n]dat esser ferias sa festa de sanctu Iohanni et de sanctu Augustino et de sanctu Marchu de Sinnis.

CXXII. De sas curadorias obligadas andari a quida de berrude.
(1)Constituim[us] et ordinam[us] qui sas curadorias et villas qui sunt ordinadas pro benne at Aristanis ad reer sa q[u]ida de berruda siant te[n]udos de benni secundu qu'est ordinadu et usadu, salvu qui cussa curadoria over villa at qui a ghitare be[n]ne in sas suprascriptas dies feriadas o festas, qui non siant tenta de be[n]ne in sas suprascriptas ferias, ma siant tenudus de torrare cussas dies qui 'll'ant ghitare qui non siant feriadas. (2)Et si tota sa muda sua illi benneret et essere[n]t dies feriadas, non siat te[n]ta de be[n]ni infini qui 'll'at be[n]ni s'atera muda sua. (3)Et icussas sente[n]cias qui s'ant dari in alcuna de cussas dies feriadas, secundu qui sunt iscriptas de supra, in qualuncha corona de loghu o de quida de berruda o de atera no[n] bagiat nen tenghat forza.

CXXIII. De nodayos.
(1)Item ordinam[us], pro bollere cessare mult[us] damnos sus quales sos subditos nostros substene[n]t per culpa et neglige[n]cia de alcunos nodayos, ordi[n]-
25r am[us] et istatuim[us] | que ciaschuno nodayu dessu Iuygadu nostru de Arbaree siat tenudo et depiat fagheri volume[n] dessas cartas et stedas c'ant faghere, su quali volume[n] no[n] siat ad minus de fogius .xv., in su quali deppiat faghere scrivere et notare totu sus co[n]tractus et testame[n]tos et inve[n]tarios et incantos et ateras cartas c'ant faghere infra dies .x. poscha qui l'at aviri levadas et factas dae ssos co[n]trahe[n]tes. (2)Et in casu que alcuno nodayo co[n]tra fagherit et esseret·illi provado, pagit per ciasch[u]na bolta l[ib]r[a]s .v. et siat tenudo de pagare et satisfaghere su damnu et i[n]teresse a sa parti qui los susteneret pro sa ditta ocaxione. (3)Et de cussu siat tenudo de faghere·[n]de rexoni su potestade nostru d'Aristanis in su officiu suo cum tres iuygantis et issos ateros officialis in su officiu issoro dogna mese una bolta, supta sa dita pena. (4)Et cussu apat loghu poscha c'at esser publicada et no[n] si intendat assas cosas passadas.

Church or to any other person, he shall pay three times as much, whatever the head slaughtered; and he shall pay a fine of a hundred soldi and an ox to the curator (*curadore*).

Article 121. On feast days.
(1)We wish and order that it be understood that the days of the feast (*sa festa*) of St John and St Augustine and St Mark of Sinis are festival (*feria*) days.

Article 122. Of the districts (*curadorias*) obligated to go to the *Quida de Berrude* (Court of Trusted Men).
(1)We decree and order that the curatorial districts (*curadorias*) and villages that are obligated to come to Oristano to hold the *Chida de Berruda* (Court of Trusted Men) are obliged to come there according to that which has been established and according to custom, except that that district (*curadoria*) or village on which it would be incumbent to come on the aforementioned holidays or feast days, during such holidays they will not be obliged to come, but they are obliged to return on the days that they are incumbent and that are not holidays. (2)And if their whole turn happens to fall on a holiday, they shall not be obliged to come until their next shift. (3)And those judgements which shall be given on any of those festival days aforesaid in the Royal Tribunal (*Corona de Loghu*) or de *Chida de Berruda*, or any other assizes, shall have no value or force.

Article 123. Of notaries (*nodoyos*).
(1)Item: we order, so that the many harms to which our subjects experience by the fault and negligence of some notaries may be lessened, we establish and order that each notary in our realm (*iuygadu*) of Arborea shall be bound to keep in a volume the documents (*cartas*) and records (*scedas*) which they shall draw up; the volume shall not be less than fifteen sheets, and in it shall be transcribed and noted all the contracts, wills, inventories, auctions and other acts which they shall produce, within ten days after they have drawn them up and acquired the contents from the contracting parties. (2)And in case the notary does not do so and it shall be proved against him so, he shall pay five lire for each time and be bound to pay and satisfy the damage and interest thereon to the party who shall have incurred the expenses for the said case. (3)And of this let our authority (*su potestade*) of Oristano in his office with three judges (*iuygantis*) and other officials in their office be held to account, once a month under the said penalty. (4)And let this [the application of the penalty] take place after it [the relative sentence] shall be published, and let it not be intended for events of the [distant] past.

Ordinamentos de salarios.
Ordinam[us] dessos salarios et paghas qui debent levare sos auditores dessa Audie[n]cia nostra et issos nodayos pro ragiones issoro.

CXXIIII. De auditores.
(1)Ordinam[us] qui sos auditores dessa Audie[n]tia nostra qui sunt assu p[re]sente o qui ant esser per inantis no[n] usint ne[n] deppia[n]t levare pro salario issoro dessas questio[n]es que 'llis at benne a man[us], ecceptu ad raxone de s[oldo]s .I. per libra.

De sas scrivanias.
(2)Ordinamus qui sos nodayus deppiant levare dae ssas scedas qui ant faghere de vendiciones o de cambio, sensa pagadores et cum pagadores, dessa butegha sua dessa nodaria, s[oldo]s .I. et dinaris .IIII.

(3)Et foras dessa butegha sua, intro imperò dessa terra, s[oldo]s .II.

(4)Et si foras de sa terra bollirint dughere su nodayu acordint·si·ndi impari de su pregiu.

(5)Et si dessas ditas cartas bollere[n]t in forma publica, si ant esser de l[ib]r[a]s .X. in iossu, deppiat levari su dictu notario s[oldo]s .VI.

(6)Et si esseret dae l[ib]r[a]s .X. in susu s[oldo]s .VII.

25v (7)Et dessa firmadura de carta de franchidadi, cu[m] testame[n]tu | et senza testame[n]tu, dae s[oldo]s .XV. infini at s[oldo]s .XXV. per testa, secundu sa chalidadi de su homini, et de sas iscedas de franchidadi soldus .II.

(8)Et de sas iscedas de p[re]stansas, acomandicias, de deposidu et de co[n]fessione et ve[n]dit[i]o[n]es de causas mobilis, sensa pagadores et cum pagadores, in sa butegha sua s[oldo]s .I.

(9)Et foras dessa butegha intro dessa terra s[oldo]s .II.

(10)Et dessas iscedas dessas allogat[i]o[n]es et libellos de dommos et de vignas et de fantis et de berbecargi[us] in butegha sua, cu[m] pagadore et censa pagadore, s[oldo]s .I. dinaris .IIII.

(11)Et foras de butegha sua s[oldo]s .II.

(12)Et dessa firmadura de ciaschuna dessas ditas cartas s[oldo]s .VI.

(13)Et dessas steas dessos testame[n]tos dae s[oldo]s .V. in s[oldo]s .X.

(14)Et dessa firmadura s[oldo]s .X. per che[n]tenaio de ciò qui ant baliri sos benes de su testadore infini s[oldo]s .XX., secundu su testamentu et issa qualidadi dessu homini.

(15)Et dessa isceda de su i[n]ve[n]tariu et firmadura dinaris .IIII. per libra de ciò qui ant baliri sos benes.

Wage orders (*ordinamentos de salarios*).
We order [the following] concerning salaries and fees to be received by our hearing (*audiencia*) and by notaries for their rights.

Article 124. Of auditors.
(1)We order that the auditors of our hearing (*audiencia*) who are operating at the present time or who will operate in the future, do not claim nor should they be paid their own wages with regard to the matters they will have to handle, except at the rate of one soldo for each lira.

Of writing offices (*sas scrivanias*).
(2)We order that notaries should be paid in respect of the records (*scedas*) that they will draw up for sales or exchanges, whether there is payment or not, if drawn up within their own offices, one soldo and four denari.

(3)And if drawn up outside their offices, but within the region (*terra*), two soldi.

(4)And if the notary is to be conducted outside the region, there shall be agreed upon the price.

(5)And if of the said papers (*cartas*) they wish to be made valid as a public deed (*in forma publica*), if relative to a value of ten lire or less, the notary should receive six soldi.

(6)And if relative to a value of ten lire and or more, seven soldi.

(7)And for the authentication (*firmadura*) of a charter of concessions (*carta de franchidadi*) whether there is a will or not, [the notary shall receive] a fee from fifteen to twenty-five soldi per person according to the condition of the person; and for drafts relating to concessions, two soldi.

(8)And for writings relating to loans, of covenants, of deposit and of public and legal declaration and for sales of movable property, whether or not there is payment, if made in the [notary's] office, one soldo;

(9)And outside the office, but within the region, two soldi.

(10)And for writings relating to leases and renting of houses, and of vineyards, and of servants (*de fantis*) and of shepherds: if made in his notarial office, with or without payment, one soldo and four denari;

(11)And outside the office, two soldi.

(12)And for the authentication of each of the said papers, six soldi.

(13)And for the drafts of wills, five soldi to ten soldi.

(14)And for authentication, [payment of] soldi equal to ten percent of the value of the testator's property, and up to twenty, depending on the will and the condition of the person.

(15)And for the draft of inventory and authentication, four denari for each lira of the value of the property.

(16)Et ciaschuno me[m]bru de testame[n]tu firmadu, secundu sa qualidadi dessu fatu, s[oldo]s .v. in s[oldo]s .x.

(17)Et dessas scedas dessas coyansas et dessa sposansa dae s[oldo]s .v. infini .x.

(18)Et dessa firmadura s[oldo]s .xx. per che[n]tenayo de ciò que at muntari sa doda, secundu sa qualidadi dessas personas, gosi sa firmadura de sa iura et dessa isposansa come[n]ti et de sas dodas.

(19)Et dessas iscedas dessos comandamentos, requestes, teneris et istasinas et appellationes dinaris .vi.

(20)Et dessa firmadura de ciasch[u]na dessas ditas cartas s[oldo]s .vi.

(21) Et dessas iscedas de sos i[n]cantos, de ciaschadunu di[naris] .iiii.

(22)Et dessa firmadura, secundu sa qualidadi dessu incanto et dessa persona s[oldo]s .xx. infini s[oldo]s .xxxx.

(23)Et dessas iscedas qui si faghint pro sus hominis qui si boghant dae prex-
26r ioni pro ciascuno paghadori s[oldo]s .i. |

(24)Et dessas iscedas dessas procuras i[n]tro de butegha s[oldo]s .i.

(25)Et foras de butegha intro dessa terra, s[oldo]s .ii.

(26)Et dessa firmadura, dae s[oldo]s tres infini in s[oldo]s .vi.

(27)Et dessas iscedas et sententias interlocutorias et compromissos, per parte s[oldo]s .ii.

(28)Et dessas sententias diffinitivas qui ant esser dae l[ib]r[a]s .x. in giosso, paghit s[oldo]s .v.

(29)Et dae libras .x. infini in l[ib]r[a]s .l., s[oldo]s .x.

(30)Et dae libras .l. infini in l[ib]r[a]s .c., s[oldo]s .xx.

(31)Et dae libras chentu in susu, s[oldo]s .xxx.

(32)Et dessa appellatione qui s'at fagheri in paraulas, s[oldo]s .ii.

(33)Et si si fagherit in scriptu secundu su volume[n] dessa scriptura, s[oldo]s .ii. infini s[oldo]s .v.

(34)Et dessos processos qui s'ant levare dae ssa corte per via de appellatione, deppiat levari su nodayu o su scrivanu dinares .viii. per carta, scrive[n]do in ciascuna carta righas .xxviii.

(35)Et dessas procuras [et] advochationes qui s'ant fagheri in corte, qui pacto non loy appat, si ssa dimanda at esser dae l[ib]r[a][s] .x. in giosso, appat su procuradore s[oldo]s .x.

(36)Et dae libras .x. infini in libras .l., appat su procuradore soldus .l.

(37)Et dae libras .l. in susu appat dinaris .vi. per libra.

(38)Et dessa firmadura, per ciaschuna dessa dictas chartas soldos binti.

(16)And each of the parts of an authenticated will, from five to ten soldi according to the value of what is contained in the will.

(17)And for writings relating to marriages or promises of marriage, from five up to ten soldi.

(18)And for the authentication of them, there shall be paid a sum equal to twenty percent of what the dowry amounts to, according to the condition of the person; likewise, for the authentication of marriage oaths and dowry covenants.

(19)And for the writings of intimations, petitions, captures, seizures, deeds of appeal, six denari.

(20)And for the authentication of the said documents, six denari.

(21)And for the drafts relating to the putting up for auction, four denari for each.

(22)And for the authentication of them, twenty soldi up to forty soldi depending on the type of auction (*incanto*) or the condition of the person.

(23)And for the draft writings which shall be drawn up concerning persons who are released from prison, one soldo for each one who pays.

(24)And for writings relating to powers of attorney drawn up in the office, two soldi.

(25)And outside the office, but inside the region (*terra*), two soldi.

(26)And for the authentication of these, from three up to six soldi.

(27)And for interlocutory writings, judgements, and compromises, two soldi for each of the parties involved.

(28)And for final judgements relating to a value of ten lire or less, five soldi.

(29)And from ten liras up to fifty liras, ten soldi.

(30)And from fifty liras up to one hundred liras, twenty soldi shall be paid.

(31)And from one hundred lire upwards, let there be paid thirty soldi.

(32)And per appeal made orally, two soldi.

(33)And if they will be made in writing, from two soldi to five soldi, depending on the length of the writing.

(34)And relative to the acts of trials of which copies will be taken from the court for the purpose of appeals, the notary or scribe shall charge a fee of eight denari per document, writing in each document twenty-eight lines.

(35)And with regard to powers of attorney and advocacy to be made before the court, without previous agreement, if the application is for cases from ten lire or less, the attorney shall have a fee of ten soldi.

(36)And from ten lire up to fifty lire, the attorney shall have a fee of fifty soldi.

(37)And from fifty lire upwards, let him have six denari per lira.

(38)And for the authentication of each of the said documents, let him have twenty soldi.

(39)Et dessa chircadura dessos actos, si si achaptat sa carta qui si faghit chircare, dinaris ses per anno, et si non si acaptat dinaris tres per annu.

(40)Et de tottu sas ateras istedas de cartas firmadas, dessa quale no '[n]di faghit me[n]sione custa Carta de Loghu, cussa persona qui los at fagheri si 'ndi acordit cu[n] ssu nodayu.

(41)Et si non si 'ndi acordat cun su nodayu, siant·indi daenante de su officiale de sa terra et icussu qui su dictu officiali ind'at sentenciari et comandare si 'ndi
26v deppiat fagheri. |

(42)Et si alcuno nodayu at esser acaptadu be[n]ne inco[n]tra a sos p[re]sentes ordiname[n]tos, pro o[m][n]i volta qui 'll'at esser achusadu et binchidu, deppiat paghare assa corte su doppiu de ciò qui at aviri levado plus.

Ordinamentos de sos salarios qui debent levare sos scrivanos de corona pro raxone issoro.

(43)Ordinam[us] qui deppiat levare de cussas personas c'ant mandare sas nunsas, per ciaschuna volta dinares .IIII.

(44)Et fassat·si paghare de ciaschuna persona qui faghirit nunsare testi[m]ongios pro ciasc[u]no testi[m]ongio pro sa polissa di[n]aris .II.

(45)Et prossu exami[n]ame[n]to de ciasc[u]no qui s'at exami[n]are, et iste[n]dat et iscrivat su narre de ciascuno testimongiu, dinaris .VI.

(46)Et fassat·si paghare dae cussas personas c'ant acomandare chertos yssoro ad alc[u]na attera persona, pro sa scriptura quando '[n]d'at fagheri dinaris .VI.

(47)Et fassat·si paghari dae cussas personas c'ant esser postos ad corona de Loghu pro chertos c'ant esser factos in sas contradas, q[ua]n[do] alcuno inde mancharit assu lassame[n]tu dessa coro[n]a de Loghu, prossa scriptura de cussa parti c'at esser benida di[n][a]ris .XII.

(48)Fassat·si paghare prossa polissa de sos chertos binchidos, quando si mandat pro faghiri·llos paghare:

(49)Dae s[oldo]s .X. infini in s[oldo]s .C., dinaris .XII.;

(50)Dae s[oldo]s .C. infini in libras .XXV., s[oldo]s .II.;

(51)Dae l[ib]r[a]s .XXV. infini in l[ib]r[a]s .L., s[oldo]s .III.;

(52)Dae l[ib]r[a]s .L. infini in l[ib]r[a]s .C., s[oldo]s .V.;

(53)Dae l[ib]r[a]s .C. infini in l[ib]r[a]s .M., s[oldo]s .X.

(54)Sos hominis qui be[n]nint pro reer chida de berrude, pro iscrivire·llos, ciaschuno [dinaris II], su qui at esser curadore et ad reer corona non paghit.

(55)Totus custos pagamentos qui s'ant fagheri si paghint dae cussa parti c'at perdere su chertu.

(39)And relative to the search of acts, if the document sought is found, the fee is six denari per year, and if it is not found, three denari per year.

(40)And relative to all other authenticated drafts of which the *Carta de Logu* makes no mention, the client shall agree with the notary.

(41)And if no agreement is reached with the notary, the parties shall appear before the official of the region, and what he shall decide and order shall be put into practice.

(42)And if any notary shall be found to be in contravention of these ordinances, for each time he shall be charged and defeated in court, he shall pay to the court twice that which he shall have received in addition.

Orders of the salaries to be taken by scribes of the court (*corona*) according to their due:

(43)We order that he shall receive from persons to whom a summons shall be delivered, four denari for each time.

(44)And he is to be paid from each person who will have witnesses summoned, two denari for each subpoena for the appearance of each witness.

(45)And for the summoning of each person who shall be examined and whose minutes shall be drawn up and written for each witness, six denari.

(46)And let him charge those persons who shall delegate their disputes to some other person, for the drawing up of the minutes, when any are made, six denari.

(47)And let him be paid by those persons who shall be summoned to the Royal Tribunal (*Corona de Loghu*) for disputes that arise in the countryside (*sas contradas*), when any person shall be absent before the dissolution of the Royal Tribunal (*Corona de Loghu*), for the writing of that part [of the hearing] that was argued, twelve denari.

(48)Let him be paid by injunction for cases won in court when there is warrant for payment:

(49)for ten soldi up to one hundred soldi, twelve denari;

(50)from one hundred soldi up to twenty-five lire, two soldi;

(51)from twenty-five lire up to fifty lire, three soldi;

(52)from fifty lire up to one hundred lire, five soldi;

(53)from fifty lire up to one thousand lire, ten soldi.

(54)The men who shall present themselves to hold (*reer*) the *Chida de Berruda* (Court of Trusted Men), to record its registration, two denari for each participant; he who shall be curator and preside over the court (*corona*) shall not pay.

(55)All such payments as shall be made, shall be paid by the party who shall lose the case.

CXXV. De sas dies feriadas.

(1)Custas sunt sas dies feriadas i[n] sas calis comandam[us] q[u]i no[n] si depiat
27r reer coro[n]a de Logu ne[n]coro[n]a de chida de berrude: |

(2)Sas dominigas de totu s'anno [et] sas festas de sancta Maria;

(3)Item totu sas festas dessos apostolos;

(4)Item totu sas festas dessus vangelistas;

(5)Item totu sas ferias dessas vignennas, ciò est dae ssa festa de sancta Maria, qui est a octo dies de cabudanni, infini a sa p[ri]ma die de sanctu Gayni;

(6)Sa festa de omnia sanctu et issa festa de sus mortus;

(7)Sa festa de sanctu Martini;

(8)Sa festa de sanctu Nichola;

(9)Sa festa de sancta Luchia;

(10)Sa festa de sanctu Anthoni;

(11)Sa Pascha de sa natividadi et octo dies depus Pasca et octo i[n]antis;

(12)Sos lunis e martis inantis de segari de petsa et issu mercuris primu infattu de carrisegare;

(13)Sa Pascha dessa Epiphania que si clamat Pascha nunsa;

(14)Sa Pascha de Ascensioni;

(15)Sa Pascha de Penthecoste cum dies .II. seguentes;

(16)Sa festa dessu Corpus de Christus;

(17)Ite[m] totu sa chida sancta et octo pusti Pascha;

(18)Sas ferias dessas messas, sò est dae .XV. de lampadas infini a dies bindichi de treulas, exceptada sa corona de Loghu de sanctu Pedru qui si reet ad voluntadi n[ost]ra et exceptadu qui si possant minare sas questiones ad voluntadi de sas partis, et issu simili qui semper si reat sa Audientia a discricioni d'issa e totu.

CXXVI. Carradores.

(1)Item, pro cessare multas fraudes que faghent et comittent sos carradores im portare vinu dae unu loghu at un'atero, ordi[n]amus et statuim[us] que nechunu carradore qui portat cuba de vinu over carrada no[n] deppiat nen presumischat dae como inantis dessu vinu qui iugheret boghare·nde nen faghire·nde boghare, nen co[n]sentire qui nechuna persona inde boghit ne 'nde biat, ne[n] dare·[n]di ad alchuna persona, ad minus de voluntadi et consentime[n]tu dessu pubillu dessu vinu. (2)Et etia[m] de[us]non loy deppiat mittere abba
27v nen attera mischo- | ladura, ad pena de s[oldo]s .C. ad opus dessa corte, per ciaschuna bolta qui co[n]tra fagherit et esseret·illis provadu, de pagare su damnu a su pubillu de su ditu vinu. (3)Et issa simili pe[n]a si inte[n]dat ad issu qui 'ndi bogharit a bier dessu vinu sensa paraula de cussu cuy ad esser su dictu vinu, be[n]ne que no[n] esseret sus carradores. (4)Et icustu capidulu

Article 125. Of feast days.

(1)These are the feast days on which we order that the *Corona de Loghu* (Royal Tribunal) or the *Corona de Chida de Berruda* (Court of Trusted Men) should not be held:

(2)Sundays throughout the year and the feasts of Holy Mary;

(3)item all the feasts of the Apostles;

(4)item all the feasts of the Evangelists;

(5)item all the feasts of the harvests, that is, from the feast of Holy Mary on the eighth of September until the first day of the month of St Gavino [October];

(6)the feast of All Saints' Day and the Feast of the dead;

(7)the feast of St Martin;

(8)the feast of St Nicholas;

(9)the feast of St Lucy;

(10)the feast of St Anthony;

(11)the Easter of Nativity and eight days before and eight days after;

(12)the Mondays and Tuesdays before carnival and the first Wednesday after carnival;

(13)the Easter of Epiphany which is called *Pascha nunsa*;

(14)the Easter of Ascension;

(15)the Easter of Pentecost and two days thereafter;

(16)the feast of Corpus Christi;

(17)item: all of Holy Week and eight days after Easter;

(18)the feast day of the Masses, that is, from the fifteenth of June until the thirteenth of July, with the exception of the Royal Tribunal (*Corona de Loghu*) of St Peter's, which is held at our will; that the Hearing (*Audientia*) may always be held at its own discretion.

Article 126. Cart drivers (*carradores*).

(1)Item: in order that many frauds which cart drivers make and commit in transporting wine from one place to another may cease, we order and decree that, henceforth, no cart driver who carries a cask of wine or keg shall either presume to draw or cause wine to be drawn, nor permit any person to draw or drink of it, nor deliver any to any person, except by the will and consent of the owner of the wine. (2)And nor shall he mix water or other liquid with it, under penalty of one hundred soldi in favour of the court for each time he shall contravene this and it be proved against him, he is to repay the damage to the owner of the wine. (3)And the same penalty shall be intended for him who shall draw wine to drink without licence from the owner of said wine, even if it be not the cart driver. (4)And this article we intend to apply to any other merchan-

bolemus que si inte[n]dat a dogna atera mercantia et ateras causas que si portari[n]t cu[m] carros over cu[m] bestias dae unu loghu ad un'atero. (5)Non los usint ixolere, ne[n] travigare, ne[n] fagheri malicia nen barattaria alcuna. (6)Et caschaduna persona possat accusare tot[us] cussas godales personas qui in ciò essere[n]t inculpados et appant·inde sa tersa parte dessa pena.

CXXVII. De logare cavallu.
(1)Volem[us], pro cessare ogna litigiu et questio[n]e qui si fagherit in allogare o dare alcuno covallo a bitura, ordinam[us] et statuim[us] que dogna persona possat allogare su covallu suo sensa qui siat tenudo [de andari] assa corte a ffagire·llu istimare, cassando ognia atero capidulu supra ciò in contrariu. (2)Et in casu qui su cavallu moreret o qui si gastarit per culpa dessu condutore over de qui 'llu covaligharit, siat tenuda de 'llu pagare at cui at esser faghendo·lu istimare per duos over .III. bonos ho[min]is de cussus qui 'll'ant aviri cognoschido.

CXXVIII. De non blastomari a Deus.
(1)Constituim[us], pro qui De[us] o[m][n]ipotenti si debet subra totas causas honorare, timire et guardare et hobedire, et ap[re]ssu sa gloriosa Virgini Madonna sancta Maria et issos apostolos et sanct[us] et sanctas de De[us], ordi[n]am[us] qui caluncha persona de caluncha co[n]ditione siat c'at blasti[m]are a Deu over a sancta Maria et l'at esser provadu siat co[n]de[n]nadu in l[ib]r[a]s .L., sos cales deppiat pagare i[n]fra dies .XV. poscha c'at esser co[n]de[n]nadu. (2)Et si no[n] pagat infra su dictu te[m]p[us], mittat·si·lli uno ammu i[n] sa li[m]ba et siat·illi tagiada pro mo[do] qui 'lla perdat. (3)Et si blasti[m]arit alcuno s[a][n]cto o sancta, siat conde[n]nado in l[ib]r[a]s .XXV., sas quales depiat pagare infra dies .XV. poscha qui at essere conde[n]nado. (4)Et si no[n]
28r paghat infra su dictu te[m]pus, mittat·si·lli unu ammu in sa limba | et cum issu siat afrustadu per totu sa terra hui ad aviri delinquido o factu su delittu et non appat atera pena.

CXXIX. De sa Charta de Loghu.
(1)Item ordi[n]am[us] qui ciasch[u]no curadore siat tenudo de aviri ad ispesas suas sa Carta de Loghu, cu[m]sa quale isso et issus iurad[us] et iuyghantes suos si possant ple[n]ariamente informare q[ua]n[do] essere[n]t a sos bisognos. (2)Et deppiant·illa levare dae ssa camera nostra et deppiant etia[m] de[us] oservare et fagheri totu cussu qui si co[n]tenit in sos capidul[us] et ordiname[n]tos qui suntu iscript[us] in sa p[re]dicta Carta de Loghu. (3)Et icussu curadore a qui at esser provadu qui no[n] avirit sa dita Carta de Logu levada et no[n]at fagheri et observare toto cussu qui in cussa si co[n]tenit pagit a sa cam-

dise and other things that are transported by wagon or with beasts of burden from one place to another. (5)They shall not dare to unpack them, or to traffic in them unlawfully, or to counterfeit them unlawfully, or to defraud them in any way. (6)And any person may accuse all of the persons who were charged with it, withholding a third part of the fine.

Article 127. Of the hiring of horses.
(1)We wish, in order that the disputes and questions which arise from the hiring out of horses for transportation may cease, [so we] order and decree that any person may hire out his horse without being required to present himself to the court to have it assessed, and every other article relating to this matter, contrary to this enactment, is therefore hereby cancelled. (2)And in the event that the horse dies or is injured through the responsibility of the handler or the one who rides it, he shall be obliged to repay it to the owner by having the latter determine its value by two or three trusted men (*bonos hominis*) chosen from among those who will have knowledge of it.

Article 128. Of not blaspheming against God.
(1)We decree, since Almighty God is to be honoured, feared, and respected and obeyed above all things, and likewise the glorious Holy Virgin Mary, and the Apostles and saints of God, we order that any person, of whatever condition he may be, who blasphemes against God or Holy Mary, and it shall be proved against him, shall be condemned to pay fifty lire, which he shall pay within fifteen days from the time he is condemned. (2)And if he does not pay within the said time, a hook shall be put through his tongue and severed so that she shall lose it. (3)And if he shall blaspheme against any saint or holy woman, let him be condemned at the rate of twenty-five lire, which he shall pay within fifteen days from the time he is condemned. (4)And if he does not pay within the aforesaid time, a hook shall be put through his tongue and he shall be whipped throughout the whole region (*terra*) in which he has caused offence or committed the crime, and he shall have no other punishment.

Article 129. Of the *Charta de Loghu*.
(1)Item: we order that every curator (*curadore*) shall be required to have, at his own expense, [a copy of] the *Carta de Logu*, from which he, his jurors and judges may be fully informed when the need arises. (2)They shall acquire it from our Chamber (*sa Camera*), and they shall also observe and put into practice all that is contained in the articles and ordinances written in the said *Carta de Logu*. (3)And the curator against whom it shall be proved that he has not acquired [a copy of] the *Carta de Logu* and will not do so, nor observe all that is contained therein, shall pay to the Chamber one hundred soldi whenever it

era per ciascuna bolta qui 'll'at esser provadu s[oldo]s .c. (4)Et deppiat su ditu curadore aviri sa dicta Carta de Logu dae ssa p[ri]ma die de corona de Plama ass'atera corona de Loghu de sanctu Marchu a sa dicta pena.

cxxx. Debitu pagadu.
(1)Volem[us] et ordi[n]am[us] qui caluncha persona adimandarit depidu pagadu over torrarit a dimandare chertu binchidu et diffinidu siat conde[n]nadu in su doppiu de cussa quantidadi qui at esser pagada over binchidu. (2)Et ciò si inte[n]dat ad icussas personas a sas quales particularime[n]te esseret fatu su ditu pagame[n]tu over qui esseret binchidu, exceptu qui essere[n]t heredes et successores de su pri[n]cipali qui de cussu pagame[n]tu et binchidura ch'esseret facta essere[n]t neglige[n]tes et no 'ndi essere[n]t certos. (3)In cussu casu non siant tenudus a paghare pena alcuna, ma si 'ndi deppiat observare secundu qui raxione si 'nd'at achaptare.

cxxxi. Maystros de lynna.
(1)Constituim[us] et ordinam[us] subra sos maystros de linna qui si fagherint maystros, bolemus qui caluncha persona a qui ant fagheri carros over arados et non esserent bene factos, per issu factu modo qui 'ndi perderent dies de servire, qui satisfassat su dampnu qui at avire su comporadore dessas dies perdidas s'est carro pro carro, s'est aradu pro aradu, s'est iuale pro iuale et de maquicia assu
28v regnu libras .v. | (2)Et anchu depiat paghare dies quantu ad perdere infini a qui 'll'appat torradu su lauro bono et sufficie[n]te. (3)Et qui no[n] inganni[n]t plus ad atteri.

cxxxii. De canes in gamma.
(1)Ordinam[us] et istatuim[us] qui caluncha pastore o pastores de brebeges, de porcos, de cabras o de vachas achaptarint, in sa gamma issoro, subra sa gamma chanis over cani, assaltigia[n]do, et no[n] bie 'llu ochirint manu a manu, illu depiant portare in manu dessu maiore dessa villa, et icussu maiore illu deppiat comandare a su pubillu de su cani qui 'llu depiat portare daenanti de su officiali et icussu officiali illu deppiat comandari qui 'llu deppiat paghare ad icussu qui at aviri recividu su damnu. (2)Et issu pubillu de su cani poy promittirit de 'llu reer bene su dictu cani, qui no[n] at faghere damnu. (3)Et si indi torrat a ffagheri, pagit assu re[n]nu prossa neglige[n]tia sua, qui no[n] lu bolfit ochire, l[ib]r[a]s .x. e morgiat su cani et paghit totu su damnu qui 'll'at aviri fatu et dare·llos pro deleadus.

shall be proved against him. (4)And the said curator shall keep the said *Carta de Logu* from the first day of the assize court (*corona*) of Palms to the other Royal Tribunal (*corona de Loghu*) of Sanctu Marchu (St Mark's) under the said penalty.

Article 130. Settled debt.

(1)We desire and order that any person who claims a debt that has already been paid or who returns to sue on a now settled or lost dispute, shall be ordered to pay at the rate of twice the amount that has been returned or with respect to which he has lost the case. (2)And this is to be understood specifically with respect to those persons to whom the said payment has been made or with respect to whom the said payment has been won in court; not so where there are heirs and successors of the principal party concerned who are negligent and have no certainty [of the balance and judgement] of the said payment or of said judicial winnings. (3)In such a case, let them not be bound to pay any penalty, but that he must behave in accordance with what the law provides in this regard.

Article 131. Carpenters (*maystros de lynna*).

(1)We decree and order concerning carpenters who become master craftsmen (*maystros*), [as] we wish that with regard to any person for whom they will make carts or ploughs and these are not made well so that the clients lose days of working service, that they shall compensate the purchasing customer for the damage suffered: if it is a wagon, the value of the wagon; if it is a plough, the value of the plough; if it is a yoke, the value of the yoke, and in addition they shall pay to the realm a fine of five lire. (2)And they shall also pay the days that they [the customers] shall have lost on the basis of a return on a good and sufficient harvest. (3)And let them not deceive anyone else any more.

Article 132. Of herding dogs.

(1)We order and decree that any shepherd or shepherds of sheep, swine, goats or cows find in their flock, dogs or a single dog attacking the flock and not killing it on the spot, they shall deliver it into the hands of the mayor (*maiore*) of the village, and the mayor shall entrust it to its master who shall deliver it to the official, and the latter shall order the master that he should pay compensation to those who have suffered damage. (2)And the master of the dog shall then promise to guard the said dog well, so that he does no more harm. (3)And if he again causes harm, he shall pay to the realm, for his negligence, if he did not intend to kill him, ten lire, and he shall kill the dog and pay for all the harm which he shall have done; and he shall pay according to what has been determined, it being considered that the dog is not tame.

[Proemio di Mariano].
(1)Nos Marian[us], pro issa gracia de De[us] iuyghi de Arbaree, co[m]pte de Gociano et bisco[n]ti de Basso, co[n]siderando sos multos lame[n]tos [qui] co[n]ti[n]uame[n]te sunt istad[us] et sunt per issas terras nostras de Arbaree et de Loghudore, prossas vignas, ortos et lavores, que si disfaghi[n]t et co[n]sumant per issa pocha guardia et cura qui si dat a su bestiame[n], cussos de qui est et qui 'llu at in guardia, prossa quali causa multas vignas et ortos sunt eremadas et multas personas si romane[n]t de lavorare, q[u]i lavorari ent, pro dubidu qui ant de no[n] perdere cusso qui 'llo ant fagheri, et bole[n]do nos providere a su utili cummo[n]i et bonu istadu de sa ge[n]te nostra, am[us] deliberado de faghere et faghem[us] sos infrascriptos ordiname[n]t[us], pro qui cussos observando et mantene[n]do, sas vignas et ortos et lavores ant romane et istare i[n] su gradu issoro et megiorare et avansare cussas de qui ant essere, et issu bestiame[n] ind'at esser megi[us] gubernadu, mantesidu et guardadu.

Ordinamentos de vignas, de lavores e de ortos.
CXXXIII. (1)Ordinam[us] qui in ciasch[u]na villa dessas terras qui ant avire vig-
29r nas et ortos si depiant, per issu officiali nostru, | maiore dessa co[n]trada, ogna annu, in su mese de frebrer, ellegere personas de bona fama et co[n]ditioni, in sa villa manna ho[min]is octo et in sa villa metzana ho[min]is ses et i[n] sa pixina ho[min]is quatro, sos quales su maiore de sa dita villa at fagheri iurare. (2)Per dogna requesta qui 'llis at esser factu, totu si 'lloy ant poder esser, et si no[n] a su min[us] tres dessos ditos iurad[us] cun su maiore dessa dita villa, ant andare a providere cussas vingnas et ortos de qui ant esser requestos. (3)Et provididos qui 'llas ant aviri, cussos qui 'llis ant parri qui siant sufficie[n]teme[n]te et benecungiadas de fossu, o de muro, o de clausura et illis at parre de recivire pro cungiada sensa fraudi [siant tenudos] de iscriviri in su chaderno qui subra cussos [s'at] ordinare. (4)Et vigna over orto qui no[n] siant cungiadas sufficie[n]teme[n]te et secundu q[u]i si co[n]tenet no[n] at aprovare ne[n] acceptare et comandare ad icussos qui ant aviri sas dictas vignas over ortos qui no[n] ant esser sufficie[n]teme[n]te cungiadas q[u]i 'llas cungint i[n]fra dies octo dae cussa die qui 'llis ad esser comandadu et etia[m] de[us]iurint de hochire et denunciare cussu bestiame[n] et accusare sos ho[min]is qui ant acaptare i[n]tro dessas dictas vignas et ortos cungiad[us] et aprovad[us] pro cungiad[us], et i[n] lavoris, secundu qui si co[n]tenit in sos capidul[us] segue[n]tes subra ciò ordi[n]ados et de andare at apersare sos damnos, (5)su quale apersu ant fagheri bene et lealime[n]te secundu qui 'llis at parri in sa conscie[n]t[i]a issoro qui esser deppiant et sensa fraudi.

[Preface (*proemio*) of Mariano].
(1)We Mariano, by the grace of God, iudike (*iuyghi*) of Arborea, count of Gociano (Goceano) and viscount of Basso (Bas), in view of the many complaints that there have frequently been—and are still being—raised in our lands of Arborea and Loghudoro, concerning vineyards, orchards and cultivations that are going to ruin and becoming impoverished because of the lack of vigilance and care that is given to the livestock on the part of the owner and those who guard them, for which reason many vineyards and orchards remain abandoned and uncultivated, and many people who would also work therein, refrain from working them, because of the uncertainty of having any produce in what they work, and desiring us to provide for the common profit and good state of our people, we have resolved to make and promulgate the following ordinances so that by observing and abiding by them, the vineyards, gardens, and cultivations, and those who own them may improve and advance them, and that the livestock may be better governed, maintained, and guarded.

Orders of vineyards, cultivations and gardens.
Article 133. (1)We order that in each village of the lands in which there are vineyards and orchards, there shall be, by our official, a senior functionary of the countryside (*maiore dessa contrada*), every year in the month of February, elected persons of good reputation and condition: in a large village, eight men; in a medium-sized village; six, and in a small village, four, who shall be made to swear by the mayor (*maiore*) of the village. (2)By request which shall be made to them, if they can all be there, or otherwise at least three of the said jurors together with the mayor of the said village, they shall go to make provision for the vineyards and gardens concerning the request that shall be made. (3)And after they have provided this, those vineyards and gardens which shall appear to them to be sufficiently well fenced by a ditch or wall or hedge, and shall appear to them to be well fenced in a sound manner, let them be bound to record them in the register which in regard to them shall be ordered to be made. (4)And such vineyards and gardens as are not fenced sufficiently and in accordance with the provisions, he shall not approve, nor accept, and shall [instead] order the owners of the said vineyards and gardens which are not sufficiently fenced, to fence them within eight days from the date on which the injunction is issued, and also they shall swear to kill the livestock and report the same, and also to report the men whom they shall find within the said vineyards and gardens enclosed with regular fencing, and in the cultivations, according to the provisions of the following articles upon this subject ordered, and to go and assess the damage; (5)the assessment they shall make properly and honestly according to their conscience that shall seem right to them, and without deceit.

CXXXIIII. Vignas et ortus.

(1)Item ordinam[us] qui ogna persona qui at avire vigna, over orto, illu deppiant cungiare over de muro, o de fossu, over de clasura, et cungiado qui at esser, illu depiant fagheri providere per issos iurad[us] p[re]d[i]ctos, qui ant esser ad ciò alletos et deputados. (2)Et ciò deppiant faghere per totu su p[re]sente mese de ap[ri]li et da inde i[n]anti ogni anno de su mese de s[a][n]ctu Gayni, bienenadu que ant avire. (3)Et providido et atprovado per issos ditos maiores et iurados i[n] su cadernu, secundu que de supra est naradu, l'at fagheri scrivire per isso maiori de sa ditta villa, qui i[n] su quaderno que avirit [et] dette[n]ne, [a] ciò qui sas ditas vignas et ort[us] qui ant esser aprovadus et recividos pro
29v cungia- | dos, scrivere si possat et acatare q[ua]n[do] at bisongiare. (4)Volemus et comandam[us] qui ciascuno maiore de ciasc[u]na dessas ditas villas hui ant aviri vignas et ortos depiant faghire unu quadernu pro ssee ognia anno, in su quali at fagheri scrivere ordi[n]adame[n]te, die a die, come[n]te, per issus ditos iurados, li at esser denunciado sas vignas et ortos aprobados et recividos pro cungiados, fague[n]do illoe scrivere sos nome[n]es de cussus iurados qui ant a providere·llos et recivire·llos pro cungiados, [et bi ant] esser istados. (5)Et cussu maiore que ad esser achatado non [aviri] factu su dictu quadernu ognia anno, over non aviri factu iscrivere sa vigna over orto qui 'lli esseret denunciada, esseret approvado et recivido pro cungiado, siat conde[n]nado, et paghit a sa camera nostra, ogna bolta qui 'lli at essere provadu over acaptado, l[ib]r[a]s tres. (6)Et icussu qui at iscriviri su dictu providime[n]tu et aprovame[n]tu appat, per ciascuna vigna over orto qui ad scriviri esser aprovadu et recivido pro cungiado, dinaris .IIII.

CXXXV. Idem.

(1)Volemus et ordinam[us] qui cussu pubillu de vigna over de orto qui at esser aprovadu et recivido pro cungiado, over arme[n]targiu, over ho[min]i suo qui siat ad istari i[n] do[m]mo sua o alcuna atera qui si achatarit pro ciò over alc[u]no dessos dictos iurados que ant acaptari bestiamen domado over rui in alcuna dessas ditas vignas over ortos aprovados pro cungiados, siat te[n]tu et deppiant, im podere suo, su dictu bestiamen ochiri over lensari, de die over de nocte, deppiant de p[re]sente denunciare a su maiore dessa dicta villa dundi sa dicta vigna over orto at esser. (2)Et si ochiri over lensari no 'ndi ad poder, denunciare l'at a su p[re]dictu maiore que lu fassat iscriviri in su p[re]dictu caderno qui at esser pro ciò ordinado, iurando cussu qui su dictu bestiame[n]

Article 134. Vineyards and gardens.

(1)Item: We order that every person who possesses a vineyard or garden shall keep it fenced either with a wall or with a ditch or with a hedge and, once fenced, he shall have it inspected by the aforesaid jurors, who shall be appointed and deputed for this purpose. (2)And this they shall do throughout this month of April and, from this date forward, every year in the month of St Gavino [October], after the harvest. (3)And when it has been viewed and approved with an annotation thereof by the said senior officials (*maiores*) and jurors in the register according to the foregoing, they shall have it recorded by the mayor (*maiore*) of the said village in the register which he shall make and keep, so that the said vineyards and gardens which shall receive approval and affirmation concerning their fencing may be reported in the register and therein found when necessary. (4)We wish and enjoin that each senior official (*maiore*) of each of the said villages where there are vineyards and gardens shall himself establish a register every year in which he shall transcribe neatly, day by day, how and what by those under oath (*sos iurados*) shall be declared to him concerning approved and affirmed vineyards and gardens in regard to the enclosures, making therein a record of the names of those jurors who shall view them and approve the validation of the fencing, having made an inspection therein. (5)And that senior official (*maiore*) who shall be found not to have drawn up the said register every year, or shall not have recorded therein the vineyard or orchard on which he shall receive declaration that it has been viewed and approved as regularly fenced, let him be condemned and pay to our Chamber, whenever, being found in default, it shall be proved against him, three lire. (6)And he who shall transcribe the said measure shall receive four denari for each vineyard or orchard which he shall have recorded as approved and validated as to fencing.

Article 135. Idem

(1)We wish and order that the owner of the vineyard or orchard whose fence shall be approved and affirmed, or his representative (*armentargiu*), or the person who, with him, shall be in his employment, or another person who shall be found deputed to do so, or any of the said jurors who shall find any tame or wild livestock in any of the said vineyards or gardens approved with respect to the fence, being in his power, be required, and shall kill the said livestock or strike them with a throwing weapon, whether by day or by night, and he shall immediately report the fact to the mayor (*maiore*) of the said village to which the said vineyard or garden belongs. (2)And if he shall not be able to kill or strike it, he shall report it to the said mayor who shall cause it to be recorded in the aforesaid register which shall be arranged for that purpose, swearing, he

ad aviri denunciado qui at factu su podere su[o] in oquire·llo et non ad possidu. (3)Et icussu pubillo de vigna o de orto o arme[n]targiu, over ho[min]i suo, qui at acatari su ditu bestiame[n] et iurare non lu bole[n]te, over que ad provado qui de voluntadi sua inde siat exidu su dictu bestiame[n] sensa illo
30r ochire, siat conde[m]pnado et paghit, pro ciaschuna bolta, a sa camera | nostra, l[ib]ras .v. (4)Et issu pubillu de cussu bestiamen qui at essere acaptado in sa dicta vigna over orto paghit pro su bestiamen domado secundu qui si contenit in su capidulu dessa Carta de Loghu de presente, de sa quali pena depiat avire su maiore de sa dita villa pro sa camera nostra sas duas partes et issa tersa appat su accusadori. (5)Et gosi si inte[n]dat pro su bestiame[n]rude comente et de su bestiamen domado. (6)Et sia creditu assu sargame[n]tu suo su dictu acusadori et denunciadore. (7)Et niente de min[us] siat tenudo de pagare et paghit su aprezu et damnu qui su ditu bestiame[n] ad aviri factu in sa dicta vigna over orto qui at aviri iscuniado per issu dictu bestiame[n], secundu qui s'at co[n]venne a dispe[n]diu suo, ceptu que si su pubillu dessa dita vigna over orto consentirit que su dictu bestiame[n] exirit dae sa dita vigna over orto sensa indi ochire over lensari. (8)Qui in cussu casu no 'ndi appat satisfacione alcuna. (9)Et si alcuno dessos p[re]dictus pobillus o armentargiu, over homini suo, over iurado, qui sunt narados de supra, acaptarit alchuno dessu dictu bestiame[n] et non lu ochirent over lensarint over non lu denunciarent, secundu qui est naradu de supra, deppiat paghare et pagit a sa camera nostra ogni bolta qui l'at esser provado, over c'at esser acatado legittimamente avire zò factu, libras quimbi. (10)Et issu bestiamen c'at esser lensado et ad morre in sa dicta vigna over orto et issu simili si intendat si morret in alcuna villa dessu castighu cue esseret sa vigna hui su dictu bestiamen ad esser lensado et gossi si intendat pro su molente comente et dess'attero bestiamen qui de supra est narado. (11)Et de presente su pubillu dessu ditu bestiamen possat aviri recursu contra assu pastore de cussu qui at debere paschire. (12)Et [si], issu factu, non avirit podere de paghare, istit in pregione infini a voluntadi dessu pubillu de su bestiamen. (13)Et intendat·si dessu bestiamen de caluncha persona siat.

CXXXVI. De su porcho mannali.

(1)Constituimus et ordinamus qui sos bonus hominis o feminas pubillos de sas
30v dictas vingnas et ortos, | armentargiu issoro over homini issoro, o iurado de sas ditas villas deputados a ciò, secundu qui de supra est narado, qui at acaptare

who shall have reported it concerning the livestock, that he has done all in his power to kill it and that he has not succeeded. (3)And that owner of a vineyard or orchard, or the representative (*armentargiu*), or one of his employees, who shall find said livestock and shall not be willing to make a sworn report of them, or who shall be proved to have voluntarily brought said livestock out of it [from the fenced areas] and not killed them, let him be condemned and pay, for each time, to our Chamber, five lire. (4)And the owner of the said livestock who shall be found in the said vineyard or garden shall pay for the tamed livestock according to what is presently contained in the article of the *Carta de Logu*; of the amount of which financial punishment the mayor of the said village shall collect two-thirds in favour of our Chamber (*sa Camera*); the third part shall be had by the accuser. (5)And, in the same manner, be it intended as much for wild as for tame livestock. (6)And let the denouncing accuser, who has sworn, be believed. (7)And no less shall he [the owner of the livestock] be bound to pay and shall pay the estimated value of the damage which the livestock shall have done in the said vineyard or garden by tearing down the fence, at his own expense according to what shall be agreed, except that the owner of the said vineyard or garden shall have consented to the said livestock going out of the said vineyard or garden without his killing or striking them. (8)In such a case he shall have no compensation. (9)And if any of the aforesaid owners or their representative (*armentargiu*) or any person in his employ, or a juror mentioned above, finds any head of livestock and does not kill it or strike it with a throwing weapon, or does not report it according to the foregoing, he must pay and shall pay to our Chamber five lire for each time it shall be proved against him, or shall be ascertained lawfully to have done so. (10)And with regard to the livestock that shall have been struck and shall die in said vineyard or garden, similarly be it understood if they die in any village of collective land (*castigu*) wherein is the vineyard in which the livestock shall have been struck, and likewise be it understood with regard to the donkey and other livestock mentioned above. (11)And the owner of the said livestock may bring a legal case, without delay, against the shepherd who shall have been in charge of bringing the livestock to pasture. (12)And if, having done so, he cannot pay, he shall remain in prison at the will of the owner of the livestock. (13)And this shall be understood of livestock belonging to any person.

Article 136. Of the tame pig.

(1)We direct and order that if the trusted men (*bonus hominis*) or the women owners of the said vineyards or gardens, or their representative (*armentargiu*) or one of their employees, or the juror (*iurado*) of the said villages deputed for that purpose, according to that which is said above, shall find any domestic

porchos manalis in alc[u]na dessas ditas vignas over ortos et si lensari [et] ochiri non l'ant poder, paghit su pubillu dessu dictu porcho su ap[re]ciu de su damnu qui at fagheri in sa dicta vigna over orto et issu q[u]i at costare a chungiare sa dicta vigna over orto et s[oldo]s tres per porcho assa camera nostra per ciaschuna volta qui 'lloy at esser achaptadu. (2)Et si non paghat, levent·si su porcho pro sa corte, sensa misericordia nixuna.

CXXXVII. Porchus de gamma.
(1)Item ordinamus que sos pubillos dessas ditas vignas, ortos, over armentargiu, o homini issoro, over cussos qui ant esser de ciò iuradus, qui ant achaptare porchos de gamma, o brebegues, o capras, in alcuna dessas dictas vignas over ortos, siant tentas et depiant ochire over levare, per ciaschuna bolta qui 'lloy ant esser achaptados, de ciaschuna gamma pegus .v. (2)Et niente de minus su pubillu de su ditu bestiamen deppiat pagare et paghit su apersiu et damnu qui cussu bestiamen at aviri fatu et cungiare ad ispendiu suo sa vigna over orto qui at esser ischungiada et soldos .xx., dessos quales appat sa camera nostra sas duas partis et issa tersa parte appat su achusadore. (3)Et alcuno dessos predictos qui ant acaptare su dictu bestiamen et at laxare de ochire over levare comente est narado, non lu at denunciare a su maiore, paghit per ogni bolta qui 'lloy ad esser acaptado over provadu legitimamente ciò aviri fatu, secundu qui si contenit in su capidulo de subra attere bestiamen. (4)Qui contra fagherit pro amore o pro timore o pro atera regione, qui si 'ndi istaret de non fagher de sas predictas causas, paghit pro dogna bolta libras quimbi.

CXXXVIII. De terra boida.
(1)Volem[us] et ordi[n]am[us] qui caluncha persona, de caluncha co[n]dit[i]o[n]e siat, at aviri terra boida i[n]castigu de vignas depiat·illi esser coma[n]dadu per issu officiali no[st]ru, maiore dessa co[n]trada, q[u]i cussa terra boida depiat po[n]ne a vi[n]gia over fageri po[n]ne et plantare·llo a vigna infra unu
31r annu, over qui 'llu bendat | o dedi a persona qui plantare·illa possat, (2)su quale comandame[n]tu depiat faggeri iscriviri, q[u]i si possat ischire q[ua]n[do] su te[m]p[us] at esser co[m]plidu. (3)Et quando, infra su ditu te[m]pus, cussu a qui at esser fatu su dictu comandame[n]tu dessa suprascripta terra no[n] plantarit over fagherit plantare a vigna, pro qui no[n] bogiat over no[n] possat, nen be[n]dat ne[n] det a persona qui po[n]ne over plantare·illa pozat a vigna, su dictu officiali sa dicta terra levet et apropit a sa corte nostra.

CXXXIX. De cungiare vigna.
(1)Constituim[us] et ordinam[us] qui ogna persona de qualuncha gradu, istadu, over co[n]ditio[n]e siat, qui at aviri vigna o terra boida in ciaschuna de sas ving-

swine in any of the said vineyards or gardens, and if they cannot strike or kill them with a throwing weapon, let the owner of the said pig pay the estimated damage he shall have done in the said vineyard or garden and the cost of the new fence, and to our Chamber three soldi for each pig, for each time he shall be found there. (2)And if he does not pay, let the pig be requisitioned from him for the benefit of the court without any discount.

Article 137. On herding pigs.
(1)Item: we order that the owners of the said vineyards or gardens, or the representative (*armentargiu*), or one of their employees, or those under oath (*sos iurados*) appointed for that purpose, who shall find swine belonging to a herd, or sheep or goats in any of the said vineyards or gardens, shall be required, and must kill or requisition it, for each time they shall be found therein, five heads of the herd. (2)And nonetheless the owner of the said livestock shall pay the damage estimated to have been done by that livestock, and shall again fence in at his own expense the vineyard or garden whose fence has been torn down, and twenty soldi of which our Chamber shall take two-thirds while the third part shall go to the accuser. (3)And any of the aforesaid who shall find said livestock and neglect to kill or requisition them as aforesaid, or shall fail to report them to the official (*maiore*) shall pay for each time he shall be lawfully found or proved to have done so, according to what is contained in the article concerning livestock of other kinds. (4)Whoever shall do otherwise out of fondness (*pro amore*) or out of fear or other reason and neglect to do the above shall pay for each time five lire.

Article 138. Of uncultivated land.
(1)We desire and order that any person, of whatever condition he may be, who has uncultivated land (*terra boida*) in a collective plot (*castigu*) of vines, should be ordered by our official of the countryside (*maiore dessa contrada*), that uncultivated land should be placed and planted as vineyard within one year, or else that he should sell it or give it to someone who can plant it; (2)the order he should have recorded, so that it may be known when the time limit will be expired. (3)And when, within the said period of time, he to whom the said order shall be enjoined concerning the said land, does not plant or cause the vineyard to be planted because he will not or cannot, nor sells or assigns it to any person who can put it or plant it as a vineyard, the said official shall requisition the land from him and forfeit it to our court.

Article 139. Of fencing the vineyard.
(1)We direct and order that every person of whatever rank, state or condition he may be, who has vineyard or uncultivated land in each of the collective vine-

nas siat tenudo de co[n]trubuhire et paghare pro rata et secundu qui '[n]de 'lli at tochare sa parti dessa cungiadura qui at fagheri.

CXL. De cungiare vingna.

(1)Item ordinam[us] qui caluncha persona c'at aviri vigna o terra boida in castigu siat tenudo de co[n]trubuhire et paghare pro rata, secundu qui '[n]de 'lli at tochari sa parti dessa cungiadura qui a[n]t fagheri cussos qui 'll'ant esser dae ladus de foras, ant aviri clasura et faghere fossu qui 'lloy at esser necessariu. (2)Et si alc[u]no de cussos qui ant aviri alc[u]na de sas ditas vignas o terra boida et no[n] ant boler paghare over at esser inposenti de paghare sa parti de su ispendiu qui s'at fagheri et ill'at torrari de su fructu qui s'at aviri dae ssas vignas qui at esser subra se, si paghit su dictu ispendiu. (3)Et si bastanti no[n] esseret assu dictu ispe[n]diu, su pubillu dessa dicta vigna siat tenudo de bender·illa infra uno mese. (4)De su p[re]ciu qui 'ndi at aviri, si 'ndi satisfassat cussa parti. (5)Et icussu qui 'll'at co[m]porare siat tenudo a ffagheri et paghare su ispe[n]diu qui ssa dicta vigna pro sa dicta cungiadura l'at tochare. (6)Et similime[n]te siat tenudo et deppiat bender cussu pubillu c'at aviri sa dicta terra boida in castigu. (7)Et si co[m]poradore non avirit et acaptare no[n] si 'ndi poderet dessa dita vigna, over terra boida, dividat·si et partat i[n]ter icussos qui ant aviri vignas in ssu suprascriptu castiu et a confinare et esser plus ap[re]ssu
31v dessa dicta vigna, over terra boida. (8)Et icussos qui sa dita | vigna over terra ant aviri siant tenudos de paghare sa parti dessu dictu ispendiu qui at tochari a sa dita vigna, over terra boida, qui at esser divisa et partida, secundu qu'est narradu de subra. (9)Si verame[n]te qui cussos qui 'll'a[n]t co[m]porare over at qui be[n]ne in parte sa dicta terra boida siant tenud[us] de po[n]ne et plantare a vigna sa dita terra i[n]fra uno anno. (10)Et si no[n] la ponet et plantat infra su dictu te[m]p[us], siat sa dicta terra dessa corte. (11)Et niente de min[us] fassat et paghit su ispe[n]diu qui assa dicta terra ad tochare in sa p[re]dita cungiadura. (12)Et icussu qui ad aviri vigna in castigu over a lad[us] de alc[u]no atero over ortos qui siat dae lad[us] de foras, qui non at esser bene co[n]giadu, depiat·si·lli comandare per issu officiali et issu iurado dessa dita villa hui at esser qui infra dies octo lu deppiat aviri co[n]giadu. (13)Et si non lu cungiant dae lad[us] suo, intraret bestiame[n] et faghit damnu in vignas over ortos dessos viginos, paghint assa corte nostra s[oldo]s .xx., emendet e satisfassat su damnu qui cussu vigino at aviri factu et recivido et appido, et issos dictos maiores et iurad[us] lu deppiant fagheri cungiare ad ispe[n]diu de cussu de qui at essere sa vigna,

yards shall be bound to contribute and pay his share, and to pay for the part of the fence which he shall make, according to his due.

Article 140. Of fencing the vineyard.

(1)Item: we order that the person who has a vineyard or uncultivated collective land (*castigu*) shall be obliged to contribute and pay his share, according to what is due to him for his own share, of the fencing that those who will be his neighbours on the outer side will make, or will have to put a fence or to dig a ditch that will be necessary there. (2)And if any of those who will have any of the said vineyards or uncultivated land, but will not want to pay or will be unable to pay, the share which shall be established shall pay it out of the proceeds from the vineyards and which shall fall under his tenure. (3)And if it shall not be sufficient to cover said expense, let the owner of said vineyard be obliged to sell it within one month. (4)From the proceeds he shall have from it, there will be satisfied his due share. (5)And he who shall purchase it will be obliged to make and pay the expenses due to him for the said fence. (6)And similarly let the owner who has uncultivated land in the collective land (*castigu*) be bound to it and must sell it. (7)And if there shall not be or be found to be a purchaser of the said vineyard or uncultivated land, the expense shall be divided and apportioned among those who shall have, in the said collective land, vineyards adjoining and next to the said vineyard or uncultivated land. (8)And those who have possession of the said vineyard or uncultivated land shall be obliged to pay that part of the said expense which shall accrue to the said vineyard or uncultivated land which shall be divided and apportioned, according to the foregoing. (9)And therefore those who shall purchase it, or to whom the part of the said uncultivated land shall touch, are bound to set it aside and to plant the said land as a vineyard within one year. (10)And if they do not set it aside and do not plant it within the said time, [then] the said land shall remain in the possession of the court. (11)Nonetheless, he shall bear and pay the expense due for the said land for the said fencing. (12)And he who shall have a vineyard in the collective land or by the side of any other, or vegetable gardens placed on the outer side [bordering on others outside the collective land] which are not well fenced, shall be ordered by the official and juror of the said village in which he shall be [resident] that within eight days he shall have fenced it. (13)And if he does not fence it on the side that is his own, and livestock penetrates it causing damage to the vineyards or gardens of his neighbours, he shall pay to our court twenty soldi and shall compensate and satisfy the damage that the said bordering neighbour shall have received and suffered; and the said senior officials (*maiores*) and jurors shall have it fenced in at the expense of the owner of the vineyard or garden, paying the labourers of the surrounding area who

over orto, dando assos servidores qui loy ant serviri approbia, plus qui per issos ateros dessa villa s'at dare et paghare dinaris duos sa die per ciaschuno, pro qui pl[us] ap[re][s]se sa causa si possat ispaciare. (14)Et si no[n] l'at boler paghare, pignorint·illi de cussu qui at montare su ispe[n]diu p[re]dictu et satisfassat sos servidores. (15)Et si non at aviri atero de poder·illi pignorare, prossa dicta vigna over orto, satisfassat dae ssu fructu dessa dicta vigna over orto, su quali fructu possant sos dictos maiores et iuradus be[n]der a tempus assu megius qui at poder, et paghit sos dictos servidores.

CXLI. De faguere lavorare sas vignas.

(1)Volem[us] et ordinam[us] qui cussos qui ant vignas, et ant avire per i[n]antes, deppiant·illas lavorare o[m][n]i anno. (2)Et si alcuna vigna esseret qui no[n] si lavorarit infra su te[m]pus qui sunt ordinad[us] in su capidulu de Carta de Loghu de Arbaree, levet·si pro sa corte. (3)Et si sa corte no[n] la lavorat over
32r fagueri la- | vorare da inde inantes per issos p[re]dictos te[m]pus ordinad[us], ne[n] be[n]dere l'at a persona over a personas qui 'lla possat lavorare, s'est vigna qui siat in castighu romanghat et siat de cussos qui ant aviri vignas in su p[re]dictu castighu et ant co[n]finare et esser pl[us] ap[re]ssa assa dicta vigna, secundo qui si contenet in su capidulo de subra. (4)Et gosi si inte[n]dat dessas vingnas dessa corte et dessas clesias come[n]ti et dessas ateras.

CXLII. Qui iscongiarit vigna o orto.

(1)Constituim[us] et ordinam[us] qui nexuna persona de qualu[n]cha istado over conditione siat deppiat over p[re]sumat ischungiare istudiosame[n]te alcuna vigna over orto qui siat cungiadu, et adprova[du] pro cungiadu per issos iurados a ciò alletos. (2)Nen etiam de[us] usit over p[re]sumat intrari in alcunas vignas subraditas over ortos qui suo non siat de te[m]p[us] alcuno, sensa paraula de su pubillu de sa vingna over orto. (3)Et qualuncha persona c'at esser acatada over l'at esser provado qui appat ischungiado studiosame[n]te alcuna de sas dictas vignas over ortos, si lo[e] at mittiri bestiame[n] paghit, per ogna bolta qui loe at esser acatadu over l'at esser provadu, l[ib]r[a]s .x. assa camera nostra et siat maxelladu et mortu su bestiami[n]i, secundu qui si contenit in su capidulo de subra, et fassat ad ispendiu suo cungiare sa dita vigna over orto. (4)Et nie[n]te de min[us] siat tenudo de pagare su ap[re]ciu et te[n]turas, secundu qui si contenit in su capidulu de subra. (5)Et siat chertido su accusadore a sagrame[n]tu suo. (6)Et si non avirit de undi paghari, istit in p[re]xioni a voluntadi de su segnore prossa maquicia, et infini at qui ad aviri satisfactu su damnu qui ad aviri factu a su pobillu de sa vigna over orto. (7)Et

shall provide their labour to a greater extent than those of the same village at the rate of two denari per day to each, so that as soon as possible the matter may be brought to an end. (14)And if he does not wish to pay, let foreclosure be imposed on him equal to the amount of the aforesaid expense and satisfy the labourers. (15)And if he shall have nothing to foreclose on, in respect of the said vineyard or garden, let him satisfy from the proceeds of the said vineyard or garden, which proceeds the senior officials (*maiores*) and jurors may sell at a propitious time at the best possible price, so as to pay the said labourers.

Article 141. Of having vineyards cultivated.
(1)We wish and order that those who possess vineyards, and shall have more afterwards, shall work them every year. (2)And if there shall be any vineyard that is not worked within the terms specified in the *Carta de Logu* of Arborea, [then] we requisition it for the Court (*sa corte*). (3)And if the Court does not cultivate it or does not have it worked from that time onwards in the aforesaid established time, and nor will it sell it to a person or persons who can work it, if it is vineyard that is in *castigu* [collective land] let it remain there and belong to those who will have vineyards in the aforesaid *castigu*, next to and adjoining the aforesaid vineyard, according to what is contained in the article above. (4)And so be it understood of the vineyards of the Court and churches as well as of others.

Article 142. Who shall tear down the fence of a vineyard or garden.
(1)We establish and order that no person, of whatever state he may be, shall dare to intentionally tear down the fence of any vineyard or garden that is fenced in, and, as such, approved by those under oath (*sos iurados*) elected for that purpose. (2)Neither shall he dare or presume to enter any of the aforesaid vineyards or gardens which are not his own at any time without the permission of the owner of the vineyard or garden. (3)And any person who shall be found therein or shall be proved to have intentionally broken down the fence of any of the said vineyards or gardens, and shall cause livestock to enter therein, he shall pay, for each time he shall be found *in flagrante delicto* or it shall be proved against him, ten lire to our Chamber (*sa camera*), and the livestock shall be slaughtered or killed according to the provisions of the article hereinabove, and he shall have the said vineyard or garden fenced at his own expense. (4)And he shall be no less obliged to pay for the damage as assessed and the penalty relating to the capture of the livestock, according to what is contained in the article above. (5)And let the accuser be believed upon his oath. (6)And if he shall not have anything to pay, let him remain in prison at the will of the lord, in relation to the penalty, and let him remain there until he has satisfied the compensation for the damage which he has done to the owner of the vineyard or garden. (7)And

icussa persona qui at esser acaptadu intro dessas dictas vignas over ortos pagit per dogna bolta, si est de te[m]p[us] de fructura, s[oldo]s .XL. et satisfassat su damnu qui illoy at aviri factu. (8)Et si non paghat infra .VIII. dies. dae ssa die qui at esser tentu, siat posto in su panghulier, et si at aviri fatu damnu cussu fructu qui at aviri levado. (9)Et si in su attero tempus dess'anno illoy intrarit alcuna per-
32v sona, paghit assa corte soldos binti. | (10)Et si non lus paghat, istit im prexoni a plachimentu nostru et assa dita pena. (11)Et non si inte[n]dat cussu ho[min]i over ho[min]is dessu pubillu dessa vigna over orto, over sos ho[min]is qui 'lloy ant intrari a llavorare sas ditas vignas over ortos over per alcuno atero modo a voluntadi de su pubillu dessa vigna over orto, (12)ne[n] etia[m] deus cussos qui ant aviri vigna in castigu over ortos a llados apare, qui de necessitadi convenit qui intrarit in su ortu dessu vigino pro passare et i[n]trare a su suo. (13)Ma chussos illoy possant intrari a ppee tantu i[n] cussu loghu qui duos bonos hominis de cussos qui ant aviri vignas in su castighu over ant aviri dessos dictos ortos, tenendo appare, ant providere qui si fassat s'aidu de i[n]trare et via de passare, (14)si veramente qui cussu qui at intrari et passare a sa vigna over orto suo, de qu'est naradu, cungit s'aidu qui 'lloy at esser ordi[n]ado, ghasi in su intrari come[n]te in su exire, qui at fagheri de passare, qui best[i]amen intrari non loy possat a sa dicta pe[n]a per dogna bolta qui 'lloy at esser acaptada over provadu. (15)Et si [a] su intrari over passare qui at fagheri a llevare aghina o araigla over fructu de atera vigna over orto qui suo non siat over illoy fagherit alcuno atero dampnu, siat conde[m]pnado come[n]te et icussos qui intrant in vignas over in ortos de ateri, ut de subra est naradu. (16)Et icusso pubillu de vigna over orto, o armentargiu o ho[min]i suo, over iurado electu a sa guardia dessas vingnas et ortos et lavores, qui 'llu achaptarint in alcuna de sas dictas vignas et ortos, siat tenudo de accusare·llu comente et issu bestiamini a sa pe[n]a qui si co[n]tenit de supra.

CXLIII. Qui venderet agresta.

(1)Item ordinam[us] qui si alcuna persona at esser achaptada be[n]der agresta over aghina furada over levada de vigna qui non siat sua paghit assa camera nostra cussa persona qui at esser achaptada bendendo·la liras .V. (2)Et issu bendidore qui at consentire over levare dessa dita aghina a dommo sua over ad atiri senza lice[n]tia de su pubillu et at·illi esser provadu et achaptadu in dommo over in ateruy, pagit l[ib]r[a]s .X. et paghit su dampnu qui at aviri fatu. (3)Et si
33r no[n] at poder | de paghare, istet in prexioni pro sa pena et pro su damnu a voluntadi nostra.

that person who shall be caught within the said vineyard or garden shall pay for each time, if it is time for the ripening and harvesting of fruit, forty soldi and he shall make good the damage he shall have done therein. (8)And if he shall not pay within eight days, beginning from the day that he shall be caught, let him be pilloried; and if he shall have done damage, let him make good the fruit which he shall have taken. (9)And if any person shall enter in a different season of the year, let him pay to the Court twenty soldi. (10)And if he shall not pay such a sum, let him remain in prison at our will and at the said penalty. (11)And this shall not be intended in regard to that man or men [in the service] of the owner of the vineyard or garden who shall enter therein, or men who shall enter therein to work the said vineyards or gardens, or for any other reason and at the will of the owner of the vineyard or garden; (12)Nor shall it be intended in regard to those who have vineyard in *castigu* land [collective land] or gardens adjoining each other, whereby it is possible to enter their own garden except by passing through their neighbour's garden. (13)But they shall be allowed to enter it on foot only if two trusted men (*bonos hominis*) of those who have vineyards in *castigu* [land] or have of the aforesaid gardens adjoining each other shall see to it that an entrance passage and a way of access be made, (14)so that he who shall enter and pass into his said vineyard or garden, of whom it has been said, shall close the entrance opening therein which shall be ordained, both at the entrance as well as at the exit when he shall pass therein, in such a manner that no livestock may enter therein, under penalty for every time he shall be found in flagrante or shall be proved against him. (15)And if, on entering or passing through it, he picks up grapes or takes away the roots of the vine or fruit of any other vineyard or garden than his own, or does any damage therein, let him be condemned as those who enter into vineyards or gardens that are not their own, as was said above. (16)And that owner of a vine yard or garden, or administrator (*armentargiu*) or man in his employ, or juror elected to guard the vineyards and crops, who shall catch him in any of the said vineyards or gardens, let him be reported as [in the same manner as one who causes] livestock to enter, and he shall be subject to the punishment aforesaid.

Article 143. Whoever sells unripe grapes (*agresta*).

(1)Item: we order that if any person shall be found selling unripe grapes (*agresta*) or grapes stolen or taken from a vineyard that is not his own, he shall pay, that person who shall be found selling them, five lire to our Chamber. (2)And the vine grower who will allow or take part of the said grapes to his house or to others without licence from the master, and it shall be proved against him and the stolen goods found in his house or elsewhere, he shall pay ten lire and compensation for the damage he has done. (3)And if he cannot pay, let him remain in prison for the penalty and for the damage, at our will.

CXLIIII. Qui esseret loghadu a vigna.

(1)Volem[us] et ordinam[us] qui nixuna persona qui at esser alogada at lavorare ad alch[u]na vingia ad te[m]p[us] de fructu over a be[n]nenare no[n] deppiat ne[n] p[re]sumat leare over portare foras dessa dicta vi[n]gia arguesta over achina per alcunu modo, sensa paraula et voluntadi de su pubillu, ad pena de pagare a su pubillu, qui at esser at lavorare over a vennenare, de maquicia s[oldo]s .x. sensa mise[ri]cordia nixuna. (2)Et satisfassat su damnu a su pupillu qui 'll'at esser factu.

CXLV. De vigna.

(1)Constituim[us] et ordinam[us] qui nexuna persona qui s'at alogare at lavorare in vingia no[n] usit ne p[re]sumat levare pro portare a dommo sua senza paraula et voluntade de su pubillu de sa vi[n]gia plus de raygla segada, nen sanas ne[n] fundos, ad pe[n]a de paghare de maquicia l[ib]r[a]s .II.

CXLVI. De vingia.

(1)Item ordinam[us] qui ciaschuna persona, de qualuncha istadu o co[n]ditio[n]e siat, qui at aver vingia in castiu over per se, siat tenudo et deppiat dogni anno, sa die de sancto Quirico, ponne su venidore over castiadore o castiadores, secundo sa vingia et comente su pubillo at plachere, uno over multos qui ant ad bisongiare a su castiu over vi[n]gia at pro see ad pena de pagare, cussu qui no 'llo at a po[n]ne, s[oldo]s .V. per ho[min]i cussus qui ant vingia in castiu. (2)Et icussos qui ant vi[n]gia a per see qui ant bisongiare benidore pro see paghit s[oldo]s .VI. pro sa mala cura sua et min[us] p[re]xu dessos ordiname[n]tos. (3)Et nie[n]te de min[us] siant tenudos infra dies .III. de po[n]ne so dito benidore over castiadore, ad pena de su doppiu de sa pena suprascripta. (4)Et issos bennidores qui ant esser in sas ditas vingnas deppiant esser satisfactos inanti qui ssu fructu dessa dicta vingia inde siat leadu. (5)Et si ciò non si fagheret, siant constrictos per sos officiales de sas villas dundi ant esser. (6)Et si veramente sos venidores de alchunas dessas dittas vingias, in su tempus qui 'll'at a guardare, si 'ndi partirit et in sa dicta vingia over vingias s'at fagher damnu in
33v su p[re]dictu te[m]p[us] qui si partirit, su dictu castia- | dore deppiat satisfagheri assu pubillu su damno qui 'lloy at esser factu. (7)Et si non at de quitheu paghare, istit in p[re]gione fini a tanto qui ad aviri satisfactu a su pubillu su da[n]no.

CXLVII. Vigna.

(1)Volem[us] et ordi[n]am[us] qui qualunca persone qui no[n] at aver vingia at esser acatado portando in domu sua, over i[n] alcun'atera parte, arguesta

Article 144. Whoever works as an employee in a vineyard.
(1)We wish and command that no person who works a vineyard as a hired labourer at the time of harvesting or grape harvesting shall dare to take or carry out of said vineyard any unripe grapes (*agresta*) or ripe grapes in any way, without the permission and without the will of the owner under penalty of paying to the owner with whom he will be working or harvesting, a fine of ten soldi without any discount. (2)And he shall make good the damage to the owner who shall have suffered it.

Article 145. Of the vineyard.
(1)We decree and order that no person who shall be hired to work in a vineyard shall dare or presume to take away to his house without the permission or will of the owner of the vineyard more than one vine strain, topped or undamaged as it may be, nor any head [of vine], under penalty of paying a fine of two lire.

Article 146. Of the vineyard.
(1)Item: we order that each person, of whatever state or condition he may be, who shall have vineyard in collective land [*castiu*] or on his own [outside the *castiu*], every year on the day of St Quirico, shall be required and must charge the vine-grower (*venidore*) or overseer or overseers according to the area of the vineyard or as the owner shall please, [with providing] one or more labourers as needed to the *castiu* or the vineyard he holds on his own, under penalty for him who does not do so, of five soldi per person relative to those who will have vineyard in *castigu* land. (2)And those who have a vineyard on their own and who will need a vinedresser shall pay six soldi for neglect and disregard of the ordinances. (3)And they shall nonetheless be required to appoint, within three days, the said vinedresser or overseer, under penalty of paying double the amount written above. (4)And the vinedressers appointed in the said vineyards shall be paid before the grape harvest takes place in the said vineyard. (5)And if this is not done, they shall be obliged to do it by the officials of the villages where they reside. (6)And in case the vinedressers of any of the said vineyards, in the time prescribed for them, go away and any damage shall occur in the said vineyard or vineyards, during the period of time in which they shall have left, the said overseer shall pay compensation to the owner for the damage that shall have occurred there. (7)And if he shall not have anything with which to pay, he shall remain in prison until he has compensated the owner for the damage.

Article 147. The vineyard.
(1)We wish and command that any person who has no vineyard shall be found to take away to his house, or anywhere else, unripe grapes (*agresta*) or ripe grapes

over achina et no[n] monstrarit de qui 'll'at aviri appida, et si cussa persone no[n] at demostrare no[n] avendo vingia, paghit cussa persone qui 'lloy ad esser acatada, come[n]ti ed icussa persone qui non mostrarit, de maquicia assa corte l[ib]r[a]s .II. pro dogna volta, come[n]ti ed icussos qui ant ad i[n]trare in vingia agiena, et nie[n]ti de min[us] paghit su damnu. (2)Et simili pena incurrant cussos at qui ad esser acatado fructura et non at aver vingia et ortos qui appant de cussa fructura, over de cussos de qui 'll'at aver appida.

CXLVIII. De fruttura.

(1)Constituim[us] et ordinam[us] qui qualunca persone de qualunca gradu, istadu, over conditione siat, non usit nen p[re]sumat levare over collire fruttura alcuna d'arbore qui siat in loghu iscongiadu co[n]tra voluntade de su pubillu, over guardianu de su p[re]dictu arbore, over arbores, ad pe[n]a de paghare, cussu qui 'lloy ad esser acatadu, over ill'at esser probadu, s[oldo]s .V. (2)Et paghit sa frutura qui 'll'at esser acatada et perdat·illa et siat·illi leada cussa propria fruttura et dadas et torradas assu pubillu dess'arbore. (3)Et supra ciò paghit su damno et sa maquicia, ciò esti: (4)si sa dicta fruttura fussi istetida leada de die paghit s[oldo]s .V. ut supra, et si esserit de nocte paghit s[oldo]s .X. (5)Et de issa prova siat crettidu su acusadore at sagrame[n]to suo, anco qui siat su pubillo, over atera persona qui i[n] cussa causa tantu pro beni qui siat parti, pro qui sa parte no[n] debet fagheri testimo[n]giu dae see istesu. (6)Però per custa causa, bolemus qui su prescriptu capitulu appat legitimu loghu.

CXLVIIII. De melloni.

(1)Item ordinam[us] qui nexuna persona, de qualunca gradu over conditione siat, no[n] usit nen p[re]sumat intrare in alcuno ortu de meloni qui siat co[n]giadu. (2)Et si alc[u]na persone illoy at intrare et illo[y] at esser acatado over ill'at esser provadu, s'est de die paghit s[oldo]s .V. et s'est de nocte pagit s[oldo]s
34r .X. et pa- | ghit su damno a su pubillu dess'ortu, et perdat su melone et siat de su pubillu dess'ortu. (3)Et per issa prova si i[n]te[n]dat qui siat cretidu a sargame[n]tu suo su accusadore. (4)Et si alc[u]no bestiamini at intrare in alcunos de sos ditos ortos qui siat cungiadu et provadu pro cungiadu per issos iurados electos at provare vingias et ortos cunyadas, su pubillu dessu ortu o ho[min]i suo o iuargiu o arme[n]targiu suo o iuradu qui 'll'at acaptare, bie 'llu deppiat ochire et denunciare·llo, secundo [qui] si co[n]tenit in su capitulu de supra dessas vingias et ortos, et icussa pe[n]a qui in su capidulu si contenit.

without being able to prove from whom he got them, and if that person [from whom they obtained them] will not be able, not having vineyard, [either] to prove [from whom he had it], then both that person who shall be so found, as well as the person who shall not be able to prove this, shall pay two lire of fine to the court for each time [that they shall be found] in the same manner as those who shall enter another's vineyard; and nonetheless let them pay for the damage. (2)And they shall incur a similar penalty to those on whom fruit shall be found and who have no vineyard and gardens producing said fruit, and likewise also those from whom they had got it.

Article 148. Of the fruit.

(1)We direct and order that any person, of whatever rank, state, or condition he may be, shall not dare or not have the audacity to take or gather fruit from a tree which is in an unfenced place against the will of the owner or of the overseer of the said tree, or trees, under penalty of paying, he who shall be found in flagrante therein or shall be proved to him, five soldi. (2)And he shall pay for the fruit which shall be found therein and taken from him, and they shall be brought and returned to the owner of the tree. (3)And in addition to this, he shall pay for the damage and the penalty, namely, (4)if the said fruit was picked by day, he shall pay five soldi as above, and if by night he shall pay ten soldi. (5)And of the evidence let the accuser be believed upon the oath of the accuser, even if he be the master or even some other person who has even a share of profit in it, thus disregarding the rule that the party to the case should not testify in favour of himself. (6)Therefore, in regard to this case, we want this prescribed article to have legitimate validity.

Article 149. Of melons.

(1)Item: we order that no person, of whatever rank or condition he may be, shall dare or have the audacity to enter any melon patch that is fenced in. (2)And if any person shall enter therein and be found therein or it be proved against him, if this be done by day, he shall pay five soldi; if by night, he shall pay ten soldi and shall pay damages to the owner of the garden, and the melon shall be taken from him and it shall be returned to the owner. (3)And by evidence it shall be understood that the complainant shall be believed upon his oath. (4)And if any livestock shall enter into any of these gardens which are fenced and whose fence has been approved by those under oath (*sos iurados*) elected to approve the fencing of vineyards and gardens, then the owner of the garden or one of his employees or the overseer of the livestock or the administrator (*armentargiu*), or the juror who shall have found it, shall there kill it [the livestock] and report it according to what is contained in the article on vineyards and gardens, the punishment provided for in the said article being applied.

CL. De faba.

(1)Volem[us] et ordinam[us] qui persona alc[u]na, de calunca gradu over conditione siat, no[n] usit ne[n]p[re]sumat intrare in alcuna terra de fa, o de xixiri, o de lupino, o de alcuno ligumine, cungiado over iscongiado, qui ssa dita terra non siat sua. (2)Et si alc[u]na persone illoe at esser acatado, over illi at esser probado, si est de die paghit s[oldo]s .x. et si est de nocte paghit s[oldo]s .xx. et paghit su damno a su pubillo de su dictu ligume[n] et perdat su legume[n]. (3)Et i[n] ssa proha, si inte[n]dat qui siat cretidu su accusadore a sargame[n]tu suo. (4)Et issu bestiami[n]i q[u]i si 'lloy at acatare si ochiat et co[n]de[n]ne[n]t come[n]ti et issu bestiami[n]i qui s'at acatare in su lavore.

CLI. Muda de boes

(1)Constituim[us] et ordinam[us] qui o[m][n]ia persona, de qualunca gradu, istadu over co[n]ditione siat, deppiat mitteri et tenne i[n] muda et guardia cussos boes domados, ruis arme[n]targi[us] qui at aver de o[m][n]ia te[m]pus. (2)Et cussos qui no[n] los ant mittiri et te[n]ne in muda et guardia in o[m][n]ia te[m]pus pagit per dogna bolta qui 'll'at esser acatadu s[oldo]s .xx. (3)Et icussu pubillu over ho[min]i o iuargiu suo qui ad aver ad te[m]p[us] de arare, over carradore qui at aver torrado alcuno iuho, deppiat sa nocte atsinare cussu iuho over iuhos qui at aver trubado cussa die ad icusso qui at esser guardianu de sos ditos boys, pro qui 'llos deressent in loghu et in parte qui non fassant damno in vingias et ortos over lavores. (4)Et icussu pubillu over ho[min]i suo o iuargio q[u]i ciò no[n] at faghere paghint per dogna bolta s[oldo]s .v. et a su pubillu dessu iuho, c'at esser mortu faguendo damno. (5)Et si no[n] loy morret, paghit
34v su damno ad qui 'll'at aver fatu et issas te[n]turas. | (6)Et s'est homini de dinaris over iuargiu, paghit su iuho qui s'at ochier a su pubillu et si non loy morret, paghit su damnu ad icussu qui 'll'at aviri factu et issas te[n]turas. (7)Et si ssu dictu ho[min]i o iuargiu no[n] averit de quitheu paghare, istit im p[re]gione infini qui at aver satisfactu sos boes et te[n]turas et damno c'ant aviri factos sos dictos boes. (8)Et dae dies .xv. de freargiu siant tenudos ciaschuno qui 'llos at aver et tenne at muda et guardia de torrare·llos ad corte.

CLII. Muda de boes

(1)Item ordinam[us] qui culla persone qui ad sa muda de sos boes et no l'at guardari et l'at refudari, tocando·li sa dita muda, paghit de maquicia l[ib]r[a]s

Article 150. Of fava beans.

(1)We wish and order that no person, of whatever rank or condition he may be, shall dare or have the audacity to enter any land not his own, fenced or unfenced, cultivated with fava beans, chickpeas, lupins or any other legume. (2)And if any person shall be found therein, or it shall be proved against him, if the fact be done by day, then he shall pay ten soldi; if by night, twenty soldi and he shall pay damages to the owner of the said legumes, and they shall be taken from him. (3)And as evidence it shall be understood that the accuser shall be believed upon his oath. (4)And the livestock that shall be found therein shall be killed, and the sentence that is applied concerning the livestock that are found in the crops shall be applied.

Article 151. Guard-shifts for oxen (*muda de boes*)

(1)We decree and order that every person, of whatever rank, status, or condition he may be, shall establish watch-shifts for tame oxen and untamed livestock gathered in herds that shall be there in every season. (2)And whosoever, in every season, shall fail to keep them under guard by watch-shifts, shall pay, for each time he shall be found wanting, twenty soldi. (3)And the owner or man or overseer of livestock whom he shall have in his employment in time of ploughing, or the cart driver (*carradore*) who shall bring back any yoke of oxen, shall deliver, on the same night, to him who shall have charge of the watch of the said oxen, the yoke or yokes which he shall have led during the day, so that they may place them in such place and part that they do not do damage to the vineyards, gardens, or cultivations. (4)And the owner or his man or his keeper of livestock who does not do this shall pay for each time five soldi, and the owner shall kill the oxen of the yoke that cause the damage. (5)And if he does not kill them, he shall pay for the damage to the one who shall have suffered it and shall pay the expenses of the capture. (6)And if he be a man paid by the day, or keeper of livestock, let him pay to the owner, by way of compensation, the yoke [of oxen] that shall be killed, and if it be not killed let him pay the damage to him who shall have suffered it, and let him indemnify the expenses of the capture. (7)And if the said man or keeper of livestock does not have enough to pay, let him remain in prison until he can pay compensation for the value of the oxen, the expenses of the capture, and the damage caused by the said oxen. (8)And, from the fifteenth day of February, let it be the duty of everyone who has and holds them [the oxen] subject to guard duty, to bring them back to the court.

Article 152. Guard-shifts for oxen.

(1)Item: we order that the person who is subject to the shifts in guarding oxen and will not exercise control [over them] and refuses to do so, shall pay a

.v. et pagit su damnu qui sos boes ant faghere in cussa iornada qui at refudadu sa dicta muda.

CLIII. De vachas

(1)Volem[us] et ordinam[us] qui dognia persone de qualuncha grado, istado over co[n]ditio[n]e siat, qui at aver vachas et ebbas illo[y] depiant tenne in sas dictas vachas vachargios et in sas ebbas asones, secundo sa quantidade de ciaschuno arme[n]to et de dognia truma de o[m][n]ia te[m]pus de s'anno. (2)Et qui co[n]tra fagheret depiat paghare, per dognia bolta qui at esser acatado over qui 'll'at esser probadu no[n]averet illoy postu bachagiu over asones secundu[m] qui est narado de supra, paghit per dognia volta a sa camera nostra l[ib]r[a]s .II., sos calis vachagios et assones siant tenudos et deppiant sas ditas bachas et ebbas colliri et gordare et tenne in sos mo[n]tes usados, qui no[n] siant in sa villa nen in abi[ta]tione de arare ne de paschere bestiamen masedo, dae ssa prima die de s[a][n]cto Saturro infini a dies .XV. de lampadas sas ebbas, et issas bachas infini assa prima die de treulas. (3)Et tando sos vachargios et asones illas deppia[n]t tenne in guardia, qui no[n] intrint in pardo de hierro. (4)Et si 'lloy intrant, siat licidu de ochire·lla gasi dessu arme[n]tu de sas vachas come[n]ti e dessas turmas dessas ebbas una tantu[m] per bolta. (5)Et icussas ebbas et bachas qui s'ant ochier in sos dictos pardos siant de sos pardargios qui 'llas ant ochier, si morret dintro desso pardo. (6)Et icussu qui
35r no[n] at mo[n]tare su bestiami[n]i qui at aver in guar- | dia, secundum qui est narado de supra, paghit a sa camera nostra s[oldo]s .XX. (7)Et issu officiale comandit a su dittu pastore qui infra dies tres depiat montare. (8)Et si no[n] obediret et fagheret su co[m]mandame[n]tu, deppiat·illu tenne et mandare a p[re]xione et fassat gordare su dictu bestiame[n]ad ispe[n]diu de so ditu pastore, qui at tenne in guardia et paschiri cussu p[re]dictu bestiamen de supra narrado.

CLIIII. De porchos

(1)Constituim[us] et ordinam[us] qui cussos qui ant aver porchos de gamma qui 'llos deppiant te[n]ne et reher do[n]nia te[m]pus foras de pardo de hierro et de mindas. (2)Et icussos qui 'lloy ant esser acatados, siant maxellados per dogna bolta de porcus dus per gamma, so quale maxello siat et deppiat esser de cusso qui 'll'at lansare, si morret in su loghu vedado, exceptu ad te[m]pus de spica. (3)Et inte[n]dat·si qui siat su principiu de su dictu te[m]pus de spica, dae ssa prima die de treulas. (4)Et dae cussa die inantis si possat tenne in qua-

penalty of five lire and shall pay compensation for the damage that the oxen will have done on that day on which the said person refused to serve on shift.

Article 153. Of cows.

(1)We wish and order that every person of whatever rank, state, or condition he may be, who shall have cows and mares, shall take care to place on guard duty for the cows of the cowhands and for the mares of the *asones* [guardians of horses/mares], according to the size of each herd, and of the drove, in every season of the year. (2)And whosoever shall contravene, shall pay for each time he shall be found wanting, or it shall be proved against him not to have appointed cowhands or guardians (*asones*) according to the foregoing, for each time, to our Chamber, two lire. Cowhands and guardians of horses shall be required and must keep together and control the said cows and mares and keep them in the mountains where it is customary for them to graze, so that they do not stay in the village or in cultivated fields subject to ploughing or for tame livestock grazing, from the first day of the month of St Saturnus [November] until the fifteenth day of June as regards mares, and as regards cows until the first day of July. (3)And, at that time, the cowhands and keepers of horses shall take care that they do not enter the meadow reserved for grazing in winter. (4)And if they enter there, let it be lawful to kill them as much if they belong to the herd of cows as to the herd of mares, one at each time. (5)And let the said mares and cows which shall be killed in the said pastures be profit for the pasture supervisors (*pardargios*) who have killed them, if they die within the pasture. (6)And he who shall not transfer to a high degree of altitude the livestock which he shall have in custody, according to the foregoing, shall pay to our Chamber twenty soldi. (7)And the official shall order the said shepherd to transfer the livestock to high ground within three days. (8)And if he does not obey and comply with the order, let him be arrested and taken to prison, and let him have the livestock in custody at the expense of the said shepherd, who shall be in charge of guarding and keeping the said livestock on high ground.

Article 154. Of swine.

(1)We establish and order that those who have pigs in herds shall keep and manage them outside the winter pasture and out of the *de mindas* pasture [closed and reserved for tame livestock]. (2)And there shall be slaughtered, for each time that swine shall be found therein, two heads per herd; the head slaughtered shall be for the profit of him who shall have slaughtered it with a throwing weapon, if it shall be killed in an interdicted place, except during the time of threshing. (3)Which period shall be understood to begin from the first day of July. (4)And from that day onward, pigs may be kept in any place they please

luncha loghu illos ad a plachere in sos Campidanos foras de pardo de hierru et d'ariolas. (5)Et comandam[us] qui in terra over in istulas no[n] si possat mittiri infini in tanto qui ssu lavore at esser totu et indi at esser carrithado et portado ad sa ariola. (6)Et si 'lloy intrant, siant maxellados per dognia gamma et pro ciascuna bolta qui 'lloy ant esser acatados, so quale maxello deppiant paghare sos pastores de sos dictos porchos. (7)Et nie[n]ti de min[us] paghit su damno qui ant aviri facto a su pubillu de su lavore et qui ssos dittos porchos ant aviri sutigado i[n] sa ditta terra et ant illoy esser vissidos per issu pubillu de su lavore over ho[min]i o iuargio suo over per alc[u]nos de sos ditos iurados, sia cretidu su accusadore a sargame[n]tu suo et issu pastore siat tenudo de dare isso maxello de porchos duos per bolta, come[n]te illoy at esser sutigado, at su q[u]i 'll'at aver bissido et accusado. (8)Et a ciò su officiale de sa villa illos deppiat co[n]stri[n]ger ad pe[n]a de s[oldo]s .c. a sa camera nostra, exceptu i[n] sos Campidanos, qui est logu istrittu, dae ssos quales logos se depiant segare et isvedare dae ssa p[ri]ma die de s[a][n]cto Guayniu.

CLV. De cabras

35v (1)Item ordinamus qui totu cussus qui ant aver crabas illas deppiant tenne over fagher tenne ad o[m][n]ia te[m]p[us] de su annu in su mo[n]te, qui non si acoste[n]t assas vingias et ortos et lavores et pardos, exceptu a te[m]pus de istadi illas possant calari ass'aba, per modo et guisa qui no[n] fassant damno. (2)Et abbadas qui 'llas ant aviri et multas·illas, si mo[n]gere·illas bolent in s'abadorgiu over in domo, et poscha illas deppiant torrare a su mo[n]te, per modo qui no[n] fassant damno. (3)Et icusso pastore qui non las boleret mo[n]tare dae ssa prima die de s[a][n]cto Guayni paghit pro sa p[ri]ma bolta s[oldo]s .x. et comandit·illu su officiale a su dictu pastore qui infra tres dies illas deppiat mo[n]tare. (4)Et si no[n]obediret, illu deppiat te[n]ne et mandare in p[re]gione et fassat gordare cussu bestiami[n]i ad ispesas de so dito pastore. (5)Et si fagheret damno cussu bestiamini in vingias o in ortos, observet·si secundum su capitulu de supra. (6)Et si in pardos ant esser acatados, per ciascuna volta si maxelle[n]t de peg[us] dus per gamma et siat de cussu qui 'll'at maxellare. (7)Et icussu qui at [aver a] maxellari et non lu maxellat pro amore o pro paura o pro atera causa qui si siat et illi at esser provadu paghit pro dognia bolta s[oldo]s .x. (8)Et de ciò siat cretidu su accusadore a sargame[n]tu suo et appat·inde sa tersa parte de sa co[n]de[n]nat[i]o[n]e su acusadore p[re]dictu.

in the [plain of] Campidano, except in winter pasture or farmyards. (5)And we order that they [the swine] may not enter [cultivated] land or into the stubble (*istulas*) as long as there is a crop in them that is loaded and brought to the threshing floor. (6)And if they enter there, let them be slaughtered for each herd and for each time they are found there, and the expenses of slaughtering shall be paid by the shepherds of the said swine. (7)And they shall no less make good the damage done to the owner of the crops and what the swine shall have destroyed in the said land; and their presence shall be ascertained by the owner, or by one of his employees, or by his keeper, or by any of his jurors. And let the one who brings an accusation on his oath be believed; and the swineherd shall be bound to deliver those of the swine slaughtered at the rate of two heads for each time, when the damage shall be ascertained, to the one who shall have ascertained and brought the accusation. (8)And, to this, the official of the village shall compel them, under penalty of one hundred soldi, to be donated to our Chamber. An exception to this is made for the Campidano, which are places where there is not a large area [for grazing]; in such places the prohibition will be enforced from the first day of the month of St Gavino (*Guayniu*) [October], the day on which the pigs must be taken away.

Article 155. Of goats.

(1)Item: we order that all who possess goats shall keep them or have them kept in every season of the year on the mountain, that they shall not come near the vineyards and gardens, crops and pastures, except that in the summer time they may bring them down to water, provided they do no harm. (2)And after they have watered and milked them, if they want to milk them at the drinking trough or at a house, afterwards they shall take them back to the mountain, so that they do no harm. (3)And the shepherd who does not want to bring them back to the mountain from the first day of the month of St Gavino [October] shall pay ten soldi for the first time, and the official shall order the said shepherd to bring them back to the mountain within three days. (4)And if he does not obey he shall arrest him and take him to prison, and the livestock shall be kept at the expense of the said shepherd. (5)And if the livestock do damage to the vineyards and gardens, there shall be observed [the orders of] the above article. (6)And if they shall be found in the pastures, let there be slaughtered for each time two livestock per herd, and let the slaughtered livestock belong to him who would slaughter them. (7)And he who would have to slaughter them and does not do so out of fondness or because of fear or for any other reason whatsoever, and it shall be proved against him, let him pay for each time ten soldi. (8)And of this let him be believed who brings the accusation on his oath, and let him who brought the accusation have the third part of the penalty imposed.

CLVI. De berbegues in pardo

(1)Volemus et ordinam[us] qui nixuna persona usit over p[re]sumat mitter berbegues in pardo de hyerro over pardo de mindas, seghados pro bestiame[n] domadu, over i[n] mindas inter lavores, pro paschiri o pro istare, excepto barigando ad iaguere qui siat licitu ad icussu qui 'llos ad paschere o duguer de passare i[n] loghu qui no[n] siat semi[n]ado. (2)Et icussa ga[m]ma qui 'lloy at esser acatada siat maxellada per dognia bolta de berbeghes dues et siant de cussu q[u]i 'll'at maxellare. (3)Et icussu qui l'at aver a maxellare et no[n] lo maxellat pro amore o pro paura o pro atera causa et illi esseret provado pagit pro dognia bolta s[oldo]s .x. (4)Et siat cretidu su acusadore a sargame[n]to suo et appat·inde sa tersa parte de sa co[n]de[n]natio[n]e.

CLVII. De apressos

36r (1)Constituimus et ordinamus simigiantimenti qui si in- | tendat et qui fagheri si depiat de ciasc[u]no de sos p[re]dictos bestiamini pe[n]as, maxellos, ap[re]tsos et co[n]de[n]nat[i]o[n]es qui s'ant acatare qui aviri[n]t fatu da[n]no i[n] su lavore, q[u]i at esser portadu et missido in sas ariolas i[n]fini q[u]i at esser levadu i[n] totu.

CLVIII. De pagare so apretso

(1)Item ordi[n]am[us] qui sos maiores et iurados, de calunca villa siat, deppiat de p[re]sente fagheri pagame[n]tu et satisfactio[n]e de su ap[re]tsu qui at esser fatu et te[n]turas qui s'ant deber paghare et fagheri·llu scriviri ordi[n]adame[n]te i[n] su quaderno q[u]i si det supra ciò ordi[n]are et te[n]ne secundu[m] i[n]su capitulu si co[n]tenet. (2)Et su maiore et iurados q[u]i s'ant acatare i[n] culpa q[u]i no[n] appant fatu satisfagher et pagare cussos dictos pagame[n]tos a sos qui 'llos debe[n]t reciviri dae ssas persones qui 'llos ant [a] reciviri et non lu fagheri[n]t, secundo qui e[st] narado de supra, siat conde[n]nado et pagit, per dognia volta qui 'lloy at esser i[n]culpado et li at esser provado qui ciò non avirit fatu, pagit a sa corte pro maquicia l[ib]r[a]s .v.

CLVIIII. De observare sos capitulos

(1)Volem[us] et ordinam[us] qui ciasc[u]no officiali de sas terras nostras i[n] cussas co[n]tradas et villas et logos qui ant aviri at officiu depiant observare et fagheri observare sensa manchame[n]tu sos dictos capidulos. (2)Et issu maiore

Article 156. Of sheep in the pasture.
(1)We wish and order that no person shall dare or presume to put sheep into the winter pasture or in a *de mindas* meadow chosen and reserved for tame livestock, or into *mindas* [meadows] obtained [unlawfully] from among cultivations, for grazing or settling unless they be made to cross there in order to take them to lie down or rest, in which case it shall be lawful for him who takes them to pasture or leads them to pass through a place which is not, however, sown. (2)And of that flock which shall be found, there shall be slaughtered two heads for each flock, and they shall be the slaughtered of him that shall slaughter them. (3)And let him who should slaughter them but does not do so out of fondness, or because of fear, or for any other reason, and it shall be proved against him, pay ten soldi for each time. (4)And let him be believed who brings an accusation upon his oath, and let him keep the third part of the fine imposed.

Article 157. Of assessments.
(1)We similarly direct and order that it [an assessment] shall be intended to be done, with respect to every kind of the said livestock which shall be found to have done harm in the crops, punishments, slaughtering, assessments, and sentences, before the crop shall be brought in and piled up on the threshing floors until it shall all be taken away.

Article 158. On paying the assessment.
(1)Item: we order that the senior officials (*maiores*) and jurors, of whatever village, shall forthwith discharge the payment and satisfaction of the assessment which shall be made and the capture [of livestock] which shall be paid; and all this shall be neatly noted on the register which shall be prepared and kept for this purpose according to what is contained in the appropriate article. (2)And the senior official (*maiore*) and those under oath (*sos iurados*) who, through culpable negligence, shall have failed to cause the said payments to be paid and satisfied by the persons from whom they are to receive them [in compensation], and shall fail to fulfil the provision, according to the foregoing, shall be condemned and shall pay, as a penalty to the court, for each time that this is charged to them, and it shall be proved against them that they have failed to fulfil the provision, five lire.

Article 159. On observing the [aforementioned] articles.
(1)We wish and order that each official of our lands in the countryside and villages and places where they shall be in charge shall observe and cause to be observed without fail the said articles. (2)And the senior official (*maiore*) or offi-

o officiali o curadore o maiore de villa qui s'at acatare over qui si 'll'at provare qui i[n] alc[u]no casu, actu vel parti de sas qui si conteni[n]t a sos capidulos de supra no observari[n]t over contra fassant, siat conde[n]nado a pagare de maquicia sensa mise[ri]cordia nixuna a sa corti per donia bolta qui 'll'at esser provadu su officiali o maiori qui contra fagheret l[ib]r[a]s .x, et icussu curadore over maiore de villa qui contra fagerit l[ib]r[a]s .v. se[n]sa misericordia nixuna. (3)Et non siat p[re]iudiciu dessas partis.

Ordinamentos de cumonis, de maxellos, de terminis e iniurias
CLX. (1)Constituim[us] et ordi[n]am[us] qui si alc[u]no ho[min]i levarit cumoni de atera persona de alc[u]no bestiame[n] et ad cussu pastore si 'lli at provari fraudu de bestia qui averit be[n]dida o donadu o mandigadu et non lu at narri a su donnu suo q[ua]n[do] ant fageri ragione i[n]tro dessu annu q[u]i fassiant ragione de su bestiami[n]i, et provari·si·lli at legitimame[n]ti, perdat su cumoni et pagit de maquicia a sa corti nostra l[ib]r[a]s .XXV.

CLXI. Cumonis
36v (1)Item ordinamus qui su cumonargio siat tenudo et depiat dari parti de casu et de lati de dogna te[m]pus qui intrada fagheret a su donno suo. (2)Et si 'lli provarit legiti[m]amenti qui sa parti no[n] darit a su donno suo, perdat su cumoni et paghit de maquicia a sa corte nostra l[ib]r[a]s .XXV.

CLXII. Cumonis
(1)Volem[us] et ordinam[us] qui nexuno como[n]argio no[n] usit ne[n] depiat levari cu[m]oni supra cumoni sensa voluntadi de su do[n]no suo et sensa lu cumbidari. (2)Et si 'llu levarit a voluntadi sua sensa lu squiri su don[n]u suo et '[n]d'esser combidadu, perdat su cumoni et paghit de maquicia a sa corte nostra libras .XXV., sas qualis l[ib]r[a]s .XXV. paghit ad cumonali cum cullo qui 'llu at desviari de 'lli dari cumoni have[n]do cumoni.

CLXIII. Comonis
(1)Constituim[us] et ordinam[us] qui si alcuno cumonargiu refudarit alcuno cumoni sensa compleri su cumoni a su te[m]pus qui inter issos at esser assig-

cial or curator, or the mayor of the village (*maiore de villa*) who shall be found or to whom it shall be proved that, with respect to any case, act, or part of the provisions contained in the aforesaid articles, they shall have failed to observe them or shall have acted contrary to them, shall be condemned to pay to the court, as a penalty and without clemency of any kind, for each time it shall be proved against them, the official or mayor who shall have acted contrary to them, ten lire; and the curator or mayor of the village, who shall have acted contrary to them, five lire without clemency of any kind, (3)and without prejudice to the parties.

Ordinances of agistment (*de cumonis*), acts of slaughtering, deadlines, and insults.
Article 160. (1)We decree and order that if any man shall enter into a contract of agistment with any other person for the raising of livestock, and if any fraud shall be proved against that shepherd concerning the beast which he has sold or donated or shall have made undue use of it, and does not account for it to his lord [the owner] when, by the end of the year, the accounts are made and the count of the livestock is taken, and it is proved against him lawfully, let him forfeit the share due to him from the agistment contract and pay to our court a penalty of twenty-five lire.

Article 161. Agistment agreements (*cumonis*).
(1)Item: we order that the agister (*cumonargio*) shall be bound and shall deliver part of the cheese and milk, at the start of each season of the year, to his lord (*donno*). (2)And if it should be lawfully proved against him that he has not delivered to his lord the part due to him, let him lose the contract of agistment and pay to our court a penalty of twenty-five lire.

Article 162. Agistment agreements (*cumonis*).
(1)We desire and order that no agister (*cumonargio*) shall dare nor shall enter into an agistment contract over a previous agistment contract without the will of his lord and without the latter inviting him to do so. (2)And if he should deliberately enter into it without the knowledge of his lord [the owner] and without his being invited to do so, let him forfeit the share due to him from the agistment contract and pay as a penalty to our court twenty-five lire; the twenty-five lire he shall pay jointly to him who shall have induced him to enter into an agistment contract over the previous contract.

Article 163. Agistment agreements (*cumonis*).
(1)We direct and order that if any agister refuses the service stipulated for the agistment without having brought it to completion within the agreed-upon

nadu et non boleret plus istari in su dictu bestiamini, su do[n]nu de su bestiamini no[n] siat tenudo de 'lli dari parti alcuna, si non complit su te[m]pus de su cumoni, salvu si cussu cumonargiu mostrarit causa legittima qui non poderit istari ad compliri su dictu cumoni. (2)Et si gasi mostrat legitti[m]ame[n]ti, qui su do[n]nu li siat tenudu de 'lli dari sa parti qui 'llis at tocari, secundu qui at aviri servidu.

CLXIIII. Cumonis

(1)Item ordinam[us] qui nixuno comonargiu de nixunu bestiamini non possat nen usit mudari su dictu bestiamini qui 'lli at esser dadu ad cumoni in atero loghu pro cuyli over pro abitari, sensa lice[n]tia de su donnu suo. (2)Et si contra fagherit secundu de supra et damnu recivirit su ditu bestiamini, siat intenudu cussu cumonargiu qui at mudari su ditu bestiamini de pagari su damnu qui at reciviri cussu bestiami[n]i a su do[n]nu suo. (3)Et si no[n] at de guiteu paghari, istet in p[re]gioni infini qui su donnu suo siat pagadu.

CLXV. Cumonis

(1)Volem[us] et ordinam[us] qui ciaschuno cumonargiu siat tenudo de faghere ragione de su bestiamini qui si 'lli at esser dadu ad cumoni a su donnu suo una
37r bolta de s'anno, sa quali ragioni depiat fagheri a dies .xv. de sanctu Gavini | a su donno suo dognia annu una bolta. (2)Et qui non at fagheri ragioni siat tenudo de pagari su damnu qui at esser factu a su donno suo in su dictu bestiamini.

CXLVI. De isviari sarachu

(1)Constituim[us] et ordinam[us] [qui] si alcuna personi desviarit alcuno sarachu qui istarit cum ateri over saracha femina pro si 'ndi andari dae domo de su padronu suo, et si 'lli at provari legitimame[n]ti, paghit cussa tali personi qui avirit desviadu o fagherit desviari paghit de maquicia a sa corte nostra l[ib]r[a]s .x., et issu damnu qui 'ndi reciverit su padrono over padrona de cussos talis terralis.

CLXVII. De su pardu

(1)Item ordinam[us] qui sas ebbas qui s'ant acatari i[n]tro dessu pardu de siidu qui su maiori de pardu et issos iurados de pardu siant tenudos de maxellari de sas dictas ebbas over qui 'llis fassat te[n]tura, de sa quali te[n]tura depiant levari s[oldo]s .x. a su pubillu de sas ebbas. (2)Ma bolem[us] qui no[n] deppiat

time between the contracting parties, and no longer wishes to attend to the livestock, the lord who is the owner of said livestock shall not be obliged to give him any part unless the service agreed upon at the time of the stipulation is brought to completion, unless the agister legitimately proves that he can no longer bring to completion what was stipulated. (2)And if he so proves according to lawfulness, that the agister is bound to give him his due share, by reason of the service actually performed.

Article 164. Agistment agreements (*cumonis*).
(1)Item: we order that no agister in charge of any livestock should dare to transfer to any other place the livestock that shall be entrusted to him, sheepfold or stall that it may be, without permission of the lord [owner]. (2)And if he contravenes this and the livestock is harmed, the agister who has transferred the livestock shall be obliged to repay the lord for the harm done to the livestock. (3)And if he has nothing to pay, let him remain in prison until the damage is made good to the owner.

Article 165. Agistment agreements.
(1)We wish and order that every agister shall be bound to make and render an account, once a year, to the owner of the livestock that shall be given to him according to the agreement. The account shall be made on the fifteenth day of the month of St Gavino [October] to the owner once a year. (2)And whosoever fails to do so shall be bound to pay to the owner for the loss which he shall have received in respect of the said livestock.

Article 166. Of the removal of a servant (*sarachu*).
(1)We direct and order that if any person induces any male servant or female servant (*saracha femina*) who is in the service of others to leave the house of their master (*padronu*), and this is legitimately proved, such person who shall have removed them or shall have caused them to be removed, shall pay to our court a penalty of ten lire, and shall pay compensation for the harm which the master (male or female) of such tenant farmers (*terralis*) shall have suffered.

Article 167. Of the pasture.
(1)Item: we order that, with respect to the mares that shall be found in the *pardu de siidu* [pasture reserved for the *iudike*], the official in charge of pastures (*maiore de pardu*) and those under oath (*sos iurados*) charged with control of pastures (*iurados de pardu*) shall be required to slaughter the said mares or they shall capture them, and from the capture they shall acquire ten soldi from the owner of the mares. (2)But we wish that the slaughtering should not be done

maxedari si no[n] abastat ad ebbas .x. in susu. (3)Et si non abastant ad ebbas .x., qui depiant levari su mayore de pardu cum sos compangios s[oldo]s .i. per pegus.

CLXVIII. De sus asones
(1)Volem[us] et ordinam[us] qui sos asones possant te[n]ne sas ditas ebbas i[n]tro dessu pardu in te[m]pus qui venit ad treulari, qui sos pardargios no[n] lis possant fagheri maxellu ne[n] te[n]tura me[n]tri qui a[n]t istari treulandu. (2)Ma bolem[us], in cantu su lavori ad esser treuladu, qui sos ditos asones depiant levari sas ditas ebbas foras de su ditu pardu, suta pena de 'llis maxellari et de 'llis fagher tentura.

CLXIX. De pardu
(1)Constituim[us] et ordinam[us] qui nex[u]na persona de sa villa qui at aviri ebba domada no[n] usit nen deppiat reere sa dita ebba intro de pardo. (2)Ma bolem[us] qui cussas talis ebbas deppiant istari foras dessu pardu, dae una parti qui no[n] fassant damnu ad cavallu domadu. (3)Et si alc[u]no cavallu domadu si ghastarit per culpa et cagio[n]i de cussa ebba, su popillu de cussa ebba siat tenudu de paghari cussu cavallu over damnu qui 'ndi reciverit su pubillu de cussu cavallu, si legittimame[n]ti i[n]d'est co[n]vi[n]tu qui per culpa de cussa ebba at apidu cussu da[n]nu.

37v CLXX. De sas ebbas
(1)Item ordinamus qui su maiori de sa villa deppiat assignari unu loghu remonidu dae una parti a sas ebbas, im parti qui cavallu domadu non v'intrit, et ponniri pe[n]a a su pubillu de sas ebbas domadas qui deppiat reere sas ditas ebbas in cussu loghu ad issos consignadu per issu maiori supraditu, suta pena de pagare a sa corte nostra qui co[n]tra fagherit l[ib]r[a]s .v. (2)Et perdat sas ebbas.

CLXXI. De pradargos
(1)Volem[us] et ordinam[us] qui sos pradargios, q[ua]n[do] ant andari a maxellari in pardu, ciò est vaca, berbegue, porchu, capra, non depiat maxellari, si non getat bogis tres. (2)Et getadu qui at aviri tres bogis et issu pastore non si aparit, possat ochiere su pradargiu de sas vacas, ad de die unu pegus su pl[us] minori qui 'lloy at esser, et ad de nocti su qui at poder. (3)Et si non bastarit ad bullos .x., non depiat maxellari, si non qui 'llos fassat te[n]tura. (4)Et si contra fagherint, pagint sos ditos pradargios pro maquicia l[ib]r[a]s .v., et dessas berbegues et dessos porcos et dessas cabras duas tantum per ciascuna gamma. (5)Et si

unless the mares reach at least ten [units] in height. (3)And if they do not reach ten units, the pasture official with his assistants shall acquire one soldo for each head of livestock.

Article 168. Of the guardians of horses.
(1)We wish and order that the guardians of horses may keep the mares within the pasture during the time approaching threshing (*ad treulari*); the officials overseeing pastures (*pardargios*) shall not be allowed to slaughter or to catch them while they are being used for threshing. (2)But we wish, after the grain is threshed, that the said guardians of horses should take the mares out of the said pasture, under penalty of having them slaughtered and captured.

Article 169. Of the pasture.
(1)We direct and order that no person of the village who shall have a tame mare (*ebba domada*) dare to, or shall, keep the said mare within the pasture. (2)But we wish that those such mares should be outside the pasture where they do no harm to the tame horse. (3)And if any tame horse shall suffer harm through the fault and cause of that mare, let the owner of that mare be obliged to compensate that horse (*cavallu*), or the harm that the owner of that horse shall receive, if it shall be legitimately proved against him that through the fault of that mare he suffered the harm.

Article 170. Of mares.
(1)Item: we order that the mayor (*maiori*) of the village shall assign to the mares a secluded place apart from where the tame horse shall not enter, and impose penalty on the owner of the tamed mares, who shall keep the said mares in that place assigned to them by the aforesaid senior official, under penalty of paying to our court five lire for contravening the provision. (2)He will also lose the mares.

Article 171. Of those in charge of common pasturelands (*pradargos*).
(1)We wish and order that those in charge of common pasturelands (*pardargios*), when they go to slaughter in the pasture cow, sheep, swine, goat, shall not proceed to slaughter unless they [first] shout out three times. (2)And having given out three cries and the shepherd does not appear, the *pardargiu* may proceed to slaughter the cows (*vachas*); by day, the smallest head they find, and by night whatever they can. (3)And if there is not enough as ten large heads, they shall not proceed to slaughter, but keep them. (4)And if they shall contravene, the *pardargios* shall pay of penalty five lire, and relative to the sheep and the swine and the goats they shall slaughter two heads of each herd. (5)And if the

sos ditos pradargios acatarint sos pastoris in su bestiami[n]i q[ua]n[do] ant andari ad maxellari et bolent pagari sa te[n]tura, qui su pradargiu, paghando·li sa te[n]tura, non siant tenudos de maxellari, anti si li fassant sa te[n]tura, sa quali deppiant levari pro sus arme[n]tos de sas vachas s[oldo]s .x. si est dae pegus .x. in susu, et dae peg[us] .x. in iosso paghit s[oldo]s .I. per testa, et de s'ateru bestiamini secundu de supra s[oldo]s .v. per gamma. (6)Et qui contra at fagheri a su dictu capitulu, secundu de supra, paghit su iuradu de pardu pro maquicia a sa corte nostra l[ib]r[a]s .I. per iuradu.

CLXXII. De pradargios

(1)Constituim[us] et ordinam[us] qui unu pradargiu solu non possat andari ad maxellari si non sunt duos assu minus et pro fagheri te[n]tura unu solu. (2)Et q[u]i co[n]tra fagherit, paghit a su curadori boe unu et s[oldo]s .xx. a sa corte nostra de maquicia.

CLXXIII. De ponni sinnu

38r (1)Item ordinam[us] qui alcuna persone non usit nen dep- | piat ponne sinnu supra sinnu nen ad fogu nen ad origla ad bestiamini alc[u]no. (2)Et si alcuna persone fagherit et ponnerit de sos p[re]dictos sinnos et esseret bestiamini de sa corte, paghit pro s'unnu .x. (3)Et si esseret de clesia o de atera persone, paghit pro s'unu .v. et [de] maquicia a sa corte l[ib]r[a]s .xxv. (4)Et si non paghat ipsu o atera persone pro se infra dies .xv. de c'at esser iuygadu, seguet·si·lli sa manu destra per modu qui 'lla perdat.

CLXXIIII. De terminis

(1)Volemus et ordinam[us] qui nexuna persone de qualunca gradu o istadu usit ne[n] p[re]sumat istrumari lacanas de terra qui sunt confinadas agenas. (2)Et qui 'ndi at istrumari et ad levari termenes, et provadu·si·lli at esser legitimamente, paghit de maquicia a sa corte nostra l[ib]r[a]s .xxv. sensa mise[ri]cordia alcuna et me[n]dat sa terra [qui] at avere istrimadu. (3)Et si non paghat infra dies .xv. de qui at esser iuygadu, seghit·illi sa manu destra.

CLXXV. De qui comporarit

(1)Constituim[us] et ordinamus si alcuna persona andarit et comporarit dae cherachu, over terrali qui istarit cum ateri, alcuna causa de su donnu suo, cussa tali personi qui 'ndi at comporari dae cussos de cussas ditas causas, isquie[n]do qui cussu non averit libertadi de ve[n]deri, siat tenudu cussu qui '[n]di at

said *pardargios* find the shepherds by the livestock, when they go to proceed to slaughter and the shepherds want to pay a fee for the capture (*sa tentura*), let the *pardargiu*, being paid the fee for the capture, not be required to proceed to slaughter, but impose on them a fee for the capture, which they shall require, for herds of cows, at the rate of ten soldi if it be from ten livestock and more, and if it be from ten and less they shall pay one soldo for each head; of other livestock, according to the above, five per herd. (6)And whosoever shall contravene the said article, according to the aforesaid, let each juror 'of the meadow' (*de pardu*) pay to our court a penalty of one lira per juror.

Article 172. Of those in charge of communal pastures (*pradargios*).
(1)We direct and order that a *pardargiu* [in charge of communal pastures] may not proceed alone to slaughter, but there must be at least two, while for capture he may also proceed alone. (2)And whoever shall contravene, shall pay into the hands of the curator, as a penalty, one ox and twenty soldi to our court.

Article 173. Of putting marks [on animals].
(1)Item: we order that no person shall dare nor shall superimpose a mark upon another mark, either by branding or on the ear, on any head of livestock. (2)And if any person shall so affix the said brands, and the livestock is of the court, [then] he shall pay, for each head, ten times the value of the head. (3)And if it be the church's or other person's, he shall pay, for each head, five times the value of the head, and in penalty twenty-five lire to the court. (4)And if he or any other person for him does not pay within fifteen days after he is judged, let his right hand be cut off so that he loses it.

Article 174. Of boundaries.
(1)We wish and order that no person of whatever rank or status he may be, dare or presume to demolish from the ground the boundary marks between his own and another's property. (2)And whosoever shall demolish or move boundary markers (*termenes*), and it shall be proved against him lawfully, he shall pay by penalty to our court twenty-five lire without any mitigation, and shall repair any damage to the land which he shall have done. (3)And if he does not pay within fifteen days after he shall be judged, his right hand will be cut [off].

Article 175. Whoever makes a purchase.
(1)We direct and order that if any person should go and buy from any servant or tenant farmer (*terralis*) who is in the employ of others, anything belonging to his lord, that such person who should go and buy from any of such persons anything of the above, being aware that they have no licence to sell, then he

comporari de restituiri su qui at averi co[m]poradu a su pubillu et paghit de maquicia l[ib]r[a]s .x. a sa corte nostra.

CLXXVI. Qui furarit

(1)Item ordinam[us] qui si alcuna persone de qualunca gradu o co[n]ditioni qui at esser provadu qui at levari over furari, ad mala voluntadi de su pubillu, dae alchunu cuyli de alcunu pastori alcunu istergiu over attera causa qui in cussu cuyli esseret et legitimame[n]ti si 'lli at esser provadu, paghit de maq[u]icia a sa camera nostra, secundu qui i[n] su capidulo de qui furat dae domo si co[n]tenit et me[n]dit su dannu a su pubillu. (2)Et si no[n] paghat infra dies .xv. de qui at esser iuygadu, seghit·si·lli una origla in totu qui 'lla perdat.

CLXXVII. Qui se allogat

(1)Volemus et ordinam[us] qui q[ua]n[do] alcuno ho[min]i s'at allogari cum
38v ateri pro serviri ad iornada et lu at i[n]ganari ad cul- | lu qui at aviri i[m]promissu cussu tali ho[min]i qui si at allogari et ad ingannari sa iornada et no[n] at serviri, siat tenudo cussu tali homini de pagari su ispendiu ad cussu ho[min]i qui lu at aviri allogadu et me[n]dit su damnu et paghit de maquicia a sa camera n[ost]ra, per dogna bolta qui si 'lli at provari, s[oldo]s .xx. per homini.

CLXXVIII. De triulari

(1)Constituim[us] et ordinam[us] qui q[ua]n[do] sos asones in te[m]p[us] de treulari ant impromittiri ad alcuna persone de treulari s'ariola et lu ant ingannari, paghi[n]t cussos talis asones over asone su despe[n]diu qui su pubillu de sa ariola at aviri factu et issos manalis qui at aviri allogadu pro sa dita ariola et paghit su damnu qui li intervenerit de su lavori et de maquicia a sa camera nostra l[ib]r[a]s .v. et siat tenudu de fagheri sa ariola de nou. (2)Et in simili pe[n]a si inte[n]dat su pubillu de sa ariola q[ua]n[do] ingannarit a su asone, qui no li lassarit treulari sa ariola.

CLXXIX. De sos bubaris

(1)Item ordi[n]am[us] qui sos bubaris de sos boes domados qui ant esser in sas villas siant tenudos sos homi[n]is de sas villas, cullos qui ant aviri boes domados, de cuniari beni su dittu bubari. (2)Et cuniadu qui at esser et provididu et bi haveret in su ditu bubare alc[u]na parti qui no[n] esseret bene cuniadu secundo sos ateros, et dae cussu loghu essirit alcuno boe et fagherit damnu, cussa persone qui tocat in parti qui no l'at haviri cuniada, secundu de supra, paghit cussa tali personi cussu damnu qui at esser factu per cussos bois et de

who has made the purchase shall be bound to return to the owner that which he has bought, and shall pay a ten-lire fine to our court.

Article 176. Whoever steals.

(1)Item: we order that if any person of any rank or condition against whom it shall be proved that he shall have taken or stolen, against the will of his lord, from any sheepfold of any shepherd any receptacle or other thing lawfully standing in that sheepfold, if it shall be proved against him, he shall pay a penalty to our court according to what is contained in the article concerning those who steal from the house of others, and he shall pay compensation to the owner for the damage. (2)And if he does not pay within fifteen days after he shall be judged, let him have an ear amputated so that he loses it.

Article 177. Those who put themselves for hire.

(1)We wish and order that when anyone shall place himself in the service of others to serve on a day-to-day basis (*ad iornada*), but shall deceive the person who has employed him and to whom he has promised [his service] and deceive him by not serving for the day, he shall be obliged to pay the expenses to the person who has employed him in service and shall compensate him for the damage, and pay as a penalty to our Chamber, for each time it shall be proved against him, twenty soldi per person.

Article 178. Of threshing (*triulari*).

(1)We direct and order that when horse-keepers (*asones*) at the time of threshing promise to any person to thresh the threshing floor and deceive him, the said horse-keeper shall pay the expenses which the owner shall have incurred and the labourers whom he shall have hired to work in the said threshing floor, and shall repay the damage which shall be proved against him relative to the [amount of] grain; and he shall pay to our Chamber a penalty of five lire and shall be required to put the threshing floor in order. (2)And likewise the owner shall incur a penalty if he deceives the horse-keeper if he does not let him thresh the threshing floor.

Article 179. Of fences for oxen (*bubaris*).

(1)Item: we order that in regard to the enclosures set aside for tame oxen to be found in the villages, the men of the villages, those who will have tame oxen, shall be bound to guard them tightly enclosed. (2)And once provision has been made for keeping it enclosed, but any part remains therein that is not as well closed as the others, and some oxen come out of it and cause damage, the person responsible for the failure to close it, according to the above, shall pay compensation for the damage caused by the oxen to the person who will have

maquicia a sa corte nostra l[ib]r[a]s .v. et paghit sa tentura qui at esser facta a sos ditos boes.

CLXXX. De sa muda de boes

(1)Volem[us] et ordinam[us] qui, pusti qui at esser missida sa muda de sos boes, et si alcuna persona de sa villa bi baturit alcunu boe furisteri a su arme[n]tu, q[u]i cussu pubillu de su ditu boe lu depiat clobari a boe istanti de sa villa. (2)Et [si], sendo clobadu secundu de supra, su ditu boe torrarit, sendo clobadu, cussu boinargiu q[u]i at aviri i[n] guardia sos ditos boes siat te[n]udu, cusu tali
39r boi[n]argiu, de torrari berbu sa note q[u]i at esser ma[n]cadu su ditu boe | a su pubillu. (3)Et si su dictu boynargiu no[n] torrarit berbu a su pubillu sa noti qui at mancari su ditu boe, qui cussu tali boynargiu siat tenudu de torrari a su arme[n]tu su dictu boe ad ispesas suas. (4)Et si no[n] lu torrarit, pagit su damnu a su pubillu de su ditu boe.

CLXXXI. De boes de mala fama

(1)Constituim[us] et ordinam[us], si in casu haverit in su armentu de sos boes domados alcunu boe qui esseret de mala fama, qui cussu pubillu de cussu boe de mala infama siat tenudo de lo clobari ad boe qui no[n] siat de mali i[n]fama. (2)Et si cussu pubillu de cussu tali boe non lu boleret clobari cussu tali boe segundu de supra, et cussu boe intrarit in alcunu logu et fagerit damnu et esseret mortu fague[n]do damnu, su boynargiu no[n] siat tenudo de lu pagari.

CLXXXII. De boynargus

(1)Item ordinamus qui si alcunu boynargiu qui haverit bois i[n] guardia li fuirit alcunu iuhu over boe dae sos boes qui teneret in guardia, cussu tali boynargiu siat tenudu qui su die qui 'lli at esser fuidu su dictu iuhu, over boe, qui su nocte qui at torrari lu depiat dari ad inte[n]diri ad su pubillu de su dictu iuhu over boe qui 'lli esseret fuidu ad malavogia sua. (2)Et si gasi faghit, su dictu boynargiu non siat tenudu ad pena alcuna. (3)Et si gasi non fagherit, secundu de supra, siat tenudu cussu tali boynargiu de torrari su ditu iuhu over boe ad ispesas suas a su arme[n]tu dessos boes domados.

CLXXXIII. De sinari su bestiamen

(1)Volem[us] et ordinam[us] qui sos officialis nostros, ciascunu in su officiu issoro, deppiat chircari, dogna annu una bolta, su bestiamini rudi, si sunt sinnados et portat ciascunu su sinnu de sos pubillos. (2)Et si 'ndi acatarit qui no[n] essere[n]t sinnados, qui cussu officiali over officialis lu deppiant levari cussas talis bestias qui no[n] ant esser sinnados pro sa corte nostra, pro qui bolem[us]

suffered it; and he shall pay a penalty to our court of five lire, and he shall pay the capture-fee (*sa tentura*) relative to said oxen.

Article 180. Of the guarding of oxen.
(1)We desire and order that when the shift of guarding the oxen has been defined, if any person of the village should introduce any ox extraneous to the herd, that the owner of the said ox shall pair it with an ox that is from the village. (2)And if, having been paired according to the foregoing, the said ox should go away, although it was paired, let the herdsman who shall have the said oxen under supervision be bound to report to the owner on the very night that said ox shall be missed. (3)And if the said herdsman fails to inform the lord on the night that the ox shall be missed, the said herdsman shall be bound to bring back to the herd, at his own expense, the said ox. (4)And if he does not bring it back he shall pay damages to the owner of the said ox.

Article 181. Of oxen with bad reputations.
(1)We establish and order, if it happens that there is an untamed and rebellious ox in the herd, that the owner of that untamed ox is bound to pair him with an ox that is not untamed. (2)And if that owner of such an ox should not pair him up with that ox according to the above, and that ox enters any place doing harm therein and should be killed doing harm, then the herdsman is not bound to pay it.

Article 182. Of ox-herder (*boynargus*).
(1)Item: we order that if any ox-herder, who has oxen in his custody, [has] any pair of oxen or a single ox which shall escape from the oxen he has in his custody, the said herdsman shall be bound, on the day that such pair or single ox shall have escaped from him, in spite of himself, to warn the master (*su publillu*) of the said pair or single ox, when, on the same night, he shall return [to his dwelling]. (2)And if he does so, the herdsman shall not be subjected to any penalty. (3)But if he does not do so, according to the foregoing, let the said herdsman be obliged to return to the herd of tame oxen, a pair or a single ox at his own expense.

Article 183. Of the branding of livestock.
(1)We wish and order that our officials, each in his own office, should search the wild livestock once a year to see whether the livestock are branded, and each shall bear the brand of its respective owner. (2)And if any are found that are not branded, that official or officials shall requisition those such beasts that are not branded for the benefit of our court, for we want each beast to be branded with

qui ciascuna bestia siat sinnada a su sinnu de su pubillu. (3)Et cullu officiali qui non l'at fagheri, secundu qui in su dictu capidulu si contenit, siat condempnadu pro sa negligentia sua a sa corte nostra in l[ib]r[a]s .x.

39v CLXXXIIII. Bestia de intradura

(1)Constituim[us] et ordinam[us] qui quando alcuna bestia de intradura ad benere ad alcunu armentu de vachas over truma de ebbas over de ateru bestiamini et cussu pastori no lu conosquirit de qui at essere su dictu bestiami[n]i, qui cussu tali pastori over pastoris lu deppiant revelari infra dies tres a sa corte nostra over a su officiali, a tali q[u]i si possat ischiri de qui at esser. (2)Et cussu pastori qui non lu at revelari, secundu qui in su dictu capitulu si contenit, siat·illu appelladu pro fura et siat condemnadu secundu qui in su capitulu de qui furat si contenit.

CLXXXV. Fura de abitacione

(1)Item ordinam[us] qui q[ua]n[do] alcuno delito over maleficiu de fura s'at faghere in habitationi, qui cussu tali maleficiu qui at esser factu si depiat dari a su cuyli qui at esser plus approbe hui at esser factu su dictu delittu. (2)Et cussu depiat provari qui 'llu at aviri factu infra dies .xv. (3)Et si non provat, paghit su damnu ad cui at esser factu et de maquicia a sa corte nostra l[ib]r[a]s .xv. (4)Et simili si inte[n]dat i[n] su ditu capitulu pro sos lavoris, q[ua]n[do] non ant isquiri qui avirit factu su damnu; (5)qui 'llu diant a su bestiamini qui ad esser plus adp[re]ssu de su lavori et cussu paghit su damnu qui at esser factu et simili sa te[n]tura.

CLXXXVI. Qui tocarit bestiamen

(1)Volem[us] et ordinam[us] qui nexuna persona de caluncha gradu o conditioni non deppiat nen p[re]sumat tocari ne[n] bortari de ladus alcuna bestia qui acatarit morta, si pastori non e[st] qui 'llu mirarit pro su sinnu. (2)Et totu cussos qui l'ant mirari et pastori non siant, paghint cussas talis personis over persona su damnu a su pubillu de su bestiamini et de maquicia a sa corte nostra, secundu qui in su capitulu de qui furat si contenit, tota borta qui si 'lli at provari legittimamente.

CLXXXVII. Qui su pastore sia cretitu

(1)Constituim[us] et ordi[n]am[us] qui su pastori siat cretidu ad sagrame[n]tu suo de sa fura et damnu qui 'lli at esser factu in su bestiamini suo, si su ditu pastori est de bona fama. (2)Et si non est de bona fama, non siat cretidu per modu nixuno.

the mark of the owner. (3)And that official who shall not do so, according to what is contained in the said article, let him be condemned for his negligence to pay to our court ten lire.

Article 184. Beast extraneous to the herd.
(1)We decree and order that when any beast foreign to the herd should come to any herd of cows or to a herd of mares or other livestock, and the shepherd does not recognise to whom the said livestock belongs, that the said shepherd or shepherds should report this to our court or to the official, so that the owner may be traced. (2)And that shepherd who does not report this, according to that which is contained in the said article, shall be charged with theft and shall be condemned according to that which is contained in the article on theft.

Article 185. Theft from cultivations (*abitacione*).
(1)Item: we order that when any crime or offence of theft shall be perpetrated at a cultivation [adjacent to the village], such crime as shall have been perpetrated shall be attributed to the sheepfold nearest to where the crime was committed. (2)And he [the shepherd of the sheepfold] shall prove, within fifteen days, who committed it. (3)And if he does not prove it, he shall reset the damage to the one who suffered it and pay to our court a penalty of fifteen lire. (4)And similarly be it understood, in this article, for the crops, when it is not known who has done the damage (5)that in such a case they shall attribute this to the livestock that will be nearest to the crop, and he [the shepherd] shall repay the damage to those who have suffered it and at the same time the capture-fee (*tentura*).

Article 186. Who touches [dead] livestock.
(1)We wish and order that no person of any rank or condition shall presume to touch, or turn on its side, any beast which he finds dead, unless there is a shepherd who recognises it by its mark. (2)And all those who claim to recognise it, but are not shepherds, such persons shall recompense the damage to the owner of the livestock and pay to our court a penalty, according to that which is contained in the article on theft, whenever it shall be legitimately proved against them.

Article 187. Let the shepherd be believed.
(1)We direct and order that the shepherd shall be believed upon his oath concerning theft and damage that shall be perpetrated against him in regard to his livestock, if said shepherd is of good repute. (2)And if he is not of good repute, let him not be believed in any way.

40r CLXXXVIII. De su cane qui fagherit damnu

(1)Item ordinam[us] et co[n]stituim[us] si in cantu alcunu cani de loru over iagaru andarit ad posta sua et fagherit damnu in alcuno bestiamini, su pubillu de cussu tali cani over iagaru qui fassat cussu damnu siat tenudu de paghari su damnu qui at aviri factu a su pubillu de su bestiami[n]i, si legittimamenti si provat qui cussu cani over iagaru avirit factu ateru damnu sensa cussu ad alcunu bestiami[n]i. (2)Et si non si provarit qui cussu cani over iagaru non avirit fatu ateru damnu si non cussu, qui su pubillu de su cani over de su iagaru, si no[n] bolit paghari su damnu qui at aviri fatu, qui det su cani a su pubillu de su bestiami[n]i, provadu qui no[n] avirit fatu ateru damnu si no[n] cussu, secundu de supra.

CLXXXIX. Qui narrit paraula criminosa

(1)Volem[us] et ordinam[us] qui si alc[u]na persona over personis narrit a atera persona alc[u]na paraula crimi[n]osa, qui cussu over cussa persone qui at narri tali paraula criminosa lu deppiat bogari in claru i[n]fra dies .VIII. (2)Et si in claru no lu bogat legiti[m]ame[n]ti, siat cussa personi ad qui at esser naradu sa dita paraula crimi[n]osa, [si est provadu], si est pro mayas, siat bruiadu. (3)Et si esserit rufiania et provadu·si·lli est legiti[m]ame[n]ti, paghit cussu ad qui at esser provadu a sa corte nostra de maquicie l[ib]r[a]s .XXV. (4)Et si cussu ad qui s'at narri cussa paraula crimi[n]osa no[n] si 'lli at provare legiti[m]ame[n]ti infra su ditu te[m]p[us], paghit cussu qui at aviri naradu et at postu ad cussa personi cussa simili pe[n]a et siat co[n]de[n]nadu, secundu q[u]i in su ditu capitulu si co[n]tenit. (5)Pro li narri mayariu, paghit l[ib]r[a]s .L. i[n]fra dies .XV. de qui at esser iuygadu. (6)Et si no[n] paghat, seguit·si·lli sa limba per modu q[u]i la perdat. (7)Et pro li narri rufianu, paghit l[ib]r[a]s .XXV.

CXC. Qui narrit corrudo

(1)Item ordi[na]m[us] qui si alc[u]na persone narrit ad atera persone corrudu over atera paraula iniuriosa qui '[n]di essirit crimi[n]i, siat co[n]de[n]nadu cussu qui at narri cussa tali paraula ad paghari a sa corte nostra l[ib]r[a]s .XV., si bi 'llu provat. (2)Et si no bi 'llu provat, l[ib]r[a]s .XXV.

CXCI. Qui fagheret ficas

(1)Volem[us] et ordi[n]am[us] qui si alc[u]na persone fagerit sas ficas over qui
40v 'llu isme[n]tirit over q[u]i 'lli narrit atera paraula iniuriosa | daenanti dessu officiali, cussu qui at faghere secundu de supra siat conde[n]nadu ad paghari assa corti nostra per dogna paraula libras quimbi.

Article 188. Of the dog that would do harm.
(1)Item: we order and decree that if any watchdog or hunting dog should go, while at their work (*ad sua posta*), and do harm to livestock, the owner of such a dog, whether a guard or a hunting dog, who does that harm shall be obliged to repay to the owner of the livestock the harm which the dog has done if it is legitimately proved that such a guard or hunting dog has already done harm, at another time than the present, to any livestock. (2)And if it cannot be proved that that watchdog or hunting dog has done any other time damage, let the owner of the watchdog or hunting dog, if he does not want to repay the damage done, hand over the dog to the owner of the livestock, it having been proved that he has done no damage other than the present one, according to the above.

Article 189. Whoever speaks criminal words.
(1)We wish and order that if any person or persons shall say to another person any criminal word [bearing and implying a criminal charge], such person who shall speak of such criminality shall make known the charge within eight days. (2)And if he does not make it known lawfully, but it is nonetheless proved what he charges, if it is for witchcraft (*mayas*), let the one against whom the charge is made be burned. (3)And if it is for thuggery (*rufiania*) and it is legitimately proved against him, let him against whom it is proved pay to our court a penalty of twenty-five lire. (4)And if, within the said time, to whom such words insinuating crime are addressed, it shall not be legitimately proved [that he has committed what in regard to him is insinuated], let the one who has made the insinuation pay such a penalty, according to what is contained in this article. (5)For having called him a sorcerer (*mayariu*), he shall pay fifty lire within fifteen days from the time he is judged. (6)And if he does not pay, let his tongue be cut out so that he loses it. (7)And for calling him a ruffian (*rufianu*) let him pay twenty-five lire.

Article 190. Whoever calls [another] 'cuckold' (*corrudu*).
(1)Item: we order that if any person calls another person 'cuckold' or another insulting word that constitutes a crime, he who shall have uttered that such word shall be sentenced to pay to our court fifteen lire, if it is proved that the content of the insult corresponds to the truth. (2)And if it is not proved, twenty-five lire.

Article 191. Who makes the fig sign (*fagheret ficas*).
(1)We wish and order that if any person makes the fig sign or asserts to be false what the other says, or says some other insulting word to him before an official, he who does this as said above shall be sentenced to pay to our court five lire for each insulting word.

cxcii. Qui narrit iniuria ad officiali
(1)Constituim[us] et ordinam[us] qui si alchuna persone narrit alcuna paraula iniuriosa ad alcuno officiali nostru fague[n]do sos factos no[st]ros over qui 'lli levarit sa prea dae man[us], cussa tali personi qui at fagheri secundu de supra pagit a sa corte nostra pro maquicia, si legiti[m]ame[n]ti ind'est bintu, l[ib]r[a]s .xxv. (2)Et si no[n] paghat infra dies .xv. de qui at esser iuygadu prossa paraula iniuriosa, si 'lli seguit sa limba. (3)Et pro levari sa prea dae man[us], segint·illi sa manu dresta.

cxciii. Qui offenderit mayori
(1)Item ordinam[us] qui si alcuna persone offenderit mayori over minori officiali nostru et illu offendet in presoni et samben '[n]di esserit et provadu·li at esser legitimamenti, siat impicadu per issa gula per modu qui 'ndi morgiat sensa misericordia nixuna. (2)Et si samben no li bogharit et li arsarit colpu, paghit de maquicia a sa corte nostra l[ib]r[a]s .l. (3)Et si non paghat infra dies .xv. de qui at esser iuygadu, seghi[n]t·illi sa manu destra per modu qui 'lla perdat.

cxciv. De bestiamen
(1)Volem[us] et ordinam[us] qui tot[us] cussos qui ant aviri bestiamen domado over rude tenghant modo de guardare·llo o fagheri·illu guardare, secundu qui in sos capidul[us] de supra est narado. (2)Et icussos boes domados et arme[n]tu de vachas domadas at aradu o covall[us] o ebbas o molentes domados, qui s'ant acatare in lavore nadu infini assa prima die de ienargiu, cussos pubillos dessu lavore hue s'ant acatare o armentargiu o ho[min]i suo over iurado de pardu tenere·llos at poder et p[re]sentare·llos a su maiore. (3)Et per ciaschaduna dessas ditas bestias paghit su pubillu, si no[n] las at aviri missidas i[n] muda o in corda o in guardia, ultra cussu qui si co[n]tenit in su atteru capidulu de mitere·llos in muda, paghit s[oldo]s .vi. per dogna bolta qui acatados ant esser. (4)Et si i[n] muda over a corda ant esser missidos over dadus a guardia,
41r paghi[n]t sos dictos s[oldo]s .vi. per | bestia su pastore. (5)Et si tenne forsi su bestiamen non si at poder, ischiri ant et conoschire de qui at esser s'at poder. (6)Et si co[n]noschire lu ant poder, benne at assu maiore de sa villa et declarare su ditu bestiamini. (7)Et declarado qui 'lli at aviri et denunciado, de sa quale denunciatione siat cretidu su acatadore a su sagrame[n]tu suo, ad fagheri paghare dae ssu pubillu de su bestiamen over pastores qui ant esser in culpa, secundu qu'est naradu, s[oldo]s .vi. per bestia per ciaschuna volta qui 'lloy ant

Article 192. Whoever says insult to an official.
(1)We direct and order that if any person shall say any insulting word to any official of ours in the performance of the duties entrusted by us to him, or shall take from his hands any property seized by us, that person who shall do the aforesaid shall pay to our court, if he is lawfully defeated in court, a penalty of twenty-five lire. (2)And if he does not pay within fifteen days from the time he is judged for the insulting word uttered, let his tongue be cut off. (3)And for removing from his hands what was seized, his right hand shall be cut off.

Article 193. Whoever offends a senior officer (*mayori*).
(1)Item: we order that if any person offends one of our major or minor officials, and if he causes him bodily offence with the spilling of blood and it is legitimately proved against him, he is to be hanged by the throat so that he dies of it, without any mercy. (2)And if there is no spilling of blood, but he shall have struck him a blow, let him pay to our court a penalty of fifty lire. (3)And if he does not pay within fifteen days after he is tried, let his right hand be cut off so that he loses it.

Article 194. Of livestock.
(1)We wish and order that all who shall have tame or wild livestock shall be sure to guard them or have them guarded, according to what is prescribed in the preceding articles. (2)And the tame oxen and the herd of cows pulling the plough, or tame horses, mares, donkeys that shall be found in cereal fields already in bud until the first day of the month of January, those owners of the cereal fields in which the said animals shall be found, or the administrator (*armentargiu*) or one of their employees or a juror in charge of the pasture (*iurado de pardu*) may capture them and present them to the senior official (*maiore*). (3)For each of said beasts, the owner of them, if he shall not have placed them under guard established by shifts, or kept them tethered, or guarded, beyond what is contained in the article of placing them under surveillance shifts, shall pay six soldi for each time they are found. (4)And if they shall have been put under guard by shifts, or shall have been kept tied or guarded, it shall be the shepherd's duty to pay six soldi for each head. (5)And if it happens that the livestock cannot be kept, they shall seek to know and understand to whom they may belong. (6)And if they can know this, let them present themselves to the mayor (*maiore*) of the village and report such livestock. (7)And after having declared and reported all that—of the truth of the said report the one who found the livestock shall be believed, upon his oath—the owner of the livestock or the shepherds who shall be responsible shall pay, according to what has been said, six soldi per head, for each time the livestock shall be detected and found, in the same manner

esser biidos et acatad[us] come[n]te et qui 'llis averit te[n]tos, de sa quale co[n]de[n]natione deppiat aver et appat su acatadore sa tersa parti. (8)Et dae sa prima die de ienargiu inante, sensa indi fagheri clamo over denu[n]ciat[i]o[n]e alc[u]na i[n]ante, lu possat et depiat lensari et ochire in su lavore qui 'll'at acatare, sensa pe[n]a, mitte[n]do boghi o faghe[n]do clamo de cusso bestiame[n] qui at aviri mortu over lensadu de presenti qui 'llu possant ischiri in sa villa o in sa habitat[i]o[n]ne, de sa quale at esser mortu si in saltu non at poder acatare personas a qui 'llu possat declarare. (9)Ma cussa die no[n] passit, s'at esser hora debita, over sa segue[n]te die, qui su ditu clamo no[n]fassat a su maiore et a sos iurados de sa villa sa bestia over bestias de qui ant esser, qui 'llas ant cognoschere su pilami[n]i, s'est de die. (10)Et s'est de nocte, no[n] siat tenudo a declarare pilami[n]i, ma declarit et narit qui avirit le[n]sadu bestiame[n] in su lavore qui 'll'at aviri le[n]zadu. (11)Et si morrit i[n]tro de lavore suo over d'atiri, siat de cussu qui 'll'at aver morto over le[n]sadu. (12)Et si morret foras de lavore, siat de su pubillu de sa bestia qui at esser morta. (13)Et pro cussos pegus qui 'lloy ant esser acatados, qui non ant esser mortos et apidos que su pubillu de su lavore no los at aviri, bene q[u]'essere[n]t le[n]sados, paghit su ap[re]ciu qui at aviri fatu in su lavore su pubillu over pastore de su bestiame[n] a su pubillu de su ditu lavore. (14)Et si at esser una bestia qui si 'lloy at acatare, cussa deppiant ochire over lensare. (15)Et si ant esser plus, duas bestias per bolta et non plus.

De bestiamen rude

(16)Et si ad esser alcuno bestiame[n] rude de sos p[re]dictos qui sunt narad[us]
41v in su capidulu de supra [qui] s'ant acatare in | lavore nadu, gosi infini a su primo die de ienargiu come[n]ti et posca, si possat et deppiat ochire seghe[n]do·l[us] dae ssu lavori, gosi foras de lavore comenti et intro de lavore, hue los ant poder conseguire in sas aydationes de sos lavores. (17)Et siant de cussos qui 'll'ant ochire. (18)Verame[n]te qui cussu qui 'll'at ochire deppiat fagheri clamu et denunciatione a su maiore et iuradus de cussa villa hue s'at ochier, secundu qu'est narado in su capitulu de supra de su bestiame[n] domado. (19)Et nie[n]te de minus su pubillu de su bestiame[n] over su pastore qui at esser i[n] culpa pagit su ap[re]ciu et danu qui su dictu bestiame[n] ad aviri fatu.

as if they had captured the livestock. And concerning the sum of this penalty, the one who shall have found the livestock shall retain for himself the third part. (8)From the first day of January onward it [the livestock] may and shall be struck with a throwing weapon and killed, without any prior notice or report being given where it shall be found, without any penalty being imposed, after he has given word or notice in regard to that livestock which he shall have killed or struck with a throwing weapon so that this may be immediately known in the village or *habitatione* [cultivated territory surrounding the village], if the livestock which shall have been killed belong to it, in the event that in the countryside (*saltu*) no person can be found to whose ownership or custody it may be attributed. (9)But let it not go beyond that day [on which the deed took place], if it is at a convenient time, or otherwise on the following day, without giving notice to the mayor (*maiore*) and to those under oath (*sos iurados*) of the village, in regard to the beast or beasts, to whom they belong, if, should it be in the daytime, they can be identified by their coats; (10)and if it is at night, he is not required to identify their coats, but only to state and say that he struck the livestock in the grain field where the beasts were actually struck. (11)And if the livestock die within the field of his [the one who found it there] or of others, let the livestock remain with the one who struck or killed them. (12)And if it dies outside the crop, let it remain with the owner of the slain beast. (13)And for those livestock which shall be found there, but which [within the crop] have not been killed, and which the owner of the grain field, did not have them, although struck, let the owner or shepherd of the livestock pay to the owner of the grain field the value of the damage which shall be estimated. (14)And if it shall be a single beast that is found there, that one shall be killed or struck with a throwing weapon. (15)And if it be more than one, two shall be killed for each time [they are found] and no more.

Of wild livestock.
(16)And if wild livestock, mentioned in the article above, shall be found in a field of sprouting grain, until the first day of January as well as thereafter, they may and shall kill it by driving them away from the grain, and this both within the crop and outside of it, where the livestock may be reached and detained in crops set for grain. (17)And the beasts shall belong to those who kill them. (18)In the case in point, the one who kills them shall give notice and report to the mayor (*maiore*) and jurors of that village where the killing is to take place, according to that which is said in the article above on tame livestock. (19)And no less shall the owner of the livestock or the shepherd who shall be responsible, pay the value and damage that the said livestock shall have done.

Bestiame[n] menudo

(20)Et si ad esser alcuno bestiamen minudo, ciò est berbegues, porcos de gamma o cabra, qui s'ant acatare in lavore nadu, depiat esser maxellada sa gamma ogna bolta de pegus .V., s'ant esser dae .X. pegus in susu, et dae .X. pegus in gioso .II. peg[us]. (21)Et paghit su damnu [et] apreciu a su pobillu de su lavore su pastore.

Porchu mannali

(22)Et issu porcho mannali qui si 'lloy at acatare lu ochiant et siat de cussu qui 'll'at ochire, si morret inante de co[m]pliri a domo de su pubillu. (23)Et si ochier no[n] lu a poder, denunciet·illu a su maiore et paghit su pubillu de su porco s[oldo]s .II. per ciasc[u]na bolta qui 'lloy at esser acatadu, et issu ap[re]ciu et damnu qui at aviri factu a su pubillu de su lavore. (24)Et siat·inde cretidu su acusadore a su sagrame[n]tu suo et appat·inde sa mesidadi de sos dictos s[oldo]s .II. sa corte et iss'atera mesidadi appat su acusadore.

Maxellos e apressos

(25)Et simigianteme[n]te si inte[n]dat qui fagheri deppiant de ciaschaduno de su bestiame[n], de pe[n]as, maxellos, ap[re]ssos et co[n]de[n]nationes, qui s'ant acatare avire fatu et fagherint dampnu in su lavore qui at esser portadu et misidu in ariola infini a qui 'nd'at esser levado in totu.

CXCV. Vingias

(1)Constituim[us] et volem[us] nos obviari et dari remedio a sa malicia de multus qui supta specie et colore de sa guardia de vignas, ortos et lavores no[n] possant tenne nen damnigiare indebitame[n]te su bestiame[n] domado over
42r rude. | (2)Ordinam[us] que nexuna persona, de qualuncha gradu, istadu over ordini siat, deppiat over p[re]sumat bestiame[n] alcuno miter in vignas, ortu over lavores istudiosame[n]te pro inte[n]tione qui 'lloy siat mortu, over te[n]tu, over levare·llu dae ssu pastu over ochire·llu in pastu pro se over pro atero, et dari ad inte[n]dere qui 'llu appat mortu over te[n]tu in vingia over orto o lavore. (3)Et icussu a qui at esser acatadu over provadu legitimame[n]ti, et inte[n]dat·si qui siat prova legittima dae unu testi[m]ongio in suso i[n] custu articulo tantu, non obstante qui dae subra narat qui siat cretidu a su sagrame[n]tu suo su acusadore, deppiat esser condemnadu et paghit per dogna bolta a sa camera n[ost]ra l[ib]r[a]s .XV. infra dies .XV. de qui l'at esser provadu. (4)Et si no[n] las pagat, siat fustighadu. (5)Et issu simili si inte[n]dat de cussu qui at mitter in pardu de siilu

Small livestock.
[20]And if there be any small livestock (*bestiamen minudo*), that is, sheep, herd swine, or goats which shall be in the field of sprouting grain, the livestock of the herd shall be slaughtered at the rate of five head if the herd be from ten head or more; otherwise, if ten head or less, two head shall be slaughtered. [21]And the shepherd shall pay the damage and the assessed value to the owner of the grain field.

Domesticated swine (*porchu mannali*).
[22]And the domesticated swine that shall be found there shall be killed, and it shall be due to him who killed it, if it dies before it reaches the owner's house. [23]And if he cannot kill it, let him report it to the official (*maiore*), and let the owner of the swine pay two soldi for each time it is found there and for the estimated value of the damage done to the owner of the grain field. [24]And let the accuser be believed upon his oath, and let the court have half of the said two soldi and the other half the accuser.

[Acts of] slaughtering and evaluations.
[25]And it is to be understood that it shall be done likewise—with respect to punishments, acts of slaughtering, appraisals and convictions—for each head of livestock that shall be found to have done damage to grain that is still to be transferred and placed on the threshing floor, until it is taken there completely.

Article 195. Vineyards.
[1]We direct and order that we will help and provide remedy against the deceitful cunning of many who, under false appearance and the pretext of guarding vineyards, gardens and crops, succeed in keeping for themselves, or unduly harming, tame or wild livestock. [2]We order that no person, of whatever rank, status, or order he may be, shall or shall dare to intentionally cause any livestock to enter the vineyard, gardens, or cultivations for the purpose of having them killed or captured or removed from the pasture or killed in the pasture for his own or another's benefit, and then give the impression that he has [legitimately] killed or captured them in a vineyard, garden, or one of the cultivations. [3]And he who shall be discovered and it shall be legitimately proved against him—and it is understood that the proof is legitimately brought by one or more witnesses, and this specifically for this article notwithstanding it was said above that it is sufficient that the accuser be believed upon his oath—he shall be condemned to pay for each time to our Chamber fifteen lire within fifteen days from the time it shall be proved against him. [4]And if he does not pay, he shall be flogged. [5]And, likewise, what is intended with regard to the one who shall

over in pardu de mindas bestiame[n] q[u]i at esser vedadu, ad intent[i]o[n]e qui 'lloy esseret maxelladu, over te[n]tu pro se over per atere. (6)Et si cussu de qui esseret su dictu bestiame[n] over su pastore non poderet avere sa dicta proa et bolerent q[u]i deberet iurare cussa persona ad qui de ciò avirit suspectu, cussa persona siat constricta a iurare qui in ciò non siat culpabili. (7)Et si 'llu iurat, siat·indi leberadu de sa dita pe[n]a. (8)Et si iurare no[n] at boler qui no[n] appat factu cussu qui su pubillu over pastore de su p[re]dictu bestiamen li at apponne, paghit sa pena qui de supra est narado et declarado.

CXCVI. De arari

(1)Item ordinamus qui nexuna persone usit over presumat arari in loghu over parti hue usit et istit bestiamen rude pro fagheri narboni over pro attero modu. (2)Et si alcuna persona illoe ararit, cussa persona qui 'll'at arare illu cungit pro si forte modu qui bestiame[n] no[n] loy possat fagheri damno. (3)Et si puro bestiamen illoy intrarit et fagherit illoy damnu, nen tenne nen ochiere si 'lloy possat nen etiam deus apersari su damnu qui ant aviri fatu, exceptu qui si poderet provare legittimamente qui istudiosamenti esseret apertu et ischungiadu per alchuna persona. (4)In su quali casu, su qui 'llu avirit apertu over iscungiadu
42v depiat pagare et satisfagere su | damnu over apreciu qui at aviri factu su bestiamini qui 'lloy at esser intradu. (5)Verame[n]te qui custu capidulu non periudichit ad icussos qui ant aviri salt[us] are[n]gados foras de aydationes de villas, ma cussos qui 'llos ant aviri sos dictos saltos et ant arari in cussos et bestiame[n] at intrari in su lavore qui 'lloy at esser, qui su pubillu de su saltu possat maxellari su diti bestiamini in su lavore, come[n]te illo podet maxellari in su pastu. (6)Et apreciu over tenturas su pubillu de su bestiamen paghare non deppiat.

CXCVII. Guardia de bestiamen

(1)Volemus et ordinam[us] qui totu sos asones, vachargios, boinargios et pastores de qualuncha bestiamini siat deppiant guardare su bestiame[n] qui ant aviri in guardia pro si factu modu qui no[n]fassant damnu in vignas, ortos over lavores. (2)Et si fagherit damnu, sos pobillos de su bestiamini deppiant paghare su damnu qui su dictu bestiame[n] at aviri factu, secundu qui de supra est narado in sos ateros capidulos. (3)Verame[n]te si inte[n]dat que su pubillu de su bestiami[n]i possat avere et appat regressu co[n]tro su pastore, lieru qui siat o servo, qui cum paraula de su donnu suo siat allogadu de su damnu qui

cause to enter into the *pardu de de siilu* [meadow reserved for the iudike] and into the meadow *de mindas* [reserved for the grazing of tethered livestock] any livestock to which access is forbidden, with the prior intention of slaughtering or capturing them for his own or another's benefit. (6)And if the one to whom the said livestock belongs, or the shepherd will not be able to bring such proof and they want to make the person on whom suspicion falls take an oath, that person will be compelled to swear that he is not guilty of this. (7)And if he swears thus, let him be discharged from punishment. (8)And if he will not swear that he has not done that which the owner or shepherd of the said livestock imputes to him, let him pay the penalty declared above.

Article 196. Of ploughing.

(1)Item: we order that no person shall dare or presume to plough in any place or part where wild livestock are wont to be, whether to make land fallow or for any other reason. (2)And if any person ploughs there, the person who will do the ploughing shall fence such land well and in a proper manner so that livestock cannot harm it. (3)And even if livestock should enter it and do harm there, they shall not be caught or killed if they pass through it, nor shall the harm done be estimated, unless it can be proved that an opening has been deliberately made in the fence by someone. (4)In which case, he who has made the opening shall pay and satisfy the damage; that is, it shall be estimated how much damage was done by the livestock that entered it. (5)And it is, of course, to be understood that this article is not to the prejudice of those who will have lands (*saltus*) arranged separately from each other outside the cultivated area adjacent to the village. But for those who will have said lands (*saltos*) and will plough in them, should livestock enter the cultivation that had been planted there, then, in that case, the owner of the land may proceed to slaughter the livestock in the cultivation just as he may do in the pasture. (6)And the owner of the livestock shall not have to pay either for the estimation of the damage or for the trapping.

Article 197. Guarding livestock.

(1)We will and command that all keepers of horses, cowhands, ox-drivers, and shepherds of any livestock shall keep watch over animals that they have in their custody, so that they do not cause damage to vineyards, gardens, or crops. (2)And if they do damage, the owners of the livestock shall make good the damage that said livestock will have done, according to what is said above in the other articles. (3)It is, of course, understood that the owner of livestock may make a demand against the shepherd, freeman (*lieru*) or servant (*servo*) that he may be, and who, with the permission of his lord (*donnu*),

su dictu bestiamini at aviri factu et qui at aviri pagadu over qui 'lli co[n]vegnat paghare et de su bestiame[n] qui 'lli at esser mortu over levadu, su quali pastore siat tenudo de paghare et paghit su dictu bestiami[n]i et damnu. (4)Et si non avirit dae unde poderet pagare, su officiali siat tenudo de tenere·llu et mandare a prexio[n]e su secundo pastore at peticione de su pubillu de su ditu bestiamini. (5)Et istit in p[re]xione infini at qui at aviri satisfactu su damnu qui ad aviri recivido de su dictu bestiamen de cussu qui 'lli at esser convintu over li convegnat pagare. (6)Et gosi si inte[n]dat de su servu qui at esser allogadu cum paraula de su donnu suo comente et de su liberu, si su donnu de su servu non at boler paghare su damnu qui at aviri recivido su pubillu de su bestiame[n]. (7)Et si aveneret qui alcuno de sos ditos pastores over guardian[us] de bestiamini si partirit over fuhirint dae ssu serviciu per damnu qui aviri[n]t fatu su |
43r bestiamini qui 'lli at esser acomandadu over per alcuna atera causa, inantes de su tempus de sa allogatione et promissione qui at aviri fattu esseret complidu, bolemus et comandam[us] qui, per tenore de su presente capitulo, qui in caluncha logu s'at poder acatare over conseghere intro dessas terras nostras qui 'llu deppiant te[n]ne et mandare·llu a p[re]xione cussu qui 'll'at aviri co[n]dutu over allogadu over procuradore over ho[min]i suo.

CXCVIII. De allogare su bestiamen

(1)Constituim[us] et ordi[n]am[us] qui sus officialis de sas terras deppiant, in cussas contradas, villas et loghos qui ant aviri ad officiu, aconsare et allogare su bestiame[n] de sa corte qui at esser in su officiu qui at aviri, qui non possat faghire nen recivire damnu in loghu alcunu, et issas terras boydas over vingias qui ant esser in castigu over ortos de sa corte faghire·llos bene aconciare e lavorari qui lame[n]tu non si 'ndi possat aviri. (2)Et icussu officiali qui in ciò ad esser negligente et in culpa deppiat paghare et paghit et satisfassat totu su damnu qui sa corte ad reciviri et at muntare pro sa neglige[n]tia q[u]i 'lloy ad averi apidu non observando sas ordi[n]ationes qui de supra sunti factas.

Fini de sus capidulus de sa Carta de Logu.

is employed in his service, for reimbursement for the damage which said livestock shall have done and which he [the lord] shall have paid or shall be obliged to pay, as well as for the livestock which shall be killed or requisitioned from him: the said shepherd shall be obliged to pay and shall pay for said livestock and damage. (4)And if he shall not be able to pay, let the official be bound to arrest and bring into prison the second shepherd [i.e., the dependent shepherd who actually manages the livestock] at the petition of the owner of the livestock himself. (5)And he shall remain in prison until he has compensated the damage caused by the livestock by reason of which he shall have been proved guilty, and [declared] what he shall have to pay. (6)And so be it understood of the servant as that of the freeman who is taken into service with permission of his lord, if the lord of the servant does not himself wish to pay for the damage done [through the servant's negligence] by the owner of the livestock. (7)And if it should happen that any of the said shepherds or overseers of livestock should depart or flee from service on account of the damage that shall have been caused by the livestock entrusted to him or for some other reason, before the time within which he is to conclude his service and fulfil his undertaking is completed, we wish and order, by virtue of this article, wherever he may be found or reached within our lands, that he who shall have held and placed him in service, or his counsellor (*procuradore*) or one of his dependents, shall arrest him and bring him to prison.

Article 198. Of the leasing of livestock.
(1)We direct and order that officials of the lands, in the countryside (*contradas*), villages, and places (*loghos*) to which they shall be entrusted for the performance of their office, shall arrange and give for hire the livestock of the court which shall be entrusted to their offices, so that they may neither cause nor receive damage in any place, and that uncultivated lands or vineyards which shall be protected (*in castigu*), or have the vegetable gardens of the court arranged and worked so that no complaint may be had. (2)And the official who shall be culpably negligent in this shall pay, and shall pay for, and indemnify all the damage that the court shall receive for the negligence therein, since he has not observed the orders that have been given above.

End of the articles (*capidulos*) of the *Carta de Logu*.

Sardinian–English Glossary

Abbreviations

adj.	adjective	indef.	indefinite
adv.	adverb	n.	noun
art.	article	part.	participle
cond.	conditional	prep.	preposition
conj.	conjunction	pron.	pronoun
def.	definite	top.	toponym
esp.	especially	v.	verb

A

a[1], **ad** (in conjunction with the definite article **su, sa**, etc., **assu, assa**, etc.), prep. 1. *at, to*; 2. introduces the personal object (accusative prepositional), **deppiant fagheri tenni et miter in pregione a su ditu debitore:** *they shall arrest and take to prison the said debtor*; 3. time: *on*, **a dies .VIII. de capudanni**: *on 8th September*; 4. *within*; 5. **a ffura**: *secretly*.

a[2] grammatical particle reinforcing the statement; its value and meaning can be rendered as *indeed, in fact*: **Maria a ssi morivit senza llos partire**: *Maria indeed died before* (the children) *were divided* or also *Maria happened to die before* (the children) *were divided*; **issu servizu ki llis poserat patre vostru ... a llu lassant**: *the service which your father assigned them, they indeed leave it*.

abadorgiu, n. *drinking trough*.

abas (abatis abbati; abbati), n. *abbot*.

abatis, see **abas**.

abastat (abastant), see **bastare**.

abba, n. *water*.

abbadas, adj. *watered*.

abbadi, see **abas**.

abbadia, n. *abbey*.

abbare, v. *to water*.

abbatia, see **abbadia**.

abi(s), n. *bee*(*s*).

abiaresu, n. *bee-keeper*.

abitacione, see **habitationi**.

 | DOI:10.1163/9789004750951_007

abitari, n. *stall.*
acabidu, n. *order, organisation, arrangement* (in a working activity).
acatadore, n. *the one who finds* (something).
acatare (acatei, adcatarus), v. **1.** *to find;* **2.** *to acquire;* **3.** *to deliver, to send;* **adcatedilli nunça et minimedi de venne:** *I had him deliver the subpoena, but he declined to come.*
acatare, v. *to find, to take, to receive, to reach.*
accatare, see **acatare.**
acceptare, v. *to accept.*
acceptu, see **exceptu.**
accessu, see **ecessu.**
acclaratoriu, n. *clearing, glade.*
accomuni: in the adverbial locution **ad accomuni:** *in common.*
acconversaresi (acconverseti), v. *to make oneself a lay brother or sister.*
accordarsi, v. *to reach agreement.*
accordiu, n. *arrangement.*
accordu, n. *agreement.*
accusadore, n. *an accuser.*
accusare, v. *to denounce, to report, to accuse.*
achina, see **aghina.**
acomandare, v. *to entrust, to place* (a minor, the cattle, any good) *under the guardianship, to delegate.*
acomandicia, n. *escrow, deposit of custody of assets.*
aconciare, v. *to set, to arrange.*
aconzadamenti, adv. *freely, without any prohibition.*
aconziu, adj. *consenting;* **esser aconziu cun:** *to settle or agree with somebody.*
acordaresi (adcordarus·nos, acordarunsi, acordat, acordint·si·ndi), v. *to agree, reach an agreement.*
acostare·si (acostent), v. *to come near.*
acrescimentu, n. *prosperity.*
actu, n. *act.*
adcatarus, see **acatare.**
addonnicaresi (addonnicaitse, adonnigadu) v. *to place oneself in the service of another lord.*
adfiiaresi (si adfìiiedi), v. *to call* (a church) *to inherit the share that a son would be entitled to.*
adimandadu, see **dimandare.**
adimandare, see **dimandare.**
aditioni, see **habitationi.**
adiungere (atungolli, aiunxi), v. *to add, to make an addition, to join.*

adiunghere, see **adiungere.**
adivisioni, see **divisione.**
adpressu, see **apressu**[1].
adprovadu, see **approvado.**
adpusti, see **pusti.**
adsoltura, see **asoltura.**
adunare (adunata) v. *to gather.*
advenit, see **avenne.**
adventura, see **aventura.**
adversu, adj: *adverse*; **adversa parti**: *opposing party* (in a legal dispute).
adviat, see **avere.**
adviamus, see **avere.**
advocadu, see **avocadu.**
advocare, v. *to exercise the functions of legal representative.*
advochationes, see **avocachione.**
aedadi, n. *age.*
afactu, prep. in the locution **afactu de**, after; **non deppiat isse iurare afactu dessus testimongios**: *he did not have to swear later before witnesses.*
affeadu (affeada, afeadas), adj. *enfeoffed*; **villa affeada**: *enfeoffed village.*
(se) afferre, v. *to make oneself a lay brother or sister.*
affrenare (affrenent), v. *to curb, to contain, to restrain.*
affurchare, see **afurcare.**
afliscaresi (s'afliscat), v. *to close, to rejoin* (said of a land boundary when it returns to the starting point).
afrustare, v. *to whip.*
afurcare, v. *to hang* (on the gallows).
agasone, n. *horse-guard, horse-keeper.*
agatare, see **acatare.**
aghina, n. *grape.*
agienu, adj. *other people's*; **fante de lectu agiena**: *concubine* (stranger, coming from the outside). See also ***aienu.***
aginariu, n. *donkey-driver.*
agitu, see **aidu.**
agravare, v. 1. *to compel*; 2. to *aggrieve, to injure.*
agresta, n. *unripe grapes.*
agustu, n. *August.*
aidu, n.; *entrance, especially of a farm enclosed by walls or hedges.*
aieno, see **aienu.**
aienu, adj. *of someone else, of other people.*
aissora, adv. *then, in the moment when*; **asora kando**: *when.* See also **asora.**

aiuda, n. *help.*
aiugere, see **adiungere.**
aiunxi, see **adiungere.**
aivi, adv. (towards) *there.*
alaterru, n. *phillyrea shrubs.*
albinathu, n. *limestone rocks.*
albinu (albina), adj. *white, whitish, light-coloured.*
albu, adj. *white.*
alcuno, pron. *some, somebody.*
alicando, adv. *ever, never.*
aligando (and Latin **aliquando**), adv. *never.* See also **alicando.**
alikis, pron. *someone.*
alinu (alinos), n. *alder tree.*
alios, pron. *others.*
aliquando, see aligando.
allegare, v. *to produce, to add, to attach.*
alletu (alletos), n. *designated to hold a certain position.* See also **ellegere.**
allogare, v. **1.** *to hire, to rent out,* **2.** *to place oneself in the employment or service of another.*
allogatione, n. **1.** *rental,* **2.** *putting oneself at service of another.*
alluari, v. *to poison* (water, e.g. with euphorbia or spurge).
altare, n. *altar.*
alteru, **altera**, pron. and adj. *other.*
altu, adj. *high.*
amante, n. *lover, concubine, mistress.*
amanti, see **amante.**
ambisuga, n. *leech.*
ambitrio, see **arbitriu.**
ambos, **ambas** adj. and pron: *both.*
amen, *amen.*
amesturare (amesturan), v. *to mix.*
amighu (amigha), n. *cohabitant, concubine.*
amittere, v. *to admit.*
ammu, n. *hook.*
amore, n. *love, out of respect for, for the sake of.*
amustrare, v. *to show.*
anathema, n. *anathema, curse.*
anbilla, n. *eel.*
anbos, see **ambos.**
anchilla, see **ancilla.**

anchu, adv. *also, even, too*; **ancu si:** *yet, although*; **nen anchu:** *not even.*
ancilla, n. *female servant.*
anco, adv. *again, also.*
andare (bat, vamus, benta, andavant, andei, andedi, andarunt, andarat, est andata), v. **1.** *to go* (to), *to leave*; **2a.** *to follow a route* (said of a land boundary or road); **2b.** *to pass, to head towards*: **3.** *to go together with, to accompany, to be following*; **4.** *to abandon* (service); **5.** *to fall to* (by rule, rightfully): **e Troodori andedi a patre: ecco a clesia:** *and Troodori was taken for his father's side*: *so he fell to the church*; **andari cun:** *to go together with, to follow*; **andari a tterra:** *to fall* (to the ground); **andari ad posta:** *to go to the place where a hunter* (or dog) *waits for game.*
angarias, n. always in the phrase: **poriglos de angarias:** *messenger or postal service employees.*
angilla, see **ancilla.**
anima (animas), n. *conscience, soul.*
animu, n. *mind, intention, will*; **cum animu deliberadu:** *with a deliberate mind.*
ankilla, see **ancilla.**
annale, n. *annual expiry date.*
anniclu, adj. *one-year-old* (horse).
anniversariu, n. *anniversary.*
anno, n. *year.*
annu (annos), n. *year.*
anquilla, see **ancilla.**
ante, prep. *before, in front of.*
antesicu, adv. *instead of, in place of.*
anti, adv. *rather, instead, but.*
antigu (antiga), adj. *ancient, old.*
anu, see **annu.**
aparc, see **appare.**
aparere (aparit), v. *to appear.*
aparigiadu, adj. *ready.*
apartenere (aparteniat), v. *to belong to.*
ape (apes), n. *bee.*
apensadamente, adv. *with a deliberate mind.*
apensadamenti, see **apensadamente.**
aperile, n. *common land* (the land of the **pauperos**). See also **pauperu.**
aperrere (apertu) v. *to open.*
apersare, see **apressare.**
apersu, see **apreciu.**
apertu, see **aperrere.**

apertenne, v. *to be entitled to*; **apertenne a sa ragione de**: *to fall under our jurisdiction of.*
apiaresos, see **abiaresu.**
apitu, see **avere.**
apostolu (apostolos), n. *apostle.*
appare, adv. *together, in common, jointly*; **a llados apare**: *adjoining one other.*
appelare·si, v. 1. *to appeal* (against a judgement); 2. *to charge* (of a crime).
appellatione, n. *act of appeal, appeal process.*
appellationibus, see **appellatione**; in the Latin phrase, **de appellationibus**: *about appeals*
applaticare, v. *to promise.*
apponerent, see **opponne.**
appi, see **avere.**
appo, see **avere.**
apponne, v. *to impute.*
apprethare, see **apressare.**
approbe, adv. *near, nearby.*
appropriare, v. *to confiscate, to forfeit.*
appus bulba, adverbial locution, *on the mother's side.*
apuste, see **pusti.**
appusti, see **pusti.**
apreciu, n. *estimation, evaluation, appraisal.* **su apreciu de su damnu qui at fagheri in sa dicta vigna**: *the assessment of the damage it will have done in the said vineyard.*
apressa, see **apressu.**
apressare, v. to *evaluate, to estimate.*
apresse, adv. *quickly.*
apressu, adv. 1. *near*; 2. *thereafter, furthermore.*
aprezu, see **apreciu.**
aprili, n. *April.*
aprobados, see **aprovare.**
aprovamentu, n. *approval.*
aprovare (aprovados, aprobados; aprovadus), v. *to approve, to prove the presence of certain qualities in the legal field.*
apud, adv. *near.*
apus, adv. and prep. 1. *near*; 2: *on the side of*; 3. *at, relating to*: **apus patre** *or* **matre**: *from the father's or mother's side.*
aqua, n. *water resource, source supply*. See also **abba.**
aquistare (aquistaremus), v. *to acquire.*
aradare (aradeit), v. *to plough, to work the land.*

aradoriu, adj. *arable, suitable for ploughing.*; **aradorias terras**: *arable or ploughed land.*
aradu, n. *plough.*
araigla, see **raigha.**
aramentu, n. *land and equipment for ploughing.*
arare, arari, v. *to plough*; **abitatione de arare**: *arable land, land for ploughing.*
aratorium, see **aradoriu.**
Arbarikesu, adj. (*person*) *from Arborea.*
arbitriu, n. always in the locution **at** *or* **in arbitriu de**: *at the will, at the discretion of.*
arbore (arbores), n. *tree.*
arcatu, adj. *curved, leaning.*
archipiscobu, n. *archbishop.*
archipiscopu, see **archipiscobu.**
arder, v. *to burn.*
arengadu (arengados), adj. *placed, aligned.*
argenthola, n. *skein* (of thread or yarn).
argento, see **argentu.**
argentu, n. *silver.*
argiola, n. *threshing floor.*
arguesta, see **agresta.**
arientu, see **argento.**
ariola, see **argiola.**
arkipiscobu, see **archipiscobu.**
arma, n. *weapon.*
armadu, adj. *armed.*
armare v. *to furnish, to fit out, to supply.*
armari (armait, aviant armada, armatu), v. **1.** *to endow, to patrimonially equip a legal entity, to constitute it patrimonially, to establish*; **2.** *to* (well) *make, to manufacture.*
armentargiu[1], n. *administrator.* See the entries with **armentariu.**
armentargiu[2], adj. in the phrase **boes ruis armentargius**: *wild oxen kept in a herd.*
armentariu de clesia, n. *administrator of a church or monastery.*
armentariu de sigillum, n. *keeper of the seal* (of the iudike).
armentariu de villa, n. *administrator of a village.*
armentario, see **armentriu.**
armentariu, n. *administrator, administrator of public or private estates*; **armentariu de logu**: *administrator of the realm, of the royal or* iudicale *treasury.* See also **armentargiu.**

armentu, n. *herd.*

arminantia, n. *ordinance, legal device.*

arminare (arminavi, arminai), v. *to issue an ordinance, a legal device.*

arquiprete, n. *archpriest.*

arramanere, see **remanere.**

arrasoni, n. 1. *reason*; 2. *farming obligation*; *obligation imposed on subjects to plough or sow*. See also **arrobatia.**

arraygua, see **raigha.**

arregere (arreiat, arreea, arregant, regant, arregendo, arreendo, regende, regendo, reendo), v. 1. *to preside over*; 2. *to hold, to administer*; 3. *to rule*; 4. *to have in hand, in possess.*

arregordare (arregordarunt), v. *to remind.*

arreire (arreeret), see **arregere.**

arrennatu, adj. (land) *directly subject to royal administration.*

arresone, see **ragione.**

arrespondere, see **respondere.**

arrivalia, n. *enmity.*

arrobadia, see **arrobatia.**

arrobatia, n. *farming obligation*. See also **arrasoni.**

arsare, v. *to raise*; **arsare colpu**: *to hit.*

arsida, see **arder.**

arte, n. *craft, craftsmanship, art.*

articulo, n. *article.*

asaghida, n. *assault.*

asaltegu, n. *assault, attack.*

ascendente (ascendentes), n. *ascendant.*

Ascensioni, n. *Ascension.*

ascuse, adv. *covertly, in secret, without knowledge.*

asinu, n. *donkey.*

asoltura, see **assoltura.**

asolvere (absolvitime, asolbendomi), v. *to allow, to grant, to authorise.*

asone, n. *keeper or guardian of horses and mares.*

asora, see **aissora.**

assaghiri (assaghirit asaghirit), v. *to assault.*

assaltigiare (assaltigiando), v. *to assault, to attack.*

assecus de totu, adverbial locution: *last of all.*

assignari, v. *to assign, to deliver.*

assolbullu, v. (from assolbere) + pron. *I permit, I release, I absolve.*

assoltura, n. *permission.*

assora, see **aissora.**

astore, n. *goshawk.*
ataxando, see **taxari.**
atazari, see **taxari.**
at(t)ere, see **atero.**
ateramente, adv. *otherwise.*
aterminare, v. *to delimit.*
atero (attero, atteru, atere, attere, atter, ateri, atteri, atiri, attiri, aturu, altero, artero), adj. and pron. *someone else, something else.*
atero, n. *other asset or substance or possession*; **atero e tantu**, adverbial locution: *as much as, likewise, the same.*
ateru[1], pron. 1. *other, another,* 2. *further, additional.* See also **atero.**
ateru[2], n. *the rest, the remaining.*
aterue, adv. *elsewhere.*
ateruy (in ateruy), adv. *elsewhere, somewhere else.*
atha, n. *slope, crag, cliff.*
at(t)iti, see **atero.**
atprovado see **aprovare.**
atrasattu, adj. (horse) *harnessed, supplied with harness.*
atsinare, see **assignari.**
attanagiare (attanagiadu, attanagando·lu), v. *to grip or compress* (as a form of torture).
attenne, v. *to observe* (e.g. the law).
attu, see **actu.**
atuntura, n. (territorial) *addition, increase.*
atungolli, see **adiugere.**
au, disjunctive conj. *or.*
Audencia, see Audientia.
Audientia, n. *hearing, tribunal.*
Audiencia, see **Audientia.**
auditore, n. *senior judge.*
ausu[1,] adj. always in comminatory formulas: *audacious, daring.*
ausu[2], n. *audacity.*
aut, see **au.**
autenticu (autenticas), adj. *authentic, valid.*
autu, autus, n. *document.*
avansare, v. *to advance, to progress.*
ave co, adv. *when.*
ave, prep. *from.*
avenne (avenit avennet, advenit), v. *to happen.*
aventura (adventura, ventura), n. chance; **per aventura** *or* **pro aventura**: *by chance, incidentally.*

avere bias, verbal circumlocution: *to have or claim rights to or over, to have the means to.*

avere (aver, averi, aviri, avire, appo, at, ait, a, hat, amus, ant, avia, avea, aviat, abiatillu, adviat, aviamus, adviamus, aviant, appi, ippi and epi (in the conditional mode forms): **kerre l'epi a serbiçu de sancta Maria:** *I would like her to serve* [the church of] *Santa Maria*; **ei commandare:** *I would order*), appit, apit, edi and eti (in the conditional mode forms: **quando s'edi suterrari:** *when he should have been buried*; **sa genaratione k'edi nasciri:** *the generation that would be born*; **onia cantu eti lassare:** *everything he would have left*); apperus, apperunt, enti and arent (in the conditional mode forms: **enti fagere:** *they would make*; **enti iskire**; *they would know*) (aviat apita, apat, avesse, averen, avendo), v. *to have*: **1.** *to possess, to own, to maintain possession*; **1b.** *to take possession as a result of purchase or exchange, to obtain*; **2.** *to have nearby*; **3.** *to arrest*: **si cussu homini … non si poderet aviri infra su dito tempus de uno mese:** *if that man cannot be arrested within the aforementioned time of one month.* In phrases: **4.** *to obtain, to derive*; **5. avereve (ivi avere):** *to be there*; **6.** it contributes to the formation of the future tense and the conditional: **sos hominis qui ant acaptare intro dessas dictas vignas:** *the men whom they shall find within the said vineyard*; **ent poder manchare:** *they might fail.* In phrases and locutions: **avere a:** *to have to, to have the right*; **avere (something) a:** *to hold something in trust* (as one holds certain functions); **avere (in pari) cun:** *to have possession of part of something* (the other part of which is owned by someone else); **avere de:** *to have something in one's own possession resulting from specific causes or actions*; **avere (children)** ***de*** + name: *to have children by* (a man or a woman); **avere de** (+ personal name): *to own by inheritance from someone*; **avere ausu:** *to dare, to have the audacity to*; **aver parte:** *to hold rights over*; **avere(ve) bias:** *to have share, rights over, means to*; **avere paraula:** *to have assurance*; **avere parçone:** *to have fate* (with); **averesinde prode:** *to have the benefit* (of something); **aviri illoe,** *to be there*; **aviri daenante de,** *to have before any officer* **aviri consigiu cum:** *to consult with someone.*; **aviri (legittime) loghu,** *to have* (legal) *force.*

avestara, adv. *from now on.*

avia, n. *grandmother.*

aviamus, see **avere.**

avinde, adv. *from there, from then.*

avio, n. *grandfather.*

avitu, see **aidu.**

avocachione, n. *legal profession, advocate.*

avocadu, n. *legal representative, lawyer.*

avu, n. *grandfather.*

avunde, adv. *from whom, where, whence.*
axendentes, see **ascendente.**
axinu (axinus), see **asinu.**
aydatione, see **habitationi.**

B

babu, n. *father.*
bacante, adj. *empty, vacant, unworked* (land).
bacca, see **vacca.**
bacha, see **vacca.**
bachargiu, n. *cow-herder, shepherd.*
bactore, see **baturo.**
badia, see **abbadia.**
bagadia n. *unmarried woman.*
bagantis, see **bacante.**
bagiat, see **baler.**
baiat, see **andare.**
bajna, n. *pond, lagoon.*
baler, v. *to valid, true, effective.*
baliri, see **baler.**
balivale, n. *bailiff, representative, executor* (of an action or order).
balle, n. *valley.*
balliclu, n. *small valley.*
bangeleu, n. *Gospel.* See also **Evangelium.**
banita, n. *cotton blanket.*
baractare, see **barattare.**
barattare (baratadu), v. **1.** *to contest, to dispute* (through legal channels); **2.** *to permute, to barter.*
barattaria, n. *deceit, fraud.*
barca (barcas), n. *boat.*
bardare, v. *to have the care and use, to take care.*
bardones, n. *parts, pieces.*
bare, see **pare.**
bari, see **pare.**
bargala, n. *grinder, millstone, press.*
bari, see **pare.**
barigare (barighat, barigando), v. *to overrun, to cross over, to exceed, to go beyond.*

barone (barones), n. *male, man* (as opposed to female or woman).
barrellu, n. *undergarment, poor and simple skirt or dress.*
bartone, see **parzone.**
basare (basadu), v. *to kiss, to invoke the grace of the judge, who grants it through the act of kissing* (the hand).
bastare (abastat, abastant, bastarit, bastanti), v. **1.** *to reach* (a certain number or amount); **2.** *to suffice, to be enough.*
bat, see *andare.*
batiri[1], v. *to bring, to lead.*
batiri[2], v. *to beat, to strike.*
bator, see **baturo.**
battorpedia, n. *livestock.*
batuere (batuer, battuere, batuier, bature, batiere, batusi, batuserunt), v. **1.** *to bring, to produce* (witnesses or documents); **2.** *to take* (away).
batuier, see **batuere.**
baturo, cardinal number: *four*; **de baturo una:** *one quarter, the fourth part.*
bau, n. *ford.*
bayat, see **andare.**
becla, adj. *old.*
bega, n. *valley.*
benas, see **ena.**
bender, v. *to sell.*
bendidore, n. *seller.*
bene[1], adv. **1.** *well, in the right way*; **dae bene in megius:** *from good to better*; **2. ben(n)e que**, conj. *although.*
bene[2], n. **1.** *good, the good, the useful, the advantageous*; **2.** *goods, properties, wares*; **3.** *donation.*
benedicere (benedixerus), v. *to bless.*
benedictione, n. *benediction, blessing.*
bendictioni, see **benedictione.**
benedictu (benedicta), adj. *blessed.*
benidore, n. *vine grower, winemaker.*
benne (be(n)nere, venghio, benit, benni, bengiat, benghat, vennet, benidu *or* a), v. **1.** *to come* (from); **benne incontra:** *contravene.* **2.** *to appear, to present oneself* (before an authority or in court), *to be present at, to show up*; **3.** *to join* (with other beasts); **4.** *to resort to.*
bennenare, v. *to harvest grapes.*
ben(n)ere, see **benne.**
benni, see **benne.**
benta, see: **andare.**

berbecargiu (berbecargius), n. *shepherd.*

berbegue, see **berbeke.**

berbeke: n. *sheep.*

berbekina, adj. *ovine, sheep's* (meat). **ficu berbekina:** *a type of small fig tree whose leaves are eaten by livestock.*

berbu, n. *word*; always in the locution **torrari berbu:** *to warn, to alert, to communicate, to claim, to reply.*

beridade, n. *truth.* See also **veridadi.**

beridadi, see **beridade.**

berruda, berrude, n. *sharp throwing weapon*; employed in the locution **corona de chida de berruda:** *court or tribunal of* **probiviri** *or* **prudhommes** *subjected to taking-turns, so called because those in attendance were equipped with a* **berrruda** *or were able to carry one.* See also **verruda.**

bervu, see **berbu.**

bestare, n. *house, dwelling.*

bestia, n. *beast, animal.*

bestiamen, n.; *cattle, livestock.*

bestiri, n. *dress.*

bi, enclitic pron. *here, there.*

bia, see **via.**

biagiu, n. *trip, travel.*

biat, see **biere.**

bicania, adv. *in replacement.*

bicanu, n. *substitute, deputy, stand-in.*

biclata, adj. (a female animal) *having given birth.*

bide, n. *vine.*

bider, see **biere.**[2]

bie, see **bi.**

biere[1] (biat), v. *to drink.*

biere[2] (viiat, vidit), v. 1. *to see*; **appala comente est a biere in su primu foliu et in sus ateros autus:** *that he maintains as can be verified in the other documents*; 2: *to realise*: **viiat ca llu podestava** *he realised that he* (the opposing party) *took over* (in the judicial debate).

biglada, see **viglata.**

biidoriu, n. *watering place.*

biidos see **videre.**

bikinu (bikinos), n. and adj. *neighbour.*

billa see **villa.**

binaiollu (binaiollus), n. *wine grower, winemaker.*

binariu (binaries), n. *vintner.*

binchidu, n. and adj. *won, the losing party in a court case.*
binchidura, n. 1. *victory*; 2. *money, collected by way of compensation, for the victory in court.*
binchere, v. *to win*; *to win in court, to obtain a favourable judgement in court.*
bindichi, cardinal number: *fifteen.*
bindiki, see **bindichi.**
bindiri, see **vendere.**
binea, see **binia.**
bingia, see **binia.**
bingna, see **binia.**
bingnas, see **binia.**
binia (binnias, bingias, bingnas, vinias, vineas), n. *vineyard.* See also **vigna.**
binkere (binki, binkerusillu, binkerant, fuit binkidu, binkidu, vinkidu), v. *to win in court.*
binkidura, n. *winning, judicial victory.*
binti, cardinal number: *twenty.*
biquanium, see **bicanu.**
birga, n. *rod* (*for measuring*); **fuste de birga**: *pertica* (unit of length); *the distance of a thrown rod* (measure of length).
bisantata, n. *the value of a besant* (*coin*).
bisanti (bisantes), n. *besant, gold coin.*
biscobu, see **piscobu.**
biscondes, see **visconte.**
bisconti, see **visconte.**
biscontissa, n. *viscountess.*
bisognu, n. *need.*
bisongiare, v. *to need.*
bissido, see **biere.**
bita, n. *life*. See also vita.
bitura, n. *transportation*; in particular: *using or hiring animals for transport.*
biu, see **vivu.**
bivu, see **vivu.**
blastomari, v. *to blaspheme.*
boe (boes), n. *ox, oxen.*
bogare (boghare, voco, bogarat, bocandonde), v. 1. *to* (*be*) *separate*(*d*); 1. *to take away*; 2. *to exempt*; 3. *to get, to bring about, to create, to extract*; 4. *to exclude*; 5. *to place the clause, the exception* (in a legal *transaction*); 6. *to draw* (*wine from the barrel*); 7. *to spill, to let* (blood) *out of*; 8. *to put or to gouge out* (the eyes); **bogari in claru (ad claru)**, *to make something clear, to make something public*; **boghare foras**: *to bring out.*

boghare, see **bogare.**
boghi, n. *voice, notice.*
bogis; see **boghi.**
boida, adj. *empty, uncultivated* (land).
bois, see **boe.**
bolere (bolio, voles, boliat, boliant, boleant, bolbillos, bolbit, volvit, bolesse, or voluerit in Latin formulae) v. *to want, will, to wish, to order, to deliberate.*
bollatu (bollata), adj. *with the seal affixed.*
bollere, see **bolere.**
bolta (voltas), n. *time, occasion.*
boltare (boltat), v. *to turn.*
boluntade, n. 1. *will*; 2. *consent*; in the phrases **a boluntade de pari** (and similar): *with mutual agreement*; **a voluntade:** *subject to the will of.* See also voluntade, voluntate.
boluntate, see **boluntade.**
bombagiu, n. *cotton.*
bona, n. *possessions, tangible goods.*
bono, adj., see **bonu.**
bonu, adj. 1. *good*; 2. *reliable*; 3. (the) *right* (thing); 4. *good, correct, valid*; 5. **homines bonus** *or* **bonu homini: prudhommes:** *trusted men* (of a certain social standing; they could serve as members of a judicial assembly or **corona**); a *or* **cun boluntade bona** (and similar) and so **ad plakimentu bonu:** *with good mutual agreement, consent.*
borce, prep. *but rather, except for, on the contrary.*
bortari, v. *to turn*; **bortari de ladu:** *to turn to the side.*
borthe, see **borce.**
bostros, see **vostru.**
boves, see **boe.**
boynargiu, n. *herdsman* (of oxen).
brasu, n. *arm*; **dare su brasu suo:** *to help, to cooperate.*
brebeges (brebegues), see **berbeke.**
breve, n. *brief, document of normative character.*
brigha, n. *brawl.*
bruiare (bruiadu), v. *to burn.*
bruncu, n. *hill*(top).
bubari, n. *cattle pen.*
bucha, n. *mouth.*
buckellu, n. *a quarter.*
buiakesu (buiakesos), n. *iudike's bodyguard, entourage.*

buiaria, n. *keeper or maker of document seals.*
bukellu, see **buckellu.**
bulba, n. *womb.*
bullada (bulladas), adj. *charter(s), with a seal affixed.*
bullare (bullarunt, bullata), v. *to affix the seal* (to a charter).
bullata, see **bullada.**
bullatoriu, n. *seal, seal punch.*
bullu (bullos), n. *large heads of cattle.*
bulvare, see **vulbare.**
burghesi, n. *citizen of a town.*
butegha, n. (notary's) *office.*

C

ca, subordinate conj. 1. *that*: introduces direct speech; 2. *because*; **dae *or* de ca**: *since*; **in qua**, *as*; **in qua directu iuyghi de Arbaree**: *as the direct iudike of Arborea.*
caballos, see ***cavallu.***
cabiça: in the adverbial locution **cabiça a**: *at the head of.*
cabiçali (cabiçalis) n. *pillow.*
cabiza, n. *end of a rope that is knotted; the end of a* **curria.**
cabizali, see **capizale.**
cabra, n. *goat.*
cabudanni, see **capudanni.**
cabudu, n. *head*; **cabudu de sa fura**: *the stolen item.*
cada, pron. *each.*
caderno, see **quadernu.**
cadernu, see **quadernu.**
cagioni, n. *cause.*
calabrike, n. *hawthorn.*
calare, v. *to descend, to go down.*
calari, v. *to bring down.*
calaridana, adj. *from Cagliari* (said of a particular type of fig).
caldu, adj. *hot.*
cale, adj and pron. *which, which one, such, as, such as.*
cali, see **cale.**
calkina, n. *lime, mortar.*
calkinare, v. *to plaster.*
calonigu, n. *canonical.*

calumpnia, n. *slander*, in the locution **sagramentu de calumpnia**: *oath of slander* (an oath by which it is sworn that one party has slandered the other).
calunca, adj, and pron. *whoever, any, whatever person, whatsoever, whichever.*
caluncha, see **calunca.**
camarlingu, n. *chamberlain.*
cambia, n. *swap, exchange contract.*
cambiare (cambiei, cambiai, cambiarus, cambiando), v. *to change, to exchange, to make exchange.*
cambio, see **cambiu.**
cambiu, n. *exchange, swap, trade-in.*
camera, n. *Chamber, Chancery, Treasury.*
campaniari(·si), v. *to agree with each other outside the court proceedings.*
campare (campit), v. *to escape.*
campu, n. *field, square.*
cana, distributive pron. *two for each one.*
canale (canales), n. *gorge, narrow valley.*
canargiu, n. *keeper of dogs.*
canariu, see **canargiu.**
canasturça: n. a type of fig.
canbiu see **cambiu.**
cancelleri, n. *chancellor, registrar.*
cande, conj. *when.*
cando, conj. *when, since.*
cane (cani, canes), n. *dog*; **cani de loru**: *watchdog* (collared dog on a leash).
canna, n. *cane (measure of length).*
cannavariu, n. *hemp field.*
cannetu, n. *reedbed, cane field.*
cannisone, n. *marsh reed.*
canone (canones), n. *canon(s), dogma.*
canonigu, n. *canonical.*
cantare (cantares), n. *cantaro* (one *cantaro* = about 40 kg).
cantu (canta, cantos, cantas), relative adj. and pron. 1. *how much* (of), *how many, what, all that*; 2. *all that*: 3. **su** *or* **sa cantu**: *as much as*; 4. *in the same way, to the same extent, as*; 5. *in respect of what*; **pro cantu**: *according to what*; **tantu quantu et que si**: *as if*; **in cantu**: *because, since,* (for) *as long as.*
capellanu, n. *chaplain.*
capidulu, n. *chapter.*
capitellu, n. uncertain meaning, perhaps: *head of, top part of a field or a* **saltu.**
capithale, see *capizale.*

capizale (capiçale, cabiçale, cabizali, cabiçali), n. **1.** *head of, top part of, the extreme edge of a field*; **2.** in the locutiontion ***capizale a***: *at the head of.*
capra (capras), see **cabra.**
caprinu (caprina), adj. *of a goat.*
caprione, n. *wild fig.*
capruficu, n. *wild fig.*
capud: **1.** in the adverbial locution **capud a pare**: *of the same value*; **2.** prep. *towards.*
capudanni, n. *September.*
capudu, n. *territorial area.*
capugosso, see capuiosso.
capuiosso, adv. *down, lower part.*
caput, n. *head of, top part of*; **caput appare *or* a pare**: *by mutual agreement.*
cardinale, n. *cardinal, papal legate.*
carica, n. *dried fig.*
carnalimente, adv. *carnally.*
carnalimenti, see **carnalimente.**
carrada, n. *keg, small wine barrel.*
carradore, n. *carter.*
carrali, adj. in the locution **sorre *or* fradri carrali**: *carnal sister or brother, of the same blood.*
carrigu, n. *charge, liability, fault.*
carrisegare, n. *carnival.*
carrithare (carrithado), v. *to carry* (on a cart).
carro, see **carru.**
carru, n. *cart, wagon.*
Carta de Loghu, n. literally, *Charter of the Realm*; *corpus of the legal norms of the realm*; *the* 'Carta de Logu.'
carta (cartas), n. *charter, deed, document proving a legal transaction*; **2.** *notarial document*; **carta bullata**: *charter with an affixed seal.*
cartolaiu, n. *register containing documents, collection of documents.*
cartula, n. *short charter or document.*
casa, see **causa.**
caschaduna, see **ciaschaduno.**
casi, see **gasi.**
cassare (cassando), v. *to cancel, to undo.*
casside, n. (hunting) *net.*
castania, n. *chestnut.*
castellanu, n. *castellan.*
castellu, n. *castle.*

castiadore, n. *guardian, watchman, custodian.*
castigadores, see **castiadore.**
castigare[1] (castigaresi, castigat, castigent, castigandollu), v. *to take care, to use taking care, to preserve.*
castigare[2], v. *to chastise, to punish.*
castigu, n. *collective land* (for vines) *guarded by caretakers or overseers paid by the landowners.*
castighu, see **castigu.**
castiu, see **castigu.**
castru, n. *boulder, outcrop, large stone(s)*; it could refer to a *nuraghe*, or maybe as well, in the plural **castros:** *enclosure for keeping livestock.*
casu[1], n. *case, event.*
casu[2], n. *cheese.*
catriclas, n. *ridges, spaces between the furrows of a field.*
causa (causas), n. *assets, property,* (owned) *goods, what one holds or owns.*
causa, n. 1. *thing*; 2. *property*; 2.1. *head of cattle*; 3. *cause, reason*; 4. *cause, legal dispute, quarrel, lawsuit*; 5. *assets pertaining to a transaction*; **cum sciò siat causa qui:** *because, since.*
cavallare, adj. *regarding horse-riders.*
cavallu (cavallos), n. *horse*; **liero de cavallu**, *free man who owns a horse and must serve at arms*; **maiore de cavallus**, *head of the horses*; *cavalry officer.*
cavillatione, n. *cavillation*; **per via de cavillatione:** *speciously.*
cchertu see **chertu.**
ce, see **ke.**
cedru, n. *cedar tree.*
censa, see **sena.**
ceptu, see **ecceptu.**
ceracho, see **zaracu.**
cerbu, n. *deer.*
cerga, n. *fee or tax collection.*
certare, see **chertare.**
certu, see **chertu.**
cessare, v. *to cease, to stop, to avoid.*
chabudu, see **cabudu.**
chaderno, see **quadernu.**
chalchi (chalchis), n. *kick*; **faghere a chalchis:** *to kick.*
chali, see **cali.**
chalidadi, see **qualidadi.**
chalighi (chalighis), n. *chalice* (*for the Eucharist*).
chalunca, see **caluncha.**

chanis, see **cane.**
charta (chartas), see **carta.**
chascaduna, see **ciascaduno.**
chentenaio, n. *(about) a hundred*, **per chentenaio:** *percent.*
chentenayo, see **chentenaio.**
chentu, cardinal number: *one hundred.*
cherachu, see **zaracu.**
cherra, conj. *when.*
cherre[1], v. *to want, to require.*
cherre[2], conj. *when.*
chertadore, n. *one who conducts a judicial dispute on behalf of another, legal representative.*
chertare (chertadu), v. *to litigate, bring a judicial dispute, debate a case, contest.*
chertari, see **chertare.**
chertido, see **credere.**
chertitu, see **credere.**
cherto, see **chertu.**
chertu, n. *litigation.*
chi, see **qui.**
chichiri, see **xixiri.**
chida (and also **kida, quida, quide**), n. *week, work shift*; **quida de berrude:** *court or tribunal of* **probiviri** *or* **prudhommes** *subjected to shifts, so called because those who attended it were equipped with a* **berrruda**, *being able to carry the* **berruda** (a sharp throwing weapon).
chircadura, n. *search, extraction* (of court documents).
chircare, v. 1. *to investigate*; 2. to *inquire.*
chircari, see **chircare.**
chirquare, see **chircare.**
chirras, n. *straw-covered enclosures for lambs or kids.*
chiteu (and variants **ghiteu, quitheu, iteu, guiteu)**, pron. *what*; in the phrase **non ad dae chiteu pagare:** *he has nothing with which to pay.*
chue, see **cue.**
chui, see **cui.**
chun, see **cum.**
chundire (at chundire, at condiri), v. *to poison the water(s).*
chungiare, see **cungiare.**
cia, n. *aunt.*
ciaschadunu, see **ciascaduno.**
ciascaduno (ciaschaduna), adj. and pron. *each, each one.*
ciaschuno, see **ciascuno.**

ciascuno: adj. and pron. *each, each one.*

cidadis, see **citadi.**

cinniga, n. *reed, rush, bulrush, field of rushes.*

ciò (and variants **sò, sciò, siò, zò**): pron. 1. *that, this, what;* **tottu ciò qui**: *all that;* **cum sciò siat causa qui**, *because, since;* **ad ciò qui**, *so that, in order that;* **ciò** *or* **zò** *or* **sò est**: *that is, namely;* **pro ciò**: *hence, therefore.*

cipiri, n. *rosemary.*

cita, see **kida.**

citadi (citadis), n. *town, city.*

citare (citado), v. *to sue.*

ciu, n. *uncle.*

ckene, see **kena** and **sena.**

ckerbiclia, see **kerviclia.**

ckertare, see **cherare.**

cki, see **ki.**[1]

ckita, see **kida.**

clamare (clamait, clamedi, clamari, clamado), v. 1. *to declare;* 2. *to sue, to call or summon as witness;* 3. *to object* 4. *to raise objections, to take exception;* 5. **clamaresi, clamandomi**: *to claim, to make a complaint, to file a complaint in court,* 6. **clamare·si**: *to be named, to have by name;* **clamare at testimongios** *or* **pro testimongio**: *to require witnesses.*

clamo, see **clamu.**

clamu, n. 1. *complaint;* 2. *notice, notification.*

claru, adj. *clear;* **bogari ad** *or* **in claru**: *to clarify, to prove;* prepositional locution **claru a**: *to, towards;* adverbial locution ***a cclaru***: *openly.*

clasura, n. *hedge;* ***ortos ad cleṣura***: *fenced gardens.*

clausura, see **clasura.**

clericatu, n. *clerical staff.*

clericu, n. *cleric.*

clerigo, see **clericu.**

clerigu: clericu.

clesia, ecclesias, n. 1. *church:* 2. *church building;* 3. *legal-economic entity belonging to a monastery;* 4. in a more general sense: *church as an institution or administrative part of it;* **festa** or **sagra de clesia**: *religious festival;* **domo de clesia**: *ecclesiastical house, sacristy.*

clesura, see **clasura.**

clobari (clobadu), v. *to pair* (the oxen).

clompere (clompet, clompit, clonpet), v. 1. *to arrive,* 2. *to join, to reach, to conclude;* 3. *to come to pay according to one's possibilities or decision* 4. *to settle an account.*

clopas, n. *pair, couple.*
clopatos, v. and adj. *coupled.*
clostra, n. *cloister.*
cludere, v. *to conclude, to rejoin.*
clusura, see **clasura.**
(in) co, adv. *where.*
(in) co[1], **quo, in quo**, adv. *where.*
co[2], **quo, in co, in quo: 1.** *as, just as, in the manner or in the extent that*; **1a.** *in the manner in which, according to what*; **1b.** ***co … et***: *insofar as*; **2.** *according to*; **2a. secundu(m) (in) co:** *according to (how)*; **dave co:** *after*; **dae co:** *since*; **de co:** *when*; **co et:** *in the same way that.*
coallos, see **cavallu.**
cobertura, n. *roof.*
coda, n. *narrow valley, gorge.*
codali, pron. *that, such.*
codike, n. *codex, document.*
codina, n. *rock, boulder.*
cogere (cogant), v. *to cook.*
cognoschere, see cognoskere.
cognoskere (cognosco, cognoskemus, connoskimus, conoskimus, connoscit, cognovimus, congnovimus, congnoscerus, gonnesserun), v. **1.** *to know*; **1b.** *to recognise, to be aware*; **1c.** *to acknowledge* (an agreement); **2.** *to inherit.*
coha, n. *tail.*
coiada, adj. *married* (woman); see **coyare.**
coiamen, n. *hide, leather.*
coiarit, see **coyare.**
coiuare, see **coiuvare.**
coiuvanthia, n. *marriage.*
coiuvare (coiuare, coiuvedi, coiuedi, coniuedi, coniuvedi, coiuvait, coiugait, coniugait, coiuarus, coiuvadu, coiuvados, coiuados), v.: **1.** *to marry, to get married, to be married* (with); **1a.** *to arrange a marriage of one person with another person.* See also **coyare.**
coladu (colados), v., past part.: *enlisted.*
colbadu (colbadas), adj. *paired, joined together.*
colivertu (colivertos), n. *social category of free men, subject to certain obligatory works or services to a lord.*
colkitra, n. *blanket, quilt.*
collare (collat), v. *to go up, to proceed, to pass, to climb* (always said of the trend of the border).
collatura, n. *passage, trip.*

colleanes, see **golleanes.**
collecta, n. *the assembly of the realm, with the iudike, ecclesiastics, curators,* **maiorales** (lords and those of high social standing); see also **sinodu.**
colletoriu, n. *meeting place* (for hunting).
collire, v. 1. *to collect*; 2. *to keep together*; 3. *to pick, to collect, to gather fruit(s).*
colliri, see **collire.**
colore, n. *colour*; in the locution **supta specie et colore:** *under the pretext of.*
colpu, n. *beating, hit.*
comandamentu (comandamentos), n. *order, intimation.*
comandare, v. *to order, to charge.*
comandicia, see **acomandicia.**
combentu, n. *agreement.*
combersaresi, v. *to make oneself a lay brother or sister.*
combersione, n. *conversion, making oneself lay brother or sister.*
combersu, see **conversu.**
combidadu, see **cumbidari.**
come, conj.; (showing) *how, as, in what way.*
comente (et), comenti (et), conj. 1. *as, in the same way*; 2. *in what condition* 3. *when, as soon as.*
comiadu, n. *licence.*
cominalimente, see **comunalimente.**
comittere (comissidu, comissu), v. 1. *to commit*; 2. *to order, to give or entrust the task.*
commandare (commandait, cumandait), v. *to order.*
commemorationem, n. *record.*
committeresi (mi committo), v. *to make oneself a lay brother or sister.*
communariu, see **comunariu.**
commo, see **como.**[1]
commune, adj. *communal.*
como,[1] adv. *now*; ***dae como inantis***: *from now on.*
como,[2] adv. and conj. *as, in the way in which.*
comonalimenti, see **comunalimente.**
comonamenti, adv. *collectively.*
comonargio, see **cumonargiu.**
comonargiu, n., see **cumonargiu.**
comonis, see **cumoni.**
compagnia, n. *company*; **in compagnia de pari**, *in company with each other.*
compangia, see **compagnia.**
compangiu (compangios, compangius), n. *companion, colleague in an assignment.*

comparare, see **comporare.**
compare, v. *to appear.*
compatre, n. *godfather.*
compellere (compellit·inde·llu), v. *to force, to obblige*; **compellere a chertu**, *to give rise to a judicial dispute, to bring to trial or to court.*
complere (complidu, complilli, clomperuntimi), see **clompere.**
compliri, see **clompere.**
compleri, see **clompere.**
compora (comporas), n. *purchase.*
comporadore, n. *buyer, the purchasing agent.*
comporare (comporadu), v. *to buy, to purchase.*
comporu, n. *purchase.*
compromissione, n. *agreement, arbitration proceeding.*
compromissu (compromissos), n. *settlement, arbitration.*
compte, see **conte.**
comunalimente, adv. *collectively, together.*
comunalimenti, see **comunalimente.**
comunariu, n. *land of common use.*
comune, always in the adverbial locution ***in comune*** or ***ad comune***: *in common.*
comuni, see **commune.**
conbentu, see **combentu.**
conbersu, see **conversu.**
concha, n. **1.** *vessel, bowl*; **2.** *valley.*
conciare, see **conzare.**
concientia, see **conscientia.**
concordia, n. *concord, agreement reached within a collegiate body.*
condace, see **condage.**
condage, n. **1.** *condaghe*; *cartulary, collection of registered deeds or records concerning legal disputes, judicial decisions, donations, exchanges*, etc; **1a.** it would also seem to indicate *a single act or document.*
condaghi, see **condage.**
condagis, see **condage.**
condague, see **condage.**
condemnare (condemnaverit, condempnaverit, condempnatus), v. *to condemn*; but above all *not to recognise, not to observe an ordinance, to ensure that it is not observed.*
condemnaptione, see **condennatione.**
condempnari (condennent, condempnadu, condemnadu, condennado), v. *to condemn.*
condempnagione, see **condennatione.**

condennare, v. *to annul, to cancel.*
condennatione, n. 1. *sentence, conviction*; 2. *fine, financial penalty.*
conditione, n. *social status.*
condoma, n. *married couple of servants.*
conduire (condutu), v. *to bring, to lead.*
condutore, n. *conductor* (of a horse).
condutu, see **conduire.**
confesare, see **confessare.**
confessare (confesedi), v. 1. *to confess, to administer confession, to collect last wills*; 2. *to recognise one's own fault*; 3. *to state ones* (last) *will in confession*, 4. *to reveal.*
confessione, n. 1. *confession* (public admission of a legally relevant fact which has consequences detrimental to the subject or favourable to the other party); 2. *legal declaration.*
confesso, see **confessu.**
confessu, n. *confessed criminal, self-confessed.*
confinadu (confinadas), adj. *bordering, neighbouring.*
confinare, v. *to border, to be adjoining.*
confine (confines), n. *border, boundary.*
confirmare (confirmo, confirmeti), v. *to confirm* (usually a donation).
confiscare (confischint, confiscadus), v. *to confiscate, to forfeit.*
confortare (confortaverit), v. *to enforce, to ensure that an ordinance is applied and observed.*
conforzare, see **confortare.**
congiadu, see **cungiare.**
coniadus, see **cungiare.**
coniugait, see **coiuare, couvare.**
coniuvedi, see **coiuare, couvare.**
connadu, n. *brother-in-law.*
connatu, see **connadu.**
connoschere, see **cognoskere.**
connoscit, see **cognoskere.**
connoskimus, see **cognoskere.**
conoschente, adj. and n. *acquaintance, well known person.*
conoschire, see **cognoskere.**
conperei, see **comporare.**
conporu, see **comporu.**
conscientia, n. *conscience.*
conscritu (conscritos), n. *enrolled* (in a list of those qualified for office).
conseghere, see **conseguire.**

conseguire, v. *to reach.*
consentiente (consentientes), n. *consenting, accessory, accomplice.*
consentimentu, n. 1. *consent*; 2. in the locution **in consentimentu**: *in complicity.*
consentire (consentivit, consentii), v. 1. *to agree,* 2. *to allow.*
consentivili (consentivilis), n. *consenting, accessory, accomplice.*
conservantia, n. *preservation.*
conservare, v. *to conserve, to maintain, to keep.*
considerare (consideradu, considerando), v. *to consider.*
consigiare, v. *to give advice.*
consigiu, n. 1. *counsel, advice with legal force*; 2. *collegiate body*; **dare unu homini pro consigiu**: *to assign for defence counsel*; **avere consigiu cum**: *to take counsel with.*
consignare (consignadu), v. *to assign.*
constituire (constituimus), v. *to direct, to dispose, to establish.*
constringhant, see **constringere.**
constringere (constringhant, constritu, constrictos), v. *to compel, to oblige.*
constritu, see **constringere.**
consumare(·si) (consumant), v. *to impoverish.*
contadu, see **contari.**
contari (contadu), v. *to count, to put into account.*
conte, n. *count* (nobility).
contenne (contenit, contennet, contennit), v. *to contain* (with reference to the chapters of the law).
contestare, v. *to contest.*
contigere (contingeret), v. *to happen.*
continuamente, adv. *frequently.*
contissa, n. *countess.*
contra, prep. *against*; in union with the verb **faghere** (**contra fassant, contra fagheret**, etc.): *to contravene, to transgress.*
contractu, n. *contract.*
contrada, n. *country, territory, district.*
contrahente (contrahentes), n. *contracting party.*
contrariu, in contrariu, n. *in contrast, in opposition.*
contribuiri, v. *to contribute.*
contro, prep. *against.*
contrubuhire, see **contribuiri.**
contu, n. *count*; in the locution **fagheri contu de**: *to account to.*
convenne (convenit, convegnat), v. 1. *to convene, to consent in court, to establish, to agree with what has been established*; 2. *to be appropriate, necessary, convenient.*

conventu,[1] n. *convent.*
conventu,[2] n. *agreement.*
conversacione, see **conversatione.**
conversare, v. *to become a lay brother or sister.*
conversaresi (mi converso, mi comberso, mi combersu, mi converto, mi combersai, conversaitsi, conversesi, conversessi, se converseti), v. *to make oneself a lay brother or sister.*
conversatione, n. *making oneself a lay brother or sister.*
converssatione, see **conversatione.**
conversu, n. *lay brother or sister.*
convertire (convertischat·si), v. *to convert, to use differently.*
convincere (convintu, convinto), v. *to prove the guilt of an accused.*
conzadore, n. *tanner of hides.*
conzare, v. *to tan hides.*
coopertu (coopertas), adj. *covered, lined.*
coperclata(s), n. *cover.*
coradoria, see **curadoria.**
coram (Latin), prep. *in the presence of.*
corbu (corvos), n. *crow.*
corda, n. *rope, cord*; **mittiri in** *or* **a corda:** *to tether with a rope.*
corgiu, n. *hide, leather.*
coriu, n., see **corgiu.**
corognu, see **coroniu.**
corona de logu, n. *hearing or judicial assembly of the realm or iudicato.*
corona de sa kida, n. *iudike's college hearing.*
corona, n. *judicial hearing; assizes in which justice is administered*; **corona (de chida) de berruda:** *a particular court of justice composed of* **probiviri** *or* **prudhommes** *subjected to taking-turns*; (so called because it was composed of men equipped with the **verrutu** *or* **berrutu**, a sharp throwing weapon, or so called (**de berruda**), or because these men were suitable for carrying weapons); **lieros de sa corona:** *free men who make up the assembly*; **corona de logu, corona de iudike:** *court, assembly presided over by the iudike*; **corona de kida de verruda:** *the judicial panel in the judicial assembly* (*or* **corona**), *formed by the* **prudhommes** (**bonos homines**), *mounted militia who had as their insignia* the **verrutu** *or* **berrutu** (throwing weapon) and were required to perform this service and public office according to a shift schedule; ***corona de***: *assizes presided over by*; **corona de sinodo**: *assizes, assembly held on Assumption Day*; ***corona de sanctu Petru***: *assizes assembly held on the feast day of St Peter*; **arreere, regere corona:** *to preside over the assembly*; **tenne corona:** *to take legal action* (against somebody): **stringere corona:** *to convene the court or assize.*

corongius, see **coroniu.**

coroniu (coronius), n. *boulder, peak of a mountain relief.*

Corpus, *Corpus* (*Christi*), n. *the body* (of Christ); **sa festa dessu Corpus de Christus:** *the feast of Corpus Christi.*

corpus, n. 1. *body;* 2. *corpse;* 3. *the body* (as opposed to the soul).

correcta, see **corrigere.**

correctione, n. *punishment.*

correre (correndo), v. *to ride, to let the horse run.*

corria (corrias), n. *ground strip with lineal measurement value.*

corrigere (corrigemus, correcta), v. *to correct, to amend, to reform* (said about the Carta de Logu).

corrudu, adj. *cuckold.*

cortaticu, n. *land relating to a farmyard.*

corte (cortes), n. 1. *property, farm complex, farmyard;* 2. *centre organised for production* (and thus distinct from mere land ownership); 3. *the residence of the iudike, his family, his entourage,* 4. *the possessions of the iudike* 5. *court, stately residence;* 5b. *archiepiscopal residence;* 6. *seat of the administrative activity of a monastery;* 7. *cattle pen.*

corvos, see **corbu.**

cosa, see **causa.**

cositas, adj. *stitched, sewn.*

costa (a), prep. *side* (of), *next to.*

costa (costas), n. (mountain) *side.*

costare, v. *to cost.*

cote, n. *pebble, stone.*

cotina, see **codina.**

cotinatha, n. *rocky.*

cottu, adj. *boiled* (said of a hide or leather).

cavalcare, v. *to ride a horse.*

covaligharit, see **cavalcare.**

covallo, see **cavallu.**

covallus, see **cavallu.**

coyada, adj. *married woman.*

coyamentu (coyamentos), n. *marriage.*

coyanza, n. *marriage.*

coyare (coyada), v. *to marry;* 2. *to get married.* See also **coivare.**

crabas, see **cabra.**

credensa, see **credenza.**

credentia, see **credenza.**

credenza, n. *belief, faith, credit;* 1. in the phrase **iurare in grughi de credentia:** *to*

take an oath on cross of belief (that is, to take an extrajudicial liberating oath made between contenders with thumb and index finger crossed); 2. **iuradu de credentia:** *trusted juror*; 3. **fagheri credenza:** *to give trust credit*; 4. **in credenza:** *on loan, by overdraft.*

credere (cretidu, creditu, cretitu, crettidu, chertido, chertitu), v. 1. *to believe, to take into consideration*; 2. to *be convinced of*; 3. in the locution **de credere:** *worthy of faith.*

creditore, n. *creditor.*

creer, see **credere.**

cretidu, see **credere.**

cretitu, see **credere.**

crettitu, see **credere.**

crimen, n. *crime.*

criminale (criminales), n. and adj. *criminal*; **cosas criminales:** *criminal cases.*

criminosu (criminosa), adj. always in the phrase **paraula criminosa:** *criminal word,* meaning *charge of criminal relevance.*

cruke, n. *cross, crucifix.*

cua, in the adv. locution **a cua:** *in secret, covertly.*

cuare (cuavat), v. *to hide.*

cuba, n. *barrel, cask.*

cubita, see **cubitu.**

cubitu, n. *cubit, length measurement* (for fabrics).

cucuru, n. *small hill.*

cucutha, n. *top.*

cue, adv., *there, in that place.*

cui,[1] dative relative pron. *to whom.*

cui,[2] see **cue.**

cuiu, cuia, relative adjective, possessive concordant in gender and number with the noun to which it refers: *whose, of whom, of which*; **si non boghant ad claru in cuia chida si at faguere su perdimentu:** *unless they prove in whose watch shift the loss will have been caused.*

cuke, adv. *there, in that place.*

culivertu, see **colivertu.**

cullu, cullo, culle, culla, cullos, pron. *that, those.*

culpa, n. *guilt, responsibility.*

culpabili (culpabilis), adj. *guilty.*

cum, prep. *with*; **cum sciò siat causa qui:** *because, since*; **cum iustu titulu:** *rightly.* See also **cun.**

cum, see **cun.**

cumbersaresi, see **conversaresi.**

cumbidari (combidadu), v. *to invite.*
cummitere (cummitendo), v. *to create unity, a connection.*
cummoni, adj. *common*; **su utili cummoni**: *the common profit.*
cumonali, adj. in the adverbial locution **ad cumonali**: *jointly to, together.*
cumonargiu, n. *soccidary.*
cumone, see **comune.**
cumoni (comonis), n. *contract of agistment.*
cun, prep. *with, together with*; **1.** it may indicate a condition accompanying an action: **cun boluntate de pare**: *by mutual consent*; **2.** it may have the sense of *long, following the same path as*; **3.** it may introduce a gerund; **a pari cun**: **et ferit a pare cun su monimento**: (the border) *rejoins the tomb*; **in pari** or **impari cun**: *together with*; **(segaresi) de pari cun**: *to divide, to separate* (a piece of land from another): **et segatsi de pare cun Zinzau**: *and it is separated from* (the land of) *Zinzau.*
cunbentum, n. *meeting.*
cuncuba, n. *mistress, concubine.*
cunda[1], adv. *there, in that place.*
cunda[2], see **cunde.**
cunde (cunda, cundos): prep. + pron. *with him or her or them.*
cundos, see **cunde.**
cunduri (de rocca), n. *short robe worn beneath clothing.*
cungiadura, n. *fence*; *the construction of a fence.*
cungiare (cuniari, chungiare, cungiadu, cuniadas, cunyadas, coniadas), v. *to fence.*
cuniadu (cuniadus), n. *enclosed cultivated land.*
cuniadura, see **cungiadura.**
cuniari, see **cungiare.**
cuniatu, see **cuniadu.**
cunsiiu, n. *counsel*, in the occurrence **fegerunt cunsiiu cun Saina Tussia, cia ipsoro**: *they took counsel with Sabina Tussia, their aunt.*
cupa, n. *barrel, cask.*
cura, n. *care, protection, surveillance, custody.*
curador, see **curadore.**
curadore (curatore, curadores, curatores), n. **1.** *curator, a legal and administrative officer (representing the iudike in the various districts or* **curatorías**); **curatore maiore**: *head* curatore, maybe *master of palace.* **2.** *guardian of minors.*
curadoría (curadorías, curatoría), n. **1.** *administrative, judicial or royal and territorial district in which the iudicato or realm was divided, subject to the jurisdiction of the* **curadore**; **2.** *safeguard: a legal arrangement whereby a person assumes the representation of a child or a minor.*

curatore (curator, curador, curatori), n. *curator, senior functionary of a district.* See also **curadore.**

curatori, see **curadore.**

curatoría, n., see **curadoría.**

curbu, adj. *curved.*

curia, n. maybe a variant of **curria** or **corria**: *measuring rope.*

curiam (Latin), n. *court.*

curte, see **corte.**

cusu, see **cussu.**

cusse: demonstrative pron. always referring to a person: *this, he, the said person.* See also **cussu.**

cussu (cusu, cusse, cussos, cussa, icussa, cussas), pron. *that, those.*

custu (icustu, custa, kusta, icusta, custos, kustos, custus, icustus, custas), pron. *this, these.*

cuyli, n. *sheepfold.*

D

da, see **dave.**

daa, see **dave.**

dadu, n. *a land tax.*

dae, prep., *from, since,* **da inde a:** *from there to*; **dae nou**: *again*; **dae hui**: *from where*; **dae ca:** *since.* See also **dave.**

daenante, prep. and adv. 1. *before, in front* (of); 2. *previously.* See also **davenante.**

daenanti, see **daenante.**

daessa, see **dave.**

dainde, adv. *from there.*

damnigiare, v. *to harm, to hurt, to wound.*

dampno, see **damnu.**

dampnu, see **damnu.**

damno, see **damnu.**

damnu, n. *damage.*

danno, see **damnu.**

dannu, see **damnu.**

dare (do, damus, dei, daili, dedi, deit, dedi, detj, det, dait, derunt, darunt, derant, avia iadu, aviat datu, dent, daret, dandomi, datu). v. 1. *to give*; 2. *to donate*; 3. *to give, to deliver*; 4. *to cede*; 5. *to give in return or in compensation*; **dare in potestate:** *to give in to someone's power*; **dare in manus:** *to give into the hands* (of); **dare disciplina:** *to make someone subject to the discipline* (of);

dare asoltura: *to grant permission*; **dare cambiu**: *to make an exchange* (with someone); **torrari a dari**: *to return, to redeliver*; **dari incontra**: *to render against*; **dari ad cumoni**: *to entrust* (in a contract of agistment); **dari ad intendere**: *to warn*.

dassare, v. *to leave*.

datu, n. *donation, charitable gift*.

datura (daturas), n. *donation*.

daunde, adv. 1. *whence*; 2. *by which, by means of which, certifying that*.

dave (+ definite article: **dassu, daessa**), prep. 1. *from, away from*; *of*; 2. with time value: *since*; 3. complement of agent or of medium or cause: *by*; **dave** ***or*** **dae co**: *after, since, because*; **dave kunde**: *after which, after that*; **da ke**: *since*. See also **dae** and **da**.

davananti, see **davenante**.

davenanti, prep. *before, in front of*.

davinde, adv. *from there, from then*.

de, di (+ definite article: **dessu, dessa, dessos, dessas**): prep. 1. *of*; 2. *from*; 3. *about*; **de mesus**: *placed among or between, in common with*; **binchidu de raxioni**: *won according to justice*; **qui non ischiat s'unu de s'atero**: *that no one may know what the others know*.

de co, conj. *since, when, where*.

de fattu, adverbial locution: *de facto*.

deber (debent, devent, deviat, deit, dedi, deppiat, depiat), v. *must, to have to, to have an obligation to* (combined with infinitive gives the value of possible or future conditional): **Et, si perunu homine suo deit molestare sa clesia**: *And, if anyone should complain to the church*.

debere, v. *to owe*.

debilitadu, adj. *maimed*.

debita, adj. *proper, appropriate*.

debitu, see **deppidu**.

debitore, n. *debtor*.

debitu, see **deppidu**.

dece, cardinal number: *ten*.

decem et octo, cardinal numeral: *eighteen*.

declarare, v. *to declare, to confess, to affirm* (officially), *to notify an authority*.

dedi, see **dari**.

defectu, n. *defect, shortcoming*.

defendere (defesu), v. 1. *to defend* (in court); 2. *to act in self defence*.

defensa, n. *defence* (in court); 2. *self defence*.

defesu, see **defendere**.

deffinire (deffinidu, diffinidu), v. *to conclude, to settle a controversy or a dispute*.

dege, see **dece.**
deghe, see **dece.**
deglutire (deglutivit), v. *to swallow.*
deinde, adv. *then.*
deleadu, adj. *restless.*
delegare (delego, delegai, delegarat), v. *to assign, to direct, to transfer.*
deliberare (deliberadu), v. *to deliberate, to sanction*; **cum deliberadu consigiu:** *with deliberate counsel.*
delictu, see **delittu.**
delinchente, see **delinquente.**
delinquente, n. and adj. *delinquent, criminal.*
delinquere (delinquido) v. *to commit a crime, to break the law.*
delinquido, see **delinquere.**
delito, see **delittu.**
delittu, n. *crime.*
demandare, see **dimandare.**
demandari, see **dimandare.**
de mesus, adv. *placed among or between, in common with.*
demostrare, v. *to prove.*
denanti, see **davenanti.**
denaris, see **dinari.**
denegare (denegarit), v. *to deny.*
dent, see **dari.**
denunciadore, n. *complainant.*
denunciare (denunciado), v. *to report, to bring something to the attention* (of a competent authority).
denunciatione, n. *complaint, denunciation, formal communication* (to a competent authority).
deo, see **ego.**
depiat, see **deber.**
depiant, see **deber.**
depidu, see **deppidu.**
deposidu, n. *deposit.*
deppidu, n. *debt.*
depus, prep. *at, along, after, by, near to.*
depusti, see **depus.**
deputadu, n. *deputed, appointed to an office.*
derectu, see **derettu.**
deressent, see **deretare.**
derettu, adv. and prep. *directly, in the direction of, toward.*

deretare (deressent), v. *to lead, to direct.*
deretu, n. (*the*) *right, that which is right.*
derredali, n. *container and capacity measurement for liquids.*
desastros, see **disastro**.
descendens, n. *descendant.*
descendere (descendant), v. *to come from.*
deseredare, v. *disinherit.*
desiderare (desiderando), v. *to desire.*
desonore, n. *dishonour.*
despendiu, n. *expense.*
destimoniu (destimonios), n. *witness*. See also **testimoniu**.
destra, locative adv. **a destra**: *right, on the right, to the right.*
destrittu, adj. in the phrase **parente destrittu**: *close relative.*
destru (destra), adj. always in the phrase **manu destra**: *the right hand.*
destruere, v. (in formulaic Latinate clause): *to destroy.*
desviari (desviadu), v. *to induce, to divert to an unlawful action.*
det, see **dari**.
determinare (determinadu), v. *to determine.*
Deus, Deu, deum, n. *God.*
deus, n. *God*; **etiam deus**, conj. (and) *also*; **nen etiam deus**: *not even.*
devangelium, n. Gospel. See also **Evangelium** and **bangeleu**.
devet, see **deber**.
deviat, see **deber**.
devito, see **deppidu**.
dexendentes, see **dixendente**.
dextra, see **destra**.
di[1], see **de**.
di[2], see **die**.
diabolus (in formulaic Latinate clauses), n. *devil.*
diaconus (diaconum), n. *deacon.*
diant, see **dari**.
dicere, v. always in formulaic Latinate clause: *to say.*
diclarare, v. *to declare, to confess, to affirm* (officially), *to notify an authority.*
dictu, v., past participle: *said, mentioned.*
die (dies), n. **1.** *day*; (**ad**) **de die**: *by day, during the day*; **2.** *day's work*, **die a die**: *day by day.*
differentia, n. *disagreement, divergence, difference.*
diffinitivu (diffinitiva), adj. in the phrase **sentencia diffinitiva**: *final judgement.*
digitu, n. *finger*, but in the only occurrence recorded in the phrase **a digitu**, the meaning is (to hunt animals) *by hand or bare-handed.*

diligentemente, adv. *properly, diligently.*
dilinquente, see **delinquente.**
dimanda, n. *application, question, request.*
dimandare (domandadu), v. **1.** *to ask*; **2.** *to seek, to request*; **3.** *to claim*; **4.** *to apply*; **5.** *to call someone to account.*
dinari (dinaris), n. **1.** *a twelfth part of a* **sollu** (coin); **2.** *money, monetary unit, denarius*; **homini de dinaris:** *man paid per day.*
dintro, adv. and prep. *in, inside.*
directu, adj. *rightful*; **iuighi Margiani padre nostru, in qua directu iuyghi de Arbaree:** *iudike Mariano, our father, as the rightful iudike of Arborea.*
diretu, see **deretu.**
diritu, n. *fee, right, tax, sum of money claimed for the trade and transport of goods.*
disastro, n. *unexpected, unintentional or accidental event.*
disciplina, n. *discipline, rule.*
discipulu, n. *apprentice.*
discordia, n. *discord, disagreement.*
discretamente, adv. *thoughtfully and accurately.*
discricioni, n. *discretion*; in the phrase **a discricioni de (issa e totu):** *at* (its own) *discretion.*
discu (discos) n. *bowl.*
diseredare, see **deseredare.**
disfaghere·si (disfaghint), v. *to go to ruin.*
diskere, v. *to learn, understand.*
dispendiu, see **despendiu.**
dispesa (dispesas), n. *expense.*
disponere (disposuerunt) (in formulaic Latinate clause), v. *to dispose.*
ditare (ditava), v. **1.** *to be due to, to belong to*; **2.** *to be up to somebody* (to do something). See also **gitare.**
dito, see **dictu.**
ditu, see **dictu.**
dittu, see **dictu.**
dividere (dividat·si, divisa), v. *to divide, to share.*
divisidu, divisidos, adj. *divided and of different opinion.*
divisione, n. *dissension.*
dixastro, see **disastro.**
dixendente (dixendentes), n. *descendant, blood relative.*
dixerit, see **dicere.**
doa, see **doha.**
doda (dodas), n. **1.** *matrimonial dowry, all assets as a contribution to marriage*;

dari in dodas: *to give in dowry*; **2.** *marriage contract stipulated with a dowry, dowry regime*; **coyari a dodas:** *to marry with a dowry.*
dogna, see **omnia.**
dognia, see **omnia.**
doha, n. *strip of land dug as a fire-trench.*
domadu, see **domatu.**
domandadu, see **dimandare.**
domatu (domatos, domados), adj. *tamed* (ox or oxen); *domesticated, trained.*
domestia, see **domestica.**
domestica, n. *farmland, or farmstead of a farm complex*; *cleared land* (derived from **domestica mansion**). See also **domu.**
domestiga, see *domestica.*
dominica, dominice (genitive case in a Latin phrase), n. *Sunday*; **dominica de palma:** *Palm Sunday.*
dominiga, see **dominica.**
domistia, see **domestica.**
domna, see **donnu.**
domo, n. **1.** *house* **1.1. domo de clesia:** *ecclesiastical house, sacristy*; **2.** *the centre of a rustic complex*; in ancient Sardinia where the **domo** was central to several rustic and pastoral houses (**domos, cortes**) with cultivated and closed lands; **3.** *home, house to be understood as a place of residence or work*; **libellos de dommos:** *agrarian contracts by which a land was given in usufruct.*
domne (Latin: feminine genitive singular): *lord.* See **donnu.**
dommo, see **domo.**
domnu (domna), see **donnu.**
domu, see **domo.**
donamentu, n. *donation.*
donare (donari, donailli, donarunt, donandi), v. *to donate, to give.*
donatione, n. *donation.*
donna, n. *lady, wife*; **donna de logu**, n. *first lady of the realm*; *queen.*
donni, see **omnia.**
donia, see **omnia.**
donnia, see **omnia.**
donnicalia, n. *domain pertaining to the iudike or a lord.*
donnicellu, n. *title used by the sons and immediate relatives of the ruling iudike*; *prince or young overlord.*
donniçellu, see **donicellu.**
donnichellu, see **donnicellu.**
donnicu, n. and adj. *property, relating to state property.*
donnigaia, see **donnicalia**

donnigellu (donnigella), see **donnicellu.**
donnikellu, see **donnicellu.**
donnigu (donniga), adj. *belonging to the iudike.*
donnu (donna, donnos), n. 1. *lord, lady*; title that is given to the iudike, lords or office-holders, bishops, archbishops, priors, **curatores**, **mandatores**, **armentarios**, **presbiteros**, etc.; the feminine is the title of the iudike's wife (also called **regina** or queen, and of women of high social standing); 2. *master, owner*, (the one who, as a lord, enters in a contract of agistment).
dono, see **donu.**
donu, n. *gift.*
doppiu, n. and adj. *double.*
dotatione, n. *donation, equipment.*
dresta, see **destra.**
duas vias, adv. *twice.*
dubidu, n. *doubt, fear*; in the phrase **pro dubidu qui**: *because of the uncertainty of.*
dubitare, v. *to doubt*; *to fear* (especially death).
dubitari; see **dubitare.**
dubitosu, **dubitosos**, adj. *difficult, uncertain, of uncertain resolution.*
dubitu see **dubidu.**
ducentas, cardinal number: *two hundred.*
dughere (dughiri, dughant·loy, dughirint), v. *to lead, to take.*
dummodo, conj. *as long as, provided that, in such a manner.*
dunde, relative adv. *whence, from which, for which.*
dundi see **dunde.**
duos (duas, dues), cardinal number: *two.*
dura, adj: *hard.*
durante, prep. and v. present participle: *during, while.*
duranti, see **durante.**
dus, see **duos.**

E

e[1], see **et.**
e[2], see **ive.**
eadem, *feminine* accusative **eandem** (Latin), pron. *the same.*
eam (Latin), pron. feminine pronoun accusative *her.*
eba, see **ebba.**
ebba, n. *mare.*

eccepto, see **exceptu.**
ecceptuadas, see **exceptare.**
ecclesia, see **clesia.**
eceptu, see **exceptu.**
eco, see **ecco.**
ecco, adv. *behold! So, so then*; **eccola** = **ecco** + pron. **la**, adv. *here or there he or she or it is!*
ecessu, n. *offence, crime, excess.*
echesiastigu, **echesiastigas**, adj. *ecclesiastical*; **regiones echesiastighas**: *ecclesiastical regions.*
ecclesia(s), see **clesia.**
ecussu, see **cussu.**
ed, see **et.**
edi, see **avere** (used in the periphrases of the conditional mode).
efectu: n. *effect, consequence*; **et appat valore et efectu**: *and have value and effect.*
ego, first person personal pron. I.
ei, see **avere** (past time).
electione, n. *discretion, choice*, in the locution **ad electione de**: *at the discretion or choice of.*
electos, see **ellegere.**
electu, see **ellegere.**
elike, n. *holly oak.*
ellegere (electu, electos); v. *to elect, to choose*. See also **alletu.**
emendare (emended), v. in the phrase **emendare su damnu**: *to pay compensation, to reimburse, to compensate for the damage.*
emere (emit) (Latin): v. *to buy.*
emmo, adv. *yes, certainly.*
ena, n. *stream, source or spring of water*; it can also refer to *low, marshy ground.*
ent, see **avere.**
eneu (enea), adj: *person (man or woman) without heirs.*
eniu, see **eneu.**
enneru, n. *son-in-law.*
ent, see **aviri.**
enti, see **avere** (in the periphrases of the conditional mood).
eo[1] adv. *through there.*
eo[2] see **ego.**
ep(p)i, see **avere.**
Epiphania, n. *Epiphany.*
episcopu, see **piscobu.**

equa (equas), n. *mare.*
erema, adj. *uncultivated* (land).
eremare (eremadas), v. *to abandon, to remain uncultivated.*
ergere (ergetsi, ergesi), v. *to climb.*
erriu, n. *river, stream, watercourse.*
escongiari, see **ischungiare.**
espalesari, v. *to make a disclosure, to reveal, to report.*
essat, see **essire.**
esser (essere, est, esti, sunti, fudi, furunt, furuntu, siat, sia, sciat, siant, esseret, fussi, esseremus, esserent, fussi istetidu *or* a, edi essere, esendo, sendo, essendo), v. 1. *to be* (copula): **erat rezone ... levare de sa causa de su serbu:** *it was right ... to requisition the property of his servant*; **fiios de ankilla de juigi sunt:** *they are the sons of the servant of the iuigi*; 2. it affirms existence, the essence itself, the pure act, without further determination: **iudike qui hat a esser de post me:** *the iudike who shall be after me*; **Custos bi furunt kerra binki:** *These men were present when I won*; 3. *to stay in, to be in a place, to be somewhere*; **essere + a:** *to belong to* (someone); in locution: **essere + a + inf.:** to be to, to need; **essere + de + inf.:** *to be to, must*; **esser in:** *to be part of, to be implicated in*; *to be in, to be employed for* (something); *to last*: **quant aet esser ipsa generatione:** *as long as the generation will last.*
essire (essit, essia), v. 1. *to come out, to join, to go forth*; **essirunt a destimonios:** *they appeared as witnesses*; 2. *to constitute*: **paraula iniuriosa qui 'ndi essirit crimini:** *insulting word that constitutes a crime.*
essirit, see **essire.**
estadea, see **stadea.**
esterminare, v. *to destroy, to make sure that something no longer exists.* See also **isterminare.**
et, conj. *and, and also, and even*; **comente et:** *as*; **quali** *or* **chali et:** *as, in the same manner*; **ver et simili:** *verosimilar, likely.*
eti, see *avere* (in periphrases in the conditional).
etiam deus, conj. *also*; **ma etiam deus via plus:** *but also, all the more*; **nen etiam deus:** *not even.*
etro, adv. *yet, still.*
eu[1], see **ego.**
eu[2], pron. *him.*
evangelista (evangelistas), n. *Evangelist.*
Evangelium, n. *Gospel.*
exaltamentu, n. *enhancement, increase.*
examinamento, n. *examination, investigation.*
examinare, v. *to examine.*

exceptare (exceptadu, exceptada, ecceptuadas), v. *to exclude, to except*; in the locution **exceptadu qui:** *excepted that.*

excepto, see **exceptu.**

exceptu, prep. and conj. *except, other than, besides, unless.*

excusa, n. *excuse, justification.*

executioni, n. *execution, implementation*, always in the locution **mandare ad executione:** *to implement, to make what has been established enforceable.*

exemplare, v. *to make a copy.*

exire, see **essire.**

exivit, see **essire.**

expresamenti, adv. *expressly.*

exstra, adv. *outside*; **in iudiciu et exstra:** *in judgement and extrajudicially.*

exterminare, see **isterminare.**

exterminatu, see **isterminare.**

F

fa, see **faba.**

faba, n. *fava bean.*

facer, v. *to make, to do*. See also **faghere.**

fachi, see **faghi.**

faço, see **faghere.**

facke, in the adverbial locution **a facke:** *openly.*

factu, n. 1. *fact, business, interest, profit*; 2. In the locutions **per issu factu modo qui, pro si factu modu qui, per issu fatu modu qui:** *so that, for such a way that, in such a way that.*

factu, in locution: 1a. **in factu:** *according*; 1b. *after*; 2. **de factu, di factu, de fatu:** *in fact*, **de facto:** *de facto* (not *de iure*).

factu, see **fattu.**

fagere (fager, fagiri, fagemi, fagire (in cond. mood, enti fagire), fakere, fazo, ffaço façu, facio, fato, faget, fagemus, fagint, faguint, fagiat, fagiamus, fakiant, faguiant; fegi, fegit, fecit, fegerus, fegerunt, fegerun, feguerunt, fekerunt, fegerat, factu), v. 1. *to do, to make*; 2. *to build*; 3. *to edit, to write, to draft*; 4. *to establish, to found*; 5. *to become*: **sos maystros de linna qui si fagherint maystros:** *carpenters who are master craftsmen* 5. in locution: **fagere liberu:** *to grant freedom to*; **fagere kertu:** *to bring legal action against somebody*; **fagere boluntade:** *to fulfil someone's will*; **fagere via:** *to take the road, to travel, to traverse*; **fager corona:** *to convene a hearing, to meet in assembly*; **fagere** + noun indicating monetary value: *to appraise*; **fagere tortu:** *to do*

someone wrong, to do what is not (considered) *right*; **fagere istorpiu:** *to damage*; *to wrong or to insult* (someone); **fagere consiiu:** *take advice from*; **su malu fageri:** *evil acting*; **contra faghere:** *to contravene, to transgress*; **fagheri lamentu:** *to file a complaint*; **fagheri briga:** *to start a fight*; **fagher defensa sua:** *to defend oneself*; **fagheri ficas:** *to make the sign of a fig* (a rude gesture made with the thumb); **fagheri habitationi impari:** *to dwell with someone, to cohabit*; **fagheri malizia:** *to counterfeit*; **fagheri mercantia:** *to engage in trade*; **faghere sa mostra:** *to parade*; **fagheri ragioni:** *to give reason, to give account*; **faker ckerbiclia:** *to compel by force*; **faker coiuvanthia:** *to agree to marry*; **faker liveru:** *to free someone from service*; **faker novu:** *to renew*; **faker turpe:** *to offend*; **faker pettita:** *to ask a female servant in marriage.*

faghi, n. *face.*

faghidore, n. *substitute.*

faha, see **faba.**

fakere, see **faghere.**

falare (falat), v. *to go down, to descend.*

falchoni; see **flacone.**

fallanza, n. *wrongdoing, adultery.*

fallidu, n. and adj. *defeated in court.*

falsidade, n. *falsehood.*

falsu, adj. *forged, false.*

falzu, falsu, adj.; *false*; **iurare falzu:** *to swear falsely*; **carta de notaiu falsa:** *false notarial charter*; 3. **mesura falsa:** *false measure*, **stadea falsa:** *rigged steelyard.*

fama, n. *fame, reputation*; **boe de mala fama:** *wild ox.*

famma, see **fama.**

famegiare, see **famigiali.**

famen, n. *food shortage.*

famigiali, n. *ancilliary worker, family member in service.*

famiia, n. *domestic servants.*

fanti, n. 1. in the phrase **fanti de lectu:** *concubine*; 2. **fantis:** *servants.*

fanxellu (fanxellos), n. *servant.*

farga, n. *millstone, crushing machine.*

fargala, n. *millstone, grindstone.*

fascas, n. in the locution **in fascas:** *in swaddling clothes.*

faschi, n. *bundle*; in the locution. **ligare in faschi:** *to bind* (e.g. hide) *in a bundle.*

fatu, n. *what one has, what one owns.*

favariu, n. *fava bean field.*

favore, n. *collaboration, aid, favour.*

favula, n. *story, lie.*

fazo, see **faghere.**

februarii, n. *February.*
fedu, n. *offspring.*
femina, n. *female, woman.*
fenariu, n. *hay field.*
fenestra, n. *window.*
fenu, n. *hay.*
fera, adj. in the phrase **abba fera:** *poisoned water.*
feria (ferias, feriis), n. *public holidays, days when judicial activities do not take place.*
feriada (feriadas), adj. in the phrase **dies feriadas:** *public holidays.*
ferida, n. *wound.*
ferre (ferit, feridu), v. *to wound.*
ferrer (si ferit, ferissi feritsi, si ferint), v. **1.** *to reach, to arrive, to come* (to); **2.** *to join with.*
ferro, see **ferru.**
ferru (ferros), n. *iron, weapon*; in the phrase **sinnare a fferro caldu:** *to brand* (hides) *with a red-hot iron.*
ferulariu, n. *field of ferula.*
festa, n. *festival, feast day.*
festivitate (Latin), n. *feast.*
fetu, n. *offpring.*
ffeu see **feu.**
ffura, see **fura.**
feu, n. *fief.*
fiat, v. *let it be*; in final formula: **fiat excomunicatu et maledictu de Deus:** *let him be excommunicated and may receive anathema by God.*
fica, n. *fig sign* (rude gesture of contempt).
fictu (fictas), adj. *standing*: **petras fictas:** *standing stones* (sometimes referring to ancient standing stones, menhirs etc.).
fictu, n. *rent*; in the phrase **terrali de fictu:** *tenant settler.*
ficu n. *fig, fig tree.*
fidado, see **fidadu.**
fidadu, adj. *endowed with trust.*
fide, n. *faith.*
fidele, n. *loyal, vassal.*
fidi, n. *faith, trust.*
figios, see **fiiu.**
figiu, n. *son, child.*
figu, n. *fig.*
fiiastru (fiiastros), n. *stepchild, stepson.*

fiiu (fiium, fiia, fiios, fiius, fiias), n. *child, son or daughter.*
filare (filent), v. *to spin.*
filiadura, n. *the part of an inheritance that relates to one of the benefactors' children.*
filiare, v. *to go on, to continue.*
filiu, see **fiiu.**
fina, prep. *until.*
fine, n. *end*; in the locution **in fine** it would seem mean *in the final stipulation that.*
fini in the locution **fini a tanto qui (infini a tantu qui)**: *as long as.* See also **infini.**
fios, n. *sons.*
firmado, v., past participle of **firmare**: *signed.*
firmadu, adj. *authenticated.*
firmadura, n. *authentication.*
firmu, adj. *fixed, settled.*
firmare, firmu: *to confirm, to subscribe.*
fisca, prep. *until, up to.*
fisca, prep. *up to.*
fittu, n. *rent*; in the phrase **terrales de fittu**: *tenants.*
flacone, n. *falcon.*
fliscare (fliscat, fliscatsi), v. said of the territorial border: *to close, to rejoin the point of departure.*
flumen, flumenes, n. *river, stream.*
foghu, fogu, fogho, n. *fire.*
fogiu, fogius, n. *sheet.*
fogu, n. *fire.*
foke, n. *mouth of a river.*
foliu, see **fogiu.**
fontana, see **funtana.**
foras, de foras, adv. 1. *out, outside*; 2. *except, with the exception.*
força: in the adv. locution **a força**: *illegally, without permission, forcibly.*
force, adv. and prep. *but rather, if not, except.* See also **borce.**
forchillos, n. *crossroads.*
forma, n. *form*; **in forma debita**: *in due form, correctly*; **forma de corona**: *mode of operation of the assizes*; **forma de iurados**: *the ordering of jurors*; **(cartas) in forma publica**: (documents) *for legal use.*
fornicare, v. *to have an extramarital relationship.*
forrithu (faker in), n. *to have a child outside wedlock.*
forrizu, n. *adultery* (esp. in the collocation of illegitimate children).

forsa, see **forza.**

forsi, adv. *maybe, perhaps, if it happens that.*

forte, adj. in the phrase **pro si forte modu qui:** *such that.*

fortunabili, adj. in the phrase **pro causa fortunabili:** *by fortuitous event, accident.*

forza, forsa, n. in the phrases: **in forza nostra:** *into our power, into our hands*; **levare per forza:** *to do violence* (to a woman); **tenne forza:** *to have value or force.*

fosadu, fossadu, n. *ditch, trench.*

fossu, n. *ditch, trench.*

fostigada, see **fustighare.**

frade n. *brother.*

fradi, see **frade.**

fradile, n. *cousin.*

fradri, see **frade.**

fraigare (fraigaat), v. *to build.*

fraile, n. *blacksmith's workshop.*

franchidadi, n. *allowance, exemption.*

franchu, adj. in the phrase **loghu francu:** *free place, exempt from the ordinary application of laws.*

francu (francos), adj. *free, exempt.*

frate carrale, n. *blood brother.*

frate de parthone, n. *co-owner of an asset.*

frate (frates), n. **1.** *brother*; **2.** of uncertain meaning, maybe *members of a group of* **libertados** (freedmen) *or* **colivertos** (freemen); **3.** *brother, monk.* See also **frade.**

frater, n. *brother, monk, friar.*

fratile, see **fradile.**

fraudare (fraudarit), v. *to defraud.*

fraudi, fraude, n. *fraud, deception.*

fravica, n. *building, construction.*

fravicatore, n. *builder.*

fraxinu, n. *ash tree.*

freargiu, n. *February.*

frebrer, n. *February.*

frevariu, n. *February.*

fronte, adv. *front of.*

fruchida, see **furchida.**

fructora, n. *fruit tree.*

fructu, n. *fruit, profit, gain*; **tempus de fructu:** *the time of harvesting or grape harvesting.*

fructura; see **fruttura.**
fruscu (fruscos), n. *butcher's broom* (*plant*).
frustadu, see **afrustare.**
fruttura, n. *fruit*; **tempus de fructura:** *time for the ripening and harvesting of fruit.*
frutu, n. *fruit* (but used collectively in reference to an *orchard or fruit tree plantation*).
frutura; see **fruttura.**
fudi, see **esser.**
fugimentu, n. *delaying, procrastination*; in the phrase (**per via de**) **fugimentu de tempus:** (*by way of*) *wasting time.*
fugire, see **fuire.**
fuire (fuivit, fuirit, fuhirint, fuidu), v. *to run away, to carry off, to flee, to escape* (said in the sense of *escaping from servile status*).
fundamentales, n. *in the phrase* **frades fundamentales:** *co-owners of a* **fundamentu.**
fundamentu, n. **1.** *estate, landed estate, real estate, building, immovable property, territorial property including land and livestock.* **2.** in some passages, this item is in correlation with **comporu** or **comporare** and would seem to have the meaning of *inherited or otherwise already possessed property* (also in relation to matrimonial law, which provides for the sharing of property acquired by spouses after marriage).
fundare (fundaverunt (Latin), apo fundadu), v. *to establish, to found.*
fundu (fundos, fundus), n. *head* (of a plant), *tuft*; *offshoot, side shoot* (of a tree); **a fundu de:** *at the foot of.*
fune, n. *rope-length, a piece of land.*
funtana, n. *fountain, well; spring.*
fura (furas), n. **1.** *theft*; **2.** *stolen goods*; **3.** in the adverbial locution **a fura** *or* **a ffura:** *covertly, secretly, fraudulently.*
furadissu (furadissa), n. *stolen goods*; **pro causa furadissa:** *concerning theft.*
furare (furait, furet, furedi, furarat), v. **1.** *to steal, to carry off, to seize*; **1a.** also in the sense of *to commit theft inside or from an institution.*
furca (furcas), n. *gallows.*
furcari, v. *to hang, to put up on the gallows.* See also **affurchare** and **infurchare.**
furcatura, n. *fork, crossroad.*
furcha, see **furca.**
furchida, n. *wooden halter* (wooden triangle put around the neck of pigs to prevent them from passing through hedges or fences).
furchillos, n. *fork on the road, crossroads.*
furicare, v. *to have an extramarital relationship.*

furisteri, adj., in the phrase **boe furisteri:** *extraneous ox.*
furoni, n. *thief.*
furrithu (faker in), see **forrithu.**
furru, n. *oven.*
furunt, see **esser.**
fusca, prep. *up to, even.*
fussi, see **esser.**
fuste albu, n. *poplar.*
fuste de virga, n. *pole* (measurement of extension).
fustes, n. *tree trunks.*
fusti, n. *rod, stake.*
fusticare, see **fustigare.**
fustigare (fustigei), v. *to flog, to cane, to whip.*
fustighare, see **fustigare.**

G

gallulesu, adj. *Gallurese, from Gallura.*
Gallulu, n. *Gallura, north-eastern iudicato of Sardinia.*
Gallure, see *Gallulu.*
gama, n. *herd of cattle.*
gamma, n. see **gama.**
ghammas, see **gama.**
gantu, see **cantu.**
gardare, see **guardare.**
gasi, adv. **1.** *so, in such a way, as much*; **2. gasi … comenti:** *both … and.*
ghasi, see **gasi.**
gedi, see **dare.**
generatione, n. *generation, posterity.*
generu, n. *son-in-law.*
genezu, n. *performance of compulsory labour due to the state or other authority.*
genezzario (jenezzariu de judigi), n. *supervisor; officer in charge of supervising artisanal work and manual labour owed to the iudike.*
genna, n. *door.*
genneru, see **generu.**
gente, n. *people.*
gercu, see **kercu.**
getadura, n. *length measurement corresponding to the distance of a thrown rod.*
getare (gittarellu, getatsi, getaitse, jetaitse, ietait), v. **1.** *to throw*, **2.** *to throw one-*

self; to drive out, to betake oneself; 2. *to drive out, to chase away*; 3. *to head towards.*

ghammas, see **gamma.**

ghasi, see **gasi.**

ghastare·si (ghastarit, gastarit), v. *to ruin, to injure oneself, to get unjures, to have an accident.*

ghitare (ietando, getadu), v. *to throw*; **getare bogis**: *to cast warning cries*; **getare a tterra**: *to throw to ground*; 2. *to be up, to be* (something) *incumbent to someone.*

ghiteu, see **chiteu.**

gholetorgiu, n. *the place of gathering for hunting.*

ghölliri, see **colliri.**

ghortellu, n. *knife.*

ghula, see **gula.**

giagaru, see **iagaru.**

giaghere, see **iaguere.**

gibulla, n. *onion.*

gienna, see **genna.**

gimilioni, n. *work obligation* (equivalent to the **arrobatia**).

ginithu bonum, n. *qualified service.*

gioso, see **giosso.**

giosso, adv. *down.*

giossu, see **giosso.**

giradoriu, n. *gutter, drainage ditch or channel.*

girare (girat, girarus, girerus, girarunt, kiraruntsi), v. 1. *to turn*; 2. in the locution **girare manu**: *to take turns in choosing, to turn, to yield the turn for choice* (always used in servant sharing); 3. *to go away or abandon* (service); 4. *to change opinion or decision*, 5. *to oppose, to object.*

giru: **in giru**, adv. *around.*

gisterru, n. *cistern, tank.*

gitare (gitat, gitavat), v. *to belong, to be entitled to*. See also **ditare.**

gitteu, pron. *that which, what*. See also **chiteu.**

glande, n. *acorn, glandiferous plantation.*

gloriosu (gloriosa), adj. *glorious.*

go, see **co.**

godales, see **codali.**

godire, v. *to benefit.*

golleanes, n. *members of a* **kita** *bound to the same service.*

gollettoriu, n. *meeting place* (esp. for hunting).

gollire, v. *to assign, to offer, to gather, to collect* (taxes).

gonnesserun, see **cognoskere.**
gordare, see **guardare.**
gorona, see **corona.**
gosi, adv. *so, as so, as such,* See also **gasi.**
gossi, see **gosi** and **gasi.**
gotale, adj. *such.*
gotalis, see **codali.**
gotantu, pron. and adv. *much.*
gracia, n. *grace*; in the phrases 1. **pro issa gracia de Deus**: *by the grace of God*; 2. **aviri gracia**: *to receive pardon, to be granted pardon* (for a crime); e.g. **In gratia de Deus et de sanctu Agustinu et de donnu meu iudike Dorgotori**: *In the grace of God and of St Augustine and of my lord, iudike Torchitorio.*
gradu, n. 1. *rank, status occupied in a social hierarchy*; 2. in the phrase **istare in su gradu issoro**: *to remain, to be kept in their good condition.*
grandissimo, adj. superlative: *very great.*
grandu, adj. *great.*
grathia, see **gracia.**
gratia, see **gracia.**
gratis, adv. *for free, at no cost.*
grisaione, n. *hedge, boundary hedge.*
grosso, adj. *intricate, controversial and difficult* (said of a court case).
grossu, see **grussu.**
gructas, n. *cave.*
grughi, n. *cross*, always in the phrase **grughi de credenza** *or* **de credentia** to indicate *an extrajudicial liberating oath made between contenders with thumb and index finger crossed.*
gruke, n. 1. *cross*, 2. *crucifix.*
grussu, adj. *large.*
guardare: v. 1. *to keep watch*; 2. *to take care.* See also **bardare.**
guardari (guardadu), see: **guardare.**
guardia, n. *custody, vigilance.*
guardianu, n. *overseer* (of gardens and orchards).
gubernare (gubernadu), v. *to govern.*
guisa, n. *way, manner*; **per modo et guisa qui**: *provided*: **per modo et guisa qui non fassant damno**: *provided they do no harm.*
guiteu, see **chiteu.**
gula, **ghula**, n. *throat.*
gulbare, n. *enclosure for livestock.*
gulvare, see **gulbare.**
guttiosa, adj. *dripping, bubbling.*

guttur, n. *path, lane.*
gutturu, n. *mountain gorge.*
guturu, n. *throat.*

H

habere (haberellu, habet, hant, habeat, habeant), see **avere**: these are mostly forms used in Latin or Latinised formulas.
habitanti, n. *dwelling.*
habitationi (habitatione, abitacione, aditioni, aydatione), n. **1.** *cultivated area in the vicinity of the village, including the village itself*; **abitatione de arare**: *cultivated fields subject to ploughing*; **2.** *dwelling.*
hat, see **avere.**
haviri (hant, haveret, haverit, havendo), see **avere.**
hec: *this* (feminine), always used in Latinising formulas.
hecco, see **ecco.**
hena, see **ena.**
herede, heredes, n. *heir.*
heredidadi, see **hereditadi.**
hereditadi, n. *inheritance.*
heres (Latin), n. *heir.*
heretamentu, n. *inheritance, hereditary succession.*
herriu, see **erriu.**
hierro, see **hierru.**
hierru, n. *winter*; **pardo de hierro**: *meadow reserved for grazing in winter.* See also **iverru.**
ho, see **o.**
hobedientes, n. and adj. *obedient.*
hobedire (obediret), v. *to obey.*
hochire, see **ochire.**
hoe[1], adv. *today.*
hoe[2], see **ubi.**
homicidiu, n. *murder, killing.*
homine (hominem homini, omine, homines), n. **1.** *man, person*; **1a.** often, and especially in the plural, the term refers to *servants*; **2.** the expression **homines bonus** must be understood to mean *men of high social standing, constituting a kind of nobility, who could serve as members of the judicial assembly, assizes or* **corona**; **3.** in the singular is most often used preceded by **perunu, neunu, alteru** with the meaning of indefinite: **ki non mi nde kertaret plus**

perunu homine (*nobody*): *that no one should make any further claims or complaint against me*; **cun levandosi ipse in pala de spiarella da omnia homini** (*anyone*): *taking upon himself the burden of answering for eviction against anyone*; **Et non fuit tale homine** (*no one, not ... anyone, no such man*) **ki nde pro·llos naredi:** *And there was not one who said to me concerning these servants*; **minimedi de venne; ne ipsa ne homine** (*anyone else*) **pro·ssa:** *but she refused to appear, neither she herself nor anyone else on her behalf and for her benefit.*

homines bonos, see **homine.**

honore, n. *honour, deference.*

hora, see **ora.**

hortu, see **ortu.**

hue, see **ubi.**

hui, hue, hoe, adv. **1.** *where* **2.** *if* (see **ubi**)

hyerru, see **hierro.**

I

iaca, n. *entrance, gateway, gate.*

iacunu, n. *deacon.*

iadu, see **dare.**

iaga, see **iaca.**

iagaru, n. *hunting dog.*

iaguere (iaguiat), v. *to lay down* (said of cattle); *to stay overnight in special pens or* **bulvares;** *to settle* (cattle).

iagunu, see **iacunu.**

iaker, see **iaguere.**

ianna, n. *gate, door.*

iata, see **dare.**

iatu, see **dare.**

ibi, pron.; proclitic **vi**, **bi**, **i**; enclitic **-ve:** *there.*

icussu, see **cussu.**

icustu, see **custu.**

idem, pron. *the same.*

ie, see **ibi.**

ienargiu, n. *January.*

ieneru, n. *son-in-law.*

ienna, see **genna.**

ietait, see **getare.**

ietando, see **ghitare.**
iettare, v. *to chase, to drive out, to head toward.*
ilike, n. *holly oak.*
ille: (always in a Latinising clause): *he.*
illi, see **illu.**
illo, see **illu.**
illoy (and variants lloy, loy, illoe, illoi, lloe), adv. *there, in that place.*
illu, illo, illos, illus, illa, illas, illi, illis, llu, llo, lu, lo, llu, lu, llo, llos, los, llus, lus, llos, llus, lus, los, lla, la, lla, llas, las, llas, lli, lli, llis, lis, personal pronoun, may be tonic, enclitic or proclitic: *him, her, them; to him, to her, to them.*
im, see **in.**
imendare (imendadu), v. *to compensate, to indemnify.*
imparare, v. *to learn.*
impare, adv. *together* See also **in pare** sub-entry **in.**
impari (unpare), adv. *together*; **faghere impari**: *to share*; **campaniari(·si) (unpare)**: *to make arrangements or to agree (with each other).*
imperò, conj. *but, however.*
impicari (impicadu, inpicado, inpicadu), v. *to hang* (on the gallows).
impressare, v. *to force, to compel.*
imprestansa, n. *loan, credit.* See also **inprestanza** and **prestanza.**
imprestidu, n. *loan.*
impromittere (impromisit, impromittiri, impromissu), v. *to promise.*
in, im, prep. *in, to, through, inside, as for as, during, in order to*; **in casu qui**: *in the event that, unless*; **1.** *in a given place or location* (also textual), *in, to, through, inside, as for as, during, in order to*; or also *to or towards a given place or location*; or also *in a given time or event*; **1a.** *at, located near*; **1b.** it indicates the place where one holds office or over which one has jurisdiction: **ego monacu Ugo, sendo priore in s'abbatia**: *I, the monk Ugo, as prior of the abbey*; **1c.** it indicates the servant of which one has ownership of a portion: **et at como sanctu Gregorii in Maria de Urri ·III· pees**: *and so now St Gregorio has three quarters of Maria de Urri*; **2.** it indicates the circumstance: **furunt in sa particione**: *they were present in the moment of the division*; **in collatura ki fegi a silva de Cercetu**: *in the trip I made to the wood of Cercetu*; **3.** *for the value of*: **deilis vacca in sollu**: *I gave them a cow worth one bezant*; **4.** *on a given occasion or event*; **5.** distributive: **·IIII· dies in setimana**: *four days a week*; **in consentimentu**: *in complicity, in joint responsability*; **in cantu**: *because, since, as long as.* In the locutions: **in casu qui**: *in the event that, unless*; **kertare in**: it indicates *the subject matter of the legal dispute*; **in forrizu**: *in adultery*; **in pake et in ketu**: *without any claims or demands from anyone*; to indicate the whole of which a fraction is owned: **su latus ki**

mi intravat: *half that of which I was entitled*; **levaresi in pala:** *to take upon onself the burden of answering for eviction*; **in giru:** *around*; **in factu:** a) *after*; b) *according to*; **in presentia:** *in presence*; **in conbentu:** *on the condition that*; **in pare:** *together*; **in cambiu de:** *in exchange for*; **intro in:** *in, inside*; **in quo, in co**, see **co¹, co².**

in co, adv. *as, in the type of, in the way in which, in virtue of which, when, after, for.*

in fattu de, adv. *after.*

in fine de, conj. *on condition that.*

inantes, inantis, inante, innantes, innantis, adv. and prep. *before*; **dae como inantes:** *from now on*; **per inantes:** 1. *previously*, 2. *in the future, afterwards.*

inanti, adv. *before all, above all.*

inanti, see **innanti.**

incanto, incantos, n. *auction.*

incertu, incertas, adj. *uncertain.*

inche, -nchi, adv. *here, there*; **nchi esser:** *to be there.*

inchurrerent, see **incurrere.**

incominçare, v. *to start* (said of a land boundary).

incontinente, adv. *immediately.*

incontinenti, see **incontinente.**

incontra, prep. *against.*

inculpare (inculpado), v. *to accuse, to blame.*

incurbaresi (incurbassi), v. *to descend, to veer towards* (said of a boundary).

incurrere (incurrant, incursu), v. *to incur.*

incursu, see **incurrere.**

inde, nde, ind', nd', pronominal or adverbial particle: 1. with genitive value: **Et det·nos·inde sa parçone sua de cussu ortu:** *and he gave us half of that garden*; 2. *concerning*: **remansitsinde Guantine Marki pro vinkidu:** *Guantine Marchi was overcome about it*; **homines … senekes, ki nde narrent sa meius beridadi kenti iskire:** *old men who would say the best information they knew about it*; **iudex inde faciat su killi ad plagere:** *The iudike shall do as he sees fit*; 3. it may have value of motion from place or removal, or also exclusion: *from there*: **foras de una terra ki nde voco:** *except a land that I exclude or remove from there.*

indebitamente, adv. *unduly.*

indictione, n. *Indiction* (chronological period of fifteen years).

indulgere, v. *to exempt.*

infama, n. *fame*; **mala (mali) infama:** *bad reputation*; **boe de mala infama:** *ox of bad character, wild ox.*

infattu, adv.; *next* **infattu de:** *following.*

inferiore (in formula of execration), adj. *in the deepest place*; **in infernum inferiore:** *in the depths of Hell.*
infernum (inferno), n. *Hell.*
infine, prep. *until, to, up to, as long as.*
infini, see **infine.**
infirmare (infirmando, infirmavit), v. *to invalidate, to fall ill, to render invalid.*
infirmitate, n. *infirmity.*
informare (informados), v. *to inform, to make aware.*
infra, prep. *within* (a given time frame).
infrascripto, adj. *hereafter or here below written.*
infurcata, adj. *fixed, embedded* (in the ground).
infurchare (infurchet, infurcadu) v. *to hang* (on the gallows). See also **affurchare** and **furcari.**
ingannari (ingannint, inghannadus), v. *to deceive.*
ingetthare, v. *to leave, start.*
ingiçare(si) (si ingiçat, si inguiçat, ingiçasi, ingiçarus), v. *to start, to begin.*
ingluttire, v. *to swallow.*
inie, **innie**, adv. *there, in the same place.*
iniquo (in a formula of Latinising execration), adj. *iniquitous.*
iniuria, n. *insult.*
iniuriosu (iniuriosa), adj. *insulting*; **paraula iniuriosa:** *insult, insulting word.*
inke, **nke:** pronominal particle, enclitic or proclitic, adv. *here, there.*
inmalavidaresi, v. *to fall ill.*
innante, prep. and adv. 1. *before, in front of, before all*; 2. *in the first place*; **da inde inanti:** *from then on*; **dave tando innanti:** *from then on*; **innati meu** *or* **suo:** *before me or him.*
innanti, see **innante.**
innocente (innocentes), adj. *innocent.*
innocentes (in a formula of Latinising execration), adj. *innocents.*
innoghi, **noghi**, adv. *here*, or also *now*; **dae noghi a:** *from now until.*
inoke, adv. *here.* See also **inoghi.**
inperadori, n. *ruler; the iudike.*
inperare, v. *to make use of, to benefit from, to take advantage.*
inpicadu, see **impicari.**
inposenti, adj. *unable to.*
inpresentari, v. *to present.*
inprestanza: n. *loan, credit.* See also **prestanza.**
inprestare, v. *to lend.*
inprovisamente, adv. *without premeditation.*
inquenivili, adj. *prone, inclined, willing to.*

inquisitione, n. *inquisition.*
insoru, see **issoro.**
insara, adv. *then, next.*
insuta, prep. *under.*
integramente, adv. *completely, totally, in full.*
intergamenti see **integramente.**
intendere (intender, intendiri, intendat, intesidu, intessida), v. **1.** *to mean*; *to understand*; **2.** *to make something known*; **3.** *to listen to.*
intenne (intenudu), v. *to be obliged to.*
intentione, n. *intention.*
inter, **intra**, prep. **1.** *among*, between; **2.** *in*, *within*, *inside.*
interesse (interesses, interessos), n. *interest.*
interlocutoriu (interlocutorias), adj. *interlocutory.*
intervenne (intervenerit), v. *to arrive, to show up.*
intesidu, see **intendere.**
intesiga adv. *in exchange.*
intessida, see **intendere.**
intestadu, in the phrase **ab intestadu** (Latin formula): *without a will, intestate.*
intica, n. *store, warehouse.*
intintu, adj. *dyed, dark, black, coloured.*
intra, see **inter.**
intrada, n. *income, profit.*
intradia, n. *income.*
intradura, n. *entrance*; **bestia de intradura:** *foreign or alien beast.*
intrare (intrareve, intravat, intradu), v. **1.** *to enter* (also *against the will of others*); **2.** *to be entitled*; **3.** *to belong to, relate to, pertain to.*
intratoria, n. *entrance.*
intregu (intreu, intrega, intrea, intreos), adj. (servant) *of a single owner whose service was full-time*; (the) *whole* (property).
intreu, see **intregu.**
intro, prep. *inside, within*; **intre pari:** *bordering, neighbouring.*
intru, see **intro.**
inventario, see **inventariu.**
inventariu, n. *inventory.*
investigare (investigando), v. to *investigate.*
iornada, n. **1.** *day*; **serviri ad iornada:** *to serve daily or on a day-to-day basis*; **2.** *working day.*
ioso, see **giosso.**
iosso, see **giosso.**
iostra, see **clostra.**

ip(p)i, see **avere.**
ipse, personal pron. (only singular and only referring to a person): *he, him.* See also **isse.**
ipsoro, see **issoro.**
ipsu, ipso, ipsa, see **issu**[2].
is, def. art. pl. *the.*
iss', see **issu**[1].
isbandidu, adj. *banished.*
isbandimentu, n. *banishment, sentence of exile.*
isbandire (isbandidu), v. *to banish, to exile.*
isbertinare (isbertinetillu), v. *to destroy someone* (from one's physical integrity).
isca, prep. *as far as.* See also **fisca.**
iscala, n. *slope, steep and craggy way, hillside.*
iscambiu, n. *change*; **in iscambiu de:** *in exchange for.*
iscaniali, n. *vessel.*
isceda (scedas), n. *notary's draft or note.*
ischarrafiare (ischarrafiarit), v. *to scratch.*
ischi, see **isca.**
ischire (ischiri, squiri, isquiri, ischiat, ischiremus, ischirint, isquiendo), v. *to know, to be aware, to make sure.*
ischovado, see **iscovare.**
isquiendo, see **ischire**
ischulpare·si (ischulparint), v. *to exonerate oneself.*
ischungiare (iscuniarit, escongiarit, ischungiadu, iscungiadu, iscuniado, ischungiada), v. *to tear down a fence*; *to remove* (by levelling it) *a ditch of demarcation.*
iscla, n. *islet, often a marshy wetland*; *land located at the confluence of waterways, lagoon.*
isclata, n. *descent, lineage.*
iscodoglare, v. *making someone confess* (through torment).
iscoiuvare, v. *to dissolve a marriage.*
iscolca, see **scolca.**
iscongiado, see **iscungiadu.**
iscongiadu, v. (past part.) and adj. *unfenced.*
iscontare (iscontandu), v. *to discount, to deduct.*
iscovare (iscovadu, ischovado), v. *to whip with the strokes of* (a plant of) *a broom.*
iscredere, v. *to disbelieve, to belie, to disappoint.*
iscripsit, see **scrivere.**
iscriptore (iscriptoris), n. *scribe, chancellor.*

iscriptu (iscritu, scriptu, scripto, iscripto), n. *written record*; **per iscriptu** ***or*** **in scriptu:** *in writing*. See also **scrivere.**

iscripturas n. *documents* or *written records.*

iscrittu, v. (past. part.) and adj. *written.*

iscrianu, see **scrivanu.**

iscrivanu, see **scrivanu.**

iscriptu, see **scrittu** and **scrivere.**

iscrivere, iscriviri, see **scrivere.**

isculpire (isculpitillos), v. *to beg, to implore, to plead.*

iscusi, adv. in the locution **a iscusi:** *fraudulently, in secret.*

iscusoria, n. *hiding place* (for objects).

isdebitare, v. *to cancel a debt.*

isettare, v. *to await.*

isfagere(si) (s'arent isfagere, isfata), v. *to ruin, to lose.*

isfata, see **isfagere.**

isforrare, v. *to annul, to delete, to repeal, to cancel.*

isfundare (isfundarit), v. *to break down a fence.*

isgirare, v. *to refute, to oppose.*

iskecatu, v. *vanished, faded, bleached.*

iski, in the adverbial phrase **cun iski de**: *being known to, having made someone aware of.*

iskire (skimus, skia, iskiant, iskivi, enti iskire), v. *to know.*

ismendare (ismendarun), v. *to prove false, to prove the fasity of something.*

ismentire (ismentirit), v. *to deny, to refute.*

ispaciare[1] (ispaciant, ispeciadu, spaciados), v. *to let wander* (e.g. livestock).

ispaciare[2], v. *to bring to an end* (with promptness).

ispacio, see **ispaciu.**

ispaciu, n. *period of time.*

ispada, n. *sword.*

ispeditu (ispeditas), adj. *free of impediment.*

ispelunca, n. *cave.*

ispendia (ispendias), see **ispendiu.**

ispendiu (spendiu, ispendios), n. *expense, cost*; **ad ispendiu suo** or **ad ispendiu de**: *at his own expense* or *at the expenses of.*

ispesa (ispesas), n. *expense*; in the locution **ad ispesas suas** or **ad ispesas de**: *at his own expense* or *at the expenses of.*

ispesoniarios, n. *tenants, sufficently free to be liable to pay rent for land.*

ispiiare (ispiiaremilu, ispiciarelu, ispiiarus, ispiiadu, spiiatu, spiiadu), v. **1.** *to release from the claims of others, to answer for eviction, to replay for eviction*; in the locution **(ponere) ad ispiiadu:** (donating something) *free of any claims*

or rights of others; 2. *to settle a question* (more or less controversial) *by agreement and mutual consent that leaves the parties satisfied in their rights.*
ispirari, v. *to expire.*
ispitale, n. *hospital.*
isponxelare (isponxelarit), v. *to violate and deflower a virgin woman.*
isposansa, see **sposansa.**
ispossedire (ispossedida), v. *to dispossess.*
isquiendo, see **ischire.**
isquire, **isquiri**, see *ischire.*
issara, adv. *then.* See also **insara.**
isse, personal pron. (only singular and only referring to a person): *he, him.* See also **ipse.**
issoro, **ipsoro**, possessive adj. and pron. *their.*
issoru, see **issoro.**
issu[1] (isso, ipso, ipsu, iso, iss', issos, issus, is, issa, ipsa, issas), full form of the def. art.: *the*: **pro issa gracia de Deus**: *by or through the grace of God,* **issu curadore c'at reer sa dita corona**: *the curator presiding over said assembly*; **issa tersa parte**: *the third part*; **et issos fiios c'at fatus sunt fiios de servu de Sanctu Jorgi et de custa libera**: *and the children he has made are servants of St George and this free woman*; **issu qui**: *that which, what.*
issu[2] (issa, issos, ipsos, ipsas), personal pron. *he, him, she, her, it, they, them.*
istadi, n. *summer.*
istado, see **istadu.**
istadu, n. *state, condition.*
istafla, n. *bracket, stirrup.*
istaios, n. *bushels* (measure of capacity).
istanti, adj. *standing, settled.*
istare (istari, istet, istit, instet, istint, istadu, istados, istandu), v., 1. *to stay, to remain, to live*; 2. *to remit, to remain* (at the discretion of someone); 3. *to reside, to dwell, to live*; 4. *to remain, to stay*; 5. *to neglect to do.* 6. *to attend*; 7. *to be, to lie*; 8. *to be someone's guest*; **istari a pane et a vinu**: *to be fed and maintained by* (someone) and, therefore, *to live with him.*
istasina (istasinas), n. *seizure, requisition, appropriation.*
istatuimus, see **statuire.**
istedas, see **steda.**
istendere (istendat), v. *to draw up or to record* (a draft).
istergiu, n. *receptacle, container, vessel, crockery.*
isterminare (esterminare, sterminare, exterminare, isturminare, exterminatu) used in the final formulae of *minatio*, v. 1. *to annul, to nullify*; 2. *to destroy.*
istesu, see **istessu.**

istessu, adj. and pron. **1.** *the same*; **2** *himself.*
istetidus, see **essere.**
istimare, v. *to assess, to estimate the value of something.*
istimonius de logu, n. *witnesses from the state, high status witnesses.*
istis, see **stare.**
isto, see **istu.**
istodiosamente, see **istudiosamente.**
istorpiu, n. *damage.*
istrampadoriu, toponym: *cliff.*
istranieri (istranieris), n. *foreigners, outsiders.*
istraniu, n. *lagoon.*
istrasinare (istraxinadus), v. *to drag.*
istraxinadus, see **istrasinare.**
istrazare (istrazarit), v. *to tear, to rip* (someone's clothes).
istrittu, adj. *not a large area* (practicable for grazing).
istrumare (istrumari, istrumet), v. **1.** *to destroy, to nullify, to ruin*; **2.** *to disband, to dissolve* (the assize).
istruminare, see **isterminare.**
istrumosa, adj. *crumbling, delapidated, in ruins.*
istu (isto, ista), pron. and adj. (always in formal utterances): *this.*
istudiosamente, adv. *deliberately.*
istula (istulas), n. *stubble, harvest stumps, chaff.*
isturminare, see **isterminare.**
isula, n. *island.*
isvedare, v. *to prohibit, to forbid.*
isviari, v. *to remove* (a servant from service to his lord).
item, adv. *likewise, moreover, also, in addition.*
iterum (in Latinising semi-formular utterance) adv. *again.*
iteu, see **chiteu.**
iua, n. *herd.*
iuale,[1] n. in the phrases **servire a iuale, servu de iuale** it indicates *a service, or servants in a state of semi-freedom, obliged to do certain tasks.*
iuale,[2] n. *yoke or pair of oxen.*
iuargio, see **iuargiu.**
iuargiu, n. *drover, overseer of cattle* (oxen).
iudicare (iudicait, iudigedi, iudicarunt, iuicarunt, iuigarunt, iudicaruntimi), v. *to judge, to establish, to decide, to impose in court, to assign, to request.*
iudike (iudicke, iudige, iudike, iuicke, iuige, iuigi, iudike, iudex, iudikes), n. *iudike*: *the ruler of the iudicato.*
iudiciu, n. *judgement, court.*

iugale, see **iuale.**
iughere (iughat·si, iugheret, iughirit), v. **1.** *to take, to bring*; **2.** *to carry* **3.** *to transfer.*
iugu: n. *yoke, pair of oxen.* See also **iuale.**[2]
iuho, see **iuhu.**
iuhu, iuho, see **iugu.**
iuigamentu, n. *judgement, sentence.*
iuigare (iuygare, iuyghare, iuighandu, iuygado, iuigadu, iuighadu), v. *to render a verdict, to pronounce a sentence, to impose in judgement.*
iuighamentu, see **iuigamentu.**
iuigarunt, see **iudicare.**
iuige, see **iudike.**
iuighante (iuighantis), n. *juror, person called to judge.*
iuyghissa, n. *queen of the iudicato or realm.*
iuigi (iuighi, iuyghi, iuyghissa, iuyghi), n. *ruler or iudike of a iudicato or realm.*
iuigi, see **iudike.**
iuike, see **iudike.**
iuker, see **iughere.**
iumpadoriu, n. *ford, place where one can traverse a watercourse, crossing point.*
iumpare: v. *to cross, to pass over.*
iumpatoriu, see **iumpadoriu.**
iunctu, see **iuntu.**
iungere, v. *to reunite.*
iunto, see **iuntu.**
iuntu[1], adj. *joint, united.*
iuntu[2], prep. *near.*
iunturas, n. *confluence* (of waters).
iuo, see **iugu.**
iura[1], n. *marriage vow.*
iura[2], n. *swearing, oath.*
iurado, see **iuradu.**
iuradu (jurados), n. **1.** *juror*; **iuradu de credentia:** *trusted juror*; **iuradu de Loghu:** *royal juror*; **iurado de pardu:** *pasture control officer.*
iurare (iurari, iurait, iuredi, iurarunt, iurandonde, iurado), v. *to swear, to take an oath, to pledge*; **femina iurada:** *betrothed woman.*
iustamente, adv. *according to justice.*
iusticia, n. *justice*; fig.: *the process of justice, judiciary*; **su loghu dessa iusticia:** *gallows, the place of execution*; **tenne sa iusticia:** *to administer justice.*
iusticiadu, see **iusticiare.**
iusticiare, v. *to execute.*

iustithia, see **iusticia.**
iustitia, see **iusticia.**
iustu, adj. *right, legitimate, reasonable*; **cum iustu titulu:** *rightfully.*
iuvale, see **iuale.**
iuvu, see **iugu.**
Iudicato, **Iuyghadu**, n. *each of the four realms or iudicati* (iudigados or iuygados) *into which Sardinia was divided.*
iuygantis (iuyghantes), see **iuighante.**
iuygare, **iuyghare**, see **iuigare.**
ive, see **ibi.**
iverru, n. *winter.*
ivi, adv. *there, in that place.* See also **ibi.**
ixolere, v. *to unpack* (*the goods*).

J

jacunu, see **iacunu**
jagunu, see **iacunu.**
janna, n. *door, entrance.*
januinos, n. *Genoese* (money, currency unit).
jenezzariu de judigi, see **genezzario.**
jenna, n. *entrance, break, valley gorge.*
jenuinos, see **januinos.**
jetaitse, see **getare.**
judice, see **iudike.**
juigi, see **iudike.**
junketu, n. *reed bed of canes.*
junpare, v. *to cross, to jump.*
juntamente, adv. *at the same time, jointly.*
junuinos, see **jenuinos.**
jurados, see **iuradu.**

K

kalunka, see **calunca.**
kando, see **cando.**
kandu, see **cando.**
ke, see **ki**[1].

ke, see **ki**[2].
keia, n. *underground cistern, grain deposit.*
kella, n. *lineage, group, group of servants from the same lineage.*
kellaridu, n. *custodian of a storehouse, administrator of a food warehouse.*
ken, relative pron. accusative: *which.*
kena, prep. *without.* See also **sena.**
kene, see **kena.**
kera, n. *beeswax.*
kerbu, n. *deer.*
kercu, n. *oak.*
kerfit, see **kerre.**
kergidore, see **kerkidore.**
kerigu, n. *cleric.*
kerketu, n. *oak woodland.*
kerkidore, n. *tax collector.*
kerkitore, see **kerkidore.**
kerku, see **kercu.**
kerra, conj. *when, as soon as.*
kerre (kereat, kerfit, kerre epi), v. **1.** *to want*; **2.** *to ask, to ask for, to demand*; **2a.** *to want someone to account for.*
kersa, n. *lentisk bush or shrub* (of the maquis); or may be *mulberry* (tree).
kertadore, n. *legal representative at a dispute; counsel, advocate, attorney.*
kertare (kertari, kertarende, kerto, kertu, kertas, kertava, kertadis, kertei, kertai, kertait, kertedi, kerterus, kertarunt), v. **1.** *to engage in a judicial dispute, to bring a case to court, to dispute, to contest, to contend, to argue with*; **1a.** *to argue in a legal case*; **1b.** *to litigate on behalf of another one.*
kertatore, see **kertadore.**
kertu, n. *litigation, judicial dispute, argument, legal case.*
kerviclia, n. this word refers to the *nape of the neck*, but occurs figuratively in the phrases: **levare a ckerviclia:** *to take away forcibly*; and **faker kerviclia:** *to compel by force.*
kervinas, adj. *something made from deer-skin leather.*
ketu, n. in the locution **in ketu:** *without any claims or demands from anyone.*
ki[1], **cki, ke, qui, que, k', ck'**: relative pron. *who, that*; **1b.** it serves to make explicit the complement of time: **sa die ki andei a Bonarcatu:** *on the day that or when I went to Bonarcado* **2.** *he who, the one who*; **3.** preceded by the definite article (**su ki**): *he who, the one who, what.*
ki[2], **ke, qui, k'**: subordinative conj. *that; so that*; **1a.** with optative value: **ki ll'apat benedicta sa parzone de donnu Piziellu:** *that he may possess blessedly the property of lord Piziellus*; **1b. da ke:** *since.*

kida, n. *shift of a job or service for the benefit of the public, or* munus publicum; *then also the whole of the members of a college required to provide this service*; 2. **(corona de) kita de verruta** *or* **berruta**: *the judicial panel at a judicial hearing or* **corona** (formed by the **prudhommes** (**bonos homines**), mounted militia who had as their insignia or emblem the **verrutu** or **berrutu** throwing weapon. These men were required to perform this service and public office according to a shift schedule); 3. *week* (services assigned to the **kita** were according to a weekly shift pattern).

kiiu, n. *edge, border.*

kimbe, cardinal number: *five.*

kiraruntsi, see **girare.**

kis, adj. and pron. *each, each one.*

kita, see **kida.**

kiteu: interrogative pron. *what?* See also **chiteu.**

kunde: An unclear entry, it would seem, from the context, to mean *after that, after all that,* but it could be the result of **dave** + **co** + **(i)nde: Dave kunde andai ad Monte sancto et deruntimi ad Araona Cucuda cun II fiios suos:** *After that, I went to Monte Santo and they gave me Araona Cucuda with her two sons.*

kusta, see **custu.**

kustos, see **custu.**

L

la, see **illu.**

laborare, v. *to work, to cultivate.*

laboratu (laborata), adj. *worked, wrought, hammered* (said of silver).

labore, see **lavore.**

labru, n. *laurel, bay tree.*

lacana (lacanas), n. *boundary marker.*

laccu, n. *stone basin, vat.*

lacu, n. *lake.*

ladicos, n. *laymen.*

lados, see **ladus.**

ladus[1] (lados), n. *half* (almost always referring to one's share of the ownership of servants).

ladus[2] (llados), n., 1. *side*; **dae ladus de foras:** *by the side of any other, located on the outer side*; **a ladus de:** *on the side of*; **dae ladus suo:** *on its own side*; **de ladus:** *on its side*; **a llados apare:** *side by side, adjoining each other.*

laicu (laicos), n. *layman.*
laigos, see **laicu.**
lamentari (lamentarit, lamentados), v. *to direct a complaint, to complain.*
lamentu, n. *complaint*; **faghere lamentu**: *to file, to report a complaint* (to a public officer).
lampadas, n. *June* (*month*).
lande, see **glande.**
landi, see **glande.**
lansare, see **lensari.**
lanzare (lanzedi), v. *to pierce* (*with a rod or spear*).
laore (laores), see **lavore.**
laoriu, n. *sown land, arable land, sowing.*
larga, n. *theft, robbery.*
largare (largarunt, ait largatu), v. *to steal* (especially animals), *to carry off, to misappropriate, to make undue or unlawful use of another's property.*
largha, see **larga.**
lassamentu, n. *dissolution.*
lassare (laxare, eti lassare, lassant, lassavant, lassando, avendomi lassadu), v. **1.** *to let, to leave, to grant, to hold*; **2.** *to bequeath* (*what is due to someone*); **3.** *to disregard, to neglect*; **4.** *to leave an office or function.*
la, see **illu.**
lata adj. in the phrase **figu lata**: *variety of white fig.*
laterati, adj. *those whose services are shared between two lords.*
lati, n. *milk.*
latus, see **ladus**[1].
lauro, see **lavore.**
lavorare (llavorare, lavorat), v. *to work* (e.g. the land).
lavore (lauro, llavori, laores, lavoris), n. *wheat, grain*; **2.** *cultivation*; **lavore nadu**: *cereal field already in bud, where the grain is sprouting.*
lavore, n. *grain.*
laxa (laxas), n. *amends, penalty.*
laxare, see **lassare.**
lealemente, see ***lealementi.***
lealimente, adv. *correctly.*
leare, see **levare.**
leberadu, see **liberare.**
lebare, see **levare.**
leberadu, see **liberari.**
lectu, n. *bed*; in the phrase **fanti de lectu agiena**: *concubine who is a stranger* (to the family).

leer (leat, ligidu lesit, lessiruntilla), v. *to read.*
leere, see **leer.**
lege[1], n. *law.*
lege[2], n. in the phrase **per meia lege**, the meaning is unclear, perhaps *halfway.*
legere, see **leer.**
legie, see **lege**[1].
legitimamenti, adv. *lawfully, according to the law.*
legitime: adv. *legitimately.*
legitimu, adj. *legitimate, prescribed by law, having legal force.*
legittimamenti, see **legitimamenti.**
legumen, n. *legume.*
leitima, adj: *legitimate.*
lençolos, see **lenzolu.**
lensari (lensare, lensadu, lensado, lenzadu), v. *to strike with a throwing weapon.*
lenthu, n. *cloth.*
lenzolu, n. *bed sheet.*
lepporariu, n. *hares' lair.*
les, see **illu.**
lesit, see **leer.**
lesseruntilla, see **leer**
letania, n. *litany.*
letu, n. *bed.*
levare (levari, lebare, leare, levat, levait, levavit, leveit, levarint, levadu, leada), v. **1.** *to take, to take away* (used very often in the division of servants), *to steal*; **2.** *to receive a payment*; **3.** *to requisition*; **4.** *to pull away, to move*; **5.** *to shirk from, to go away from, to abandon* (service); **6.** *to take something as payment for an exchange*, or *as compensation for a wrong*; **7.** *to take what is due*; **8.** *to withdraw from service, to divert from service*; **9.** *to take something from someone*; **9a.** *to take away* (servants) *from service to use them for another service*; **9b.** *to illegally appropriate*; **10.** *to require as a tax*; **11.** *to take a direction, to reach*; **12.** *to acquire a copy.* In phrases: **levare appus:** *to take what is due to the owner from the father or mother* (in the division of children of servants whose parents are servants of different lords) **levare pro salario:** *to ask as salary or wage*; **levare per forza muleri:** *to do violence to a woman*; **levare pro mugere:** *to take a women in wife*; **levare a força:** *to commit robbery, prevarication*; **levaresi in pala:** *to take upon oneself the burden of answering for eviction*; **levare prestanza, acomandicia, deppidu:** *to get a loan or a debt, to borrow, to have as a deposit in escrow, to contract any debt by overdraft*; **levare appellatione** *or* **levare processu:** *to make an appeal or to request the proceedings*; **levare mesura:** *to take the measure*; *to calibrate*; **levare cumoni:** *to enter*

into a contract of agistment; **levare a biu:** *to take* (an animal) *alive*; **levare a ckerbiclia:** *to take away by force.*

levatura, n. *taking away, seizure.*

levorare, see **lavorare.**

li, see **illu.**

libellu (libellos), n. *enphyteusis, rental agreement* (of land from a lord).

liberari[1], (liberadu, leberadu), v. *to release, to acquit.*

liberari[2], v. *to deliberate, to render a sentence.*

liberatione, n. *deliberation, resolution.*

libertadi, n. *licence, right.*

libertadu (libertados), n. *freedman, freed servant but required to perform certain services.*

libertaresi (se furunt libertatos), v. *to have oneself set free*; or maybe better: *to join the* **collivertos.** See **colivertu.**

liberu (lieru, liere, libera, livera, liberos, liveros), n. *free, free man*; 1. *free man, non-servant, of free social status*; 2. *free worker* (but dependent employee); 3. **liberu maiorali:** *free lord*; 4. **liberu muniariu:** *a free person but required to provide special services to the iudike*; 5. in the plural, **liberos**, may mean **colivertos:** *free persons subject to certain impositions or work performance, and organised in collegiality and sodality.*

libra[1] (libras), n. *pound, measure of weight.*

libra[2] (libras, lira), *n. lira, currency unit.*

libru (libros), n. *book.*

licentia, n. *licence, permit, authorisation.*

licidu, see **licitu.**

licitu, adj. *lawful, permitted, legal.*

liere, see **liberu.**

liero, see **liberu.**

lieru, see **liberu.**

ligadore (ligadores), n. *hide binder.*

ligare (lighare lighant): v. *to tie, to bind.*

ligata, adj. *tied.*

lighare (lighant), see **ligare.**

ligidu, see **leer.**

ligone: n. *hoe.*

ligumen(e), see **legumen.**

limba, n. *tongue*; **morrer kene limba:** *to die without having made a will.*

limide (limides), n. *border, boundary.*

linna, n. *wood, carpentry*; **maystros de linna:** *carpenters.*

lintha, n. *line, rod* (for measuring); *strip of cultivated land on the side of a hill.*

linu, n. *linen.*
linya, see **linna.**
lis, see **illu.**
lite, n. *litigation, dispute.*
litera, n. *letter.*
litigante (litigantis), n. *disputant.*
litigiu, n. *quarrel, dispute.*
littu, n. *wood, woodland.*
livastrina: adj. *pure white.*
livertatos, n. *freedmen.*
livertu (liveratos), n. *freedman.*
livra, n. *pound.* See **libra**[1].
lladus, see **ladus.**
llu, lu, llu, llo, lla, llas, dative **lli, llis, li, lis:** personal pron., enclitic or proclitic: *him, her, it, them,* dative *to him, to her, to it, to them.*
locu, see **logu.**
loe, adv. of place reduced and atonal form of **illoi** *or* **illoe:** *there.* See **illoy.**
logare, see **allogare.**
loghadu, see **allogare**
loghu, see **logu.**
logu, n. 1. *the iudicato, the realm*; 2. *the components of the* **corona de logu** (assembly presided over by the iudike), or *any case of the royal council*; 3. *place, country*; **loghu iscongiadu:** *unfenced place*; **loghu dessa iusticia:** *site of execution, gallows*; **aviri (legitime) loghu:** *to have* (*legal*) *force*; see also **logusalbadori.**
Logudore, Lugudorre, n. 1. *Logudoro, the north-western region of Sardinia*; 2. *iudicato or realm also known as the realm or iudicato of Torres, and or or its territory in that region.*
logusalbadori n. it is the **lociservator:** *deputy and on-site representative of the iudike.*
lompere (lompet), v. *to arrive.*
longu (longa), adj. *long, extensive* (almost always in toponyms): **Billalonga; Serra longa; sa terra longa dessas petras.**
loru, n. *leash*; always in the phrase **cani de loru:** *watchdog.*
los, lu, lus, l, see **illu.**
loy, see **illoy.**
lu, see **llu.**
lunis, n. *Monday.*
lupino, n. *lupin bean.*
lus, see **illu.**
lutu, n. *mud.*

M

ma, conj. *but, however, rather.*
Madonna, n. *Madonna, the Virgin Mary.*
madrassa (madrassas), n. *mattress.*
madrigues, see **matrige.**
magellare, see **maxellare.**
maghellare, see **maxellare.**
maghellos, see **maxello.**
magine, n. (exclusively in execration formulas): *physical integrity* (of a person).
magistru, n. *master* (of an art, or of a skill).
magna, see **mannu.**
magnale, see **mannali.**
maiale, n. *pig, barrow* (castrated male pig).
maiali (maialis), see **maiale**
maiolariu maiore, n. *head pig-keeper.*
maiorarle (maiorales), n. *leaders, heads, chiefs, lords*; **liberu maiorali:** *free lord* (of high social status).
maiore[1], n. **1.** *a person entrusted with an office or function, with precedence over his employees*; **maiore de regnum**: *royal maiore*; **1a. maiore de siillu**: *keeper of the seal, the highest official or senior officer who oversaw the assets of the realm* (certainly in the kingdom of Torres, but probably in the other three realms); **1b. maiore de sa villa:** *major, head of a village*; **1c. maiore de pardu**: *the officer in charge of pastures*; **1d. maiore de cavallus:** *royal horse officer*; **1e. maiore de portu:** *senior port official*; **1f. maiori de scolca:** *head of the ward; district's senior functionary* **1g. maiore dessa contrada:** *senior officer who has jurisdiction over the countryside*; **maiori de equas**: *master of the horses*; **1h. maiore de gulbare**, n. *head of a livestock enclosure*; **1i. maiore de isolca**, n. *chief of the guard*; **2.** *pre-eminent man* (of high standing).
maiore[2] (maior), adj. **1.** *greater*; **maiore parte**: *the majority*; **2.** in toponyms: *bigger or major*: **Sii maiore; Solas maiore; Patru maiore.**
maioria, n. *jurisdiction of a lord or mayor.*
maistru, n. *master* (*craftsman*); **maystros de linna**: *carpenters.*
maiu, n. *May* (*month*).
major, see **maiore**[2].
malavida, adj. *ill.*
malavogia, adv. *in spite of oneself, unwillingly.*
male, n. *evil, crime.*
male, adv. *ill, badly.*

maledictione, n. (always in formula of execration): *anathema, curse, damnation.*

maledictu, adj. (in formula of execration): *cursed, damned.*

maleditione, see **maledictione.**

maleficiu, n. *crime, misdeed.*

malesiosamente, adv. *fraudulently, maliciously.*

mali, see **male.**

malicia, n. *deceitful, cunning*; in the phrase **fagheri malicia:** *to counterfeit* (a product and pass it off as good).

malu (mala, malos), adj. *bad, poor, harmful*; **mala cura**: *bad and poor care*; **de mala (in)fama**: *of bad reputation*; *wild and untamed animal*; **ad mala voluntadi**: *against the will of*; **malu fageri**: *evil acting.*

malufactore, n. *wrongdoer.*

malum, adj. *bad.*

malvagiu (malvagios), n. *evil-doer, wicked.*

mama, **mamma**, n. *mother.*

manacaresi, v. *to become a monk.*

manacu, n. *monk.*

manago, see **monagu.**

manale, see **mannali.**

manali (manalis), n. *manual laborer.*

manca, n. *left*; and **a manca** adv. *to or on the left.*

mancamentu, n. **1.** *loss, subtraction*; **2.** *damage*; **3.** *fail, default.*

manchamentu, see **manchamentu.**

manchare (manquit, mancharit, mancadu), v. *to be absent, to miss.*

mandare (mandari, mandat, mandadu), v. **1.** *to send, to deliver, to notify*; **2.** *to delegate, to ask*; **3.** *to summon, to trial*; **mandare a *or* in prexione**: *bring into prison*; **mandare in manu de**: *to deliver into the hands of*; **mandare ad executioni:** *to send for execution, to let (something) go into effect.*

mandatore (mandadores), n. **1.** *deputising officer*; **2.** *legal representative*; **3.** *attorney.*

mandicare, v. *to make use of, to profit from*. See also **mandigare.**

mandigare (mandigadu), v. **1.** *to eat*; **2.** may be also *to exploit, to make use*; **3.** *to have the usufruct.*

mandra (mandras), n. *fenced meadow.*

manka, see **manca.**

mannali, adj. always in the locution **porcho mannali**: *domestic swine.*

mannu (manno, manna), adj. **1.** *big, great, large, serious*; **2.** in the phrase **terra manna**: *the continent, the mainland* (as opposed to the island).

manquit, see **mancare.**

mansionem, n. *dwell, home.*
mantadura (mantaduras), n. *fur, coat.*
mantenni (mantenne, mantesidu, manthesida, mantenendo), v. *to maintain, to administer, to govern.*
manthenni, see *mantenni.*
manu (manus), n. 1 *hand*; 2. generally: *in or by the hand(s) of, in the ownership or power of*; **a** *or* **per manu de:** *at the hands of*; **ponne in manu:** *to place in the hands, in the ownership or in power of, to deliver, to place in the sight of*; **girare manus:** *to turn, to take the turn, to yield the turn for choice* (used in the division of servants); **aviri in manu:** *to be appointed at, to be in charge of, to be responsible*; **manu a manu:** *immediately, at once,* on *the spot*; **benne a manus:** *to handle, to take care* (of something).
maore, see **maiore.**
maquicia, n. 1. *offense subject to fine, to a financial penalty*; 2. *fine, financial penalty.*
maquicie, see **maquicia.**
marchare (marchint), v. *to brand or mark an animal or hides.*
marchesu, see **markesu.**
marcho, see **marchu.**
marchu, n. *brand, mark.*
mare, n. *sea*; also meaning of *fishpond* and *lagoon* (esp. of Mare Pontis), but also said of the *sea* itself.
marghine, see **margine.**
margine, n. *edge.*
maridu, n. *husband.*
maritu, see **maridu.**
markesu, **markeso**, **marchesu**, n. *marquis* (always referring to William, marquis of Massa and iudike of the realm of Càlari under the name of Salusio IV from around 1187 to 1214, and iudike of Arborea around the turn of the century).
martire (martires), n. *martyr.*
martis, n. *Tueday.*
marzu, n. *March.*
mascare, v. *to offend.*
maschus, see **maschiu.**
maschiu, n. and adj. *male.*
masciones, see **masone.**
masclu, see **maschiu.**
masculos, see **maschiu.**
masedo, adj. *tame, domesticated.*

masognu, see **masoniu.**
masone, n. 1. *flocks of cattle, livestock*; 2. *enclosure.*
masoniu, n. *cattle shelter, paddock.*
mastriu, n. *master* (of an art, trade or skill).
mata, n. *plant, tree.*
mater, n. *mother.*
matre, n. *mother.*
matricas, see **matrige.**
matrige, n. *sow.*
matrikes, see **matrige.**
matrikis, see **matrige.**
matrona, n. *wife.*
matta, n. *tree, maquis* (macchia mediterranea).
maxedari, see **maxellare.**
maxellare (maxellat, maxellados, maxellada), v. *to slaughter.*
maxello, n. *slaughter.*
maya (mayas), n. *witchcraft, magic.*
mayariu, n. *sorcerer.*
mayore, see **maiore.**
maystru, see **maistru.**
maystus, see **maistru.**
me (mimi mi): tonic and atonic pron. *me.*
mecu, pron. *with me, against me.*
mediu (media), n. *half.*
megiorare, v. *to improve.*
megius (megios), comparative adj. *better*; in the locution **dae bene in megius:** *from good to better.*
megu, see **mecu.**
meighina (meighinas), n. *medicine.*
meioramentu, n. *improvement.*
meiu, n. *middle* (*of*), *by half*; in the locution **per meiu:** *in the middle of.*
meius comparative adj. *better.*
mela, n. *apple.*
melioramentu, see **meioramentu.**
meloni (melone, melloni), n. *melon.*
melloni, see **meloni.**
membro, see **membru.**
membru, n. 1. *member, limb* (of the body); in the locutions, **membru particulari:** *minor member or limb of the body*; **membru principali:** *main member or limb* (of the body); 2. *part of a document.*

memoria (memoriam), n. *record of act or fact of legal significance.*
memoria, n. *memory, record.*
mendari (mendat), v. **1.** *to amend;* **2.** *to repair, to make reparation, to compensate* (for damage).
mense, n. *month.*
mensione, in the phrase **faghere mensione:** *to make mention.*
mentre, mentri, conj. *while;* **mentre qui:** *so long as.*
menudo, see **menudo.**
mercante, n. *merchant.*
mercantia, n. *merchandise,* **fagheri mercantia:** *to practise trade.*
mercede, n. *grace, mercy.*
merchedantis, see **mercante.**
mercuris, n. *Wednesday.*
meretrice (meretrices), n. *prostitute.*
merkede, n. *thanks.* See also **mercede.**
merkee, see **mercede.**
mersare (mersent), v. *to reap* (wheat).
mesa, n. *half.*
mese, n. *month.*
mesidadi, n. *half.*
mesinu, n. *container, receptacle.*
messare (messadu), v. *to harvest, to reap* (wheat).
messas, n. *the harvest.*
messer, n. *sire, lord.*
mesu (mesus, mesa), n. and adj. (the) *half;* **de mesus:** *placed among or between, in common with.*
mesura, n. *measure.*
meta, adv. *very, very much.*
metatu, n. *enclosure, pigsty.*
metzanu (metzana), adj. *middle, of medium size.*
meu (meo, mea, meos, mias), possessive adj. and pron. *my, mine;* substantivised: (all) *that is mine.*
meyghu, n. *physician.*
mi, see **me.**
mimi, see **me.**
minare (minando), v. **1.** *to lead* (a horse); **2.** *to transact, to deal with.*
minda (mindas) n. *pasture* (closed and reserved for tame livestock).
minimança, n. *waiver* (to appear in court), *contumacy, in contempt.*
minimançça, see **minimança.**
minimanza, n. in the locution **a minimanza:** *in absentia, in default.*

minimare (minimait, minimedi), v. *to fail, to renounce, to withdraw, to be or remain inferior or defeated in judgement.*

ministrari, v. *to administer.*

minore, adj. *minor, younger.*

minori, adj. 1. *minor, of lower grade*; 2. *smaller*; 3. *minor, underage.*

minudo, adj. in the phrase **bestiamen minudo:** *small cattle, small livestock.*

minudu, adj. *small* (cattle).

minus adv. and adj. *little, least*; in the locutions, 1. **niente de minus:** *nevertheless*; 2. **prossu minus** *or* **assu minus:** *at least*; 4. **de minus:** *fewer*; 5. **ad minus de**[1]: *less than*; 6. **ad minus de**[2]: *except, unless.*

minus prexu, n. *disregard, negligence.*

minutu (minutos), adj., see *minudu*; in the phrase **dinaris junuinos minutos:** *Genoese silver coins.*

mio, see **meu.**

mirari, v. *to watch over* (e.g. livestock).

mischoladura, n. *mixture.*

misericordia, n. *mercy, leniency, grace, discount.*

misi see **mittere.**

missidu, see **mittere.**

missa, n. *Mass.*

missas, n. *harvest, crops.*

missu, **misso**, n. *messenger.*

mitire, see **mittere.**

mitteri, see **mittere.**

mittere (miter, mittiri, mitter, mitire, mitteri, mittat·si·lli, misi, missidu, misidu, mittendo), v. 1. *to put*; 2. *to add, to mix*; 3. *to stick*; **mittere a trumentu**, *to torture*; **mitteri et tenne in muda:** *to keep under guard*; **miter in pregione:** *to take to prison, to imprison*; **mitire in possessione:** *to put in possession*, **mittere in manu de:** *to entrust to.*

miu, see **meu.**

mmodo, see **modo.**

mobili (mobilis), adj. in the phrase **causa mobili:** *movable property.*

modo, see **modu.**

modu, n. 1. *way, manner*; 2. *custom*; in the phrases: **in alcuno modo:** *in any way*; **per modu qui:** *so that*; **per issu factu modo qui:** *in such a way that*; **tenne modo:** *to have, to find a way to*; **assu modu sardischu:** *according to Sardinian custom or law.*

mogere, see **mugere.**

moiant, see **molere.**

moiu (moios), n. *bushel, unit of dry measurement.*

mola, n. *millstone, grindstone.*
molente, molenti, n. *donkey.*
molere (moiant), v. *to grind.*
moliare (moliat), v. *to turn* (said of the border).
molici, n. *lentisk, lentisco.*
molinu (molinos), n. *mill.*
monachu, see **monagu.**
monacu (monacus, manacos), see **monagu.**
monagu (monigu, monacu, monacus, manago, monagos, managos), n. *monk, friar.*
monasteriu (monasterio, monasterium, monasterju), n. *monastery.*
mongere, v. *to milk.*
monigu, see **monagu.**
monimentu, n. *sepulchre, tomb.*
montare, v. *to transfer to a high degree of altitude, to a high ground.*
monte, n. *hill, mountain.*
monticlu, n. *hill.*
montiglu, see **monticlu.**
montonargiu, n. *dunghill, dump.*
monumentu, see **monimentu.**
morgiat, see **morre.**
morimentu, see **monimentu.**
morre (moriat, morivit, moriit, morrunt, morgiat, mortu), v. 1, *to die*; 2. *to kill.*
mortaia, n. *funeral service, exequies*; **pannu a mortaia:** *funeral cloth.*
mortale, adj. *mortal*; always in the phrase **perunu homine mortale:** *no mortal man:* to indicate *no person*, in formulated sentences.
morte, n. 1. *death*; 2. *killing, murder.*
morti, see **morte.**
mortu (mortus), adj. *dead*; n. in the phrase **festa de sus mortus:** *the feast of the dead.*
mostra, monstra, n. *exhibition, review of free men armed with weapons and horses.*
mostrare (mostrat mostret monstrarit), v. 1. *to show* (something to test it); 2. *to prove.*
mover, v. *to move*; in the phrase **mover chertu:** *to move quarrel, a judicial dispute.*
muda, n. *shift of cattle surveillance service according to a shift rotation system,* and therefore, *the group of people who constituted and did that shift*; **mitteri et tenne in muda:** *to establish watch-shift concerning tame oxen.*

mudari (mutamus), v. 1. *to change, to exchange*; 2. *to transfer*.
mugere (mugeri), n. *wife, married woman*.
mughere, **mugheri**, see **mugere**.
muiere, see **mugere**.
muierile, adj. *feminine*.
muleri, see **mugere**.
muliere, see **mugere**.
multu[1] (multos, multas), adj. *much, many*.
multu[2], adv. *much, a lot*.
mundu, n. *world*.
munga, see **mungia**.
mungia, n. *lower public service*.
muniariu, adj. in the phrase **liberu muniariu**: *nominally free person obliged to perform particular services for the iudike*.
munimentu, see **monimentu**.
munistere, n. *monastery*.
muntare (at muntare), v. *to amount, to sum up, to quantify*.
mura, n. *blackberry, blackberry bush*.
muradu (murados), adj. *surrounded by walls or brambles*.
muraiolu, n. *mason, bricklayer*.
murikersa, n. *mulberry*.
muristere, n. *monastery*.
muro, n. *wall*.
murta, n. *myrtle* (berry or shrub of myrtle).
muru, n. *wall*.
musuleu, n. *tomb*.
mutacione, n. *change, changing*.
mutamus, see **mudare**.
mutare (mutamus), see **mudari**.
muteclariu, n. *field of rockrose bushes*.
muteclu, n. *cistus, rockrose*.

N

nanti, see **innanti**
narado, see **narre**.
narboni, n. *fallow land* (first adapted to cultivation, or worked after a rest period).
narre (narri, naras, naravant, narai, narei, narrai, naredi, narrunt, narrent, nar-

rando, narado), v. 1. *to say*; 2. *to tell, to report, to make known*; 3. *to attest*; 4. *to name, to have by name, to be called*; 5. *to utter*; 6. *to produce evidence, to declare, to state, to oppose*, 7. *to account*; 8. as a noun, **su narri**, *declaration, testimony.*

narri, see **narre.**

nasariu, see **nassariu.**

nasker, v. *to be born.* See also *nasciri.*

nassariu (nassarju, nassarios), n. *weir, fishpond.*

nassu, n. *nose.*

natale, n. *natal, birth day, anniversary.*

natias, (a) nnatias, n. *according to the order of birth*, (always used in the locution **a nnatias**, which is used in connection with the division of servants' children between different owners, according to the order of their birth and the ownership of their parents): *in order of age.*

nativitadi, n. *Nativity*; **Pascha de sa natividadi:** *Christmas.*

nde, see **inde.**

ne, see **nen.**

nebode, n. *grandchild.*

nebodi (nebodes), see **nebode.**

nebodorum, n. genitive pl. (in Latin formulas): *of grandchildren.*

nec, see **nen.**

necessariu (necessarias), adj. *necessary.*

necessitadi, n. in the adverbial locution **de necessitadi:** *necessarily.*

nechunu (nechuna), see **nexuno.**

necta, see **neta.**

negligencia, see **negligentia.**

negligensia, see **negligentia.**

negligente (negligentes), adj. *negligent, careless.*

negligentia, n. *negligence, carelessness.*

negociante (negociantes), n. *merchant.*

negosantis, see **negociante.**

negotium, n. *business, shop, sale.*

negunu, see **nexuno.**

nemos, pron. *no one.*

nen (*ne, ni, n, nec*) (Latin): negative coordinative conj. *nor, neither*; **ni … ni:** *neither … nor*; **nen anchu:** *not even.*

nepode, see **nebode.**

nepote see **nebode.**

nepotorum, n. genitive pl. (in Latin formulas): *of grandchildren.*

neunu, pron. *no one.*

nepode, see **nebode.**
neta, see **netta.**
netta, n. *granddaughter, niece.*
neunu (neuna), pron. *nobody.*
nexuno, nexun, pron. *nobody.*
nchi, see **inche.**
ni, see **nen.**
niente, nienti, pron. always in the locution **niente de minus:** *nevertheless.*
nigella, adj. *black.*
nisi, conj. (in Latin formulae): *except, unless.*
niu, n. *nest.*
nixunu (nixuna), see **nexuno.**
nke, see **inke.**
nnatias, see **natias.**
nnou, see **novu.**
nnovu, see **novu.**
nnurake, see **nurake.**
no, adv. of negation: *not, no.* See also **non.**
noa, see **novu.**
nobu, see **novu.**
nocte, nocti; see **notte.**
nodaiu, n. *notary, scribe.*
nodayu, nodayo, see **nodaiu.**
nodaria, n. *notariat, notarial office or profession*; **butegha dessa nodaria:** *notary's office.*
noe, nnoe, cardinal number: *nine.*
noghi, see **innoghi.**
nois: personal pron. *we, us.* See also **nos.**
nomen (nomenes, nomines), n. *name*; in the Latin incipit formulae as: **in nomine Dei; in nomine Domini:** *in the name of God*; *in the name of the Lord.*
nomine, see **nomen.**
non obstante, non obstanti, conj. and prep. *despite, nevertheless, notwithstanding.*
non, no, adv. of negation: *not, no.*
nonnu: n. honorary title for clergy: *monk.*
nontho, n. *envoy, representative* (in a transaction).
nos: personal pron. *we, us.*
nostru nostro, nostra, nostros, nostras, nostri (genitive in Latin formulas), pron. *our.*

notabili, adj. *visible, evident.*
notaiu, see **nodaiu.**
notare[1], v. *to note.*
notare[2], see **notariu.**
notaresi, v. *to present oneself.*
notariu, notario, n. *notary, scribe.* See also **nodaiu.**
note, noti, see **notte.**
notte, n. *night* **de nocte tempus:** *during the night;* **su de noti chali et issu de di:** *both by night and day.*
nou, see **novu.**
novellu, n. *calf under one year old.*
novu (nova, novos, novas), adj. *new;* **fagere o fraigare a (n)nou:** *to renovate, to rebuild,* **dae** *or* **de nou:** *again.*
nuke, n. (*wall*)*nut.*
nullu[1] (nulla), adj. *void, null, annulled.*
nullu[2] (nullum, nulla), pron. *no, no one, not any* (thing), *nobody.*
numen, see **nomen.**
nunça, see **nunza.**
nunça, see **nunza.**
nunçadore, n. *bailiff, he who delivers summonses.*
nunçare (nunçailla), v. *to sue, to summon, cite before the court.*
nunsa, see **nunza.**
nunsare, see **nunçare.**
nunthare, v. *to convene, to announce, to call to justice.*
nunza, n. 1. *citation, summon in court;* 2. **Pascha nunsa:** *Epiphany, the Easter of Epiphany.*
nunzadore, see **nunçadore.**
nunzadu, see **nunçare.**
nunzza, see **nunza.**
nurachi, see **nurake.**
nuracke, see **nurake.**
nuracki, see **nurake.**
nuragi, see **nurake.**
nurake, nuracke, nuraki, nuragi, n. *nuraghe* (Bronze Age tower or structure).
nuracki, see **nurake.**
nuragi, see **nurake.**
nutricare, v. *to feed, to raise, to bring up* (*a child*).
nuverare, v. *to count up, to reckon.*

O

o, **ho**, disjunctive conj. *or*

obediret, see **hobedire.**

obera (oberas), n. the original meaning of this word was *working day*, but it may also refer to *a unit of value, perhaps linked to the economic worth of a working day*: **Comporeilli a Terico Puliga parzone sua quanta aviat in icussu ortu. Et fegindelli ·vi· oberas inter peza et casu et complilli:** *I bought from Terico Puliga his share of that garden. And I paid him for the value of six working days given in meat and cheese and settled the account.*

obierit, v. *to die* (Latin indicative future perfect, but here with value of future eventuality).

obligare (obligadu), v. *to oblige, to constrain, to bind,*

observare (observada, observando), v. *to enforce, to fulfill* (the law), *to observe.*

obstante, see **non obstante.**

obviare (obviasserun), v. *to meet.*

obviari, v. *to help, to provide remedy.*

ocaxione, see **occasione.**

occasione, n. *cause, reason.*

occidere (okier, okisit, ociserat), v. *to kill.*

ochaxione, see **occasione.**

ochire (ochiri, ochiat), v. *to kill.*

ockidere, see **ochire.**

ochier, **ochiere**, see **ochire.**

ockisura, n. *murder, killing.*

octo, cardinal number: *eight*; **decem et octo**: *eighteen.*

oe, adv. *today.*

offendere (offender, offendet, ofendet, offesidu offensida), v. **1.** *to offend*; **2.** *to hurt, to wound.*

offensida, see **offendere.**

offesidu, see **offendere.**

offerre (offerremi, oferrimi, offerimus, offerin, me offersi), v. *to offer*; reflexive: *to offer oneself as a lay brother or sister.*

officiale, n. *officer.*

officiali, see **officiale.**

officiu, n. **1.** *office, duty and task related to the job, office or post held, profession*; **durante in su officiu issoro** *or* **in sos officios issoro**: *in the performance of own duties*; **aviri at officiu:** *to be in charge in*; **2.** *divine office*; **3.** (funeral) *office and service.*

offizio, see **officiu.**

ogna, **ogne**, see **omnia.**
ognia, **ogni**, see **omnia.**
ogui, n. *eye.*
oi, see **oe.**
oiastru: n. (*tree*) *oleaster, wild olive.*
okidere, see **ochire.**
olidone, n. *strawberry tree, corbezzolo.*
oliva, n. *olive.*
olivellu, n. (toponym): *wild olive.*
omine, n. *man*. See also **homine.**
omnes, adj. and pron. *all, every, everyone.*
omni, adj. and pron. *all, every.*
omnia (ogna, ognia, ogni, ogne, dogna, dognia donnia, donia, dogni), adj. and pron. *all, everything, everyone, every, each*; **sa festa de omnia sanctu:** *the feast of All Saints.*
omnibus, (dative plural) adj. and pron., see **onnia.**
omnipotente, adj. *Almighty* (God).
omnium genitive pl.; **omnibus** (dative plural): adj. and pron. *all, every*(body). See also **omnia.**
onnia, see **omnia.**
operaiu, n. *worker, overseer of work.*
operas, see **obera.**
oppone (oppostu), v. *to oppose.*
opponnere, see **opponne.**
oppostu, see **opponne.**
opus, n. *work, work performance, profit, favour, need, necessity of work, servile manual labour*; **ad opus de:** *in favour of.*
ora (hora, oram), n. *hour, time.*
orbitu, n. *rural path.*
ordinadamente, **ordinadamenti**, adv. *precisely.*
ordinamento (ordinamentos), n. *ordinance.*
ordinare (ordinavi, ordinamus, ordinadu), v. *to order, to prepare, to establish, to ordain, to command.*
ordinatio (nominative), **ordinatione** (accusative) (in Latinising clauses), n. *order, ordinance.*
ordinatione, n. *order, decision, provision.*
ordine (ordines), n. *order, row of vines.*
ordini, n. 1. *order, provision, will*; 2. *social order or class*; 3. in the phrase **su ordini dessa ragoni:** *according to that which the principles of law require.* See also **ordine.**

orfanu (orfana, orfanos), n. *orphan* (male).
origla, n. *ear.*
origa, see **origla.**
oriu, n. *barley.*
ormedu, n. *elm tree.*
orriina, n. *barley field.*
orriola, see **ariola.**
orriu, see **oriu.**
orroglu, n. *piece, chunk*; or, perhaps, also *ruin.*
orrubiu, adj. *red.*
orrudunda, see **rodunda.**
ortale, n. *vegetable garden.*
orto, see **ortu.**
ortu, n. (vegetable) *garden*; **ortu d'abis**: *beeyard.*
oru, n. *edge, verge, side.*
orvitu, see **orbitu.**
osca, adv. *after, later on.*
oservare, see **observare.**
over, **overo**, disjunctive conj: *or, or rather.*
oviare, v. *to meet.* See also **obviare.**

P

pacare, v. *to pay.*
pace, n. *peace.*
pacificamenti, adv. *without opposition, without any dispute.*
pacifichamente, see **pacificamenti.**
pacifichu, adj. *peaceful.*
pacto, n. *agreement.*
padre, see **patre.**
padro, see **padru.**
padronu, **padrono**, n. *master*; **padrona**: *mistress.*
padru, n., see **pardu.**
padule (paules), n. *swamp, marsh.*
paeccadu, n. always in the formula **pro remissione de sos paeccados meos:** *for forgiveness or remission of my sins.*
pecados, **pecadus**, see **peccados.**
peccados, n. *sin.*
peccatos, **pecactos**, see **peccados.**

paga, n. *payment.*
pagadore, n., *payer, guarantor.*
pagamentu, n. *payment.*
pagha (paghas), n. *wages, fee.*
paghadori, see **paghadore.**
pagare (pagari, pagat, pagit, pagadu), v. *to pay.*
paghare (paghari, paghat, pagharit, paghando), see **pagare.**
paghi, see **pace.**
pagu, adv. *little, a very small amount*; **acateillos ... kena serbire force pagu**: *I found them ... they did not render any service except a very small amount.*
paguit, see **pagare.**
pahura, see **paura.**
paiu, n. *pair, couple.*
pake, see **pace.**
pala[1] (palas), n. 1. *shoulder*: in the singular it is used exclusively in the locution **levaresi in pala**: *to take upon oneself the burden of answering for eviction.*
pala[2], n. *slope.*
pala[3]. adv. *behind.*
palatiu, n. *palace.*
palesamenti, adv. *overtly.*
palesi, adv. *overtly.*
palisimenti; see **palesamenti.**
palma, n. it is used exclusively in the locution **dominica de palma**: *Palm Sunday.*
palmas, n. *palms.*
palmu (palmus), n. *span, handwidth* (unit of length).
palu, n. *stake.*
panghuliere, **panghulier**, n. *pillory.*
pani, n. *bread*; in the phrase ***istari a pani et a vinu de***, literally, *being on bread and wine,* that is: *to be fed and maintained by someone.*
paniiu, see **panilio.**
panilio (servu de), n. (co-opted, but partially free) *servant.*
panilo, see **panilio.**
pannu (pannos), n. *cloth, dress.*
panpinu, n. *vineleaf.*
paperu, see **pauperu.**
paradisu, **paradisum**, n. *paradise.*
paragula, n. *word.* See also **paraula.**
paramentu, (paramentus), n. *vestment.*
parare, v. *to pay for, to acquire, to buy.*

paraula (paraulas), n. **1.** *word, permission, licence, authorisation*; **2.** *mandate, proxy, authorisation*; in the phrases, **senza** or **per paraula de:** *without or with permission*; **dare paraula:** *to give promise or assurance* **paraula criminosa** *or* **iniurosa:** *insult, criminal or insulting word* (bearing and implying a criminal charge); **in paraulas:** *orally, verbally.*

parçone, see **parzone.**

parççoni, see **parzone**

parçzoni, see **parzone.**

pardargiu (pardargios), see **pradargiu.**

pardassus, see **pradargiu.**

pardu (pardo, pardos), n. **1.** *meadow, communal pasture land kept as grassland*; **iuradu de pardu**, see *pradargiu*; **maiore de pardu:** *officer overseeing pastures who collaborates with the* **pradargios** *and supervises their work*; **pardu de siidu** *or* **siilu:** *meadow reserved* (for a lord); **pardo de hierro:** *meadow reserved for grazing in winter*; **pardo de mindas:** *pasture closed and reserved* (for tame fettered livestock or for sowing).

pare, adv. always in locution: **in pare:** *together*; **de pare: segaresi de pare:** *to cut out* (into its surface) *or to separate itself, excising itself from another surface*; **ladus a pare:** *half for each*; **a plakimentu bonu de pare, cun** *or* **ad boluntade bona de bare:** *by mutual agreement, with mutual satisfaction*; **capud a pare:** *for the same equal* (economic) *value*; **ispiiaresi de pare:** *to resolve by mutual agreement*; **(essere) bikinos de pare:** (to be) *near each other*; **afliscaresi a pare:** *to return to, to rejoin with the starting point* (said of a land boundary).

pari, see **pare.**

parente (parentes, parentis), n. *relative*; **parente destrittu:** *close relative.*

parerent, see **parri.**

pares (pari, paris), adv. *together*; **2. partire pares:** *to divide half by each*; **3. fagersi pares:** *to join with*; **in compagnia de pari:** *in company with each other*; **intre pari:** (border) *in common with others.*

pargiant, see **parri.**

pari[1], see **pares.**

pari[2], adj. and n. *equal*, person *of the same and equal rank.*

pari[3], adj. in the Latin phrase: **agentes et consentientes pari** (i.e. equal) **pena puniuntur:** *agents and consenting agents or accessories are punished with equal punishment.*

pariamentu, n. *compensation.*

pariare, v. *to compensate, to settle the score.*

paris, see **pares.**

parit, see **parri.**

parixente, adj. *identifiable.*
parladu, n. *prelate.*
parre (parrer, parit, ant parri, pargiant, parerent), v. 1. *to appear, to seem, to be deemed*, 2. *to be of the opinion.*
parrer, see **parre.**
parrere (parit, pariat, parsit), see **parre.**
parsit, see **parre.**
parte[1], n. 1. *part, portion, fraction, share*; 2. *administrative division corresponding to the curatorial disrict*; 3. *share, division* (of land or services); 4. *area, place*; 5. *limb, part of the body, member*; 6. *parties, litigants in court* 7. in Latin clauses: *fate, destiny*: **et appat parte cum iniquo Herode**: *and share his fate with the iniquitous Herod*; in locution: **dae parte de**: *in lieu of*; **per parte**: *for each one*; **pro parti de**: *from*; **in parti**: *in part, partly*; **aviri parti in**: *to be involved in*; **sa maiore parti de**: *the majority.*
parte[2], n. *territorial part, equivalent to* Logu, *iudicato, realm or a district of it.*
parthimentu, n. *division, separation, apportioning.*
parthire, v. *to divide, to share, to apportion.*
parthithione, n. *division, separation, apportioning.*
parthitura, n. *division, separation, apportioning.*
parthiu, n. *division, separation, apportioning.*
parthone, n. *part of, subdivision.*
parti, see **parte.**
particione, n. *division* (used for dividing servants).
participantes, n. *participants, attendees.*
participare, v. *to participate.*
participe (participes), n. *co-participant.*
particulari, adj. in the phrase; **membru particulari** *minor limb of the body, as the hand or the finger*. See also see **membru.**
particularimente, adv. *mainly*, specifically: **ciò si intendat ad icussas personas a sas quales particularimente esseret fatu su ditu pagamentu**: *And this is to be understood specifically in relation to persons to whom such payment has been made.*
partidu (partidus), n. *judgement, determination, resolution*; **dari a partidus**: *to seek for a judgement in judicial disputes.*
partidura: n. *division* (of servants).
partimentu, n. *division* (of servants).
partione, n. *division* (of servants).
partire[1] (parço, partent, partiat, partiamus, partiant, partivi, partirus, partant, partindo) v. 1. *to divide*; **partire cun**: *to share*; 2. *to acquire part of a product of economic activity as an exaction of a tax right*; 3. **partire in pare** or **de pare**: *to*

stand on the boundary, to divide or share the boundary between two properties; **esserer partido:** *to be divided in judgement* (in court).
partire[2] (partit·si, partidos), v. *to leave, to go away, to move away.*
partithone, n. *division, separation, apportioning.*
partitione, see **paticione.**
partjone., see **parzone.**
paru, n. *purchase, acquisition.*
parzitura, n. *division, separation, apportioning.*
parzone, n. **1.** *part of, subdivision*; **2.** *part of an estate or inheritance, or territorial extent*; **2a.** *share accruing in a division of children of a servant couple in the respective property of two different owners.*
parzoni, see **parzone.**
parzzoni, see **parzone.**
Pasca de maiu, n. *Easter Sunday.*
Pascha, Pasca, n. **1.** *Easter*; **2. Pascha de sa natividadi:** *Easter of Nativity, Christmas*; **3. Pascha dessa Epiphania:** *Easter of Epiphany*; **4. Pascha nunsa:** *Epiphany*; **5. Pascha de Ascensioni:** *Easter of Ascension*; **6. Pascha de Pentecoste:** *Easter of Pentecost.*
paschere, v. *to graze, to lead the cattle to pasture.*
paschire (paschit), see **paschere.**
paschiri, see **paschere.**
pasificamenti, see **pacificamenti.**
pasker, see **paschere.**
passare (passit, passado), v. **1.** *to pass, to go beyond, to cross*; **2.** *to go by* (the time); **cosas passadas:** *past facts*; **2.1. infini ad passadu de:** *after, until the end.*
Passassione, n. Unclear meaning, possibly *the servants in the property of the monastery* **cun testimonios tota passassione de clesia et cun colivertos quantos ie furunt:** *all the servants of the church being witnesses and with all freedmen present there.*
pastinu, n. *newly planted vineyard.*
pastore, pastori, n. *shepherd.*
pastu, n. *pasture, grazing, unworked land.*
patire (patischat, ppaciente), v. *to suffer*; **pena alcuna non patischat:** *not be subject to any penalty*; **persona ppaciente**, *person having been injured.*
patischat, see **patire.**
ppaciente, see **patire.**
patre (patri, padre, padri, patrem, patres), n. *father.*
patrona, n. *female patron.*
patronu, n. *patron.*
patru, patro, see **pardu.**

paules, see **padule.**
pauperu, pauperum, paperu, n. *minor landholder* (in a village; not from a high social class, but not necessarily poor).
paura, n. *fear.*
paximentu (paximentos), n. *pasture.*
peale, n. in the locution **a peale de:** *at the foot of, below.*
peccadu (peccatos), n. *sin.*
peccator, n. *sinner.*
peccatos, see **peccadu.**
pecos, n. *heads of cattle.*
pecter, see **petere.**
pectus, n. *chest.*
pecuiare, see **peguiare.**
pecuiu; see **peculiu.**
peculiu, n. 1. *money*; 2. *livestock.*
pedale, n. *foot*; **a(ssu) pedale de:** *at the foot of.*
pedaniu, n. *pedestal of a barrel.*
pedati, n. and adj. *servants owing a quarter service to each of the four masters.*
pede, n. 1. *foot, base*; 2. *quarter, quarter service* (of a servant).
pede (pedes), see **pee.**
pedire (pedivili, pedindomi), v. *to ask, to request.*
pedra, see *petra.*
pee (pees), n. 1. *foot*; 2. *the fourth share or portion of a servant's property*; **a pees (de):** *at the foot of, below*; **a ppee**, *on foot.*
peghugiare, see **peguiare.**
peghu (peghus), see **pegus.**
peguiare: *private, of private property*, (something) *that is private property* (of someone); 2. *one's personal estate.*
pegus (pegos), n. 1. *beast, head of cattle*; 2. (hunted) *game or prey.*
pelle (pelles), n. *animal fur, skin, leather, hide.*
pena (penas), n. *penalty, punishment, sentence, sanction, fine, penalty.*
pendenti, adj. *pendant, pending, indefinite*
penedentiare (penedentiedi, penedentiait), v. *to confess, to give sacramental penance, to collect last wills.*
penetenthia, see **penitentia.**
penitentia, n. *confession* (of sins), *confession, penitence.*
pensadamente, adv. *intentionally, with premeditation.*
penetenthiare, see **penedentiare.**
Penthecoste, n. *Easter of Pentecost.*
per, prep., 1. *for, about, throughout, in, to, in order that, during, by, as*; in the

locutions: **per ispaciu de:** *for a period of*; place: *all over*; time: *for*; cause: *by, at*; means or instrument: *by, at*; **per inantes**[1]: *previously*; **per inantes**[2]: *in the future, later*; **per issu factu modo qui (pro issu fatu modu qui):** *so that*; **per (a)ventura:** *by chance, accidentally*; **getadura de birga per parte:** *for the space of a rod cast* (length measurement for each of the two part measuring); **boleant tenne·illu per sa persona:** *they wanted to arrest him, detaining him in person.*

percontrare, v. *to ask, to demand.*

percussione (percussions), n. *beating.*

perdere (perder, perdat, perderet, perdiremus, perdidas), v. **1.** *to lose, to suffer a loss*; **2.** *to lose the case* (in court); **3.** *to be deprived of*; **3.1.** *to lose a limb* (of the body); **3.2.** *to be deprived of something*; **4.** *to forfeit, to give up, to suffer the breaking of a contract*; **5.** *to lose time, days.*

perdimentu, n. *loss, damage.*

perdittu, see **predictu.**

perdonare (perdonai, perdonarunt), v. *to forgive, to remit, to pardon, to condone.*

perigulosu (perigulosa), adj. *dangerous, serious* (injury).

perigulu, n. *danger.*

periudicare (periudichit, periudischat), v. *to be prejudicial to, to prejudice, to invalidate.*

periudiciu, see **preiudiciu.**

permutadu (permutada), adj. *changed.*

però, conj. *but, however, though.*

perpetrare (perpetradu), v. *perpetrate.*

perpetuum, n. in the locution **in perpetuum:** in *perpetuity, forever.*

persona, n. **1.** *person*; **2.** (in) *himself*; **et boleant tenne·illu per sa persona:** *they wanted to arrest him, detaining him in person*; **iusticiare in persona:** *to sentence to death*; **in persona,** *bodily.*

persone, personi, see **persona.**

pertenencia, n. *appurtenance, what is pertinent, surrounding a property or territorial entity.*

pertenenthia, see **pertenencia.**

pertenere (pertenet, pertinent), v. *being pertinent to* or *surrounding a property or territorial entity.*

pertinenti, adj. *due*; **sa parti pertinenti ad issos:** *their due share.*

pertinere, v. *to be entitle to.*

pertunghere (pertungherit), v. *to make an opening, to break through* (the wall).

pertusita, adj. *pierced.*

pertusu (pertusa), adj. *pierced*; toponym: **Petra pertusa**, top. *Pierced Stone.*

perunu (peruno, peruna), adj. *nobody, not any.*

pervengiat, see **pervenne.**
pervenne (pervengiat), v. *to come up.*
pesare(si), v. *to get up, to erect.*
pesari (pesat, peset), v. 1. *to call to*; 2. *to rise.*
pesentinu, n. *velvet fabric* (of Piacenzan origin).
petere, v. *to request, to demand, to ask, to seek, to petition.*
petha, see **petsa.**
petholu, n. *piece* (of land).
pethone, n. *compensation.*
peticione, n. *petition.*
petire (petiili), v. see **pedire.**
petra, n. *stone, rock, boulder, stony material.*
petrosa, adj. *rocky.*
petsa, n. *meat*; in the locution **segari de petsa:** *carnival.*
pettitura, n. *request, petition.*
piazza, see **plaza.**
piccinnu, see **pikinnu.**
pichinno, see **pikinnu.**
picinnu, see **pikinnu.**
picinu, see **pikinnu.**
piciu, see **pizinu.**
pietosu (pietosas), adj. *compassinate, charitable.*
pignorare (pignorint·illi), v. *to foreclose, to seize, to confiscate.*
pikinnu, n. and adj. *small, little, baby, youngster.*
pilamini, n. *pelage, coat* (of animals).
pilu (pilos), n. 1. *pelage, coat* (of animals); 2. *hair.*
pinnus, n. *pledge.*
pintana, n., *seedbed, land* (ready for cultivating).
piperas, n. *snakes.*
pira (piras), n. *pear* (tree).
pirastru, n. *wild pear.*
pisanischu, adj. *Pisan.*
Pisanos, n. *Pisans.*
piscare, v. *to fish.*
pischina, n. *pool of water, waterhole, marsh.*
piscina, see **pischina.**
piscobu, n. *bishop.*
piscopu, see **piscobu.**
piskinale, n. *marshland.*
pismaresi, v. *to complain, to protest.*

pisque, n. *fish.*
pisquera, n. *fishpond.*
pisquina, see **pischina.**
pithinnu, see **pikinnu.**
piu (pias), adj. *pious.*
pixinu, see **pizinu.**
pixiu, see **pizinu.**
pizinu, n. and adj. **1.** *minor* (child); **2.** *lesser, slight*
pizzariu, n. *upland.*
plaça, see **plaza.**
plachimentu, n. in the phrase **a plachimentu de:** *at discretion or at will of.*
pladigait, see **platigare.**
pladigarunt, see **platigare.**
plagere (plaguiat, plagit, plaguit, plagende), v. **1.** *to please, to be liked, to be enjoyed, to wish*; **2.** *to seem right, to be agreeable*; **3.** *to be at someone's will*; **4.** *to agree*; **4a.** in the formula **plagendonos a pare:** *by mutual agreement*; **ad plaghere de:** *at the consent or at the discretion of.*
plagit, see **plagere.**
plaguit, see **plagere.**
plakere (plakit, plakiat, plakerunt), see **plagere.**
plakimentu, n. *consent, accord*; in the formula **a plakimentu bonu de pare:** *in mutual agreement.*
plakitare, v. *to promise.*
plama, n. *palm*; in the phrase, **corona de plama:** *assizes of Palm Sunday.* See also **palma.**
plantare (plantat), v. *to plant* (with or as).
planu, n. *plain.*
plassa, see **plaza²**.
platicu, n. *promise.*
platigare (platicai, pladigarunt), v. *to promise, to pledge, to guarantee.*
plaza¹, n. a *not large plot of land adjacent to the* **domu.**
plaza², n. *square.*
plenariamente, adv. *fully, thoroughly.*
plenos, adj. *full.*
plevanu, n. *parson, parish priest, vicar.*
Plominos, **Plominus**, n. *place near Càlari* (Cagliari); *the iudicato of Càlari.*
plubica, adj. *public* (*road*).
Pluminus, see **Plominos.**
plus, adv. **1.** *more, further*(*more*).; **2.** *several*; **3.** *still more*; **4.** *in addition*; **4.** preceded by the definite article it forms the relative superlative; **5.** in the locutions **non plus:** *no more*; **5.2. via plus:** *all the more.*

pobillu, see **pubillu.**
pobulu, n. *people.*
pochu, pocha, adj. *inadequate, scarce.*
poder[1] (podet, podiat, potuit, pozat, possant, pozant, posant, pozint, pozat, pozamus, pozant, pozint, possidu), v. *can, to be able, to have the opportunity or the chance to.*
poder[2], **podere**, n. 1. *power, possibility*; **in podere suo:** *being in one's power*; **faghere su podere suo:** *to do all in one's power.*
podestade, see **potestate.**
podestava, see **potestare.**
podiat, see **poder(e)**[1].
polissa, n. 1. *subpoena*; 2. **polissa de sos chertos binchidos:** *order for payment for successful judicial cases.*
polliricata, adj. (mare) *that has foaled, calved.*
pomu, n. 1. *fruit*; 2. *orchard*, 3. *fruit tree.*
ponere, see **ponne.**
ponne (ponio, ponnemus, ponemusillu, poniat, posi, posit, poserus, poserunt, apo postu, poserat, ponnet, ponendollos, ponendomi), v. 1. *to donate*; 2. *to establish, to arrange, to order*; 3. *to impose*: especially, but not exclusively, *in court*; 4. *to set oneself, to dispose oneself, to put oneself, to start* (to do something); 5. *to place someone in an office or function*; 6. *to plant, to plant* (a land) *as a vegetable garden, orchard*, etc; 7. *to put, to place*; 8. *to indicate, to make use of, to assign* 9. *to appoint*; 10. in the phrases: **ponne in manu(s) de:** *to place in the ownership or power of, to deliver, to place in the sight of*; **ponere a destimoniu:** *to call as witness.* **ponere a postu:** *to make an appointment, to call a meeting*; **ponere corona:** *to convene a hearing*; **ponere in fattu:** *to pursue, to chase*; **ponere in manu de:** *to entrust to*; **ponere in pegnu:** *to make a pledge*; **ponere in pena:** *to establish as a fine*; **ponere muru:** *to put up a wall*; **ponere opus:** *to work, to labour*; **ponne boghi**, *to give notice*; **ponne foghu**, *to light a fire*; **ponne pena**, *to sanction, to punish*; **ponne sinnu**, *to brand*; **ponni a sagramentu**, *to enjoin the oath*; **ponne a trumentu**, *to torture*; **ponne in su panghuliere**, *to put to the pillory.*
popillu, see **pubillu.**
populare, n. *collective property* (of a village).
populum, n. *people.*
porcariu, n. *swineherd, swine-keeper, overseer of a pig-farm.*
porchargiu (porcargios), see **porcariu.**
porcho, porchu, see **porcu.**
porcinu, see **porkina.**
porco, see **porcu.**

porcu, n. *pig, swine*; **porcho mannali**: *domestic swine*; **porchos de gamma**: *pigs in herd.*
poriglos (poriglus), n. always in the phrase **poriglos de angarias** (see the entry): *co-owners, for a given share, of a horse subject to the* **angaria**, i.e. *the messenger service.*
porkile, n. *pigsty.*
porkina (petha), adj. (meat) *of pig.*
porta, n. *gate, entrance.*
portare (portat, portadu, portando), v. *to take* (away), *to bring, to carry, to deliver.*
portorariu, n. *tax collector.*
portu, n. *port*; **corona de portu**: *assizes governed by a port officer*; **maiore de portu**: *senior port officer.*
portu, n. *port.*
pos, see *post.*
posca, adv. *after.*
poscha, see **posca**.
possediri (possedidu), v. *to possess, to own.*
possessione, possessioni, n. **1.** *possession, real estate*; **2.1.** in the locution **mitire in possessione de**: *to put in possession of.*
possidu, see **poder**[1].
post, adv. and prep. **1.** *after,* **2.** *behind,* **3.** *beyond,* **4.** *from or by someone.*
posta, n. in the phrase **andari ad posta sua**: *to go to the place where the hunter or the dog awaits the game.*
postea, adv. *after.*
postu, n. *date, appointment, day agreed and set for court.*
postura, n. *donation, gift.*
potere, see **poder**[1].
potestade, n. *power, authority, podestà.*
potestare (potestent; potestando), v. **1.** *to have power, to rule, to govern*; **2.** *to take over, to dominate, to gain superiority over someone.* **viiat ca llu podestava**: *he realised that he* (the opposing party) *took over* (in a judicial debate).
potestate, see *potestade.*
poveru, n. and adj. *poor.*
poy, adv. *after.*
ppaciente, see **patire**.
ppoder, see **poder**[1].
ppoveros, see **poveru**.
pradargiu (pradargos), n. *officials in charge of communal pastures.*
pradu, see **padru**.

pratu, see **padru.**
prea, n. *seized property, a taking possession of an item, property, or person legally or by force; confiscate.*
preare, v. *to seize and retain in custody of the law; to confiscate.*
prebiter, see **prebiteru.**
prebiteru, n. *priest.*
preciu, n. *proceeds.*
precontare (precontait, percontait, precontait, percontedi), see **pregontare.**
preçu, see **prezu.**
predare, v. *to subtract, to steal.*
predictu, **predicto**, see *predittu.*
perdittu (predita), adj. *aforesaid, mentioned above.*
pregare (pregavant, pregai, pregaitimi): v. *to beg, to pray, to implore.*
pregione, **pregioni**, n. *prison.*
pregiu, n. *price.*
pregontare (pregontaremi, pregonteillu), v. *to ask, to question, to request, to interrogate.*
pregontu (pregontus), n. (report of) *interrogation.*
pregu, n. *prayer.*
preidaru, see **prebiteru.**
preideru, see **prebiteru.**
preitero, see **prebiteru.**
preiteru, see **prebiteru.**
preiti, n. *priest.* See also **prebiteru.**
preiudiciu, n. (anything) *that is detrimentral.*
premiu, n. *reward.*
presbiter, see **prebiteru.**
presbiteru, see **prebiteru.**
prescriptioni (prescriptiones), n. *prescription,* **prescriptione de tempus:** *usucapion.*
prescriptu, n. *prescribed.*
presentare (presentarint), v. *to present.*
presente, n. and adj. 1. *present, the present time*; 2. *he who assists or participates directly in something*; 3. *this, this present* (chapter, order, etc.), *what is being talked about*; **de presente:** *immediately*; **assu presente:** *at the present time*; **su presente:** *the present.*
presenti, see **presente.**
presentia, n. *presence,* always in the location **in presentia de:** *in the presence of, before.*
presone, see **pregione.**

presse, n. *haste, urgency.*
pressona, see **persona.**
prestansa, see **prestanza.**
prestanza, n. *loan, credit.*
prestare (prestait, prestadu), v. *to lend.*
presumere (presumat, presumischat), v. *to presume, to dare.*
presumischat, see **presumere.**
pretender(·si) (pretender s'at): v. *to allege, to claim, to oppose.*
prethu, see **prezu.**
pretio, see **prezu.**
previderu, see **prebiteru.**
previteru, see **prebiteru.**
prexione, prexioni, prexoni, see **pregione.**
prexu, n. *value, consideration*; **minus prexu:** *disregard, negligence.*
prezare, see **apressare.**
prezatura, n. *appreciation* (of market value).
prezu, n. *price, amount paid.*
priga, adj. **1.** *weak*; **2.** *slow* (said of the flow of a spring).
prima, see **primu.**
primarga, see **primargiu.**
primargiu (primargia), adj. and. pron. *the first* (time), *the first time.*
primariu, adj: **1.** *the first*; **2.** *first-born*; **3.** *primary or first* (cousin); **in primariu:** *primarily, chiefly.*
primis, in the adv. locution **in primis:** *first of all.*
primo, see **primus.**
primu, adj. *the first.*
primus 1. adj. *the first*; **2.** adv. *firstly.*
principali, adj. **1.** *main participant, principal*; **membro principali:** *main member or limb* (of the body).
principiu, n. *beginning.*
prior, see **priore.**
priore, n. *prior.*
priorissa, n. *prioress.*
privare (privadus), v. *to deprive of property, to dispossess.*
pro, prep. (that forms articulated prepositions with the definite article, **prossu, prossa, prossos, prossas**): *for, about, with regard to, by, from, as, instead of*; *in relation to, about*; **pro parti de:** *from*; **pro ispacio de:** *for a period of*; **pro aventura:** *by chance*; **pro testimonios:** *as witnesses* **pro qui** *or* **que** *or* **ca:** *because, for the fact that*; **pro ciò:** *hence*; **pro modu qui:** *so that*; **pro icussu modu qui:** *in the same manner as.*

pro·llu, see **pro.**
pro·ssu, see **pro.**
proa, see **prova.**
proare, see **provare.**
probadu, **probado**, see **provare.**
probe, see **prope.**
procedere (procedat), v. *to proceed.*
processu (processos), n. *record of proceedings.*
procura (procuras), n. *power of attorne.*
procuradore, n. *attorney.*
procuradori, see **procuradore.**
procurationi, n. *office or activity of attorney or prosecutor.*
procuratore, see **procuradore.**
prode, n. *pro, advantage, benefit*; **prossu prode**: *as a guarantee.*
proe, see **prode.**
progitteu, pron. 1, *why*; *the reason for*, 2. *since*; *because.*
proha, see **prova.**
promissione, n. *promise.*
promitere (promitiat), see **promittere.**
promittere (promittirit), v. *to promise.*
pronomen, n. *surname.*
prope, **a prope de**, prep. *near.*
propriu (proprios, propria), *own* (that belongs to).
prounde, relative conj. *for which, so.*
prova, n. *evidence.*
provare (provari, proare, provadu), v. *to prove.*
providere (provididu), v. 1. *to provide*; 2. *to inspect, to view.*
providimento, see **providimentu.**
providimentu, n. *foresight, provision*; 2. *measure* (act by which a necessity is provided for).
provigione, n. *decision, resolution.*
provincia (provincias), n. *province.*
provisioni, see **provigione.**
proxima, adj. *pregnant.*
proximu, adj. *next coming.*
pruna, n. *plum* (tree).
pubillu (pobilus), n. *master, owner, holder.*
publica, see **publichu.**
publicamente, adv. *publicly.*
publicare (publicari, publichit, publicada), v. *to publish.*

publichu, **publicha**, adj. *public*; **(cartas) in forma publica**: (charters or writings drawn up as) *a public deed for legal use*.
pubuliaina (pubulianas), n. *poplar woodland*.
puçu, see **puzu**.
pugnare, see **punnare**.
pullerigada, see **polliricata**.
pulletru, n. *foal*.
pumora, see **pumura**.
pumu, see **pomu**.
pumura, n. *fruit orchard*.
punire (ponidu), v. *to punish*.
puniuntur, v. in Latin phrase *to punish* ('they will be punished').
punnare, v. *to try*.
pupillu, see **pubillu**.
puriles, n. and adj. *boys, lads*.
puro, conj. in the locution **puro qui**: *provided that*; **si puro**: *even if*.
puru[1] (puros), adj. *righteous, honest*.
puru[2], conj: *also, too*.[1]
pus, prep. *after, besides*. See also **post**.
pusco, conj. *since, because*.
puspare, adv. *over all, as a whole, overall, in its entirety*
pusti, adv. 1. *after*; 2. (to be) *in the retinue of*.
puteca, n. *store, depot*.
puthancaru, n. *marsh, bog*.
puthu, see **puzu**.
puzu (puzus), n. *well, reservoir*.

Q

qua, see **ca**.
quaderno, see **quadernu**.
quadernu, n. *register, notebook*.
quadrupedia, n. *quadruped* (livestock).
quale (quales), see **cale**.
quali, see **cale**.
qualicunu (qualicuna), pron. *somebody*.
qualidadi, n. *quality, value, condition*.
qualunca, see **calunca**.
qualuncha, see **calunca**.

quando, see **cando.**
quanta (quantas), see **cantu.**
quantidade, quantidadi, n. *amount, quantity, size.*
quanto, see **cantu.**
quantu, see **cantu.**
quantu, see **cantu.**
quartu (quarta), adj. *fourth.*
quatro, cardinal number: *four.* See also **baturo.**
quaturpenna, n. *quadrupeds*; *livestock.*
que, see **qui.**
que, see **ki**[1] e **ki**[2].
quercu, see **kercu.**
questione, n. *question, dispute, proceeding.*
questioni, see **questione.**
qui, see **ki.**
qui[1], **que, chi, qu, ch**, relative pron. *who, whom, that, the one who.* See also **ki**[1].
qui[2], **que, chi, qu, ch'**, conj. *that, than*; maybe also *if.* See also **ki**[2].
quia, see **ca.**
quida, see **chida.**
quimbanta, cardinal number: *fifty.*
quimbi, cardinal number: *five.*
quindeci, cardinal number: *fifteen.* See also **bindichi.**
quini, pron. *he or him or they or them who(m).*
quirquidore, see **kerkidore.**
quis, pron. always and exclusively in Latin formulas of execration or benediction, preceded by *et* (*et si quis*): *anyone*: **Et si quis ista carta audire eam voluerit et nostra ordinatione confortaverit, habeat benedictione de Deus et de sancta Maria et de sanctu Petru de Bidoni:** *And if anyone wishes to observe* (the provisions of) *this charter and apply it, may God, Holy Mary and Saint Peter of Bidonì bless him.*
quitheu, see **chiteu.**
quo[1], see **co.**
quo[2], in Latin context in Sardinian phrase: relative pronoun in ablative of price: pro **eo pretio quo**: *at the same price with which.*
quod, conj. in Latin context in Sardinian phrase: *that.*
quoiuvanthia, n. *marriage, wedding.* See also **coiuvanthia.**

R

radicariu, n. *area where canes are left to grow.*

ragione (ragiones, raxiones, resone, rexioni), n. 1. *Law, justice, jurisdiction, trial*; **secundo ragione** *or* **a ragione:** *according to the law, lawfully*; **apertenne a sa ragione de:** *to fall under the jurisdiction of*; **faghere ragione**, *to render an account of*; **dimandari sas raxiones:** *to claim his own right*; **faghere raxioni:** *to administer justice*; **istare a sa raxioni:** *to put oneself back to justice, to submit to justice, to grarantee*; **reere** *or* **tenere rexioni:** *administer justice*; 2. *Right* or *title claimed on an asset*; **regiones echesiastighas:** *ecclesiastical rights, goods or territories over which the Church has rights*; 3. *tax, tribute*; 4. *reason, argument*; **non est ragione:** *it is not right that*; **ad raxone de:** *at the rate of*; *account, counting*; **a resone de:** *for the price of.*

ragioni, see **ragione.**

ragionibilimente, adv. *by right.*

ragoni, see **ragione.**

raigha, n. *fence post, root of the vine.*

raizone, see **ragione.**

ramanent, see **remanere.**

ramasit, see **remanere.**

ramenere (ramanet, rammanent, ramannint), see **remanere.**

rankidas, adj. *rancid, sour* (taste).

rasone, see **ragione.**

rata, n. *installment, payment, share.*

rathone, n. *right, reason* (in the subjective sense); **per rathone de:** *in return*; **in rathone de:** *provided that.* See also **ragione.**

raxione, see **ragione.**

raxone, see **ragione.**

raxonivili, adj. *reasonable.*

raygla, see **raigha.**

raygha, see **raigha.**

raygua, see **raigha.**

razone, see **ragione.**

rebellaresi (sse rebellait): *to rebel, to abandon unduly servile condition.*

receptare (receptarit), v. *to give receptivity.*

rechonoschimentu, n. *acknowledgement.*

recivere, see **recivire.**

recivire, reciviri, recivir (recivido), v. 1. *receive*; 2. *to take delivery*; 3. *to approve.*

reciviri, recivir (recivido), see **recivire.**

reclamare, v. *to reclaim, to call back.*

reclamo, n. in the phrase **andare a reclamo**: *to file a* (judicial) *complaint*; *to make a complaint to the authorities*.
reconventione, n. *reconvention, counter-claim*.
recordacione, see **recordatione**.
recordantia, n. *written record for memory*.
recordare, v. *to recall, to remember*.
recordari·si (recordari·si·ndi, recordarit), v. *to remember*.
recordaria, n. *written record for memory*.
recordatione, n. *written record for memory*.
recordu, n. *record, memory*.
recursu, n. *complaint*; **aviri recursu contra**: *to bring suit against*.
redangiu, n. uncertain meaning, may be *possession, ownership*.
reer, reere (reet), v. **1.***to preside over*; **2.** *to hold, to administer*; **3.** *to rule*; **4.** *to have in hand, in possession*. See **arregere**.
refudari (refudadu), v. *to refuse*.
rege (rex, regis, regum), n. *the iudike, king*.
regenthia, n. *work tools, equipment*.
regere, see **arregere**.
regina, n. *the wife of the iudike, queen*.
regione, see **ragione**.
registrare (registradas), v. *to register*.
regnare (regnante), v. *to reign, to rule*; **regnante iudike Mariano**: *in the reign of iudike Mariano*.
regno, see **rennu**.
regnu, see **rennu**.
regordatione, see **recordatione**.
regressu, n. *reimbursement*.
reher, see **reer**.
religiosu (religiosos), n. *religious*.
remanente, n. *remainder*.
remanere (ramanet, rammanent, ramannint, arramanint, remasit, remansit, arramasit, remaserunt, remaneat, remagnat, remaneant), v. *to stay, to remain*: **1.** *to remain in ownership*; **2.** *to recede, to desist from action*; **3.** *to turn out* (to be).
remedio, n. *remedy*.
remittere (remittat), v. *to trade* (for); in the locution **remittere in iscambiu** *to trade, to replace*.
remonidu, adj. *closed, inaccessible*.
render, v. *to render*; **render testimonianza**: *to bear witness, to testify, to witness*.
rengnu, see **rennu**.

rennu, **renno**, n. 1. *the realm, the kingdom, the* iudicatu; 2. *state or public property, the Tresaury.*
renobare, see **renovare.**
renovare (renovola), v. *to renew, to confirm a provision, an arrangement.*
replubigha, n. *republic, the state.*
representari, v. *to present.*
requeder (requederent, requestu, requesto), v. *to request, to convene.*
requesta (requestes), n. *request, instance.*
requestu, **requesto**, see **requeder.**
rere, see **reer.**
res, n. Latin *res*, in the phrase **in res**: *in the matter of, with reference to.*
reservare (reservando), v. *to safeguard, to protect*; **reservandu qui**: *unless.*
resone, see **ragione.**
responder, **respondere** (respondet, respondat), v. *to answer* (before the court), *to respond* (and or or challenge) *in court*
restare (resta), v. *to stay, to rest, to remain.*
restituiri, v. *to return.*
restitutioni, n. *restitution.*
rethone, see **rathone.**
retinere, v. *to requisition, to keep in delivery.*
reu (reos), adj. *guilty, culprit.*
revelari, v. *to reveal, to report.*
revertere (revertamus), v. *to return.*
rex, see **rege.**
rexione (rexiones), n. *region, land.*
rexone (rexones), see **ragione.**
rexioni, see **ragione.**
rezone, see **ragione.**
ribu, n. *river, stream*. See also **erriu.**
righa, **righas**, n. *line.*
rispondere, v. *to reply, respond.*
riu, see **ribu.**
rivu, n., see **ribu.**
robadore, n. *robber.*
robaria, n. *robbery.*
rocca (cunduri di), n. *short robe worn beneath clothes.*
rodunda, adj. *round.*
romanere, v. *to stay, to remain.*
romanne (romannet, romanent, romangat, romanghat, romangiant, romasidos, romanendo), v. *to remain, to stay*. See also **remanere.**

rrecivire, see **recivire.**
rregnu, see **regnu.**
rubiu, adj. *red.*
ruclare, v. *to cross.*
rude, adj. *wild.*
rufiania, n. *pimping.*
rufianu, n. *pimp, thug.*
ruge, see **cruke.**
ruginas, n. *ruins.*
rui, see **rude.**
ruys, see **rude.**
ruviu, see **rubiu.**

S

sa, see **su.**
sabunare (sabunent), v. *to launder* (clothes).
sacerdote, n. *priest, minister.*
sacrare, v. to *consacrate.*
sacrathione, n. *consacration.*
sagra, n. *feast, religious festival.*
sagradu (sagrada), adj. *sacred.*
sagramentu, n. 1. *oath*; **sagramentu de calumpnia:** *oath of slander* (an oath by which it is sworn that one party has slandered the other); **ponni a sagramentu:** *to enjoin the oath.*
sagu, n. *heavy woollen cloth.*
salariu, n. *wages.*
sale, n. *salt.*
salina, n. *saltpan.*
salitare, v. *to safeguard, to care.*
salsa, adj. *brackish* (water).
salto, see **saltu.**
saltu n. *land, tract of land* (sparsely inhabited and little cultivated), *often of great extension*; *unworked or poorly worked land, pasture, countryside, woodland.*
salvu[1], adj. *safe.*
salvu[2], prep. *except*; **salvu si** *or* **qui**: *except.*
samben, n. *blood*; **maquicias de sanben**: *crimes of blood punishable by a fine.*
sambini, see **samben.**

sanare (sanavi), v. *to be healed or cured.*

sanbani, see **samben.**

sanben, see **samben.**

sanare, v. *to heal, to cure.*

sanctu, n. and adj. *saint*; **chida sancta:** *Holy Week*; **festa de omnia sanctu:** *feast of All Saints.*

sanitate, n. *health.*

santu, see **sanctu.**

sanu (sanas), adj. *undamaged, entire.*

sara, adv. *then, in that circumstance.* See also **insara** and **issara.**

sarachu (siracha), see **zaracu.**

saracu, see **zaracu.**

sardischu (sardischo, sardischa sardisca), adj. *Sardinian*; **assa sardischa, assu modu sardischu:** *according to Sardinian jurisdiction*; **secundu ussanza sardisca:** *according to Sardinian legal usage or custom.*

Sardos, n. *people from Sardinia, Sardinians.*

sardu, adj. *Sardinian.*

sargamento, see **sagramentu.**

sargamentu, n. *oath*; **sagramentu de calumpnia:** *oath of slander: an oath by which it is sworn that one party has slandered the other*; **ponni a sagramentu:** *to enjoin an oath.*

sas, see **su.**

satisfacione, n. *compensation.*

satisfaction, see **satisfacione.**

satisfaghere (satisfagheri, satisfagher, satisfagere, satisfahiri, satisfactu), v. *to satisfy, to compensate.*

satisfaghumentu, n. *compensation.*

saviu, savios, n. *judicial adviser*; **sos savios dessa corte nostra:** *the wise men group of judicial counsellors.*

scala, see **iscala.**

scedas, n. *notary's draft or note.* See also **isceda.**

sciat, see **esser.**

scientimente, adv. *deliberately.*

sciò, see **ciò.**

scolca, n. 1. *guardhouse*; 2. *administrative division within the* **curatoría**, *small village.*

scribere (scribo, scribemus, iscripsit), see **scrivere.**

scriptore, n. *writer.*

scriptu, scripto, see **scrivere.**

scriptura, n. *document, record, written form.*

scrittu, n. and v. (past part.): *written.*
scrivania (scrivanias), n. *notary's office, registry office.*
scrivanu (scrivano, iscrianu, iscrianos, iscrivanos), n. *scribe.*
scrivere (scrivire, scriviri, iscriviri, scriptu, iscriptus, scrivendo), v. *to write, to record, to draw up.*
se[1], see **si**[1].
se[2], see **si**[2].
secare, v. *to extract, alienate* (a piece of land for concession).
secidu, see **seer.**
secatura, n. *tract of land for alienation.*
secretamente, adv. *secretly, without one knowing about the other.*
seculum (seculi, seculo): in Latin formulas: (time of) *worldly life, earthly world.*
secundo[1]: (secunda), adj. *second.*
secundo[2], see **secundu.**
secundu, secundum, prep. **1.** *in accordance with, according to, equated with, as, so as*; **2.** *following, according to.*
secus, adv. and prep. *behind.*
secutare, v. *to pursue, to chase, to reach.*
see, see *se.*
seer (seerent, secidu), v. *to mount or ride on horseback.*
segadura, segatura (de rennu), n. *a land extract* (from a given territory according to the course of the boundary); *transfer of a piece of royal property to private individuals as a beneficiary* (because it was alientated from the iudike's estate).
segare[1] (seghit·si·lli, seghit·illi, seguit, seghent·illi, segint·illi, segadu, segado), v. **1.** *to break, to tear*; **2.** *to alienate* (land), *amputate, to cut off*; **3.** *to top, to trim.*
segare(si)[2] (sego, si segat, segatsi, segando), v. **1.** *to alienate* (said of a territorial extension, with certain boundary development); **1a.** *to alienate* (a territory or territorial extension from a larger one); **segare da(v)e rennu**; see also **segadura de rennu**: *conferring royal or iudicale property* (to private individuals as beneficiary property because it was taken out of the iudike's estate).
segari de petsa, n. *carnival.*
segatura, see **segadura.**
seghire (seghidus, seghendo·lus), v. *to follow, to pursue.*
seghundo, see **secundu.**
segnore (sengore, sengores), n. *lord, master.*
seguente, adj. *following, thereafter.*
segundu, see **secundu.**
seguritade (seguritades), n. *safety.*
segus (a segus, de segus), adv. and prep. **1.** *afterwards, last*; **2.** *behind.*

sella, n. *saddle.*
semare (semet), v. *to remain maimed.*
semida, semita, semitta, n. 1. *path*; 2. and in particular *paths bordering an estate or farm*, and thus, by extension, *enclosed land of an estate* itself, *a farm bordered by paths.*
seminare (seminado), v. *to sow.*
semmu, adj. *maimed.*
semper, adv. *always.*
sempiternum, in sempiternum, adv. *forever.*
(a) **sempiterru**, adv. *forever, for all eternity.*
semu[1], adj. *odd* (*not even*): *the unit remaining, in odd number, in the equal partition of the total account of several units*; **et Orçoco remansit ad accomuni ca fuit semu:** *and Orçoco remained in common because it was odd* (in the division count).
semu[2], adj. *maimed, disabled* (person).
semute, prep. *except for.*
sena, prep. *without*; it can give negative value to infinitive, **lavore messadu over senza messare:** *harvested or unharvested grain.*
sendo, see **esser.**
sene, see **sena.**
seneke (senekes), adj. *old man or men, elder*(*s*).
sengoria, n. *lordship.*
sengore (sengores), see **segnore.**
seniores, n. *elders*; in formal Latinising clause: *the twenty-four authors of the Old Testament* (Apocalypse, IV, 4 as interpreted by St Jerome).
sentencia, n. *judgement, the act by which the court concludes a legal dispute.*
sentenciari, v. *to sentence.*
sententia, see **sentencia.**
sentiri (at senter, sentendo), v. 1. *to hear, to listen to*; 2. *to feel.*
sensa, see **sena.**
senudu, see **sinodu.**
senza, see **sena.**
sepe, n. *hedge.*
sepellire, v. *to bury.*
septe, cardinal number: *seven.*
ser, n. *sir, sire, lord.* See also **messer.**
serachos, see **zaracu.**
serbiciu, see **serbizu.**
serbire, see **servire.**
serbithiu, see **serbizu.**

serbithu, see **serbizu.**

serbizu, n. 1. *servile work*; 2. *work due for fiscal purposes or in compensation*; 3. *funeral office.*

serbu, see **servu**[1].

sere, see **ser.**

serra, n. *ridge.*

serviciali (servicialis), *domestic servant.*

serviciu, n. (work) *service.*

servidore (servidores), n. *servant, labourer, employee.*

serviente, n. *utensil.*

servire (serviri, servat·si·lla, servidu), v. 1. *to serve, to perform servile work, to give due time in work* 2. *to be useful for*; 3. *to make use of, to keep, to keep something while maintaining possession of it*; **dies de servire:** *days of working service*; **serviri ad iornada:** *to serve per day or on a day-to-day basis.*

servithu, n. *servitude, due time given in work.*

servitiu, see **serbizu.**

servitiu*m*, see **serbizu.**

servizu, see **serbizu.**

servu[1], n. *servant* (who owes time in work); *unfree agricultural labourer*; **servu de clesia:** *servant that legally belongs to the church*; *a servant that belongs to an ecclesiastical institution.*

servu[2], n. *deer.* See also **cerbu.**

servu de paniliu (panilo, paniiu), n. *partially free man who must give partial service to the iudike or a lord, villeins.*

ses, cardinal number: *six.*

setimana, n. *week.*

settumana, see **setimana.**

sfertas, adj. *grafted.*

si[1], **ssi, sse, s', sibi:** proclitic and enclitic or tonic personal pron. 3rd person sing. and plur. 1. *himself, themselves*; 2. reflexive dative: *for or to himself or themselves*; 3. indicates reciprocity: **acordarunsi sus homines de corona:** *the men of the hearing agreed with each other*; 4. with passivating value: **su corpus se devet sepellire per manu dessos monacos**; *the body is to be buried at the hands of the monks*; 3. ethic dative: **regendosilla custa carta a cua:** *keeping this charter secretly*; **pro godiresilla in vita sua:** *to enjoy it in his life*; 4. in the pronominal conjugation: **sendesi biu:** *being alive*; **Maria a ssi morivit senza llos partire:** *Maria indeed died without dividing them.*

si[2], conj. 1. hypothetical: *if*; 2. interrogative: *if, whether*; 3. in the phrases: **salvu si:** *unless*; **anchu si:** *if even.*

si[3], adv. in correlation with *co*: *just as*: **non potuit razone torrare si co li kereat ipse:** *he could not account for it just as he* (the other) *wanted to.*
si[4], adv. *so, in this way, in such a way, thereby*; **pro si forte modu qui**: *well in a proper manner such that*; **pro si factu modu qui**: *so that*; **si veramente qui**: *unless, provided that*; **si qui**, *so that.*
sciat, see **esser.**
siat, **sia**, **siant**, see **esser.**
sibi, see **si**[1].
sicut: adv. and conj. Latinate, *as well as.*
sientimente, see **scientimente.**
sigillum, n. *seal* (*of a document*).
signadu, see **sinnari.**
signu, see **sinnu**[1].
siidu, see **siilu.**
siilu, n. *seal*, always in the phrase **pardu de siidu** or **siilu**: *communal pasture.*
silba, see **silva.**
silva, n., **1.** *woodland, forest* (for hunting) **2. silvas (nosta o de curadores)**: *collective hunting* (called or summoned by the **curatore** or by the iudike); **3.** *hunting party* (in a woodland).
simana, n. *week.*
simigante, see **simigiante.**
simigantemente, see **simigiantemente.**
simigiante, adj. *similar, resembling, alike, corresponding.*
simigiantemente, adv. *similarly, likewise, in like manner.*
simigiantimenti, see **simigiantemente.**
simili: **1.** adj. *similar, the same*; **2.** adv. *similarly*; ***ver et simili***: *verisimilar, likely.*
similmente, adv. *similarly.*
similimenti, see **similmente.**
simul, **simul cum** *or* **cun**, prep. *together.*
sinari, see **sinnari.**
sine, prep. *without.*
sinkeras, adj. *sane, lucid.*
sinna (sinnas), n. *boundary marker.*
sinnali, n. *boundary marker.*
sinnari (sinnare, sinari, sinnadu, sinnado, signadu), v. *to mark, to brand.*
sinnata, adj. *registered, inscribed.*
sinno, see **sinnu**[1].
sinnu[1], n., **1.** *mark, brand*; **2.** *scar*; **3.** referring to livestock: *size.*
sinnu[2], n., *sense, good judgement, wisdom, discernment.*
sinodo, see **sinodu.**

sinodu, **sinodo**, n. *the assembly of the iudicato, with the judge, ecclesiastics,* **curatores**, **maiorales** *and the people, for political, financial, judicial or even religious purposes*, the same as **collecta**.
sinotu, see **sinodu**.
siò, see **ciò**.
siracha, see **zaracu**.
sire, see **ser**.
sive, conj. Latinate *or*.
skia, see **iskire**.
skimus, see **iskire**.
sò, see **ciò**.
so, see **su**.
so, see **su**.
sociu, n. *soccidary*.
socra, n. *mother-in-law*.
socroniu, n. *son's or daughter's father-in-law*.
socru, n. *father-in-law*.
solamente, adv. *only*.
soldadu, n. *soldier*.
soldo (soldos, soldus), n. *solidus coin, money*.
solennidadi, n. *formality, formal practice*.
solere (solint), v. *to use, to usually happen*.
sollu (de dinari), n. *real solidus, monetary unit, the actual coins, cash, bezant, solidus* (coin).
solo, see **solu**.
solu, adj. *alone*.
sonnu, n. *dream*.
sorasta, see **sorrastra**.
sorike, n. *mouse*.
sorrastra, n. *female cousin*.
sorre, n. *sister*; **sorre carrali**: *carnal sister, of the same blood*.
sorri, see **sorre**.
sorti, adv. *by chance*.
sos, see **su**.
sotzus, see **sociu**.
spaciados, see **ispaciare**[1].
specie, n. *appearance*; **supta specie et colore**: *under the false appearance and under the pretext*.
spendere, v. *to spend*.
spendiu, see **ispendiu**.

spiiare, see **ispiiare.**
spiiatu, see **ispiiare.**
spica, n. *ear of wheat*; **tempus de spica:** *time of threshing* (beginning on 1st July).
spiiadu, see **ispiiare.**
spiritus, n. *spirit.*
sposansa, n. *marriage, promises of marriage.*
squiri, see **ischire.**
ssancta, see **sanctu.**
ssanta, see **sanctu.**
ssantu, see **sanctu.**
sse, see **si**[1].
sserbire, see **servire.**
ssi, see **si**[1].
ssu, see **su.**
stadea, n. *steelyard.*
stadu, n. *status, social condition.*
stalla, n. *stable.*
stara, adj. *now.*
stare (staresi, staant, stavat, stetit, steterunt, fudi stetida, istis), v. *to stay, to reside.*
statuire (statuimus, istatuimus), v. to *establish.*
steas, see **steda.**
steda (stedas, steas), n. *notarial draft, preparatory drafting of a document.* See also **sceda** or **isceda.**
steriu, see **istergiu.**
sterminare, see **esterminare.**
strada, n. *street* (paved road).
strilige (striliges), adj. *desiccated, dry.*
stringere (strixi), v. *to convene* (a judicial assembly).
strixi, see **stringere.**
studiosamente, studiosamenti, adv. *intentionally.*
su, sa, sos, sas: def. art. (reduced form of **issu**, see the entry): *the*; **2.** antecedent of the relative pron. *the one or that* (*which*) **et sa binia ki lli derant … et issa c'apit de fundamentu, et adiunsit *sa* c'appit de conporu:** *and the vineyard they had given him … and the one he already owned, and he added the one he had by way of purchase*; **2a. su ki:** *what, that which*; **3.** as an anaphoric pron. **Gantine de Lacon, su de Nuroço:** *Gantine de Lacon, the one from Nuroço*; **3b.** it implies an antecedent personal pronoun implicit in the verbal morphology: **custu partimentu amus factu, sos donnos, a bene:** *this division we,*

the lords have made for the sake of good; **3c.** it contributes in forming ordinal numerals: **et issu de dece**: *the tenth* (**dece** means *ten*).

sua, see **suo.**

subdictos, see **subditu.**

subditu (subditos, subdictos), n. *subject.*

subra, see **supra.**

substenent, see **sustenere.**

subta, prep. **1.** *under; below*; **2,** *under the jurisdiction of*; **supta specie et colore**: *under the pretext of.* See also **supta.**

succedere (succedat, sussedat), v. *to succeed, take over property.*

successor, see **successore.**

successore (successors), n. *successor.*

sucta, prep: *below.*

sue (sues, suis), n. *sow.*

suegher, v. *to macerate, to tan* (leather).

suergiu, see **sueriu.**

sueriu, n. *cork, cork oak.*

suetore (suetoris, suetores), n. *macerator, tanner.*

sufficiente (sufficientes), adj. **1.** *sufficient*; **2.** *of good and sufficient quality, suitable, adequate.*

sufficientemente, adv. *sufficiently.*

sufficienti, see **sufficiente.**

suis, see **sue.**

sulcu, n. *furrow.*

sunt, see **esser.**

suo (sua, suos, suas, suu): possessive adj. and third-person pron. *his, her, their.*

suparpare, adv. *one on top of another.*

superbia, n. *pride, arrogance, haughtiness.*

superclare, v. *to be above, superior, to overtake.*

supra, prep.**1.** *on, upon, above, over*; **1.1. supra ciò**: *in relation there to*; **1.2.** *over a previous one*; **1.4. subra se**: (the proceeds) *from its own* (management of the vineyard); **2. de supra**: *what is said above, what is aforesaid*; Latin **ut supra**: *as said above*; **secundu de supra**: *as said above.*

supraditu (subraditas), adj. *aforesaid.*

suprascriptu (suprascripto, suprascrita), adj. *above written.*

supta, see **subta.**

sus[1], see **suo.**

sus[2], see **su.**

suso, see **susu.**

suspectu, n. *suspicion*; **aviri suspectu**: *to suspect.*

sussedat, see **succedere.**
sustenere (substenent, susteneret), v. *to support, to bear the costs.*
susu, adv. *upwards.*
suta, sutta, see **subta.**
suterrari, v. *to bury.*
sutigare (sutigado), v. *to destroy, to wear out.*
sutta, see **subta.**
suu, see **suo.**
suveriu, see **sueriu.**
suvile, n. *pigsty.*

T

tagiare (tagit, tagiada), v. *to amputate, to cut off or out*; **siat·illi tagiada sa testa per modu qui 'ndi morgiat:** *let his head be cut off so that he dies.*
tale, adj. and pron. *such, such a one, someone, the aforesaid*; **a tali qui:** *so that*; **in tali casu:** *in such a case, if so.*
tali (talis), see **tale.**
tamariske, n. *tamarisk* (tree), *salt cedar.*
tando, adv. 1. *then, at that moment, on that occasion*; 2. *therefore*; **dae tandu:** *since then.*
tandu, see **tando.**
tanti, see **tantu.**
tanto, see **tantu.**
tantu[1], adv. *only*; **infini a tantu qui, infini in tanto qui:** *until*; **tantu quantu et que:** *as much as*; **atero e tantu:** *likewise, and so* (the same), *also.*
tantu[2] (tantas), adj. *so much, so many.*
tantum Latin, adv. *only.*
tavernaiu, n. *tavern keeper.*
tavernayos, see **tavernaiu.**
taxari (atazari, ataxando), v. *to tax, to fix a fee for the payment of a tax or of a tax fixed for compensation*; **atazari sos ispendios:** *to establish the amount of the expense.*
templu, n. *church*; (the entry, occurring only once, appears to be the name of the church of *Santa Corona d'Errivora*, modern Riòla, as it was attached to a Templar hospital).
temporale, n. 1. *season* (of the year), *time*; 2. *weather, atmospheric phenomenon*; **secundu qui fudi usadu per temporale:** *in the manner used seasonally.*
temporali, see **temporale.**

tempus (tempos), n. 1. *time, period of time*; 2. *era, period of time*; 3. *time of the year*; 4. *weather*; **de nocte tempus:** *in nightly time, during the night.* **benne assu tempus:** *to come within the set time limit*; **dimandari tempus:** *to ask for time, to ask for an extension*; **fugimentu de tempus:** *wasting time* (with dilatory conduct).

tenendo, see **tenne.**

tenere, see **tenne.**

teneri (teneris), n. 1. *capture*; or maybe 2. *rights to the lawful seizure of livestock.*

tenghat, see **tenne.**

tenne (tennet, tensierunt, tenghat, teneret, tenerent, tenudo, tenudu, tentu, tenendo), v. 1. *to hold*; 2. *to detain, to arrest, to capture*; 3. *to keep* (and guard); 4. *to have, to possess, to take possession of, to be at disposal by*; 5. *to border* (in this sense used mostly in the gerund with participial value); 6. riflexive **tennesi:** *to consider oneself*; **tenendo appare**, *adjoining each other*; **essere tenudo de** *or* **a** *or* **pro:** *to be bound to*; **tenne sa iusticia:** *to administer justice*; **mitteri et tenne in muda:** *to subject* (the oxen) *to a surveillance regime*; **tenne corona:** *to hold or to preside over a court, an assizes*; *to appeal to court*; **tenne modo:** *to have a way*; **baliri et tenne:** *to have value.*

tennere, see **tenne.**

tenneru, adj. *soft.*

tenni, see **tenne.**

tenore, n. *way of doing*; in the phrase **per tenore de:** *by virtue of.*

tenpus, see **tempus.**

tensierunt, see **tenne.**

tentura, n. *capture* (of cattle, usually caught grazing illegally): and thus, *the penalty imposed on the owner of the cattle and the costs for the capture.*

terali, see **terrali.**

termen (terminis, termenes, terminus), n. 1. *deadline, time limit*; 2. *boundary, boundary marker, limit.*

terra (terras), n. 1. *land, country, territory, parcel of land*; 2. *arable land*; 3. *territory of the iudicatu*; 4. *earth*; **terra boida:** *uncultivated land*; **terra manna:** *the mainland* (as opposed to the island); **terra d'agrile:** *ploughland.*

terrafirma, n. *the mainland* (as opposed to the island).

terrale, see **terrali.**

terrali, n. *tenant, settler* (holding land on lease from the lord), *agricultural worker*; **terrali de fictu:** *tenant settler.*

terramanesos, n. *those from the mainland, inhabitants of the mainland.*

terramangeso, see **terramanesos.**

terramangiesu, terramangieso, see **terramanesos.**

terramangessu: sse **terramanesos.**

terrania, adj. *of land.*
terraticu, n. *arable land.*
terrazola, n. *plot of land.*
tersu (terza) adj. *third.*
terza, see **tersu.**
tesone (tesones), n. *net for trapping birds.*
tessere (tessant), v. *to weave.*
testa, n. *head*; **per testa**: (for) *each one.*
testadore, n. *testator.*
testamentu, n. *will, last will and testament.*
testes, abl. **testibus**, n. *witnesses.*
testificare (testificadu), v. *to testify.*
testificatione, n. *testimony, deposition.*
testimongio, n. *witness*; **per *or* a testimongios**: *by testimony.*
testimonianza, n. in the phrase **render testimonianza**: *to give testimony.*
testimonio (testimonios), see **testimoniu.**
testimoniu (testimonius), n. *witness.* See also **destimoniu.**
testimonzu, see **testimoniu.**
thancas, n. (enclosed) *lands.*
theraccos, n. *babies, young children.* See also **zaracu.**
thinnigas, n. *canes, reeds.*
thiriccas, n. *siliquas* (silver coins).
thithiclos, n. *udders, breasts.*
thiu, n. *uncle.* See also **ciu.**
thuccare, v. *to transfer.*
thurpu, adj. *blind.*
ti: personal pron. *you, to you.*
tija, n. *lime, tilia. linden* (tree).
timangia, n. *incense.*
timire, v. *to fear, to be afraid.*
timore, n. *fear.*
tirare (tirarit), v. *to pull.*
titimalu, n. *euphorbia, spurge* (plant).
titulo, see **titulu.**
titulu, n. *title,* always in the phrase **cum iustu titulu**: *rightfully.*
tocari (tocat, tocando·li), v. **1.** *to touch*; **2.** *to due, to be due, to be up, to be entitled to.*
toctos, see **totu.**
toctue, see **tottuve.**
toctuve, see **tottuve.**

tollere (tolliant), v. 1. *to remove*; 2. *to divert*; 3. *to subtract*; 4. *to demand, to extort.*

torrare (torrari, torreindelli, torredi, torraimi, torrarunt, torrent, torraret, torrarint), v. 1. *to return, to go or come back*; 2. *to return, to give back*; in locution **torrare verbu** *or* **berbu**: *to answer, to challenge* (in court), *to have a word with, to complain, to explain, to report, to give notice*; **torrare razone**: *to account* (for).

tortu[1] (torta), adj. *crooked, curved.*

tortu[2], **tuturu**, n. *wrong, injustice, unjust action*; in the phrase **a tortu** *or* **a ttuturu de**: *against the will of*; **a tortu**: *without having the right, unjustly.*

toscho, n. *venom, poison.*

tosighu, n. *toxic poison.*

toto, see **totu.**

tottota, adv. *all, whole, entirely.*

tottuve, adv. 1. *along*; 2. *keeping the same direction.*

totu, **toto totus tota**, adj. and pron. *all, totally, the whole quantity, completely, entirely completely, every, each time.*

tottu, see **totu.**

totue see **tottuve.**

totuve, see **tottuve.**

tottuve, 1. prep. *along*; 2. adv. *keeping the same direction*; adv. 3. *everywhere.*

trabuda, n. *tribute.*

tractare (tractarit, tratarit), v. *to conspire.*

tractu, see **tratu.**

traditore, n. *traitor.*

traginu, n. *stream, flow.*

traitore, see **traditore.**

tramudare (tramudu, tramudeilli, tramudessi, tramudarus, tramutarus, tramutavimus), v. 1. *to exchange, to swap*; 2. reflexive: *to change course of action* (in legal action): **resposit et tramudessi**: *responded and changed line and defence strategy.*

tramudu, n. *exchange, swap.*

tramutare, see **tramudare.**

tramutu, see **tramudu.**

tranquillu, adj. *tranquil.*

tratarit, see **tractare.**

trattadu, n. *conspiracy.*

trattadu, see **tractare.**

tratu, prep: *except.*

trauda, n. *tribute.*

travessare, v. *to traverse, to cross, to cut through.*

travessaria, adj. *traversal.*
travessu, adv. *across.*
travigare, v. *to traffic, engaging in illicit trafficking.*
travigho, n. *transit, passage.*
traycioni, n. *treason.*
tremisse (tremisses, tremises), n. *tremissis* (coin).
tres, cardinal number: *three.*
treulari (treuladu, treulandu), v. *to thresh.*
treulas, n. 1. *July* (*month*) 2. **tempus de treulas:** *threshing time.*
tridicu, n. *wheat.*
trigonia, n. *administrative or diocesan district.* Used only of Barbária, it seems to be a synonym of **curatoría.**
triticu, n. *wheat.*
triulari, see **treulari.**
trubare (trubado), v. *to lead* (cattle).
truma (turmas), n. *flock, drove.*
trumentu, trumento, n. *torture*; **mittere (o ponne) a trumentu:** to *submit to torture.*
tudentimi, see **tutare.**
tudore (tutores), n. *guardian* (entrusted with the guardianship of someone).
tudoria, n. *guardianship, defence.*
turma, n. *the army,* or perhaps *the cavalry of the iudike.*
turmas, see **truma.**
turmentu, see **trumentu.**
turpe, n. *wrong.*
turre, n. *tower.*
tutare (tutarus, tudentimi), v. *to bury.*
tutela, n. *guardianship.*
tuti, see **totu.**
tutores, see **tudore.**
tuttue, see **tottuve.**
tutturo, n., see **tortu**
tuturu see **tortu.**

U

ube, see **ubi.**
ubi, relative adv. *where, when.*
ue, see **ubi.**

ufficiale, see **officiale**.
ulpinu (ulpina), adj. *fox, frequented by foxes.*
ultimu (ultimas), adj. *last*, in the phrase **ultimas voluntadis:** *last wills.*
ultra, prep. *over, beyond, in addition.*
ultramare, adv. *overseas*, in *the mainland.*
ultramari, see **ultramare**.
ulumetu, n. *elm wood.*
ulumu, n. *elm* (tree).
umpare, adv. *together, in equal part.*
un, see **unu**.
unde, relative adv. *from where, from which, whence, with or by which.* See also **dunde**.
undi, see **unde**.
uniskis, pron. *each one.*
unnu, see **unu**.
unore, n. *honour, deference.*
unpare, see **impari**.
untha, n. *ounce* (weight).
uno, see **unu**.
unu[1] (un, una), indef. art. *a, an*;
unu[2], cardinal number: *one*; **s'unu cum satero:** *with each other, against each other*; 3. **ad unu ad unu:** *one by one*; 4. **pro s'unu ·v· (chimbe):** *quintuple, the fivefold*; **de baturo una, de quimbi unu:** *one fourth, one fifth.*
unuchis, pron. *each one.*
urbidu, n. *track, narrow country path lined with vegetation.*
urvitu, see **urbidu**.
usadu, adj. *used, in use.*
usansa, see **usanza**.
usanza, n. *custom, legal usage, customary law.*
usare[1] (usat, usit, usadu), v. 1. *to operate, to exercise* (an office, a profession); 2. *to use*; 3. *to be wont*; 4. In the phrase **secundu qu'est usadu:** *according to habit; according to custom*; 5. **usadu:** *customary, according to use, habit.*
usare[2], **usit**, v. *to dare, to presume.*
usque, prep. (Latin) *until*, (until) *to, up to.* See also **fisca**.
ussanza, see **usanza**.
usu, n. *custom.*
ut, adv. always in the Latin phrase **ut supra** *or* **ut de subra:** *as mentioned above, as provided above.*
ut, conj. *so that, in order to.*
utili, n. *profit, advantage.*

uve, relative adv. *where, when, with regard to.*
uxore, **uxor**, *n. wife.*

V

vacante, adj. *empty, not cultivated.*
vaca, see **vacca.**
vacca (bacca, vaccas, baccas, bacas), n. *cow.*
vacha, see **vacca.**
vachargios, n., see **bachargiu.**
vadu n. *crossing-ford* (of a stream). See also **bau.**
valere, v. *to have value.*
valiclu, see **valliclu.**
valle, n. *valley.*
valliclu, n. *small valley, glen.*
valore, n. *value, validity.*
valsente (valsenti), n. *capital, economic availability, sum, wealth*; in the phrase. **aviri valsente de libras**: *to dispose of a sum amounting to ... lire.*
valsuda, n. *value, cash equivalent.*
vamus, see **andare.**
vangelista (vangelistas), n. *Evangelist.* See also **evangelista.**
vangeliu, n. *Gospels*, see also **Evangelium** and **bangeleu.**
vardones, n. *parts, pieces.*
varellu, see **barrellu.**
varicare. v. *to pass, to go beyond.*
varicatione, n. *death, passing away.*
variedadi, n. *diversity, change.*
varrellu, see **barrellu.**
varietadis, see **variedadis.**
vedare (vedadu, vedado), v. *to forbid, to interdict.*
vedere see **vetere.**
ve: enclitic form of **ive**, see **ibi.**
vel, conj. Latin **or.**
vender, **vendere**, see **bender.**
vendicione (venditiones), n. *sale.*
vene, n. *benefice.*
venenu, n. *poison.*
venerent, see **benne.**
venghio, see **benne.**

venidore (venidores), see **benidore.**

venit, see **benne.**

venne, see **benne.**

vennenare, see **bennenare.**

vennerent, see **benne.**

venner, see **benne.**

ventosa, adj. *windy.*

ventura, see **aventura.**

ver, adj. in the locution **ver et simili:** *likely, credible.*

veramente, adv. 1. *truly*; 2. *in the specific or particular case, so that, of course*; in the locution **si veramente (qui)**, *unless, if indeed it is the case.*

veranu, n. *summer.*

verbeke, n. *sheep.* See also **berbeke.**

verbu, verbum, n. *word*, but it is used exclusively in the locution **torrare verbu:** *to answer, to contest, to reply*, always (in the context of judicial action, or at any rate of litigation or dispute).

veridadi, n. *truth*; **mostrare beridadi:** *to prove the truth.*

verideru (veriderus), adj. *true, truthful.*

veritate, see **beridade** and **veridadi.**

vero, adv. Latin: *otherwise, however.*

verruda, n. in medieval Sardinian, and in particular in Arborea, **verruda** is always used in the expression **(corona de) kita de verruta** (or phonetic variants **verruda, berruta, berruda**); by it, it is meant the judging college in the judicial assize (or **corona**), formed by *bonos homines*, militiamen on horseback, who had the **verrutu** or **berrutu** (a sharp weapon, a throwing rod) as their insignia; these men were required to perform this public service and office according to a rotation rhythm. See also **berruda.**

verruta, see **verruda.**

vertudi, n. *virtue.*

veru, adj. *true.*

verveke, n. *sheep.*

vestare, n. *abode, dwelling.*

vetere, adj. *old, ancient.*

vi, v', see **bi.**

via (bia, bias), n. 1. *street, road, way*; 2. **bia de logu:** *main road*; **averevi bias in:** *to have a share in*, or *to have right to something*; **per** *or* **in via de:** *by, by means of, for the sake of*; **via plus:** *also the more*; **duas vias:** *twice.*

viagiu, see **biagiu.**

vicanos, n. *substitute.*

vicarius, n. *vicar.*

viclata, see **viglata.**
vida, n. *life.*
videre (bissido, vissidos, biidos), v. *to see, to check, to ascertain, to detect.* See also **biere.**
vidit, see **biere**[2].
vidua (viduas), n. *widow.*
vigino, n. *neighbour.*
viglata, adj. *a cow that has calved.*
vigna (vingia, vingna, bingnas) n. *vine, vineyard.* See also **binia.**
vignenna, vignennas, n. *grape harvest.*
vigore, n. *vigour*; **per vigore de:** *by virtue of.*
viiat, see **biere**[2].
vikinos: n. *neighbours.*
villa, n. *village, village population, territory of a village*; **villa de foras:** *peripheral village*; **villa affeada** or **villa in feu:** *enfeoffed village, village held in fief.*
vincitura, see **binkidura.**
vinea, see **vigna.**
vingia, see **vigna.**
vingna, see **vigna.**
vinia, see **vigna.**
vinker, see **binkere.**
vino, see **vinu.**
vinu, n. 1. *wine*; 2. in the locution, **istare a pani et a vinu suo:** *to be fed and maintained by him or someone*; that is: *to be fed and maintained by someone.*
virga, see **birga.**
virgini, n. *virgin*; **Virgini Madonna sancta Maria:** *the Holy Virgin Mary.*
virgo, n. *virgin, the Virgin Mary.*
viridadi, see **veridadi.**
visconte, n. *viscount.*
visdominu, n. *bishop's representative.*
vissidos, see **biere**[2].
vita, see **vida.**
viva, adj. **viva voce**, *verbally*. See also **vivu.**
viver, see **vivere.**
vivere, v. *to live.*
vivu (biu), adj. *alive*; **mare vivu:** *open sea, at sea.*
vocare, v. *to call, to call together, to call back, to take possession of.*
voce, n. **viva voce:** *viva voce, verbally*. See also **boghi.**
voco, see **bogare.**
voe, see **boe.**

volemus, see **bolere.**
volere, see **bolere.**
volitravu, n. *swamp, bog.*
volta, see **bolta.**
voluerit, see **bolere.**
volumen, n. 1. *volume*; **fagheri volumen:** *to keep in volume*; 2. *amount, length, extent size.*
voluntade, n. *will, consent, authorisation, discretion, goodwill*; **a voluntadi sua:** *willfully, of his own free will*; **contra voluntadi sua:** *unintentionally*; **ad mala voluntadi de:** *against the will of*; **ultimas voluntadis:** *last will.* See also **boluntade.**
voluntadi, see **voluntade.**
voluntate, see **voluntade.**
volvit, see **bolere.**
vorthe, see **borce.**
vos: personal pron. *you.*
vostru, possessive adj. and pron. *your(s).*
vulbare, n. *enclosure for livestock.*
vulpe, n. *fox.*
vulvare, see **vulbare.**

X

xixiri, n. *chickpea.*

Y

yagharu, see **iagaru.**
ymagine, see **magine.**
yssoro, see **issoro.**
ysula, see **isula.**

Z

zaracu, n. 1. *minor, boy, baby, young man*; 2. *servant.*
zò, see **ciò.**

Bibliography

Manuscript Sources

Archivio Diocesano Storico di Cagliari
- 'Carte volgari'
- *Liber Diversorum*, 1/I serie [A]; 2/I serie [E]

Archivio Capitolare della Chiesa di San Lorenzo (Genoa)
- Cartulario PA, cc. 17b–18a (34b–35a); 18a (35a–35b) [duplicate]
- Cartulario PB, cart. 9b–10a

Archivio Capitolare di Pisa
- Fondo Diplomatico, no. 69

Archivio della Certosa di Calci (Pisa)
- Pergamene, II serie/634 (30 maggio 1226)

Archivio di Stato di Pisa
- Fondo Diplomatico, R. Acquisto Coletti (10 maggio 1212)

Archives Départementales des Bouches-du-Rhône (Marseille)
- Fond Saint-Victor, 1 H 88, nos 427 (Greca); 428

Biblioteca Universitaria di Cagliari
- Aleo, J., *Sucessos generales dela Isla y Reyno de Sardeña. Tomo segundo* (Cáller [Cagliari], 1694). Sala Piccola 6.3.49. Also available on microfilm (Pos. 899-1/3)
- *Carta de Logu d'Arborea*, Inc. 230
- 'Carta de Logu dell'Arborea', Ms. 211
- 'Condaghe di Santa Maria di Bonarcado', Ms. 277

Biblioteca Universitaria di Sassari
- 'Condaghe di San Pietro di Silki', Ms. 95

Bodleian Library
- 'The Laudian Acts'. Ms. Laud Gr. 35

Printed Sources

Accardo, Aldo. 'L'invenzione della storia sarda nelle *Carte d'Arborea*'. In *Le carte d'Arborea: falsi e falsari della Sardegna nel XIX secolo*, ed. L. Marrocu, 331–343. Cagliari, 1997.

Amari, Michele. *Biblioteca arabo-sicula; ossia Raccolta di testi arabici che toccano la geografia, la storia, le biografie e la bibliografia della Sicilia*. Turin, 1880–1889.

Baratier, Édouard. 'L'inventaire des biens du prieuré Saint-Saturnin de Cagliari dépendant de l'Abbaye Saint Victor de Marseille'. In *Studi storici in onore di Francesco Loddo Canepa*, vol. 2, 41–74. Florence, 1959.

Baudi di Vesme, Carlo, ed. *Codex diplomaticus Ecclesiensis*. Turin, 1877.

Besta, Enrico. *La Sardegna medioevale: le vicende politiche dal 450 al 1326*. Vol. 1. Palermo, 1908.

Besta, Enrico. *La Sardegna medioevale: le istituzioni politiche, economiche, giuridiche, sociali*. Vol. 2. Palermo, 1909.

Besta, Enrico, and Pier Enea Guarnerio. *La Carta de Logu de Arborea. Testo con Prefazioni illustrative*. Sassari, 1905.

Besta, Enrico, and Arrigo Solmi. *I condaghi di San Nicola di Trullas e di Santa Maria di Bonarcado*. Milan, 1937.

Blancard, Louis, and Carle Wescher. 'Charte sarde de l'abbaye de Saint-Victor de Marseille écrite en caractères grecs'. Bibliothèque de l'École des chartes 35 (1874): 255–265.

Blasco Ferrer, Eduardo. *Storia linguistica della Sardegna*. Tübingen, 1984.

Blasco Ferrer, Eduardo. 'La carta sarda in caratteri greci del secolo XI: revisione testuale e storico-linguistica'. *Revue de Linguistique Romane* 66 (2002): 321–365.

Blasco Ferrer, Eduardo. *Crestomazia sarda dei primi secoli*. 2 vols. Nuoro, 2003.

Blasco Ferrer, Eduardo. 'Sardo antico'. In *Manuale di linguistica sarda*, ed. E. Blasco Ferrer, P. Koch and D. Marzo, 119–136. Berlin, 2017.

Bonazzi, Giuliano, ed. *Il condaghe di San Pietro di Silki: testo logudorese inedito dei secoli XI–XIII*. Sassari, 1900.

Boscolo, Alberto ed. *Le fonti della storia medioevale. Orientamenti*. Sassari, 1964.

Brook, L.L., Francesco Cesare Casula, Maria M. Costa, Anna M. Oliva, Romeo Pavoni, and Marco Tangheroni, eds. *Genealogie medioevali di Sardegna*. Cagliari and Sassari, 1984.

Bussa, Italo. 'L'armistizio tra regno d'Aragona e giudicato d'Arborea (1388)'. *Quaderni Bolotanesi* 41 (2021): 103–128.

Cannas, Vincenzo Mario. *San Giorgio di Suelli. Primo vescovo della Barbagia orientale. Sec. X–XI*. Cagliari, 1976.

Carta Raspi, Raimondo ed. *Condaghe di S. Maria di Bonarcado*. Cagliari, 1937.

Carta Raspi, Raimondo ed. *Condaghe di S. Nicola di Trullas*. Cagliari, 1937.

Casula, Francesco Cesare. 'Sulle origini delle Cancellerie giudicali sarde'. In *Studi di Paleografia e Diplomatica*, eds F.C. Casula and L. D'Arienzo, 1–99. Padua, 1974.

Casula, Francesco Cesare. 'Rassegna dell'Istituto di Storia medioevale della Facoltà di Lettere dell'Università di Cagliari'. *Medioevo: Saggi e Rassegne* 1 (1975): 61–140.

Casula, Francesco Cesare. 'Giudicati e curatorìe'. In *Atlante della Sardegna*, eds R. Pracchi, A. Terrosu, and M. Riccardi, 94–109. Rome, 1980.

Casula, Francesco Cesare. 'Aggiornamento e note storico-diplomatistiche al *Codex Diplomaticus Sardiniae* di Pasquale Tola'. In *Codex Diplomaticus Sardiniae*, vol. 1, 2nd edn, ix–xxxvi. Sassari, 1984.

Casula, Francesco Cesare. *La Carta de Logu del Regno di Arborèa: traduzione libera e commento storico*. Cagliari, 1994.

Cau, Ettore. 'Oralità e scrittura nel Medioevo'. In *La Sardegna*, ed. M. Brigaglia, vol. 1, 5–24. Cagliari, 1982.

Cau, Ettore. 'Peculiarità e anomalie della documentazione sarda tra XI e XIII secolo'. In *Giudicato d'Arborea e Marchesato di Oristano: proiezioni mediterranee e aspetti di storia locale, Atti del I Convegno Internazionale di Studi (Oristano, 5–8 dicembre 1997)*, ed. G. Mele, 313–422. Oristano, 2000.

Castellaccio, Angelo Aldo. 'Il diritto della Sardegna medioevale: dalle consuetudini alla forma scritta'. In *La civiltà giudicale in Sardegna nei secoli XI–XIII*, 127–142. Sassari, 2002.

Castellaccio, Angelo Aldo. 'I regni giudicali e il diritto statuale: le *Carte de Logu*'. In *Scritti editi e inediti*, 197–212. Sassari, 2022.

Contini, Gianfranco. 'La seconda carta sarda di Marsiglia'. *Studia Ghisleriana*, serie 2, 1 (1950): 61–79.

Cortese, Ennio. *Appunti di storia giuridica sarda*. Milan, 1964.

Cortese, Ennio. *Il diritto nella storia medievale. Il basso Medioevo*. Rome, 1995.

Cossu Pinna, Maria Giuseppina. 'La carta pisana del 1 marzo 1230'. *Biblioteca Francescana Sarda* 1 (1987): 41–49.

Cossu Pinna, Maria Giuseppina. 'Le carte d'Arborea alla Biblioteca Universitaria di Cagliari'. In *Le carte d'Arborea: falsi e falsari della Sardegna nel XIX secolo*, ed. L. Marrocu, 195–210. Cagliari, 1997.

Crasta, Paola, Alessandro Soddu and Giovanni Strinna. 'Un'inedita carta sardo-greca del XII secolo nell'Archivio Capitolare di Pisa'. *Bollettino di Studi Sardi* 3 (2010): 5–42.

de Vico, Francisco. *Historia general de la isla y reyno de Sardeña*. Barcelona, 1639 [repr. Cagliari, 2010, ed. F. Manconi].

de Vico, Francisco. *Leyes y Pragmaticas reales del reyno de Serdeña*. Naples, 1640.

Delogu, Ignazio. 'Introduzione'. In *Il Condaghe di San Pietro di Silki*, ed. G. Bonazzi, 38–41. Sassari, 1997.

Delogu, Ignazio. 'Donnos, servos, appatissas e priores nella più grande "Cronaca" del Medio Evo sardo: il *Condaghe di S. Pietro di Silki*'. *Sacer* 8 (2001): 145–171.

Di Donato, Flora. *La costruzione giudiziaria del fatto: il ruolo della narrazione nel processo*. Milan, 2008.

Di Tucci, Raffaele, ed. *Il condaghe di S. Michele di Salvenor. Testo inedito*. Cagliari, 1912.

Fadda, Bianca. 'Le pergamene relative alla Sardegna nel Diplomatico Coletti dell'Archivio di Stato di Pisa'. *Archivio Storico Sardo* 42 (2002): 1–91.

Fadda, Bianca, and Mariangela Rapetti. 'Cartulari del Mediterraneo occidentale: il caso dei condaghi sardi'. In *From Charters to Codex: Studies on Cartularies and Archival Memory in the Middle Ages*, eds R. Furtado and M. Moscone, 135–158. Turnhout, 2019.

Falchi, Marietta, ed. *Le carte volgari dell'Archivio Arcivescovile di Cagliari*. Edizione digitale. RE.I.SAR. https://www.reisar.eu/category/carte-volgari-dellarchivio-arcivescovile-di-cagliari/. 2025.

Falkenhausen, Vera von. 'Greek and Latin in Byzantine Italy (6th–11th Century)'. In *A Companion to Byzantine Italy*, ed. S. Cosentino, 541–581. Leiden, 2021.

Feissel, Denis. 'Écrire grec en alphabet latin: le cas des documents protobyzantins'. In *Bilinguisme gréco-latin et épigraphie*, eds F. Biville, J.C. Decourt and G. Rougemont, 213–230. Lyon, 2008.

Fernández-Aceves, Hervin, Alex Metcalfe and Marco Muresu. 'Discovery, Invention, and Supposition: Three Case Studies from Medieval Sardinia'. In *The Making of Medieval Sardinia*, eds A. Metcalfe, H. Fernández-Aceves and M. Muresu, 17–41. Leiden, 2021.

Frank, Barbara, and Jörg Hartmann, eds. *Inventaire systématique des premiers documents des langues romanes*. 5 vols. Tübingen, 1997.

Gallinari, Luciano. 'The Sardinian *Giudici* between Historical Memory and Identity. A Matter of *Longue Durée*?'. In *Sardinia from the Middle Ages to Contemporaneity*, ed. L. Gallinari, 29–44. Bern, 2018.

Gallinari, Luciano. 'Some voices on institutional, cultural and personal ties from within a Mediterranean island society with a Byzantine matrix: the *Giudicati Sardinia* (11th–14th centuries)'. In *Forms of Unfreedom in the Medieval Mediterranean*, eds M.F. Lopes de Barros and C. Almagro Vidal, 49–70. Évora, 2021.

Gallinari, Luciano. 'The *Iudex Sardiniae* and the *Archon Sardanias* between the sixth and eleventh century'. In *The Making of Medieval Sardinia*, eds A. Metcalfe, H. Fernández-Aceves and M. Muresu, 219–226. Leiden, 2021.

Guérard, Benjamin, ed. *Cartulaire de l'abbaye de Saint-Victor de Marseille*. Vol. 1. Paris, 1857.

Haug, Henrike. 'The Struggle for Sardinia in the Twelfth Century: Textual and Architectural Evidence from Genoa and Pisa'. In *A Companion to Sardinian History, 500–1500*, ed. M. Hobart, 215–227. Leiden, 2017.

Lai, Roberto, and Marco Massa, eds. *S. Antioco da primo evangelizzatore di Sulci a glorioso protomartire "patrono della Sardegna"*. Monastir, 2011.

Lalinde Abadía, Jesús. 'La "Carta de Logu" nella civiltà giuridica della Sardegna medievale'. In *La Carta de Logu d'Arborea nella storia del diritto medievale e moderno*, eds I. Birocchi and A. Mattone, 13–49. Rome and Bari, 2004.

Lazzeri, Gerolamo. *Antologia dei primi secoli della letteratura italiana*. Milan, 1954.

Lupinu, Giovanni, ed. *Carta de Logu dell'Arborea: nuova edizione critica secondo il manoscritto di Cagliari* (*BUC 211*) *con traduzione italiana*. Oristano, 2010.

Maninchedda, Paolo. *Medioevo latino e volgare in Sardegna*. Cagliari, 2007; 2nd edn, Cagliari, 2012.

Marongiu, Antonio. 'Sul probabile redattore della *Carta de Logu d'Arborea*'. *Studi economico-giuridici della R. Università di Cagliari* 27 (1939): 19–32.

Martini, Pietro. *Pergamene, codici e fogli cartacei di Arborea*. Cagliari, 1863.

Martini, Pietro. *Appendice alla raccolta delle pergamene dei codici e fogli cartacei di Arborea*. Cagliari, 1865.

Mastruzzo, Antonino. 'Un "diploma" senza Cancelleria, un "re" senza regno: strategie documentarie di penetrazione coloniale in Sardegna'. *Bollettino Storico Pisano* 77 (2008): 1–32.

Mastruzzo, Antonino. 'Una postilla sarda'. *Bollettino Storico Pisano* 78 (2009): 169–171.

Mattone, Antonello. 'Le *Carte d'Arborea* nella storiografia europea dell'800'. In *Le carte d'Arborea: falsi e falsari della Sardegna nel XIX secolo*, ed. L. Marrocu, 25–152. Cagliari, 1997.

Maxia, Mauro, ed. *Il Condaghe di San Michele di Salvennor: edizione e commento linguistico*. Cagliari, 2012.

Mele, Giampaolo. 'I condaghi: specchio storico di devozione e delle tradizioni liturgiche nella Sardegna medievale'. In *La civiltà giudicale in Sardegna nei secoli XI–XIII. Fonti e documenti scritti*, 143–174. Sassari, 2002.

Merci, Paolo. 'Le origini della scrittura volgare'. In *La Sardegna*, ed. M. Brigaglia, vol. 1, 11–24. Cagliari, 1982.

Merci, Paolo, ed. *Il Condaghe di San Nicola di Trullas*. Nuoro, 2001.

Mimaut, Jean-François. *Histoire de Sardaigne*. Vol. 1. Paris, 1825.

Monteverdi, Angelo. *Testi volgari italiani dei primi tempi*. Modena, 1941.

Motzo, Bachisio R. 'La donazione dell'isola sulcitana a S. Antioco'. *Archivio Storico Sardo* 13 (1921): 75–89.

Murgia, Giulia, ed. *Carta de Logu d'Arborea: edizione critica secondo l'*editio princeps (BUC, Inc. 230), Milan, 2016.

Orrù, Michele. 'Byzantine Administrative Influence in Medieval Sardinia'. In *The Making of Medieval Sardinia*, eds A. Metcalfe, H. Fernández-Aceves and M. Muresu, 160–169. Leiden, 2021.

Ortu, Gian Giacomo. 'Establishing Power and Law in Medieval and Modern Sardinia'. In *A Companion to Sardinian History, 500–1500*, ed. M. Hobart, 228–251. Leiden, 2017.

Orunesu, Salvatore. *Quale Carta de Logu: nuove ipotesi sul codice arborense: dal proemio contraffatto ai capitoli di Ugone III*. Lecce, 2024.

Paulis, Giulio. *Lingua e cultura nella Sardegna bizantina: testimonianze linguistiche dell'influsso greco*. Sassari, 1983.

Paulis, Giulio. *Studi sul sardo medioevale*. Nuoro, 1997.

Paulis, Giulio. 'Greco e superstrati primari'. In *Manuale di linguistica sarda*, ed. Eduardo Blasco Ferrer, Peter Koch and Daniela Marzo, 104–118. Berlin and Boston, 2017.

Paulis, Giulio. 'Sociolinguistic Dynamics and Dynastic Names in Byzantine and Early Medieval Sardinia'. In *The Making of Medieval Sardinia*, eds A. Metcalfe, H. Fernández-Aceves and M. Muresu, 293–313. Leiden, 2021.

Perria, Lidia. 'La carta sarda di S. Vittore di Marsiglia: scrittura e tradizione bizantina in Sardegna nell'età giudicale'. In *Chiesa, potere politico e culturale in Sardegna dall'età giudicale al Settecento*, ed. G. Mele, 361–366. Oristano, 2005.

Petrucci, Armando, and Antonino Mastruzzo. 'Alle origini della *scripta sarda*: il *Privilegio Logudorese*'. *Michigan Romance Studies* 16 (1996): 201–214.

Puncuh, Dino, ed. *Liber privilegiorum Ecclesiae Ianuensis*. Genoa, 1962.

Putzu, Ignazio Efisio. 'Il repertorio linguistico sardo tra tardo-antico e alto medioevo. Un breve status quaestionis'. In *Itinerando. Senza confini dalla preistoria ad oggi*, ed. R. Martorelli, vol. 1, 497–518. Perugia, 2015.

Roncaglia, Aurelio. 'Le origini'. In *Storia della letteratura italiana. Le origini e il Duecento*, ed. E. Cecchi and N. Sapegno, 3–269. Milan, 1965.

Saba, Agostino. *Montecassino e la Sardegna medioevale*. Montecassino, 1927.

Scanu, Antonina, ed. *Carta de Logu. Riproduzione dell'edizione quattrocentesca conservata nella Biblioteca Universitaria di Cagliari*. Sassari, 1991

Schena, Olivetta. 'Le scritture del condaghe di Santa Maria di Bonarcado'. In *Miscellanea di studi medioevali sardo-catalani*, 42–73. Cagliari, 1981.

Schena, Olivetta. 'La carta sarda in caratteri greci: note diplomatistiche e paleografiche'. In *Sardegna e Mediterraneo tra Medioevo ed età moderna*, eds M.G. Meloni and O. Schena, 329–343. Genoa, 2009.

Schena, Olivetta. 'Archives and Documents Pertaining to the History of Medieval Sardinia'. In *A Companion to Sardinian History, 500–1500*, ed. M. Hobart, 51–67. Leiden, 2017.

Serra, Patrizia. 'La donazione di Barisone I all'abbazia di Montecassino'. In S. *Elia di Montesanto: il primo cenobio benedettino della Sardegna*, eds G. Strinna and G. Zichi, 117–131. Florence, 2017.

Serra, Patrizia, ed. *Il* Libellus Judicum Turritanorum. *Storia. Testi e commenti*. Cagliari, 2024.

Simbula, Pinuccia F., and Alessandro Soddu. 'Forme di servitù e mobilità dei servi in Sardegna nel basso Medioevo'. In *Migrazioni interne e forme di dipendenza libera e servile nelle campagne bassomedievali. Dall'Italia nord-occidentale alla Catalogna*, eds R. Lluch Bramon, J.P. Garçon and P. Le Pogam, 361–394. Cherasco, 2015.

Simbula, Pinuccia F., and Alessandro Soddu. 'Nuove riflessioni sulla *Carta de Logu* di Arborea'. In *Medioevo e Mediterraneo: incontri, scambi e confronti. Studi per Salvatore Fodale*, 179–194. Palermo, 2020.

Sini, Francesco. 'Influssi del diritto romano sulla "Carta de Logu" di Arborea'. In *La Carta de Logu d'Arborea nella storia del diritto medievale e moderno*, eds I. Birocchi and A. Mattone, 50–96. Rome and Bari, 2004.

Sini, Francesco. 'Diritto romano nella *Carta de Logu* d'Arborea: i capitoli "De appellationibus" e "De deseredari"'. In *Giudicato d'Arborea e Marchesato di Oristano: proiezioni mediterranee e aspetti di storia locale, Atti del I Convegno Internazionale di Studi* (*Oristano, 5–8 dicembre 1997*), ed. G. Mele, 983–1012. Oristano, 2000.

Soddu, Alessandro. 'I *pàperos* ("poveri") nella Sardegna giudicale (XI–XII secolo): eredità bizantine, echi carolingi, peculiarità locali'. *Acta Historica et Archaeologica Mediaevalia* 29 (2008): 205–255.

Soddu, Alessandro. 'Il potere regio nella Sardegna giudicale'. In *Linguaggi e rappresentazioni del potere nella Sardegna medievale*, ed. A. Soddu, 31–88. Rome, 2020.

Soddu, Alessandro. 'Il decretorum doctor Filippo Mameli tra Papato, Regno di Ungheria e Giudicato di Arborea (XIV secolo)'. *Rivista Storica Italiana* 136 (2024): 888–939.

Soddu, Alessandro. 'Il trattato di pace tra Giovanni I d'Aragona ed Eleonora d'Arborea (1388–1390)'. *Pandemos* 2 (2024): 1–33.

Soddu, Alessandro. 'Brevi, Statuti e "*Cartas de logu*" nella Sardegna tardomedievale'. In *La libertà di decidere: Da Cento a Cento 1993–2024. Trent'anni di studi sugli statuti*, eds E. Angiolini, B. Borghi, R. Dondarini and F. Galletti, 409–422. Florence, 2025.

Soddu, Alessandro, and Giovanni Strinna, eds. *Il condaghe di San Pietro di Silki*. Nuoro, 2013.

Solmi, Arrigo. 'Ademprivia—Studi sulla proprietà fondiaria in Sardegna'. *Archivio giuridico "Filippo Serafini"* 72 (1904): 411–447 [repr. in *Il feudalesimo in Sardegna. Testi e documenti per la storia della questione sarda*, ed. A. Boscolo, vol. 4, 49–144. Cagliari, 1967].

Solmi, Arrigo. 'Le carte volgari dell'Archivio Arcivescovile di Cagliari: testi campidanesi dei secoli XI–XIII'. *Archivio Storico Italiano* 5, no. 35 (1905): 273–330.

Solmi, Arrigo. 'Le carte volgari dell'Archivio Arcivescovile di Cagliari: note illustrative'. *Archivio Storico Italiano* 5, no. 36 (1905): 3–65.

Solmi, Arrigo. *Studi storici sulle istituzioni della Sardegna nel Medio Evo*. Cagliari, 1917; 2nd edn, Nuoro, 2001.

Spano, Giovanni. *Ortografia sarda nazionale. Ossia grammatica della lingua logudorese paragonata all'italiana*. 2 vols. Cagliari, 1840.

Spanu, Pier Giorgio. 'I possedimenti vittorini in Sardegna'. In *Committenza, scelte insediative e organizzazione patrimoniale nel Medioevo* (*De Re Monastica I*), ed. L. Pani Ermini, 245–279. Spoleto, 2007.

Spanu, Pier Giorgio, and Raimondo Zucca. I sigilli bizantini della Σαρδηνία. Rome, 2004.

Strinna, Giovanni. 'La carta di Nicita e la *clausula defensionis*'. *Bollettino di Studi Sardi* 2 (2009): 7–22.

Strinna, Giovanni. '"*Litteris semigraecis ac barbaris exarata monumenta*": sulla *scripta sarda* in caratteri greci'. *Archivio Storico Sardo* 52 (2017): 9–47.

Strinna, Giovanni. 'The Earliest Charter Sources from Medieval Sardinia'. In *The Making of Medieval Sardinia*, eds A. Metcalfe, H. Fernández-Aceves and M. Muresu, 314–342. Leiden, 2021.

Tanfani Centofanti, Leopoldo. 'Due carte inedite in lingua sarda dei secoli XI e XIII'. *Archivio Storico Italiano*, serie 3, 13 (1871): 357–376.

Tangheroni, Marco. 'La "Carta de Logu" del Giudicato di Cagliari'. In *La Carta de Logu d'Arborea nella storia del diritto medievale e moderno*, eds I. Birocchi and A. Mattone, 204–236. Rome and Bari, 2004.

Tola, Pasquale. *Codex Diplomaticus Sardiniae* (*CDS*). 2 vols. Turin, 1861–1868.

Turtas, Raimondo. 'The Sardinian Church'. In *A Companion to Sardinian History, 500–1500*, ed. M. Hobart, 177–214. Leiden, 2017.

Virdis, Maurizio, ed. *Il Condaghe di Santa Maria di Bonarcado*. Nuoro, 2003.

Virdis, Maurizio. 'Le prime manifestazioni della scrittura nel Cagliaritano'. In *Judicalia*, ed. Barbara Fois, 45–54. Cagliari, 2004.

Virdis, Maurizio. 'Sociolinguistica storica nella Sardegna medievale: fra dialettologia e filologia'. In *Il sardo medioevale*, eds G. Paulis, I. Putzu and M. Virdis, 11–34. Milan, 2018.

Virdis, Maurizio. 'Language and Vernacular Writing in Medieval Sardinia'. In *The Making of Medieval Sardinia*, eds A. Metcalfe, H. Fernández-Aceves and M. Muresu, 343–357. Leiden, 2021.

Wagner, Max Leopold. *Dizionario Etimologico Sardo*. 3 vols. Heidelberg, 1960–1962 [repr. Nuoro, 2008].

Zanetti, Ginevra. *I Camaldolesi in Sardegna*. Cagliari, 1974.

Zedda, Corrado. 'A Revision of Sardinian History between the Eleventh and Twelfth Centuries'. In *A Companion to Sardinian History, 500–1500*, ed. M. Hobart, 115–140. Leiden, 2017.

Onomastic Index

For ease of use, some orthographic variants in the original texts, especially for the letters *ç*, *z*, and *th* have undergone a degree of harmonisation in the index. For example, *ç* is here rendered as *z*; *sancti* and *sanctu* appear as *San* etc. Minor localities and micro-toponyms have not been referenced. Please also note the following abbreviations:

B.	Bonárcado (Condaghe of)
CdL.	Carta de Logu
CV.	Carte volgari
loc.	locality
mod.	modern
S.	Silki (Condaghe of)
top.	toponym

T

Printed by Libri Plureos GmbH in Hamburg, Germany

9 789004 741133